# THE
# GOVERNOR
# AND THE
# COLONEL

*A Dual Biography of William P. Hobby
and Oveta Culp Hobby*

## DON CARLETON

BRISCOE CENTER
FOR AMERICAN HISTORY
THE UNIVERSITY OF TEXAS AT AUSTIN

DISTRIBUTED BY TOWER BOOKS, AN IMPRINT
OF THE UNIVERSITY OF TEXAS PRESS

Requests for permission to reproduce material from this work should
be sent to:
Office of the Director
Dolph Briscoe Center for American History
University of Texas at Austin
2300 Red River Stop D1100
Austin, TX 78712-1426

∞ The paper used in this book meets the minimum requirements of
ANSI/NISO z39.48-1992 (r1997) (Permanence of Paper).

Library of Congress Control Number: 2020943676

# CONTENTS

# BOOK THREE: THE COLONEL

# INTRODUCTION

February 1929 was a bleak month for former Texas governor William Pettus Hobby. His beloved wife, Willie Cooper Hobby, was gone from his life forever—taken away by an apparent cerebral hemorrhage. He was suddenly and terribly alone. Fifty-one years old and childless, Will had also lost his closest sibling, Edwin. Will's colleagues at the *Houston Post-Dispatch*, where he was managing editor, tried to distract him from his sorrow, but their efforts were largely unsuccessful. His friend and employer Ross Sterling, one of the founders of the Humble Oil Company, who was now publisher of the *Houston Post-Dispatch*, made a special effort to console Will, but the shock of Willie's death was too severe, the loss too great. No matter how deeply Will threw himself into his newspaper work or visited with old friends, he inevitably had to return to his house on Lovett Boulevard in Houston's Montrose Addition, surrounded only by photographs and other artifacts of his life with Willie.

Willie was the college-educated, politically sophisticated daughter of the former East Texas congressman Samuel Bronson Cooper. She and Will, the son of the late attorney and former state legislator and judge Edwin Hobby, had been married for nearly fourteen years at the time of her death. The couple had been close friends long before their marriage. Willie had been at Will's side when he was owner and publisher of the *Beaumont Enterprise*, the leading newspaper in southeast Texas. She had been his counselor and booster when he campaigned successfully for two terms as lieutenant governor. And Willie was with him when he unexpectedly became governor as the result of the impeachment of James "Pa" Ferguson. A supporter of women's suffrage, Willie strongly influenced Will to support and sign the 1919 state law that allowed women to vote in Texas primaries. After the Hobbys moved to Houston and Will became editor of the *Post-Dispatch*, they had worked together in political campaigns and civic good works. Both had been deeply involved in the 1928 Democratic National Convention held in Houston. And now Willie was gone.

—

Soon after his wife's death, Will decided to publish a tribute book in her honor filled with quotes from the large number of family, friends, and business and political leaders who had rushed condolence messages to him after the news of her sudden passing. As Will sorted through the stack of cards, letters, and telegrams that had piled up on his dining room table, he found a brief message of sympathy from Miss Oveta Culp, the attractive, twenty-four-year-old daughter of Will's friend Isaac Culp, an attorney whose second tenure in the state legislature had overlapped with Will's time as governor from 1917 to 1921. Will had met Oveta, a native of Killeen, Texas, in 1919 when she was a precocious fourteen-year-old assisting her father during a legislative session. In the years that followed, Will had watched Oveta grow up. She had become well known in Texas government and political circles as an eighteen-year-old bank examiner for the state banking commission, as the twenty-one-year-old parliamentarian of the Texas House of Representatives, as a political campaign worker for several candidates for local and state office, as secretary of the State Democratic Women's Club, and as an attention-grabbing volunteer worker at the 1928 Democratic National Convention. When Will received Oveta's telegram expressing her condolences on the death of his wife, Oveta was back in Austin serving another term as parliamentarian of the Texas House.

Oveta Culp's telegram might have been the spark that motivated Will to contact her—an action that would result in their becoming romantically involved before the end of 1929 and in their marriage slightly more than one year later. Will and Oveta, the "Hobby Team," soon forged an intimate personal and professional relationship. They would be the proud parents of one son and one daughter, both of whom would become important figures in their own right. Oveta and Will's marriage would eventually lead to the establishment of a pioneering media business, substantial personal wealth, and membership in Houston's power elite. And, linked together through shared knowledge of and devotion to public service and journalism, they would play an influential role in the transformation of Houston into the fourth-largest city in the United States.[1]

As individuals, Will Hobby and Oveta Culp Hobby have been the subjects of separate biographies, but until now there has been no comprehensive biography linking and integrating their lives. Will was one of the pioneers of Texas journalism, and he oversaw one of the most legislatively significant governorships in Texas history. His early success as a newspaper publisher and politician is critical to an understanding of Oveta Culp Hobby's later success on the national stage. And during the first fifteen years of their marriage, Oveta and Will were close partners in all of their business and civic activities. One did not act without the other. During World War II when Oveta took her place on the national stage as the founding commander of the Women's Army Corps, and later when she became only the second woman to serve in a presidential cabinet, Will's encouragement and support were essential to her success. Oveta survived Will by more than thirty years, and she continued to be active in business and public service long after his death. Throughout her last three decades, Oveta continued on the course set and shaped by her partnership with the man she always called "Governor."

To understand the background of the historically significant partnership between the man and the woman who became the Hobby Team, one must begin with Will Hobby, who achieved most of his noteworthy accomplishments in politics and business long before his marriage to Oveta.

# BOOK ONE

---

# THE GOVERNOR

# EDWIN HOBBY

B y the time of his death in Houston in 1964, William "Will" Pettus Hobby Sr. had lived a long life deeply connected to politics and journalism. For more than six decades Will had served as a successful and innovative reporter, editor, and publisher of two influential urban daily newspapers. For six years he had given up his role as a journalistic monitor of governmental power to be a wielder of that power, first as lieutenant governor and then as governor of Texas.

Politics and journalism have long roots in the Hobby family, going back to Will's great, great, grandfather, Wensley Hobby Jr., whose ancestors, William and Anne Hobby, had migrated to Boston from Wales in the mid-seventeenth century. Wensley owned a dry goods business in Middletown, Connecticut. During the American Revolution, Wensley served on the public committee that enforced trade laws in Connecticut for the Continental Congress. He was also among the leaders of a group of fellow patriots who investigated and monitored the activities of Middletown residents who remained loyal to the British monarchy. According to family history, President George Washington appointed Wensley the first postmaster of Middletown, and he operated the post office from his residence on the town's main street. Wensley's son, William Johnson Hobby, migrated to Augusta, Georgia, in 1789 when he was twenty-three years old. Two years later, William married Sarah Elizabeth McKinne. William Johnson Hobby's career in journalism and politics foreshadowed that of his future great-grandson, William P. Hobby Sr. He served as the town's mayor and for many years edited and eventually owned the *Augusta Chronicle*, Georgia's most influential newspaper in the early nineteenth century. William was described by one observer as one of "the prominent representatives of pioneer journalism in Georgia."[1]

In 1830, one of William and Elizabeth Hobby's children, Alfred Martin Hobby, took a residence in Macon, Georgia, where he married Anna Eliza Slade Danelly, the widow of the former mayor of Macon, Captain William Danelly. Alfred and Anna named their first child Alfred Marmaduke Hobby, who was born in 1836 in Macon. At some point between

1836 and 1840, Alfred and Anna moved with their young son to the Florida Territory's capital, Tallahassee, where Edwin, their second son and the future father of William P. Hobby Sr., was born in 1843 or 1844. Anna gave birth to their youngest child, Barney, in Jacksonville, Florida, in 1846.[2]

In the mid-1840s, Alfred and Anna relocated with their family to the Apalachee Bay outpost of St. Marks, which had become a busy cotton-shipping port for Tallahassee after the towns were connected by rail in the late 1830s. When Alfred died in 1848 or 1849, Anna Hobby, now twice widowed, took her family to Madison, Florida, located in the heart of the Florida Panhandle's thriving long-staple-cotton-growing region fifty-six miles northeast of Tallahassee.[3]

In 1857, Anna and her three sons—twenty-one-year-old Alfred Marmaduke, thirteen-year-old Edwin, and eleven-year-old Barney—made their way to Galveston, the main gateway for new settlers to Texas. The Hobbys were among the more than four hundred thousand people who migrated to the state in the 1850s. The Texas economy was flourishing due to a worldwide cotton boom that continued throughout the decade. That boom attracted new infusions of investment capital, as well as large numbers of migrants from other slave-holding states who acquired land to grow cotton. The Lone Star State was enjoying its highest level of prosperity in its short history as part of the United States. The Hobbys were eager to take advantage of the economic bonanza.[4]

Soon after arriving in Galveston, Alfred, who was now head of the family and Edwin's role model, persuaded a local investor to fund his mercantile store in the newly established town of St. Mary's, located on the shore of Copano Bay on the Gulf Coast of Texas. Alfred believed the site had the potential to become a cotton port, a potential that unfortunately was never fulfilled, largely because ocean-sailing ships had great difficulty navigating the shallow bay. Anna Hobby and her younger sons, Edwin and Barney, moved with Alfred to St. Mary's, where they were among the town's earliest residents. Soon after they arrived, Alfred used the money he had raised in Galveston to pay for the construction of a two-story wooden building facing the bay. He named the structure the Hobby Building. The family's general store operated on the ground floor. The members of the local Masonic Lodge rented the second floor. The business flourished. Alfred Marmaduke Hobby was listed in the 1860 US Census as possessing a "$20,000 personal estate," the equivalent of over half a million dollars in 2019.[5]

In addition to tending to his successful business operation, Alfred was active in local politics. Refugio County's commissioners appointed him the county's notary public. He was described in one historical account as having been "a silver-tongued orator, as well as a man of letters." Alfred put his oratorical skills to work on behalf of his primary political cause: the right of slave owners to preserve and extend their system of human bondage into new territories.[6]

While it cannot be determined for certain if the Hobbys were slave owners, it is almost certain they were. There were enslaved people in St. Mary's, and Alfred and Edwin's fierce defense of slavery suggests they had practical reasons for that position. The brothers helped to organize a St. Mary's chapter, or "castle," of the Knights of the Golden Circle (KGC), a secret society founded in Lexington, Kentucky, in 1854. The KGC's name came from a grandiose proposal that called for Havana to serve as the capital of a new slave empire. With Havana at the center, a great or "golden" circle 2,400 miles in diameter would include Maryland, Kentucky, and southern Missouri to the north, all of the states to the south of them, a portion of eastern Kansas, most of Texas and Mexico, all of Central America, the northern part of South America, and all of the West Indies. The society's goal was to raise a private army to forcibly unite the entire region of the "golden circle" into a giant slave empire, one with a global monopoly on sugar, tobacco, and cotton. The resulting political entity would dominate the Western Hemisphere and ensure the preservation of slavery. The KGC planned to invade and conquer Mexico as the beginning of its efforts to create their slave empire. Texas was among the strongholds of the KGC, with "castles" in several locations, including Houston, Galveston, Austin, and San Antonio. The fantasy of a global empire went nowhere, and the KGC disintegrated with the onset of the Civil War. Nevertheless, the KGC played a vigorous role in stirring up sentiment in Texas for secession.[7]

Alfred took a leadership role in the local KGC chapter, with Edwin following in his older brother's footsteps, serving as secretary of the "castle." One of their best friends, Judge Charles Arden Russell, who lived in nearby Helena, was a knight officer. As a secret society, the knights had their own set of rituals, and members communicated with each other by code. In his correspondence with Judge Russell during the secession crisis, Edwin was careful to write his letters in the knights' special code.[8]

As the slavery debate intensified and talk of secession increased, the Hobby family earned a reputation in Refugio County as "the soul of the State's Right faction." Alfred in particular was known as an "able leader and moreover a fighting man" and "a typical Southern fire-eater," the latter a term used to describe those who took the most extreme proslavery and prosecession positions in the years before the Civil War.[9]

Abraham Lincoln's election as president in November 1860 convinced the fire-eating Hobbys the time had come for Texas to secede from the Union. Alfred and Edwin joined their associates in the KGC and other secessionists in Texas to demand that Governor Sam Houston call a special convention to vote on secession from the Union. The antisecessionist Houston rejected their demands. On December 3, 1860, a group of prominent Texas political figures led by Oran Roberts, chief justice of the Texas Supreme Court, placed announcements in the state's newspapers of a special election to be held on January 8, 1861. Every Texas county was called on to elect delegates to a secession convention to meet in Austin. The secessionists ignored Governor Houston's opposition and held the election anyway. By early January, the secession movement was sweeping the South. South Carolina had already seceded from the Union, and four other slave states were convening their own secession conventions.[10]

Alfred Hobby declared his candidacy to be the convention delegate from Refugio County as soon as the election date was announced. His leadership of the local secessionist movement made him the obvious choice, and he easily won election. On January 28, he was among the 177 delegates who assembled in the state capitol to debate and vote on the secession ordinance. With slave owners comprising 72 percent of the delegates, passage of the ordinance was preordained. Along with his friend and fellow KGC leader Judge Russell, Alfred was among the most vocal and active delegates in favor of secession. On February 1, their two votes joined those of 164 other secessionists who voted for the ordinance. Only eight delegates cast ballots against leaving the Union. Despite passage of the ordinance, Texas had not yet formally seceded. The ordinance required that it be submitted to a popular referendum, to be held on February 23.[11]

The convention's vote to secede led to the resignation of antisecessionist state legislator Henry Kinney, one of the founders of Corpus Christi, whose district included St. Mary's. Alfred Hobby, who had been one of the strident voices critical of Kinney, decided to run in the special election in February 1861 to fill the legislative vacancy created when Kinney resigned. Running on a proslavery, secessionist platform and as the recent victor of the election to be a delegate to the secession convention, Alfred was victorious. After serving the remainder of Kinney's term, Alfred won reelection to a full term in the Texas House in November 1861.[12]

On February 23, the statewide referendum on secession passed by a landslide, 46,154 to 14,747. The Texas Secession Convention reassembled on March 2, 1861, to officially withdraw the state from the Union it had joined only sixteen years earlier. The convention also passed a measure for Texas to join the newly formed Confederate States of America, which required all state officers to swear an oath of allegiance to the Confederacy or resign from office. When Governor Sam Houston refused to take the oath or resign, the convention declared his office vacant, and Lieutenant Governor Edward Clark assumed the governorship.[13]

Texas's new Confederate government created a Committee of Public Safety to confiscate federal property and force the removal of Union troops from the state, which was accomplished peacefully. With civil war apparently unavoidable, the committee also called for the formation of local militias to prepare for the state's defense. Alfred Hobby rushed back to St. Mary's, where he and Edwin helped assemble the St. Mary's "Rough and Ready" Home Guard.[14]

War did come in April 1861 with the Confederate attack on Union forces posted at Fort Sumter in South Carolina. As the war progressed, Alfred continued his service in the state legislature while Edwin, only seventeen, stayed close to home and trained with the local militia. When the Texas Legislature passed a military conscription act, Alfred resigned his seat in the legislature and returned to St. Mary's. In May 1862, he organized and was appointed commander of the Eighth Texas Infantry Battalion, with the rank of colonel. The battalion, which was composed largely of Refugio County residents, became well known as Hobby's Eighth Texas Infantry. For a brief period, eighteen-year-old Edwin

Hobby was a private in Company B, serving as Alfred's assistant. Within weeks, however, Alfred had Edwin promoted to captain and commander of Company D.

The Union Navy blockaded most Confederate ports soon after the start of the war, but Texas ports remained open. It wasn't until the summer of 1862 that Union naval forces arrived in the western Gulf of Mexico to halt cotton exports and to seize strategic points on the Texas coast, including wharf areas and military outposts guarding entrances to the bays. When the Union Navy gained control of Aransas Bay in early July, General Hamilton Bee ordered Alfred's battalion to protect the forty miles of Gulf Coast between Corpus Christi and the village of Lamar. Alfred moved his men to Corpus Christi, where he established his headquarters, reinforced the local militia garrison, and waited for an attack. His force, which included Edwin, consisted of seven hundred men, including militia volunteers and his five companies.[15]

A few weeks after Alfred and Edwin arrived in Corpus Christi, a Union naval force seized five Confederate naval boats. Before dawn on August 18, Alfred responded with an artillery attack on the Union boats anchored near shore, hitting two of them and forcing their withdrawal. The next day a small force of Union marines landed a mile from Alfred's artillery. After a fierce battle, during which Alfred suffered a minor head wound, the marines withdrew. Ignoring his wound, Alfred stayed with his troops until the end of the battle.[16]

Alfred Hobby's soldiers won the battle, but Corpus Christi's port remained blocked. In October 1862, after Union forces captured Galveston, General John Bankhead Magruder, commander of the military district of Texas, ordered Alfred's battalion to Houston, where they joined troops transferred from other brigades and made plans to recapture Galveston. During the early hours of January 1, 1863, Alfred and Edwin were members of a contingent of Magruder's troops that streamed across the railroad bridge from the mainland to Galveston in a surprise attack. The Confederate forces prevailed after heavy fighting that claimed nearly three hundred casualties. Recognizing Alfred's outstanding performance in the battle, Magruder had him commissioned as a colonel in the regular Confederate Army. Galveston returned to Confederate control, but like Corpus Christi, the port remained under Union blockade until the end of the war.[17]

Alfred and Edwin Hobby remained in Galveston with other members of their battalion until the end of 1863. Early in 1864 General Magruder ordered the Hobby brothers and their battalion to leave Galveston and head to northeast Texas. Alfred and Edwin barely survived the brutal battles at Mansfield and Pleasant Hill in northern Louisiana. The Confederates suffered heavy casualties in the campaign but successfully prevented the Union Army from capturing Shreveport and northeast Texas.[18]

Among the Southern casualties in the campaign in northwest Louisiana was General Tom Green, a former clerk at the Texas Supreme Court who had been an ally of Alfred and Edwin in the prosecession movement and in the secession convention. The Hobbys renewed their friendship with Green when they linked up again during the campaign in Louisiana, where Green commanded the Confederate cavalry. His death shook the

Hobbys badly. When Edwin heard the news about Green's death, he penned a poem in tribute to his late friend with the title "To the Beloved Memory of Major-General Tom Green," which was published in Galveston on May 26, 1864.[19]

After the campaign in northern Louisiana, Alfred and Edwin were transferred back to Houston, where they remained until war's end. They both mustered out of the Confederate Army of the Trans-Mississippi on May 22, 1865. Two months later, while still in Houston, they received federal pardons as a result of President Andrew Johnson's highly controversial policy of issuing blanket pardons to thousands of ex-Confederates. After they were pardoned, the Hobby brothers joined their mother, Anna, at their residence in St. Mary's. By this time, Alfred and Edwin were pessimistic about the economic future of St. Mary's as a port. In addition, while Alfred was stationed in Galveston in 1863 he had fallen in love with a local woman named Gertrude Stiles Menard, and he decided to move back to the island city to marry Gertrude and open a general store. Alfred and Edwin liquidated their family mercantile business and relocated to Galveston. The decision to leave St. Mary's proved to be a wise one. In the 1870s that coastal town experienced a series of devastating hurricanes that resulted in its abandonment by all but a small contingent of residents. In Galveston, Alfred opened his general store and then married Gertrude Menard in July 1867. He and Gertrude later moved to New Mexico, where Alfred was killed in a wagon accident in 1881.[20]

During the war, Edwin had developed a strong interest in the law. Late in 1865, he decided to move to Houston with his mother to apprentice with an attorney to prepare for his law exam. While Edwin was studying the law, he met and courted Eudora "Dora" Adeline Pettus, a college-educated, twenty-two-year-old private tutor. Born in Lunenburg County, Virginia, on September 11, 1843, Dora was the daughter of Dr. John Richard Pettus and his wife, Mary. Dora, her sister, Laura, and her brother, William, migrated with their parents to Tennessee, then later settled in Marlin, Texas, in November 1855. Three years later, the Pettuses resettled in Fort Bend County, Texas. Not long after he arrived in Fort Bend County, Dr. Pettus invested in several parcels of land in Richmond, the county seat. The family homesteaded near Walker's Station, located a few miles east of Richmond and twenty-five miles southwest of Houston. Situated on the fertile bottomlands of the Brazos River, Walker's Station flourished because of its location on the Galveston, Harrisburg, and San Antonio Railroad. A guide published in 1878 described Walker's Station as a "thriving little town" and an "important shipping point for cotton, sugar, corn. . . . At or near Walker are located some of the largest sugar houses in the state." Dr. Pettus did well in his new home. Two years after settling in Texas, he owned a 471-acre plantation, estimated to have a cash value of $10,500. He also employed an overseer and owned twenty-four enslaved workers. "Pettus Place" eventually grew in size to more than one thousand acres, with a third of that in timber. The affluent and well-educated Pettus family was well known in Fort Bend County. Dr. Pettus sent Dora to be educated at the female department of Baylor College in Independence, Texas, which later became the University of Mary Hardin–Baylor in Belton, Texas.[21]

After a brief courtship, Edwin and Dora were married on February 20, 1866, at Christ Episcopal Church in Houston. A few months later, Edwin appeared at an examination hearing where three lawyers appointed by the district court judge questioned him about his knowledge of the law. Edwin passed the examination, and the district court granted his law license.[22]

Because Houston in the late 1860s had an excess of lawyers, it was a difficult place for a newly minted attorney to make much of a living. Which might have been the reason the newlyweds decided in 1867 to relocate to East Texas to tiny Peach Tree Village in Tyler County, ninety miles to the northeast of Houston. Edwin's reasons for his choice of a new home can only be surmised. Land was cheap in this isolated and undeveloped area, which attracted migrants from the Deep South states of the former Confederacy who were escaping places devastated during the Civil War. Perhaps Edwin selected Peach Tree Village because of friendships forged with fellow soldiers during the Civil War, as hundreds of men from Tyler County served in the Confederate Army. The more likely explanation was that Edwin learned he would be one of the only attorneys in the county, which would give him the opportunity to build a law practice without the intense competition he faced in Houston. Whatever the reasons, Edwin decided to make a new home and legal practice in the Piney Woods of East Texas.

Early in 1867, Edwin and Dora Hobby loaded Edwin's law books and their family belongings into a wagon and with Edwin's mother, Anna, made the one-hundred-mile trek from Houston over primitive dirt roads to their new home in Peach Tree Village. Located near the upper Neches River in Tyler County in southeast Texas, Peach Tree was in a rugged area known as the Big Thicket, one of the most biologically diverse areas in North America. It was a wild area full of swamps, bayous, pine savannahs, and sand hills that neither Spain nor Mexico ever managed to settle. Before the lumber industry clear-cut wide areas of the pine forest, the thicket covered over one million acres, stretching about twenty miles across at its widest and about forty miles long, with the Sabine River as its eastern boundary and its southern boundary south of Sour Lake. Its northern and western borders were less well defined. A tribe of Alabama Indians established Peach Tree Village when they settled in the area in the early 1800s after Europeans drove them out of the region that is now the state of Alabama. Before settlers from the United States pushed them from the area in the late 1830s, Peach Tree had an estimated one thousand Native American residents.[23]

Edwin's decision to settle in Peach Tree was a professional gamble. The entire county had fewer than five thousand inhabitants, and most of those residents supported themselves on small subsistence farms. A railroad would not reach the county for another fourteen years. The economy of Tyler County, like most of East Texas, continued to struggle from the impact of the Civil War, and money was scarce. The county seat and largest town, Woodville, was still occupied by federal troops.[24]

As it developed, however, Edwin's decision to settle in Peach Tree Village was a fortunate one. The village was located at the intersection of two heavily trafficked trails.

One trail stretched from Houston and the Gulf of Mexico to north-central Texas. The other began at Alexandria, Louisiana, and continued west to San Antonio, the largest city in Texas. By the time Edwin and Dora arrived in Peach Tree, migrants who were headed west and south and traders peddling their goods to the newly settled villages and towns connected by these important trails were generating enough business to support the establishment of a general store, cotton gin, gristmill, saloon, church, post office, and small private academy. The growing village needed an attorney, and Edwin soon became the town lawyer. In addition to providing routine legal services such as wills and probates, Edwin also specialized in land law, particularly land titles, which required him to make frequent trips to the county courthouse in Woodville, where he eventually opened a law office.[25]

It was also Edwin's good fortune that the little village of Peach Tree attracted three other families—the Coopers, the Kirbys, and the Sterlings—who would forge strong, lifelong business and political ties with each other and with the Hobbys. Edwin and Dora became close friends with members of each of those families in Peach Tree.

Edwin's relationship with these families began with Samuel Bronson Cooper. A few months after his birth in Caldwell County, Kentucky, in 1850, Bronson and his parents, Elizabeth and Reverend A. H. Cooper, moved with his uncle and aunt to Peach Tree Village. When Reverend Cooper died three years after the family settled in East Texas, Bronson and his mother moved in with her brother, Sam Frazer, who had a farm near the village. Bronson grew up as a member of his uncle's household and worked on the farm while attending the common school in Woodville. The economic devastation that followed the Civil War left his aging uncle destitute, forcing Bronson at the age of thirteen to get a job in the general store to help support his mother and uncle. After three years, Bronson had saved enough money to pay for a year of school at the Masonic High School in the town of Moscow in nearby Polk County, after which he then moved to Woodville to work as a clerk in the general store.[26]

Edwin Hobby, who was a friend of Bronson's uncle Sam, had taken an interest in Bronson when he was still a young boy. Edwin's law business in Woodville was prospering, and he was looking for office help. It was clear to Edwin that the young man had intellectual curiosity and ambition. He recruited Bronson, who was ten years younger than Edwin, to help him in the office. Edwin served as Bronson's mentor and guided him in reading law. Bronson also continued to work in the store, which he eventually bought from his employer.[27]

Edwin also formed an important friendship with fellow Confederate Army veteran John Thomas Kirby, his wife, Sara, and their son, John Henry. The Kirbys were also close to the Coopers. One source describes Bronson Cooper as John Henry Kirby's "benefactor and idol." While in school in Woodville, John Henry ran errands for Edwin and Bronson while also working in the tax collector's office. After John Henry's graduation in 1879, Bronson paid for him to attend classes for a year at the Methodist-affiliated Southwestern University in Georgetown, Texas. The Kirby family's next-door neighbors in Peach Tree, the William Sterlings, also befriended the Hobbys. Sterling, known to his friends as Uncle Billy, operated a gristmill and a cotton gin, and it is likely he was one of Edwin's clients.[28]

Edwin and Dora's family underwent a number of changes during this time. Their first child, Helen, had been born in 1867. A son, whom they named Alfred, obviously after Edwin's older brother, followed in 1869. Another daughter, Mary, was born in 1871. A third daughter, Laura, would join the family in 1873. On September 26, 1870, around the time Bronson Cooper began his apprenticeship with Edwin, Dora's father, Dr. John Pettus, died in Fort Bend County. Edwin's mother, Anna, continued to live with the family, while Dora's mother remained with her son at Pettus Place.[29]

In 1872, when Bronson Cooper passed his law exam, he sold his store and joined with Edwin and William Perry Nicks in a law partnership. When Edwin established the new law firm, he and Dora moved their growing family to Woodville. Edwin and his partners became leading political figures in Tyler County within months of opening their law practice, which soon led to Edwin's election to the Texas Senate in December 1873 to represent the district that included most of the Piney Woods area of southeast Texas. Edwin's campaign was part of the Democratic Party's successful effort to take control of state government away from the Republicans, who had implemented and administered the Reconstruction laws that were much despised by the former rebels. These so-called Redeemers sought to restore white supremacists to power, turn back every legal gain made by formerly enslaved Texans, and drastically reduce the power of state government. The Democrats won a majority in both houses of the legislature. The race for governor pitted former military enemies against each other. A Confederate Army veteran, Richard Coke, easily defeated incumbent Republican governor Edmund J. Davis, who had served as a brigadier general in the Union Army. Claiming voter fraud, Davis refused to vacate his office.[30]

When Edwin made the journey from East Texas to Austin in early January 1874, he found himself in the middle of a major constitutional crisis. A few days before his arrival, the Texas Supreme Court invalidated the December 1873 general election, which voided Edwin's election as well as that of his legislative colleagues and their gubernatorial ally, Coke. The Democrats, many of whom were former members of the Confederate Army, ignored the court's ruling and moved forward with their plan to convene as the new legislature. When Edwin and his fellow Democrats entered the capitol, they discovered that Davis had ordered the doors to the House and Senate chambers on the second floor to be locked. The Travis Guards and Rifles, a group of Confederate Army veterans who had served as a unit in the war, had been reorganized a few days earlier as a paramilitary unit to help support Democratic efforts to regain control of state government. With aid from the Travis Guards, the Democrats soon located keys, unlocked the doors, and organized as the Fourteenth Legislature of the State of Texas.[31]

Edwin Hobby not only actively participated in these events at the capitol, he also played a leading role in the legislative proceedings that followed. One of the first items of business was to settle a dispute over the seating of Walter Burton, a black senator from Fort Bend County. Senator William Wood from Leon County asserted that Burton, who was a Republican, had won his election by fraud as result of the misprinting of names on the ballot. Wood's protest was a transparent attempt to seat the white Democrat whom Burton had defeated. Edwin rejected Wood's argument and defended Burton from the floor of the Senate. Senator Jewett Davenport of Bell County joined Edwin to argue that Burton should be recognized as the duly elected senator. Hobby and Davenport prevailed, and Wood's protest was defeated by a vote of fourteen to eleven. Burton, a staunch defender of the rights of freedmen, would go on to serve four consecutive terms in the Senate.[32]

Among Edwin's fellow senators was his friend John Ireland, whom Edwin had met when both men were serving in the Confederate Army on the Texas Gulf Coast. On the opening day of the Senate session, Edwin rose from his seat to nominate Ireland for election as president pro tem, which under the Texas Constitution of 1869 was the Senate's presiding officer until a newly elected lieutenant governor could be sworn into office. Ireland was elected by unanimous vote. Edwin also submitted a resolution to aid news coverage of the Senate by locating "suitable seats . . . to be assigned to reporters from the press." The Senate adopted his resolution.[33]

On January 19, after President Ulysses S. Grant refused his request for federal intervention, Edmund Davis resigned as governor, giving the Redeemers total control over Texas government. Richard Coke was inaugurated governor and Richard Hubbard lieutenant governor. As the first regular session of the legislature proceeded, Edwin was appointed chair of the Enrolled Bills Committee and a member of the Public Buildings and Internal Improvements Committees. As a member of the latter committee, Edwin introduced a bill to improve navigation on the Sabine and other rivers in southeast Texas, a project his future son, Will, would continue more than thirty-five years later.

When the legislature adjourned on May 4, 1874, Edwin returned home as a well-regarded and popular senator among his colleagues. He went back to Austin in January 1875 to attend the second session of the Fourteenth Legislature, where the primary issue was the Constitution of 1869, which was much despised by former secessionists as a document the Radical Republicans had imposed on the state. Edwin and the majority of his colleagues were convinced that the 1869 Constitution gave the governor too much power and had expanded the reach of state government at the expense of local authority. Governor Coke asked the legislature to pass a bill to establish a convention to write an entirely new constitution. Edwin, who led the movement in the Senate in support of the governor's request, submitted a joint resolution "providing for a constitutional convention, to assemble in the city of Austin."[34]

After much debate, a compromise was made to let voters decide in a statewide referendum whether or not a constitutional convention should be called. The voters did approve, which led to a constitutional convention in Austin from September to November 1875. The delegates eventually produced a document that decentralized state government, reduced the power of the governor, limited the legislature to biennial meetings, and essentially established a commission form of government managed by independently elected officials. This new constitution was approved overwhelmingly in a popular referendum on February 15, 1876.[35]

At the end of the legislative session in 1875 Edwin ended his partnership with Cooper and Nicks and moved his family to Moscow, a logging and sawmill town in central Polk County, Texas, where he opened his own law office. Moscow was not a prosperous place in the 1870s. It had not recovered from the loss of the cotton plantation economy and the end of enslaved labor. The Polk County seat, Livingston, was fifteen miles to the south of Moscow, requiring Edwin to make a thirty-mile round trip over bad roads whenever he needed to file deeds and attend court hearings.[36]

On March 26, 1878, not long after settling in their new home, Dora gave birth to the Hobbys' second son, William "Will" Pettus Hobby, named after Edwin's grandfather and Dora's Pettus family. Less than one month after Will's birth, Edwin traveled to Austin to attend a new legislative session. Edwin had retained his Senate seat despite his move to Polk County because the county was in his senatorial district. The new constitution reduced Senate terms from six years to four years and required that half of its members stand for reelection every two years. The senators drew lots to determine whose term would end in two years and whose would end in four years. Edwin drew one of the four-year lots, which extended his senatorial term to 1880. The fifteenth legislative session was among the most important in Texas history. It organized fifty-four new counties in West Texas, overhauled the state's civil code, allocated one million acres of state land as an endowment to benefit the planned University of Texas, and reorganized the state courts. Edwin took the leadership role in judicial reorganization, authoring a bill to create the court of appeals. The legislature also elected Governor Richard Coke to the US Senate before adjourning the session.[37]

With his senate term extended until 1880, Edwin made the trek back to Austin in January 1879 to attend the sixteenth legislative session. Because of Coke's election to the US Senate, Lieutenant Governor Richard Hubbard served as the state's chief executive for a few days until Oran Roberts succeeded him. One of the major accomplishments of this legislature was an extensive revision of the civil statutes, the penal code, and the code of criminal procedure. Edwin, who served on the Senate's law committee, submitted the bills revising the penal and criminal codes. Because of the respect Edwin had earned as a senator, his colleagues elected him president pro tem of the Senate on January 24, 1879. Early in the session, Governor Roberts informed Edwin he would appoint him judge of the Thirty-First Judicial District, which included San Jacinto, Polk, Angelina, Hardin, Liberty, and Chambers counties. For Edwin, a judgeship was a dream come true, a position he had long wanted. He eagerly accepted the governor's offer, but it meant he would have to resign from the Senate at the end of the session.[38]

When Edwin announced his decision to leave the Senate, Edwin's colleagues went to the floor to make speeches stating their disappointment at his departure and expressing their gratitude for his service. The senator from Huntsville, James Burnett, in the oratorical style typical of the time, declared, "In parting with Senator Hobby we all trust his public life will not terminate, but that he may be called to a position for which his ability and learning as a lawyer, his executive abilities and his conscientious Christian manhood so eminently fit him." In his response, delivered from the dais of the Senate, Edwin stressed that he had no "language to express my appreciation of the honors conferred upon me by this Senate. I have to say that I shall part from you with unspeakable regret, proud indeed of your friendship, grateful for your kindness."[39]

Edwin soon earned a reputation as an energetic and dedicated judge with deep knowledge of the law, especially Texas's difficult land law, which was entangled in a confusing mishmash of overlapping legal traditions dating back to the Spanish colonial era. It was a subject Edwin had studied intensely from the beginning of his law practice. In 1883, he made his knowledge and experience in land law widely available when the Gilbert Book Company of St. Louis published his book, *A Treatise on Texas Land Law*. Hobby's book provided an analysis of the colonization land laws and the empresario systems of Spain and Mexico, how they applied to Coahuila and Texas, and how they were legally interpreted after Texas was annexed by the United States. *A Treatise on Texas Land Law* immediately became the standard work on the topic and was soon commonly known to the legal profession as "Hobby's Land Law."[40]

In 1881, a year after Edwin became a district judge, Dora gave birth to their third son, Paul. On August 8, 1883, a fourth son, Edwin, was born. As Dora raised her seven children and took care of household matters, Judge Hobby busily traveled throughout his judicial domain and held court in the six county seats in his district. Dabney White, a historian of East Texas whose father was a friend of Hobby's, wrote a fascinating description of the colorful judge that was published in *Frontier Times* in 1933. White recalled that Judge Hobby was "a little man physically, yet he wore a Prince Albert coat, a big black, slouch hat and high-heeled boots. He also wore red flannel underwear, a prevailing custom." White also noted, "Judge Hobby, while District Judge, frequently walked from one courthouse to another."[41]

While Edwin was making a name for himself as a jurist and an author, his former law partner, Samuel Bronson Cooper, won the 1880 election to replace Edwin as senator in District One. The Peach Tree Village political network continued to solidify. Cooper brought his protégé, John Henry Kirby, to Austin as his secretary. Kirby had recently completed a year of studies at Southwestern University, made possible by Cooper's sponsorship. After Cooper's election to a second term in the Senate, his colleagues elected him president pro tem, and he subsequently appointed John Henry Kirby the Senate's calendar clerk. During the regular and called sessions of the Seventeenth and Eighteenth Legislatures, Cooper was one of the leaders of the conservative Democrats who strengthened and extended the legal system supporting white supremacy and restricting the power of state government. Among Cooper's successful legislative initiatives was his bill granting 1,280 acres of state land to any Confederate veteran in Texas who had been disabled by wounds suffered during the war. The benefit was also extended to the widows of Confederate soldiers who had been killed in the war.[42]

Cooper decided to leave the Senate after completing his second term. In 1882 the Sabine and East Texas Railroad had laid a line from Beaumont north through the entire length of Tyler County. Two years later, the Missouri, Kansas, and Texas Railroad constructed twenty-nine miles of track across the northern part of the county. These rail connections made possible the exploitation of the timberlands by lumber and other wood-related industries. Predicting that Tyler County's economy was ready to flourish, Cooper wanted to take advantage of the legal business the boom was certain to generate. To help him, Cooper made John Henry Kirby his law partner. Kirby had studied law while working for Cooper in the capitol. The legal team of Cooper and Kirby soon prospered. During these years a widely distributed book featuring profiles of "representative men of Texas" declared that Bronson Cooper was "considered to be one of the best lawyers . . . in this state."[43]

By 1886, with the economy growing from the rapidly expanding lumber industry in the region, Edwin's caseload as a judge had increased to such an extent that he decided to move his family to Livingston, the Polk County seat, where most of the trials he presided over were held. After he moved to Livingston, the Texas Legislature reorganized his judicial district into the new Ninth District Court. In 1888, Edwin resigned as district court judge to serve as associate judge on the court of appeals.[44]

The Hobby children attended the Livingston public school, which held classes in two rooms in the Masonic Lodge the first three years after the family moved to town. In 1888, classes moved to a newly constructed building erected to serve exclusively as a school. Ten-year-old Will was a favorite among his teachers, who encouraged his interest in history and politics. Local historian Emma Haynes interviewed residents of Livingston who recalled that young Will loved to stand on a dry-goods box to deliver speeches to anyone who would listen. One of Will's favorite public performances was his passionate recitation of Thomas Campbell's poem "Hohenlinden" about a battle during the Napoleonic Wars. At the time, the poem was a favorite of many teachers of history, reading, and grammar, who required their students to memorize and recite it. Those students who excelled were chosen to declaim Campbell's poem, as well as others, to school assemblies held on Friday afternoons at the end of the school week. Parents who attended these performances were greatly amused as little Will, with "clinched and shaking fist," would mangle the word "artillery" as he shouted out Campbell's verse: "And louder than the bolts of heaven far flashed the red artillder."[45]

Many years later, Will recalled that as he progressed in school he became an avid reader. His favorites included the works of William Shakespeare and the novels of Charles Dickens, James Fenimore Cooper, Mark Twain, and Bret Harte. Will also loved history. He eagerly read biographies of George Washington, Thomas Jefferson, Abraham Lincoln, and Robert E. Lee. And as was the case with many boys his age, Will loved to hear his father recall his experiences on the battlefields in Corpus Christi, Galveston,

*Edwin Hobby as a state judge, ca. 1888.*

and northern Louisiana during the Civil War. Years later, in speeches Will delivered after he became a public figure, he often drew on the stories Edwin had shared about his experiences defending the "Lost Cause." Will, like so many white Southerners, never questioned the righteousness of the cause, which in the decades after the war was no longer explained as a fight to preserve slavery but instead as a struggle for "states' rights." The courage of the soldiers who fought and died for that cause was the inspiration that shaped the rhetoric of most Southern politicians of his generation, including Will. As important as Edwin's war experiences were in shaping Will's worldview, an equally important influence on Will was his father's recollection of the trials over which he presided, the attorneys' legal arguments, and the often fascinating human interest stories that were involved in the cases.[46]

Edwin's judicial career received a boost when Governor James S. Hogg appointed him to the vacant position of presiding judge of the Commission of Appeals on April 15, 1891. That promotion was short-lived, however, as voters rejected his bid to continue as the court's presiding judge in fall 1892. The defeat also ended his tenure as a judge on the court. Edwin might have lost his race because of the political tumult stemming from the Populist Party's insurgency against Governor Hogg that year. The Populist Party was strong in some parts of Edwin's region, and he was a strong supporter of the governor. Whatever the reason, Edwin's loss, which deeply disappointed the fourteen-year-old Will, resulted in his father's decision to move his family out of Polk County and start a new life in the bustling city of Houston, a move that would profoundly shape Will's future.[47]

After his disappointing defeat, fifty-two-year-old Edwin Hobby found himself unsure about what direction he should next take in his career. Five of his children were now adults, but he still had three sons—Will, eleven-year-old Paul, and nine-year-old Edwin—to support at home. Judge Hobby had presided over a court for more than thirteen years, and he left the bench as a respected legal expert. He could continue to practice law in Livingston or even return to Woodville to open a new practice, but a more attractive opportunity soon appeared. It came from Edwin's old Peach Tree Village network, specifically from John Henry Kirby.

By 1890, Kirby was a wealthy man. He owned two of the largest timber companies in Texas, and he hoped to diversify, possibly into the railroad business. When Bronson Cooper decided to run for US Congress, he and Kirby ended their law partnership and Kirby moved his headquarters from Woodville to Houston. By the beginning of the 1890s, Houston had become the third-largest city in Texas, ranked behind only San Antonio and Galveston. Houston was growing so rapidly, it would soon overtake Galveston in population. Kirby knew he could better carry out his plan to organize a railroad from Houston instead of a small town in the Piney Woods. He also wanted to invest some of his profits in the city's real estate market and take advantage of the rising property values. As Kirby later noted, Houston was the right place at the right time for an optimistic and fearless entrepreneur: "Money is in abundant supply and interest rates are easy."[48]

By the time Edwin Hobby lost his election in 1892, Kirby was firmly established with an office in Houston's Commercial National Bank. Ever since his move to Houston, Kirby had urged Edwin to leave Livingston and join his law firm. Kirby's enterprises needed the services of an outstanding land lawyer, and he had deep trust in his old family friend. The timing was perfect. Edwin knew Kirby's offer was a great opportunity, plus he knew Houston well: it was where he had read law and where he and Dora were married. Their eldest son, Alfred, was studying medicine at the Houston Infirmary and daughter Laura Aline was teaching school in the city. Edwin accepted Kirby's offer.[49]

In February 1893, Edwin and Dora and their three youngest children boarded a train of the Houston East and West Texas Railway in Livingston for the trip to Houston. Many years later, when Will recalled the family's departure from Polk County, he said he was unhappy about leaving Livingston and anxious about living in the "big city." Although Houston's population was a little less than thirty thousand in 1893, Livingston's

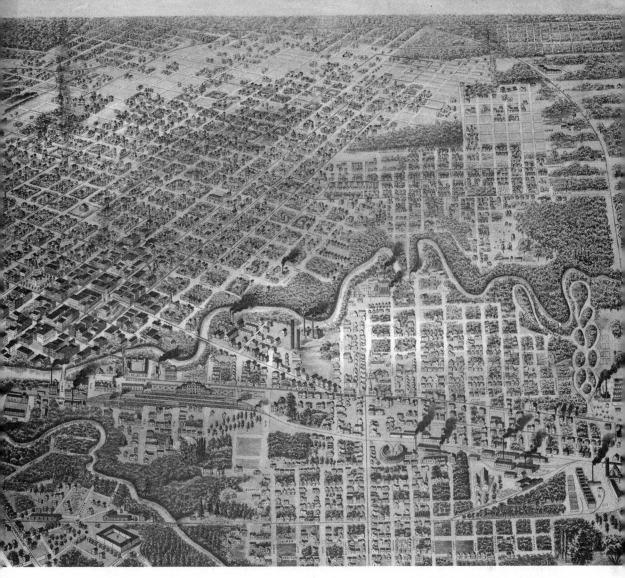

*Bird's-eye view of Houston, 1891, near the time Edwin Hobby moved his family to the city.*

population only numbered in the hundreds. Relative to Livingston, Houston qualified as a "big city."

Will remembered that the train ride was slow and uncomfortable. To many passengers who traveled on the Houston East and West Texas Railway, the initials H. E. & W. T. were often described derisively as standing for "Hell Either Way You Take It." When the Hobbys finally arrived in Houston, Will was shocked by how bright the electric lights were in the large and busy railroad depot. Livingston had neither electricity nor telephones. Houston had become the largest rail center in Texas by 1893, with twelve major rail lines stretching out like spokes on a bicycle wheel in every direction from the city's core. The Hobby family hired a carriage to take them to the Tremont Hotel, where they would stay until Edwin could find suitable living quarters. Will recalled that as the carriage made its way to the hotel, he was intrigued by the nightlife on the streets: "Men were hawking hot tamales and popcorn. Swarms of people were still up, walking and laughing and talking. Lights were still on everywhere. It was nothing like . . . Livingston."[50]

Edwin soon rented a house at 1713 McKinney Street, a few blocks from the Union Station train depot. The family later moved to a larger house at 1417 La Branch Street, and Dora's mother, Mary Pettus, moved in with them. A month after Edwin arrived in Houston, John Henry Kirby gave him the job of organizing a railroad company—the Gulf, Beaumont, and Kansas City—to link his East Texas pine holdings to the shallow-water shipping docks in Beaumont. Financed by Kirby's investment partners in Boston, the railroad began operation in 1896. It ran north from Beaumont for fifty-three miles to Jasper County. Kirby soon extended the railroad from Jasper to San Augustine as a separate company called the Gulf, Beaumont, and Great Northern Railway. In 1900, he sold the entire line to the Atchison, Topeka, and Santa Fe and bought East Texas timberland with the profit. The Texas Development Board in Dallas would later note, "The building of this railroad was the greatest boon in furnishing an outlet to the markets of the country for the great virgin pine forests of East Texas."[51]

The national economic depression that began with the Panic of 1893 slowed progress on Kirby's railroad project. He was fortunate to have had his investors' money in the bank before the depression worsened, which allowed him to move forward with the project, but the depression severely reduced Kirby's income and his law firm's business. As a result, Edwin's hope that his partnership with Kirby would enrich the family failed to materialize. He was grateful that Kirby had the financial resources to weather the severe economic collapse, which continued to support Edwin's base salary, but his overall income was much less than he had anticipated.[52]

Edwin also missed the work he performed as a judge, especially the decision-making role. He had remained active in the affairs of the Texas Bar Association and kept up his relationships with the leading lawyers in the state. In early 1895, Edwin returned to the judiciary, but not as a judge. Thanks to connections in the legal profession, as well as help from his old Peach Tree Village friend and former law partner Congressman Samuel Bronson Cooper, Edwin was appointed master of chancery by the US Court for the Southern District of the Indian Territory, which became the state of Oklahoma in 1907. Due to a massive backlog of cases, the court appointed masters of chancery to conduct hearings and then report their findings as a way to speed up the legal process. Edwin's court was located in Ardmore, Indian Territory, where he opened an office and rented a room in a boardinghouse. Dora, Will, and Will's two younger brothers remained in Houston while Edwin commuted back and forth from Ardmore. Edwin resigned from Kirby's law firm, but the two old friends continued to do business. In Ardmore, Edwin joined with a group of local businessmen to organize the Ardmore Street Railway Company, with Kirby among the investors.[53]

While Edwin was trying to make his way professionally and take care of his family's finances, his son Will was attending classes as a freshman at the Houston Normal School.

The school was housed in a temporary building while the red brick Houston Central High School was being built on Caroline Street, a few blocks away from Will's home. The city's leading newspaper, the *Houston Post*, was renting space in the Larendon Building at 1111 Congress Avenue, next door to Will's school.[54]

Gail Borden Johnson, grandson of Gail Borden Jr., who was a pioneer of the Texas newspaper industry as well as an inventor who developed the process for condensing sweetened milk, established the *Houston Evening Post* in 1880. His newspaper struggled from the start, eventually ceasing publication in 1884. In April 1885, it reappeared as the *Houston Post* after it was bought by a group of investors led by J. L. Watson. Watson, who held a majority of the stock, assumed duties as business manager and hired Colonel Rienzi M. Johnston to serve as editor. The *Post* flourished under Watson's business guidance and Johnston's journalistic skills.

As he walked to school in the mornings, Will often stopped at the Larendon Building to see the bundles of morning newspapers tumble out of a chute from the second floor to the ground. The papers were loaded on horse-drawn wagons and distributed around town, while newsboys grabbed bundles to peddle on the street. At the end of the school day, Will would head straight back to the Larendon Building and loiter around the entrance of the *Post* in the hopes of talking to the editors and reporters as they came and went. He was especially happy to meet the locally famous Marcellus E. Foster, one of the *Post*'s star reporters recruited by Colonel Johnston.[55]

Will began to spend almost as much time in front of the *Post* building as he was spending at school. He not only got to know the reporters, editors, and other staff, he also met famous people whom others could only read about in the newspaper. One was world boxing champion "Gentleman Jim" Corbett, whom a *Post* sportswriter obligingly took to Houston Central High School to visit one of Will's classes. Another reporter took Will to Houston's Grand Central Station to see the Apache leader Geronimo, who was being transferred as a prisoner from Alabama to Fort Sill in the Indian Territory. These and other incidents removed any doubt Will had about his future course in life. He knew that he did not want to study law like his father, or go to medical school like his brother Alfred. A position in one of John Henry Kirby's companies could have been arranged easily, given his family's connections. None of these possible career paths held any attraction for Will Hobby. He decided that nothing could keep him from being a newspaperman, even if that meant leaving high school before graduating.[56]

Early one morning in 1895, Will met twenty-one-year-old Alabama native A. E. "Eddie" Clarkson, cousin of publisher J. L. Watson. Eddie had a job in the *Post*'s circulation department. He and Will soon became close friends. The ever-smiling and easygoing Eddie was soon like a member of the Hobby family, often enjoying Dora Hobby's home-cooked meals at their home on La Branch. Will sometimes volunteered to run errands for Eddie and helped him with other chores around the *Post*. On Saturday afternoon, March 2, 1895, while Houstonians were celebrating Texas Independence Day, seventeen-year-old Will made his usual journey to the *Post* to visit Eddie. On that day, Clarkson persuaded Watson to offer Will a full-time job as an out-of-town circulation clerk at a salary of eight dollars a week. Will was eager to accept the offer but he needed his father's approval, which would have to wait until Edwin's next visit home.[57]

Undoubtedly aware of his son's almost daily visits to the newspaper, Edwin could not have been surprised by the job offer. Will later recalled that his father was reluctant to approve Will leaving school but finally consented when Will promised to continue his studies that coming September. Not only did Edwin understand how important this offer was to Will, he also knew the family could use the extra income. Edwin was still doing legal work for John Henry Kirby on a part-time basis and spent several weeks a year in the Indian Territory hearing cases as a master in chancery, but the country's economy had not yet rebounded from the Panic of 1893, and money was tight. Will was convinced Watson's job offer was his golden opportunity to fulfill his dream of becoming a reporter. Will was assigned to work in a tiny cubbyhole in the mail room, where he maintained the *Post*'s out-of-town circulation lists and handled complaints about delivery service. September 1895 came and went and he remained at the *Post*. Despite his promise to his father, Will later admitted that he'd had no intention of going back to school.[58]

The *Houston Post* was a great fit for young Will Hobby, but a promotion was slow to come. He remained stuck in the *Post*'s circulation department for three years. Despite his low position, Will made friends with his heroes in the newsroom, including Jim Quarles, the *Post*'s fiery legislative reporter; columnist Marcellus E. Foster, whose pen name was "MEFO"; and columnist William Sydney Porter. Editor Rienzi Johnston hired Porter in October 1895, five months after Will went to work at the paper. Mid-thirties in age, Porter had held a number of jobs, including ranch hand, clerk in the Texas General Land Office in Austin, bank teller, and editor of the short-lived *Rolling Stone* humor magazine. At the *Post*, Porter demonstrated his skills as an imaginative wordsmith whose writing exhibited a dry, understated humor. His column, at first called Tales About Town, and later Some Postscripts, quickly became one of the newspaper's most popular features. Porter worked in a small cubicle on the second floor of the Larendon Building. Will often went upstairs from his clerk's desk to visit with Porter, whom he admired and liked. He sometimes ran errands for Porter and occasionally went with him to dinner when they both worked late.[59]

One morning in June 1896, a stranger entered the front office of the *Post* and asked where he could find Mr. William Sydney Porter. Will was happy to direct him to Porter's desk upstairs. Will and his colleagues were stunned when the man walked up to Porter and declared he was under arrest for alleged embezzlement of the First National Bank in Austin. After his father-in-law posted his bail, Porter left his wife in Houston, fled to New Orleans, and wound up in Honduras. He returned to Texas a year later and was tried and convicted. After imprisonment for three years, he moved to New York City, where he wrote under the pseudonym O. Henry and became one of the most prolific and famous writers in American history.[60]

In May 1897 an event occurred that would eventually lead to Will's promotion. The newspaper's owner and publisher, J. L. Watson, died of tuberculosis. His only heir was his five-year-old son, Roy. Through his will, Watson created a trust to manage his estate's assets, including the *Houston Post*. Watson had named three men to serve as his son's trustees and to operate and manage the newspaper until his son reached the age of twenty-five: business manager G. J. Palmer, Colonel Rienzi Johnston, and prominent Houston banker Henry F. MacGregor. Colonel Johnston assumed the position of president and editor in chief of the *Post*, with Palmer taking care of business matters. MacGregor, who would later amass a fortune as a Houston real estate developer, served as treasurer.[61]

Colonel Rienzi Johnston's ascension would prove crucial to Will's future. Born in Sandersville, Georgia, in 1849, Rienzi Johnston joined the Confederate Army in his early teenage years as a drummer boy, but by war's end he was an infantryman. After the war, he worked at a newspaper in Savannah, Georgia, and then eventually made his way to Texas and became editor of the newspaper in Crockett in 1878. In his early years in Texas, Johnston was restless as a newspaper editor and publisher, moving from one town to another in a short period of time. He worked briefly for the *Austin Statesman* in 1880 before being hired as the capital correspondent for the struggling *Houston Post*. Five years later, he was appointed editor in chief of the newly resurrected *Post*. By this time, Johnston's friends were addressing him as "Colonel," a reference to the manners, dress, and opinions attributed to the stereotypical "Southern aristocratic gentleman," an image the thirty-six-year-old Johnston carefully cultivated.[62]

Will Hobby later noted that Johnston was as interested in politics as he was in journalism. Within weeks of his arrival in Houston, he began to write and publish his political views in a steady stream of strongly worded editorials that not only attracted readers in the city but also were reprinted in newspapers throughout the state and across the South. Popular interest in Johnston's editorials helped to increase the *Post*'s advertising and circulation and placed Watson's newspaper on a sound financial footing. Ross Sterling, governor of Texas in the early 1930s, recalled, "Under the editorship of Rienzi Johnston . . . the *Houston Post* played a leading role in the most memorable Texas political campaigns since Reconstruction days."[63]

By the time Will Hobby went to work at the *Post* in 1895, Johnston was an influential figure in Democratic Party affairs in Texas and the South. He was a Democratic Party "Regular," which meant that in the tumultuous campaigns of 1892 and 1896, he opposed the party's populists and vigorously supported the Democrats' conservative, business establishment faction. After delivering the keynote speech at the August 1896 Democratic State Convention in Fort Worth, Johnston used the *Post*'s editorial page as a platform from which to rally the conservative cause against the populists, who had significant support in Texas. In 1898 leaders of the Texas Democratic Party's conservative wing tried to persuade Johnston to run for lieutenant governor, but he declined, arguing that he would have more influence as editor of the *Post*. Johnston was a prominent figure in Houston's political and civic affairs. He could be found almost daily in the "old" Rice

Hotel, as he sat in his favorite chair in a prominent place at the hotel bar, lecturing his friends, associates, and hotel guests about politics and international affairs. And when the weather permitted, the Colonel would conduct his seminars while sitting in a rocking chair on the sidewalk in front of the hotel.[64]

Colonel Johnston, who knew Will's father and was a close friend of John Henry Kirby's, began to take an interest in Will and eventually became his mentor. Johnston had a reputation for spotting young men who had an affinity for politics and whom he could help develop as journalists. He knew that Will came from a politically involved family, and he was much impressed with young Hobby's energy, enthusiasm, and ambition. Soon after he took control of the *Houston Post*, the formidable Johnston promoted Will to cashier, working at the business counter and manning the cash register. A year later, Johnston placed Will in a better job in the advertising department, where he solicited ads and maintained accounts. By this time, the *Post* had moved into rented space in the McIlhenny Building at the corner of Fannin and Franklin Streets. With the Colonel's patronage, Will's future at the newspaper now appeared bright.[65]

In 1897, as Will climbed the promotional ladder at the *Post*, Edwin's work as a master of chancery in the Indian Territory had increased to such an extent that he and Dora moved to Ardmore. After his parents left Texas, Will rented a room at the Hutchins boardinghouse, within walking distance of the *Post*. His brothers Edwin and Paul, who were both employed as debt collectors, continued to live in the Hobbys' house on La Branch. This arrangement lasted less than a year. Will's father's health declined while he and Dora were in Ardmore, and they returned to Houston. Will moved back home at that point.[66]

At nine thirty on the morning of November 1, 1899, Edwin suffered a heart attack and died at his home. The judge was fifty-six years old. The family arranged for his burial in Houston's historic Glenwood Cemetery overlooking Buffalo Bayou. Rienzi Johnston was one of Edwin Hobby's pallbearers, along with some of Edwin's old legislative and judicial colleagues. Judge Hobby's passing marked the end of an era in the family's history. As the new century began, Will embarked on his own journey to business success and significant accomplishments in public service that far exceeded his father's legacy. But first, the newspaper world called.[67]

## CHAPTER 2

# NEWS AND POLITICS

At the beginning of 1900, Will was still selling ads and managing accounts for the *Houston Post*, but he yearned to be a reporter. He was living at home with his mother, Dora; grandmother Mary Pettus; and brothers Paul and Edwin. With a job at a Houston bank, Edwin was beginning a career as a banker, while Paul was working as a debt collector for the *Houston Post*. In April, Will did something unusual for an employee with his fairly low position at the newspaper. With help from his friend Eddie Clarkson, Will borrowed $1,000 (equivalent to nearly $28,000 dollars in 2019) to purchase ten shares of *Houston Post* stock from Colonel Rienzi Johnston. Will was confident that the *Post* was on a firm financial footing and that it would only continue to grow and prosper along with Houston. Will's stock purchase deeply impressed Johnston. It demonstrated Will's loyalty to the *Post* and his confidence in Johnston's stewardship.[1]

Will's initial foray into politics also caught Johnston's attention. In the winter of 1900 the campaign for mayor of Houston was a bitterly fought affair between the incumbent, urban progressive Samuel Brashear, and Irish immigrant and conservative former mayor John Thomas Browne. Brashear ultimately won reelection that April. During the campaign, Colonel Johnston, who was no progressive, harshly criticized Brashear's reform administration and praised Browne in the editorial pages of the *Post*. After the mayoral election, Brashear's supporters submitted a resolution at the Harris County Democratic Convention that called for the convention to condemn the *Houston Post* and, indirectly, Colonel Johnston for the attacks on Brashear. The losing candidate, Browne, made a motion to table the anti-*Post* resolution. In defense of his patron and the *Post*, Will spoke from the convention floor in support of Browne's motion. In the first political speech of Will's career, he argued forcefully against the Brashear resolution, pleading for party harmony. Colonel Johnston listened to Will's speech with considerable interest. He was less interested in harmony than Will, but he was impressed with Will's performance. Johnston later acknowledged the event convinced him Will might have a future in politics.[2]

With his personal financial investment in the *Houston Post* and his first public appearance as a political activist that summer of 1900, Will's year was off to a memorable start. But within a few months, two of the most monumental events in American history would occur, events that had a significant long-term impact on the city of Houston, on the *Houston Post*, and ultimately on Will himself. The first was the great hurricane that struck Galveston Island in September 1900. The second was the Spindletop oil well strike on the outskirts of Beaumont in January 1901, which ushered in the petroleum era in world history.

The hurricane that hit the upper Texas coast on Saturday morning, September 8, was the worst natural disaster in US history, killing an estimated eight thousand people and destroying or severely damaging much of the city of Galveston. It also caused major flooding and extensive damage to buildings in Houston, but because of that city's location fifty miles inland, the city escaped the catastrophic destruction and loss of life Galveston suffered. The many structures damaged in Houston included the *Post*'s building, which had a large section of its roof ripped off and several windows blown out. The storm surge from Galveston Bay flowed up Buffalo Bayou into the streets of Houston's central business district. Many streets were impassable because of downed trees, telephone poles, and fencing.[3]

Will was working at the *Post* the morning of the storm, and he had to wade through the streets in waist-high water to get to his home on La Branch Street. After he confirmed that his family was safe and the house was largely intact, he returned to the *Post* that evening to help get the next day's paper out. He found the entire staff had gathered in a dry area in the building to put together the next day's edition, which was dominated entirely by news reports of storm damage in Houston and various towns in the greater Houston region. Ominously scarce in those reports, however, was information about conditions in Galveston. The four bridges connecting the mainland to the island were destroyed, and all telephone and telegraph lines had been cut by the storm. Documentable information was sketchy at best, but there was the certainty that the city had been devastated, with high loss of life.

The journalists at the *Post* acquired their first detailed information about conditions in Galveston early on Sunday morning, when to their surprise some eyewitnesses arrived at the building. One was Tom South, the *Post*'s freelance correspondent in Galveston. South arrived "bare footed and drenched to the skin." Based on these eyewitness reports, the *Post* was able to publish one of the first newspaper accounts of the disaster. The headline was appropriately apocalyptic: "THE FATE OF GALVESTON: The Most Appalling Calamity in the History of Modern Times Has Befallen Galveston." A day after this first account, M. E. Foster and a team of *Post* reporters traveled by steamer from Texas City to Galveston, where they set up headquarters in a downtown building and sent a steady stream of news dispatches back to Houston.[4]

Although Will was not yet a member of the *Post*'s news staff, he was in the middle of the chaotic and exciting effort to get the Galveston storm edition out to the newspaper's readers. If he had any doubts about his goal to become a news reporter, they were certainly erased by the great Galveston storm. The disaster had another, although indirect, impact on Will Hobby's life. The destruction caused by the storm convinced a number of Galveston's important businessmen to move to the safer shelter of Houston. The resulting boost to Houston's economy and population growth meant the ultimate end of Galveston as a major urban center. And as Houston grew and prospered, so did the *Post* and Will's career prospects.

On January 10, 1901, four months after the Galveston hurricane, petroleum engineer Anthony Lucas struck oil at Spindletop Hill south of the town of Beaumont, located eighty miles east of Houston. The discovery well immediately produced one hundred thousand barrels of oil a day, not only making Beaumont a boomtown almost overnight but also transforming the economy of the city of Houston, which in turn expanded the business of the *Houston Post*. Colonel Johnston sent M. E. Foster to Beaumont to cover the Spindletop story. Foster caught oil boom fever and invested a week's salary to buy an oil lease option, which he soon sold for a $5,000 profit. Within weeks of the oil strike, Will Hobby's desk was covered with ads placed by newly organized companies, many of them "wildcatters," seeking buyers for their stock. As advertising sales increased, the number of pages in the issues of the *Houston Post* nearly trebled and its profits soared.[5]

Will's skilled handling of the new source of advertising was duly noted by business manager G. J. Palmer and, more important, Colonel Johnston, who wanted to expand the *Post*'s business coverage as a result of the oil discovery. In August 1901, Johnston asked city editor M. E. Foster to promote the twenty-two-year-old Will to be the *Post*'s commercial editor and reporter for business and market news at a salary of $22.50 a week. Will had finally achieved his goal to join the news staff. Working from a rolltop desk in his cubicle at the *Post*, Will covered the development of the Spindletop oil field and other discoveries nearby.[6]

Will's new job came during an exciting time in the economic history of Houston and southeast Texas. He reported on the cotton business, which still dominated the local economy, and on the expansion of the area's railroads and the establishment of new banks. Will interviewed the region's leading bankers, railroad executives, and important oil company entrepreneurs, including Joseph S. Cullinan, Howard Hughes Sr., and Walter B. Sharp, all of whom lived in Houston during this period of rapid economic growth driven by the oil discoveries. Will also made frequent trips to Beaumont to cover the founding of such future corporate giants as Gulf Oil, the Texas Company (Texaco), and—of special interest to him—the Humble Oil Company, whose founders included Ross Sterling, the grandson of Peach Tree Village's "Uncle Billy" Sterling. Will's interview with Ross Sterling gave him the opportunity to renew his connections with the Sterling family and to get to know Ross, who had grown up in Anahuac after his father left Peach Tree Village. This connection with Sterling would later play a significant role in Will's professional career.[7]

During this exciting time in Houston's history, President William McKinley paid an official visit to the city on May 3, 1901. McKinley, a Republican who had recently been inaugurated to his second term, was on a goodwill railroad tour of many of the Southern states he had not carried in the election of 1900. Will was among the thousands of Houstonians who gathered on the city's streets to welcome McKinley as he rode in a parade through the business district accompanied by Texas governor Joe Sayers. It was the first chance Will had to see a sitting president of the United States. McKinley shocked white Houstonians when he briefly stopped his parade to accept flowers and hear a speech of praise from representatives of African American churches in the city. After the parade, Will was part of the *Post*'s team of reporters who covered McKinley's speech in the city auditorium, which attracted an audience of more than five thousand people. Perhaps as a counterpoint to his special visit with some of Houston's African American religious leaders and their congregants, McKinley applauded the former Confederate States for their strong support of the recently ended war with Spain. After his speech, McKinley departed for Austin, San Antonio, El Paso, and points west. On September 6, during his visit to the World Exposition in Buffalo, New York, McKinley was shot by an assassin and eventually died from his wounds.[8]

In August, M. E. Foster gave Will an assignment that led to his second promotion that year. Aware that Will's father had worked for John Henry Kirby, Foster asked Will to cover a testimonial dinner in honor of Kirby's impressive business and civic achievements. Foster also asked Will to write a biographical profile of Kirby. Will was delighted to get the assignment to interview his father's former law partner, and he knew he would have Kirby's full cooperation. Undoubtedly, Colonel Johnston played a role in Will getting the Kirby assignment. Johnston, who was a friend and political ally of both John Henry Kirby and Kirby's mentor, Bronson Cooper, served as the toastmaster for the testimonial dinner. The colorful Kirby, whose business had survived the economic depression of the mid-1890s, had formed one of the biggest lumber companies in the South and was organizing the Houston Oil Company, at that time the largest company ever chartered in Texas. In 1895, he had founded a town in Jasper County that took the name Kirbyville in his honor. He had made $1 million through real estate investments on Houston's Main Street. The tall, blue-eyed, ruddy-cheeked Kirby was a gregarious and brash man. He lived in one of Houston's landmark mansions, where he hosted lavish parties while wearing a white suit with a red carnation pinned to his lapel, looking the part of an antebellum plantation owner.[9]

Will later recalled that his coverage of the dinner and his profile of Kirby was the biggest story he wrote while business editor. The *Post*'s headline for Will's article about the dinner, which was held at the Rice Hotel and attended by three hundred dignitaries, declared it "the greatest banquet ever given in Texas." Kirby gave Will a candid interview full of details that he had not previously discussed in public. Will wrote that Kirby's achievements were "the triumph of a big mind, an indomitable will, and a tireless energy, and are an encouraging example to the youth of the land that merit can and will win!"

*John Henry Kirby in the early 1900s.*

Impressed with Will's informative and entertaining story about Houston's most prominent citizen, Colonel Johnston and M. E. Foster gave it four full pages in the *Post*. The positive reaction the *Post* story received from its readers benefitted both Foster and Will. Johnston promoted Foster from city manager to managing editor of the *Post*, and Will was given much wider responsibilities as a general assignments reporter, with a welcome boost in salary.[10]

M. E. Foster's tenure as managing editor was short-lived, however. Foster held progressive political views that inevitably led to serious clashes with the conservative Rienzi Johnston. Foster supported women's suffrage, prohibition, and "clean city government" reform, the issues dominating the progressive agenda. He also had a sympathetic view of labor unions. Johnston opposed progressive reforms and disliked unions. Foster resigned after he had a heated falling-out with Johnston only two months after becoming the *Post*'s managing editor. Foster used the money he had made from his Spindletop oil field gamble and other investments to buy the moribund *Houston Herald*, which he renamed the *Houston Chronicle*. The *Chronicle*'s first issue appeared on the afternoon of October 14, 1901. Foster's new paper became the progressive voice of Houston and quickly became a serious rival to the *Post*.[11]

At the beginning of 1902 Colonel Johnston hired antiprohibitionist Clarence Ousley to replace Foster as managing editor. Ousley had been editor of the *Galveston News* and then owner and editor of the *Galveston Evening Tribune*, but he had lost everything in the Galveston storm, including his home and newspaper plant. Colonel Johnston made Will assistant managing editor, and Will became Johnston's protégé and "personal companion." The twenty-four-year-old Will became something like an adopted son to the grizzled old newspaper publisher. He was a frequent visitor to the Johnstons' spacious family home in the city's newly developed Westmoreland Addition, an exclusive neighborhood where many of Houston's most prominent citizens had purchased houses. Johnston often invited Will to keep him company at his residence during the occasional times when Johnston's wife, Mary Elizabeth, was away from Houston.[12]

Will not only became Colonel Johnston's close friend and professional associate, he also became his political confidant. In June 1902, Colonel Johnston arranged for Will to be appointed to the Platform Committee at the Harris County Democratic Party Convention, where under Johnston's tutelage Will helped write the convention's resolutions. Will and Colonel Johnston were also selected to be the county's delegates to the state convention in Galveston, where Johnston, who was also a member of the Democratic National Committee, was among the leaders of the antisuffrage and antiprohibition forces.[13]

A year after taking the job at the *Post*, Clarence Ousley resigned and moved to Fort Worth to start a newspaper called the *Fort Worth Record*. When Ousley departed at the beginning of 1903, Colonel Johnston appointed Will the *Post*'s interim managing editor until he could find a permanent replacement for Ousley. Will helped Johnston oversee the move of the *Post*'s offices and printing equipment to a building it purchased at Travis Street and Texas Avenue. Will, now in his midtwenties, was eager to prove to Colonel Johnston that he could perform the managing editor's job. His age, however, worked against him. As longtime *Post* editorial editor Ed Kilman noted many years later, "[Johnston] wasn't going to entrust the managing editorship to [Will] permanently until and unless he proved himself well qualified for the important job."[14]

Instead of Will, Colonel Johnston hired the much more experienced New England native George McLelland Bailey as the *Post*'s managing editor. Bailey, a forty-year-old

Washington correspondent for the *Galveston News*, was a skilled editorial writer with a special talent for imaginative word use. Despite his initial disappointment, Will was pleased when Colonel Johnston assigned Bailey control over the *Post*'s editorial page, including writing the newspaper's editorials, which was Bailey's preference. Will was appointed city editor with responsibility for managing the newsroom. In effect, Will was the managing editor without the formal title. Will was finally in the position he had wanted since he went to work for the *Post* in 1895.[15]

Will Hobby and George Bailey made a good team. Will was the news hawk, while Bailey served as Colonel Johnston's conservative political voice. He issued a steady stream of editorials denouncing prohibitionists, suffragists, and Republicans and supporting states' rights and white supremacy, carefully couched in paternal terms. Bailey and Colonel Johnston made it clear that the *Post* supported the government's imposition of Jim Crow–era segregation ordinances, such as those enforcing racial segregation on Houston's streetcars. The *Post* also supported the passage of the poll tax in 1904, which effectively removed 7,500 citizens—mostly black—from the city's voting rolls. Colonel Johnston and

*Col. Rienzi M. Johnston, 1913.*

Will were both admirers of US senator Joseph Bailey of Texas, a vocal white supremacist. In a speech made in Brownwood in 1904, Senator Bailey criticized President Theodore Roosevelt for inviting African American educator Booker T. Washington to the White House, declaring, "I believe more in the purity of the Anglo-Saxon race than I do in the principles of democracy." Will Hobby left little public record documenting his position on these Jim Crow laws, but he was a man of his time, place, and culture, and it can be assumed that he shared Colonel Johnston's views on race.[16]

With Colonel Johnston's encouragement, Will continued to be politically active.

Along with future Harris County judge Chester Bryan, Will helped organize the Young Men's Democratic Club of Houston, for which he served as president. In 1904 he was again elected a delegate to the Texas Democratic Party's state convention. Will had powerful friends who played leading roles at that meeting, including Congressman Samuel Bronson Cooper and John Henry Kirby. One of his new friends was Frank Andrews, an influential Houston attorney who was chairman of the Democratic Party's state executive committee. Andrews was close to both Cooper and Colonel Johnston, and he was Kirby's lawyer. He appointed Will secretary of the party's executive committee after Will had been one of the leaders of the effort to secure the chairman's post for Andrews. The convention, which was held in Houston, also reelected Colonel Johnston to a second two-year term as the Texas Democratic national committeeman and renominated Colonel Johnston's friend, Joe Bailey, for US Senate. The convention completed its business by declaring its support for Alton Parker as the Democratic presidential nominee.[17]

Bronson Cooper chaired the Texas delegation to the Democratic Party's national convention in St. Louis, held during the much-celebrated 1904 World's Fair. The party nominated Judge Parker as its presidential candidate, but the incumbent Republican president Theodore Roosevelt easily defeated Parker in the general election. Although Will Hobby supported Parker, he wasn't terribly upset by Teddy Roosevelt's victory. During the Spanish-American War, Roosevelt had stopped in Houston with his famed "Rough Riders" during a trip on the Southern Pacific Railroad from San Antonio to Tampa, Florida, from where they would embark for Cuba. Will, who was still a circulation clerk at the *Post*, went to the train depot with *Post* reporters to see Roosevelt and his cavalry. They were pleased that Roosevelt took a few minutes during the stop to give a brief but characteristically enthusiastic speech about the war. Will was much impressed with what he saw of Lieutenant Colonel Roosevelt at the time.[18]

On August 15, tragedy struck the Hobby family. Will's twenty-three-year-old brother, Paul, died in Beaumont of a typhoid infection while he was working for John Henry Kirby's lumber company. Will and his sister Mary were with Paul at the time of his death, and Will accompanied Paul's body back to Houston on the Southern Pacific train. Will's brothers, Dr. Alfred Hobby and Edwin, came from Dallas for the funeral. Edwin had recently moved to Dallas, where he took a position with the Gaston National Bank. Will was still living with his mother, Dora, in the house on La Branch. After Paul's death, however, Will and his mother moved to a house a few blocks away at 1712 Capitol Street. His sister Mary, who had a job as a stenographer for John Henry Kirby's lumber company, moved in with her mother and brother.[19]

During the winter and early spring of 1905, Will continued to work as the *Post*'s unofficial managing editor while George Bailey was busy with the editorial sections of the paper. In April, however, Will finally had his opportunity to prove to Colonel Johnston that he was qualified to have the actual title of managing editor.

Will occasionally worked late into the night manning the newsroom night desk. On the evening of April 24, 1905, he answered a telephone call from a man who identified himself as a railroad dispatcher at the Southern Pacific depot in Houston. The dispatcher told Will that he had received a wire sent on the Southern Pacific Railroad's closed communication system from a fellow dispatcher at the station in Hempstead, Texas, located about fifty miles northwest of Houston. The wire stated there had been "one hell of a shooting." Congressman John Pinckney had been killed, and at least three other men were dead or dying. The dispatcher told Will that he was giving him the scoop on the story because he was an avid reader of the *Houston Post* but that the call had to remain confidential.[20]

Will was stunned by the news, but he immediately understood the magnitude of the story. He knew Congressman Pinckney from his work with the Harris County Democratic Party. Will called the Southern Pacific depot office in Hempstead, and the dispatcher confirmed the story and admitted that he was the person who had called the *Post*. Hobby then called the Hempstead telephone exchange. The operator confirmed the report and gave him additional information. Will tried to call some of his friends in Hempstead but was unable to reach anyone. He then telephoned his best reporter, Pat Daugherty, and told him to go to Hempstead as fast as he could. Hobby called other staff members to come to the office to check the files for a picture and biographical sketch of Pinckney and to contact anyone they knew in Hempstead to gather more information.

At 3:00 a.m., Daugherty called Will from Hempstead and confirmed that Congressman Pinckney, his brother Thomas, a Hempstead lawyer named H. M. Brown, and a farmer named J. E. Mills were all dead. Two men were wounded, including Pinckney's secretary, R. E. Tompkins. Daugherty told Will that the congressman, who lived in Hempstead and was an ardent prohibitionist, had tried to stop a fight at the Waller County Courthouse. He and other prohibitionists were attempting to pass a resolution calling for Governor Samuel Lanham to send the Texas Rangers to enforce a recently enacted local-option prohibition law that was being ignored by local bar owners. The fight started when attorney H. M. Brown hit Pinckney's secretary, R. E. Tompkins, in the head with his pistol while the secretary was speaking at the courtroom podium in favor of the resolution. Brown's attack initiated a brawl, which quickly escalated into a gunfight. Brown's son, Roland, shot the unarmed Pinckney. The congressman's secretary shot Roland's father, H. M. Brown, and then was shot by someone else. Roland Brown also caught a bullet, but he survived.

Will took his notes from Daugherty's report and wrote the news story, which he sent to press at 6:00 a.m. He devoted the entire front page to the sensational news, which gave the *Post* a major scoop. He also ensured that his delivery boys got the paper to the train depot as rapidly as possible to distribute the *Post* throughout southeast Texas. Will took advantage of his reporter being the first on the scene and mined the exclusive information Daugherty had gathered to keep the story on the front page for several days. For one edition, Will directed the *Post*'s illustrator to sketch a drawing of the shooting scene and a diagram indicating where each body had fallen and the locations on the bodies where the bullets had hit. The *Post* sold thousands of extra newspapers the day the story broke and for several days afterward. The paper also enjoyed an increase in the number of its subscriptions. Many years later, Will looked back on the Pinckney affair as one of his greatest newsbreaks. After a sensational trial, the murderers were acquitted. As a result of the episode, Hempstead was known for many years as "Six-Shooter Junction."[21]

Will's skillful management of the Hempstead story convinced Colonel Johnston that the time had come to give him the official title of managing editor. Will had finally attained his professional goal, something he could only dream about back in the days when he would hang out in front of the *Post* building on his way to and from school. George Bailey retained his job as the editorial page editor and columnist. Johnston also promoted Pat Daugherty to city editor. One of Will's longtime colleagues in the newspaper business, Hugh Nugent Fitzgerald, later wrote that Will "climbed the . . . ladder under the tutelage or training of Col. Johnston. He filled every desk in the editorial department of the *Post* until he became managing editor. He must have filled the positions . . . most acceptably, for Col. Johnston was a glutton for work and he expected the members of his staff to fill their assignments to the very letter of instruction."[22]

Will hit his stride as editor, attracting widespread attention with his vigorous coverage and imaginative presentation of major stories. In a front-page story on March 4, 1906, Will announced that the popular former Texas governor James S. Hogg had died the day before in Houston. A few years earlier, Will had met Hogg during a visit Hogg made to the *Post* to see his friend Colonel Rienzi Johnston. The *Post*'s front page was dominated by an eye-catching graphic of black crepe wrapped around a map of Texas. Will allocated three pages to the story inside that day's paper, which was another high-selling edition. In October, Will's coverage of and involvement in a sensational debate staged in Houston's city auditorium between Senator Joseph Bailey and former Texas attorney general Martin McNulty Crane also added to his growing stature as a newspaper editor and political activist in southeast Texas.[23]

Native Mississippian Joe Bailey was an attorney in Gainesville, Texas, who was elected to US Congress in 1890. Famed as a spellbinding orator and skilled parliamentary tactician, Bailey was one of the most popular as well as most controversial political figures in Texas during the 1890s and the first twelve years of the twentieth century. In 1900, after serving two terms as the Democratic minority leader in the House of Representatives, the Texas Legislature elected Bailey to the US Senate. Bailey was an archconservative who opposed nearly all of the reforms associated with the progressive movement, especially prohibition, women's suffrage, and the referendum. Will and his patrons Bronson Cooper, Rienzi Johnston, and John Henry Kirby were among Senator Bailey's political allies. As Will noted many years later, Colonel Johnston "worshipped at [Bailey's] shrine." Kirby was especially close to Bailey, who represented Kirby in a controversial legal case in which Bailey earned $149,000 in legal fees.[24]

The reason for the debate between Bailey and Crane in Houston in 1906 was the revelation that Bailey had worked in Texas as a lobbyist for the Waters-Pierce Oil Company while serving as a member of Congress. In 1897, when Martin McNulty Crane was attorney general of Texas, he sued the Waters-Pierce Oil Company in state district court, charging that the company was secretly controlled by John D. Rockefeller's Standard Oil Company trust. Texas antitrust laws banned Standard Oil from operating in the state. Although Waters-Pierce lost the case, it continued to do business in Texas after claiming it had broken ties to Standard Oil. When its permit was set to expire in 1900, the company hired Congressman Bailey to lobby key public officials to renew the permit, which was done in 1901. The negative popular reaction to the permit renewal eventually led to a legislative investigation of Bailey's role in the affair as the attorney for Waters-Pierce. The investigation determined that Bailey's fee was proper and not a conflict of interest.[25]

In 1906, the Texas Attorney General's Office discovered that Waters-Pierce remained under the control of Standard Oil, contrary to its previous claims. Attorney General Robert Davidson not only filed a new antitrust suit against the company, he also reopened the corruption case against Bailey, alleging that Waters-Pierce had paid Bailey a $100,000 retainer to help the company circumvent the state's antitrust laws. In August 1906 the state Democratic convention ignored these charges and renominated Bailey for a second term in the Senate. Nevertheless, Davidson's lawsuit threatened to derail Bailey's reelection by the Texas Legislature. In October, Bailey embarked on a statewide speaking tour to defend his reputation. It was this tour that took him to Houston in October 1906, where he agreed to debate his old nemesis, Martin McNulty Crane, about the charges against him.[26]

Will and Colonel Johnston saw Bailey's appearance in Houston as a potential boost for his reelection campaign. They also understood that a debate between the fiery Bailey and the former attorney general who had filed the original lawsuit against Waters-Pierce would be a spectacle that would generate widespread popular interest and sell newspapers. Will used the pages of the *Houston Post* to promote the event, dramatically declaring that it would be the "debate of the century."[27]

Colonel Johnston was one of the three members of the Bailey debate committee, while Will helped with arrangement details. Both men were among the leaders of the delegation that cheered for Bailey when he arrived in his private Pullman car at the Houston train depot early on the afternoon of October 6. The welcoming party was a who's who of the Houston civic and business establishment, including John Henry Kirby; upcoming young entrepreneur Jesse Holman Jones; former congressman Tom Ball and his law partner, Frank Andrews; influential attorney and banker James A. Baker Sr.; former mayor O. T. Holt; and former state legislator and corporate lawyer Jacob Wolters. Johnston and Ball accompanied Bailey in a large horse-drawn carriage that took them from the depot to the Rice Hotel, where a large crowd had gathered to greet the senator.[28]

Bailey was considered to be the finest orator in Congress, with some claiming him the equal of William Jennings Bryan. Historian Claude Bowers observed that in an era when politicians were judged almost as much by their oratorical talents as by the positions they took on issues, "no man drew greater crowds [than Bailey] to the gallery on the announcement that he would speak. His voice was as melodious as a fine organ. His eloquence was both powerful and persuasive." Bailey's reputation and Will's promotion of the debate worked; the auditorium crowd was standing room only. Will hired a dozen public stenographers to work in shifts to record every word of the debate, and he used newsboys to deliver the transcripts to the *Post*'s rewrite editors in the city room. The front and four additional pages were reserved for the story. He also assigned the *Post*'s artist to make sketches of the debaters. Will's authorized biographer, James Clark, later claimed, "Hobby had organized and directed coverage that represented one of the major feats of Texas journalism." Although Clark's assessment was an obvious exaggeration, Will's management of the news coverage was impressive.[29]

The event began late because of a squabble between Bailey and Crane about the order of program. Bailey eventually agreed to let Crane open and close the event. Crane opened with the charge that John Henry Kirby had paid Senator Bailey $225,000 to lobby the federal government for help with some of his projects and that the senator made a large profit from selling Kirby's lumber company bonds to the railroads. Bailey admitted that he had worked as Kirby's legal counsel and that he had been paid for the job, as any hardworking American would expect. Bailey had agreed to let Crane make the concluding statement of the event only if no time limit would be set for their remarks. It soon became apparent why Bailey wanted no time restriction. It allowed him to drone on for several hours until past midnight, giving up the stage only after many members of the exhausted audience had filed out of the auditorium. Crane's closing statement was made to an almost empty auditorium.[30]

In his account of the debate in the next day's *Houston Post*, Will declared Bailey to be the clear winner. He made no attempt to be objective. The headline announced, "Bailey Acquitted Himself Well in the Debate with Crane." Will also stressed, with another headline, how magnanimous Bailey had been in allowing Crane to open and close: "Bailey Conceded All to the Opposition." Written in the exaggerated manner of the day, the story declared, "Senator Bailey has come before the largest audience ever assembled for a political meeting in this state, has met his accusers, has replied to them in detail, has proved that some who charge him are not blameless in their own lives. He has answered slander with a statement of facts . . . and the people there believed him. The people . . . have indorsed [*sic*] him." Marcellus Foster's *Houston Chronicle* saw the event differently. Foster was an anti-Bailey man, which was one reason he and Colonel Johnston had split. He praised Crane's performance, conceding nothing to Bailey.[31]

Bailey survived this controversy. The legislative investigation of his relationship with Waters-Pierce concluded Bailey had violated no laws but that his actions raised major ethical issues. Nevertheless, the legislature returned him to the US Senate in January 1907. In the state's antitrust suit, however, the court ruled that the Waters-Pierce Company had violated Texas's antitrust laws. The court also canceled the company's permit to do business in the state and penalized it with a $1,623,000 fine. The Waters-Pierce affair plagued Bailey for the remainder of his career. Uncomfortable in an increasingly progressive, pro-women's-suffrage, and prohibitionist Democratic Party, Bailey eventually resigned from the Senate in 1913, while remaining politically influential.[32]

The *Post*'s coverage of the Bailey-Crane debate brought much attention in southeast Texas to Will's work as an editor, and it was widely noted in Texas newspaper circles. Will's rising status in Houston and his close friendship with John Henry Kirby were highlighted in November 1906 when Will attended the gala wedding of Kirby's daughter Bess May at Christ Episcopal Church. The *Post*'s coverage of the wedding, the city's social event of the year, made a point of noting that Will gave Kirby's daughter a "handsomely bound" family Bible for a wedding gift, one that "brought forth expressions of tender appreciation" from the bride when it was unwrapped.[33]

Will's success as managing editor attracted the attention of a group of lawyers and businessmen in Beaumont. In May 1907, Walter Crawford, a Beaumont attorney and political activist, took the Southern Pacific passenger service from Beaumont to Houston to meet with Will in his office at the *Post*. Crawford had graduated from the University of Texas Law School in 1894 and moved to Beaumont to practice law. He and Will had worked together on the state Democratic executive committee. Crawford and four other prominent Beaumont citizens owned Beaumont's morning newspaper, the *Enterprise*, which they had rescued from bankruptcy in 1905. The newspaper, established in 1880, was not competing well with the city's afternoon paper, the *Beaumont Journal*. It had also suffered from the faltering economy in Beaumont resulting from the decline in production at Spindletop.[34]

Crawford surprised Will by making him an attractive business proposition. Crawford and his partners had purchased the *Enterprise* because they saw it as a bargain and a potentially good investment, but they had no interest in managing a newspaper. They also felt that its current editor was not up to the task of competing with the *Journal*. Crawford had traveled to Houston not only to offer Will the job of managing editor of the *Enterprise* but also to offer him half ownership of the company, with an opportunity eventually to own all of it. They offered half of the *Enterprise*'s stock to Will at a lower price than they had paid. Crawford also promised Will a starting monthly salary of $200, which was higher than his pay at the *Post*.[35]

Will was pleased with Crawford's generous offer. He thanked him and said that he needed to think it over. Will immediately arranged a meeting with Rienzi Johnston to tell him about the offer and to seek his advice. Will was flattered by Crawford's comments, but he was reluctant to leave the *Post*, which had been his professional home for twelve years. He halfway hoped Johnston would talk him into staying at the *Post*. Will later recalled Johnston's words: "You know how much I'd hate to lose you, son, but you have a good opportunity here. In time I think you'd succeed to my place, but I hope it would be a good long time. You might reach the top more quickly on the *Enterprise* and maybe make more money." Will also believed that Colonel Johnston liked the idea of having his protégé and political ally running a daily newspaper in Beaumont. Will received the same advice from John Henry Kirby, whose timber empire and oil holdings surrounded Beaumont. Kirby could certainly see the potential advantages for his business and political interests with Will running the *Enterprise*.[36]

There was also a personal reason why Will found Crawford's offer attractive. The city was well known to Will because his father's old friend Congressman Bronson Cooper and his family lived there. Bronson and his son, Sam Jr., had a law practice in the city. The younger Cooper was also Beaumont's city attorney. Perhaps more important, Will was attracted to the Coopers' oldest daughter, Willie, who was still living with her parents and whom he had known since childhood. Will had traveled frequently to Beaumont to visit the Coopers, especially Willie. In addition, Will had covered business developments in the Beaumont area for the *Post*.[37]

Because of the strong encouragement from his patrons Johnston and Kirby, Will's friendship with Willie Cooper, and the realization that this was a golden opportunity for him to run his own newspaper at the young age of twenty-nine, Will eagerly accepted the offer. As promised, Crawford and his partners sold Will 50 percent of the *Enterprise* stock. On June 11, the *Beaumont Enterprise* announced that new management would soon be revealed. Five days later, the *Enterprise* published the news that Will Hobby had taken the position of managing editor, with "full control of the publication of the paper."[38]

As Will busily made arrangements to move to Beaumont, his mother, Dora, and his sister Mary, who was still working for John Henry Kirby, relocated to a house at 1104 Chartres Street in Houston. Will's sister Laura also moved in with her mother and Mary. Before Will left for Beaumont, his colleagues at the *Houston Post* gave him a silver cup with his initials engraved on the front as a going-away present. As a formal send-off, Rienzi Johnston hosted a "thank you and good luck" dinner at what was then the top restaurant in Houston, Café Sauter, at Travis and Preston Streets. The next day, Will boarded the eastbound Southern Pacific train to Beaumont, where he would fulfill his dream of being a newspaper owner.[39]

# CHAPTER 3

# THE BEAUMONT ENTERPRISE

Will Hobby arrived at the new Southern Pacific passenger station in Beaumont on June 7, 1907, after a three-hour train ride from Houston. First settled in 1835 on the west bank of the Neches, Beaumont was a small, sleepy lumber and rice mill town of about nine thousand people when oil was struck at Spindletop Hill in 1901. That oil strike set off an unprecedented economic boom in Beaumont and the adjoining Gulf Coast area. Almost overnight, Beaumont became, at least temporarily, the oil capital of the world. Money and people soon flowed into Beaumont as well as oil, the latter at a rate of one hundred thousand barrels a day. The boom spread to the Piney Woods of East Texas when wildcat drillers struck oil in the Saratoga and Sour Lake fields, both less than forty miles northeast of Beaumont. During the three-year period after the Spindletop strike, the city's population reached a peak of fifty thousand. By 1904, however, production from Spindletop and from the other fields with shallow wells began to fall dramatically and the economy stalled. Beaumont's population dropped by more than half. By the time Will moved to the city, its population had fallen to approximately twenty thousand. This economic decline was a major reason behind the *Beaumont Enterprise*'s receivership.[1]

By outward appearances, however, Beaumont—which its civic boosters promoted as the "Queen City of the Neches"—seemed to be a thriving and prosperous town in 1907. The Spindletop boom had enlarged the central business district with a number of substantial brick and stone structures three and four stories tall, which gave the city a much more urbane appearance than other cities in Texas with similar populations. The six-story Perlstein Building, the city's first "skyscraper," was under construction on Pearl Street. Three hotels that predated the Spindletop discovery dominated the area around the train depot. The largest was the Crosby Hotel, considered the finest in southeast Texas; its customers, including Will Hobby, who had stayed there many times while covering Beaumont for the *Houston Post*, thought it might be the finest in the state.

The Crosby Hotel's Acme café and bar, advertised as "a gentleman's resort frequented by the better class of people," was favored by Beaumont's leading businessmen, who gathered there to exchange information and make deals. Jake Nathan's Department Store ("Nathan Sells for Less"), a two-story structure located across from the train station, was the town's largest clothing store. Jake Nathan would become one of Will's most important advertising clients. Electric-powered streetcars rolled on several miles of steel track through the central business district and out to the Spindletop oil field. New houses for the middle and upper classes, including the impressive McFaddin-Ward mansion, lined the streets extending from the downtown area. Keith Park, where popular open-air concerts were held in the summer at the circular bandstand and where political candidates spoke and held rallies, was the center of much of the city's outdoor social life.[2]

John Henry Kirby owned and operated three large lumber mills strung along the Neches riverfront near the Beaumont docks and the Southern Pacific Railroad depot. The mills, which employed a total of one thousand workers, were shipping out four hundred million board feet of lumber annually to customers worldwide. South of the river docks, on the west bank of the Neches, the Sisters of Charity of the Incarnate Word had built the city's hospital, Hotel Dieu, with wood beams donated by an East Texas lumberman. Farther down the Neches River, the Security Oil Company's refinery operated twenty-four hours, seven days a week. The refinery employed 250 people, many of whom lived in the company's barracks or its boardinghouse near the refinery. Surrounded by several thousand acres of rice fields, Beaumont promoters could also boast of having the three largest rice mills in the country.[3]

Beaumont's leading citizens were optimistic about its future. Even with the economy struggling, the city's voters had recently passed a bond issue to build two modern public schools, primarily to serve the children of oil field workers. Will Hobby was quick to share that optimism, and he was determined that his newspaper would play a key role in breaking Beaumont out of its economic slump. Will embraced the idea that one of the most important roles the newspaper could play was that of active and vocal promoter of the economic interests of the city and surrounding region.

Urban boosterism, instead of investigative reporting, was the prevailing ethos of newspaper publishers during the late nineteenth and early twentieth centuries, especially in the relatively new towns west of the Mississippi River. Boosterism was seen as one of the essential strategies for a city to create business opportunity and wealth. The idea was to attract railroads; to establish and sponsor fairs, exhibitions, and pageants to advertise regional products and build tourism; to improve streets and utilities to enhance business operations; and, in the case of towns near water, to dredge ship channels and harbors to create ports. The main goal was to attract more residents, which would improve the local real estate industry, increase property values, promote the construction business, and expand the tax base.[4]

Will Hobby also knew that his newspaper's survival depended on advertising from local businessmen, a strong motivation for him to give allegiance to the prevailing

*Postcard bird's-eye view of Broadway Street in Beaumont, 1908.*

economic order. Will had been well educated about the role of the newspaper as a city promoter during his years at the *Houston Post*, and he was skilled at using his newspaper for that purpose. As John Henry Kirby explained to one of Beaumont's most powerful business leaders, "[Will] is very anxious to have his newspaper reflect the sound business sentiment of Beaumont and be at all times in harmony with her broad-gauged and public-spirited citizens." In turn, Will hoped Kirby would be a frequent visitor to Beaumont, "as it always does me good and I hardly think it necessary for me to add that when I can render you any service here, I am subject to your commands."[5]

As he settled into his office in the *Enterprise*'s three-story building on Mulberry Street, Will outlined his plans for the paper in meetings with his investors, banker A. L. Williams, furniture merchant B. Deutser, attorney and former state senator Robert Greer, and insurance agent and city alderman P. A. Heisig. Will also had discussions with Beaumont's leading business, civic, and political leaders, including First National Bank president Colonel W. S. Davidson, wealthy land developer and oilman W. P. McFaddin, businessman and investor "Captain" William Wiess, attorney Leon Sonfield, Sun Oil Company executive and chamber of commerce president J. Edgar Pew, and railroad developer R. C. Duff. Will wanted to know how these prominent citizens would define the city's most important development needs, which the *Enterprise* could promote. Walter Crawford, who served on the board of directors of Beaumont's Gulf National Bank, was Will's initial connection to this influential group.[6]

These local business elites convinced Will that dredging the Neches River through

Sabine Lake to give Beaumont shipping direct access to the Gulf of Mexico was the city's most pressing need. A deep channel would make Beaumont a major distribution center for southeast Texas and southwest Louisiana, thus linking the city directly to the economy of its surrounding region. Will quickly realized that he and his newspaper could play a key role in the promotion of this dredging project, which would enhance the reputation of the *Beaumont Enterprise* in the business community and, hopefully, attract more advertising. If successful, the project would also greatly boost the region's economy, which would increase the newspaper's circulation and produce even more advertising revenue. Will's decision to become directly involved in the deepwater port project, however, would eventually have an unintended result. It would help make him the lieutenant governor of Texas.

The catastrophic hurricane of 1900 had devastated Galveston, but Beaumont still faced strong business competition from Port Arthur, founded only twelve years earlier by railroad developer and oilman Arthur Stilwell, for whom the city was named. Port Arthur had completed a ship canal in 1899 with funds invested by Stilwell's private company. Houston, located on Buffalo Bayou, and Orange, situated on the Sabine River, had plans to build their own ports and shipping infrastructure. Beaumont's business establishment understood that the city had to move as quickly as possible to dredge the Neches, build an inland seaport, and establish the city as the terminus of rail lines carrying oil, timber, and rice.[7]

The citizens of Beaumont had dreamed of a ship channel since the 1850s, but it was too expensive a project to be supported privately. The city's docks and wharfs on the Neches River were able to accommodate barges and small boats with shallow drafts that could transport shipments of lumber, rice, and oil to Sabine Lake, into which the Neches emptied before reaching the Gulf. But Sabine Lake had filled with centuries of silt until only three feet of draft remained for vessels, restricting the size of ships that could serve Beaumont. Without a water transportation alternative, railroads were able to charge higher than standard rates for shipping out of Beaumont, which was the terminus for bulk shipments of lumber from East Texas, cotton and rice from nearby farms, and oil from the new fields. Cheaper transportation rates were essential if Beaumont and its surrounding industries and farms were going to be competitive.

A serious effort to secure federal funds to dredge a channel to reach deep water began in the late 1890s after Bronson Cooper was elected to represent Texas's Second District in Congress. In 1904, Cooper finally secured two separate appropriations totaling $535,000 to construct a canal to connect the mouths of the Neches and Sabine Rivers to Taylor Bayou, the terminus of the Port Arthur Canal. The project was stalled for two years, however, after San Augustine attorney and political progressive Moses L. Broock defeated Cooper in the 1904 Democratic primary. Broock rode to victory largely on the charge that Cooper, who had served six consecutive terms as Beaumont's congressman, was "a tool for J. H. Kirby" and his northern investors. Cooper returned to Congress after winning the Democratic primary in March 1906 in a campaign managed by his son, Sam Jr.

When Will moved to Beaumont, Cooper was serving on the powerful House Ways and Means Committee, and the funds for the canal project had been released. The project was completed in February 1908.[8]

Cooper was among those who encouraged Will to use the editorial and news columns of the *Enterprise* to help generate community enthusiasm and support for Cooper's bid for federal funds for the deepwater port project. Cooper agreed that a deeper dredging of the channel took precedence over all other issues because it was the key to significant economic expansion. Now that he was back in Congress, Cooper was trying to get another appropriation to accomplish that goal. John Henry Kirby also advised Will to work on the project. No one had a greater stake in the future of Beaumont's economic development than Kirby, who needed a deepwater port to ship his lumber products to market and to save an enormous amount of money in railroad freight charges. At one point, Kirby even urged Will to meet with the head of the Santa Fe Railroad to persuade him to build a rail line from his "lumber district" in East Texas to Beaumont. He believed the Santa Fe would be attracted to Beaumont if efforts to build the deepwater project succeeded.[9]

Armed with the wish list of the city leaders and Bronson Cooper's advice, Will's first editorial as publisher of the *Enterprise* announced that under his management, the newspaper's primary agenda would be to promote efforts in Beaumont to take better advantage of the

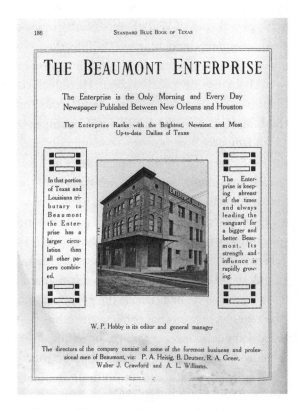

*The new* Beaumont Enterprise *building, 1908.*

economic developments that had occurred after the Spindletop oil strike, starting with the deepwater port project. Will's goals also included support for other urban improvements, including the completion of the Intracoastal Canal to New Orleans, municipal development of land along the Neches River, and rail connections to Waco, the trade and agricultural center of the Brazos Valley.[10]

Will's most immediate task was to regain the subscribers and advertisers the *Enterprise* had lost to the *Journal* and turn the *Enterprise* into a profitable business. The experience he had gained working in every department of the *Houston Post* served him well. On the news side, he redesigned the paper and devoted more of its column space to local and regional stories, often with the kind of attention-grabbing headlines he had used successfully in Houston. On the business side, Will was determined to make the *Enterprise* a two-state newspaper, with significant readership and advertising in the towns between Houston and New Orleans. The Southern Pacific Railroad had frequent and dependable early morning service going east and west from Beaumont that could deliver the *Enterprise* to subscribers and newsstands along its route. Beaumont also enjoyed frequent rail service on the Frisco and the Gulf, Colorado, and Santa Fe Railroads that traveled north and northwest. Will took advantage of these rail connections by arranging for daily editions of the *Enterprise* to be shipped to the towns and villages of the pine forests of Will's home country in lower East Texas.[11]

An energetic thirty year old, Will worked seven days a week. He attended business luncheons, dinner celebrations, weddings, funerals, and every other event or activity that would help him promote the paper. He rode the trains to publicize his newspaper in Lake Charles and Lafayette, Louisiana, and in the Piney Woods areas he had known well as a child. He tapped into his experience working in the business and circulation department of the *Houston Post*, personally selling ads and peddling subscriptions. And he was a tireless editorialist, publishing his views on a wide range of civic and political issues.

Only one month after Will took control of the *Enterprise*, he wrote editorials urging his friend John Henry Kirby to run for governor of Texas in 1908. After Will sent Kirby a clip of one of those editorials, Kirby responded that he sincerely appreciated "the splendid way in which you had me handled and yet I am a little apprehensive about this gubernatorial talk. My ambition is primarily to be of value to my country . . . and yet I think to seek the governorship is a laudable ambition in any citizen." Hobby quickly responded that he had "feared the gubernatorial mention would embarrass" Kirby, but "the thought has so often come to my mind . . . that I could not suppress it and I have heard some talk since . . . that the ideas advanced made some impression along the lines intended." Kirby eventually decided not to run.[12]

An early editorial stance of Will's caused some unintended trouble with one of Beaumont's most powerful business barons, the venerable "Captain" William Wiess. In September 1907, Beaumont scheduled a controversial referendum on a new city charter that proposed to establish a commission form of governance for the city, a progressive reform that had originated in Galveston after the devastating hurricane. Will initially supported the new charter, but after reading the final version of the text he changed his mind. He announced his opposition in an editorial, arguing that it was a "makeshift" document that would not create an actual commission form of government. The referendum generated widespread and heated debate in the city. Will's editorial displeased Captain Wiess, who was one of the leading supporters of the new charter. Aware of Will's close relationship with Kirby, Wiess asked Kirby to "have a talk" with the young new editor of the *Enterprise*. Kirby, who lived in Houston, had no strong feelings about the charter, but he did telephone Will to share Wiess's unhappiness. After Will explained his position, he asked Kirby to make it clear to Wiess that his stance against the charter was nothing personal against Wiess and that Will was eager to maintain good relations with him. Kirby assured Will that he would smooth Wiess's ruffled feathers. Kirby's call alarmed Will, although it did not change his opinion about the inadequacies of the charter.

Kirby subsequently wrote Wiess, stating that Will "seemed very anxious to please you in whatever he did. He said he had taken hold of the *Enterprise* with the expectation and hope that he would tie the business interests to him and that he would at all times have the support of such men as you; that you had always been his friend and that he did not wish his attitude at the present time to disturb in any respect your cordial relation; but he said, believing that his position was right he didn't think that even you would continue your respect for him should he change his attitude at this time." Kirby also flattered Wiess and said he had assured Will that Wiess was "too entirely broad-gauged to hold him responsible for defending his convictions even though you might radically differ with him in his conclusions." This letter placated Wiess. Appreciative of Kirby's intervention, Will wrote Kirby that "like everything you take a hand in, it was with skill and good results that you handled the matter for me in which Capt. Wiess was interested. I regret very much that the conditions arose which placed Capt. Wiess and myself on opposite sides."[13]

Will's hard work promoting the *Enterprise* and cultivating relationships with Beaumont's elite quickly paid off. Readership increased dramatically. Unfortunately, the stock market crash on Wall Street in October set off the Panic of 1907 and delivered another blow to Beaumont's economy. As a result, businesses in the city were forced to slash their advertising budgets, which sharply reduced the paper's advertising revenue. Despite the healthy increase in subscriptions, the *Enterprise* remained unprofitable. Through the end of 1907 and into the early months of 1908, Will struggled to meet his payroll and pay his bills. The newspaper once again faced bankruptcy.

Will's close relationship with A. L. Williams, the president of Gulf National Bank and one of the *Enterprise*'s investors and directors, provided a safety net. Despite the contraction of the money supply and the reduction of bank reserves, Williams's bank managed, reluctantly, to cover the "hot" payroll checks Will was sometimes forced to write. The *Enterprise*'s payroll check overdrafts caused Williams deep anxiety, and at one point he warned Will that he could no longer cover his bad checks. Faced with an empty bank account and an immediate need to fund a $2,000 payroll, Will took a deep breath and wrote the checks on Williams's bank anyway. On one occasion when Will issued another round of checks despite having insufficient funds, Will decided to leave town before the *Enterprise*'s staff could cash their checks to escape the wrath of his banker. He hopped on the Southern Pacific's Sunset Limited bound for New Orleans, a city he had visited frequently and knew well. He remained there for a few days, as he later recalled, hoping "to give the storm time to blow over." Unable to locate or contact Will, the bank honored his checks. Years later, Will admitted that at that point he faced ruin, because he "didn't know whether the bank would cash the checks or not. But it did. And it wasn't thirty days until we turned the corner." Luckily for Will, economic conditions finally improved in 1908. Beaumont merchants bought more ads, and the *Enterprise* began to make enough money to at least pay its expenses, if not make a profit.[14]

Beaumont's economic recovery received a boost on January 29, 1908, when the nine-foot-deep Sabine-Neches channel finally opened. Will joined the official party that made a trip down the river on the steam yacht *John Henry Kirby* to celebrate completion of the channel. He was also among the happy business leaders on the reception committee that welcomed the small revenue cutter *Windom* when it docked at Beaumont's Main Street wharf. In the spirit of boosterism, Will's headline in the *Enterprise* declared that the arrival of the *Windom* was the "greatest water event in the history of Beaumont," which was not too much of an exaggeration. At high tide, the water at Beaumont's docks reached a depth of eleven feet, which soon made it possible for smaller seagoing vessels to make the voyage from Sabine Lake, including the tugboat *Higgins* and the steamer *Nicaragua*.[15]

Will published a forty-eight-page special edition of the *Enterprise* on May 5, 1908, to celebrate Beaumont's progress toward becoming a seaport, as well as to bring more attention to his newspaper. He wrote an editorial arguing that no matter how important the new nine-foot channel was to the city, Beaumont still needed a channel twenty-five feet in depth to allow larger ships with greater load capacity to navigate their way from the Gulf of Mexico. Will soon earned a reputation among his fellow newspaper editors as an innovator because of his imaginative use of attractive special promotional editions, which his subscribers stashed away in trunks and closets to keep as souvenirs. This large special edition of the *Enterprise* also signified the end of the *Enterprise*'s financial problems. Soon after its publication, Will was able to gain majority control of the newspaper by purchasing the stock owned by R. A. Greer and A. L. Williams, the latter undoubtedly relieved at this positive turn of events. This buyout increased Will's holdings to 70 percent, placing him solidly in control.[16]

The effort to get additional federal funding for a deeper dredging of the Neches River had begun a few months earlier. As both Senator Bailey and Congressman Cooper were lobbying their fellow members of Congress to support an appropriation to deepen the channel, Will and his business friends were optimistic about their chances to score a quick victory. Given Will's close political and social connections to Bailey and Cooper, Beaumont's business and political leaders were delighted to have him take an active personal role in the effort.

This early optimism proved premature. The effort to get the channel dredged would be much more difficult and take longer than anyone anticipated. Vigorous opposition soon arose from a variety of special interests, including business tycoon John "Bet a Million" Gates, who had taken control of Arthur Stilwell's Port Arthur company. "Uncle Joe" Cannon, the Speaker of the US House, informed Bronson Cooper that he was against the channel project on the grounds that such public works projects were too expensive and not the business of the federal government. In March 1908, Cooper was surprised when attorney Martin Dies Sr., a former resident of Cooper's old political base, Tyler County, ran against him in the Democratic primary. Having no substantive policy differences with Cooper, Dies's campaign largely focused on allegations that Cooper was a pawn of wealthy John Henry Kirby. Dies, who had been Cooper's campaign manager in 1906, opposed Cooper to spite Kirby, with whom he had a financial dispute. Kirby warned Cooper that Dies was "an adversary . . . both capable and unscrupulous." To practically everyone's shock, including Cooper's, Dies won the election by only 311 votes.[17]

Cooper's defeat was a major disappointment for Will, and it was seen as a significant setback to the effort to secure funding for the deepwater channel, especially because Cooper had been in line to be chairman of the House Ways and Means Committee. Because Cooper's term as congressman did not end until March 1909, he continued to fight for the channel project for the remainder of his time in office. Prior to losing the primary, Cooper persuaded the Army Corps of Engineers to send its district engineer to Beaumont to inspect the new nine-foot channel to understand why it should be deepened to twenty-five feet. The plan backfired, however, when the engineer submitted a confidential report to Washington arguing against the project. As a result, the Corps of Engineers continued to stall.[18]

In January 1909, frustrated by the federal government's inaction, Will and other Beaumont businessmen decided that a different strategy was needed. Will did some research and discovered that in 1904, the Texas Legislature had passed a constitutional amendment, subsequently approved in the general election, that gave the legislature the power to authorize the creation of local taxing districts. These districts could issue bonds to finance flood control, drainage, and navigation improvement projects on the state's rivers and streams. Will believed that this amendment could be used to benefit their deepwater project. If Beaumont could create a navigation district and pass a revenue bond to provide funds for the dredging project, the federal government would be more likely to appropriate the money needed to complete the project.[19]

The first step was for the legislature, empowered by the constitutional amendment, to pass an act authorizing local navigation districts. Will's fellow campaign leaders, especially Colonel Davidson, thought his idea had merit. After all, nothing else seemed to be working. They agreed to take the fight to Austin. They also believed that joining forces with business leaders in Orange would strengthen their chances for success. John Henry Kirby had observed, "The rivalry between Beaumont and Orange . . . is friendly because they are both in the same boat and must depend on the same means for the development of their future shipping. I have no doubt that . . . Port Arthur would knife Beaumont or Orange if they had the opportunity." Will subsequently met at the Orange Elks Hall with a delegation of prominent Orange community leaders, led by lumber barons Lutcher and W. H. Stark and attorney J. W. Link. The Starks, Link, and the other prominent business leaders in Orange agreed to work with Will to get legislation authorizing navigation districts for both cities. A former mayor of Orange and a close associate of Kirby, Link would be one of Will's most effective allies in the effort to secure legislative support.

Link eventually moved to Houston, and in later years he and Will would continue their association there.[20]

Will had already planned to cover the January 1909 legislative session for the *Enterprise*, but he now decided to mix journalism with politics, an activity in which he had gained much experience by this point. While reporting on the legislative session, he would also lobby legislators to pass the bill creating the navigation districts. He traveled to Austin when the legislative session began on January 12, 1909, and received his press credentials, which gave him access to the floor and a seat at the press table of both houses of the legislature. Will arranged meetings with the members of the House and Senate whose support was essential for the passage of the navigation district bill. One of those members was Sam Rayburn of Fannin County, one of the legislature's rising stars. Rayburn would be elected Speaker of the Texas House in 1911, followed two years later by his election to Congress. He eventually became Speaker of the US House of Representatives. Will's meetings with Rayburn, who pledged his support for the bill, began a personal relationship that would last until Rayburn's death fifty-two years later.[21]

When Rienzi Johnston told former congressman Tom Ball about Will's plan, Ball gathered a group of Houston Ship Channel advocates to meet with Houston mayor Baldwin Rice. They persuaded the mayor to appoint a committee to join Will in lobbying the legislature to create the navigation districts, which would benefit Houston's own effort to create a deepwater port. The mayor appointed Tom Ball and corporate attorneys W. H. Wilson and T. H. Stone to go to Austin to help Will. Now aided by a powerful group of allies, Will faced little opposition in Austin. With East Texas senator E. I. Kellie of Jasper leading the effort in the Senate and the endorsement of Governor Tom Campbell, the navigation district bill quickly passed both houses in February under an emergency clause. When Governor Campbell signed the bill on February 20, 1909, he sent the signing pen to Will in recognition of the crucial role he had played in getting it passed, even though he was not a member of the legislature.[22]

Will had returned to Beaumont in early February before the legislature voted on the navigation district bill. Confident of its passage, Will met with the chamber of commerce's board of directors to plan their next step. They decided to send Will and a small delegation of other chamber members to Washington to work with Senator Bailey and Congressman Cooper, the latter now a lame duck but still with influence in the House of Representatives. Together they would lobby Congress to pass a bill to fund the deepwater channel project. Cooper's successor, Martin Dies, would not take his seat until March 4. Dies had not yet revealed his position on the matter, but his campaign comments had hinted that he opposed using federal funds for the project. Will and Bronson Cooper therefore were eager to move as quickly as possible to take advantage of Cooper's final days in the Congress.

Cooper, Hobby, Colonel Davidson, and the other members of the Beaumont deepwater committee spent much time with members of the House Rivers and Harbors Committee pushing the bill. On February 9, Cooper reported to Kirby that he had "carefully looked after all the local affairs affecting the District and I have been diligent in that. For the past week I have had a fight on with Mr. Burton, Chairman of the Rivers and Harbors Committee [and] I have to contend with . . . John W. Gates." In his hope to develop Port Arthur at Beaumont's expense, Gates was in Washington to oppose Beaumont's efforts to dredge the Neches channel.[23]

A compromise was reached that also benefitted Port Arthur. On February 24, after including a provision to deepen the channel at Port Arthur from twenty-five to thirty feet, Cooper succeeded in getting the bill through the House. Senator Bailey was able to get passage in the Senate with significant help from Texas's other senator, Charles Culberson, the minority leader. Securing Culberson's help took some effort, not because of his opposition but because Culberson was almost disabled by alcoholism and frequently absent from the Capitol. On March 2, 1909, President Theodore Roosevelt signed the bill in one of his last acts as president. Bronson Cooper had made his last legislative contribution to his district. When he returned to Beaumont he was greeted with a homecoming party and Will's editorial in the *Beaumont Enterprise* praising his record of public service.[24]

After Congress passed the bill, Will traveled back to Beaumont to help plan and launch a bond petition drive scheduled for April 28. The legislation authorizing the navigation districts required that a certain percentage of the district's taxpayers had to sign a petition calling for the bond election before it could be held. If enough citizens signed the petition, the Jefferson County commissioners could move forward to create the district and then set a date for the bond election. Will's next task was to manage the program to gather the required number of petition signatures. With help from Walter Crawford and his law partner, Leon Sonfield, Will took charge of the effort to promote the petition signing. Late on the night of April 14, Will had walls, trees, and fences throughout Beaumont quietly covered with posters declaring "D.W.C. 28." The words were printed in fire-engine red. The poster had no other words or explanations. When the residents of Beaumont left their houses the next morning, they saw the mystery posters nearly everywhere they looked. On April 25, Will published a front-page story in the *Enterprise* explaining that the letters and numbers on the posters stood for "Deep Water Campaign April 28." The signs had been posted to alert citizens that the petitions calling for a bond election would be circulated throughout the city on April 28 and then submitted to the county commissioners. The announcement was accompanied by stories explaining why the bond election was important and how passage of the bonds would bring great economic benefits directly or indirectly to all the citizens of Beaumont.[25]

On April 28, Will personally directed the effort to gather volunteers to circulate the bond election petitions. He arranged for the city's fire alert siren to blast five times at 8:00 a.m. to signal the start of the drive, and then to blast every time two hundred people had signed the petition. After garnering more than four thousand names—far more than legally required—the petitions were submitted to the county commissioners court. The commissioners created the navigation district and then approved a $498,000 bond issue election, scheduled for July 8, 1909. After a major publicity campaign led mainly by the

*Enterprise*, an overwhelming majority voted in favor of the bond issue. The day after the election, Will published a celebratory sixty-eight-page edition of the *Enterprise* to announce the victory.[26]

On August 12, Will wrote Kirby, "We certainly have the waterway project in fine shape now, for when the bonds voted by such a big vote are sold, we will have the money to get 25 feet. . . . I am confident the government will take hold of this waterway and give it the support and development needed and it will take very little to make the facilities far greater than either New Orleans or Galveston." In an editorial, Will urged the navigation district to issue and sell the bonds as soon as possible. There was no time to waste. The struggle to deepen the channel, once thought to be an easily attainable goal when Will first became involved, was now entering its third year. Will and his business allies feared that the community might become apathetic and lose interest if the slowly moving campaign took much longer.[27]

In September 1909, two months after passage of the bond issue proposal, the War Department's district engineer, Captain A. E. Waldron, informed Beaumont that the size of the bond issue would not produce enough money to fund the entire project. Leaders of the channel-dredging campaign would have to find additional funding before the War Department would begin the project. Even if Beaumont raised the necessary funds, Captain Waldron would continue to oppose the project, warning the secretary of war that it was a boondoggle, a waste of federal time and money. He argued that there was not enough heavy industry in the region to justify a deeper channel. Without Bronson Cooper in Washington to push the matter, Congress failed to allocate any additional money for the project during the fall 1909 session, and the federal government took no further action.[28]

At the beginning of January 1910, Will and Beaumont's other business leaders decided to take another long train trip to Washington to once again lobby Congress for federal funding. When the delegation arrived in the capital, Will went directly to his friend Senator Joe Bailey. While Bailey was deeply embattled politically as a result of the continuing controversy over his business dealings, his struggles were more of an issue back in Texas than in Washington. The senator remained a valuable ally in Congress. Senator Culberson, whose problems with alcohol continued, still supported the project, but he was no longer an effective legislative ally. Will was pleased, however, that he was able to secure a pledge of support from Congressman Dies, the man who had replaced the invaluable Bronson Cooper.[29]

After three weeks in Washington, Will realized that the fight to get federal funds was going to be more difficult than he had hoped. Deciding to devote his full attention to the task, Will and the chamber of commerce committee members returned to Beaumont at the beginning of February to allow Will to make arrangements at the *Enterprise* to return to Washington for an extended time. Will delegated many of his duties at the newspaper to his talented right-hand man, circulation manager Jim Mapes, whom Will had hired in 1908. He then returned to Washington accompanied by James Weed, a Beaumont oilman, professional civil engineer, and former employee of John Henry Kirby. Weed's engineering expertise proved to be a major help in Will's meetings with the army engineers. Will's mission to Washington lasted three months. To maintain public interest, Will sent regular dispatches back to Beaumont on his progress, which the *Enterprise* printed as the publisher's column from Washington. He finally returned to Beaumont in late May after persuading the War Department to send yet another inspection team in September to evaluate the need for the channel.[30]

Following his return to Beaumont, Will had the *Enterprise* publish a series of editorials urging the community to do all that it could to impress the federal engineers who would conduct the inspection. In an *Enterprise* editorial on July 30, "Prepare for the Engineers," Will argued it was "no time to sit still and let these engineers come here and form their own conclusions and go away." That editorial was followed the next day with another declaring "Beaumont Needs Deep Water." When the army engineers arrived in Beaumont on September 21, a sixty-page special edition of the *Enterprise* showcasing Beaumont's businesses and industry welcomed them to the city. Will joined officials from Beaumont's chamber of commerce to give the engineers a boat tour of the Neches and Sabine Rivers all the way to the Gulf.[31]

Following the tour, the engineers held hearings in Beaumont at which local proponents of the channel testified about the need to deepen the channel. The speaker who made the most impact was governor-elect Oscar B. Colquitt, a former newspaper publisher, member of the Texas Railroad Commission, and close political ally of Will Hobby, Rienzi Johnston, John Henry Kirby, and Bronson Cooper. During the previous summer, Will had managed Colquitt's gubernatorial campaign in Jefferson County, which Colquitt carried easily in the primary election in July. Colquitt told the engineers that as a member of the Railroad Commission, he had knowledge that the absence of competition from ocean freighters resulted in the railroads overcharging Beaumont industries for transporting their freight. He also argued that there was already more than enough industry in the Beaumont region to justify the deepwater dredging project. The existence of an inland seaport would create even more industry.[32]

Colquitt's testimony, in addition to what the engineers had learned on their tour, turned the trick. They submitted a report to the War Department stressing that the project merited federal funding. In addition, the engineers pointed out that the completion of the Panama Canal, which was due to open within the next few years, would greatly increase Gulf shipping traffic further and justify the building of additional ports on the Gulf Coast. Panama City, Florida, had been founded in 1909 for that same reason. When Will received the news that the engineers recommended federal support for the deepwater project, the *Enterprise* sponsored a major celebration in Keith Park.[33]

Bolstered by the army engineers' favorable report and recommendations, Will returned to Washington in December 1910 with Colonel Davidson. They worked closely with Joe Bailey to convince the members of the Senate Rivers and Harbors Committee to allocate the necessary funds to deepen Beaumont's ship channel. Martin Dies did the same work in the House of Representatives, much aided by Texas congressman John Nance "Cactus Jack" Garner of Uvalde. Garner had recently become a member of the Democratic Party leadership in the House. Garner was a political ally of Rienzi Johnston, whom he had met when both served in the Texas Legislature. Colonel Johnston had given Garner crucial political support in 1903 during his tough first campaign for Congress. With his close ties to Colonel Johnston, Garner was a strong and dependable ally of Will's in the deepwater lobbying effort. Getting federal money for the Beaumont project was no violation of Garner's legislative principles. He was a vigorous practitioner of pork barrel politics who once declared that while other members of Congress worked to "bring the bacon" back home to their districts, he worked on bringing back the "whole hog."

In February 1910, Will's years of hard work finally paid off. Largely as a result of Joe Bailey's efforts, Congress voted to approve more than $500,000 for channel-deepening projects in Beaumont and its nearby neighbor Orange, contingent on both cities providing matching funds. President Taft signed the appropriation bill on March 1, 1911.[34]

Work began on the Neches-Sabine channel on March 15, 1912, nearly five years after the start of the deepwater campaign. It took four years to complete. In 1920 the channel was widened and deepened. The Port of Beaumont, which was made possible by the deepwater campaign, skillfully led and managed by Will Hobby, eventually became the fourth-busiest in the United States in tonnage shipped. To a large extent, Will Hobby deserves credit for this achievement. He had used his newspaper to heavily promote the campaign; he had developed the crucial strategy that ultimately led to victory; he had put his influential political connections to effective use; and he had tirelessly devoted a major part of his time lobbying the Texas Legislature, the War Department, and Congress on behalf of the deepwater project. In later years, in a life full of achievements, Will always considered the Neches-Sabine canal one of his proudest.[35]

# CHAPTER 4

---

# MISS WILLIE

Will's revival of the *Beaumont Enterprise* and his tireless labor on behalf of the city's deepwater port project made him one of Beaumont's leading citizens. He was a fixture at the daily luncheons in the Crosby Hotel's dining room attended by a small group of Beaumont's other business and political leaders, including the locally powerful and influential W. P. McFaddin and Captain William Wiess and his sons, Harry and Perry. In its 1910 yearbook, the Beaumont Chamber of Commerce praised Will's newspaper for "consistently boosting Beaumont on all occasions." The chamber later elected Will to a one-year term as its president.[1]

Will's civic prominence was enhanced by his editorial promotion of other city projects. The *Enterprise* helped persuade the Frisco Railroad to move its repair shops from Louisiana to Beaumont, advocated successfully for a bridge to be built across the Neches River to Orange, and urged the federal government to complete the Intracoastal Canal to New Orleans. Will and clothing merchant Jake Nathan served on the executive committee of the chamber of commerce that planned Beaumont's ambitious six-day Southeast Texas Fair, which had its successful grand opening in November 1909. And his *Beaumont Enterprise* continued to boost the city and its port. One of the hopes held by many of the city's leaders was that the US Navy might build a naval base in the area. When the navy dispatched three shallow-draft torpedo boats up the Neches to Beaumont in November 1909, Will sent a reporter to interview the flotilla commander. The resulting story quoted the naval officer as observing that the Neches was "one of the finest rivers it had ever been his pleasure to encounter." That quote, along with a story about the naval visit, was featured prominently in the *Enterprise*. Hopes for a naval base were destined to be unfulfilled.[2]

Will's editorials also promoted city infrastructure and public safety projects that would enhance business prospects, such as paving streets and roads to accommodate the growing number of automobiles, working with the railroads to remove and reroute downtown grade crossings bisecting and disrupting the business district, building additional city docks and improving existing ones, and constructing new fire stations and an interurban line to Port Arthur.[3]

Will was in an enviable position. He owned an attractive home at 1168 McFaddin Avenue, one block north of fashionable, tree-lined Calder Avenue. He enjoyed the widespread respect of his fellow citizens in Beaumont, controlled his own newspaper, and was finally making good money. Under the skilled management of Jim Mapes, the *Enterprise*'s circulation had tripled, as had its paid advertising space. The newspaper had become an influential news source in the southeast Texas–southwest Louisiana region. Its letterhead boasted that the *Enterprise* circulated "in more exclusive territory than [any] other paper in Texas or Louisiana" and that it was "the Paper of Three Cities" (Beaumont, Orange, and Port Arthur). Its promotional literature also claimed that it was the "Paper of the Lumber, Rice, and Oil Belts of Texas and Louisiana." The Temple, Texas, *Pythian Banner-Knight* noted that the *Beaumont Enterprise* "has become one of the best pieces of newspaper property in the state under Mr. Hobby's control. . . . [I]t has graduated into a paper of large proportions and great influence in eastern Texas and western Louisiana." At one point in 1912, Will's interest in Louisiana even led him to explore the possibility of buying the *New Orleans Item*, but the asking price deterred him.[4]

Will's increasing visibility in Texas newspaper publishing circles, his deep involvement in public affairs in Beaumont, and his close ties to John Henry Kirby, Rienzi Johnston, Samuel Bronson Cooper, and other influential members of the conservative faction of the Texas Democratic Party drew him ever deeper into politics. Will was an elected delegate to the party's local and state conventions, and he chaired the Jefferson County campaigns of the candidates that he and his allies favored, particularly Senator Joe Bailey and Governor Oscar Colquitt.

Will's relationship with Rienzi Johnston, with whom he remained personally close after he moved to Beaumont, gave Will one of his most important political connections. Colonel Johnston served on the Democratic National Committee from 1900 to 1912. A friend of three-time presidential nominee William Jennings Bryan, Johnston was considered as a potential candidate for vice president on Bryan's ticket in 1908. When Johnston's name was floated as a vice presidential possibility, a newspaper editorial noted that in Texas Johnston had "wielded a powerful political influence for a quarter of a century."[5]

Will's friendship with Governor Colquitt, who had given effective testimony to the army engineers during the hearings on the deepwater port issue, would also have a significant impact on Will's political future. Colquitt, like Will, had a background in journalism. He published newspapers in the Texas towns of Pittsburg and Terrell, and he was one of the owners of the *Fort Worth Gazette*. Colquitt was elected governor in 1910 after serving terms in the Texas Senate and on the Texas Railroad Commission. Will not only supported Colquitt's 1910 gubernatorial candidacy with editorial endorsements in the *Enterprise*, he also managed Colquitt's Jefferson County campaign. After Colquitt won the Democratic nomination, Will attended the Democratic State Convention in Galveston, to which he brought "Bailey for Senator" and "Colquitt for Governor" buttons that he distributed to the delegates. Colquitt could not attend the convention because of the death of his son, but he later wrote Will a warm letter asking him for twelve of the buttons, signing the letter, "Your friend."

Will also worked on Colquitt's behalf in his reelection campaign in the spring and summer of 1912. That campaign turned out to be a bitterly fought one, largely because of the prohibition issue. A fervent antiprohibitionist, Colquitt's election as governor in 1910 had been a major setback for the prohibition movement. As a result, prohibition supporters recruited a "dry" opponent, Texas Supreme Court justice W. F. Ramsey, to run against Colquitt. The political fight against "demon rum" in Texas had roots going back to the late nineteenth century, and it had led to the passage of "local option" laws giving individual counties, municipalities, and precincts the authority to ban alcohol. During the late 1890s and early 1900s, numerous areas in rural North Texas and East Texas had used local option laws to outlaw alcoholic beverages. South Texas and most of the urban areas of Texas, including San Antonio, Dallas, Houston, Galveston, and Beaumont, remained solidly "wet." Two powerful lobbying organizations, the Anti-Saloon League and the Texas Brewers Association, funded and directed opposing sides of the political battle.[6]

The crusade in Texas to prohibit the selling and consuming of alcoholic beverages was part of a larger national movement that eventually led to the Eighteenth Amendment to the US Constitution. The battle against booze was also an integral part of the political agenda of the progressive movement, especially in Texas and the rest of the South. A reaction to the rapid changes resulting from the nation's transformation from a predominantly rural to an urban society, the progressive movement was an attempt to solve the two major problems its followers believed threatened American democracy: the growing power of corporate monopolies and trusts—epitomized by the Standard Oil Company—and the increasing discontent of the lower economic classes, especially among urban industrial workers. The movement embraced a wide variety of individual reforms, including those to make the process of government more democratic, such as the direct election of US senators and the adoption of the initiative, recall, and referendum. But the progressives, especially those on the urban side of the movement, also had a social agenda that sought to eliminate poverty, disease, and crime. Reformers believed that the widespread availability of alcohol in the form of liquor, beer, and wine was one of the major causes of those social evils and that its prohibition would significantly improve social conditions and help ensure law and order, especially for citizens in the lower economic classes. Middle-class progressives in Texas and other Southern states believed that liquor was also a major cause of unrest and discontent among African Americans and a cause of rape, lynching, and political corruption related to race. So prohibition was one of the most important, if least understood, of the reforms on the progressive agenda. The progressive movement, like most social and economic reform efforts, was not monolithic, and prohibition was one issue that divided its adherents. Prohibition was not popular among the urban, labor, and immigrant elements of the movement, but the old-stock white, Anglo-Saxon, middle-class, and conservative protestant and evangelical church members who dominated the movement in Texas were particularly aggressive advocates of the reform. In the coming decade, from 1910 to 1920, prohibition would dominate politics in Texas.[7]

Will Hobby, who enjoyed his liquor, felt that prohibition was a significant political distraction that diverted attention from more critical issues in Texas. "There are other things that need attention in this state," Will told his friends. "The prohibition question ought to be laid aside." Although he opposed a statewide prohibition amendment, Will did support local option, but only reluctantly. His position reflected the majority opinion in Beaumont, which remained "wet." Will's conservative political allies, especially John Henry Kirby and Colonel Johnston, believed prohibition was a path that led to socialism and governmental infringement on individual freedom, but Will's views were not that extreme.[8]

Colquitt was against statewide prohibition, but like Hobby, he did not oppose local option laws. Nevertheless, Texas prohibitionists considered him to be solidly "wet," labeling him "Oscar Budweiser." Colquitt also opposed most of the progressive reform agenda. During his first term as governor, he vetoed a progressive reform mandating an eight-hour workday for men on state construction projects. He also strongly opposed progressive election reforms that had the purpose of taking power away from political bosses and their organizations, including the initiative, referendum, and recall. The initiative enables citizens to bypass their state legislature by placing proposed laws and, in some states, constitutional amendments on the ballot. The referendum is a process in which a legislature refers a proposed law to the voters, or a law is placed on the ballot as the result of a voter petition drive. Recall is a procedure that allows citizens to remove and replace a public official before the end of a term of office.[9]

In this era, when racist attitudes and Jim Crow laws were pervasive elements of the social and political environment, Colquitt and his opponent both engaged in racist rhetoric. For example, in one campaign speech, Colquitt pledged his support for the "White Man's Union" groups that had been organized in several counties in South Texas to prevent black Texans from voting in the 1912 election, with violence if necessary. Judge Ramsey countered with equally racist statements.[10]

Colquitt defeated Ramsey in the July 1912 primary by approximately forty thousand votes, with significant support from South Texas and the larger cities in Texas, including Houston, Dallas, San Antonio, and Beaumont, where the antiprohibition sentiment was strong. Will attended the Democratic State Convention in San Antonio in mid-August as both a Colquitt delegate and a journalist covering the proceedings for the *Enterprise*. Because Texas was a one-party state, Colquitt easily won the general election in November without having to campaign.[11]

In that year's presidential campaign, loyal Democrat Will Hobby supported the party's nominee, New Jersey governor Woodrow Wilson, but he and his conservative political allies had not favored Wilson's nomination. Although Wilson straddled the fence on the hot-button issue of prohibition, he generally represented the views of the progressive wing of the national Democratic Party. The year before the presidential election, Will printed an editorial in the *Enterprise*, written by Bronson Cooper, complaining that Wilson was too progressive and criticizing him for his support of the initiative, referendum, and recall. "The conservative element in the Party will not stand for such radicalism," Bronson declared. Wilson, however, had the solid support of Texas progressives, led by Dallas attorney Thomas Love and Austin attorney Thomas Watt Gregory, who opposed the conservatives on many issues. Despite their disagreements, both factions united to send a pro-Wilson delegation to the Democratic National Convention in Baltimore. At the convention, the forty delegates from Texas voted as one block on every ballot for Wilson, who finally won the nomination on the forty-sixth ballot. Wilson carried Texas easily in the general election and won the presidency by defeating incumbent president William Howard Taft and third-party candidate Theodore Roosevelt, who split the Republican vote.[12]

Two months after Wilson's election as president, the scandal-plagued Joe Bailey denounced the progressive takeover of the Democratic Party and resigned from the US Senate before his term was over in March 1913. Governor Colquitt appointed Rienzi Johnston to replace him until the Texas Legislature could meet to elect Bailey's successor. Johnston hoped to serve out the remainder of Bailey's term, but many members of the legislature were eager to put Texas congressman Morris Sheppard in the Senate. Sheppard was one of the nation's strongest advocates for prohibition and a solid supporter of Woodrow Wilson. Johnston was neither. Colquitt declared he would not support "Morris Sheppard . . . for the reason that Sheppard did not support me. Col. Johnston has been a consistent friend and supporter of mine and he has rendered the Democratic Party of Texas ten times more valuable service than Sheppard." When Colquitt launched a vigorous lobbying campaign on Johnston's behalf, Will Hobby traveled to Austin to help his old patron, but to no avail. The legislature elected Sheppard.[13]

While Will was focused on managing the *Enterprise*, pushing the deepwater port project, and being politically active, his younger brother and closest sibling, Edwin, was enjoying success as a banker in Dallas. Their older brother, Alfred, who had a medical practice, and their sisters Laura Aline and Mary Hobby Amis also resided in Dallas. Their mother, Dora, had moved to Dallas to be near those offspring, but she occasionally traveled to Beaumont to stay with Will. With so many of his family in Dallas, Will made frequent trips to that city. As a result, he forged a number of friendships with several Dallas businessmen, most of whom he met through his brother Edwin.[14]

Now in his midthirties and still a bachelor, Will was actively involved in Beaumont's social scene. He joined in the community's annual Fourth of July barbecue and celebrations at Keith Park and attended balls and parties at the Beaumont Country Club, perched on a hill overlooking the Neches River, and at the Neches Club, which was located downtown on the top floor of the five-story Kyle Opera House. He also enjoyed taking visitors on "pleasure excursions" up the Neches River on covered motorized barges that advertised (in the over-the-top chamber of commerce boosterism typical of the time) that the trips through the Big Thicket provided scenery "comparable to the Rhine River."[15]

Observers began to notice that frequently Will Hobby's female companion at these social affairs was the blonde, blue-eyed Willie Chapman Cooper, the charming and sophisticated daughter of Samuel Bronson Cooper Sr. It eventually dawned on their friends that the two were romantically involved. Will and Willie were exceedingly quiet about their relationship.

Willie and Will had known each other since early childhood in Tyler County because of the close relationship between their families. Bronson Cooper had married Phebe Young, the daughter of a Methodist minister, in October 1873. Phebe's family always called her by her nickname, "Daughtie." Their first child, Willie, was born in Woodville, Texas, on June 19, 1876. She was nearly two years older than Will Hobby. When she was fourteen, Willie left the Piney Woods of East Texas to attend North Texas Female College in Sherman (later known as Kidd-Key College). The curriculum of the college emphasized the fine arts, particularly music education. She graduated two years later as valedictorian of her class.[16]

Willie graduated in 1892, a few months before her father was elected to his first term in the US Congress representing Texas's Second Congressional District, which included Beaumont and much of East Texas. At the time of his election, Bronson Cooper was serving as collector of internal revenue in Galveston. John Henry Kirby and the managers of Kirby's lumber company played a key role in Cooper's successful election campaign in East Texas, as they would in Cooper's subsequent bids for reelection. Willie moved with her family to Washington, DC, and soon became her father's office secretary. The vivacious, attractive young Willie quickly became a prominent figure in the social life of the capital. Two years after moving to Washington and at only nineteen years old, she was listed in the city's social register, which described her as a well-read young woman who "devoted considerable time to music and painting." The register also claimed, rather extravagantly, that because Willie worked so closely with her influential father, she had become a "power in the politics of the nation" and was "well known in the most important political, diplomatic, and artistic circles." She was characterized in a magazine article as having a "brilliant mind, a quick wit, and a magnetic personality." One of her father's associates was quoted as saying that Willie was a "clever politician" who had practically "inherited" her political skills due to her immersion in the legislative culture of the Capitol.[17]

Willie also helped tend to the Cooper family's close relationship with John Henry Kirby. In April 1900, when her father became gravely ill while home in Beaumont, she sent a personal note to Kirby urging him to visit her father. "Papa is quite sick and seems to be growing worse every day, so mother asked me to write you this note to tell you of his condition and to insist on your coming over to see him at once, if possible," she wrote.

"I am sure your very presence would be very encouraging to Papa, for he is so despondent, something so unusual for his philosophic nature and he has such great confidence in you." Later that fall, when Houston's civic promoters selected Kirby to be "King Nottoc" (King Cotton) for the "Notsuoh" (Houston) festival, the city's new Mardi Gras–like event, Willie dispatched another personal note to Kirby. She informed him that she would attend the festival, "delighted at the prospect of paying homage to King Nottoc and I shall depend on you for the introduction! Whenever I can serve you, please don't hesitate to call on me. It is a pleasure I assure you. I can never forget the many kindnesses you have shown me. With love to all, I am your friend."[18]

Willie was a member of a highly political family. In 1907 one of her two sisters, Margaret, married Henderson M. Jacoway of Little Rock, Arkansas, who was later elected to Congress. Her youngest sister, Bird, married S. W. Sholars, a state representative in the Texas Legislature from Woodville. Willie's brother, Samuel Bronson Cooper Jr., worked in Washington as secretary to Senator Charles Culberson and Congressman Samuel Lanham during the early 1900s while he attended law school at Georgetown University. He later served in the Texas Legislature. And of course, her father was a widely respected congressman, especially among the members from the former states of the Confederacy. As Willie ran her father's office, she was at the center of his business and thus became well known to his fellow congressmen. One of Bronson Cooper's friends described her as being "brilliant, learned, well-poised, and well-minded." The latter attribute was considered a necessity for any woman who wished to have a visible presence in public life during this era.[19]

After Bronson Cooper lost his bid for a seventh term in Congress in the election of 1904, he, his wife, Daughtie, and Willie, who was then twenty-eight, moved back to their permanent residence in Beaumont. Although Will was working at the *Houston Post*, he spent a lot of time in nearby Beaumont to cover stories for his newspaper, which made it possible for him to maintain his close relationship with the Coopers. When the voters returned Bronson Cooper to Congress in 1906, Willie went back to Washington to resume her work as his secretary, but she and her father returned to Beaumont whenever the Congress adjourned for several weeks or for the summer. The Coopers maintained a residence in Beaumont at 1096 Calder Avenue at the corner of Forrest.[20]

While Bronson was in Congress, he continued to practice law. Beginning in 1904, he partnered with his son, Sam Jr., whom the family called "Bubber." The team of Cooper and Cooper, working out of an office in Beaumont's Alexander Building, became one of the city's leading law firms. After Will took over the *Beaumont Enterprise* in 1907, he was a frequent visitor to the Cooper residence whenever Bronson and his daughter were in town. When Will was in Washington from January until May 1909 lobbying Congress for the deepwater project, the Cooper residence in the capital was his home away from home. Willie was his guide to the city, and he accompanied her to parties and receptions given by members of Congress and prominent federal officials. He even went with Willie and her best friend, Florence Stratton, to a White House reception hosted by President

Theodore Roosevelt during his final months in office. Stratton was also from Beaumont and was a columnist for Hobby's competition, the *Beaumont Journal*. According to a 1915 newspaper story, it was during this time that Will and Willie began their romance: "As [Will and Willie] grew up, they separated but frequently met, and finally, when Mr. Hobby came to Beaumont about seven years ago, they were thrown much together, and the friendship of childhood days was renewed, and ripened rapidly."[21]

When his final term in Congress ended in March 1909, Bronson Cooper returned to Beaumont with his family. He resumed his law practice, but bitter about his defeat and

*Samuel Bronson Cooper as a member of US Congress, 1896.*

still harboring political ambitions, he had no enthusiasm for it. With Willie living back in Beaumont, she and Will were able to spend much more time together. The Cooper residence on Calder Avenue, where most of Beaumont's affluent residents lived, was conveniently located around the corner from Will's house on McFaddin Avenue. The Cooper residence featured a wood-paneled study and library, stocked with almanacs, histories, novels, and books of poetry. Among the well-thumbed volumes were the complete works of James Fenimore Cooper, Sir Walter Scott, and Robert Burns. Will made use of and enjoyed his access to the Cooper family library.[22]

Bronson Cooper's time in Beaumont was cut short in 1910, when President Taft appointed him to the National Import Appraisal Board with headquarters in New York City. Functioning as a court with nine lawyers as members, the board reviewed the import duties collected by the US Customs Service, with jurisdiction in all sections of the United States, which required frequent travel to various port cities, including Tampa, New Orleans, and Galveston. It was challenging but prestigious work.[23]

The appointment was a much-welcome development for the Cooper family. After his reelection defeat in 1908 and the loss of his congressional salary, Cooper's financial situation was desperate. He was heavily in debt and unable to make mortgage payments on his investments in real estate and timberlands. Cooper was unable to blame his financial difficulties entirely on bad investment choices. "You, knowing my weaknesses," Cooper admitted to Kirby in a letter written in 1896, "will conclude that I have wasted my money in gambling, and in this there is some truth."[24]

Service on the appraisal board was nearly full-time work, so Bronson and Daughtie Cooper rented an apartment in Manhattan, leaving the big house on Calder Avenue in Beaumont in the care of their unmarried son, Bubber. Bronson, however, maintained Beaumont as his legal residence. Willie and her younger sister, Bird, moved with their parents to New York City, but Willie kept a room at the family's house in Beaumont, where she spent much time, undoubtedly because of Will. During her lengthy stays in Beaumont, Willie accompanied Will to social events, often with Florence Stratton in tow. When Willie was living in Manhattan, Will took the long railroad trips to the Northeast to be with her. The couple took advantage of the city's diverse entertainments, especially its nightlife. After Daughtie died in 1911, Willie spent more of her time in Manhattan and served as her father's hostess for dinner parties and his escort to other social events in the city.

By 1913, Willie was spending most of her time back in Beaumont as her romantic relationship with Will deepened. Neither was the type to show public affection. In addition, both were deep into their thirties during a time when the cultural norm was to marry at a much earlier age. The couple began to talk seriously about marriage and finally set a tentative wedding date in May 1914. They kept their decision private, although it's likely that Willie told her family and Florence Stratton, and Will shared his plans with his brother Edwin. There was an important reason why they decided to wait until 1914 to marry. Will was being urged by his Beaumont friends to run for political office. His successful effort to fund Beaumont's deepwater project had generated much favorable notice in the state's newspapers, especially in East and South Texas. In addition, through his active involvement in the affairs of the Texas Press Association, Will had made friends with a number of the state's most influential publishers and managing editors, including those who were also suggesting he might have a future as an elected office holder. With his growing public visibility, Will's family, friends, business associates, and members of his political network, including Walter Crawford and Rienzi Johnston, began to encourage him to run for public office. Will was somewhat conflicted about the prospect, but if he did become a candidate, he thought it best he not be caught up in a campaign early in their marriage. Willie, who had grown up in the political world, understood the situation well. They decided to wait until the political possibilities worked themselves out. Nonetheless, the odds seemed to be against his running for election in 1914, so a spring marriage remained on their calendars.[25]

Will was no stranger to politics. He had lived his life surrounded by men whose lives were deeply involved in public affairs. When he was a young boy, his father had fascinated him with stories of his political exploits as well as those of Will's uncle Alfred Marmaduke. Will's strongest interest as a newspaper editor was in the political world. It was common during this era for newspaper editors and publishers to move back and forth between elected office and the newsroom. So it is no surprise that Will was more than a little interested in running for state office. And crucially, Willie did not discourage the idea.

But if Will ran for public office, which one would it be? Some of Bronson Cooper's old supporters urged him to run against Representative Martin Dies Sr., but Will had no interest in being a member of the US Congress; his preference was a state office. After serving the traditional two terms as governor, his friend Oscar Colquitt would not be a candidate for reelection in 1914, which meant there would be no incumbent in the governor's race. But Will apparently gave little consideration to running for governor for several reasons, one being that a number of John Henry Kirby's friends were trying to persuade Kirby to be a candidate for governor. Another was Will's realistic understanding that although he had become a public figure in southeast Texas, serious candidates for the highly visible position of governor typically were much better known statewide than he was. The position of lieutenant governor, which more frequently attracted lesser-known candidates, would also be vacant in 1914, making a race for that office an attractive option. Other possibilities included running for the Texas House or for the Texas Senate, a position his father had held. Not having a law degree ruled out attorney general and the judiciary.

By the beginning of 1914, Will remained undecided about his political future despite his growing interest. No particular public office was obvious, and much depended on the decisions of others who might be candidates. In the meantime, he and Willie kept their marriage plans on a tentative schedule, contingent on developments in the coming months that could not be predicted.

## CHAPTER 5

———

# THE CAMPAIGN

# OF 1914

In November 1913, a little-known attorney and banker in Temple, James E. Ferguson, announced he would run for governor in the July 1914 Democratic primary. Texas Democratic Party leaders didn't take Ferguson's candidacy seriously at first, but Ferguson, who adopted the campaign nickname of "Farmer Jim," soon demonstrated a talent for fiery, populist-style oratory. As one observer noted, a Ferguson speech could "electrify and sway audiences to the near frenzy of a wild mob!" Ferguson quickly began to attract large crowds of farmers to his speeches. His growing appeal was the result of his promise to help the increasing number of economically distressed and exploited tenant farmers who had been generally ignored by state government. In 1914 tenants operated slightly more than half of the state's farms, and most were "mired in poverty." Ferguson's platform was simple and plainspoken: "Whereas, I, James Ferguson, am as well qualified to be Governor of Texas as any damn man in it; and Whereas, I am against prohibition and always will be; and Whereas, I am in favor of a square deal for tenant farmers: Therefore, be it resolved, that I will be elected."[1]

Ferguson's candidacy and his focus on improving the lives of the state's tenant farmers surprised the leaders in both of the Democratic Party's dominant factions, who expected prohibition to be the crucial issue of the 1914 election. Ferguson was considered to be antiprohibition, but in his campaign speeches he generally downplayed the issue, arguing that voters were tired of the constant battle between "wets" and "drys." Instead, Ferguson focused his attention on populist reforms to alleviate the plight of the state's tenant farmers. At the start of his campaign, however, Ferguson's admission that he would veto any prohibition legislation if he became governor confirmed the suspicions prohibitionists had about him. Ferguson's attempt to avoid the issue during the campaign did not fool antiprohibitionists either. Texas brewers eagerly rallied behind Ferguson with money and support.[2]

By spring 1914, Ferguson's surprising popularity drove other antiprohibition candi-

———

dates out of the campaign. His populist rhetoric alarmed many conservative Democratic leaders, even the antiprohibitionists, including Rienzi Johnston, who urged John Henry Kirby to run against Ferguson. Kirby declined. One of Johnston's friends later recalled that Colonel Johnston "never had any use for James E. Ferguson. He did everything in his power to prevent [Ferguson's] nomination." Johnston considered Ferguson a dangerous socialist and an irresponsible demagogue. When Ferguson emerged as the major challenger to attorney and former progressive congressman Tom Ball of Houston, a vocal prohibitionist, Johnston surprised many of his friends by throwing his support to Ball. Although Johnston was antiprohibition, he and Ball were friends. Johnston was willing to tolerate Ball's "dry" position rather than see Ferguson become governor. Many of the Colonel's antiprohibitionist friends criticized him for supporting Ball. Johnston wrote Oscar Colquitt that he had anticipated that his support of Ball would be "misunderstood and probably unjustly attacked in this campaign, but I believe I have done the right thing and future events will vindicate my course. We have been prone to speak of the fanaticism to be found in the prohibition ranks of Texas, but I am now forced to conclude that there is just as much, if not more, intolerance in the anti ranks."[3]

While the gubernatorial battle between Ferguson and Ball dominated newspaper headlines across the state, the press was paying little attention to the race for lieutenant governor. As the filing deadline approached, the only candidate was fifty-year-old state senator B. B. Sturgeon, a prominent defense lawyer and former district attorney in Paris, Texas. Sturgeon, a William Jennings Bryan Democrat and a gifted orator, was also a "militant" prohibitionist whom one of Will's associates described as "a witch-burning dry."[4]

Sturgeon was well known in northeast Texas due to his role as Lamar County Attorney in the arrest of Henry Smith, an African American man who was alleged to have murdered a four-year-old white child named Myrtle Vance in Paris in 1893. Denied a trial or legal counsel, Smith was tortured and burned alive in the county square in front of ten thousand eager spectators, including large delegations from Dallas and Fort Worth. Local law enforcement officials, including Sturgeon, not only failed to intervene but also informally sanctioned the entire affair. In 1908, Sturgeon was elected to the state Senate and reelected in 1912.[5]

Rienzi Johnston and his conservative allies, including Houston attorneys Jacob Wolters and Frank Andrews, John Henry Kirby, Oscar Colquitt, Clarence Ousley, and Houston insurance executive John L. Wortham, were alarmed that the prohibitionist Sturgeon would take the lieutenant governor's office by default in the absence of a viable opponent. With "dry" Tom Ball heavily favored to defeat Ferguson, it seemed likely that the prohibitionists soon would control the offices of governor and lieutenant governor. In that event, they would finally have a golden opportunity to persuade the legislature to pass a statewide prohibition law, despite the likelihood that the courts would rule such legislative action unconstitutional.[6]

Faced with the unhappy prospect of either prohibitionist Ball or the demagogic

Ferguson becoming governor, Johnston switched his attention to finding a "wet" candidate for lieutenant governor who would serve as a bulwark against whichever man became the state's chief executive. With strong encouragement from John Henry Kirby, Johnston turned to his friend and protégé Will Hobby as the person to challenge Sturgeon. Despite being characterized by one of his newspaper colleagues as "one of the last persons who might have been expected to run [for lieutenant governor] considering his lack of legislative service," Will was receptive to Johnston's proposition. Running for a state office had been on his mind for several months. The real question had been what office he should seek, and Johnston and Kirby had given him the answer. With Will now almost ready to jump into the race, he and Willie decided to postpone their wedding until after the election.[7]

Walter Crawford also urged Will to enter the race. He knew Will didn't want to give up his newspaper to run for office, but Crawford assured him he could serve as lieutenant governor without having to resign as editor of the *Enterprise*. Will would only have to be in Austin when the legislature was in session, which the state constitution limited to 140 days during the biennial regular session. Will's friend Colonel R. C. Duff, the railroad entrepreneur who had also been close friends with Will's father, joined Crawford in trying to persuade Will to put his name on the ballot.[8]

Despite the urging of his friends and his interest in serving in state government, Will told Johnston that before making a final decision he would go to Dallas to get the advice of his brother Edwin, now cashier of the Security National Bank. After the *Enterprise* finally began to make a profit, Will and Edwin had bought the *Waco Morning News* in 1912 for $75,000. Will persuaded John Henry Kirby to be his outside investor and to guarantee a loan the brothers borrowed for part of the purchase price. The Hobby brothers had hoped to use their newspaper to promote a railroad line between Waco and Beaumont to transport agricultural products, primarily cotton, to Beaumont's new port, but the railroad plan was soon abandoned. After two years of ownership, the newspaper turned out not to be as profitable as Will and Edwin had expected, and they decided to sell it. The Hobbys reached an agreement in late January 1914 to sell the *Waco News* to Artemus Roberts, founder of Waco's Amicable Life Insurance Company. The sale netted them a $10,000 profit.[9]

In May 1914, Will traveled to Dallas to pay off the loan he had received to purchase the Waco paper. While in Dallas on May 30, which was the day before the deadline for filing as a candidate in the July primary, Will and Edwin met with a group of antiprohibitionists allied with outgoing governor Colquitt. Rawlins Colquitt, the governor's son and a member of Colonel Johnston's conservative faction in Houston, organized the meeting, which was held in the bar on the ground floor of the Oriental Hotel. The six-story Oriental was the finest hotel in Dallas at the time, featuring ornate Italian marble floors and a grand staircase in the lobby, all surrounded by a near jungle of potted exotic plants. It was a favorite meeting place for local politicians and business leaders. And not surprisingly, Dallas's antiprohibitionists especially enjoyed the Oriental's huge barroom.

Rawlins Colquitt was one of the leaders of the antiprohibition forces in Texas. He was superintendent of agents for the Texas Guarantee Life Insurance Company in Houston. Will's good friend Jacob Wolters, another one of the state's most important antiprohibition leaders, was a member of the Texas Guarantee Life Insurance Company's board of directors. In 1911 Rawlins had played a prominent role in the fight to defeat the statewide prohibition amendment to the constitution, working with Wolters, who served as the head of the organization opposing the amendment, and Colonel Johnston, the campaign's chief fundraiser. Rawlins was also a friend of Will's brother Edwin.[10]

The group of antiprohibition leaders that Rawlins assembled shared Colonel Johnston's concerns about what would happen if "wet" candidate Ferguson became governor and hard-line prohibitionist Sturgeon became lieutenant governor. It would be an even worse situation for the "wets" if Tom Ball beat Ferguson and teamed with Sturgeon. Everyone, including Will, agreed that Sturgeon must not become lieutenant governor by default. Will had recently written an editorial in the *Enterprise* making that same argument. Although Will was strongly inclined to enter the race, he shared with the group his concerns that he was not as well known as Sturgeon because of Sturgeon's service in the legislature and his prominent ties to the William Jennings Bryan presidential campaigns in 1900 and 1908. Rawlins and his associates assured Will that because of his service as secretary of the Texas Democratic Party, he was well known and highly respected by party leaders. As secretary, he had become acquainted with most of the county and district committeemen in Texas, and he was liked and admired by his colleagues in the Texas newspaper business, most of whom could be counted on to endorse him. He would also have a lock on the "wet" vote.[11]

After an hour of discussion, Will finally asked his brother if he thought he should enter the race. Edwin urged Will to run. With Edwin on board, Will agreed to be a candidate for lieutenant governor. Immediately after the meeting, Rawlins rushed off a handwritten note to his father, Governor Colquitt: "Got tired of waiting on others to announce for Lt. Gov—Hobby sent his name in this P. M. Leave tonight for Houston." Only a few hours before the signing deadline, Will filed the paperwork for his name to appear on the ballot.[12]

Will called his managing editor at the *Enterprise* to give him the news about entering the race, while Rawlins informed the *Dallas News*. The next morning, the *Dallas News* headline read, "Hobby in Race for Lieutenant Governor." The story noted, "For several days there has been considerable speculation upon the possibility of Mr. Hobby announcing. He has received many requests from various parts of the state and has been urged by his friends to become a candidate. He thought it over carefully and said last night that he had mailed . . . an application. . . . He is a well known newspaper man both in and out of Texas." The Dallas newspaper reported that Will had declined "to discuss political issues in advance of the formal announcement he will make shortly." The Associated Press distributed the news about Will's candidacy to newspapers throughout the state, which was reported positively by many of the state's newspaper editors. The editor of the

*Coleman Democratic-Voice* noted, "Being an efficient journalist, it follows, naturally, that [Hobby] would make an efficient lieutenant governor."[13]

A few days after Will's announcement, Rawlins wrote another letter to his father. "I was instrumental in this of course and cannot but believe that it is for the best interests of our friends," he said. "Had he not announced we would have just handed the place over to Sturgin [*sic*] on a silver platter. I could not consent to this." Rawlins added that Ferguson's campaign manager, John McKay, phoned him as soon as he heard about Hobby's announcement and complained that his candidacy would be a "dreadful mistake, and that [Ferguson] . . . would not support" Hobby. Rawlins replied that he couldn't see how Ferguson "had any say so" in the matter. He pointed out that "Jim [Ferguson] had announced without asking anybody about it" and that "Will Hobby had the same right" that Jim had.[14]

When Will's train arrived in Beaumont, Willie and a delegation of his friends led by Walter Crawford met him at the station. They walked across the street to the Crosby Hotel to discuss strategy. Crawford agreed to be Will's campaign manager, and they spent an hour making general plans for the campaign. Crawford stressed to Hobby that Sturgeon would be a tough opponent. They should assume that Sturgeon's colleagues in the Texas Senate would support him and that his campaign would contrast his years of public service and extensive legislative experience with Hobby's lack thereof.[15]

In an attempt to straddle the middle ground between the dominant progressive faction and his conservative patrons, Will decided to campaign in favor of the progressive reforms he found reasonable while ignoring the progressive position on prohibition and suffrage. The legislature had passed a bill that placed an amendment on the ballot to allow statewide prohibition. The battle over that amendment was certain to be heated and emotional, and Will had no desire to get caught up in that whirlwind. As historian Lewis Gould noted, "The boyish Hobby was caught between the demands of former wet loyalties and the imperatives of the altered political situation" brought about by the growing popularity of prohibition as a progressive reform. Will and Walter Crawford decided to downplay the issue and released a statement to the press that Will Hobby was not taking a position on prohibition.[16]

Will also made a strategic decision to ignore the women's suffrage issue in his campaign, although not because he opposed giving women the right to vote. He supported suffrage. Willie was a vigorous women's suffrage advocate, and Will's position had been greatly influenced by his wife's views on the issue. She had developed a strong interest in the issue of women's rights and suffrage when she was living in New York City. She had studied short-story writing at Columbia University, but at that time, women could not attend Columbia as regular students. They had to enroll in Columbia's special Collegiate Course program, which required them to study at home. The only time women could mix with male students was when exams were given. Willie was angered by the rule that she could take tests with men but not attend classes with them. Willie also attended special club forums in Greenwich Village to hear lectures on the social and political issues of the day, including presentations in favor of women's suffrage. Some of her female friends in New York were public school teachers. "When I realized the big injustice of paying men more than women for equal services rendered in the public schools of New York," Willie stated years later, "I became an enthusiastic advocate in aiding women in securing their rights and have since worked hard for suffrage." She became a suffragist and spoke on the subject at salons and other forums around Manhattan.[17]

As the daughter of a former congressman, however, Willie understood the need for a pragmatic campaign strategy. A newspaper story published later about Willie noted that she was a better politician than Will. "If she had been a man," the story stressed, "she would have been a congressman or a governor or a senator." Will saw the suffrage issue as another dangerous distraction that he preferred to avoid. In his view, the suffrage issue would be resolved one way or the other on its own. And as a practical matter, the fact that women could not vote meant that he didn't have to worry about a vote that didn't exist.[18]

The items on the progressive agenda that Will thought were more important than suffrage, prohibition, and other moral and social justice causes were the less controversial "efficiency and modernization" goals, which had the purpose of enhancing the business environment through improvements in the infrastructure, including constructing highways, paving old dirt roads, and building bridges and port docks. He favored state aid to encourage home ownership and to make it possible for more tenant farmers to own land, actions that he believed would expand the economy as well as make socialism and populism less attractive political options. Will also supported increased state funding to improve public schools to better educate young Texans who were needed for skilled jobs in an increasingly urban state. In addition, Will agreed with progressives who believed in "better government" reforms that would protect entrepreneurs and small businesses from the unfair practices of corporate monopolies and powerful special interest groups. Those reforms included campaign finance laws prohibiting corporate political donations, legislation to require runoff elections in the event that no candidate won the majority vote in the regular primary, and other reforms aimed at preventing corruption in local and state governments.[19]

Although Will's positions on these matters closely matched those of Jim Ferguson, he did not want to be linked to the "wet" Ferguson or the "dry" Tom Ball. Journalist Ed Kilman, a longtime friend and employee of Will's, later observed that Will ran for lieutenant governor as a free agent. "Although having an ultra-dry adversary and being liberally disposed himself, he drew support largely from the anti-pro[hibition] ranks," Kilman noted. "But on the other hand he had known Colonel Ball well as a congressman and in politics, and was his good friend."[20]

Will officially launched his campaign on June 14, 1914, only six weeks before the primary election. With campaign time short, Will and Crawford decided to concentrate their efforts in North, Central, and West Texas. Will was already well known in his home base in the southern part of East Texas, which included the Beaumont area and Houston, and he had a network of friends and associates in the region who would serve as proxy campaigners. John Henry Kirby was among those friends who provided significant help in East Texas. "I am very interested in your campaign," Kirby told Will. "No doubt it would be very pleasing to you to preside over the body in which your father rendered such distinguished service." Because Will took a neutral stance on prohibition during the campaign, he was able to attract support from both sides of the issue. One pro-Ferguson newspaper editorialized, "In the main [Hobby] is in line with that of Mr. Ferguson and is quite pleasing to the Ferguson supporters." On the other side, the strongly prohibitionist *Hamilton Herald* published an editorial declaring that Will was "an anti-prohibitionist, but he is a good, clean, fair man, and would make a good Lieutenant Governor. Don't be too hidebound. There are lots of good men who don't agree with you on every question."[21]

Colonel Johnston helped Will's cause with supportive editorials in the *Houston Post*. "The *Post* can speak for him as one of its own family," Johnston wrote in one editorial, "for it was under its own roof that he received the training that has in later years brought him into the front ranks of his profession." The *Post*'s popular columnist Judd Mortimer Lewis mailed letters to editors throughout the state. The *Temple Mirror* noted in one of its issues that Lewis had "sent out a bunch of letters asking his friends who are members of the Press association to support Will Hobby of Beaumont for Lt. Governor. The *Mirror* is going to support Mr. Hobby. Judd, we believe in you and glory in your supporting your old comrade of the *Post*." William Mayes, the incumbent lieutenant governor who was not seeking reelection, owned a chain of newspapers in west-central Texas. Mayes and his newspapers also supported Will Hobby.[22]

The pro-Hobby editorials probably stemmed from Will's positive relationship with the state's newspaper publishers and editors. "Here was their . . . chance . . . to elect a newspaper man to an important office," Kilman later wrote. "Even the country papers joined actively in his campaign." The value of the support that Will received from most of the newspapers in Texas cannot be discounted. In an era before radio, television, and social media, newspapers were practically the only source of news. Every small town had at least one newspaper, while the cities had at least two, and some had three or more. And the opinions expressed on the editorial page were much more influential than would be the case in the future, when multiple sources of opinion and news would overwhelm society. Another journalist, when recalling the 1914 campaign, noted, "Col. Johnston and the newspaper tribe of Texas, with few exceptions, backed Hobby to a successful finish."[23]

Despite the editorial support for Hobby, the colorful and quotable "Pa" Ferguson and the passionate debate over the statewide prohibition amendment dominated newspaper coverage of the 1914 campaign and largely distracted public attention from the Hobby-Sturgeon race. International developments, including the assassination of Archduke Ferdinand and his wife in Sarajevo two weeks into the campaign, Austria's subsequent declaration of war against Serbia, and the ongoing revolution across the border in Mexico, also diverted the attention of Texans from state politics.

*Will Hobby's lieutenant governor campaign card, 1914.*

As the campaign moved toward its climax, Will received encouraging reports from Dallas, where Edwin was coordinating campaign efforts in North Texas, and from Colonel Rienzi Johnston and Rawlins Colquitt in Houston. John Henry Kirby told Will, "Everything I hear about your race is encouraging. I find no opposition to you in East Texas. You are doing right to devote your time to North Texas." Because of those positive reports, Will grew confident that he would defeat Sturgeon decisively. Walter Crawford, however, was less sanguine. Based on reports from around the state, he warned Will that the prohibitionists in the rural areas of North and West Texas were working extremely hard for Sturgeon and that the election results were likely to be close. When Democratic Party voters went to the polls on July 25, Jim Ferguson easily defeated Tom Ball in the governor's race, despite the Wilson administration's widely publicized endorsement of Ball. A large majority of voters also rejected the statewide prohibition amendment, a stunning setback for the prohibition movement. As the returns gradually trickled in, it became clear that Crawford's caution was warranted. As midnight approached, Hobby and Sturgeon were in a dead heat with approximately 34,000 votes each. It took two days to determine that Will had won the election. In the final tally, Hobby received 211,197 votes to Sturgeon's 203,441. When the news of his victory finally reached Will's campaign headquarters in Dallas, Edwin sent a telegram to Willie, who was in Beaumont: "YOUR LOVER IS ELECTED . . . COME UP AND CELEBRATE."[24]

Will failed to attract as many votes as he had hoped in South Texas, but he enjoyed wide victory margins in "dry" areas of East Texas, especially in his home territory of Tyler and Polk Counties. Will also carried the cities of Beaumont, Houston, Dallas,

El Paso, and San Antonio, indicating that his win was an urban victory over the rural prohibitionist vote. Hobby received approximately twenty-five thousand fewer votes than Ferguson did in his race. In addition, Ferguson won more votes than Hobby in "dry" North Texas, probably because of Ferguson's pledge to help tenant farmers, a position Will supported but largely ignored in the campaign. Because of his narrow win, it is difficult to determine if Will's neutral position on prohibition helped or hurt him. With antiprohibitionist Ferguson's victory and the defeat of the statewide prohibition amendment, 1914 turned out not to be a prohibitionist year, despite expectations. The antiprohibition triumph would prove transitory, however, and Will would be forced to confront the issue in the future.[25]

Despite the narrow win, Edwin Hobby declared a few days after the election that he was "thoroughly satisfied with the results of the primary . . . considering the limited time from the date of announcement until the primary, which was only fifty-three days against his opponents' eleven months active campaigning." Edwin, who had been mildly favorable toward prohibition, was "not sorry" that statutory prohibition was defeated. In a letter to his fiancée, Sadie Webb, Edwin admitted, "The intolerance of the preacher politician had dampened my ardor somewhat on this question."[26]

As news of the horrific war erupting in Europe dominated the front pages of the state's newspapers in mid-August, the Democrats held their state convention in El Paso. In his acceptance speech as the party's nominee for lieutenant governor, Will claimed that his election and the defeat of the statewide prohibition referendum were clear signs from the voters that it was time to get past the prohibition issue. "I will devote my time and my efforts to the material and general up-building of the state," Hobby declared, "and to the suspension of liquor agitation, and all of those things that bring about factional and political strife."[27]

Will Hobby, James Ferguson, and the rest of the Democratic slate easily won the November 1914 general election over token opposition from the Republicans. Assured of an easy victory, Will spent the fall preparing for his new job, busily arranging for Jim Mapes and others to manage the *Enterprise* while Will was in Austin during the legislative session. His preparations for assuming the duties of lieutenant governor also included a trip with Willie and Edwin to Washington, DC, and New York City to promote investment in Texas businesses. While in Washington, they met with members of the Texas congressional delegation, many of whom Willie had known during her time as her father's secretary. In Manhattan they took the opportunity to spend time with Willie's father, Bronson Cooper. While in town, Will was interviewed by the *New York Times*. He urged Wall Street to invest in Texas and noted that the state had gotten a bad reputation among large investors because of its antitrust laws and trust-busting actions. Will sought to reassure Wall Street that the state's financial laws were reasonable. Similar laws were being passed by the Wilson administration, and there was great opportunity for investors to profit under existing statutes.[28]

On January 10, 1915, after Will's return from his and Willie's expedition to the East

Coast, thirty of their Beaumont friends honored them with a banquet at the Crosby House. Walter Crawford presided as toastmaster. Will was celebrated as the first citizen of Jefferson County ever elected to a statewide office. In his toast, Judge Frederick C. Proctor, who was general counsel for Gulf Oil, declared that it was reasonable for Will's friends to believe he would be the next governor of Texas. Proctor's prediction would turn out to be prescient.[29]

*Governor James "Pa" Ferguson, ca. 1915.*

# CHAPTER 6

# LIEUTENANT GOVERNOR HOBBY

A t noon on January 19, 1915, Associate Supreme Court Justice Nelson Phillips administered the oath of office to James "Pa" Ferguson, who became the twenty-sixth governor of Texas. The ceremony was held in the chamber of the Texas House of Representatives before a boisterous, standing-room-only crowd jammed into the upper galleries. Many of the audience had arrived in Austin that morning from Temple, Texas, in a special eight-car train covered in bunting, flags, and signs to celebrate the inauguration of Temple's native son as governor.

After Ferguson was sworn, Will Hobby stepped forward to take his oath as lieutenant governor. Retiring governor Oscar Colquitt and acting lieutenant governor Quintus Watson stood behind Will on the House Speaker's platform. Will then signed the official written copy of his oath, and Justice Phillips affixed the Great Seal of the State of Texas to certify it. The president pro tem of the Texas Senate, C. W. Nugent, then stepped forward and introduced Governor Ferguson, who gave his inaugural address.[1]

Ferguson's speech was brief and revealed none of his legislative agenda. Instead, he asked that all three branches of state government work in unison and harmony. The most memorable moment in his address came when Ferguson declaimed to the legislature,

> If you love me, and I love you,
> Nothing can cut our love in two.[2]

After Ferguson's address, the new lieutenant governor stepped forward and gave his inaugural speech, which was described as "brief and scholarly." Will referenced the Great War in Europe, now in its seventh month. He stressed that the monarchy-ruled "Old World," which was "torn with grief and red with blood," had unleashed war on the people of Europe, while America, ruled by the elected representatives of the people, was "full of peace and progress." Will declared that the inaugural ceremony itself was symbolic of how democracy worked in America. Will then spoke modestly of his role as lieutenant governor, stressing that he would play only a small part in the administration and that his job was "just a 'twilight' office lingering between the departing shadow of the Governor and the scintillating star of the Senate." Will ended his speech with an indirect reference to the political battle over prohibition. He urged the legislature, the courts, and the governor to join him in moving past divisive issues so they all could work in harmony to "advance the material welfare of Texas." In Will's unspoken view, the defeat of the statewide prohibition amendment and Ferguson's focus on his populist agenda gave the new legislature the opportunity to move forward, free of the liquor question.[3]

In some ways, the new lieutenant governor was unlike any of the men who had preceded him. Will was the first native Texan to be elected to the office and the first from Jefferson County. At the age of thirty-six, he was the youngest lieutenant governor. It was Will's first elected office, and he had no experience as a legislative leader. The Senate was not unknown territory to Will, however. He had grown up surrounded by men who had intimate knowledge of the Senate and how it worked. As a teenager, he had spent many hours talking to his father about his experience in the Senate. One of his mentors, Bronson Cooper, was a former senator, while another of Will's patrons, John Henry Kirby, had served as the Senate's calendar clerk. Will had also gained extensive personal experience working with Senate committees and individual senators when he was lobbying on behalf of Beaumont's deepwater channel.

When Will took office in 1915, the office of lieutenant governor was not the powerful position it would become after World War II. The powers of the lieutenant governor did not extend much beyond those enumerated in the Constitution of 1876. As John Henry Kirby advised Will three days prior to his inauguration, as lieutenant governor he was "not in a position to influence legislation officially and you have no veto power and no vote . . . except in case of a tie but you can wield a tremendous influence by discussing the pending measures freely with the Senators." As president of the Senate, however, the lieutenant governor did hold some influence over proceedings. Every session, senators also passed what were called "simple resolutions" that conferred authority on the lieutenant governor to hire staff and take care of other matters needed to perform his duties as presiding officer. Later in the twentieth century, at the beginning of each session the Senate would pass special rules that delegated the power to appoint the chairs and other members of standing committees to the lieutenant governor. In Will Hobby's years as lieutenant governor, however, the Senate committee on committees still performed that function.[4]

The constitution gave the lieutenant governor the power to break tie votes taken during regular sessions and to debate and vote on bills whenever the Senate was convened as a committee of the whole. Otherwise, the lieutenant governor's only other constitutional duties were contingent on events beyond his control: serving as acting governor whenever the governor traveled out of the state and assuming the duties of governor in the event of the governor's death, resignation, or removal from office. As a result of his earlier experiences lobbying the legislature, Will was well aware of the limited duties of his new position.

One of Will's predecessors as lieutenant governor, Martin McNulty Crane, frustrated by the job's limitations, observed, "The truth is that the office of Lieutenant Governor ordinarily takes little more of a man's time than that of being a State Senator." Crane also described the job as "punishment" because the lieutenant governor was "compelled to sit and listen to so many speeches, remaining silent when he so much desires to enter the controversies." Will approached his job with confidence. Sitting in a large swivel chair on the dais overlooking the Senate chamber, he presided over the Senate with enthusiasm and quiet humor, making certain the business at hand proceeded smoothly, which it did more often than not under his patient guidance, and earning the respect and friendship of most of the members.[5]

Will's first session as lieutenant governor went extremely well. The Thirty-Fourth Legislature had an unusually ambitious and full agenda that was deeply influenced by the progressive movement, a situation that worried Will's conservative backers, who expected Will to slow down, if not block, the progressive agenda. A few days before the legislature convened, Kirby warned Will, "I predict a stormy session . . . and you are going to have to keep your wits about you at all times . . . to check the firebrands and men of limited information." Kirby feared that the progressives would push bills that would "burden and repress industry." He argued, "Most legislators advocate the strangulation of every sensible enterprise and . . . hold that all men are selfish and insincere and dishonest except themselves." Kirby's fears proved to be real, as the legislature tackled a wide variety of progressive issues, including more equitable taxation, increased support for rural schools and higher education, creation of new courts, establishment of free county public libraries, and land title reform. Women's suffrage had also become an active legislative issue by 1915, but efforts to pass a constitutional amendment failed to win the required two-thirds majority in the House, so no action on that issue was taken in the Senate. The fight to win women the right to vote, however, was far from over.[6]

Despite Kirby's advice, Will did nothing to hinder the passage of progressive legislation, although he had limited options even if he had tried. Except for a weeklong battle over mandatory public school attendance (a bill opposed by rural interests) that featured a five-day filibuster, the legislature enjoyed an unusually harmonious session. Even the mandatory school attendance fight was eventually resolved to most of the members' satisfaction. A law with progressive roots was passed that required all children between the ages of seven and fourteen to attend school for a minimum of one hundred days. The legislature passed other bills providing state aid to rural schools (part of the mandatory attendance compromise) and granting authority to the counties to create boards of education and to levy taxes. Another progressive-inspired act created the Austin State School for adults with mental disabilities.[7]

The Thirty-Fourth Legislature ended its regular session on March 20. As productive as the legislature had been, it was still unable to complete its agenda within the constitutionally imposed number of days that the legislature was allowed to meet. The Texas Constitution grants the governor power to convene the legislature in a special session if necessary to complete unfinished legislative business, to enact measures necessitated by an emergency, or for other reasons the governor deems necessary. Shortly before the end of the regular session, Governor Ferguson informed Will Hobby and Speaker John W. Woods that he would call a special session to meet late in April to enable the legislature to deal with unfinished business. With this knowledge, Will adjourned the Senate "sine die" and immediately departed for Beaumont by train. There was a special reason for Will's rush to get home. He and Willie had planned to be wed in New Orleans in April, but the called special session now forced them to alter their plans. After Will returned to Beaumont, he and Willie decided to reschedule the wedding ceremony for a still to be determined date in May, if not sooner. With the wedding postponed once again, Will returned to Austin in late April for the special session.[8]

In the called special session, the legislature passed a bill creating the Texas Forest Service. It also increased appropriations and approved a new construction program for the state's colleges and universities. To pay for these new expenditures, the legislature more than doubled the ad valorem tax rate. The legislature's generous support of the state's colleges and universities had strings attached. Governor Ferguson and his legislative supporters imposed tight controls on how college administrators could spend state appropriations. Ferguson also insisted that the budgets for the state's colleges and universities be itemized, listing every employee and their salaries as a line item. After a strong lobbying effort by W. J. Battle, acting president of the University of Texas, and some of the university's influential graduates and supporters, the appropriations bill was amended to authorize the university's board of regents to adjust the itemized allocations in the event of altered circumstances. Although strongly opposed to the amendment, Governor Ferguson grudgingly signed the bill but publicly chastised President Battle and his administration for their lobbying effort. Nevertheless, the seeds were planted that would lead to a historical confrontation between the governor, the University of Texas and its alumni, and the legislature. The results of that confrontation would change Will Hobby's life forever.[9]

Other than the tax hike, which generated the usual protests from antitax groups, and the dustup over the university's line item budget, most of the legislature's actions received widespread public approval. Will was given credit for his patient skill in guiding these progressive bills efficiently through the Senate. And for the folks back home, Will—with the aid of friendly senators—nudged a bill along to create a new court of civil appeals in Beaumont.[10]

Eager to have a spring wedding in New Orleans before the heat and humidity became unbearable, Will finally saw an opportunity during a long-weekend legislative break to make the trek to Louisiana to have the ceremony. Will loved New Orleans and had many friends there. With Willie's father, Samuel Bronson Cooper, back in Beaumont during a long break in the New York Board of Appraisers court schedule, Will and Willie wanted to take advantage of his availability.[11]

Will hurried from Austin to Beaumont on Wednesday, May 12, and at noon the following day, he and Willie boarded the Southern Pacific's famed Sunset Limited train at the line's depot in Beaumont, bound for New Orleans. A large group of family and friends accompanied them, including Will's brother Edwin, Bronson Cooper, Willie's sister Bird Sholars, and Willie's brother, Sam Jr. Other members of the wedding party included Colonel Rienzi Johnston, Walter Crawford, state legislator Louis J. Wortham, Harris County judge Chester Bryan, R. C. Duff, Rawlins Colquitt, Beaumont businessmen and investors in the *Beaumont Enterprise* Bernard Deutser and R. A. Greer, and Willie's best friend, Florence Stratton. Willie's other sister, Margaret, and her husband, Arkansas congressman Henderson Jacoway, who lived in Dardanelle, Arkansas, joined the wedding party in New Orleans. Will and Willie and their guests took their lodgings at the famed St. Charles Hotel near the French Quarter.[12]

At 6:00 p.m. on Saturday, May 15, with the venerable Samuel Bronson Cooper giving away the bride, Will Hobby's long alliance with the Cooper family was officially sealed in matrimony in suite 501. Reverend Shepard Halsey Werlein, the prominent minister of the First Methodist Church in New Orleans, officiated. Werlein had served as pastor at Houston's Shearn Memorial Church during the 1880s. Florence Stratton was Willie's bridesmaid, while Edwin Hobby served as Will's best man. After a romantic relationship stretching back nearly a decade and two years of planning and postponements, Will Hobby, thirty-seven years old, and Willie Cooper, thirty-nine, were now married.[13]

Because it was the wedding of the lieutenant governor of Texas, news of Will's marriage to Willie Cooper received widespread newspaper attention in Texas. The news was also featured in the New Orleans newspapers and in other newspapers throughout southern Louisiana. The Associated Press carried the news, and of course the *Beaumont Enterprise* and the *Houston Post* featured it prominently. Most of the stories featured individual photographic portraits of both the bride and the groom. Four different portraits of Willie dressed stylishly in the latest fashion illustrated the news stories. The portraits reveal an attractive woman with delicate facial features, a beautiful and full head of hair, and captivating eyes. A story in the *New Orleans Item* described Willie as wearing "a large black hat at the wedding." A headline in the *New Orleans Times-Picayune* proclaimed, "Lone Star's Lieutenant Governor Elopes: W. P. Hobby Comes Here to Wed Miss Willie Cooper." The *Times-Picayune* reported, "It was the wish of both parties that the ceremony be simple." The parlor where the ceremony occurred was "beautifully decorated with lilies and palms." The story also noted that because of Will and Willie's "social prominence" and the "interest in the nuptials throughout Texas . . . much local interest was shown and a large number of prominent Orleanians called at the Hotel St. Charles during the day to pay their respects." Louisiana governor Luther Hall was among the visitors. The governor "warmly congratulated . . . Hobby and his bride, having personally known the former for some time. Many prominent state people gathered [at the hotel] en route to Baton Rouge for the extra session of the Legislature displayed their interest in the Texas wedding."[14]

With the legislature still in session, the Hobbys' stay in the Crescent City was brief. On Sunday night, May 16, the wedding party departed New Orleans on the Sunset Limited back west to Beaumont. Because Will and Willie had kept their wedding plans quiet, it was a surprise to many of their friends and acquaintances in Beaumont when the *Enterprise* published the news. After a brief stop in Beaumont, the newlyweds traveled to San Antonio, where they spent the night of May 18 at the St. Anthony Hotel and visited with several friends. The next evening, the Hobbys were met by a small delegation of legislators when their train arrived in Austin.[15]

Will's modest and self-deprecating personality and his skilled and fair manner of dealing with the members of the Texas Senate had made him a popular figure in the capital. After his return to Austin with his attractive and politically savvy bride, his friends staged a series of events celebrating their marriage. On the morning of May 20, the Senate held a special program in their honor. With Will and Willie seated on the presiding platform on the floor of the Senate chamber, they were presented with a set of sterling silver hollowware, including a large meat platter with an inscription stating that it had been presented to "Lieutenant Governor W. P. Hobby and wife, from the officers and employees of the Texas Senate, 1915." The names of each of the members of the Senate were engraved on the back of the platter. A small delegation from the House of Representatives presented them with other pieces of the hollowware set. After the gift presentations, Will stood at the podium to declare that he was "always glad to receive a message from the House, and in this instance I shall be glad to ask that the senate concur without amendment!"

A week later, Governor Ferguson and his wife, Miriam, graciously hosted a late evening reception at the Governor's Mansion in honor of the Hobbys. Former congressman and governor Joe Sayers and his wife were special guests. A newspaper account of the event observed that Willie was "bright, charming, and winsome," with a "gracious and pleasing personality. She . . . has traveled much and come into contact with the brilliant political and social life of the nation's capital and is well suited to be the helpmate of a man with political aspirations."[16]

When the called special legislative session finally adjourned on Friday, May 28, 1915, Will and Willie returned to Beaumont and moved into a house on Broadway within walking distance of the *Enterprise*'s offices. Because the state constitution mandated that the legislature meet only once every two years in regular session, and with terms of office for statewide officials two years in length, Will's official work as lieutenant governor was now over. Because the legislative session was widely praised as a success, it was apparent that Will would have little or no opposition if he chose to run for a second term. Because he had greatly enjoyed his work during the two legislative sessions of 1915, it was an easy decision for him to make to run for another term in office, especially with his primary election in July 1916 virtually assured. With no legislative sessions until January 1917,

Will could now devote the next eighteen months to his new marriage, his newspaper business, and his civic activities, while also making public appearances at venues of his own choice to keep his name in the state's newspapers.[17]

In the months following their wedding and before the primary election of July 1916, the Hobbys publicly supported Willie's brother Sam Jr. in his campaign for the legislature in a special election in July 1915. Sam's victory returned him to the Texas House after a six-month absence. He had served in the Thirty-Third Legislature from 1913 to January 1915. The Hobbys also made several appearances in southeast Texas, including a weekend in Galveston in mid-July 1915 attending the island city's Cotton Carnival. After the great hurricane of 1900, Galveston had been rebuilt in one of the major engineering feats of the era. To protect from future storms, most of the city's houses and buildings had been elevated seventeen feet on top of sand that had been pumped in from the floor of the Gulf. A three-mile-long concrete seawall seventeen feet in height had been constructed to stop storm waves from surging over the city. During their visit to Galveston, the Hobbys, Rawlins Colquitt and his wife, and Willie's Beaumont friend Florence Stratton went on a four-hour ride on Galveston Bay on the quarantine boat *Alice* to view the new lighthouse and jetties. The Hobbys also attracted public attention as they rode in a VIP car in the Cotton Carnival's main parade.

News reports noted that one of the reasons for the carnival's success that year was Galveston's celebratory mood about the city's continuing recovery from the disaster of 1900. Three weeks after the carnival's end, however, a hurricane packing 120-mile-per-hour winds unleashed a sixteen-foot storm surge on the city. The seawall limited the death toll and damage, but eleven people died and all major streets were flooded. The storm marked the end of Galveston's hopes to compete commercially with Houston, as many of its leading businesses soon relocated to the city's neighbor to the north.[18]

A veteran of the political scene in Washington, DC, Willie Hobby eagerly played her role in Will's publicity efforts. In mid-October she traveled to Houston to participate in the newly established Texas Woman's Fair. As the guest of Mayor Ben Campbell, she rode in an open car to lead a parade through downtown Houston. When they arrived at the building on Texas Avenue in which the fair was being held, Mayor Campbell presented Willie with the keys to the city and she gave the keynote speech to officially open the fair. Her speech left no doubt where she stood—and by implication, where the lieutenant governor stood—on the issue of women's suffrage. Willie noted that it had been "a slow process to gain for [women] the recognition that would be given to men who performed even the same deeds. That time is passing . . . and now the enlightened thought of the day is beginning to accord to her a place of equality in the economic, industrial, and political affairs of the world. Such an exposition as the Texas Woman's Fair is a substantial demonstration . . . that women are capable of meeting any and every responsibility that may be given them." Willie's forceful endorsement of suffrage received much attention in the press.[19]

In November 1915, the Texas Associated Press Managing Editors Association, meeting in Beaumont, elected Will their president. As the association's leader, Will's main goal was to create a Texas election bureau to provide more timely local election returns to the public. Will had been deeply frustrated by how slowly the votes had been reported during his own election. With critical support from the Associated Press, Will's proposal became a reality in time for the statewide election in 1916. The Associated Press and the managing editors of the leading newspapers in Texas established an election tabulation bureau in Dallas to gather and report voting results to their newspapers. The bureau's work was a major success and was widely praised.[20]

In his efforts to stay in the public eye, Will did not neglect his hometown, especially as he still had a newspaper to promote. His record as one of Beaumont's most effective civic boosters was enhanced when the newly expanded and renamed Southeast Texas State Fair opened in the spring of 1916. Will had worked diligently to make the event one of the largest regional fairs in the state. Accordingly, when the fair opened on a site east of the city, Will served as the principal speaker at the opening festivities. In his speech, Will enthusiastically hailed the "magnificent" port of Beaumont, now "open to the commerce of the world." Afterward, Will and Willie mingled with the large crowd touring the grounds, enjoying the carnival rides and visiting the displays of agricultural products and prize livestock.

A few weeks after that appearance at Beaumont's fair, the Hobbys led a local delegation to greet the Italian steamer *Lampo* as it arrived at the new deepwater Port of Beaumont. The *Lampo*, which filled its tanks with oil products from the Magnolia Oil Company's dock, was the first oceangoing ship to navigate the now twenty-five-feet-deep Neches River channel. The event set off a major celebration that evening in Beaumont, at which Will and Willie were the center of attention.[21]

In May 1916 Will returned to Galveston, which had barely recovered from the hurricane of the previous September. He delivered the featured speech observing the twenty-third anniversary of the death of Galveston businessman and philanthropist Henry Rosenberg. Will's speech was in harmony with the main tenets of the progressive movement, especially the idea that social reform was necessary to prevent epidemics, crime, and civic unrest and disorder. "If we are to progress, we must do it together and nobody must be left behind," Hobby declared. "If we let the poison of filthy disease percolate through the hovels of the poor, death knocks at the palace gates. If we fail to provide education, the consequences of ignorance strikes us all and there is no escape."[22]

Will then attended the Jefferson County Democratic Party Convention, where he led support for a resolution endorsing the reelections of Governor James Ferguson and President Woodrow Wilson. The convention passed another resolution, over Will's modest objections, calling for him to run for governor in 1918. The delegates also endorsed Will's election to a second term as lieutenant governor. Will's widely praised performance in his first term and his status as an incumbent fended off all potential opponents in the Democratic primary. With the Republican Party not a factor in Texas, Hobby's victory in the general election in November was assured.

When Governor Ferguson took a trip out of state for a few days in June, Will became acting governor, as required by the Texas Constitution. He and Willie traveled to Austin with a group of their Beaumont friends to celebrate the largely honorary designation with several receptions and parties. The day after the celebration, Will lectured to a group at the University of Texas assembled by former lieutenant governor Will Mayes, who had recently organized the university's journalism department. Will Hobby told his audience that he had been in the "game" of journalism since the age of fourteen and had filled "every desk in the office." He spoke of how valuable the new journalism program would be to the newspaper business, stressing that there was "no opportunity for owners to teach new men" how to be reporters. Stating that reporters were the most important members of any newspaper staff, Will emphasized that it was crucial they should strive always to be accurate and honest. "The making of a newspaper is a fascinating business," Will added, "and it gives the broadest field for observing human endeavor. The newspaper reflects the life, heart, and hopes of the community."[23]

Having no opponent, the Democratic primary election on July 22, 1916, was basically a nonevent for Will, as he won renomination by default. When John Henry Kirby's general manager sent Will his congratulations on the primary victory, Will replied that he had "tried [it] both ways and I am willing to impart to you the confidential information that a race without opposition is the best. The people always act intelligently under those circumstances."[24]

To James Ferguson's unpleasant surprise and chagrin, however, prohibition activists refused to abandon their cause despite their election setbacks in 1914. They recruited the politically obscure Charles H. Morris, a banker from Winnsboro, to oppose Ferguson in the primary. Seeking to revive their movement, prohibitionists ignored leaders such as Tom Ball who warned against challenging Ferguson. In addition to his support for prohibition, Morris attacked the legislature's tax increase and "extravagant" spending, perennially popular issues for nearly all Texas politicians seeking election. More significantly, the Morris campaign circulated rumors about corruption in the Ferguson administration.[25]

On primary-election day, Ferguson was reelected by a majority of about sixty thousand votes. But the opposition to Ferguson, which included a number of voters who were not prohibitionists, surprised many political observers, including Will. The *Beaumont Enterprise* supported Ferguson editorially and published several favorable news stories about the governor's performance during his first term. It was apparent, however, that the rumors about corruption in the governor's office and the general popularity of Morris's prohibition and antitax stances had been more effective than expected. The corruption rumors would haunt Ferguson's second term. The results also foreshadowed the return of prohibition as a powerful political issue and the increasing strength of the suffrage movement.[26]

With obvious signs that the cause of prohibition was experiencing a revival in Texas, Hobby officially continued his neutral position on the issue. His words and actions, however, revealed that he leaned strongly toward the antiprohibition side. In an editorial in the *Enterprise* on November 16, 1916, Will declared his opposition to a provision on the ballot of an upcoming local election that would outlaw the sale of liquor in Jefferson County. Will argued that the law would not stop anyone from drinking. Its real outcome, he stressed, would be to put some local store owners out of business while enriching liquor dealers in Galveston and Houston by forcing Beaumont's drinking citizens to travel to the stores in those nearby cities. This argument was not one that the prohibitionists could accept, of course, but it allowed Will to treat the issue as a strictly local economic matter while staying out of the debate over statewide and national prohibition. Will's argument against prohibition in Jefferson County prevailed, and the antiliquor proposition was defeated.[27]

Despite the surprising results of the gubernatorial election, the US Senate campaign dominated newspaper coverage of the Texas primary election of 1916. This election was the first held since the passage of the Seventeenth Amendment to the US Constitution, which mandated the direct election of US Senators by popular vote, the novelty of which seized the attention of voters. In the primary, former governor Oscar Colquitt won the most votes but he lacked a majority, which forced him into a runoff with the incumbent senator Charles Culberson. John Henry Kirby supported Culberson, but Will Hobby and the *Enterprise* supported Colquitt. Will had nothing personal or political against Culberson, but his loyalty was with his family's friend, Colquitt, who had also given significant aid to Will when he was campaigning for the Sabine-Neches ship channel. And, as previously discussed, Oscar Colquitt's son, Rawlins, had played a key role in recruiting Will to run for lieutenant governor. In addition, Will was well aware of Culberson's severe alcoholism, which was not well known among the public in Texas. The senator's drinking problem had made him ineffective as a representative of Texas's interests in Congress. The chief issue in the Senate campaign was Woodrow Wilson's reelection as president. Declaring Wilson's administration "a complete failure," Colquitt opposed Wilson's nomination for a second term and he openly supported Germany in the European war, which won him major support from Texans of German heritage, who were critical of Wilson's obvious pro-English sympathies. Culberson, however, was a strong Wilson supporter, and the vast majority of Texas voters, including Will Hobby and James Ferguson, favored the president's reelection. Like most Texans, Hobby's sympathies were decidedly with the British and the French.[28]

Assuming that Ferguson would support Colquitt, Hobby wrote him a letter three days after the first primary election stressing that Colquitt needed the governor's help in the runoff. Because Hobby was going to Dallas to meet with Colquitt, he asked Ferguson if there was any advice or information that Ferguson would like Hobby to pass along. As an indication of his friendly relationship with Ferguson, Hobby closed his handwritten letter with a warm "best wishes and congratulations [on Ferguson's reelection]—your friend, W. P. Hobby." Ferguson, however, endorsed Culberson, who easily won the runoff.[29]

As 1916 drew to a close, Will continued to be popular with his colleagues in the newspaper business. He was elected to a second term as president of the Associated Press Managing Editors Association, whose members praised his leadership in establishing the voting-returns bureau. Will and Willie looked forward to their return to Austin to begin Will's second term as the lieutenant governor of Texas. Although there were clear indications that there was increasing popular unhappiness with Governor Ferguson because of the rumors of corruption and his increasingly heated criticisms of administrators and faculty at the University of Texas, Will maintained a friendly if not close relationship with him. As inaugural day approached, Will gave every indication that in the coming session the governor and the legislature would continue to make progress in their effort to improve the state's public schools, expand its road system, and improve its business climate.

What Will couldn't foresee was the degree to which Ferguson's growing problems would culminate in a political crisis that would profoundly change Will Hobby's life.

# CHAPTER 7

# THE UNELECTED GOVERNOR

In a ceremony in nearly every detail the same as the inauguration two years earlier, Governor James Ferguson and Lieutenant Governor Will Hobby took their oaths of office in the House chamber on January 16, 1917. Ferguson's inaugural address differed little in content from the one he gave at the beginning of his first term; both were vague and lacking substance. As he had two years before, Will devoted a portion of his speech to the Great War in Europe, now well into its third year. He stressed the superiority of American democracy over "those old and crumbling monarchies on the other side" of the Atlantic Ocean. Because of violent incidents on the border, Will also contrasted Texas with Mexico. "While the pretended republic to the south of us is trailing in the dust of tyranny and ignorance," Will declared, "we are growing stronger in the shining light of progress."[1]

Sitting in a chair on the floor of the House was a new member of the Texas Senate, Colonel Rienzi Johnston, who listened with pride to his former "cub" reporter's inaugural speech. The Colonel had been elected to the Senate in the July 1916 Democratic primary. The venerable "Old Man," as his staff at the *Houston Post* referred to him (but not to his face), ran for the Senate so he could fight against prohibition, an issue that was gaining renewed popularity.[2]

Will had arrived in Austin anticipating a successful and relatively peaceful legislative session. Those expectations soon evaporated, however, as the legislative session became immersed in a heated feud between Governor Ferguson and the University of Texas. Ferguson remained angry at university president William J. Battle for opposing Ferguson's budget demands during the previous legislative session. The governor's hostility deepened during the primary campaign in the early summer of 1916 when he discovered that several university faculty and staff members were actively opposing his reelection. He was convinced that an elite faculty clique composed of progressives who opposed him and supported prohibition and women's suffrage had taken control of the university. As a result, Ferguson demanded that the board of regents fire President Battle and appoint a replacement whom he approved. Instead, the regents enraged the governor further by hiring Robert E. Vinson, president of the Presbyterian Theological Seminary in Austin, without consulting him. After Vinson assumed his position, Ferguson ordered the new president to fire the faculty members who had campaigned against him. When Vinson refused the governor's demand, Ferguson threatened to punish the university when the new legislature convened in January 1917.[3]

The traditional explanation for Ferguson's actions has been that he was anti-education. But as historian Lewis Gould noted, at the start of Ferguson's first term he declared his intention "to do something about the pitiful and backward condition of the public schools. Nearly fifteen percent of the population [in Texas] over the age of ten was illiterate. Ferguson wanted to devote more state resources to the public schools." The argument that Ferguson was opposed to education is unconvincing. During Ferguson's administration, the state established—with his encouragement—Sul Ross College, Stephen F. Austin College, and South Texas College (later renamed Texas A&I but now called Texas A&M–Kingsville). The state also purchased three private colleges that were renamed East Texas College, Tarleton State College, and Arlington State College. In addition, the budgets for the Texas College of Mines (now the University of Texas at El Paso) and Prairie View College were given generous increases. But the governor also complained that too much money was being diverted to the state's institutions of higher education and that the University of Texas "was growing too large and too powerful." The governor's criticism of the University of Texas was not about higher education; it was about taking revenge on his political enemies at the university.[4]

Ferguson's attack on his enemies at the university became a public matter early in the legislative session in 1917, when he announced that faculty and administrators were guilty of financial abuses. After an investigation, the legislature cleared the university of Ferguson's charges. Moreover, a House committee also investigated Ferguson's financial affairs. Charges had been made that Ferguson had committed fraud in the way he had financed some of his properties in Bell County. The committee decided the governor's behavior, while questionable, did not warrant further action. But the controversy not only continued, it got worse.[5]

Throughout the spring and summer of 1917, a complicated and dizzying series of interrelated events occurred that included the dismissal of six members of the university's faculty and staff, Ferguson's veto of the university's budget, and his indictment on charges of misapplication of public funds and embezzlement by a Travis County grand jury. After his indictment, Ferguson posted bond and then announced he would run for a third term as governor, although he also told friends and associates he would run against the incumbent Morris Sheppard in the 1918 US Senate election. While this political circus was underway in Austin, the United States declared war on Germany on April 2. Historian Gould has noted that the Ferguson controversy dominated newspaper coverage in Texas throughout the summer of 1917, even overshadowing to some degree the entrance of the United States into World War I.[6]

In the meantime, members of the Texas House and Senate did what they could to carry out their legislative duties in the regular session and one called session. Aside from passing an important bill to create the state highway department and the increases in the number of state-funded colleges, the Thirty-Fifth Legislature accomplished little else of permanent value by the time it adjourned the regular session in March and the first called session in May 1917.

Throughout this tumultuous period, Will Hobby quietly carried out his duties as president of the Senate. Publicly he remained silent and essentially avoided involvement in the Ferguson affair, despite the fact that his political allies, especially Colonel Johnston, were vocal in their condemnation of the governor. Will had not been close to Ferguson before the controversy, but he had supported Ferguson's reelection in 1916, and he enjoyed a friendly relationship with the governor and his wife. Although Ferguson's impeachment seemed unlikely in the spring of 1917, Will understood that he was in the extremely sensitive position of being next in line as governor if Ferguson was impeached. He wisely chose to stay away from the controversy.

In addition, Will had decided early in the 1917 session that he would not run for a third term as lieutenant governor. His friends were encouraging him to run for the US Senate, but that was not a realistic option in Will's mind. Senator Morris Sheppard faced reelection in 1918, but Will did not relish the idea of opposing a popular incumbent senator whose strongest base was in Will's own East Texas. Texas's other senator, Charles Culberson, would not stand for reelection until 1922. The only other public office that interested him was governor, and that also seemed unobtainable at this point. Will assumed Ferguson would break political tradition and run for a third term as governor, although he also knew Ferguson had hinted that he might make a bid for the US Senate. Despite Ferguson's troubles, he would be a formidable opponent in whatever race he entered. Ferguson had a huge following of voters in rural Texas, and running against the oratorically gifted demagogue was not an attractive prospect to Will.

With no obvious pathways open to any public office that he would consider, Will accepted that after his second term as lieutenant governor was over, his immediate future would be focused on the *Beaumont Enterprise*. He also had thoughts about acquiring the rival newspaper the *Beaumont Journal* and merging it with the *Enterprise*. At this point, however, another opportunity unexpectedly presented itself. In early March 1917, Will was delighted to learn from his friend Thomas Love, a former Speaker of the Texas House of Representatives whom President Wilson had appointed assistant secretary of the treasury, that he was on US treasury secretary William Gibbs McAdoo's list of candidates for the position of secretary and director of the newly established Federal Land Bank in Houston. This was a job that Will wanted. Will had met Tom Love through their mutual involvement in the Texas Democratic Party. Although Love was a fervent prohibitionist, he and Will had other interests in common that allowed them to ignore their differences on that issue.[7]

Congress had established the Federal Land Banks in 1916 as part of the Federal Farm

Loan Act. Governed by the Federal Farm Loan Board in Washington, the banks were established to provide low-interest loans to farmers who were having difficulty getting credit from commercial banks. It is likely that Secretary McAdoo chose Will for this position at the Federal Land Bank in Houston because of the role Will had played in February 1917 to push through the legislature a bill to make it legal for trust funds and savings banks to invest in bonds from the Federal Land Bank. When Governor Ferguson refused to submit the bill to the legislature, McAdoo appealed to Will for help. He wrote Will on February 16, 1917: "Can you not have a bill introduced and put through the Legislature covering this matter?" Aware of Ferguson's troubles, Wilson's treasury secretary told Hobby he was "not trying to start a campaign against Governor Ferguson or his position. The matter is of such importance that I think it ought to be considered by the legislature." Will was soon able to get the measure through the Texas Senate, with the House following suit. Ferguson signed the bill. A grateful McAdoo thanked Will for "this patriotic action on the part of the great state of Texas as represented by the Legislature and yourself."[8]

On March 24, three days after the end of the regular session of the legislature, McAdoo notified Will that he was appointing him to the farm land bank board. Before he received word of his appointment, Will had planned to attend his mother's birthday party on March 26 in Dallas, but this news caused him to cancel the trip. When Will wrote Dora to apologize, he explained that he had to be in Houston "to participate in organizing the Farm Loan Bank—will be there most of the time until April 15 or 20 when will go to Austin for another month."[9]

After working in Houston to help organize the Federal Land Bank, Will returned to Austin to preside over the Senate's first called session. The main order of business was a budget for the University of Texas. Despite, or perhaps because of, the governor's attack on the university, the legislature substantially increased the appropriation, sent it to the governor's office for his signature, and then adjourned on May 17. Declaring that it was time for all Texans to "face the issue and determine whether this State shall let the autocratic, educated high brows control its policies," Ferguson vetoed the budget on June 7, setting off a firestorm of protest. Reacting to the protests, Ferguson told the press he did "not care a damn what becomes of the University of Texas. The bats and owls can roost in it for all I care."[10]

As the controversy continued and calls for Ferguson's impeachment spread across the state, Will traveled to Austin on June 29 for a meeting with the governor and three other members of a special committee to select a location for the newly funded West Texas A&M College, which had been established during the recent legislative session. The other committee members were F. W. Doughty, commissioner of agriculture; Fred Davis, commissioner of education; and Frank Fuller, Speaker of the House. When they cast their secret ballots, Governor Ferguson, whose assistant opened and counted the votes, declared that Abilene, which was Ferguson's choice, had been selected by a vote of three to two. Will, who had voted for Amarillo, agreed to join with the other members to

*University of Texas coeds protesting Governor Ferguson's
veto of the university's budget, 1917.*

make the selection unanimous. When the committee members left the governor's office, Speaker Fuller told reporters he had not voted for Abilene, although he declined to say which location he had favored. A problem arose when Will Hobby and F. W. Doughty disclosed publicly that they had not voted for Abilene either, which meant that only two members of the committee had voted for Abilene. The confusion about the vote made newspaper headlines around the state. Fuller believed that Ferguson had misreported the vote in favor of his choice. He proposed that the committee meet again to cast voice votes, but Ferguson ignored Fuller's request. Instead, he called Will, who was doing Federal Land Bank work in Houston, and claimed Fuller had admitted that he did vote for Abilene. Ferguson asked for Hobby's consent for the governor's office to issue a statement that all of the committee members agreed that the selection process had been "regular, honest, and square." Instead of checking with Fuller first, Hobby agreed to issue the statement. Outraged and embarrassed, Speaker Fuller now joined with those calling for Ferguson's impeachment. The confusion over the actual vote count eventually led to the legislature's repeal of the bill to create West Texas A&M.[11]

Except for his involvement in the West Texas A&M controversy, Will Hobby continued to refrain from involvement in the protest against the governor. Privately, however, Will realized that Ferguson might be impeached, a possibility that worried him, as Ferguson's removal from office would make Will governor. He was conflicted by the prospect because he did not want to be an unelected governor as a result of such controversial and historically unique circumstances. In addition, Will found his work with the Federal Land Bank to be deeply satisfying, and he did not want to give it up. His involvement in the bank's operations not only gave him the opportunity to help hard-pressed small farmers, but it also brought him into contact with a number of business leaders in Houston and southeast Texas with whom he made friends and forged potentially useful business connections. John W. Canada, the editor of the *Southland Farmer*, a monthly agricultural magazine published in Houston, became acquainted with Will after his appointment to the Federal Land Bank board. He reported to a friend, "Hobby has been associating with some fundamentally sound men . . . in the bank and it has been of value to him."[12]

Early in June, before the meeting in Ferguson's office to select the location for the new college, Will had asked the bank's legal counsel if he could remain secretary and board member if he became acting governor in the event that the Texas House passed articles of impeachment against Ferguson. The attorney advised Will that because his position as acting governor would be temporary, he could take an official leave of absence from his bank duties and not have to resign. In a letter to Assistant Treasury Secretary Tom Love, however, Will pointed out that "if there be any condition . . . under which I would succeed to the office of Governor it would be necessary for me to resign [from the bank board]," because of the constitutional requirement that the governor cannot hold another civil, military, or corporate office. Will stated that "the other members of the Board of Directors of the Bank here are not only willing but anxious for me to remain in the office of Lt. Governor." In his letter to Love, he added, "It is a most deplorable situation in the State affairs of Texas." He predicted that unless university president Robert Vinson and "several professors" resigned, "unquestionably there will be no money to run the University next session. It is unbelievable, but it is true."[13]

A month after Will's letter to Tom Love, the controversy around Ferguson took a new and even more serious turn. On July 21, 1917, Ferguson was called to testify before the Travis County grand jury that was examining charges he had illegally used public money. Two days later, wealthy Houston businessman Will Hogg, a former regent of the University of Texas and a progressive whose father was the late governor James S. Hogg, arranged a meeting between Speaker Fuller and Will Hobby in Houston. Hogg had become the leader of a group of former students who had organized in an effort to force the governor to sign the university's budget. At the meeting, Fuller claimed that after the controversy broke about the disputed vote for the site for West Texas A&M, Governor Ferguson had tried to bribe him to say that he voted for Abilene. Hogg then persuaded Hobby and Fuller to sign affidavits stating they both had voted against Abilene as the site for West Texas A&M. As one of Ferguson's opponents on the University of Texas faculty later noted, "[When] they got Fuller and Hobby together, and when they compared notes the Governor's troubles began in good earnest. It seems the irony of fate that Ferguson should have lied to the only two men in the state who had the legal power to bring him to account for his meaness [*sic*]." With the affidavits in hand and Fuller's bribery accusation, Hogg urged Speaker Fuller to issue a call for House members to assemble in Austin for a special session to file a bill of impeachment charging that Ferguson had tried to bribe Fuller. The Speaker issued the call immediately after his meeting with Hogg and Hobby.[14]

Hogg informed a few of his allies in the anti-Ferguson group about his meeting with Speaker Fuller and Lieutenant Governor Hobby. Because Will had kept his feelings about the Ferguson controversy largely to himself, some of Hogg's allies were concerned that Will might threaten to refuse to serve as acting governor if Ferguson was impeached and that such a stance might persuade a majority of senators to vote against Ferguson's removal. On July 25, magazine editor John Canada, who had published editorials calling for Ferguson's impeachment, wrote to University of Texas professor Alexander Caswell Ellis, one of the faculty members Ferguson was trying to dismiss, and assured Ellis he had the "distinct . . . impression that Hobby has just as little use for Ferguson as [Speaker] Fuller has. Much as the work appeals to [Hobby], I think that he would resign from the land bank to take up the duties of governor in case Ferguson is impeached."[15]

Ferguson's problems increased substantially on July 27, when the Travis County grand jury indicted him on a total of nine charges of misapplication of public funds, embezzlement, and the diversion of a special fund. The impeachment movement was gaining momentum with each passing day. In Dallas, as soon as Edwin Hobby heard about the indictments, he wrote Tom Love, who was in Washington, that "the political situation has become very acute in Texas. The whole thing on my mind is just how this situation will affect Will. I want Will to do his full duty and take the office [of governor] while the impeachment trial is being conducted by the Senate. At the same time, I want him to be able to resume his position with the Federal Farm Loan Bank in the event that he does not have to fill the Governor's office the rest of the term."[16]

Edwin asked Love to tell Secretary of the Treasury McAdoo about Will's situation and its possible impact on his service at the Federal Land Bank. Reflecting the pressure and stress that Edwin and his brother felt about the Ferguson controversy and its impact on his brother's immediate future, Edwin also told Love that Ferguson always had a contingent of Texas Rangers around him as guards. He was worried that if Ferguson was impeached he might refuse to give up his office and rely on men he had appointed to be Rangers to use force if necessary to keep him there. Edwin's concerns were such that he asked Love to talk to Secretary of War Newton Baker about sending army troops from Fort Sam Houston in San Antonio to the capitol in Austin to physically remove Ferguson from his office if necessary. Because he had more intimate knowledge about conditions in Austin than Edwin, it is doubtful Will shared his brother's alarmist concerns about possible violence. It is highly unlikely he would have encouraged Edwin to seek an unconstitutional federal military intervention. It is much more plausible that with the controversy's potential impact on Will's service on the farm loan bank board, he would have supported Edwin's request to Tom Love that he return to Texas "during the next two weeks as the situation is pretty hot and your judgment would, no doubt, be very valuable."[17]

The Speaker's call for the House to meet in special session was on questionable legal grounds, as the Texas Constitution restricts that power to the governor exclusively. Ironically, Ferguson himself solved that problem for his enemies on July 30, when he issued his own call for a session to convene, ostensibly to reconsider the university's budget and, hopefully, to take most of the steam out of the impeachment effort. As members of the House assembled in Austin for the special session, Will made preparations for Ferguson's possible removal from office. He requested advice from Texas attorney general B. F. Looney, who had his own gubernatorial aspirations, about whether or not he would have to resign from the land bank board if he became acting governor. Looney advised Will that if the House impeached Ferguson, Will would have to vacate his position as president of the Senate and serve as acting governor during Ferguson's trial in the Senate. He would not have to resign from the board as long as he served as acting governor, but if Ferguson lost his trial in the Senate and was removed from office, Will would become governor and would have to resign from the board. After he received Looney's ruling, Will sent a request to Treasury Secretary McAdoo through Tom Love asking if McAdoo would approve his remaining on the board while serving as acting governor. McAdoo had no objections.[18]

The House convened on August 1. Ignoring the official reasons Ferguson gave for calling the special session, the House immediately organized as a Committee of the Whole and initiated hearings on the impeachment of the governor. Will was convinced the House would impeach Ferguson, but he told Tom Love that "it looks very doubtful in the Senate. It appears the liquor machine is going into the fight . . . to save the governor and that of course is likely to be effective."[19]

An editorial in the *Temple Mirror* declared the paper's opposition to Ferguson's impeachment. The editorial added, however, that if Ferguson was removed from office, "Will Hobby was more than qualified" to be governor. The *Mirror* was especially taken with Willie Hobby. "The *Mirror* is strong for Will Hobby . . . but stronger still for Mrs. Will Hobby, as a Governor's wife. . . . There is no shadow of a doubt . . . as to [Willie's] fitness to be First Lady of Texas . . . for she is splendidly educated, highly accomplished, and blessed with an unusual abundance . . . of plain old common sense." Willie clipped the editorial and placed it in her personal scrapbook.[20]

By the middle of August, after hearing testimony from a wide variety of witnesses, including Speaker Fuller, the effort in the House to oust Ferguson seemed to falter. Many of the House members seemed uninterested in Ferguson's personal financial affairs, and the Speaker's accusation of bribery proved problematic because of Fuller's own inconsistent and contradictory testimony. At this point, however, the ever self-confident Ferguson foolishly ignored the advice of his attorney and agreed to testify before the House. Under intense questioning by former attorney general Martin McNulty Crane, the House's astute chief counsel for the impeachment hearings, Ferguson mentioned, almost as an aside to an unrelated query, that in the previous April he had borrowed $156,000 (equal to more than $3 million in current value) from friends to pay personal debts. When Crane asked Ferguson who had given him the loan, Ferguson declined to answer. Despite increasing public pressure, after the hearing Ferguson continued to refuse to reveal his benefactors. His enemies quickly spread rumors throughout the state that he had received the loan from a "foreign source," possibly even from the German kaiser.[21]

The reality was that Ferguson, who was struggling financially, demanded and received the loan from Texas brewers. His power over the brewers stemmed from his threats to call a special session of the legislature to pass statewide prohibition, which would put the brewers out of business. As Lewis Gould has pointed out, Ferguson's action "was a kind of gubernatorial extortion, but what were the brewers to do?" Ferguson wanted to keep the loan a secret; if he decided to run against the prohibitionist leader Morris Sheppard for the US Senate in 1918, the news of the loan would be fatal to his chances.[22]

As it turned out, the knowledge that Ferguson had been loaned a large amount of money from a source he refused to identify proved fatal to Ferguson's career. On August 24, 1917, the House of Representatives approved twenty-one individual articles of impeachment against Ferguson and then submitted the articles to the Senate the following day, making Will Hobby the acting governor of Texas. A plan for Will to take the oath of office as acting governor was quickly abandoned when the attorney general pointed out that the plan would remove him as lieutenant governor. If Ferguson eventually escaped conviction by the Senate, Hobby would not be able to reassume the post of lieutenant governor and he would no longer have an office in state government.

Two days after he became acting governor, Will was feeling pressure from the quickly moving events. He wrote his mother, Dora. "As you know," Will said, "I have gone through a siege the last few days and I cannot think of much else than this large responsibility that now rests upon me." He made a promise to visit her in Dallas "when this thing is over or if I have to stay [I] will want you to come down, for in times of stress I am always anxious to see you."[23]

On August 29, Will's first official action as acting governor was to call "an extraordinary session" of the Thirty-Fifth Legislature to convene on August 30. Will's call included several items for legislative consideration. He asked the legislature to pass bills to aid cotton farmers whose crops were being destroyed by a plague of bollworms and other farmers who were suffering from a severe drought; laws to protect men who had been drafted into the military from civil suits while in the service; and, most important, a bill for the Senate to meet as a "High Court of Impeachment to conduct the trial of James Ferguson."[24]

The third called special session convened on August 31. Now that Will was acting governor, the Senate's president pro tempore, W. L. Dean, became the Senate's presiding officer and chaired Ferguson's impeachment trial. Will allowed Ferguson to remain in the governor's regular office, and Ferguson and his wife continued to reside in the Governor's Mansion. Will and Willie lived in a suite in the Driskill Hotel.[25]

The Senate spent three weeks considering the charges against Ferguson, whose removal from office was far from certain at the beginning of the trial. Will was in a sensitive and awkward position and did not want to appear eager to drop "acting" from his title at Ferguson's expense. He kept away from the press during the proceedings and did only what was legally required as acting governor. In private, Will's friends and associates bombarded him with advice and observations, and he had a stream of confidential meetings with his closest colleagues, among them John Henry Kirby. "You

*Will Hobby appearing before a joint session of the Texas Legislature shortly after becoming governor following Ferguson's impeachment, 1917.*

have been called to high duties," Kirby told Will. "This is the time when you need the counsel and support of your real friends [who] could help you and I know your nature and disposition well enough to know that you will seek their advice and to a large extent rely upon their counsel." Kirby stressed to Will that he should "behave with dignity and act with caution, indulging in no sensationalism." Will also received regular phone calls from Kirby. Not surprisingly, his old patron and mentor Colonel Johnston, now a state senator, was also among those Will relied upon for guidance. The sixty-eight-year-old Johnston was one of the strongest advocates in the Senate for removing Ferguson from office. The *San Antonio Express* noted that during Ferguson's trial, Johnston had proven to be "a pillar of strength" to Will Hobby, whom Johnston had "raised" as a newspaperman at the *Houston Post*. Although Will was not nearly as close to Will Hogg as he was to Johnston, Hogg was also among those who peppered Hobby with advice. "As soon as Ferguson is ousted," Hogg cautioned in one of his letters to Hobby, "then the pressure for appointments and re-appointments will be tremendous. I think every known hench-man or political appointee of Ferguson's now in office should be replaced as soon as opportunity is presented."[26]

The pressure on Will reached its zenith in the last ten days of Ferguson's trial. On September 19, Will wrote John Henry Kirby's attorney in Houston, Frank Andrews. Referring to Ferguson's likely removal, Will pleaded, "If this thing happens I would like you to come up *the night of that day* if you can conveniently arrange it for there are some things I would like to talk about. *Yours in haste.*" Two days later, Will informed Tom Love, who was still in Washington, that Ferguson's conviction by the Senate now seemed certain. He was now giving thought to the "delicate and difficult things I will have to deal with and of course it will take a good deal of time and a lot of investigation to determine what is best." Accordingly, he asked Love for his opinion about reappointing one of the men Ferguson had appointed to the state industrial accident board. As these sensitive and unceasing discussions behind closed doors continued, Will wrote to Dora. "My Precious Mother, I have never been so busy in my life . . . but I think of you every day and wish you were with me."[27]

On September 22, 1917, the Texas Senate voted to sustain ten of the twenty-one charges against Ferguson that the House had passed. According to Lewis Gould, there seemed "little doubt that without the revelations about the loan, Ferguson would not have been removed from office. The case for ousting Ferguson was not as strong as it appeared to his enemies, and a political compromise could well have been worked out that would have allowed the Governor to serve out the last year of his term." Ferguson's removal from office became official on September 25. The Senate also voted to make Ferguson ineligible to hold any office of honor, trust, or profit under the State of Texas. Claiming that the trial had been a "kangaroo court," Ferguson issued a statement declaring that he "did not have the same chance of securing an impartial jury as is given a 'nigger' crap shooter or a 'nigger' bootlegger." Rienzi Johnston retorted in an editorial in the *Houston Post*, "It was the desire of money which wrought the ruin of James E. Ferguson—and not politics nor prohibition, nor personal enemies." Ferguson officially resigned as governor the day before the Senate announced its decision. He argued that because he had resigned before being impeached, the ban on his holding any other public office was inoperative. The courts disagreed with Ferguson's interpretation, but that would not keep Ferguson from making another run for governor.[28]

The Senate's decision made Will Hobby the twenty-sixth governor of the state of Texas. At thirty-nine, Will was the youngest man to hold the office. It was proposed to have Hobby sworn in as governor at a joint session of the legislature, but Senator O. S. Lattimore raised a constitutional objection. He argued that according to the Texas Constitution, Hobby automatically became governor when Ferguson resigned. Although the swearing-in ceremony was canceled, Will did make an appearance before a joint session of the legislature and was greeted by a standing ovation.

While the Senate was conducting its trial of Ferguson, the Texas House worked on the legislation Will had listed in his call for a special session. They also passed a new budget for the University of Texas, which the Senate approved after Ferguson's trial was over. There was no doubt that Will would sign the university's budget. Even before the Senate convicted Ferguson, Will Hogg had written to the superintendent of schools in Tyler, "If Governor Ferguson is convicted and ousted from office, I have no doubt Governor Hobby will lend his official approval and assistance to any sensible and definite program which the friends of higher education may offer." Will signed the university's budget act almost as soon as it landed on his desk.[29]

The controversy stemming from the Ferguson affair generated heated and emotional debate throughout the state. Ferguson remained popular with his core of voters, but Will Hobby's ascension to the governor's office was generally met with enthusiastic approval and tangible relief. An editorial in the *Dallas Times Herald* illustrated Will's widespread popularity in newspaper circles: "Every once in a while we hear somebody say, 'Well, Will Hobby is a pretty good sort of a fellow; he will make an honest Governor, but we must not expect anything brilliant from him.' But that is an incorrect estimate of the man, as time will prove. Mr. Hobby . . . is one of Texas' greatest editors. He is president of one of Texas' most successful daily newspapers, the *Beaumont Enterprise*. He has earned his money and his position honestly."[30]

# CHAPTER 8

---

# THE WAR GOVERNOR

A few weeks after Will became governor he gave an exclusive interview to Anne Austin, a syndicated newspaper columnist. Austin wrote that she had expected to meet "a magnetic human dynamo" but was disappointed to find a "short, stocky, almost pudgy" man who would pass unnoticed in any other situation. Austin reported that Will's answers to her questions were brief and unenlightening. "I tried to pierce the veil of inanities," she wrote, by pointedly asking Will what he planned to do as governor. He didn't immediately answer and instead sorted through papers on his desk, shifting and rearranging them. Finally, he spoke slowly: "Well, I'm going to do a day's work every day. A man can do no more. It is a big job. I am ... holding the reins and doing what seems to be my duty each day." To Austin, it seemed obvious that Will, who had not planned or expected to be governor, was in awe of the task before him.[1]

Will Hobby was acutely aware that he had become governor at an inauspicious time, and that he was an unelected governor as well, with Jim Ferguson and his allies referring to him as the "accidental governor." When he suddenly assumed the duties of governor, Will faced a wide range of difficult issues, including the revival of the prohibition cause; the rapidly growing women's suffrage movement; Texas Ranger violence against Tejanos on the Mexican border; horrific lynching of African American Texans; deep labor unrest in the state's oil fields, timber industry, and seaports; and a severe drought and boll weevil infestation devastating the state's agricultural sector. Adding to the pressure, the United States had entered the Great War in Europe and the War Department was demanding that the state play a significant role in the war effort, including providing young men to fill manpower needs and serving as the location for a large number of training bases.[2]

As Will Hobby thought about how to deal with these pressing issues, he soon concluded that his priority had to be the war effort. One of Will's first actions as governor was to bring Texas into compliance with the national military conscription program. The

---

distractions of impeachment had hampered the state's implementation of the draft. In addition, Ferguson had opposed the national Selective Service Act and had done little to implement it in Texas. From his office in the capitol, Will organized and for several months supervised the state's selective service efforts. He eventually appointed John C. Townes Jr. to serve as the supervisor of the selective service law.[3]

Prohibition, however, was not on Will's priority list. Considered dead as recently as the election of 1916, the issue had been given new life with the removal of the "wet" Ferguson. Despite Will's lack of interest in prohibition and his annoyance over its impact on state politics, the issue was hard to ignore. The day after he became governor, temperance leaders demanded that he call a special session to pass statewide prohibition. Will quickly found a convenient excuse to decline those demands. After the Ferguson affair, the legislature had created a special commission to investigate state agencies and educational institutions. Will pleaded that he needed to wait for the commission to complete its investigation before he could call a special session. He knew, however, that he would not be able to keep the anti-alcohol crusaders at bay for long.[4]

As he faced these formidable issues and the pressure mounted on him to take action, Will was keenly aware that the main burden in addressing these problems fell on his shoulders. He had been thrust into the governor's office after the constitutionally prescribed biennial session of the Texas legislature. Unless Will called a third special session, the legislature would not meet again until January 1919, which was nearly sixteen months away. Will knew that a gubernatorial call for a special session was never popular. The sessions were costly to the state budget, and they interrupted the private lives and business affairs of part-time, poorly compensated legislators. As an "accidental" governor, Will was particularly sensitive about exercising one of the office's most critical powers.

Another pressure on Will was the question of his future political plans. Would he run for a term of his own as governor? He needed to make the decision soon. The next Democratic Party primary election would be held in less than a year. Earle B. Mayfield, a member of the Texas Railroad Commission, had already announced his candidacy for governor. From comments Will made to friends during the first few weeks he was governor, his own decision was far from being made. Unlike the position of lieutenant governor, the governor's job was full-time. Will loved his life in the newspaper business and needed time as governor to see if the job could justify giving up journalism for possibly as much as five years.

Facing these pressures and problems, Will moved forward with his work as governor of Texas, making his first public speech as the state's chief executive on October 6, 1917, at the East Texas Fair in Tyler. The *Galveston News* claimed a record-breaking crowd composed mainly of farmers gathered to hear their new governor. At the beginning of his speech, Will connected with the locals by pointing out that his father, Edwin Hobby, had been a regular visitor to Tyler thirty years earlier when he served as a judge on the commission of appeals. Will's speech focused on Texas's contribution to the war effort, the issue on which he would concentrate in the first months of his governorship. Will made his priorities clear, declaring he would be "guided in every thought and every act by what will contribute most to the success of our army and navy forces." He promised to make the operations of government as efficient as possible in order to make every dollar available for the support of the war effort. "We can whip the world," Will said, "but it is going to take time and money and the largest and best equipped and most powerful army the world has ever known." Will praised Woodrow Wilson and declared his full support for the president's hope to "make the world safe for democracy." Winning the war, Will claimed, would bring the values of the Declaration of Independence to every nation, making the United States the "liberator of mankind and the emancipator of the world."[5]

Although Will was in pro-Ferguson territory, he took the gamble of touting the fact that he had signed the university's budget, describing it as the "proudest act of my life" and that the "money could not be spent in a worthier cause." But Will also stressed that, like Ferguson, it would give him "equal pleasure to approve a bill that will help education in the lower grades," especially in the rural areas. In a final reference to the impeached governor, Will promised the audience that every citizen could be assured that his government "was being administered honestly."[6]

Giving his speech in one of the "dry" strongholds in East Texas, Will had neglected to declare a position on his least favorite issue: prohibition. But Will did respond to a challenge from the prohibitionist Earle Mayfield, who claimed he would withdraw from the gubernatorial race if Will would call a special session of the legislature to enact a statewide prohibition law. Ignoring the prohibition basis of Mayfield's offer, Will's public response was to declare that as governor he was "not open to any propositions from politicians or candidates. Whenever I get ready to trade, I will do my trading directly with the people of Texas and not with anyone else."[7]

Will's Tyler speech was published in many of the newspapers in Texas and praised in a number of editorials, but newspapers that supported prohibition noted Hobby's failure to speak about the issue. "From the standpoint of the prohibitionist the disappointing feature of the Governor's speech is not what was said, but what was not said," one newspaper argued. "There was . . . no allusion to the liquor evil or its suppression." The editorial promised that if Will sought election in 1918 and proved he was not a "dry," a strong prohibitionist would run against him. Earle Mayfield, who had already declared his candidacy, reacted to Will's fence straddling by issuing a public statement that Will would "work his own destruction if he thinks for a moment he can run with the hare and bark with the hounds on the prohibition question."[8]

Despite his strong desire to avoid the issue, Will's "dry" friends urged him to support the cause by calling a special legislative session to pass a statewide prohibition law. A local option law was already on the books, and several cities and counties had banned the sale of liquor within their jurisdictions. But prohibitionists wanted alcoholic beverages outlawed in every nook and cranny of the state, including in those areas such as San Antonio, Galveston, and most of South Texas where prohibition was decidedly unpopular. "Prohibitionists expected the new governor to quicken the pace of reform," Lewis Gould noted, "but recognized that [Hobby] would not easily accede to their demands. Marriage to the daughter of Congressman S. B. Cooper and friendships with R. M. Johnston, J. H. Kirby, and Frank Andrews ushered him into the inner circles of Texas conservatives." According to Gould, the "boyish" Will Hobby was caught in a political vice between "former wet loyalties" and the demands of the increasingly powerful prohibitionists who viewed his motives with "distrust and skepticism," with the result that Will's early months as governor were marked by "indecision and vacillation."[9]

US treasury official Tom Love was one of Will's most fervent prohibitionist friends. Several days after Ferguson's impeachment, Love and his wife traveled to Austin to visit Will and Willie in the Governor's Mansion. The visit was ostensibly social in purpose, but Love had another agenda. Love, who was closely tied to the pro-Wilson Democrats in Texas, urged Will to run for governor in 1918 and pledged his active support. But he warned Will that his ultimate fate would depend on the position he took on the liquor question. Love urged Will to remove the issue by having the legislature pass the statewide prohibition act.

Tom Love continued the pressure after he and his wife returned to Washington. He wrote Will, "The people of Texas are through with the liquor traffic. It is dead and the people want it buried . . . at the earliest possible moment." He argued that "there are almost no anti's left, outside of foreign-born Mexican and Negro voters and those financially interested directly or indirectly in the liquor traffic." Love also predicted that Ferguson would run against Will in 1918 despite the legislature's ban on his holding public office. Noting that much of Ferguson's appeal was in rural areas, especially among tenant farmers, Love argued that if Will would call a special session, he could also have bills submitted to help tenant farmers buy their own farms and give rural public schools funding equal to urban schools, thereby co-opting Ferguson's most popular causes. Passing those reforms before the opening of the gubernatorial campaign in 1918, Love argued, would be "more easy for you to do now than it is likely to be, even after your reelection." He flattered Will by telling him that he was blessed with the "ability to easily do great things. You ought to do them now while you can and run for reelection on a record of superb accomplishment rather than rely upon your . . . personal popularity. I am fearful that . . . personal popularity will count for infinitely less than we now think possible."[10]

Will waited three weeks before responding to Love. A meeting with Love's boss, Secretary of Treasury McAdoo, on October 21 prompted the response. McAdoo was in Dallas to speak to an audience of several hundred people in an effort to sell war bonds. Will introduced him at the event. Reporting to Love about McAdoo's speech, Will took the opportunity to stress that he would continue his focus on the war effort. "I shall try to continue such a campaign as will cause the people of Texas to understand the full meaning of this war," Will wrote. He told Love that he had given serious consideration to calling a special session but felt it best to wait until after the first of the year to develop his plans. His ultimate goal, Will stressed, was to "remove [prohibition] as a factor in Texas politics." Although he did not reveal how he would accomplish that goal, Will implied that the issue might take care of itself without his direct involvement. That obviously was his hope. He noted that the issue was being rapidly settled at the local level, with several counties voting for prohibition within their jurisdictions. "These [local elections] may be a factor in helping me reach a decision."[11]

A month later, Will informed Love that he had consulted with other prohibitionists and they approved of his cautious approach. They had advised Will that a federal constitutional amendment pending in Congress would settle the issue "at the earliest possible time." Its passage would relieve Will of having to take any action that might hurt his election prospects. Will reiterated his intention to concentrate on the war effort and provide relief to areas suffering from the drought, "where the distress is great." He assured Love that he would decide after the first of the year if he should call a special session in the spring or "go to the people with my propositions" during the campaign. If he won the primary election in July, he would call the legislature into session and put his proposals into effect.[12]

Will's explanation failed to placate Love. Frustrated by Will's prevaricating, Love turned to Edwin Hobby. He warned Will's brother that he feared "a serious mistake is being made [in] the Governor's treatment of the liquor question." Complaining that Will was showing a "disposition to straddle" on the liquor issue, Love claimed that many prohibition activists believed the governor was being unduly influenced by Rienzi Johnston, John Henry Kirby, and "possibly Colquitt." "The political contest in Texas in 1918 will be decided upon the liquor issue," Love argued. "I never wanted anything political quite so strongly in my life as I now want to see your brother re-elected [*sic*] Governor of Texas."[13]

Despite intense pressure from Love, Will tried to remain neutral, but it came across to many as indecisiveness. On New Year's Day 1918, he wrote Love, asking why he should "take a chance on spoiling things before the primaries by calling a special session? Still I may call a special session and will let you know pretty soon." Love's response was to repeat his earlier expression that his "chief interest" was to see Hobby get elected. But he also admitted, "Of course, I am for prohibition above all things."[14]

While Will was attempting to thread his way safely through the activists on both sides of the emotional issue of prohibition, he was forced to deal with a serious episode of labor union strife in the oil fields. On November 1, 1917, after oil producers refused to discuss oil field worker grievances with representatives of numerous Gulf Coast union locals, approximately ten thousand men in seventeen oil fields in Texas and Louisiana went on strike. After federal mediation failed to end the strike, the oil producers spread rumors that the "radical" Industrial Workers of the World (IWW) and possibly German spies were responsible for agitating the workers to strike. Little evidence exists that the IWW played any role in the strike, and there is no evidence of German involvement. Not a friend of labor unions, Will was strongly opposed to labor strikes. His closest political mentors and patrons, John Henry Kirby and Colonel Johnston, as well as his good friends Ross Sterling and Judge F. C. Proctor, Gulf Oil legal counsel, were rigidly opposed to unionism. Kirby had fought collective bargaining in the timber industry for years, and he had a special animus for Big Bill Haywood and his IWW. Sterling's Humble Oil Company as well as Gulf Oil were two of the companies most affected by the strike.[15]

Will's friends in the oil industry moved quickly to ask for the governor's help in suppressing the strike. On November 2, Harris County sheriff M. Frank Hammond sent Will a telegram declaring that he would not be able to protect nearby oil fields from "I. W. W. or alien enemies." The sheriff's telegram was soon followed by a formal request from Ross Sterling in his position as president of the Texas Independent Producers Association. Sterling later recalled, "I asked Governor Hobby to intervene. Hobby prevailed on the commanding general at Fort Sam Houston in San Antonio to send troops to the Southeast Texas oil fields to protect the [nonunion] workers from violence at the hands of strikers." The army agreed to Will's request as a war measure. Armed soldiers were soon patrolling the oil fields to maintain peace at the drilling sites and to ensure that oil would continue to flow to support military needs. While the strike continued until the early months of 1918, Will's role in the affair ended, as it became a federal matter when the army occupied the fields. Oil producers won a major victory over the union. Nearly one-fourth of the strikers lost their jobs. Within several months, however, in an effort to discourage additional labor unrest, the Gulf and Humble Oil Companies raised worker pay rates and provided company-owned housing to employees, among other new benefits. Although Will was able to escape this particular episode of labor strife relatively unscathed, it would not be his last confrontation with the labor union movement.[16]

To bring more public attention to his focus on the war effort and to thank the army for its help with the oil worker strike, Will accepted an invitation from the War Department to meet with military commanders in San Antonio and inspect some of the bases that had been established in that city. On November 9, Will and Willie visited Fort Sam Houston, Kelly Air Field, and Camp Travis. At Kelly Field, which had opened only seven months earlier, they watched army aviators demonstrate their flying skills. One of the aviation instructors took a delighted Will Hobby on a brief flight over the base in an open-cockpit plane. The Hobbys brought a contingent of reporters with them, resulting in headlines in newspapers across the state, such as one in the *Austin Statesman* proclaiming, "Governor Flies in Airplane." Once safely back on the ground, he and Willie attended a dinner with several army generals and a visiting US senator from Ohio named Warren G. Harding, whom Will would meet again when Harding was back in Texas as the president-elect.[17]

A few days after his return to Austin, Will learned that James Ferguson had announced he would run for governor in the 1918 Democratic primary. It was not an unexpected development. A month after his removal from office, Ferguson established a weekly newspaper, the *Ferguson Forum*, to give himself a public platform to counter the hostile coverage he was getting from most of the newspapers in the state. When he announced his candidacy, Ferguson declared that the main issue in the campaign would be the battle of the "so-called educated few against the great democratic many." His election hopes were given a boost when a judge dismissed most of the indictments against him and the district attorney decided to drop the others. According to Lewis

Gould, "discussions of whether Ferguson had been vindicated raged in the press for several months, but the outcome of the trials allowed him to persuade many voters that the impeachment was unfair."[18]

Ferguson's announcement and seeming legal vindication put additional pressure on Will to make a decision about running for governor. By late November, Will had become increasingly comfortable in his role as governor. His closest friends and political allies, especially Rienzi Johnston, John Henry Kirby, Ross Sterling, and Frank Andrews, were urging him to run. And with the "wet" Ferguson's announcement, many of Will's more moderate prohibitionist critics quickly realized that he represented their best chance of keeping Ferguson from returning to the governor's office, where he could use his veto power over any prohibition measures passed by the legislature. In December, Congress passed the Eighteenth Amendment to impose prohibition on the nation and sent it to the states for ratification. It was likely that Ferguson, who still enjoyed the support of the powerful brewing industry, would oppose ratification. Despite the legislature's prohibition against Ferguson holding public office, his allies still dominated the state Democratic Party's executive committee, and they placed his name on the primary ballot. "Pa" Ferguson remained popular with his core supporters: white farmers who constituted the vast majority of the rural vote in a state where agricultural interests remained powerful. Will rejected advice that he go to court to remove Ferguson's name from the ballot. He felt that if he prevailed in the primary, his victory would be stained by such an action.[19]

By Thanksgiving 1917, Will had decided to enter the governor's race, but he and Willie kept it private. Will deeply respected his wife's judgment and he understood that she was one of his strongest assets. It was unthinkable that he would enter the campaign without her agreement. The authors of a book on the First Ladies of Texas noted, "The Hobbys' intimate friends testified to the truth of his dependence on her counsel." Willie had made a positive impression on the public ever since she and her husband moved into the Governor's Mansion in early October. Because the Fergusons had left the residence a mess when they moved out, Willie brought in some splashy new furnishings, including a Victorian walnut bedroom suite. She placed a French Empire straight chair and an old spinning wheel in the Sam Houston Room, where she also hung a framed letter written by Sam Houston in which he discussed an Indian treaty. Willie had a new bathroom constructed, and she had steam heat installed throughout the residence, changes that were somewhat controversial due to their cost. When asked by a reporter if her husband's political career might be hurt when the public learned how much money she had spent for the new heating system, Willie laughed and replied that she preferred to be warm for the year remaining in her husband's unelected term than to freeze for the next three years if he won his own term. When a reporter told Miriam Ferguson about the improvements, she replied, "I'm awfully glad she's having a bath put in. Goodness knows the place needs improving. I just wonder where she got the money. I hope she will keep on improving it. It will be more comfortable for us when we get back into the mansion."[20]

During these early days of his gubernatorial tenure, Will also tended to the normal duties of his office, which included filling vacancies in the judiciary and other official positions the governor is empowered to fill on a temporary basis until an election can be held. One of those vacant offices was district attorney of Harris County. John Crooker, the previous DA, had resigned when he joined the army after the United States entered the Great War. For his replacement, Will chose James Anderson Elkins, an attorney Will had met when Elkins was living in Huntsville and serving as Walker County judge. Will's father had known Elkins's father when the latter was sheriff of Walker County. After leaving office as county judge, Elkins had practiced law in Huntsville. Aware that Elkins was eager to move his practice to a bigger playing field, Will had encouraged him during

*Will and Willie Hobby in the front yard of the Texas Governor's Mansion, ca. 1918.*

the summer of 1917 to move to Houston to join with Will Vinson to establish Vinson and Elkins, which eventually grew into one of the largest law firms in the United States. Elkins had been in Houston only a few months when Will Hobby appointed him to serve out the last year of Crooker's term as DA. Elkins refused the appointment, explaining that he left Huntsville to get away from criminal law. "Jim, that may be true, but we are at war," Will argued. "There are two Army camps in Harris County, which is conducive to a crime wave. I want one with your background and experience, and [not] one who is politically ambitious. I don't want to shame you, but it's your patriotic duty and I think you ought to serve." Elkins finally accepted the appointment on the condition that he could resign as soon as he completed the last year of Crooker's term, which was from January 1, 1918, until the end of the year.

After Elkins completed his term as district attorney, he never again held public office, but his year in office gave him access to the city's most influential business and political leaders, which ushered him in to Houston's civic and political power elite. After Elkins left the district attorney's office and Will Hobby was still governor, their relationship was strengthened even more when Will urged the Prairie Oil Company to retain Elkins as their attorney. Will advised Elkins that the oil company could "be developed into a wonderful organization, profitable to the owners and beneficial to the trade and to the state." Elkins eventually parlayed that relationship into a major financial gain, as Prairie expanded through mergers to become Pure Oil of Chicago, at one time the largest independent oil company in the nation. Elkins eventually became a director as well as legal counsel for the company. In the years to come, Elkins would not forget the role Hobby had played in his rise to wealth and power.[21]

As the new year approached, Will turned more of his attention to his as yet unannounced election campaign. He assumed that his likely primary election opponents from the prohibition side, Railroad Commissioner Mayfield and Attorney General Looney, would split the vote of the most fervent prohibitionists. Will's base consisted of a coalition of moderate "dry" progressives like Martin McNulty Crane and "wet" conservatives like Colonel Johnston, Ross Sterling, and John Henry Kirby. He also counted on the support of influential graduates of the University of Texas, no matter if they were wet or dry. Ross Sterling later noted he had found "common ground with Hobby in political enmity for 'Farmer Jim' Ferguson. I had some business dealings with Ferguson and as a result, I despised him." Will believed these anti-Ferguson leaders and the voters over whom they had influence would put prohibition aside and unite to keep Ferguson out of office.[22]

After he and Willie celebrated Christmas and New Year's, Will announced on January 6, 1918, that he was a candidate for an elective term as governor. Walter Crawford agreed to serve as his campaign manager. Assured of support from his longtime political allies in the party's conservative faction, Will reached out to influential leaders on the progressive side whose support he would also need. Those leaders included men with whom Will had only recently established political ties, including Will Hogg of Houston and Martin

McNulty Crane, both of whom had contempt for Ferguson but also had been active opponents of Will's controversial friend, former senator Joe Bailey.[23]

Will began to court Will Hogg, who was living in New York City during this period, assiduously by mail. A week before announcing he would enter the race for governor, he wrote Hogg that he shouldn't make himself "so scarce around the capitol, because I wanted to see you ever since the rat-killing. I heard Mrs. Hobby say a few days ago how much it would please her to have you with us some time. There are many matters I would be pleased to speak with you about." Will Hobby reminded Will Hogg that his father, Edwin Hobby, had been an enthusiastic supporter of Governor James S. Hogg, Will Hogg's late father. "I am glad we are friends, not only for our own sakes, but for our fathers' sakes." Reacting positively to Hobby's courting, Hogg soon distributed letters to his friends declaring that he was "in favor of electing Mr. Hobby. He is honest." Hogg also sent word to Hobby that he was with him "heart and soul." Nevertheless, Hogg confided to one of his friends that Hobby was trying too hard to satisfy everyone, which was a "mistake most men make in politics."[24]

Will Hobby had clashed with Martin McNulty Crane back in 1906, when Will sided with Joseph Bailey at the time Crane was accusing Bailey of corruption. That was now ancient history. The Ferguson affair had brought Will and Crane together. Crane, a friend of Will's brother Edwin, had served as the legislature's chief counsel for Ferguson's impeachment. Pledging his support, Crane assured Will that his downplaying of the prohibition issue was "entirely satisfactory" to him. But he also suggested that if Will called a special session before the primary election, he should throw the prohibition issue on the legislature and persuade its members to "tax the saloons out of existence," which would destroy the liquor industry and spare Will the difficulty of having to deal with a politically divisive statewide prohibition bill that might threaten his election. He also agreed with Will's plan to "regard the war question as paramount to all other issues."[25]

Tom Love, like Hogg and Crane, also abhorred "Farmer Jim" Ferguson. But for Love, prohibition transcended all other issues. Will knew he had Love's backing, but he also knew he could easily lose that support if Love ever decided that Will was not helping the cause sufficiently. Will was aware that his support among the "drys" was soft, which made it even more important that he keep Tom Love in his camp. Will's friends were reporting that a few members of the prohibition leadership were restlessly searching for a more zealous supporter of their cause to run for governor. An influential prohibitionist in Galveston informed Martin Crane that some of his "dry" friends were "picking Hobby as a 'Hobson Choice' out of the gang that has announced for Governor." He urged Crane to enter the race as an alternative to Hobby. Crane ignored this request.[26]

Despite intense pressure from Tom Love and the grumblings from "dry" supporters, Will held to his initial decision to base his election campaign on support for the war against Germany, with a major emphasis on the need for patriotism and loyalty. Because of Ferguson's continuing refusal to identify the source of the $156,000 loan and his popularity in German American areas of Texas, Walter Crawford, Frank Andrews, and

Will's other campaign advisors believed the impeached former governor was vulnerable to demagogic charges that his loan came from German interests, possibly even the kaiser himself. Will apparently agreed.

This campaign strategy was unveiled at the official launch of Will Hobby's candidacy at Dallas's Oriental Hotel on January 19, 1918. Newspaper accounts reported that the participants included "several hundred men representing Democratic leadership in every section of Texas," including John Henry Kirby, Colonel Rienzi Johnston, Houston attorneys Frank Andrews and James A. Elkins, Huntsville's state senator W. L. Dean, Austin banker and University of Texas regent George W. Littlefield, and Texas Press Association secretary Sam Harbin. Walter Crawford, who served as master of ceremonies, opened the event by declaring it had been called to support Will Hobby, the man who would "make Texas safe for Democracy" while also assisting "Woodrow Wilson to make the world safe for Democracy." Other speakers included Kirby, who noted that he had known Will Hobby "from babyhood and he has never done or said anything that a man should not do or say." Kirby pleaded for activists on both sides to "lay aside factional differences and continue him in office." Colonel Johnston also urged "wets" and "drys" to put aside their disagreements and devote their energies to winning the war. Senator Dean, a major leader of the prohibitionists, claimed that the prohibition question was "near its settlement and greater things demand our attention." When one speaker asked if the prohibitionists in the audience who also supported Will Hobby for governor would stand, a reporter noted that half the audience stood.[27]

Robert E. Knight, president of the Texas State Fair and a member of the Texas State Council of Defense, gave the keynote address. The council, which had been established by the legislature in April 1917 at the request of Secretary of War Newton Baker to encourage patriotism, promote the purchase of war bonds, help recruit soldiers, and maintain enthusiasm and support for the war effort in general, was destined to play a controversial role in the campaign. Knight's speech was a red meat harangue against Germany, with strong implications that anyone who opposed Hobby's election was not only unpatriotic but also guilty of giving aid and comfort to the enemy in a time of war. Knight proclaimed that in his service as lieutenant governor and then governor, Will Hobby had "exhibited those lofty traits of patriotic purpose and devotion that have characterized the greatest patriots in our history." It was an early warning to Ferguson that his loyalty and patriotism would be severely questioned in the coming political battle.[28]

One member of the audience at the Dallas event sat at her table with a pad and pencil, scribbling notes and listing the names of attendees. Those around her probably assumed she was a reporter, but instead she was monitoring the meeting for Minnie Fisher Cunningham, president of the Texas Woman Suffrage Association. The thirty-five-year-old Cunningham, one of the first women in Texas to earn a degree in pharmacy, had recently opened an office in Austin and was planning a major effort to win Texas women the right to vote in primary elections, which in a solidly one-party state was the only election that counted. Once that right was established, Cunningham and her allies believed they could use their voting power to achieve full suffrage. Cunningham was gathering information on Will Hobby and all other potential candidates for governor to determine whom her rapidly growing organization would support. Her informant duly sent Cunningham her notes, with the heading, "Names of the Men Present at the Meeting in Dallas, January 19, 1918." Women's suffrage was another hot-button issue Will Hobby preferred to ignore because his conservative friends, including Colonel Johnston, opposed it. As a result, the issue went unmentioned at the rally in Dallas. Will soon learned that Cunningham and her colleagues would not be ignored.[29]

# CHAPTER 9

# PROHIBITION, SUFFRAGE, AND LOYALTY

The rally in Dallas on January 19 publicly launched Will Hobby's gubernatorial campaign, but instead of hitting the campaign trail, Will returned to his office in the capitol to try to placate his prohibitionist supporters without angering the conservatives. Prohibition leaders were generally ignoring the call to put aside the issue for the duration of the campaign, and they continued to demand that Will call a special session to pass a statewide prohibition bill. Will Hogg was among those pushing Hobby on the issue. "Anyone who says that the liquor question is out of this campaign or can be eliminated by anything except decisive legislation," Hogg lectured Hobby, "is either a poor political prophet or a self-seeking schemer." Hogg argued that passing statutory prohibition was the only way to eliminate an issue that was dominating political debate.[1]

Will opposed a legislated statewide ban on alcohol, but he had no objection to the legislature placing a prohibition amendment to the state constitution on the general election ballot. Will confided to his friend Thomas Perkins, a former state senator who owned a newspaper in North Texas, that although he was "an Anti-Prohibitionist and was elected as such," nevertheless, he would not oppose prohibition if "it is the will of the people; and I know of no other way to settle it than by vote of the people." That vote could only be done by an election for or against a prohibition amendment to the Texas Constitution. But because the voters had rejected a similar amendment in 1916, the more zealous prohibitionists were against trying that approach again.[2]

The danger to Will's election chances was not that prohibitionists would support Ferguson. The threat was that one or more prohibitionists would run against him. Concerned that Ferguson could win the primary because of a split vote spread among several "dry" candidates, prohibition leaders also wanted a special legislative session to pass a so-called majority primary law requiring a runoff election between the two top vote getters. The law then in place gave the victory to whichever candidate won a plurality, instead of a majority, of the votes.[3]

One of Will's conservative advisors, Frank Andrews, believed that Will might be able to satisfy most, if not all, of the prohibitionists with a compromise approach. Secretary of War Newton Baker and other members of the Wilson administration had publicly expressed their concern that young and supposedly innocent army draftees were being debauched and corrupted by the saloons and brothels springing up near the military training bases around the country. Texas had nearly half of the country's military camps (nineteen) and most of its airfields (nine), housing more than a quarter of a million troops in bases scattered around the state. Andrews proposed that Will call the legislature back to Austin to pass a law to close the saloons near every military base in order to protect soldiers from alcohol abuse and immoral behavior. Because of the large number of bases, the practical result would be the extension of prohibition to many of the "wet" areas of Texas. Andrews believed this would please conservatives, as the law could be considered a patriotic war measure, while it would please prohibitionists by expanding the number of "dry" areas in the state. Because the Texas Constitution allowed prohibition on a local option basis, 199 of the 254 counties in Texas were already dry, while another 43 were mostly dry. A zoning bill would also avoid a contentious legislative battle over whether to pass a statewide prohibition law or a constitutional amendment. Will was impressed with Andrews's advice.[4]

Andrews was not alone in urging this specific solution to Will's prohibition conundrum. Will Hogg also advised Will Hobby that he could "well afford" to submit a prohibition zone law to the legislature as a war measure. "Texas has twice as many camps and soldiers to safeguard as any other State in the Union," he noted. "You are familiar with the local difficulties near all camps." Tom Love advocated a similar approach, except he recommended a specific distance of ten miles for the liquor-free zones around the bases.[5]

Will quickly grasped that this "prohibition zoning" plan could be an acceptable solution to his dilemma. He decided to issue the call for a special session, but only if he could get additional support from President Wilson's administration. As Will told Love, he feared he could lose the conservative, antiprohibition vote while he "might gain nothing for the pros, but lose a great deal politically." He asked Assistant Secretary of the Treasury Love to ask President Wilson or Secretary of War Baker to send him an official message "recommending and urging that such a law be passed in Texas for the protection of the soldiers. If the constituted military authorities would advise me to this effect, I do not see how anybody could oppose the legislation." Hobby asked Love to keep his request confidential; he wanted to "not be known" in the matter.[6]

Love duly sent the request to Secretary of War Baker, who promptly dispatched a telegram to Will asking that the legislature ban alcohol from a ten-mile zone around military camps. In a second telegram sent soon after the first, Baker told Will that if the legislature would pass an alcohol-free zone bill, "the State of Texas will have made a contribution to the welfare of the army of no mean proportions." Baker added to the pressure on Will by threatening that the army might move its large training camp from San Antonio if conditions there did not improve.[7]

Will now had his political protection, but he continued to worry about his conservative base. Prohibitionist Martin Crane understood Will's predicament, but he believed Will could have it both ways. He wrote Will that he appreciated that he did not want to appear to the conservatives to be "flopping to the pros overnight." He also knew that Will was especially concerned about offending his mentor, Colonel Johnston. He reminded Will that although Johnston was not a prohibitionist, he was "as much opposed to the liquor dealers and brewers' reign as I am." Will replied that he was "extremely anxious to do something, but I do not want to do the wrong thing."[8]

Armed with an official request from the War Department, Will called a special session of the legislature to convene on February 26, 1918. Before making the call, Will asked Tom Love and former Texas House Speaker Chester Terrell, who was an antiprohibitionist, to draft two bills. One would establish a prohibition zone around military bases; the other would outlaw brothels near those same bases. Will contacted his key allies to justify his actions. He explained that the secretary of war had asked him to call the session simply "to improve the moral conditions surrounding the army camps." It was a patriotic act, not a move toward statewide prohibition. Will assured his base that he would continue to oppose statewide and national prohibition.[9]

Under the Texas Constitution, only the governor can decide what items the legislature can consider during a called special session. Tom Love recommended that Hobby ask the legislature to ratify the Eighteenth Amendment to the US Constitution, which Congress had passed the previous December and sent to the states for formal ratification. Martin Crane asked Will to add a "dual primary" bill that would require a runoff election in the event that no candidate received a majority of votes in a primary election. He also wanted a bill to ban impeached state officials from being on a primary election ballot. Crane argued it would prevent Ferguson from "annoying the public with his black guardish utterances" and "trying to embarrass better men than he is." Will agreed to Love's and Crane's requests, except for the latter's call for legislation banning Ferguson from running for public office.[10]

Will also received multiple requests to place women's suffrage on the special session agenda. Most of those requests came from Minnie Fisher Cunningham and her associates in the suffrage movement, but Will Hogg also pressured Hobby on the subject. Not only did Hogg support suffrage, he also believed that if the special session gave women the right to vote in party primaries, Will Hobby would receive the overwhelming support of the newly enfranchised women voters against Ferguson, who was openly hostile to suffrage. Hogg's argument failed to convince Hobby. "[I have] always been in favor of woman suffrage," he told Hogg, "but do not think it well to give them the right to vote suddenly in the primaries in July, and much would not be accomplished since they have not paid poll taxes this year." Hobby intended to remain neutral in the matter. He told another supporter, John Davis, that he was "in favor of woman suffrage but . . . the Governor's office while I am the occupant will not be used for or against ratification of the [federal] prohibition amendment or either to the suffrage amendment, because these are matters to be settled entirely by the wisdom of the Legislature."[11]

Will's public silence about women's suffrage understandably led movement leaders to question his support for their cause. Judith McArthur and Harold Smith, the coauthors of a biography of Minnie Fisher Cunningham, have noted that before he became governor, Will Hobby had "never made any public declaration on either side of the suffrage question." As already noted, however, Will did not oppose suffrage, and it was well known that Willie Hobby strongly supported it. Will and Willie marched in lockstep politically as well as in all other matters. Also, Will's editorial decisions at the *Enterprise* reflected his friendly position on the issue. When the United Kingdom passed the first women's suffrage law in 1916, Will devoted much favorable attention in the *Beaumont Enterprise* to its possible impact on the United States. Under Will's editorship the *Enterprise* also gave extensive and positive coverage to developments in the suffrage movement in the United States, which was not the editorial path taken by newspaper editors who were hostile to suffrage. As was the case with prohibition, Hobby's fence straddling on suffrage was largely due to his fear of offending some of his closest conservative associates, especially Colonel Johnston, John Henry Kirby, and Joe Bailey, each one a vocal opponent of giving women the right to vote.[12]

When the legislature convened on February 26, Will's list of items led with the request for prohibition in a ten-mile zone around military bases and camps. The list also included proposals for antiprostitution vice laws to "protect" soldiers (an item demanded by the Texas Women's Anti-Vice Committee) and relief for drought-stricken areas. Conspicuous by its absence, however, was a women's suffrage bill. Will maintained his neutral stance despite intense pressure from Minnie Fisher Cunningham and others. He even rejected a formal offer from the Texas Equal Suffrage Association executive board to endorse his election and make their statewide organization available to his campaign in return for his placing suffrage on the special session agenda. The pressure became so intense, however, that Will eventually told Cunningham he would add a primary election suffrage bill to the agenda if a majority of members of both the House and the Senate signed a petition asking him to do it.[13]

At this point, Cunningham shrewdly played her James Ferguson card. She knew the prohibition faction in the legislature did not want to risk a Ferguson primary victory resulting from multiple dry candidates splitting the vote. "Bypassing the obdurate Hobby, [Cunningham] made a deal," McArthur and Smith noted: "the vote for women in return for women's votes." Cunningham asked Representative Charles Metcalfe, a rancher from San Angelo and a suffrage ally who also supported Hobby, to line up members to sign the petition Hobby demanded. When Metcalfe asked for assurance that her organization could turn out the female vote for Hobby, Cunningham sent him a letter declaring, "Whomever the women of Texas concentrate on in the July primaries, that man is just as good as elected. But without us, it is Ferguson with a plurality."[14]

*Minnie Fisher Cunningham, 1928.*

Metcalfe agreed to Cunningham's request, but he warned her to stay away from the legislature while he persuaded members to sign the petition. He feared that her lobbying would only antagonize many of the legislators. Armed with Cunningham's list of members who were known to support suffrage or were undecided, Metcalfe gathered the required number of signatures and submitted the petition to Will requesting that he add a women's suffrage primary election bill to the special session agenda. Will, who now had the political cover he needed, agreed to the request. With several cosponsors, Metcalfe submitted a primary suffrage bill, which included a provision waiving the 1917 poll tax for women voters. The legislature passed the bill and Will Hobby signed it on March 26. Texas women still did not have the legal right to vote in the general election, but being able to vote in the Democratic primary now gave them the opportunity to cast their ballots for candidates who were assured of victory in the general election in one-party

Texas. Historians Judith McArthur and Harold Smith have observed that the suffrage bill "was a bargain of political expediency made possible by a factionalized Democratic Party and [Cunningham's] shrewdness in exploiting this rift."[15]

Although Will's wife was publicly silent as the legislature worked on the suffrage bill, those who were knowledgeable about their relationship were well aware of the key role Willie played in Will's decision to sign the bill. The *Houston Chronicle* later noted that Willie "had more to do with political and governmental development than was ever recorded." Although Will clearly expected to attract the women's vote in the upcoming primary election because of his approval of the bill, his support of suffrage was not simple political expediency. It was sincere. The day before he signed the primary suffrage bill, Will wrote a private letter to Willie's father, Bronson Cooper, stating he had been "in favor of woman suffrage for several years because I have considered it an inevitable development in the . . . progress of events." He argued that in the past twenty-five years, women had taken an essential role in the operation of most businesses and professional enterprises. He believed it was inevitable that they would become a factor in the political affairs of the country. "I am convinced that a majority [of the people of Texas] are in favor of it, and therefore the Governor of the State should approve what he thinks is the will of the people, unless it conflicts with his conscience, and in that event, he should resign."[16]

On the first day of the special session, Will submitted his bill to prohibit liquor sales and prostitution in a ten-mile zone around army camps. Framing those acts as strictly patriotic war measures instead of progressive reforms, he avoided having to take a stand on prohibition. He hoped this compromise would protect him from the wrath of his wet friends. He also believed it unlikely that any dry legislators would openly oppose zoned prohibition that protected soldiers because those opponents would be "classed as a traitor or alien enemy." Will attached to his bill Secretary of War Newton Baker's statement that President Wilson had the power to impose dry zones around camps but that the president preferred "the people of Texas solve this problem." Will also asked the legislature to make a decision about ratifying the Eighteenth Amendment to the US Constitution, which would impose prohibition on the entire country. Will added the issue to the special session agenda without taking a position on the matter. He justified his action as a step required by Congress's submission of the amendment to the states, not as an indicator of his preference in the matter. The legislature quickly ratified the amendment during the first week of the session. It also passed the bill banning alcohol sales and brothels within a ten-mile zone around military bases, as well as a bill placing the proposition of statewide prohibition on the general election ballot in November. Will signed the latter bill reluctantly, with the justification that it was the citizens of Texas who should make the decision.[17]

Will's strategic neutrality failed to satisfy some of his conservative friends, especially the staunch antiprohibitionist Joe Bailey, who believed Will had sold out his dry allies simply to win the gubernatorial election. Angered by Will's actions, Bailey tried to recruit candidates to run against Will in the Democratic primary. Years later, Will admitted that Colonel Johnston, Rawlins Colquitt, and John Henry Kirby were also angered by his handling of the prohibition legislation but that they "had thrown up their hands in disgust and said they guessed they would continue to back him even if he joined the German Army." Will's legislative strategy, which aimed to win the support of as many prohibitionists as possible for his election campaign without alienating his conservative base, was severely criticized by other observers. A reporter for the *Dallas News* complained to Will Hogg, "Hobby is lamentably weak. His readiness to be all things to all people for the sake of votes is disgusting a good many men."[18]

Despite these complaints, Will's election chances were given a boost when the legislature passed the dual primary bill on March 22, 1918, a bill that Will actively lobbied the legislature to pass. Will and his supporters had been concerned about Ferguson's ability to attract a solid block of rural voters that could carry him to victory with only a plurality of ballots cast if other candidates entered the race and split the anti-Ferguson vote.[19]

Having passed laws to protect undoubtedly grateful military personnel from booze and "lewd" women, the Texas Legislature took another significant step that its members justified as essential to the state's support of the war effort: passage of a law to enforce patriotism. This draconian legislation was the product of war hysteria. As Adam Hochschild has noted, "The moment the United States entered the war in Europe, a second, less noticed war began at home. Staffed by federal agents, local police, and civilian vigilantes, it had three main targets: anyone who might be a German sympathizer, left-wing newspapers and magazines, and labor activists." The Texas law made it a felony if any person used "language in the presence and hearing of another" or wrote or published language "disloyal and calculated to bring into disrepute" the United States, the flag, any branch of the military, or "any officer of the United States." The law included a provision making it illegal to display, or even to own, a flag of any enemy country or to "mutilate, deface, defile, tramp upon, or cast contempt upon either by words or act" the US flag. A violation was a felony punishable by not less than two years or more than twenty-five years in prison. The bill, passed on March 4, 1918, was officially titled House Bill 15, but because of Will Hobby's strong and active support, it soon became known to the public as the "Hobby Loyalty Act." Will did not embrace the title but he did not reject it either. He saw that his close association with the effort to enforce loyalty and fight subversion played into his strategy to make his support of the war a major campaign asset. Will signed the bill on March 11, 1918, and it became effective that same day.[20]

The Hobby Loyalty Act was not more or less repressive than the laws passed by the US Congress or by eleven other states during the war, but repressive it was. The Texas Supreme Court would rule the act unconstitutional in 1920. President Wilson inspired the federal legislation in his speech to Congress on April 2, 1917, when he asserted that Germany had recruited and planted spies and launched subversive activities in unsuspecting communities and in offices of the government and industry throughout the nation. Congress subsequently passed the federal Espionage Act, making it a crime for any person to support or favor the cause of any country with which the United States was at war. Under its provisions, an individual could be arrested if his or her speech or writing could be construed as having done harm to the United States government, regardless of whether the criticism was based on fact or whether or not the criticism was intended to cause harm. Congress amended the Espionage Act in May 1918 with the Sedition Act, which criminalized a wider range of dissent. For example, the federal law made it illegal during wartime to willfully speak, print, or publish any disloyal, profane, scurrilous, or abusive language about the form of government of the United States or its Constitution, military, or flag. The Wilson administration also encouraged the creation of civic organizations at the local and state levels to watch for individuals who indicated any signs of disloyalty and to report them to law enforcement authorities whenever such individuals were identified. The administration's encouragement inspired state and local governments to enact and implement their own loyalty laws.[21]

The Hobby Loyalty Act was a response to this federal encouragement. While James Ferguson was still governor, the secretary of war had urged the states to form Councils of Defense to direct local efforts to support the war. The Thirty-Fifth Texas Legislature responded by passing legislation on May 14, 1917, to establish the Texas State Council of Defense, composed of thirty-eight members appointed by the governor. The state council subsequently created local councils throughout Texas to work on a wide range of matters related to the war effort, including sanitation and medicine, labor, and food supply and conservation. The state council and its versions at the local level would also become the most effective enforcers of the Hobby Act and therefore became involved in the upcoming gubernatorial primary election.[22]

With the passage of the Hobby Loyalty Act, Will's main goals for the special session were accomplished. After the legislature adjourned, Will proudly reported to Secretary of War Baker that eight measures in support of the war effort had been enacted: the ten-mile prohibition zone; the outlawing of prostitution around army camps; the mandatory quarantine and treatment of venereal diseases; a requirement to invest all of the state's funds in government securities; "the severest disloyalty act that could be adopted"; and an appropriation of $350 million to raise a new National Guard division for border protection and for service in Europe if necessary. Assistant Secretary of the Treasury Tom Love also passed information about these legislative achievements to President Wilson.[23]

With the exception of the bill placing statewide prohibition to yet another popular vote in the general election in November, Will Hobby was deeply satisfied by the results of the special session. A few days before it ended, he told Bronson Cooper that the legislature had passed ninety-five laws in only thirty days and that Will believed the session was the most successful in Texas history. He wrote Martin Crane, "[The session] has brought approval and satisfaction to a great majority of the people of Texas. The approval is more extensive than I expected. I enjoy greatly the sensation of feeling that I have to this extent carried out the will of the people whom I serve." Tom Love was equally pleased with the results and their potential usefulness to Will's election campaign. He urged

Edwin Hobby to send a press release to the Associated Press to ensure wide publicity about Will's active support of the war effort. Love admitted that because of the zone ban on liquor, "the Governor has lost some friends," but he felt that Will's legislative work to aid the nation's war endeavor would "get some of them back."[24]

The positive public reaction to the legislative session defeated the efforts of Joe Bailey and the more extreme prohibitionist leaders to recruit candidates to run against Hobby in the primary. Earle Mayfield and Attorney General B. F. Looney both withdrew their candidacies. The gubernatorial race was now down to two: Will Hobby and "Pa" Ferguson. A gloating Martin Crane wrote Will: "May I not say to you this morning that I told you so? You are now the only man in the game with Jimmie [Ferguson]. This is what I thought would be the effect of things you have done."[25]

On April 5, soon after the end of the special session, the US Congress passed the Third Liberty Loan Act authorizing the sale of bonds to help pay for the war. Each state was expected to launch its own campaign to urge its citizens to purchase the bonds during the six-week period between April 6 and May 19. This development gave Will an idea. His main campaign strategy was to stress his hard work to support the American war effort while raising questions about James Ferguson's loyalty. Will believed he could add to his reputation as a war patriot by taking a visible and active role in leading the bond drive. He decided to delay the start of his active campaign for more than five weeks while he focused his time exclusively on the war bond effort—all the time making certain that the newspapers took full notice of his decision to place country above his personal political ambitions. When Martin Crane heard about Will's decision to delay the start of his campaign, he expressed his concern that it would not give Will time to act quickly enough to create his county organizations. Will assured Crane that he planned to mount an "aggressive campaign" and that he would "make the issue" of Ferguson "so clear that none will fail to understand."[26]

During the special session and the third Liberty Loan drive, the politically astute Willie Hobby carried out her duties as the First Lady of Texas and the mistress of the Governor's Mansion, while Will's staff made certain the newspapers reported on her domestic activities, which focused on support of the war effort at home. She planted and maintained a "war" garden on the mansion grounds that was eagerly covered by the newspapers, which kept their readers informed about the progress of Willie's beets, beans, potatoes, and peas. The *Austin Statesman* reported that she visited the garden "every morning to see if any boll weevils have appeared. Yesterday Mrs. Hobby, properly gowned for gardening, came out with a hoe and posed for a picture. Just at present the onions seem to be more flourishing than anything else."[27]

In newspaper interviews, Willie carefully pointed out that the Hobby household was conforming strictly to all war measures in the conservation of food and other commodities. She stressed that she made many of her own clothes. In spite of her fondness for entertaining, she noted she had placed a moratorium on such affairs while the war continued and said, "Social entertainment would be out of place in a world torn by war."

The only exception was the visit of Margaret Wilson, President Wilson's daughter, for whom Willie hosted an open house and reception at the mansion.[28]

The *Austin Statesman* published a lengthy profile of Willie that reported her volunteer work for the Red Cross: "[She] spends much of her time at the surgical dressing rooms making bandages and doing other important work there." In April, Willie walked with the Red Cross delegation in the parade that traveled on Congress Avenue from the Colorado River to the capitol. One reporter wrote that Willie did not march at the head of the parade, "nor was she seated with the high officials in the reviewing stand, but she marched along with the other earnest workers, wearing the blue veil that showed service. Many of those who looked on did not even recognize the Governor's wife among the marchers." Willie traveled with Will on a number of inspection tours of the state's military camps; served on the Texas Library War Council, which distributed books to soldiers; and worked as a member of the Women's Division of the State Council of Defense. She also participated in the Liberty Loan drive, which came to a successful conclusion at the end of April, largely due to the intense effort of the highly organized women's suffrage and antivice groups led by Minnie Fisher Cunningham, who chaired the state's Liberty Loan women's committee.[29]

As the loan drive came to an end, Will finally turned his attention to the battle with Jim Ferguson. He informed Walter Crawford that he would be ready to go out on the campaign trail by May 11. Hoping to tap into the hostility that many influential University of Texas graduates had for Ferguson, Will told Crawford to recruit one hundred members of the University of Texas Ex-Students' Association to cover the state in "a mass formation" to make speeches, with a concentration on places where Ferguson had already campaigned. This was welcome news to many of Will's campaign activists, who were concerned that he had wasted valuable time. Will's former colleagues at the *Houston Post*, editorial editor George Bailey and managing editor Colonel Johnston, were worried that delaying the campaign for the Liberty Loan drive might have done irreparable harm to Will's election chances, as it allowed Ferguson to campaign around the state and make charges against Hobby that went unanswered.[30]

Will also appealed to Will Hogg, who was living part-time in New York City, to come back to Texas to help rally university graduates. He told Hogg that Ferguson's followers were "making as much noise as a lot of roosters in a barnyard when they get on a crowing spree." Knowing that a threat to the University of Texas was the best way to get Hogg's attention, Will Hobby warned that Ferguson was promising to keep the university budget permanently at $250,000 if he won the election.[31]

Despite Will Hobby's warning, Hogg remained in New York. Nevertheless, he urged Will to take the fight to Pa Ferguson, a man Hogg despised. "Go right after the hellhound with hammer and tong," Hogg stated, "and never let up until every voter in the state had an opportunity to know the real facts about him. I would start right out with the slogan that 'Jim Ferguson is a common crook.'" Will accepted Hogg's advice. The fight was now on.[32]

# CHAPTER 10

# "SOS CALL TO TEXAS WOMEN"

W ill chose McKinney, the county seat of Collin County in North Texas, as the location for his first campaign speech. Collin County was an area dominated by small farms, many of which were operated by tenants, Ferguson's core group of supporters. But the county, like most of North Texas, was also a prohibitionist stronghold. By opening his campaign in McKinney, Will was trying to gauge his strength with Ferguson's farmers as well as with the prohibitionists, who might still be unhappy with his opposition to a statewide prohibition law.

When Will launched his campaign, the war in Europe was beginning to turn against Germany and its allies, and patriotic fervor in Texas had intensified. Following Will Hogg's advice, Will Hobby was prepared to use every issue he could find against his opponent—including trying to match Ferguson's own demagoguery. Will and his advisors were convinced that his best campaign strategy was to focus on the patriotic work he had performed to support the war effort, but they also decided that an effective tactic would be to hit Ferguson with the "loyalty issue" and anti-German hysteria. Rumors had spread widely that the $156,000 loan that a still-unidentified source had given to Ferguson was from the German American Alliance, an organization the brewing industry had financed before the war. Will believed that if Ferguson continued to refuse to identify who had given him the loan, it would be easy to claim that the source had connections to the German government, which meant Ferguson was colluding with the enemy. This tactic would place Ferguson in a difficult position. He could remain silent and leave himself vulnerable to charges of allying with the enemy, or he could reveal the source, which Will and his associates believed would likely give them another potent campaign issue. Will avoided any direct reference to Ferguson's mysterious loan and any charges that the impeached governor had been disloyal. He would rely instead on his campaign surrogates to make accusations and to spread rumors that the German kaiser had loaned Ferguson the money.[1]

Will's appearance in McKinney attracted a large and friendly crowd that filled the courthouse square. His speech followed his campaign strategy of emphasizing support of the war instead of advocating specific legislation. He declared that the federal government had called on all Texans to give "money and men" to the war effort. "Texans, your very existence as a free people is the stake for which you are fighting," he claimed. "German success means German domination. The Hun oppression is more unspeakably barbarous than any other cruelty the world has ever known. . . . [D]eath is preferable to the slavery the German Kaiser would impose."[2]

Will's debut in McKinney was judged a success by his supporters, who had worried that their candidate's lack of charisma and his less than dynamic oratorical skills would hurt his election chances when contrasted with "Pa" Ferguson's entertaining public performances. Before Will's appearance in McKinney, Edmund Travis, a reporter for the *Austin Statesman*, complained to Will Hogg that "it is yet to be seen what Hobby can do on the 'stump,' but, as you know, he is not an orator; neither can he be a 'rough-neck debater' like his opponent." W. W. Woodson, a prominent banker in Waco who disliked Ferguson more than he liked Hobby, complained, "Hobby is a weak candidate and gains his support because he is the lesser of two evils; as he has no personal magnetism and will not be able to make a speech that will be effective in its delivery. I feel quite sure that there will be very little left of Hobby when Mr. Ferguson gets through with him." A columnist for the *El Paso Herald* wrote that Will was "not the sort of man to slap you on the back and call you 'Bill,' neither is he the sort of a man you'd do that to. There can be a crowd of people, all talking for dear life . . . and Hobby would be the only man who would be saying nothing." The journalist added that Will was "soft of speech and smiles little." Those were not the normal attributes of a successful politician. Despite the grumbling of some editors, the vast majority of the state's newspapers supported Will's candidacy, as they had his campaigns for lieutenant governor.[3]

In his McKinney speech, Will displayed a folksy, humorous, and easygoing style that was balanced by a self-confidence that was well received by the audience and cheered his advisors. At the beginning of the campaign, the plan had been for Hobby to remain in Austin most of the time and make few speeches. But Walter Crawford and Will's other close advisors persuaded him to alter that strategy. In his speeches, Ferguson had spread information around the state that Hobby was, as one of his friends noted, "bashful, timid, and afraid to go before a crowd and could not make a speech at all." Will's performance in McKinney demonstrated that even though he was no William Jennings Bryan, he was an effective speaker in his own way. The decision was made for Will to "remain on the 'stump' continuously" and to travel throughout the state until the election.[4]

The call to keep Will out on the campaign trail proved to be a smart one. In the cities, he could give conservative speeches demonstrating his detailed knowledge of public policy issues to urban business leaders. In rural Texas, he could share charming and humorous anecdotes that appealed to small-town merchants and farmers. One of his favorite stories he often told when speaking to small-town crowds was about a candidate who campaigned in a county seat in East Texas. He appeared at the courthouse square on a Saturday, when the farmers were in town buying supplies and visiting their friends. The politician found a wagon to stand on to address the crowd, but he spoke for such a long time that every farmer but one had left by the time he finished. The candidate looked at the remaining farmer and thanked him for staying. "Now, pray tell me, my friend," he asked, "what was in my speech that held you here after all the others departed?" The farmer replied, "You're standing on my wagon."[5]

At one point in the campaign, Will himself was speaking at a courthouse square in East Texas when an elderly man in the crowd who had known Will years earlier when he lived in Polk County called out to him, "Will, just where do you stand on this here prohibition thing?" Without a pause, Will immediately responded, "Oh, I'm all right on that, Joe! What's the next question you have?" At another rally, Will admitted to the crowd that Ferguson was calling him a short, fat, and ugly man. "My opponent says I was slighted by the Creator and that I am a mental weakling," Will said. Referring to charges that Ferguson had used public money for his personal needs, Will then declared, "My friends, when the good Lord created me, He at least gave me the ability to tell the difference between my own money and the money of the people of Texas."[6]

As Will's bid for election went forward in late May, his campaign advisors were receiving disturbing reports that Ferguson's rallies were attracting large crowds. Walter Crawford and many of Will's prominent supporters feared Ferguson might be building an insurmountable lead. Crawford wrote Will Hogg that Ferguson was attracting labor as well as farmers. "He appeals to their ignorance," Crawford charged, "and seeks to arouse their prejudices and passions, to array class against class." Galveston banker W. L. Moody Jr. complained, "Greatly to my astonishment, the Ferguson sentiment seems very strong in Texas, and many good people are for some inconceivable reason, announcing for him." This news produced much anxiety within the Hobby campaign headquarters, particularly for Crawford; Edwin Hobby; James A. Harley, a former state senator whom Will appointed as adjutant general; and Harley's assistant, former state representative Walter Woodul. Their concern led them to make a politically ruthless and probably illegal decision to bring a newly created special unit of the state's fabled Texas Rangers into the campaign.[7]

The Texas Rangers had a long history dating back to 1835. They had fought at the Battle of San Jacinto, played a key role in General Zachary Taylor's army during the Mexican War, served in the Confederate Army during the Civil War as a mounted regiment known as "Terry's Texas Rangers," and had worked with the US Army to eliminate Native American tribes from the Texas frontier. Many of Teddy Roosevelt's Rough Riders during the Spanish-American War came from the Ranger force. They had also been effective in bringing a semblance of law and order to the Texas frontier regions in the late nineteenth century. As a result of this almost legendary history, aided by skilled self-promotion, the Rangers enjoyed great popularity in Texas. By the early 1900s, however, the Ranger force had become something of an anachronism. The frontier no longer existed, but many

Rangers continued to practice frontier justice, which was to shoot first and investigate afterward. As relics of a "Wild West" that had disappeared, the Rangers had been reduced in size to a few hundred men by the time the United States declared war on Germany in 1917. The Great War, however, soon created fear in Texas that Germany would use Mexico as a conduit into the United States for spies and saboteurs. Tensions were made worse by Germany's clumsy and unsuccessful efforts to entice Mexico to its side by promising the return of Texas, New Mexico, and Arizona to Mexico if the Germans won the war.[8]

In addition to the fear of German meddling in Mexico, government officials in Texas had to deal with difficulties on the border resulting from the revolutionary chaos in Mexico from 1910 to 1920. During those years, Mexico was something of a "failed state," to use a more contemporary term. The result was a major escalation of lawlessness, especially Mexican banditry, on both sides of the border. Several Texans were murdered, businesses and ranches were raided, and at least two trains were derailed and robbed, with passengers shot by the bandits. Some residents in South Texas responded by taking vengeance on citizens of Mexican descent—most of them innocent of any crimes—with beatings, shootings, lynching, and the torching of their homes and farms. Many Tejanos fled to Mexico for safety. Some sources estimate that as much as half of the Mexican American population of South Texas fled into Mexico during the worst period of reprisals.[9]

In response to the fear of Mexican collusion with Germany, as well as to an increase in outlawry along the Rio Grande, the legislature passed the Ranger Home Guard Act in the fall of 1917, which authorized an increase in the number of Rangers to a maximum of one thousand members. After he signed the bill on October 15, 1917, Will gave the newly expanded Ranger force the primary responsibility of patrolling the Mexican border. Aware that the Rangers had been accused of committing crimes and abuses in the years prior to his becoming governor, Will made an effort to prevent illegal behavior. After he signed the bill expanding the force, Will told his newly appointed adjutant general James Harley to examine the backgrounds of all the new Rangers carefully, especially to determine if any had criminal records.[10]

Despite Will's efforts to screen the newly appointed Rangers, with a large number of them deployed to the Rio Grande, many still engaged in what Robert Utley aptly described as "thuggery" against innocent Tejanos and other citizens. The Rangers frequently used extrajudicial measures, including illegal searches, arrests, and jailing without hearings; whippings and floggings; and cold-blooded executions of several Mexican nationals who were never charged or tried for a crime. In December 1917, Rangers stationed in the Brownsville area killed Toribio Rodriguez, a Mexican policeman, by shooting him in the back. When the grand jury in Cameron County refused to indict the Rangers for murder, R. B. Creager, a prominent attorney in Brownsville and a leader of the Republican Party in Texas, sent a message to Will claiming there was overwhelming evidence the Rangers had murdered Rodriguez. On Will's orders, Adjutant General Harley discharged the Rangers who were involved in the shooting. The dismissed Rangers had been under the command of the notorious Captain Monroe Fox, who openly condoned the criminal behavior of many of his men. The dismissals failed to stop Fox's illegal actions and violations of human rights.[11]

Early in the morning of January 28, a month after Fox's men killed the Mexican policeman in Brownsville, a group of about ten Texas Rangers under Fox's command joined with US cavalry troopers and several local ranchers to round up approximately fifteen Mexican men and boy residents of the border village of Porvenir in Presidio County. The villagers were marched to an area south of the village and murdered in cold blood. The killings were retaliation for a raid by Mexican bandits on the nearby Brite Ranch, during which the bandits hung and slit the throat of the local mailman. A subsequent investigation revealed that the villagers in Porvenir had no connection to the bandits who raided the Brite Ranch. They were simply picked out at random and killed to serve as examples to other Mexicans living in the area. The tragic irony was that the innocent villagers had also been victimized by bandits from across the border.[12]

Captain Fox tried to whitewash the murders in a report he sent to Austin about the affair, now known as the "Porvenir Massacre." Fox, who was not present when the incident occurred, claimed his men had come under gunfire when they were passing by the village and returned fire only in self-defense. But Adjutant General Harley soon received a report from an attorney in Marfa who claimed that the Rangers and their accomplices had killed innocent men and boys. Harley gave this information to Will Hobby, who ordered Harley to investigate. The adjutant general determined that the villagers were innocent and had indeed been murdered. After Will received Harley's report, he fired five of the Rangers who had been at Porvenir and disbanded their company at the beginning of June.[13]

On June 14, as Will was out on the campaign trail, Walter Crawford brought him newspapers that had reprinted an item that had originally appeared in the Marfa, Texas, newspaper on June 11. The story prominently featured an open letter to Will Hobby from Captain Fox announcing his resignation from the Ranger force. Fox charged that Will, "just to gain some Mexican votes," had fired five courageous and dedicated Rangers who had bravely served under his command along the border. Contradicting his earlier explanation, Captain Fox said he had ordered the execution of the villagers, whom he claimed had carried out the raid on the Brite Ranch and were armed and dangerous when his men tried to arrest them. Fox also called on voters to elect James Ferguson to rid the state of Will Hobby.[14]

Fox's letter outraged the lawyer in Marfa who had reported the killings in Porvenir to Harley. The attorney sent a letter to Walter Crawford complaining, "[Captain Fox] is a snake in the grass. He has been secretly working for Ferguson all the time. Everybody here knows that these Mexicans were not bandits. He knows that the Mexican vote here, what few will vote, is for Ferguson . . . and it is a joke to claim that firing these rangers was for the purpose of influencing the Mexican vote." Will ordered Adjutant General Harley to strike back at Fox.[15]

On July 3, 1918, Harley issued a public statement that was published in newspapers throughout the state. Harley explained that after a "thorough investigation," the evidence proved that the Mexicans had been killed "while in the custody of [Fox's] men after they had been arrested and disarmed." Addressing Fox directly, Harley explained that he and Governor Hobby were "not interested in your political views when a question of the honor and decency of the state is involved. The lawless ranger has no place on the border, where international complications can be brought that will hamper progress in the war in Europe." Harley emphasized that "every man whether he be white or black, yellow or brown, has the constitutional right to a trial by jury, and that no organized band operating under the laws of this state has the right to constitute itself judge and jury and executioner. . . . We are fighting a world war now to overthrow ruthless autocracy and do not propose to tolerate it here at home."[16]

According to Harris and Sadler, Fox was "discredited" by Harley's letter, but no legal actions were ever taken against anyone for the crime. Will had taken strong action to punish the Rangers involved in the Porvenir incident, including disbanding their company, but as governor, Will had no prosecutorial authority. Only local authorities could take legal action. Will's efforts to tame the Rangers ultimately proved futile, as abusive incidents continued. A number of Ranger critics claimed they continued because Captain William M. Hanson, the investigating officer of the adjutant general's office, protected any Ranger who was accused of committing crimes. In nearly every case of Ranger abuse that made it to Will's desk, however, Will took quick action to punish the culprits by ordering them dismissed from the force.[17]

In later years, Will admitted he was not surprised by the complaints made against the Rangers in South Texas during 1917 and 1918. "Most of the recruits were inexperienced and, in some cases, incompetent," he recalled. "Their activities were not always in keeping with the traditions of the Ranger service." Will's characterization was an understatement, given that some of the Rangers engaged in criminal behavior, including murder.[18]

Will's problems with the Rangers on the border did not deter him from using the force for his own political purposes. Back in November 1917, a month after the Ranger Home Guard Act became law, Will had created the Loyalty Secret Service Department as a special unit of the Rangers, consisting of four companies of men, most of them from outside the Ranger organization. The men Adjutant General Harley appointed to the Loyalty Service were nominated by the sheriffs in each of the state's 254 counties. The sheriffs were instructed not only that the nominees had to be well-known patriots but that they also had to be "reliable" in partisan political matters. After the special session of the legislature passed the Hobby Loyalty Act in March 1918, members of the special unit, which became known as "Loyalty Rangers," were assigned the job of enforcing the act's provisions. Loyalty Rangers policed their counties to ferret out any pro-German sentiment and to crush "the least hint of subversion." Captain Hanson, who was a Hobby supporter, was placed in charge of the day-to-day operations of the service. He oversaw the tracking of alleged revolutionary and subversive activities, the pursuit of fugitive draft evaders, and the prevention of armed incursions from Mexico.[19]

Two months prior to the primary election in July 1918, the Hobby campaign's reaction to the news that Ferguson was attracting huge crowds to his rallies led to Harley's directions to Captain Hanson to put the members of his special Ranger unit to work on the Hobby campaign. Hanson followed orders. His Loyalty Rangers distributed Hobby campaign literature as part of their duties. Hanson asked Adjutant General Harley to provide his men with "a bunch of Hobby literature and that a letter be addressed to each one of them asking their opinion as to whether Governor Hobby will carry that county . . . and their opinion as to how is the best way to carry it in case it is doubtful." According to historian Darren Ivey, "Quite often the only loyalty [the Loyalty Rangers] ensured was to Hobby's election campaign." Harris and Sadler claim that the Loyalty Rangers "formed a statewide political network. As the all-important Democratic primary approached, Hanson spent more of his time quietly working for Hobby's election." In addition to setting up a statewide network of pro-Hobby Loyalty Rangers, Captain Hanson recruited Hobby supporters to organize local Hobby Clubs.[20]

Although no evidence has been found to document Will's direct approval or involvement, it is obvious that he had to have known about this situation. Harley took his orders directly from the governor, and he and Woodul had frequent meetings with him. And it was a tradition in Texas that the governor had special control over the Texas Rangers. According to Harris and Sadler, the Texas Rangers had long been seen as the governor's "personal police . . . often being sent to intrude where they were not wanted and thus fueling resentment that local rights were being trampled." Harris and Sadler note that Governor Hobby "took a much more hands-off approach toward the Rangers" than previous governors and that he gave Adjutant General Harley "a great deal of latitude in running the organization." But they also conclude that Hobby knew the Rangers were being used to support his gubernatorial campaign.[21]

It is difficult to determine how much influence the activities of the Loyalty Rangers had on election results, but there is ample evidence to support claims that the Rangers discouraged and suppressed voting in German American and Mexican American communities where Ferguson was popular. Unfortunately, severe discrimination against Hispanic Texans stretched back to the rebellion against Mexico in 1836. But except for the Civil War years, when many German Texans opposed secession and the Confederate cause, Germans in Texas were generally spared the level of bigotry suffered by Mexican Texans. That changed when the United States declared war on Germany, which unleashed a wave of anti-German hysteria not only in Texas but also in other areas of the nation. At the start of the war, ethnic Germans in Texas numbered well over 200,000 out of a total state population of approximately 4.6 million people. As Robert Utley has pointed out, these German Texans "felt the sting of suspicion and discrimination." The Loyalty Rangers were often the instruments of this discrimination and harassment. Some of the worst examples of such harassment occurred in May and

June in the towns of Snyder and Sweetwater in west-central Texas. Fifty farmers, most of whom were of German descent, were arrested for violating the Hobby Loyalty Act. The men had formed a local branch of the national Farmers and Laborers Protective Association, which was a pacifist agricultural cooperative. The Loyalty Rangers accused them of being socialistic troublemakers. One of the farmers was killed during the arrest. The farmers were charged with sedition for protesting the military draft law and for criticizing the US president and the Congress. When they were tried in September, all but three were acquitted.[22]

The Hobby campaign had worries about the political situation in the borderlands other than the brutal behavior of the Ranger force. There was deep concern that the *patrones*, the political bosses who ruled the region and who were antiprohibition and anti–women's suffrage, would throw their support to Ferguson and manipulate the Hispanic vote in his favor. As one study of voting practices in the region noted, electoral fraud along the border "was not just a tradition but an art form. As a generalization, it can be asserted without much fear of contradiction that everyone elected to public office in South Texas during this period . . . benefitted from electoral fraud."[23]

Ferguson, however, had alienated Jim Wells, the *patrón* of South Texas who was the most influential of the political bosses. As a result, Wells reluctantly declared his support for Will Hobby, and he helped persuade other political bosses in South Texas to do the same, including A. Y. Baker in Hidalgo County and the Guerra family in Starr County. Ranger captain Hanson and Brownsville attorney and state legislator José T. Canales, a Tejano from an old landowning family in the Rio Grande Valley who was campaigning for Hobby, also worked with Wells to bring the Guerras over to their side. Twelve days before the primary election, Canales reported to Walter Crawford at the Hobby campaign committee headquarters in Dallas that he and Hanson had succeeded in getting the Guerra family "to throw all of their influence for Governor Hobby *and we feel sure that Starr County will vote strongly for Hobby.*" He added that it would be best if their meeting with the Guerras "be kept secret until after the election." Canales's law partner, Oscar Dancy, also wrote a letter to Crawford, assuring him of Jim Wells's support. "When the votes are counted down here," Dancy declared, "you will find the precincts controlled by Judge Wells will give a *unanimous vote* for Governor Hobby."[24]

But the political boss of Duval County, state senator Archie Parr, was a major Ferguson supporter who rejected the pleas of Canales and Captain Hanson for him to support Hobby. In retaliation, Hobby's friends in Parr's senatorial district recruited Hobby supporter D. W. Glasscock, a lawyer and former legislator from McAllen, to run against Parr, who was seeking reelection to the Senate in the July primary. Parr used electoral fraud that depended on bloc voting by Mexican Americans to maintain his power and control over Duval County. Glasscock, who had good reason to fear that Parr would steal the primary with inflated returns, persuaded Hobby to order the Texas Rangers to monitor the election in that county as well as in Mexican American precincts in Cameron and Hidalgo Counties. Hobby and Crawford well understood the danger in Duval County.

Charles Flato, Caesar Kleberg's close business partner and political operative, wrote Crawford, "I do hope you will arrange some way to protect the Duval County election box from their customary illegal votes."[25]

Harley ordered the Rangers to South Texas, where they did more than monitor the election. They gave direct assistance to the Glasscock campaign. For example, Rangers were alleged to have helped Glasscock activists discourage Mexican Americans in Corpus Christi from voting by telling them that they would go to prison if they were illiterate and tried to vote. When the election was held in July, Parr submitted the vote returns from Duval County for the Senate race. The count was 1,303 votes for him and 23 for Glasscock. When the Duval vote tally was added to results from the other counties in the Senate district, Parr emerged with a 118-vote majority over Glasscock. A Ranger investigation soon uncovered massive voter fraud in Duval County, but a judge who was friendly to Parr issued a ruling in Parr's favor, declaring him the victor by a margin of 624 votes.[26]

While Crawford, Harley, and Captain Hanson were focusing on South Texas, the Hobby campaign didn't ignore an even more important group, the newly enfranchised (at least for party primaries) women voters. By the end of May, Will's supporters were busily organizing "Hobby Clubs" around the state. These clubs proved valuable to the campaign, but not nearly as valuable as the parallel network of Women's Hobby Clubs organized by Minnie Fisher Cunningham, Hortense Ward, Jane McCallum, and their associates in the Texas Equal Suffrage Association and the Texas Women's Democratic League. Cunningham had promised to turn out the women's vote for Hobby if women were given the right to vote in party primaries. She kept her promise. The Women's Hobby Clubs provided strong grassroots support for the campaign. Members energetically worked at getting out the vote. They conducted house-to-house canvasing, handed out campaign literature on street corners, instructed women in marking ballots, and informed women that they did not have to pay a poll tax but that they had to register before they could vote. The literature they distributed included a flyer declaring, "Women Can Vote in Texas in July, 1918. How, When, and Where They Can Cast Ballots." In addition, Women's Hobby Clubs in towns and counties all over Texas provided women speakers in support of Hobby to as many women's clubs and groups as they could identify and reach. Some Hobby Clubs formed speakers' committees that gave talks during the lunch hour in areas where significant numbers of women worked. Cunningham and her associates also recruited suffragist Annie Webb Blanton, a professor of English at North Texas State Normal College whose brother was Congressman Thomas Blanton, to run for state superintendent of public instruction. The goal was not only to get a woman elected to state office but also to use her candidacy to attract more women to the voting booth. Blanton also campaigned for Will Hobby at the same time she campaigned for herself. In July, she informed Hobby's headquarters, "Wherever I go, I am speaking to big crowds and am speaking in support of Governor Hobby's candidacy, too. Hundreds of women tell me that they had not intended to vote, but mean to do so now, in order to

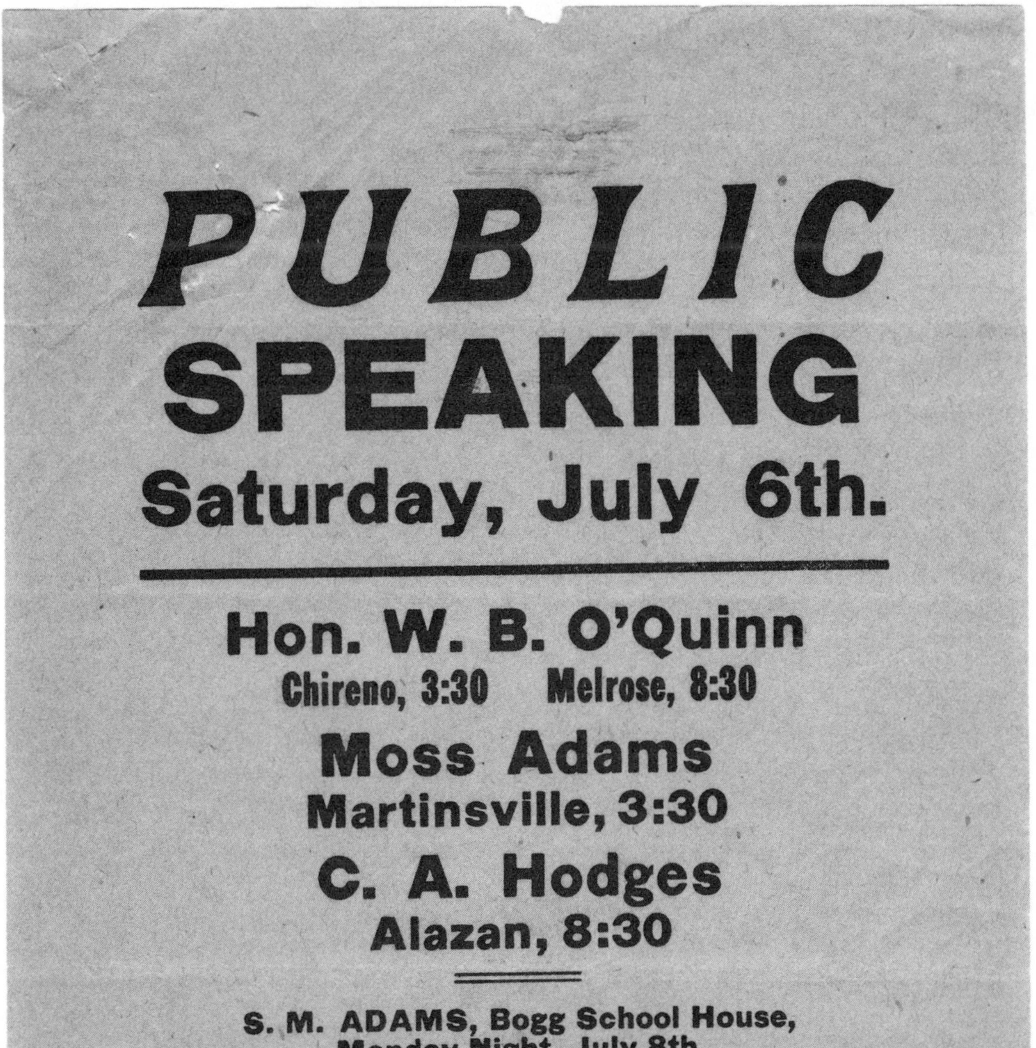

# PUBLIC
## SPEAKING
### Saturday, July 6th.

---

## Hon. W. B. O'Quinn
**Chireno, 3:30    Melrose, 8:30**

## Moss Adams
**Martinsville, 3:30**

## C. A. Hodges
**Alazan, 8:30**

===

**S. M. ADAMS, Bogg School House,
Monday Night, July 8th**

---

The above speakers will speak in the interest of

# Gov. Hobby
**Candidate for Governor**

**LADIES are especially invited to be present
and hear the issues discussed as they are to have
the equal responsibility in the election of officers**

Redland Herald, Printers

*For next Saturday the circular will
have 9 speakers and Points — Pres.*

---

*Handbill for Will Hobby's 1918 campaign with a special invitation to Texas's new women voters.*

*Annie Webb Blanton, ca. 1918.*

vote for me." Blanton won her primary bid and went on to become the first woman to be elected to statewide office in Texas.[27]

Working full-time on the campaign, Cunningham coordinated her activities with Walter Crawford, who wanted her to "visit as many of the sections of the state as possible during the campaign, for I know that such visits will be 'as bread cast upon the waters.'" A skilled public speaker, Cunningham initially concentrated her efforts on East Texas. By late June, Cunningham's work in East Texas was so effective that Crawford asked her to cut short her time there and instead concentrate on Dallas, where Will's campaign was now largely focused. A resident of Galveston, Cunningham also organized the Women for Hobby campaign on the island, recruiting local women to manage and operate it while she traveled around the state. Her effort in Galveston included forming an automobile committee "to take busy mothers and elderly women to register" to vote.[28]

The Texas Equal Suffrage Association (TESA) circulated campaign material to women throughout the state declaring, "Vote for Hobby and you will vote right and for the man who gave Texas women the Vote." Another TESA flyer described Hobby's accomplishments benefitting women: "A dry Texas. Our boys in camp protected from liquor and vice. The primary suffrage [and] the vice law requiring registration for certain diseases for the protection of the homes and the youths of the land. There are many other measures passed at the instance of Governor Hobby that deserve our support and approval. Won't you start a Hobby Club in your community? Do your part towards the reelection of the man who has been the friend of the women and children of this State. DO IT NOW."[29]

The efforts of Cunningham and her allies in the TESA proved effective beyond the Hobby campaign's expectations. Martin Crane, who served on the TESA's Legal Defense Committee, informed Crawford that the Hobby campaign chairman in Hill County reported Women's Hobby Clubs in thirty-six of the forty precincts in his county. Crane also noted that the Hobby chairman in Abilene predicted that Ferguson "will get a big surprise . . . on election day. The women are taking a very active interest and most of them are for Hobby . . . in spite of the fact that their husbands were for Ferguson." Crane also reported that the TESA had registered sixteen thousand women voters in Dallas County. He added that the TESA told him, "The wife of the Judge [in the East Texas town of] Canton who . . . is a Ferguson appointee will vote for Hobby even if her judgeship supports Ferguson."[30]

Cunningham and the TESA's tireless efforts caused deep alarm in the Ferguson campaign headquarters. In a letter to Ferguson, State Commissioner of Pensions J. C. Jones reported that a women's committee had been formed to visit every woman in Texas who could vote in the primaries. He claimed that if a woman refused to support Hobby, she would be threatened with being "black-listed." Jones felt "this is a fine recommendation for woman suffrage and if this is the kind of democracy to lead to victory, God pity the old party under the regime of Woman Suffrage." Confronted with such an outpouring of support for Hobby, Ferguson's campaign tried to divide women along rural-urban lines. In his speeches, Ferguson urged farm women not to be influenced by the "pink tea" women of the cities, "who would rather nurse a poodle dog than a baby." In a speech in Houston, Ferguson referred to Cunningham and her associates as a "class of women who would rather raise trouble than to raise a family."[31]

In their efforts to keep Jim Ferguson from returning to the Governor's Mansion, Cunningham and her cohorts in the TESA and the Texas Women's Democratic League eagerly adopted the Hobby campaign's tactic of associating Ferguson and his supporters with pro-German disloyalty. The Women's League produced and distributed a brochure, "S. O. S. Call to Texas Women," which proclaimed, "Every true Texan must help to bring down the Kaiserism in Texas." The brochure charged that the so-called German brewing industry in Texas was spreading imperial German propaganda while supporting Ferguson for governor.[32]

The Hobby campaign, which included the Loyalty Rangers, also handed out literature that accused Ferguson of having ties to German agents and propagandists. As for the mysterious $156,000 loan, Hobby's supporters charged, with no evidence, that the kaiser had ordered the Texas brewing interests to give Ferguson the loan as his pay for doing his bidding. The Hobby campaign claimed that on orders from Kaiser Wilhelm, Ferguson tried to install political science professor Lindley M. Keasby as president of the University of Texas in the summer of 1917. Keasby was a pacifist faculty member who had publicly opposed the United States' entrance into the war. He had joined the faculty in 1905 and had an impressive record as a published scholar and popular teacher. Will Hobby's supporters spread rumors that the German government had planted Keasby in Texas with the mission to spread German "kultur." There is no evidence to support those charges, and the university's regents never seriously considered appointing Keasby president. According to historian William Nicholas, "Keasby was a professional activist, but he apparently did nothing to indoctrinate his students with pacifist ideas." Nevertheless, the university's regents dismissed Keasby from his position in July 1917 because of speeches he had made outside of the classroom denouncing the war. He moved to Arizona and never taught again.[33]

The Ferguson campaign reeled under the barrage of these anti-German attacks. Ferguson's county campaign chairmen reported that local voters were raising troubling questions about the veracity of the accusations, especially about the mysterious loan for an amount of money that all but a few of his supporters could only dream about. Ferguson tried to fight back. Denying that the kaiser or anyone in the German government had given him the controversial loan, Ferguson promised to donate $1,000 to the Red Cross if Will could prove the charge. Will responded that he would be pleased to make the donation to the Red Cross himself if Ferguson would tell from where he had borrowed the $156,000. Ferguson ignored Will's challenge.[34]

Will was drawing large and enthusiastic crowds to his campaign appearances. His speech in San Antonio's Beethoven Hall drew three thousand. One of the attendees reported to Walter Crawford, "The Governor's effort here last night surpassed the expectations of his most enthusiastic friends. His reasons for urging prohibition measures in aid of the war put the audience in a high state of excitement." A rally in Corsicana on July 1 attracted ten thousand people, an impressive number for that location and during the heat of the summer. One of Will's campaign assistants told Tom Love, "When [Hobby] finished, they picked him up and put him on a table and the cheers lasted ten or fifteen minutes." By early July, with Election Day fast approaching, Will made several campaign stops in the Texas Hill Country, including a Fourth of July speech in Johnson City in front of the Blanco County Courthouse, where he was introduced to the crowd by state representative Sam Ealy Johnson. Afterward, Sam hosted dinner at his house for Will and a group of local politicians. As was traditional, Sam's children had their meal at a table in the kitchen. But Lyndon Baines Johnson, Sam Johnson's ten-year-old son and the future president of the United States, loved political talk, so he hid underneath the large table in the dining room to listen.[35]

The Hobby campaign cost slightly more than $80,000. Will and his brother Edwin together contributed $11,865. But his biggest contributors included not only his friends Frank Andrews, John Henry Kirby, Reinzi Johnston, Will Hogg, and Thomas Love but also other wealthy members of the Democratic Party's establishment from both sides of the prohibition issue. Will's fundraising efforts were bringing in an impressive number of small donations to supplement those he was receiving from his well-to-do friends and allies. Typical of the letters small donors sent to the campaign was one from a train dispatcher in Palestine, who wrote that he wished he "could subscribe more in this fight for an honest and patriotic governor against a corrupt and vicious tyrant." Another voter sent the Hobby campaign ten dollars with a note declaring that the money was to support "good government, especially in favor of a man who can note the difference between his own funds and the funds of the State."[36]

Will's fear that he would alienate his conservative financial backers by his support of the prohibition zones and women's suffrage proved unfounded. Any concerns conservatives might have had about Will's courting of prohibitionists and suffragists were far outweighed by their intense dislike of Ferguson as well as his pro-unionism and rural populism. In addition, Will had been careful to preserve his longtime personal relationships with many of the most influential conservative leaders, such as antiprohibition stalwart Jacob Wolters, a German Texan who brought many of his German friends to Will's side. And of course, conservative members of his father's old Peach Tree Village network, especially John Henry Kirby, remained loyal. Kirby, who rigidly opposed prohibition and women's suffrage, urged his associates to ignore those issues in the campaign. Citing Will's anti-union actions in the oil field strike as an example, Kirby assured his conservative friends that they could trust Will Hobby to do the right thing as governor. The main objective, Kirby declared, was to defeat "[the] criminal and bastard" Ferguson.[37]

The attacks on Ferguson's patriotism, his refusal to reveal the source of his loan, and the highly organized grassroots efforts of the women's suffrage organizations took their toll on Ferguson's campaign. But Will Hobby as a personality made a significant contribution to his own cause. He proved to be an entertaining speaker with a low-key style. He was also a tireless worker, eagerly seeking votes in every corner of the electorate. For example, late in the campaign, Will spoke to a large crowd in Waxahachie. He took a midnight train from Austin that was scheduled to stop at Waxahachie at 6:30 a.m. When the train arrived, he realized he was early enough to make a campaign visit to a little town about fifteen miles to the north, where he could shake a few hands and then board the interurban back to Waxahachie in time for his rally. Will stayed on the train and jumped off when he arrived at the Red Oak station. As he walked through the station, the ticket agent recognized him and insisted on taking him around Red Oak to meet the residents and visit some homes. Hobby happily accepted her offer. Once he had visited most, if not all, of the residents of that small, north-central Texas town, he hopped aboard the interurban and made it back to Waxahachie in time for the rally. Years later, Will described that visit to Red Oak. Chuckling as he remembered the episode, Will recalled that when the election results were reported, he learned he had won every vote cast in Red Oak.[38]

By mid-July Will and his campaign team were confident of victory. One of Will's campaign workers reported to Tom Love, "Ferguson's campaign seems to be disintegrating, and the information is that Hobby will receive an enormous majority of the whole vote." Walter Crawford wrote to Frank Andrews, "We are hearing very excellent reports from all over the State, and I believe [Hobby] is going to win by an unprecedented majority." Referring to South Texas, Crawford added that matters looked good, "provided, of course, we can secure a fair count at the ballot boxes, which matter we have to leave very largely to our friends in the local communities."[39]

Will closed his campaign with a swing through North Texas, followed by a visit to Galveston, where he gave his final campaign speech on July 26. He and Willie traveled home to Beaumont to cast their votes. Thanks to the primary suffrage law, this was Willie's first election. All that was left for them to do was go to the *Beaumont Enterprise* offices to monitor the telegraph and wait patiently for the election results. A crowd of local supporters gathered outside the building to watch voting returns projected on a sheet hung on a wall. The wait was brief. Vote counts soon revealed that Will had won by a landslide. He crushed Ferguson 461,479 to 217,012, the largest majority a gubernatorial candidate had ever received in the Texas Democratic primary. Will won 232 of the 254 counties and seven of the largest cities in Texas, most by substantial majorities. Ferguson carried the wet stronghold of San Antonio and the surrounding German Texan counties, as well as seven lumber industry counties in East Texas, where John Henry Kirby's efforts to suppress union organizing among his workers cost Will his old home territory. In South Texas, Will's problems with Archie Parr cost him Duval and McMullen Counties, but the reliable "boss of bosses" Jim Wells, as promised, delivered the other counties in the region.[40]

The well-organized effort by Minnie Fisher Cunningham and her allies was a decisive factor in the election's outcome. The press reported a heavy turnout of women at the polling booths, and their votes obviously played a key role in Will's victory. During one seventeen-day period, Cunningham's organization registered 386,000 women to vote. Hobby supporters were well aware of the contributions Cunningham and her volunteers had made. One Hobby supporter sent a telegram to Cunningham conveying "sincere congratulations for your wonderful work—greatest victory since Battle of San Jacinto."[41]

Ferguson later conceded that women had apparently voted against him by a ten to one margin. Embittered by this development, Ferguson tried to make the case that allowing women to vote was illegal because the recently passed statute giving them that right was unconstitutional. That argument, however, went nowhere. His problems deepened a month after the election when the Internal Revenue Service filed income tax evasion charges against several members of the brewing industry. During testimony, witnesses revealed that representatives of the brewing industry had arranged the $156,000 loan to Ferguson. In 1924, Ferguson's attempt to run again for governor was thwarted by a Texas Supreme Court ruling that his impeachment and the legislature's ban on his holding public office were both legal and final.[42]

Will's campaign had also been helped by his successful effort to hold together the uneasy coalition of prohibitionists and antiprohibitionists, which was only possible because leaders of both factions feared and detested James Ferguson. Will recognized that some of his leading supporters from the progressive wing of the party were silently unenthusiastic about his candidacy. Two years after the primary election, as his term as governor was nearing its end, Hobby wrote a revealing letter to Frank Andrews complaining about the "gang at Dallas," which included Tom Love and Martin Crane. Will told Andrews he realized that what "rankles . . . some of them" was that he had become governor without their "being able to direct the tide" and that they had supported him "not because they loved me more, but because they loved Ferguson less."[43]

Will and Willie returned to Austin early in the morning of July 30. As their train pulled into the passenger depot, Willie opened the curtains on the window of their compartment to discover a large crowd had assembled on the platform to welcome the victorious couple back to the capital. As the crowd cheered and waved, a brass band struck up "Hail to the Chief" as the Hobbys stepped out onto the platform. University of Texas President Robert Vinson stood on a baggage truck to laud Will Hobby as the leader of a "peaceable revolution" that had defeated the university's nemesis, James Ferguson. Playing the inevitable song "Dixie," the band led the crowd in a parade that escorted the Hobbys up Congress Avenue to the Governor's Mansion. Assured of victory in November's general election, Will and Willie returned to the historic mansion contemplating how they would spend the coming fall, which for Will included planning his agenda for the new legislative session that would convene in January 1919. Although it would be six months before Will would be inaugurated to his own term as governor, he was no longer viewed as the "accidental" chief executive of Texas.[44]

Less than one month after their triumphant return to the Governor's Mansion, the Hobbys' thoughts about the future were interrupted by the shocking news that Willie's father, sixty-eight-year-old Samuel Bronson Cooper, had died in New York City on August 21 after taking ill at his home the night before. The cause of death was judged to be acute indigestion, but it is likely Bronson died from a heart attack. After conducting appraisal board hearings on the West Coast early in 1918, Bronson had spent most of the spring and early summer at his house in Beaumont and at the Governor's Mansion in Austin. He remained in Texas long enough to vote in the primary in July and had been with Will and Willie in Beaumont when they celebrated Will's victory. Before returning to New York, Bronson had promised he would be in Austin in January to attend Will's inauguration. Only two weeks earlier, Will had received a letter from a friend who was serving in New York City in the Supply Division of the army. His friend reported that he had seen Bronson Cooper while walking on upper Broadway in Manhattan near Cooper's apartment at 501 West 110th Street. He wrote to Will that Cooper had been full of excitement about Hobby's election victory.

A telegram informed Willie that her father had become ill; a second telegram soon followed delivering the news of Bronson's death. As soon as he received the news, Will ordered the flag over the capitol to be lowered to half-mast in memory of his father's old friend and protégé and Will's father-in-law. Will and Willie traveled to Beaumont, where they stayed at the Crosby Hotel, the site of many parties and meetings they had attended with Bronson and his wife, Phebe. John Henry Kirby canceled business meetings in New York City to rush to Beaumont for the funeral. Cooper's funeral service was held on Sunday afternoon, August 25, at his home at 1096 Calder Avenue in Beaumont. Hundreds of people attended the burial service in Beaumont's Magnolia Cemetery. Honorary pallbearers included John Henry Kirby, Texas Railroad Commissioner Allison Mayfield, Texas Supreme Court Justice Nelson Phillips, Colonel Rienzi Johnston, and *Houston Post* editorial editor George Bailey. Bronson Cooper's burial marked the end of a significant phase of Will and Willie Hobby's lives.[45]

# CHAPTER 11

# THE TEXAS
# RANGERS

As summer slowly faded into autumn in 1918, Will and Willie Hobby were in Beaumont recovering from the grueling primary campaign and coping with the death of Bronson Cooper. When not at home with his grieving wife, Will was at his office at the *Beaumont Enterprise*, where Jim Mapes had skillfully managed the day-to-day operation of the newspaper while Will carried out his duties as governor in Austin. Will was able to monitor wire reports from Europe about the progress of the Allied armies as they launched a series of assaults on the Germans that would lead to an armistice later in the fall. Will also used this break from his duties in Austin to plan his activities for the last four months of his initial term as governor.

The first item on Will's fall agenda was the Texas Democratic Party's state convention in Waco in September, where he and his political supporters would finally take control of the party away from Ferguson. There was also important work for him back in Austin, including the tedious job of filling vacant state offices that were the result of Ferguson appointees resigning after their leader had been defeated in July. In addition, the state's cotton farmers were urging Will to go to Washington to lobby on their behalf. Will also gave thought to the upcoming legislative session convening in January 1919 and the various issues that were certain to dominate, including the expansion of women's suffrage to include general elections and a growing controversy over the activities of the Texas Rangers. Finally, with the Great War apparently moving toward its end, Will predicted military demobilization would necessitate state action to ease the return of Texas soldiers to civilian life.

Because of his decisive victory over Ferguson and the now-complete domination of the party by the prohibitionists, the state convention in Waco turned out to be a "love fest," as one reporter characterized it, instead of the contentious battle between "wets" and "drys" that had marked previous conventions. In his keynote speech as the newly anointed head of Texas Democrats, Will called for party unity and continued support of the war. But he could not avoid noting that those who had called him a "political accident" were now suffering from a "political catastrophe."[1]

The convention was not completely free of controversy. "Drys" were certain the Eighteenth Amendment would make prohibition the law of the land before the end of 1919, but Minnie Fisher Cunningham and other leaders of the suffrage movement were not as confident about the success of their cause. As a result, suffrage delegates urged the convention to pass a formal resolution calling for ratification of the Nineteenth Amendment. When Cunningham asked Will to submit and endorse the resolution, he declined, arguing that a vote might disrupt the otherwise harmonious meeting. Will was keenly aware that his conservative mentors and supporters might have given up on trying to kill prohibition, but they still had hopes of stopping women's suffrage. Cunningham warned Will that she and her allies were prepared to wage a fight on the convention floor for as long as it was necessary to get their suffrage resolution submitted and passed. In an attempt to avoid a disruptive floor fight, Will sent an emissary to meet with Cunningham to persuade her not to push for the resolution. When Cunningham was told that a battle over the resolution might unnecessarily jeopardize Will's political future, she quickly retorted, "If he doesn't support this amendment, he doesn't have a future." Faced with Cunningham's firm refusal to give up, Will agreed to let the resolution go forward. The convention proceeded to endorse the Nineteenth Amendment after a short but heated debate, with no negative impact on Will.[2]

After the state convention, Will turned his attention to the customary promotional duties of the governor's office, including delivering the featured speech at the annual meeting of the Texas Bankers' Association in Dallas. He continued to urge support for the war, issuing a call for more Texans to register for the military draft. He also led the effort to sell more war bonds in what would be the last Liberty Loan drive of the war.[3]

In late September and early October, Will met with representatives of Texas cotton farmers who were alarmed by the news that the Wilson administration was considering fixing the market price of cotton. Through their representatives in Congress, wheat farmers in the American West were putting great political pressure on President Wilson to either remove the price controls on wheat or place the same controls on cotton, which had escaped federal price-fixing. Cotton prices had increased 400 percent since 1917, while wheat prices had been held down to a set rate. Wheat-farming interests were in an uproar over what they considered to be Wilson's preferential treatment of the Southern cotton-growing (and solidly Democratic) states. As the nation's largest producer of cotton, Texas had a major stake in the price of that commodity. A federally imposed price ceiling was most unwelcome, especially with the state suffering from a drought that had reduced the size of that year's cotton crop.[4]

During the time Will was in Waco attending the Democratic Party's state convention, delegates who represented the large cotton growers persuaded him to lobby the Wilson administration on their behalf. The delegates told him that if political pressure from the wheat states forced Wilson to set cotton prices, they wanted Will to urge the president to fix the price at a level that would cover their production costs, plus "a small or reasonable profit." When he returned to Austin, Will telegrammed President Wilson that Texas had no objection to fixing the price of cotton if it was necessary to the war effort, but he argued the price should not be fixed so low that it would ruin the business interests of the state. He reminded Wilson that Texas was the leading producer of cotton in the United States and that cotton was the "commercial backbone" of the state.[5]

Tom Love urged Will to come to Washington to meet with President Wilson and other administration officials to discuss the growing controversy over cotton prices. Love also suggested that it would be good for Will, now assured of being governor for another two and a half years, to renew his relationship with several Texans who held important positions in the administration. Will accepted Love's advice. Not only did he see the potential political usefulness of the trip, he was also eager to leave Austin for a few days to escape the pressure he was under from the large number of individuals who were seeking appointments to state jobs. Many of the job requests came from Will's closest supporters and friends. Frank Andrews asked Will to appoint their mutual friend, Fort Worth insurance company executive, newspaper publisher, and historian John L. Wortham, to the State Penitentiary System Commission. "The insurance business does not seem to me to have a very promising future outlook until the war is over," Andrews told Will. "[Wortham] is a man of intense loyalty [and] has been your friend from the beginning." Will agreed that Wortham should receive an appointment, but he decided instead to appoint him to the University of Texas Board of Regents, a prestigious appointment but one without financial compensation. Will left several of Ferguson's appointees in their positions. That choice surprised and disappointed some of his friends, who feared that Ferguson appointees would be disloyal to their new governor. Will explained that in some cases Ferguson had appointed competent and honest men to state positions, and he saw no reason to replace them simply because Ferguson had put them in their jobs.[6]

Will also took care of his close allies in the newspaper industry, several of whom he appointed to state commissions and college boards of regents. He appointed former journalist Walter Woodul to the post of assistant adjutant general. Raymond Brooks, who was a reporter at the *Beaumont Enterprise*, served as Will's chief of staff. One observer noted, "The presence of these and other journalists in the administration," combined with his open-door policy for all reporters, assured a "favorable climate" for Will in the capitol press corps. Will's appointments also pleased most of his political allies. "It is indeed refreshing to read the announcement of such appointments," Tom Love wrote Will. "They indicate that indeed Texas has been redeemed."[7]

By September 30, Will was ready to make the trip to Washington to meet with Wilson. He wrote his mother that he was eager to go. "I am so anxious to get rid of this political atmosphere and the supplicants for positions and endorsements," Will stated, "that I will be glad indeed to spend two or three days on the train." Will and Willie, accompanied by Florence Stratton and Edwin and Sadie Hobby, left for Washington on October 1.

Before his departure, Will met with his old mentor, Colonel Rienzi Johnston, who was serving as president pro tem of the Texas Senate. As Hobby's former position of lieutenant governor was vacant due to Ferguson's impeachment, Colonel Johnston would serve as acting governor for the several days Will would be out of state. He and Will had a drink to celebrate the event.[8]

Tom Love, who had lined up a number of appointments in Washington for Will, met the Hobbys at the train station. Because Willie was well known in the capital as a result of her days serving as her father's aide and escort during his years in Congress, the *Washington Times* published her photograph and announced her arrival. During his busy week in the capital, Will met President Wilson, Secretary of State Robert Lansing, War Industries Board chairman Bernard Baruch, and Provost Marshall General Crowder. His visit with Baruch, who was a wealthy Wall Street tycoon, went especially well. The two men remained in touch for several years after this initial meeting. Will also visited some of the Texans who were serving in the Wilson administration, including presidential advisor Colonel Edward M. House, Postmaster General Albert S. Burleson, Secretary of Agriculture David Houston, Attorney General Thomas Watt Gregory, and Clarence Ousley, Will's former colleague at the *Houston Post* who was serving as assistant secretary of agriculture. In these meetings, which Willie also attended, Will was able to cover a wide range of issues important to Texas, including the use of the Texas National Guard to patrol the border with Mexico as well as the cotton price issue. Love later wrote Will that his visit had accomplished "untold good" for Texas interests, especially for the state's cotton farmers.[9]

After the Hobbys returned to Austin, Will issued a statement to the press predicting the Wilson administration would not set cotton prices. That prediction proved to be correct. He also declared that it was obvious that Texas was enjoying more influence in Washington than it had ever had, with a significant number of Texans playing important roles in the cabinet and other offices of government. "The influential judgment and clear-headed vision of Colonel E. M. House of Austin is recognized everywhere," Will stated.

While Will was in Washington, the German government sent a request through the Swiss embassy for a meeting to discuss an armistice on the basis of President Wilson's Fourteen Points. Although Wilson rejected the offer, it was an exciting moment that signaled the end of the war was near. Will had been thrilled to be in Washington when the news broke about the German proposal. He told the press back in Austin that Wilson would go down in history with George Washington as one of the two greatest presidents: Washington because he had established the principles of the American republic and Wilson because he applied those principles worldwide. Will proclaimed that Wilson had a "surpassing ability and broad conception of human rights," and he predicted that the president would play the dominant role whenever the peace conference was held.[10]

Will and Willie had planned to remain in Washington for a few days longer and then to go to New York City for an extended visit, but they canceled the trip and returned to Austin early because of news that the deadly "Spanish flu" epidemic that was sweeping the world and killing millions had worsened in the northeastern states. They were alarmed to learn on their arrival in Austin that influenza had spread to Texas. The situation was dire. One source estimates that at the height of the epidemic in Texas in October and November, as many as nine thousand men stationed at the state's military bases died of the flu. In Austin alone, ten or more people were dying from the flu every day. The situation was so bad that Colonel Johnston, in his capacity as acting governor, issued a proclamation urging the temporary closure of all places of assembly in the state, including theaters, churches, and schools. Soon after his return from Washington, Will was struck with a case of the deadly disease. Although he was among the fortunate who survived, he was ill for several weeks. His illness was severe enough in early December to spark rumors that he might resign from office or that he was close to death. Willie, who nursed and watched over her husband, managed to escape the highly contagious disease.[11]

Early in the morning of November 11, news reached the Governor's Mansion that an armistice had been signed and the Great War had ended. Will, confined to his bed because of his illness, released an official statement, declaring that the armistice meant "a peace with complete victory. Win the war has been the guiding thought in every act of my administration. Prepare for peace is the task to which we should give our efforts now and I shall subordinate all things else to that."[12]

Will's recovery was excruciatingly slow, and he was bedridden and miserable for the remainder of November. Nonetheless, the business of the governor's office continued, as his staff and various functionaries streamed into the Governor's Mansion to bring him paperwork to sign and to ask him to write letters to help with one minor matter after another. Not all of the business was minor. Almost as soon as the armistice was signed, the US Army began to demobilize, releasing a flood of discharged soldiers back into civilian life. Texas had more than its fair share of these discharged soldiers returning home. University of Texas School of Law dean John C. Townes Jr., whom Will had appointed head of the Texas Selective Service, was concerned that thousands of these military veterans would be unable to reclaim their former jobs. He feared that the situation could lead to social disorder. Townes asked Will to create a governor's "reconstruction" organization, using some of the $350,000 in unused funds that the legislature had allocated for support of the Texas National Guard, which would not be needed with the war coming to an end. Townes noted that it was unlikely that the federal government would do anything to help the soldiers and that it would be up to the states to take action. He was worried that if veterans remained unemployed, they would become "disgruntled and we will find a condition of discontent tending toward socialism and other 'Isms.'" Townes, who was as anti-labor-union as Will, warned the governor that labor leader Samuel Gompers had recently been in Laredo, where he had declared that organized labor "would fight any effort to reduce wages" that had been raised during the war. "The attitude of organized labor," Townes argued, "will certainly lead to a very disturbed domestic condition."[13]

Townes, whose son Edgar was general counsel for the Humble Oil Company in 1919, was expressing a great fear that was spreading among the leaders of American industry about the influence the Bolshevik Revolution in Russia might have on American workers. Will, alarmed by the news of this "grave and important problem," asked Townes to go to Houston "at the earliest possible moment" to meet with Frank Andrews and cobble together a program for Will to consider. Townes and Andrews advised Will to keep the Texas Council for Defense in operation until June 1919 for the purpose of providing assistance to returning soldiers. Will accepted the proposal. The council's main role was to urge employers to rehire men who had left their jobs to enter the military and to encourage prospective employers to give veterans preference when hiring new employees. Employer compliance was entirely voluntary, however. The program did nothing to prevent a major strike in Galveston in 1920 in which Will Hobby, as governor, would be deeply and controversially involved.[14]

At the end of November, Willie was worried that as long as Will remained in Austin, where he was easily accessible to state officials, he was not going to get the rest he needed to recover his health. She persuaded him to go with her to Beaumont until he returned to full strength. Her plan succeeded; Will was fully recuperated by late December. He was well enough to travel to Dallas with Willie to spend a quiet Christmas Day with his mother. They returned to Austin immediately after Christmas, but they canceled the traditional New Year's Day reception at the mansion. Willie was preserving Will's strength, and with the influenza epidemic still raging, people were avoiding large social gatherings.[15]

When Will was in Beaumont recovering from influenza, the *Houston Post* was undergoing significant changes that would ultimately have a major impact on Will's future. Colonel Johnston, who was still serving as president pro tem of the Senate, was forced to retire from his position as editor of the *Post*. As a trustee of the estate of Julius Watson, the late owner of the *Post*, Johnston had served as the newspaper's editor since Watson's death in 1896. In May 1917, Julius Watson's Princeton-educated son, Roy, assumed control of the *Post* when he turned twenty-five, as his father's will had stipulated. For eighteen months the young Watson served as the president of the Houston Printing Company, the legal entity that owned the *Post*, but he let Johnston and George Palmer continue to run the newspaper. Watson, however, was a Christian Scientist, and he strongly disapproved of Johnston and Palmer's editorial and business policies. In December 1918 he took Johnston's position as editor of the *Post* and remained as president of the Houston Printing Company. The "Colonel" was allowed to continue as chairman of the board. Watson immediately banned all ads in the *Post* for patent medicines, wildcat oil stock, liquor, wine, beer, and yeast, all of which were major sources of the newspaper's income. Unhappy with Watson's changes, Colonel Johnston soon resigned from the company. Rienzi Johnston had worked at the *Post* for thirty-four years and had played a key role in helping Watson's father create the newspaper. Acknowledging his debt to Johnston for his stewardship of the *Post* for more than two decades, Watson granted him a $5,000 annual pension for life.[16]

A week before Will's inauguration, the legislature had to address two issues before the ceremony could be held and the new session could proceed. The first was the disputed election of Archie Parr, whose victory was under challenge in the Senate. His opponents, who were Hobby supporters, were denying the legitimacy of his narrow victory in 1918 and were demanding a vote on whether he should be allowed to serve. Ordinarily, this matter would not have involved the governor, but to Will's great discomfort, Rienzi Johnston led the effort to seat Parr and he expected Will's open support. Caught between his strong disapproval of the corrupt "Boss of Duval County" who had supported Ferguson for governor and his loyalty to a mentor and longtime friend, Will refused to take a public position in the controversial matter, even going so far as to refuse to meet with Johnston to discuss the issue. The situation was especially difficult for Will because of his concerns about Johnston's state of mind after his recent removal as editor of the *Houston Post*. After a heated debate, the Senate voted sixteen to fourteen to seat Parr, with Colonel Johnston casting the deciding vote that avoided a tie. Parr would remain in the Senate until 1934.[17]

Despite this disagreement, Will's close friendship with Colonel Johnston survived. Only two months before the legislature convened, Colonel Johnston had been grateful to Will for appointing Johnston's ne'er-do-well, thirty-three-year-old son Harry as a captain of the Texas Rangers Headquarters Company at Camp Mabry in Austin. It was an appointment Will would soon regret, however. A few months later, Will was forced to fire Harry Johnston and two other Rangers after they participated in a drunken brawl and gun battle in Austin in which one Ranger shot and killed another Ranger. Will's dismissal of Harry Johnston, however, did not result in a break with Colonel Johnston, who was fully aware of his son's problems. Colonel Johnston remained in the Senate until January 12, 1920, when Will appointed him chairman of the state prison commission.[18]

The other issue that the legislature had to confront before the inauguration was the Texas Ranger problem. On January 15, Brownsville representative J. T. Canales, who was serving his seventh term in the legislature, created a major stir in the capitol when he introduced House Bill 5. The bill called for strong measures to reform the Ranger force and bring an end to the extrajudicial methods many Rangers had long employed in South Texas. Declaring that the Texas Rangers had "committed crimes equal to those of the Germans in Belgium right here in our own civilized state," Canales filed nineteen separate charges of serious Ranger irregularities and crimes, including the Porvenir Massacre, the murder of the Mexican policeman in Brownsville, and several other incidents in South Texas. Canales also charged Captain Hanson with covering up Ranger crimes. Except for a general reference to Ranger political activities, Canales's bill ignored the Hobby campaign's use of the Rangers in the Democratic primary in 1918. Canales, of course, had not only campaigned for Will Hobby in South Texas but he had also worked with Captain Hanson to organize Starr County, located on the Rio Grande between Laredo and McAllen, for the Hobby campaign. Starr County was the domain of *patrón* Gustavo Guerra and his family, who ruled the area with an iron hand.[19]

After Canales filed his bill, the House and Senate passed a concurrent resolution creating a joint committee to investigate Canales's charges. The joint committee held

*Texas Rangers, ca. 1920.*

hearings from January 31 to February 13 and issued an official report on February 18 that revealed a number of well-documented occasions of serious misconduct by various Rangers, including murder. The report demanded the dismissal of any Rangers involved in the incidents who were still on duty. The report also acquitted Captain Hanson and other Ranger commanders of the charge of partiality and unfairness in carrying out their duties. Despite the well-known use of Rangers by the Hobby primary election campaign, the report not only cleared Governor Hobby and Adjutant General Harley of any improper conduct, it also praised their administration of the Rangers.[20]

The legislature used the committee's report to revise HB 5 and passed the bill on March 31. Will quickly signed it. The Ranger reform act increased pay at all levels of the force as a means to attract higher quality candidates, and a new appointment process was created to better screen applicants. Soldiers who had received honorable discharges were to be given preference in hiring. The act also prohibited the Rangers from interfering with the work of local law enforcement officials, although the Rangers retained the authority to make arrests in all jurisdictions in Texas. HB 5 reduced the Ranger force to a total of seventy-five men. As the war had ended, the Special Rangers and Loyalty Rangers had already had their commissions revoked before HB 5 was passed. HB 5 was generally successful in restoring the reputation of the Rangers as a professional law enforcement organization. In 1935, the legislature transferred the Texas Rangers from the governor's office to the newly created Texas Department of Public Safety.[21]

At noon on January 21, 1919, Will Hobby took the oath of office as governor of Texas, finally shedding the "unelected" label. Will's fellow newspaper publisher W. A. Johnson was sworn in as lieutenant governor, a position that had remained vacant since Ferguson's impeachment in 1917. Chief Justice Nelson Phillips administered the oath to both men. As was his style, Will's inaugural speech was brief and largely a reflection on the past year. Referring to the fact that the primary suffrage bill had made it possible for women to vote in the Democratic primary election and that the women's vote had helped to elect him, Will declared himself proud that "for the first time the voice which speaks in this historic hall on this occasion is the voice of all the people, the men and women of Texas alike." This statement was met with loud cheers and extended applause from the women who packed the galleries.[22]

The remainder of Will's speech was a reflection on the tumultuous previous year, one he characterized as "a stormy one . . . because of all that war could engender." He declared that the election of 1918 had settled the issues of prohibition and suffrage, "questions that have divided the people of this commonwealth for many years." He also noted that the "devastating" drought and the "death-dealing" influenza had beset his administration "with thorns and thistles at every turn." The remainder of his speech was mostly filled with praise for the victorious Allied armies in Europe, who, Hobby declared, would never have prevailed over the "Huns" had it not been "for the fact that [General] Pershing and the boys in khaki were near at hand and to the tune of 'Dixie' and 'Yankee Doodle' were heading towards the Rhine."[23]

Soon after his inauguration, Will submitted to the legislature his proposals for the thirty-sixth session, including a $10 million construction program for new buildings at Texas A&M University, the University of Texas, and the state's teachers' colleges; merging the court of criminal appeals with the supreme court; creation of a State Board of Control to streamline the state's budget system; clarification of the state libel laws to better protect journalists who reported on the actions of public officials; a state-funded low interest, long-term loan program to support the purchase of small farms and homes with special terms for returning military veterans; and new laws to regulate the booming oil and gas industry, including conservation laws to be enforced by the Texas Railroad Commission and an act giving pipeline companies the power of eminent domain. Will also urged the legislature to increase support for public schools, which he called the "bulwark of free government." All of his proposals were eventually passed in one form or another, with the oil and gas legislation serving as the basis for state regulation of the energy industry for decades to come.[24]

Will's legislative success can be explained to some extent by his skill at forging friendships with individual members, who appreciated his talent for calm deliberation and his even temperament. Hugh Fitzgerald noted that as governor Hobby "never lost his temper. He never lost his poise. He avoided the snags. *He carried on.*" He also avoided high-pressure lobbying tactics, never acted rashly, and often sought the opinion and advice of trusted advisors, such as Frank Andrews, Walter Crawford, and his brother Edwin. And as a newspaperman himself, Hobby also had an open-door policy with the capitol press, which served him well when he wanted to promote legislation he supported.[25]

After serving as lieutenant governor for three years, Will also had a solid understanding of the concerns and needs of individual legislators. Will rarely attached a draft of a bill when he submitted a specific request to the legislature. He made it clear to the members that he preferred they write their own bills. Will later said that "almost invariably" after he made a request for a law, legislators would meet with him and his staff to discuss a bill, and they would produce a draft together. At that point, Will would show his own draft to the legislators to use in their discussions. As a result, Hobby usually knew in advance the details of the most important bills submitted to the legislature, many of which contained his own text. That process let members take personal credit for writing the bill, instead of simply being seen as a "message boy" for the governor, while also making it possible for Will to get most of his legislative agenda accomplished. He was happy to let others take the credit as long as he got his bill passed.[26]

While the joint committee investigated the Rangers, the legislature proceeded with its normal business of passing laws, including bringing closure to two long-standing issues: prohibition and suffrage. Although Will declared in his inaugural address that both issues had been settled, the fact was that prohibition and women's suffrage required additional action to bring them to final resolution. The Eighteenth Amendment, which would impose prohibition on the entire country, would go into effect in January 1920, but prohibitionist stalwarts in the Texas Legislature, led by Senator W. Luther Dean, were unwilling to wait that long to make the entire state dry. They launched an effort to have the legislature submit a prohibition amendment to the state constitution to a popular vote in May.

Will was reluctant to endorse Dean's plan, because national prohibition would make the state's amendment redundant. But Senator Dean had endorsed Will in the 1918 primary and had helped the governor in a number of legislative and appointive matters. Gratitude for Dean's support won out over any reluctance Will had about his bill. He pledged his support for its passage. But Will was not too shy to ask Senator Dean for something in return: his support for an increase in funding for the state's public colleges and for a women's suffrage bill. Dean agreed to the trade. The legislature passed Dean's bill and set May 24 as the date for the voters to accept or reject the state amendment.[27]

A similar legislative scenario played out for women's universal suffrage. Over the objections of the prosuffrage activists and organizations, the legislature, with Will's support, passed a bill on February 5 to submit for voter approval a state constitutional amendment granting full suffrage for women. At the time, the US Congress was still debating the Nineteenth Amendment granting women the right to vote. Suffrage supporters in Texas opposed putting the issue to a popular vote. Every suffrage referendum previously held in the South had lost, and there were fears that a failed referendum in Texas would hurt the battle in Congress to pass the Nineteenth Amendment. Women's voting rights leaders were also angered that the legislature placed the amendment on the May 24 referendum ballot, giving suffragist activists little time to raise money and campaign for its passage. Will supported the referendum bill despite these objections. He asked for a state amendment, but with an early submission date that gave the supporters of women's suffrage little time to mount an effective campaign.[28]

The amendment included a rider prohibiting foreign-born individuals from voting until they had achieved full naturalization. The law in force at the time allowed alien residents to vote in Texas. It was obvious that the legislative opponents of suffrage added the alien voting ban to the amendment as a way to defeat it, as the voters who would be disenfranchised by its passage were eligible to vote against it. Cunningham was angered so much by the referendum bill that she spread word she was "determined to torpedo" Will Hobby's political future if he decided to run again for governor. Despite her unhappiness with the governor, Cunningham attended the ceremony in the Texas Senate chamber on February 5 when Will signed the suffrage amendment referendum act. A photograph was taken of Will signing the bill in the Senate chamber, surrounded by Cunningham and other supporters of women's suffrage. That widely published photographic image has often been incorrectly labeled in textbooks as Will signing the bill that gave Texas women the right to vote.[29]

With the hot issues of prohibition and women's suffrage addressed if not completely resolved, the legislature focused on less controversial bills. After the legislative session was adjourned on March 19, prohibitionists and suffrage activists turned their attention to the upcoming referendum election.

Two weeks before the Thirty-Sixth Legislature ended its regular session, the members took a break from regular business to participate in the governor's inaugural ball. Originally scheduled for January 21, Will had postponed the traditional ball until March 3 with the explanation that the legislature should immediately begin work on an unusually long list of items before taking time for a ball. While that was the official justification, it's likely that the winter's great influenza epidemic and the reluctance to host large gatherings were more of a factor. Prior to the ball at the Driskill Hotel, Will and Willie hosted a reception at the Governor's Mansion for members of the legislature and other friends. Attendance was estimated to be in the hundreds, straining the capacity of the

*Will signs the suffrage referendum act in the Texas Capitol, while a skeptical
Minnie Fisher Cunningham looks on from his left, February 5, 1918.*

mansion, with guests flowing out onto the building's grounds. At one point a power
failure plunged the event into darkness. Willie had the staff light candles and the party
continued in candlelight. The reception was such a success that the Hobbys were late for
the inaugural ball, delaying the Grand March into the ballroom until nearly midnight.[30]

There was one guest invited to the reception and ball whose absence distressed Will, and that was his mother. The details are unknown, but for some reason Dora declined the invitation. Apparently her decision was not due to infirmities or health reasons but because of hurt feelings, perhaps because of perceived neglect by her son. A week after the ball, Will wrote a letter to Dora that more than hints at the source of the problem and provides a window into Will's relationship with his mother. Telling her that he was sorry she had not come to the reception and inaugural ball, Will wrote, "I cannot be happy when I am not in communication with you for so long a time and now when I have so many things on my hands is when I want your presence, your words, and your love and affection. I knew you must feel aggrieved and if so I want you to feel otherwise. I am miserable without something to show that your heart is beating with mine. When it comes to the innermost depths of my heart I love you better than all else." He urged Dora to come to Austin to stay with him and Willie at the mansion as soon as the legislature adjourned.[31]

It's not known if Dora made the trip to Austin in March, but Will and Willie visited her in Dallas in mid-April after they spent a few days relaxing at a resort in Mineral Wells, eighty miles west of Dallas. Mineral Wells, which was famous as a spa resort and "medicinal" mineral water source from the 1890s until the 1940s, was a favorite getaway place for the Hobbys. At the height of its popularity, the town featured more than four hundred wells from which foul-tasting water heavy in mineral content was drawn. Thousands of bottles of "Crazy Water" from the wells were shipped all over Texas and the South. After he became governor Will had taken up golf, and he took advantage of the free time in Mineral Wells to shoot a few rounds. Will's golfing buddies in the legislature jokingly accused him of learning to play golf only to have the opportunity to chew tobacco away from Willie, who strongly disapproved of the habit. Will confessed to his golf partners that Willie had discovered a half-eaten plug of tobacco in his pants pocket one morning after a golf game, and as a result he had spent a brief time in Willie's "dog-house."[32]

The inaugural reception was the largest but not the only event the Hobbys hosted at the Governor's Mansion during the late winter and all of spring 1919. Will and Willie had declared a moratorium on parties and entertainment at the mansion during the Great War, but peace and a noticeable diminution in flu infections allowed them to reopen the mansion for events. Under Willie's guidance, thousands of guests filled the mansion during the first six months of the year as they attended a constant round of parties and official functions. Those guests included an impressive number of prominent citizens, such as President Wilson's trusted advisor and counselor Colonel Edward M. House, J. P. Morgan's celebrity daughter Anne Morgan, and Wilson's vice president Thomas Marshall. Some of Willie's family also flocked to the mansion to attend parties and stay as overnight guests. Willie's sister Margaret Jacoway and her two children stayed with the Hobbys in the Governor's Mansion for a few days. Sam Young, Willie's first cousin on her mother's side, was a frequent guest. Willie and her brother, Sam Cooper Jr., were close to the twenty-two-year-old Sam Young, who had grown up with them. And Will had become fond of Sam Young as well. While serving in the army at Fort Sam Houston in San Antonio in 1918, Sam Young took advantage of his three-day passes to make frequent trips to Austin to stay in the mansion with his cousin, whom he called "Sis Willie." At Willie's request, Sam wore his first lieutenant's army uniform and stood at attention by his uncle Samuel Bronson Cooper's casket during the funeral service in Beaumont.[33]

According to a history of the First Ladies of Texas, Willie invited a wide range of ordinary citizens as well as celebrated figures to the mansion. "Willie had a flair for pleasing all manner of guests," the historical account noted. "Her concern and skill enabled her to make people from all levels of society feel welcome and wanted." For example, Willie held receptions to bring attention to the work of young Texans involved in civic and educational activities. An event she hosted for members of a youth agricultural organization attracted statewide newspaper coverage. Willie's favored guests, however, were female students at the University of Texas, for whom she gave numerous teas and tours of the mansion. After the Hobbys left state government to return to Beaumont in 1921, one newspaper declared, "As mistress of the executive mansion, Willie Cooper Hobby was one of the most popular and winning women that has ever presided since the stately building was erected."[34]

Willie's closest friend, Florence Stratton, was often her cohost for the receptions and dinners at the mansion when Will was called away for business. Florence was at Willie's side, for example, as they stood beneath a large Confederate flag suspended above the entrance hall to the mansion and greeted members of the United Daughters of the Confederacy to a formal reception. The group was holding its national convention in Austin, and Will gave the welcome address opening the meeting. Florence also served as Willie's cohost for an afternoon reception at the mansion for the Texas Division of the Daughters of the American Revolution, while Will played golf, although he did give the keynote address to the organization's state convention in Austin that night. On this occasion, Florence Stratton greeted guests as they entered the mansion and then directed them to the room where Willie awaited them.[35]

Stratton had moved from Beaumont to Austin when Will became governor in 1917. She was a constant presence at the mansion, and she also traveled with the Hobbys. Willie met her in 1907 when Florence began her career at the *Beaumont Journal* as its society editor. Although Willie was five years older than Florence, the friends had much in common. Both were independent, college-educated, prosuffrage, socially adept, and worldly women who shared a strong interest in social affairs, journalism, government, and politics. When the Hobbys moved back to Beaumont in 1921, Will gave Florence a job at the *Beaumont Enterprise*. She eventually published several books, including a local history, *The Story of Beaumont*, and *Favorite Recipes of Famous Women*. The latter book featured recipes Willie Hobby had collected during her years as Texas's First Lady.[36]

Throughout the spring of 1919, prosuffrage organizations campaigned to persuade male Texans to vote for the suffrage amendment in the referendum election on May 24.

Will, however, focused his efforts on conducting ceremonial duties of governor, including meeting in Laredo with the governors of two Mexican border states on April 7, attending the Battle of the Flowers Fiesta in San Antonio on April 21, and giving a speech in Houston on April 23 to help promote an exposition at W. C. Munn's, the largest department store in the city at the time.[37]

When the special referendum election on the constitutional amendments was held on May 24, foreign-born Texans flocked to the polls to preserve their right to vote, which meant they had to vote against the suffrage amendment to keep from being disenfranchised. Suffrage proponents had thought they could win the votes of many of the men returning from military service, reasoning that their experience in a war supposedly fought to defend democracy might have made them more appreciative of the need to expand democratic rights in their own country. Most of these men, however, were not eligible to vote because they had not paid their poll tax. To remedy that problem, Cunningham and other suffrage leaders persuaded Will to call a special session of the legislature to pass a law permitting these veterans to vote in the special election even if they had not paid their poll tax. That temporary poll tax waiver was passed in the session, which lasted from May 5 until May 9. Despite that and all other efforts made by suffrage proponents, the amendment was rejected by a margin of twenty-five thousand votes, mainly because women could not vote in support of their own cause.[38]

Armed by the defeat of the referendum, antisuffrage members of the legislature demanded that Will Hobby submit a bill to a special session of the legislature to repeal the law that allowed women to vote in party primaries. Hobby rejected their demands, arguing that the primaries and the general election were separate issues and that the law giving women the right to vote in primaries had been "in the interest of good government and accorded simple justice to all our citizenship."[39]

The women's suffrage amendment to the Texas Constitution failed, but a victory was not long in coming. On June 4, Congress passed the Nineteenth Amendment and sent it to the states for ratification. Despite her husband's foot-dragging on the issue, Willie demonstrated her strong support by traveling to Washington to attend the ceremonial signing of the amendment. Three weeks later, when Will called a special session of the legislature to pass an appropriations bill and address other issues, including a law to enforce the Eighteenth Amendment, women's suffrage leaders demanded he include ratification of the Nineteenth Amendment among the items to be considered. Even though Willie had made a public show of her support of the amendment by going to Washington, Will at first declined the request, arguing that it would complicate the appropriations process. This indicates some difference of opinion between Will and Willie, not about the need for the amendment but about how quickly to move, and is an example of Will's cautious nature. Nevertheless, under intense pressure from women's suffrage organizations (and possibly Willie), Will relented. The House of Representatives passed the ratification bill quickly. There was strong opposition in the Senate, but after heated debates and attempts to kill the bill through parliamentary maneuvers, the

Senate passed the ratification bill on June 25 by a vote of nineteen to ten. Texas became the ninth state and the first Southern state to ratify the Nineteenth Amendment.[40]

Now that Texas had ratified the amendment, and perhaps to placate Willie, Will lobbied other states to join Texas in ratification. He gave speeches in Oklahoma and Tennessee urging the legislatures of those states to finish the job. When only one more state was needed to ratify the amendment, Will wired the Tennessee Legislature and argued, "The right of women to a voice in the affairs of their government has been won by faithful and efficient service and I trust that Tennessee whose history is entwined with the history of Texas . . . will join with Texas, the first Southern state to ratify, and make possible the full and complete citizenship of women throughout the Union." On August 27, 1919, Tennessee was the thirty-sixth state to pass its ratification bill, which finally established women's suffrage as the law of the land. Will immediately dispatched a letter of thanks and congratulations to Albert H. Roberts, the governor of Tennessee. On September 4, 1919, Will proclaimed an official state holiday to celebrate the passage of the women's suffrage amendment.[41]

Before the legislature ended its third called session on July 22, it completed its work on prohibition. Because the statewide prohibition amendment had passed in the referendum in May, the legislature needed to enact an enforcement law to carry out the amendment's provisions. Senator Dean authored the bill, which quickly became known as the "Dean Law." Because the prohibitionist senator had kept his promise to Will to support increased funding for public schools and women's suffrage in exchange for Will's support of the state prohibition law, Will told Dean he would sign his bill. When he gave Dean the news, Will smiled and pleaded, "Don't make it too drastic, Luther." Years later, when Senator Dean laughingly recalled the meeting, he noted that Will was a man who supported prohibition but didn't practice it.[42]

Will was justly proud of the legislative accomplishments of 1919. In addition to the Dean Law and ratification of the Nineteenth Amendment, the legislature had acted on a wide range of other business, including the passage of a landmark bill to conserve oil and gas resources, another to fund free textbooks in the public schools, and one to establish the Texas State Library and Archives Commission. It also passed a budget for the coming two fiscal years, although with a significant reduction in overall funding from the prior biannual allocation.[43]

# CHAPTER 12

---

# RED SUMMER

The legislative sessions of 1919 were among the most productive in the state's history, but that success was achieved while Texas and many other areas of the United States were suffering through shameful episodes of racial bigotry, horrific mob violence, and xenophobia.

Historian Adam Hochschild has pointed out that after the United States entered the war in Europe in 1917, millions of Americans rushed to spurn anything German. Families named Schmidt quickly became Smith. German-language textbooks were tossed on bonfires. "Hamburger" was now "Salisbury steak" and "German measles" were "liberty measles." The fighting in Europe was over by the end of 1918, but much of the mindless xenophobia resulting from war propaganda lingered, some of which attached itself to Will. When the annual budget for the University of Texas landed on Will's desk for his signature in the summer of 1919, Will shocked the university and its prominent graduates by vetoing, without warning, the appropriation for the Department of German Languages. Will's veto was in reaction to news that the university's board of regents had dismissed Professor Eduard Prokosch, the German Language Department chairman and a distinguished linguist. The former US ambassador to Germany James Gerard had accused Prokosch of being a propagandist for Kaiser Wilhelm. Gerard made his charges in his book *Face to Face with Kaiserism*, published in 1918. Citing a German-language textbook Prokosch had authored, Gerard claimed the text was slanted to compare Germany favorably to the United States. For example, Gerard was outraged by Prokosch's statement that Germany was a union of states, like the United States. Gerard ludicrously argued that American students would take that statement to mean that Germans had the same civil liberties as Americans. Among Gerard's many complaints about the textbook was Prokosch's inclusion of the lyrics to the German anthem "Die Wacht am Rhein." Though no one charged Prokosch with subversive teaching or with disloyal activity while on the university faculty, Gerard's complaints persuaded the university's regents to remove the professor from the faculty.[1]

---

Apparently, Prokosch's dismissal reminded Will that the university had a department that taught the German language, which he found unacceptable. He justified his veto by declaring that teaching "our American children Americanism is better than the practice of teaching them Germanism." Using Prokosch as an example, he argued that hiring German language teachers provided an opportunity for those instructors to spread foreign propaganda. In a careful nod toward the voters in the German communities in Texas, however, Will carefully explained that his veto was not meant to be an affront to the "true and loyal American-German citizens of Texas." Why Will took this stance is difficult to explain. Whatever political gain he thought he could enjoy was insignificant. He had just won election, and it's clear he had little interest in running for reelection in 1920. Whatever justification he had for eliminating the German Language Department, it failed to resonate with a legislature eager to let go of the extreme patriotic fervor that the war had unleashed. Astonished by Will's action, university president Vinson pleaded with the legislature to restore funding, arguing that Prokosch was no longer on the faculty and that the study of the German language was of "real value." The legislature agreed with Vinson and overrode Will's veto. Eduard Prokosch went on to serve as the Distinguished Sterling Professor of Germanic Languages at Yale University.[2]

Will's involvement in Texas's public educational institutions included his service as chairman of the state textbook commission. Under Will's guidance as chairman, the commission decided early in 1919 that it would not approve any textbook for use in the public schools that included "criticism of the Christian religion." When news of this ruling reached influential Galveston rabbi Henry Cohen, he urged Will to replace "Christian religion" with the words "any recognized religion." Cohen wrote Will, "The justice of this is apparent and needs no argument." His letter included an editorial clipped from the *Jewish Monitor*, which was published in Fort Worth, calling for the revision. Cohen offered to come to Austin to make his case before the commission. Will replied that he had read his letter "with much interest" and that he believed Cohen's position to be correct. Will called a meeting of the textbook commission and asked his fellow members to approve Cohen's request, which the commission did by a unanimous vote. The textbook commission also ruled that it would not approve any textbook for the public schools that expressed any "sentiments unfriendly to the South or to the Southern Confederacy, or to Texas." The word "unfriendly" was not defined. Neither Will nor Rabbi Cohen nor anyone else expressed objection to that rule, and it remained.[3]

These examples of intolerance paled, however, in comparison to the epidemic of lynching and other forms of racial murder and related violence that swept through Texas and many other sections of the nation in 1919. In the months between May and November of 1919, more than three dozen cities across the United States, including Washington, DC, and Chicago, experienced race riots that resulted in the deaths of hundreds of Americans, the vast majority African Americans. The root cause of this violence was deeply embedded white racism, but it was triggered by social and economic conditions immediately after the Great War, including unemployment, housing shortages, economic recession, labor unrest, and a growing fear of socialist and Communist subversion stemming from the Bolshevik Revolution in Russia. In addition, a large number of African American men had served in the military and been sent to Europe to fight. When many of these soldiers returned home, they were unwilling to tolerate the systemic racial oppression and segregation practiced by whites in most of the country, especially in the South. Many of these returning black soldiers, joined by other black citizens inspired by the veterans, fought back when attacked by white rioters, resulting in the deaths of a number of whites, which led to even more riots and lynching. During this period, white mobs lynched a large number of African Americans. One source has estimated that lynching averaged one per day during 1919. Hundreds of African Americans who escaped extrajudicial executions and murder were given lengthy sentences in prison by all-white juries, almost always after court hearings that mocked any definition of due process. The bloody events that occurred in 1919 caused James Weldon Johnson, civil rights activist and field secretary of the National Association for the Advancement of Colored People, to label it the "Red Summer."[4]

Texas did not escape the Red Summer. The racial violence that blighted much of 1919 made an earlier appearance in Texas than it did in most of the country. A major race riot occurred in Houston during the night of August 23, 1917. More than one hundred soldiers who were members of an all-black army battalion based at Camp Logan (now Memorial Park) mutinied and marched downtown to confront the local police in reaction to white harassment and numerous humiliating racist incidents, including an assault on a respected black military policeman by white Houston policemen. In the melee that followed, fifteen whites were killed, including five policemen, and nearly a dozen were seriously injured. Four black soldiers were killed. It was the first race riot in US history in which more whites were killed than blacks. The army quickly transferred the battalion to a camp in New Mexico. After military trials were conducted in San Antonio, nineteen black soldiers were hanged and sixty-three were given life sentences.[5]

The Houston race riot occurred the night before the Texas House of Representatives approved the articles of impeachment against Governor Ferguson. Will Hobby was not yet acting governor. The governmental chaos in Austin and Will's conscious attempt to keep a low public profile removed him from any involvement as a state official in the tragic events in Houston. But when the racial violence of Red Summer erupted in Texas in 1919, Will was forced to act.

The first major racial incident in Texas that year took place on January 13, 1919. The county attorney and district judge of Hill County, located about sixty-five miles south of Dallas, sent an urgent message to Will requesting that he dispatch Rangers to Hillsboro, the Hill County seat, to protect an African American man who was scheduled for trial and was being held in the county jail. The message stated that the prisoner was in imminent danger of being lynched and that the local sheriff had declared not only that he would not harm white citizens in any attempt to prevent the lynching, but also that he opposed any attempt by Texas Rangers to protect the man. According to historians Charles Harris and Louis Sadler, "Governor Hobby did not share the sheriff's tender solicitude for the good citizens—and voters—of Hill County and ordered a detachment of six Rangers to Hillsboro on January 14." The Rangers were able to protect the accused man during the trial, which resulted in his conviction by an all-white jury. As soon as the Rangers left Hillsboro, however, a mob pulled the man from his jail cell and lynched him. As usual, no one was indicted or arrested as a result of this murder.[6]

Later in the spring, Will had better luck in helping with a dangerous situation in Tyler, where the local authorities were concerned about an imminent threat of a race riot. He immediately sent Rangers to Tyler. A riot was averted and calm was restored. But Tyler would prove to be an exception. As spring became summer, at least twenty-five major race riots broke out in towns scattered across the country, including in the northeast Texas town of Longview.[7]

In the days before it was transformed by the discovery of the giant East Texas oil field in the 1930s, Longview was a small community dominated by cotton and lumber. In the summer of 1919, the town had a population of approximately 5,700, one-third of which were African Americans. In June, a young black man named Lemuel Walters was jailed for allegedly having an affair with a white woman from the nearby town of Kilgore. On June 17, soon after Walters was jailed, the local county sheriff willingly turned Walters over to a white mob, which took him out of town and shot him dead. A month after Walters's murder, a leader of the black community in Longview was beaten, and racial tensions reached a crisis level, culminating on the night of July 10 in a firefight between members of a white mob and blacks who were attacked by the mob. By dawn's light, several houses and other buildings in the black section of town had been burned by the white mob.[8]

Early the next morning, Gregg County judge E. M. Bramlette and Sheriff D. S. Meredith reached Will Hobby on the telephone and informed him that local law enforcement officials were unable to control the situation. They urged the governor to send Texas National Guard units to Longview to restore order. Will immediately ordered eight Texas Rangers and one hundred guardsmen to Longview. The same day that Will received the phone call from Longview, Sheriff Meredith shot and killed a black man under mysterious circumstances, although Meredith claimed it was in self-defense. That shooting led Longview's mayor to ask Hobby for more aid to bring the situation under control. Will quickly dispatched a contingent of 150 additional National Guardsmen. He also placed Longview and Gregg County under martial law, beginning at noon on Sunday, July 13. Texas Rangers arrested seventeen white men on charges of attempted murder. Twenty-one black men were arrested, charged, and taken by National Guardsmen to Austin temporarily for their own safety. But no one, white or black, was ever tried. Once order had been restored, Will lifted the martial law order at noon Friday, July 18.[9]

A few days after martial law ended in Gregg County, a white mob lynched a black man in Gilmer in Upshur County, fifteen miles north of Longview. Fearful that the lynching would lead to a race riot, a judge in the county telegraphed Will and requested that he

# LYNCH-MURDER IN NORTH TEXAS
# AND MANY HOMES ARE BURNED!

## THE OCEAN CABLE CAUGHT A WHALE

**The Limit in Fish Stories Has Just Been Received from Far-away Chile**

### LEVIATHAN HELD EIGHT MONTHS

Cable Wouldn't Work—Repair Ship Sent Out Fishing—Dragged to Surface Whale with Three Turns of Cable Around Its Body.

## FRESH OHIO NEWS

**Written by The Old Reliable Gazette's Correspondents Throughout the State**

What Our People Are Doing Each Week—Church, Personal, Social, Lodge, Literary and Musical—Marriages, Deaths, Etc.

### EDITOR WM. DUBOIS FAILED

But Editor Wm. Monroe Trotter Continues to Fight For Us in France.

## "YELLOW JOURNALISM"
## SAID TO BE THE CAUSE

A Hot Reception Tendered Lynch-Murderers Who Sought Jones at Midnight.

## FAKE ROBBERY GAME FAILS

Thieving Agent of Wisconsin Corporation Nearly Got Away With Bundle

### HOW HE WAS BAMBOOZLED

Editor Wm. Monroe Trotter

Major W. T. Anderson

### DOINGS OF THE RACE

### AN N.A.A.C.P. PRESIDENT

### A WOMAN GAVE $10,000

A Member of the Race, too—Real Estate

### His License Revoked:

### HOTEL DALE GUESTS

Cape May City, N. J., July 13th, 1919.

### WILSON WELCOMES ABYSSINIAN ENVOYS

Mission Congratulates U. S. on Victory; Brings President Valuable Gifts.

send Rangers to investigate the lynching and to prevent further violence. The next day, Will ordered Captain William Hanson and three other Rangers to Gilmer. According to one account, "The Rangers' mere presence helped to restore order." Unlike most of these incidents of racial violence and lynching, the Ranger investigation resulted in the arrest of five white men who were indicted on the charge of murder. None of these men were convicted.[10]

At the end of July, news reports of major race riots in cities such as Chicago and Washington, DC, arrived in Will's office. The riot in Washington lasted four days, forcing President Wilson to mobilize the National Guard to restore order. In Chicago, the riot began on July 27 and continued for nearly two weeks. Estimates of deaths ranged from 38 to 50, with 537 badly injured. Several thousand Illinois National Guardsmen were sent to Chicago to end the violence. Denying or ignoring that the obvious causes of the riots included white racism, racial segregation, lynching, unemployment, and poverty, rumors soon spread that Communist agitators directed by the Bolsheviks in Russia were responsible for "stirring up our Negroes." Even the venerable *New York Times* spread false claims and published a story with the sensational headline, "Reds Try to Stir Negroes to Revolt."[11]

The day after publication of the *New York Times* story alleging Communist involvement in race riots, Will Hobby made a formal request to US attorney general A. Mitchell Palmer that the Justice Department investigate the possibility of a "Bolshevik influence at work in an organized way to incite race trouble in the South." Palmer had issued a statement to the press that he "feared that 'the Negro is seeing red,'" and that both Russian and American Communists would find fertile ground among black Americans. Will informed Palmer that he had initiated through the Texas adjutant general's office an investigation of Bolshevik agitation in Texas. He asked Palmer to direct the San Antonio branch office of the Bureau of Investigation (as the FBI was then called) to help the Texas Rangers in the investigation. Will told Palmer that Bolshevik elements in Texas were making "the negroes believe that they are not being treated fairly and are being discriminated against by the white people," and that these Bolshevik agitators were trying to work the black population into "a frenzy against the government, both State and Federal." He added, "Negro newspapers in the South and throughout the country . . . together with the propaganda carried out by Negro speakers, I believe, is financed and prompted by some sinister source." Will wanted the authorities to identify that source.[12]

After asking for help from Attorney General Palmer, Will ordered Adjutant General Harley to organize a meeting of sheriffs at the Rice Hotel in Houston to discuss how the Texas National Guard and the Rangers could assist them during this period of racial unrest. The meeting, which was led by Ranger Captain Hanson, took place on August 23. Instead of addressing what steps could be taken to prevent lynching, which had caused most of the riots in Texas, Hanson led a discussion about how local law enforcement authorities could suppress black agitation and demands for equal rights. Hanson told the sheriffs that black newspapers and magazines had "inflamed the negroes, which naturally lead to race troubles." No specific actions resulted from the meeting, but the sheriffs left Houston confident that the governor's office and the Rangers would support any action they took to suppress black rights.[13]

The US attorney general was overwhelmed with requests similar to Will Hobby's, especially from Southern politicians, and was undoubtedly more concerned about possible Communist influence in the big cities of the North than in places like Texas, where there were few, if any, "Red agitators." The best that Palmer could do for Hobby was to send vague instructions to his field office in San Antonio to "cooperate fully" with the investigation in Texas. In addition, Palmer accused the National Association for the Advancement of Colored People (NAACP) of inciting the Longview riot and recommended that Will order the NAACP's state chapter to disband. Later that August, when the national headquarters of the NAACP learned that Palmer was recommending that the state of Texas ban the organization, the association's officials sent their executive secretary, John R. Shillady, a white man, to Texas to evaluate the situation and determine what legal steps the NAACP could take to defend itself.

Soon after Shillady arrived in Austin on August 20, he sought a meeting with Will, but the governor was out of the city. After Shillady visited with officers of Austin's NAACP chapter on August 22, he was walking back to the Driskill Hotel when an automobile pulled up to the sidewalk. Travis County judge Dave Pickle, Constable Charles Hamby, a man named Charles Pierce, and one or two other men got out of the car. Pierce asked Shillady why he was stirring up "our Negroes." When Shillady replied, "You don't see my point of view," Pierce yelled, "I'll fix you so you can't see," and punched Shillady in the eye. Pickle, Hamby, and the other men joined in the assault, beating and kicking Shillady severely until he cried for mercy. They dragged the bloody and badly bruised Shillady into their car and drove him to the Austin rail station, where they put him on a train to St. Louis and warned him not to leave the train while it was still in Texas. When the NAACP sent a message to Will demanding an investigation of the incident and the arrest and punishment of the offenders, Hobby responded that the only "offender" in the incident was Shillady and that the beating was punishment for his offenses. "Your organization can contribute more to the advancement of both races," Will told the NAACP, "by keeping your representatives and their propaganda out of this state than in any other way." When the NAACP received Will's response, it sent a telegram to President Wilson: "The [NAACP] respectfully inquires how long the Federal Government under your administration intends to tolerate anarchy in the United States?" Shillady's attackers admitted their involvement to a reporter for the Associated Press. Judge Pickle emphasized that they had acted as private citizens who had simply decided to give Shillady "a good thrashing on general principles." None of the culprits were arrested or punished.[14]

Soon after the attack on Shillady, Will gave a speech at the Shelby County Fair in the little town of Timpson in deep East Texas. Addressing a receptive white audience, Will declared that he believed in "Texas for Texans only" and that he was in favor of "sending any narrow-brained, double-chinned reformer who comes here with the end of stirring up racial discontent back to the North where he came from with a broken jaw if necessary." He stressed that he had "warned that New York society [the NAACP] that Texas is not a healthy climate for those who come down here from eastern States to poison the minds of the negroes and attempt to interfere in the relations of two races who are living side by side in peace and contentment and perfect understanding." By the time Will gave his speech in Timpson, dozens of African American citizens had already been lynched or burned at the stake in Texas in 1919, while many others had been brutally beaten or had their homes burned to the ground. Historian Lewis Gould noted, "Hobby's response, part of a national mood in this period, indicated how little the limits of white tolerance for black activity had been extended during the war years." It also revealed the unsurprising fact that Will's racial views, which were typical of his generation of Southerners, were learned behavior shaped by his family's Southern heritage and his East Texas upbringing. Will's overall views about his fellow black citizens, especially his servants, were paternalistic and not Klan-like, and he certainly abhorred communal disorder. Nevertheless, the reality is that Will's actions were rooted in racism and the creed of white supremacy. Political leaders from President Wilson on down the governmental ladder shared those views to one degree or another. From a twenty-first-century perspective, however, no matter how widely shared or how relatively moderate Will's racial views might have been, his reactions to the Red Summer of 1919 were not among his finest moments.[15]

# CHAPTER 13

# MARTIAL LAW IN GALVESTON

As the racial violence of the Red Summer subsided in Texas at the beginning of autumn 1919, Will turned his attention to the more mundane business of being governor. More than a year remained in his term, and he was determined to spend that time productively. The next regular session of the Texas Legislature would not convene until January 1921. He anticipated, however, that he would need to call a special session at some point before the Democratic primary in July 1920.

The main pressure on Will was the question of whether or not he would run for reelection. He had little interest in waging another election campaign or serving another term as governor. Although Will's skills as a campaigner had surprised even his closest friends, the introverted side of his personality kept him from enjoying the experience. In addition, because public office was costing him financially, he was eager to reenter the private business sector on a full-time basis. This lack of enthusiasm was an open secret among some of the leaders of the Texas Democratic Party, including former House Speaker Pat Neff, who had decided during the summer of 1919 to run for governor in 1920, with the expectation that he would not have to oppose a popular incumbent. Many of Will's supporters, however, were urging him to make another run. After Will received a letter from Abilene judge Harry Tom King pleading with him to stand for reelection, Will admitted that he did not find the prospect of another campaign appealing, "because of the expense and labor and because my campaign pledges have been redeemed." Nevertheless, Will told the judge that he would wait until late fall or early winter to make a final decision. As Will continued to weigh the pros and cons of serving another two years as governor, his financial situation emerged as the most important factor in his decision. Three weeks after his letter to Judge King, Will confided to his brother-in-law, Henderson Jacoway, that he was concerned about the "personal cost to me of holding the office [of governor]."[1]

Will's financial problems forced him to turn his attention back to his business affairs, which eventually outweighed all other factors in his decision not to run again. He told one of his friends, "I cannot afford financially to hold [the governor's office] any longer." He admitted as much to Bernard Baruch, the famed Wall Street investor and unofficial advisor to Woodrow Wilson whom Will and Willie had met in Washington in the fall of 1918. Will later told Baruch that as his term as governor was ending, he was "naturally thinking of personal affairs and private business more than has been the case for some years." He observed that after his election in 1918, his time had been "absorbed more than the usual extent on public business, because of the precarious period during my term and culmination of political issues." Will told Baruch that he was satisfied that during his term as governor the prohibition and women's suffrage issues, "which for a long time divided the people of Texas" had been "finally disposed of." As a result, Will stated, "I am particularly glad to retire and I am anxious to continue along constructive lines, but in private business, rather than public business."[2]

Will's financial situation was not the only factor influencing his decision. Another was the tradition that Texas governors served no more than two terms, a custom that had been observed by every governor elected under the Constitution of 1876. Because Will had served fifteen months of James Ferguson's second term as governor and then had won his own two-year term, he was generally perceived to be serving his second term. That perception was one Will shared.[3]

Will privately informed some of his closest friends and political allies about his decision, including Frank Andrews, Walter Crawford, Tom Love, and Martin Crane. His fellow progressives in the Democratic Party persuaded Will to delay a public announcement. Progressives who were strong supporters of the Wilson administration were alarmed by the unwelcome resurfacing of Will's old political ally, former senator Joe Bailey, who was making speeches around the state vehemently denouncing Woodrow Wilson, the League of Nations, women's suffrage, prohibition, the direct election of US senators, and the progressive wing of the Democratic Party. Bailey did not identify Will by name in his attacks, but as Will later recalled, as governor he was "the titular head" of the party in Texas, and "there could be little uncertainty that Bailey was delivering a direct ultimatum and challenge to [me]." Progressives worried that Bailey might enter the governor's race. They hoped that if Bailey believed he would have to campaign against Will, who was popular and had the strong advantage of incumbency on his side, it might be enough to sway Bailey from being a candidate. As a result, Will agreed to keep publicly silent about his decision not to run, or at least to wait until Bailey announced his own intentions. But Will made it clear to his confidants that he had no intention of changing his mind about returning to his newspaper in Beaumont.[4]

Despite Will's decision not to be a candidate in 1920, he continued to make campaign-like appearances and speeches stressing his accomplishments as governor and the Wilson administration's success in Washington. These speeches were partially in response to Bailey's widely publicized attacks. On August 28, while he and Willie were guests of honor at an annual "Old Settlers" ranching festival in the West Texas town of Van Horn, Will refused to say if he would run for another term as governor, but he gave a speech

*Will at the "Old Settlers Ranching Festival" in Van Horn, Texas, August 28, 1918.*

criticizing Bailey. Although he stopped short of referring to Bailey by name, he called him out as a "calamity howler" who wanted to "stop the stride of Texas for education, home ownership, material progress, moral progress, and intellectual progress" that Wilson and Texas progressives had initiated. The highlight of the festival in Van Horn featured a parade of cowboys from area ranches riding on horseback through the center of town, wearing silk shirts with specific colors to represent their individual ranches. One group wore red shirts that caught Will's eye. When he stopped a cowboy to compliment him about his clothes, the rider took his shirt off, gave it to Will, and then rode down the street shirtless. For years Will made this episode a staple of the talks he made at the formal dinner events over which he presided, typically as an example of Texans willing to give the shirts off their backs to the needy, even when they weren't asked.[5]

After leaving Van Horn, the Hobbys traveled to Cleburne, where Will made a luncheon speech in which he accused Bailey, again not by name, of wanting to turn the clock back twenty-five years to "retard the progress of the State." Will later pointed out to James Clark that he did not pick the fight with his old personal and political friend Joe Bailey, who as a US senator had done much to help get congressional support for Beaumont's deepwater port. It was Bailey who initiated the attack on Will's accomplishments as governor, no matter how indirect the attacks might have been. Will's reaction to Bailey's unrestrained criticism of his record as governor was an indication of the shift in Will's political views toward progressivism and away from those of his rigidly conservative longtime friends, such as Rienzi Johnston, Oscar Colquitt, and John Henry Kirby. Will had once joined Johnston, Kirby, and his late father-in-law, Bronson Cooper, in fervently supporting Bailey and his ultraconservative positions. During his time in elected office, however, Will had eventually endorsed women's suffrage and prohibition, and he had become an enthusiastic advocate for spending the funds necessary to improve the public schools, even if taxes had to be raised. He had also become a strong supporter of Woodrow Wilson and his version of progressivism, which Wilson called the "New Freedom." Wilson's foreign and domestic policies and progressive reforms at both the federal and the state levels were anathema to Bailey and Kirby.[6]

Wilson's proposal for the creation of a League of Nations was another point of disagreement between Will Hobby and Kirby. When Kirby groused to Will about his support for the league, Will's response illustrated not only his evolving political outlook, especially in foreign policy, but also his continuing respect for his old friend and his desire to maintain their friendship. Assuring Kirby of his and Willie's "warmest Love" for their "dear friend," Will explained, "I am in favor of a League of Nations to restore order, put an end to war, bring about permanent peace, and suppress anarchy and bolshevism." He then concluded with a statement he knew would appeal to Kirby, who believed Wilson was pushing the country toward socialism. "I am in favor of a league of States," Will declared, "to prevent a Washington-run government and . . . centralized authority upon those things which concern the domestic affairs of States and of citizens." The latter statement was not dissembling on Will's part. He disagreed with Kirby's opposition to

*Will Hobby breaks ground at Rice Institute for a pecan tree planting
as a memorial to Americans who died in the Great War. General John J.
Pershing looks on from Will's left, February 5, 1920.*

such progressive reforms as women's suffrage, but he agreed with his old friend that it was the role of state government to make decisions about those matters, not the federal government. Will's Wilson-style progressivism on some issues did not make him a fan of big government, as it did many other Wilsonians who later played key roles in Franklin D. Roosevelt's New Deal. Despite Kirby's differences with Will on several issues, it had no effect on their relationship. Kirby wrote Will a few days after he received Will's letter defending the League of Nations. "Please . . . know that however much I may differ from you on public questions," Kirby stated, "you will always hold a permanent and prominent place in my affections."[7]

As Texas progressives had expected, on February 18, 1920, Joe Bailey formally declared that he was a candidate to be the Democratic Party's nominee for governor. When Bailey made his announcement, he also stated his intention to make the Democratic Party precinct elections in May a referendum on both the Wilson and Hobby administrations. The precinct elections would decide whether the conservative Bailey faction or the progressives would control the Texas delegation to the party's national convention in San Francisco later in the summer. Bailey decided not to run for election as a delegate to the national convention because he needed to remain in Texas to campaign for governor. Instead he named Judge William Poindexter as his personal candidate for election as an at-large delegate. Bailey expected Poindexter to head an anti-Wilson delegation to the convention in opposition to the bid of William Gibbs McAdoo, Wilson's son-in-law, for the presidential nomination.[8]

By the time of Bailey's announcement, two pro-Wilson progressives, former attorney general B. F. Looney and House Speaker R. Ewing Thomason, had joined Pat Neff as candidates for governor. Bailey's announcement and the entrance into the governors' race of candidates acceptable to Texas progressives freed Will from his promise not to declare his own intentions. When Will revealed his decision to the public, he declared that Neff, Thomason, and Looney were all "well qualified in character and ability" and that each would stand behind Wilsonian principles. In his statement, Will made no mention of his financial ambitions or his desire to return to his newspaper. He explained that he did not want to complicate matters "by entering a race which would confuse many . . . who supported me so loyally two years ago and who are now divided in their allegiance between several candidates for governor."[9]

Although Will did not endorse any of the candidates publicly, he preferred his friend and political ally Thomason. Will did make it clear he would not endorse Joe Bailey, who Will declared had "assailed the administration of which I am the head and whose mandate I hold." Because of Bailey's attacks on his record as governor and his intention to send an anti-Wilson Texas delegation to the national convention, Will also declared that he would run as a delegate at large in May's precinct election and campaign to send a pro-Wilson delegation from Texas. He accepted Bailey's challenge to make the precinct elections a referendum on his gubernatorial record. "I am anxious for the people to determine this issue," Will stated, adding that he would not claim he had "been faultless or free of mistakes" in his administration of the state's affairs, but he was proud of his "achievements and measures that have advanced the material and moral progress of Texas."[10]

Progressive Democrats rallied behind Will's leadership in the fight against Bailey's attempt to control the Texas delegation. Frank Andrews was among the anti-Bailey leaders in Houston. "I want you to know from me," Andrews wrote Will, "that I shall take great pleasure in doing anything possible to advance your interests to head the delegation." Will's brother Edwin joined with Martin Crane and Thomas Love in North Texas to organize voters to attend local precincts to vote for pro-Wilson delegates. Edwin also helped plan a mass rally of Texas Democrats in Dallas on March 6 to denounce Bailey and to defend the Wilson administration. Will went to Dallas for the meeting, which was attended by eight hundred enthusiastic pro-Wilson Democrats. Much of the energy fueling the anti-Bailey movement came from former prohibitionist leaders and activists, as well as from the women leaders of the suffrage movement, none of whom had any love for Bailey. One speaker at the meeting received loud cheers and extended applause when he vilified Bailey as a "complacent reactionary who puts property above humanity."[11]

On May 1, the progressives routed Bailey's supporters at the precinct meetings, giving Will Hobby's local candidates all but 49 of the 1,250 precincts. When the county conventions were held, Bailey's supporters carried only a dozen of Texas's 254 counties. Delighted by the results, Will wrote Houston attorney and developer George Howard that the outcome was "very encouraging to me and did my heart good." All three of Bailey's gubernatorial opponents urged Will to head the Texas delegation to the national convention, but Will declined. He was satisfied with Bailey's failure to capture and control the delegation. Tom Love, Will's close ally, was elected Democratic national chairman from Texas.[12]

Victorious in the convention delegation battle, Will gave in to demands from the state's public school leaders that he call a special legislative session to address an acute statewide shortage of teachers. Low salaries had forced large numbers of teachers to leave the profession. Will had been reluctant to bring the legislature back to Austin, but a severe outbreak of pink boll worm infestation in nine counties changed his thinking. The federal Department of Agriculture threatened to stop the movement of cotton from Texas if the state did not impose quarantine areas in the counties the worms had infested. A quarantine of the state's most valuable agricultural commodity would have a ruinous impact on the economy. When the legislature convened in special session on May 20, Will listed the boll weevil problem and the teacher shortage as issues he wanted the legislature to address. By the time the legislature adjourned on June 18, the measures it passed included acts creating zones in which growing cotton was temporarily prohibited. The legislature also allocated $4 million to make it possible for local school districts to raise teacher salaries, and it added $1 million to the original appropriation for state colleges and universities. A $6 million budget surplus made these new appropriations possible. Will signed the emergency appropriation bills as soon as they hit his desk.[13]

A few days after the end of the special session, Will and Willie traveled with the Texas delegation to the Democratic Party's national convention in San Francisco, which convened on June 28. The delegation was uncommitted to any presidential candidate, but Will, who was attending as an observer and not a delegate, and most of the delegation wanted to draft former treasury secretary William Gibbs McAdoo, Wilson's son-in-law. At one point, some of the Texans tried to promote Will's nomination for vice president, but Will quickly and firmly stopped the effort. After a fierce convention floor battle, Ohio governor James Cox finally won the presidential nomination on the forty-fourth ballot. Before adjourning, the convention selected New York's Franklin D. Roosevelt as the vice presidential nominee. Cox's nomination was unpopular with many in the Texas delegation because of his well-known opposition to prohibition, but that presented no problem for Will, who was not a prohibitionist. Will was pleased with Cox's nomination, especially because Cox was a fellow newspaper publisher. In later years, Cox would create the Cox Enterprises news media conglomerate.[14]

Will returned to Texas after the national convention ended on July 6. With the primary election a little more than two weeks away, the gubernatorial race was reaching its climax. Will stayed out of the campaign and refused to publicly endorse any of Bailey's three opponents. He remained in Austin, where he monitored a difficult labor union strike in Galveston. The primary-election day was July 25. As expected, Bailey finished slightly ahead of Pat Neff, but he failed to win a majority, forcing him to face Neff in a runoff. This turn of events undoubtedly irritated Bailey considerably, as he had been a vociferous critic of the recently passed law that required runoffs in primary elections when no candidate had won a majority of the votes. Thomason, who finished third, and Looney, who finished fourth, quickly announced their support of Neff. Will continued to play no role in the campaign, but he did tell the press a few days before the election that he was going home to Beaumont to vote for Pat Neff.[15]

With fellow progressives Looney and Thomason out of the race, Neff benefitted from a united effort by the progressive faction. On Election Day, August 28, Neff defeated Bailey by more than seventy-nine thousand votes. As Lewis Gould has noted, Bailey's defeat represented "a last stand of Texas conservatism of the old style . . . and it marked the end of Bailey's statewide influence." The Bailey wing of the party withered. Many of his staunchest supporters faded away with him, including the aging Colonel Rienzi Johnston, who no longer had a newspaper platform, and John Henry Kirby, who switched his party loyalty to the Republicans. Bailey moved to Dallas, where he opened a law office. He died suddenly in 1929 while giving a speech in Denison.[16]

During the gubernatorial campaign in the spring and summer of 1920, Will was forced to deal with major controversies that ultimately required him to activate units of the Texas National Guard for police duty at both the Texas-Oklahoma border on the Red River and on Galveston Island.

The problem in North Texas stemmed from the discovery of oil along the southern bank of the Red River in 1918, which initiated an oil boom in the area around Wichita Falls. The shallow Red River meanders and alters its course between the two states, resulting in a shifting borderline. Oil companies drilled wells on the Texas side as close to the river as possible and, in some cases, in the water. Private property owners and spokespersons for the Indian tribes on the Oklahoma side of the border claimed that oil was being drained illegally from their property. These competing ownership claims on wells in the disputed land along the river soon escalated into a major clash not only between Oklahoma and Texas, but also with the federal government, which was also claiming royalty rights. The contested land was 160 acres on the south side of the river, the site of several oil wells generating $1,000 per day in royalty revenue for the State of Texas. Oklahoma claimed that most of the oil-producing land was within its state boundary. The Texas Legislature disagreed and passed a resolution directing the governor and the attorney general to ask the US Supreme Court to settle the matter.[17]

In early March 1920, heavily armed landowners on both sides of the Red River were threatening to resort to violence to protect their property rights. Oklahoma governor James Robertson dispatched state police to patrol the north bank of the river. Responding to demands from Texas's independent oil operators and from legislators representing North Texas, Will Hobby sent Texas Rangers and a unit of the Texas National Guard to the disputed area on the south bank of the Red River. Will ordered the troops not to "surrender the land" to anyone until the US Supreme Court ruled on the dispute. Will declared that the "territorial integrity of Texas will be maintained and this state will not surrender territory over which it has exercised sovereignty and of which it has been in actual and unquestioned possession for eighty-four years." Tensions were soon lowered when a meeting in Fort Worth between Will and Texas attorney general Calvin Cureton and representatives of Oklahoma and the federal government produced an agreement to pull the Oklahoma state police and Texas's guardsmen away from the border. Despite a series of Supreme Court rulings, the border dispute proved to be a long one. In 1991, the state legislatures of Oklahoma and Texas finally created the Red River Boundary Commission and charged it with establishing a fixed and permanent boundary. Congress approved the boundary in 2000 by passing the Red River Boundary Compact Act.[18]

Will later recalled the Red River dispute with wry amusement. He noted that when he sent the National Guard to the Red River, a federal judge ordered him to appear in court to explain his decision. Will asked Attorney General Cureton if the federal courts had jurisdiction in the matter. Cureton advised him that "more than likely" they did. When Will asked Cureton what the judge could do if he refused to appear in court, the attorney general replied that he could be cited for contempt and even jailed. Cureton also pointed out that legal maneuvering could delay Will's appearance in court for as long as two years. "Then I won't go," Will recalled saying. "This summons orders the Governor of Texas into court—not Will Hobby. In two years I will be out of office. The next governor can have the honor." Will remembered thinking that the prospect of going to jail might deter some of the gubernatorial candidates from running, but "the field was getting a little crowded, anyway." The judge's order was rescinded after Will attended the peace meeting in Fort Worth.[19]

Later in the spring and summer of 1920, Will was confronted with a much more serious situation in Galveston. On March 12, 1,600 members of the International Longshoremen's Association (ILA) went on strike against the Mallory and Morgan steamship companies, the two lines that dominated shipping at the city's port. The strike in Galveston developed into a dramatic, six-month-long confrontation between the ILA, the two steamship companies, and "open shop" forces eager to suppress unionism.[20]

Dockworkers in Galveston had long worked under "closed shop" contracts with the Mallory and Morgan steamship lines that required the two dominant shipping companies to hire only union members. Those workers had to remain in the union in order to keep their jobs. These closed-shop agreements, which were common in the shipping business, gave unions significant power when negotiating with business management.

After the end of World War I, organized labor launched a series of strikes to demand higher wages and better working conditions for its members. These strikes in turn spurred anti-union business and civic leaders to initiate an anti-open-shop political movement. Their efforts quickly gained momentum throughout the country, including Texas. In 1919 Beaumont's business community organized the Southwestern Open Shop Association, the state's first. Within two months of its founding, the association had succeeded in ending all closed-shop agreements in Beaumont. The movement soon spread from Beaumont throughout the state in 1919 and 1920. Will Hobby, who had no love for labor unions, supported the Southwestern Open Shop Association's work in Beaumont, and his newspaper printed editorials lauding its activities.[21]

The steamship companies attempted to end the strike and destroy the ILA in Galveston in two ways: hiring white strikebreakers, or "scabs," to do work previously performed by black ILA locals and employing black scabs to replace workers in all-white locals. Because black and white ILA locals had a long record of sharing dock work cooperatively in Gulf Coast ports, the companies' exploitation of the race issue created an atmosphere in which racial violence appeared inevitable. In addition, the scabs were harassed and threatened by some of the strikers, although most of the incidents were relatively minor. The Galveston police force, whose members were unionized, and a majority of the members of the Galveston city commission, who had been elected the year before with support from the unions, sided with the strikers. As a result, local law enforcement officers often left strikebreakers unprotected from union harassment.

Will Hobby became involved in the strike because of the fear of racial violence and the absence of police protection for strikebreakers. In an effort to prevent violence, Galveston mayor H. O. Sappington and the sheriff of Galveston County, Henry Thomas, sent an official request to Will on May 13 for a detachment of Texas Rangers to protect the strikebreaking nonunion workers and to help prevent a race riot. Will immediately sent four Rangers to Galveston to patrol the Mallory and Morgan docks.

On May 14, the Mallory steamship company announced that it would relocate its terminals to Port Arthur and cease operations in Galveston indefinitely, while the Morgan Company hinted that it also was considering such a move. The shipping company announcements were followed by an invitation from a group of civic clubs and business associations in Houston for Mallory and Morgan to move their operations to that city. The Houston offer included a pledge that the companies would have no union problems at its port. These developments caused alarm among Galveston's business leaders, who began to pressure Will Hobby to take even stronger action to help end the strike. Members of Galveston's city commission, however, assured Will that outside assistance to maintain order was not needed, because the local police force had the situation under control.[22]

Meanwhile, the Texas Chamber of Commerce, which had taken a leadership role in the state's open-shop movement, realized that the Galveston strike could be used to end the closed shop in that city. A success in Galveston, which was one of the bastions of union activity in Texas, would provide the movement with a major victory that could help spread the cause throughout the state. On May 29 the board of directors of the Texas Chamber of Commerce declared war on the closed shop by passing a resolution opposing strikes, boycotts, picketing, the minimum wage, and "class rule by either labor or capital." Four days later, the chamber sent a delegation to Austin that included three businessmen from Galveston to present a petition to Will Hobby, asking him "to provide adequate protection to citizens of Texas in the port of Galveston while in pursuit of their work, even to the extent of declaring martial law."[23]

The chamber's committee was surely aware of Will's hostility toward the union movement before it met with him in the governor's office. Will's negative view of labor unions had been shaped and influenced by his mentors, Samuel Bronson Cooper, Rienzi Johnston, and most especially John Henry Kirby. The list of Will's largest financial donors when he ran his successful race for governor in 1918 was a who's who of anti-union Texas business leaders, including not only Kirby and Johnston but also bankers Nathan Adams and George W. Brackenridge; oilmen Lee Blaffer, Ross Sterling, and J. S. Cullinan; rancher Caesar Kleberg; attorneys and corporate lobbyists Frank Andrews, James Elkins, and Jacob Wolters; and Galveston cotton and sugar entrepreneur I. H. Kempner. Each of these donors either actively promoted the open shop in Texas or otherwise opposed the labor movement in words or action.[24]

The meeting with the governor went well for the delegation from the chamber of commerce. The next day, Will telegraphed an ultimatum to Mayor Sappington that threatened to impose martial law on the city unless police protection was not immediately given to strikebreakers. Will set a deadline of June 5 and then ordered twenty-nine units of the Texas National Guard to assemble in Houston to prepare for a move into Galveston. He also sent the newly appointed adjutant general A. D. Cope to Galveston to assess the situation and to determine if martial law was required. Will most likely expected Cope's report to provide him with the justification for the decision to intervene in the strike. With the legislature still in special session, Will requested an emergency appropriation of $100,000 to pay the cost of sending National Guard troops into Galveston if necessary. The legislature approved his request, but a few members gave speeches on the floor of the House chamber denouncing Will for planning to impose martial law. The state representative from Galveston, Lee Brady, expressed his strong resentment that state troops were being subsidized with public money to "jog down the throats [of Galveston's] citizens the Open Shop Association."[25]

On June 4, 1,500 union members passed a resolution at a mass meeting in Galveston denouncing Will Hobby's threat to impose martial law. The pro-union Galveston city commission also voted to protest Will's threat, claiming that the strikers were acting in a lawful and peaceful manner. Ignoring the protests, Will Hobby declared martial law in Galveston on June 7 and sent in one thousand National Guard troops under the command of his good friend, oil company lobbyist, and campaign donor General Jake Wolters. Decades later, Will Hobby's biographer, James Clark, claimed that by the time Will gave the order, the strike had deteriorated into "a bitter gang-type war on the freight-clogged docks." The evidence fails to support Clark's statement. There were few known incidents of violence on the docks and strikebreakers were efficiently moving freight in and out of the port, a fact confirmed by Will Hobby's personal representative in Galveston, Adjutant General Cope. The May 1920 port shipping records reveal that two months into the strike, freight shipments actually increased over shipments documented in May 1919.[26]

But Clark's claim that many observers were worried that the strike might cause race riots was accurate. The Galveston docks were one of the few workplaces in Texas where black and white laborers maintained a fragile coexistence, cooperating as union members and performing the same type of work in close proximity—although still racially segregated. Agents of the steamship lines and open-shop activists were among those who spread rumors that because hundreds of black workers were taking part in the strike, race riots were imminent, and that white vigilante groups were forming to take matters into their own hands. As the strike took place less than a year after the end of the Red Summer of 1919, spreading such rumors was an effective tactic in the effort to justify intervention by the Texas Rangers and the National Guard.[27]

Will later claimed that a day or two before he declared martial law, Adjutant General Cope warned that the situation in Galveston was "hopeless without state interference," which led immediately to his imposition of martial law. Only two days before Will declared martial law in Galveston, however, the union-friendly *Houston Press*, which supported the strikers, described Cope as being hopeful about conditions in the city. According to the *Press*, Cope said that "freight was moving on the Mallory docks" and that "the mayor and the chief of police have assured me that the fullest police protection will be given workers on the docks and going to and from their homes." These contradictory statements have never been squared.[28]

The city commissioners, the Galveston Dock and Marine Council, and the state's labor press all charged that the true motive behind Will's decision to order troops to Galveston was to destroy union effectiveness and to guarantee an open-shop labor market. The headline in the June 7 edition of the *Houston Press* declared, "Open Shop War Is On." Historian Joseph Abel argues, "Simply put, Hobby's aim in declaring martial law was the establishment of an open shop in Galveston." With the National Guard deployed on Galveston's docks and beachfront, a group of businessmen proceeded to charter the Galveston Open Shop Association on June 10 and announced that the closed-shop system would no longer be tolerated in the city. That same day, Will Hobby, noting the establishment of the Open Shop Association, wrote Adjutant General Cope that he had informed the Galveston Wharf Company and the Mallory and Morgan steamship companies that the labor situation in Galveston was now under control. He said the state was protecting the rights of every citizen "desiring to work" and the "property rights" of Texans. Will ordered Jake Wolters to restore commerce on the Galveston wharfs to full capacity.[29]

On July 4, Wolters told the *Houston Post* that it was "necessary to keep [the National

Guard in Galveston] because the city officials are backing up the strikers." He claimed that the city government had been elected with the support of Galveston's black voters, who, Wolters declared, were "the worst and most insolent in Texas." According to Joseph Abel, pro-union citizens of Galveston soon realized that martial law had been imposed to accomplish three goals: to make Galveston an open-shop city, to displace the labor-backed city and county government officials who had defeated the business establishment candidates in the 1919 election, and to keep black workers "in their place."[30]

On July 15, Will took steps to help achieve one of those three alleged goals when he suspended the mayor, city commissioners, and police force for failing to maintain the peace and protect citizens. Jake Wolters explained to the press that the governor had taken such an extreme action because Galveston's elected city officials were not "faithfully" executing "the laws of this state." The police were disarmed, and Jake Wolters and his officers took control of the courts and jails. The mayor, city attorney, and commissioners continued to perform routine duties, but their authority over law enforcement was terminated. The city commissioners filed a suit against Governor Hobby, General Wolters, and the Texas National Guard to have their law enforcement authority restored, but Judge Robert C. Street of the Fifty-Sixth District Court dismissed the case, ruling that the governor had the constitutional right to declare martial law. Soon after that ruling, one of Galveston's private citizens whom National Guardsmen had arrested for a traffic violation sued Will Hobby in the federal Southern District court, challenging the constitutionality of the governor's martial law order. The federal court also upheld Hobby's action, ruling that "the governor has the constitutional right to proclaim martial law when it is required for the enforcement of the law. He is the exclusive judge of the existence of such conditions as make this necessary."[31]

As the military occupation continued into late summer 1920, some members of the poorly trained National Guard were involved in incidents in which they abused local citizens, two of them resulting in accidental deaths. In addition, many of the increasingly bored young men who constituted the majority of the troops began to enjoy their access to the bootleg liquor, gambling, and prostitution prevalent on the island, despite General Wolters's attempts to close down speakeasies, casinos, and brothels. As historian Joseph Abel has noted, the troopers "were partaking in vice rather than ridding the city of it." This behavior, along with other numerous incidents of arrogant and insensitive actions taken against law-abiding citizens, created ill feelings about martial law among a wide range of Galveston's residents, including those in the business community who had at first supported it. Unhappy Galveston citizens who had no direct connection to the strike began to bombard Governor Hobby, Speaker Thomason, and members of the legislature with complaints about the situation.[32]

The most embarrassing and troubling problem for Will, however, was Jake Wolters's attempt to silence the progressive and prolabor Scripps-Howard newspaper the *Houston Press*. Its editor, G. V. Sanders, was a relentless critic of Wolters, Hobby, and martial law. In one front-page story, Sanders compared Wolters with General Erich Ludendorff, who had commanded the German Army in the Great War. Sanders denounced Hobby's martial law order in an editorial. "Governor Hobby has been led into a number of bonehead plays during his administration," Sanders complained, "but his declaration of martial law is by far the worst of all." Wolters did not take Sanders's criticisms well. His troops confiscated copies of the *Houston Press* circulating in Galveston, arrested merchants who sold the newspaper in their stores, and on one occasion assaulted one of the newspaper's reporters.

The attack on the *Houston Press* came to its climax on the night of August 30, when three of Wolters's National Guard officers attempted to kidnap editor Sanders as he was leaving the Houston Country Club. Bystanders, including some prominent Houston business and civic leaders, were able to prevent the abduction, and city police arrested the officers, who were dressed in civilian clothes. An investigation revealed that Wolters's chief aide, Colonel Billie Mayfield, had issued an order to the guardsmen "to arrest Sanders . . . for writing and circulating highly incendiary literature calculated to precipitate serious trouble in the zone of military law." This incident caused outrage across the political spectrum. Houston's mayor A. E. Amerman sent a telegram to Will complaining about the "very foolish stunt." In a newspaper interview, Houston city attorney Kenneth Krahl criticized Will severely and demanded that the governor take immediate action "to clean out the whole bunch" in the National Guard "guilty of [this] outrage." Even Will's former employer, the *Houston Post*, denounced Wolters and his officers, describing their actions as "an unwarranted abuse of military authority. . . . [T]here is or ought to be no military despotism in this State."[33]

Mayfield took responsibility for the incident, and Wolters relieved him of his duties. The three officers who attempted to kidnap Sanders were acquitted in their court martial trial on the grounds that they were following orders. When Colonel Mayfield was also acquitted, Will restored him to his commission in the Guard. James Clark later described the attempted kidnapping as a "most embarrassing incident . . . for Hobby," who blamed it on the "overzealous efforts" of Mayfield and his three officers. Clark admitted that Will was stung by the almost unanimous condemnation he received from his newspaper friends, who "roundly denounced this abortive expedition."[34]

The kidnapping scandal and the unfavorable press it generated, the growing impatience among Galveston's citizenry over being policed by the ill-prepared National Guard, the loss of business in the recreational tourism segment of the local economy, and the mounting cost of the military occupation to the state treasury all combined to put Will Hobby under tremendous pressure to end martial law. He searched for a way out of the mess. The Nineteenth Amendment to the US Constitution unexpectedly and indirectly provided him that way out.

The women's suffrage amendment had become law after the February deadline had passed in Texas for voters to pay their poll tax, which meant that Texas women had not had an opportunity to pay the tax and therefore were ineligible to vote. In response to this legal quandary, Texas attorney general Calvin Cureton ruled that the amendment had voided the state's poll tax statute, making it possible for any otherwise qualified person to vote whether they had paid the tax or not. Cureton's ruling alarmed a number of local election officials and politicians who depended on the poll tax to help suppress the vote of African American citizens, which was the reason the poll tax had been passed in the first place. As a result, local election officials pressured Will to call a special session of the legislature to clarify voter eligibility issues.

This unexpected problem gave Will an idea. He realized that a special session would make it possible for him to have an open-port law passed that would weaken the dock-workers' union and help end his Galveston problem. But such a bill was certain not only to attract opposition from pro-union legislators but also to draw intense protest from the labor unions and the newspapers that supported them, such as the *Houston Press*. To shorten the period of time opponents of the bill would have to organize against it, Will decided not to list the issue on his initial agenda for the legislature. He preferred to spring the open-port bill on the legislators as they gathered in Austin.

On September 14, a week before Will announced his decision to end martial law in Galveston, he issued an official call for the legislature to meet in a fourth special session on September 24 to correct the women voter eligibility problem. Will's recommendation was for the legislature to pass a law to extend the poll tax payment deadline to fifteen days prior to the election, giving women time to pay the tax and making it possible for them to vote but also keeping the tax in place to help reduce the African American vote. A number of newspapers questioned the necessity for the special session, but the *Houston Chronicle* supported Will's action, stressing that it was necessary to "protect" the voting process, which was an unstated warning that the black vote would be increased if the law remained uncorrected.[35]

The same day Will issued his call for a special session, he quietly asked Attorney General Cureton's office to draft text for a bill that would grant the governor "superior jurisdiction for police purposes over everything that is an integral part of a Port . . . without martial law and without taking on the burden" of having to deal with the local government "where a port happens to be." The act would define what "constitutes a crime in connection with the interference of workers engaged at a Port, and enables the State to remove their trial from local influences."[36]

While the attorney general's staff drafted the port bill, Will received word from Galveston that a group of the city's leading citizens were taking actions that would help him out of his martial law predicament. On September 16 an informal committee of the city's religious, labor, business, and civic leaders proposed a solution it hoped would persuade Will to end martial law. He had traveled to Galveston on July 21 to meet with a small group of local judges and lawyers to determine how soon martial law could be ended. That meeting led to the formation of the committee that now offered him a solution. They proposed that the troops could be removed if Will would appoint a Texas Ranger to command the city's police department. They also proposed that the Ranger commander be accompanied by a supporting contingent of Rangers. The committee pledged to serve in an advisory capacity to help mediate any problems between business and labor that might arise in the near future. With the Open Shop Association's success at ending the closed-shop arrangements on the docks and the steamship companies no longer threatening to move to another port, Will eagerly accepted the committee's proposal.[37]

On September 21, Will announced that martial law would be lifted on October 1. He also ordered Texas Ranger captain Joe Brooks to take to Galveston "a sufficient number of officers and men as will be necessary to enforce the laws of the State . . . and to keep open those arteries of trade which are essential to . . . business in Texas." He added that Brooks was to "assume control and authority over the police department and all peace officers [in Galveston] both regular and special, promptly at twelve o'clock, midnight, September 30." This action would allow Jake Wolters and his National Guard units to withdraw from Galveston on October 1.[38]

On September 22, the day after announcing the end of martial law and only two days before the special session convened, Will surprised the legislature by adding an "Open-Port Law" to the agenda. Several legislators immediately protested the addition because a special session would not allow much time to scrutinize the bill and it gave opponents little time to organize. Legislative critics of the port bill included Will's friend, Speaker Thomason, who called its provisions "dangerous." Will later added two other items to the agenda: a bill to prevent large packing and oil mill corporations from taking control of the state's locally owned cotton gins and a bill to amend the antitrust law to allow farmers to organize cooperatives for marketing their cotton. Aware that many members of the legislature had a keen interest in addressing agricultural issues, Will raised the specter of the union problems in Galveston having the potential to hinder the shipping of crops to market during a time when the nation was experiencing an economic recession. He warned that it was "more important than ever to keep this port [Galveston] open now to move the various crops of Texas and to prevent the farmers from sustaining heavy losses."[39]

The legislature passed the Hobby Open-Port Law in late September 1920, despite the opposition of Speaker Thomason and the small number of pro-union legislators. Jake Wolters withdrew his National Guard units from Galveston on October 1. The following day, October 2, the special session adjourned after enacting only two of the four major bills Hobby had requested: the Hobby Open-Port Act and the suffrage election bill, which extended the deadline for payment of the poll tax until October 22, making it possible for women who paid the tax to vote in November's general election.[40]

The Hobby Open-Port Act made it virtually illegal for dockworkers and others to engage in strikes deemed by the governor to be harmful to commerce. Will's actions resulted in a clear victory for open-shop advocates. Texas Rangers remained in Galveston until January 1921 to supervise the police department. The striking dockworkers slowly returned to work between December 1920 and July 1921. They received a pay increase, but it was far less than what they had demanded when they went on strike in March 1920. The dockworkers also had to accept an open-shop contract that permitted the hiring of nonunion workers. Martial law and the Hobby Open-Port Act utterly demoralized the members of Galveston's labor unions, including the police union. By 1924 company unions had replaced Galveston's ILA locals and the labor union movement in Texas was in disarray. It would not recover until the 1930s, when Congress passed the Wagner Act guaranteeing workers the right to organize and bargain collectively and prohibiting management from engaging in unfair labor practices.

In his history of the *Houston Post*, which was published in the early 1950s, Ed Kilman called the Hobby Open-Port Act the "most sensational and controversial legislation" of Will Hobby's administration. The law was in effect for less than two years. In November 1922, the Texas Court of Criminal Appeals ruled that the act violated the Fourteenth Amendment of the US Constitution barring the states from restricting the basic rights of citizens.[41]

# CHAPTER 14

---

# MEXICO

By early October 1920, all that remained of Will Hobby's formal legislative duties as governor was to transfer his gubernatorial authority to Pat Neff in January 1921. With the legislature no longer in session and Pat Neff the governor-elect, Will was a lame-duck governor. But he was not entirely finished with electoral politics and his role as head of the Texas Democratic Party, especially with a presidential campaign in progress. Throughout September and October 1920, Will traveled the state making speeches in support of the Cox-Roosevelt ticket. On September 8, Will addressed the Texas Democratic State Convention meeting in the auditorium of the First Baptist Church in Fort Worth. The *Fort Worth Record* called his speech the "outstanding event of Wednesday morning's session." When the governor mounted the platform, the audience rose and cheered enthusiastically for several minutes. Hobby "delighted the delegation with his witty references to the primary campaigns recently concluded. . . . His points were all the more appreciated because his facial expression never altered, no matter whether his remarks were serious or jocose." In an indirect reference to Joe Bailey's defeat, Will declared, "Democracy has triumphed in Texas and with that triumph equal . . . justice . . . has been given to all our citizens by the ratification . . . of [women's] suffrage." He predicted a "Democratic tidal wave that will sweep our nominees James M. Cox and Franklin D. Roosevelt into office."[1]

Three weeks later, Will issued a proclamation on his official gubernatorial letterhead calling on the Democrats of Texas to make "liberal" contributions to the Democratic National Committee's campaign fund. He argued that for the Cox and Roosevelt ticket "to be properly presented to the people of the United States . . . funds are necessary. The call is urgent." The conservative *Chicago Tribune*, which was supporting the Republican presidential candidate, Ohio senator Warren G. Harding, charged in an editorial that Will's proclamation "has all the appearances of a state document. It is presumed that such expense for its publicity was paid from the state treasury, and, if so, it was a violation

---

of the spirit, if not the letter of the law." Will ignored the editorial. Senator Harding won an overwhelming victory on November 2, despite Will's prediction, and any questions about Will's alleged misuse of state funds were quickly forgotten.[2]

Will refused to let his lame-duck status keep him from performing the ceremonial, promotional, and civic leadership duties of his office during the last three months that remained in his term, including a visit with President-Elect Warren Harding. Certainly the most noteworthy and colorful of these activities was a series of unlikely meetings and public events with Álvaro Obregón, the president-elect of the Republic of Mexico, in October, November, and December 1920.

That Will Hobby would end his days as governor of Texas as a friend of a revolutionary leader of Mexico did not seem possible as late as April 1920. The long-standing and bloody troubles between Texas and Mexico stretched back to 1836, but the revolution that broke out in Mexico in 1910 that overthrew the dictator Porfirio Díaz began an especially tumultuous period of bad relations that lasted for more than a decade. Like every governor of Texas in the decade of 1910 to 1920, Will Hobby was forced to confront episodes of violence and displacement at the border, many of them involving the Texas Rangers. As a result, Will had developed a hostile and militant view of the nation on Texas's border. In August 1919, Will sent a message to US secretary of state Robert Lansing urging an American military intervention "to pacify Mexico . . . to relieve a bad condition on this continent." At a dinner given in Will and Willie's honor in El Paso on August 30, 1919, Will explained that when he had called for intervention, he meant armed intervention. At a press conference held a few weeks later, Will repeated his demand for the US Army to invade Mexico to restore order. His bellicose remarks made headlines in newspapers across Texas. Will's extreme statements provoked the members of San Antonio's Pan-American Round Table into sending a resolution of protest to President Wilson, stating its members "regretted exceedingly" Hobby's attitude toward Mexico and adding that the majority of Texas women "have no wish for unnecessary warfare."[3]

This criticism had no effect on Will, who knew that most of the Anglo Texan population viewed Mexico unfavorably. He continued his rhetorical attacks on September 27, 1919, at an event in East Texas. He declared that the "lives and property of American citizens should be protected and made safe in Mexico." He proposed that the United States had an obligation to Western civilization to send an "ample army" into Mexico, "not for conquest but to police and pacify a land that is tributary, and make it livable and make it safe for all human beings within its borders." That fall he repeated his call for an invasion of Mexico in speeches at other events around the state, although criticism of his warmongering caused him to put more stress on the humanitarian need for intervention. "It is a question," Will said, "of saving women and children who are starving." Editorial reactions in Texas newspapers were mostly positive.[4]

Will maintained his hostile stance toward Mexico well into 1920. In April, the Venustiano Carranza government requested permission for two army generals and their staffs to travel as civilians from Nogales to Mexico City via El Paso. The State

Department informed Will of this request and stressed that it had no objection, as armed troops would not be involved in what would amount to a brief trip through El Paso to the Mexican railhead in Juárez. The department asked Will to approve the request. Will, however, announced that he was "unalterably opposed" to the movement of any Mexican military officials "across Texas soil" because it would "endanger the lives and property of American citizens along the border, to a large extent at the mercy of the bandit forces" that opposed the Mexican federal government. Hobby's decision was widely approved in Texas.[5]

Perhaps the person who exerted the most influence on Will's negative view of Mexican affairs was San Antonio businessman Francisco A. Chapa, who was on Will's personal staff as a lieutenant colonel in the Texas National Guard and who served as Will's advisor on Mexico. Born in Matamoros, Mexico, and educated as a druggist, Chapa was a naturalized US citizen who established a successful drugstore business in San Antonio. He eventually diversified his business interests, including publishing an influential Spanish-language newspaper, *El Imparcial*. Although Chapa was a Republican in a state totally dominated by Democrats, he was described as "the most powerful Hispanic politician in Texas for more than a decade." Despite his allegiance to the Republican Party, Chapa worked closely with the Democratic Party's conservative faction, with whom he shared opposition to prohibition, suffrage, and Woodrow Wilson. He served on the personal staff of three Democratic governors: Oscar Colquitt, James Ferguson, and Will Hobby. Chapa was widely believed to control the Mexican American vote in San Antonio, and he was credited with swinging that vote to Colquitt and Hobby in their campaigns for governor. Chapa was an ally of the South Texas political bosses and senior Texas Ranger officers, such as Ranger captain Will Hanson. When the legislature held hearings on Ranger abuses in late winter 1920, Chapa criticized the investigation as being unfair to the Rangers.[6]

As an admirer and supporter of the deposed Mexican dictator Porfirio Díaz, Chapa was a foe of all leftist factions in the Mexican Revolution. According to historians Harris and Sadler, Colonel Chapa "was always waist deep in Mexican revolutionary plotting." In 1912, while serving as an aide to Governor Colquitt, he was convicted of violating US neutrality laws because of his active involvement in a conspiracy with Porfirio Díaz's former minister of war, General Bernardo Reyes, to overthrow the government of Mexican president Francisco I. Madero. Senator Joe Bailey eventually persuaded President Taft, who had family ties in South Texas, to grant Chapa a pardon, which allowed him to remain on Governor Colquitt's personal staff.[7]

While Hobby's hostile view of Mexico's revolutionary government was influenced by a number of factors, Chapa's role cannot be overstated. He not only played a significant role in shaping Will's negative attitude toward Mexico, he also helped cause a dramatic and almost sudden shift in Will's views in the opposite direction. That shift came about because of a forty-one-year-old, one-armed, former revolutionary general from Sonora, Álvaro Obregón. A colorful, gregarious, innovative military tactician and savvy politician, General Obregón won national fame in 1914 for a skillfully directed and brutal military campaign to defeat the forces of President Victoriano Huerta and bring Venustiano Carranza to power. Obregón later won victories in 1915 over Emiliano Zapata's forces in the Battle of Puebla and Francisco "Pancho" Villa at the Battle of Celaya. In the latter conflict, a bomb blew off Obregón's right arm, earning him the nickname "El Manco de Celaya" (the One-Armed Man of Celaya). Obregón eventually fell out with Carranza and retired to his chickpea farm in Sonora in 1916. In 1920 he joined the revolt against Carranza, which eventually led to Carranza's assassination as he fled Mexico City. In September 1920, General Obregón won the presidency by an overwhelming majority of the popular vote. His inauguration was scheduled for December 1, 1920.[8]

One of President-Elect Obregón's most important goals was to restore diplomatic relations with the United States, which President Woodrow Wilson had terminated in 1917. Mexico faced an extremely difficult economic situation. It was obvious that one of the keys to alleviating the financial crisis would be the renewal of trade and investment relations with the United

*General Álvaro Obregón, president of Mexico.*

States, which depended on formal diplomatic recognition. Obregón knew he had to repair Mexico's badly mangled relationship with the US states on his northern border, chiefly Texas. Making friends with Will Hobby would be a good start. Soon after his election, Obregón sent messages to Will, Arizona's governor Thomas Campbell, and New Mexico's governor Octaviano Larrazolo, requesting a meeting in El Paso with Obregón, his wife, and the governors of Chihuahua and Sonora to discuss how to improve relations between their states and the Mexican government. Obregón suggested that the visit should occur on October 7 and 8, while El Paso was staging an international exposition.

Francisco Chapa was a supporter of Obregón and helped persuade Will to go to El Paso to meet the Mexican president-elect.[9]

After a long train ride from Houston, where they had attended the national convention of the Confederate Veterans Association, Will and Willie arrived at El Paso's red brick Union Depot on Thursday morning, October 7. The train from Ciudad Juárez carrying Obregón's large party, which included Provisional President Adolfo de la Huerta, had arrived a day earlier, greeted by a crowd of ten thousand people. Because of bandit raids and military battles in Juárez and other border towns during the Mexican Revolution, Obregón's train was the first passenger train to cross the border in eight years. The Mexican delegation and the US gubernatorial entourages were all lodged at the city's premiere hotel, the Paso del Norte.

Immediately after their arrival in El Paso, the Hobbys learned that the city's chapter of the League of Women Voters was having a meeting at the hotel, so they decided to make an unplanned visit. The *El Paso Times* reported, "Although the governor is known to be a most loyal supporter of equal suffrage, his appearance at the meeting . . . came as a complete surprise to most of the members." When the meeting's chairperson asked Will to address the gathering, he gave brief remarks about how proud he was to have supported the women's suffrage movement. "The Lone Star shines brighter in our flag since we have exact and equal justice for all citizens," Will declared.[10]

Obregón, Huerta, and the governors of Chihuahua and Sonora met with Will and Governors Campbell and Larrazolo at the hotel late that afternoon. The convivial president-elect of Mexico quickly made a positive impression on the Americans. Wearing a bowler hat and a tailored business suit that was designed to bring attention to his missing right arm, Obregón vividly retold the story of how, after his arm had been blown off during battle, he and his aides desperately searched for the detached limb. "I was helping them myself," Obregón said as he laughed. "It's not so easy to abandon such a necessary thing as an arm." He explained that the arm was finally found when an aide pulled a gold coin from his pocket and the arm slithered from where it had landed and the hand grabbed the coin. Will, who enjoyed self-deprecating humor, was so amused by this story that he repeated it to friends for years afterward. This initial meeting was judged a success by all participants. Will especially enjoyed getting to know New Mexico governor Larrazolo, a progressive Republican who had lived for several years in El Paso before moving to Santa Fe, New Mexico. He and Will had something in common beyond being governors. Both had used their state guards to suppress labor strikes.

The US governors hosted a gala banquet in Obregón's honor at the Paso del Norte the evening of October 7, ending a long and exhausting day. When it was his turn to speak at the banquet, Will revealed how meeting with Obregón had changed his attitude toward Mexico. "The old feeling that existed when Texas and Mexico were one has continued," Will declared. "I invite all Mexicans to come to Texas as visitors and friends. We look upon Mexico and the United States as pals in the same great brotherhood of republics." He promised to use his influence with the Wilson administration to encourage recognition of Obregón's government. An El Paso resident who was an associate of New Mexico's senator Albert Fall reported to the senator that Hobby's meeting with Obregón was "a big International Love feast . . . about the largest I ever saw a [M]exican receive in El Paso or *any* where else."[11]

Another meeting was held late the next morning, followed by a luncheon where Obregón gave a speech in which he thanked Will Hobby for his expression of friendship. The president-elect declared his desire to develop "the most cordial relations with America" and stressed his intention to resolve all of the issues that had created hostile relations between their two countries. By this time, Will was completely taken with Obregón. He told the press that he wanted the United States and Mexico to be "pals" and the "Mutt and Jeff of the Western Hemisphere." After lunch, Will urged Obregón to attend the State Fair of Texas in Dallas on October 15 as his special guest. Obregón accepted the invitation. On the final day of their stay in El Paso, the Hobbys and Governors Larrazolo and Campbell crossed the Rio Grande to attend a bullfight in Laredo, Mexico, as Obregón's guests.[12]

Accompanied by an entourage of one hundred Mexican officials and businessmen, President Obregón arrived in Dallas by train on October 15, where he was met and welcomed by the Hobbys. The next day, which was declared "International Day" at the state fair, Will and Willie escorted Obregón and his party on a tour, including of Mexico's official exhibit touting its mines, agriculture, and industries. While reviewing Mexico's exhibit, a band reputed to be "the most popular band in Mexico" serenaded the president-elect and the Hobbys. Because of rumors of a plot to assassinate Obregón, the Dallas Police Department surrounded the touring party with extra security that included several Texas Rangers. To mark the occasion, the next morning's edition of the *Dallas News* featured a twelve-page special section in Spanish describing Obregón's tour of the fairgrounds. Copies of the special section were distributed to Obregón and all members of his party.[13]

After the tour, the Hobbys hosted a banquet in Obregón's honor that included many of Dallas's civic, political, and business leaders. Will delivered the banquet's opening speech and referred to the Wilson administration's reluctance to recognize Obregón's government. "So far as Texas is concerned General Obregón is already recognized," Will declared. "He has been recognized . . . for his record as a soldier, statesman, and for his devotion to his people, and is recognized now as the friend of Texas and of the United States. And since we have seen him in Texas the easier he is to recognize and the better he looks to us." Newspaper reports noted that Will's remarks visibly moved Obregón. After Hobby spoke, Obregón followed with a declaration that Mexico would honor all of its legal foreign debts, but that US recognition of his government would need to precede the payment of debt. He also stressed that although Mexico desired good relations with its neighbor to the north, it would not "become a province of . . . the United States."[14]

The banquet was followed the next morning with a breakfast hosted by a coalition of Dallas civic organizations. Obregón departed Dallas that afternoon for a brief visit to Fort Worth on the way back to El Paso. As a gesture of friendship, Will assigned Adjutant General Cope, Colonel Chapa, and Jake Wolters to accompany Obregón in a private railcar on Southern Pacific's Sunshine Special back to the border. Two days after Obregón left Dallas, Will helped to organize a meeting between Dallas newspaper editors and publishers, Mexican commerce minister Jacinto Treviño, and a group of Mexican newspaper publishers in an effort to improve news communications between the two countries. Will accompanied Treviño on a train to Eagle Pass the following day, where they met with officials of the Southern Pacific and the Mexican Railroad to discuss restoration of through train service to Mexico City from Eagle Pass.[15]

Will promised Obregón he would urge the Wilson administration to recognize his government, and he kept that promise. On October 21, he sent a telegraph to President Wilson urging him to restore diplomatic relations with Mexico. In his message, which he released to the Associated Press for national distribution, Will argued that there was "no longer any reason for withholding recognition." He admitted that only "a year ago the situation in Mexico to me seemed hopeless. Today it is rich in promise and the viewpoint is entirely different. I have no doubt of the good intentions of the administration under . . . Obregon. There is cooperation in maintaining peace on the border." He added that he had "personally" heard Obregón "declare for the payment of all debts and for the adjustment of every claim in accordance with the practice of international law." The Wilson administration, however, remained silent about recognizing Obregón's government.[16]

Will continued his last round of ceremonial activities as governor, which included a trip with Willie to Waco on October 30 to speak at the opening of the Texas Cotton Palace Festival. That morning, Will led the opening parade by driving a truck with its rear bed filled with bales of cotton. A long line of horse-drawn wagons followed Will's truck. One wagon drew special attention and applause from the spectators standing along Waco's main street. Sitting on cotton bales on the wagon were African Americans dressed like slaves, which one newspaper story explained was meant to recall the happy "old plantation days by Southern negroes." At a dinner in Will's honor after the parade, cotton festival officials presented to Will a silver "loving cup" filled with wine. Governor-Elect Pat Neff sat next to Hobby at the dinner. As the silver cup was passed around the head table, each guest took a sip. Even Neff, a Baptist and stout prohibitionist, was reported by the local newspaper to have "quaffed a deep draught" of the wine, after which he turned to Will Hobby and said, "It might be a little strong for you, governor!" While the Hobbys were in Waco, Willie inaugurated the festival's "tea room." A news story noted that Willie made a point to go "from table to table" to meet each woman there.[17]

The Hobbys had planned to go to Beaumont to vote in the presidential election on November 2, but Will felt ill while they were in Waco, so they returned to Austin and were unable to cast their votes for the losing Cox and Roosevelt ticket, which was crushed by the Republican ticket of Warren Harding and Calvin Coolidge. Whatever the reason for Will's feeling unwell, it proved to be nothing serious. By November 6 he was cosponsoring and promoting an American Legion fundraising effort to build a veterans' hospital in Kerrville on land Will's friend and campaign donor Charles Schreiner and his son had given for the purpose. The project was estimated to cost $350,000. By early November the American Legion had raised $150,000 of the needed amount. Will took a strong personal interest in the project and was eager to see it accomplished before he left office. To raise the remainder, he issued a proclamation declaring November 6 as "American Legion Memorial Hospital Tag Day." The proclamation was printed on flyers and distributed statewide. As Will had done ten years earlier when he promoted Beaumont's deepwater port bond vote, he devised a public relations stunt to get the attention of potential donors. He arranged for the army to fly a fleet of warplanes out of Kelly Field in San Antonio to drop the flyers over towns throughout the state. The campaign goal was easily met. The State then leased the facility to the federal Veterans' Bureau, which eventually purchased and incorporated it into the federal system of veterans' hospitals. The American Legion made it clear to the press that the hospital would not have been built without Will Hobby's efforts. One of Will's proudest accomplishments, the hospital continues to serve as a unit of the Veterans Administration.[18]

Immediately after Warren Harding won the presidency, he and his wife, Florence, traveled to Brownsville, Texas, for a vacation of golfing and tarpon fishing as guests in the home of attorney Renfro B. "Gus" Creager, a South Texas oil and land speculator who headed the Texas state Republican committee. The Hardings were accompanied by their wealthy socialite friends Ned McLean and his wife, Evelyn Walsh McLean, the owner of the famed Hope Diamond; Ohio native Frank Scobey, a San Antonio businessman and Republican who was one of Harding's closest friends; and three US senators who were Harding's golfing and drinking buddies. When the president-elect arrived in Brownsville, he wired an invitation to Will to meet with him at Creager's home, which Will accepted. The Hobbys, accompanied by Florence Stratton, Colonel Chapa, and a few other friends, arrived at Brownsville on November 16, where they were greeted by a crowd of several hundred well-wishers, as well as the Fourth US Army Cavalry Band from nearby Fort Brown, which played "Hail to the Chief" as Will and Willie stepped out of their railcar.[19]

Will was driven from the train depot to Brownsville's Manhattan Café to speak at a Rotary Club luncheon in his honor. He entertained the standing-room-only crowd at the Manhattan Café with his now well-rehearsed repertoire of folksy jokes delivered with a straight face. The local newspaper reported that Will kept the audience in laughter as he related some of his "East Texas" anecdotes, including one about a political meeting in Will's home county in East Texas, which he recycled from Samuel Bronson Cooper. Will said that Cooper had been on the stage of a school auditorium chairing an informal political meeting when someone in the audience moved that the temporary organization be made permanent. When the motion was made, Will said, "a slow witted delegate inquired of one of the more prominent" members of the audience what the difference was between temporary and permanent. The prominent citizen, Will continued, "was slightly under the influence of the flowing bowl, but possessed an acid tongue. Viewing the questioner with an unfocused eye he drawled, 'Well, Hank, I'm drunk—that's

*Will Hobby with President-Elect Warren G. Harding, Port Isabel, Texas, 1920.*

temporary. You, well you're a damned fool and that's permanent.'" When asked by one of the Rotarians why he had not visited Brownsville since becoming governor, Will replied with his trademark wry smile that it was because "you never invited me."[20]

After the luncheon, Will and Willie and their entourage were driven to the Creager residence, where Harding and his wife greeted them on the front porch of the house. A large group of still photographers and newsreel camera operators recorded the arrival. After posing for the photographers, Creager, Harding, Frank Scobey, and Ned McLean escorted Will Hobby and his party into the house, where the men took seats in the front room to chat about Texas politics and the recent presidential campaign. New Mexico senator Albert Fall and Mexican diplomat Elias Torres, who had arrived at Creager's house shortly before the Hobbys, were already seated in the front room. Torres had worked in Washington, DC, for Mexican president Carranza. After Obregón's allies assassinated Carranza, Torres quickly switched his allegiance to Obregón. While the men made themselves comfortable, Florence Harding and Evalyn Walsh McLean escorted Willie and Florence Stratton to the parlor. William Thornton, a *Dallas News* reporter who accompanied the Hobbys, later noted that the women "got into a pleasant and animated conversation with Mrs. Hobby, who was never more charming. The women enjoyed it immensely."[21]

As they sat in front of the fireplace, Harding and Scobey recalled having dinner with Will and army officers at Kelly Field in San Antonio a couple of months after Will became governor in 1917. Laughing, Harding remembered the occasion well. An army pilot had taken Will for a flight the afternoon before the dinner, and the army generals who hosted the event had kidded Will that he should become an army pilot after he left the governorship. Will and the president-elect also swapped ribald jokes and stories, of which Harding apparently had a limitless supply. Journalist Thornton reported that Harding, whose face was tanned and reddened by his time in the sun at Point Isabel and on the golf course, was "in an unusually affable frame of mind. Some of his campaign yarns had strong words in them," Thornton wrote, which caused Governor Hobby to laugh "uproariously."[22]

Senator Fall and diplomat Torres soon redirected the conversation to the reason for their visit, which was to persuade the president-elect to recognize the Obregón government. Will Hobby, fresh from his meetings with Obregón, and Colonel Chapa joined in this effort. The Associated Press later sent an unpublished report to Frank Scobey that claimed Senator Fall's efforts were part of an influence-peddling scheme that also involved Colonel Chapa. The details are murky, but the report alleged the Mexican government had secretly agreed to pay Senator Fall and his coconspirators to persuade Harding to recognize the Obregón government. Fall, who was fluent in Spanish, had close connections to officials in high positions in the Mexican federal government. According to the report, Fall's coconspirators also included Colonel Chapa's good friends Texas Ranger William M. Hanson and Frank G. Huntress, editor of the *San Antonio Express*. The roles Hanson and Huntress were supposedly playing in this scheme were not detailed, but the AP report claimed that Colonel Chapa hoped Harding would appoint him US ambassador to Mexico.[23]

The AP report did not allege, nor is there any evidence, that Will Hobby had any involvement in the scheme. In his long life as a businessman and politician, there was never even a hint of Hobby ever being involved in corruption of any type. One of the reasons Will was so disgusted with Jim Ferguson was Will's belief that his impeached predecessor had engaged in shady deals while in office. Harding's close friend Frank Scobey also argued in favor of recognition, but he was outraged by the allegations made against Fall. Suspecting that they were true, he reported them to Harding. The president-elect dismissed the report as preposterous. Fall's attempt to persuade Harding to restore diplomatic relations with Mexico failed, mainly because Obregón refused to guarantee that the Mexican government would prohibit the future expropriation of any US business properties, especially those of oil companies. Until new evidence is uncovered, the accuracy of the AP report will remain unknown. Fall, however, proved to be no stranger to corruption. Harding later appointed Fall his secretary of the interior. While serving in that post, he was convicted of accepting bribes and sent to prison for his role in the Teapot Dome oil lease scandal.[24]

Following their meeting with the Hardings, Will and Willie went to Fort Brown, where they bundled up in warm coats in the cold weather to watch a parade of the Fourth Cavalry in Will's honor. Afterward, the Hobbys and their party made the short trip across the border into Matamoros to meet with the mayor and other officials, including the commander of the local militia. *Dallas News* reporter Thornton wrote that the visit was "like turning back the pages of history. The Mexican soldiers were like those pictures in the annals of the long ago . . . in nondescript uniforms, all blanketed up to their noses and holding their arms at present. A bugler blared a fanfare and the Americans wended their way through a dark hall, mounted the stairs and were soon in the commandant's office, barely furnished and a window pane missing, the cold wind pouring through." At his meeting with Will Hobby, Matamoros's mayor gave a brief speech about letting "bygones be bygones" between Mexico and the United States. He then escorted the Hobbys and their companions to a local café for a reception. Thornton reported that several unnamed members of Will's group decided to take advantage of being in prohibition-free Mexico, so they "made a quiet get away to one of the nearby bars and had a real drink." Thornton did not say if Will Hobby was among those who trekked to the bar.[25]

On November 18, the Hobbys and their party boarded Harding's private train, which departed for Kingsville, where Caesar Kleberg took them on a tour of the King Ranch. After the tour, the Hardings continued on their train to New Orleans, while the Hobbys went on to Austin. In a newspaper interview after the trip to Brownsville, Will noted that Harding had given him "a very hearty welcome, the Senator is plain and courteous, easily met, and very agreeable." Will stated he was encouraged that Harding, despite being a Republican from Ohio, had promised he would be president of "all sections of the country. "I believe the Senator will carry out his expectations," Will said. "He is a man of broad-mindedness and has the qualities . . . that the country needs in a president at this time. He has the qualities of greatness and I expect him to prove a great president." Will's optimism about Harding would turn out to be misplaced. His administration was awash in scandal, and although he has his defenders, most students of his presidency have ranked him among the worst presidents in US history.[26]

As Will had expected, when he returned to Austin on November 18 he received an official invitation to attend Obregón's inauguration in Mexico City on December 1. The Mexican government would pay all of his and Willie's expenses while they were in Mexico, and it would make a special train available for the Hobbys for the trip to the capital. From El Paso, Elias Torres followed up with a telegram to Colonel Chapa in San Antonio informing him that he had arranged for the International and Great Northern Railroad (I&GN) to make two Pullman cars available to the Hobbys and their guests for their trip from Laredo to Mexico City. Obregón's invitation indicated that Will could bring with him as many guests as he wanted to accommodate, so the Hobbys invited nearly sixty people to travel with them to the inauguration. The guest list was made up largely of journalists and political, business, and academic leaders, including University of Texas regents Joseph Kemp, Lutcher Stark, and H. A. Wroe; university faculty member and scholar of Latin American history Charles Hackett; Texas assistant attorney general Alvin Owsley; and Austin businessman Edgar Perry. Also in the Hobby party were Will's brother Edwin; Edwin's wife, Sadie; Willie's brother, Sam; and her friend Florence Stratton.[27]

As Will prepared for the trip, he informed the US State Department about his plans and asked for their advice on how to deal with the Mexican government officials with whom he would be meeting. The State Department, which was annoyed that Will and so many other prominent US citizens were going to attend Obregón's inauguration, gave Will a stern warning not to let his presence at the inauguration give the Mexican government the impression that the United States was planning to reestablish diplomatic relations.[28]

Will's train left Austin on November 26 for San Antonio, where he and his guests stayed overnight. The next day the Hobbys and their Austin companions were joined by other members of their delegation, including Mississippi governor Lee M. Russell and Alabama governor Thomas Kilby. They all boarded the special I&GN train, with the Hobbys settling down in George W. Brackenridge's luxurious private railcar named the Fern Ridge, which the wealthy San Antonio banker made available to them for the journey to Mexico City and back. When Hobby's train arrived in Laredo, they were surprised by news that the I&GN Railroad had decided not to allow its dining car to enter Mexico because of fear that bandits might seize it. After two and a half hours of hurried negotiations, the president of a local Laredo bank, who was also the president of the Texas Mexican Railroad, deposited a cashier's check for $60,000 with the I&GN as a security bond for the dining car. The railroad returned the check when the train returned to Laredo ten days later. The Hobbys' train then proceeded to Mexico City, with stops at Monterrey, Saltillo, San Luis Potosí, and Querétaro to pick up additional guests. By the time the train arrived at the Colonia depot in Mexico City on the morning of November 30, there were more than two hundred passengers aboard.[29]

General Obregón and his wife greeted the Hobbys' delegation at Colonia station with a military band playing the Mexican and US national anthems, as well as the inevitable "Dixie." From the Colonia station, the Hobbys were treated to an automobile tour of Mexico City before they were delivered to the Princess Hotel. Will and Willie's first day in Mexico City turned out to be a lengthy and exhausting one. Soon after they had unpacked and settled into their hotel room, they were taken on a tour of Mexico's national museum. The Hobbys barely had time to take a nap before changing into their formal clothes to attend a banquet in Obregón's honor at the National Palace that evening.[30]

Obregón gave the Hobbys places of honor at the banquet. Will was seated next to the foreign ministers of Argentina and Chile, while Willie sat next to the retiring provisional president, Adolfo de la Huerta. At Obregón's request, Will was among the guests who gave brief remarks at the banquet, which made him the first American to make an address at the inauguration of a Mexican president. A reporter from the *Dallas News* noted that "a great deal of attention is being paid to [the] Texans, in fact, more so than to delegations from other states." After the banquet, Obregón was sworn into office a few minutes after midnight on December 1, 1920, before a joint session of the Mexican Congress.

The evening after the inauguration, the Mexican government staged a show at the national theater featuring music and dancing by performers in costume. Will and Willie sat in a special box seat with Governor-Elect Pat Neff and his wife, Myrtie, who had journeyed with other guests to Mexico City from Laredo on a separate train from the Hobbys. Will took this opportunity to become better acquainted with Neff, whom Will did not know that well despite having sat next to him in Waco at the hectic luncheon opening the Texas Cotton Palace the month before. Neff, in turn, was eager to have the chance to visit with Will away from Austin to discuss the issues that Neff, who had been away from legislative politics for over fifteen years, would have to face as the new governor. The mutually respectful relationship they forged in Mexico City, although never close, would last until Neff's death in 1952. Neff would later appoint Will to the board of regents of the newly established Texas Technological College (now Texas Tech University) in Lubbock in 1923, and they had an occasional correspondence over the years. And when Will was in Austin while Neff was still governor, Will often dropped by Neff's office for a chat. During one of Will's visits with Neff at the capitol, Neff pointed to a high stack of documents on his desk and complained that he was being overwhelmed with paperwork. "Governor," Neff said to Hobby, "I understand that you used to find time to take the afternoon off from this job and play golf. I want to know how you did it." Hobby replied, "Well, Governor, after you have been here a little longer, you will make only half as many mistakes as when you work all day."[31]

The morning after attending the performance at the national theater, on December 2, Will and his Texas delegation visited Chapultepec Castle, at that time the official residence of the president of Mexico. Will laid a wreath at the nearby tomb of the Niños Héroes, the young cadets who had jumped to their deaths instead of surrendering to the US Army in 1847 during the Mexican War. In brief remarks at the tomb, Will declared that time had erased "the bitterness between the two republics," to be "replaced with warm friendship and mutual understanding." The ceremony was followed by a luncheon in the castle. Will would later say that the visit to Chapultepec Castle was "among the memorable experiences" of his trip to Mexico City. After the ceremony at Chapultepec, the Hobby delegation visited the US embassy to meet with the chargé d'affaires, George T. Summerlin, who would later serve as the protocol chief for Franklin D. Roosevelt's White House. The United States had no ambassador in Mexico City because it was withholding recognition of Obregón's government. The *Dallas News* story about the Hobby delegation's visit with Summerlin pointed out that even though the embassy was legally US territory, "the Eighteenth amendment did not exert a gloomy influence."[32]

A nearly continuous round of receptions, luncheons, banquets, and parties dominated the last couple of days the Hobbys and their companions spent in the Mexican capital. Newspaper stories about these affairs frequently made special note of the positive impression Willie made on everyone she met, describing her "effortless poise" and "polished manners." Among the most notable of the last round of events was a formal banquet at the Chapultepec Restaurant on December 3, where President Obregón gave a speech expressing his sincere hopes for peaceful relations between the United States and Mexico. The president repeated the pledges he had made during his visits to El Paso and Dallas that Mexico would welcome foreign capital and investments once diplomatic relations between the two countries were restored. The following day, Will Hobby, Pat Neff, and the other US governors who attended the inauguration hosted a farewell banquet in honor of Obregón and his closest associates in the government. Will, who was among the banquet speakers, admitted that he had once been characterized as an "enemy" of Mexico. "There have always been ties of friendship between the U.S. and Mexico and when these have been broken it has been due to a temporary misunderstanding, or to a degree of impatience. We have come here with the hope that as a result of our visit it will be impossible for any misunderstanding to ever occur again."[33]

The Hobbys and the Texas delegation left Mexico a few pounds heavier and thoroughly exhausted from the nonstop partying. Ultimately, little of substance came from their expedition, with one exception. After arriving in Mexico City with Will Hobby, University of Texas Latin American historian Charles Hackett learned that the famed bibliophile and collector of historical documents and rare books Genaro García had died on November 26, the day the Hobby delegation departed Austin for Mexico. Hackett was informed that García's widow had tried to sell his extensive rare book library to the Mexican government but the offer had been refused. Seeing an opportunity to improve the University of Texas's library holdings, Hackett met with Will and university regents Kemp, Stark, and Wroe and explained the collection's value and how it would enhance the university's reputation. Will and the three regents granted Hackett permission to secure an option from the widow García for the university to purchase the collection. After an appraisal by university librarian Ernest Winkler, the university eventually purchased the García collection in 1921. It served as the basis for the future Nettie Lee Benson Latin American Collection and ultimately led to the university's Latin American Studies program becoming internationally renowned.[34]

President Obregón's strenuous effort to win US recognition of his government by wining and dining the Hobbys and the three thousand other Americans who came to Mexico City for his inauguration failed, at least in the short run. After they returned to Texas, Will and his brother Edwin continued to urge their friends in the Wilson administration to persuade the president to recognize Obregón, but their pleas were ignored. On December 8, Edwin wrote a letter to President Wilson's son-in-law, William Gibbs McAdoo, emphasizing that Obregón had stressed to the American visitors in Mexico City that he was eager to appoint a commission to meet with US representatives at any time to negotiate a mutually beneficial treaty of recognition. Edwin urged McAdoo to persuade US secretary of state Bainbridge Colby to send a commission to Mexico, with McAdoo as the chairman to negotiate such a treaty. President Wilson, however, left office in March 1921 without addressing the issue. Warren Harding also refused to restore diplomatic relations. Not until Calvin Coolidge became president after Harding's sudden death in 1923 did the United States recognize Obregón's government and then only after Obregón finally agreed to sign a treaty in which he pledged not to expropriate American oil company property in Mexico.[35]

Will and Willie celebrated their last Christmas in the Governor's Mansion with Will's mother, Dora, and other family members. Will spent his final days as governor gathering files and memorabilia from his office in the capitol, while Willie made arrangements to move their personal belongings back to their house on Calder Avenue in Beaumont. A news columnist from New York traveled to Austin in December and subsequently wrote a column about the governor. "We found Governor Hobby the most popular governor from an Austin viewpoint of any governor ever elected in Texas," the enthralled writer declared. "Hobby has made a splendid governor." The columnist claimed that he could find "no adverse criticism of Hobby," which was an assertion the state's labor leaders and the still formidable faction of Ferguson supporters would certainly challenge. The reporter, however, did capture Will's quiet, cautious, and collaborative governing style, observing that Hobby had "made no blunders. He has the judgment and good sense to profit by the advice of his friends. He was safe and dependable and the Legislature and the people learned to trust his judgment. Above all he possesses character, integrity, and honesty." The writer also noted that political activists he interviewed in Austin were urging Will to run against four-term incumbent US senator Charles Culberson in 1922. "[Hobby] is going to be a strong man if he decides to enter the contest."[36]

There was much speculation about Will challenging Culberson in the upcoming Senate race, but the idea never interested Will. After five years of public service, and entering middle age, Will was eager to leave elected office and return to the newspaper business, both for financial and personal reasons. Before he left Austin, Will tended to some final business as governor. His last recommendation to the legislature was for approval to move the university campus to a tract of land on the east bank of the Colorado River in West Austin that his friend, philanthropist George W. Brackenridge, had donated for that purpose. Will's advocacy in favor of the move was to no avail. The university remained in its original location.[37]

Will also hosted the first racially integrated wedding conducted in the Governor's Mansion. When the Hobbys moved into the mansion in the early fall of 1917, they brought their African American maid, Savannah Pearl, with them from Beaumont. During Will's tenure as governor, Savannah fell in love with the longtime head porter of the capitol, an African American man known as "General Jackson" who was popular with the legislators. Several days before the Hobbys were scheduled to move back to Beaumont, Savannah asked Willie if she and General Jackson could get married in the mansion's servants' quarters on Sunday, January 15. Willie, who according to one source "was widely admired for her gracious friendliness to strangers, employees, and servants at the Mansion," easily won Will's approval for the wedding. Before the ceremony was held, however, the Hobbys decided to move it to the front living room of the mansion, with both white and black guests in attendance. Not only was this the first racially integrated wedding at the mansion, it might also have been the first racially integrated event ever held there. Will and Willie served as the ceremonial witnesses. After the wedding vows were exchanged, the African American preacher solemnly declared, "And now, in the presence of the Governor of Texas and God Almighty, I pronounce you man and wife."[38]

Will also issued a few last-minute pardons of prison convicts. Because he had exercised his pardon power extensively during his tenure as governor, Will received much criticism from rigidly strict law-and-order supporters. One observer concluded, "But for the fact that there was no hint of corruption in it, his pardon record would have been scandalous. He would not let anyone of whose guilt he had doubt suffer the extreme penalty or remain in prison, no matter how great the popular outcry against him." The criticism stung Will. He later directed James Clark to go to some length to explain, "not to apologize for," his policy in his biography. Before and during Will's years in office, the governor's pardon power was absolute. Will granted pardons to more than 1,500 prisoners and paroled an additional 200. Will's generous pardon policy was based on his awareness of the flaws in the criminal justice system that too often convicted and imprisoned innocent people or condemned individuals who had committed minor transgressions to long and unfair sentences. As Will later told James Clark, he "conceived it to be as much his duty to give deserving convicts a second chance as it was to see that the undeserving paid their debt to society in full."[39]

Soon after he became governor in 1917, Will created a committee to tour the prisons a few weeks before Christmas to identify prisoners who were good candidates for a pardon and who had no friends or relatives to intercede for them. Selecting from the committee's list of candidates, Will announced on Christmas Day pardons for thirty-five "forgotten men." He continued this Christmas Day pardon ritual throughout his years as governor. One of Will's longtime friends later recalled, "[Hobby] also felt deeply about the families of the convicts. He instituted provisions for paying convicts for their labor to prevent their families from becoming destitute. He tightened up the procedures for hiring out or paroling prisoners to farmers. Before this, some parolees had been 'lost' to the prison accounting system and they became virtual indentured servants to the farmers."[40]

When Will issued his last set of Christmas pardons in December 1920, one of the prisoners he freed was an African American man named George Hightower who had been convicted of murder. Hightower had become a convict trustee and was assigned to the Governor's Mansion, where he worked as a yardman during the years the Hobbys occupied the house. Will and Willie got to know and respect Hightower as a hardworking, kind, and responsible person. After Will pardoned Hightower, he took him to Beaumont, where George worked for the Hobby family for more than fifty years. A few years after Will left office, the governor's absolute pardon power was eliminated with the creation of the Texas Board of Pardons and Paroles.[41]

Near the end of Will Hobby's governorship, Martin McNulty Crane assured Will that his administration had been "unusually successful. You have accomplished more in the one and a half terms which you have held than any other Governor has accomplished in the past twenty-five years." Crane's reference to the past twenty-five years was his way of saying that Will Hobby had been the best governor of Texas since the administration of the esteemed Jim Hogg. The record supports Crane's judgment. Of the six men who served as governor after Hogg, Will Hobby's productive accomplishments are rivaled only by those of Tom Campbell, a protégé of Hogg's who was governor from 1907 to 1911.[42]

Will Hobby's term in office coincided with World War I, and historically important and controversial political and social issues came to a head while he was governor, most significantly prohibition and women's suffrage. The manner in which Will handled his assumption of gubernatorial duties after the removal of Jim Ferguson from office; his leadership during World War I, when the state became the training ground for tens of thousands of soldiers; and his scandal-free administration are praiseworthy. His three and a half years as governor were marked also by the passage of a wide array of notable laws relating to women's suffrage, prohibition, education, the criminal justice system, the oil and gas industry, agriculture, and other areas over which state government has responsibility. With the exception of prohibition, a cause that he never really supported, Will deserves much credit for the passage of these laws, either because he actively encouraged their adoption during regular sessions of the legislature, because he submitted them for specific consideration during called special sessions, or simply because he did not veto them. Although Will made a point to keep the process obscure for strategic reasons, in a few cases successful legislation was drafted in his office or drafted at his request by trusted advisors such as Frank Andrews. But as has been the case for all governors of Texas, the laws passed during his administration were also achievements of the legislature. This is a judgment with which Will Hobby readily agreed. But Will Hobby deserves more credit for the legislation that was passed during his administration than he has historically received. He was not passive in his relations with the state legislature. His lack of charisma and flamboyance and his calm, quiet, and deliberative manner of administration have obscured the key role he played in governing Texas in partnership with the legislature.

From the perspective of the early twenty-first century, however, some of Will's other actions as governor are easily criticized. His use of the Texas Rangers for political purposes, his response to the violence of the "Red Summer," his support of the anti–civil liberties "Hobby Loyalty Act," and his veto of the German Language Department at the University of Texas fall on the negative side of any balance sheet evaluating his years as governor. Will's imposition of martial law in Galveston during the port strike and his strong support for the unconstitutional anti-union legislation that followed are undoubtedly viewed favorably by those who are hostile to labor unions, but for individuals who are pro–labor union, Will's actions are black marks on his record.

As has been the case for most of the individuals who have had executive governmental powers at the local, state, and federal levels, Will Hobby's performance had its pluses and minuses. Nevertheless, his overall record should be seen as positive, and his administration must be recognized as one of the most productive and activist in Texas history.

BEGAN CAREER AS CUB REPORTER UNDER THE DIRECTION OF Col. R. M. JOHNSTON

FROM MANAGING EDITOR OF A BIG DAILY TO LT. GOVERNOR

SUDDENLY FOUND HIMSELF BEING SWORN IN AS GOVERNOR TO SUCCEED FERGUSON —

RETIRED OF HIS OWN DESIRE — A SUCCESSFUL ADMINISTRATION NOTED FOR ITS ENACTMENT OF CONSTRUCTIVE LEGISLATION.

HOBBY'S WAR ADMINISTRATION SAW 2 00,000 TEXAS BOYS ENLISTED.

WILLIAM P. HOBBY

FREE TEXT BOOKS AND COMPULSORY EDUCATION —

STATE AND NATIONAL PROHIBITION ENACTED.

JOHN BARLEYCORN

VOTE

WOMAN SUFFRAGE FORMALLY RATIFIED.

*Will Hobby's gubernatorial record as viewed by an admiring journalist.*
*From Hugh Nugent Fitzgerald,* Governors I Have Known.

# CHAPTER 15

# ROSS STERLING AND THE POST-DISPATCH

T he day after Pat Neff's inauguration on January 18, 1920, Will and Willie Hobby returned to Beaumont and moved into a house at 1215 Calder Avenue, near Willie's old family residence, where her brother, Sam, still lived. Will refurbished his old office at the *Beaumont Enterprise*, where he resumed his former duties as owner and publisher. His business manager, Jim Mapes, had done an outstanding job guiding the *Enterprise* while Will was governor. Mapes had also become part owner of the newspaper when he bought out Will's initial investors, Walter Crawford, Bernard Deutser, and Paul Heisig, in 1920. Will remained the majority stockholder, with his brother Edwin owning the third-largest block of *Enterprise* stock.[1]

Beaumont's population had grown to forty thousand, more than doubling in size since Will first took the reins of the *Enterprise* nearly fifteen years earlier. Under Mapes's direction the newspaper's circulation had increased as the city grew. It continued to be the dominant news source for the area stretching from Beaumont to Lake Charles, Louisiana, although the rival *Beaumont Journal* was challenging that dominance. The *Enterprise*'s continuing success can also be credited to young journalist Alfred Jones, whom Will had recruited from M. E. Foster's *Houston Chronicle* in 1915 to serve as the newspaper's managing editor. The *Enterprise* was flourishing and the company was profitable, providing Will with a steady income. The newspaper's accounting records no longer exist, but it is likely that the *Enterprise* had not paid Will a salary while he was governor. His name was not on the *Enterprise*'s masthead during the gubernatorial years, and his diminishing financial resources while he served as governor played a determining role in his decision not to run for reelection. With the paper prospering, Will wisely decided to keep Mapes in control of day-to-day business operations as general manager, with Jones guiding the editorial and news side of the *Enterprise*. This administrative arrangement freed Will to be involved in other businesses, although he continued to direct the editorial views of the *Enterprise*.[2]

In the 1910s, Will became enamored with the money-making potential of water power to generate electricity for utility companies and to store water to sell for agricultural irrigation. While he was lieutenant governor, he had been one of the investors in an $8 million irrigation and hydroelectric project on the Devils River in Val Verde County in West Texas that failed because of the remoteness of the site. His participation in that project was well enough known in Austin to inspire Jim Ferguson to refer repeatedly to Will as "Water-Power Hobby" during the 1918 gubernatorial campaign. After Will moved back to Beaumont he searched for new business opportunities. Constructing and owning an investor-funded dam to generate and sell electricity was among the possibilities he considered. He also explored opportunities in the newspaper publishing, banking, and insurance businesses. Only a month after he left the governor's office, Will sought investment partners with the capital to fund a waterpower project, start a new insurance company, or even purchase the *Enterprise*.

Will initiated his quest for investors by renewing his acquaintance with financial tycoon Bernard Baruch. Will wrote the wealthy and influential financier in early February 1921 to remind him of their earlier visit and how much he and Willie had enjoyed their conversation. He informed Baruch that he was no longer governor of Texas and that as a result he was now concentrating on business opportunities. "It seems to me that you mentioned some interest in waterpower and newspaper propositions," Will wrote. "I own a very profitable newspaper at the present time and there are some water projects in Texas capable of development along most profitable irrigation lines, also for waterpower use. I simply wanted to know if you would be interested in any of these things and if you know of any source which might be interested in the promotion and development of such projects." Baruch answered that he had "no present expectation to go into any form of business." He politely added, "Nothing would give me greater pleasure in case I decided to go into business than to be in association with you."[3]

While Will searched for new business opportunities, he continued to be involved in civic projects that the *Enterprise* boosted, such as persuading the Beaumont Temperance Club, now without a cause as a result of the Eighteenth Amendment, to donate their four-story building to serve as a new city hall. Will also returned to the project that had gained him public attention more than a decade earlier: the Neches-Sabine deepwater ship channel. He assisted the successful effort to fund a project to deepen the channel to a depth of thirty feet to accommodate the largest oceangoing ships. That project was easier to fund than the initial effort, because the channel had proven its value during the war. The federal government had established a major shipbuilding factory on an island in the Neches River to the east of Beaumont that produced a large number of wooden-hull ships for war service. After the war, the government sold the shipyard to a steel company that continued to construct commercial ships at the site.[4]

Within weeks after his return to Beaumont, Will took serious notice of the growing popularity of his rival newspaper, the *Beaumont Journal*, which the Marsh-Fentress newspaper chain had purchased in 1918. As a fellow publisher and political candidate,

Will was well acquainted with journalist Charles Marsh and businessman E. S. Fentress, the Waco-based owners of the company. Marsh and Fentress also owned the *Austin American* (which later became the *Austin American-Statesman*), which had covered Will during his last two years as governor. Will decided the best way to deal with the increasingly successful *Journal* was to buy it. He traveled to Waco in late March to make the pitch to Marsh and Fentress. The Waco businessmen had purchased the *Port Arthur News* a few months earlier, and they were more interested in developing that property, especially as it had no real competition in that city, unlike the *Journal*. They agreed to sell the *Journal* to Will in May 1921.[5]

After the purchase, Will experimented with an unusual operational arrangement. He moved the *Journal*'s staff to the building that housed the *Enterprise*, and he continued to publish the *Journal* as a separate publication distributed in the morning, while the *Enterprise* continued as an afternoon paper. This created one of the first combination morning and afternoon papers in the country. He also kept the editorial departments of both newspapers separate and urged them to compete with each other when gathering the news. This arrangement worked well. Both papers were moneymakers.[6]

While Will negotiated with Marsh and Fentress in mid-April 1921, his brother Edwin sent a message urging him to come to Dallas as soon as possible. Their mother was desperately ill and near death. Will suspended his negotiations with Marsh and Fentress in Waco and took the train to Dallas. He was able to spend a few days with Dora before she died on April 26, 1921, at the age of seventy-seven. She was buried in the historic Oakland Cemetery in South Dallas.[7]

A few months after Dora's death, a post office was opened next to a general store in eastern Fort Bend County about two miles north of the IG&N Railroad. The post office was named in honor of Will Hobby because it was near Dora Pettus's old family plantation. Because of the named post office, the unincorporated village became known as Hobby, Texas. Never having more than about thirty residents, the town of Hobby disappeared after World War II, and the area was eventually covered by suburban development.[8]

Soon after Will's return to Beaumont, some of its citizens formed a chapter of the Ku Klux Klan, which quickly grew into a formidable organization. Founded nationally in 1866 by white supremacists, the organization had largely disappeared after the former leaders of the Confederacy regained political power in the South in the late 1870s. The Klan enjoyed a major revival nationally after the end of the First World War. This second coming of the Klan was not only in support of white supremacy, it was also nativist, anti-Catholic, and anti-Semitic. Many of its members enforced a strict version of Victorian moralism and engaged in flogging and tarring and feathering of individuals who had been accused of adultery, gambling, and bootlegging. Like most progressive businessmen, Will abhorred the Klan's prejudices and methods. He also believed the masked and hooded members had a negative impact on local business conditions and instead of suppressing crime, their violent extralegal actions were destructive of law and order. Accordingly, Will, Jim Mapes, and Alfred Jones denounced the vigilante group in the *Enterprise*'s editorial pages and published unfavorable news stories reporting the violent activities of its members, including a rash of pistol whippings and lashings. The *Enterprise*'s opposition to the Klan, however, did not include banning the vigilante group from the advertising pages of the newspaper. In September 1921, after the Klan publicly tarred and feathered a local physician who had been accused of performing abortions, the *Enterprise* sold the Klan a page in the newspaper justifying their actions.[9]

Despite the *Enterprise*'s public criticism of their activities, the Klan grew rapidly in Beaumont as well as in other cities throughout Texas. In 1922 the Klan staged a parade and rally in Beaumont that attracted a crowd of thirty thousand spectators. That same year, Klan political candidates won nearly every public office in Beaumont. Most of the Beaumont city police force and the Jefferson County Sheriff's Department were members. Even some of the Protestant clergy joined the Beaumont KKK, including Dr. A. D. Ellis, rector of St. Mark's Episcopal Church, who had served briefly as Grand Dragon, or state leader, of the Klan in Texas.[10]

With more than one hundred thousand dues-paying Klan members eligible to vote, the KKK also became a major political force statewide, which they demonstrated in the US Senate race in the summer of 1922. Incumbent US senator Charles Culberson, alcoholic, aging, and ill, sought reelection to a fifth term in the 1922 Democratic primary. Because it was well understood in Texas political circles that Culberson carried too much negative baggage to win the Democratic primary, James Ferguson decided to challenge the incumbent senator. The legal ban on Ferguson running for state office did not apply to a federal office. Fearful that Ferguson might win an easy victory over Culberson, Will Hobby's longtime political supporters made a concerted effort to persuade him to enter the Senate race, certain that he could take Ferguson down again. But Will had no interest in serving in the US Senate, and he had even less interest in enduring another campaign against the vitriolic Jim Ferguson.[11]

With Will's decision to stay out of the race, many anti-Ferguson progressives backed Will's former colleague at the *Houston Post*, Clarence Ousley, while others decided to stick with the vehemently anti-Klan Culberson, despite his obvious flaws and weaknesses. Three self-admitted members of the Klan, including Railroad Commissioner Earle B. Mayfield, also entered the race. Mayfield won the most votes on Election Day, July 22, but he lacked a majority, which forced him into a runoff against Jim Ferguson, who had come in second. Culberson had placed third, ending his Senate career after twenty-four years. Pat Neff, who maintained a neutral position on the KKK, easily won the nomination for a second term as governor against token candidates.[12]

Will and his progressive friends were now in a difficult position. They were faced with having to choose between Earle Mayfield, an active member of the KKK, and their longtime nemesis "Pa" Ferguson, who despite all efforts and wishes, refused to disappear from Texas politics. Although Will was anti-Klan, he was even more anti-Ferguson. Before becoming involved in the KKK, fervent prohibitionist Mayfield had entered the governor's race against Will because of his correct perception that Will was soft on the liquor issue. Mayfield eventually withdrew his candidacy and endorsed Will. Mayfield and Hobby weren't friends, but they weren't enemies either. The idea of Ferguson serving as one of the US senators from Texas was intolerable to Will. On July 30, 1922, he released a statement endorsing Mayfield. Ferguson's election, Will declared, would be "a step backward" in the "progress of democracy and the forward march of Texas." When he learned of Will's public endorsement of Mayfield, Ferguson gave a speech in Georgetown claiming outrageously and without any evidence that Mayfield and "Water-Power Hobby" had attended a party together on the San Gabriel River in 1919 where "they got drunk as boiled owls." In what has to be the most ludicrous charge ever made against Will Hobby, Ferguson claimed that Mayfield and Hobby "got naked and run [*sic*] up and down the banks of this river in that condition until forced to stop by the local officers at Georgetown."[13]

Mayfield overcame Ferguson in the runoff election in August by slightly more than fifty-two thousand votes. He then defeated independent candidate George Peddy in the general election in November, giving one of Texas's seats in the US Senate to a leader of the KKK. By 1925, however, Klan membership in Beaumont and in the rest of Texas began to decline drastically, as did KKK membership in other areas of the nation. By the end of the 1920s the organization had lost membership to the point of insignificance.[14]

In the spring of 1922, Will and Willie informed their friends and acquaintances in Beaumont that they were moving to Houston. Dora Hobby's death the year before had a profound effect on Will. Many years later, Will recalled to James Clark that his mother's passing caused "not so much a dissatisfied as an unsatisfied feeling" about his life in Beaumont, which caused him and Willie to reassess their course. The reevaluation was not about their marriage, which was successful and deeply fulfilling to them both. It was their yearning for more than Beaumont could offer them. After being the First Family of Texas, which included the exciting experience in Mexico City and the meeting with President-Elect Warren Harding in Brownsville, the Hobbys found Beaumont a little too small and unexciting. Willie had family, good friends, and a long history in the southeast Texas city, but she had greatly enjoyed the exciting years she had spent in Washington, DC, and Manhattan with her father and the three and a half years she had been First Lady of Texas. Will believed he had taken the *Enterprise* as far as the size of Beaumont warranted and that he didn't want to "spend the rest of his life deepening the Sabine-Neches ship channel."[15]

Will not only longed for a bigger arena, he also sought new opportunities to enhance his wealth. There was an attractive opportunity only eighty-seven miles to the west of Beaumont, in Houston, the city Will considered his hometown. The "Bayou City" was booming economically and experiencing rapid growth because of its ship channel, its growing involvement in the oil industry, and the efforts of its sophisticated and imaginative business elite. It was well on the way to becoming the largest city in Texas and the second-largest in the South. A building spree was taking off in the downtown area. This attractive business environment had already lured a few of Will's Beaumont friends to

Houston, including oilman Harry Wiess, one of the founders of the Humble Oil Company, and Will's family friend Ross Sterling, another member of the Humble Oil founding group. And, of course, his old patron John Henry Kirby had his main office in the city.

Before he moved to Houston, Will gave total authority over the *Enterprise* and the *Journal* to Jim Mapes. Will retained his majority ownership of the newspapers, but he assumed the role of an investor instead of an active participant in their management. In 1931 Will sold his stock in both newspapers to Mapes, who operated them until his death five years later.[16]

Will was unsure of the exact direction he wanted his career to take after moving to Houston, but he was confident that his fame and good reputation as governor coupled with his extensive connections would provide him with several options. As he later told James Clark, he was "in no hurry [to decide]." He wanted to "take a long-needed rest and look around awhile." Nevertheless, there was one business opportunity in Houston Will had already decided to take before he left Beaumont, and it played a key role in his decision to move.[17]

Sometime in late 1921, George Christie, an attorney and longtime employee of John Henry Kirby's lumber company in Beaumont, persuaded Will to be his partner in a new business enterprise to be named "Christie and Hobby." The new partners formed two insurance companies: the Oilman's Reciprocal Association and the Security Union Casualty Company. The Oilman's Reciprocal Association was an unincorporated group of subscribing members who exchanged contracts of indemnity as a type of self-insurance. Security Union was a traditional insurance company offering casualty and workmen's compensatory policies. Will's interest in the insurance business was not new. A year before Will entered into a partnership with Christie, he had sought John Henry Kirby's opinion about the profit potential for selling liability insurance to oil companies. Among John Henry Kirby's many enterprises was his Lumberman's Reciprocal Association. Kirby was enthusiastic about the idea. "I urge you to persevere in the effort," he advised Will. "As soon as you are ready for business I hope you will give the Kirby Petroleum Company . . . an opportunity to become subscribers." Kirby became one of Will's first investors.[18]

Will's role in the Christie and Hobby enterprise was to attract clients, not to manage the companies. He left the business office to Christie, who had been Kirby's auditor and comptroller. While he was governor, Will had established a long list of contacts from which he now drew to solicit business. In addition to Kirby, Sterling, and Wiess, Will had forged solid relationships with a number of Houston's most important business-men, including Judge Jim Elkins, Joseph Cullinan, Jake Wolters, Will Clayton, Howard Hughes Sr., Will Hogg, and Frank Andrews. The latter became Christie and Hobby's attorney as well as an investor and an active solicitor of clients for the firm. For example, Andrews teamed with Will in a successful effort to persuade Humble Oil board members Harry Wiess and Will Farish to give Christie and Hobby's new reciprocal insurance company some of its business. That effort was aided by a trip Andrews made to New York City to pitch to executives of Standard Oil of New Jersey, Humble's corporate owner. After his meeting with Standard of New Jersey in May 1922, Andrews sent Will a telegram: "Closed up with Humble today. Things look better."[19]

Frank Andrews's effort to sell reciprocal insurance to the Texas division of the Western Union Telegraph Company, although unsuccessful, is a good example of how Will's pro-business record as governor was also used to win clients. In October 1922, Andrews wrote his friend Ralph Kimball, one of Western Union's legal counsels, that Will's new reciprocal insurance company was seeking his company's liability and compensation business. His pitch was candid. A corporation such as Western Union should feel gratitude toward Will, Andrews stressed, because of his "stand for the law enforcement in Texas while he was Governor" during the Galveston longshoremen's strike in 1919. "The laws were enforced and property rights were protected," Andrews wrote. "I feel like the . . . business of this state should rally to his assistance now so that it may not be said that a man who faithfully . . . performs his duty is promptly repudiated by those who are beneficiaries of it." Undoubtedly, this same plea was made to Standard of New Jersey, as well as to other large corporations. In the case of Western Union, however, it seems that the argument failed to persuade.[20]

Will's contacts helped the business to expand rapidly, aided as well by Houston's overheated economy. Jim Elkins was another one of Will's most active supporters. While he was governor, Will had played a role in bringing Elkins to prominence by appointing him district attorney and by making an important connection for him in the oil industry. Grateful, Elkins eagerly promoted Will and Christie's new enterprise. He distributed circulars to his growing list of corporate clients informing them that he was "very much interested in the success of Gov. Hobby's [insurance] company, and if you can give him this business, we will appreciate it very much."[21]

Will eventually added other businesses to his portfolio, including the Interstate Trust Company, which he and his investors chartered as a holding company in Delaware. One of his partners was former University of Texas law school dean John C. Townes, who became vice president. Will served as the company's president. Will also accepted a business offer from another friend of John Henry Kirby's, former US congressman from Waco R. L. Henry, an ultraconservative states' rights advocate who had been a political ally of Samuel Bronson Cooper. A year after losing a race for governor as a Ku Klux Klan candidate in 1922, Henry broke with the Klan and moved to Houston to practice law. He was general counsel of Southern Oil and Refining Company when Will arrived in the city. The former congressman persuaded Will to invest money in Southern Oil and to serve as its corporate secretary.[22]

Will also used his extensive network of contacts to solicit clients for his Security Union Casualty Company. One of those contacts was Bernard Baruch. Will had maintained contact with Baruch despite his unsuccessful effort to get him involved in his waterpower schemes. During the war Baruch and J. P. Morgan purchased the Texas Gulf Sulphur Company, which mined sulfur deposits on the Texas Gulf Coast. By the mid-1920s, the company was one of the largest producers of sulfur in the world. Will was eager to have Texas Gulf Sulphur as a workmen's compensation policy client for his insurance company. When he and Willie traveled to New York City in March 1925, they visited Baruch, who had recently sold his stock in the company at an enormous profit. Although Baruch was no longer officially associated with Texas Gulf Sulphur, Will knew he still had influence with its management. Will asked Baruch if he would call the company's president to recommend that it buy its workmen's compensation insurance from Security Union. Baruch agreed to make the recommendation.

Six months later, Will wrote Baruch that he "had never been able to get favorable consideration on the [Texas Gulf Sulphur] matter and while I do not wish to burden you concerning it, if you think you can be of any assistance, I will appreciate it." It took Baruch nearly two months to reply: "I put my recommendation for your company, and am sorry they have not acted upon it. I shall speak further about the matter." After one year had passed, Texas Gulf Sulphur had still not responded to Will's solicitation. On November 15, 1926, he wrote Baruch: "We have, so far, been unable to get the insurance of the Texas Gulf Sulphur Company. I shall thank you if you can be helpful to us in this matter." Baruch responded two weeks later with bad news. "If I had had my way," he said, "you would have had the insurance of the Texas Gulf Sulphur Company a long time ago, but unfortunately I cannot get it for you."[23]

When Will and Willie moved to Houston, they initially rented an apartment at the Rice Hotel downtown. Will developed his business opportunities while Willie became involved in Houston's women's clubs and organizations, including the Houston League of Women Voters and the Daughters of the American Revolution. Explaining her active involvement in Houston's Literature and Culture Club, she confided to her friend Anna Pennybacker, who was a leader in the national women's club movement and an author of a popular textbook on the history of Texas, that she was "hungry for more time to read the things that are worth reading; to understand spiritual values. I have made up my mind that from this time on I shall MAKE time to read each day something that feeds my soul." Willie was also active in Houston's First Methodist Church, and she worked with the Bluebird Circle to raise money for sick and indigent children. "God has been good to me," she told Florence Stratton. "I want to be worthy of these blessings; I want to share them with others; I want to be a help to those who need assistance."[24]

Happily for Will, a much more exciting opportunity that included a salary and the chance to be involved in the newspaper business soon appeared, thanks to Ross Sterling. Sterling had recently sold some of his Humble Oil stock for $8 million. In November 1923 he used some of that cash to purchase the nearly insolvent *Houston Dispatch*, a morning newspaper in direct competition with the *Houston Post*. The *Dispatch* had been in existence for only a few months and was in serious financial trouble. Soon after he acquired the *Dispatch*, Sterling hired Ray Dudley and Dale Rogers, two young friends of his who were familiar with the business, to run the newspaper. He appointed Dudley, who had been oil editor at the *Houston Post*, president. Rogers took the position of vice president. Sterling moved the *Dispatch* offices to the main floor of his Humble Company

Building, and he began the construction of a printing plant nearly a mile away at a site on the corner of Polk and Dowling Streets.[25]

To better compete with the rival *Houston Post*, Sterling hired the *Post*'s top editorial talent, George Bailey, who was unhappy with the *Post*'s editorial policies. Sterling also raided the *Houston Chronicle* staff, hiring the popular poet and humorist Judd Mortimer Lewis and one of Houston's star reporters, Charlie Maes. With these major additions to its editorial staff, the *Dispatch* not only became profitable, it also took subscriptions and advertising away from the *Post*, which soon began to lose money, forcing it to close its evening edition.[26]

In the summer of 1924, as the *Post* continued to lose money, Roy Watson made it known that he might be willing to sell the Houston Printing Company. This information found its way to the immensely wealthy California newspaper baron William Randolph Hearst, who offered Watson a little more than one million dollars for the *Post*, more than twice the value of its actual physical assets. As attractive as Hearst's offer was, Watson preferred to keep the newspaper under local ownership if at all possible. He asked his attorney, Wharton Weems, to meet with Sterling to see if he would buy the *Post* for the same amount of money Hearst had offered. "I snapped the offer up without making an inventory or an audit of the *Post*'s books," Sterling later recalled. The merger removed one of Sterling's competitors from an overcrowded field. It was the highest price ever paid for a newspaper in Texas up to that time.[27]

At the time that Sterling purchased the *Post* on July 29, 1924, the newspaper had a circulation of about forty thousand, which was a poor showing in a city with a population of two hundred thousand. As Sterling later noted, it was "pretty badly run down at the heel, but it was a paper with a noble past and unlimited future possibilities. It had the established name and good will" in the community. Sterling combined the *Post* and the *Dispatch* into one publication, the *Houston Post-Dispatch*. He took the position of chairman of the board and appointed Ray Dudley vice president and general manager. But he also needed a president, and he had no doubt about whom he wanted to fill that post. As Sterling later wrote in his memoir, he never had any candidate other than Will Hobby. "I had known Hobby as governor; in fact, I had supported his candidacy for that office," Sterling stated. "When I looked about for an experienced, successful newspaperman to take the helm of the *Post-Dispatch* and steer it through the shoals of reorganization, William Hobby was just the man I needed." This was a dream come true for Will, who eagerly accepted Sterling's offer. He also bought a block of stock in the newspaper, as did Ray Dudley. They joined with Sterling as the largest stockholders in the newspaper, but of the three, Dudley was the junior partner. Sterling observed that his bringing Hobby to the *Post* "would prove to be the most significant change for its future."[28]

Will's return to the newspaper that had started his career continued the link between the Hobby and the Sterling families that began back in Peach Tree Village. Will's father, Edwin Sr., had been a good friend of Ross Sterling's father, Benjamin Franklin Sterling, and grandfather, William Sterling, when they all lived in Peach Tree Village. After Edwin

*Ross Sterling, ca. 1920s.*

moved his family to Woodville, Ben Sterling relocated to Anahuac, Texas, where Ben's son, Ross, was born in 1875. Edwin Hobby Sr. had maintained ties with the Sterling family until his death. John Henry Kirby, another Peach Tree native, had also maintained the close ties he had forged with the Sterlings in his youth. In addition, Ross Sterling and his wife, Maud, were good friends with Willie Hobby, whose father, Bronson Cooper, had his own ties to little Peach Tree Village. Ross Sterling's hiring of Will Hobby in 1924 continued the friendship and familial network that had originated in Tyler County in the late 1860s. That network of relationships, which had entwined the life stories of the Hobbys, the Kirbys, the Coopers, and the Sterlings for nearly sixty years had now led to one of the most significant events in Will Hobby's business career.

Will restored another link to his past by bringing his journalistic and political mentor Colonel Rienzi Johnston back to the newspaper. As soon as he made his deal with Ross Sterling, Will persuaded Sterling to appoint Johnston to the *Post-Dispatch* board of directors. Johnston had left the *Post* a few years earlier after a falling-out with publisher Roy Watson. Will Hobby told his biographer James Clark that he "owed much" to Johnston, whom he characterized as a "sagacious, able newspaperman and political seer . . . who had been [his] mentor and faithful friend for thirty years." Johnston soon became the wise sage of the board of directors, but his tenure was cut short by his death on February 28, 1926, at the age of seventy. Rienzi's troubled son, Harry Johnston, whom Will had been forced to dismiss from the Texas Rangers, died a year later. Those deaths, however, did not end Will's relationship with the Johnston family. Two decades after Rienzi Johnston's death, Will continued to repay his debt to the Colonel by hiring his daughter, Mary Elizabeth, and his grandson, Harry Johnston Jr., as reporters for the *Post*. Both hires were based as much on talent as they were on Will's loyalty to Colonel Johnston's memory. After excelling at the *Post*, Mary would later distinguish herself as editor of *Fortune* magazine, while Harry would rise to the position of editor at the *Post*.[29]

Will became president of the *Post-Dispatch* on July 29, 1924, when the purchase was made final. The following day he settled into his new office on the third floor of the old *Post* building at the corner of Texas and Travis Streets in downtown Houston. This was familiar territory. Nearly twenty years earlier he had helped Colonel Johnston move furniture and printing equipment into the building after Johnston had purchased it. Will Hobby and Ray Dudley sat across from each other at a big mahogany desk they shared in Roy Watson's ornate former office. Years later, when he recalled those days working across the desk from Will Hobby, Dudley observed that Will could "sit longer without saying anything than anybody I ever knew," and that he could "ask shorter questions that take longer to answer than anyone I ever worked under." These office arrangements were temporary. Ross Sterling's renovation of a building at the southwest corner of Polk and Dowling Streets was completed in March 1925. The building housed his new printing press and served as the temporary headquarters for the combined newspaper staff. The business and editorial staff would later move to Sterling's new twenty-two-story Houston Post-Dispatch Building in downtown Houston.[30]

Because Sterling was eager to see the first copies of the new *Houston Post-Dispatch* out on the streets, Will, Ray Dudley, and their team hurriedly gathered and edited material from the wire services and their local reporters to produce that first issue, which appeared on Friday morning, August 1, 1924, only three days after the purchase. The newsstand price was five cents a copy. The front page featured Sterling and Hobby's joint "Statement of New Officers," in which Sterling declared, "The owners of the *Houston*

*Post-Dispatch* will double their efforts to make it a more powerful agency for good, a newspaper with more news, better features, and more circulation, a credit to Houston, a benefit to the people it serves and a greater factor for the moral advancement and civic betterment of Texas." In his statement, Will said that he was filled with the "ardor and the zeal which comes with a new opportunity for service." His goal was a newspaper that measured up "to the best standard of journalism of the best American cities, keeping step with Houston's progress, helping every cause that is good."[31]

The readers of that first issue saw the headline "Defense Seeks to Have Experts Placed on Stand," a report on the sensational Leopold and Loeb murder trial in Chicago and Clarence Darrow's efforts to spare the two confessed killers from death sentences by claiming they were mentally ill. Readers also saw a large number of advertisements placed by local merchants welcoming the new *Post-Dispatch*, including a large ad purchased by Sakowitz Bros. clothiers declaring that the Palm Beach suits offered for $11.50 each in their big clearance sale were "as New as the Houston Post-Dispatch." Readers that morning would also notice the reappearance of the lucrative patent medicine ads Christian Scientist Roy Watson had banned from the *Post* years before.[32]

On the editorial page, popular poet and columnist Judd Mortimer Lewis happily noted "the lineup of old friends and new" in the management of the combined newspaper. Lewis named "Ex-Governor Hobby who was managing editor through many happy years of our service," and Charlie Maes, "who has worked his way up from cub reporter to be one of the South's best managing editors." Lewis noted that Ray Dudley had been "doing leg-work on the paper eleven years ago." The columnist also identified an "old friend" of his who was a new friend of the *Post-Dispatch*, "R. S. Sterling, whom we would like to tell you more of, but who reads the column and would be embarrassed. We are so proud we strut in our sleep." Thus was launched the version of the newspaper with which Will Hobby and his family would be identified as employees and eventually as sole owners for sixty years.[33]

Sterling made it clear to Will Hobby and Ray Dudley that he was willing to spend as much money as it would take to make the newspaper a success. He admitted that he was the liberal spender, throwing money at whatever he thought would advance the *Post-Dispatch*, and that Will Hobby was the "conservative element, the balance wheel" keeping the newspaper on a firm financial basis, which included searching for potential revenue from a highly unusual source. Two weeks after printing the first copy of the *Post-Dispatch*, Will sent a proposal to Mexican president Álvaro Obregón, who was nearing the end of his term, stating that for a fee of $60,000, his newspaper would publish a series of stories touting the commercial "advantages and opportunities" in Mexico for Houston investors. No record of a response has surfaced, but it appears that Obregón passed up this opportunity. No articles boosting investment or business opportunities in Mexico appeared in the paper.[34]

As Will and his colleagues were busy trying to get out the first issue of the new *Post-Dispatch*, officials were still counting ballots cast during the Democratic Party primary election on July 26. As usual, the contest for governor had attracted the most attention from the public and the press. The leading candidates included Lieutenant Governor T. Whitfield Davidson, former lieutenant governor Lynch Davidson, Ku Klux Klan leader and district court judge Felix Robertson, and James Ferguson's wife, Miriam "Ma" Ferguson. The latter entered the race after her husband lost his lawsuit to lift the ban on his running for state office. When the final count was certified, Judge Robertson and Ma Ferguson were the top two vote getters. With no one receiving a majority of the votes, Robertson and Ferguson would face each other in a runoff election on August 23. Once again, Will Hobby was forced in an election campaign to choose between a leader of the despised KKK and Jim Ferguson, whose wife was obviously his surrogate in the race.[35]

In his memoir, Ross Sterling noted that both the *Post* and the *Dispatch* had supported Houstonian Lynch Davidson in the primary and that his defeat presented the *Post-Dispatch* with a difficult editorial problem. "'Fergusonism' was as repugnant to me as it was to Will Hobby," Sterling recalled, "so neither one of us wanted any part of Mrs. Ferguson's candidacy. On the other hand, we did not want the Klan candidate as our political bedfellow." But Sterling also noted that M. E. Foster of the *Houston Chronicle* had accused both the *Post* and the *Dispatch* of having Klan sympathies when under their previous owners. "I wanted to keep the reincarnated paper's skirts clean," Sterling stated. Sterling and Will Hobby decided their newspaper would "take no stand on either side." Sterling declared their neutral position in a signed editorial, explaining that "the alternative to a Klan governor is Jim [Ferguson]; the alternative to Jim is a Klan governor. What is a good citizen to do in a situation like that?"[36]

M. E. Foster realized that the new *Post-Dispatch* was going to be formidable competition. Part of his response was to launch an editorial campaign attacking the *Post-Dispatch* for taking a neutral stance in the primary runoff. Foster, who had waged an unrelenting editorial war against the Klan, implied that the *Post-Dispatch*'s publisher as well as its president were friendly to Robertson and the KKK. Sterling and Hobby were quick to respond to Foster's criticism. As Sterling later observed, Foster "found out that in tackling us, he had grabbed hold of a bear." Clearly relishing the fight, the *Post-Dispatch*'s chief editorial writer, George Bailey, fired off a series of editorials attacking Foster and the *Chronicle*. According to Sterling, Bailey was capable of writing an editorial "that left an odor of burning hide on everything it touched." During the month before the runoff election, Sterling went to Bailey's office every day at noon to help with the editorials. "Governor Hobby joined us in concocting the daily acid throwing," Sterling recalled. "Our editorials were so searing that the *Chronicle* publisher finally phoned and said he was ready to call a truce." How much this fight affected reader loyalty is unknown, but it is apparent that both sides enjoyed the journalistic fray.[37]

On August 23, 1924, Miriam Ferguson defeated Judge Robertson for the Democratic nomination for governor, mainly because the progressive wing of the Democratic Party opposed the Klan more than they disliked the Fergusons. Nevertheless, progressive unhappiness about the prospect of the Fergusons returning to the Governor's Mansion led to an effort to persuade voters to cast their ballots for the Republican candidate, George C. Butte, in the general election in November. The forty-seven-year-old Butte, a highly respected dean of the University of Texas School of Law, had an impressive record of nonpartisan public service. Progressives soon rallied to his side, and the *Post-Dispatch* joined them. Sterling, Hobby, and Bailey collaborated in writing the editorial endorsing Butte. "The clear-cut issue," they wrote, "is honesty and righteousness in government. Only the issue of Fergusonism and the menace it offers to decent government remains." The voters had defeated the Klan's candidate, they declared, so "now let them eliminate Fergusonism. This can be done by selecting George C. Butte—a Christian gentleman, a patriot, a clean-minded and clean-tongued exemplar of private and public righteousness."[38]

Miriam Ferguson won the general election in November by a wide margin, largely because of overwhelming support from the state's rural precincts, the Fergusons' dependable strongholds. Butte attracted three times more votes than any other previous Republican candidate in Texas history, and with the exception of San Antonio's Bexar County, he carried the state's largest urban counties. The 1924 general election was the first time Will Hobby publicly supported a Republican candidate for a major political office. It would not be the last.[39]

*Miriam "Ma" Ferguson, ca. 1930.*

# CHAPTER 16

# THE DEATH OF MISS WILLIE

By the beginning of 1925, Ross Sterling's new *Post-Dispatch* was a profitable enterprise, although it continued to trail the *Houston Chronicle* in number of subscribers and ads. Despite the newspaper's profits, Sterling had a long way to go before he could begin to recoup his million-dollar-plus investment. Will Hobby, however, had no doubts about Sterling's financial situation and his commitment to the newspaper. Sterling's wealth increased considerably in February 1925, when he resigned from the board of the Humble Oil Company and sold his remaining stock in the company to Standard Oil, increasing his net worth to $22 million.[1]

After Sterling left the Humble Company, he turned his attention to another project that would have an additional long-term impact on Will Hobby and his family. In the early 1920s, Sterling's teenage son, Ross Jr. ("Little Ross"), became a ham radio operator, which developed into a keen interest in the rapidly developing commercial radio business. After his father purchased the *Houston Post*, Ross made frequent trips to the Iris Movie Theater located next to the Post Building, where he hung around the studio of WEAY, a low-watt radio station owned by Will Horowitz, who also owned the Iris. Horowitz had rented space on the top floor of the Post Building for his station's transmitter ever since WEAY had made its first broadcast in 1922. The station's antenna wiring stretched from the roof of the Iris to the roof of the Post Building.[2]

Convinced by his visits to WEAY that this new medium had commercial possibilities, Little Ross enrolled in a radio class at the YMCA in downtown Houston. The instructor, Alfred Daniel, had founded and was still operating another one of the earliest radio stations in the city, WCAK, and he was also involved in another pioneering station, WEV. Shortly before the elder Sterling merged the *Post* and the *Dispatch*, Little Ross and Alfred Daniel persuaded Sterling to spend $25,000 of his newly gained Humble Oil money to purchase radio transmitting equipment and launch a new five-hundred-watt broadcast station. After Sterling purchased the equipment from the Westinghouse Company, it was placed in storage and left uncrated until it could be moved to the *Post-Dispatch*'s new printing plant at the corner of Polk and Dowling Streets. Sterling planned to set up the station and turn it over to Little Ross, with Alfred Daniel serving as announcer and program director. That plan came to an end in 1924, however, when Little Ross died at the age of seventeen as a result of complications from surgery.[3]

Stunned by his son's premature death, Sterling quickly lost interest in his radio project. The transmitting equipment had gathered dust in storage for about a year when Alfred Daniel sought Will Hobby's help to persuade Sterling to proceed with the project. Will was enthusiastic about the future possibilities for commercial exploitation of radio. He was aware of how much Amon Carter and his *Fort Worth Star-Telegram* newspaper had benefitted from launching radio station WBAP in 1922. The *Dallas Morning News* was also having great success with its WFAA radio station, launched shortly after WBAP's first broadcast in 1922. Will had a hunch that whenever radio became more sophisticated at delivering the news, it would give the newspaper business serious competition. He later told James Clark that he "preferred to see Houston radio grow up as a partner of his newspaper, not as a rival."[4]

When Will and Alfred Daniel made their pitch to Sterling, they suggested that the new radio station could serve as a living monument to Little Ross's memory. That idea had deep emotional appeal to Sterling. He agreed to move forward. He gave Ray Dudley the job of setting up the broadcasting operation and directed him to construct a penthouse on the roof of the newly renovated Post-Dispatch Building at Polk and Dowling to serve as a broadcast studio. On Will's recommendation, Sterling hired G. E. Zimmerman, who had set up KFDM in Beaumont, to serve as the station's general manager. Alfred Daniel was appointed head announcer and program director. Once the US Commerce Department approved Sterling's request to use KPRC ("Kotton Port Rail Center") as his new station's identification call letters, everything was in place for the first broadcast.[5]

On May 9, 1925, Will Hobby ran a front-page story in the *Post-Dispatch* announcing that KPRC would go on the air at 8:00 p.m. that evening with entertainment provided by three bands, including the forty-five-piece Humble Oil Company orchestra. Alfred Daniel opened that first broadcast with the words "Hello, folks, everywhere." He then introduced Will Hobby, who served as the broadcast's master of ceremonies. In his opening statement, Will declared that the *Post-Dispatch* would use KPRC to promote "good will" and provide the "widest circulation of the truth" as well as "give pleasure to and benefit the people." Other guests on the first broadcast included Houston mayor Oscar Holcombe and *Post-Dispatch* columnist Judd Mortimer Lewis, who would host a regularly scheduled children's program on the station.

Because few Houstonians owned radios, Sterling, Dudley, and Hobby distributed simple crystal sets with earphones at no charge to new subscribers of the *Post-Dispatch*. The crystal sets were wired to receive only one radio station: KPRC. The city's merchants complained about the competition from the free crystal sets, but they soon realized that the *Post-Dispatch*'s giveaway efforts increased their sales of regular radios. The newspaper eventually distributed more than twelve thousand sets. "Thus, we killed two birds with one stone," Sterling recalled. "We simultaneously built a listening audience and the newspaper's circulation." The *Post-Dispatch*'s circulation grew from approximately 40,000 when the station went on the air to 54,700 in 1926, a gain of approximately 37 percent. Sterling later claimed that by the end of 1925 the newspaper's advertising space had increased more than any other newspaper in the country during that same period. Whether Sterling's claim was accurate or not, profits did climb. To celebrate, Sterling treated the newspaper staff to dinner at the San Jacinto Inn, a popular restaurant famed for its seafood and Southern-style fried chicken, located next to the San Jacinto Battlefield.[6]

KPRC soon became an important vehicle of news and sports reporting as well as a popular source of entertainment. In 1926 Sterling relocated the broadcast studios to his new Post-Dispatch Building at the southeast corner of Texas Avenue and Fannin Street in downtown Houston. The station's transmitter would be moved to a tower near the town of Sugar Land in Fort Bend County in 1929. The station garnered major attention and additional listeners as a result of broadcasting the Tunney-Dempsey world championship heavyweight boxing rematch in September 1927 over loudspeakers to twelve to fifteen thousand people assembled at the outdoor theater in Houston's Hermann Park. But the development that gave KPRC its biggest boost in listeners occurred in

*KPRC Radio tower house, Sugar Land, Texas, 1929.*

January 1928, when the station became an affiliate of the newly established National Broadcasting Company (NBC), which sent a wider range of broadcast content over the wires to the KPRC transmitter. Soon, few homes in Houston were without a radio, and with no effective competition, KPRC began to turn a nice profit. Sterling later admitted that he had initially seen radio as "a plaything," but less than ten years after it went on the air, KPRC was earning more money than the *Post-Dispatch*. The station also became an important way to promote political campaigns. When Sterling later ran for governor, Will persuaded him to make aggressive use of the new communication medium to promote his candidacy. In his memoir, Sterling noted, "[I] had never dreamed that [radio] would play an important role in my political career. I would be the first Texan to go on the air in a political race, and the first to take a 'sound truck' along on a campaign tour to amplify my speeches."[7]

KPRC eventually gave the *Post-Dispatch* such an advantage over Houston's two other daily newspapers that in 1937 wealthy real estate developer and banker Jesse Holman Jones, who by then had purchased the *Houston Chronicle*, acquired a broadcasting station of his own, which had the call letters KTRH ("Kum to the Rice Hotel"—which Jones also owned). Ironically, when Sterling spent $25,000 to buy the original equipment for KPRC, Jesse Jones told him he had "gone crazy" to spend that much money for a radio station.[8]

Almost as soon as Miriam Ferguson was inaugurated governor in January 1925, the *Houston Post-Dispatch* and the *Fort Worth Star-Telegram* became the leading newspaper critics of the Ferguson administration, which they correctly perceived as a continuation of Jim Ferguson's aborted second term. With Sterling's blessing, Will Hobby and George Bailey wrote editorials condemning the Fergusons at every opportunity, which increased with each passing month of Miriam Ferguson's administration. The new governor quickly became immersed in one controversy after another, including accusations that her husband was selling pardons and was involved in contract kickbacks and bid rigging in the State Highway Commission. Although the accusations against the Fergusons were never proven, the *Post-Dispatch* reacted to every allegation of wrongdoing with a scathing editorial or a prominent news story. Amon Carter's *Star-Telegram* followed suit with equally harsh commentary. In response, the Fergusons, who were well aware that both Hobby and Carter continued to enjoy alcoholic beverages in their private lives, took out ads in newspapers offering a $500 reward to anyone who could provide information to the police that would lead to the arrest and conviction of the two "millionaire" newspaper publishers (unnamed) who were known to be frequent violators of the prohibition laws. It was clearly understood that the Fergusons were targeting Will Hobby and Amon Carter, although they had overestimated Hobby's net worth. Apparently no one claimed the reward.[9]

Despite more than a year of turmoil, including threats by several members of the legislature to initiate impeachment proceedings against her, Miriam Ferguson announced on February 27, 1926, that she would run for reelection. This news fired up Will Hobby and Ross Sterling, who soon increased their editorial attacks on the Fergusons. Rienzi Johnston's death the day after Ferguson made her announcement only intensified Will's determination to do everything he could to help defeat her. Sterling later recalled that Will eagerly led the *Post-Dispatch*'s "offensive" against the Fergusons, which "was by no means an unpleasant job for Governor Hobby to battle his old political enemy, Jim Ferguson." Sterling added that Hobby's zeal was partially in tribute to "his old journalistic mentor, R. M. Johnston." When Attorney General Dan Moody, who had first attracted public attention as an anti-Klan crusading district attorney, announced his candidacy for governor on March 6, Sterling later recalled that he "threw the full force of the *Post-Dispatch* behind Moody's candidacy for governor, along with my all-out personal and financial support. I told the boys running the paper not to spare the horses or the newsprint. They carried out my wishes with a vengeance." Former attorney general Lynch Davidson of Houston also announced his candidacy for governor, but Will Hobby and Ross Sterling preferred Dan Moody, which angered Davidson. "The *Post-Dispatch* had championed his cause in the 1924 race," Sterling noted later, "but I now felt that Davidson had had his chance and it was Moody's turn."[10]

During the primary campaign for governor, which lasted from March until July 1926, Will worked closely with columnist George Bailey and editorial writer Paul Yates to fill the pages of the *Post-Dispatch* with attacks on the Fergusons. "Nearly every day," Sterling recalled, "the *Post-Dispatch* greeted the dawn with a militant editorial blasting 'Fergusonism.'" Will gleefully printed anti-Ferguson letters from the newspaper's readers. Unlimited space was devoted to news reports and articles about the campaign—all of them negative about Governor Ferguson and positive about Moody. The *Post-Dispatch*'s editorial cartoonist, Bert Blessington, drew unflattering caricatures of both of the Fergusons, while Moody was always depicted in heroic fashion. As Sterling noted in his memoir, it seemed that the Fergusons were always drawn with horns and Moody with a halo. Hobby and Sterling also made effective use of their new radio station, KPRC, which broadcast the speeches of several anti-Ferguson and pro-Moody supporters.

Moody's campaign appearances were given front-page, highly laudatory coverage; the Fergusons' speeches were ignored. Will Hobby assigned *Post-Dispatch* political reporter Boyd Gatewood to cover all of Moody's campaign appearances. Gatewood not only understood that all of his news stories would have to be pro-Moody, but, according to Sterling, the reporter also served as Moody's "unofficial press agent and publicity counselor, helping him plan his strategy and his speeches." One typical Gatewood story, which was printed on the front page of the *Post-Dispatch*, announced, "Moody Applauded by Thousands at Mass Meeting." Hobby and Sterling even made a few campaign appearances with Moody, including a major event in Will's old home territory, Polk County, which attracted a huge audience. The ever-combative Jim Ferguson fought back, frequently including virulent diatribes in his speeches against Hobby and Sterling and the *Post-Dispatch*, which he called the "Pest-Disgrace."[11]

Hobby's old political allies Oscar Colquitt, Jake Wolters, Tom Love, Will Hogg, and other progressive Democrats, as well as the publishers of most of the major urban news-papers in the state, including the *Houston Chronicle*, the *Fort Worth Star-Telegram*, the *Dallas Morning News*, and of course Will's own *Beaumont Enterprise-Journal*, also worked hard to defeat Miriam Ferguson. When one of the bitterest political campaigns in Texas history finally ended on Election Day, July 24, Dan Moody led Miriam Ferguson by more than 125,000 votes, missing a majority by only 1,771 votes and forcing him to face Ferguson in a runoff. Lynch Davidson placed a poor third. After a controversial runoff campaign in which the *Post-Dispatch* continued its attacks on the Fergusons, thirty-three-year-old Dan Moody defeated Miriam Ferguson by more than 200,000 votes.[12]

Hobby and Sterling attended Dan Moody's inauguration on January 18, 1927, where Hobby joined former governors Joseph Sayers, Oscar Colquitt, Pat Neff, and Jim Ferguson on the inaugural platform. Will later recalled that the Fergusons were understandably tense and unhappy, making the pre-ceremony gathering awkward for everyone. Three weeks after Moody's inauguration, he appointed Ross Sterling chairman of the scandal-ridden Texas State Highway Commission. Sterling found such a mess in the highway department that he decided to work full-time in Austin to sort it all out. He told Will that it could take him most of two years to clean up the department. In the meantime, the *Post-Dispatch* and KPRC Radio were exclusively Will's to run. He was more than prepared for the opportunity. His assumption of sole administrative control over his and Sterling's media holdings would unexpectedly continue until the end of Will's life nearly forty years later.[13]

With Ross Sterling away and the war against the Fergusons over for at least two more years, Will busily occupied his time with the rapidly growing KPRC and an increasingly successful *Post-Dispatch*. With Jim Mapes managing the *Beaumont Enterprise-Journal*, Will had little if any involvement in its affairs. The spring, summer, and early fall of 1927 passed calmly and uneventfully. He and Willie moved into the newly opened Plaza Hotel Apartments on Montrose Boulevard. Willie, who was described by a news report at the time as "an astute politician in her own right," continued her active involvement in a wide variety of civic and social affairs in Houston, particularly in the League of Women Voters. With no political campaigns or other journalistic crusades to lead, the Hobbys were able to take time off for pleasure. When Ross Sterling took a break that summer from his work at the Highway Commission, Will and Willie accompanied Ross and his wife, Maud, on a sightseeing and shopping expedition to Manhattan. They also traveled to Mineral Wells for a few days of soaking in hot mineral water at their favorite bathhouse.[14]

A sad event in late fall of 1927 brought an end to what had been a happy and satisfying year for the Hobbys. On November 22, Will received the shocking news that his brother Edwin had died suddenly in Kerrville at the age of forty-four. With Edwin's passing, Will lost his closest sibling, friend, and trusted counselor. Will had sought Edwin's advice in nearly every significant decision that Will had made as an adult. It was Edwin to whom Will turned when he was trying to decide if he should make the run for lieutenant governor. Edwin had been a trusted political advisor and advocate, and he had partnered with Will in several business deals. Will grieved deeply for his brother. Many years later, he admitted to James Clark that the shock of his brother's unexpected death plunged him into depression. Will coped with his grief by immersing himself "into the day-by-day routine of newspaper making."[15]

As the election year of 1928 approached, Will was widely discussed in the state's newspapers as a likely candidate for the US Senate against the unpopular incumbent, Earle Mayfield. Will firmly rejected these pleas to enter the race. He had his dream job, which was running the *Houston Post-Dispatch* and KPRC Radio. He had no ambition to serve again in any elected position, especially in the US Senate, and he was still mourning his brother's recent death. Will's deep interest in politics had not dissipated, however. As a newspaper publisher and former governor, he relished his role as an influential political figure and fixer, as well as his reputation as a wise political sage, even though he was not yet fifty years old. He would play this political role for the rest of his life. Accordingly, Will was pleased to be involved in the biggest political event in Houston's history up to that time: the 1928 Democratic National Convention.[16]

In January 1928, Jesse Jones made the winning bid for Houston to host the Democratic National Convention in June. Jones secured his bid with a $200,000 check (approximately $2.5 million in 2020). This would be the first national political convention held in the South since before the Civil War and the first ever in Texas. Jones then teamed with the City of Houston to construct a new all-wood convention hall, longer than three football fields and with six acres of floor space, making it 33 percent larger than Manhattan's Madison Square Garden. The hall was large enough to host the thousands of delegates, party officials, members of the press, and spectators who were expected to attend. The entire project was completed in only four months.[17]

New York governor Al Smith, a Catholic who was a vocal critic of prohibition, was the leading contender for the presidential nomination. Smith's religion, his antiprohibition stance, and his status as a "Yankee," alarmed many Texas Democrats, especially the strong prohibitionists, who soon expressed their opposition to his nomination. Some threatened to walk out of the convention unless it sent a rigidly prohibitionist, anti-Smith delegation to the national convention. Initially Governor Moody aligned with the anti-Smith forces, declaring that he would fight against the nomination of any candidate who advocated repeal of the Eighteenth Amendment. Concerned about this deep division among Texas Democrats and its potential to hurt the party's chances in November's general election, Will Hobby and Martin McNulty Crane cobbled together a compromise position to unify the party and avoid a disastrous factional dispute at the party's state convention to be held in Beaumont in May. After some squabbling with die-hard prohibitionists, Will succeeded in getting Smith's opponents to agree to a plan in which the Texas delegation would be bound to vote for Jesse Jones as Texas's favorite-son candidate for the presidential nomination. This would make it possible for Texas to send an anti-Smith delegation to Houston without openly attacking Smith. After the first ballot, individual delegates would be free to vote for Governor Smith, Jesse Jones, or any other nominated candidate. Once again, Will Hobby had played a critical role in maintaining unity in the Texas Democratic Party and preserving party loyalty. It was a role he would abandon in the future.[18]

Early in April, Will joined with Ross Sterling, wealthy cotton trader Will Clayton, and Will Hogg to serve on Houston's Executive, General Finance, and Arrangements Committees for the national convention, which held meetings in the Houston Club and worked until shortly before the convention opened in late June. Will also took charge of the operation to distribute convention tickets and passes. Willie Hobby served on committees that helped make arrangements for the twenty-five thousand plus visitors expected to come to Houston from every section of the country. Because there was a shortage of hotel rooms in the city, Willie's committee recruited Houstonians to provide rooms in their homes to accommodate delegates. Will later told James Clark that although he had met and become acquainted with Jesse Jones not long after the Hobbys moved back to Houston six years earlier, working with Jones to prepare for the national convention was their first close association. "Out of it," Clark noted, "came a lasting friendship built on mutual regard and appreciation." Will's friendship with Jones, a six-foot-three-inch-tall, multimillionaire developer, banker, and national Democratic Party leader would play a major role in Will's future.[19]

The newly constructed Sam Houston Hall was dedicated on Sunday, June 23, with speeches by Mayor Oscar Holcombe and Jesse Jones and brief remarks by Edith Wilson, Woodrow Wilson's widow, who was close friends with Jesse Jones and his wife, Mary Gibbs Jones. Will and Willie Hobby were among the seventeen thousand people filling the hall, most of them Houstonians. News about the dedication ceremony filled the front page of the *Post-Dispatch*, which also featured a large portrait of Mary Jones, who was identified as the "Democratic Hostess."

Will and Willie accompanied Ross and Maud Sterling to attend the opening ceremonies for the national convention on Tuesday, June 26. The convention was the biggest political event in Texas and possibly the entire South in the 1920s. Will had all of the *Houston Post-Dispatch* reporters on duty that night and throughout the four days the convention was in session, reporting on speeches and disputes among the state delegations and conducting interviews with prominent visitors, such as famed movie and radio star Will Rogers. Bernard Baruch was among the celebrated visitors, which gave Will Hobby an opportunity to reconnect with the Wall Street financier. Will persuaded Baruch to grant an interview to one of his reporters. KPRC Radio also provided full-time coverage of the convention.[20]

The organizational meeting of the Texas delegation at the Lamar Hotel was among the events Will's reporters covered in detail. The delegation voted to make Governor Moody its chairman and to confirm the deal that Will Hobby had brokered that required the delegation to cast all of its forty votes for Jesse Jones for president. This decision was not pro forma, however. For several weeks, Will Hogg had led an intense effort to oppose voting for Jones, whom he accused of having a long record of shady and unethical business

*Delegates celebrate on the floor at the Democratic National Convention in Houston, June 1928.*

practices. Hogg had earlier quit the executive planning committee in protest of what he called Jones's "delusions of grandeur as a candidate for the presidency." His campaign against Jones resulted in a few of the Texas delegates voting against the agreement, which nevertheless passed.[21]

On Wednesday, June 27, Franklin D. Roosevelt, the Democratic candidate for governor of New York, gave the principal speech nominating Al Smith for president. The following night, Smith won the nomination on the first ballot, with Texas casting its forty votes for its favorite-son candidate, Jesse Jones. After Smith's victory, the Texas delegation stubbornly refused to change their votes to make his nomination unanimous. The next day the Democratic National Committee, eager to balance the ticket with a Southerner, offered Jones the vice presidential nomination, but he declined the offer. The nomination went instead to Arkansas senator Joe T. Robinson. The convention adjourned on June 29 on a note of disharmony. In the telegram Al Smith sent to the convention accepting his nomination, he declared his opposition to prohibition and his intention to make significant changes in the laws enforcing the Eighteenth Amendment. Although no fan of prohibition, Will criticized Smith's statement as an unnecessary provocation certain to stir up strong opposition in Texas and the rest of the South. To Will, it was a clear signal that the Democratic presidential ticket faced a difficult campaign against Republican candidate Herbert Hoover.[22]

During September and October 1928, Will and Willie worked almost full-time for the Smith-Robinson ticket, even traveling to the northeastern states to make appearances in support of the campaign. Will attended the Texas Democratic Party's state convention in September, where he joined with Jesse Jones to stop a move to withdraw support for Al Smith for president and to endorse Herbert Hoover. Despite the effort of Hobby, Jones, and Moody to maintain unity, a large group of disgruntled Democrats formed an organization to campaign for Hoover, earning for themselves the name "Hoovercrats." At the state level, Will supported Governor Dan Moody's bid for a second term against the little-known Fort Worth attorney L. J. Wardlaw, a candidate James Ferguson had persuaded to run. The US Senate race featured the controversial incumbent candidate Earle Mayfield, who was also supported by James Ferguson. Mayfield attracted several opponents, including Judge Thomas Blanton, former suffrage leader Minnie Fisher Cunningham, and Will's favored candidate, Congressman Thomas Connally. In one of the races for the state Senate, Will was confronted with a difficult situation after publicly declaring his support in an editorial in the *Post-Dispatch* for Houston attorney Walter Woodul, his former assistant in the adjutant general's office. Will was unhappily surprised when John Henry Kirby announced that he was also entering that same Senate race. Kirby's declaration forced Will to print an editorial in the *Post-Dispatch* explaining that despite his great admiration and respect for Kirby, it would not be honorable for him to retract his support for Woodul. He pledged, however, that the *Post-Dispatch* would make no statements critical of Kirby during the campaign. On Election Day Woodul narrowly missed winning a majority of the vote, which forced him into a runoff battle with Kirby. Will was rescued from this awkward situation, however, when Kirby decided that he could not win and withdrew from the race.[23]

Will's candidates for governor and US senator both won their primary battles, although Connally had to defeat Mayfield in a runoff election. Dan Moody won his nomination easily in the first primary. Both men proceeded to victory against token candidates in the general election in November, while Herbert Hoover won the presidency in a landslide over Al Smith, much to Will's disappointment if not surprise. Hoover was the first Republican ever to win the state's electoral votes. He even carried Smith's home state, New York.[24]

Only one month after Dan Moody's reelection as governor, Will began to test the level of public interest in the possibility that Ross Sterling might run in the 1930 Democratic primary to be Moody's successor. Newspapers statewide were praising Sterling for cleaning up the mess in the Texas Highway Department. His reputation as one of the founders of the hugely profitable Humble Oil Company as well as his successful merger of the *Houston Post* and the *Houston Dispatch* and his establishment of KPRC Radio were much admired by the state's business community. The Hobbys and the Sterlings traveled to Beaumont in early December to help open the South Texas State Fair. Both Will and Ross were asked to give speeches at the opening ceremony, which was being covered by a large contingent of news reporters. Will spoke first, and then he introduced Ross Sterling by declaring that the audience should note that they were hearing from "one governor in retrospect and another in prospect." The press described Will's statement as having the effect of dropping a bombshell on the audience, which erupted in cheers and prolonged applause. It was the first time a serious public remark had been made that Ross Sterling might be a possible candidate for governor. The wire services spread the news throughout the state, and the response was overwhelmingly positive. The 1930 Democratic primary was still more than eighteen months away and Sterling had not yet decided to run for governor, but Will was working hard to persuade him.[25]

The Hobbys celebrated the end of 1928 in Houston, enjoying a host of parties and dinners, including a Christmas event for the staff at the *Post-Dispatch* and a reception and New Year's feast at Ross and Maude Sterling's mansion. Sterling had temporarily returned to Houston from his work with the Texas Highway Commission in Austin to take part in the holiday observances. Will took advantage of Sterling's presence to discuss the coming year's goals for the newspaper and KPRC Radio. The economy was continuing to boom, which promised another profitable year for both enterprises. Will was also looking forward to his work as an investor and a member of the board of the Braeswood Development Corporation, which had recently been organized by Houston banker George Howard. The Braeswood Corporation was developing a deed-restricted housing addition on 456 acres located barely outside the Houston city limits at the intersection of two major roads, Main and Bellaire, about a mile south of Rice University. Will was attracted to the development because of John Henry Kirby, who had sold the land to the corporation and then became one of the investors. George Howard planned Braeswood as a garden suburb of expensive country houses designed in the English manorial style on large lots facing curvilinear streets lined with live oak trees. Will had decided to purchase the first lot in the development with the intention of building a new home for him and Willie.[26]

The bright promises Will expected to be fulfilled in the coming months collapsed tragically two weeks into the new year. On January 13, the Hobbys were spending a quiet Sunday afternoon at their home at 506 Lovett Boulevard in the Montrose neighborhood when Willie complained to her husband that she felt ill and that she was going to lie down on the bed until she felt better. She died quietly in her sleep at 1:00 a.m. on January 14, the victim of a massive stroke. Willie's death at the age of fifty-one shocked her many friends in Houston and around the state. She had seemed in perfect health and in good

*Willie Cooper Hobby's portrait as First Lady of Texas, ca. 1918.*

spirits and had continued to be busily involved in club work and the League of Women Voters until the day before she became ill.[27]

As the news about Willie's death quickly spread to Austin, Governor Dan Moody ordered the flag over the state capitol lowered to half-mast. Both houses of the newly convened regular session of the Forty-First Legislature passed memorial resolutions and then adjourned in her memory. There was widespread sadness over the sudden passing of such a highly respected and well-liked former First Lady of Texas. A number of newspapers printed editorials lamenting Willie's death. The *Brownwood Bulletin* observed that it was "said by intimate friends that much of the success of the Hobby administration—and it was successful in many respects—was due directly to the wisdom and political experience of Mrs. Hobby." The *Houston Chronicle* noted, "Her friends called her 'Miss Willie.' She was known for her great sense of humor, charm, and warmth."[28]

Miss Willie's funeral on January 15 was held in the home she had shared with Will. Flowers filled every room in the house. Reverend A. Frank Smith, a locally prominent Methodist minister, presided as Willie was gently "laid in earth" at Houston's historic Glenwood Cemetery. Her grave was buried under a mountain of flowers. In the days immediately following Willie's death, Will received a large number of telegrams, letters, and cards from family, friends, politicians, and business associates eulogizing Willie and expressing their sorrow at her death. Willie's longtime maid Savannah Jackson, who had been married in the Governor's Mansion and was now living with her husband in Austin, wrote to Will: "Mrs. Hobby was my best friend. She understood my problems and helped me both with sympathy and money. We had many happy times together." John Henry Kirby's message was typical of their longtime friends: "I mingle my tears with yours and with those of her sisters and her brother who loved her no less than I." Will carefully culled and edited these and other quotes and printed them in a small tribute booklet to Willie that he had privately published and distributed to friends and family. In the preface Will wrote, "These expressions are put in printed form so I may pass them on to those I believe will read and understand. . . . As precious to me as their words are I feel they knew the story of her worth and virtues only in part while it was given to me to know it all."[29]

A couple of years after Willie's death, Will donated to the Texas Governor's Mansion a sterling-silver, footed flower bowl of ornate design that he had purchased in New York as a gift for his wife. It had been one of her favorite things. Will had the bowl engraved, "In memory of my beloved wife, Willie Cooper Hobby, whose presence graced the Governor's Mansion, 1917 to 1921. W. P. Hobby."[30]

# Tributes

*in memory of*

## WILLIE COOPER HOBBY

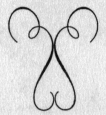

*Title page of tribute book to "Miss Willie," 1929.*

——

# BOOK TWO

# WILL AND OVETA

# CHAPTER 17

# MISS OVETA CULP

It was while Will was shifting through the large stack of condolence messages he was organizing for Willie's tribute book that he noticed Miss Oveta Culp's telegram with its brief message of sympathy. Will and Willie had befriended the young Miss Culp after she moved to Houston in 1926 and took a job as a clerk at the *Post-Dispatch*. In future years, Will and Oveta would give different accounts of how and when they met, but by the end of 1929 they would be romantically involved.[1]

Will and Oveta later claimed that they had first met soon after Oveta began work at the *Houston Post-Dispatch* during the spring of 1926, but it is clear that Will had known of Oveta as far back as 1919, while he was governor. Will and Oveta also gave the impression that their romance developed sometime in the spring of 1930, more than a year after Willie's death, but the evidence documents that a love affair existed by November 1929. It can be assumed that the contradictory stories Will and Oveta gave over the years about when their romantic relationship began stemmed from their concern that the public might not approve of their starting a love affair soon after Willie's passing, a concern more likely to have been Oveta's, who was more concerned about proper appearances than Will. In a Southern society influenced by Victorian mores, widows were generally expected to formally grieve for a couple of years before embarking on another romantic relationship. Although Oveta was not a widow, she would not have wanted to foster the idea she had somehow violated any code of proper behavior. Men, however, were not burdened by that stricture. Their difference in age—Will was fifty and Oveta was twenty-four—might also have encouraged them to push the date of the beginning of their relationship forward a year. More important than how they met and when their romance began, however, is who this beautiful and precocious young woman was, a woman who so soon after Willie's death would become Will Hobby's wife, the mother of his children, his closest friend, and eventually his famed professional partner who would leave her own mark on the history of the United States.[2]

Oveta Hoover Culp was born in the Central Texas town of Killeen on January 19, 1905. That January day is also Confederate general Robert E. Lee's birthday, which in that era was a date celebrated throughout Texas with parades and special events. The day before Oveta's birth, the Texas Daughters of the Confederacy held a celebration in the chamber of the Texas Senate in honor of General Lee and his role in the "Lost Cause." Lee's birthday would later become an official state holiday. In an interesting coincidence—at least, it's assumed to be a coincidence—Oveta would give birth to her first child on January 19, 1932, and to her second on January 19, 1937. The fact that Oveta and her children were all born on the same day and month and that it was also Robert E. Lee's birthday became something of an interesting bit of family trivia.[3]

Oveta's father, Isaac "Ike" W. Culp, was thirty-four years old when she was born, and her mother, Emma Elizabeth Hoover Culp, was twenty-three. Oveta was their second child; five more children would follow. According to family tradition, Emma Culp named Oveta for a fictional Cherokee Indian who was a character in a popular romance novel. "Oveta" was allegedly the Cherokee word for "forget," but Cherokee language sources do not support that. Another version is that Ike and Emma chose "Oveta" because it rhymed with Juanita, the name of her older sister, who was born in 1902. It might be that both stories are true. What we do know for certain is that Oveta's name was misspelled and mispronounced throughout her life.[4]

The Culp family appears to have originated in Germany, where their name was Kolb. Sometime in the seventeenth century, a Kolb family or families migrated to Britain, where they changed their surname to Culp. Some of their descendants eventually migrated to England's colonies in America. Oveta's great-grandfather, Josiah Culp, was born in Tennessee in 1819. When he was a teenager, Josiah migrated to Texas and served as a soldier in the Texas Army of rebellion against Mexico. The Republic of Texas granted him 640 acres of land for his service. In 1841 Josiah married Illinois native Rachel Eaton in a village on the Neches River. Two years later, Josiah and Rachel made their way to Central Texas and settled on Josiah's land grant. One of Josiah and Rachel's six sons, John Robinson Culp, Oveta's grandfather, was born in Limestone County, Texas, on September 1, 1846. In August 1869 he married eighteen-year-old Kentucky native Nancy Ann Miller, Oveta's paternal grandmother. John and Nancy Culp made their home on a farm in Coryell County, where they grew cotton on land that is now part of the sprawling Fort Hood army base. The Culps eventually had seven children, six boys and one girl. One of their sons, whom they named Isaac, was born on September 22, 1870. He was Oveta's father.[5]

Ike Culp grew up on his family's cotton farm near his grandparents' residence. His grandfather, Josiah, died in 1879, and his mother, Nancy, died in 1887, when Ike was seventeen. After Ike finished his secondary schooling in Coryell County, he studied law at the University of Texas for one year before returning home to continue legal studies under the guidance of a local attorney. In 1898, at the age of twenty-eight, Ike was elected to the Texas House of Representatives, where he served on the Judiciary, State Affairs, and Public Building and Grounds Committees. He also served on the special committee that investigated the mismanagement of the state reformatory in Gatesville. After serving one term in the legislature, Ike passed the bar exam in 1900 and moved to Killeen, Texas, to practice law and to buy and sell real estate. It was in Killeen that he met and courted twenty-year-old Emma Hoover, a member of a prominent Bell County family. They married on August 21, 1901.[6]

Emma Hoover's father, Andrew Jackson Hoover, was a native of Tennessee and a Civil War veteran who had served in the Confederate Army's Tenth Tennessee Cavalry. Andrew's unit fought in Georgia, where he was captured at Peach Tree Creek near Atlanta in July 1864. After spending six months in a Union prisoner of war camp in Ohio, he was sent to Richmond in a prisoner exchange. A year after the end of the war, Andrew migrated to Texas through the port of Indianola, eventually settling in Williamson County, where he married native Texan Cordelia Atkinson, Oveta's maternal grandmother. Andrew and Cordelia Hoover moved to Killeen in 1889, where they eventually had five children, including Emma, Oveta's mother, who was born on August 4, 1881. Emma grew up in an affluent family. Her father had acquired more than 2,300 acres south of Killeen and had a stable of horses, a flock of sheep, and large herds of cattle. He eventually became vice president of First National Bank of Killeen and a stockholder in the Killeen Independent Telephone Company.[7]

Andrew Hoover's son-in-law, Ike Culp, also found success in Killeen. His law practice, which he formed with J. H. Evetts, flourished, and his forays into other business enterprises, which included drugstores in Killeen and Wolfe City, proved lucrative. Ike also acquired large tracts of land in West Texas and in the Texas Panhandle. A published profile of Ike in 1911 stated he had "gained recognition as an able and versatile trial lawyer" and, like his father-in-law, Andrew Jackson Hoover, had become one of Bell County's most prominent businessmen. The article declared that Ike was a "man of marked executive ability" and "a public-spirited citizen." That judgment was probably based, at least partially, on Ike's record as Killeen's city attorney for several years and as Killeen's mayor for one term. Ike and Emma were characterized as "popular factors in connection with the best social activities in Killeen." The Culps' home, which was recognized as "a center of gracious refinement and hospitality," was described as an attractive frame house located on a quiet street shaded by hackberry trees. The Culp home was also always full of kids. Ike and Emma had six children who survived childhood: Juanita, Oveta, Ike Jr., Jackson Robinson, Texas Evetts, and Lynn. A seventh child named John Harris died at the age of two. Ike named his third son, Texas Evetts, after his law partner, J. H. Evetts.[8]

Many years after Ike's death, when his daughter Oveta was a nationally known figure, *Time* magazine published a biographical article about her. The editors dispatched a reporter to Killeen to talk to elderly residents who had known her father. They told *Time*'s reporter that Ike Culp was "a rawboned, fiery-tempered lawyer, a Baptist, a Prohibitionist, a politician and a lover of horses." It was claimed that Ike always carried a small double-barreled derringer for his protection because Killeen was a rough, frontier-like place where it was not uncommon for disputes to be settled violently. Ike also bought a matching derringer as a gift for J. H. Evetts, who apparently never carried it.

Texas Culp, who was one of *Time* magazine's sources for its story about his sister Oveta, recalled an incident when a man attempted to stab J. H. Evetts in the back, but Evetts was able to fight him off. The attacker had sought revenge because Evetts had successfully defended a young man who in an act of self-defense had killed the owner of one of Killeen's pool halls. Evetts's attacker was an associate of the pool hall's owner. The town's billiard parlors had a well-deserved reputation for being centers of vice and brawling. After the attack on his law partner, Ike Culp and other town leaders ordered one of the pool hall owners to close his business and leave town, but the owner refused. Texas Culp told *Time* that "a few nights later someone planted a charge of dynamite in the pool hall after closing hours and people were picking up cue balls all over that side of town." In another incident, one of Killeen's residents who apparently held a grievance against Ike and Evetts went to their law office, which was located on the second floor of the building, and began to curse them in a loud voice. Evetts calmly walked up to the angry man and threw him down the stairs.[9]

The old-timers who talked to *Time* magazine believed Ike Culp favored Oveta above his other children, and they recalled that much of his attention was focused on shaping and directing her development. There was a consensus that Ike was the person who had the greatest influence on Oveta as a young girl and that despite his strongly held religious beliefs that stressed that women were to be submissive to men, Ike taught Oveta she was the equal of any man. Oveta later recalled that her father taught her she "could turn the world around just as well as any of my brothers."[10]

Ike's advice helped to build in Oveta a strong degree of determined self-confidence, a personal trait she exuded throughout her life. Ike's influence could be discerned in numerous characteristics Oveta exhibited as an adult. For example, she shared her father's love of horses. Caring for horses and riding were among her favorite pastimes both as a child and as an adult. In her youth, Oveta enjoyed the summer evenings when she would go to her family's corral and watch Ike work and control his horses. Ike would crack a whip and make the horses strut around him in a circle. Based on Oveta's reputation for her obsession with order and control when she was an adult, a reporter for *Time*, engaging in a bit of pop psychology, concluded that Ike's demonstration of the control he had over his horses was a "lesson not lost on Oveta."[11]

Oveta was raised in a pious family. Ike was an ordained Baptist minister who served for a time during the early 1900s as pastor of Killeen's Baptist Church of Christ, which was built the year of Oveta's birth. A photograph still exists of Ike waist-deep in the Lampasas River, holding the back of the neck of a church member as he readies to dunk him underneath the water to baptize him in front of the congregation standing on the riverbank. The baptism took place in front of his church, which was located next to a cemetery on a four-acre lot on the edge of the river. Over the years Ike held several tent

revivals outside the church. Oveta's mother, Emma, was also a devout Baptist and, like her husband, firmly believed in the prophecies of the book of Revelations. When Oveta was growing up, she often heard her father declare that according to the Bible the earth was fated to be destroyed by fire. When Halley's Comet made its spectacular reappearance in 1910, the newspapers were filled with stories that the earth would pass through the comet's tail. One astronomer even warned that the comet could destroy all life on earth. Despite his belief that the end of the world was foreordained and inevitable, Ike wasn't certain Halley's Comet was the way the prophecy was to be fulfilled. To be safe, on the day the earth was to pass through the comet tail, Ike frantically raced around Killeen in his horse-pulled wagon buying up all the ice in town. Neighbors soon noticed that Ike had stacked the ice in mounds around his house in case the comet was not the prophesized "end of days" firestorm but merely a temporary threat to his family. As it turned out, there was no fire, only a beautiful display of "shooting stars" that night.[12]

Living in such an environment, it's not surprising that Oveta and her siblings were caught up in their family's religious obsessions as children. Oveta later recalled that as a child she wanted to grow up to be a Christian missionary to China, where the natives needed to be brought to Jesus. Although she never followed that path, her brother Texas Evetts did become a prominent evangelical preacher. But as a child, Oveta was enthralled by her charismatic father's religious orations, which inspired her to write and deliver her own youthful sermons. Some of her childhood friends later recalled that Oveta often "played preacher" for the neighborhood kids, giving "spellbinding" sermons and conducting church services in a neighbor's backyard. When Oveta was eight years old, she was baptized, and she later claimed she had read the Bible three times by the age of thirteen.[13]

One of the copies of the Bible Oveta read might have been the copy she won in a contest in school when she was in the sixth grade. Early in the school year, the teacher told Oveta and her classmates that at the end of the semester she would reward the class's best speller with a beautifully printed Bible with their name inscribed in it. Years later, *Time* reported the story this way: "A self-assured little girl came forward from her desk and in a firm, quiet voice told the teacher she might as well go right ahead and inscribe the Bible with her name. Pig-tailed Oveta Culp wasn't being brash or smart-alecky; she knew she was the best speller, and was merely stating what she regarded as inevitable. At term's end, Oveta won the Bible."[14]

A favorite story of Oveta's was one from her childhood that illustrated how literally and seriously she took her parents' religious instruction. When she was six years old, Oveta was attending Sunday school one morning at Killeen's Missionary Baptist Church when a member of the Woman's Christian Temperance Union visited her class and asked every child to sign a pledge to never drink alcohol. After signing the pledge each child was given the union's white ribbon to pin to his or her clothes. Little Oveta, however, caused a stir when she adamantly refused to sign it. Church members quickly relayed the news of Oveta's stubborn refusal to her "Grandmere" Cordelia Hoover, with whom Oveta was living at the time. As Oveta walked up on the porch of her grandmother's house, the passionately prohibitionist Cordelia, who was known as "Delia" to friends and family, stood behind the screened door waiting for her granddaughter with a switch in hand.

Marguerite Johnston, a staff writer at the *Houston Post* who was close to Oveta, later retold the story. "Punishment was swift," Johnston said. "Oveta took her switching in icy indignation. For two days she spoke only when spoken to. Finally Grandmere broke down and prepared to have it out with this small, unrepentant sinner." She asked Oveta if she hadn't expected to be punished for refusing to sign the pledge. Oveta replied that she had. Delia asked her grandchild why she wasn't speaking to her if she knew that her behavior had been unacceptable. "Because you didn't ask me why I refused to sign,"

Oveta replied. "I did not know what that word temperance meant and I couldn't promise something I wasn't sure I could do." Johnston observed that Oveta's grandmother "had the wisdom to apologize."[15]

The "official" reason that Oveta was living with her "Grandmere" at this time was because of a promise she had supposedly made to her late grandfather, Andrew Jackson Hoover. Shortly before his death, Andrew, who was concerned that his widow would be lonely after his passing, had asked Oveta, who was five years old, to live with Delia. Ike and Emma agreed to Andrew's request. While that explanation was the one Oveta gave to reporters later in her life, on at least one occasion she admitted to a close friend that there was another reason she moved into her grandmother's house. In 1942, Oveta told her friend Emily Newell Blair that when she was in her preadolescence, she frequently heard her parents and perhaps other family members compare her unfavorably with her older sister, Juanita. As a result, she admitted to being something of a "problem child" who was unhappy, not only about the constant attention her parents were giving to her older sister, but also about the negative comments they often made. "Too bad," she would hear them say, "that Oveta is not pretty, like Juanita," or "Too bad that Oveta is not good, like Juanita." She told Blair that she stuttered badly and was painfully shy, although some of the anecdotes about her childhood behavior contradict her claim that she suffered from shyness. Nonetheless, Oveta appears to have been frustrated and resentful because of what she perceived as her parents' preference for Juanita. Ike and Emma likely asked Delia to let their "problem" child stay with her. Delia was alone and she could devote more time to "correcting" Oveta's bad attitude and habits than Ike and Emma. Apparently, Oveta lived with Delia, whose house was close to Delia's daughter and son-in-law's home, until she was nearly fourteen.[16]

Oveta told Blair that during those years, Delia treated her as a "contemporary, an equal in age and in intelligence," and that she was able to confide her "ambitions and resentments" to Delia. Her grandmother, however, was not one to coddle. She taught Oveta that the Culps and the Hoovers had a reputation in Killeen as community leaders and that she must behave accordingly. Her grandmother was a strongly independent woman, "determined and wise" in the manner of the women who grew up on the frontier. And she was not averse to bucking the local code of formal religious behavior. When Grandmere died in Temple in January 1940 from esophageal cancer, Oveta and Will Hobby attended the funeral in Killeen. The Baptist preacher who presided at the funeral repeated over and over again, "Sister Hoover may have had her own ideas." She might not have strictly followed Baptist beliefs, he declared, but "Sister Hoover had her convictions and followed them." As Oveta and Will were being driven home to Houston, Will observed, in his typically dry way, "It sounded to me almost as if the minister was apologizing for your grandmother." Oveta replied that she thought he was and added, "Grandmother would have loved it."[17]

Many years later, Oveta told *Houston Post* journalist Marguerite Johnston that she had come to realize that the arrangement of living with her grandmother "was not fair to either of us. Grandmere was too old to take on a small child. And I was too young to profit as much as I might have from her upbringing." Oveta, however, did credit her grandmother for coaching her to speak without the Texas drawl that was considered déclassé within Oveta's social circle beyond Texas borders when she was an adult. Cordelia also worked with Oveta to help her conquer the stuttering problem she had as a child.[18]

Even though Oveta was living with Cordelia, she was not a stranger in her family's home. She might have spent the nights and mornings with her grandmother, but she ate most of her evening meals with her parents and siblings, where she enjoyed hearing Ike's comments about local and state politics. As early as the age of ten, instead of chasing boys, like her sister Juanita enjoyed doing, Oveta loved to go straight to her father's law office after school, where she thumbed through his law books and read the profoundly dull official journals of the Texas Legislature and the equally tedious *Congressional Record*. She spent many hours sitting with her father in his office as he discussed legal issues and politics with his precocious daughter, building in her a deep and lifelong interest in the law and in government. Remarkably, Oveta learned at an early age how to help her father in preparing his legal briefs, and by the beginning of her teen years she had become one of Ike's confidants and advisers. It was during those visits to Ike's office that he coached Oveta on her oratorical skills, although she seemed to have had a natural affinity for public speaking that was apparent to her family and friends at an early age.[19]

Oveta's equally precocious older sister, Juanita, had similar skills and shared with Oveta a love for performing in public. According to their younger sister, Lynn, Oveta followed Juanita's lead whenever they did things together. It's likely it was Juanita's idea for them to perform skits for the public on the large stage of Killeen's Texas Theater, which was also the town cinema. As a result, friends of the family later recalled that everyone in town knew who the "pretty" Culp girls were.[20]

According to her childhood acquaintances in Killeen, Oveta's zest for public speaking and theatrical performances led her to enter the local Chautauqua chapter speech contest. When Oveta's presentation won the prize, the Chautauqua managers were so impressed with her performance that they offered her a contract to go on the touring circuit. The offer thrilled Oveta because the Chautauqua movement was at the height of its popularity at the time. One can assume that she had stars in her eyes as a result. Ike and Emma, however, did not. They were appalled by the idea of their pretty little girl going out on the road to perform. They declined the offer. As Oveta later recalled, they refused to even glance at the contract.[21]

Oveta, however, remained undaunted. Recruiting other kids, she organized her own local performing tour group called the Jolly Entertainers. This time she had her parents' approval and support. The Jolly Entertainers toured nearby towns, performing skits at local benefits to raise money for churches to buy organs and pianos. From all reports, Oveta's little touring troupe gave polished and entertaining performances. As a public figure later in life, Oveta would put to effective use the valuable experience she gained from her youthful performances onstage, as well as the coaching in public speaking she received from her father and grandmother.[22]

Ike might have been Oveta's dominant role model, but her mother also played a significant part in shaping Oveta's development. Like most women of her time, Emma Hoover Culp carried out the household's day-to-day domestic chores and was the primary caregiver for her children. But the stories her children later recalled document that Emma, like her mother, Cordelia, was a strong and independent woman who had her own projects outside of home and church. One major activity was her charitable work in support of the economically distressed families in her community, especially at Thanksgiving and Christmas. With Juanita and Oveta as her helpers, she gathered and distributed food and clothing to the needy.[23]

A photograph portrait of Emma and Ike made sometime in the late 1890s reveals that Oveta looked like her mother. The portrait also shows Emma wearing a large feathered hat, apparently one among many of the hats that Emma collected and wore to church and for special occasions. That Emma owned hats and probably wore one whenever she was out in public was not unusual for the time. In the United States in the first decades of the twentieth century, every fashion-conscious woman wore a hat when outdoors, particularly on special occasions. But it seems that hats were one of Emma's favorite clothing interests and may be the main reason Oveta developed her own strong affinity for hats, which became one of her stylistic hallmarks.[24]

Robert Pando retells a story told by the owner of a hat store in Killeen who recalled that as a young girl Oveta was one of her best hat customers. When Oveta was in her early teens, she went alone to the hat store to shop for a new chapeau. After trying on several, she selected a turban with a veil, which was a hat style commonly worn by older women. The hat store owner attempted to talk Oveta into buying a straw hat that was more appropriate for her age, but Oveta had no interest in the hats worn by teenage girls during that era. The hat seller finally gave in and suggested that Oveta take the turban to Emma to get her reaction. The shop owner assumed Emma would not approve Oveta's choice and that she would have to return the hat, but Oveta kept her turban.[25]

During World War II, Oveta returned to Bell County to make a widely publicized appearance as head of the Woman's Army Corps. By this time, she was well known for her distinctive hats. As Oveta stood at the podium and looked over her audience, she spotted her old acquaintance, the hat shop owner. They later reminisced about Oveta's visits to her hat store. When Oveta recalled buying the turban, she explained that it was at a time when she was writing and delivering sermons and that she "just had to look a bit older—and the hat made her feel sophisticated."[26]

Oveta's sister Lynn, who was nine years younger than Oveta, once asked her mother what Oveta was like when she was young. Emma replied, "Oh, Lynn, Oveta was never young." In later years, her siblings and family friends in Killeen recalled that Oveta was the most serious and studious little girl in town, never showing much interest in playing children's games. "Oveta was a very private person," Lynn recalled. "She never dated."

Lynn's recollection that Oveta "never" dated is a slight exaggeration, but she dated rarely. For one reason, most of the boys in Bell County thought she was more intelligent than a girl should be. A few times, Juanita paired her sister with boys she knew in Temple, but Juanita couldn't make the boys interesting to Oveta or vice versa. After returning home from a disastrous double date in which Oveta spent much of the time revealing the depth of her knowledge about some subject, Juanita advised her sister, "If you have to think, Oveta, do you have to think out loud when you are with a boy?"[27]

Emma and Ike often urged Oveta to go to the movies or to go fishing with them on the Lampasas River on Sunday afternoons, but she was usually too busy with her backyard church services or reading the Bible or the popular fiction, histories, and political and government publications she accumulated. Oveta's voracious reading habit eventually led her to accumulate a library of more than 750 volumes by the time she was a young adult. The titles ranged from biographies of Thomas Jefferson and Alexander Hamilton to the poetry of Edna St. Vincent Millay, as well as *Cases of Common Law Reading* and the *Congressional Record*.[28]

In 1918, Ike decided to reenter the state legislative political arena after an eighteen-year absence from the Texas House of Representatives. As a widely known and respected civic and business leader in Bell County, Ike easily won the Democratic nomination in the same primary election in which Will Hobby, his future son-in-law, won the party's nomination for governor. As a Democrat, Ike's victory in the November general election was pro forma.[29]

As staunch prohibitionists and supporters of women's suffrage, Ike and Emma supported Will Hobby in his race against James Ferguson for the gubernatorial nomination in 1918. Emma not only worked for her husband's nomination that summer, she also worked in the Hobby for Governor campaign as a member of Bell County's Hobby Club. With the newly passed legislation allowing women to vote in the party primaries, Emma joined the effort to get as many women registered to vote as possible, confident they would cast their ballots for Hobby. She trekked across the county distributing Hobby for Governor literature and urging women to vote. One of Oveta's most vivid memories was of her mother leaving the house for the political trail when the older girls were canning peaches. "I can see her open the screen door and I remember exactly what she had on," Oveta recalled. "She was wearing a pale blue suit and a white straw hat and high, laced white boots. She was pulling on her gloves and she turned to my sister [Juanita] and me and said, 'Girls, you'll have to look after the peaches. I'm going out to campaign for Will Hobby.'"[30]

After Ike Culp won the general election in November 1918, he moved his family and his law office from Killeen to nearby Temple, the rapidly growing town in Bell County that served as a center for two major rail lines, the Santa Fe and the Missouri, Kansas, and Texas. His law practice, which included both civil and criminal cases, grew into one of the largest in Bell County.[31]

Ike took his seat in the Texas House of Representatives in mid-January 1919. According to various accounts published over the years, Ike supposedly took fourteen-year-old Oveta with him to Austin. Reporters and other writers frequently claimed in newspaper and magazine profiles of Oveta published when she became a national figure that she was Ike's chief helper and advisor while he was serving in the legislature. It was claimed that instead of enrolling Oveta in the local public schools, Ike hired private tutors, possibly students or faculty from the University of Texas, to continue her education. Working with tutors in the evenings allowed Oveta to attend daily legislative sessions, where she sat next to her father every day and studied the proceedings. Oveta never bothered to cor-

rect those stories until late in her life, when she wrote to a student who was working on a senior thesis about her life. She told the student, "Contrary to what has been printed elsewhere, I did not accompany my father to Austin and sit by his side during each day of the legislative session. I did visit him at every opportunity and had a great interest in the legislative process, but I was a school girl in Temple High School at that time."[32]

*Ike Culp as a member of the Thirty-Sixth Texas Legislature, 1919.*

The Thirty-Sixth Texas Legislature was one of the busiest and most productive in the state's history, as it confronted a host of important issues, including prohibition and women's suffrage. Because the list of items on the agenda was long, Will Hobby had to call four special sessions after the regular session adjourned on March 19, 1919, to deal with them all. During the summer break from school, Oveta did accompany her father to the session held from June 23 to July 22. At some point in his first term, Ike felt that Oveta had adapted well enough to her new surroundings in the capitol to take on a low-level job as a clerk. Earning money wasn't the issue. Ike probably thought Oveta had too much time on her hands, and he knew that his serious and studious daughter would welcome the challenge. Although only fifteen, she had the office work skills of someone older. One observer at the time described her as "a thin girl, with great serious eyes, a high brow, and a large mouth which opened over extremely white teeth." Ike was a friend of El Paso legislator Robert Ewing Thomason, who was serving as Speaker of the House for the Thirty-Sixth Legislature. Because the Speaker's office was in charge of all job appointments in the House, Ike asked Thomason if he would give Oveta a job as a clerk for one of the committees during the second called special session that summer. In an oral history interview conducted at the LBJ Library in 1968, Thomason recalled that he was "happy to grant [Ike's] request. . . . [Oveta] proved to be a very efficient clerk and has been my friend ever since."[33]

Because Ike had already served one term in the legislature twenty years earlier, he was not a novice legislator. He was an active member who missed few votes, and he had a reputation among his fellow members as a hard worker who was well informed about the issues before the legislature. Ike was also a friend of Governor Hobby, who was grateful for Ike and Emma's work in Bell County in support of his campaign against Ferguson in the 1918 primary. Because of his friendship with the governor, Ike was able on at least one occasion to persuade Hobby to submit to the legislature a special act to aid one of his clients in an inheritance matter.[34]

Although Ike was close to Speaker Thomason, he did not use that connection to author any notable legislation. Ike, however, excelled at weakening bills that displeased him by putting an editor's sharp pencil point to specific words in the text of a bill and then submitting his edited version as an amendment. For example, a bill was proposed to make it a misdemeanor crime for anyone "who shall permit" a dog to run loose that was known to kill sheep. He revised the bill to state "who shall willfully and maliciously permit" a dog to run loose, thus making it much more difficult to prosecute the accused because of the requirement to prove intent.[35]

After the legislature's second called session adjourned in midsummer 1919, Oveta returned with her father to their home in Temple, where in September she enrolled for her senior year in Temple High School. Oveta soon withdrew from school, however, because of a dispute with the principal. Her sister Lynn later recalled that the principal had reviewed a copy of Oveta's speech before she was scheduled to read it to a school assembly. Lynn neglected to say what the speech was about, but the principal disliked the subject and told Oveta she would have to write on another topic. Angered by the principal's objection, the "headstrong" Oveta walked out of Temple High and never returned. With Ike's support, Oveta transferred to Baylor Academy, the secondary school operated by Mary Hardin–Baylor College in Belton, located about eight miles from Temple.[36]

Oveta's father had long harbored ambitions to be lieutenant governor, and probably governor beyond that. He had lost a bid to be lieutenant governor in 1900. In spring 1920, Ike decided not to run for reelection to the legislature and instead announced his candidacy for lieutenant governor in the Democratic primary in July. As a result, Oveta worked for Ike's campaign in June and July during her summer break from Baylor Academy. Ike, who had little name recognition outside of Central Texas, lost the primary election to wealthy Houston businessman and state senator Lynch Davidson. Although Ike was now a lame-duck member of the Texas House, he still had legislative responsibilities to fulfill. In late September he traveled back to Austin, with Oveta in tow, to attend the special session that Will Hobby called to resolve the poll tax payment problem that the women's suffrage act had created. This contentious session was the one in which Will succeeded in having his Galveston port law enacted.[37]

Because Oveta was with her father at the special session, which lasted from September 21 to October 2, she missed the fall semester at Baylor Academy. She continued her efforts at self-education through intensive reading. In January 1921, with Ike no longer in the legislature but now working full-time in Temple, she enrolled for the spring semester at Baylor Academy. She ended her course of study at the secondary school in May and apparently never received a high school diploma. Whether or not that is accurate, Oveta nevertheless was admitted to Mary Hardin–Baylor College in Belton for the fall semester of 1921. If she did lack a high school diploma, she might have had to pass an entrance exam for college, but this is unknown. Historian Robert Pando's research revealed that Oveta was listed officially as an "irregular" student at Mary Hardin, which might have been an institutional category for individuals who were on a nontraditional course of study and possibly not pursuing a degree plan. Whatever the reason might have been for this classification, Oveta's class attendance was intermittent. At one point during her time at the small women's college, she taught speech and helped students stage plays at the high school in the nearby town of Rogers, but the record is unclear about whether or not this brief teaching job was part-time, or if it required Oveta to drop out of school. And according to people whom *Time* interviewed in the early 1950s, after Oveta's experiences in Austin attending legislative sessions and working for a committee, "school was a big bore. She frequently skipped classes." Although she would later take law school classes in Houston, Oveta's formal schooling was over, but not her efforts to learn. She would be an autodidact her entire life.[38]

After two years of being out of office, Ike was eager to regain his legislative seat. In May 1922, he filed as a candidate for state representative from his old district in the Democratic primary election to be held in July. Once again Oveta worked full-time in her father's campaign. After Ike won his primary, she continued to take classes at Mary Hardin–Baylor in the fall of 1922 but withdrew from school in January 1923 and returned with her father to Austin. Oveta had managed to get through three semesters at the college, but she never returned as a student. As one of her associates later observed, "[Oveta] was more interested in the legislature than she was in her courses at that little college."[39]

On January 9, 1923, ten days prior to celebrating her eighteenth birthday, Oveta sat next to her father at his desk on the floor in the grand chamber of the Texas House of Representatives for the official opening of the Thirty-Eighth Texas Legislature. Pat Neff was now beginning his second term as governor. Having made her first appearance at the capitol four years earlier at the young age of fourteen, Oveta was a familiar face among Ike's closest colleagues in the legislature, including Lee Satterwhite, a representative from the Texas Panhandle who would later serve as Speaker; future Texas attorney general Robert Lee Bobbitt, representing the district that included Laredo; and Wright

Patman, a legislator from northeast Texas and a future powerful member of the US Congress. Ike's circle also included the representative from Blanco County, Sam Ealy Johnson, the father of future president Lyndon Baines Johnson. Oveta's relationship with the Johnson family would last throughout her life.

Speaker R. E. Seagler, whom Ike had befriended during the Thirty-Sixth Legislature, appointed Ike to the powerful House Committee on Revenue and Taxation, while Oveta was given a job as a clerk for the House Jurisprudence and Judiciary Committee. The Thirty-Eighth Legislature adjourned its regular session on March 14 and then reconvened the next day for a special called session that lasted only one day. It is not known if Oveta returned to Temple with her father after the end of that brief special session, but at some point during 1923 she began to live in Austin full-time. The legislature met in two additional back-to-back special sessions that year from mid-April until June 24, which meant Ike also had to be in Austin for most of the spring of 1923.

Now that Oveta was residing full-time in Austin, she was able to audit classes at the University of Texas Law School and to work briefly as a cub news reporter for the *Austin Statesman* while she continued to help her father during the special sessions that spring. The Thirty-Eighth Legislature adjourned for the final time in mid-June. With no legislative work available to her that summer, Oveta was able to secure another full-time job at the capitol. The Thirty-Eighth Legislature had split the Texas Banking and Insurance Department into two separate entities, one for regulating insurance companies and the other for banks. Oveta got a position at the newly reorganized banking department, working for state banking comptroller Charles O. Austin to codify state banking laws and regulations.

Oveta's duties soon included fieldwork helping state auditors close failed banks, an assignment that caught her off guard, as she had received no training for the job. Because of the large number of small-town banks in trouble because of the economic recession in rural Texas in the mid-1920s, the Banking Department hadn't been able to keep up with the need to examine accounts and evaluate the banks' financial health. In desperation, the head of the State Banking Department walked over to Oveta's desk one day and announced, "Miss Culp, I need for you to go on the road and examine some banks." When Oveta protested that she wasn't a bank examiner, the department head said, "Now you are." In an interview with *Texas Monthly* writer Harry Hurt in 1978, Oveta later noted that what she observed during her fieldwork made a lasting impression on her. "I remember very vividly going into those towns where the banks were closing," she said. "The people were terrified, but the banks could not stay open because there simply wasn't enough money. . . . I think that experience of seeing the banks close and the people so afraid made me a very conservative person."[40]

Oveta attracted much attention as a pretty eighteen-year-old working in the male-dominated environment of the capitol. Because of banking investments in Dallas, Cleburne, and Beaumont, Will Hobby and his brother Edwin were frequent visitors to the Banking Commission's office on the first floor of the capitol. It is likely that he saw Oveta during those visits. An eighteen-year-old woman working in a position with important responsibilities in such a small office environment would have been hard to miss.

Oveta had an active social life from 1923 to 1925, going on dates to movies downtown and to dances and basketball games on the University of Texas campus with some of the up-and-coming young men in Austin. Nevertheless, she also continued the pattern she had set as a serious and studious young girl in Killeen and Temple who was more involved in her work and studies than in frivolous leisure-time activities. While Ike Culp was in the legislature, he carefully monitored Oveta's dating. According to *Time*, whose reporter might not have understood Texas exaggeration, "Old Ike Culp took to carrying a long-bladed, switch-back knife in his pocket, ostensibly to pare his nails, but word got around the legislature that he intended to use it on any young man who attempted to get smart around Oveta."[41]

Based on research and interviews its reporter conducted in 1953, *Time* claimed that the men Oveta dated during these years included twenty-nine-year-old Silliman Evans, future owner and publisher of the *Nashville Tennessean*, who was working as capitol correspondent for Amon Carter's *Fort Worth Star-Telegram* during the legislative sessions of 1923. *Time* also reported that Oveta dated twenty-four-year-old James V. Allred, who was in Austin during the legislative session in 1923, successfully lobbying Governor Neff for the unexpired open position of district attorney at Wichita Falls. Oveta's relationship with Allred might have been more serious than her others. Allred was a future attorney general and governor of Texas. Independent Texas oilman J. R. Parten, who was a close political advisor of Allred's, later recalled, "[Oveta] and Jimmy Allred used to be sweethearts, before he married Jo Betsy." Parten frequently traveled to Austin from 1935 to 1939, when Allred was governor. He occasionally saw Oveta, who by then was married and living in Houston, visiting in Allred's office. "Oveta was . . . his former flame," Parten said. "They were very good friends."[42]

Oveta seems to have been a heartbreaker. University of Texas law professor Frank Bobbitt, the brother of Ike's friend Representative Robert Lee Bobbitt, was among one of Oveta's more fervent suitors. Oveta might have met him when she was auditing classes at the law school. Frank Bobbitt would be killed in an accident in 1933. At the time of his death, one of Oveta's friends, Jessie Ziegler, reported the news to her mother. "A man who used to be desperately in love with Oveta, Frank Bobbitt fell from a second story porch and was killed last week," Ziegler wrote. "It must have touched Oveta to hear of Frank's death. He loved her very much and wanted to marry her."[43]

Bob Poage was another young man whose heart would be broken by Oveta. His father, William Allen Poage, was a prosperous rancher and cattleman from Waco who served in the legislature from 1917 until his death in 1920. Bob Poage, who was six years older than Oveta, might have met her when he went with his father to Austin for the special session of the Thirty-Sixth Legislature in the summer of 1919. They probably did not date, however, until Poage won his own term to the Texas House in 1924, where he served until 1929, when he lost his bid for election to the Texas Senate. Like Frank

Bobbitt, Bob Poage fell in love with Oveta and proposed marriage to her, but she was not interested. Poage was a rancher as well as a lawyer in Waco. By the time they were dating in the late 1920s, when Oveta would return to Austin during sessions of the legislature, she was deeply involved in a whirlwind of activities in the big city of Houston and had no intention of living out her life on a ranch in Central Texas or in the town of Waco, which was only thirty-three miles from the Culp family home in Temple. Not long after it became clear to Bob Poage that Oveta was not going to marry him, he wrote to her, "Oveta, I sincerely loved you. . . . I know that I am a better man and will always be, for having known and loved you." Poage eventually won a seat in the Texas Senate and then later served forty-two years in the US Congress.[44]

Despite all of the attention from the likes of Silliman Evans, James Allred, Frank Bobbitt, and Bob Poage, Oveta remained independent and unmarried, focused on broadening her cultural horizons and professional options, which included a possible life in politics. Members of the Austin news corps were well aware that Oveta's popularity with the males around the capitol was tempered greatly by her keen focus on a possible political future. Journalist W. Boyd Gatewood, whose weekly column Tips on Texas Politics was carried by several of the state's newspapers, informed his readers that there was a popular young woman working in the capitol named Miss Oveta Culp. He added, "With her, romance is a pleasant diversion and politics an abiding passion."[45]

Ike Culp had decided in May 1924 not to run for another term in the legislature. With no other special called legislative sessions on the governor's agenda, Ike returned to his law practice in Temple. His daughter, however, was now firmly ensconced in her Banking Commission job and tending to her social life in Austin. Back in Temple, Ike Culp watched his daughter's energetic pursuit of a life outside the constraints of marriage and domestic duties. On her twenty-first birthday, January 19, 1926, he wrote Oveta a birthday message on old letterhead of the Judiciary Committee of the Texas House that listed her name as clerk. Stressing how proud he was of her, Ike wrote, "Dear Daughter: you have been a great comfort to me and I am looking forward to greater things in the future." Ike expressed his hope that Oveta would eventually find a suitable husband, but one who would give her the freedom to follow her dreams. "I want you not to go through life an unmarried woman," Ike wrote, "but I want you to be sure you are making a selection that 1st be *your* equal from an intellectual standpoint, 2nd congenial, and 3rd that [he] love and honor you, Papa." It appears likely that Oveta paid close attention to her father's advice and wishes for her future. The letter was among only a few letters from this period of her life that were found in her papers after her death nearly seventy years later.[46]

With her father as her role model and having been immersed in politics and the legislative process most of her young life, Oveta was eager to follow his example and develop her own career in public affairs. She soon made a connection that would help her take an important step toward that goal and lead her to the city with which she would be closely identified for the rest of her long life.

## CHAPTER 18

# PRECOCIOUS PARLIAMENTARIAN

A t some point in 1925, while Oveta was working in the capitol, she became friends with Ross Sterling's sister, Florence Sterling, who was in her early fifties when she met Oveta. A native of Anahuac, Texas, "Flo" Sterling had worked closely with her brothers, Ross and Frank, as they and their partners organized and developed the Humble Oil Company. For several years Flo Sterling served on Humble's board of directors and was the corporate secretary until she retired from the company in 1925 to help manage the Sterling family's investments. The enormous success of Humble Oil, especially after it came under the control of Standard Oil of New Jersey, made Flo Sterling a wealthy woman. After her retirement, that wealth made it possible for Sterling to work full-time for the rest of her life in support of her political and educational causes. Her ideas about public policy were far more progressive than those of her brother Ross, a difference that did not seem to affect their relationship.[1]

Flo Sterling was among the leaders of a number of organizations that promoted women's rights and encouraged women to be politically active, especially in support of her favored causes: progressive government, strong prohibition and drug-enforcement laws, and world peace. The organizations she led included the Texas branch of the Woman's Christian Temperance Union, the Houston Suffrage League, the Houston League of Women Voters, and the Texas Women's Democratic League. As one of the tireless workers and leaders in support of the Nineteenth Amendment, Sterling famously hired a brass band and then led it and her fellow suffragists down Houston's Main Street in celebration of the amendment's adoption in 1920.[2]

Oveta's relationship with Flo Sterling was one of the important turning points in Oveta's life. As their friendship grew, Flo identified Oveta as a young woman with much promise, one whom she could mentor professionally and enlist in her progressive crusade. Flo persuaded Oveta to move to Houston late in the fall of 1925. As historian Kelli Walsh has noted, Oveta's move to Houston "was a life-changing decision for Culp, both personally and professionally."[3]

THE WOMAN'S VIEWPOINT
HOUSTON, TEXAS

FLORENCE M. STERLING

Vol. 1     WEDNESDAY     DECEMBER 12, 1923     No. 1

Oveta quit her job at the State Banking Commission and moved temporarily into Flo Sterling's mansion on Hawthorne Street in the fashionable Westmoreland section of Houston, located a little more than a mile to the southwest of downtown. Flo Sterling's mansion had ample room for Oveta, who brought her 750-volume personal library, stored in several lockers, with her. Soon after moving into Flo's house, Oveta rented a room in a boardinghouse on Westmoreland Street, near Ross Sterling's place and a few blocks from Will and Willie Hobby's house at 506 Lovett Boulevard. A few weeks after Oveta relocated to Houston, Flo got her a job as secretary to the Houston League of Women Voters, where Flo was in her final year as president.[4]

Oveta also briefly performed some part-time clerical and copyediting work for Flo Sterling's monthly magazine, the *Woman's Viewpoint,* before it ceased publication at the end of 1926. Written and edited by an all-female staff, the *Woman's Viewpoint* featured articles about the achievements of professional women and editorials stressing the obligation those women had to be involved in civic and political affairs. Sterling's worldview, as revealed in the *Woman's Viewpoint* editorials, had a major influence on Oveta's positive attitude about balancing work and marriage and the professional possibilities that were beginning to open up to women in the 1920s.[5]

Oveta's duties for the League of Women Voters left her plenty of time for another job. When Sterling offered to find Oveta a position at her brother Ross's newspaper, the twenty-year-old Oveta eagerly agreed. She began work at the *Post-Dispatch* in December 1925 as a clerk in the circulation department. Over the years, different versions of the story about how Will and Oveta first met circulated. According to Will, he met Oveta in the summer of 1926, when Ike Culp called and told him that Ike's daughter was working for the *Post-Dispatch*. He asked Will "to keep an eye" on her. Will promptly summoned Oveta up to his office and introduced himself in his "naturally brusque manner and gave her a start. She thought she was being fired." Many years later, Oveta explained that her meeting with Will at the *Post-Dispatch* was not the first time they had met. Will had been a friend of her family "all her life," and she stated she had met Will when her father was in the legislature. Oveta also claimed later that it was not a call from her father that alerted Will to the fact that she was working at the *Post-Dispatch*. A family friend from Killeen was visiting Will in his office at the newspaper, and he told Will that he wanted to see Ike's daughter Oveta Culp, which alerted Will that "a young woman he had remembered as a growing girl" was now working for him. No matter how it happened, Will was well aware of Oveta by the summer of 1926. He later told the *New York Daily News*, "It was politics, strangely enough, that brought us together. She had a grasp of it even then that amazed me and there's nothing I would rather do than talk politics. Beautiful girl, too."[6]

Oveta continued to seek ways to further her education. Having left Mary Hardin–Baylor after only three semesters, she was aware that her education was incomplete. Her years working with her father in his law office and her firsthand experience observing how the laws were legislated had given her thoughts about becoming an attorney, which is clearly the reason Oveta audited law classes at the University of Texas. A friendship with Houston attorney Hortense Ward, one of the first women to pass the bar exam and practice law in Texas, also motivated Oveta to continue her studies. Ward had been an ally of Minnie Fisher Cunningham and was an ardent suffragist and prohibitionist. In 1918 she helped organize the Hobby Clubs for women and served as the chair of the club in Harris County. After he defeated Jim Ferguson in the Democratic primary, Governor Hobby appointed Ward to the state's Industrial Accident Board. Oveta later recalled that Ward "took a great interest" in her. "She'd call and say, 'let's have lunch.'" These lunches would be at the Rice Hotel.[7]

The only law school in Houston, the private South Texas College of Law, had opened three years before Oveta moved to the city. It gave Oveta an opportunity to continue her study of the law, as the college's classes were held at night. Her efforts remained informal, however, because she never enrolled as a regular student, possibly because of her lack of college credits. Instead, Oveta audited law classes at South Texas College, beginning in the spring semester of 1926 and, except for a break in 1927, continuing until 1929.[8]

Oveta did not complete her quest to become a lawyer. She never received a degree, and she did not take the bar exam, which she later regretted. When she was in her late sixties, Oveta responded to a reporter's compliment about the several honorary degrees universities had awarded her by saying degrees that had been "earned" instead of being honorary were more worthy of praise. "I'm sorry I didn't [get a degree]," she noted. "I don't think a piece of paper makes an education although I do wish I had gone ahead and [graduated]."[9]

In later years, the fact that Oveta did not have a high school or college diploma was frequently obscured and sometimes inaccurately stated in the various biographical sketches written by journalists, press officers, and even some of her staff after she became a public figure. Many assumed Oveta's formal education matched her obvious talents and achievements, and they mistakenly credited her with high school and college diplomas. While she was working at the State Banking Commission, the *Austin City Directory* listed her job as "attorney." According to biographer Robert Pando, "Most of the time, [Oveta] corrected these inaccuracies, sometimes she did not, allowing even such vaunted fact-checking publications as *U.S. News & World Report* and the *New York Times* to print flawed curricula vitae." Unhappy about news reports that stated Oveta was a graduate of the University of Texas, the university sent an official letter to *Time* magazine to correct the record. "Your story . . . is totally incorrect. Mrs. Hobby has never received any degree whatsoever from this institution." *Time* published the letter.[10]

Oveta was soon leading an extremely busy life in Houston, filling her days and nights with working at her job at the *Post-Dispatch*, taking care of her secretarial duties for the League of Women Voters, and sitting in on law classes in the basement of the downtown YMCA, where the South Texas Law School was located. Kelli Walsh makes the point that at this stage of her life, Oveta was a member of that "generation of women who evolved from suffragists to so-called modern women. She reached adulthood during the Roaring Twenties, when women began expressing themselves with shorter hair and skirts, enrolling in college, and seeking independent personal lives prior to marriage." Flo Sterling also supported the idea that a woman could lead a life outside of marriage. According to Walsh, "[Oveta] embraced all of the newfound privileges of public womanhood. Like others of her generation, [she] did not identify herself as a feminist; rather she believed that if she supplied the ability, opportunity would find her."[11]

With 1926 being an election year, Oveta eagerly added politics to her already crowded agenda. Texas attorney general Dan Moody, who was from Oveta's former home region in Central Texas, entered the governor's race that March in opposition to the incumbent, Miriam Ferguson. Oveta volunteered in his Houston campaign office and served as the office secretary. When Moody held a rally in Houston in late May that attracted a large crowd, Oveta helped with the arrangements. Moody eventually defeated Ferguson in a runoff election in August.[12]

In May 1926, Read Granberry, the first and only person who had ever served as House parliamentarian in the Texas Legislature, resigned from his post to accept a job as an instructor in the Department of Electrical Engineering at the University of Texas, leaving House Speaker Lee Satterwhite with a problem. It was widely assumed that at some point after the Democratic Party primary in July, Governor Miriam Ferguson (whether or not she won reelection) would have to call a special session of the legislature. That meant Satterwhite had to find someone to replace Granberry, who essentially had invented the position and codified most of the procedural rules. There were no obvious candidates for the job, but it occurred to Granberry that Oveta Culp might be the answer to Satterwhite's problem. Granberry had gotten to know Oveta when she worked for the House Jurisprudence and Judiciary Committee, and he knew she had been fascinated with the procedures Granberry had developed that made the House function in an orderly fashion. She was also familiar with the overall legislative process. He recommended to Satterwhite that he offer the job to Oveta, despite her lack of experience. If she accepted the offer, Granberry promised to make time late in the summer to tutor her. Satterwhite was an old friend of Ike Culp and knew and was impressed by Oveta. He agreed to Granberry's recommendation. Satterwhite contacted Oveta in Houston, and she accepted his offer.[13]

Coincidentally, in 1914, when Granberry was only fifteen years old, John Henry Kirby had urged newly elected lieutenant governor Will Hobby to hire Granberry as his private secretary. Granberry had worked in the Thirty-Third Legislature as a page for Speaker Chester Terrell when Kirby was serving as a state representative. Kirby had become Granberry's patron. "There is a boy in Austin . . . whose name is Read Granberry," Kirby wrote Will, "who will make an application to you for the position. Read is . . . as bright as a dollar, quick as chained lightening, and dependable as Truth. I am very fond of the boy but I am likewise fond of you, and in urging you to give him consideration I know that I am doing a favor to both." Will decided, however, to give the job to one of his *Beaumont Enterprise* staff members. As a result, the new Speaker of the Texas House, John William Woods, hired Granberry to be his secretary at the beginning of the Thirty-Fourth Legislature in January 1915. It was during that session that Granberry suggested to Woods that the Speaker needed a parliamentarian. Woods agreed, and Granberry became the first person to hold the position.[14]

The parliamentarian's duties include guiding the Speaker on proper responses to parliamentary inquiries and points of order. The role requires an intimate knowledge of the complex, and in some ways arcane, procedural rules and regulations of the Texas House. Oveta had spent years reading legislative journals as well as observing Read Granberry's work as House parliamentarian. She already had a general understanding of *Robert's Rules of Order*, the most widely used set of parliamentary procedures, and she was not daunted by the prospect of having to learn what many people considered to be the tedious and boring details of the process. The rules Oveta found in parliamentary procedure were a perfect fit for her personality, which was attracted to order, efficiency, and control. The position also made her a highly visible member of the Speaker's team, as she had her own chair on the platform next to the Speaker's podium. That visibility was enhanced when Satterwhite gave her the additional appointment of secretary to the Speaker. The job paid the equivalent of approximately $100 per day in 2017 value. This was exciting and heady stuff for a young woman in an era when women had only recently been given the right to vote. Shortly after Oveta was appointed House parliamentarian, the Associated Press declared, "No young woman of her age in the United States is filling more responsible political positions than Oveta Culp. Not yet 21 years old, Miss Culp knows the ins and outs of Democratic politics far better than the average legislator."[15]

Oveta resigned from the *Post-Dispatch* in August 1926, left Houston, and moved into the Bradford Apartments on Colorado Street in Austin to begin the process of learning her new job. During that month she made frequent trips back to Houston, where she continued to be involved in local Democratic Party politics. She was selected to be a delegate from Harris County to the party's state convention in San Antonio on September 8. Oveta made her political debut when her fellow delegates elected her convention secretary. After her election, the diminutive and poised twenty-one-year-old drew much attention from the audience when she gave a short speech thanking them for their vote of confidence.[16]

Immediately after the state party convention adjourned, Governor Ferguson called a special session of the Texas Legislature to convene on September 13, which required Oveta to return to Austin to devote full attention to her new job. When the House convened, the representatives voted unanimously to confirm Oveta's appointment. After her confirmation, Speaker Satterwhite invited Oveta to the podium and asked her to speak. Fashionably dressed as usual, and wearing one of the turbans that had become an integral part of her stylistic image, she gave a brief speech thanking the members for having confidence in her ability to do the job. Oveta was more than ready for the challenge, and she flourished in the position. By the time the special session adjourned on October 8, she had earned the respect of Speaker Satterwhite and the other members of the House leadership.[17]

When the special session ended, Oveta remained in Austin at the request of state representative Robert Lee Bobbitt of Laredo, who was slated to succeed Satterwhite as House Speaker when the regular session of the Fortieth Legislature convened in January 1927. Bobbitt, who was another old friend of Ike Culp, asked Oveta to continue to serve as the House parliamentarian and to serve as his private secretary. When the regular session convened on January 11, 1927, House members reconfirmed her appointment. She served in her typically efficient manner until the legislature adjourned on March 16, 1927. During this session, members of the House learned that Oveta was the go-to person not only for obtaining information about procedural matters but also for getting legislative requests to the Speaker. A state political news reporter during this period later

*Oveta Culp serving as parliamentarian of the Texas House of Representatives,
Speaker Lee Satterwhite presiding, ca. 1926.*

claimed, "More House members went to [Oveta] with their requests for action on bills
and other problems than went to the [S]peaker himself. If you asked any disinterested
representative who knew the most about the work of the House he probably would have
replied 'Miss Culp.'"[18]

Oveta's appointment as Speaker Bobbitt's secretary was reported in a story in the
*Post-Dispatch* that included a photograph of her on the Speaker's rostrum with Bobbitt. With this publicity and her visibility in the state capitol, Oveta was now becoming
something of a minor public figure. Oveta later noted the impact her job had on her
future: "If I hadn't been parliamentarian other things would never have sparked." Many

years later, Waco newspaper editor Frank Baldwin, who served as a state representative in the Fortieth Legislature, recalled how much influence Oveta had gained with the Speaker. While giving a guest lecture to a journalism class at Texas Tech University in 1927, during a break in the session, Baldwin had severely criticized several of his fellow members of the legislature. When the news about Baldwin's incendiary remarks made its way back to Austin, some of the targets of his rhetoric tried to remove him from the legislature. Speaker Bobbitt sought to derail the resolution. Oveta helped him by issuing a procedural ruling as parliamentarian that killed the effort. Baldwin later jokingly noted that he never forgave Oveta for saving his legislative position. "I was a cinch to be impeached," he recalled, "and it would have been an honor."[19]

After the legislature ended its regular session in March 1927, Oveta moved back to Houston, where she once again rented a cottage from Florence Sterling on Westmoreland Street, knowing she would soon have to return to Austin, as Governor Dan Moody intended to call a special session in May. The special session convened on May 9, 1927, and Oveta moved back to Austin, where she rented a room in a house at 1205 Castle Hill on the west side of town. She continued in her post as parliamentarian and secretary to Speaker Bobbitt until the session ended early in June. The next regular session would not be held until the Forty-First Legislature convened in January 1929.[20]

Freed from any requirement to be in Austin for another eighteen months, Oveta returned to Houston in the summer of 1927 and took up residence in another rental cottage near Flo Sterling's house. Oveta quickly resumed her whirlwind of activity, going back to work at the *Post-Dispatch*, increasing her visibility in the Democratic Party organization, and renewing her affiliation with several women's organizations, including the Women's Democratic Club of Houston, whose members elected Flo Sterling to a term as president.[21]

Oveta's political involvement increased substantially in January 1928, when Flo Sterling helped her get an appointment as the executive secretary of the Texas Democratic Women's Club, which had a statewide membership of fifteen thousand. Although it was a part-time job, Oveta's service gave her an opportunity to expand her network of influential women, which helped broaden her intellectual and cultural horizons. By far the most important of these new friends was wealthy Houston socialite Estelle Boughton Sharp, the fifty-six-year-old widow of oilman Walter Sharp. Sharp and Howard Hughes Sr. had cofounded the Sharp-Hughes Tool Company. Sharp also helped Joseph Cullinan organize the Texas Company, which later became Texaco. He died in 1912 at the age of forty-two, leaving Estelle with a fortune that she tapped for philanthropic and progressive social-welfare causes.[22]

Oveta came to Estelle's attention at the local Democratic Party's annual "Jefferson-Jackson" dinner in February 1928. Oveta gave a speech that urged women to register to vote and to pay their poll tax to make it possible for them to play a larger role in formulating public policy. Sharp was impressed by Oveta's presentation and her poised delivery. She approached Oveta as the event ended and said, "Miss Culp, thank you for speaking up on the point. We must get to know one another." Oveta accepted Sharp's invitation to join her women's study group, and Oveta soon became an active participant. The wealthy and worldly Sharp, a native of Michigan who had attended Oberlin College before marrying Walter Sharp, quickly became one of Oveta's most influential mentors.[23]

Historian Debra Sutphen has described Estelle Sharp as a "tall, exquisitely dressed woman of regal bearing, whose intellectualism, innate style, and taste for the exotic made a lasting impression on Oveta." Years later, Oveta recalled that Estelle (whom she always called "Mrs. Sharp") opened her eyes to "the great issues of the world. She was interested in the mind and the thinking process. She organized a study group and saw to it that we learned about important national and international issues."[24]

Willie Hobby was also a regular attendee of Sharp's study group, and she was an active member of the Texas Democratic Women's Club. Early in the spring of 1928, Willie joined with Estelle Sharp and Flo Sterling to support the passage of the club's resolution urging the legislature to lower the age for free public education from seven to six years old. To work on behalf of that resolution and to support other reforms championed by the membership, Willie, Florence, and their associates in the club persuaded Oveta, their dynamic, young, articulate, and ambitious executive secretary, to run for the state legislature in the July 1928 primary election.[25]

Will Hobby's *Houston Post-Dispatch* duly reported the news that Oveta Culp would be a legislative candidate. Oveta decided, however, to wait until 1930, apparently thinking that because of her age, the time was not yet right for her candidacy. Instead, Oveta decided to work in the Houston campaign office of Congressman Tom Connally, an old family friend from Central Texas who was mounting what would be a successful primary race against the controversial incumbent US senator Earle Mayfield. Will and Willie Hobby were also actively involved in the effort to elect Connally and undoubtedly encountered Oveta at the Connally headquarters in Houston.[26]

Oveta was also elected a delegate to the Democratic Party's state convention in Beaumont in May 1928, where Will Hobby played a major role by helping hammer out the compromise that pledged the state delegation's support for the presidential nomination to Jesse H. Jones. After Oveta's election as a delegate to the state convention, the *Post-Dispatch* ran yet another feature about her. The news story, referring to her service as House parliamentarian, noted Oveta had occupied "several positions of distinction" and that she already had enjoyed "a most unusual career due to a gift of leadership and very keen ability."[27]

When the Democratic Party held its national convention in Houston in June 1928, Oveta was not about to miss the biggest political event in Houston's history. She was released from her usual duties at the state Democratic Women's Club to work full-time in the citywide effort to prepare Houston for the event, as well as to attend the convention sessions and key committee meetings. Oveta later characterized her role as "only a flunky," carrying out a range of menial tasks, which might have accurately described much of her work. But she also had some important duties thanks to her influential patrons Florence Sterling and Estelle Sharp. Perhaps Oveta's most significant assignment was to run one of the convention's major special events, a breakfast in the rooftop room at the Rice Hotel sponsored by the National Democratic Women's Club in honor of the club's national president, Emily Newell Blair, and Woodrow Wilson's widow, Edith Bolling Galt Wilson. The breakfast guests included other party notables, such as Texas governor Dan Moody, Houston mayor Oscar Holcombe, and the state's favorite-son candidate, Jesse H. Jones.[28]

Oveta also appeared before the convention's executive committee on June 8 to request financial support for entertaining the various Democratic national committeewomen and other women leaders, including delegates, who would attend the convention. Will Hobby was a member of the committee and was present when Oveta made her request. Oveta explained that the local chapter of the Democratic Women's Club also wanted to host a luncheon for five hundred guests at the Rice Hotel, with a reception afterward. She estimated the cost to be approximately $2,000. The committee, however, denied the request. The breakfast event that Oveta arranged at the Rice Hotel might have been held as an alternative to this luncheon.[29]

Despite Oveta's understated observation that she only worked as an errand runner, the comely young woman attracted considerable attention from the press and the male delegates as she dashed around the convention puffing on Chesterfield cigarettes. Kelli Walsh has observed that as "a young Southern woman, Oveta Culp was learning the politics of impression management. Almost every article written about Oveta Culp made note of her appearance." At one point, she sported a yellow clothing ensemble featuring twenty-seven strings of beads and a fashionable, snug-fitting turban. One newspaper and one magazine story about the convention noted that Oveta Culp, who was described as having gray eyes, an "eclectic taste," and elegant manners, occupied "positions of distinction that scores of veteran politicians would cherish." News reports revealed that Oveta had declared she was a "staunch exponent of Thomas Jefferson, Tom Connally, W. P. Hobby, Dan Moody, Al Smith, and William Penn." The inexplicable reference to the founder of Pennsylvania went unexplained, but it might have been connected to one of the books on American history that Oveta liked to read during these years. More important was the inclusion of Will Hobby in that list of her heroes, which is clear evidence that by the summer of 1928, if not earlier, she had become an admirer of the former governor, whom she had placed in her personal pantheon with Thomas Jefferson and William Penn.[30]

When the convention ended with Al Smith as the Democratic presidential nominee, Oveta went back to work on Tom Connally's campaign for the US Senate, which Connally won in the primary a month later. Oveta wasted little time in transferring her political work to the Houston campaign office of Al Smith, where she was given assignments to speak at meetings of various women's groups in Houston in support of Smith's candidacy. After Smith's defeat in November, Oveta worked throughout December 1928 on conservative judge Walter Monteith's mayoral campaign to defeat incumbent Houston mayor

Oscar Holcombe. Monteith accused Holcombe of "profligate spending" and of initiating unnecessary public works. Monteith and his brother, Houston attorney and lobbyist Edgar Monteith, grew up in Bell County and were old friends of Ike Culp's. Will Hobby had appointed Walter Monteith a district judge in 1919. When he defeated Holcombe in the city election in January 1929, Monteith offered Oveta the job of assistant to the city attorney, Sam Neathery. By the time of Houston's mayoral election, however, Oveta had returned to Austin to serve as House parliamentarian in the Forty-First Legislature for the new Speaker, Wingate Barron.[31]

Despite her legislative job, Monteith's offer appealed to Oveta because of her interest in the law and the opportunity it provided for her to be in the thick of the political action at city hall. Oveta was now thinking seriously about running for the legislature in 1930. The assistant city attorney position would be an important addition to her resume and would provide some public visibility. But she did not want to leave Speaker Barron in the lurch, especially in the early days of the legislative session. Monteith solved Oveta's problem by agreeing to delay her appointment until after the legislature adjourned in mid-March. Oveta gladly accepted the offer. Monteith had to wait well beyond March, however, as Governor Moody called multiple back-to-back special sessions that stretched into July 1929.[32]

The end of the last special legislative session finally freed Oveta to focus on her job as Houston's assistant city attorney. When she returned to Houston, Oveta moved in with *Gargoyle* magazine reporter Ruth West at 5 Asbury Street, located on the north bank of Buffalo Bayou across from exclusive River Oaks, the newly built elite neighborhood developed by Will Hogg. Oveta had met West when the latter published an admiring profile of Oveta for the magazine in August 1928. West's house was a short drive along Buffalo Bayou to Houston's city hall. Oveta lived on Asbury Street for more than a year. She could occasionally be seen out in the front yard raking the bountiful pine needles from the trees surrounding the house into piles and then burning them in bonfires. Her friends noted that when she worked in the yard and when she was at the office, she had a habit of softly humming songs (often "Ol' Man River") "a bit off-key." Parked in front of the house was her faded-blue, old Ford coupe with fenders that rattled as she drove it down Houston's streets.[33]

Oveta was eager to pursue her dream of getting a law license while also continuing to cultivate the connections she had forged in the women's club network. She was also ready to explore the possibilities of a career in politics.

# CHAPTER 19

# "I CANNOT WRITE
# YOU HOW MUCH
# I LOVE YOU"

Will Hobby's pursuit of Oveta Culp began in earnest in summer of 1929, when she was spending most of her time in Houston instead of Austin, working in the county attorney's office. Years later she recalled seeing Will occasionally that summer and fall, but only with other friends, never alone. At some point, she remembered, they "just kind of struck up." Oveta also claimed that in the beginning she didn't realize Will's intentions were romantic in nature. This seems less than credible. Kelli Walsh has observed, "It is hard to believe a woman so insightful to the world of politics was oblivious to the fact the Governor was courting her." While Oveta might not have realized the depth of Will's interest, Will was certainly aware of it. His courtship of Oveta was intense. Will was greatly attracted by Oveta's beauty, humor, and intelligence. He also admired the way she projected a self-confident determination and independence, which were characteristics he had respected in Willie. And, as was the case in his relationship with his late wife, Will shared with Oveta a strong interest in politics and government. In other words, it is apparent that Will found strong, smart, and politically savvy women deeply appealing. It is also safe to assume, based on future developments, that Will yearned to have children, and the object of his affection was the right age for childbearing.[1]

Will was soon expressing his love to Oveta in a way she couldn't have misunderstood. Late in November, while on a trip to Washington and New York to conduct business for KPRC Radio, Will wrote a series of letters to Oveta. "As soon as I left you," Will wrote, "I realized the melancholy days have come." In a tongue-in-cheek reference to Oveta's informal study of the law, Will asked her to prepare a brief telling him how she was going to spend the coming weekend. "You need not cite precedent or other cases . . . as much as you are in the habit of doing that. I shall find contentment in the thought that even if I am not satisfied with where you are, I am satisfied with what you are." He ended the letter with an unambiguous, "I love you." In a letter from New York the following week,

Will could not have been more clear: "I cannot write you how much I love you." Despite Will's passionate declarations of his love for her, Oveta was not yet ready for a serious relationship. "I never thought about a romance," Oveta admitted years later. "I was quite busy and I really didn't have marriage on my mind."[2]

As soon as Will returned from the Northeast, he temporarily suspended his pursuit of Oveta to take a long-planned deer-hunting trip to Ross Sterling's huge Chupadera Ranch, located on the Rio Grande in southwest Texas. This was Will's first Christmas since Willie's death eleven months earlier. Oveta spent Christmas with her parents back in Temple. Sterling's stag retreat had become an annual affair attended by prominent and influential state officials, judges, and leading business and civic leaders, who took the opportunity while isolated out on the ranch to talk politics and hatch business deals while enthusiastically imbibing in forbidden alcoholic beverages easily smuggled in from Mexico. During this holiday outing, Dan Moody tried to persuade Sterling not to run for governor in 1930. Moody was giving serious thought to standing for a third term, and he was trying to avoid a match against Sterling, but Moody's effort was unsuccessful.[3]

The retreat included not only Governor Dan Moody but also Jesse Jones, cotton entrepreneur M. D. Anderson, Houston banker R. M. Farrar, the presidents of three major railroads, two federal judges, and an army general. Sterling's ranch partner and manager was Uvalde businessman Dolph Briscoe Sr., father of future Texas governor Dolph Briscoe Jr. Will traveled from Houston with Jones, Anderson, and Farrar in a private railroad car to the remote village of Catarina, the rail station nearest to the ranch. Chupadera's headquarters was an hour drive from Carrizo Springs, the nearest town of much size.[4]

After a day of hunting, Sterling and his guests, whom he called the "deluxe deer-slayers," gathered for a heavy supper of wild game, followed by rounds of "refreshments" around the fireplace of the main ranch house. In his memoir, Sterling observed that these gatherings "naturally evolved into tall tale-telling contests." After a few drinks, Jesse Jones told the group that while he was out alone with one of the hunting guides, he had taken a shot with his handgun at a squirrel scampering many yards away on the other side of a creek. He claimed that he had aimed his shot fifty feet high in the air to allow for the bullet to fall over the distance and that he had hit the squirrel in the head. Sterling also delighted in playing practical jokes on his guests, especially Will Hobby, who delighted his companions with wisecracks in response to the jokes Sterling played on him. "At the end of that hunt in 1929," Sterling recalled, "I had the boys take a buck I had killed from the cooling house and load it on the car for Governor Hobby, whose buck had let him down. As it was being tied on, Hobby cracked, 'I hadn't thought I hit him [with] that third shot.'" Sterling would lose his much-treasured ranch three years later during the Depression.[5]

After Will returned to Houston from his Chupadera Ranch outing, he barely had time to visit Oveta before she had to travel to Austin in mid-January to serve as the House parliamentarian for a special called session. The deepening national economic crisis forced Dan Moody to call the special session to address a major state budget deficit. The legislature failed to address all of the issues Governor Moody asked them to resolve, so he called the legislators back to work on February 19, the day after they ended the fourth session. They remained in session until March 20.

Because these multiple special sessions required Oveta's presence in Austin from late January through most of March, Will made frequent trips to the capital to be with her. There is no doubt that by this time he and Oveta had become a couple. When the legislature finally adjourned in March, Oveta traveled with Will to Dallas to meet his brother Alfred and sister Laura. While they were in Dallas, Oveta decided to remain in the city for a few weeks to work for the gubernatorial campaign of James Young, a sixty-four-year-old former US congressman from Kaufman County. How Oveta knew Young is unclear, but he was apparently a friend and former legislative colleague of Oveta's father. We can be fairly certain that Oveta's connection with Young was not through Will, who was a vigorous and enthusiastic supporter of Ross Sterling's not-yet-official bid for governor. Although Sterling would not announce his candidacy until May 30, Will was well aware that his patron would enter the race, so he would not have had any reason to further Young's interests. Nevertheless, either Will had no problem with Oveta working for one of Ross Sterling's competitors for governor or, more likely, he knew better than to try to dissuade her. Will, who by now was desperately in love with Oveta Culp, made frequent trips between Houston and Dallas on the fast Texas and New Orleans Sunbeam Special to be with her. During those visits, Will kept Oveta busy in the evenings, escorting her to dinners, symphonies, movies, and other events.[6]

While Oveta was working at Young's campaign headquarters, she became better acquainted with attorney Sarah T. Hughes, whom Oveta had met in the fall of 1929 in Houston at a state conference of the Texas League of Women Voters. By then, Oveta had become a rising star in the organization. The league invited Oveta to give the luncheon speech at the Rice Hotel, which she titled "Women in Elected Offices." A newspaper story featuring a headshot of Oveta wearing a stylish turban reported, "A prominent place on the program is occupied by a Houston young woman, Miss Oveta Culp." Sarah Hughes also spoke at the conference.[7]

Hughes was a young woman with career ambitions in politics and the law similar to Oveta's. Like Oveta, Sarah Hughes was contemplating a run for the state legislature in the 1930 Democratic primary in July. Both women faced filing deadlines in May. Several of the activists in the Texas League of Women Voters, including Oveta, Sarah Hughes, and Minnie Fisher Cunningham, were part of a wave of women who sought political office in the 1930s as a way to advance and promote progressive reforms deemed especially important to women. Hughes did become a candidate in 1930. She won a seat in the legislature and eventually was elected a state district judge. In 1961 President Kennedy appointed her a federal judge. Hughes secured her place in history by giving the presidential oath of office to Lyndon B. Johnson aboard Air Force One at Love Field in Dallas on November 22, 1963, the only woman to swear a president into office.[8]

Finally deciding to join Hughes and the other women who had entered the election arena that year, Oveta returned to Houston in late May and filed as a candidate for the legislature in a district in Harris County where the incumbent, Captain J. Lewis Thompson, had decided not to run for reelection. Oveta later claimed she made her decision after learning that the only other likely candidate was rumored to be a member of the Ku Klux Klan. "I thought, I can't let that happen," she said. "I'd lived in the county just long enough to qualify. So I took out my dollar and filed." Despite her claim that she had decided to be a candidate to further a cause, Oveta also admitted to one reporter that she had always wanted to be a member of the legislature. "Even when I was too young to understand what it meant, when my father used to tell me about it, I thought it would be a wonderful thing to do," she said. "And now that I've seen something of the work at first hand and know what an opportunity it holds for serving Texas, I want more than ever to do it."[9]

This was another of Oveta's decisions that Will Hobby either supported or at least didn't oppose. Because of Will's active and open support of Oveta's independent governmental and business activities after their marriage, it can be assumed that he approved of Oveta's decision to run for the legislature. Will was deeply involved in helping Ross Sterling plan his campaign for governor, but he made certain that Oveta's campaign received free and favorable publicity with a story in the *Houston Post-Dispatch*. On June 24, 1930, the newspaper announced her candidacy in a story with the headline, "Oveta Culp to Carry Family Banner in Race," which emphasized her father's service in the legislature and as mayor of Killeen.[10]

Houston attorney Ruth Hastings, one of the members of Oveta's network of women's club members, served as Oveta's campaign manager. Oveta had met Hastings in Austin when the latter was attending law school at the University of Texas. Oveta also enjoyed the support of her patrons Flo Sterling and Estelle Sharp, who provided financial backing as well as connections to other prominent Houstonians. First-term state representative Helen Moore of Texas City also served as one of Oveta's close advisors. Moore and Oveta had met at the Texas Democratic Party's state convention in 1926. Moore, whose husband had developed the Texas City oil-refining port on Galveston Bay, had been vice president of the Texas Equal Suffrage Association and head of the Women's Committee of the Hobby Campaign Club in 1918.[11]

Early in the campaign, Oveta, Moore, and Hastings understood that they needed to counter charges that twenty-five-year-old Oveta was too young and inexperienced to serve in the legislature. In what appears to be a planted story, one newspaper printed an interview with Oveta featuring the headline, "Miss Oveta Culp Experienced in Field She Seeks." In an indirect reference to her sixty-year-old opponent, Oveta stressed that the "old dream dreams" while the "young see visions," and she pleaded that the legislature needed more young members to provide a balance between young and old. To help counter charges that she was too inexperienced to serve in the legislature, Oveta told a reporter from the Associated Press that as her father's assistant and later as

OVETA CULP

IS LEGISLATIVE CHOICE OF H⁣ ⁣⁣
COUNTY WOMEN

parliamentarian, she had spent as much time on the floor of the Texas House chamber as many elected members. Oveta's campaign platform indicated how much she shared the views of her progressive women patrons and associates. She called for improvement of the state's institutions of higher education, expansion of the public highway system, passage of meaningful prison reform, and strengthening of law enforcement agencies. She also opposed the Ku Klux Klan and pledged to support any bills providing for the protection of women and children.[12]

Oveta's opponent was attorney John Mathis Sr., who had previously served as a representative from Washington County when Will Hobby was governor. Mathis had relocated his law practice from Brenham to Houston in the early 1920s. Initially, Oveta had nothing against Mathis. She later claimed that she liked her opponent and would have supported him in the race if he had not been an alleged Klan member. Her attitude soon changed, however, when she learned that some of Mathis's supporters were spreading a rumor that she was a member of the women's version of the Ku Klux Klan, an absurd charge given Oveta's close alliance with progressive women political activists who were adamantly opposed to the Klan.[13]

When the spurious rumor about Oveta's Klan membership reached Helen Moore, she wrote Oveta that it was ironic that Mathis's supporters were spreading the rumor, considering the widespread belief that Mathis was himself a member of the secret society. Moore advised Oveta that it was possible that the false charge was intended "to get the hounds off [Mathis's] own trail" and to attract Catholic voters. Pointing out that the KKK was "poison to Catholics," Moore urged Oveta to appeal for help from the head of the Catholic Society of Texas to counter the charge. The rumormongering so annoyed Flo Sterling that she wrote an editorial for the *Houston Mirror* officially endorsing Oveta's election, despite the newspaper having a policy of never endorsing political candidates. Sterling stated, "Religiously, morally, and intellectually Miss Culp has no superiors, and will do credit to any position she may be called upon to fill."[14]

Oveta later admitted that despite the rumormongering and absurd allegations the campaign was "such fun." She also confessed to being naïve. "I thought my opponent was being such a gentleman," she said. "I was new at this, so I didn't know any better. We spoke in the back of trucks. Each time there was a group to speak to, we drew lots to determine the order of speaking, and he always said, 'I'll let the lady speak first.' And I did. And after I spoke, he got up, and he was such a good speaker, very witty. Anyway, when he got up to speak, he'd say in dramatic, hushed tones, 'I think you should know that this lady is a parliamentarian!' And there would be the great hush." Mathis had borrowed one of James Ferguson's favorite ploys, in which he would scare his rural, uneducated audiences with the charge that his opponents were "utilitarians" and "epistemologists." It's not possible to know how effective this tactic was in Houston, where voters were more likely to know the actual meaning of such terms.[15]

Oveta was able to attract the support of a number of prominent Houstonians to her campaign. It's likely that Will Hobby played a crucial role in getting some of that support. A few days before the primary election, Will's longtime acquaintance Colonel Tom Ball broadcast a strong endorsement of Oveta in a radio address. In addition, Captain Thompson, the legislator she was hoping to succeed, issued a public statement calling for Oveta's election. Despite the strenuous campaign effort, favorable newspaper coverage, and endorsements from several influential Houstonians, Mathis won an easy victory over Oveta. Losing to Mathis was a major disappointment. Oveta had expected to win, but instead she attracted slightly less than 40 percent of the vote. The memory of this bitter defeat would stay with her for many years in the future, ending permanently her ambitions for elected office. After a brief rest, she returned to work in the Houston city attorney's office, briefing lawyers, writing opinions, and drafting city ordinances.[16]

While Oveta had been busy with her race for the legislature, Will was deeply involved in Ross Sterling's campaign for governor. When Sterling announced his candidacy on May 30, he faced ten other candidates, the most serious being Miriam Ferguson, Thomas Love, Lieutenant Governor Barry Miller, former US senator Earle Mayfield,

James Young, and Texas senator Clint Small. Dan Moody eventually decided against running for a third term. In an oral history that journalist Ed Kilman conducted in the late 1940s, Sterling implied that he didn't make the decision to run for governor until a few days before he announced his candidacy. The evidence is clear, however, that he and Will Hobby had been preparing for his campaign for several months. Although Sterling had been coy about his intentions, he surprised no one when he finally announced.[17]

Will served as one of Sterling's main advisors during the short campaign in June and July. Except for a trip to Fort Worth in mid-June to attend a strategy meeting with Sterling, he remained in Houston to oversee the *Post-Dispatch*'s barrage of pro-Sterling news stories, while the candidate traveled throughout the state giving speeches. Will also continued to court Oveta while advising her about her own campaign tactics. June was an extremely hectic time for them both as they immersed themselves in electoral politics. Oveta's friend and supporter Helen Moore referred to their busy campaign schedule when she invited them to come to Texas City for a break. "Any time you and Governor find time to spare for a trip phone me," Moore wrote. "If it was Sunday afternoon as you suggested we could take a boat ride and have supper out." Moore's letter also confirmed that their friends now considered Oveta and Will to be a couple.[18]

On July 23, as the primary campaign was coming to a close, Will and Oveta attended a mass rally for Ross Sterling at Houston's Sam Houston Hall that featured speeches by Colonel Tom Ball and Jesse Jones as well as Sterling. At that point it was obvious that with eleven candidates in the race, former governor Miriam Ferguson would attract more votes than any of her opponents but that she would fall far short of winning a majority. The only question was who would come in second place and qualify as Ferguson's opponent in the runoff: Ross Sterling or West Texas state senator Clint Small. In the election three days later, Miriam Ferguson won a plurality of the votes, but as predicted, she fell short of a majority. Ross Sterling prevailed over Small to win a place in the runoff election scheduled for August. Will and the other members of Sterling's team were confident of victory, especially when three of the defeated candidates—Clint Small, Tom Love, and James Young—along with Governor Moody, announced their support for Sterling.[19]

The runoff campaign featured the usual histrionics and demagoguery typical of the Fergusons. In one campaign speech, Jim Ferguson declared that Ross Sterling, who had not completed his high school education, "could neither read, write, nor think." He charged that at campaign appearances in Amarillo and Lubbock, Sterling "sat on the platform like a rhinoceros and never opened his mouth. He had somebody else make his speech." In reality, Sterling had suffered a bout of laryngitis and had lost his voice. Acutely aware of the pro-Sterling editorials in the *Houston Post-Dispatch* and of the fact that his old foe Will Hobby was directing the newspaper's attacks on his wife's campaign, Jim Ferguson called the newspaper the *Houston Post-Disgrace* in his speeches.[20]

Despite Jim Ferguson's fiery rhetoric and vigorous campaigning, Sterling defeated Miriam Ferguson in the runoff election on August 24 by nearly ninety thousand votes. Confident that Sterling would prevail, Will was in Washington, DC, on the day of the election to meet with officials at the Federal Radio Commission to discuss KPRC business. When the election returns came in, Will sent Sterling a telegram stating that with "the exception of one, your election is the most gratifying to me in the history of our state."[21]

In September 1930, Will served as chairman of the Platform and Resolutions Committee at the Democratic State Convention in Galveston. He joined a group of Sterling's other key advisors, including Dan Moody, Jake Wolters, Tom Love, state senator Walter Woodul, and Santa Fe Railroad general counsel John Darrouzett, to shape the policies of the incoming Sterling administration. Sterling later recalled that Will was "the guiding spirit" of that effort. The result was a platform calling for one of Will's favorite causes: statewide highway development planned by the Highway Commission in Austin and paid for with state tax revenue instead of funding from local county governments.[22]

The general election in November 1930 was the usual pro forma affair for Texas Democrats enjoying the benefits of a one-party state. There had been no need to campaign for statewide offices, and Sterling easily won election as governor. On December 30, 1930, Sterling's friends held a preinaugural testimonial dinner in his honor in Houston at the Rice Hotel banquet room, attended by seven hundred guests. After a long bout of speechmaking by several of the city's business leaders, Will, who was serving as the master of ceremonies for the event, presented Sterling with a handsome carving set on behalf of the Knife and Fork Club, the official sponsor of the event. As Will handed the set to Sterling, he declared, "We know you will not use the knife at the pie counter or the fork in the appropriation bill, but we want you to use it in carving for yourself a name in the Hall of Fame."[23]

Will and Oveta traveled to Austin in mid-January 1931 as Oveta reassumed her post as House parliamentarian for the newly elected Speaker, Fred Minor, while Will attended Ross Sterling's inauguration. It was during this stay in Austin that Will and Oveta decided to marry. Years later, Oveta recalled the moment Will asked her to marry him. She told Harry Hurt, who was writing her profile for *Texas Monthly* in 1978, that Will told her, "You know, we really ought to go talk to your mother and father." Oveta asked, "What for?" Will responded, "Well, I'd like to ask them for your hand in marriage." Oveta replied, "Well, you'll have to ask *me* first." Will did, and Oveta said yes. Oveta later observed that her courtship with Will had been more about "intellect and politics than flowers and candy."[24]

When Will proposed to Oveta, he might have been concerned about the fact that he was remarrying so soon after his late wife's death and that he was twenty-seven years older than his fiancée. Oveta apparently had no concerns about this age difference. At least there is no documentation of any concerns she might have had. As discussed earlier, however, there is evidence Oveta had some social unease about marrying Will so soon after Willie's death. That latter concern motivated Will to get the blessings of Willie's family. A few days after Oveta accepted Will's proposal, they traveled to San Antonio to have dinner at the St. Anthony Hotel with Willie's favorite first cousin, Sam Young. With Willie's death only two years past, Will was eager to get informal approval from one of

Willie's closest relatives to remarry. Why he sought approval from Young instead of from Willie's brother, Sam Cooper Jr., is unknown. Sam Jr. was still living, although he would die within the next year. It might be that Will felt closer to Young, whom Will had known since Young had been a teenage errand boy for the Gulf National Bank in Beaumont and who had spent many nights in the Governor's Mansion with Will and Willie.[25]

At the time Will and Oveta met with Sam Young, he was fast becoming a leading figure in El Paso banking and civic circles. While Willie was still living, Will had helped Sam make important business contacts in Houston. Sam eventually became a major player in statewide banking circles, and he worked closely with Conrad Hilton to expand the Hilton Hotel chain. Will asked Young to meet him in San Antonio so that he could introduce Young to "this young lady I'm planning to marry." Years later, when Young recalled the evening, he said, "[I] recognized in Oveta the charm and intellectual vigor that had captivated [my] old friend." As dinner ended, Young proclaimed, "So what are you folks waiting for?" Will and Oveta would remain friends with Young another fifty years, and in Oveta's case, until Young died in 1987.[26]

Will gave *Waco News-Tribune* reporter Raymond Brooks, who had been his secretary when he was governor, the news scoop about his and Oveta's wedding plans. When Brooks's story was published on February 14, the news quickly spread through the capitol. The newly elected attorney general, Jimmy Allred, who was one of Oveta's former boyfriends, was quick to express his best wishes. Another one of Oveta's former suiters, Bob Poage, who was now serving in the Texas Senate, scrawled a handwritten letter to Oveta in which he stressed his love for her and expressed his regret that their relationship was over. "Oveta, I know that I am a better man and will always be, for having known and loved you, and now that it is over I want you to know that you are the finest type of intelligent womanhood."[27]

The news surprised and concerned some of Will's old friends, and some called the upcoming wedding a "Hollywood marriage," a negative term predicting that a marriage was doomed to be of short duration because of the age difference. Comments were also made privately that their difference in physical appearance was an additional imbalance in the relationship. Will was five foot, eight inches in height (although he was taller than Oveta), and the words "rotund" and "jug-eared" were occasionally used to describe him. Oveta, of course, was as admired for her beauty as she was for her intelligence.

Oveta's friends, on the other hand, warned her that marrying Will was no guarantee of high social status or financial comfort, because they felt that at the age of fifty-three, Will's best days were behind him. At the time of their marriage, a decade had passed since Will had held political office, and he had no further political ambitions. More problematic, however, was Will's financial condition, which had begun to deteriorate in late 1930 because of the Depression. Some of Oveta's friends were aware of that.[28]

Oveta later admitted that Will's and her friends were surprised at the match, but their surprise didn't last long because "the marriage worked. We liked each other a great deal. I always felt so at ease with him." As historian Kelli Walsh has observed,

*Portrait of Oveta Culp by*
*Vera Prasilova Scott, ca. 1931.*

the marriage seemed to be an odd pairing by conventional standards but that Will and Oveta "bonded over their shared love of politics and Texas." Another historian, Debra Lynn Sutphen, noted that Will Hobby was also "a kind, gracious, and witty man with an infectious sense of humor who was loved and respected by nearly all who came in contact with him. He became the single most influential person in Oveta's life." In addition, Will gloried in Oveta's ultimate rise to the stature of a national figure. "The age difference worked to Oveta's advantage," Walsh noted. "Because her husband was older and professionally established, his young, ambitious wife did not threaten his ego, and she was free to work long hours and travel as needed to advance their business and her professional profile."[29]

Will and Oveta decided to have their wedding at her parents' home in Temple on February 23, 1931. Oveta later revealed that her intention had been to take a brief break from her duties as parliamentarian to get married. Her plan was to return to the capitol immediately after the wedding and reassume her job. Will, however, had a different idea. He went to Speaker Fred Minor, another old legislative friend of his, and persuaded Minor to release Oveta from her job as parliamentarian. Will said nothing to Oveta about this arrangement until the night before the wedding. It was not a happy moment when Will told her that she no longer had the parliamentarian's job and that Minor had lured Read Granberry back as her replacement. She soon saw a newspaper story proclaiming the news that "Read Granberry now 'pinch hits' as parliamentarian since Oveta Culp married former Gov. W. P. Hobby." In one of her writings about Oveta, *Houston Post* journalist Marguerite Johnston claimed that Oveta remained displeased about this incident for many years afterward.[30]

The dustup over Will's meeting with Speaker Minor might have angered Oveta, but it didn't interfere with the wedding plans. After Ike and Emma Culp hosted a luncheon for Will and Oveta and close family members at the Kyle Hotel in Temple, the couple exchanged their marriage vows at 3:30 p.m. on Monday, February 23, 1931, in a private ceremony at the Culp home at 1219 South Fifty-Fifth Street in Temple. As the guests assembled in the reception room of the Culp family home before the ceremony, Ike Culp observed that his daughter was stylishly dressed in a spring ensemble fashioned from a design by the famed Parisian couturier Jean Patou. He pulled Will aside and teased him, "Will, she's going to embarrass you. She doesn't give a hang about clothes and doesn't dress up the way she should." The guest list was restricted to members of the Culp and Hobby families, including Will's oldest brother, Alfred, and his youngest sister, Laura Aline, who had traveled from Dallas to attend. The ceremony was far different in the type of service, the setting, and the size of the audience from Will's marriage to Willie in New Orleans almost sixteen years earlier.[31]

A minister from the First Baptist Church in Temple presided. Oveta was still officially a member of the church, but her days of preaching sermons in the backyards of friends and dreaming of becoming a Christian missionary were long over. Oveta's religious beliefs had evolved from the raw, hellfire evangelism of her preacher father to a liberal theological worldview that brought her to Unitarianism in the late 1920s (as her opponent in the race for the legislature had correctly charged!). As Robert Pando notes, it's probable that Oveta asked for the Baptist minister to perform the wedding ceremony as a courtesy to Ike and Emma and her brother, Texas Culp, who had become a Baptist evangelist. Oveta's Unitarianism seems to have been short-lived. By the 1940s she and Will self-identified as Episcopalian and their beliefs were solidly ecumenical. Neither she nor Will was a regular church attendee, nor did they openly express religious views. In his youth Will had occasionally attended services at a Methodist church, and he sometimes listed Methodism as his religious affiliation, but when asked about his religion Will typically answered that it was the Lord's Prayer and the Sermon on the Mount.[32]

After the wedding reception, the newlyweds drove off in Will's car, with Oveta at the wheel, as Will told everyone they were going on a tour of various spots in Texas, with San Antonio as their first stop. But it appears that instead they went straight to Oveta's apartment in Austin, where they spent the night, and then on to their new home in Houston. Oveta's friend Jessie Ziegler, a former reporter for the *Houston Post-Dispatch* whom Ross Sterling brought to Austin to serve as his executive secretary, wrote her mother, "Oveta and the Governor fooled everyone into believing they had gone to San Antonio and spent the night [instead] . . . until 11 am Tuesday in their apartment. Rather clever of them."[33]

When the Hobbys arrived in Houston in late February 1931, they settled into Will's two-story house at 2115 Glen Haven in the Braeswood Addition near Rice Institute. Will had built and moved into the house a few months after Willie's death. Designed by architect Harry D. Payne, the structure featured six bedrooms, four baths, a grand entryway, and a large dining room. Will had developed the Braeswood Addition with George Howard and other investors in the Braeswood Development Corporation. Will and Oveta's move into their beautiful new home might have been with feelings of trepidation. The Depression had devastated the housing industry, which was a severe threat to Will's investment in Braeswood. The Hobbys, undoubtedly excited newlyweds, had married at an economically inauspicious time. They would soon be facing daunting financial circumstances.[34]

# CHAPTER 20

————

# THE HOBBY TEAM

In the prologue to his classic work *The Age of Roosevelt: The Crisis of the Old Order*, Arthur Schlesinger Jr. described the Great Depression as a "fog of despair" that "hung over the land." Schlesinger wrote, "Factories that had once darkened the skies with smoke stood ghastly silent . . . families slept in tar paper shacks and . . . one-fifth of the pupils in public schools were suffering from malnutrition." In 1930, nearly 1,400 banks had failed in the United States. In the spring of 1931 that number spiked as another wave of bank closings swept the country. More than six million men and women, one out of every four American workers, were unemployed by the beginning of 1931.[1]

In the year that followed the stock market crash in October 1929, Houston's banks remained open and the city generally weathered the economic storm. But as national consumption of commodities declined in 1930 and 1931, cotton, lumber, rice, and sulfur piled up in Houston and Galveston warehouses and oil products filled nearly every storage tank. Shipping at the Port of Houston slowed precipitously, resulting in a ripple effect of wage reductions and job layoffs and a corresponding drop in household purchasing power. Renters struggled to make lease payments. Mortgage, business, and personal loans were going unpaid. Although Houston eventually managed to avoid the worst effects of the Depression, it still suffered a serious economic downturn in the first years of the 1930s.[2]

Will Hobby was not immune to the financial illness spreading rapidly through the region. He was on the verge of bankruptcy when he married Oveta, and his fiscal woes only worsened in the months immediately after they moved into their new house on Glen Haven. The Braeswood Development Corporation was soon forced into bankruptcy, which significantly added to Will's growing financial woes. The Hobbys managed to retain ownership of the house, however, and they continued to make it their home for several years.

Perhaps due to her youthful resiliency, her strong work ethic, and her inherent self-

————

confidence, as well as her sincere affection for her new husband, Oveta reacted to this financial crisis as a challenge she would help her husband overcome. When later recalling these difficult early years of their marriage, Oveta said, "It would have been easy for Will to have taken bankruptcy. But we weren't going to do that." Oveta's use of the word "we" in this context is noteworthy. Although she had played no role in the business decisions Will had made prior to their marriage—decisions that had placed him on the edge of bankruptcy—it was a challenge they would confront together. As a newspaper profile noted, Will and Oveta's marriage "was a working partnership from the start." Their friends, associates, and, eventually, the public would soon recognize Will and Oveta as the "Hobby Team." And in the story of his life that Will later dictated to James Clark, he was careful to title one of the book chapters "The Hobby Team." It was an apt description of the relationship they would have for the rest of Will's life.[3]

Now married to a former governor of Texas, Oveta, as a good friend later noted, "went after her wardrobe as she had her house, as a business. The result was the sudden blooming of an already attractive woman into a stunning one." A new hairdo emphasized her oval face, and "well cut clothes outlined a junior-miss figure." Oveta had no intention of being a housewife, and Will obviously had no expectation that she would be one. She continued her volunteer club and political work, including serving as president of the Texas League of Women Voters for a one-year term. But Oveta also wanted a real job. Accordingly, Will soon gave her a research editor's position at the *Post-Dispatch*.[4]

While juggling these various activities, Oveta found time early in the spring of 1931 to travel to Temple to see her parents and to Austin to visit with her many friends in the capitol. Jessie Ziegler reported to her mother that "*Oveta is in town*. She looks fine and is doing a little lobbying as well as *Hobbying*." Oveta's lobbying might have been with Will's patron, Governor Sterling. Ziegler, who was Sterling's personal secretary, also reported that Oveta "looks so rested, tho' she says she hasn't gotten any sleep at all since she has been in Houston. She says [Will] is the kindest person in the world and all kinds of fine things about him. She is busy up here—everybody wants to entertain her one way or another. The governor is coming Thursday and they are going to Washington for a few days, and then she is going alone to New York to visit [former *Houston Gargoyle* writer] Ruth West and other friends. It's a great life. I almost envy her."[5]

As it turned out, Will was unable to join Oveta in Austin, and the trip to Washington and New York was canceled. In another letter to her mother, written on April 9, Ziegler reported, "Oveta rushed home late last evening after a call from Houston that Governor Hobby was quite ill with chills and fever and had a nurse. I don't know how true that is but she was crying when she left—nervousness, mostly, I guess. Don't say anything about his being sick to anyone as she asked me not to mention it." Will recovered from his illness quickly. Twelve days later, he served as master of ceremonies at outdoor events at the San Jacinto battleground for the observance of the ninety-fifth anniversary of Sam Houston's victory over General Santa Anna on April 21, 1836. Oveta sat in a section reserved for local and state officials and their spouses as Will stood at a podium on a platform and guided the festivities, which included his reading an official message from Governor Sterling.[6]

Soon after San Jacinto Day, Oveta canceled a trip to Austin because of an attack of nausea. Jessie Ziegler wrote her mother that Oveta was ill with a stomach bug, but that was a misdiagnosis. She was suffering from morning sickness. Twenty-six-year-old Oveta was pregnant. At the age of fifty-three, Will was going to be a father for the first time. The baby, who was due in January 1932, didn't slow Oveta down, however. She continued to work full-time at the *Post-Dispatch* while tending to her duties as president of the Texas League of Women Voters.[7]

By mid-1931 Will's personal financial woes had worsened, largely because of the failure of the two insurance companies he had organized with George Christie, which left him $200,000 in debt (nearly $3 million today). After the stock market crash in 1929 it became clear that Christie, whose contract with Will allowed him to pocket 10 percent of the gross profits from each of the companies, had spread the business too thin, especially with an unwise expansion into California. As one observer later noted, money flowed from Christie's pockets like it was water. Security reserves were nearly depleted, and there were long delays in paying insurance claims. When unpaid claims reached a total of $800,000 in the summer before Will and Oveta married, the state insurance commissioner and attorney general placed the companies in receivership and all employees were dismissed. The reinsurance companies with which Security Union had done business demanded that Christie, but not Will, be indicted for fraud. In addition, Christie had borrowed heavily to create the stock company that he formed with Will, and Will naïvely signed notes secured by the stock, leaving him with the debt. The affair was a public embarrassment for Will because he had allowed his name to be used prominently in the effort to attract business.[8]

Christie's business malpractices, which resulted in the tragic loss of financial support for insured workers who had been badly injured on the job and the widows of men killed while working, affected Will deeply and greatly added to his humiliation. Although few blamed him for the fraud, he was criticized for his blind trust in Christie. Weldon Hart, a longtime reporter for the *Austin American-Statesman* and a publicist who became a good friend of Will's during his years as governor, later noted, "[Will] loved his friends and trusted them perhaps too much, for some of them let him down rather badly." Will's troubles first became publicly known during the 1930 gubernatorial campaign between Sterling and Miriam Ferguson when Jim Ferguson included the news in a campaign speech for his wife at Houston's minor-league baseball stadium. Houston attorney Wright Morrow, who was appointed receiver for both of the failed insurance companies, later noted, "Governor took it in stride [but] it was a body blow."[9]

Will took another financial hit when the Southern Oil and Refining Company filed for bankruptcy. R. L. Henry, who was one of Will's partners in that company, shot himself in the head with a pistol on July 9, 1931. Henry's suicide was widely understood to have been the result of the severe depression he had suffered from his financial losses. During one of

Will's visits at the capitol with Governor Sterling and Jessie Ziegler during this period, he shared his worries about his financial situation with them, afterward prompting Ziegler to write her mother that "it sounds as if he isn't so prosperous. Who is now anyway?" Many years later, when Will was looking back on his business career, he admitted that the collapse of his insurance enterprises in addition to the Braeswood Corporation's bankruptcy "represented the greatest trial and embarrassment" of his life.[10]

Adding to the misery was a steep decline in the *Post-Dispatch*'s revenue. Ross Sterling's wealth, which had served as a critical source of support for the newspaper, was under great pressure because of the money he had borrowed to finance speculative building ventures in downtown Houston before the stock market crash. Those structures included the new twenty-two-story home of the *Post-Dispatch* and the twenty-one-story Sterling Building. Even as Sterling prepared to assume the office of governor in January 1931, Will and Sterling's accountants were warning him that he was facing serious economic difficulties. Will had to give the new governor the bad news that the *Post-Dispatch* would have to close shop if it didn't get an infusion of cash soon. Revenue from advertising and subscriptions had fallen to the point where they no longer covered operational expenses. Sterling responded by having the newspaper's parent entity, the Houston Printing Company, float a $600,000 bond issue to raise the cash the *Post-Dispatch* needed to stay in business. The bonds secured by a deed of trust to the *Post-Dispatch* and to Sterling's personal business assets were sold to two banks in Dallas and to one in Houston for resale. Sterling also persuaded his friends at Humble Oil, including his brother Frank, to advance him $225,000 on royalties from an oil lease Sterling owned and had subleased to Humble. The company also paid Sterling a $175,000 bonus for the sublease.[11]

Sterling's economic distress was exacerbated by a severe reduction in rental income from the high-rise office buildings he had constructed in downtown Houston. He fought to stay solvent, but an avalanche of financial problems overwhelmed him. Although the *Post-Dispatch* had never been much of an income source for Sterling, it not only had now ceased to be a source of any income, it also absorbed what remained of Sterling's cash reserves. Sterling's ultimate downfall came in the fall of 1931, when another wave of bank failures swept the nation, threatening some of Houston's weaker banks, including his Houston National Bank. Early in the Depression, Sterling had loaned money through his bank to several friends who were sinking in their own debt and in need of help. Many of those friends were unable to repay the loans. Sterling also borrowed several hundred thousand dollars from Houston National in his own name to make payments on his mortgages and other debts. He was unable to repay the loans, which left Houston National Bank with $800,000 in bad debt. Rumors spread that the total of bad loans exceeded the amount of money Houston National Bank had on deposit, which caused some of its customers to withdraw their cash from the bank.[12]

Will soon was forced to call for help from Willie's cousin Sam Young, who ran the El Paso National Bank. Young's bank was holding its own, despite the Depression. Will had opened an account at the new bank after Young had organized it in 1925 as a token of his support. Will told Young that the *Post-Dispatch* was now in dire need of financial help. He needed a short-term $40,000 loan because the payroll was coming due before the revenue from upcoming ads could be collected. Without asking for collateral, Young deposited the money in Will's account at the El Paso bank, making it possible for Will to meet his payroll. Will paid off the loan when his advertisers paid their bills. The entire experience, unfortunately, was not a new one for Will. It was a repeat of his early days at the *Beaumont Enterprise*, when he had faced a similar shortage of cash with which to meet the payroll.[13]

As Sterling later recalled, the total of these problems pushed him into the "harrowing last stages of my own transformation from a multimillionaire into a poor man." Sterling believed he could still save Houston National Bank, but the imminent failure of another Houston bank, the Public National Bank, soon set off a chain of events in late fall 1931 that resulted in Sterling's financial downfall, which included his loss of the *Houston Post-Dispatch*.[14]

Throughout the summer of 1931, Jesse H. Jones, the city's most powerful and influential businessman, who had purchased Houston's National Bank of Commerce in 1926, nervously monitored the increasingly precarious condition of Public National Bank and Sterling's Houston National Bank. By Friday, October 23, Jones concluded that those two banks were going to fail as soon as the following Monday, which would likely set off a panic in which customers would try to withdraw the money they had on deposit at their banks, setting off a chain reaction that could threaten all of the banks in Houston, including his own. Jones decided to do whatever he could to prevent these two bank failures and a subsequent run on the city's banks.[15]

On Sunday afternoon, October 25, Jones held an emergency meeting in his office on the thirty-third floor of the Gulf Building with the presidents and many of the board members of the major banks in the city. Jones informed the group that drastic measures should be taken to head off the city's looming banking crisis. The meeting was contentious, as the presidents of two of the banks insisted that Public National should be allowed to fail even if that led to Houston National's failure. They argued that Public National had been badly mismanaged and everyone involved should suffer the consequences, including their innocent customers. Jones and his allies, however, continued to make the case that if one bank failed, it was likely to cause a general panic with dire consequences for them all. The meeting lasted all night, finally ending at five o'clock on Monday morning, when everyone agreed to fund a pool of money to keep the two banks open for at least that day, which would give the bankers a little more time to reach some kind of permanent solution to the problem. During the recess, Jones was able to persuade the holdout banks to agree to his plan.[16]

When Jones and his fellow bankers reconvened late that same Monday afternoon, the meeting included Will Hobby, who was acting as Ross Sterling's agent, as well as lawyers representing Galveston's Moody and Seagraves Interests, the owners of Public National Bank. Bank examiners had determined that it would take $1.25 million to save Houston

National Bank, but the smaller Public National was a lost cause and would need to be merged with another bank that could absorb its bad loans but keep its depositors' money safe. Jones and his colleagues told Hobby that the group had agreed to pay off Sterling's $1.25 million in debt. In return, however, Sterling would be required to place virtually all of his assets in a trust, including his Chupadera Ranch, his buildings in downtown Houston, and his majority stock in the Houston National Bank. The fate of Sterling's stock in the Houston Printing Company, which owned the *Houston Post-Dispatch*, was to be negotiated, but it was unlikely he would be able to retain ownership, as the size of his debt might not be covered by the sale of his other assets. Jones's National Bank of Commerce was selected to serve as trustee of Governor Sterling's assets. The "Advisory Committee under the R. S. Sterling Deed of Trust to the National Bank of Commerce" was organized to guide Jones's bank in managing those assets. First National Bank executive John T. Scott agreed to chair the advisory committee, which included Jesse Jones and Roy Farrar.[17]

Sterling's bank stock, which was being held by Jim West and three other Houston banks as security for his personal loans, was sold to Joseph F. Meyer Jr., Houston National's principal creditor. Sterling's former associates at Humble Oil purchased his property at the Port of Houston for $405,000, which Sterling applied toward his $1.25 million loan debt. Meyer agreed to keep the bank open and operating as normal, but he refused to make the purchase unless Sterling's remaining $800,000 debt at the bank was liquidated. Jessie Ziegler later quoted Will Hobby as saying, "The Houston National Bank changed hands under fire. Joseph Meyer would not take it until every penny of the governor's paper was disposed of—in other words, they did not want any of it." Sterling's trust agreed to Meyer's demand and used proceeds from the sale of Sterling's assets to pay off the debt. Jones was willing to subsume Public National Bank into his National Bank of Commerce and absorb its deposits and liabilities, but only after twelve of the financially sound Houston banks contributed to a guaranty fund to cover bad loans. Six of the banks also deposited a total of $1.4 million in Jones's bank to protect against a run on his bank.[18]

The deal was hammered out before dawn on Tuesday morning, October 26. Jesse Jones called Will Hobby to give him the news. He explained that he was giving the *Post-Dispatch* the scoop over the *Chronicle* because it was important to spread this information as soon as possible to assure the customers of Public National Bank and Houston National Bank that their deposits were safe. Jones asked Will to delay publication of that morning's edition of the *Houston Post-Dispatch* until Jones could release an official statement announcing the action the bankers had taken. Will received Jones's statement, and the headline was spread across the front page of the *Post-Dispatch*.[19]

Jones, who also coveted control over Sterling's newspaper and radio station, told Will Hobby that the advisory committee had decided that Sterling's controlling stock in those properties, which totaled 8,864 shares, also had to be sold. Five banks in New York City, Chicago, and elsewhere, were holding Sterling's *Houston Post-Dispatch* stock (which included KPRC Radio) as collateral for some of his loans. That stock sale would be delayed until the bank deals had been completed and a purchaser for the *Post-Dispatch* could be found. Will, who was understandably worried about how the sale of the *Post-Dispatch* would affect his immediate future, took this news to Sterling, who replied that he intended to negotiate with Jones to prevent the sale. If he failed, he would try to persuade Jones to sell the newspaper to someone who would agree to keep Will as president. In the meantime, Sterling encouraged Will to try to patch together financing to make his own bid to buy the newspaper stock. This was a tall order, given the poor state of Will's own financial resources, but Will, who had long dreamed of owning the *Post-Dispatch*, decided to give it a try.[20]

Will secured enough loan pledges to allow him to make an offer to buy a majority of Sterling's stock and then assume payments on Sterling's loans at the banks that held the stock as collateral. On October 29, Will informed the advisory committee that he had reached an agreement with Governor Sterling—subject to the committee's approval—to purchase most of his stock for $551,550, which would give him control of the *Post-Dispatch*, but only barely. Sterling's trust would hold the remaining 4,178 shares of Sterling's *Post-Dispatch* stock, which it could sell to pay some of Sterling's debt. The advisory committee tentatively agreed to Will's proposal but without further explanation delayed final approval. On October 31 Jessie Ziegler, who was in Austin, reported to her mother that Governor Sterling had gone to Houston and was "in a huddle with Jesse Jones . . . so I don't know whether the [*Post-Dispatch*] will remain the governor's or not." She reported a rumor that "one man wanted to buy the paper but not retain Hobby and that Governor Sterling wanted Hobby taken care of."[21]

Will's loan agreements had expiration deadlines, and he was under pressure to get the deal approved quickly. He wrote the advisory committee on November 2, 1931, requesting final approval as soon as possible. Will stated that he would be "greatly embarrassed and put in a very unfavorable position aside from losing the benefits that might accrue to me from the purchase, if the trade is not consummated and I sincerely trust that it may be closed as made." The advisory committee delayed its decision on Will's offer to give Jesse Jones time to find someone to serve as a front for Jones to gain control over the *Post-Dispatch* and KPRC Radio. As Will waited through most of November for a decision, Jones finally found his front man, oil and insurance entrepreneur J. E. "Jack" Josey, who was a longtime friend of Jones, Sterling, and Hobby. Jones loaned Josey and his brother Robert slightly more than $1 million to form an investment company to purchase all 8,864 shares of Sterling's stock in the Houston Printing Company. By holding the loan the Josey brothers used to make the purchase—a loan that Jones could legally call back at any time—Jones in effect took control of Sterling's media properties.[22]

Journalist Weldon Hart, a good friend of Will Hobby's, later noted that Jack Josey was merely a "front for the deal since no one except the Jones Interests put up any money or had any appreciable amount of stock" in the purchase. Jones, who also owned the *Houston Chronicle* and KTRH Radio, concocted this subterfuge as a way to dodge accusations that he now controlled the city's main news sources. Although the *Houston Press*, owned by Scripps-Howard, was still in operation, it was a poor third in circulation, had no Sunday edition, and, as a tabloid-style publication, lacked the editorial prestige that the *Chronicle* and *Post* enjoyed. Another probable reason Jones hid his ownership of the *Post-Dispatch* and KPRC was the federal restriction on the number of radio licenses that one person or corporation could own in a given listening area. Despite the attempt at secrecy, other Texas newspaper publishers soon determined that Jones was the actual owner of the *Post-Dispatch*. In November 1932, *Austin American-Statesman* publisher Charles Marsh wrote Colonel E. M. House that he had just learned "that both the Houston newspapers are now controlled by Jones. Ex-Governor Hobby, editor of the *Post*, is Jones' employee."[23]

Possibly as a response to Sterling's demands, Josey retained Will's services as president of the newspaper. It's likely that it was an easy decision for Josey to make. Will had met Jack Josey in Beaumont when Josey owned a grain and feed store and Will was publishing the *Enterprise*. Josey had gotten rich in the oil and insurance businesses and had relocated to Houston. He had remained friends with Will and supported him in his races for lieutenant governor and governor.[24]

Ross Sterling was devastated by the loss of his properties. He agreed that the Public National Bank would have failed if it had been left alone and that it was proper for Jones and his allies to prevent that. But Sterling later claimed that his Houston National Bank "was as safe as it could be. There never was a run on my bank. But I was the one who suffered. I had to pay for lots of loans I had taken out for other people, fair-weather friends, in whom I had misplaced confidence." Despite Sterling's claims, the evidence supports the charge that he had mismanaged his bank. Sterling's business practices were more typical of the oil wildcatter that he was than those of a conservative banker. His good friend and fellow banker Roy Farrar described Sterling as a "jazz banker" who took excessive risks and disregarded "the rules of banking." Sterling claimed that Jesse Jones had carried out a plot to ruin him by persuading Jim West and his other creditors to call in his loans when it hadn't been necessary. The result was that West was able to gain control of Sterling's ranch and Jones and his banker friends were able to eliminate Sterling as a business competitor. Sterling was also aware that Jack Josey had cooperated in that effort by merely acting for Jones in buying the *Houston Post-Dispatch*.[25]

Two weeks after he acquired Sterling's stock in the *Post-Dispatch*, Jack Josey wrote a letter to Sterling, whom he had known for more than twenty-five years, saying that he didn't want Sterling to feel he had "intentionally harmed or hurt" him by buying the stock. He explained that Jesse Jones and Will Hobby, "whom I have regarded as among your best friends[,] told me that you had turned a part of the stock over to your Committee for sale and I made the Committee an offer through Mr. Jones. I had no idea you would object to my buying the control." Josey also told Sterling that he would have visited with him to explain the situation, but he had learned Sterling was telling people that Josey "was acting for other parties and working with them to ruin you." Josey pleaded that "nothing could be farther from the truth. Mr. Jones does not own one dollar of the block of stock I bought and no one else does except members of my own family." While it was true that Jones did not own any of the stock, Josey's statement that he had not acted as a front for Jones was a falsehood. Probably more honest was Josey's pleading that he "would not enter into a conspiracy to harm you in any way. I think you have made one of the greatest Governors the State has ever had." Somewhat disingenuously, however, Josey also offered to sell half of his *Post-Dispatch* stock back to Sterling "at the price I paid for the stock and we will hold control together." Obviously, Sterling was not in a financial position to accept the offer, and Josey had to have known it.[26]

Will wrote an editorial that was printed on the first page of the *Post-Dispatch* announcing that Josey had purchased the paper. He praised Sterling and pledged that the *Post-Dispatch* would continue to "get all the news and present it straightforwardly and accurately." A separate news release was distributed announcing that Will Hobby would remain in "complete charge" of the paper as president of the Houston Printing Company and as publisher of the *Post-Dispatch* and that he would have unfettered editorial freedom. In reality, this development resulted in little change for Will. As James Clark later noted, "Hobby had virtually been in control while Sterling worked on the Highway Commission and then in the governor's job." Will did make one major change. On February 1, 1932, he dropped *Dispatch* and restored the newspaper's original name: the *Houston Post*. He later admitted he had never liked the name *Post-Dispatch* but hadn't complained, in deference to his patron Ross Sterling. Will also had practical reasons for the name change. It was as the *Houston Post* that the newspaper had originally gained its reputation, and he knew that many Houstonians never referred to it by any other name than the *Post*.[27]

Josey's acquisition of the *Post*'s stock gave him legal responsibility for Sterling's debts to the five banks holding that stock as collateral. After examining the account books and facing payments on Sterling's stock debt, Josey (probably at Jesse Jones's request) ordered Will to cut expenses, primarily through staff layoffs and salary reductions. Accordingly, Will called a meeting with his editors and reporters in the *Post*'s city room to explain the tough economic situation and the need to take additional austerity measures. He promised to do all he could to keep the newspaper going, but staff layoffs meant they would all be working shorthanded, and that success depended on their hard work as well as his. Longtime *Post* staff member Ed Kilman later recalled that it was the only time he had ever seen Hobby "address the news men collectively like that. The boys didn't say much then, but the chief's simple appeal touched them deeply, and I thought at the time that there wasn't a one in the bunch who wouldn't have gone to hell for Governor Hobby. They came through; the paper survived and with the upturn of 1934–35 it began to look up."[28]

Will's staff layoffs did not include Oveta, of course, but from the Christmas and New Year's holidays to early February, she went on leave from her duties at the newspaper. The Hobbys' baby was due in mid-January, and Oveta agreed to slow down and prepare for the child's arrival. That much-anticipated event occurred at eight twenty in the morning on January 19, 1932, which was also Oveta's twenty-seventh birthday. The newborn, eight-and-one-half-pound boy was named after his proud father. As the son of a popular former governor and the current president of the *Houston Post*, William Pettus Hobby Jr.'s birth and infancy received much more public attention than that given the average child. The *Houston Chronicle* published the news first, scooping Will's own newspaper.[29]

The *Chronicle* also released to the public a picture of William Jr., only one month after his birth, proclaiming that it was the "first newspaper picture of Col. W. P. Hobby, Jr." The *Chronicle*'s reference to baby Hobby as "Colonel" came from Governor Sterling's official announcement that he had appointed him an honorary colonel in the Texas National Guard. The tongue-in-cheek pronouncements continued with Will's old friend and political ally Jacob Wolters, who was commander of the state's Guard units, releasing a public statement that he was assigning William P. Hobby Jr. to the headquarters staff of the Texas National Guard's Fifty-Sixth Cavalry Brigade. The *Dallas Morning News* joined in the fun and published an editorial that pointed out, "At present, the Colonel's uniform is basically that of Mahatma Gandhi," a reference to Gandhi's habit of wearing a simple loincloth called a dhoti. Another Texas newspaper noted that Will's son "was born on Robert E. Lee's birthday, on Joan of Arc's birthday, and on Mrs. Hobby's birthday. He ought to be a political personality some day. Also, the lad might turn out to be a newspaper personage. His father is editor of the *Houston Post* after having spent a lifetime in the newspaper business."[30]

Will and Oveta's friends were quick to congratulate the couple on the birth of their first child and predicted that he was destined to have a great future. John Henry Kirby wrote to Oveta, "Knowing the mother who will train him, I have no hesitation in predicting that forty years hence he will occupy the White House as its master." Oveta's former boyfriend Jimmy Allred, now Texas attorney general, sent a handwritten note to Will: "Congratulations! Just heard about the new 'President of the United States.'" Another of Oveta's former boyfriends, Bob Poage, continued the theme that a future president had been born. In a telegram to Will and Oveta, Poage conveyed the congratulations of "an old bachelor to the father and mother and future president. Nineteenth of January has always been a great day for the South and especially for the Culp Family."[31]

Other friends predicted that a future governor or senator had been born. Florence Sterling wrote that she was "so happy to know W. P. Hobby Jr. has arrived. May he grow to be the Governor of Texas and United States Senator." Tom Love also sent his "hearty congratulations on the new Governor," while Senator Tom Connally sent the newborn a message for his scrapbook, warning him, "Young man, you will have the responsibility of carrying on a splendid tradition because of the distinction of your parents on both sides of the house." Governor Sterling and Dan Moody cosigned a telegram to Will, stating that they were "wondering just what size hat it will now take to fit you." On behalf of Governor Sterling's entire staff, Jessie Ziegler sent a message addressed to the newborn Hobby, using the name "Bill," which would be the name his friends would use to differentiate him from his father. "Dear Bill," Ziegler wrote, "we understand you arrived in Houston today to be the permanent guest of Governor and Mrs. Hobby. You certainly have good taste in picking such splendid and able parents, and greeting them on the anniversary of the birth of Robert E. Lee. We hope that you will follow in the footsteps of your illustrious parents and keep the name Hobby in the hearts of as many Texans as they have theirs." Will reacted to all of this attention by confessing to Oveta that if he had known "babies were so popular, I would have put them in my [campaign] platform."[32]

Oveta was soon back at work. Will hired a registered nurse to stay with the baby while Oveta was at her desk at the *Post* during the day. By mid-March, she and Will were spending time in Austin, visiting Ross Sterling and other friends in the capitol. In a letter to her mother, Jessie Ziegler reported that "Oveta and Governor came in to say howdy to us all this morning. She had on a rather roomy coat in black and white with a bloused effect, and she looked as big as all outdoors. She looks mighty fine in the face, though. Her skin is very soft and delicate looking and she looks so well." Referring to the sensational national story about the March 1 kidnapping of famed aviator Charles Lindbergh's baby, Ziegler noted that Oveta "did not have the baby with her and in view of the Lindbergh affair I can't see how she could run off from him. She still talks about the baby as if he was a new puppy."[33]

Even with the help of a nurse, Oveta found it hard to balance motherhood with work. In an interview she gave to the *New York Daily News* in 1953, Oveta admitted she had believed she could handle being a businesswoman and a wife and mother all at the same time but that "in the early years it was sometimes difficult." There were additional reasons for the stress. She recalled that the "Depression was on, profits were nil," and she still had to do a "great deal of the household work" herself after office hours. Having a child also forced her to go through some emotional adjustments. Oveta's intense drive and her zeal for work, along with her obsession with order, were interfering with her need to bond with little Bill. And Will was having his own problems at the *Post*. Jack Josey, who was acting as Jesse Jones's surrogate, had ordered Will to make additional reductions in staff that went beyond what Will believed was necessary to keep the newspaper afloat. Will's increasing discomfort with the severe budget cuts was obvious to his friends, which led to rumors that he might leave the newspaper.[34]

One way Oveta coped with her new domestic situation was to set aside some time to relax, exercise, and clear her mind by going horseback riding and skeet shooting. Because of her father's influence, Oveta had developed a love for target shooting and horseback riding when she was a young girl, and she became skilled at both. One of her companions who often accompanied her on shooting expeditions later recalled that she was "a great shot." But horses were her real love. After she moved to Austin and then to Houston, she only occasionally found time in her busy schedule to ride. After she married Will, however, she was able to spend more time enjoying the sport, often with her husband. The Hobbys' house on Glen Haven was conveniently located near horse stables with easy access to riding paths in spacious Hermann Park. Oveta took advantage of being close to the stables and could often be seen riding on the park's bridle trails.[35]

Early in July 1932, Oveta was on an early morning ride when her horse suddenly bolted, tossing her to the ground. She suffered a badly broken leg, a shattered right wrist, and deep bruises to her right hand, nerve damage in one arm, and numerous cuts and abrasions from head to toe, which required her to be hospitalized for several days. After she was released from the hospital, Oveta was confined to home and disabled for several weeks. Adding to her worries, Oveta's brother Jack was arrested in San Antonio while she was still in the hospital. Jack had been forging her name to checks for several months, and when he refused to stop, Oveta filed a complaint with the police, who caught him trying to cash two of the checks.[36]

Oveta was out of circulation for slightly more than two trying months, which restricted her involvement in the Democratic primary election and the probable runoff. Ross Sterling's campaign for a second term as governor was in full throttle. He was engaged in a difficult struggle with his opponent, former governor Miriam Ferguson, who once again was her husband Jim Ferguson's proxy. Oveta had planned to work for Sterling's campaign, but her accident made it difficult. Unable to handwrite letters because of her crushed right wrist and injured arm, Oveta dictated her messages to a typist and then scrawled her signature with her left hand. She sent one of these messages to her friend Jessie Ziegler on July 18, 1932, to convey her apologies for not being able to work in Governor Sterling's campaign. Referring to the election date, Oveta assured Jessie that she felt "sure the result on the 23rd will please us all very much." She added that she hoped Jessie would visit her in Houston and ended the letter with, "MUCH LOVE, Oveta." The affectionate closing caught Ziegler's attention. In a letter to her mother, she said, "Get the 'much love'? Oveta is always like that when she is calm and not in such a hurry to accomplish something. When she is aggressively doing something, she loses her sweetness in her desire to accomplish something. Like all of us, she has a sweet nature as well as another side."[37]

While the gubernatorial election continued during the last half of July and the first half of August, Oveta endured a painfully slow recovery. She had lines in her arm and leg to drain fluid, and she remained bedridden. Nevertheless, she managed to do some work for the Sterling campaign from her bed at home. She made telephone calls to his wealthy supporters asking them to contribute money to the campaign. She examined Houston's precinct voter lists closely and then called precinct leaders to urge them to get Sterling's voters to the polls on the runoff-election day. Oveta's refusal to slow down caused her physician to warn Will that she needed to take it easy. The doctor felt that because of the serious nature of her injuries, it might take a few months before she could walk. Undaunted and undefeated, Oveta ignored her physician's warning and continued to work from bed. Dictating copy to a stenographer, she wrote book reviews for the *Post*'s book page, and she had *Post* staff members bring her reference books from the Houston Public Library so that she could continue research for an article she was writing for the newspaper.[38]

This was an extremely frustrating time for Oveta. She awoke one morning and insisted to Will that she was going downstairs even though her leg was in a rigid cast. She was so insistent that Will and her nurse gave in. With their help, she crawled to the stairway and sat on the top step. As the nurse held the leg that was in a cast, she inched down each step until she got to the ground floor, where Will and the nurse helped her get in a wheelchair. Will asked his wife how she thought she was going to get back upstairs. She replied that she didn't care because she was going to stay out of bed for a while. Will eventually called the *Post* printing plant and asked two of his workers to come to the house. They carried Oveta back upstairs in the wheelchair.[39]

While Oveta's injuries forced her to remain bedridden, Will was boosting Sterling's reelection effort with laudatory editorials in the *Houston Post* and friendly news coverage of Sterling's campaign. Miriam Ferguson won a plurality in the first primary election in late July, but Sterling attracted enough votes to place second over several other candidates and to qualify for the runoff election. Despite hopes that Sterling would prevail by picking up enough of the ballots cast for the anti-Ferguson candidates, Ferguson managed to win a narrow victory over Sterling in the runoff. The vote count was so close that it took several days to determine the outcome. Miriam Ferguson was eventually declared the winner by a little more than three thousand votes. Sterling filed a lawsuit claiming voter fraud, but the courts ruled against him. In the general election in November, Sterling supported the Republican candidate, Orville Bullington, while Will and the *Post* took a neutral position. Bullington waged a spirited campaign, but Ferguson prevailed.[40]

At the beginning of September, Jessie Ziegler reported to her mother that Will had told Ross Sterling that Oveta would probably have to wear a built-up shoe when she was back on her feet and that her wrist might be stiff the rest of her life. "Poor girl," Ziegler wrote, "she must feel terrible not to be able to go anywhere or do anything and the prospect of being crippled the balance of her life. I'm so sorry for her. If she was mighty, she surely 'fell,' but I am not one to be glad that she had to come 'down to earth' by such a route." Nearly a month later, however, Will was able to bring better news about Oveta to Sterling and his staff. Jessie reported to her mother, "Governor Hobby was in today and said that Oveta, while she had to wear a high top shoe, was getting along nicely but her arm was still practically useless. Her fingers are still numb and kind of useless." According to Ziegler, Will also candidly admitted that there had been one benefit from Oveta's forced confinement to home: "He said that Oveta had gotten to love the baby [Bill] and that while she had fought against it, she just had to succumb to the little darling."[41]

Balancing on crutches and wearing a special shoe and braces on her fractured wrist and broken leg, Oveta returned to the *Post* and to her volunteer civic work at the end of September, hobbled but mobile and surely happy to be back in action. It may be that Oveta made a special effort to get on her feet because of her desire to see and possibly meet Huey P. Long, the notorious US senator from Louisiana who was scheduled to travel to Houston to attend the football game between his beloved Louisiana State University (LSU) Tigers and the Rice Institute Owls.

When Houston mayor Walter Monteith learned that Senator Long would be coming to the city for the football game, he asked Will to join him at the train depot to greet Long and to give the senator a key to the city. Will was serving as a substitute for Governor Sterling, who had declined Monteith's invitation to meet Long. His excuse was that he was too deeply involved in his lawsuit contesting Miriam Ferguson's victory to spare the time. But that was a convenient out. In 1931, when Long was governor of Louisiana, he and Sterling had clashed bitterly over a bill Long wanted the Texas Legislature to pass declaring a moratorium on the planting of cotton. Sterling angered Long by leading the opposition against the moratorium. Sterling had also denounced Long for his attacks

*Huey Long and the Louisiana State University marching band in Baton Rouge, Louisiana, 1934.*

on Standard Oil of New Jersey, which controlled Humble Oil. Will had no objection to standing in for Sterling, because he had long-standing ties to Louisiana dating back to his days in Beaumont and he still had many friends in New Orleans, the city where he had married Willie.[42]

Senator Long and Louisiana governor O. K. Allen arrived in Houston from Baton Rouge early in the morning of October 1 on one of three special trains LSU had chartered for a large number of its faculty, several members of the state legislature, four hundred students, its football team, the 140-person marching band, and a contingent of prominent alumni. When the LSU trains arrived in Houston, the marching band disembarked from its coach, set up sheet music stands on the platform, and played the school fight song, "Hold That Tiger," and marching tunes as the football team and the other passengers stepped off the trains. The band continued to play as Mayor Monteith and Will Hobby and a large crowd of Houstonians waited patiently for Huey Long to emerge from his private railcar. When Long, who was called "Kingfish" by his enthusiastic supporters, eventually staggered out of his railcar, it was obvious he had enjoyed a large number of alcoholic beverages on his way to Texas, no matter that prohibition was still the law. After the mayor and Will Hobby welcomed the senator, Long immediately lined up the LSU band in marching formation and led it on a parade from the train station to the Rice Hotel, where the contingent from Louisiana was staying.[43]

After the parade, Mayor Monteith and Will Hobby took Senator Long in a chauffeured limousine to the mayor's house for a brunch honoring Long. In his memoir, Bill Hobby shared his father's story about that day. While the trio were on their way, "Senator Long clapped my father on the knee and, blowing his whiskey breath in my father's face, [and] asked: 'Hobby, are you a friend of [Governor] Sterling's?'" Will Hobby replied that he certainly hoped so. Referring to Sterling's lawsuit contesting Miriam Ferguson's victory, Long said, "Tell Sterling to keep his ass out of the courthouse. Being counted out is the same as being voted out. I know. I've done it both ways."[44]

Oveta was not invited to the breakfast at the mayor's house because of doctor's orders and Will's concerns about not hampering her recovery from the horse-riding accident. She was determined, however, to see the famous "Kingfish." There are conflicting versions of how Oveta carried it off, but she did succeed in getting to Monteith's house to meet Long. One account is the one Oveta told her daughter-in-law, Diana Hobby. According to this version, Oveta dressed up as a waitress and crashed the stag brunch and reception. In his memoir, Bill Hobby tells a slightly different version of the story, which he attributes to his father, about Oveta wearing a waitress's dress and serving coffee as a way to meet Huey Long. The waitress story may indeed be accurate, or at least some aspect of it; however, Oveta was still wearing a heavy leg brace and was dependent on crutches for mobility when Long was in Houston, which casts doubt on both versions.[45]

A more likely version of this incident was the one Al Shire, a longtime employee of the *Houston Post*, reported many years later. Shire transcribed a number of stories Oveta told her editors during editorial meetings. According to Shire's account, Oveta was asked to host a reception for Huey Long when he came to Houston, but she refused, probably because she was still on crutches. "So someone else gave a reception. . . . It was for men only," she recalled. "I told Governor that since there was a side porch, I'd just go in that way and sit there. I wanted to see Huey Long." Her reference to sitting down on the side porch was probably because she recalled that she was still on crutches. Two of her friends were with Oveta on the porch, probably to help Oveta get around. As the group watched the party through the open windows on the porch, Oveta noted that "[Long] was quite intoxicated." Suddenly Long stumbled forward as the French doors to the porch opened. Oveta said that Long stared at her and asked, "Wellll, whooo are youuuuu?" When someone told him she was Governor Hobby's wife, Long asked, "An' where'd he fin' youuuu?" Someone jokingly responded, "In an orphan asylum, Senator." Long mumbled, "[Will Hobby] married a second time and found her in an orphan asylum. Wunnnerful! No kinfolks!" Bill Hobby's version of this incident says that it was his father who said he found her in an "orphanage." Yet another version states that it was Long who said, "Pretty little thing. Where did you find her, in an orphanage?" The significance of this incident, no matter which of those versions is correct, is that the story reveals a playful and mischievous side of Oveta that has often been ignored. It also indicates how determined Oveta could be when she set her mind to do something, even on crutches.[46]

After the reception, Huey Long continued his shenanigans that afternoon by happily leading the LSU band around Rice's football field at halftime. In a bit of an understatement, the Associated Press noted, "The Kingfish had quite a day in general." The Rice Owls defeated LSU by a score of ten to eight in a game described by the Associated Press as "gaudy with suspense and thrills."[47]

# CHAPTER 21

# WORKING FOR
# "MR. HOUSTON"

After Oveta returned to work at the *Post* in October 1932, her injuries began to heal more quickly than her physicians had expected. She was able to toss her crutches aside late that month, and she happily shed the wrist and leg braces soon thereafter. Oveta still had difficulty using her right hand and her arm remained numb, but she had the services of a stenographer to whom she could dictate her letters and text for her articles in the *Post*. As it turned out, she was able to walk without having to wear a special shoe, as her doctor had feared. The only visible reminder of the accident was a long surgical indenture in her wrist that she carried for the rest of her life.[1]

Oveta's mobility and stamina improved enough during October and early November to allow her to work in support of the presidential ticket of Franklin D. Roosevelt (FDR) and his vice presidential nominee, Texas's native son John Nance Garner. The Hobbys had initially supported House Speaker "Cactus Jack" Garner's bid for the Democratic nomination for president in 1932. When Will was governor he had several meetings with Garner, who had served as a US congressman from Texas since 1903. He and Garner had mutual political allies in South Texas. In the spring of 1932, Will published several editorials and stories in the *Post* favorable to Garner and critical of FDR. One editorial, "Ambitious New York," questioned the wisdom of nominating Roosevelt, who was governor of New York, because that state's Al Smith and John Davis had both lost their presidential elections. The editorial also pointed out that Democratic presidential candidates had carried New York only once during the last thirty-six years. George Lynn, managing editor of the *Santa Barbara Daily News*, sent a clipping of the editorial to Will's friend former treasury secretary William Gibbs McAdoo, who was leading the Garner campaign in California. "The Houston Post—Hobby's paper—is plugging the cause hard almost every day," Lynn wrote McAdoo. "The attached clipping is representative of their attitude." When it became apparent that FDR would win the nomination at the Democratic National Convention, Will assumed Garner would prefer to remain as

Speaker of the House instead of serving as vice president. He lobbied his associates in the Democratic Party to put McAdoo on the ticket as FDR's running mate. Garner surprised Will, however, by accepting the vice presidential nomination.[2]

After FDR won the party's nomination, the Hobbys readily shifted their support to the New York governor, joining the vast majority of Texans who were eager to defeat Herbert Hoover and restore the Democratic Party to power in Washington. Will had met and was impressed by FDR during the Democratic convention in Houston in 1928. Oveta had been in the convention stands to hear FDR's "Happy Warrior" speech nominating Al Smith for president and had found it inspiring. Accordingly, both were enthusiastic as well as active supporters of the Democratic presidential ticket, and the editorial pages of the *Houston Post* openly reflected that. Although it was clear that Texas was safely in FDR's camp and that 1932 was going to see a national Democratic sweep, Oveta nevertheless devoted considerable time on the telephone to raising money for the campaign. Oveta's efforts were reported to Eleanor Roosevelt, who wrote Oveta a letter of appreciation. "I am so glad to hear that you are doing such good work in the campaign," the future First Lady wrote, "and I very much appreciate your doing it." Future events would bring Oveta into closer contact with the Roosevelts, especially with Eleanor.[3]

Jones was not interested in any effective competition between the *Houston Chronicle*, the profitable newspaper he openly owned, and the *Houston Post*, which he silently controlled. By the time of the presidential campaign in 1932, Will Hobby had become increasingly dissatisfied with the *Houston Post*'s new ownership arrangement. He was getting along well with Jack Josey, but Jesse Jones held in collateral all of Jack Josey's stock in the Houston Printing Company, and he was calling the business shots for the newspaper. The main problem Will had with Jones was his refusal to modernize the *Post*'s equipment and facilities and to take other measures to improve the newspaper. Will knew those improvements were essential to his efforts to increase the *Post*'s circulation and make the paper profitable. Improvements would cost money, however, which meant they weren't made, much to Will's frustration. According to Jessie Ziegler, a prominent Houston lawyer visited Governor Sterling's office in August 1932 and told Sterling and Ziegler that Will "would probably be looking for another job on January 1st." Ziegler reported this news to her mother: "I have suspicioned [Will's resignation] for some time and believe I told you when the paper was sold to Josey that Hobby wouldn't continue long." Given her closeness to Sterling, Ziegler's "suspicion" was undoubtedly based on Sterling's speculations. This situation raises the question of why Jesse Jones bought the *Houston Post* if he had no intention of making it profitable. It is reasonable to assume that Jones acquired the *Post* to keep it out of the hands of other owners who might have had the resources to challenge the dominant position his *Houston Chronicle* enjoyed. Other complex financial issues, including possible tax implications, might have played a role.[4]

Ultimately, Will decided not to leave the *Post*. In January 1932, President Herbert Hoover had appointed Jesse Jones to the board of the newly authorized Federal

Reconstruction Finance Corporation, which was a full-time job. Jones and his wife were now living in a hotel in Washington, DC, but he was aware of Will's unhappiness with his situation at the *Post*. In December 1932 Jones allowed Will to buy a large block of the Houston Printing Company's twenty-five thousand shares of stock, thus giving him a strong stake and more of a voice in the company's direction, although not majority control. Will Hobby and Eddie Clarkson, his close friend and business associate of nearly forty years, signed a loan/purchase agreement with Jack Josey for Will to buy eleven thousand shares and for Clarkson to buy one thousand shares of stock in the *Post*'s parent company, leaving Josey with thirteen thousand shares. The purchase was financed by a loan from Josey to Hobby and Clarkson, with their shares turned back to Josey as collateral. The agreement gave Josey unrestricted legal power to sell his and Hobby and Clarkson's stock to another party. That same day, Josey signed an agreement with Jesse Jones, who was in Houston for the Christmas holidays, giving him a five-year option to buy all of the twenty-five thousand shares of Houston Printing Company stock owned by Josey, Hobby, and Clarkson for a token price of $25,000. If and when Jones exercised his option, he would own all of the Houston Printing stock that the banks were holding as collateral. Jones would still owe the banks for the debt the collateral had secured.[5]

The arrangement made it possible for Will to own—at least on credit—a major portion of the *Houston Post*'s stock, as well as for Jack Josey to keep his promise to allow Will complete freedom over *Post* editorial and news coverage. It also placated Will for the time being, although he continued to chafe at the financial restraints Jones imposed on his efforts. He and Oveta now turned their full attention in the new year of 1933 to the *Post*, with Will managing the news and editorial staff and monitoring business affairs while Oveta performed a variety of jobs, including book reviews and some editorial work.

When working with his editorial writers and department heads during these years that he was in control of daily operations, Will's management style was to make suggestions and hints instead of issuing orders. As Weldon Hart, one of his former reporters, later noted, Will listened to his staff carefully while they debated a problem but spoke only when his opinion had been fully formed. "Although never trained for the law," Hart said, "he had the ability to get a lot of information with few questions, and he could say a lot in very few words." According to Hart, Will's speaking manner was "direct and terse without being rude," and when he ended his telephone calls he usually said "okeydokey" instead of "goodbye." In conversation he did more listening than talking and often disposed of a subject under discussion in one or two sentences. "His grasp of a situation was phenomenal."

Hart also recalled that Will, who had a "merry, elfin smile on his face most of the time," was "a gentle and kind man who never knowingly harmed anyone." Because of Will's respect for the feelings of his staff, he hesitated even to call one of them to his office. A new secretary around the executive suite would be puzzled when "Governor" asked in a somewhat uncertain tone, "Did Joe want to see me?" The new secretary would eventually catch on. Actually, Governor wanted to see Joe. The secretary would discreetly transmit

*Jesse Jones with architect Alfred C. Finn, 1928.*

the message, and Joe would drop by the office. Governor would then cordially talk to Joe about whatever he needed to talk to him about, happy he had avoided the possibility of offending Joe by ordering him to his office.[6]

With Oveta now fully recovered from her injuries, she renewed her involvement in club work, civic matters, and larger public policy issues, especially in the national movement to repeal the Eighteenth Amendment. Will Hobby had never been a fan of prohibition, and like millions of his fellow countrymen, he ignored the law. Oveta, however, was raised in a religious, conservative, and anti-alcohol family. At some point Oveta turned against prohibition, perhaps when she moved to Houston, or, more likely, when she began her relationship with Will Hobby. Her change of heart about the Eighteenth Amendment was shared by millions of Americans, including its initial supporters. By the early 1930s it had become clear to many Americans that the Eighteenth Amendment, which Herbert Hoover had called the "noble experiment," was a failure. In the decade since its passage, prohibition had played a strongly negative role in the national economy—one that some historians believe exacerbated the Depression. There was a major decline in the amusement and entertainment industries. Restaurants failed because liquor sales had generated the profits necessary for many of them to stay in business. Thousands of jobs were eliminated, including those in the brewing and distillery industries and in saloons. One of the most profound unintended consequences was major loss of tax revenue at the local, state, and federal levels. It has been estimated that the federal government lost approximately $11 billion in tax revenue during the prohibition era, a huge sum in 1920s dollars. Among other serious problems, the amendment also resulted in widespread police corruption and growth in organized crime. The large number of people being arrested overwhelmed the courts. Prohibition had been meant to foster temperance, but it actually resulted in increasing alcohol consumption. Even previously fervent prohibitionists concluded that the amendment had too many unintended consequences.[7]

The movement to repeal the Eighteenth Amendment gained serious momentum early in 1932. After the Texas Legislature placed a prohibition repeal referendum on the ballot for the general election in November 1932, Will Hobby made speeches and wrote editorials exhorting voters to support repeal. He also urged the Democratic Party to include repeal on the platform for the presidential election in November 1932. The state referendum passed by a margin of four to one. It was clear that public support of prohibition in Texas had declined drastically.[8]

In February 1933, a month before FDR's inauguration as president, Congress passed the Twenty-First Amendment to repeal the Eighteenth Amendment and sent it to the states for ratification. A month later, Oveta joined the Women's Organization for National Prohibition Reform (WONPR), founded in New York City by influential conservative socialite and Republican National Committee member Pauline Morton Sabin. WONPR's mission was to coordinate the effort at the state level to pass the Twenty-First Amendment by the constitutionally required three-fifths of the states. Oveta was attracted to WONPR not only for its cause but also because of Sabin and her associates, which included a group of prominent women in the Northeast.

Sabin was the type of leader Oveta aspired to be. Prohibition historian Daniel Okrent describes Sabin as being "as intelligent as she was beautiful, as energetic as she was elegant." She "engaged the Republican Party with the same vitality she brought to her luminous social life." Like Oveta, Sabin had initially been a prohibitionist, but she turned against it when she concluded that it had resulted in widespread "political dishonesty, cultural dislocations, and contagion of crime." According to Okrent, Sabin made the repeal movement "respectable, even fashionable." When it was "elegant, refined, fabulously wealthy Pauline Sabin" criticizing prohibition, it helped "other women to find their voices." Even though Sabin was an actively partisan Republican, she endorsed FDR for president because of his support for repealing the Eighteenth Amendment. By 1933, WONPR had more than 1.3 million members, with Oveta Hobby one of them.[9]

Within days after Oveta joined WONPR she took a leadership role in Houston's local chapter, which was chaired by Annie Bonner, the socially prominent wife of Frank Bonner, a longtime business associate of John Henry Kirby and an old friend of Will's. When Oveta learned that Pauline Sabin was organizing a national conference in Washington, DC, for members representing state chapters, she volunteered to serve on the Texas delegation. After Annie Bonner notified WONPR national headquarters in New York, a staff member sent a letter to Oveta stating that the organization was "happy to know you will be one of our Texas representatives" and that Pauline Sabin was appointing her to the Committee of Political Activities, "which will be one of the most important committees at this Conference." The national office also assured Oveta that she would be "inspired by the sincere, outstanding women who are working for this *constructive temperance* cause."[10]

When Oveta arrived in Washington on April 4, 1933, she paid a visit to Jesse Jones and his wife, Mary. By this time, it was widely understood that FDR would soon appoint Jones as chairman of the Reconstruction Finance Corporation. The president made the appointment a month later. After Oveta's visit, Jones reported back to Will that he and Mary were "delighted to see Oveta. She was looking fine and very spiffy." After her visit with the Joneses, Oveta spent two days in the thick of things at the convention, which was held at the Mayflower Hotel. She participated in the WONPR general and topical sessions and the meetings of the Political Activities Committee, and she met and was impressed by the dynamic Pauline Sabin. Oveta's involvement was mentioned in wire service press reports, which might have been her first, albeit small, appearance in the national press. When Oveta returned to Houston, she reported to the chair of the Texas WONPR chapter, Dallas civic leader Florence Rodgers, that the most important session of the conference was about liquor control. "I believe I secured some information that will be of great help in determining what plan we shall adopt in Texas to control the sale and use of liquor."[11]

At the next meeting of Houston's WONPR chapter in early May, Oveta gave a report on the national convention and the organization's plans for lobbying states that had not yet ratified the Twenty-First Amendment. She recommended that the Houston chapter adopt the convention's recommendations about how liquor should be regulated after the end of prohibition and present them to Governor Miriam Ferguson. Oveta also presented these recommendations to the Texas Federation of Anti Prohibition Clubs, a men-only organization led by John Henry Kirby and managed out of his office in the Kirby Building.[12]

On December 5, 1933, Utah became the thirty-sixth state to ratify the Twenty-First Amendment, resulting in the repeal of the Eighteenth Amendment, the only constitutional amendment ever rescinded. The "noble experiment" had ended in failure as a national prohibition, although some individual states, including Texas, kept their "dry" laws. Texas did not end statewide prohibition until 1935. With the adoption of the Twenty-First Amendment, the Women's Organization for National Prohibition Reform dissolved, its mission accomplished. Oveta turned her attention to other activities, but her brief involvement with WONPR gave her a taste of involvement in public policy matters at the national level. In addition, Oveta's exposure to Pauline Sabin, and to the prominent and socially sophisticated women associated with Sabin's organization whom Oveta met and admired, was one of several important experiences that played a role in shaping Oveta Culp Hobby as a public figure.[13]

On Mother's Day in 1933, the *Post* published a large photographic portrait of Oveta holding her fifteen-month-old son as part of a special feature that included the portraits of five other mothers posing with their children. The caption noted that the photo was Oveta's first public appearance with her "fine young son, William Pettus, II." The publication of Oveta's portrait with her child was not the first time her photograph had appeared in the local press, but it was significant nonetheless. It was now obvious that Oveta Culp Hobby had joined the ranks of Houston's prominent citizens. It also signified that Oveta was a woman who could do it all. She was a wife, a workingwoman, a community activist, and a mother. That image, and not a false one, was one that Oveta would cultivate for the rest of her life.[14]

Although Oveta had written book reviews, conducted research, and contributed special articles to the *Post* for a couple of years, she lacked an official title as editor. That oversight was addressed in October 1933, when Jack Josey agreed to her appointment as editor of the *Post*'s Sunday book page. She promptly expanded the scope of the section, contributing her own reviews and assigning books to other writers. This new job title gave Oveta a heightened degree of cultural and intellectual credibility, while her status as a former governor's wife, her ever-growing network of political connections, and her involvement in a range of public causes drew Oveta into a widening circle of the professional, cultural, and political elite in her city and state, as well as in Washington and New York.[15]

As one of her biographers, Debra Sutphen, noted, Oveta had adopted the "lifestyle expected of an influential city newspaper publisher's wife." During these years of her increasing public visibility, the deeply image-conscious Oveta continued to work on improving aspects of her public persona. Although her grandmother had helped her shed most of her Central Texas drawl, she hired tutors for elocution and public speaking lessons. Her friend and longtime *Houston Post* employee Marguerite Johnston later observed that Oveta developed the "well modulated, clean articulation of an educated Southern gentlewoman. She never spoke or laughed loudly, but when she spoke, people listened. She had presence. Her sense of humor: Naughty, yes, but never bawdy."[16]

With Will's enthusiastic encouragement and support and with the help of nannies they hired for their son, Oveta worked to broaden, in Sutphen's words, her "innate sense of style and formality" and her "eye for beauty and love of cultivation." She improved her general knowledge of music, dance, architecture, and decoration, and she eventually

*Oveta Culp Hobby
in the mid-1930s.*

began to collect antique silver. And as Sutphen also notes, "With [Oveta's] typical unbridled enthusiasm [she] spared no effort in educating herself thoroughly on each subject." Oveta joined the Junior League and became a patron of the Houston Symphony and the Houston Museum of Fine Arts, eventually becoming a major donor and a member of the board of directors of the museum. Not surprisingly, given her love of performance when she was a young girl back in Killeen, Oveta got involved in Houston's budding live theater scene, even acting in amateur theatricals at Houston's Little Theater. At one point she played the role of Mrs. Clandon in George Bernard Shaw's comedy *You Never Can Tell*. In the middle of this frenzy of learning, Oveta decided to take Spanish language lessons. When Lynn Culp recalled the whirlwind life her older sister lived in these years, she said, "Oveta made every hour of her time count. She didn't waste a minute." When Oveta discovered that Velma Soule, the society writer at the *Post*, not only spoke Spanish but also wanted to lose weight, Oveta persuaded Soule to go with her to the Houston Country Club early every morning to swim for exercise. After the swim, Soule tutored Oveta in Spanish. At the end of each lesson, they went to their jobs at the *Post*.[17]

After Lynn Culp graduated from high school in Temple in May 1934, she accepted Will and Oveta's invitation to move to Houston and room at their house on Glen Haven while she attended business school. She wound up staying with Will and Oveta for nearly two years while attending classes. During that time, Lynn helped out by babysitting young Bill, occasionally with the help of Lyndon Johnson's brother, Sam, who worked at a Houston bank. "I used to go with [Oveta's] sister a little bit down there [in Houston]," Sam later recalled. He claimed that after he brought Lynn home late one night, Oveta wouldn't let them get together again unless it was to help Lynn babysit Bill, which he recalled required changing "that kid's diapers."[18]

Many years later, Lynn said that when she was living with Will and Oveta, she could see that her sister "worked as hard as anyone I've known in my life," noting that Oveta would drive herself to the *Post* at seven in the morning. "Sometimes it was 9 o'clock at night before Oveta came home, and it was not unusual to see the light was still on in her room late at night while she continued to read and work." According to Lynn, Oveta seldom took breaks from her work at the *Post* and often had a brown-bag lunch at her desk, while Will preferred to lunch at his club.[19]

On September 18, 1934, three months after Lynn Culp took up residence in Houston, their father, Ike Culp, died after being ill for more than a year. During the summer of 1933, Oveta had rushed to Temple after her mother called with the warning that Ike was near death. Will followed Oveta to the Culp home a couple of days later. When Ike recovered enough to be out of danger, Will returned to Houston, leaving Oveta to remain for a few days at her parents' house. On his way to Houston, Will stopped by the capitol to visit with political friends. Jessie Ziegler, who by then was working for the State Highway Commission, reported to her mother that "Governor Hobby had been en route home from Temple where Oveta was called to her father's death-bed." Ziegler added that "Governor," in his typically laconic and dry-witted way, told her that his father-in-law "fooled us and got well instead."[20]

After Oveta's appointment as an editor, she and Will began to develop and shape the roles each would play at the *Houston Post* in the coming years. Will concentrated on overall management issues and politics, while Oveta was more interested in general news coverage and in developing more imaginative and innovative special features. Occasionally, she authored editorials for the *Post*, including one with the title "A Plea for Tolerance," which expressed her concern about political and cultural intolerance in American society. Will focused his interest on politics more than on philosophical and cultural issues. Sharing a strong interest in politics with her husband, Oveta also worked closely with him to plan the *Post*'s political coverage and candidate endorsements.[21]

A memorandum Oveta wrote to Will during the county and city election campaigns in August 1936 provides a good example of the role she had taken at the newspaper, despite her official title of book page editor. The document outlined her ideas about the political and editorial role the *Post* should play in the seven days before Election Day. She recommended that the *Post* begin with a major editorial on the Sunday before voters cast their votes on the following Saturday. Monday's edition would feature a story about legislative candidates, to be written by the newspaper's political reporter Ed Kilman, whose article, Oveta stressed, "should be informative as to the fitness of the men rather than editorial in style." Tuesday's edition would feature a story on their favored candidate for sheriff, Norfleet Hill, which would include an explanation of a sheriff's civil duties in addition to law enforcement. "Many voters," Oveta advised Will, "feel that the man quickest on the draw makes a good sheriff." A *Post* story on Wednesday would be about Mayor Oscar Holcombe's bid for reelection, featuring comments about him by leading citizens, followed by a general news story on Thursday about some other political candidate still to be determined, and then on Friday an editorial in support of all of their endorsed candidates. Oveta stressed to Will that they had "stuck" their necks out by endorsing certain candidates and therefore "we ought to keep pushing" their candidacies. A final story on Saturday morning, which was Election Day, would urge people to go to the polls. She even suggested the title of the editorial: "Vote Houston."[22]

Although she had no formal position at KPRC Radio, Oveta also paid attention to its political programming, recommending to Will that on the day of the election in August 1936 KPRC should make hourly announcements reminding people to go vote. The announcements "should be done in some attractive manner," Oveta noted, adding that the radio staff had "overworked the usual approach." She advised her husband that if the program director, Kern Tips, "was told in time, continuity writers could prepare something more interesting and less blah" than their usual material.[23]

The "Hobby Team" also became increasingly involved in a wide variety of community projects and institutions in Houston. They joined the boards and committees of several cultural, civic, and welfare organizations. Oveta also became an advocate for the less fortunate in her home city. She accepted an appointment to the State Committee for

Human Security, which lobbied the legislature for appropriations for support of blind and dependent children, and she served as Texas chair of the Women's Committee for the Mobilization of Human Needs. She helped organize the "Women's Crusade," a temporary club of society women that raised money to fund and create a Houston community chest to help the needy. She later served on its board, which oversaw the distribution of funds to twenty-eight human service agencies in the city. This experience inspired Oveta to write a special series of articles for the *Post* on community welfare, which focused on the issues of health care, child welfare, and the need to merge social agencies for the sake of efficiency.[24]

Immediately after Houston suffered a devastating flood in December 1935, Oveta was the only woman member of a blue-ribbon committee of prominent Harris County citizens who successfully lobbied the state legislature to help fund a flood-control district. Although Will was not on the committee, he was also involved in the lobbying effort. During the 1937 legislative session, he and Governor Allred had a brief falling-out over Allred's refusal to support the flood-control district. The legislature passed a bill authorizing the City of Houston to use tax money for flood-control projects, but Allred vetoed it. The Senate overrode the veto, but the override stalled in the House. Will and Oveta's strong connections in the legislature played a key role in securing state support for their cause after Allred's term in office ended. Eventually, flood-control dams were constructed on the upstream section of Buffalo Bayou, and the lower bayou was deepened and paved to channel floodwater more effectively into Galveston Bay. Although relatively successful in the short term, apocalyptic flooding from Hurricane Harvey in 2017 would demonstrate the system's inadequacy in the face of unrestrained and ill-planned urban development.[25]

Oveta also played a leadership role in the campaign to raise a $1 million endowment ($17 million in 2019) to support the University of Houston, which had become a private school after separating from the Houston Independent School District. She agreed to serve as cochair of the fundraising committee with independent oilman Hugh Roy Cullen. The campaign reached its goal. Oveta's work in support of the University of Houston began a significant relationship between the Hobby family and the university that continued long after it became a state school in 1964.[26]

Oveta also found time in her busy schedule to accept the growing number of speaking invitations she received as she gained a reputation as an informed, articulate, and mildly provocative speaker. Many of her speeches focused on the role of women in civil society and in the workplace. A typical presentation was one she gave to the Art and Interest Forum luncheon sponsored by the Junior League in San Antonio in 1934. Speaking on the topic of "Political Education for Women," Oveta argued that active citizenship was an essential responsibility for everyone in a democracy, including women, and that to be effective citizens it was critical for women to be as knowledgeable as possible about the legislative process and the function of government at all levels. Aware of her elite audience, Oveta stressed that women of "some advantage" had a special obligation to be active citizens and to be leaders in the community.[27]

As dictatorial governments gained power, restricted civil liberties, and violated human rights in Europe and Asia in the 1930s, Oveta shared the alarm of many of her colleagues in the newspaper business about the potential influence these totalitarian systems might have on traditional American democratic values, including, of course, freedom of speech and the press. Beginning in the mid-1930s, Oveta expressed her concerns in several speeches warning against the danger of authoritarian ideas taking root in America. In January 1938, when religious organizations were leading a movement against the "gangster" movies coming out of Hollywood, Oveta gave a speech to the Houston Council of Federated Church Women in which she cautioned against overzealous censorship of the film industry. "We have seen how censorship began in Germany, Italy, Russia, and Spain," Oveta told the council. "The same force that imposes censorship of pictures, newspapers, books and magazines can impose any other form of censorship, even the censorship of religion. It is far better to take a few of the evils that lurk in an uncensored life than to be compelled to bear the curse of a completely censored existence." Oveta advised her audience that if they found a particular movie morally offensive, the wisest course for them to take was to not go to the movie. "The future of pictures is what we make them," she argued. "If the box office receipts show that the American people appreciate artistic productions over the gangster picture, we will get fine pictures." Oveta's stance against censorship would never waver, as she would demonstrate years later during the "Red Scare" of the 1950s.[28]

Early in 1936, while Oveta was in the middle of her almost frantic schedule working on civic projects, giving speeches, reading and reviewing books, and managing the *Post*'s book section, she decided to write a book on parliamentary procedure. Because of her experience as the parliamentarian of the Texas House of Representatives, she was aware of the lack of a simplified, easy-to-use manual that any type of organization could reference to guide formal meetings. She also believed that the rules of parliamentary procedure should be taught in high school. Her goal was to write a book that not only could be put to practical use by organizations but also could serve as a supplementary textbook for high school classes in government or business.

To avoid distractions as she researched and wrote her book, Oveta moved into an isolated office on the first floor of the Post Building. She had *Post* staff members bring her stacks of reference books from the Houston Public Library about the US Constitutional Convention, the procedural rules of the British Parliament, and the deliberative procedures adopted by the League of Nations and the newly formed parliamentary governments of nations created by the Versailles Peace Conference. As she drafted the manuscript, she decided to give it the working title of "Mr. Chairman," which survived as the book's final title. For advice about how to structure the book for use as a school textbook, Oveta sought help from Harriet Binion, a faculty member at Central State Teachers College in Edmond, Oklahoma. The manuscript went through several drafts during the spring of 1936.[29]

For a few days in March, Oveta's strict focus on *Mr. Chairman* ground to a halt when her four-year-old son, Bill, became seriously ill, possibly with influenza. Consisting of body aches, high fever, and chills, Bill's condition gave Will and Oveta a real fright, especially with their memories of the Spanish flu epidemic of 1919. Both stayed at home while Bill slowly recovered. Their colleagues at the *Post* monitored the situation closely, sending them flowers, cards, and cookies. When Bill was finally out of danger, Judd Mortimer Lewis, Will's old friend and the *Post*'s longtime columnist and poet, published a poem in the *Post* titled "I Am So Glad." Lewis wrote, "I am so glad to know your little feet will tread the ways of life and make them sweet. For those who love you so, who bent above your bed of pain . . . and through each terror-stricken day and night gave of their strength to help you win the fight."[30]

Oveta had other interruptions that March. After her sister Lynn moved into her own residence in Houston, Oveta and Will leased out their house on Glen Haven and moved to apartment 12F in the Lamar Hotel in downtown Houston. Built in 1927 by Jesse Jones, who kept a residence on the sixteenth floor even during the years he lived in Washington, the Lamar was a power base for Houston elites, with suites permanently rented to major figures in oil, politics, and banking. The Lamar was also the home of the KPRC broadcast studios, which had been moved to the hotel in 1935. Another interruption to Oveta's work on her book resulted from Jesse Jones's insistence that she accept an appointment to the advisory committee to the commission in charge of the state's official celebration of the centennial of Texas's independence from Mexico in 1836.[31]

On March 2, 1936, Oveta and Will traveled to the campus of Sam Houston State Teachers College (now Sam Houston State University) in Huntsville to attend an official Texas Centennial event, which celebrated Jack Josey's donation to the State of Texas of an 1858 structure known as the Steamboat House. Sam Houston had died in the house in 1863. Josey purchased it in 1933 and in 1936 donated it for use as a state museum in honor of Sam Houston. Governor Allred attended the event, along with Governors Philip La Follette of Wisconsin and Hill McAlister of Tennessee. Will served as master of ceremonies and spoke briefly in front of a crowd of ten thousand people and over a live radio broadcast on the statewide Texas Quality Network. Will declared that he was pleased to be in Huntsville, a town whose native sons, including Jack Josey and Judge Jim Elkins, had made significant contributions to the development of the city of Houston. At one point in Will's speech he turned, and glancing at the three governors who were sitting on the platform behind him, he observed that he had attended political conventions where you could see one governor and three platforms, but this was a rare opportunity to look at one platform and see three governors.[32]

After the event in Huntsville, Oveta went to San Antonio to participate in another celebration cosponsored by the centennial commission and the Daughters of the Republic of Texas. The event was in honor of the men who had died on March 6, 1836, defending the Alamo garrison against the Mexican Army. New York governor Herbert Lehman asked Jesse Jones, who was scheduled to be the event's speaker, to present the New York state flag at a special ceremony in which the flags of the states and foreign nations where individual defenders had been born would be given to the Alamo. New York native Captain John Forsyth had been among those defenders. Because of a schedule conflict in Washington, Jones was unable to travel to Texas. Oveta agreed to serve as his replacement. After arriving by train in San Antonio on the night of March 5, Oveta spent all of March 6 participating in the various events of the day and evening. She attended a Catholic mass at the Alamo chapel in the morning and then spoke on Jones's behalf at the official luncheon following the mass. That afternoon, she presented the New York state banner at the flag ceremony. In the evening, Oveta was among the guests of honor at a dinner hosted by the archbishop of San Antonio. Afterward, she wrote Jones, "I wish that you could have been there. It is putting it mildly to say that the persons in charge of the celebration were disappointed that you could not be there to help in the flag waving. The Celebration was really unusually effective. The Catholic Church held Pontifical Mass during the morning. There were archbishops and bishops to burn—or so the Ku Kluxers would have said. I was so important all day with escorts and national guards as military aides. I spoke at a luncheon meeting where I bespoke your greetings and regrets. I was so set up with my importance as your representative."[33]

# CHAPTER 22

# THE ROOSEVELTS AND AN ESCAPE FROM DEATH

A s she was finishing the first drafts of her parliamentary rules book, Oveta shopped the prospectus to several publishers in New York but found no takers. She eventually found success with the Economy Publishing Company, a regional press located in Oklahoma City that specialized in the textbook market. With a book contract in hand, Oveta had the manuscript nearly completed by the end of May 1936. At this point, Oveta had additional motivation for getting the book finished as soon as she could. She and Will had learned in May that their second child was on the way, with a due date in January 1937. Oveta was determined to send a finished manuscript to her publisher by mid-June, but that schedule was soon delayed by a terrifying accident.[1]

Running for a second term in 1936, Franklin D. Roosevelt (FDR) eagerly accepted Jesse Jones's invitation to make a "noncampaign" expedition to five different cities in Texas in June as the highlight event of the centennial celebration. The president agreed to make Houston his first stop, where he would dedicate the cornerstone of the towering monument commemorating the Battle of San Jacinto. The presidential party, which included Eleanor Roosevelt, Jesse Jones, and Senator Morris Sheppard, arrived in Houston by special train the morning of June 11. As the Roosevelts took their seats in the back of the limousine convertible for their drive through downtown Houston, they were handed a copy of the *Houston Post* with Will Hobby's above-the-fold banner headline "HOUSTON WILL WELCOME ROOSEVELT TODAY." Large portraits of the president and the First Lady appeared below the headline. Members of the presidential party were driven slowly through the city to a dock on the Houston Ship Channel, where they boarded boats that took them to the San Jacinto battleground. As Jones's guest, Will boarded the boat carrying FDR, while Oveta traveled with Eleanor Roosevelt and her party on the yacht *Sumoria*, where they had an opportunity to have a long chat and get acquainted.[2]

*President Franklin D. Roosevelt speaking in the Cotton Bowl, Dallas, Texas, 1936.*

Following the ceremony at San Jacinto, FDR departed on a Southern Pacific train bound for San Antonio, where he gave a speech at the Alamo and then traveled on to Austin. The Hobbys, Jesse Jones, and the latter's secretary, Joe Toomey, took an overnight train to Dallas, arriving on the morning of June 12. They joined the president and his entourage at the Texas State Fair Grounds, where FDR addressed a high-spirited crowd of fifty thousand at the Cotton Bowl. Afterward they attended a luncheon for the president and the First Lady at the Adolphus Hotel and then accompanied them to Oak Lawn Park (now Turtle Creek Park) to attend FDR's official unveiling of a statue of Robert E. Lee. After Jones gave the formal speech honoring Lee's memory, the president went by train to Fort Worth, where he and Eleanor spent the night at their son Elliott's home.[3]

Jesse Jones arranged to return to Houston on a single-engine, six-passenger Vultee V-1AD executive airplane that the United Gas Company of Shreveport, Louisiana, made available to him. The Vultee V-1AD was the same model of aircraft that American Airlines was using at the time. The Hobbys accepted Jones's invitation to fly back with him, despite a vow the Hobbys had made after their son's birth never to fly on the same airplane together. Approximately twenty minutes after the airplane took off from Love Field, a fuel line leaked at seven thousand feet, shutting down the engine and igniting a fire that quickly spread into the cockpit. One of the pilots, Eugene Schacher, stepped out of the cockpit and yelled at his passengers to fasten their seat belts to prepare for an emergency landing. As he returned to the cockpit, he slammed the door shut to prevent flames from spreading to the passenger cabin. Undoubtedly terrified, Will and Oveta, Jesse Jones, and his secretary nevertheless remained outwardly calm and followed instructions. While Schacher fought the flames, the other pilot, twenty-eight-year-old Eddie Hefley, who had been a pilot since the age of fifteen, took the airplane into a steep nosedive traveling at an airspeed of 275 miles per hour. The pilots managed to crash-land the airplane in a cotton field a few miles west of the town of Ferris, about twenty miles south of Dallas. As the aircraft skidded 150 yards, the engine broke loose from the fuselage. The force of the crash sprang the cabin doors open, allowing Joe Toomey, Jesse Jones, and Eugene Schacher to escape quickly from the burning wreckage, while Oveta pulled her stunned husband from his seat and out the door. Hefley, however, remained trapped in the cockpit. While Oveta tended to Will, who was laid out on the ground, Jones, along with a badly hurt Schacher, rushed back into the fiercely burning fuselage and pulled the severely burned Hefley out of the aircraft. With everyone out of

*Wreckage of the airplane carrying Jesse Jones and the Hobbys*
*that crashed in a cotton field south of Dallas, 1936.*

the burning plane, Oveta commandeered a farmworker's automobile and drove Hefley to a doctor's office in Ferris. From there, ambulances were quickly dispatched to bring Will Hobby, Jones, Toomey, and Schacher back to town to receive first aid.

Although only Hefley and Schacher had been injured seriously, it was decided to transport everyone to St. Paul's Hospital in Dallas by ambulance, except for Jones, who was driven to the hospital in a private car. When everyone arrived at St. Paul's, Jones, his shirt splattered with blood, helped attendants take the pilots to the emergency operating room. At the insistence of the doctors, Jones reluctantly agreed to be hospitalized. Because Oveta was calm and stoic when she arrived with Will in an ambulance, the medical staff failed to realize she had been aboard the plane. They left her alone while they tended to the others. Will had a cut above his right eye and suffered multiple bruises, but he had no broken bones or other serious injuries. The Hobbys also agreed to spend the night in the hospital. Although Oveta was largely unscathed, the doctors wanted to keep her under observation because of her pregnancy.[4]

The next afternoon Jesse Jones's friends at the Missouri Pacific Railroad made a private railcar available to transport him, Toomey, and the Hobbys back to Houston. It was a melancholy trip back home. They were grateful to have survived with relatively minor cuts and bruises, but they remained shaken and deeply worried about Schacher and Hefley. They all knew their lives had been saved by the pilots' courageous actions and flying skills. As Jones noted later, "If the [pilots] had not stuck to their posts, we all would have been killed." The gloom deepened as their train rumbled farther south toward Houston. During a brief stop at a rail depot, Will received a telegram informing him that Jim Mapes, his old friend and business partner at the *Beaumont Enterprise*, had died suddenly from a heart attack on June 12, the same day of the airplane crash. Afterward, Jones admitted they were all "a little down" as they made their way home, which was an unusual confession of emotion from that typically stoic man. As their train arrived in Houston, however, their feelings were lifted somewhat when Jones received a telegram from a doctor at St. Paul's Hospital informing them, "Hefley in good spirits this morning, improving satisfactorily. Hope you are feeling okay. Better take it easy for a few days until fully recovered."[5]

News of the accident had quickly made its way to FDR's train as it passed through Indiana on its way back to Washington. Concerned about Jones's condition, the president insisted on hearing from Jones himself that he was okay. Eleanor Roosevelt sent a telegram to Oveta from the presidential train. "The President and I were distressed to see that you were slightly hurt in the plane accident," the First Lady stated. "It must have been a terrifying experience and I hope that neither of you suffered anything serious. It was very nice to see you in Texas and I hope we will meet again before too long." Eleanor Roosevelt's hope to see Oveta "before too long" would be fulfilled in a way neither one of the women could have predicted at the time.[6]

The day after Will and Oveta and Jesse Jones arrived back in Houston, they were stunned by the news that copilot Schacher had died from smoke inhalation and burns.

Before leaving Dallas, they had all visited Schacher in his hospital room and went to the train station thinking that he would survive but not Hefley. To everyone's surprise, Ed Hefley survived the crash, although he remained in the hospital for three months. When he learned of Schacher's passing, Jones wrote a eulogy that he published on the front page of his *Houston Chronicle*. "Such courage, such fortitude, such endurance, it has never [before] been my privilege to witness," Jones wrote. "I pray to God for the knowledge to understand for what purpose He saved my life by sacrificing yours." Jones wrote Arthur Hays Sulzberger, the president of the *New York Times*, that "it was a miraculous escape, and the odds against a safe landing were probably a million to one. . . . [T]wo more clearheaded pilots could not be found, nor men with more stamina and fortitude. They were literally in a furnace for the time required to descend more than a mile." A grateful Jones paid Schacher's and Hefley's, as well as Toomey's and the Hobbys', medical and hospital bills. He also helped Hefley financially, and he provided a lifelong stipend to Schacher's widow.[7]

The airplane crash left a lifelong mark on the Hobbys. Thinking about the devastating impact their joint deaths would have on their children, they decided never again to fly together on the same airplane. On June 11, 1937, Will and Oveta sent a telegram to Jones in Washington noting the first anniversary of the crash. "The common bond that will ever hold our friendship is stronger as we count back a year," they wrote. Several months later, as their chauffeur Cecil McBride was taking the Hobbys out on a drive, he overheard Will tell Oveta, "We were sure lucky to come out of that plane crash alive." "Yes, we were," Oveta replied. "Obviously, God has more work for us to do." Vivid memories of the crash remained etched in Will's mind for the rest of his life, resurfacing at odd times. On the day in April 1953 when Oveta was sworn in as a member of President Dwight Eisenhower's cabinet, McBride drove the Hobbys from the White House to Oveta's Washington apartment. He recalled that Will told Oveta he had "come out of that crash a lot better than you did." Oveta replied that she didn't know what he was talking about. "I'm talking about that plane crash," Will said. "I came out a little bit better than you. This is the second hard job you've gotten from Washington, and I haven't had even one yet."[8]

Still suffering from the aftereffects of the airplane crash, Oveta turned her focus back on *Mr. Chairman*. She sent the finished manuscript to her publisher on July 1, only a month later than she had originally planned. When her contact at Economy Publishing Company asked Oveta about her schedule for working on the book galleys, Oveta warned him she was "still under the care of the doctor and am not able to be at my desk." Nevertheless, she managed to plow through the galleys quickly and returned them at the beginning of August, after which she and Will departed for a vacation in California to recuperate from the accident.[9]

Economy Company published *Mr. Chairman* in early October 1936. The publicity release described the book as a simplified version of parliamentary law. Oveta was a tireless promoter of her book. She hired journalist Paul Wakefield, who was a former aide to Governor Ross Sterling, to publicize *Mr. Chairman*. Wakefield persuaded several newspapers to conduct author interviews and also to have their book editors review the book. Wakefield contacted Vann Kennedy, Austin bureau chief of the International News Service, and he agreed to distribute news about the book on the organization's mail service. Wakefield also succeeded in getting a review in the *Austin American-Statesman*. "Would-be students of parliamentary law have long been looking for just such a book as Mrs. Hobby has prepared," the *Statesman*'s reviewer wrote. "A book as simple as this one should have a wide appeal now that almost everyone is connected with some organization and must know something of the fundamentals of parliamentary procedure."[10]

After *Mr. Chairman* was published, Oveta began writing a column for the *Post* about parliamentary procedures, using material from her book. The column, which served as an ongoing advertisement for *Mr. Chairman*, made regular appearances in the *Post* until April 1937. Oveta was interested in marketing her book to the general public, but her main goal was to sell *Mr. Chairman* to the public schools for use as a supplemental textbook. She lobbied the Texas School Book Committee of the State Board of Education to adopt *Mr. Chairman* as an official textbook. Oveta recruited prominent administrators at the Houston Independent School District, including the influential business manager H. L. Mills, Assistant Superintendent of Schools J. O. Webb, and Director of Curriculum W. W. Kemmerer, to lobby the members of the textbook committee on behalf of *Mr. Chairman*. These men in particular

*Cover of Oveta Culp Hobby's book,* Mr. Chairman, *1936.*

had important connections to school districts statewide, and each knew members of the state textbook committee. Mills had two friends on the State Board of Education, to whom he wrote letters in support of Oveta's book. Skipping details about the contents of *Mr. Chairman*, Mills made a simple political argument in favor of its adoption. "My good friend [the] wife of Governor Hobby, has submitted her book [for state adoption]," Mills wrote. "It would be a mighty fine book for the schools of Texas."[11]

While Oveta's campaign to persuade the state to adopt *Mr. Chairman* as a textbook continued through the fall of 1936, she and the Economy Publishing Company were pleasantly surprised when the book managed to sell out its first small print run in

February 1937. Her publisher soon decided to print a revised, second edition, which encouraged Oveta to intensify her effort to have the book adopted by the state in 1937. At one point, Will enlisted the aid of his old friend Lieutenant Governor Walter Woodul. At Will's request, Woodul wrote a letter to Senator Clay Cotton, who was a member of the textbook committee, urging him to pressure his fellow committee members to vote for the adoption of *Mr. Chairman*. Woodul followed through, telling Senator Cotton that he thought "the book would be most effective in the classroom. I have no other interest excepting that Governor and Mrs. Hobby are my friends," he explained, "and I am interested in the schools getting good books." Despite Oveta's politicking the committee declined to adopt *Mr. Chairman*.[12]

Oveta refused to take no for an answer. In the fall of 1938 the textbook committee had new members who she believed would have a more favorable view of *Mr. Chairman*. After orchestrating another lobbying effort with the help of her friends in the Houston Independent School District administration, she finally persuaded the committee to adopt *Mr. Chairman* as a seventh-grade textbook. With this victory, Oveta turned her sights on having *Mr. Chairman* adopted in the public schools in Louisiana, New Mexico, and Arizona, but that effort failed, as did her attempt to get a New York trade press to publish a more sophisticated and rewritten version of *Mr. Chairman* that had the working title "How and When in Parliamentary Law." No other versions of the book were ever published, but Oveta continued for several years to promote the second edition. She closely monitored sales reports, and she maintained a detailed list of how many books each school district in Texas had purchased. By September 1940, Oveta's publisher reported that sales had reached thirty thousand. She continued to receive royalty checks well into the 1940s.[13]

On January 18, 1937, Oveta took a break from promoting her book to check into Hermann Hospital to prepare for the delivery of her second child. The baby girl was born the next day, Tuesday, January 19, which was Oveta's birthday as well as that of her son, Bill. According to Bill Hobby, Will named his daughter Jesse Oveta Hobby, in honor of his friend Jesse H. Jones, without telling his wife before having the name entered on their daughter's official birth certificate. "Mother was not happy. She detested Jesse Jones," Bill Hobby recalled. "Mother issued orders that my sister's name would be Jessica, and that's what she was called her entire life." Bill claimed his mother disliked Jones for a number of reasons, including his overbearing personality and shady business dealings, but chiefly because of the way he restricted the Hobbys' efforts to improve the *Post* to make it competitive with the *Chronicle*. Her dislike of Jones, which she kept private, was deepened a year later when she and Will negotiated their purchase of the *Post*.[14]

Will did not share his wife's feelings about Jones. During the twelve years Jones served in the Roosevelt administration, he and Will met for lunch nearly every time Jones was in town, and Will would meet with Jones during his visits to Washington to lobby members of the Texas congressional delegation or to consult with Federal Communications Commission staff about regulations affecting KPRC Radio. Will also kept Jones informed of banking issues and developments in Texas, as well as Texas newspaper reactions to Reconstruction Finance Corporation policies and actions. Oveta's and Will's starkly contrasting feelings about Jones were one of the few examples of a serious difference of opinion existing between them.[15]

Oveta's objections to naming their daughter after Jesse Jones might also have stemmed from a concern that it might give people the wrong idea about her own relationship with the man known as "Mr. Houston." If Oveta did fear the possibility of scandalous rumors of sexual impropriety, those worries were well grounded. A rumor did soon spread that Jessica was named for Jesse Jones because Jones was her actual father. Because it was well known that Jones had engaged in at least one extramarital affair, the rumor did not seem preposterous in light of Jones's own history. A bachelor until the age of forty-six, Jones had had an affair with Mary Gibbs Jones, the wife of his nephew, Will Jones. Mary eventually divorced Will Jones and married Jesse in 1920. Another factor that fed the rumor was the physical contrast between Will Hobby and Jesse Jones. Jones was a six-foot-tall, wealthy, and politically powerful Houstonian whom some people considered handsome. Will Hobby was short, jug-eared, and rarely, if ever, characterized as being attractive. Will often engaged in self-deprecating witticisms about his appearance. It would not be the first time in history that a young, beautiful, sophisticated, and ambitious woman like Oveta would find it advantageous to be the lover of a powerful friend who was also her employer, especially since her own husband was not considered physically attractive.[16]

The Oveta-Jesse love affair gossip was largely confined to the higher circles of Houston's society until 1954, when Jack Guinn, a disgruntled former reporter for the *Post*, published *The Caperberry Bush*, a combination science fiction/historical novel with characters and a setting partially inspired by Guinn's real-life experiences working for the Hobbys. Its characters include newspaper publishers Calhoun DeQuincey Duncan and his wife, Mrs. Duncan, who are obviously based on Guinn's former employers, Will and Oveta Hobby. In the novel, Calhoun, who is thirty years older than Mrs. Duncan, gave up visiting his newspaper office in the 1930s, "when he named his wife assistant publisher and let her run it." In *The Caperberry Bush*, the Oveta Culp Hobby figure has an affair with an extremely wealthy friend modeled on Jesse Jones.

*The Caperberry Bush* was a moderately successful book, but it ultimately had little impact on Oveta's reputation, although it did revive the old gossip in Houston about her relationship with Jesse Jones. Its publication also resulted in an additional rumor that the Hobbys suppressed its distribution, which historian Robert Pando has documented as untrue. Although out of print, *The Caperberry Bush* is available in the various libraries in the Houston area and in 2018 could be purchased readily from a number of online sources.[17]

The salacious rumor, which was spread far and wide, undoubtedly upset both Will and Oveta, especially in the early days of its appearance, but it seems their wise reaction was simply to ignore it, and for obvious reasons it was never denied or mentioned in the *Post*, the *Chronicle*, or even the tabloid *Houston Press*. The people closest to Oveta have always rejected the rumor's veracity. "I knew that woman as well as I know my own mother," said Oveta's longtime assistant Peggy Buchanan. "It was a good rumor, but simply not true. Oveta Culp Hobby was the most moral person I ever knew." Bill Hobby also dismissed the rumor, arguing that anyone who knew his mother found the idea "preposterous. . . . [The rumormongers] obviously didn't know my Mother." In 1978, when author Harry Hurt III interviewed Oveta for a lengthy profile in *Texas Monthly*, Oveta not only denied ever having an affair with Jones, she also made the unlikely claim that she had never heard the rumor, despite the publicity generated by *The Caperberry Bush* and other published references to the gossip, including a story in *Time*. "Mr. Jones and I were friends," Oveta told Hurt. "We seldom discussed the business of our newspapers, but we talked a great deal about politics and government."[18]

For a couple of weeks after Jessica's birth, Oveta remained at home in the apartment at the Lamar Hotel to recuperate and bond with the baby. Even during this period she continued to work, busily revising *Mr. Chairman* for its second edition. Oveta was soon back in her office at the *Post*, with Bill and infant Jessica under the care of nannies. Her return to work was interrupted when both her husband and their son suddenly became ill with an apparent case of influenza. Oveta remained at home for several days to care for her husband with help from a nurse and a nanny for the children. As a result, Oveta was late in getting the revised manuscript of *Mr. Chairman* to her publisher. Embarrassed by her tardiness, Oveta wrote her publisher an apology: "Governor Hobby's illness was far more serious and protracted than we had any idea that it would be. To add trouble to trouble, my son, William, has been quite ill again." She promised to have the revised manuscript in the mail within the week.[19]

Fully recovered from his illness, Will presided once again at the April 21 ceremonies at the San Jacinto battleground, while Oveta gave one of the celebratory speeches. Will's old rival, former governor James Ferguson, made a surprise appearance at the celebration. Recalling the event many years later, Will noted that for the first time in nearly twenty years, he and "Pa" Ferguson had a long and friendly chat, reminiscing about the 1914 campaign and characters and places they had known as they sat together at lunch and shared a platter of fried chicken and Gulf trout. The next day the *Post* ran a photograph of the two men as they sat together at the picnic table.[20]

After Jessica's birth, Will and Oveta decided the Lamar Hotel was not a suitable place to raise a family and their hotel suite was not large enough to accommodate an additional child. When the renters' lease to the Glen Haven house expired late in the summer of 1937, the Hobbys reclaimed possession and remodeled and enlarged it. They had already moved some of their furniture back when a fire broke out on the first floor. The house was saved, but the damage was extensive enough to delay their return for several weeks while the house was being repaired. The Hobbys were forced to find temporary living quarters in the Rice Hotel, as they had already given up their suite at the Lamar. They finally moved into their newly remodeled home on Glen Haven early in 1938.[21]

With the second edition of *Mr. Chairman* in print by the fall of 1937, Oveta turned her full-time attention back to the *Houston Post*, where Jack Josey agreed to promote her to assistant editor. The new job duties allowed her to remain as editor of the book page, but she now assumed official responsibility for other areas of the newspaper. As staff member Ed Kilman later noted, Oveta soon streamlined "styles of presenting the news and editorial matter" and introduced plans "for efficiency and economy." Drawing from and inspired by her experiences as a regular member of Florence Sterling's and Estelle Sharp's study groups, Oveta also wrote a series of special features on current international developments and their historical context for the newspaper's Sunday editions. Oveta's new job title and her growing prominence in the newspaper industry caught the attention of the American Society of Newspaper Editors, which elected her to a full membership. She was thirty-two years old and only the second woman to be elected a member. When Oveta traveled to New York to attend her first meeting of the society, she learned that the convention's opening dinner would be held in a men's club. Following instructions, she entered the club through the back door and then was guided by a club staff member through the kitchen to get to the dining room. When she cracked open the double doors in the kitchen to peer into the dining room, she saw nothing but men. She closed the doors and confessed to her escort that she didn't know if she had the nerve to go out. Iowa newspaper publisher and *Look* magazine founder Gardner Cowles Jr. saw Oveta peek out from behind the kitchen doors. He rushed into the kitchen, gave Oveta a warm welcome, and then took her arm and escorted her into the dining room to her table. It was a kindness Oveta never forgot.[22]

After her promotion to assistant editor and then election to the American Society of Newspaper Editors, Oveta's climb up the *Post*'s executive ladder quickened. In March 1938, the newspaper's board of directors appointed Oveta executive vice president. Oveta learned about her promotion from Jack Josey, who continued to serve as board chairman. Josey asked Oveta to attend a board meeting but didn't tell her why. When she arrived, Josey announced, "Young lady, we've just elected you executive vice president." Oveta later claimed that this unexpected news shocked her to the extent that her only response was "Why?" Josey replied that because the board realized she was guiding the day-to-day work of the newspaper, they decided "to give you the authority to do what you've been doing already." It's unknown whether Will knew about or participated in this decision beforehand. It's possible that he was also surprised. Because Jesse Jones still had total control over the newspaper, Jones would have had to approve such a significant promotion, and it's probable it was done at Jones's suggestion.[23]

No matter who made the decision, it enabled Oveta to assume responsibility for most of the newspaper's operations. Will, who was sixty, continued to make overall policy decisions, and he remained involved in the newspaper's editorials. But he continued to spend most of his time on political interests and community projects, including time-consuming service as chairman of the Houston Chamber of Commerce Highway Committee, which worked on the modernization of the Houston-Galveston regional road system. The committee also played a key role in lobbying for the construction of a new straight route highway between Dallas and Houston, which later became US Highway 75.[24]

Once Oveta had executive control over the *Post*'s newsroom and editorial offices, she quietly made a noteworthy change in one aspect of the paper's content: its coverage of Houston's African American community. Under Oveta's direction, the *Post* began to print more news of importance to black Houstonians. And in a major break with Southern journalistic tradition, she ordered that the word "Negro" not be used to identify citizens in news stories unless the specific story was one that showed African Americans in a positive light. She also issued orders that a respectful "Mr." or "Mrs." be placed before the names of black individuals mentioned in any story, column, or editorial. Oveta's Southern newspaper colleagues warned that the new policy would enrage the *Post*'s readers and drive off subscribers and advertising. Those problems failed to materialize. Protests were few and the newspaper's circulation actually increased. Not long after Oveta's policy change, a reporter slipped the word "nigger" into a news story, aided either by carelessness or maliciousness on the part of an editor. Telling her staff that she was "personally offended" when she found the word in the story, Oveta immediately called an editorial meeting and told her team that heads would roll if the word appeared in the newspaper again.[25]

By the spring of 1938, the Hobbys were now directing the *Houston Post* at every level except the most critical one, and that was ownership, something Will had coveted for nearly fifteen years. That long dreamed of goal would soon become a reality.

# CHAPTER 23

# A DREAM FULFILLED

While Jesse Jones was living in Washington, DC, and was deeply involved in his work as chairman of the federal Reconstruction Finance Corporation, he still kept a close watch on his personal business interests back in Houston, including both of Houston's major newspapers and radio stations. In August 1936, Jones exercised his option to acquire nearly all of the shares in the Houston Printing Company, the legal entity that owned the *Houston Post* and KPRC Radio. Nevertheless, several banks continued to hold those shares as collateral for Jones's loans. Late in 1938 Jones decided to take the *Post* and KPRC off his account books. He paid off the debt and regained the stock shares the banks had held as collateral, which cleared the way for him to sell those properties to his preferred buyers, Will and Oveta Hobby. According to Bascom Timmons, Jones took this action despite the *Post* and KPRC being "moderately profitable." Timmons wrote that Jones was philosophically opposed to newspaper monopolies and that he believed the city of Houston would be better served by the *Post* and KPRC if they had new owners who could give the properties more attention than he could.[1]

Jesse Jones's purported philosophical unease about monopolies was not evident in his business dealings, however. Jones owned Ross Sterling's former media properties for nearly eight years with no apparent concerns about it being a monopoly. The Sterling Trust, which he essentially controlled, could have sold the *Post* and KPRC to other purchasers at the time Sterling's assets were being liquidated. There is evidence that the trust did have an offer from an unidentified independent source, possibly newspaper tycoon William Randolph Hearst, who had tried to buy the *Post* in the early 1920s, but that offer was rejected. After Jones gained control of the paper, he prevented Will Hobby from modernizing the printing plant and making other improvements that might have made the *Post* more competitive with the *Chronicle*. Timmons's statement about the *Post*'s financial condition was also inaccurate. The *Post* was not "moderately profitable" when Jones sold it. The newspaper was operating at a loss. It had failed to earn a profit for several years, largely because of payments on loans from banks in Chicago, New York, Dallas, and Houston, which held the *Post*'s capital stock as collateral. As a result, the *Post* had been under the continual threat of foreclosure on its stock in the late 1930s.[2]

Whatever guided "Jesus" H. Jones (the name FDR called Jones behind his back) in this matter, instead of putting the properties on the open market, he made what was essentially a private sale to Will and Oveta Hobby. He might have done that as a favor to the Hobbys, who were his friends. It's also possible that by doing so he was keeping the *Post* out of the hands of Hearst, who had the deep pockets necessary to make the *Post* a formidable competitor to Jones's *Chronicle*. Jesse Jones's decision to sell the *Post* to the Hobbys was obviously good news to them. Will had long dreamed of buying the newspaper with which he had been associated most of his adult life and that he had managed for almost seventeen years. And, of course, the *Houston Post* had become an integral part of Oveta's life as well. She had been involved off and on with the *Post* for nearly fourteen years. It had become an important platform for her own writing and opinions, and it had made her a local celebrity.

When the Hobbys began negotiations with Jones to buy the *Post* and KPRC Radio, they soon found that "Mr. Houston" was not going to let something like friendship interfere with a good business deal. Because Jones insisted on extremely difficult terms and conditions and the Hobbys needed time to make their own financial arrangements, the negotiations were protracted, lasting from late summer 1938 until December 1939. During that time, Jones gave Will and Oveta permission to take the steps necessary to improve the *Post*'s value, which not only improved the Hobbys' chances to attract additional financing but also gave Jones justification to increase the sale price. Using Jones's money, which he included in the final price of the newspaper, the Hobbys replaced the *Post*'s outdated printing equipment with a high-speed Scott printer capable of printing forty-five thousand editions per hour. They hired architects to design a two-story, $175,000 addition to the plant. To attract new subscribers, the Hobbys introduced new sections on entertainment and local news. They reduced the length of hard news stories and editorials with tighter writing and careful editing to free space for more advertising.[3]

While Will negotiated with Jones, Oveta was busy with activities away from the *Post*. At the opening of the Forty-Sixth Texas Legislature in January, Emmett Morse was elected Speaker of the Texas House of Representatives. Morse was a Houston real estate developer who had served for twelve years as one of the city's representatives in the state legislature and was an old friend of the Hobbys. He asked Oveta to come to Austin to help him organize the House committees, get the session started smoothly, and serve temporarily as his parliamentarian. Oveta, who was still actively promoting *Mr. Chairman*, might have seen her brief return to parliamentary work as a marketing opportunity. She and Will had also planned to lobby the Forty-Sixth Legislature to get the Harris County flood-control district bill passed after its failure in the previous regular session. The invitation to come to Austin was a help to Oveta as well as to Morse, and she

*Four former Texas governors attending the inauguration of W. Lee O'Daniel at Texas Memorial Stadium in Austin, January 1939.* Left to right: *Ross Sterling, Pat Neff, O'Daniel, James Ferguson, and Will Hobby.*

readily accepted it. She worked with Morse for three weeks before returning to Houston. This was the first time Oveta had served as parliamentarian since 1931.[4]

Late in the fall of 1939, the Hobbys finally reached an agreement with Jones to buy the *Houston Post* and KPRC Radio for $2,167,000 (more than $37 million in 2019). The deal was closed on December 30, 1939, while Jones and his wife were in Houston for the Christmas holidays. To finance the Hobbys' purchase, Jones loaned them $950,000 at a 6 percent interest rate. Dallas banker and civic leader Fred Florence, president of the Republic Bank, loaned the Hobbys $1,162,500 at a 4 percent interest rate. Will paid the remaining balance from his and Oveta's own funds. Annual payments were set at a minimum of $200,000 for a period of fifteen years. Any of the newspaper's annual net earnings over $200,000 had to be applied to the debt. At Jones's insistence, the agreement included the provision that an accounting firm approved by his National Bank of Commerce would be allowed to monitor the *Post*'s business records to make certain excess earnings were being applied to debt payments. The Hobbys were not allowed to declare or pay dividends on stock or pay bonuses to themselves or to any other officers, directors, stockholders, or employees. Especially galling to the Hobbys was Jones's stipulation that until the debt was paid off, they and other *Post* and KPRC executives could not increase their salaries over what was paid to them for the year 1939 unless Jones gave his written consent. As Oveta later observed about Jones, "[He] got great enjoyment out of getting the best of people."[5]

Bascom Timmons claimed that Jones sold the *Post* and KPRC "on such easy terms as to enable the ex-governor to pay for it out of the earnings of the paper." But the written agreement itself counters the claim that the terms were "easy." Because the *Post* was losing money, payments were going to be difficult to make at the rate and interest demanded. In her book *Houston: The Unknown City*, Marguerite Johnston noted, "It was assumed in Houston that Jones had given the Hobbys a very generous deal because he thought it wrong for both major newspapers to be under one ownership. In truth, Jones made the same stiff business provisions in selling the *Post* to his friends that he would have made to anyone else." In later years, Oveta denied that she and Will had purchased the *Post* from Jones, claiming instead that "legend to the contrary," they bought it directly from Ross Sterling. The reason for Oveta's false denial is unclear, but it might have stemmed from popular accounts alleging Jones had essentially given the newspaper to the Hobbys, which in turn played into the scurrilous rumors about Oveta's personal relationship with Jones.[6]

Will and Oveta accepted the onerous terms. They realized that it might be the only opportunity they would have to own the *Post*. Oveta admitted to Will, "It's too much, but it's the only game in town." The *Post* became the Hobbys closely held private company, with no stockholders, free from federal securities regulators. Although Jack Josey no longer had a major stock investment in the Houston Printing Company, the Hobbys valued his basic common sense and business acumen. They asked him to continue his services as chairman of the board, and he agreed. Oveta later recalled that she and Will "were both very concerned" about buying the newspaper and radio station at that time, "particularly when the paper was losing money." Oveta also shared with some of her employees at the *Post* that buying the newspaper was "an awesome financial challenge." She and Will "had to stay on top of every department to be sure we didn't waste ten cents."[7]

At the beginning of 1940, Will, now in his early sixties, began to turn more of the management of the newspaper over to Oveta, who soon celebrated her thirty-fifth birthday. Will retained the title of publisher, but as Oveta admitted in an interview with the *New York Telegram*, she "ran things." Oveta stressed her leadership was Will's "idea" and that he was "quite content with her management of the paper." Although Oveta was in charge, Will continued to exert a quiet influence over the newspaper. Wearing his bow tie and a dark suit with the coat sleeves slightly pulled up, sporting a gold watch chain and a shock of hair down over his right eye, he often visited with staff to give advice, praise, and encouragement. Will's longtime editorial page editor Ed Kilman later observed, "[Will Hobby] had a way of getting everything a fellow had and I often wondered how he did it. I doubt if Governor Hobby ever fired anyone in his life. It just isn't in him."[8]

While Oveta assumed more authority over the daily operation of the *Post*, Will tended to his banking and other investments and to his civic and political interests. Because he had never learned to drive a car, every workday around 9:00 a.m., Cecil McBride, who lived in an apartment above the garage at the Hobbys' home on Glen Haven, would drive him to the *Post*'s offices at the corner of Polk and Dowling Streets southeast of downtown. Three days a week, McBride delivered Will first to the Rice Hotel to get a shave (he never shaved himself). During World War II, when gasoline rationing was in effect, Will often kept the limo in the garage and rode to work on a city bus. One day he was running late for an important meeting at the chamber of commerce. As he stood on a street corner waiting for the bus, a milk truck stopped for a red light. Smiling and waving his hat at the driver, Will asked if he was going downtown. When the driver said yes, Will asked if he could hitch a ride. "Sure, hop in," the friendly driver replied, and Will stepped up into the truck cab and rode it to his meeting. One of his editors was standing on the sidewalk outside the building where the chamber was holding its meeting when he was shocked to see a milkman deliver the former governor of Texas to his destination.[9]

Will and Oveta had adjoining offices at the *Post* and the door separating them was seldom closed. Oveta was usually at her desk much earlier than Will, usually driving herself to the *Post* after leaving Jessica in the care of a nanny, while one of the house staff drove Bill to Kinkaid School, a private coed school. Because Will didn't like for Oveta to drive, he sometimes persuaded her to let another one of their employees, Vernon Wiley, drive her downtown. On those occasions, the newspaper staff would see Will and Oveta leave the *Post* together at the end of the day, walking arm in arm to the street, where Cecil McBride would be waiting in Will's Cadillac limousine to take them home.[10]

As their friend journalist Weldon Hart later noted, with "the Jones Interests . . . off their necks," the Hobbys were finally free to make significant changes at the *Post*. Oveta oversaw physical improvements in the printing plant, and she initiated cost-saving procedures. Oveta had the newspaper's format redesigned to make it easier to read. She hired talented new editors and writers and gave them a relatively free hand, while maintaining daily contact with the managing editor and the other executives. Few details escaped her view. For example, she banned the word "honeymoon," which she strangely thought referred to the marriage wedding bed, and told her editors to replace it with "wedding trip." Her editors undoubtedly scratched their heads when they received that command. She discontinued the printing of pictures of attractive young women on the front page of the Sunday edition and later hired a female editor to handle all news of special interest to women. In an interview with the *New York World Telegram* while attending an annual convention of the American Newspaper Publishers Association in New York City, Oveta observed that her changes had "proved particularly popular with the women—and they are the ones running things. [laughing] Sometimes a man's nose gets out of joint on women's news." The story in the *World Telegram* included a picture of Oveta wearing one of her trademark hats; this one was shaped like a bird's nest, with a little stuffed bird in it. Oveta's tireless efforts soon paid off. The *Post* enjoyed an increase in subscribers and advertisers, and within a year the paper was operating at a profit for the first time in a decade.[11]

Oveta soon earned a reputation not only as an intelligent and visionary newspaper editor but also as a ruthless administrator. And more ideas about how to promote the newspaper and improve its contents continued to flow out of her hyperactive mind. At one point, as she was reminding Will how successful some of her ideas had been, her ever-patient husband told her, "Dear, a woman with as many ideas as you have is bound to run across a good one every now and then." Will was Oveta's most trusted advisor during this period when she was transforming the newspaper. Oveta later noted that around the end of 1940, when the *Post* was attracting a lot of new attention in Houston, she and Will went to a cocktail party. She recalled, "People were picking at me all night complaining how they didn't like this and that in the paper." On their way home, she told Will that it wasn't worth going out to social events at night. "Will chuckled," Oveta remembered, "and said, 'When they quit talking, that's when you'd better begin worrying. When people tell you things like this, it shows they care what the *Post* is doing. And our job is to keep them caring.'"[12]

While Oveta was reorganizing the *Post*, she and Will didn't neglect KPRC Radio, which was still broadcasting from the Lamar Hotel. Unlike the *Post*, the radio station had been making money. In 1934 it had joined with WFAA (Dallas), WBAP (Fort Worth), and WOAI (San Antonio), the major radio stations in the state, to form the Texas Quality Network. Special telephone lines connected the stations to allow simultaneous broadcasts and shared programming. The network eventually expanded into the states adjoining Texas, and it proved to be a profit booster for all of its radio partners. Will and Oveta made frequent visits to KPRC's studios and offices. Jack McGrew, the station's program director and later vice president, recalled that their visits "never frightened us. [Governor] knew our names and those of our families, and he stopped to chat with us before he went in to see Kern Tips," who was general manager of the station. "We loved Governor's stories and ready wit," McGrew said. Oveta also "took particular pains to speak to (and visit with, if time permitted) every member of the staff she encountered."[13]

McGrew also noted that Oveta played a role in all major decisions at KPRC, especially the one to create a news radio operation, which made KPRC one of the first stations in the country to furnish regularly scheduled newscasts. Oveta agreed to have a KPRC staff member work at the *Post* to gather the newspaper's wire service information and use it to prepare daily radio news reports. McGrew, who joined KPRC in April 1936 after working in radio in Beaumont and Austin, often was the KPRC staff member assigned that duty. As a result, he recalled, he "began to see Mrs. Hobby more frequently and began to understand even more clearly her key role in both the newspaper and radio operations."[14]

The expansion of the *Post's* circulation and the subsequent return to profitability, combined with KPRC's success, made it possible for the Hobbys to make an early escape from their draconian financial agreement with Jesse Jones. While they struggled to make the newspaper profitable in 1940, they often only made payments on interest and not on the principal of their loans. According to Bill Hobby, at one point Will had a meeting with one of his bankers to plead for relief from that month's interest payment. The banker was sympathetic, but given the newspaper's financial condition, his advice was for Will to jump out of the banker's office window on the upper floor of a downtown building. Although this undoubtedly was an example of Will's style of humor (or the banker's), the reality was that Will was having extreme difficulty making payments.[15]

As soon as the *Post* and KPRC became dependably profitable, Will devised a plan to refinance the deal he had made with Jones. Will traveled to Dallas to meet with his banker friend Fred Florence, whom he had met years earlier through his late brother, Edwin. Will and Oveta had worked with Florence while he served as president of the Texas Centennial Exposition in Dallas in 1936. Florence had loaned the Hobbys more than half of the money they needed to swing the original agreement with Jones, and he had charged less interest than Jones. Florence and his rival, Nathan Adams of the First National Bank in Dallas, had pioneered the business of commodity loans, mainly oil and gas in the East Texas field. Will had expectations that Florence would take the risk and offer a new financing deal, especially now that the *Post* was making a profit. Florence agreed to refinance the loan, but he declined to make it for the entire amount. "Will, you're publishing a newspaper in Houston," Florence said. "You ought to do your banking in Houston. But if you have any problems with those country bankers down there, show them this." Florence then wrote his loan terms on his personal letterhead and signed it. Will took Florence's loan memorandum back to Houston, where he presented it to his old friend Judge James Elkins, who had added banking to his growing business empire. His First City National Bank was quickly becoming a financial powerhouse. Will had played a key role in getting Elkins established in Houston in 1917, and Elkins was not ungrateful. He agreed to loan Will the rest of the money he needed to pay off his loan from Jones. In the coming years the Hobbys would rely heavily on credit from Fred Florence's and Judge Elkins's banks to finance the expansion of their media properties.[16]

Americans anxiously watched events unfold in Europe in the fall of 1939 as Nazi Germany invaded Poland and Europe was quickly engulfed in what would soon become a world war. They also prepared for a presidential campaign and election. FDR, who remained popular with a majority of the American people, had served the traditional two terms and showed no inclination to run for an unprecedented third term. It appeared that American voters would be tasked with electing a new president while also hoping to stay out of the war.

With the Democratic Party presidential nomination seemingly wide open, Will eagerly endorsed Jesse Jones for the job. He declared that preference in late May 1939 in a speech introducing Jones at a special joint session of the Texas Legislature. He admired the work Jones had done as the head of the Reconstruction Finance Corporation (RFC) to help the American business community. In his speech, Will stated that under Jones's leadership, "[The RFC] has done more in the fight against the Depression than any other agency of government," which included the rescue of the nation's banking system. In private, Jones was interested in the presidency, but he made no effort publicly to get the nomination. Responding to Will's endorsement, Jones said, "I would say to you, Governor Hobby and to others, that I have no political ambitions, no expectations, no hopes." His statement, of course, left open the possibility that Jones would accept the nomination if offered. That hint soon encouraged a few influential boosters, including FDR's son, Elliott, former chairman of the National Democratic Committee James Farley, and newspaper tycoon William Randolph Hearst to promote Jones as a presidential candidate.[17]

Jones, however, eventually realized that despite FDR's refusal to announce his candidacy for a third term, the president had every intention of being renominated. In the summer of 1939, FDR appointed Jones to be the head of the Federal Loan Administration, a powerful position that gave Jones authority over ten major federal loan agencies, including the RFC. Because Will Hobby understood that Jones was not going to challenge FDR for the nomination, he switched his support to John Nance Garner. But it soon became apparent to Will, who was undoubtedly counseled by Jesse Jones, that FDR was assured of winning the nomination at the national convention in Chicago. Nevertheless, a significant number of the members of the Texas delegation insisted they would oppose FDR's nomination, which would result in a contentious battle between them and the pro-Roosevelt delegates from Texas. As he had done in the past when Texas Democrats faced a threat to party unity, Will led an effort to bring harmony by persuading the two sides to support Garner as Texas's favorite-son candidate during the first ballot at the convention and then to support FDR's nomination in the balloting that would follow.[18]

FDR easily won renomination for president at the national convention in Chicago in August. Will Hobby had hoped that Roosevelt would select Jesse Jones as his running mate, but much to Will's chagrin, FDR picked the liberal secretary of agriculture Henry Wallace instead. FDR's nomination presented the Hobbys with a quandary. For the first time in both of their lives, they decided they could not support the 1940 Democratic presidential ticket. Will and Oveta were lifelong, loyal Democrats and well-known party activists and leaders. Will, of course, had been a Democratic lieutenant governor and governor of Texas, and he was a highly influential figure in the state party for nearly two decades after leaving elected office. Oveta had been a candidate for the state legislature as a Democrat, and she had held several posts in local and state Democratic Party organizations. But in 1940 their party loyalty would not hold, at least not to the national ticket.

They decided to oppose FDR's 's bid for a third term. Will's anti-Roosevelt position would be expressed quietly, while Oveta's was overt.[19]

Their decisions were not made lightly. They had supported FDR's election in 1932 and reelection in 1936 with enthusiasm. Will and Oveta had met the president and the First Lady, and they had liked and been impressed with both. The Hobbys spent time with the Roosevelts when they came to Houston to dedicate the San Jacinto Monument in 1936. Oveta accompanied Eleanor Roosevelt on a boat excursion down the Houston Ship Channel on that occasion. Will also visited briefly with FDR in May 1937, when the president arrived in Houston by special train after his ship landed at Galveston at the end of a presidential fishing trip in the Gulf of Mexico. When the Hobbys were in Washington, DC, in late January 1938, Will visited with Jesse Jones while Oveta accompanied House Majority Leader Sam Rayburn and Vice President Garner to a meeting at the White House with FDR and Speaker William Bankhead. During that visit the president questioned Oveta about business conditions in Texas. In April 1939 Oveta was among a group of newspaper editors who attended an off-the-record discussion with FDR in the State Dining Room of the White House. As she left the White House, reporters who hadn't attended the meeting quizzed her about what the president had said to the editors. Oveta simply smiled and replied, "Off the record."[20]

The Hobbys had enjoyed their visits with the Roosevelts during the 1930s, but they didn't favor the prolabor, social welfare, "big government" direction FDR took after he began his second term in 1937. Especially troubling to the Hobbys was FDR's controversial judiciary reorganization bill, popularly known as the "court-packing plan," in which the president tried to persuade Congress in February and March of 1937 to pass legislation to make it possible for him to pack the US Supreme Court with pro–New Deal justices who he hoped would not rule any of his programs unconstitutional. This proposed legislation greatly alarmed the Hobbys and many other public figures, including Vice President Garner, most of the Texas congressional delegation, and other Southern Democrats. Opinion polls indicated that the bill was unpopular with the public, and it was a turning point in the relationship between FDR and many conservative Democrats, including the Hobbys.[21]

Will's support of FDR had diminished even earlier than 1937 because of FDR's Agricultural Adjustment Act of 1935 and his support of prolabor legislation, among other programs, which Will opposed on the grounds that they constituted federal interference in private enterprise. "I don't feel [Will Hobby] could be described as a 'New Dealer,'" Will's journalist friend Weldon Hart has written. "He did not seek government participation as such in controlling the welfare of citizens. He looked upon government as having an obligation to provide ways and means for helping themselves with a minimum of interference after that." In his own memoir, Will's son, Bill, was more blunt: "Make no mistake—my father was no liberal."[22]

Nevertheless, James Clark has noted that although Will's "warm support of the New Deal had cooled noticeably," he was "still friendly until FDR came out with his 'court-packing plan.'" Initially, the *Houston Post*'s editorials about FDR's court reorganization effort were cautiously worded and admitted that some judicial reform might be warranted, but they also suggested that packing the Supreme Court would set a dangerous precedent that could threaten the concept of separation of power between the three branches of the federal government. "But as the weeks passed and the extent of the Roosevelt plan was revealed," Clark observed, "Hobby's attitude became one of firm opposition."[23]

Oveta opposed the "court-packing plan" for the same reasons her husband opposed it, but she was more vocal in expressing her fear that it could be a first step toward totalitarianism in the United States. In 1937, totalitarianism seemed to be taking over the world, with Fascist governments in Italy, Spain, and Portugal; Nazi dictatorship in Germany; Stalinist terror in the Soviet Union; militarist control in imperial Japan; and dictatorships in Eastern Europe, South America, and Asia. There was an understandable concern in the United States about potential authoritarian trends in the federal government, concerns that were fueled by several ultraconservative political pressure groups.

In 1937, Oveta was still writing book reviews for the *Houston Post*. When the Roosevelt administration submitted its court-packing bill to Congress that February, she happened to be reviewing Sinclair Lewis's political novel *It Can't Happen Here*, which had been published a little more than a year before. Lewis's novel was inspired by Adolph Hitler's rise to power in Germany, as well as the demagogic career of the late Huey Long, who had been assassinated in 1935. In the novel, a Huey Long–type populist and demagogue named Windrip is elected president and quickly imposes a fascist dictatorship on the United States. *It Can't Happen Here* became an instant best seller. Oveta was interested in the novel. Not only had she met Huey Long in Houston in 1932, she had closely followed his career through her and Will's friends in New Orleans, most of whom opposed Long. Oveta saw Lewis's novel as a warning that totalitarianism was possible even in the United States, which made her even more concerned about the impact of FDR's court-packing bill.

When the Texas Federation of Women's Clubs invited Oveta to speak at its annual convention in Houston in March 1937, she decided, with the court-packing controversy much on her mind, to speak about the need for Americans to be alert to the totalitarian threat to liberty. She borrowed Sinclair Lewis's book for the title of her talk. Citing the examples of Italy and Germany, Oveta argued that the citizens of those countries had remained passive, telling themselves, "It can't happen here," even while dictatorships were being imposed on them. She claimed that the same thing could happen in the United States because Americans hold their "heritage lightly. We neglect that which our forbears nourished and held in trust for us." In an indirect but obvious reference to FDR's court-packing plan, Oveta warned that maintaining the balance of power between Congress, the presidency, and the Supreme Court was essential to the preservation of individual freedom. It was the responsibility of all Americans to remain on guard against any governmental action that could threaten liberty, Oveta argued. Accordingly, any proposed legislation should be closely examined and evaluated rationally, not emotionally, to determine if it would "endanger the wealth of liberty you hold in trusteeship." If legislation did seem to pose a danger, it was every citizen's duty to "oppose it with all the strength and ingenuity" at their command. Oveta reminded the women's club members that they had made great progress in the fight for equality under the law and that it was women who stood to lose the most under a totalitarian government, because "their long years of struggle to be citizens of their country in their own right will go for naught."

The audience gave Oveta a standing ovation, and afterward she received a number of compliments about her speech. Pleased with such a positive reaction, Oveta printed her speech as a pamphlet, which she distributed to friends, associates, and a select group of editors at newspapers around Texas.[24]

FDR's court-packing legislation eventually died in the Senate, but it and the "liberal" social and labor policies the administration advocated during the president's second term seriously damaged FDR's relationship with many conservative Democrats, including Will and Oveta Hobby. For the Hobbys, the result was that they now considered themselves politically independent. "Now I have come to the opinion that I shall never again say: 'I am a Democrat' or 'I am a Republican,'" Oveta declared in an essay she wrote during this period. "'Our country, right or wrong' for me can never be translated: 'My party, right or wrong.'" She and Will still found it difficult to leave their party to vote for a Republican presidential candidate. Will had voted in nine presidential elections beginning in 1900, and he had never cast a ballot for the Republican candidate for president, although he had considered voting for Theodore Roosevelt in 1904. Accordingly, despite their disenchantment with the liberal wing of the Democratic Party, if FDR failed to seek a third term, the Hobbys had hoped to support one of the party's conservatives, preferably Jesse Jones, but John Nance Garner or James Farley would also have been acceptable to them.[25]

Two unexpected developments in the summer of 1940 made the Hobbys' decision much easier. One was the Republican Party's surprising nomination of Indiana utilities executive Wendell Willkie as its candidate for president. Willkie was an attractive alternative to FDR for the Hobbys. He was a former Democrat who had only recently switched to the Republican Party because he believed FDR was antibusiness. That was a view the Hobbys shared with Willkie, despite Jesse Jones's influential role in the administration. In addition, Willkie was not a member of the ultraconservative and isolationist Robert Taft–Arthur Vandenberg faction of the GOP, which was important to Oveta, who was a strong internationalist. And Oveta, if not Will, also liked that while Willkie was a critic of the growing size and power of the federal government under FDR, he was generally supportive of some New Deal programs, including Social Security, that had become hugely popular with voters.[26]

What proved decisive for the Hobbys, however, was FDR's nomination for a third term, which broke the two-term tradition established by George Washington. Years later, Will Hobby admitted to James Clark that he was "flat-footedly opposed to a third term."

The decision was made. Will and Oveta would break from the national Democratic Party and vote for Willkie for president in 1940, while continuing to support Democratic candidates in Texas, especially those running for the US Senate. With a few exceptions, this was the political path Will and Oveta would follow for the rest of their lives.[27]

Lyndon Baines Johnson (LBJ), the son of Will's friend Sam Ealy Johnson, was one of those Texas Democrats whom the Hobbys supported. Will had met LBJ when Lyndon was a kid hiding under his parents' dining table listening to Will and his father swap political gossip with local Blanco County officeholders. Oveta met LBJ for the first time in April 1937 when he was running for Congress in a special election to replace the late congressman James P. Buchanan. When LBJ traveled to Houston to seek support from the "Governor," Will asked Oveta to join the meeting. Oveta later recalled that she was strongly impressed with LBJ. He struck her as "a very personable and handsome young man [who was] very knowledgeable about governmental processes." When LBJ left Will's office, Will turned to Oveta and said, "That's a young man to watch. He will go far." Oveta later told an interviewer, "You know, all young men who were running for office usually came to see my husband because he had a great interest in young people seeking public office. And my husband was always glad and willing to counsel any young man who wished to come to see him, and I'm certain that he did give [LBJ] advice." Soon after the election, Will sent LBJ a letter congratulating him on his "splendid victory." He added that he was especially pleased "on account of your father who is my good friend."[28]

At the time that Will and Oveta decided to vote for Willkie in 1940, the Hobbys had a written policy that executive officers of the *Post*, including themselves, were not allowed to make political statements other than on the editorial pages of the paper. And while the *Post*'s editorials during the campaign were critical of various Roosevelt administration policies and actions, the newspaper did not endorse either candidate out of respect for Will's friend Jesse Jones, who was making speeches over national radio networks that not only criticized Willkie but also staunchly defended FDR's business policies and his decision to run for a third term.[29]

Oveta complied with her own policy, but she nevertheless worked actively for the Willkie campaign. In late August, she sent word to the Wendell Willkie for President campaign office in New York City that she was supporting Willkie's candidacy as a private citizen and was available to work behind the scenes for the campaign in Texas. She stressed, however, that she had to be cautious because of the *Houston Post*'s editorial policy. "I can't begin to tell you how enchanted I was to hear you are for Willkie," responded Martha Cross, a Willkie Club leader in New York. Near the end of September, Oveta reported to the Willkie campaign that she was "doing all that I can for Mr. Willkie in Texas" and that she believed "we are making progress." She was quietly working with a small group of fellow Houstonians who were opposed to Roosevelt, some of whom were longtime friends of the Hobbys. The group included James Elkins; Mike Hogg, the brother of the late Will Hogg; and oilmen Jim Abercrombie, Hugh Roy Cullen, and Jim West. With Elkins taking the lead, he and Hogg helped organize Texas Democrats for

Willkie, for which Hogg served as chairman. Except for Mike Hogg, most of the members of the Texas Democrats for Willkie had long ago left the national party, while some, like Cullen, had long been steadfast members of the Republican Party.[30]

The ultraconservative Hugh Roy Cullen proved to be more of a problem than a help to the campaign. Although he was working hard to defeat Roosevelt, he wasn't particularly happy with Willkie, who he felt was too liberal. Much to Oveta and Will's displeasure, when Willkie made a campaign visit to Houston, Cullen released a statement denouncing Willkie's internationalist foreign policy stance, which resulted in a public spat between Cullen and Willkie. In response to oilman Cullen's criticism, Willkie told a press conference, "You know, the Good Lord put all this oil in the ground, then someone comes along who hasn't been a success at anything else, and takes it out of the ground. The minute he does that he considers himself an expert on everything from politics to petticoats." This would not be the last time the Hobbys, Oveta in particular, would be unhappy with Cullen's political shenanigans.[31]

Oveta's quiet work for the Texas Democrats for Willkie organization mainly involved privately conducted fundraising and helping write and distribute pro-Willkie literature, as well as sending notices to Texas newspapers whenever Willkie scheduled radio talks over national networks. Between that and managing the *Post*, Oveta had little time for anything else. Apologizing to Willkie's national headquarters for not sending them timely reports about the situation in Texas, Oveta explained, "Frankly, between the office and the campaign, there has been no time to keep abreast of current mail." Not only did Oveta try to keep the Willkie organization informed about the campaign's work in Texas, she also gave them press and public relations advice. When Willkie appeared in a newsreel and declared that the city of Chicago could "go to hell" after he made a speech there in mid-September, Oveta asked the national headquarters to tell Willkie to refrain from using profanity. The remark, Oveta complained, had been "a great hump to get over in the Bible belt."[32]

Two days before Election Day, Oveta wrote a letter to Willkie's national campaign headquarters that expressed her strong feelings about the importance of the Willkie campaign and why she was working hard to defeat FDR. The night before, she had listened to Willkie address a final mass campaign rally in Madison Square Garden that had been broadcast over a national radio hookup that included KPRC. "Listening to Mr. Willkie in Madison Square Garden last night was an appreciative reminder of what you and many others are doing in this campaign to restore America to Americans," Oveta wrote. "We have no hopes of carrying Texas," she admitted, "but we felt that we should make every effort possible to poll a large protest vote. There is nothing to do now but pray, and I am sure a great many are doing that." Oveta's letter confirmed that she and Will did not view the Willkie campaign as a temporary break from the Democratic Party. "We should like to think that this effort will in time make Texas a two-party state."[33]

There was an amusing sidenote to the Hobbys' efforts for Wendell Willkie. Their son, Bill Hobby, who was now a precocious eight-year-old student at Kinkaid School in Houston, wrote a paper during the presidential campaign that he titled "An Account of National Affairs." In what was perhaps an early indication he would develop some political views that differed from his parents', Bill wrote that because of the war in Europe, America "must have a leader who can build up a defense and offense. Franklin D. Roosevelt is the man for the job! He is eligible for a third term. As many of us say, 'We shouldn't swap horses in the middle of the stream.' *We don't want Wendell Willkie.*"[34]

On November 5, as Oveta expected, Roosevelt and his running mate, Henry A. Wallace, trounced Willkie in Texas. They won thirty-seven other states, garnering 449 electoral votes to Willkie's 82. While the final results weren't close, FDR did win eight fewer states than he had won in 1936, surely giving Will and Oveta a small degree of satisfaction.[35]

A few days after the election, Oveta wrote a letter to the Willkie national campaign leaders thanking them for their overall efforts and their help with the Texas campaign. Her letter included a promise to remain vigilant in monitoring any trend toward authoritarianism in the White House: "We hope that the people who worked so hard will remain intact as a nucleus to serve as an articulate and watchful group during the coming years." Oveta also sent a telegram to Willkie, declaring that his campaign had been "an inspiration, a tonic. It furnished the much needed note of persistence in our task of being a watchful and articulate group."[36]

Ironically, despite their unsuccessful effort to help defeat FDR's bid for a third term and their worries about authoritarian trends in Washington, world events would soon draw the Hobbys not only back into the Roosevelt camp, at least temporarily, but, in Oveta's case, directly into the president's administration.

# CHAPTER 24

---

# "PETTICOAT ARMY"

By the beginning of 1941, Nazi Germany had occupied most of Western Europe. Although the United Kingdom was holding its own in the air war known as the Battle of Britain, that nation was still facing a dire threat from Adolph Hitler's submarines in the North Atlantic. In Asia, the Imperial Japanese Army, which was continuing its military adventure against China, had recently occupied French Indochina. In the United States, President Franklin Roosevelt was exerting intense diplomatic pressure on Japan to withdraw its forces from Southeast Asia, while also doing all that he could to help the British, despite the legal restrictions Congress had imposed on his efforts through the Neutrality Act. Nevertheless, Congress had passed the Selective Service Act in September 1940, and young American men were being drafted into the military in large numbers. The likelihood that the United States would soon be at war was increasing with each passing day.

Within weeks after Roosevelt won reelection to an unprecedented third term, the Hobbys put aside political partisanship. They directed the *Houston Post* to print a series of editorials that called on all Houstonians to unite behind the president in support of his efforts to prepare the country's defenses. "The President is offering the nation a leadership that its safety demands it accept and follow," one *Post* editorial declared. "It is high time that the people with one accord join in supporting the President." With his experience as a war governor in 1917 and 1918, Will understood the need for national unity in the face of the military menace from abroad. Oveta had long been concerned about the hypothetical danger of authoritarianism at home, but she understood the threat from Germany and Japan was real and immediate.[1]

As war in Europe and in Asia dominated headlines in the *Houston Post* that fall of 1940, life continued as usual for the Hobby family. Comfortably settled in their newly refurbished and remodeled house on Glen Haven, Jessica (soon to be four years old) and Bill (soon to be nine years old) were tended to by nannies, longtime Hobby servants, and

---

*Will with his five-year-old son, Bill, in 1937.*

their father, while Oveta focused much of her time on the *Post*. This is not to say that Will was at home all the time and not busy with his own projects, or that Oveta neglected her children. Of the two parents, however, Will was more of a presence at home than was his wife. Nonetheless, Oveta closely monitored her children's activities, including Bill's (Oveta preferred to call him William) education at Kinkaid School, where he was a fourth grader in the fall of 1940.

The family's return to the house in Braeswood was a happy development for Bill, who enjoyed rabbit hunting in a nearby field with George Hightower, the African American prison trustee whom Will Hobby had pardoned while he was governor. By this time, Hightower had worked for the Hobby family for twenty years as a handyman, gardener, and, along with Vernon Wiley and Cecil McBride, as one of their three chauffeurs. Will, who was readily available to his son during this period of Bill's boyhood, loved to take Bill to the KPRC Radio studios in the Lamar Hotel, where the fourth grader would be wide-eyed with wonder at the flashing lights, the tangle of wiring, the microphones, and all of the other electronic gadgetry. Will also took his son with him on trips to Austin, where they swam in Barton Springs and visited Will's old friends, including colorful cotton baron and developer Edgar "Commodore" Perry and T. C. "Buck" Steiner, a former rodeo star, law officer, and movie stuntman who owned the Capitol Saddlery, a famed boot and saddle shop on Guadalupe Street.[2]

Young Bill suffered from pollen allergies that became so severe in the fall of 1940 that he developed chronic sinusitis. His doctors advised Will and Oveta that a dry climate could dramatically improve their son's health. They recommended enrollment in one of the boarding schools in the deserts of the Southwest. Like Oveta when she had been a child, Bill also had a stuttering problem, which his sinusitis seemed to make worse. A family friend suggested to Oveta that she and Will should take a look at Green Fields Prep School for Boys, a boarding school in the desert near Tucson, Arizona. In January 1941, after reading the school's catalog and reviewing references from parents whose children were students there, Oveta and Will enrolled Bill in Green Fields. After Will traveled to Tucson early in February to check on Bill, he and Oveta were convinced they had made a good decision. Bill spent the spring semester in Arizona and then returned to Texas at the end of May, and his parents enrolled him in the Rio Vista summer camp in the Texas Hill Country.[3]

After getting her son settled in at summer camp in June 1941, Oveta traveled to Washington, DC, to consult with Federal Communications Commission staff about regulatory issues of concern to KPRC Radio. One morning during her visit to Washington, Oveta was surprised when a staff member in the Department of War called her hotel room and asked if she could attend a meeting at the army's Bureau of Public Relations. She later recalled that she didn't understand why the army was inviting her to a meeting, but she agreed to attend out of curiosity. The army officer chairing the meeting was Lieutenant Colonel Ernest Dupuy, chief of the planning and liaison branch of the army's newly organized Bureau of Public Relations. Dupuy had been a newspaper reporter in New York City before beginning a career in the army at the start of World War I. In June 1941 Dupuy and his staff were struggling with a major public relations problem resulting from the first peacetime draft law Congress had passed nine months earlier. The wives, mothers, and girlfriends of draftees were flooding the War Department with an average of ten thousand letters a day, complaining about their men being called away from their jobs and family relationships. Many of the letter writers also expressed concerns about the welfare and safety of the draftees. They asked questions about the kind of food the draftees were being fed, what kind of recreation they were allowed, the availability of religious services, and the quality of health care. Some letters included specific complaints draftees had made to their families about army life.[4]

The War Department, fearful that it was facing a significant public relations disaster that could result in desertions and bad morale, asked Major General Robert C. Richardson, the head of the army's Bureau of Public Relations, to develop a plan to address the problem. General Richardson gave the assignment to Colonel Dupuy, who queried his contacts in the newspaper industry for recommendations about who could advise him on how the army could best respond to the women who were bombarding the army with their questions and worries. While he was trying to find a suitable advisor, Dupuy came across news stories from the *Washington Herald* and the *New York World Telegram* about Oveta. The Washington newspaper published a story about Oveta's attendance at the American Newspaper Publishers Association's annual meeting in Washington in April 1939, where she had attracted news media attention as the only woman attending the meeting. The *Telegram* story included Oveta's comments about the changes she had made at the *Houston Post* to attract more women readers. Dupuy wondered if Oveta might be the answer to his quandary. When he learned she would be in Washington in early June, he decided to invite her to meet with him to discuss the army's "woman" problem.[5]

At their meeting, Dupuy explained to Oveta the potential public relations disaster confronting the War Department. Oveta suggested that the army should establish a special branch, preferably led by a woman with professional public relations experience, that could develop and direct a campaign to educate the nation's women about the positive aspects of life in the army and the necessity for building up the military to defend against foreign threats to the country's security. Impressed with Oveta's ideas and style, as well as her experience as a newspaper executive, radio station owner, and community leader, Dupuy realized that not only should the army organize such a branch, it also should ask her to lead it. "Apparently he had sort of cast around the country," Oveta said years later, "to see if he could find a woman . . . to communicate with the women of the country to tell them the necessity for the peacetime draft, for the types of training the men had to have."[6]

Colonel Dupuy asked Oveta if she would consider serving as a consultant to the army if a decision was made to organize a women's branch of the public relations bureau. Oveta replied that she would like to help in some capacity, but because the position would require her to be in Washington for an extended time, she was concerned about the impact it would have on the *Post*. She needed to give the idea more thought. Oveta did agree, however, to take a sample of letters women had sent to the army back to Houston, where she would compose template language for the bureau to use when responding to such mail. She also agreed to draw up an organizational plan for the women's branch, as well as to submit a list of ways women could support the military effort in the event of war.[7]

A few days after Oveta returned to Houston, she received a letter from Colonel Dupuy informing her that General Richardson had approved establishing the women's unit in the Bureau of Public Relations as she had recommended, which would have the official title of Women's Interest Section. He thanked Oveta for the "sound advice and . . . valuable time" she had given him at their meeting. He then added, "[General Richardson] has asked me for recommendations as to who should head it. So . . . I would like to learn . . . whether or not you would consider heading the Section, either in de facto or in an advisory capacity. Will wait your reaction with much interest."[8]

Oveta was intrigued by the army's offer. After thinking it over, she decided the job was an unusual opportunity to contribute to the country's defense preparations in an area in which she had some expertise. She also saw it as a chance to gain valuable personal experience that could potentially benefit the *Post*. It was also a temporary appointment, which meant she would not be away from her family for more than a few months at most. She obviously discussed the offer with Will, who encouraged her to take the job for patriotic reasons. He assured her that the children and the *Post* would be in good hands in her absence. Oveta sent a letter to Dupuy stating she had a strong interest in the job but only in "an advisory capacity." She agreed to return to Washington on July 18 to meet with him to discuss the details. She also sent Dupuy an outline of an organizational chart she had promised him during their meeting in Washington, as well as her recommendations on how to carry out a publicity campaign, which, she argued, should have the goal of building "constructive attitudes" among American women about the need for the peacetime draft. Her plan was to generate publicity by sending press releases to local newspapers about "routine Army news translated into terms of woman reader interest." That informational effort could be enhanced by inviting women reporters who worked near military camps to act as liaisons between their newspapers and the public relations bureau. Oveta also recommended that the publicity campaign stress the important role women could play in the national defense program. In addition, Oveta suggested that the section could also educate women about the "disciplinary, recreational, and occupational training phases of military service."[9]

When Oveta met with Colonel Dupuy and General Richardson in Washington in late July, they persuaded her to serve as the chief of the new women's section in the army's Bureau of Public Relations. Her acceptance was with the understanding that she would serve as a federal employee on a "dollar-a-year" compensation basis, that she would hold the position for no more than four months, that she could appoint one of her staff members at the *Houston Post* as her personal assistant, and that she would be able to return to Houston for one week each month. Richardson allowed her up to two months to complete unfinished business in Houston before she reported for duty. The general submitted Oveta's employment conditions, as well as the organizational chart and campaign proposals she had drafted, to Secretary of War Henry L. Stimson. The secretary soon approved them. On July 28, 1941, the army appointed Oveta "Expert Consultant to the Secretary of War," with the official title of "Chief, Women's Interests Section, Planning and Liaison Branch, Bureau of Public Relations."[10]

The army's announcement of Oveta's appointment was widely noted in the press with stories that emphasized that not only did a woman now hold an important administrative job in the Department of War, which was extremely unusual, but that she also was working on women's issues, not previously perceived to be an area of concern to the military. Her own newspaper broke the news in Houston on July 31 with a headline declaring, "Oveta Culp Hobby Named War Dept. Woman's Editor." The Associated Press story about Oveta's new job included a photograph of the petite and photogenic thirty-six-year-old Texan posing at a desk holding a telephone receiver to her ear while looking at the camera. "The army has selected a woman editor to interpret the activities of the military to wives, sweethearts, and mothers," the AP reported. "She is Mrs. William P. Hobby of Houston, Texas, a youthful and attractive newspaper executive." Newspapers across the country published the AP photograph over captions that variously read, "Mrs. Hobby Gives Woman's Slant to Army News," and "To Interpret Army for Women." One story noted that Oveta was deeply knowledgeable about the "women's viewpoint. Her selection is viewed as a tacit recognition by men in the masculine profession of arms that there is such a viewpoint." Unaware that Oveta had accepted the appointment for a token "dollar-a-year" salary, the *New York Herald Tribune* reported that Oveta "was called into service so suddenly she doesn't know what her title will be—if any—nor what her salary will be, if any." The *Tribune* also reported inaccurately that she would be "working directly with Henry L. Stimson, Secretary of War, in a consultative capacity."[11]

Despite the *Tribune*'s claim, Oveta would not be reporting directly to the secretary of war. Instead, she would be responsible to General Alexander "Day" Surles, the highly regarded commander of a brigade of the First Armored Division stationed at Fort Knox. When Oveta was negotiating with General Richardson and Colonel Dupuy about the women's section position, Surles was in Kentucky organizing and preparing to take command of the new Sixth Armored Division. However, on August 6, the army gave General Richardson a new assignment as commander of the army's Seventh Corps in Alabama and then called Surles back to Washington as General Richardson's replacement as head of the Bureau of Public Relations. It was the same job Surles had held in the mid-1930s, when he was on the staff of army chief General Douglas MacArthur.[12]

When Oveta accepted the position at the War Department, she retained her position as vice president of the *Post*, which allowed her to continue to have an assistant back in Houston, Helon Johnson, who was on the newspaper's payroll. Oveta resigned from the various boards and other positions she held in Houston and statewide. Because Oveta would eventually spend only ten days a month back home, her mother moved to Houston to take care of three-year-old Jessica. Bill was sent back to Green Fields School in Tucson in September.[13]

Will correctly assumed that as one of the only women working as an administrator in the War Department, Oveta would inevitably attract much public attention, especially because her unusual duties required frequent interaction with the press. He also knew that newspapers would be eager to publish photographs of an attractive woman working

(WX1)WASHINGTON, Aug. 1—WOMAN EDITOR TAKES OVER WAR DEPARTMENT DESK—
TO INTERPRET ARMY ACTIVITIES FOR WIVES, MOTHERS AND SWEETHEARTS,
MRS. WILLIAM P. HOBBY, EXECUTIVE VICE PRESIDENT OF THE HOUSTON POST,
HAS BECOME "WOMAN'S EDITOR" OF THE WAR DEPARTMENT'S BUREAU OF PUBLIC
RELATIONS. (SEE WIRE STORY)(AP WIREPHOTO) 1941 (HEW61818CPG)

*The army heavily publicized Oveta Culp Hobby's appointment at the War Department,*
*as shown by this wire service photograph nationally distributed in 1941.*

in what was basically an all-male military environment. He therefore was determined she should have a large enough wardrobe that photographs would show her wearing a variety of stylish dresses. Will called Oveta's sister Lynn and asked her to take Oveta to Ben Wolf's Fashion, a store in downtown Houston, to shop for new clothes but not to tell Oveta it was his idea. "Once I got [Oveta] into the dressing room, she was lost," Lynn remembered. "She was almost like a child; it was charming." They remained in the store until closing time because Oveta couldn't make up her mind about which dresses to buy. With Oveta's agreement, Lynn gathered several dresses to take home to show "Governor" and let him decide. "So we got him settled in the library," Lynn recalled, "and he watched her model those dresses with a huge smile. I believe she kept all of them. And Governor caught me alone a few days later and said, 'Lynn, you sure did teach her well.'" As Will had predicted, news stories about Oveta invariably commented on her stylish appearance.[14]

Oveta moved into a small apartment in the Lanier Place section of Northwest Washington and reported to work the first week in August 1941. The War Department assigned her an office in the massive and awkwardly named Munitions Building, located on the north side of the National Mall at Twenty-Sixth and Constitution Avenue, which also housed the offices of the secretary of war. Her first task was to recruit three veteran women journalists to help her respond to letters, write press releases and brochures, and carry out other duties. Because Oveta was eager to get the women's section up and running as quickly as possible, she appointed three veteran reporters whose work she admired and whom she knew through her own involvement with the national and regional press associations. Emily Newell Blair, a contributing writer for *Liberty* magazine whom Oveta had met at the Democratic convention in Houston in 1928, was appointed chief of staff. Genevieve Forbes Herrick, the former Washington correspondent for the *Chicago Tribune*, assumed duties as information officer. Lily Shepard, a journalist who had several years of experience as a reporter for the *New York Herald Tribune*, took charge of radio news. Velma Soule, former women's editor of the *Houston Post*, came with Oveta from Houston to serve as her executive assistant.

On October 13, Oveta hosted a meeting in Washington with the leaders of the nation's twenty-one largest women's clubs to explain that the task of her office was to inform women about how the army cared for its men. She outlined her plans for carrying out that mission. Army chief of staff General George Catlett Marshall spoke off the record at the meeting, which was when the general met Oveta for the first time. Utilizing the connection she had made with Eleanor Roosevelt that dated back to 1936, Oveta persuaded the First Lady to give a luncheon speech at the Raleigh Hotel to the women's club leaders stressing the importance of the Women's Interest Section and urging them to do all they could to help Oveta meet its goals. Mrs. Roosevelt hosted a tea at the White House after the luncheon. Oveta also recruited the women's club leaders to join an advisory council to help guide her work.[15]

Oveta later recalled that the first months on the job were difficult: "It was new, all new. We had to start from scratch; no precedents, no files, not even a pencil." She soon learned that an administrative job in the army was vastly different from running her own business. At first she was frustrated that many of her decisions had to be vetted by faceless bureaucrats before they could be implemented, although she eventually learned to be patient, if not happy, with bureaucratic strictures. A magazine article about Oveta noted, "Red tape irked her at first. But she learned to cut through it in her quick, determined way, and admits that sometimes it keeps her from making mistakes."[16]

Another adjustment Oveta had to make was following minor army rules and regulations that governed activities she had always controlled herself. Oveta had been on the job a little more than one month when Colonel Dupuy scolded her for failing to provide

*General George C. Marshall in Washington, DC, talking to leaders of national women's organizations who were assembled by Oveta Culp Hobby, 1941.*

the army with an address where she could be contacted in an emergency whenever she was back in Houston. Dupuy also informed Oveta that bureau regulations required her to sign a book on the receptionist's desk whenever she left the office and again when she returned. Dupuy's lecture undoubtedly raised Oveta's blood pressure, especially when he asked, "Will the Women's Interest Section please get military?"[17]

Despite these bureaucratic annoyances, Oveta and her staff moved quickly to produce and distribute a vast quantity of brightly colored brochures, pamphlets, and flyers with a "frequently asked questions" type of feature. Answers were provided to the most common questions they received about why the draft had been necessary and what kind of training and living conditions men would experience in the military. The army liked Oveta's material, but not everyone did. A *Vogue* story about Oveta's project criticized her "pastel booklets" for reading "as though they were meant for ten-year-old minds [and] are written in the mealy-mouthed style that withers writing in practically all newspaper women's pages."[18]

Oveta's office also wrote and distributed scripts for news commentators to use on the radio and in newspaper columns, and her staff composed as many as four pages of news stories a week for release to newspapers nationwide. Because Oveta was aware that this literature could easily be overlooked in the flood of press releases the government delivered to the media, she developed a strategy to make it more likely that her target audience would get the information she wanted them to have. Her experience at the *Post* had taught her that newspapers were more likely to print a story if it involved individuals who were from the community. Accordingly, her staff noted the names and hometowns of individual men featured in army base newspapers whose stories illustrated points her office wanted to make about what the military was like for these men. A story would be written about that individual soldier and then submitted to his hometown newspaper.[19]

Oveta also went on the road to hold press conferences and to speak at local women's club meetings, where she conducted question-and-answer sessions. She attracted large audiences to these events, including one in Minneapolis in November that drew seven hundred to a luncheon. The week before, she had traveled to New York City to address the annual conference of the National Council of Women; to Corpus Christi, Texas, to speak to the Texas Newspaper Publishers Association; and to Houston to attend the dedication of the Houston Municipal Garden Center, which was sponsored by more than one hundred women's garden clubs in the greater Houston region. The latter visit gave her the opportunity to stay with her family for a week. As a newspaper editor and columnist with extensive experience as a public speaker, she was able to deliver her message effectively. She was skilled at providing safe and simple answers to difficult questions, such as when she was frequently asked about the quality of the food being served to the army's draftees. Her standard answer was, "It's getting better all the time," which was a dodge that nevertheless seemed to satisfy her audiences. A magazine writer who accompanied her on one of these trips wrote, "From her office she speeds via airplane to [begin] a speaking tour that takes her thousands of miles from the Capital. Here we find her explaining to a group of clubwomen the need of equipment for a day room in a nearby Army camp. The women promise to furnish what the Army does not provide. At the close of the meeting she holds a fifteen-minute question period."[20]

By the fall of 1941 there were well over one million men in the US Army. "For every one of those men," Oveta said in a newspaper interview, "there are four or five women—mothers, wives, sisters, sweethearts—who are closely and personally interested" in their welfare. It was her job to tell those women what they wanted to know about the "boys" in the army. One of the admonitions Oveta frequently repeated during her meetings with women's groups was that army morale would be greatly improved if everyone would stop crying "Oh you poor brave boys" to the soldiers. Instead, she asked the women to toughen up. "Keep your handkerchief in your pocket and ask them home to dinner," she suggested. "Women as well as men have to stop talking about what can't be done—and do it. This is going to take us all, and all we can give. No effort is too small to be unimportant; no effort is great enough to be complete."[21]

Oveta's efforts attracted considerable media praise. Six weeks into her job, the *New York Sun* judged her job performance a success, noting her achievements "were being nationally recognized as a bang up score for women in the defense effort." Colonel Dupuy later claimed that the Women's Interest Section was the "most vital method of molding the opinion of women" of the United States in support of the military during the war.[22]

Oveta's success with the Women's Interest Section soon drew her into the battle to create a Women's Army Corps. The idea for such a unit had been discussed ever since the start of World War I, but it had languished because of opposition by Congress, the War Department, and the army. A month after General George Marshall assumed his duties as chief of staff of the army in September 1939, he ordered planning to begin for a women's unit, with the general idea that it would be organized along the same lines as the Civilian Conservation Corps. Its members would not be officially in the army and would not serve in uniform. Opposed by most of the officers in Marshall's command, the idea was shuttled around the War Department for a couple of years without any meaningful progress.[23]

The idea took on new life, however, as the German Army overran Western Europe and Japan expanded its war on China in 1940. Massachusetts congresswoman Edith Nourse Rogers led the cause. She had served in the American Red Cross in France in World War I and had been active in veterans' affairs after succeeding her husband in Congress in 1925. She had long advocated the creation of a women's unit of the regular army. On May 28, 1941, Representative Rogers submitted a bill to Congress to authorize the army to establish a women's corps, but it was met with intense opposition from the War Department, the army, and most of the Southern congressional delegation. As with all newly proposed legislation impacting the budget, the Rogers bill was referred to the Bureau of the Budget for a cost analysis. The bureau was also a place where the bill could be buried quietly.[24]

The Rogers bill lingered until the fall of 1941, when General Marshall, almost alone among his colleagues in the War Department, announced his support. "I regard the passage of this bill at an early date as of considerable importance," Marshall informed Congress. "Women certainly must be employed in the overall effort of this nation." According to his biographer, Forrest Pogue, General Marshall greeted the Rogers plan "with enthusiasm rather than apprehension. He saw no reason . . . to train men as telephone operators or typists when most of those jobs in civilian life were handled by women." Pogue also argues that Marshall's support stemmed from an additional source. He was influenced by the fact that many women were eager to join the army to support the war effort, which appealed to Marshall's egalitarian passion for democratic ideals.[25]

Despite General Marshall's "vigorous support" for women to serve in the army, the Bureau of the Budget continued to hold up the Rogers bill. In mid-November, Oveta attracted General Marshall's attention when she reported a conversation she had had with Eleanor Roosevelt, who wished to know if the Rogers bill would permit women to be involved "in anti-barrage activities and similar fields of endeavor in which women are now being used in England." Marshall had been impressed with the way Oveta had orchestrated the gathering of women's club leaders soon after her arrival in Washington, and he was pleased by the success of her public relations efforts in the weeks following that meeting. Marshall now realized that Oveta, who obviously had connections to the First Lady, could be a skillful advocate for the women's corps. Her knowledge of women's problems, her strong relationship with women's organizations, and the fact that she was known to favor women's service in the military made her an obvious candidate to serve as a lobbyist for the cause with Eleanor Roosevelt as well as with Congress. On November 14, he sent a handwritten note to the army's personnel office, which had the responsibility for planning how the army would organize and administer the women's corps if it passed Congress: "Please utilize Mrs. Hobby as your agent to smooth the way in this matter through Mrs. Roosevelt."[26]

Oveta not only had Eleanor Roosevelt actively involved in the campaign to create a women's unit in the military, she also established a communications pipeline between the First Lady's office and the Women's Interest Section, which resulted in a stream of memoranda flowing back and forth between their respective offices, including on at least one occasion involvement by President Roosevelt. Marshall asked Oveta to give his planners assistance on public relations matters that might arise about the Rogers bill. He also appointed her as the War Department's representative for the negotiation sessions with the Bureau of the Budget. Most important, General Marshall asked Oveta to determine which army jobs women could perform with the least amount of special training and to incorporate her findings in an organizational plan for the women's unit. Eager to help in an effort she ardently supported, Oveta educated herself thoroughly about the legislation and all of the related issues. She had the attention of not only the First Lady but also the widely admired and influential chief of staff of the army.[27]

On Friday, December 5, after Oveta submitted her draft of the women's corps planning report to General Marshall's office, she headed to Houston for the holidays. She intended to return to Washington after New Year's Day to finish her fourth and last month as head of the Women's Interest Section of the Bureau of Public Relations. She also planned to continue to help persuade the Bureau of the Budget to release the Rogers bill to Congress for hearings. On her way to Houston on December 7, Oveta stopped over in Chicago, where she was scheduled to meet that afternoon with the Associated Women of the American Farm Bureau Federation, which was holding its national convention at the Sherman Hotel. As she stepped into Chicago's municipal airport terminal after her flight arrived at noon, she was surprised to find agitated news reporters waiting for her. The entire airport seemed to be full of people scurrying through the gateways. A reporter from the isolationist *Chicago Tribune* called out for her reaction to the Japanese attack on the US naval fleet at Pearl Harbor. Oveta's immediate thought was that the *Tribune* reporter was trying to trick her. His "America first" newspaper had criticized her appointment to the Bureau of Public Relations, claiming it was part of FDR's alleged propaganda scheme to persuade the US public to support his plan to "drag" the nation into the war. Oveta, fearing the reporter was trying to get her to make a provocative statement that the newspaper could take out of context, kept cool and didn't answer. When other reporters confirmed the attack, Oveta rushed to a pay telephone and called Will. They both agreed she should cancel her trip to Houston and return to Washington, but not before fulfilling her commitment to speak to the women's group that afternoon. The presiding officer of the event later wrote Oveta to tell her how much the members appreciated her "brave effort" and her "self control" while speaking to the group on the day of the attack on Pearl Harbor: "In fact, we have always felt that the fine manner with which you carried on in that dramatic moment did much to keep our people gathered there, under control."[28]

After Oveta returned to Washington from Chicago, she met with Colonel Dupuy and General Surles to discuss the possibility that she might need to remain at her post longer than she had initially agreed. That decision depended on the role her office might play now that the nation was at war. It was clear that the mission of the women's section of the Bureau of Public Relations would change. After the Japanese attack on Pearl Harbor, it was assumed that it would be obvious to all women why men were being drafted. Dupuy and Surles agreed that the new mission for the women's section would be to rally American women to support the war effort and that if Oveta remained at the bureau, her role would probably change as well. While Oveta was trying to decide if she would stay in Washington, events in the War Department and in Congress essentially made the decision for her.

With war now a reality, the Bureau of the Budget finally sent Representative Rogers's Women's Army Corps bill to Congress on December 11. The Rogers bill was gaining support among many members of Congress, but there was strong opposition from the Southern delegations. General Marshall was aware he would need all the help he could muster to get the bill passed. Recognizing that Oveta could play a key role in that effort, he asked her to stay in Washington to work with him and his staff for as long as it took to get Rogers's proposed legislaton through Congress, even though it might take several months. Marshall's plea was all Oveta needed to make her decision. She agreed to stay. When Oveta informed Marshall of her decision, he personally transferred her from the army's Bureau of Public Relations to the personnel section of the general staff, where she would report directly to him.[29]

After she received her new assignment, Oveta flew from Washington to Houston on December 21 to spend nearly two weeks with Will and the children over the holidays. Bill, who was back from Green Fields School in Tucson, was returning to Kinkaid School in Houston for the spring semester of 1941. A news story about Oveta's visit to Houston included a quote from her nine-year-old son, who vowed he would never be a journalist, because "Mother is, and she has to work too hard."[30]

While Oveta was home for the holidays, Secretary of War Stimson sent his official endorsement of the Rogers bill to Congress on December 24, while Representative Rogers amended the bill to make it more palatable to the army. The House Committee on Military Affairs scheduled a hearing for January 21. When Oveta returned to Washington on January 10, Marshall asked her to testify at the hearing to outline her proposal for the organization of the women's army unit and to explain the rationale for substituting women for men in noncombat roles. Oveta immersed herself in research, and she prepared for her testimony with help from John J. McCloy, the assistant secretary of war, and members of Marshall's staff. On the morning Oveta was scheduled to testify, General Marshall asked her to come to his office prior to the hearing. He asked if she had ever testified before a congressional committee, and she replied that she had not. When he asked if she knew what she was going to say, she pulled a written statement out of her purse and handed it to him. Marshall read her testimony and then ripped it up and tossed it into the wastebasket. "Now I want to give you a piece of advice," he said. "When you go to testify before a congressional committee, you say what you have to say." He did not want her to rely on a prepared statement. Oveta replied that there were many questions the committee members might ask that she would not necessarily know how to answer. She admitted that she was "about as unmilitary a person as ever existed." Marshall continued to lecture her about how to deal with the committee, ending the meeting with only a few minutes to spare before she was to testify. Oveta dashed to a car waiting outside the Munitions Building and was driven to the Capitol by one of Marshall's staff officers.[31]

At the hearing, Oveta argued that the army could not rely on "haphazard, unorganized voluntary assistance" from the nation's women. "The Army needs a trained, disciplined and readily available" corps of women. She explained that the army's general staff planned to organize ten companies, each composed of two hundred women in the ranks and four women officers. Male officers would train the students at the first training school, while women officers would train the subsequent classes. Oveta concluded her testimony by arguing somewhat audaciously, "General Marshall, who is, after all, chief of staff, has told me that he wants this legislation on the books. If the Army feels the necessity for such a corps, it must be a good idea." One newspaper account of Oveta's testimony stated,

"Wearing a tight fitting black coat that had broad bands of mink shaped like epaulettes on the shoulders and a hat as smart as any pre-1940 Paris model, the chic Southerner elicited smiles and soft-spoken questions from the Military Affairs committeemen."

The House committee members treated Oveta with respect and generally refrained from making tired sexist remarks and jokes about women soldiers, but two members couldn't help themselves. One asked if the proposed women's unit was going "to start a matrimonial agency." Another asked how the army would handle the "fact" that many of the women recruits would only want to do the "glamorous jobs" and would refuse to do laundry, cooking, or other menial work. Before Oveta could answer, Ohio Republican Frances Bolton, the only woman on the committee, quickly and effectively ridiculed it, sparing Oveta from possibly offending the congressman with her answer. It would not be the last time Oveta would have to endure such remarks. Oveta's performance at the committee hearing impressed its members as well as the media, but most important, it impressed General Marshall. "I found out that this remarkable woman had been the parliamentarian of the Texas Legislature for years," Marshall later recalled. "She should have been teaching me."[32]

As the Rogers bill navigated through the House of Representatives, some of its members revealed their deeply embedded sexism. One representative solemnly declared, "[It is] a reflection on the courageous manhood of the country to pass a law inviting women to join the armed forces in order to win a battle. Take the women into the armed forces, who then will do the cooking, the washing, the mending, the humble homey tasks to which every woman has devoted herself?" The Senate also had its share of critics, mostly Southerners, who issued ludicrous and misogynistic statements in their attacks on the Rogers bill. Among the worst offenders was South Carolina senator Ellison "Cotton Ed" Smith, who had a well-earned reputation as a demagogue and a virulent racist. Smith declared that the formation of women's units in the army and navy would be "one of the most deplorable steps ever taken by this nation," eventually leading to the "downfall of the country." It would result in "disrespect for womanhood [because] all this nonsense about how many girdles and brassieres and things the women are going to wear will cause us to lose our modesty."[33]

Despite the vocal opposition from some members of Congress, Marshall believed the Rogers bill would be passed. In the event of the bill's passing, he wanted most of the structure of the women's corps in place so that no time would be wasted in getting the unit operational. He created a preplanning group, with Oveta as its head, to plan recruiting procedures, training necessities, and the administrative structure for the corps. Marshall also dispatched Oveta to Ottawa and Toronto, Canada, from March 5 through March 10 to meet with leaders of the Canadian military's women's units, as well as with British women officers who were visiting Canada. Her mission was to assess the experience of the British and Canadian women's services, which were well established by that date, and to learn what had worked and, most important, what had not. Oveta discovered that the initial opposition in Canada and the United Kingdom was based on the same arguments that were being made in US Congress. Despite all of the dire predictions, the women's units had proved so valuable that the Canadian and British governments authorized a vast increase in their numbers. Oveta's visit to Canada gave her a wealth of information that proved extremely useful to her as she continued her work.[34]

In late January, Marshall directed the army's personnel division (known as G-1) to write a job description for the head of the proposed women's army unit. The description required the director to be a woman "of an active temperament" between thirty and fifty years old, with experience managing both women and men, and no link to any political pressure group. Marshall asked Oveta, Congresswoman Rogers, and G-1 to submit a list of nine candidates they could recommend for the position. Oveta's list included successful business executives and college administrators but no social or political leaders. G-1 recommended three candidates, with Oveta at the top of the list. The colonel in G-1 in charge of preplanning later stated that Oveta's name was first on the list because he had "never known a finer executive, man or woman." Congresswoman Rogers submitted only one name: Oveta Culp Hobby.[35]

At the end of February 1942, Marshall arranged a meeting with Oveta, ostensibly to review her nominees. When she entered the general's office, he had her list in his hands. He went to the point immediately. "Thank you for this list," he said, "but we want you to head the corps." Surprised, Oveta replied, "General, I have no military knowledge, none." Marshall pointed out that no other woman did either. Marguerite Johnston later claimed that Oveta declined the offer at first. But Oveta told Forrest Pogue, Marshall's biographer, that she explained to the general she "would to talk to my husband about it and I did." Will was in Washington at the time. When Oveta told him about Marshall's request, he urged her to take the job: "Any thoughtful person knows that we are *in* this war. Every one of us is going to have to do whatever we are called upon to do." Will was comfortable with the management team he and Oveta had in place at the *Post* and at their radio station, which operated under his general supervision. He also had the care of their children well in hand.[36]

With Will's blessing, Oveta accepted General Marshall's offer. On March 18, 1942, he submitted Oveta's name to Secretary Stimson as his choice for the position of director of the yet to be created women's corps. He told Stimson preliminary arrangements for the organization of the corps had to be made in rapid fashion "in order to handle the inevitable avalanche of applications and suggestions, along with strong pressures to influence the appointment of candidates for the head of the Corps." Because of the outstanding work Oveta had already carried out as the leader of the planning group, she could move quickly to organize the corps once Congress passed the Rogers bill. Marshall explained that Oveta "had displayed sound judgment and carried out her mission in a manner to be expected of a highly trained staff officer. She has won the complete confidence of the members of the War Department Staff." A separate G-1 recommendation noted Oveta's "personal energy, magnetism, sincerity, and idealism," as well as a "certain stubborn determination in pursuing major issues." To head off the inevitable political lobbying by powerful members of Congress to have prominent constituents be considered for the job of heading the women's unit, Marshall urged Stimson to "endeavor to obtain an early decision of the President in this matter" in advance of the bill's passage. Stimson approved the recommendation and sent it to FDR the same day he received it from Marshall.[37]

Although the Rogers bill had not yet passed, the news media covered Oveta's activities, including her trip to Canada, which was heavily publicized by the Canadian press. In addition, many of the publishers and managing editors of the major urban newspapers already knew Oveta through her involvement in their national associations. In early April, Sidney Fields, whose popular column Only Human was featured in the tabloid *New York Daily Mirror*, published an interview with Oveta. "If the Women's Army bill becomes law," Fields wrote, "Mrs. Hobby is likely to be the first major to lead the U.S. Army in skirts." He described Oveta as a "shy exact woman" who had the "warm face and earthy understanding of a farmer's wife, and a passion for hats, hair-dos, law, government, ideas, words." Oveta told Fields that a women's corps would play a vital role in the military effort: "In this war, women have to carry more than their own weight. So far, we've been all sail and no ballast." Fields observed that when she was deep in thought, Oveta had a habit of running her fingers through "a well-set, beautiful hair-do. People around her despair because as soon as she has her hair brightly set and someone asks her a tough question, Mrs. Hobby will run her hand right through it. The pompadour wilts. The friends wince. Mrs. Hobby carries on." A story published a week later in the Hearst-owned *New York Journal American* quoted Oveta as saying the women's unit would not be "a pink tea affair, for there are real jobs for these women to do—jobs they can do better than men."[38]

Like most of the news stories about Oveta that would be published in the coming years, the *Journal American* and *Daily Mirror* profiles made a point of referencing her physical attributes, clothing, and feminine qualities. The *Journal American* described Oveta as being "of medium build," with "dark curly hair" and a combination of "charming femininity and cool efficiency." Another news story noted that "Mrs. Hobby is about the height movie directors favor for their feminine stars" and that her figure would look good in uniform. Despite the superficiality of the issue, Oveta's good looks and pleasant femininity did play an important role in her selection to be head of the women's corps. Robert Pando has noted that even Representative Edith Rogers supported Hobby's candidacy to some degree because she thought Hobby would "look the part," which she believed was essential to the successful start-up of the corps. One of the unstated reasons for this preference for a leader who was physically attractive and who exhibited strongly feminine qualities, in addition to being married and having children, was the fear that opponents of women serving in the military would accuse the women's unit of being a haven for "male-hating" lesbians. And indeed, such charges, usually implied or insinuated, were made, although there is no record of Oveta ever being the target of such accusations.[39]

The news media stressed Oveta's attractive physical appearance throughout her tenure in the army, sometimes to an absurd extent. When she was touring the women's corps training camp in Iowa, the Associated Press asked its photographer to photograph her in a "swim suit standing on the diving board of the [women's corps] pool." An army press officer vetoed that idea, with the explanation that there would be no "cheesecake of the boss." Members of the public duly noted the newspapers' obsession with Oveta's looks, inspiring one woman to submit a poem to her local newspaper:

> I'm not a WAAC, I'm not a WAVE
> Yet I'm a patriotic slave
> I'm saving grease, flattening each can
> I'm one of those women "behind the man"
> I'm selling bonds in a theater lobby—
> But why can't I look like Oveta Culp Hobby?[40]

Oveta and her colleagues on the preplanning committee worked long hours in April and early May 1942, hurriedly trying to put together an organization that Congress had yet to authorize. As Mattie Treadwell, the official historian of the Women's Army Corps, later noted, Oveta found herself in an unusual situation. She was the "unannounced head of a nonexistent office" that was working on a project that depended on legislation that might not pass. The War Department added to her burden when it carried out a major reorganization of the entire department, dropping Oveta two levels down in the administrative hierarchy and removing her from General Marshall's direct command. Marshall told Oveta to come to him if any problems surfaced that she could not resolve under the new reporting structure, but aware of the political dangers of going outside of the chain of command, she rarely took advantage of that privilege. Undaunted, she and her team did manage to put in place a number of essential elements that would be necessary to the operations of the proposed women's corps, including recruitment procedures; discipline, promotion, and discharge regulations; and a final table of organization designating units and the purpose of each unit. Oveta and her team also worked on needs that ranged from finding a suitable training base site for the women recruits to designing uniforms, headgear, and the type and composition of work clothes and footwear. The latter task turned out to be more difficult than expected, because the army was clueless about the clothing needs of women.[41]

In March of 1942 the House of Representatives passed the Women's Army Corps bill by a vote of 249 to 86. And on May 14, 1942, the Senate passed the bill by a vote of 38 to 27, but only after Representative Rogers dropped her plan for the women to be full members of the army with the same pay and benefits as men. She agreed to a compromise to make the Women's Army Corps an auxiliary instead of a regular unit of the army. On May 15, President Roosevelt signed the Rogers bill, approved Oveta's appointment, and issued an executive order establishing the corps. Although the bill authorized a total of 150,000 members, the executive order limited enlistment to no more than 25,000 women in the initial recruitment drive. After the president signed the bill, Secretary of War Stimson announced his appointment of thirty-seven-year-old Oveta Culp Hobby as director of the newly authorized Women's Army Auxiliary Corps (WAAC) with a rank of major. Her salary was $3,000 a year, with an additional housing allowance of $100 a month. To head off any political attempts to force the army to appoint someone else to the job, Stimson's announcement of Oveta's appointment was made almost simultaneously with FDR's signing ceremony. Eleanor Roosevelt held a press conference immediately after her husband signed the bill. She expressed her deep satisfaction that the bill had become law, but she also "deplored the fact that it did not contain an antidiscrimination clause." She added, however, that she was "vastly relieved" that Oveta Culp Hobby would head the women's corps. She was certain that Oveta would extend to African American women the equal treatment the Constitution guaranteed them.[42]

On Saturday morning, May 16, 1942, Major General Myron C. Cramer, judge advocate general of the army, administered the director of the WAAC's oath of office to Oveta Culp Hobby. Oveta raised her white-gloved right hand and repeated the oath as camera flashes lit up the room. To signify how important this new and unprecedented women's corps was to the War Department, Secretary Stimson and General Marshall stood closely at Oveta's side to be more easily photographed with her. Congresswoman Edith Nourse Rogers, who was celebrating the attainment of a goal she had labored hard and long to achieve, was present, as was Will Hobby, who sat silently in the back row. George Dixon of the *New York Daily News*, who didn't know that Oveta's husband was simply being his typically laconic and unassuming self, reported, "If ever a man looked as if he was saying to himself what-the-hell-am-I-doing-here, it was Mr. Hobby." This was a serious misreading of Will's demeanor. After interviewing Will, a correspondent for the *Rocky Mountain News* reported, "William Pettus Hobby is genuinely proud of his wife's new job. He thinks she is showing the spirit American women want to show for war work."[43]

After she took the oath of office, Oveta turned to Secretary Stimson and declared that she was "aware of the honor and obligations of this appointment. The task you have assigned me is a great opportunity for service, its fulfillment a solemn responsibility. I will give to it all the devotion, all the strength and whatever ability I possess." Because of the large number of photographers and newsreel cameras, Oveta had to repeat taking her oath and her remarks several times so that all could get good pictures from different angles. Newsreel film of Oveta taking the oath of office was projected on movie theater screens across the nation. Secretary Stimson later wrote in his diary, "There was such a crowd anxious to see her that the meeting took place in the room where press conferences were held and all the photographers were there and [they] generally had a field day."[44]

Immediately after the ceremony, the War Department's Bureau of Public Relations held a press conference to give reporters an opportunity to question Oveta about her plans for the WAAC. General Marshall and General Surles joined her to provide support and to answer questions about matters outside Oveta's scope of duties. Oveta had worked late into the previous night with Genevieve Forbes Herrick to prepare. They had made

*Will and Oveta Culp Hobby with US Representative Edith Nourse*
*Rogers after Oveta was sworn in as director of the WAAC, 1942.*

a list of potential questions and then composed and rehearsed the answers, paying close attention to the sexist, sensational, and silly queries they expected from some of the male journalists.

As Oveta anticipated, the press peppered her with questions ranging from the frivolous to the scornful in tone. They included questions about what type of underwear the WAAC members would be issued ("not yet decided"); whether WAACs would wear khaki-colored panties (question ignored); whether they would be issued girdles ("yes, if required"); whether they would be allowed to wear makeup and nail polish ("yes, if inconspicuous"); and what would happen if a WAAC got pregnant ("discharged, married or not"). Famed news columnist and author Damon Runyon, referring to the "rather idle questions" reporters asked Oveta, judged that she "disposed of the questions quite tactfully." A wire service reporter likewise noted that Oveta "handled herself excellently. She was direct, forthright, composed, and as candid as could be. She made a good impression." When Oveta was asked about what rules were in place to regulate dating between WAAC members and male army personnel, Oveta turned to Generals Marshall and Surles for a response, but neither man could answer the question, because the issue had not been considered by either of them. Marshall finally managed to explain he hadn't been out in the field lately and didn't know. A female reporter from the Associated Press wryly observed, "It was a day never before seen in that stronghold of stouthearted men: the U.S. War Department."[45]

After the press conference, General Marshall invited Will and Oveta to come to his office. Oveta later recalled, "We all went in, and [Marshall] said, 'I know that any man must have great trepidation about his wife's taking such an assignment, but I want to tell you . . . that the Secretary of War and I mean to give her added support in doing what we know will be a very difficult job.'" Will replied, "General Marshall, I had intended to seek an appointment with you to discuss this very thing because I know that it will be a very difficult thing to form a Women's Corps and to make [it] acceptable to the Army and to the population not accustomed to the idea."[46]

The news that the US Army now had a woman officer for the first time in its history provided content for numerous newspaper columnists. In his column, Damon Runyon declared that he was "highly gratified by the organization of the WAACs. I think, too, that no better selection of a leader could have been made than Mrs. Oveta Culp Hobby of Texas." Runyon described Oveta as a "splendid type of American womanhood and a lady of considerable intelligence and ability. The WAACs represent the greatest recognition in the U.S. of the importance of women since they were given the vote." As for WAACs dating soldiers, Runyon suggested that "we just relax and let nature take its course." He also warned that any man who makes a WAAC the "object of jesting . . . should be sure of their own military status."[47]

Elisabeth May Craig, Washington correspondent for the Gannett newspapers, described the event as "Hollywoodian" because of the many movie cameras at the press conference. "And I was sore because [Edith Nourse] Rogers was ignored," Craig complained. "Nobody even mentioned the author of the bill, who had spent months of hard work getting it through Congress. Nothing happened, until at the end, when they brought up Rep. Rogers and took one picture of the two together." Malvina Stephenson, correspondent for the *Tulsa World*, noted that Oveta was "a good looker and a clever talker" who had "a national reputation as a newspaper executive but not until she emerged out in front of Uncle Sam's first 'soldierettes' did she really steal the spotlight. She's the type around whom stories grow and grow. Mrs. Hobby is a strong personality and most people have very decided opinions about her." Stephenson also stressed, "[Representative] Rogers is impressed with Mrs. Hobby and thinks that Mrs. Hobby will 'look the part' of a clever leader, a quality that can't be underestimated in getting the corps off to a good start. [It's the] old story of 'beauty and brains,' but it's still a rare combination, although Mrs. Hobby has a good share of both."[48]

Most of the news reports of the event were accurate, but there were exceptions. The International News Service reported inaccurately that Oveta was a graduate of the University of Texas School of Law and "one of the first women lawyers in Texas." The *Washington Star* declared that Oveta was a graduate of Baylor University and a former two-term member of the Texas Legislature. These widely spread errors went uncorrected and became a staple of biographical sketches of Oveta for years to come. Nearly all of the news coverage was favorable, although many headline writers couldn't resist titles featuring words and phrases such as "Petticoat Army," "Wackies," "Fort Lipstick," and "Doughgirl Generalissimo." Not all of the editorial columns were as positive, however. The most offensive was in the *Miami News*, which compared the WAAC with "the naked Amazons . . . and the queer damozels [*sic*] of the Isle of Lesbos." In a rare example of her commenting on a matter that she might have been better off ignoring, Oveta responded angrily, understandably, to the *Miami News* editorial, declaring, "WAACs will be neither Amazons rushing to battle, nor butterflies fluttering about." Other editorials were unabashedly misogynistic. A favorite argument was the WAAC violated the sacred tradition that the function of women during a war was to have babies. One editorial writer feared that the WAAC would give mothers the opportunity to abandon their infant children. Although those editorials were outrageous and offensive, the negative editorials published in the African American press stemmed from a not unreasonable concern that the army had appointed a director of the WAAC from Houston, Texas, where racial segregation was rigidly observed. The *Pittsburgh Courier* worried that as a white, Southern woman, Oveta Hobby would inevitably discriminate against African American women.[49]

*Washington Post* publisher Eugene Meyer and his wife, Agnes, hosted a cocktail reception in Oveta's honor the evening following the ceremony. The Meyers had become friends with the Hobbys through their mutual involvement in the newspaper publishers' national association. The party was featured prominently in a story in Meyer's newspaper that included photographs of Oveta wearing one of her attention-grabbing hats and posing with Vice President Henry Wallace. The *Washington Post* reporter described Oveta as "slender, vivacious and dynamic." Many of the who's who of the nation's capital attended, including Speaker Sam Rayburn, Representative Edith Rogers, Representative Lyndon B. Johnson, and several other members of Congress; Supreme Court chief justice Harlan Fiske Stone; a number of generals and admirals; Alice Roosevelt Longworth; famed photographer Edward Steichen; poet Carl Sandburg; columnist Walter Lippmann; and the Meyers' daughter and son-in-law, Philip and Katharine Graham. A few days later, Speaker Rayburn honored Oveta with a luncheon in his private dining room in the Capitol, which was attended by the congressional leadership from both parties. When Rayburn asked Oveta to speak, she took the opportunity to stress how much she needed the support of Congress in her efforts to organize the WAAC.[50]

When Oveta received her first WAAC uniform a few weeks later, she wore it to a meeting with General Marshall. After she arrived at his office and they exchanged salutes, the army chief of staff reached into a drawer in his desk and took out an eagle-shaped, silver pin designating the rank of colonel, telling Oveta that now he had something appropriate to put it on; it was time for her to wear the symbol of her new rank. He announced that from this moment on, she was to be addressed as Colonel Hobby, even though she was not officially in the army. The newly minted colonel was now better armed to address the daunting challenge of organizing the Women's Army Auxiliary Corps, while also working quietly to have her new corps moved from its auxiliary status to that of a regular unit of the army.[51]

# BOOK THREE

# THE

# COLONEL

CHAPTER 25

---

# THE "LITTLE COLONEL"

On Monday morning, May 18, 1942, Oveta Culp Hobby walked into her office in the Munitions Building as the commander of an army auxiliary corps with only one member: herself. She did have a small support staff of regular army officers, including one colonel from the adjutant general's office to serve as her in-house legal counsel and another colonel who worked as finance officer. Those two colonels helped guide her way as she plunged ever deeper into the dense bureaucracy of the US Army and the War Department to organize the WAAC. Velma Soule had returned to Houston soon after Oveta resigned as chief of the Women's Interest Section. The army soon came to Oveta's aid by permitting her to add thirty-seven civilians to her staff, including Helen Gruber, the wife of army general William Gruber, to manage her schedule and to help with other tasks. She soon had her team of assistants busily at work.[1]

Army historian Mattie Treadwell later described Hobby's office as chaotic during its first month of operation as it "swarmed with new clerks, insistent visitors, and hurrying staff members." The telephones rang constantly and "boxes of supplies were stacked in corners." The "insistent visitors" included journalists and magazine writers eager to do stories about and conduct interviews with this new woman military commander and those who would soon join her corps. Business executives, members of Congress, and miscellaneous VIPs also jammed the small waiting area outside Oveta's office, eager to give her advice or recommend favored constituents for admission to the first officer class.[2]

Oveta's job was completely new in US military history. There were no precedents for her to follow, and the initial set of regulations, which were makeshift and had been hastily written while the Rogers bill was making its way through Congress, had to be thoroughly revised now that the corps was a reality. Oveta's task had been made even more difficult in February, when the War Department decided to push her corps further down the chain of army command. She and the WAAC were transferred from George C. Marshall's general staff to the vast bureaucracy of the newly organized Services of

---

347

Supply command, led by fifty-year-old General Brehon "Bill" Somervell, a West Point graduate and engineer who had served during World War I. As a civilian from 1936 to 1940, Somervell had directed New York City's Works Progress Administration, where he oversaw the construction of LaGuardia Airport, among a host of other major New Deal projects. The ambitious, sharp-tongued Somervell had a knack for making enemies, particularly Secretary of the Interior Harold Ickes, who viewed Somervell as a "ruthless" and "vindictive" man who harbored dictatorial instincts. Described by one of his colleagues in the army as "impatient, tense, and decisive," Somervell also had a reputation as an ambitious empire builder whose ultimate career goal was to succeed George Marshall as army chief of staff, a goal that went unmet. Although Somervell frequently and openly disagreed with Marshall's decisions and directives, Marshall respected Somervell's abilities, ignored his ambition, and came to depend on his talent for getting the job done, including supervising construction of the Pentagon, the War Department's massive new headquarters.[3]

Somervell soon pushed Oveta even lower in the hierarchy by placing her under his longtime deputy, General Wilhelm Styer, the chief of administrative services. Somervell and Styer, neither of whom were friendly to the concept of women serving in the military, soon became major obstacles in Oveta's effort to build the WAAC. Oveta now found she was submerged three echelons below General Marshall's office. In addition, the fact that the WAAC was *of* the army but not *in* it was an ambiguous status that created major operational headaches. Because they weren't officially members of the army, Oveta and her staff were denied access to the technical services normally provided to all army units. She was forced to prepare the WAAC budget for presentation to Congress without help from the army's budget specialists who typically provided such services. The budget was a highly complicated process for which neither she nor her fiscal officer had any training or experience. Other examples of technical procedures Oveta had to develop and decisions she had to make without the administrative support of regular army units included the writing of basic documents that had to comply with the army's complex personnel regulations and the evaluation of, in Oveta's words, "endless, bewildering blueprints" for housing at training bases. Other essential tasks also pressed on her. Oveta later recalled that she and two of her assistants "worked all one night until nine the next morning" drafting the recruiting literature.[4]

Oveta and her staff had a multitude of other organizational and administrative details to sort out, and, sometimes, to fight for approval, including seemingly trivial matters, such as the official WAAC insignia and the design and composition of uniforms and hats. The heraldic section of the army Quartermaster Corps, for example, recommended a beelike creature as the official insignia for the WAAC, but Oveta complained that it looked like a "bug" and rejected it, stating she did not want to be known as the "Queen Bee." She eventually accepted an insignia that represented the profile of Pallas Athena, the Greek goddess of just wars.[5]

Choosing an insignia was easy relative to other decisions, but selecting the WAAC uniform was not. Mattie Treadwell noted that it was a "most troublesome" problem that "soon assumed difficulty out of all proportion to its importance." The War Department delegated responsibility to the quartermaster general for the uniform's design and fabric. That office formed a committee that included Oveta and some of her staff, who were often outvoted. The committee invited well-known designers, directed by a vice president of Lord & Taylor, to submit sketches of uniforms for the committee to consider. This process was largely futile because the quartermaster general rejected most of their recommendations. For example, one designer proposed leather jackets, but the quartermaster general opted for less expensive cotton. Another designer recommended pleated skirts, but the quartermaster general vetoed that idea as consuming too much cloth. The committee agreed on shirts with ties but rejected slacks in favor of skirts. Oveta supported that decision because she considered slacks too masculine, which she feared would cause "unfavorable public comment." A designer recommended a blue uniform, but Oveta, whose ultimate goal was to make the WAAC part of the regular army, insisted from the start that the women's corps uniform be identical in color to that of the regular army, with a similar design. The quartermaster general agreed with Oveta. The final result was a khaki uniform that was in harmony with the men's army clothing.[6]

The choice of a hat for the WAAC was also the cause of much debate among committee members. The quartermaster proposed a foldable "overseas" or "garrison" cap patterned on the type worn by male soldiers. Oveta strongly opposed that hat because several private civilian women volunteer organizations had adopted it, and she did not want the WAACs to be mistaken for those groups. Instead, the committee chose a kepi, a hat worn by the French military, including General Charles de Gaulle, the leader of the Free French Army. It had a flat, circular top and a short, stiff, horizontal visor. Although Oveta did not select the kepi and was not fond of the design, it soon became known as the "Hobby hat." The hat proved cumbersome and unpopular with the enlisted women. One recruit complained to *Time* that the hats were "terrible." "They were designed for Mrs. Hobby," the recruit stated erroneously. "She's the only one they look smart on." Eventually, the so-called Hobby hat was replaced by other designs, including a version of the garrison cap.[7]

In her first weeks as corps director, Oveta had only one prototype uniform: the one on which General Marshall had pinned her colonel's eagle. This was largely because she was the only member of the WAAC, but also because of delays in manufacturing and distributing the final version of the uniform. Having only one uniform during this early period, Oveta was forced to pack an electric fan and iron when traveling to make it possible for her to wash, dry, and iron the shirt and skirt every night. The famed, nationally syndicated newspaper columnist Drew Pearson reported during this period that news photographers went to a radio studio to take photos of Oveta while she broadcast a call for women to volunteer for the WAAC. When the photographers arrived, Oveta was dressed in a stylish dress, not in the khaki uniform they had expected. Oveta explained to the disappointed photographers that her only uniform was at the cleaners, which forced her to wear civilian clothes for the radio broadcast. The photographers agreed to come back when Oveta could pose in her uniform.[8]

Instead of relying on the Quartermaster Corps to deliver government-issued clothing that didn't fit her perfectly, Oveta soon decided to purchase her own uniforms, specially tailored by Saks Fifth Avenue. A few of her officers did likewise. As one observer noted, Oveta soon cut an imposing figure as she strode "purposefully through the War Department, trimly clad in her dress uniform and her 'Hobby hat.'"[9]

With most of the multitude of organizational and operational details either decided or making their way slowly through the army bureaucracy, Oveta turned her attention at the end of May to the recruiting of 440 officers for the WAAC. The Women's Interest Section, now headed by Emily Newell Blair, and the section's advisory council, which Oveta had organized the previous fall, proved invaluable in this effort by working at the community level to attract recruits. Historian Brenda Moore has concluded that the advisory council was "perhaps the War Department's single most important vehicle for reaching the thousands of women who would eventually put on the uniform."[10]

Oveta understood that an officer staff needed to be in place before she could recruit for the enlisted ranks. The set of regulations establishing eligibility requirements for officers had been drafted before the Rogers bill was passed. All officers had to be high school graduates between the ages of twenty-one and forty-five, no shorter than five feet and no taller than six feet, not less than 105 pounds, and able to pass physical and intelligence tests comparable to those given to prospective officers in the regular army. The critical task of finding a suitable training facility for the first class of WAAC officer candidates had also been completed during the preplanning period. Initially, old Civilian Conservation Corps camps, several college Reserve Officers Training Corps training areas, and even state fairgrounds were considered, but they were ruled out for various reasons. Finally, in late April, the army made Fort Des Moines, a former army cavalry post in Iowa, available to the WAAC. Although Iowa's winter weather was not ideal and the post was located far from Washington, DC, the Fort Des Moines facility was suitable in all other aspects, with red brick barracks that could house one thousand women and a large parade ground. Because of the decision to bring African American women into the corps, an additional plus was the camp's location in a section of the Midwest that was free of Jim Crow racial segregation laws and had no record of racial strife.[11]

The fact that members of Congress, high-ranking army officers, and a variety of influential public officials pressured Oveta to select their favored candidates greatly complicated recruitment. By the time of the June 4 deadline, more than 30,000 women had applied. After the recruiting stations administered aptitude and intelligence tests and physical examinations, the number of candidates was reduced to 4,500. Oveta then sent personal representatives to participate in the final screening interviews at the local level. They returned to the WAAC office in the Munitions Building with boxes filled with photographs of the candidates, their applications, and comments from members of the interviewing boards. The army's history of the WAAC claims that Oveta personally read all of the applicant files. She later recalled four days of "careful, almost prayerful, work of making the final selections." More than 99 percent of those chosen had been employed in civilian positions, and 90 percent had attended college. Twenty-four percent were thirty-six years old or older.[12]

Oveta's recruiting efforts attracted the attention of several popular magazines, including *Vogue*; the *New York Times Magazine*, which featured Oveta's portrait on its cover; and *Life*, which also ran a full-page photo of Oveta, with an army recruiting poster on the wall behind her. Congress's passage of the WAAC bill unleashed a deluge of requests by women seeking officer's commissions. "The response was terrific," *Life* reported. "Women of infinite variety scrambled to enlist in the first cadre. There were college girls and career women, shop girls and stenographers, housewives and widows." Applications had to be submitted to army recruiting stations. Local newspapers reported a wide range of unexpected applicants, including a Native American woman dressed in full tribal regalia, a sixteen-year-old runaway, and a "wild-eyed mother brandishing a pistol and demanding to get to the front." *Vogue*'s July 1942 article "She's in the Army Now" was snarky, condescending, and full of factual errors and innuendo. "Oveta Culp Hobby has the biggest job of any woman in the country," it noted. "Her enemies, who have been poking at the appointment, say that Director Hobby got there through politics, through the artful ways of Secretary Jesse Jones of Texas. They say that she wears absurd hats. They say that she has a calculating, cash-register mind. They say that she ought to stay home in Houston, Texas, minding her beautiful whitewashed brick house, her two children, her husband. They say that Washington society, the part that really counts, ignores her. Much of this is undoubtedly true. She has had no social time in Washington, one of the reasons is because she planned it that way."

*Vogue* even called Oveta's publication of young Bill's reviews of children's books in the *Houston Post* as "a bit of nepotism." The article does end with one positive sentence, stating, "[Her] two notable characteristics are her fine, healthy regard for facts and plain dealing" and her "simple calm." And as a high-fashion magazine, it is no surprise that the article pointed out that the WAAC uniform blouse had plastic buttons, the slip was rayon, and the "panties" were cotton.[13]

While Oveta was busy making her selections for the first WAAC officers' school, General Marshall decided to expand the size of the corps. He ordered Oveta to select an additional 860 women after she had chosen the initial class of 440. Because army manpower needs were growing rapidly, Marshall realized the WAAC was going to play an important role in providing noncombat replacements for men needed in the field. He made a decision to have another officer school class as soon as the first class graduated. Oveta made her final selections for the first class of officers late at night on June 30. The 440 women she chose were given two weeks to get their affairs in order before reporting to Fort Des Moines for the three-month training course. Because of the manpower shortage in the army, however, the length of the course was soon reduced to six weeks.[14]

As Oveta and her staff were evaluating applications and making selections for the officers' training camp, various African American organizations, including the National Association for the Advancement of Colored People (NAACP), the National Negro Council, and the National Council of Negro Women, criticized her appointment as director. They were concerned that Oveta was from a Southern, racially segregated city and that therefore she would discriminate against African American women. The National Negro Council declared it had "little or no confidence that justice would be meted out to colored women" by a director whose record and background indicated she was "imbued with the mores and undemocratic practices of a State like Texas." The organizations called on Secretary Stimson to appoint African American educator Mary McLeod Bethune, who was also director of the National Council of Negro Women, as Oveta's assistant director to oversee the recruitment and job assignments of black women. FDR's response was to appoint Bethune to be a special assistant to the secretary of war for racial matters.[15]

Oveta reacted quickly to the charges that she was racially prejudiced. Two days after the National Negro Council published their complaints about her appointment, she announced that the first group of officer candidates would include at least forty black women. In addition, because the army was racially segregated, at least two of the first companies would be all-black units. Black officers would serve in administrative positions, not in menial jobs. The ratio of black to white WAACs would be the same proportion as in the regular army. Oveta also dealt quickly with reports that some army recruiters were discriminating against African American women who wanted to file applications. A week after the War Department created the women's corps, an NAACP youth council in Winston-Salem, North Carolina, sent her a telegram complaining that the local recruiting officer was refusing to accept black applicants. Oveta immediately dispatched a telegram to the accused army recruiter directing him to accept applications from African American women. She followed that telegram with one to the youth group and reported that the situation had been corrected. Despite her efforts, however, claims of racial discrimination by recruiters continued to arrive at WAAC headquarters.

A few weeks after the first complaint, another African American woman from that state wrote a letter to Oveta stating that a recruiter had refused to give her an application. Oveta responded that there was nothing that could be done because the application deadline had passed. The woman then sent the letter to Dr. Bethune, who forwarded it to Oveta, asking for an explanation. In her reply, Oveta acknowledged the validity of the woman's complaint but noted that unfortunately all of the applications had been processed and the candidates selected. She regretted "exceedingly that at this late date there is nothing which can be done." Aware that these racial issues would continue to generate major criticism from African American organizations and unfavorable stories in the black press, to an extent that they could hinder the development of the corps, Oveta met with Dr. Bethune on July 21, 1942, at Fort Des Moines to seek her guidance in selecting African American women officer candidates and in smoothing their way as members of the corps. As a result, she and Bethune forged a mutually respectful relationship. Bethune soon persuaded the National Negro Council to withdraw its objections to Oveta's appointment.[16]

To underscore her commitment to racial fairness, Oveta gave a speech to students at the predominately black Howard University in Washington, DC, about her recruitment of African American women to serve as officers and her plan for organizing companies of enlisted African American women. In her speech, which was widely reported in the press, Oveta cited the valuable help and advice Dr. Bethune had given her, emphasizing that Bethune was one of her "good friends." Oveta praised the patriotism that African American volunteers had demonstrated in their recruiting interviews and quoted from the application letters of black women who held advanced college degrees as proof of their qualifications and talent. She also understood the importance of having an African American woman on the WAAC command staff in Washington, DC.

When the first class of forty African American women officers graduated from Fort Des Moines, Oveta selected one of the graduates, Harriet West, to serve on the command staff. The forty-two-year-old West had been an assistant to Dr. Bethune at the Bureau of Negro Affairs, and she had worked with Oveta as a civilian member of the WAAC planning staff. Oveta promoted West to the rank of major and eventually placed her in charge of investigating incidents of racial discrimination in the corps, among other duties. Oveta also supported the selection of Charity Adams as the highest-ranking African American in the women's unit. Adams rose eventually to the rank of lieutenant colonel and commanded the only black women's corps battalion to go overseas. While Oveta's racial views were liberal compared to those of many of her white friends, colleagues, and fellow officers, she was unwilling to call openly for racial integration in the army. As documented in her official correspondence, she preferred to apologize for the army's segregation rules rather than criticize them. African American WAACs continued to face acts of blatant racism and discrimination for the entirety of the war. Although the army ended segregation of housing at Fort Des Moines by the end of 1942, it strictly enforced racial segregation in WAAC housing, training, and recreational facilities in other camps.[17]

On June 13, 1942, Will and the children arrived at Oveta's newly leased house near the Sidwell Friends School off Wisconsin Avenue, where they stayed for most of the summer. Will had remained with Oveta for a week after her oath-taking ceremony on May 16, and then he returned to Houston to bring Jessica and Bill back to Washington. Earlier in the year, Will had one of the family chauffeurs drive Oveta's sporty Lincoln Zephyr from Houston to Washington for her to use, although she rarely drove it herself and instead used the services of an army driver. Will made use of the car and a private driver to take the children sightseeing while Oveta spent long hours working in her office preparing for the upcoming officer training camp.[18]

When a reporter for the *Rocky Mountain News* learned that Oveta's husband was back in Washington, she contacted Will and persuaded him to sit for a lengthy interview. She and her newspaper were aware of the interest readers had in this man, a former governor of Texas, who was "allowing" his wife to join the army and leave him to tend to their two children. Prior to the interview she called some of Will's friends in Texas for background. They told her that Will "always talks quietly, works quietly, and gets things done." During her visit with Will, he made it clear he had encouraged his wife to accept the appointment. "He does seem sure she's doing the part she should in this war," the reporter stated. Will also assured the journalist that the children were being well taken care of and that they were spending the summer with their mother in Washington. He added that his six-year-old daughter was "a beauty like his wife" and that his ten-year-old son was obsessed with model airplanes. "The thing [Will Hobby] obviously likes best about himself," the reporter noted, "is the fact that he has been a newspaper man almost all of his life." She questioned him about his tenure as governor and the issues he had confronted when in office. "He was proud of signing the bill giving women the right to vote in Texas, although you have to ask him before he admits it. Mr. Hobby is a modest man." Oveta joined the discussion soon after it began. When the reporter mentioned Will's modesty, Oveta responded, "The Squire always is reticent about himself." She then turned to "Governor" and asked, "Did you tell her what you are doing for war work?" When he simply answered "no" and made no additional comment, Oveta explained that Will was serving on the federal "alien enemy board" in Houston.[19]

To be with Oveta in Washington that summer, Will had taken temporary leave from his duties as a member of the Houston unit of the federal Alien Enemy Hearing Board. At the beginning of 1942, the Department of Justice established "alien enemy boards" in each of the nation's federal judicial districts. Texas was the site of four boards, including the one in Houston. The boards had the responsibility for deciding if individual citizens of Germany, Japan, or Italy—the countries with which the United States was now at war—who were in the custody of the immigration authorities should be released, paroled, or interned for the duration of the war. Each of the Alien Enemy Hearing Boards consisted of three civilians from the local community, one of whom had to be an attorney. The Justice Department asked Will to serve as one of the nonattorneys on the Houston board and he agreed. Oveta was worried that at the age of sixty-four he might be taking on too much work, but Will explained that it was one of the ways he could support the war effort. Service on the board was an unglamorous and thankless job. Each member had to make decisions that could send individuals to prison whose only crime, in most cases, was that they were judged to be sympathetic to the wartime enemies of the United States. Too often those decisions were based on little evidence other than the national identity of those under suspicion. Will later recalled that the process of judging each alien reminded him of the difficult deliberations he had conducted for clemency petitions when he was governor. He continued to serve on the Houston board until the end of the war.[20]

After Oveta had selected the 440 women candidates, she traveled to Iowa to oversee the opening of the first WAAC officers' camp at Fort Des Moines on July 20, 1942. Besieged by demands from the news media and eager to cover the first military training camp ever held for American women, Oveta reluctantly agreed to host a press conference. She was relieved to have the expert aid of Vann Kennedy, a native Texan and an old friend of the Hobbys who had helped promote Oveta's book on parliamentary procedure when he was the Austin correspondent for the International News Service. Kennedy joined the army in 1942 and was assigned to the Bureau of Public Relations. The press conference was held outdoors in the sweltering midsummer heat and was attended by a swarm of reporters and photographers from nineteen newspapers and several wire service organizations, as well as cameramen from six movie newsreel companies. Some male members of the news media continued to treat the idea of women in military uniform as something akin to the two-headed calves at state fair freak shows, asking Oveta frivolous questions ranging from what type and color of panties the women would be wearing to what rules for dating were in place. Mattie Treadwell described the journalists as being in a state of "near hysteria," with news photographers invading the barracks "in search of the still elusive WAAC underwear." Oveta was pleased to have a few women reporters present who asked more serious questions about the training course, housing conditions at the camp, and the kind of assignments the women officers could expect after they graduated. Oveta had well anticipated the circus atmosphere and generally sarcastic nature of many of the questions and concluded the conference without giving the press any quotes they could sensationalize. She also declared that at the end of the camp's opening day, the army would enforce a two-week news blackout and reporters would not be allowed on the grounds. Although this decision angered many members of the press and generated some negative publicity, Oveta was determined to protect her women officer candidates' privacy as they adjusted to army life.[21]

In the weeks immediately preceding the opening of the camp, Oveta had insisted she would attend and go through the same training as her officer candidates. General Marshall, however, vetoed the idea, with the explanation that it would violate the army system of rank for her to go through basic training with officers who would be under her command. In addition, the army couldn't afford for her to take that much time away from the work of organizing the corps. Denied her opportunity to experience army training, Oveta nevertheless remained at Fort Des Moines during the first week it was in operation to monitor how well the women were being brought into military life. On July 23 she had the camp commandant, Colonel Don Carlos Faith, assemble the women on the fort's spacious parade ground for a general inspection and for her to address them before she returned to Washington. Dressed in her well-pressed WAAC uniform, "Hobby hat," and sturdy, low-heeled walking shoes, Oveta looked in control, except that she also immediately revealed how much she still had to learn about the army. As she stepped out onto the parade ground and began to walk at a quick pace to inspect her regiments, she failed to salute the flag, which was a violation of long-standing army protocol. Walking slightly behind her, Colonel Faith called out as discreetly as he could, "The flag, the flag!" Oveta immediately stopped and snapped her hand up to her hat.[22]

When she completed her inspection, Oveta stood on a platform and for the first time addressed her WAACs as a group, each of whom were now dressed in their new uniforms and hats. "You are the first women to serve," Oveta proclaimed. "Never forget it. . . . You have just made the change . . . from the individualism of civilian life to the anonymity of mass military life. You have taken off silk and put on khaki. And all for essentially the same reason—you have a debt . . . to democracy, a date with destiny. . . . From now on you are soldiers, defending a free way of life. You wear the uniform of the Army of the United States. Respect the uniform. Then the world will respect all that the Corps stands for."[23]

After Oveta left Fort Des Moines, she and Will traveled to New York City on August 23, taking Bill with them and leaving Jessica in Washington with a nanny. While in New York, they took time to sit for a long interview with a group of reporters in their room at the Savoy-Plaza Hotel. Oveta told the journalists that Jessica was too young "to know what this business is all about, but she's old enough to know that she doesn't like my uniform." That remark prompted one reporter to ask Bill what he thought about his mother's uniform. "The uniform's all right," the ten-year-old answered. "What I like is aviation. Yes, sir! I really like aviation." He then "rattled off" a description of "every known American fighting plane." Oveta told the journalists that she had been delighted to have her husband and the children with her that summer, but that Will would have to make do alone with Bill and Jessica during the coming winter. When someone suggested that Oveta's absence from her domestic duties must be difficult for Will while also managing his newspaper and radio properties, Will stressed that he employed a governess for Bill and Jessica, as well as a cook and other household staff. "Mr. Hobby doesn't mind," one reporter wrote. "In fact, he said . . . '[Oveta] didn't have to ask my permission to join the Army. Anything she does is all right with me. We're all proud of her. She's doing her duty.'" The reporters noticed that Oveta's "eyes brightened" when Will stated that the *Houston Post* staff missed her. She replied that she also missed the *Post* but declared, "You'd be surprised—I manage to keep an eye on what's going on."

Most of the media attention was on Will, who was described as a "stocky man . . . with the kind of complexion one would see on a cowboy or a sea captain. He doesn't talk a lot, his conversation running toward giving polite and direct answers to questions." When a reporter asked Will how it felt to have a famous wife, Will replied, "Doesn't feel any different. She's always famous with me." That "laconic" response gave the *New York Times* its headline for the story: "Mr. Hobby, Impressed but Not Awed by Famous Wife, Comes to Town." That evening Oveta and Will attended Irving Berlin's patriotic musical *This Is the Army*. After the show, Berlin took them backstage to meet the cast members.[24]

When the Hobbys returned to Washington after their brief break in Manhattan, Will and the children soon departed for Houston, while Oveta went to WAAC headquarters to focus her full attention on a surprising problem. When the corps was established, most of the army base commanders had made it clear they had no interest in having WAACs assigned to their bases, largely because they didn't understand what skilled jobs the women were capable of performing. In addition, no plans had been made to send WAACs overseas. Oveta was shocked when she picked up a copy of the *New York Times* from her desk and read an interview with General Dwight Eisenhower, who recently had been sent to London to take command of US Army forces in the European theater. Discussing his organizational plans for his headquarters in London, Eisenhower mentioned he would request that a contingent of African American WAACs to be sent to England "to perform duties such as car driving and secretarial work and also to provide companionship to thousands of Negro troops" stationed there. The *New York Times* story reported that the army was eager to solve a "problem" for their black troops in England. "Negroes on leave wander disconsolately," the story claimed. "One of [the black soldiers] remarked, 'There's no hot music and none of our girls.'" The army thought that having African American WAACs in London would solve that problem by providing companionship to black male troops.[25]

Oveta was stunned by this news. She and her colleagues had worked hard to avoid the women's corps being seen as an escort service to entertain male soldiers. She soon dispatched a strongly worded message to Eisenhower through a contact she had in the War Department, informing the general she would oppose a request for African American WAACs to be shipped to Europe to be "scattered in uncontrolled small field units near male Negro troops." Eisenhower apparently realized his mistake. His headquarters abandoned the idea, issuing a statement declaring that "colored" WAACs would not be requisitioned until "such a time as the War Department" decided it was a "necessity."[26]

Oveta, accompanied by Will, traveled to Iowa to preside over the graduation ceremony for the WAAC's first officer class on August 29. She and Congresswoman Rogers, who were accompanied by three army generals, also made speeches to the newly minted officers. General Marshall sent a telegram to Oveta for her to read aloud at the ceremony on his behalf welcoming the women into the army, despite the fact that they weren't officially in the army. Marshall's understandable misstatement reflected the confusing and problematic situation Oveta and her corps faced as an auxiliary of the army instead of an official unit.[28]

After the graduation of this initial WAAC officer class, Oveta assigned eighteen specially chosen members to serve on her headquarters staff in Washington. Several of those officers would make important contributions to the corps in the coming years, including Harriet West. But for Oveta, the most significant new member of her command staff was Betty Bandel, a thirty-year-old graduate of the University of Arizona and a former reporter for Tucson's *Arizona Daily Star*. Oveta first met Bandel on September 17, 1942, soon after the latter arrived in Washington. During the years she served as an officer in the women's corps, Bandel kept a diary that is a prime source of behind-the-scenes information about Oveta's work as head of the women's unit. The diary documents Bandel's first impression of the woman she would often simply refer to as the "Director" or the "Little Colonel." Bandel confided to her diary that Oveta was "up close, what she seems to be from afar. [She is] simple, intense, sincere, intelligent, womanly." Oveta was attracted to Bandel's background as a journalist and to her obvious enthusiasm for the corps, and she quickly came to appreciate Bandel's intelligence, practicality, and sense of humor. She invited Bandel to join her for a coffee break, where the two "got into a fine discussion of books and philosophy and things," Bandel noted in her diary, concluding that Oveta was "all right." Oveta thought Bandel was "all right" as well. Eight days after meeting her, Oveta appointed Bandel to be her personal aide. As historian Mattie Treadwell later noted, Bandel's duties expanded "beyond those of an aide"; she also became the director's "right-hand" assistant who carried out a wide variety of tasks, and she became one of Oveta's most trusted confidants.[29]

On September 15, at the same time that Oveta was meeting Betty Bandel, the army "dropped a veritable blockbuster on WAAC headquarters," according to Mattie Treadwell. The army directed Oveta to make plans to expand the corps to more than one million members. Soon after issuing the directive, General Marshall sent two staff officers to meet with Oveta to determine how this huge expansion could be implemented. Oveta stressed her firm belief that the WAAC could never reach that goal by depending on volunteers. A draft would be necessary, which would be a radical step Congress was highly unlikely to take. In addition, Oveta made it clear that it would be extremely difficult for her to increase the WAAC by any significant degree, much less to a million women, if she had no real authority over the corps. This news came as a shock to Marshall's staff officers, because neither they nor General Marshall had known about Somervell's decision to take most of Oveta's command authority away from her.[30]

Two days after this meeting, General Marshall directed General Somervell to restore Oveta's command powers, including authority over the camp at Fort Des Moines. "I also find that the WAAC has been fitted into the [Services of Supply] somewhat on the same basis as the Military Police," Marshall wrote Somervell. "For a new organization . . . composed entirely of women, I think this is not an effective arrangement," Marshall stated, adding that it would be important for some time to maintain a direct relationship between Oveta and all WAAC units after they had been organized. As there was "too much that is entirely new and that demands a woman's point of view," Marshall had his staff make changes in regulations to "obviate some of the apparent difficulties." He also ordered Somervell to provide more assistance to WAAC headquarters. "I had gotten the impression that Mrs. Hobby was becoming too heavily involved and rather overworked," Marshall wrote, "so I had her in the other day to see how things were going. It appears to me that she has been rather engulfed in a mass of detail." He told Somervell "to find her a good officer" to relieve Oveta of "many time-consuming details." Somervell acted promptly and assigned retired regular army colonel Thomas Catron to WAAC headquarters to serve as Oveta's executive officer. Catron's assistance proved invaluable in gaining badly needed control over the workflow streaming into Oveta's office.[31]

Soon after Marshall restored Oveta's command authority over the WAAC training camp at Fort Des Moines, she learned of clothing problems the army's division of Services of Supply was causing at the camp. Army regulations forbade requiring enlisted personnel to wear clothing that was not issued to them free of charge. Accordingly, the WAACs at Fort Des Moines were issued bras. Senior male officers objected, however, with the explanation that it would be favoritism to give the WAACs any articles of clothing that male soldiers were not given. An army colonel in Services of Supply issued a memorandum stating that the proper physical appearance of WAACs could be obtained by exercise and good posture and not by "surgical contraptions." If the army was issuing bras to women, then "such devices could well be considered for the officers and enlisted men." Services of Supply then ruled that to avoid favoritism against men, bras would not be issued to women. "Actually, the brassieres the Army had bought for the first class were so stiff and uncomfortable that few women wore them," army historian Mattie Treadwell later noted. "Most preferred to use part of their $21 a month to buy more comfortable ones in civilian stores."[32]

A more serious clothing problem arose, however, when an early winter storm hit Iowa in late September, blanketing the camp in snow and plunging the temperatures below freezing. The frigid temperatures remained for several days, creating extremely uncomfortable living conditions. Heating units had yet to be installed in the barracks or in any of the other buildings, and Services of Supply had not shipped winter clothing to the women trainees. The average temperature in the barracks and classrooms hovered slightly above the freezing mark. A wave of respiratory illnesses swept the camp, and training sessions were postponed. When she received the news about these conditions, Oveta, accompanied by Betty Bandel, flew to Iowa. As soon as they arrived at the camp they quickly determined that the environmental conditions were unacceptable. When Oveta discovered that the army had issued winter coats to the men in the camp but not to the women, she went to her quarters and changed to summer clothing in solidarity with her trainees. Not only did Oveta share in the discomforts of the out-of-season clothing, she also caught the respiratory bug that was circulating through the camp.

Confident she would have General Marshall's support, Oveta telephoned her superiors in Services of Supply to protest the situation, as Mattie Treadwell later noted, "in a manner that evoked a promise to expedite clothing shipments without delay." Discovering that there was a surplus stock of enlisted men's winter overcoats in storage at a neighboring army base, Oveta ordered the commander of that base to ship the coats immediately to Fort Des Moines, even though the garments were sized for men. With Marshall's support, the coats arrived and were distributed that same day. Marshall's biographer later described the scene at Fort Des Moines after the coats arrived: "Looking rather like children dressed in their papas' overcoats, [Oveta's] WAACs drilled in overlong outerwear, not smartly but warmly." Because the trainees were scheduled to graduate from the camp a few days after Oveta arrived, she remained long enough to preside at the graduation ceremonies. After she returned to Washington, Bandel wrote to her mother, "I wish I could give you a real idea of what the Colonel is like. She is much loved. . . . I have never known anyone with a deeper sense of responsibility than the Colonel has—she says she only acquired it when her children were born. It shows up in little ways—telling me to wear my winter uniform because of the cold." Bandel also told her mother that Oveta's decisive action to get warm clothing to her WAACs was an example of "how the Little Colonel works. She spoke at graduation in the big old riding

*Oveta Culp Hobby (left) and Betty Bandel
(right) at Fort Des Moines, Iowa, 1943.*

hall—in summer uniform—and personally presented diplomas. . . . [T]he girls were eating out of her hand."[33]

In late September 1942, when US military forces were fighting the Japanese at Guadalcanal in the Pacific and the German Army was surrounding Stalingrad in the Soviet Union, FDR asked his wife to go on a mission to the United Kingdom. Eleanor Roosevelt's biographer, Blanche W. Cook, has written that "part of her task would be to use her personal warmth and diplomatic magic to fortify the Anglo-American alliance" and to help raise the morale of the US troops stationed in the United Kingdom. Cook also pointed out that because Eleanor Roosevelt (ER) had pressured her husband to give her a more formal role in war work, he also might have sent her on this mission in response to those pleas. The founder and head of the British Women's Voluntary Service was Lady Reading, whose birth name was Stella Isaacs. A decade after the war, she became the first woman to take a seat in the House of Lords in her own right. She asked Queen Elizabeth, the wife of King George VI, to issue ER a formal invitation to come to England to observe the role that British women were playing in support of the British war effort. The US ambassador to the United Kingdom, John Gil Winant, sent ER a message that he and Lady Reading would make all necessary arrangements for her visit and serve as her primary hosts.[34]

One of ER's main tasks for her trip to the United Kingdom was to evaluate how the British people were holding up and how they were integrated into the war effort. She also planned to tour some of the recently established US troop camps. In addition, the First Lady was interested in visiting the British women's service installations and meeting with the service's officers. As Oveta later stated, ER wanted "to study the work of the British Women's Services and to learn of the types of work women can do best and can learn most rapidly." ER telephoned Secretary Stimson on September 16, 1942, and told him she was planning a visit to England in mid-October. She asked if Colonel Hobby "might be going over some time" to England, because she "would be glad" if Oveta "happened" to be there during at least part of her stay. Stimson understood that this was the First Lady's indirect way of asking that Oveta be sent to the United Kingdom to inspect the women's service posts with her. He replied that he would check with General Marshall about Colonel Hobby's schedule. After Marshall received Stimson's call, he sent a hand-delivered memorandum to Oveta, sealed in a "personal and confidential" envelope, as ER's trip was a secret. The memo informed Oveta of ER's call to Stimson. "As I understand it," Marshall explained, "she did not have in mind that you would be a member of her party, but rather that when she was visiting women's military or naval organizations that you might join her." Marshall was in favor of Oveta making the trip for more reasons than one. "I have had in mind that it would be profitable for you to see what the British have done and . . . I do think that it would be an excellent thing if you were brought into more intimate contact with Mrs. Roosevelt and this seems just such an opportunity."[35]

This was an invitation Oveta was happy to receive. She telephoned Marshall, who had asked her to call him instead of writing, and told him she would immediately make plans to make the excursion. Marshall asked her to come to his office that same day to discuss the trip. It was during this meeting that Oveta complained about losing her command authority over WAAC units and Marshall agreed to restore that authority. It was also at this meeting when Marshall determined that Oveta was exhausted from overwork. As a result, Marshall agreed to her request to bring her aide, Betty Bandel, with her on the trip to England. Much to Oveta's surprise and pleasure, Marshall also told her that Stimson would be able to arrange passage for her and Bandel on ER's flight across the North Atlantic.[36]

The expedition with ER would be Oveta's first trip overseas, which was an exciting prospect by itself, but in 1942 transatlantic air travel was still a novelty with some element of danger. In addition, the First Lady's party would travel by air across the North Atlantic at a time of the year when weather conditions could be difficult, not to mention the fact that the area over which they would fly was a war zone. This reality understandably tempered Oveta's excitement. After all, she had escaped a nearly fatal airplane crash, and the terror of that day remained a vivid memory. Although she had long ago conquered any fear of flying she might have once had, this trip was in an entirely different category from domestic air travel. As usual, Will supported Oveta's decision, but they both agreed that it would be good for her to pay a quick visit to Houston to see the kids before she went on the highly secret trek across the Atlantic. To make the trip to Houston an official duty, Will arranged for the Houston Chamber of Commerce to host a reception in her honor at the Rice Hotel on October 1, where, dressed in full uniform and "Hobby hat," she gave a brief talk about the mission of the WAAC. Underscoring the semiofficial purpose of Oveta's visit, Speaker of the US House Sam Rayburn gladly dispatched a telegram to the chamber of commerce leaders congratulating them on hosting the reception and asking that he "be remembered kindly to [Oveta]."[37]

On October 21, Oveta and Betty Bandel arrived in New York City and met Eleanor Roosevelt and her party at New York Municipal Airport (later named LaGuardia), where they went out onto the airport's water dock to board an eighty-feet-long, sixteen-feet-wide, four-engine, long-range commercial seaplane named the Sikorsky Excambian. The seaplane would take them on a nonstop flight to the Republic of Ireland, where they would board another airplane to England. Although the commercial firm American Export Airlines operated the flight, the US Naval Air Transport Service had contracted the company exclusively to fly VIP civilians who were on assignment to the United Kingdom. The seaplane could accommodate a maximum of sixteen passengers. For security as well as personal comfort, the War Department had decided to send ER (code name "Rover") and her party on a commercial aircraft. A military airplane was more likely to attract enemy fighter planes, and such aircraft were not outfitted for comfort. The Excambian was furnished as a luxury liner of the sky, with sixteen individual bunk beds placed in private, wood-paneled cabins and a kitchen that served meals made from scratch.[38]

This particular expedition to the UK was a memorable one for ER, who wrote about it in her memoir, *This I Remember.* She recalled arriving at the airport "at the appointed time, together with Colonel Oveta Hobby" and Oveta's aide, Betty Bandel, for the nonstop commercial flight ("one of the first to be made") to Foynes, Ireland, a village with a seaplane dock on the navigable Shannon River. ER's personal secretary, Malvina "Tommy" Thompson; a State Department courier; and the vice president of American Export Airlines rounded out the passenger list. Two flight crews were also on board, as the flight was approximately twenty-four hours in length.[39]

When the seaplane lifted up from the East River, ER and her companions had to keep the curtains drawn over their windows until they were over Cape Cod. As they flew over Newfoundland, Greenland, and the open waters of the North Atlantic, ER later recorded that she and Oveta and their companions were "luxuriously taken care of." At one point, the pilot caused some excitement when he alerted his passengers that they were passing over a large convoy of Allied ships bound for Great Britain. They all went to the seaplane's large windows to gaze down to the ocean below to catch a view. ER wrote that the ships were "little tiny specks on the ocean," noting, "It was hard to believe that those ships were in danger and that some of them might suddenly be torpedoed."[40]

During the long flight over, the crew initiated Oveta and Betty Bandel into the "Short Snorter Club." The initiation was a ritual in which flight crews in the air above the Atlantic signed dollar bills, which were then called "short snorters." These short snorters conveyed good luck to soldiers crossing the Atlantic. The initiated, usually all the passengers on a flight, signed the banknotes to become members of the "club." All members of the club were supposed to carry their signed dollar bill with them at all times, and if asked by another member if he or she was in the club, they were required to produce their signed dollar bill as proof. If the member did not have the dollar with them, they had to either buy every short snorter member present a drink or pay them a dollar. Oveta and Bandel duly signed their dollar bills and carefully stashed them in their purses.[41]

The flight of the Excambian was uneventful, but the landing on the Shannon River, which was obscured by fog and driving rain, caused the passengers a few tense moments. The seaplane landed safely but became stuck in the mud of the shallow part of the tidal river as it approached the seaplane dock. A small boat motored out from shore to take ER and her party to the dock. David Gray, the US ambassador to Ireland and ER's uncle, was in the boat. In her memoir, ER wrote that Ambassador Gray was "much concerned over my having to land" in Ireland because of the troubled relations between the two countries. The Irish had refused to take sides in the war and had even demanded that US troops leave Northern Ireland. As a result, the United States had an official policy called "absent treatment." The Irish government was kept at arm's length and official visits by American VIPs were strongly discouraged, although diplomatic relations were never broken. In accordance with this policy, the United States did not inform the Irish government that the First Lady and the director of the WAAC would pass through the country on their way to Great Britain. Even Ambassador Gray had not been told of ER's visit until the night before she arrived in Foynes.[42]

The secret arrival in Ireland of the famous wife of the president of the United States was sensitive enough, but the military status of Oveta and Betty Bandel was a more serious concern. International law prohibited the presence of a combatant nation's military personnel in a neutral country. For that reason, Colonel Hobby and Lieutenant Bandel had not been listed on the flight's passenger manifest. In her memoir, ER wrote, "Ambassador Gray made sure that our military ladies were unmilitary in dress; if they had gone ashore in military uniform they would have been interned [by the Irish government]." Warned about this issue before they departed from the United States, Oveta and Bandel had left their uniforms and hats in their baggage and were wearing high heels and black suits as they stepped carefully into the open boat as it bounced up and down in the river. There was no reason for Oveta and Bandel to take a chance, but sympathetic Irish officials typically looked the other way in those situations if the individuals were Americans. That sympathy was not granted the British, however. As ER observed, "It was a bit of a farce because Irish authorities closed their eyes." The rain continued to pour, drenching everyone despite the presence of the ambassador's large open umbrella. ER later recalled that as the cold rain fell on the group, she realized she had made the mistake of stowing away her raincoat and umbrella in her luggage stored inaccessibly in the wings of the plane. "The hat that I had bought new for the trip was ruined," she lamented, "and I looked a bit bedraggled when I got on land." "Bedraggled" also described her wet and cold WAAC companions.[43]

Ambassador Gray and his wife hurriedly and quietly transported ER, Oveta, and the other members of their group to the office of the American Export Company, where they ate a hot breakfast and tried in vain to dry off. Ambassador Gray told them that bad weather had forced the cancellation of their flight to England and that another would be scheduled for the next day. Gray offered to house them overnight (and secretly) at the US embassy in Dublin, but Eleanor declined the invitation because it was a 150-mile trip from Foynes to Dublin and she feared she might be recognized. Instead, the US consul at Foynes arranged for the First Lady to spend the night at the nearby castle of Anglo-Irish nobility Lord and Lady Dunraven of Adare, who could be trusted to keep her visit secret. The US consul found lodging for Oveta and Bandel in a local inn, where they signed the register as American civilians. On the way to the inn they were taken on a drive through the countryside. At one point, Oveta had the driver stop at a convent, where she purchased some lace items.[44]

When the weather cleared late the next morning, British prime minister Winston Churchill dispatched an airplane to Foynes to fly ER, Oveta, Betty Bandel, and Malvina Thompson to Bristol, England. The airline executive, accompanied by the State Department courier who had delivered his diplomatic pouch to Ambassador Gray, flew back to New York on the return flight of the Excambian. As ER's airplane made its landing approach in Bristol, the passengers were able to get their first glimpse of a bombed city. ER later recalled that they were all shocked "to see the areas of rubble and to look down the streets and see no house left standing." The American ambassador to the United Kingdom, John Gil Winant, met the airplane at the Bristol airport. Winant, a former college professor and three-term liberal Republican governor of New Hampshire, was an old friend of ER's. The entourage boarded a special private train, also sent by Churchill, which took them to London's bomb-damaged Paddington Station to be greeted officially by the king and queen. When ER asked Winant why they weren't flying directly to London, he told her that court etiquette dictated the king and queen could meet visitors at train stations but not at airports. During the two-hour train trip, Winant met with ER and Oveta to go over their official schedules, which had been approved by the queen and Lady Reading. He explained that the First Lady and Malvina Thompson would be the guests of the royal family at Buckingham Palace that night, and then they would move to Winant's personal apartment, with a staff for all their needs. Winant explained to Oveta and Bandel that since they were not officially members of a "state visit delegation," they would not be able to stay at the palace. Their lodging would be at Claridge's Hotel in Mayfair, which was full of American officials and military brass.[45]

On October 23, King George VI, dressed in the powder-blue uniform of a marshal in the Royal Air Force stood with Queen Elizabeth on a special red carpet as the train bearing ER and her three companions steamed into London's Paddington Station. British journalists, who were veteran observers of the monarchy, noticed that the royal couple seemed nervous "as they checked their watches and paced about Paddington Station while huge crowds thronged the streets to greet the first lady." As ER, with Ambassador Winant close behind, descended from the train to be received by the king and queen, Oveta remained a discreet distance behind, waiting on a signal from Winant to step from the train. After the king and queen and ER exchanged greetings, the First Lady introduced them to Oveta, who was dressed stylishly in a black hat, overcoat, and dress. The greeting party at the station included army general Dwight Eisenhower, naval admiral Harold Stark, British foreign secretary Anthony Eden, and Lady Reading.[46]

As ER departed the station with the king and queen to Buckingham Palace for the night, General "Ike" Eisenhower and his chief of staff, Walter "Beetle" Smith, cheerfully greeted Oveta and Betty Bandel on the station platform. General Marshall had sent word to Eisenhower that his headquarters staff should make a temporary office available to Colonel Hobby and provide whatever assistance she might need while in London. As Oveta later recalled, when Eisenhower walked up to her, she "managed as snappy a salute as I could. General Eisenhower looked me over, and said, 'I expected you in uniform.' I had a mental picture of myself sitting in a guard house, eating bread and water, but the general quickly understood my problem." With a mischievous grin, the general joked that he was happy to finally meet the colonel who had scolded him over the African American WAAC matter. Oveta blushed, somewhat embarrassed, but she appreciated Eisenhower's gentle reference to the affair. Eisenhower was "the nicest overgrown Iowa farm boy I ever met," Bandel wrote in her diary, not realizing that Ike was from Kansas. He was "big and booming and straight from the shoulder." Oveta and Bandel accepted Ike's invitation to join him and Beetle Smith for lunch at the Dorchester Hotel. As they entered the restaurant, the women surprised Ike by stepping aside and letting him go in first because he outranked them. Unaccustomed to entering a room ahead of his female guests, Ike "howled" with laughter and declared that "where he came from a lady was a lady" and not a member of the military, where rank overruled traditional rules of etiquette in male/female relations.[47]

After lunch, Oveta and Bandel were driven around London to see all the famed historic sites, including Hyde Park, the Houses of Parliament, London Bridge, and the Tower. After the tour, Oveta and Bandel checked into Claridge's, where they were assigned a two-bedroom, two-bath suite on the fifth floor with a living room, complete with a desk with push buttons to summon the maid and the valet. When they entered the luxurious suite and observed the amenities, Oveta laughed, turned to Bandel, and remarked, "Wouldn't it be wonderful to be rich all the time?" After they unpacked, Oveta and Bandel went to a bookstore and bought a copy of G. K. Chesterton's *A Short History of England*, sections from which Oveta read aloud to the literary-inclined Bandel before they went to bed.[48]

On her second day in London, the king and queen invited Oveta to a luncheon in honor of the First Lady. Keenly aware that this was a long way from Killeen, Texas, Oveta was in awe of the setting and the occasion. When presented to the king and queen, she curtsied while in her WAAC uniform, which was a minor breach of military rules and a violation of the American tradition of not bowing to royalty. ER later admitted she was surprised that US Army "colonel" Hobby would curtsy to a foreign monarch, but she understood it was well intended, and nothing further was said about the faux pas. During the reception prior to lunch, Oveta had the opportunity to chat with the queen about Oveta's plans for bringing American women into the US military. The queen's questions revealed her keen interest in the matter.

Following the luncheon at Buckingham Palace, the king and queen took ER on a tour of bombed-out East London, while Oveta linked up with Bandel and three US Army officers sent by Eisenhower to help them set up at a small temporary office in a US Army building. At Eisenhower's headquarters, Oveta noted how badly they needed clerical and telephone operator help as she observed a colonel typing his own memoranda using the one-finger method. Before she and Bandel left headquarters, they met with Eisenhower, who asked Oveta if she would please send him the two companies of WAACs General Marshall had promised him for clerical support. Oveta knew about Marshall's promise. In August she had sent Colonel J. Noel Macy to London to gather information for her to use in making the assignment, but other business had kept her from following through. She promised to look into the matter after she returned to Washington.[49]

That night, Oveta and Bandel attended a dinner at their hotel hosted by Ambassador Winant, whom they found attractive. Bandel wrote in her diary, "We were both much taken with that stern old Vermonter, with his sad, granite-like, shy eyes of a thinker." Other women also fell for Winant, who had been Joseph Kennedy's replacement as the American ambassador. At the time of the dinner, Winant was having a discreet affair with Winston Churchill's daughter, Sarah. Winant's dinner party included Eisenhower and a number of British dignitaries. Betty Bandel's diary documents an incident about Oveta being badly in need of a cigarette after everyone had been seated and were chatting before waitstaff began serving dinner. Traditional British etiquette dictated that one could not smoke until the host toasted a drink to the king. "Oveta was dying for a cigarette," Bandel wrote, "so she gestured inquiringly across the table to [Eisenhower, a fellow smoker] who called out, 'Mr. Ambassador, are we going to toast the King?'" Winant replied that he would not make a toast. Ike then "reached in his pants pocket, hauled out a package of cigarettes, and sent it spinning across the table practically into Oveta's lap."

Later during the dinner, Ike looked directly at Oveta and "boomed out" loudly, "Are you a short snorter?" Oveta answered that indeed she was before realizing she had left her signed dollar bill in her other purse in the hotel room upstairs. Ike, who could tell by the look on her face that she didn't have the short snorter with her, "gleefully" told her it was going to cost her several dollars if she didn't produce the signed dollar bill in two minutes. "But he reckoned without the Colonel," Bandel recalled. "[Oveta] shot out of the staid dining room at a dead run, scattering British dignitaries like quail, tore to the lift and up to our rooms . . . got the bill and was back down inside the time limit." A few days later, news reached London that the US and British Armies had made landings on the coast of northwest Africa. Oveta would later recall with admiration how at ease Eisenhower had been at this dinner and on the other occasions when they were together as he waited for the start of Operation Torch, the first major American military operation in the European theater of the war. Now that the invasion had been announced, Eisenhower told Oveta he also needed to take a few WAAC officers with him to North Africa to work on his staff.[50]

From this point on, Ike and Oveta Culp Hobby maintained a deep and respectful friendship that would ultimately have a significant bearing on Eisenhower's nomination for the presidency in 1952 and would last until Eisenhower's death in 1969. Several years after the war ended, Ike told Oveta that his mind often went "back to the day I first met you in London, in 1942 I suppose it was, when you came over there as head of the [WAAC]. . . . But you were the first one that sold [the WAAC] to me. I must say it proved itself, under your leadership, to be one of the finest organizations that the Army has ever had." It would not be unreasonable to presume that Oveta, consciously or not, felt a strong and favorable comparison between the two men named Ike who played significant roles in her life: Ike Culp and Ike Eisenhower.[51]

Once the official luncheons and dinner parties were over, Oveta and Bandel began a series of tours of British women's war service stations in London and other areas in England. "We spent days . . . traveling to their many training centers, hotels, and military installations," Bandel wrote in her diary. "The number of jobs the British women are filling is really amazing." She and Oveta rose at six thirty every morning and headed out for tours soon after. Elspeth Duncan, an English civilian hired by the US Army, served as their guide and driver as they motored through the English countryside that was flush with beautiful fall colors. All road signs had been removed because of fear of a German invasion, so Duncan frequently had to pull over to the side of the road so that she and Bandel could study a map in an attempt to find the way to their next destination. One morning while in London, Duncan drove her two congenial American "clients" through the market district. "As we crept along between the push-carts," Bandel wrote, "the car door was suddenly opened and a grinning Cockney thrust three apples inside, saying 'For America.' Apples are so scarce, his gift was like a gift of gold."[52]

On another day, Winston Churchill's wife, Clementine, took Oveta and ER to the headquarters of the British Air Transport Auxiliary (ATA). The ATA had a large number of American men and women pilots on its staff. The ATA's mission was to ferry newly built planes from the factory to battle stations. Oveta was amazed to discover that the ATA had nearly one hundred women pilots. ER later recalled that during this trip with Clementine Churchill, she saw "girls learning how to service every kind of truck and motor car and to drive every type of vehicle; I even saw girls in gun crews, helping the men to load the guns. I visited factories in which women did every kind of work." Oveta was equally impressed by what she observed. One small thing that caught her eye were toilet kits that contained combs, clothes, brushes, and other useful articles issued to the women at the quartermaster's store. Her WAACs did not have such kits. She told Bandel that she knew it would be a struggle, but she intended to have army Services of Supply issue similar kits to the women's corps members when she returned to the States.

That same day, as they toured an Auxiliary Territorial Service (ATS) camp in London, air raid sirens began to blare. The Germans obviously knew that the First Lady was in the general area. Newsreel footage of her arrival in London had already been shown in British movie houses, and the newspapers had covered her public appearances extensively. After a relatively long lull in German air raids, the Luftwaffe suddenly assaulted a wide area around the ATS camp with an entire day of attacks that were more of a nuisance than destructive. While the bombs fell in the distance, ER continued to address the women at the camp "without faltering, thereby winning the admiration of several thousand girls." As ER and Oveta left the camp, the women in the ATS "lined up along the driveway—they cheered and sang 'For She's A Jolly Good Fellow.'"[53]

A week into their stay in England, a correspondent for the British Press Service accompanied Oveta and Bandel while they toured another ATS camp. "A pretty woman in a trim two-tone brown uniform walked along the parade ground here," the correspondent wrote. "A British sergeant glanced casually at her as she passed, caught site of the spread eagles of a U.S. Army colonel, stiffened and snapped into a smart salute. Mrs. Oveta Culp Hobby . . . returned the salute just as smartly and continued her tour of inspection."[54]

After constant requests by newspaper reporters for Oveta to hold a press conference, she finally set aside time to answer questions during a visit to one of the ATS camps. In her opening statement, Oveta told the press she was at the camp to gather information on the business of running a women's army: "I'm here to learn. You've been in it so long and you can teach us a lot. We're still, to use an American phrase, green to the army.

*Oveta Culp Hobby* (far right) *with Eleanor Roosevelt* (far left) *inspecting provisions issued to the British Auxiliary Territorial Service during their mission to the United Kingdom in 1942.*

But we're learning." By now she had become used to frivolous questions about women soldiers and their undergarments and dating habits. In this regard the British press was little different from their cohorts in the United States. The only question that caught her slightly off guard was one about the contents of her ever-present leather shoulder purse. She smiled and replied that it contained a vanity case, an officer's identification card, and "the usual things a woman carries in her purse." She ended the conference when reporters asked her to identify the "things" women usually carried in their purses. Afterward she joked to Betty Bandel that she didn't want to tell the reporters that her purse contained a couple of her beloved Hershey's chocolate bars. Aware of the severe food rationing in the United Kingdom and the nearly total absence of chocolate, Oveta had stuffed her luggage with Hershey bars before she left the United States. She willingly shared her supply with Bandel.[55]

At one point, Oveta and Bandel accompanied the First Lady and her close friend Lady Reading on a daylong expedition through Kent that included stops at Canterbury and Dover. During this trip, Lady Reading arranged for ER and Oveta to meet an English farmer who had attracted much publicity by naming one of his pigs "Franklin Pig." A photograph of ER cuddling the pig was printed widely in the British newspapers, and it eventually made its way to the US press. Oveta diplomatically managed to avoid the opportunity to pose with "Franklin Pig."[56]

Far more important was the time Oveta was able to spend talking to Lady Reading, which delighted ER. For years the First Lady had admired Reading's work with the Women's Voluntary Service, and she was eager for Oveta to emulate it with the WAAC. According to biographer Blanche Cook, ER and Oveta had "a chance to see all that Reading and her allies had accomplished, and learn how completely women were trained and how vigorously they worked—with respect and dignity—at their many tasks, in every service." The value of the British example was not lost on Colonel Hobby. At a press conference in London the day after her trip with ER and Lady Reading, Oveta emphasized how much she was impressed with the way women were being used in the war effort in Britain. She declared her intention to recommend to General Marshall that the WAAC should adopt many of the features of the British system. "As much as I'd read and heard from Americans and Englishmen who returned from England," Oveta stated, "I had no picture of what the British women are doing. What I've seen here makes it come alive."[57]

Oveta and Bandel ended the English portion of their mission on November 11, 1942, when they flew with ER and Malvina Thompson to Northern Ireland for breakfast with members of the British Army's women's organization in Belfast and then toured a naval hospital in Londonderry. After lunch, they flew to the airfield at Prestwick, Scotland, from where they made their way to Edinburgh to tour the city. Oveta and Bandel then said goodbye to ER and Thompson, who returned to London for another few days before going back to Washington. Oveta and Bandel then traveled back to Glasgow, where they were scheduled to take a plane to the United States. Because of bad weather, the flight was delayed for four days, which left Oveta and Bandel unhappily stuck in Glasgow, a city Bandel decided was "the world's dirtiest." She marveled at Oveta's constant good cheer despite the awful food and gloomy weather. She noted in her diary that Oveta had a "peculiar inability to cry over spilt milk. She has the most amiable spirit under adversity I have ever seen. The moment a disappointment occurs, some peculiar something happens in her mind to bring all her gaiety to the surface. She shoves her hat back on her head, sticks out her lower lip, and says, 'Come on, my pet, let's go to a movie.'" One evening they attended a production of a Gilbert and Sullivan "light opera." Oveta also spent some of the time shopping. Her purchases included a long-stem churchwarden pipe for one of her brothers and some English silverware for herself. Bandel later noted that one night she and Oveta became so bored sitting in the lobby of the hotel that they stuffed the pipe full of tobacco and smoked it, much to the "amusement and amazement" of the army major who was their escort. "The L. C. [Little Colonel] told her husband about it," Bandel added, "and he thought it was very funny."[58]

Oveta and Bandel finally escaped Glasgow on November 16, 1942, on an uneventful flight back to New York. The entire expedition to the United Kingdom had lasted three weeks. On their trip back to the United States, Oveta and Bandel talked about how bad the food had been. Oveta concluded that if the British would "just give up boiling everything to death they would begin to make some headway." Bandel noted in her diary that they had eaten potatoes and cabbage three times a day: "We promised to never again eat cabbage."[59]

Oveta returned to Washington physically exhausted but mentally energized. The trip across the North Atlantic at close quarters with Eleanor Roosevelt had provided Oveta with an opportunity to become better acquainted with the First Lady, and it strengthened their ties, which in turn would be useful to Oveta in her dealings with the secretary of war and the army brass. After ER returned to Washington from Britain, Oveta sent her a handwritten note on her personal stationary, writing, "I was thankful to know of your safe arrival." She also expressed her appreciation for the opportunity to accompany ER on "that never-to-be-forgotten journey to learn at first hand the many things that will be so valuable for the WAAC. I should also like you to know that I appreciated more than I am able to express, the privilege of knowing you better." Oveta's meetings with the British royal family and the strenuous tours of women's army operations in England, Scotland, and Northern Ireland were all landmark experiences that broadened her culturally and intellectually. From a practical perspective, most valuable of all was what she had learned about how the British had developed a role for women in their military, especially what had gone wrong as well as what had gone right. And from a long-term perspective, she had made an important connection with Dwight "Ike" Eisenhower that would play a significant role in both of their political futures.[60]

# CHAPTER 26

# FIGHTING THE ARMY

Oveta's trip to the United Kingdom filled her mind with ideas about how to guide the WAAC to build it into an effective force in support of the army. Much of this newly gained knowledge, however, would go to waste in the coming months because of the army bureaucracy's rejection of most of Oveta's recommendations, which resulted, in many cases, in the same mistakes the British had made. Oveta's bureaucratic problems began as soon as she arrived back in Washington, when she was informed of a severe supply problem at Fort Des Moines and at a new WAAC training camp at Daytona Beach, Florida. When she had departed for England almost a month earlier, Oveta thought she had taken care of the clothing and equipment supply issues in Iowa. As soon as she sat at her desk after her return, however, she learned that new recruits were arriving once again with no winter clothing available. Recruiters had made the situation worse by telling the new recruits to take only one outfit of clothing with them. Women arriving from southern and southwestern states wore light summer clothes, unaware that Iowa was already well into an early cold and damp winter. Respiratory illnesses had spread throughout the camp once again, while the women trainees shivered miserably in their classrooms and in their barracks, hampering their training and dragging down morale. The problem at Daytona Beach, which was scheduled to receive recruits within days, was not cold weather but the complete lack of any uniforms and equipment, as well as inadequate housing.[1]

Oveta checked her staff office records and confirmed that they had made the appropriate requests and requisitions in a timely manner. She then worked the telephones, trying to dislodge from the army's supply bureaucracy winter clothing for Iowa and almost everything necessary for the camp in Florida. Her effort was cut short, however, when General Somervell ordered her to report immediately to Fort Leavenworth, Kansas, to lecture at the Command and General Staff School "on the proper administration of WAACs." Before she departed for Kansas with Betty Bandel, Oveta asked Colonels Don

Faith and John A. Hoag, commanders of the camps at Fort Des Moines and Daytona Beach, respectively, to come to WAAC headquarters in Washington to attend a meeting with her regular army staff support officers, Colonels Harold P. Tasker and Thomas B. Catron. In what was later described as a "stormy session," Oveta made it clear she expected these army officers to rattle every cage in the effort to secure winter clothing for her women trainees. According to the minutes of the meeting, Colonel Hobby went immediately to the point. When Colonels Catron and Tasker expressed reluctance to pressure Somervell's staff, Oveta stated firmly and clearly, "Let me straighten out the position of this headquarters. You are given a job to do and a time schedule to do it on, and when your equipment does not come through I want to know about it." She concluded the meeting by declaring, "I will say another thing: you will find a lot of people with a bureaucratic frame of mind [in the army] that would kill anything new unless you fought for it. It is my job to fight for it." This tough talk to four veteran, high-ranking army officers came from a woman who technically was not even in the army. Nonetheless, all four followed Oveta's orders. They were able to stop the army from sending women to the two camps until it provided proper clothing, and they sent instructions to recruiters to tell the women to bring enough clothing to wear for several months. But supplies and equipment still did not come.[2]

On November 19, immediately after Oveta gave her lecture at Fort Leavenworth, she and Betty Bandel flew to Dallas and then on to Houston, where Oveta gave a late-afternoon speech at the Lamar Hotel to the statewide conference of the Texas Parent Teacher Association. Afterward, she went home to be with Will and the children. By this time, only a few days after their return from the United Kingdom, Oveta and Bandel were in a deep state of exhaustion. Bandel, who was a guest at the Hobbys' home, later wrote to her mother that "L. C. [Little Colonel] is now spending the first evening she has had with her family in ages. The Governor is a fat, round little man who at first glance looks like a typical Babbitt, and at second—when his eyes suddenly open, as an idea in the conversation catches his interest—is anything but. He has a host of friends all over Texas who know only the obvious side of him . . . and a few who know the other side." Bandel noted Will's reputation in Houston as a man with important business and political connections. Referring to the phrase used by Ali Baba to magically open the mouth of a cave that held treasure, Bandel wrote that Will Hobby's name was "'Open Sesame' in these parts." Bandel closely observed the Hobby children, writing, "Jessica is a little tow-head show-off, full of appeal, who is nearly six. . . . William is ten, but be-spectacled, manly, quiet, inclined to inform his mother, 'But, Mother, you couldn't have seen a Boeing over England. It must have been some other ship.'" Bandel was amused that William hadn't liked the wallpaper Oveta had selected for his room, "so aided and abetted by his father, he went down and changed it to an entrancing design covered with airplanes—as a 'surprise' for his mother. It really goes awfully well with the room, and his mother is tickled." Bandel also recorded that Will and Oveta's house on Glen Haven was, "despite its size . . . a real home—lovely tapestries and rugs and paintings, mixed with family pictures, nice books."[3]

The next morning after a late breakfast, Oveta and Bandel learned that FDR had issued an executive order to increase the size of the WAAC force from 25,000 to 56,000 by July 1943, and as soon as possible after that to increase it to the limit of 150,000 previously authorized by Congress. Despite her fatigue this surprising news caused Oveta to cut short her visit with Will and the children, and she and Bandel rushed back to Washington. At this point there were 16,000 women in the WAAC, with 7,000 having completed their training. When a full-scale expansion had been discussed back in September, Oveta had warned the War Department that 150,000 women could not be recruited on simply a volunteer basis. A draft would be necessary. Aware that Congress would not look favorably on drafting women into the military, Secretary Stimson firmly rejected the idea. Now two months later, Oveta hastened back to her office to ask the War Department how she was supposed to recruit 40,000 women into the WAAC in six months when she and her team were having serious difficulty persuading women to join an auxiliary force that denied them any of the benefits or status that men in the military enjoyed.

When she returned to Washington, Oveta learned that the War Department hoped to meet the new recruiting goal by hiring a major New York public relations firm to launch a glitzy Madison Avenue–style publicity campaign early in the coming year. To accommodate the anticipated increase in the size of the WAAC, the army would need to build several new camps. General Somervell's staff had decided they would aid Oveta's recruiting efforts by constructing special barracks with new amenities that included bathtubs instead of showers, beauty parlors, lounges, recreation halls, and other improvements. During the meeting when a group of Somervell's staff officers explained these plans to Oveta, one of them admitted his unhappiness about providing camp beauty parlors because he considered them an unnecessary feminine frivolity. When Oveta quickly pointed out that every army base had a barbershop, the officer was unable to counter her observation. Despite the army's promises, however, few of these advertised amenities would ever be provided.[4]

Oveta also learned she had a more immediate problem than the new recruitment goal. She was angered to discover that badly needed wintertime supplies and equipment were still being withheld from Fort Des Moines. She immediately telephoned General Somervell's chief of staff, Major General Wilhelm D. Styer, whose office was down the hall from WAAC headquarters. According to official WAAC historian Mattie Treadwell, who based her account on interviews with Oveta's staff members who witnessed the incident, what Oveta said to General Styer on the telephone "was not recorded, but observers reported that it was sufficient to bring General Styer down the hall" to her office. Treadwell wrote that Oveta had threatened to submit her resignation to General Marshall and Secretary Stimson if Services of Supply did not get winter supplies to Fort Des Moines within a few days. While still in Oveta's office, General Styer, who admitted that the matter had been badly mishandled by his staff, made telephone calls to subordinates, who quickly dispatched an emergency procurement of winter clothing to the camp. After the war, one of the generals in the army's Services of Supply who had been on the wrong end of similar telephone calls from Oveta told a newspaper reporter, "[She is] the prettiest booby trap in Washington. She looks as soft and feminine as a dove and she thinks and acts like a high-powered dynamo."[5]

Although Styer's action addressed the immediate needs in Iowa, Oveta continued to have major problems with General Somervell and his military bureaucrats until the end of her command. The decision to double the size of the WAAC by July 1943 only increased those difficulties. "We are undergoing terrific changes of policy and plan because of the sudden lifting of our 25,000 ceiling," Betty Bandel wrote her mother. "[Oveta] has a true newspaperwoman's 24 hour deadline sense, and the way War Department people will take a week or two to make up a plan drives her wild. She would be the last one to advocate sloppiness or error, but, as she often says 'we can dot the i's after the war is over.'" These supply shortages played a factor in the poor public image of the WAAC, because the women who were enduring these difficulties sent letters back home and these complaints were being printed in local newspapers. Although it was obvious to Oveta and her staff that General Somervell was less than enthusiastic about the WAAC, they also realized he had one of the most difficult jobs in the army's command structure. As one WAAC officer later noted, it was Somervell's responsibility to supply millions of American troops worldwide with everything "from bullets to boots, sandwiches to stamps, cots to coffins. In his eyes, women who needed bras were not going to be placed at the head of the line." Nevertheless, Somervell's actions, or inaction, proved to be a continuing problem for the WAACs.[6]

Oveta did manage to win some battles with the army. Three high-ranking officers from the air corps met with Oveta on Thanksgiving Day, November 26, to discuss how the WAACs could help their mission and how many WAACs might be made available to them. When Oveta asked if the WAACs allotted to the air corps could attend specialized training schools as well as receive on-the-job training, the officers told her that could not be done because WAACs were not part of the army. Oveta was determined that WAACs be given the opportunity to serve in specialized and highly trained jobs, of which the air corps had a larger number than the army ground forces, so she expressed her disappointment at this answer. One of the officers replied that given her bad attitude, it might be best if the army created a separate women's organization for the air corps, presumably with a more pliable commander than her. Oveta was reluctant to go outside the chain of command to General Marshall with her problems, even though he had invited her to do so, but this incident enraged her so much that she felt she had to complain to him. The news she delivered to Marshall on the morning of November 27, 1942, clearly annoyed him. He immediately dispatched a memorandum to General George Edward Stratemeyer, chief of the army air staff under the command of General Henry "Hap" Arnold. Marshall told Stratemeyer that he believed one of his officers "took up with Mrs. Hobby the question of her attitude toward a separate women's organization for the Air Corps. I don't like the tone of this at all. I want to be told why they cannot train these women. . . . I don't wish anyone in the Air Corps office to take up without my personal knowledge any question of organizing a separate unit, nor any discussion of it except with me first." That ended any thoughts of the army air force creating its own women's corps.[7]

That night after her morning meeting with General Marshall, Oveta was able to enjoy a brief and welcome break from her difficulties with the army. Concerned about his wife's physical condition after such a backbreaking travel schedule, Will had left the children in the care of Oveta's mother back home in Houston and flown to Washington to join Oveta for Thanksgiving. Because of Oveta's meetings with the army air force officers at WAAC headquarters on Thanksgiving Day and her determination to meet with Marshall the next day, the Hobbys decided to delay their observance of Thanksgiving until the following evening. They hosted a quiet dinner at Oveta's apartment, with Betty Bandel and Helen Gruber as their guests.[8]

Oveta's break from her battles with the army was short lived. When she returned to her office after her delayed Thanksgiving dinner, she was informed that Somervell's staff had proposed a regulation to grant honorable discharges to married WAACs if they became pregnant while in the corps, but that unmarried women would be dishonorably discharged for "pregnancy without permission," which was the same action taken when military personnel were convicted of violating military or civilian law. Oveta recognized that the regulation was not only unfair but also legally untenable. Obviously, there were laws against rape, incest, and even adultery, but there was no such thing as an "illegal" pregnancy, either in military or in civilian law. Accordingly, Oveta submitted a request to Somervell to have the proposed regulation rewritten to allow an honorable discharge for unmarried pregnancy under a category labeled as "unsuitability for the service."

According to Mattie Treadwell, when officers on Somervell's staff questioned the need for the change, they were "forced into hasty retreat" when Oveta asked if married pregnant women would be required to provide legal proof that their husband was the father of their child. She also argued that male soldiers who fathered illegitimate children should be dishonorably discharged if the policy remained unchanged. Unable to produce a rational counterargument and undoubtedly preferring to avoid getting any deeper into such a sensitive subject, the army dropped the idea. Any WAAC, married or unmarried, who became pregnant would receive an honorable discharge.[9]

At the same time that Oveta was fighting against "pregnancy without permission," a near disaster brought the difficulties of the WAAC's nonarmy status to the forefront. In mid-November, Allied forces continued to capture large swaths of North Africa, including Algiers, where General Eisenhower established his headquarters. Feeling that Algiers was secure from enemy action, he asked Walter Bedell Smith to arrange for General Marshall to send him five WAAC officers to provide his headquarters with badly needed clerical and telephone operational support. He was tired of watching army majors inefficiently typing orders and other communications with one finger. He also requested that the WAAC officers be fluent in the French language to help his staff communicate with local authorities. The army had already scheduled two companies of WAACs who had volunteered for overseas duty to be shipped to England. General Marshall informed Oveta of Eisenhower's request and asked her to select five of her best French-speaking officers out of those units to be the first WAACs to go to the battle zone in North Africa. Complying with Marshall's request, Oveta found five volunteers fluent in French who were willing to accept the assignment.[10]

A few days after Thanksgiving, Oveta was deeply distressed to learn that a German U-boat had torpedoed and sunk the ship carrying her five officers as it neared the coast of North Africa. She was relieved when informed that all five of the women had survived without injury. Three had found safety in a lifeboat, and the crew of a British destroyer had pulled the other two out of the water. This near catastrophe highlighted the danger of sending WAACs to a war zone without the protections accorded members of the army. Oveta was quick to make the point to the War Department that plans to use the WAAC overseas were untenable as long as the corps was an auxiliary instead of an official part of the army. Not only was it unfair to ask her corps members to place themselves in harm's way while denying them war zone extra pay and medical, life insurance, and pension benefits, but it would also be a public relations disaster if the public realized the WAACs would have to pay for their own hospitalization if injured or wounded, and that if captured they would not have the legal rights of military prisoners of war. If killed they would not be allowed the honor of an official military burial. Oveta was able to share these concerns with one of her most important allies, Eleanor Roosevelt, when she and Betty Bandel were invited to dinner at ER's private "hideaway" apartment in the Kalorama section of Washington the evening of December 2.[11]

Eisenhower quickly realized he needed more than five WAACs, fluent in French or not, to provide badly needed basic clerical services. It was a problem that would continue to plague his headquarters for many months to come. At one point, Eisenhower sent a message to General Marshall explaining, "From every source there is a constant cry for trained . . . secretaries and stenographers. It has become almost impossible to find a satisfactory clerk or stenographer among the enlisted men. I understand that one of the difficulties about sending the WAACs overseas is the type of accommodation given them on ships. I would . . . pack them in exactly as I would a troop unit whenever it was necessary to ship them to a theater."[12]

On December 9, when Eisenhower's chief of staff, Beetle Smith, asked Oveta to organize additional WAAC units to be shipped to North Africa, she told Smith she could not agree "to send them in submarine-infested waters, in battle conditions, as long as they are not members of the Army." Smith replied, "Well, of course, you know I am going to take this to the Old Man," meaning General Marshall. Unaware of the urgent pleas Eisenhower had made directly to Marshall, Oveta went to Marshall to voice her opposition to the request. Marshall overruled her objection. "He looked at me and said, 'Hitler won't wait,'" Oveta later recalled. "He said, 'Are you unhappy?'" She replied, "No, sir, I am not unhappy, I have an order and I will carry it out." Marshall then told Oveta he was making his personal airplane available for her to fly to the training center at

Daytona Beach, Florida, where newly trained women's corps members were waiting for their assignment, which was to be North Africa. "I know it troubles you to send [them] over there," Marshall acknowledged. He told her to call the WAAC officers and enlisted women together and tell them, without identifying where they were being sent, that she had been ordered to send most of them into "hazardous conditions." Marshall told her to inform these WAACs that she would have to select those who would have to go but that she preferred to send volunteers instead.[13]

That same afternoon, after her meeting with Marshall, Oveta and Betty Bandel flew in his airplane to Florida. That night, Oveta addressed the three hundred WAACs who were waiting for their orders. In her official history of the women's corps, Mattie Treadwell wrote that after Oveta explained to the assembled women the potential perils of going overseas, she asked, in a manner "spectators called reminiscent" of Colonel William Barrett Travis's speech at the Alamo, for volunteers to step forward from their formation. All but two of the three hundred women came forward. The two WAACs who stood still had disabled parents who were dependent on them. "At this," Treadwell wrote, "Director Hobby was unable to continue speaking and hastily sought privacy in a broom closet." Oveta later said that the incident was "something I will never forget." The army eventually sent two hundred of the volunteers to North Africa, where they joined Eisenhower's staff and served as switchboard operators, clerks and typists for the postal directory service, and stenographers and drivers for Eisenhower and his staff. Years later when Oveta reminisced about this episode, she admitted that Marshall knew his decision to send the WAACs to North Africa "was absolutely right, this should be done," but that he also knew how badly she felt about the decision. His solution, however, "made it easy for me. That way I felt right about it." It was a prime example of the respect Marshall had for Oveta Culp Hobby, even when he had to overrule her.[14]

According to Forrest Pogue, the near disaster off the coast of North Africa made a strong impression on Marshall, who realized the WAAC would never be "fully accepted or completely effective until it was a full-fledged part of the Army." Oveta also used the episode in her lobbying effort to make the corps a regular part of the army. She and her staff wrote policy papers arguing that the army's goal of recruiting a WAAC force of 150,000 was not "even remotely possible under the Auxiliary system," because of the lack of benefits and the low pay. The navy's women's corps (Women Accepted for Volunteer Emergency Service, or WAVES), enjoyed benefits the army had denied to the WAACs, and they were being paid much higher salaries. A WAAC force of 150,000 was also going to be difficult to manage. The army had no more legal control over WAACs than it had over civilians. Because the members weren't in the army, they were not subject to military law, and thus no legal discipline could be imposed to control behavior. The first round of volunteers, who were largely motivated by patriotism and a sincere desire to play a role in winning the war, in most cases followed orders out of a strong sense of patriotic duty. The larger the corps became, however, the less likely its new members would be imbued with that same esprit de corps.[15]

In mid-December, after spending two days in New Orleans attending a conference, Oveta took a break from work and traveled over to Houston to spend the Christmas holidays with her family and, hopefully, to get a few days' rest. But that hope was only partially fulfilled. While Oveta was home, she and Will took the opportunity to have a christening ceremony for Jessica and Bill, with Dr. Ernst William Bertner and his wife, Julia, and Harry and Olga Weiss serving as the children's godparents. Oveta and Will also attended an evening rally at Sam Houston Coliseum to celebrate the successful effort to raise $86 million to build a new battle cruiser, the *Houston*, to replace the cruiser of the same name that the Japanese Navy sank in the Battle of Sunda Strait the previous March. Secretary of the Navy Frank Knox also attended and spoke, as did Jesse Jones. Because the money raised in Houston was more than was needed to pay for the ship, the remaining funds were applied toward the cost of a new aircraft carrier, which was named the *San Jacinto*. Earlier that same day, the Business and Professional Women's Club of Houston hosted a banquet in Oveta's honor at the Rice Hotel, attended by five hundred guests.[16]

Oveta's sister Lynn joined the Hobbys for lunch at the Houston Club while Oveta was in town. The Hobbys and their driver picked Lynn up at her house. When she stepped into the car, Lynn was stunned to see Oveta wearing her WAAC uniform. Lynn exclaimed, "Oveta, what are you?" Oveta answered, "I'm a colonel." Lynn then burst into tears. Oveta consoled her sister, "Don't cry, Lynn. I'm going to be the best colonel you have ever seen!" When they arrived at the Houston Club, Lynn later recalled, "[We] walked into that huge, noisy room which was filled with people. We had to wait a few moments for our table, and that room suddenly became very quiet, and then some people stood up, looking at Oveta in her uniform, and they began applauding. Soon everyone in that room was on their feet applauding. We went to our table, and people started coming over to speak to her. Soon they were standing in line. She was so appreciative. But I don't think she got a bite to eat that day."[17]

While Oveta was in Houston, she received word that General Marshall had publicly announced his support for making the WAAC an official part of the army. Eager to take advantage of the momentum Marshall's endorsement had given the proposal to give the women's corps military status, Representative Rogers moved quickly to revise an earlier version of her own bill and submit it to Congress by mid-January, which was less than a month away. When she sent word to Oveta that she needed her help to write the bill, Oveta decided to return to Washington immediately after Christmas Day to help the congresswoman meet her deadline and to make sure the bill included provisions Oveta wanted. She called Betty Bandel, who was spending Christmas with her mother in Arizona, and asked her to return early to WAAC headquarters to help draft the bill. Oveta and Bandel were back in Washington by December 31, where they spent the evening at army colonel J. Noel Macy's apartment celebrating the New Year. Macy was a journalist who served as the WAAC public relations officer. Bandel recorded in her diary that when the clock struck midnight, they raised their champagne glasses and "toasted the WAAC, and the army, and each other, and sat and talked until 2:30 am."[18]

By now, Bandel had become Oveta's closest friend and companion in Washington, despite the fact that Oveta was Bandel's commanding officer. That didn't seem to matter to Oveta. The two had bonded during the expedition to the United Kingdom, and Bandel's diary documents how close they had become. When they traveled together, which was often, they would share a hotel room and often stayed up "to the wee hours of the night" engaging in "long-winded discussions of life and art and the modern economic system." Their late-night talks sometimes caused Oveta to sleep later than normal, causing Bandel to joke, "The boss says I am a deterrent to the war effort." In a letter to her mother, Bandel reported that on one trip, she and Oveta were walking away from their airplane, and Bandel, as Oveta's aide, was carrying all their coats and bags. "[Oveta] started to take some away from me, and I said, 'Now, now, mustn't do it.' She said 'Daw-gonn-it Betty, that may be the Army's idea, but it isn't mine. Army or no Army, you aren't going to make me look like a clown. Here, give me some of that junk.'" Oveta grabbed half of the load, and as Bandel noted, they went "wandering out" of the airport "like two civilized grown women, instead of like the traditional commanding officer and aide. She will play army just so long, and then will balk—especially when she thinks they are being silly."[19]

During the first ten days of January, Oveta, Bandel, and other staff teamed up with Representative Rogers to draft the bill. Getting the job done on time required long hours and intense concentration. Bandel wrote her mother that they were working from eight thirty in the morning straight through to seven at night, when they broke for a meal, followed by a long evening of more work. They got the bill drafted by January 11, in time for Rogers to file it on January 14, 1943. Their effort received a major boost two weeks later when Secretary Stimson, who had long opposed integrating the WAAC into the army, reversed his position and announced his support. The proposed legislation, now referred to as the WAC (Women's Army Corps) bill, sailed through the Senate, which passed it on February 15. But the bill faced stiff opposition in the House of Representatives, where it was shunted off to a House committee where it could be delayed or killed.[20]

Marshall, Stimson, Eisenhower, and other brass in the War Department had dropped their opposition to the women's corps becoming a regular part of the army largely because of their growing awareness of the valuable contributions the members of the corps were making to the war effort. Eisenhower in particular had developed an appreciation for their work. Ike's driver in North Africa was a sergeant in the WAAC and his headquarters was filled with highly productive WAAC clerical staff. The help that the small contingent of WAAC officers had already provided his staff headquarters in North Africa had convinced him women were not only more than capable of war work, they were also as courageous. The five WAACs who had been fished out of the sea had not requested to be returned to the States, despite their harrowing experience. In a letter to his wife, Mamie, Ike noted that every woman he had talked to in the WAAC, as well as in the British Auxiliary Territorial Service, reflected "an attitude that seems to be characteristic of all women . . . in this region. They want to get close to the front." He admired their resolve, writing, "The women seem more casual with respect to danger than do the men. These particular ones want to get up as close as possible to do their stuff." Their attitude was in contrast to "many of my officers [who] are quite willing to take cushy jobs far from the sound of bombs and bullets."[21]

As already discussed, Marshall had long supported the idea of a Women's Army Corps, but only as an auxiliary. He shared Eisenhower's respect for the contributions women were making in the war, and, like Eisenhower, he admired their bravery. When Marshall learned that the five WAACs who had been fished out of the sea in November had lost all of their personal clothes when their ship sank, he obtained a list of the items and asked his staff to reimburse the women for their loss. The staff had to give him the bad news that because the WAACs were not actually in the army, there was no legal way to reimburse them. Marshall then personally paid for and forwarded new clothing to replace what the WAACs had lost. He refused their offer to repay him. In January 1943 during the Casablanca Conference, Marshall was able to get the five WAACs included among the guests for the dinner hosted by FDR and Churchill, where the women were recognized for their bravery.[22]

An equally significant factor in changing Marshall's mind about the WAACs, however, was his increasing respect for Oveta's leadership in making the corps a success. Oveta's leadership skills included knowing how to lobby for a cause, even if it was indirectly aimed at the chief of staff. At Marshall's request, Oveta had assigned several WAACs to serve on his staff, including a sergeant, Marjorie Payne, who became one of his official chauffeurs. When Oveta told Payne about her new duties, Oveta pointed out that the job would place her in a unique position of access to the chief of staff. She stressed that Payne should be aware at all times that she had "the highest spot of any WAAC" and that Marshall "will see the WAAC through you." Payne proved her worth. After the war, Marshall expressed his "respect and admiration" and "high regard" for her service.[23]

The Casablanca Conference was another landmark event for the women's corps. The five French-speaking WAAC officers Oveta had sent to North Africa provided much of the clerical and other office help that the US delegation needed. Their outstanding performance made a strong impression on FDR. The near loss of those five WAACs off the shore of North Africa underscored the inequity of asking these women to volunteer for hazardous duty without the protection of benefits enjoyed by men in the military. And as a practical matter, the War Department had finally awakened to the increasingly obvious impossibility of greatly expanding the women's corps without making it a legal unit of the army. Marshall's and Stimson's support suddenly made things happen.

With the WAC bill now in Congress, Oveta, accompanied as usual by Bandel, flew to Fort Leavenworth, Kansas, on January 11, where the Oveta gave a speech at the Command and General Staff School. As an indication of how much support General Marshall gave Oveta, they were flown to Kansas in General Marshall's plane, piloted by his personal pilot. Marshall had told Oveta she could use his plane whenever he didn't need it, and during this period he was on his way to the Casablanca Conference.

On February 2, Oveta joined Mildred McAfee, the commander of the navy's WAVES, at a forum on "Women and the War" at New York City's Town Hall. Speaking at the forum, Oveta referred to Louise Anderson, one of the five WAAC officers present at the Casablanca Conference. Only a few months earlier, First Officer Anderson had been a secretary in Denver. Oveta said, "I don't know exactly how many miles it is from Denver to Casablanca, but I do know the trip was a long step forward in the annals of feminine history. Women's place is still in the home, but today the American women, thousands of them, have left their homes, and thousands more will leave them, to help keep those homes free and happy."[24]

With the WAC bill stalled in the House of Representatives because of opposition from misogynistic Southern Democrats, Oveta embarked on a series of widely publicized trips and public appearances to bring attention to the important work the corps was performing. On February 11, three days before Oveta embarked on her road tour, she had lunch with Eleanor Roosevelt at the White House. ER had agreed to go with Oveta to Fort Des Moines, the first stop on Oveta's itinerary. Over lunch Oveta and ER discussed the upcoming trip and what role the First Lady would play as they toured the training camp. When Oveta and ER arrived at Fort Des Moines on February 14, they were met by a large contingent of the news media, which resulted in favorable stories throughout the country about the WAAC training facility. An impressive precision march on the parade ground by 2,800 officer candidates capped off the visit. The First Lady, who gave speeches at the post theater and at Drake University in Des Moines, thought the day was a great success. Afterward, she wrote Oveta, thanking her "for all you did to make the trip comfortable and pleasant. I think you are doing a grand job and I congratulate you."[25]

After their long day at Fort Des Moines, ER and Oveta went to Kansas City to inspect the WAACs studying at the radio and television school and then to Columbia, Missouri, where ER left the plane to give a speech at Stephens College, while Oveta traveled on to Dallas to stage another publicity event. Will and Bill met her there. The next day, Oveta met with reporters from the Dallas–Fort Worth newspapers and radio stations, followed by a chamber of commerce luncheon arranged and hosted by the Hobbys' old friend banker Fred Florence. Attended by five hundred of the city's business and civic leaders, the event provided another staged news photo opportunity, in which Oveta administered the WAAC oath to forty-five women recruits, who were organized into a newly created unit called "Hobby's Texas Platoon." The next morning Oveta and Will took a train to Houston, where Oveta spoke at the launching of the USS *Snowden* at the Brown Shipbuilding Company's docks.[26]

After a four-day break at home with Will and the children, Oveta boarded a Southern Pacific train on February 22, headed west from Houston to Los Angeles. After a nearly three-day journey, she arrived in Los Angeles, where she addressed a meeting of the advisory council of the Women's Interest Section at the Biltmore Hotel and held a press conference for the Los Angeles news media. From there, Oveta took a train to Salt Lake City, where she spent two days meeting with the press, staging photo opportunities,

*Oveta Culp Hobby and Eleanor Roosevelt with Colonel Homer Munson,*
*General Marshall's personal pilot, at Des Moines, Iowa, 1943.*

visiting with WAACs stationed at Fort Douglas, and giving speeches to the Utah members of the Women's Interest Section advisory council and women faculty at the University of Utah. Oveta's western tour next took her by train to San Francisco, where she met with WAACs at Fort Mason, visited a recruiting station, and held yet another press conference. Her visit to the Bay Area had one particularly notable moment. On March 2, she was the center of a major publicity event at one of Henry Kaiser's shipyards in the nearby city of Richmond. As movie newsreel cameras recorded the event, Oveta dedicated the new Liberty-class cargo ship *William B. Ogden* by smashing a bottle of champagne on its hull.

Because of the tradition that only women can dedicate ships, Oveta thus became the first US military officer in American history to do so.[27]

Oveta finally returned to Washington on March 6, in time to prepare for her testimony at House Military Affairs Committee hearings on the WAC bill on March 9 and March 16. Oveta told the committee that after almost one year of operation, the WAAC force had reached a total of slightly more than 45,000, which was far short of the authorized quota of 150,000 but double the initial allotment of 25,000. She stated that the four specific jobs for which the WAACs were first enrolled had grown to more than 140 because the army had quickly realized the value of their work and how they had freed men to go from office work to battle stations. She also cited the example of how one WAAC unit of 56 women at one army base had replaced 128 men in post office, personnel, and records work. Oveta was pleased to report to Congress that after an initial rough start bottle-necked by inadequate facilities and lack of supplies, the army had solved most of those problems and had accelerated its training program by opening seven new schools in the past four months. Recruits were now coming out of training at the rate of 4,500 a week.

Oveta also told the committee that the WAAC could never reach its full potential unless it was integrated into the army. As long as the WAACs were denied the same privileges enjoyed by the WAVES and women marines, recruitment would be severely hampered. Unlike all other members of the armed services, the WAACs were even denied the right to free postage for their letters home. The news media, including *Time* magazine, judged Oveta's performance both impressive and effective. Oveta later recalled that she was much cheered by the presence of El Paso congressman R. Ewing Thomason on the House committee. Not only had the congressman been one of her father's old friends when Ike Culp served in the Texas Legislature and Thomason was Speaker, but Thomason had given Oveta her first job as a clerk for a legislative committee when she was only fifteen years old.[28]

Two days after Oveta gave her testimony to Congress, she and Bandel flew to New York City to meet with the Writers' War Board. The board had been organized at the request of the Department of the Treasury to write scripts to promote the sale of war bonds. Chaired by best-selling mystery writer Rex Stout, the board included the literary critic Clifton Fadiman, sports writer and novelist Paul Gallico, and Pulitzer Prize–winning historian Margaret Leech. Oveta asked the board for advice about writing strategies that might be employed to enhance the WAAC public image and boost recruiting. Bandel later wrote that the group responded with "many extremely helpful ideas," but she didn't provide details. She did note, however, that "as usual, [Oveta] won them all" over.[29]

After meeting with the writers' board, Oveta and Bandel checked into the Savoy-Plaza Hotel on Fifth Avenue. While Oveta paid a visit to Mayor Fiorello La Guardia and his wife, Marie, Bandel went to a salon to have her hair done. Later that same day, Will Hobby arrived in New York by air, and he joined Oveta and Bandel for dinner and a play on Broadway. At dinner, Will surprised Bandel when he made a comment about a change in her appearance: "Governor, who is far beyond noticing such details, asked,

'Say—haven't you done something different to your hair?'" When Bandel later related this incident to her mother, she added, "Someday I must find a way to tell the Little Colonel and her nice little fat round husband what they have meant to me."[30]

Although Oveta had downplayed it during her presentations to the House committee, the biggest difficulty the WAAC faced was that many in the public failed to take seriously the need for women to serve in the military. A story published in *Time* a few weeks after Oveta testified in Congress reported that studies had revealed that the main resistance to WAAC recruiting "is not among women, but among the men in every woman's life—American men are notoriously softheaded about their women." *Time* called the attitude "sentimental slavery." Newspapers that had long opposed FDR encouraged public criticism of the WAAC by claiming the corps was simply another dangerous New Deal social experiment, while evangelical clergy preached that the corps was inherently immoral and "un-Christian."[31]

Opponents of women having an active role in public life, much less being in the army, could not have missed the positive press Oveta was generating in the spring of 1943. To fight back and to enflame popular opinion enough to affect members of Congress, some opponents, both in concert and as individuals, initiated a slanderous rumor and gossip campaign. It included the dissemination of obscene jokes, cartoons, and salacious false stories about rampant promiscuity, out-of-marriage pregnancy, adultery, and lesbian behavior in the women's corps. The allegations about lesbianism were especially problematic for Oveta and her staff officers, because they had always been concerned that opponents of the WAAC would raise questions about the sexual orientation of corps members. A fear of WAACs projecting a "mannish" appearance was one reason Oveta had vetoed trousers as a uniform option. WAAC training procedures emphasized femininity and sexual restraint, and corps publicity had stressed the middle-class, "normal" status of corps members. In their postwar memoirs, some former WAACs recalled the "trick" question that psychiatrists asked them during their psychological evaluation. The question "Do you like women?" had presented a dilemma. The recruits worried that if they answered "yes," they might be accused of being lesbians; if they replied "no," they risked being labeled "antisocial." Obviously, some WAACs were lesbians, but given the heavy stigma against and even illegality of that sexual orientation at the time, there is no way to determine how many. The important point is that there is no record indicating or even suggesting that lesbianism presented a "problem" within the corps. In addition, the accusations about sexually immoral behavior were often contradictory, as some gossip stressed rampant heterosexual misbehavior while other rumors emphasized equally rampant homosexual behavior.[32]

The rumors and gossip first began to be noticed on the Atlantic Coast and then spread throughout the country. The most prevalent rumors claimed that 90 percent of the WAACs were prostitutes, that 40 percent had become pregnant and large numbers of them had been shipped back from overseas posts, and that army physicians were rejecting all virgins who were trying to enlist. Oveta received reports that some WAACs had resigned when their parents, who were upset about the rumors, had called them to come home. Oveta and her staff soon determined that one factor that encouraged the scurrilous gossip was the public behavior of a few civilian women who were wearing uniforms similar in style to those worn by the WAACs, including not only civilian war workers but also prostitutes. Some of the women war workers were wearing their uniforms when they got drunk in public bars, while others were seen picking up men for obvious sexual encounters. In addition, it was learned that prostitutes were purchasing WAAC-like uniforms to wear when standing outside the gates of military bases while they solicited clients. In an attempt to address this problem, Oveta requested the army's Services of Supply to ask clothing manufacturers and retail stores to stop manufacturing and selling uniforms that looked like WAAC clothing. Her request was denied. Oveta asked the army's Bureau of Public Relations for advice on what public steps she should take to counter the slanderous gossip. Concerned that publicity would spread the rumors even more widely, the bureau advised her to ignore the rumors and to refrain from making public statements about the situation.[33]

Reluctantly agreeing to remain silent, Oveta turned her attention back to her publicity campaign in support of the WAC bill and to monitoring its progress in the House of Representatives. At the beginning of April, Secretary Stimson's office notified her that in the middle of the month President Roosevelt would conduct inspection tours of the marine base at Parris Island, South Carolina, and the army base at Fort Benning, Georgia, followed by a brief visit to his "Little White House" in Warm Springs, Georgia, on April 17. FDR also planned to stop at Fort Oglethorpe, Georgia, located near the Georgia-Tennessee border, to inspect the Third WAAC training camp. FDR's visit, which was his first tour of a WAAC camp, would not be publicized, and no advance notice would be given to the newspapers. Oveta was to keep this information as confidential as possible.[34]

At the time that the War Department notified Oveta of FDR's plan to visit Fort Oglethorpe, she had already made arrangements to escort several members of the Writers' War Board on tours of the training camps at Des Moines and Oglethorpe, followed by a visit to a WAAC contingent at Fort Dix, New Jersey. The army's Bureau of Public Relations, which was coordinating the tour, agreed that Oveta should go forward with the tour, but she would have to keep the writers in the dark about the president's visit while they were at Fort Oglethorpe. On April 15, Oveta and Betty Bandel flew in a military aircraft to New York, where they picked up the writers and proceeded to Iowa. After spending the night at Fort Des Moines, they flew south to Chattanooga, where the writers and Bandel remained to have lunch while Oveta was driven to Fort Oglethorpe to prepare the WAAC camp for the arrival of "a very important visitor" the next morning. Bandel and the writers arrived at Fort Oglethorpe later that afternoon, where they were treated to a dress parade by the WAACs. Oveta informed the camp band that they were to gather early in the morning at the camp entrance prepared to play the "Star-Spangled Banner" and other tunes. WAAC officers were instructed to have their companies assembled on the parade grounds and prepared for another march. The reason for these arrangements was kept a secret.[35]

Aware that the WAACs would guess who their important visitor was going to be, Oveta asked Fort Oglethorpe's commander, Colonel Hobart Brown, to seal the base that night. Early Saturday morning, April 17, Oveta and Colonel Brown and his aide were driven to a small train depot at nearby Chattanooga, Tennessee, to greet the president. After Secret Service agents transferred the president's special convertible limousine off the train, FDR asked Oveta and her accompanying army officers to join him in the open car for the drive to Oglethorpe. At FDR's request, Oveta sat next to him in the rear seat. Back at the camp, the WAACs assembled in tight formation in front of the main buildings next to the parade ground, waiting for the president. They soon heard the roar of the motorcycle escort leading an automobile packed with Secret Service agents, followed by FDR's convertible, which stopped in front of the fort's headquarters building. Oveta stepped out of FDR's car and stood nearby as Colonel Brown called the WAAC battalion officers over to be introduced to the president. Betty Bandel later described FDR's arrival to her mother: "The 21 gun salute sounded, and the WAACs—the most excited kids you ever saw—let out a roar of welcome and the band struck up the National Anthem. . . . It was a perfect spring morning . . . and 24 companies of WAACs gave a simply perfect review. The President said the band played the National Anthem better than any band he ever heard. He seemed tremendously impressed—grinned, and complimented the Director and said it was 'a great show.' Falla [Fala, FDR's Scottie dog] got loose and raced over to join the WAACs—he was mobbed and seemed to love it. Almost as soon as it began, it was over. The big open car swept off the field and away, the companies were dismissed and everybody let out a whoop."[36]

Oveta returned to the train depot with the president, while Bandel and the contingent of writers followed in other cars. Oveta, Bandel, and their entourage continued on to Chattanooga, from where they flew in two small military planes to Fort Dix, the last stop on the tour. At Fort Dix, Oveta presided over a national radio broadcast that featured remarks by the writers' board members about what they had seen on their tour. After the broadcast, Oveta accompanied the group on a flight to New York, ending the expedition.[37]

Oveta's main focus in spring 1943 continued to be the effort to promote the positive contributions the WAAC was making in support of the army, with a hope that the public would pressure Congress to pass the WAC bill, which remained stalled in the House. Her promotional efforts in April included travel to New York City to give a lecture about WAAC training at a conference on manpower mobilization and a trek to Pittsburgh to address a large gathering of mothers of WAAC recruits. Early in May, Oveta took her publicity tour back to Chattanooga to address the city's chamber of commerce. After an inspection tour of the WAAC training camp at Fort Oglethorpe, Georgia, and of WAAC units serving at Camp Ruston and Fort Polk, Louisiana, Oveta flew on a military plane to Houston, where she had an opportunity to stay with Will and the children. While in

Texas, she and Will, with Bill in tow, traveled on May 7 to Belton, where Oveta was the guest of honor at a formal banquet at her mother's alma mater, Mary Hardin–Baylor College, where Oveta had briefly been a student. Attended by five hundred guests, the event, broadcast on a nationwide radio hookup, included speeches by Texas governor Coke Stevenson, Fort Hood commander Major General A. D. Bruce, and Houston mayor Otis Massey, each of whom praised Oveta's service to the nation. The next day, General Bruce guided the Hobbys on a tour of Fort Hood, where Oveta visited with the base's WAAC contingent. On May 9, the Hobbys were in Waco, where Baylor University president and former Texas governor Pat Neff presented an honorary doctorate to Oveta. Because

*Oveta Culp Hobby and President Roosevelt at Fort Oglethorpe, 1943.*

Oveta was in her distinctive WAAC uniform, Neff gave her the doctoral hood folded, remarking that it would be unpatriotic to drape it over her uniform.[38]

When Oveta returned to Washington on May 10, she continued her promotional blitz by joining with Congresswoman Edith Rogers at Bolling Field Air Base to screen an army signal corps film about the WAAC in celebration of the first anniversary of the women's corps. Four days later, Oveta addressed the annual luncheon of the Texas State Society. Because most of the Texas congressional delegation and their staff members attended the event, Oveta took advantage of the occasion to do some lobbying. She noted that there were now 62,500 WAACs assigned to 120 military posts in the United States and that 200 WAACs were now on duty at Eisenhower's North African headquarters. Although there were now five training facilities in operation around the country, the army's request for WAACs was far beyond the number of WAACs available. She stressed that it would be unlikely the demand for more WAACs could be met without making the women members of the army. Texas congressman Wright Patman, who supported the WAC bill, inserted the speech into the *Congressional Record*.[39]

To mark the WAAC's first anniversary, Betty Bandel, who obviously had developed a discrete crush on her commanding officer, wrote Oveta an affectionate letter on May 15, 1943:

My very dear: My thoughts turned to all the miraculous events which have made up the pageant for the past year for me, and to the Corps, and so—inevitably—to you. . . . If we were tonight on one of our customary frantic "grand tours," you would at this moment be driving me to bed with horrible threats as to the hour for arising, and I would be lingering at the door, thinking up one more excuse for not yet putting out your light, and being quite unable to say what was in my heart about your first anniversary, and the Corps. But you would know. Every place I look, I see the Corps—and therefore you. . . . Just as you know my weaknesses, I think I know your foibles. I love them almost better than your virtues. And knowing them again I know how great your triumph is. . . . What is your triumph, really? To have made it work, to have given the army sixty thousand women soldiers . . . ? Not at all. Lots of people could have done that. What is it then? I am sure that you have remade a whole chunk of American lives. . . . They will never walk the same, they will never speak the same, they will never think the same as they did a year ago. Remember that Retreat Parade, in the sunset at Des Moines the other night, and the look of the women who marched toward you? They had something of you—of your remarkable innocence (so at odds with your worldliness in little matters), and of your remarkable faith, and your softness and your hardness, and of your communion with an ideal reality. Americans worship things seen—and you have been the thing seen to these women. Good night. God bless and keep you, for yourself, for the children, and Governor, for me, but most of all for the sixty thousand. With all my love, Betty.[40]

Oveta returned to Texas on May 19. The next day she and Will traveled to Huntsville, where the Hobbys' friend and business partner J. E. Josey, who was a member of the State Teachers Colleges of Texas board of regents, arranged for her to give the commencement address at Sam Houston State Teachers College. The college also celebrated Oveta's accomplishments by presenting her with an honorary degree. The next day Oveta inspected the WAAC unit at Ellington Field, located between Houston and Galveston, before she returned to Washington on May 24.[41]

Oveta's lobbying campaign got a major boost when the Columbia Broadcasting System invited her to be on its *CBS Playhouse* radio program. Broadcast over its national network on May 30, the program featured popular conductor Andre Kostelanetz and his orchestra. Oveta remained in Washington and spoke through a hookup to the CBS studio in New York City, where fifty women had gathered to be inducted into the WAACs as part of the show. After Oveta swore the new recruits into the corps, she gave a speech urging other women to step forward and serve their country as these new WAAC inductees had done.[42]

Oveta's exhausting efforts for the WAAC continued unabated throughout June 1943. From June 2 through June 4, after Catholic bishop James E. Cassidy publicly criticized the WAAC as a "serious menace to the home and foundation of a true Christian and democratic country," Oveta gathered ten prominent Catholic, Jewish, and Protestant religious leaders to fly with her on a military plane to Fort Des Moines and Fort Oglethorpe to inspect the camps and conduct religious services. Impressed by what they saw and heard on their visits to the training camps, the religious leaders signed a statement supporting the WAAC program and praising the character and moral values of the women in the corps. Oveta distributed the statement to the parents of WAACs who had expressed to WAAC headquarters their concerns about the rumors.[43]

Oveta's schedule for the remainder of June included a three-day visit back at Fort Oglethorpe in Georgia, a nationwide radio broadcast from Cleveland on the Mutual Broadcasting System to promote recruiting, an appearance before the House Military Affairs Committee, a return to Fort Oglethorpe, a nationwide radio broadcast from Detroit in support of the war bond drive, a speech at the Mayflower Hotel in Washington to the advisory committee of the Women's Interest Section, and a speech in Massachusetts to the annual conference of the National Federation of Women's Clubs. On June 12, she made her fourth trip that month to Fort Oglethorpe to escort twelve generals, including the inspector general, the quartermaster general, and the surgeon general, on an inspection tour of the WAAC camp.[44]

In the middle of this flurry of travel, Oveta somehow squeezed in a four-day visit to Hollywood to be a consultant for a twenty-one-minute Warner Bros. movie short about the WAAC titled *Women at War*. Starring Faye Emerson and Dorothy Day, the loose plot focuses on three women who join the WAAC for varied reasons and the contributions they make to the war effort. After a lunch with movie mogul Jack Warner and other studio officials, Oveta had a cameo role in one scene in which she addressed a graduating class of WAACs that included the movie's main characters.[45]

As Oveta's publicity efforts were peaking, the opposition suddenly struck back. On June 28 the tabloid *New York Daily News*, which in this era was a conservative, anti-Roosevelt journal published by tireless New Deal critic Joseph Medill Patterson, gave nationwide attention to what had previously been only whispered gossip about sexual promiscuity and perversion in the WAAC. The tabloid's nationally syndicated and popular columnist John O'Donnell, who was also the *Daily News* Washington bureau chief, wrote a column in which he made the false claim that Oveta had made a "super secret agreement" with "high ranking military officials" to issue supplies of contraceptives and prophylactics to the WAACs "so that they could fulfill the 'morale' purposes for which the Army had really recruited them." O'Donnell's claim was apparently based on the fact that a few months earlier the surgeon general had held a secret meeting with civilian doctors to discuss the possible issuance of condoms and birth control to all WAAC personnel. These birth control items were already being distributed to male military personnel. The surgeon general did not inform Oveta or any other WAAC planner about the gathering, and no policy had resulted. When she learned about the meeting, Oveta was outraged and complained to General Somervell, who readily agreed to kill any such proposals that might surface in the future. That was the end of the matter. So despite O'Donnell's claim, no such agreement had ever existed. His column was as much an attack on the Roosevelt administration as it was on the WAAC.[46]

According to the Women's Army Corps historian, the column and the news it generated caused "distress, anger, and humiliation," not only throughout the corps but also with the families of corps members. Oveta shared in that reaction. As soon as she read the column, Oveta met with WAAC headquarters staff to inform them. As she spoke, she began to cry and was unable to continue the meeting. Oveta knew immediately that this column could not be ignored. It would be necessary to issue a public denial to reassure the WAACs and their families. She believed the existence of the WAAC was at stake. The army and the War Department leadership agreed. They not only approved her request to respond, but with approval from the FBI they also ordered military intelligence to conduct an investigation.[47]

Denials were quickly issued to the news media. Oveta declared, "There is absolutely no truth" to O'Donnell's allegations. Secretary Stimson denounced the charges as being "completely false" and a reflection on the "whole of American womanhood" that could hurt the morale of men on the battlefront. Even General Somervell, whose bureaucratic rigidity and hard-nosed practices continued to cause operational difficulties for the WAAC, denounced the columnist. The WAACs, Somervell stated, "are your and my daughters and sisters and are entitled to respect." When an Alabama congressman suggested that the dirty jokes and rumors were simple "traveling salesman jokes" and that WAACs needed a better sense of humor, General Marshall told the press that the members of Congress might not feel that way if such stories were circulated about their wives and daughters. According to his biographer, "no wartime criticism infuriated Marshall more than these attacks." He sent a private message to Oveta assuring her of his "complete confidence in the quality and value of the organization which has been built up during the past year under your leadership. I wish you would assure your subordinates of the confidence and high respect in which they are held by the Army." Representative Edith Nourse Rogers denounced O'Donnell for spreading "gossip of the most scurrilous sort." Angry denials also came from the White House. At a press conference, Eleanor Roosevelt claimed that the rumors were the work of the enemy, "a lot of Nazi propaganda." She stated the Germans were "naturally interested in discrediting an organization which released so many men for the fighting fronts." When reporters asked FDR to make a comment, he said it was obvious it was "a deliberate newspaper job." Columnist O'Donnell, FDR charged, had simply obeyed "orders from the top," referring to the anti-Roosevelt publisher, Joseph Medill Patterson.[48]

Perhaps more effective than these strongly stated denials were the facts and figures the War Department and the army released to the press that disproved the damaging allegations. An examination of WAAC medical records for the year revealed that the incidence of WAACs diagnosed with sexually transmitted infections was close to zero. Although the rumors claimed that five hundred pregnant WAACs had been removed from duty in North Africa and returned to the United States, Oveta documented that only three women had returned. One, who was married, had become pregnant before she entered the corps, one had gall bladder illness, and a bomb had injured the other. At Representative Rogers's request, Oveta appeared at a House committee meeting and provided other statistics that rebutted the rumors. Her presentation was so effective that the committee issued a statement of support for the WAAC program and condemned the rumormongering as "cowardly, contemptible, and despicable."[49]

After an extensive ten-week investigation, Military Intelligence confirmed that the "secret agreement" O'Donnell had written about was fabricated. When the army demanded O'Donnell retract his story, the columnist soon complied, but he continued to claim that the unidentified source for this information was "reliable." In his report to Oveta, General George Veazey Strong, the army's chief of staff for intelligence, described the rumors as "the outward manifestation of a psychological adjustment the American public is undergoing in regard to women in uniform." General Strong stressed that the slander campaign was the result of popular prejudice, not army policies, enemy propaganda, or misconduct by WAACs. "Off-color stories about female soldiers," Strong reported, "furnish a lively topic of conversation in all walks of life." The rumors had been spread thoughtlessly, he argued, but without subversive intentions.[50]

WAAC recruiters, however, conducted a separate investigation that revealed an additional source of rumors: army personnel. As historian Ann Elizabeth Pfau has argued, the WAAC image problems largely stemmed from rumors emanating from the army itself. "As a group, servicemen were far more hostile toward the corps than was the American population generally," Pfau noted. "Many insisted that women were out of place on Army bases, and those who feared losing their noncombat job assignments to WAACs were particularly antagonistic." This finding did not surprise Oveta. For several months prior to the publication of O'Donnell's column, she had received a number of reports about widespread antagonism among army personnel toward WAAC members. In addition, the recruiters reported that they were hearing complaints from the wives of army personnel who feared that their husbands were having affairs with WAACs, while fiancées of men in the military worried that WAACs might threaten their marriage prospects. It was obvious this hostility was hurting the recruitment drive. In an oral history interview conducted after the war, General Marshall told an anecdote that illustrated a common attitude held by many of his staff officers. During a meeting Marshall was having with Oveta in his office, one of his officers entered and announced in a shocked tone that he had recently observed a WAAC officer and an enlisted man walking on a sidewalk holding hands. He asked Oveta how she felt about such outrageous behavior. Oveta responded in a matter-of-fact voice, "Well, they have been doing that for about a thousand years, haven't they?" Marshall was humored by her response, recalling that it "was a complete retort."[51]

A few years after the war, Oveta admitted to Women's Army Corps historian Mattie Treadwell that as she looked back on the slander campaign, she realized that it was "inevitable." She realized that bringing women into such a traditionally male bastion had been an event of significant social change and that she had underestimated how much of an impact it would have on the army as an institution. "I feel now," Oveta told Treadwell, "that nothing we might have done could have avoided it."[52]

Throughout the month of June, Oveta continued her public effort to discredit the slander campaign. On June 20 she traveled to Manhattan to take part in a nationwide radio broadcast from NBC's studio in Rockefeller Plaza. The program featured the famed conductor Arturo Toscanini conducting the NBC Orchestra. During the concert's intermission, Oveta appeared onstage and urged her radio audience to support the American war effort by purchasing bonds. She ended her remarks by reading a famous passage from *The American Crisis*, Thomas Paine's pamphlet written during the American Revolution. As she quoted Paine, some of her listeners undoubtedly also thought of the difficulties she was facing in the current slander campaign. "These are the times that try men's souls," she read. "The summer soldier and sunshine patriot will, in this crisis, shrink from the service of their country; but he that stands it now deserves the love and thanks of man and woman." Five days later she addressed a meeting of the Women's Interest Section advisory council at the Mayflower Hotel in Washington, DC, where she "vehemently" denounced the rumors and gossip as false. She admitted that in a force with 150,000 members, there were some members who had violated accepted standards of behavior, but the percentage was tiny. In the matter of sexually transmitted infections, which rumors had claimed had spread through the women's corps in epidemic proportions, Oveta explained that the percentage of WAACs who had been diagnosed with venereal disease was miniscule compared with how many men in the army were being treated for those illnesses. She repeated those facts a week later at a meeting of the General Federation of Women's Clubs in Swampscott, Massachusetts, where she once again called the rumors "malicious and untrue. Americans resent the arrogance of those individuals who spread such rumors in the press by distorting facts to obtain startling effects."[53]

Despite the official denials issued from the War Department and the White House and all of the speeches and the overwhelming evidence Oveta presented to the public, the rumors that WAACs were prostitutes or lesbians persisted. Even after the war ended, religious publications, including *The Missionary Worker* and *The Evangelical Beacon*, continued to print stories with sensational captions such as "Astounding Degeneracy" that repeated the slanderous gossip and rumors. Some of those publications featured a photograph of Oveta in her Women's Army Corps uniform, with the false claim that Oveta was the source for many of the accusations, including those O'Donnell had made in the *New York Daily News*. The fact that O'Donnell had retracted his story was ignored.[54]

If the goal of some of those who were spreading rumors was to defeat the Women's Army Corps bill in Congress, that effort failed. The House finally approved the bill, but with a number of provisions that differed from the Senate version. The joint conference committee eventually cobbled together a bill that both houses accepted, although the final version included provisions to which Representative Rogers objected. For example, the joint conference committee rejected Rogers's request to raise Oveta's rank from colonel to brigadier general. The final bill dictated that the rank of colonel would continue to be the highest rank in the WAC. Rogers had also opposed the requirement that the women's corps would have to be disbanded no later than six months after the end of the war, the severe restriction on the number of women who could be commissioned as officers, and the prohibition against WAC officers having command authority over any male army personnel unless that authority was approved by superior male officers. Less controversial was a ban against women being assigned to combat duty.

Oveta was willing to accept all of these provisions as long as the bill made her women actual members of the army with benefits. The final version of the bill accomplished that goal. Congress granted WACs full army benefits and privileges, including dependency allotments and eligibility for GI Bill of Rights benefits. WACs would now be sent overseas under the protection of international law if they became prisoners of war, and they could receive hospitalization and death benefits while on duty. Congress finally passed the legislation on June 28, 1943, and President Roosevelt signed it on July 1. After a period of transition ending on September 1, 1943, the Women's Army Auxiliary Corps would no longer exist. Eleanor Roosevelt noted, "Oveta Hobby and her WAAC had demonstrated that women could do almost every job in the Army except fight—and could probably do that, too, if they had to. [Oveta] had to do a lot of nudging, a lot of hard work, and a lot of tactful persuading to bring this about."[55]

As soon as the Rogers bill became law, Will Hobby decided to travel to Washington to be with Oveta on July 5, when she took her oath to become the director of the new Women's Army Corps. Helon Johnson, a *Houston Post* employee whose official job was to serve as Will Hobby's executive secretary but who in reality was spending most of her time as Oveta's personal assistant, wrote Oveta on July 2 that the Hobbys' cook, Alberta, was generously giving her personal ration book to Will to bring with him to Washington. "[Alberta] thought you might like to have it for extra things since Governor is going to be there for a few days," Johnson wrote. With the children away at summer camps in the Texas Hill Country, Will decided to remain in Washington with Oveta for the rest of July. He had Johnson ship to Oveta a box of canned meats, tomatoes, peas, vegetable shortening, and several other food items that were hard to find because of wartime rationing. When *New York Post* reporter Marjorie Hansen interviewed Oveta after the oath-taking ceremony, she asked Oveta why Bill and Jessica weren't also in Washington with her. She replied, "Last summer when they were with me in Washington was the only summer they didn't spend on the ranch. And much as I'd like them with me again, Washington is no place for them. There's such a problem with housing and the heat. They're much better off on the ranch."[56]

On Monday, July 5, 1943, a day after his arrival in Washington, Will Hobby watched as General H. B. Lewis, acting adjutant general of the army, gave Oveta her oath as the first female colonel in the history of the US Army and the director of the newly created Women's Army Corps. As he had done when Oveta had been sworn in as director of the WAAC fourteen months earlier, General Marshall, her chief patron, stood by Oveta's side as she took her oath. General Somervell also stood with Oveta. Given his less than enthusiastic support of the idea of women in the army, which would continue to hamper Oveta's work to develop the WAC, it can be surmised that he stood with her because Chief of Staff Marshall wanted him there. Despite Somervell's misgivings, it was a landmark moment in women's history, one that signified the beginning of an official, and eventually permanent, role for women in the US Army.[57]

Oveta Culp Hobby being sworn in as commander of the WAC, 1943. Generals Marshall (middle) and Somervell (far right) stand behind her.

Best Wishes From Henry Modell
CHAIRMAN LOCAL DRAFT
BOARD #144

## CHAPTER 27

———

# "HOBBY'S ARMY"

After Oveta took her oath as a colonel, she directed her attention to converting her auxiliary corps into a regular unit of the army by September 1, the date when the WAC was authorized to begin operations. Her most critical task was to persuade as many members of the WAAC as possible to enlist in the new corps. Auxiliary corps members were not legally required to transfer to the WAC, but if they did want to join, they had to submit reenlistment paperwork within sixty days to avoid additional vetting and training.

The job of organizing a new corps immediately became more difficult than Oveta had anticipated. Now that she was an army officer, she found herself in a new position in the army bureaucracy. She continued to report to army Services of Supply under General Somervell's command, but she would no longer have direct command over all corps members, which significantly diminished her authority. As WAAC director, Oveta had been at the head of a direct chain of command, but with the women's corps now in the regular military, the army's standard chain of command went into effect. WAC officers would now report directly to the army's base commanders instead of to the women's corps director. Male army commanders soon stepped forward to assert their authority over the women in their units. General Eisenhower was among them. Annoyed by the WAAC rule prohibiting social relations between WAAC enlisted members and male army officers, he sent a memorandum to General Everett Strait Hughes, his deputy theater commander, in June 1943. "I understand that the WAACs are now in the Army," Ike wrote. "If this is true, it appears to me that regulations governing their authorized social contacts and recreational facilities in the theater become a prerogative of the Theater Commander. I see no reason why an enlisted WAAC should not be free . . . to choose her social contacts from among officers or enlisted men according to her own desires. All I am trying to show is that these problems should be approached as much from the standpoint of natural history as from stiff-necked military tradition." Hughes responded

———

that Colonel Hobby was insisting the relationship that existed between supervisors and their staff members in civilian life, which discouraged their associating on the same social level, should also be observed in the army. Hughes told Eisenhower that his answer to Oveta was, "Nonsense! You will have to think up a better story than this if you want to clarify a situation which is becoming more complicated every day." The WAAC non-fraternization rule was rescinded.[1]

Not only was Oveta's command authority downgraded, she also had newly focused job duties that largely entailed serving as a liaison between the women's corps and other government and military entities, including the navy's WAVES, the coast guard's SPARS, and women marines; nongovernment organizations, such as the American Red Cross, the American Legion, and the United Service Organizations (USO); the news media; and the general public. She would continue to provide testimony about WAC matters at congressional hearings and respond to the constant stream of queries and requests from individual members of Congress that were submitted through letters, telephone calls, and personal visits to her office.

One of Oveta's time-consuming responsibilities would be to provide the army and the War Department with a series of detailed reports called staff studies that focused on WAC activities and problems. But Oveta's most time-consuming and frustrating duty was her work with the public, most of whom did not understand that Oveta no longer had command of all members of the WAC. Her office was soon overwhelmed with daily deliveries of large bags of mail from parents, husbands, and other relatives and friends of individual WACs who had questions and special requests or who expressed concerns about their loved ones' living conditions and assignments, matters over which Oveta had no authority. In addition, WAC headquarters received thousands of requests from the public for autographed photographs of Oveta, reporters demanded face-to-face interviews, public service organizations invited her to speak at luncheons and banquets in locations spanning the country, and museums and libraries asked for artifacts such as uniforms, hats, and documents for preservation in their historical collections.[2]

Betty Bandel, who had been promoted to the rank of major, was now serving as staff director for the WACs attached to the army air force, so Oveta brought in Captain Jessie P. Rice to replace her. Rice was a forty-two-year-old native of Georgia, a former history teacher, journalist, and sales manager who had attended the WAAC's first officer training camp. Within a month, Oveta had Rice promoted to the rank of major, and eventually Rice would become WAC deputy director. According to historian Mattie Treadwell, "For the next 20 months . . . she was to be, next to Col. Hobby, the chief author of WAC policy." Rice's primary role was to lead recruiting, but she also helped Oveta write responses to the most serious public queries, while Oveta had sole responsibility for relations with Congress and the White House. Oveta's role as liaison with the other women's military organizations was accomplished via monthly lunches with their commanders, with whom she developed close relationships. The army's Public Relations Bureau also helped with the news media and photo requests.

No matter what administrative system or division of duties Oveta concocted, the workload was staggering, sometimes requiring twelve to fourteen hours in the office, often seven days a week. A *Time* profile on Oveta during this period noted, "She spares herself no work. Husband [Will] Hobby has to go to Washington if he wants to see her. She is at her office before 9 o'clock, gets home around 7:30. . . . Frequently in the evening she pores over a stack of work in her . . . private moments among the soft tan Chinese hangings of her living room." That pace and the stress it caused began to take a major toll on both Oveta's and Jessie Rice's health. Although Oveta made frequent pleas to General Somervell for additional staff to deal with this work, her requests were denied, a pattern Somervell would continue during the first year of the WAC's existence.[3]

Oveta focused on the task of convincing the current WAACs to transfer to the WAC and of persuading entirely new recruits to join. She flew to Long Island, New York, the morning of July 6, 1943, to stage a media event at Mitchel Field to publicly launch that effort. Advertised as her first official act as the WAC director, Oveta reviewed a contingent of women from the 703rd Post Headquarters Company. Dressed in their freshly pressed jackets and khaki skirts, the WAACs passed in review before Colonel Hobby as the yellow-colored company flag was lowered in salute and army air force planes flew overhead. A large group of news reporters and photographers gathered to observe Oveta as she walked around the base for three hours, saluting her troops "snappily," as one of the journalists noted. A photo op was staged of her talking to a WAAC who was driving a tractor-like vehicle used to tow planes. She then visited with WAACs who were learning how to operate "Link Trainers," the army's main flight simulator for training pilots to fly blind at zero weather conditions. Oveta posed for more photographs as she removed her hat to put on earphones at the Link Trainer control table. Afterward, the director had lunch in the mess hall with the women's corps contingent, followed by a press conference with reporters from the New York City newspapers. When Oveta arrived at the mess hall, the WAACs were standing in formation outside. As the diminutive woman they all referred to as the "Little Colonel" approached, the female troops sang "Shine On, Harvest Moon."[4]

To promote the new version of the women's corps, Oveta granted several interview requests while she was at Mitchel Field, including one from *New York Post* reporter Marjorie Hansen that was distributed to newspapers around the country. Almost by script, Hansen stressed the point so important to Oveta and her staff, that WAACs who would soon be members of the army were not only steadfast professionals, they were also feminine. Hansen observed that "despite" being an army officer and a prominent business woman, "Col. Hobby still retains her charm and graciousness, her quick, quiet manner of speaking, her soft, charming Texas accent, her flashing smile and friendliness." According to Hansen, one of the WAACs declared, "It means so much to us to realize that we have not only a militant woman at the head of our organization but one who is feminine, too." The *New York Post* reporter added that Oveta had given up "her pet extravagance: frivolous hats and hair-dos." Nevertheless, she was smartly dressed in her "tailored khaki gabardine suit with its bright insignia" and "wearing dark tan rayon stockings, sturdy brown brogues designed for comfort and utility, leather shoulder-strap bag, and tan chamois-suede gloves." And despite being "one of the prettiest women in the news today . . . Col. Hobby is probably the only woman in the U.S. who tries not to smile for a cameraman. She believes such pictures of her smiling detract from the seriousness of the work of the WACs. Her eyes snap with pride as she talks about the [WACs]." Hansen also emphasized that although Oveta Culp Hobby was now an army colonel, "she still thinks of home and her children frequently. And after the war—her eyes light up at the thought and she declares eagerly, 'I'm going home as fast as I can; I'm going to sit on my front porch and rock and rock. I'm just going to sit and enjoy myself. Yes, I'm going back to my family and business.'"[5]

In mid-July, Oveta returned to Texas, where she inspected newly organized WAC units at the four major army bases in San Antonio. After the last event, at Kelly Field, she made an overnight stop at home in Houston, from where she made two nationwide radio broadcasts. On July 20, she flew to New York City, where she was the guest speaker at an Advertising Club luncheon hosted by Mayor Fiorello H. La Guardia. The club's war activities council was helping to recruit WACs in the New York City area. When Mayor La Guardia introduced Oveta, he stated that Congress might have commissioned "Colonel Hobby," but "only God could give anyone so much charm." He also declared that the army needed more women to volunteer for duty in the WAC. "The only kind not needed is a woman who can't do anything," La Guardia joked, "and, of course, we have none of those in New York City." In her address, Oveta provided details about the 155 categories of noncombat specialist jobs that women were filling for the army. She also pointed out that sixty-five thousand WACs were at 244 posts, camps, and stations in North Africa and England. Stressing that there was an urgent need for many more women to volunteer, she pleaded for eligible women to join the corps as a way for them to make a significant contribution to the nation's war effort. Notably, this event was the first time the Advertising Club had allowed the wives of its members to attend one of its luncheons.[6]

In early August, Oveta continued her grueling travel schedule with an airplane flight to the WAC training camp at Fort Des Moines, immediately followed by an excursion to Missouri to escort a group of twenty-eight leaders of prominent women's organizations on a tour of WAC housing and mess facilities at Jefferson Barracks, Camp Crowder. She urged the women leaders to use the information they were provided on the tour to help promote WAC recruiting. From Missouri, Oveta flew to Commerce, in northeast Texas, to attend a ceremony at East Texas State Teachers College in which US House Speaker Sam Rayburn received an honorary degree. After the ceremony, Oveta administered the WAC oath to nearly four hundred women attending the Army Administrative School at the college.[7]

Oveta's nonstop travel and frantic work schedule finally caught up with her while she was in Texas in early August. She became ill with extreme fatigue and was hospitalized in Houston for a few days. The Hobby family physician, Ernst "Bill" Bertner, determined that Oveta was suffering from a thyroid condition, which was causing anemia and fatigue. He prescribed levothyroxine pills for treatment. After her release from the hospital, she went home to the Glen Haven house, where she remained for several days until she had regained her strength enough to return to her duties in Washington in mid-August. Deeply concerned about Oveta's health, Will decided that he and the children would stay with her in Washington and spend most of the fall in her spacious, antiques-filled apartment. She had moved to the prestigious Westchester Apartments on Cathedral Avenue, the largest luxury apartment complex in Washington, in August 1942. Oveta's illness was kept out of the newspapers until she was back in her office in the Pentagon. The Associated Press reported that Oveta was "looking refreshed and well after a summer illness" and that she had assured reporters she would "stick to her job . . . until the war's end."[8]

Several days after Oveta and her family arrived in Washington, Will, now sixty-five years old, suddenly took ill and was hospitalized on September 18. He had surgery five days later. The nature of Will's medical problem remains unknown, but it was the beginning of a very gradual decline in his general health that would continue off and on for another two decades. Betty Bandel reported to her mother that Oveta was "simply worried to death" about Will and was spending "sleepless nights running out to the hospital to see him, trying to dig up a nurse . . . and getting somebody to look after young Jessica, who went off her feed the way children will when things are upset around them. You have some idea of what that one woman shoulders, aside from what I consider the most trying job in the War Department." Bandel also noted that she had seen Oveta go to important meetings at the War Department "when she would have to pull herself up and out of her chair by holding on to the edge of her desk—and yet she went into it [and] no one in the room would have dreamed she was anything but sailing along at the top of her form, full of energy, strength, composure. Don't ever tell any of this to anyone—she never even tells people in the office of her family obligations."

Adding to Oveta's exhausted state at this stressful time was a trip she made to Chattanooga, Tennessee, while Will was still in the hospital and facing surgery. Several months earlier, she had agreed to serve as the commencement speaker at the summer school graduation ceremony at the University of Chattanooga. Although she had been able to cancel or postpone some of the events on her schedule, the trip to Tennessee was one she decided she had to make, so she flew south on September 22. After her well-received speech was delivered, the university's administration surprised her with an honorary doctor of laws degree. Oveta was able to fly back to Washington in time for Will's surgery on September 23.[9]

The operation was a success and Will recovered quickly from his surgery. Two days after the operation, he sent a telegram to Jack Josey. "I am doing fine," Will said. "The operation has worked out favorably and expect to be well in a few days and will come home in a couple of weeks." Will was released from the hospital on September 30. Oveta was happy to report to Will's sisters and friends that he was doing "extremely well."

Will and Bill soon returned to Houston, but Jessica, who was minded by a nanny during the day, remained with Oveta in Washington until Christmas.

Although her own health was fragile, Oveta restarted her hectic travel schedule, making promotional and recruiting trips in October and November to Saint Paul, Minnesota; Oklahoma City; Philadelphia; Pittsburgh; Indianapolis; Columbus, Ohio; New London, Connecticut; and Chattanooga, and three to New York City. On one of the trips to New York in October, Oveta appeared on singer Kate Smith's popular radio hour program on ABC's national network to make an appeal for more women to join the WAC. The Associated Press distributed a photo of Oveta dressed in her WAC uniform, posing with Smith.[10]

In New York City that October, a columnist for the *New York Journal American* followed Oveta to the Institute of American Women's Military Services, where she had lunch with a group of WACs at the club's cafeteria-style canteen. The columnist reported, "[The] militarily glamorous . . . comely queen of the WACs" caused a commotion when she sat with some of the enlisted women. "Not even Frank Sinatra could have thrilled the girls more," the columnist wrote. "[They] were starry-eyed at the opportunity of shaking hands with the famous WAC leader." The *Journal American* also noted that Oveta "munched" on chow mein and ice cream with chocolate sauce. The latter dessert "must have endeared the Colonel to her 'girls,'" the columnist added, "since they are all avid patrons of the club's soda fountain concoctions. Now when anyone raises an admonishing zinger as one of the [WACs] 'dig in' to a syrupy soda she'll be able to come back with a snappy 'What's good enough for the Queen, is good enough for me.'"[11]

Despite her grueling schedule, Oveta did not forget her continuing, if unofficial, relationship with the *Houston Post*. While she was traveling back and forth between Washington and New York in fall 1943, she took time to choose what Christmas gifts she and Will would send to the ninety-two *Houston Post* employees who were serving in the military, two of whom were women. Sixteen of the employees were stationed overseas. Helon Johnson thought that Oveta wanted to give the staff members who were overseas a gift instead of a Christmas bonus and wrote Oveta that she had found toilet dopp kits at a price of $5 each and "game sets" for $18.65. Charlie Maes, the *Post*'s general manager who was running the newspaper's day-to-day operations, assured Oveta that the total cost for both items would not be as much as the amount given as bonus money to the employees the year before. "I did not have in mind that our Christmas presents to the troops overseas would take the place of our Christmas bonus," Oveta replied. "I still want to give the bonuses and the gift was to be extra for those overseas. Perhaps the 'jeep kit' is just the thing. I certainly want to remember every one of our staff who is in the hospital this Christmas. I would like to write each of them a personal note."[12]

As Oveta promoted the WAC to the public, Jessie Rice carried the largest share of the administrative side of recruiting. She devised a recruitment campaign called the All-States Plan that depended on the active help of state governors. Each would recruit a WAC company composed of women from their respective states, and each company would have its own special flag and armband linked to its state identity. General Marshall sent a letter to each governor to encourage participation in Rice's campaign. By early fall, it became clear that recruiting goals, including those set for the number of WAACs whom Oveta hoped to lure into the WAC, were not going to be met anytime soon. By the beginning of September, enrollment was less than half of the 150,000 members Congress had authorized. The lackluster recruitment results were a special concern to the War Department, because the army was experiencing a manpower shortage that it hoped the WACs could help alleviate with an expanded pool of recruits, freeing more men for duty in combat zones. General Marshall estimated that the army had an immediate need for as many as 600,000 WACs, which was 450,000 more women than the Congress had authorized and an impossible target under the best of circumstances.[13]

To aid recruitment, the War Department had hired the Young and Rubicam advertising agency in July to plan a public campaign. Famed pollster George Gallup agreed to conduct opinion polls to learn more about public attitudes toward women serving in the army to address any negative issues that might be affecting recruitment. The survey revealed that individual reasons WAACs were giving for not remaining in the corps included emotional and physical problems; family issues; competition from industry and from the other women's services; dissatisfaction with job assignments, including the low likelihood of overseas deployment; impatience with army bureaucracy and rules; unsuitable WAAC commanders at bases; open hostility toward WAACs by army personnel; the slander campaign that many of the women found humiliating; and, in the case of African Americans, the likelihood of being stationed in the segregated South.[14]

Nearly fifteen thousand members of the WAAC eventually decided against enlisting in the new women's corps. The federal War Manpower Commission (WMC), which was independent of the War Department, also added to Oveta's recruiting difficulties. The WMC prohibited WAC recruiters from being active in the regions that the WMC had designated as having labor shortages that could be alleviated by hiring women workers. Those designated regions covered half of the country. The War Department protested the WMC's restrictions, but the protests were rejected.[15]

Another problem stemmed from Oveta's demand that the WAC should have higher standards for women than those for men in the army. She reasoned that less-qualified men could do jobs in supply or construction as ordinary unskilled laborers. Typically, women lacked the physical strength for such labor-intensive work, so higher standards were needed to assure that every woman who became a WAC would have a job that utilized her specific skills.

By the time the special reenlistment effort was over on September 1, 1943, 75 percent of the WAACs had transferred over to the WAC. When all the negative factors are considered, the 75 percent reenlistment figure is not a bad number, but it was still a major disappointment. Early that autumn, Oveta had to endure a press conference in her Pentagon office with a small group of reporters who asked pointed questions about the recruitment figures. One reporter reminded Oveta that early in the summer she had predicted, "Women will come marching—shoulder to shoulder—to serve their country. I predict that all America will be proud of them." When asked for an explanation for the recruiting shortfall, Oveta responded that she didn't believe it was "so strange that there are no[t] more women in uniform. Add up all the services, WACs, WAVES, SPARS, Marines and the various nursing corps and you get a sizable number of women who volunteered. I don't think it's a bad figure."[16]

*Time* magazine, however, pointed out that only one woman out of every 300 had volunteered for all of the US women's military services. In contrast, the number of Canadian women who had volunteered for their services was one out of every 150. *Time* also claimed that Nazi Germany was delighted by the recruitment shortfall, observing that Radio Berlin "had gloated over 'totally inadequate' women's Army enlistments in the U.S." The *Time* article continued, "Oveta must often wonder, what is the matter with U.S. women? One of the answers is: U.S. men—who have always preferred their women in the home." *Time* also claimed, "[Women] themselves have plenty of excuses and confused rationalizations. . . . [T]he majority of American women simply felt no sense of personal responsibility" for helping the war effort. "Colonel Hobby could beat her iron-grey, smartly coiffured head against that blank wall until she was groggy," the influential magazine argued. "She could launch advertising campaigns, promise recruits they could pick their own post, camp or station, get Army generals themselves to appeal to U.S. young women to help [but] they were not listening."[17]

*Time*'s evaluation of the WAC recruiting situation was a bit unfair. It failed to consider how radical the idea of enlisting women into the military was at the time and what a major challenge to long-prevailing cultural attitudes it signified. The number of women who joined the WAC was not insignificant. In fact, Jessie Rice's recruiting campaign brought in slightly more than ten thousand new recruits by the end of 1943. While it was far below the army's needs, it was the highest number of recruits the women's corps had ever attracted in a six-month period.

Only one month after its negative story about WAC recruiting, *Time* published another story that had a much more positive tone. In its January 17, 1944, issue featuring Oveta on the cover, the magazine happily pointed out that WACs were now filling 239 different kinds of jobs in the army. "In some cases," *Time* reported, "[women] have filled them better than men. Among other things, WACs are opticians, surgical technicians, chemists, surveyors, electricians, radio repairmen, control-tower operators, boiler inspectors, riveters, welders, tractor mechanics, balloon-gas handlers, [and] dog trainers."[18]

Despite recruiting more than ten thousand new WACs in the fall of 1943, Oveta and Rice were now more convinced than ever that the large number of WACs the army needed could never be attracted on a volunteer basis. As Oveta had argued several months earlier, only a draft could accomplish the army's goal of adding six hundred thousand women to its ranks. Oveta reiterated this point to General Marshall, adding that based on a recent Gallup Poll, 70 percent of the public would accept a women's draft if it was restricted to single women and if it would keep fathers from being drafted. Nevertheless,

*Oveta Culp Hobby on the cover of* Time, *January 17, 1944.*

she also understood how exceedingly difficult it would be to get a women's draft bill through Congress, a view shared by General Marshall and his staff. In addition, Congress would need to authorize an increase in the size of the WAC from 150,000 to 600,000. That would be an easier political task than a women's draft, but nearly meaningless if women weren't going to volunteer. Early in 1944, Oveta told the press, "What happens on the question of Selective Service [women's draft] depends on how long the war lasts. I do not think there is any thought of it in Congress at this time."[19]

Stripped of her command authority over WAC units at the various army camps and having little influence over policy, Oveta's attention and time continued to be dominated by recruiting and related issues, as well as by bureaucratic political warfare with Somervell and his staff officers, particularly General Joseph Dalton, commander of the army's Military Personnel Division. Beginning in the summer of 1943, when Congress established the WAC, Somervell and Dalton continued to ignore or reject nearly all of Oveta's policy and staffing recommendations, even some that were endorsed by General Marshall. In November, Marshall recommended that a WAC officer be appointed commandant of the Fort Oglethorpe training camp to improve the base's supply situation and health conditions. Somervell's staff ignored the recommendation. That same month, Somervell rejected Marshall's directive to promote new WAC lieutenant colonels from the WAC ranks. Instead, Somervell informed Oveta that she should give socially prominent civilian women direct commissions as lieutenant colonels and that he would choose the women. Oveta chose to ignore Somervell's recommendation. Their bureaucratic battles would continue into the early months of 1944.[20]

Early in December 1943, army air force commander General Henry "Hap" Arnold, who was among the strongest supporters of the WAC, asked General Benjamin Franklin Giles to take Oveta on an expedition to London and the Mediterranean in January 1944 for inspection tours of WAC operations and pep talks to the women stationed there. Giles, a congenial native of Mineola, Texas, was serving as head of the Ninth Army Air Force Troop Carrier Command in Europe. Much to Oveta's satisfaction, Giles also asked Betty Bandel, as head of air force WACs, to accompany her. Oveta's travel was also intended to generate news stories about the jobs WACs were performing in the European theater of the war. Gallup Polls revealed that one of the problems hindering WAC recruitment was the perception that the women were doing menial and boring jobs, stuck away in remote bases in the United States away from the action. It was hoped that the publicity about the duties WACs were carrying out in Europe and North Africa would help change that perception.[21]

Facing an extended trip overseas, Oveta was able to take a rest and relaxation break for the Christmas holidays. On December 21, Oveta, with seven-year-old Jessica and her nanny "Miss Moore" in tow, traveled by train to Houston, arriving on December 23. After a quiet holiday, Oveta returned to Washington immediately after New Year's Day to prepare for her trip to London and points beyond. When she arrived at her Pentagon office, she told Betty Bandel and Jessie Rice that Jessica was developing into a headstrong young girl. On Christmas, Oveta was reading in the living room when she overheard Jessica attempting to make a telephone call. Apparently unable to get a dial tone, Jessica slammed the telephone down on its base and exclaimed, "Goddamn it, it's broken!" Oveta's reaction was to state in a calm voice, "I gather the phone is broken." Jessica replied, "You heard what I said." To which Oveta responded, "Jessica, I have said 'damn' many times in my life, but I don't believe I have ever taken the name of the Lord in vain. I think you had better go upstairs and ask God to forgive you." Jessica replied, "God is busy. It's Jesus's birthday." Jessie Rice asked Oveta what she did after Jessica made that observation. Oveta replied, "Do? I sat there. What would you have done?"[22]

While humorous, the episode with Jessica on Christmas Day could have only under-scored Oveta's awareness, and perhaps guilt, about her extended absence from her children during their formative years. In a letter to her mother, Betty Bandel shared an incident where she and Oveta were being driven to a meeting in Washington. On the way, they saw "some little dirty ragamuffins playing on the street . . . one with his socks all down and his hair every which way," Bandel wrote. "In a moment [Oveta] was a flood of tears. She wants one thing after this war—to get back to Governor, and William and Jessica, and run her home again." But Bandel knew Oveta well. "Of course," she added, "being the [Little Colonel], she couldn't be there a month before she would be into something extra-curricular—but after all she is executive vice president of a big newspaper, which is a fairly good-sized job to add on to running a home."[23]

Oveta had the comfort of knowing that Will was spending as much time with the kids as he was giving to the *Houston Post*. She and Will also had the luxury of a full-time staff to tend to cooking, chauffeuring, lawn care and gardening, household chores, and childcare. And Oveta's mother came from Dallas from time to time to stay with Bill and Jessica.

In addition, Oveta had the services of the dutiful and efficient Helon Johnson, who had been a *Houston Post* employee since 1932. Will Hobby brought Johnson up from her position in the auditing department in early 1942 to be his executive secretary. Johnson's duties soon included serving as Oveta's "right hand" back in Houston. Oveta directed Johnson by telephone and through frequent correspondence and telegrams on everything Oveta needed to be done back in Houston. Johnson paid Oveta's personal department store and hotel bills, renewed her driver's license, and tended to her health, making sure that the prescription for thyroid-pituitary pills that Dr. Bertner had written could be filled in Washington. She also sent Oveta monthly revenue reports for KPRC Radio and circulation numbers for the *Post* and passed on news about staff members at the newspaper.[24]

Helon Johnson also managed the Hobbys' household, including the maid and the cook, and passed on to the cook Oveta's instructions about what meals to prepare for Will and the kids. In one letter, Oveta asked Johnson to tell the cook "to prepare menus by the week . . . taking into consideration three balanced meals a day and also the ration problem. Tell her not to be skimpy with portions. . . . Do this each week and make sure there is enough and variety." Johnson shipped foods to Oveta that were difficult to find in Washington, at one point sending her a supply of sausage. Oveta's attention to detail was clearly apparent in a letter she wrote Johnson asking her to ship a couple of cases of food that the cook had home canned, specifying exactly eighteen cans of black-eyed peas, eighteen of corn, eighteen of string beans, twelve of carrots, thirty-six of tomatoes, eighteen to twenty-four jars of hominy, and two gallons of ketchup and two gallons of chili sauce. After Oveta received the shipment, she reported to Johnson, "I opened a can of tomatoes the day before last and found it to be most delicious corn! You might mention the labeling to the people putting it up." Oveta had been sending smoked turkeys as presents to friends and associates, so Johnson told her she was reserving more for Christmas. Johnson also reported that she had no luck "having the tamales canned. If I can find about six or eight cans of tamales and can get enough points to buy them, could you use them with the brick chili?" Oveta replied she would "love" to have them.[25]

Johnson also shopped for shoes, clothes, and toys for Bill and Jessica. In March 1943 Johnson informed Oveta, "The dressmaker has finished with one of Jessica's dresses and it is just darling. She made the dress and panties for $4 and I don't believe we could beat that price and get the nice work that she has done." Johnson's help with the kids included buying the Christmas and birthday presents Oveta gave them. When Johnson was preparing for Christmas in October 1943, she wrote Oveta, "Mrs. Hobby . . . are you going to get Jessica a doll this year? The Toy Shop where we bought her things last year has gotten their dolls and do have some very pretty ones. Jessica told me that she didn't want a baby doll this year, that she wanted one in 'evening clothes.'" A month later, Johnson reported that most of the Christmas shopping had been done. "We have gotten William's chemistry set," she wrote, adding that "I got Jessica's doll Friday and I surely do hope that you are going to like it." And then, just before Oveta and Jessica returned to Houston for the holidays, Johnson reported that Bill had made a last minute request ("last minute" because Oveta always wanted these tasks completed early). "William told me that he wanted me to go with him to do his Christmas shopping," Johnson reported, "so we are going Thursday evening after school. Since the stores will be open Thursday night, that will give us more time." Bill would later fondly remember the Captain Midnight secret code badge he received one Christmas during the war as his favorite toy.[26]

On January 9, 1944, Oveta, Betty Bandel, and General Giles flew on an Air Transport Command airplane to Iceland and then on to London, where the city's newspapers immediately reported their arrival. This was Oveta and Bandel's first trip back to the United Kingdom since their expedition with Eleanor Roosevelt in October 1942. In London, Oveta reconnected with US ambassador John G. Winant, who hosted a lunch in her honor. Afterward, Oveta agreed to a series of newspaper interviews with the US press, including the Associated Press and the *New York Times*, as well as live on-the-air interviews with the Armed Forces Radio Network and CBS Radio. These interviews, of course, were in line with the purpose of the trip: to bring more public attention to the jobs WACs were doing overseas. When the *New York Times* reporter asked if WACs would go to Western Europe after the invasion of the Continent, which was expected to occur that spring or summer, Oveta confirmed there was an "excellent chance" a contingent would be sent to France after Allied forces had secured their positions on the ground. She pointed out that General Eisenhower would determine the role the WACs would play in France, but as they were already working near the front lines in Sicily and the Italian peninsula, she thought they might do the same in France. When the reporter asked Oveta if WACs would be given special treatment because of their gender, she firmly rejected the idea, explaining that Congress had prohibited any combat role for the women but that some WACs were working very near to battle zones. She also confirmed that there had been a few incidents of WACs balking at going overseas but that she had refused to intervene on their behalf. "They're in the Army, and they're soldiers," she stressed, "and if they are needed they are going."[27]

The army also invited a reporter for *Time* to follow Oveta and Bandel as they inspected the three WAC battalions at the Eighth Army Air Force bases scattered around England. Before she departed on her tour, Oveta had a private meeting with General Eisenhower in his headquarters. Ike had developed a deep respect for Oveta, and he greeted her warmly. Oveta responded in kind, the little flare-up over rules governing social relations between enlisted women and male army officers long forgotten. Ike stressed that his experience working with the women's corps in North Africa as well as at his headquarters in London, where he was surrounded by WAC clerical staff, had made him a strong supporter of the corps. He told Oveta that WACs were doing such valuable work that he could use as many as possible in Europe to support his troops after the invasion. Oveta explained the recruiting problem she was facing, but she pledged to do all she could to get Ike the WAC force he needed.[28]

Eisenhower would later pay tribute to the WAC and Oveta by staging a major public event in London on May 14 to mark the second anniversary of the women's corps. Eisenhower and several high-ranking officers of the US and British Armies, including his chief of staff General Walter Bedell Smith, Army Air Corps general Carl Spaatz, Eighth Army Air Force general Jimmy Doolittle, and Royal Air Force chief marshal Sir Arthur Tedder, reviewed a parade of the nearly one thousand WACs who were on duty in England with the Eighth Army Air Force. A contingent of British women serving in the Auxiliary Territorial Service marched with the WACs, the first time the American and British women had paraded together. Ike made certain that the news media understood that the parade was his way of showing support for the women in the army as well as a way to recognize the outstanding job Oveta had done to organize and manage the WAC. He cabled her that he was "proud of the women in khaki" and urged her to "keep up the good work."[29]

After her meeting with Eisenhower, Oveta rejoined Bandel to meet with the five officers who had been rescued from the sea after a German U-boat sank their transport ship off the shore of North Africa. When Eisenhower moved his headquarters back to London to prepare for the upcoming invasion of Normandy, he brought the WAC officers

*Oveta Culp Hobby, Betty Bandel (left), unidentified WAC officer, and General Jimmy Doolittle at the headquarters of the Eighth Army Air Force in England.*

with him and promoted them to a higher rank. He now had seven WACs on his personal staff, three of whom were involved in the highly secret planning for the invasion.[30]

After visiting Eisenhower's headquarters, Oveta embarked on her tour of WAC units at bases outside of London. *Time* reported, "Trim Colonel Oveta Culp Hobby found everything in order. She saw erect, well-dressed girls drawn up for parade." *Time*'s reporter also observed that the living quarters for members of "Hobby's army" were either "huts heated by a single stove, or some drafty English country house. Only a few hundred WACs working in London were lucky enough to live in greater comfort." The story stressed that WAC pay "was low. The hours were long. Discipline was strict." There were also bombings during which they had to "bolt from their barracks, crouch in a slit trench and duck back to bed at the 'all clear' signal."

Oveta explained to *Time* that slightly more than 3,000 WACs were serving in the European theater of operations, with 2,000 in Africa, 350 in Italy, and the remainder in England. Small contingents were also on their way to New Caledonia and India. She stressed that all WACs were enduring the same rigors as male military personnel "with dignity and firm morale" and that they had survived the organizational mistakes the corps had made when it first launched. Of the three thousand WACs in Europe and Africa, only three had gone AWOL. Oveta claimed that WACs had learned their important jobs in England "with a speed which amazed U.S. and British officers," including operating switchboards and teleprinters, making maps, assessing combat films, and "sweating out" the fate of bombing missions as they waited in the flight control rooms at their air bases for bomb crews to return. Oveta declared that the WACs had "distinguished themselves as nice-looking, hardworking, cheerful girls and that commanding officers had recognized their work by pleading for more of them." With an eye to the WAC recruitment drive back home, she emphasized that the WACs in England also managed "to have some fun" taking in the historic sights and enjoyed "more dates than they had ever had in their lives."

*Time*'s correspondent also interviewed some of the WACs whom Oveta had met during her tour. The women reported their great disappointment "over the tales from home that WAC recruiting had fallen down. They favored conscription for women. They asked: 'What's the matter with them? Don't they want to live?'" *Time*'s coverage of Oveta's tours produced a highly favorable view of the WAC for the magazine's large readership back in the states. "The Colonel indeed had reason to be proud of her overseas troops," the popular magazine concluded.[31]

After nine days in the United Kingdom, Oveta, Bandel, and General Giles flew on an army air corps plane to North Africa to inspect WAC units on duty in Algiers. The night before they left, Betty Bandel, who was sharing a suite with Oveta at Claridge's, gave Oveta a collection of letters from the members of the WAC headquarters staff back in Washington wishing her a happy thirty-ninth birthday, which would be the next day. Oveta and Bandel were trying to get some sleep before meeting Giles at the air base from which their flight would depart very early the next morning. Oveta was already in bed when Bandel brought them to her. Bandel wrote her mother, "I could see she was very homesick for her two little bambinos [whose birthdays were also the next day]. I think her staff's thoughtfulness touched her very much. She called me her 'third child,' which is as near as she ever gets to saying 'thank you.'"[32]

The flight carrying Oveta and her companions took off from the base in England shortly after midnight on January 19. No announcement was made to the news media. The nighttime departure was for security reasons. Although its strength had fallen off considerably by early 1944, the German Luftwaffe was still a threat to the flight path the aircraft would follow from Britain to Algiers. Bandel later recalled that after making the flight during a "magnificent moonlit night," they landed in the morning at an army air base in Morocco and were greeted by "a blue sky, and fleecy white clouds, and hot piercing sun." They were taken to a villa near the airport for breakfast and then returned to their plane to fly to Algiers. When the flight landed that afternoon, Major Westray Battle Boyce, head of the WACs in North Africa, other WAC officers, and a group of army air corps brass met them at the airport. At this point, the army issued press releases to the Allied journalists in Algiers announcing this portion of Oveta's tour. From the airport a WAC driver took them to a local movie theater, where Oveta addressed a contingent of her troops. She thanked them for their fine work and said they had earned "high praise from male commanders to whose units they were attached." Afterward, Oveta was able to use her connections as a newspaper publisher to persuade the United Press news service to send happy birthday greetings to William and Jessica by wire to the *Houston Post*. Her busy day concluded with an evening cocktail reception hosted by Major Boyce and attended by high-ranking army officers.[33]

The next morning Oveta staged a photo opportunity with WAC private Margaret "Peewee" Maloney of Rochester, New York, who on General Eisenhower's order was the first woman to win a soldier's medal in US history. The previous November, Maloney had saved the life of an army private by pulling him from a burning pool of gasoline at a supply depot in Oran. She had used her body to smother the flames, suffering severe burns on her arms and legs. As Oveta noted, it was one of the rare occasions when she posed for a photo with one of her WACs who—at four feet, eleven inches—was shorter than she was. Afterward, Oveta agreed to do an interview with a *New York Times* correspondent, who revealed to readers the previously unreported news that Oveta would tour WAC units near the battlefront in Italy after departing Algiers. When asked if the WAC recruiting campaign had been a flop, Oveta denied it and declared that the effort had gone "remarkably well in the last three months." She added that more WACs would be serving overseas but for the lack of room on the ships due to the priority given to transporting soldiers to war zones. The reporter mentioned that an unidentified Republican senator had blamed the WAC uniform for keeping down enlistment and asked if a uniform change was being contemplated. Oveta smiled and replied, "I would doubt it. We have quite a supply on hand."[34]

On January 20, Oveta, Bandel, General Giles, and Major Boyce flew across the Mediterranean to Naples, Italy. From the air, Giles pointed out the bomb-devastated communities along the coast between Salerno and Naples. On the day Oveta and her party landed in Naples, the Allies launched a major offensive against the German Army in the area around Cassino, only sixty miles to the northeast. Oveta and Bandel were driven to a Fifth Army field evacuation hospital located near the battlefront where wounded soldiers were being treated. Bandel reported to her mother that it was "a scene I will never forget." Oveta later recalled, "The wounded began arriving . . . and the hospital couldn't begin to take care of the casualties. I said to one of the nurses, I can give shots and my aide can learn. I'll never forget one of those young men saying, 'Miss, give the shot to my buddy here; he's in much worse shape than I am.'" Later, while visiting the Fifth Army's forward field headquarters, Oveta found a camouflaged trailer that was staffed entirely by women who were running the command's telephone operations. At the field headquarters, an army colonel told Oveta and Major Boyce that the WACs were giving their rations to the starving children outside the camp and denying themselves proper nutrition, which was beginning to show in their work. He urged Oveta to ask the

*Oveta Culp Hobby and General Mark Clark at his headquarters in Italy, 1944.*

women to stop giving their food away. Oveta assembled the WACs, told them they were on a critical mission, and said they were failing their duty by not remaining strong and healthy. They had to eat their meals. "I was stern," she later said. "You know, very stern. And I walked off and dissolved in tears."[35]

Oveta's itinerary next took her back across the Mediterranean to recently liberated Tunisia. She, Bandel, Giles, and Boyce were taken to a large, Moorish-style, stucco villa in the art colony Sidi Bou Said, fifteen miles north of Tunis, where they would spend the night. The villa was perched high above a bay of the Mediterranean Sea, located between an Arab village and a mosque, with terraces below. They could hear the calls to Muslim prayers very clearly. When they arrived at the villa, which also housed several US and British Army generals and colonels, Oveta picked up an orange off the ground in the grove next to the villa and she and Bandel playfully tossed it back and forth. They were awestruck by the beauty of the village, with its distinctive buildings painted in blue and white and its gorgeous view of the sea. Oveta later remarked that while she and Bandel were in the village, it was difficult to imagine that terrible battles were being fought in Italy to their north. Sixteen high-ranking American and British officers joined them for dinner. Early the next morning, Oveta and her party were taken back to Tunis, where they inspected the quarters of a contingent of recently arrived WACs, who were housed in a large building in the center of town. As Oveta and her companions walked out of the building after completing the inspection, the entire troop of WACs gathered on the balcony above them and sang "God Bless America." Oveta later recalled, "The first thing we knew there was a handful of American soldiers staring at the first American girls they had seen in a long while. Then, in typical fashion, they began to point out the individual girls . . . to establish their preference. After this, they joined in the singing."[36]

From Tunis, the army treated the group to a side trip to Cairo, where Oveta toured the Great Pyramid while riding a camel, while her army escort Major Wally Burgoyne and Betty Bandel rode donkeys. Cairo was the last stop on their tour. Leaving General Giles in North Africa, Oveta and Bandel began their long trek home. The Air Transport Command's South Atlantic air ferry route took them to Khartoum, Sudan; Accra, Ghana; and then to the US air base at Mallard Field in Dakar, Senegal, where they spent the night sleeping under mosquito netting and covered with mosquito repellent. From Dakar, they flew on a C-54 aircraft 1,800 miles across the South Atlantic Ocean to Belem Field, the US air base in Natal, Brazil. At Belem, Oveta and Bandel were housed for one night in the nurses' quarters at the base, where the showers were located outdoors in an enclosed patio. Bandel later noted that the showers were "where you calmly take a cake of soap and prance out under the sun and/or stars, turn on the faucet, and take a shower . . . with nothing around you but space for more people to take a shower next to you. I asked [Oveta] what she thought they did when it rained, and she said, 'Not turn on the faucet.'"[37]

After flying from Brazil to Waller Field on the Caribbean island of Trinidad and then to Puerto Rico, Oveta and Bandel arrived back in Washington, DC, on the night of February 2. They had traveled more than twenty-nine thousand miles in twenty-six

*Oveta Culp Hobby, with Major Wally Burgoyne, takes*
*a camel ride at the Great Pyramid, Egypt, 1944.*

days. The day after their return to Washington, Oveta had a press conference where she announced that when the Allied armies invaded northwest Europe (which was believed to be imminent) and established well-defined front lines and field units, she expected that WAC units would follow close behind. In a reference to the importance of WAC recruiting efforts, she admitted that there were still not enough WACs in England, which had compelled the US military to hire British women to make up the shortfall.[38]

Two days after Oveta returned from her trip, she gave a speech to the Congressional Wives Club about her trip to North Africa and Italy. She outlined in detail the various jobs WACs were performing with the Eighth Army Air Force in England and the Fifth Army in Italy. As she later recalled, "I told those women exactly what conditions were in Italy—the wounded . . . everything." She shared with the wives of the members of Congress that the WACs were proving "infallibly that the Corps is accomplishing the purpose for which it was formed. These women have shown that they are useful and necessary assets in war."[39]

The day after her speech, General Marshall's office ordered Oveta to meet with the chief of staff immediately. Oveta quickly realized she had not followed War Department policy, which required preclearance of speeches to any political group, especially to the wives of members of Congress. She thought, "Well, it's all caught up with you finally." When she went to Marshall's office in the Pentagon, he asked her if she had cleared her speech with the War Department. She admitted she had not. To her surprise and relief, Marshall responded, "Thank God! My phone rang all night, and it hasn't stopped this morning. Those women told their husbands, and the senators and representatives have been calling me, asking what Congress can do about the war. Don't you ever let anyone in the War Department clear a speech for you in the future!"[40]

The First Lady, who was well aware of WAC recruiting problems, also wanted to bring attention to Oveta's visit to Europe and North Africa as a way to highlight the positive aspects of service in the WAC. She invited Oveta to the White House for tea on February 8 to discuss how she could best help the recruiting cause. Because ER's press conferences received much more news media attention than any conference Oveta could host, Oveta suggested that she could attend the press conference ER had scheduled at the White House on February 14. At some point during the conference, ER could ask Oveta a question about her recent trip to tour WAC encampments in England. ER agreed, and at the conference she invited Oveta, who was sitting in the audience, to come up to the podium. ER asked Oveta if she had heard any WACs in England complain about discomforts they might be experiencing. Oveta replied, "No, not anywhere. I didn't see a one who wanted to come home until it was over, not a one!" She also noted that there were three WAC sergeants on General Mark Clark's staff in Italy that worked in a camouflaged outpost: "They wouldn't swap jobs with anybody." Oveta's plan worked. The wire services and the *New York Times* reported her comments in their stories about ER's press conference.[41]

After her extended tour overseas, Oveta was unable to return to Houston to see her family because of the pressure to focus on the WAC recruitment effort, but she continued to receive a steady stream of detailed letters from Helon Johnson about the kids. On February 17, Johnson informed Oveta that Bill, who was in his last semester at Kinkaid School before entering St. Albans School in Washington in September, had received his Boy Scout uniform. "William . . . is just thrilled beyond all words," Johnson reported. "He said that none of the boys who had recently joined had been able to buy their uniforms so you can imagine how proud he will be when he goes to the meeting tomorrow night in his full uniform." These letters had to be reminders to Oveta that she was missing many important moments in her children's young lives. That awareness must have added to the stress that was affecting her so severely. That emotional strain would increase in the coming months, as the war neared its end.[42]

# CHAPTER 28

---

# "WOMEN WHO STEPPED UP"

Oveta returned in February 1944 from her extended tour of WAC posts in England and the Mediterranean filled with pride about the valuable support the members of "her" corps were providing to military operations. She was also physically exhausted by the trip and emotionally frustrated by her constant struggle with General Somervell and his bureaucracy in the army's supply arm, now called the US Army Service Forces, which continued to reject her requests and ignore her complaints. The WAC force totaled 62,000 that February, not only falling far short of the needs of the army but also much less than the 150,000 troops authorized by Congress. Oveta believed that her lower place in the army hierarchy and the resistance and disrespect she was receiving from some of the officers in Army Service Forces were significant obstacles to WAC recruitment.[1]

Another medical emergency in the family added to Oveta's stress and exhaustion, but this time it wasn't Will who was sick. Soon after Oveta returned from the Mediterranean, an attack of appendicitis sent young Bill into surgery. Oveta made a hasty flight to Houston in time for his operation and stayed a couple of days while he fully recovered. While she was at home with time to give her problems in Washington more thought, Oveta decided she had to confront Somervell about her deep frustration with his army bureaucrats. When Oveta returned to her WAC headquarters in the Pentagon, she met with Somervell to outline the issues she had with his officers, especially Military Personnel Division chief General Joseph Dalton. She also asked for clarification of her status within Somervell's command. The general told Oveta to submit her complaints to him in writing. Because Oveta had anticipated such a request, she had already drafted a document outlining her issues, which made it possible for her to submit the memorandum to Somervell within hours after their meeting. She attached to the memorandum a detailed addendum with a list of her policy papers that General Dalton had rejected, including his denial of important personnel requests. Oveta assumed Somervell would bury the documents in his files, but the general sent the material straight to General Marshall, along with the surprising recommendation that Oveta and her staff should report directly to the general staff instead of to the service forces. Somervell admitted to Marshall that he now fully realized Oveta was responsible for WAC policies that were applicable on an army-wide basis and that the current reporting structure was inefficient. Somervell also might simply have wanted to get Oveta out of his hair.[2]

Whatever the reasons, Oveta was victorious. Marshall gave her the welcome news that she would be reporting to his general staff, effective March 1, 1944. It was not a difficult decision for Marshall to make. He had grudgingly accepted her assignment to Services of Supply as part of the army's reorganization plan because it had seemed an obvious place for the WAC as an organization. George Marshall was an old-school army man who was reluctant to buck his own planners for the sake of one person he admired, especially one who also happened to be an attractive woman he was pleased to be around. Somervell's recommendation was likely all that Marshall needed to justify what he wanted to do anyway. The record does not reveal if Oveta and her staff popped any champagne corks and made celebratory toasts, but no one could blame them if they did. When she heard about the organizational change, WAC lieutenant colonel Anna Wilson wrote to Oveta, "The news is very good news indeed. The fact is that it is the answer to a very insistent prayer of mine. . . . I'm sure you'll now be able to operate more freely and as one who has seen those early struggles, I am delighted for you—and for all of us." WAC official historian Mattie Treadwell later noted, "From this time throughout General Marshall's tenure of office . . . attention to women's welfare was to be the rule rather than the exception." Oveta later recalled that Marshall "was one of the greatest friends we ever had." As Marshall himself said in a private letter to an old acquaintance in February 1944, "I am probably the strongest Army advocate of the WAC organization and I am fully convinced that a great deal of the work of the Army can be done better by women than by men."[3]

To note that General Marshall had not only a high regard for Oveta's skills as a leader but also a personal attraction to her as a woman is not to suggest any romantic involvement between them. Neither person was wired that way. Dean Acheson, who later served as Marshall's deputy when the general was President Truman's secretary of state, famously recalled that Marshall once confided to him he had "no feelings except those reserved for Mrs. Marshall." The army chief of staff was aloof in his personal relationships. As Eisenhower once noted, Marshall was formal even with his close associates, although he was capable of lighthearted banter with those who were closest to him, including Oveta. He was not a first-name-basis person. He famously showed his irritation when President Roosevelt called him "George" during a cabinet meeting. Remarkably, FDR never called him by his first name again, at least not in public or in front of others. For Marshall, it was always "Mrs. Hobby," and Oveta reciprocated by always calling him "General Marshall."

Marshall's probity and dedication to duty were widely recognized. He seems to have evoked a mixture of fear, awe, and devotion from those under his command, but as one scholar has noted, Marshall "also had a sense of proportion and humility, and an aversion to self-aggrandizement and self-promotion." These were all personal qualities that Oveta valued in others, and they were qualities she tried to emulate in her own life. Their mutually respectful relationship, which continued until Marshall's death in 1959, was certainly made possible by Oveta's professional talents, but it was also an example of the personal skills Oveta possessed that allowed her to navigate easily in such a rigid man's world.[4]

Debra Sutphen has observed that Oveta used her "beauty, intelligence, and charm to her advantage in dealing with men . . . allowing her to move easily and successfully among those at all levels of power." To Eleanor Roosevelt, Oveta was a "thoroughly practical politician. So far as other women are concerned, she has pretty much gone it alone. . . . She is not much of 'a woman's woman,' although there is nothing catty about her. But she learned her politics from men and wouldn't know how to play the game any other way." Oveta's longtime executive assistant Peggy Buchanan told Sutphen that Oveta "never used any 'feminine wiles' with people she worked with. [She] was never flirtatious in any way." Many years after the war, when Oveta's daughter, Jessica, was asked about how her mother functioned effectively in male power structures, Jessica answered that Oveta "enjoyed the game—the sexual politics—it was fun for her [and] she was good at them." To Jessica, her mother had an almost inherent ability to use her feminine charms to her advantage when operating in male-dominated political, governmental, and business endeavors, while also carefully preserving her image as a no-nonsense and deeply serious professional. As *Time* noted when it profiled Oveta in a cover story in 1953, "Through [her directorship of the WAC], Oveta managed to seem both completely military and completely feminine."[5]

Although Oveta's transfer to the general staff was a welcome development, it happened at the same time as the publication of a report that was highly critical of WAC leadership and its recruiting problems. The report was not how Oveta wanted to launch her new reporting status. Issued early in March, it was compiled and written by Samuel W. Meek, vice president of the prestigious J. Walter Thompson advertising agency. Meek's firm was a fierce competitor of the Young and Rubicam ad firm that the army had hired in summer 1943 to devise an advertising strategy to boost WAC recruiting. The so-called Meek Report claimed the WAC public relations effort had been poorly developed and led—a direct criticism of Oveta. The report unfavorably contrasted the WAC campaign with the WAVES recruitment program, with Meek claiming that the women's naval corps had a superior public image because, among several factors, its uniforms were more attractive than those worn by the WACs. The WAVES, unlike the WAC, had granted officer commissions directly to women based on their national prominence instead of merit, which generated positive stories about the WAVES in the society pages of major city newspapers. Oveta had earlier ignored a similar suggestion by General Somervell. Supported by the knowledge that General Marshall had always insisted that WAC officers come out of the enlisted ranks, she had maintained a strict merit system for commissioning officers in the WAC.[6]

After reading Meek's report, General Marshall asked Oveta to meet with him and Meek in Marshall's office on March 15. Meek presented his survey results, which he alleged revealed the failure of WAC leadership in the recruitment campaign. Oveta had not been shown the report prior to the meeting and was blindsided by Meek's claims. Aware that she had been caught off guard, Marshall gave a copy of the report to Oveta, despite Meek's objections, and asked that she study the findings and write a response. Meek, a member of the navy's civilian advisory committee, was a socially prominent resident of Manhattan who seems to have wanted to secure some of his society women friends prestigious, short-term officer appointments in the WAC.

Meek had tangled with the wrong adversary. Oveta and her staff quickly deconstructed Meek's report to reveal that nearly all of his allegations were unfounded. The so-called public survey was based on the views of a tiny sample of women who were students at elite private schools in the northeastern states. Oveta was also well armed with polling data from George Gallup that contradicted Meek's findings. The only charge with which Oveta agreed was the highly subjective one that the WAVES uniform was more stylish and thus more popular with women than the WAC uniform. Oveta was acutely aware of that problem.[7]

Oveta immediately perceived that General Marshall's request for a formal response to the Meek Report was an opportunity to bring to the army's chief of staff all of the proposals Somervell and his generals had suppressed during the past two years, proposals that Oveta had been reluctant to take to Marshall because of the rules governing the chain of command. Treadwell later observed that Oveta's response to the Meek Report "was to rank as perhaps the most important WAC policy paper" produced during the war. Oveta's report detailed how Somervell and his staff had rejected her proposals to address the most important problems Meek mentioned in his report. In particular, Somervell had ignored her suggestions for improving public relations and the serious issue of army officer hostility toward the corps, which played a key role in the decision by a number of WAACs to not reenlist. In other words, the problem was the army, not Oveta's leadership.[8]

Oveta's report to General Marshall stressed that the hostile attitude of soldiers toward women in the military service and the apathy that unmarried, nonworking women had about the war were the two most significant deterrents to WAC recruiting. She also attached to her report several examples of scurrilous material circulated during the slander campaign, most of which Marshall had not seen, although he had been aware of the gossip and had commented about it at a congressional hearing. But for Marshall, the most shocking information was a long compilation of anti-WAC statements that army officers of high rank had made to their soldiers as well as to the public. The list included Marshall's commander of Army Ground Forces, three-star general Lesley J. McNair (who would be killed later that summer by friendly fire during Operation Cobra in Normandy). All but one of these officers commanded combat troops on the battlefronts and therefore had no experience working with WACs and no personal knowledge of how well they performed their duties.

Oveta argued that these hostile attitudes would never change as long as influential army officers made public statements such as those she had documented. She suggested that the army launch an education campaign and that generals be ordered to clear their statements and speeches about the WAC with the special public relations group before issuing or speaking them.[9]

Wary of outside interference by uninformed civilians, Somervell told Marshall he objected to most of Oveta's recommendations, especially the ones calling for increased authority for Oveta, the creation of a WAC advisory board, and the order for generals to get clearance from the board before making public statements about the WAC. If anything, Somervell argued, Oveta's authority should be reduced, not increased. As for the board, it was unnecessary and might give "WAC leaders" too much control over WAC affairs. General Surles agreed. When Marshall shared these objections with Oveta, she reacted strongly. Tired of two years of Somervell's obstructions, she responded frankly that his attitude was "not in accord with fact or experience" and that WAC public relations under Somervell had been "unfortunate . . . and will continue to be unsatisfactory" unless her recommendations were accepted.[10]

Oveta's forceful argument convinced Marshall, who appreciated candor in his subordinates. He accepted nearly all of her recommendations and ignored Somervell's suggestion that Oveta's authority be reduced. The general rejected Somervell's and Surles's protests against the advisory board. Marshall directed General Surles to help Oveta organize the board, which would be chaired by Colonel J. Noel Macy and composed of twelve officers (six male and six female). He also directed Surles to work with the board to produce news stories and photographs that presented the WAC as a success, showing the women performing jobs necessary to the war effort while also retaining their femininity. But Marshall rejected Oveta's request that generals be required to clear their WAC-related statements with the special public relations group. Somervell had advised Marshall that if he felt it necessary to send a message on this issue to the general officers, it should not be in the form of an order, but as an official letter reminding them of the critical importance of the WAC to the army.

Marshall agreed with Somervell that a letter rather than an order should be issued, but instead of sending the letter only to his generals, he distributed it to all commanding officers, and his message was much more forceful than Somervell preferred. Marshall's letter stated he had received reports "indicating that there are local commanders who have failed to provide leadership and have in fact made evident their disapproval of the Women's Army Corps." He noted that the attitudes of the enlisted men "have quickly reflected the leadership of their commanders, as always." He ordered his commanders to see that "the dignity and importance of the work women are performing are recognized." He stressed it was imperative that every member of the army understand that his position on the importance of the women's corps was the official policy of the War Department and that it had to be "supported by strong affirmative action." The clear implication was that any future transgressions violating that policy would not be tolerated.[11]

After Marshall reassigned Oveta to the general staff, her workload continued at a backbreaking pace. Soon after the transfer, her chronic thyroid illness flared again, made worse by overwork and stress. She also suffered from a serious throat ailment that temporarily took away her voice. Her army physician determined her state of health was becoming "increasingly precarious" and ordered her hospitalization at Walter Reed General Hospital in Washington. After a brief stay at Walter Reed, Oveta returned to work, only to be forced to reenter the hospital a few days later. This pattern of going in and out of Walter Reed eventually convinced army doctors to order her to San Antonio for six weeks of hospitalization and treatment at Brooke General Hospital and then "to an address known only to her family with orders that not even policy matters could be communicated to her." This unknown address, of course, was her home on Glen Haven in Houston, as her doctors knew. Oveta entered Brooke Hospital on July 1 and remained there for two weeks.[12]

When word began to spread about Oveta's health woes, the army's Bureau of Public Relations told the news media that she was "doing fine" and enjoying a rest "after traveling a lot recently." General George Beach, commanding officer of Brooke General Hospital, confirmed to reporters that Oveta had been diagnosed with extreme exhaustion, adding that "Col. Hobby's condition is very good. It is not thought she will be in the hospital very long." When Lieutenant Colonel Anna Wilson, one of the WAC's most highly respected officers, heard the news about Oveta's hospitalization, she sent her a message: "We are so sorry that you found it necessary to submit to an enforced vacation. It is no doubt doing just what you needed—giving your system a chance to rebuild its energy—and we all hope you will let rest and Nature do a complete job before you return to the office."[13]

Oveta's health issues came at a particularly difficult time for the WAC because of a widespread morale problem that became apparent in August and continued until the end of the war. Oveta and Jessie Rice characterized the problem as "war weariness" or "war fatigue," which was a general decline in patriotic fervor for the war among the rank and file. This decline manifested in several ways, including a large increase in uniform violations, untidiness, and behavior resulting in disciplinary action. As one WAC complained in a letter to Oveta that summer after she read Oveta's quote in the press saying that the nation should appreciate the work WACs were doing, "We don't want appreciation; we only want to go home."[14]

With these indications of a decline in morale in the corps, Oveta feared that illness and her ever-present exhaustion were degrading her ability to give proper attention to her duties. She decided it might be best for the WAC that she give up her post. When she entered the hospital in San Antonio, Oveta informed her deputy, Colonel Jessie Rice, who was serving as the unofficial head of the WAC in Oveta's absence, that she planned to submit her resignation to General Marshall. Rice succeeded in talking Oveta out of resigning, arguing that her departure would have a seriously detrimental impact on morale in the corps, which was already becoming "demobilization-conscious" as Allied victories continued to mount in Europe and in the Pacific. Rice also enlisted General

Marshall's help to keep Oveta from feeling guilty about her absence. A telephone call from Rice to Marshall on July 27 resulted in Marshall immediately dispatching a letter to Oveta. In his usual formal style, Marshall wrote that he was "disturbed that you follow the conventional reaction of all the higher officials in the War Department to the effect that you think a minimum of absence is sufficient for the purpose of a complete rehabilitation. Please do not make that mistake," Marshall pleaded, "which invariably has serious consequences." He added that "ten days of the present Washington heat will break down a good constitution, let alone someone who has felt the urgent necessity for a rest." Rice's pleas and Marshall's letter accomplished their goals. Oveta backed away from her decision to resign.[15]

After Oveta's physicians released her from Brooke General Hospital on July 14, she rested at home in Houston for a month. When she returned to Washington in mid-August, she enrolled Bill in the highly regarded St. Albans, an all-boys college prep school located near the National Cathedral and run by the Episcopal Church. Oveta and Will were impressed with the school and decided that it would be a perfect place for their son. St. Albans is a boarding school, which meant Bill could remain as a student there whenever Oveta left the WAC and returned to Houston. Back at her desk in the Pentagon by August 21, Oveta gradually took on a limited amount of work while continuing to receive medical treatment. Despite her ongoing health problems, she sent a memorandum to General Miller White, assistant chief of staff for personnel, to report that she expected "now to be able to finish out the war. I hope that it will not be too long." White, who was one of Oveta's best friends among the army's general staff, sent an "unofficial" handwritten note to Oveta. "I take it that means they found nothing serious wrong with you," White wrote, "and that I may expect you back to help me carry the load . . . with the old sparkle in your eye and bloom in your cheeks." He added that while Oveta was on leave he had learned from Jessie Rice that Oveta "had requested recruiting figures and she sent them. That was a direct disobedience of orders on your part—I told her hereafter she was to tell you that recruiting during the next five weeks is none of your business." Despite a brief recovery, Oveta's health issues flared again in mid-October 1944, forcing her to undergo what was described by the War Department as a "minor operation" at Walter Reed Hospital. The procedure was effective enough that by November she had recovered her health sufficiently to return to work full time.[16]

Now that her headquarters was part of the general staff instead of the Army Service Forces, Oveta was able to focus more attention on congressional matters, public relations, and the new WAC advisory board, as well as working with Jessie Rice to alleviate the "war fatigue" problem within the ranks. In addition, the role and treatment of African American women in the WAC, which had been an issue that had waxed and waned ever since the beginning of the corps, required more of Oveta's attention in the fall of 1944. African American WACs continued to experience rigid racial segregation when stationed at army bases in the South, which was no surprise to anyone.

What was not expected was overt racism at the highest levels of command in the Pentagon. At the time Oveta was reassuming her duties late that fall, Jessie Rice took a group of African American WACs to meet with Major General Stephen Henry, the general staff officer who had command over the women's corps. A native of Dallas, Texas, and a graduate of Southern Methodist University, Henry was a heavily decorated bomber pilot who had flown seventy combat missions in Europe and the Mediterranean. During the meeting, which had been called to express concerns about racial incidents in the South where African American WACs were based, General Henry stunned the women by his use of "racially insensitive language" when referring to black corps members. The details are unknown, but it can be surmised that Henry used the obscene racial epithet for an African American. Rice and the other WACs walked silently out of the general's office, and then Rice returned alone, protested his language, and submitted her resignation, declaring, "Sir, your staff officer just went out—and a citizen of the United States walked in." When Rice reported the incident to Oveta, she immediately offered her own resignation to General Henry, who quickly apologized for his racist language and asked the two women to withdraw their resignations, which they did.[17]

At one point, Eleanor Roosevelt complained to Assistant Secretary of War John J. McCloy about the humiliating treatment of black WACs assigned to Camp Shelby in Hattiesburg, Mississippi. When McCloy sent the complaint to Oveta for a response, she informed McCloy that she had decided to end the assignment of African American corps members to bases in areas where "Jim Crow" laws were in place or where race relations were volatile until "local conditions both on the base and in the vicinity" were suitable for WACs to serve. ER also told McCloy that she was receiving complaints from the NAACP and other civil rights organizations that African American WACs were being kept from overseas assignment because of racial prejudice. When McCloy passed this complaint to Oveta, she responded, "[I share] Mrs. Roosevelt's feeling concerning overseas service for Negro members of our Corps," but she explained that her hands were tied. Because of army command procedures, she lacked the authority to send anyone overseas. Only the theater military commanders could requisition personnel, and "no Negro WACs had been requisitioned." After McCloy passed Oveta's response to Eleanor Roosevelt, ER decided to send a letter to Oveta to express her concerns about the issue. She asked Oveta if "colored WACs are going to get a chance to serve overseas. They are very anxious to go and I should think now they would be very useful in some of the places where there are colored troops." Oveta responded that she agreed that black corps members should have a chance to serve in the theaters of war. She would try to identify a situation where there was a manpower shortage overseas that she could convince the general staff that African American WACs could alleviate.[18]

In February 1945 Oveta found a staffing shortage in England that African American WACs could relieve. A lack of manpower had resulted in more than three million pieces of mail piling up in London, sometimes delaying delivery for months and causing morale problems among soldiers on the battlefront who were desperate for news from their families and friends. Oveta worked with the general staff to organize a postal battalion composed of 855 African American WACs to go to Britain to solve the mail backlog problem. At Oveta's recommendation, the army selected Major Charity Adams to serve as battalion commander. On February 3, 1945, Oveta traveled to the New York City waterfront to demonstrate publicly her support of their assignment and her confidence in the women's ability to do the job. In uniform and standing alone on a platform on the dock, she saluted Charity Adams and her battalion as they were ferried out to the famed luxury liner *Île de France* to be transported to Britain. Once the battalion reduced the mail backlog in England, the army transferred the unit to Rouen, France, where they soon took care of another postal backlog. The army later praised Major Adams and her unit for efficiently resolving their mail problems in England and western France. Adams was promoted to the rank of lieutenant colonel, which made her the highest-ranking black officer in the WAC. As historian Brenda Moore has noted, "The only black WAC unit to serve overseas during the war would never have been selected for the assignment if it had not been for the pressure of black activist groups," but Oveta's positive response and direct involvement facilitated that assignment. "By bidding bon voyage to Maj. Charity Adams and her troops, Hobby made an important public gesture."[19]

By late 1944 Oveta's tangible accomplishments as WAC director, as well as her skillful presentations at committee hearings and her deft and diplomatic handling of constant requests from members of the Senate and the House on behalf of their individual constituents, had gained her much favorable attention among some members of Congress. As a result, Louisiana congressman Overton Brooks, with support from General Marshall and Secretary of War Stimson, led a campaign for authorization to promote Oveta to the rank of major general. Much to Marshall's disgust, the effort failed, the victim of continuing opposition to women serving in the military by a few powerful Southern representatives. Marshall later noted that the Southern congressmen "would kiss a woman's hand and give her an orchid but not consent to military rank."[20]

One of Oveta's allies and admirers from General Marshall's staff, Major General Miller G. White, wrote a letter to General Marshall on December 19, 1944, urging him to award Oveta the Distinguished Service Medal as partial compensation for Congress's refusal to raise her in rank. White had worked with her during the two years he was assistant chief of staff for personnel, but he was now serving in Italy. He admitted to Marshall that he was "stepping entirely out of channels" to make his request and that it would require an exception to the decoration policies Marshall had established. Nevertheless, White argued that an exception was justified. "I do not need to tell you what she has done, or the obstacles and discouragements she has overcome," White wrote. "You know these perhaps better than I. However, I observed her work closely for two years and my admiration for her sound judgment and tact, her great moral courage and her high ideals grow steadily. . . . I have known few people in my life whom I would be willing to classify as 'nobility,' yet if I were required to list the few I have known, I think I would inscribe

Colonel Hobby's name close to the top. If the award is made, it . . . should, if possible, [be made] while she is still in uniform." For Marshall's consideration, White included in the letter his draft of the award citation.[21]

White's letter convinced Marshall, whose quick decision indicated that it was an action he might have already been contemplating. Secretary Stimson approved Marshall's recommendation, also in rapid fashion, and the War Department announced on New Year's Eve 1944 that it would award the army's most prestigious noncombat medal, the Distinguished Service Medal, to Colonel Oveta Culp Hobby.

On January 8, 1945, Secretary Stimson pinned the Distinguished Service Medal on Oveta's uniform in a brief ceremony in his Pentagon office. She was the first woman to receive the award, which has the third-highest prestige of all of the army's decorations. Will Hobby joined Generals Marshall and Hap Arnold and other high-ranking army officers at the ceremony. General White told Oveta, "Since our friends on the hill won't let us pin stars on you, this is the next best thing." The award stated, "Without the guidance of precedents in U.S. military history to assist her, Col. Hobby . . . planned and supervised the selection and training of officers and the preparations of regulations.

*Secretary of War Henry Stimson congratulating Oveta Culp Hobby on being awarded the Distinguished Service Medal at the Pentagon, January 8, 1945.*

The soundness of basic plans and policies promulgated is evidenced by the outstanding success of the Women's Army Corps." In an editorial, the *New York Herald Tribune* declared that because Oveta was "once a newspaper woman herself," her medal "fills us with professional as well as patriotic pride. . . . [I]t is a token not only of her own exceptionally meritorious service but also of the loyal service of the WACs she commands." Oveta would receive several honors during her long life, but she always said that she treasured the Distinguished Service Medal above all others because it had never before been given to a woman.

The many letters of congratulations Oveta received included one that had a special meaning to her. Mary McLeod Bethune, who had been an invaluable advisor to Oveta on racial matters related to the women's corps, wrote, "No one can appreciate more sincerely than I, the success that has come to you. . . . I have watched with prayerful eyes and understanding heart and mind, your forward strides in this great movement." Referring to Oveta's efforts to secure fair treatment for African American WACs, Bethune assured her that she knew "that all has not been done that you wanted done, but you have been blazing the way in a very courageous manner." Bethune also recognized the pathbreaking role Oveta was playing in support of women's rights, pointing out that her earning the Distinguished Service Medal "is another mark showing the real progress of the women of America."[22]

When General White sent his letter to Marshall requesting that Oveta be given the Distinguished Service Medal, neither he nor Marshall showed it to her. The carbon copy remained in White's own files, which he took with him when he retired from the army years later. In August 1972, when he was cleaning out his old files, White rediscovered the carbon copy and sent it to Oveta. "I withheld it from the waste-basket and decided to let you destroy it," he wrote to Oveta. "It brought back many memories to me." Oveta was deeply touched. "My dear friend," she replied, "how wonderful to hear from you. I do thank you for sending me your letter to General Marshall. I have no intention of destroying it; on the contrary, I shall keep it always. It brought a flood of memories to me, too. I was moved to recall your kindness to me and how much I relied on your sensitive judgment."[23]

Will Hobby remained in Washington after Oveta's medal ceremony to attend FDR's inauguration to a fourth term as president. He was invited as the special guest of his old friend Jesse Jones, whom FDR had appointed secretary of commerce in 1940, while also keeping him as head of the Reconstruction Finance Corporation. Will accepted the invitation because of a natural curiosity about such a historical event and out of respect for Jesse Jones, but not as a sign of support or high regard for Roosevelt. Will had abandoned his support for FDR years earlier. Even after Oveta joined the Roosevelt administration in 1941, the *Houston Post* printed a stream of anti-Roosevelt editorials written by the *Post*'s conservative editorial editor, Ed Kilman, who most certainly was representing the political viewpoint of his employer. In 1944 Hobby's newspaper gave its enthusiastic editorial support to the "Texas Regulars," the conservative anti-Roosevelt faction in the Texas Democratic Party that included many of Will's old political allies. Will kept his personal opposition to FDR quiet in 1944 because of Oveta's nonpartisan job as head of the WAC, as well as his own feeling that it would be best not to change presidents at such a critical stage in the war. But as he told his biographer, James Clark, that "did not mean that he had weakened in his opposition to New Dealism."[24]

Because of FDR's failing health and the somber and austere wartime atmosphere, his fourth inauguration was conducted on the south portico of the White House instead of at the Capitol. The ceremony was brief, with no inaugural parade or gala balls. Saturday, January 20, was a bitterly cold day in Washington, with a layer of ice and snow covering the ground. Will was among a tightly packed crowd of five thousand who watched the ceremony from the South Lawn of the mansion, while Jones stood with a small crowd of other dignitaries on the portico a few feet away from where Chief Justice Harlan Stone administered the oath of office to FDR. For easy and convenient access to the ceremony and to allow Oveta and Bill to have a partial view of the event, Will rented a room in the Hotel Washington, located across the street to the east of the White House. Oveta and Bill, who had recently enrolled at St. Albans, were able to grab a spot on the hotel's outdoor rooftop restaurant and bar from where they tried to get a view of the inauguration. Bill wrote about that day in his memoir. "You could actually from the roof of the hotel see the back portico of the White House," he recalled. "My mother and I were up on the roof using binoculars to see what little we could of the ceremony."[25]

After the ceremony, FDR hosted what one guest later described as a "skimpy" buffet luncheon in the State Dining Room for cabinet members, congressional leaders, Supreme Court justices, and more than 1,700 other dignitaries and their guests, who scattered throughout the White House trying to find a place to sit and eat. Will rejoined Jesse Jones at the luncheon, and they walked in the line where FDR sat to greet his guests as they passed on the way to the buffet. As the exhausted and visibly frail president watched the crowd gather to stand in the receiving line, he looked at his son, Jimmy, who had stood by his side to help his father stand during the inauguration: "Jimmy, I can't take this unless you get me a stiff drink. . . . You better make it straight."[26]

Because of the crowded and semichaotic conditions at the White House, Jones and Will decided to skip the buffet and go to the Shoreham Hotel for a more comfortable and quiet lunch. What happened after that is somewhat unclear because of contradictory published accounts, but it appears that Will accompanied Jones to his office, where they were joined by Jones's longtime assistant, Norman Baxter; undersecretary of state and fellow Houston businessman Will Clayton; Supreme Court justice Stanley Reed, who had once served as the Reconstruction Finance Corporation's legal counsel; and one or two other Jones confidants. What these men talked about remains undocumented, but it would be safe to speculate that at some point they discussed the likelihood that FDR would remove Jones as secretary of commerce. Jones's biographer Steven Fenberg has written that Jones "had not been told officially but he knew" that FDR planned to take that step. Harry Hopkins, a longtime New Deal administrator and close friend of the Roosevelts, had told him.[27]

A telephone call from Grace Tully, the president's White House assistant, interrupted the discussion in Jones's office. Tully asked Jones to come to a meeting with FDR at noon the next day, which was Sunday, January 21. A messenger from the White House arrived a few minutes later with a letter from the president to Jones informing him that he was being removed as secretary of commerce to allow the outgoing vice president, Henry A. Wallace, to have the job. Jones had assumed he would be replaced, but not by Wallace, whom he despised. "When my father came back to the Hotel [Washington]," Bill Hobby later recalled, "he told us how extraordinarily cordial the President had been to Mr. Jones" at the inaugural reception but that the subsequent dismissal letter he received from Roosevelt had "infuriated and humiliated Jones." When Jesse Jones met with FDR in the Oval Office on Sunday, the president offered Jones an ambassadorship to his choice of countries, but Jones refused the offer.[28]

The incident not only outraged Jesse Jones, it also angered Will and deepened his opposition to the Roosevelt administration. When Will returned to Houston, he guided the *Houston Post*'s outraged editorial reaction to the incident. "It is a pity to replace a man of Mr. Jones's distinguished ability with a left-wing ne'er-do-well in this critical hour of the nation's history," the *Post*'s editorial page declared, "especially as a mere political reward for [Henry] Wallace's political support of the fourth term ticket." Oveta's exact reaction to this incident, however, seems not to have been documented. Of course, she was still Colonel Hobby, director of the WAC, and she would not and did not criticize her commander in chief in public. Oveta's political views tended to be slightly more progressive, although not in all areas, than those of her husband. And Oveta did not totally share her husband's positive view of Jesse Jones. She certainly admired Eleanor Roosevelt, even though she did not agree with many of the First Lady's political views. Their trip together to the United Kingdom in 1942 had given Oveta an opportunity to see the First Lady in close quarters, and she had been impressed with what she saw and heard. She had also enjoyed her ride in the back seat with FDR and her chat with him during his visit to Fort Oglethorpe. But whatever Oveta's view was of the president's dismissal of Jesse Jones, it remained private.[29]

President Roosevelt died of a massive cerebral hemorrhage on April 12, 1945, at his retreat in Warm Springs, Georgia, stunning and saddening the nation. And those mourners included Will and Oveta Hobby, as well as Jesse Jones, each of whom recognized that a giant in American political history had passed. Even Jesse Jones, whom FDR had angered deeply, declared that Roosevelt "pulled us through the Depression and was a great leader in war. We have lost a great man in his death, which we all deplore."[30]

On Monday afternoon, May 8, less than a month after FDR's death, Oveta and her staff received the much-anticipated but not unexpected news that Nazi Germany had finally surrendered to the Allies on May 8, 1945, ending the war in Europe that had begun nearly six years before. The celebration in Oveta's Pentagon office was relatively brief, however, as everyone's thoughts now focused on the war in the Pacific. Ten days later, Oveta traveled to New York City to review 1,200 WACs as they marched through Times

*Twelve hundred WACs parade before Oveta Culp Hobby in New York City's Times Square for the third anniversary of the corps, May 1945. Note the 550-pound cake in the foreground.*

Square in a parade celebrating the third anniversary of the women's corps and promoting war bonds. Will made the trek to Manhattan to be with her at this deeply satisfying event in which she stood on a raised platform and saluted her corps members. The event featured Oveta using a sword that had once belonged to the Marquis de Lafayette to cut slices of a 550-pound birthday cake and serve them to the first group of bond purchasers. At the ceremony, Oveta told the press that although the war in Europe was over, she was "still hopeful of being able to continue" as WAC director. "Until everybody can get out of the Army—I won't. . . . No matter what you've heard, I'm staying in until the Pacific war is over."[31]

Only one month later, Oveta's stated plan became untenable. Her health, as well as Will's, suddenly turned for the worse. Will learned that he had to undergo yet another surgery, while Oveta's army physician advised her she would need to be hospitalized once again because of her thyroid problem. In addition, General Marshall asked her to go on an extended tour of WAC bases in the Pacific, which would be unwise and difficult given the state of her health. Oveta had completed her assignment to draft the plan for the rapid demobilization of the WAC, which was based on her strong conviction that the corps should be disbanded as soon as possible after the war. She opposed the continuation of the WAC, feeling that the public wanted the women released as soon as it was practicable. After the demobilization plan was completed and approved, no unfinished business or unresolved issues remained for her as director. As she contemplated Will's as well as her own health problems, she made the long-postponed decision to leave the WAC. The difficult, three-year struggle to organize and build the women's corps and to defend it from its enemies, both inside and outside the military (while also being separated from Will and the children), had taken a major mental and physical toll on the "Little Colonel." Her friends noted that her dark hair was now frosted with silver and, although still attractive, she had lost some of her youthful look. Will had tried to ease the strain, including concealing some of his less serious physical problems from her. He and the children had called Oveta every day she was in Washington, but the long hours, the bureaucratic warfare, and the emotional distress caused by the vicious slander campaign had pushed her to the limit of endurance.[32]

The increasingly precarious state of Oveta's health had been common knowledge within a limited circle of the general staff, but she decided to resign rather than seek a medical discharge (for which she met eligibility rules) so that Secretary Stimson could immediately appoint her successor. Oveta submitted her resignation in writing to Marshall on June 26, 1945. Marshall reluctantly accepted it, but he understood the circumstances. Her resignation letter made no mention of her health issues but instead focused on the successful completion of her mission to organize the women's corps. She explained that when she had agreed to go to Washington to organize the Women's Interest Section of the Bureau of Public Relations in 1941, she had intended to be there for only a few months. Those "few months" turned out to be more than three years. Her mission was now completed. It was time for her to return to her family.[33]

The War Department agreed with Oveta's recommendation that her replacement should be forty-three-year-old lieutenant colonel Westray Battle Boyce. A native of North Carolina, Boyce joined the women's corps in 1942 as a supply sergeant and rose rapidly through the ranks to become head of WACs in North Africa. Boyce had accompanied Oveta on her tour of WAC units in North Africa and Italy in January 1944. That August, Oveta transferred her to the staff at WAC headquarters in the Pentagon. Boyce was appointed deputy director in May 1945. Although Jessie Rice had served ably as deputy director, especially during Oveta's frequent bouts of ill health, Rice had developed her own extremely serious health problems and was forced to give up her position as deputy in April. She had been diagnosed with breast cancer, which would result in her death soon after the end of the war.[34]

Worried about the effect the director's resignation might have on WAC morale, the army delayed the public announcement until mid-July. General Miller White asked Oveta to undergo her final physical exam at the Pentagon dispensary instead of at Walter Reed Hospital because it would attract less attention. The army also wanted to give Colonel Boyce a month to better establish her command before announcing Oveta's resignation.[35]

The evening of the day she submitted her resignation from the army, Oveta hosted a dinner at her apartment in the Westchester. The guests included some of the members of Oveta's social circle in Washington: House Speaker Sam Rayburn, Attorney General Tom Clark, Congressman Mike Monroney, FCC Director Paul Porter, and native Texan and University of Texas graduate Hope Ridings Miller, a *Washington Post* reporter and columnist. Oveta greeted her guests at the door in the first evening dress she had worn since the war began. When her guests expressed their surprise that Oveta was wearing civilian clothes, she announced that she had resigned earlier that day and that her uniform had been "shelved." All were sworn to secrecy. Betty Bandel, Oveta's closest friend in the corps, was also among the first to know about Oveta's resignation. After the army released the news, she wrote to her mother that "[Oveta] had to do what . . . I have feared she might have to do at any time for the last 12 months: go home. Her own health has been anything but good for long months. . . . I have never felt so sorry for anyone. She fought through the battle of wondering whether she should leave, for her own health, six months ago, and had determined to stay on until the end [of the war]." Bandel also felt sorry for Oveta's replacement, Westray Boyce, "who . . . only knew about it three days before it all happened."[36]

The War Department finally announced Oveta's resignation at a press conference in the Pentagon on July 12, 1945. Will Hobby, who had flown to Washington to be with Oveta after her decision to resign, was present at the announcement. With Secretary Stimson and General Marshall in Germany attending the Potsdam Conference with President Truman, Acting Secretary of War Robert Patterson hosted the event. Patterson admitted to reporters that Oveta "had to fight many obstacles in promoting a program that was unique in the history of the Army, but she did it with great distinction." Colonel Boyce, whom Patterson introduced at the press conference as Oveta's successor, declared, "The hearts of 100,000 women who served under her will record the image of Colonel Hobby as the symbol of the corps." Much progress had been made in the effort to take seriously the role of women in the army since Oveta had taken her oath as a colonel in the WAAC three years earlier, but some things hadn't changed. At the press conference, a reporter asked Oveta if she had "bought any new civilian hats?" Normally tolerant of such trivial questions, Oveta immediately made her displeasure evident: "Do you mind if I don't end this conference on a note of levity?" Oveta then said goodbye, embraced Westray Boyce, Jessie Rice, and Betty Bandel, and, as reported by *Time*, "patted her carefully coiffed, blue-tinted hair and, moist-eyed," departed from the Pentagon with Will at her side.[37]

Will had arranged for medical aides to take Oveta by stretcher from the Pentagon and then transport her to Union Station, where the Hobbys took the train to New York City. Oveta was admitted to Doctors Hospital for rest and treatment of anemia and exhaustion. She remained there for two weeks. A few days after Oveta left Washington, Hope Ridings Miller wrote in her news column Capital Talk that Oveta's retirement "has left a deep sense of personal loss in Capital officialdom. In my many years of watching women in public office, I have never seen one accomplish her tasks with more efficiency, grace and dignity than has Oveta Hobby."[38]

In an editorial about Oveta's resignation, the *New York Herald Tribune* declared that she had "richly earned her retirement. . . . In the three years of her command the corps has served in virtually every theater of the war and enlisted the encomiums of our top flight soldiers. And now, at forty, she has resigned her most distinguished post to be close to her 'family and business.' Let us acclaim her and congratulate them."[39]

News of Oveta's resignation did not go over well with many of the WAC rank and file, largely as a result of the Associated Press's edited version of her announcement statement. The army's press release stated that her mission of organizing the corps had been completed, but nearly every news story reprinted the AP's version, which by leaving out the words "of organizing the Corps" implied that Oveta was leaving because she felt that the war was essentially over and it was time to go home. A large number of WACs asked, if the director's mission was ended, why wasn't their mission also finished? Many of them expressed that view in letters to family and friends, and even in letters to the editors of their hometown newspapers and to their representatives in Congress. Parents wrote letters to the army denouncing Oveta for resigning when their daughters were unable to leave. WAC commanders in the field reported widespread displeasure among corps members, not only about Oveta's resignation but also about the failure to replace her with Jessie Rice, who was widely admired and much better known to the rank and file than Westray Boyce. Rice's cancer diagnosis had not been publicized, and it was unknown to members of the WAC. In her history of the WAC, Mattie Treadwell noted, "The total effect on the Corps soon became quite serious."[40]

Because she had not wanted a medical discharge, Oveta had chosen to keep her health problems confidential. She had not mentioned health in her resignation statement. But when she learned about the widespread anger in the corps over her departure, Oveta realized her mistake. She released a public statement explaining that her poor health was the main cause of her departure and that she had entered the hospital in New York City on the day of her resignation. Another statement from the army explained that Jessie Rice had her own serious health issues. These explanations helped calm the ranks, and, as Treadwell has stated, "within a few weeks the normal routine of WAC life had been resumed."[41]

Imperial Japan announced its unconditional surrender on August 15, 1945, a little more than one month after the army announced Oveta's resignation. On the day World War II ended, Oveta was out of the hospital and resting back at her home in Houston. She later remarked that had she known how suddenly Japan would be defeated, she would have tried to delay her hospitalization and postpone her departure from the WAC.[42]

The Women's Army Corps began demobilizing immediately after the surrender of Japan. Although no member of the WAC died as a result of being near the battlefront, sixteen women were wounded and awarded the Purple Heart. Twenty-seven won the Bronze Star, recognizing bravery or meritorious service. By the end of 1946, fewer than ten thousand women remained in the corps, with most of those women requesting that they be allowed to continue their service. Oveta Culp Hobby, the talented staff she had assembled to work with her, including Betty Bandel, Jessie Rice, Westray Battle Boyce, and Harriet West, and the thousands of women in the corps who had performed their duties effectively convinced the military leadership that the WAC should be a permanent component of the army. The legislation creating the WAC had included the provision that it had to disband no later than six months after the end of the war, which was determined to be June 1, 1946. In November 1945 the War Department, at the urging of Generals Eisenhower and Jacob L. Devers and especially air corps commander Spaatz, among others, asked Congress to make the WAC permanent.

Ironically, Oveta and her successor, Colonel Boyce, and all of the officers on Oveta's staff opposed the continuation of WAC, largely because they believed the WAC would lack a logical mission in the peacetime army. Eisenhower, however, who now was serving as army chief of staff, understood that in a world where war remained a real threat, the army could not afford to revert to its prewar levels and that the WAC would have a necessary mission. Air corps general Spaatz declared, "If I have anything to do with it, there will be a place for women in the Regular Air Force." Due to the typical bureaucratic holdups in the War Department, the legislation was not submitted to Congress until April 1947, while the WAC, given a temporary extension by Congress, continued to function at a much-reduced level. The same hard-core obstructionists in Congress who opposed the women's corps when it was first proposed held up approval of the army's request for fourteen months. Finally, on June 12, 1948, the Women's Army Corps became a permanent part of the army, an arrangement that lasted until 1978, when the corps was abolished and women were accepted into all but the combat units of the army.[43]

Oveta's impressive record as the organizer and the director of both versions of the women's corps was considered an outstanding success from nearly every quarter. Congresswoman Edith Nourse Rogers deserves the most credit for pushing and shoving the Congress and the military into creating the women's corps in the first place. And Rogers's success would not have been possible without the strong support of Secretary of

War Stimson and General George Marshall. But once Congress agreed to authorize the women's corps, it was Oveta Culp Hobby, aided by her army advisors, who organized it literally from scratch, guided it through the jungle of a military bureaucracy filled with men who were often openly hostile to her cause, sustained it during the vicious slander campaign, and, by the time of her resignation, left a fully functional and vital organization that the army had recognized it could not do without. Despite her relatively young age when she went to Washington in 1941, she had already gained extensive political experience through her work with legislative committees and as parliamentarian in the Texas House of Representatives. She benefitted greatly from the sage political advice of her husband, who was a willing and eager tutor who encouraged and supported her career. Her work editing and publishing a major daily newspaper provided her with valuable experience in managing a complex and sometimes controversial business. Oveta's many years of work in women's clubs, charitable organizations, and professional societies provided experiences she drew upon as a leader of an all-women's organization.

Most important, perhaps, was Oveta's inherent talent and natural ability as a leader. Despite her diminutive physical stature, she possessed the type of command persona that is an essential element of successful military leadership. She knew to choose her battles, to fight for what she perceived to be attainable, and to shift to alternative goals when necessary. She did her homework, paid attention to detail, and often worked deep into the night to prepare for congressional hearings, press conferences, and presentations to the army brass. Oveta was skilled at articulating a cause both in writing and speaking. She also enjoyed the personal qualities that created and maintained solid relationships with peers and subordinates. As historian Kelli Walsh has noted, Oveta Culp Hobby led by example, and her performance as head of the WAC "promoted the idea that femininity and competence were synonymous."[44]

Journalist Marguerite Johnston, one of Oveta's closest friends, believed Oveta was changed by her experience as organizer and leader of the WAC. Johnston felt that by the time Oveta resigned from the army, she had "a keener appreciation of the problems of women in a man's world—problems which had never been forced to her attention in her life in Austin or Houston. She developed an abiding awareness of the barriers many women have to surmount." Johnston added, "Those who knew her best felt that Oveta gained an even deeper understanding and sympathy for humanity in general." Many years after the war, Mattie Treadwell, who had served as an officer in Oveta's command, concluded, "Any success the Corps had was due to [Oveta's] efforts, and to her character and personality. All who worked with her praised her energy, magnetism, sincerity, and idealism. All cited her diplomatic ability combined with stubborn refusal to give up on major issues affecting her enlisted women." In 1954, Treadwell's assessment was seconded by Eleanor Roosevelt. "How well [Oveta] handled the job [as head of the WACs] may be attested by the fact that we now have women in every branch of our military services, in uniform, receiving the same pay and rating as the men, performing almost every type of duty except combat," the former First Lady observed. "A great deal of the credit belongs to Oveta Hobby."[45]

In a newspaper interview soon after the war, Oveta discussed what she believed her army experience had taught her. She said that having multiple duties of equal importance forced her to learn how to organize her time more effectively. She learned that she could accomplish more by doing "one thing at a time, trying to put first things first." Recalling the slander campaign, she admitted that another valuable lesson was to discover how it felt to be on the receiving end of highly critical newspaper articles that she knew were based on inaccurate reporting. Oveta stated that she had always insisted to her journalists at the *Post* that they report the news fairly and accurately, but her experience during the slander campaign reinforced her commitment to that standard even more.[46]

Forty years after Oveta resigned from the WAC, Ruth Cheney Streeter, who had served as the commander of the US Marine Corps Women's Reserve, wrote a letter to Oveta expressing her view of the impact their respective organizations had made in the long-term struggle for equal rights for women. "You and I were in some strange way more than comrades in arms, as we shared the exigencies of the times," Streeter said. "I have talked to and heard from many WACs in these intervening years, and each one has expressed in some way her feeling that she had shared in a very great experience. I, for one, shall never forget the courage and valor of those women, and I hope each one realizes her place in history. I think that we sensed even then that in future years, more and more doors would open to women, as indeed we have seen take place, as a result of that participation."[47]

Perhaps the most lasting tribute Oveta would receive for her contribution to the American military effort in the Second World War was the decision to select one of her quotes to be chiseled in stone in 2004 and preserved permanently on a wall of the World

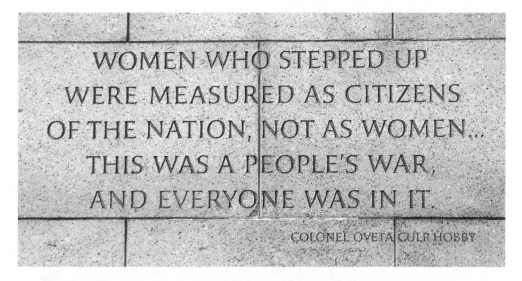

*"Women Who Stepped Up," World War II Memorial, National Mall, Washington, DC.*

War II Memorial on the National Mall in Washington, DC. Oveta's words join those of Franklin D. Roosevelt, Harry S. Truman, Dwight D. Eisenhower, Chester Nimitz, and Douglas MacArthur. Her inscription, which echoes the words Will Hobby uttered to her when he encouraged her to accept the army's request for her to go to Washington in 1941, reads:

WOMEN WHO STEPPED UP
WERE MEASURED AS CITIZENS
OF THE NATION, NOT AS WOMEN . . .
THIS WAS A PEOPLE'S WAR,
AND EVERYONE WAS IN IT.

# CHAPTER 29

## AROUND THE WORLD IN THIRTEEN DAYS

Oveta returned to Houston in August 1945, eager to reengage fully with the business and civic life she had mostly abandoned in the summer of 1941. Much had changed for her as well as for Houston during the war. She returned to a city on the verge of a massive economic and population boom. The needs of modern war had rapidly expanded the region's petroleum production and spawned completely new industries in chemicals and metals. The Texas Gulf Coast, with its cheap fuel and varied resources, proved to be a natural location for the new petrochemical industry. In 1940 the chemical industry employed 180 people in Houston; that number increased to 20,000 shortly after the war, as the Houston region became the center of the fastest-growing industrial area in America. This boom in chemical and related industry growth was paralleled by a massive expansion in all facets of Houston's urban development, which doubled the city's population. The boom created entirely new wealth, while also vastly increasing the financial resources of the already affluent. The Hobbys, although not as wealthy as nouveau riche independent oilmen like Hugh Roy Cullen and Glenn McCarthy, were among those whose wealth would take off during these postwar years.[1]

Oveta left Houston in 1941 as one of the city's more prominent residents, but she had not been well known outside of her town and state. She came home as a national figure. The period between the fall of 1945 and 1953, when Oveta would be called back to government service in Washington, were the years when she and Will became Houston's most visible power couple. The *New York Times* called her "undoubtedly the city's First Lady." The official welcome home that Houston gave Oveta at the end of the war symbolized the rise in her reputational status in Houston.

On September 14, 1945, Houston's business and political elite hosted a dinner in her honor in the Rice Hotel ballroom attended by more than seven hundred people. As a sign of the prominence Oveta had garnered as the path-breaking "Little Colonel," the NBC radio network broadcast the dinner's program nationwide. President Truman and

General Marshall sent messages praising Oveta's service as commander of the Women's Army Corps (WAC). The president praised Oveta for contributing "so unselfishly and with such great distinction to the war effort of our nation." Marshall's message declared that Oveta's "firm leadership and unselfish purpose were a tremendous factor in the outstanding success of the [WAC]." A week after the event, Marshall wrote Oveta a private letter explaining that he and his wife had been on vacation in the Adirondacks. Before he left Washington, he had intended to record a message to be broadcast on the radio, but NBC would not permit any prerecorded statements. "The fact that I was at Potsdam [for Oveta's departure from the WAC] and in the mountains [for the dinner in Houston] was most unfortunate and disappointing . . . for I had a strong feeling that you deserved much better of me. You made a great sacrifice in your effort which I hope will not prove costly to your future health."[2]

When Houston lawyer and banker George Butler referred to Will Hobby in his speech lauding Oveta, the audience gave "Governor" a standing ovation, which he acknowledged with a bow. At the time, Will was involved in yet another of his many civic activities, as chairman of a project to sell $55 million in bonds to improve Houston's streets and flood control. Oveta's successor as WAC director, Colonel Westray Battle Boyce, also spoke at the dinner. Earlier that day, Colonel Boyce had arrived in an army airplane at Houston's Ellington Field, where Will and Oveta greeted her. When Oveta gave Colonel Boyce a hug and a kiss after she stepped from the airplane, the colonel told reporters, "She may be in civilian dress, but to me and to the rest of the WACs she's still 'The Boss.'" When it was Oveta's turn to speak at the dinner, she referred to Will as "my partner, my friend, my husband." She compared her WACs to pioneer women crossing the plains, but her final remarks looked to the future. She urged the audience to join in the important effort "to turn the inventions and discoveries of this war to the good of mankind." And she challenged her fellow Texans and countrymen to direct "the great energies used in making war to making peace and establishing virtues of Freedom. We must build skyscrapers and discover poets. We must return the dignity of man to its former high station. Let us consider and treat him as he truly is . . . 'made in the image of God.'"[3]

Oveta's return to Texas set off a flurry of reports in the press that she would be a candidate for governor in 1946. She was quick to deny those rumors, telling reporters she was "much too busy" managing her newspaper and radio station and tending to the needs of her family to run for political office. That denial was not a ruse. Brimming with self-confidence gained from her successful tenure as director of the WAC, Oveta was eager to put that administrative experience and knowledge to work at the *Houston Post* and KPRC Radio. Of the two, the *Post* was the one that most needed her immediate attention. During the war, the *Post* had suffered, like the newspaper industry in general, from newsprint shortages, gasoline rationing, tax issues, the loss of veteran staff members to military service, and a reduction in advertising. At one point during the summer of 1942, while Oveta was busy organizing the first officers' training camp of the women's corps, she and Will quietly gauged the prospects for selling the newspaper either outright or attracting an investor to join them as a minority owner. Will hired Allen Kander, a broker who specialized in arranging the sale and purchase of newspapers, to test the market. Nothing came of the effort, and it was terminated in October 1943.[4]

Will had guided the general affairs of the *Houston Post* during the years Oveta was in Washington, but she had still paid attention to the newspaper, not only through Will but also by communications with Helon Johnson and with visits to the Post Building during her trips back to Houston. That attention often led to involvement in operational details. While in Houston for Christmas in 1944, Oveta decided that the lighting in the printing plant was inadequate. She asked General Manager Charlie Maes to hire an electrical engineer to inspect the facility and then send the engineering report to her WAC office in Washington. After two months passed and no report arrived, Oveta wrote Helon Johnson. "What have they done about the lighting facilities at the plant?" she asked. "I talked to Mr. Maes about it when I was home and I would like to have a report of progress."[5]

Although Oveta continued to monitor her newspaper while she was in Washington, it wasn't possible, desirable, or appropriate for her to divert much of her attention away from the women's corps. For practical reasons, neither Oveta nor Will was in a position to manage the day-to-day operations of either of their two media properties. Much of the burden of running the *Post* fell on the shoulders of Will's good and loyal friend Charlie Maes, who started out as a "cub" reporter for the *Post-Dispatch* in 1924. By 1945, Maes had been the newspaper's dependable general manager for nearly two decades. His steady hand guided the paper throughout the war as Will battled health problems and traveled back and forth from Houston to Washington to be with Oveta. Ed Kilman, a hard-core conservative anti–New Dealer whom Ross Sterling hired as a political reporter in 1925, managed the editorial page. Arthur Laro, whom Will had hired away from the *Houston Press* in 1938, was the highly capable city editor. Harry Johnston Jr., grandson of Will's mentor Rienzi Johnston, was Laro's assistant editor.[6]

In an interview with the *New York Herald Tribune* a month after she reassumed her position at the *Post*, Oveta stated, "For the last several years newspapers have had a good excuse for failure to cover all the news. They could point to the short supply of paper. But in a few months the honeymoon will be over." She argued that with the war over, newspaper subscribers would expect more expansive and more readable coverage, from world news to local. "The newspaper of the next few years," she added, would have to be "better departmentalized—easier to read—better illustrated, better printed. In short, a quality product."[7]

Oveta quickly acted to make the *Post* the kind of newspaper she predicted postwar readers would demand. Improving the bottom line, of course, provided the primary motive for making changes: no readers, no advertisers, no profit. The *Post* had suffered a decline in net profits from 1944, when earnings totaled $340,000 (nearly $4.8 million in 2018 dollars), to 1945, when the total was $277,500 ($3.9 million in 2018). Oveta promoted Arthur Laro to managing editor, reporting directly to her, and Harry

Johnston Jr. assumed Laro's duties as city editor. Under Oveta's direction, Laro increased the *Post*'s coverage of national and international news. He also weeded out some of the older reporters, firing twelve, and replaced them with younger journalists to "pep up" the "staid old *Post*." The replacements included top young talent Laro lured away from the *Houston Press*. Other newcomers included Alabama native Marguerite Johnston, who had been Washington correspondent for two Birmingham newspapers. Oveta had met Johnston when Oveta was director of the WAC. Johnston would soon become Oveta's close confidant, and she would play an important role in reshaping the *Post*'s news coverage. Other fresh faces included former war correspondent George Fuermann and farm and ranch reporter Leon Hale. Both would become two of the paper's most popular columnists for many years to come.[8]

Oveta and Will soon made other changes at the management level. Charlie Maes was made assistant to the president, but Maes soon left the *Post* to start up a new weekly news publication. His replacement as general manager was Lloyd Gregory, who would leave after two years and be replaced by Howard Baldwin. Other changes occurred with the passage of time. Jack Josey, who had continued to serve on the *Post*'s board of directors, died in April 1945, and popular columnist and poet Judd Mortimer Lewis, who had worked at the *Post* since 1900, passed during the summer of 1945. The Hobbys also reorganized the Houston Post Company to unify the newspaper and radio station as one legal entity. Helon Johnson, still working as Will's executive assistant, was elected a member of the new board of directors.[9]

Houston was one of the most competitive newspaper towns in America. It was the only city in the South that had three major daily newspapers: the *Post*, the *Houston Chronicle*, and the *Houston Press*. For many years, Jesse Jones's *Chronicle*, an afternoon paper, had been more profitable than the *Post*. Jones had placed ownership of the *Chronicle* in his charitable foundation, the Houston Endowment, after he founded the endowment in 1937. That move exempted the *Chronicle* from having to pay federal income taxes. The *Post*, on the other hand, was taxed like any other business, which reduced its profit in contrast to the *Chronicle*. The *Houston Press* also had to pay federal income tax, but as part of the Scripps-Howard national newspaper chain, it had more financial resources to draw from than did the *Post*. The *Press* did not publish a Sunday edition, and it was a sensationalist tabloid newspaper, so its subscriber base differed from both the *Post* and the *Chronicle*.

These personnel changes and other improvements in the newspaper soon brought positive results, although Houston's explosive postwar population growth and economic prosperity certainly played a major role in the *Post*'s improved financial situation. The newspaper's circulation grew steadily from a little more than 116,000 in 1945 to 137,000 in 1946 and then continued to expand every year after that, reaching 176,210 in 1952. More important was the growth in advertising space, which brought in more revenue and made it possible for Will to pay off the loans he had received in 1940 to pay his debt to Jesse Jones. The *Post*'s profit by the end of 1946 was nearly $919,000 ($11 million in 2018 dollars), which was a happy increase for the Hobbys of nearly $600,000 over the previous year's profits. By 1949 the *Post*'s net profit was $208,000, equal to $3.5 million in 2018.[10]

The *Houston Post*'s growth during the last half of the 1940s caught the attention of Jake Butler, the *Chronicle*'s vice president and business manager. Butler informed Jesse Jones, "We have some keen competitors over at the *Houston Post*. Both Governor Hobby and Mrs. Hobby take an active part in the selling of their newspaper in the advertising field, and they are tough competition. They, like all morning newspapers, have the natural advantage for out-of-city circulation, and there isn't anything we can do about it." The *Chronicle*'s managing editor, Emmet Walter, sent an additional warning to Jones. He told him the Hobbys had launched an aggressive subscription drive for the *Post* on their popular radio station, KPRC, and they had significantly increased the amount of news coverage in the paper. "A higher percentage of news content gives the paper more pages with large chunks of reading matter," Walter stated. "This leads the reader to believe he is getting more reading matter than in a paper which has only a column or so on most pages," which was the *Chronicle*'s style. He explained that for the *Chronicle* to equal the *Post*'s amount of reading matter, it would require about two additional pages daily and Sunday. He urged Jones to approve a more intensive drive for subscribers and to take other measures or they risked losing their position "as the leading paper in Texas."[11]

It was during these years that Oveta's obsession with control and efficiency became most evident, both at home and at work. Although those traits had been apparent since her childhood, it wasn't until she left the WAC that she was finally able to give free rein to those impulses. During the first few years of their marriage, she had happily deferred to Will when major decisions had to be made at the *Houston Post*, but by the time Oveta went to Washington in 1941, she had assumed more and more authority. The army, of course, was a step backward in terms of her freedom to control her work and surroundings, despite her being the WAC director. She provided leadership, but it was leadership without much authority. That lack of control, as well as her frustration with the inefficiencies caused by military red tape and General Somervell's obstructions, undoubtedly contributed to her health problems during the war.

Once she was back in Houston, Oveta quickly reassumed her role as the dominant figure in the *Post*'s management. One of the *Post*'s editors during this period noted that after the war Oveta "took over as publisher," and the staff had no doubt about who was in charge. Leon Hale recalled that after he joined the staff, "I began to learn that you didn't simply work for *The Houston Post*. You worked for Oveta Culp Hobby, and don't you forget it because she was keeping up with what you did that she liked, and what she didn't like." David Westheimer, who later earned fame as the author of the novel *Von Ryan's Express*, joined the *Post* staff soon after the war. He later recalled that Oveta would be the only woman present at editorial meetings, which rarely included Will. "We stood when Mrs. Hobby came into the room, and again when she rose," he recalled. "Someone always held her chair. Mrs. Hobby said little, but on all important matters, she made the

*Will Hobby inspecting a new supplement to an edition of the* Houston Post
*at the printing plant with Paul Tanner, head pressman, October 1952.*

final decision." When a *Time* reporter was in Houston to write a personality profile on Oveta, an unidentified *Post* staff member told him that Oveta's "calm demeanor almost never deserts her. When she is displeased, her expression telegraphs the clue: her warm smile vanishes, and is instantly replaced by a frosty stare."[12]

Although Oveta was clearly in charge at the operational level, Will didn't retire or disappear. He continued to be a decision maker on larger business matters, and he would play a key role in their move into television and their decision to build a new printing plant. Will's management style, however, was in stark contrast to Oveta's. He had always been slow to make changes in personnel and he was extremely reluctant to dismiss anyone. He was passive when faced with difficulties over which he had little control, believing that many problems would simply go away if ignored. During one crisis at the newspaper years earlier, Will told an assistant not to panic: "Sometimes you just have to tie things down and let 'er blow."

One of the *Post*'s reporters recalled a humorous incident that illustrates Will's calm persona. The reporter and her daughter were walking down a street in downtown Houston when they saw Will buy a newspaper from a coin-operated rack on the sidewalk. "Governor . . . was standing near the rack with the paper in his hand. A woman came by and looked at the Governor standing glumly by. She said, 'I started to get my paper off the rack, but I'll take yours.' His expression didn't change. He gave her his paper and took her nickel."[13]

Will's age and health issues began to take a toll in the years after the war, and he increasingly deferred to Oveta in most matters, but he remained involved in the *Post*'s editorial endorsements and political pronouncements. Will and Oveta continued to work as the "Hobby Team," but it was Oveta who issued the orders. As KPRC Radio executive Jack McGrew later recalled, "We knew the direction from the top was seamless. Governor and Mrs. Hobby were a team in the very best sense of the word. Which of the two might have made a specific decision we neither knew nor cared."[14]

As Oveta took charge of the *Post*, her personal traits came more to the fore, settling into a pattern that largely defined her personality for the rest of her life. David Westheimer recalled Oveta as being "gracious and open to suggestions but very precise about what she wanted done. The occasion demanding, she could be firm [but not] unreasonable in her firmness." Westheimer soon discovered that Oveta kept well informed about who was working at her newspaper. "She knew us all by our first names and used them." One time he was pulled away from his normal job and given the assignment to cover a ceremony that Oveta was hosting. A *Post* photographer asked him to hold a light a certain way for him while he took a picture of her, but Westheimer pleaded that he didn't think he could hold the light properly. Convinced that Oveta didn't know his name, Westheimer was shocked when Oveta smiled and said, "David, I didn't think there was anything you couldn't do."[15]

During the postwar years, *Time* noted that Oveta's life in Houston moved "with the precision of a metronome." Her day began at 6:00 a.m. After dressing, she held weekly meetings with her four household staff to issue assignments and instructions about how their work was to be done. A reporter for the Associated Press observed that Oveta consulted several "well-thumbed" cookbooks from her kitchen library for menus for the day's meals. "And if the cook doesn't understand exactly, Mrs. Hobby can tell her just how much lemon to use in Hollandaise sauce." Will told a reporter who was doing a story about his wife that she was "a very efficient woman. She has always run her house by remote control from wherever she is." By 8:15 a.m., Oveta would telephone one of her two secretaries at the *Post* to issue directions for the work of the day. Afterward, Oveta's chauffeur drove her to the *Post* (she gave up driving after her return to Houston), usually arriving around 10:30 a.m., where she would sort through her mail and then meet with business department heads. Her two well-trained assistants were able to take care of much of the paperwork that came through the door. One of them told *Time* that Oveta could be "completely ruthless in dealing with detail. She can center her attention on the immediate problem and completely eliminate everything else." On a table near her desk fashion magazines were placed side by side with the *Wall Street Journal* and a framed, signed photograph of General George C. Marshall. On a bookshelf a statue of Pallas Athena, whose head was the emblem of the WAC, sat in a prominent location. Oveta had not forgotten the women who served under her command, nor had they forgotten her. Nearly every day, she received wedding announcements, cards announcing baby births, and personal letters from former WACs.[16]

After lunch, which she took at home, Oveta was back in her office by 2:30 p.m. for conferences with editorial staff and for other meetings, usually related to her civic activities. At the editorial meetings, Oveta would occasionally remind her staff about a lesson she had learned in the army. "I learned how it feels to be on the receiving end of newspaper writing," she would say. "In the WAC I saw how much harm can be done by half-truths—not by malicious half-truths but merely half-truths." As a result she insisted that the *Post* should always be fair in reporting. Although her writers couldn't argue against that objective, some of them would later argue that her obsession with fairness too often resulted in the newspaper's avoidance of controversy and a failure to report on the activities of close friends and associates. Oveta typically ended her workday a few minutes after 6:00 p.m., leaving her desk, as one of her secretaries noted, "as clean as if a vaccum [*sic*] cleaner has been over it."[17]

Peggy Buchanan, Oveta's personal assistant, later recalled, "Mrs. Hobby was always well-organized. 'If you're not three weeks ahead, you're behind,' she would say. She would begin planning for Christmas in September." At one point, Oveta imposed a task-management system on the *Post* staff developed by the Booz Allen Hamilton consulting firm. She made out her daily schedule on four three-by-five index cards. One card was for her housekeepers, one for her office staff, one for her driver, and one for herself. The system was highly touted as a way to improve efficiency and productivity. Every task was prioritized and placed on an "Action Time" schedule to be handled or completed by certain dates. Oveta even applied the "Action Time" management strategy to her commute back and forth from home to work, as well as on her travel out of town. She carried a custom-made, double-handled calfskin bag that she designed to house her business papers and her purse. The bag was stuffed with papers on which she worked while she was traveling on trains and planes or in her chauffeur-driven car. Now a committed Episcopalian, Oveta also carried a copy of the Book of Common Prayer in her bag wherever she went. Buchanan recalled that Oveta was "so pleased with the success of this work schedule at the [*Post*] that she applied 'Action Time' to her own life—including the garden. Even the vegetables were put on a schedule." Oveta's focus on work even intruded on her bedtime. One friend described her as a "fitful sleeper" who kept a notebook on the table beside her bed and that she frequently made notes as she woke during the night.[18]

Oveta didn't ignore KPRC while she was retooling the *Houston Post*, but the radio station was flourishing under the guidance of general manager Kern Tips. Broadcasting was not her forte, so she and Will generally deferred to Tips's and Jack McGrew's judgment on radio matters. Tips was one of the most highly regarded radio executives in Texas, as well as being a famed sportscaster who specialized in calling Southwest Conference football games on the radio. McGrew noted that he and Tips were "given freedom to operate in what we thought to be the best interests of our audience, the stations and the licensee. Our judgments were seldom questioned and when they were, our arguments were fully and thoughtfully weighed. To be frank, I do not recall any situation in which our position was overruled or even seriously questioned [by the Hobbys]."

A little more than a year after Oveta returned to Houston, Kern Tips resigned to go into the advertising industry. It didn't take her long to find a replacement. During fall 1941, when Oveta had been leading the Women's Interest Section, she had met Jack Harris, a young executive at WSM Radio in Nashville, Tennessee, who was in Washington to help organize and manage the radio division of the army's Bureau of Public Relations, which Oveta used to disseminate information to the public about army life. She soon was impressed with Harris's work, and they became friends. After the United States entered the war, Harris joined the army and was commissioned as a colonel. During the last year of the war, he served as General Douglas MacArthur's radio and press communications officer in the Pacific, directing radio coverage of the final phase of the Philippines campaign and Japan's surrender. After the war Oveta kept up with Harris, who returned to his position at WSM Radio. When Kern Tips told the Hobbys he was leaving KPRC, Oveta immediately thought of Harris. Her contacts in the radio industry advised her that Harris would never leave Nashville, so she gave up the idea. After Oveta and Will interviewed several candidates who didn't measure up to their expectations, Will encouraged Oveta to contact Harris, who accepted her invitation to visit Houston. After spending a day with the Hobbys, Harris accepted their offer to take the job of general manager of KPRC. He reported to work on January 25, 1947. Hiring Harris would become one of Oveta's most significant personnel decisions. As she recalled many years later, that meeting with Harris in 1941 had been "one of the most fortunate days" of her life.[19]

With a substantial increase in the *Houston Post*'s profits matching a rise in profits at KPRC, Will and Oveta saw a significant rise in their personal wealth, which in turn gave them the means to acquire a residence more in keeping with their ascendency up the city's economic and social ladder. When their house on Glen Haven was damaged by a fire while Oveta was directing the WAC, Will and Oveta decided to remodel and sell it. In 1944, during their search for a new residence, they learned that the former home of the late Joseph Cullinan, the founder of the Texas Company (Texaco), was available. The mansion was located on a seven-acre lot at 2 Remington Lane in the exclusive Shadyside neighborhood, adjacent to the campus of Rice Institute and across South Main Street from Hermann Park. Built in 1919 and designed by the regionally prestigious architect John Staub, the mansion was one of the most imposing houses in Houston at the time. It was a sixteen-thousand-square-feet, three-story, rambling Georgian red brick structure with twenty-seven rooms, including five bedrooms, two dressing rooms, a music room, a drawing room, a garden room, a large dining room, a library, two maid's rooms, and several bathrooms and powder rooms. There was a large terrace on the second floor and an elevator to the two upper floors. A smaller side house contained a cardroom, a powder room, a drawing room, a bathroom, and an office. The property also included a tennis court, but the Hobbys soon sold that to a neighbor. Oveta hired Staub to restyle and update much of the mansion, including some of the exterior ornamentations that she felt were too garish. A few weeks after they purchased the property, Oveta wrote her mother that the renovation was "going very slowly but we have hopes of its being finished within the next sixty or ninety days. I know when it is finished it will be worth the trouble and waiting we have had."[20]

Because of the heavy traffic on Main Street, which was only one hundred feet from the house, the Hobbys built a wall along the street side of the property to muffle the noise, which continued late into the night. Oveta chose to decorate the house herself instead of employing a professional decorator. She filled the residence with antique furniture, statuary, paintings, vases, Georgian silver, and rare books that she had collected as she traveled around the country and overseas. She and Will decided to make the third floor of the mansion a home office where Will could work at a large desk with a view of several tall oak trees in their yard. At the *Post*, Oveta and Will had adjoining offices, but his went largely unused as the years passed and his health continued to decline.[21]

Will and Oveta obviously purchased the Cullinan mansion to serve as their private residence, but they also intended to use it for social and business receptions and dinners. Jack McGrew later recalled that company parties at the mansion were major events for the staff. And there was no doubt who was in charge. Will, who had no interest in the details of planning dinners and receptions, left such decisions to Oveta, as he had deferred to Willie before her. "[Mrs. Hobby] went to extraordinary lengths to prepare for these business parties to make our people and guests comfortable." Depending on the purpose of the event, Oveta would bring in either KPRC (for visiting NBC officials, for example) or *Post* staff (for visiting wire service executives) to help her prepare a

*Will and Oveta Hobby host NBC Radio star Dinah Shore and her husband, George Montgomery, at the Hobby mansion on Remington Lane, Houston, April 1946.*

detailed guest list. They also gathered information about the business connections the guests might have with the Hobbys, as well as the names of their spouses and the names and ages of their children. A day before the event, Oveta and Helon Johnson would meet with staff to rehearse for the event. At the parties, Oveta stood in the foyer to greet each guest personally. If the occasion was related to KPRC, Jack Harris stood with her. If it was a *Post* event, an executive from the newspaper stood beside her. The executive on duty was expected to help Oveta identify any guest whom she did not know. She occasionally excused herself to discreetly consult a guest information sheet that she hid in a book in the shelves lining the corridor leading to the family dining room. "All of this attention paid off, of course," Jack McGrew later recalled, "in the unfailing success of these affairs." The Hobbys' dinner table could seat twenty, but they typically had no more than sixteen guests because Oveta preferred that the table not be crowded. Yellow roses, an Oveta favorite, usually decorated the table. According to household staff member Cecil McBride, Oveta "was not a steak person," preferring fish or chicken to be served at her dinners. Oveta also took great pleasure in serving fresh vegetables, including string beans, romaine and Bibb lettuce, green peas, and broccoli that her staff grew in the garden on the mansion grounds.[22]

During the years immediately after the end of the war, Oveta cultivated a taste for modern art (Modigliani), symphonic music (Bartók), and high fashion (Valentina). She told friends and family that her art collections were for her private enjoyment and satisfaction, not for status seeking. Oveta's grandson Paul Hobby recalled that she "never owned a painting or piece of furniture without knowing a tremendous amount about whatever it was. [She] liked fine things because they pleased her, not because other people admired them." Famed art collector and museum founder Dominique de Menil, who became a friend of Oveta's after Dominique and her husband, John, moved from Paris to Houston after the war, later noted that she could not recall Oveta ever bringing attention to her art or discussing it whenever the Menils visited the Hobbys' mansion. According to close family friend and art historian Susan Barnes, Oveta "was a discerning, adventurous, private art collector." Her collection, which she displayed at the mansion and at her office at the *Post*, would eventually include some of the most outstanding artists of the twentieth century, including works by Picasso and Matisse and a Modigliani gouache titled *Caryatid*.[23]

It was also during these postwar years that Oveta became the only woman member of Houston's "8F crowd," an informal group that constituted the city's power elite establishment from the early 1940s until the early 1960s. There were other well-known and influential women of wealth in Houston, including oil-fortune philanthropists Ima Hogg, Nina Cullinan, and Ella Fondren, among others (Florence Sterling had died in 1940), but their activities were largely focused on cultural and educational matters. None were as deeply involved in business, civic, and political power brokering as Oveta Culp Hobby.

The "8F crowd" got its name (which was used by outsiders when referring to the group but never formally used by its members) from the fact that their gatherings, usually in the evenings but frequently also at lunch, were held in the 8F suite of Jesse Jones's Lamar Hotel in downtown Houston. Suite 8F, located eight floors below Jones's apartment, which occupied the entire top story, was leased to the Brown and Root construction conglomerate controlled by brothers Herman and George Brown, who were the key members of the group. Before he moved to Houston, Herman Brown had operated from Austin, while his younger brother George guided company business in Houston. Because he was in Houston on a regular basis, Herman leased the suite to serve as his headquarters whenever he came to town. After Herman moved to his own house in Houston, the company kept the suite as a convenient and private meeting place for the group.

*Oveta Culp Hobby chats with fellow "8F crowd" members Herman Brown (left) and Jim Abercrombie (middle), 1957.*

Besides Herman and George Brown, who had a lucrative political alliance with Lyndon B. Johnson, the core members of 8F were Gus Wortham, who was founder of the highly successful American General Insurance Company and whose father had been a friend of Will's; Judge James Elkins, another old friend of Will's, who controlled Texas's largest law firm, Vinson and Elkins, and whose City National Bank was the second-largest financial institution in Houston at the time; and, of course, "Mr. Houston," Jesse Jones. Will Hobby, known to all as "Governor," was the most popular member of the group. Brown and Root lobbyist Posh Oltorf, who was a distant cousin of Will's, was a frequent visitor to the 8F suite. He later recalled that Will "had the driest wit" of any of the 8F crowd. "So much of Governor can't be captured in a book, because he talked with his eyes and his little throw-away lines. He was such a delightful man."[24]

The other members of the 8F group fluctuated as business and personal affairs demanded, with politicians in particular coming and going, but there was a stable outer circle of businessmen who were strongly allied financially, socially, and politically to the core members of the 8F group and who helped to leverage the group's influence. That outer circle included W. Alvis Parish of the Baker Botts law firm and head of the Houston Lighting and Power Company; Warren S. Bellows, owner of the city's largest construction firm, whose client list included most of the members of the 8F group; James S. Abercrombie, an independent oilman and owner of Cameron Iron Works; Hines Baker, president of the powerful Humble Oil Company, which was controlled by Standard Oil of New Jersey; and Lamar Fleming of the cotton firm Anderson, Clayton, and Company.[25]

Oveta was welcomed into the inner circle after her return to Houston in 1945. It was clear to the other members that Will and Oveta were partners in every respect. She had earned her reputation as a power broker during her tenure in Washington, and it was obvious she would be taking the reins of the *Houston Post* and KPRC Radio from Will. Every core member of the 8F group, especially Jones and Elkins, were long-time personal and business associates of the Hobbys, and George Brown's relationship with Will and Oveta would deepen in the coming years. The members of the 8F circle respected Oveta's business acumen, political instincts, and understanding of public opinion. They also trusted her.

A set of photographs in an October 1946 article in *Life* magazine titled "Booming Houston" signified Oveta's ascendance into Houston's power elite. One of the pictures featured Will and Oveta sitting on a couch in their executive office at the *Post* below a large oil portrait of Oveta in her WAC uniform. Subtitled "Texas' Biggest City Is Suddenly Growing Bigger and Wealthier," the *Life* article identified Oveta as "one of the first citizens of Houston." In the opening lines of the feature, Oveta was quoted: "I think I'll like Houston . . . if they ever get it finished." It was one of her most often published quotes, and it quickly became part of the city's promotional lore. Native Texan Stanley Walker, writing in the *New Yorker*, claimed Oveta borrowed the comment from William Sydney Porter, who made the statement when he was writing for the *Houston Post*. The quote was also one of Oveta's favorites, one that she used occasionally in speeches at events celebrating landmark events in the city's business development. She repeated the statement when she was the featured speaker at the opening of the massive, eight-story, $13 million Foley's department store in downtown Houston on October 20, 1947. The ceremony and open house attracted two hundred thousand people.[26]

Although the men in 8F obviously welcomed her participation in their deliberations, it wasn't Oveta's style to join them when they played cards or drank whiskey in the late afternoons, which undoubtedly was her colleagues' preference. She much preferred to play her role at lunch meetings with her peers in Houston's downtown clubs or in private rooms at expensive restaurants. Like Jesse Jones, who was still spending much of his time in Washington, Oveta did not have to be physically present in the 8F suite to be considered an integral part of the group.[27]

Journalist Theodore White, who later gained fame for his *Making of the President* book series, analyzed local power structures in Texas in the early 1950s for *Reporter* magazine. He noted the existence of autonomous "self-winding" cliques in the state's urban centers that he characterized as the "local aristocracy of enterprise and commercial achievement." He argued that these people ran the cities as if the cities were clubs in which they constituted the nominating committees and the electorate at large acted as "the herd." White labeled these leadership groups "local businessmen's machines." White's analysis aptly described Houston's 8F group, except for the fact that it included one woman.[28]

Contrary to widely prevalent myths, Houston's most powerful leaders during the post–World War II years were not oilmen. The members of the 8F crowd were entrepreneurs whose wealth came from traditional business enterprises—banking, insurance, publishing, construction, and real estate—that tended to be more stable and predictable than the oil industry. They all had direct or indirect business ties to the oil economy, which was the engine driving the city's boom, but there was no single stereotypical "wildcat" oilman among them. This was mainly because wildcatters by definition were major risk-takers not inclined to collaborate with others. Members of the 8F group and their close associates, generally (but quietly) looked down on Houston's immensely wealthy wildcatters, such as Hugh Roy Cullen, "Silver Dollar" Jim West, and Glenn McCarthy, as uncouth know-it-alls and loudmouths. Jesse Jones particularly disliked Hugh Roy Cullen, a Republican critic of Jones's role in FDR's administration who frequently opposed Jones on local civic issues, such as the need for city zoning. Nevertheless, a few of the 8F group, including Will Hobby, enjoyed socializing with Glenn McCarthy, the so-called King of the Wildcatters. McCarthy was a frequent participant in Jesse Jones's poker games. He attracted national attention in 1949 when he built and operated Houston's glamorous 1,100-room Shamrock Hotel. The hotel featured the Cork Club, a Manhattan-style cabaret where local gossip columnists occasionally spotted Will and Oveta seated with McCarthy.[29]

Despite the fact that Houston's 8F group subscribed to the tradition of rugged individualism and cultivated images of the "loner" and the Horatio Alger myth of the

*Will Hobby* (left) *and Jesse Jones* (middle) *visit with Glenn McCarthy*
(standing), *at his home in Houston, October 1946.*

self-made man, they constructed a tangled web of interlocking commercial arrangements, eagerly took advantage of opportunities to grab federal money for business projects, and consulted one another frequently about political, civic, and business matters.
Judge Elkins served as the crucial link in these interrelationships. He had legal and
financial connections with almost every member of the group, especially the Hobbys,
for whom Elkins had long served as a banker as well as their personal legal advisor. For

example, when Humble Oil offered an oil lease to the Hobbys in February 1945 on land Oveta inherited from her father, she sent the proposal and contract directly to Judge Jim Elkins for his guidance.[30]

Elkins's law firm represented the Browns' Texas Eastern Corporation, which owned and operated lucrative natural gas lines extending from Texas to the Northeast, and he was on Brown and Root's board of directors. Elkins was also a major stockholder and director of Gus Wortham's American General. The Browns and Wortham, in turn, served on the board of directors of Elkins's bank, and Wortham was a director of the Browns' Texas Eastern Corporation. Jesse Jones and Judge Elkins had each loaned $75,000 to Wortham to help found American General, which had become the largest insurance company in the South. And, of course, the Hobbys had a long and complicated but close relationship with Jesse Jones.[31]

One writer has referred to suite 8F as "one of the secret capitals of Texas." Watergate special prosecutor and prominent Houston attorney Leon Jaworski, who was close to this inner circle, later recalled, "There was a time when Jesse Jones . . . would meet with Gus Wortham, Herman Brown and maybe one or two others and pretty well determine what the course of events would be in Houston." Typically, the 8F group would form a general committee with perhaps from twelve to twenty other persons who had influence or special interest in a particular matter, such as a mayoral election. The composition of the general committee would differ slightly with each election, since some members of the group had no interest in school board elections, while others might not care about municipal or legislative elections. The general committee would form two subcommittees, one to nominate candidates and another to raise money. Each committee member was expected to do all he could to help elect the chosen candidates.[32]

An example of how the 8F group operated was their involvement in Houston's mayoral race in 1952 in which the incumbent, Oscar Holcombe, was running for reelection to his fourth consecutive two-year term. The 8F group decided it might be time to bring a new face to city hall. They met with the mayor and his main opponent, former county judge Roy Hofheinz, to determine if the latter merited their money and support. Attending the meeting were Will Hobby, the Brown brothers, Judge Elkins, Gus Wortham, and *Houston Chronicle* editor Emmet Walter, who was representing Jesse Jones. Speaking for the group, Herman Brown told Holcombe it would be best if he withdrew from the race. After questioning Hofheinz, they decided to endorse him over the other remaining candidates. Holcombe had already printed his campaign literature, but that did not matter. After the meeting he publicly announced his retirement. Hofheinz won the election against his main opponent, Louie Welch.[33]

The gubernatorial race in the Democratic primary in 1954 is another example of 8F political influence, but on this occasion Will took the lead. Allan Shivers, a friend of the Hobbys for many years, was completing his second term as governor and was seriously considering running for a third term, which was unprecedented in Texas, where no governor had served more than two terms. Shivers and his advisors were concerned that the 8F group, especially Will Hobby, might not be happy about his breaking the two-term tradition. It was well known that Will had always strongly favored maintaining the two-term tradition, which was among the reasons Will decided against running for reelection himself in 1920, even though technically he had only served one term of his own. When Shivers's concerns got through to the 8F group, Will offered to alleviate the governor's worries, and he did it in his own distinct manner. As he later told James Clark, the telephone conversation was brief: "Allan, this is Hobby. I hear you are going to run for a third term. I think it is a good idea." After Shivers thanked him, Hobby hung up. The endorsement had been delivered. Shivers, as expected, won reelection.[34]

During her tenure as director of the WAC, Oveta's portrait had graced the cover of *Time*; she had been profiled in dozens of other national news publications, many with photographs of her posing in uniform and "Hobby hat"; she had spoken on nationally broadcast radio programs; and she had been the focus of numerous newsreel stories screened in movie theaters throughout the country. In the years immediately following the end of World War II, Oveta continued to be a prominent and well-respected national figure. As a result, she was bombarded with requests to be the keynote speaker at a wide variety of events, including national conventions of professional and patriotic organizations. Because of her focus on the *Houston Post* and KPRC, she was unable to accept most of the invitations. She also continued to suffer from bouts of her thyroid problem that sapped her energy. In the summer of 1946 another flare-up forced her to decline an attractive invitation from the *Chicago Tribune* to speak in that city. The *Tribune* had asked for Jesse Jones's help in getting Oveta to accept their invitation, but Jones reported that "Governor" had informed him that Oveta "has not been particularly well and may not feel up to it."[35]

Oveta was able to take advantage of a few opportunities that she realized would either help maintain her status as a national figure, which contributed to the reputation of her newspaper, or relate to some special personal interest. For example, she was the featured speaker at the annual convention of the National Council of Jewish Women, which was held in Houston in March 1946. This meeting was important to Oveta because it gave her the opportunity to express publicly her fears about the aggressive intentions of the Soviet Union in China, Iran, and Eastern Europe, and it allowed her to declare her strong support of the newly established United Nations (UN). Her comments were published in newspapers across the country. Oveta's internationalist outlook underpinned her deep interest in the UN, which was demonstrated by pro-UN editorials in the *Post*, despite editorial editor Ed Kilman's dislike of the international body; Will, who had supported the League of Nations, was neutral (at best) about the UN. In June 1946 Oveta traveled to New York City to cover sessions of the UN held at its temporary site in Flushing Meadows while its members were drafting the Universal Declaration of Human Rights. The *Post* duly published her reports. In one of them, Oveta noted that observing the sessions was "something like watching a chess game between powerful antagonists."[36]

In April 1947 the American Society of Newspaper Editors elected Oveta to a three-year term on its board of directors. She was the first woman to be given that distinction and the only woman to serve on the board until the 1970s. The most influential media entrepreneurs and executives in the United States now recognized Oveta as a peer, and their major advertisers took notice. Pan American Airways (Pan Am) was among the latter. In early 1947, Pan Am announced its first commercial flight route circumventing the globe. The flights would be on the company's newly purchased fleet of Constellation aircraft. To publicize their new service, Pan Am decided that the first flight, which would be scheduled nine days prior to the beginning of regular service, should be filled with the publishers and editors of important news media companies, including Oveta Culp Hobby.[37]

Slated to embark on June 17 from New York City's LaGuardia Airport and to terminate back in New York on June 30, Pan Am's flight would be in the air a total of ninety-three hours, plus time for stopover tours and meetings in most of the cities the plane would visit. Oveta enthusiastically accepted Pan Am's invitation. Her internationalist views, which had been fostered in Estelle Sharp's salons and forums two decades earlier, had only deepened as a result of her service as director of the WAC and her expeditions to Europe and North Africa during the war. Under her guidance, the *Post* was publishing editorials and commentaries supporting America's active involvement in world affairs and criticizing the isolationist tendencies in the Republican Party represented by US senator Robert A. Taft of Ohio. She made a decision from the start that she would be a journalist on the trip and that she would question, listen, observe, and report what she had learned in a series of articles for the *Post*. The well-written and insightful series gave proof that she had, indeed, developed solid journalism skills.[38]

The ambitious itinerary was especially attractive to someone as curious about the world as Oveta. The Constellation airplane *America*, with a crew of ten, would lift off from New York City's LaGuardia Airport, with a refueling stop at Gander, Newfoundland, before landing in Ireland. From there, the itinerary included stops in London, Istanbul, Dhahran, Karachi, Kolkata, Bangkok, Manila, Shanghai, Tokyo, Guam, Wake Island, Honolulu, and San Francisco. The passenger list was another attractive feature for Oveta. Her companions included her good friends Gardner Cowles Jr., publisher of several newspapers and *Look* magazine; Roy Howard of the Scripps-Howard newspaper chain, owner of the *Houston Press*; and Helen Rogers Reid, president of the *New York Herald Tribune*. The list also included Frank Gannett, publisher of the influential Gannett newspaper chain; Marshall Field, publisher of the *Chicago Sun*; Erwin Canham, editor of the *Christian Science Monitor*; Maurice Moore, board chairman of Time Life; and editors and publishers from the *Cleveland Plain Dealer*, the *New Orleans Item*, the *Chicago Tribune*, the *Baltimore Sun*, and the *Nashville Banner*. The mayor of San Francisco, Roger Lapham, was also a passenger. To highlight the importance of the expedition for Pan Am, Juan Trippe, the charismatic founder and chairman of the company, accompanied the group. Trippe had an additional purpose for this special flight other than publicity. He was lobbying Congress for Pan Am to be designated the official American flag carrier for overseas travel, a plan opposed by Trans World Airlines (TWA) and American Airlines. He hoped this excursion would win him editorial support for his efforts.[39]

Pan Am went to great lengths to publicize the flight. The company sponsored a special broadcast over the CBS and NBC radio networks covering the departure, which featured famed announcer and commentator Lowell Thomas as master of ceremonies. After a buffet luncheon, Oveta joined her fellow passengers on the tarmac to hear speeches by the mayors of New York City and San Francisco about how commercial air travel would link their cities to the other leading cities of the postwar world. As an orchestra performed music associated with the countries included on the itinerary, Lowell Thomas introduced each individual passenger as he or she walked up the stairs and boarded the plane. Oveta wrote in her notebook that at two o'clock on the afternoon of June 17, "the great ship roared to life, lifted itself with great ease and pushed toward the far horizons."[40]

After brief refueling stops in Gander, Newfoundland, and Ireland, the aircraft flew to London, the first major destination on the *America*'s route. Oveta was curious to see if the city had changed much in the more than three years since her last visit when she was director of the WAC. One of the highlights of the stop was a meeting with Prime Minister Clement Attlee at 10 Downing Street, which included US ambassador Lewis Douglas. Oveta described Attlee as "cordial but cautious. He gives the impression of being very timorous and wary." Afterward, the Americans were hosted at dinner by newspaper baron Lord Beaverbrook and other London newspaper publishers. Oveta noted, "The food situation in England is still tight. We had three courses but no bread of any kind. One may either have a sweet or bread. That night we had a sweet." As a dedicated Anglophile, Oveta reported to her readers in the *Houston Post*, "It is well for us to remember as we consider Britain's economic and social ills that she was at war for six years. Offer her understanding and aid, because when the blue chips are down, England and the U.S. treasure essentially the same fundamental principles of government and stand side by side under the banner of human freedom."[41]

From London, *America* flew to Istanbul, Turkey, where Oveta and company spent a portion of the day touring the city's grand mosques. She was impressed with the city and with former premier Kemal Atatürk's modernization of Turkish society. "Turkey as a nation does not want Communism," she concluded. "Don't count her in the Russian sphere if the democracies stand together." Shortly after midnight, the passengers returned to the Constellation for the takeoff to their next destination, Dhahran, the American-constructed town in Saudi Arabia where the Arabian-American Oil Company (Aramco) had drilled its first successful oil well on the Arabian mainland and had located its field headquarters. American executives of Aramco met the airplane at the airport, which was built and operated by US Army Air Force personnel, and drove the party in a caravan of cars to company headquarters, where they provided them with a "bountiful" breakfast and a lecture about their operations. Company officials told the Pan Am passengers that Saudi oil production was "negligible" compared to production in the United

States but that its reserves were enormous and ready for full exploitation. They explained that the Saudi people were simple and unfriendly nomads, fiercely resistant to change, obsessed with their Muslim religion, and living in the most primitive of conditions. Aramco's operations impressed Oveta and her colleagues, who were delighted that the United States controlled the country's oil. She proudly noted, "The modern Aladdins [many of them Houstonians] are bringing 'black gold' out of the oil lakes beneath the sands." Oveta was "thrilled," she later wrote in one of her *Houston Post* articles, to see American "know-how operating in such a primitive country and serving as representatives of American standards of culture, sanitation and commercial relations."[42]

From Saudi Arabia *America* flew to India, with stops in Karachi and Kolkata. The impending independence of India and Pakistan from Britain on August 15 was the dominating topic during their visit. The day the flight landed in Karachi the city was declared the capital of the newly established nation of Pakistan. Oveta did not like what she saw in either city. "Much testimony has been given on the sub-standards of health, sanitation and nutrition in India," Oveta noted. "My stay was brief but overwhelming. The lack of mirth, the apparent hopeless resignation to poverty and degradation on many, many faces depresses one to the point of morbidity." She added, "The future of India as a self-governing country is not hopeless, but it is a far distant objective."[43]

On June 22, Oveta and her fellow passengers arrived in Bangkok, Thailand, direct from India. Oveta was shocked by the contrast with what they had seen in India. "We were not prepared for the incredibly beautiful temples and palaces in Bangkok," she later wrote. "Bangkok is a completely charming oasis in the East. It is clean, it is peaceful, and it is independent." Although the official name of the country had been changed from Siam to Thailand nearly a decade earlier, Oveta continued to use the old name. She concluded, "Siam falls into the category of countries I want to go back to."[44]

The Constellation *America* departed Bangkok at five o'clock in the afternoon for Manila, where it arrived at midnight at Nichols Field, a US Air Force base. Referring to the Philippines' former status as an American territory and as a major battlefield during the war, Oveta observed that after landing, the Pan Am group "had the feeling of being home again." That feeling of being "back home" quickly dissipated as they saw Manila in the daylight. She observed, "About 70 [percent] of the city is destroyed. The walled city is almost level. Little has been done to reconstruct the roads." Oveta and her companions met with American ambassador Nathaniel Davis, who warned that land mines left over from the war had been discovered at the end of the runway on which their Pan Am plane had landed. They could hear the mines being detonated as he gave them this news. They also met for more than two hours with President Manuel Roxas at Malacañang Palace. She noted that the Filipino president was "a very impressive person. He is able, factual and disarmingly frank." Roxas hosted a dinner for the group later that evening at the palace. Oveta was convinced after talking with Roxas that under his leadership the Philippines would be an "important clinic for the development of democratic ideals in the Orient." Roxas, however, would be dead from a heart attack only a year after this meeting.[45]

The next stop was Shanghai, the largest city in civil-war-torn China. Soon after the aircraft landed, the Pan Am passengers were divided into two groups to board a pair of DC-3s operated by the Chinese National Airlines, which then flew to Nanking, capital of the Republic of China, where they met with Generalissimo Chiang Kai-shek and his US-educated wife, Soong Mei-ling. Oveta had met Chiang's wife in 1943, when Oveta was directing the WAC and Madame Chiang was in Washington lobbying for congressional support for the Nationalist Chinese war effort against Japan. "The Generalissimo appears to be a modest person," Oveta reported. "He is extremely nervous [which is] reflected in both his speech and in the constant way he moves his foot and ankle." She noted that an official interpreter was present but that "Madame Chiang rephrased the questions to the Generalissimo and at times interrupted to further interpret for her husband." After meeting with Chiang Kai-shek and other members of his government, Oveta concluded that the war against Mao Zedong's Communist forces was "going very badly for the Nationalist government. Underneath the Oriental urbanity one could sense the tension and great uneasiness." It also seemed to her that "democracy in China is at this time stalemated. I had the feeling democracy has gone as far as it can without cutting loose from its feudalistic moorings." She was critical of the way the Nationalists were running the country. "Programs of reform are being blocked by the selfishness of a few members of the government leadership. Around this government there seems to be a vacuum. Almost separate and apart seem the people of China." Nevertheless, Oveta argued that the United States had to continue its support of the Nationalist regime. "Whichever way the decision goes [in the civil war]," she declared, "at this time it is extremely important for the U.S. to remain in contact with the government in opposition to Communism."[46]

Oveta and her traveling companions soon returned to Shanghai, where they spent the night before boarding the *America* and flying to Tokyo. The flight to Japan included a low pass over Nagasaki and then Hiroshima, "where vast areas of ruins were mute reminders of the atomic bomb," Oveta later wrote. "We shall not soon forget the emotions these pictures produced." The aircraft also made low passes over Tokyo before landing. Nearly two years after the war, the devastation remained widespread. Oveta later reported to her readers in Houston that "the destruction of Tokyo is about 70 percent. In one area alone, during one B-29 raid, 100,000 people died. Our people seem to make a distinction between the destruction of the atomic bomb and the destruction of these deadly effective raids of the B-29's." Oveta noted that the destruction caused by the atomic bombs "moved me no more than the devastation and destruction I saw in Tokyo. Modern warfare, with or without the atomic bomb, is destructive beyond one's capacity to understand without actually seeing the destruction and learning the number of casualties. Instead of discussing the ethics of the atomic bomb, we should be discussing the ethics of warfare itself."[47]

They landed in the Japanese capital at noon on June 26. With Japan still under US military occupation, the Pan Am passengers found themselves in a military environment as soon as they disembarked from the Constellation. To her delight, the first thing Oveta spotted as she walked down the stairs off the plane was a "smartly turned out WAC band" on the tarmac, which immediately struck up the national anthem. Lieutenant General Robert Eichelberger, commander of the Eighth Army, greeted the party on behalf of General Douglas MacArthur, the military governor of Japan. Army drivers took Oveta and her traveling companions to the Imperial Hotel, where they spent the night.

After lunch at the hotel, one of Oveta's former WAC colleagues, Lieutenant Colonel Mera Galloway, arranged for her and Helen Reid to meet with a group of sixty Japanese women, which included writers, educators, and labor union activists, as well as members of the Japanese legislative body, the Diet. Many of the women had been educated in American colleges. They discussed how their newly granted right to vote could be used to help address Japan's economic, social, and political problems. Oveta told them she had a personal connection to the issue of women's suffrage in the United States because her husband had signed the state law giving women the right to vote in primary elections when he was governor of Texas. That evening Oveta and a few other members of her group had dinner at the home of famed *Life* magazine photojournalist Carl Mydans and his wife, Shelley. Both had been in the Japanese prison camp Santo Tomas in the Philippines.

The next morning, three Japanese women reporters interviewed Oveta and Helen Reid for a Japanese movie house newsreel. They discussed the peace treaty at that time being negotiated between the Allies and Japan and the American attitude toward the Japanese. Later, Oveta went with her group to have lunch with General MacArthur and his wife, Jean, at the US embassy. Oveta admired the MacArthur art collection on display at the embassy, most of which they had collected since the end of the war. Jean MacArthur told the group how their silver collection had been saved when the Japanese occupied their quarters in Manila. It was stored in a chest, and one of the Filipino servants told the Japanese officers that it contained the ashes of General MacArthur's father. The chest remained unopened and the silver undiscovered. Oveta noted that the luncheon was "a simple but delightful affair." General MacArthur sat between Oveta and Helen Reid at table. Obviously aware that he was speaking to influential members of the American news media, MacArthur put on quite a performance. Oveta wrote that the general had "a great flair for the dramatic. The stage lost a great player when he was enrolled at West Point. Strategist, thespian, and statesman are combined in this man."

Oveta took careful notes throughout this performance. MacArthur answered questions about the food situation in Japan, and he gave them details such as the average amount of calories provided to the population and how much whale oil was available for fat. "Japan is now faced with a food crisis of the first magnitude," Oveta later reported. "General MacArthur told us that substantial food imports would be necessary until October. Unless these provisions are forthcoming, he believes five million people will starve." MacArthur also discussed the status of the peace treaty, the economic situation, reparations, and the purging of war criminals from the industrial leadership. Oveta was shocked when MacArthur, a conservative Republican, stated that he was controlling

Japan's foreign exchange rates for trade purposes, which she called "a first class example of a regimented economy." Her firm opposition to government interference in business, which was among the reasons she and Will had withdrawn their support from FDR, was made evident. Ironically, MacArthur, hardly a New Dealer, was imposing New Deal–style reforms on the Japanese because they worked, a fact that was lost on Oveta. "That thing called private enterprise must be a stranger [to MacArthur]. Sounds like the brilliant theories of some of the long-haired boys, doesn't it? Such a policy is bound to wreak such havoc that it will be changed shortly."[48]

When MacArthur asked Oveta what impressions the trip had made on her, she complained that every country wanted the United States to give them money to solve their postwar problems. She told MacArthur she was "extremely troubled. I did not believe dollars would solve some of the governmental problems we had encountered." The general agreed with Oveta, despite his free spending of dollars in Japan at a rate of $500 million a year (nearly $6 billion a year in 2018 dollars). "Dollars won't buy democracy," MacArthur declared. "Unless the people want democracy and we are willing to work to make it function, dollars are dross."[49]

Pan Am's Constellation took off from Atsugi air base a few minutes before midnight on June 27, bound for distant Honolulu. Despite her concerns about MacArthur's adoption of New Deal–type policies in Japan, Oveta left the country feeling that it was "our best postwar occupation" and that she wished Germany "had fared as well." After refueling stops on the islands of Guam, Wake, and finally Midway, where the travelers observed the large flocks of gooney birds and enjoyed breakfast in the officers' dining room at the naval station, *America* landed in Honolulu midafternoon on Saturday, June 29. As the plane approached the airport, it made a slow and low pass over Pearl Harbor and Hickam Airfield, giving Oveta and the other passengers clear views of the area. Oveta was surprised to see that the Pearl Harbor naval base was located adjacent to the air base. "The proximity of [Hickam] to the harbor," she noted, "is the answer to 'Why couldn't the planes get off the ground?'" The airfield had been hit at the same time Pearl Harbor was attacked.[50]

The stop in Hawaii lasted only ten hours. A *Honolulu Star-Bulletin* story about their visit featured a large photograph of the group wearing leis around their necks, holding pineapples and sticks of sugarcane, and posing in the airport terminal with a welcome party of local female hula dancers dressed in grass skirts. After clearing customs, Oveta and other members of the group spent a half hour being interviewed by the reporters from local radio stations and newspapers who had been gathered by Pan Am's local publicist. From the airport the visitors were driven to the Royal Hawaiian Hotel to attend a reception hosted by Hawaii's acting governor Oren E. Long, followed by dinner with the public relations director of the Hawaiian Sugar Planters Association and the director of the territory's Economic Foundation. By this point, Pan Am's special passengers were exhausted and eager to get back to the US mainland. Armed with stacks of pamphlets and information sheets about Hawaii, they returned to their aircraft at midnight and were in the air thirty minutes later. Having seen or heard little, Oveta's reporting in the *Houston Post* about this stop on their journey was based almost entirely on the literature she brought back with her, which focused on the efforts of Hawaii to become a state (she favored statehood), with additional comments on the condition of the island's pineapple and sugar industries.[51]

The *America* landed in San Francisco shortly after noon on June 29, ten and a half hours after departing Honolulu. They were met by a crowd of Pan Am employees, reporters, and city officials, the latter of whom were also welcoming back San Francisco mayor Roger Lapham. Oveta participated in a press conference in the airport terminal, where reporters quizzed her and other members of the party about conditions in the cities they had visited. She restricted her observations to the situation in China, declaring that it was clear to her it was "facing an extremely grave situation" because of the civil war. But she refused to say what Chiang Kai-shek had discussed with them because, she said, "he spoke entirely off the record." Oveta and her companions departed San Francisco at midnight and arrived in Chicago midmorning, where they remained for only two hours. Finally, on June 30, 1947, Pan Am's around-the-world expedition returned to New York City's LaGuardia Airport thirteen days after it had begun.[52]

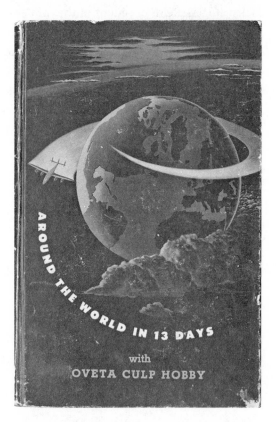

*Cover of Oveta Culp Hobby's privately published account of her thirteen-day trip around the world in 1947.*

When Oveta returned to Houston, she gathered her notes and wrote a series of articles about the trip, which included her observations about conditions in each city and country she visited. Published in the *Post*, the series was well received. Her friends and associates around the country asked for copies. The requests were numerous enough to persuade Oveta to privately publish the series in a book: *Around the World in 13 Days*. Frank Gannett also published his own version of the experience, titling his book *Winging 'Round the World*. Although Oveta's visit to each location was much too brief to give her in-depth insights, the experience nevertheless was a valuable one that exposed her to countries and regions such as Turkey, Saudi Arabia, and the subcontinent of India that in those days were far off the path of normal tourist traffic but would become increasingly important to the United States. The expedition had given her the opportunity to have face-to-face discussions with significant personalities, such as Clement Attlee, Manuel Roxas, Chiang Kai-shek and his influential wife, and Douglas MacArthur. These were people whom it would have been difficult for her to meet and interview under most circumstances.

The experience also gave Oveta the opportunity to make valuable new connections in the news-publishing world as well as strengthen old ones. In the latter category was Helen Rogers Reid, president of the influential *New York Herald Tribune*. Reid was a moderate Republican and a friend of Governor Thomas Dewey who would join forces with Oveta in 1952 in the effort to secure the Republican presidential nomination for Dwight Eisenhower. Among Oveta's new friends was the *Christian Science Monitor* editor Erwin Canham, who would play a role in Oveta's appointment as an alternate delegate on the US delegation to a UN conference held in Geneva the following year. Altogether, Oveta's trip "around the world in 13 days" proved to be well worth her time and energy.[53]

# CHAPTER 30

# KPRC-TV

T he *Houston Post* and KPRC Radio reaped increasingly large profits during the late 1940s and early 1950s, partly due to the successful managerial changes Will and Oveta had made soon after the end of the war. On the family front, the children were busy on their own. Bill lived in Washington, DC, where he was a student at St. Albans until he graduated in 1949 and returned to Houston to enter the Rice Institute. Jessica was in private school in Houston and increasingly involved in her passion for horse shows and horse-riding competition. During these years, Will continued to contend with illnesses that occasionally put him in the hospital or confined him to his bed at home. Although Will's health was infirm, he still managed to remain active as Houston's unofficial toastmaster and after-dinner speaker, not only because of his place in the city's power structure but also because of his sharp wit and folksy storytelling ability that drew from a deep store of East Texas folklore.[1]

One of Will's favorite dinner stories in these years was a yarn he had picked up as a young man from an old publisher friend from Galveston, who told him that when he was a kid reporter he received word that Sam Houston was dying at his home in Huntsville. Will's old friend had written stories denouncing Sam Houston for his opposition to Texas seceding from the Union, so he was leery of visiting the famed hero of the Texas Revolution. Nevertheless, he knew the former governor's death would be a major story he could ill afford to miss. So the young reporter and another journalist who had also criticized Sam Houston traveled to Huntsville together for mutual protection. As they sat on deathwatch in the front yard of Houston's home, they were told that the old warrior wished to see them. Will's friend assumed that Houston wanted to reconcile with his two former critics. When they entered the bedroom, Houston motioned them to come to his bed. He asked the reporters to stand on opposite sides of his bed because, Houston said, "I've always wanted to die like Christ—between two thieves."[2]

During these years, when Houston's construction boom was in overdrive and attracting national attention, Will presided over the official ground breakings for several local land-mark buildings and structures, including the $5 million Ezekiel Cullen Building at the University of Houston and the eighteen-story Prudential Insurance Company Building across the street from the Texas Medical Center. At the luncheon for the dedication of the Prudential Building, where Will served as master of ceremonies, he noted, "Houston has reached the point where a ground-breaking has to be mighty unusual to get any attention at all—all we ask any more is, who is digging the hole?" Will also kept busy as a speaker introducing honorees at award dinners and at special events celebrating important visitors who came to Houston. Will especially enjoyed presiding at the annual April 21 celebration of Sam Houston's victory over Santa Anna and his army in 1836 at the Battle of San Jacinto. In 1948 Will was a notable participant in the celebration when it featured the permanent docking of the recently decommissioned battleship *Texas* on a newly dredged portion of the Houston Ship Channel adjacent to the San Jacinto battle-ground. Under Will's direction, the *Houston Post* and KPRC Radio had been among the businesses that led the fundraising effort to bring the battleship to Houston to serve as a museum and as a memorial to Texas war veterans.[3]

Will's public activities also included his favorite civic causes, especially the expansion and improvement of Houston's road and highway system, which included serving as chairman of the Houston Chamber of Commerce's Highway Committee. Because of his many years as an advocate for a modern freeway between Houston and Galveston, he was especially proud in August 1952 to speak at the dedication ceremony for the Gulf Freeway, the new access-controlled main highway between the two cities. He was also called on to turn the first shovel of dirt for the symbolic start of the construction of the four-thousand-foot-long Baytown–La Porte Tunnel under the Houston Ship Channel. The tunnel, which in the 1980s was replaced by a bridge, was another "good roads" project Will had long called for in the editorial pages of the *Post*, just as he had boosted the project to bring deep water to Beaumont when he owned the *Enterprise*.[4]

Will and Oveta also took their initial steps into the world of philanthropy by activating the Houston Post Foundation, the family's charitable enterprise they had founded in 1940. The Hobbys made their first foundation grant in January 1946 to the Houston Community Chest, which for many years to come was the recipient of the foundation's largest annual donation. In 1947 they gave their philanthropy a new name: the Hobby Foundation. The foundation would eventually become a significant source of funding for cultural and educational causes in Houston, with Rice University; the Museum of Fine Arts, Houston; and the Houston Symphony being among its main beneficiaries.[5]

While Will was busy with his activities in Houston, Oveta remained in demand on the national stage, accepting honors and receiving invitations to speak at conventions or to serve as a trustee, a board member, or an officer in various organizations. The University of Missouri gave Oveta its Honor Award for distinguished service to journal-ism, and Bard College presented her with an honorary degree. The members of the Southern Newspaper Publishers Association honored Oveta by electing her president of the association. It was the first time a national newspaper group had elected a woman president.[6]

Although Oveta declined most of the invitations to serve as an officer or board member for various organizations, a few were important to her, and she happily accepted them. Among those was an invitation from fellow newspaper publisher Helen Reid to serve on the board of directors of the recently established Reid Foundation in New York, which provided funds for journalism students to study abroad. Oveta agreed as well to serve on the national council of the Atlantic Union Committee, which had been organized to support the idea of an "Atlantic union" between the United States, Canada, and the nations of Western Europe. Oveta also accepted an invitation from her esteemed friend George C. Marshall to serve on the advisory committee for his campaign to raise $67 million for the American Red Cross.[7]

In early 1948 Oveta received an invitation that she didn't hesitate to accept. President Truman asked her to serve as a first alternate delegate on the official contingent representing the United States at the UN Conference on Freedom of Information in Geneva, Switzerland. Truman made his request on the recommendation of William Benton, the assistant secretary of state for public affairs. Benton, the publisher of the *Encyclopedia Britannica* and a significant figure in the advertising industry, knew Oveta through their mutual involvement in national advertising associations. Benton would soon leave his position in the State Department to run for the US Senate in Connecticut. Before he returned to private life, he agreed to President Truman's request that he serve as the chairman of the US delegation to the UN conference. *Christian Science Monitor* editor Erwin Canham, one of Oveta's fellow travelers on the Pan Am trip around the world, was another member of the ten-person delegation. Canham also recommended Oveta's appointment to Truman.[8]

On March 12, 1948, Oveta, accompanied by *Houston Post* reporter and friend Marguerite Johnston, sailed on the *Queen Elizabeth* to the United Kingdom. She and Johnston then flew to Geneva, arriving a few days before the conference convened on March 23, 1948. Because she was the primary alternate delegate, Oveta planned to attend the opening and every working session that followed in case she had to replace one of the regular delegates. In that event, she wanted to fill the vacancy as a fully informed member. As it developed, she replaced her friend Erwin Canham, who was called back to the United States in the final days of the conference. The UN conference was the first attempt on the international level to formulate a basic set of principles governing the right to collect, disseminate, and publish news. Oveta and her colleagues in the delegation, most of whom were in the news industry, were pessimistic about accomplishing much, given the rapidly deteriorating relationship between the Soviet Union and the United States. Before he departed for Switzerland, Chairman Benton sent a message to Truman telling him that although he would do his best, he agreed with the president's warning that he "should not expect much from this forthcoming Geneva Conference." Erwin Canham later wrote that the American delegation went to the conference in Geneva "with meager expectations" because of obstruction by the Soviet delegation. This concern was deepened by the Communist coup d'état in Czechoslovakia that occurred a few weeks before the conference convened. The Communist Czechoslovakian government moved quickly to shut down the independent press.[9]

The American strategy in Geneva was to orient the conference to the concept of "freedom of information" instead of "obligations of the press," which the Americans knew would be interpreted and implemented as legal controls. At the beginning of the conference the American delegation introduced a draft resolution on the general principles of freedom of information. They also submitted a multipart proposal that called for an international convention to persuade as many nations as possible to sign a charter guaranteeing journalists greater access to news events and greater freedom in news transmission. The American delegation proposed nonrestrictive remedies (as opposed to legal controls) for abuses committed by the press, based primarily on the moral responsibility of information agencies. The plan provided for the right of "official correction," whereby a government could submit its refutation of damaging press reports to the secretary-general of the UN. The United States, however, was unwilling to grant the UN wide authority for investigatory or coercive powers. During the debates about the American proposals, Oveta got a firsthand preview of the coming Cold War as the Soviet delegation heatedly opposed most of the resolutions, offering amendments that would cripple freedom of expression. Nevertheless, much to the surprise of the delegation, all of the American proposals were adopted in one form or another, some substantially intact, others in varying degrees of modification. Canham later characterized the results as "excellent."[10]

Although the totalitarian regimes that were among the signatories would ultimately ignore the agreements reached in Geneva, the conference did bolster the cause of press freedom in the democracies, as well as in some nations where that freedom existed precariously. Oveta, who was pleased with the results, found the experience valuable because it was the first time she had been immersed in the intricacies and back and forth of deliberations at the international level. The conference also solidified her long-held internationalist outlook and support for the United Nations. She and Johnston remained in Geneva the entire month the conference was in session. Soon after adjournment on April 21, they made their way to England and boarded the historic luxury Cunard liner the *Queen Mary* bound for New York. It was during this lengthy stay and journey back home that Oveta and Johnston bonded and established a close relationship that lasted for the remainder of Oveta's life.

A few weeks after her return to the United States, Oveta gave a speech at the annual meeting of the Advertising Federation of America in Cincinnati about her experience at the conference. She pointed out that because the United States and most of the other delegations believed in the principle of freedom of information as a "basic human right—man's right to know . . . about his government and its dealings with other nations," the conference was able to pass resolutions that reaffirmed the critical importance of a free and independent press to a democracy. She also stressed that freedom of information was critical to the US effort to spread positive information around the world about itself to counter Communist propaganda. "The rest of the world needs to know about America," she declared. "If the world is to know the facts, we must give them the facts." Oveta later published her entire speech in the *Houston Post*.[11]

When Oveta returned to Houston, she received an invitation to contribute to another public policy project. This one was from a former president, Herbert Hoover, who sent her a telegram asking if she would, as "one of the leaders in the last war," serve as a consultant for the Commission on the Organization of the Executive Branch. Because Hoover was serving as chairman and playing an active and highly visible role in its deliberations, the news media referred to it as the Hoover Commission. The Republican-controlled Eightieth Congress created the twelve-member commission in mid-1947, ostensibly to make the federal government more efficient by eliminating duplicate and obsolete agencies. But in reality, congressional Republicans, confident that Truman would lose the presidential election in November 1948 to Thomas Dewey, intended to use the commission's report as a legislative blueprint for dismantling Roosevelt's New Deal after the GOP regained the White House. The enabling legislation granted full authority to the commission to recommend the elimination of government activities. As a historian of the Hoover Commission later noted, Hoover's staff and consultant positions were largely filled by political conservatives, "many of whom wanted to chop away at past liberal gains in public power, to turn many Government business activities over to private enterprise, to reorient administrative law procedures in a pro-business direction, and to oppose Truman's national health insurance program."[12]

Oveta and Will had been early supporters of the Hoover Commission's stated as well as unstated goals, and they made their endorsement clear in *Post* editorials. Soon after Congress authorized the commission, Oveta delivered a speech at Columbia University's American Press Institute praising the commission's plan to eliminate waste in federal programs. Hoover, who played a direct role in the selection of appointees, undoubtedly knew of Oveta's views in favor of reducing the size and reach of the federal government. In this era, when news clipping services were used widely, Hoover probably knew about the *Houston Post* editorials praising his work. As a resident of Manhattan, it is also likely he knew about Oveta's speech at Columbia University endorsing the commission and his leadership. In his telegram, Hoover assured Oveta it would be "a great service to the country and a great satisfaction to the Commission if you would consent to serve in this capacity. I [do] not anticipate that it would require a great deal of your time." Oveta's response to Hoover's invitation was concise and direct: "I am glad to serve."[13]

Hoover's initial request was for Oveta to serve as an outside consultant to evaluate a report on the effect and progress of the consolidation of the armed forces, but Hoover soon broadened her role with an appointment to the commission's advisory panel. Oveta took her role seriously and quickly immersed herself in the commission's work. She spent much of the summer and early fall of 1948 in Washington doing commission business.

Later in the fall, however, she took a break to work on Thomas Dewey's presidential campaign. Harry Truman's upset victory over Dewey in November, however, stunned Hoover and the Republican congressional delegation and upended their plan to use the Hoover Commission to dismantle FDR's New Deal agencies and programs.[14]

After Truman's surprise victory, which included Democratic control of Congress, Hoover revealed his pragmatic side. He altered the commission's political goals by agreeing to produce a report more closely aligned with the president's focus on government reorganization for greater efficiency instead of on the Republican anti–New Deal agenda. A week after the election, Hoover held a press conference in which he announced that the job of the commission was "to make every Government activity that now exists work efficiently. It is not our function to say whether it should exist or not, but it is our function to see if we cannot make it work better."[15]

The Hoover Commission submitted its recommendations to Congress in a series of reports beginning in February and ending in May 1949. According to a history of the commission, the recommendations "provoked spectacular public and congressional acclaim, breaking the impasse between Truman and Congress over reorganization." Oveta accepted the shift in goals. She served on the citizens' committee that was organized to win public support for the adoption of the commission's final proposals. To promote the commission's recommendations in Houston, Oveta organized a committee of prominent local citizens that included Hugh Roy Cullen, Jesse Jones, Will Clayton, and famed surgeon Dr. Michael DeBakey. She also directed *Post* editorial writer Hubert Mewhinney to write a series of articles summarizing and explaining the Hoover Commission report favorably. Using her contacts with leading publishers in the newspaper industry, Oveta persuaded seventeen other newspapers around the country to reprint Mewhinney's articles. She also published the series in a pamphlet that the *Post* distributed throughout Texas. In April 1949, the *Post* sponsored a contest for high school and college students in Houston and the surrounding area that awarded federal savings bonds to the students who wrote the best letters to members of Congress about the need to adopt the Hoover Commission's recommendations. The *Post* awarded the savings bonds to the contest winners at a luncheon sponsored by the League of Women Voters. When a newspaper trade magazine writer asked Oveta why the *Houston Post* was taking such an active role in touting the Hoover Commission, Oveta replied that not only was the commission's work "news worthy," the newspaper also had an obligation to educate its readers about the commission's recommendations in support of good government.[16]

On June 16, 1949, Congress passed legislation authorizing the implementation of six of the Hoover Commission's major recommendations, including the reorganization of the Departments of State and Labor and the Office of the President. The legislation also created the General Services Administration. Thus, with Hoover's support, Truman pushed through Congress the most extensive reorganization program in US history. As William Pemberton has noted, Truman achieved more than the streamlining of the executive branch: "He had carefully and successfully protected the New Deal's

*Pencil sketch of Oveta Culp Hobby, late 1940s.*

reform programs from postwar conservative onslaughts, one of which had been the Hoover Commission."[17]

Several other commission recommendations, including one to consolidate a hodge-podge of federal education, health, and social welfare agencies into one major department, failed to pass. In December 1949, Oveta attended the Hoover Commission's "Reorganization Conference" at the Shoreham Hotel in Washington to bring public attention to the failed recommendations. In what by now was a common occurrence for her, Oveta's presence at the conference garnered considerable news media attention. The *New York Times* printed a large photograph of Oveta with two other conference leaders standing by a large fake cracker barrel labeled "Hoover Report." After Hoover gave the keynote address, Oveta was among the speakers chosen to make follow-up speeches. She urged America's "women homemakers" to organize in their local communities to promote the passage of the remaining recommendations.

The part of Oveta's speech that attracted the most attention from news media was subtitled "The Private Life of a Can of Beans." As she held a can of beans in her hand, Oveta pointed out that the beans were an example of how entangled homemakers were in the various activities and regulations of the federal government. She declared that the average housewife probably believed that the only direct contact she had with the federal government was the Postal Service. That was an illusion, Oveta stated, pointing out that it was likely that every housewife had at least one can of beans in her pantry. She then explained that the particular can of beans in her hand was a common but well-known national brand that was heavily advertised. The Federal Trade Commission regulated that advertising. The can itself was made of steel, and the production of that steel was subject to federal labor regulations. The manufacturer shipped the beans by rail, which fell under Interstate Commerce Commission regulations. It was likely that federal agencies had loaned money to the farmers who grew the beans, had guaranteed a minimum price for the beans, and had provided the farmer advice about the most productive way to raise the beans. The beans might also have been raised on land irrigated by water from a federal dam project reservoir, which might have brought the bean farmer into contact with the Army Corps of Engineers, the Federal Power Commission, and the Bureau of Reclamation. The American housewife's relationship to the federal government, Oveta declared, "is as direct and immediate as a mustard plaster."

Oveta charged that the increasingly complex federal bureaucracy, as demonstrated by her example of a can of beans, had led to "chaos and waste" and "an over-planned economy, an over-governed nation, and an over-spent budget." The federal government, she added, was "a little bit like a Humpty-Dumpty who has grown so corpulent and ungainly that he has lost his original agility. It is important that we reduce Humpty-Dumpty and put him back into efficient trim before he runs any danger of falling." Congressional adoption of all of the Hoover Commission's recommendations to reduce the size of the federal government, Oveta argued, would be a major step forward in the effort to bring order to chaos and an end to waste. The statement about "an over-planned economy, an over-governed nation, and an over-spent budget" became one of her favorites, and she used it in numerous speeches afterward.[18]

Throughout 1950 Oveta continued to speak publicly in support of the commission. She spoke at the annual convention of the American Newspaper Publishers Association in New York in April, where she claimed government waste was growing "infinitely worse" with each passing year and called for the elimination of unnecessary government departments. She argued that making government smaller could allow a lower income tax rate, which was a necessity "if venture capital is to be free to provide an expanding economy in the United States." She asked her fellow newspaper publishers to join her in a "crusade" on behalf of the commission's recommendations.[19]

Despite these efforts, the campaign to implement all of the Hoover Commission's recommendations eventually failed. After Dwight Eisenhower became president in January 1953, he created a second Hoover Commission, but Congress rejected its proposals. Nevertheless, Eisenhower would eventually succeed in implementing one of the Hoover Commission's recommendations: the creation of the Department of Health, Education, and Welfare.

While Oveta was working with the Hoover Commission and tending to her other projects, she also helped guide the writing of the official history of the Women's Army Corps. Under the supervision of Major General Orlando Ward, the chief of military history, the army undertook a massive effort to document every aspect of the army's role in World War II. The project would eventually produce seventy-eight volumes under the overall title *The United States Army in World War II: Special Studies*. General Ward assigned the job of researching and writing the history of the WAC to thirty-three-year-old Mattie Treadwell, a native Texan who had joined the Women's Army Auxiliary Corps in 1942 and had attended the first officer-training school at Fort Des Moines. She had served on Oveta's personal staff, and then she later became Betty Bandel's assistant in the WAC's air corps division. Treadwell was still an officer in the WAC when she began her research in late 1945. It would take nearly seven years to complete. Although she left the army in November 1947 with the rank of lieutenant colonel, Treadwell continued her project as a federal civil service staff member and as an officer in the army reserve.[20]

*The Women's Army Corps*, like every other volume in the series, was an in-depth study, dense with factual information about events, decisions, personnel, and any other topic related to the subject. Treadwell received significant help from Betty Bandel and Helen Woods as well as Jessie Rice, but Oveta also served as Treadwell's silent and unofficial advisor from the beginning of the project. As the first director of the women's corps, Oveta's input was obviously necessary and critical to the accuracy and scope of the book, but she didn't want the public to know how deeply she influenced the historical narrative as well as Treadwell's interpretations of decisions and events in which Oveta was directly involved. She feared that public knowledge of her involvement in Treadwell's work would cause critics to question the book's objectivity about her role as director. Treadwell assured Oveta that she would not be credited with officially approving the contents of the history, nor would it be suggested that it represented her opinions.[21]

In June 1948, after nearly three years of deep research in the army's voluminous official records, Treadwell sent copies of early drafts of her manuscript to Oveta for review. Oveta read them closely, suggesting—and getting Treadwell to make—extensive revisions and corrections. Treadwell also conducted an oral history interview with Oveta in August 1948 in Houston. After the interview, Treadwell wrote Oveta. "It was wonderful to see you," she stated. "The history and I have taken a new lease on life." It took

Treadwell longer than she had hoped to send the last half of the manuscript to Oveta. "I have been disappointed in my attempt to get the entire manuscript to you," Treadwell wrote, explaining that her writing, typing, and proofing had been "exasperatingly slow." She sent five chapters to Oveta in November 1950, but the final six chapters remained unfinished for several months. Nevertheless, Treadwell hoped Oveta would review the latest chapters. After Oveta reviewed the drafts, she assured Treadwell that she "had done a thorough and highly readable job, and I am glad that the history of our WAAC should have been in such capable and sympathetic hands." Treadwell also sent portions of the manuscript in draft form to General George Marshall for his comments. Marshall was surprised by the sections that detailed the headaches the army bureaucracy had given Oveta, particularly in the areas of supply and recruitment. He wrote her to ask if she had actually encountered those problems. Oveta's reply to her good friend, the former army chief of staff, was, "No, more."[22]

Treadwell finished the last draft of her manuscript in March 1952, but it took the army two years to publish the 841-page book. The first page of *The Women's Army Corps* featured a formal photographic portrait of Oveta Culp Hobby sitting at her desk and dressed in her WAC uniform. In her preface, Treadwell explained that "Col. Oveta Culp Hobby has not only commented upon the manuscript, but has answered specific questions and has given me generously of her time in discussing puzzling references." But as promised, she neglected to state that Oveta had also revised some of the text. Well received by reviewers when published, Treadwell's work is the indispensable source for all other studies related to the story of the WAC as an organization and Oveta Culp Hobby and all of the women pioneers who served in the army in World War II.[23]

While attending the annual meeting of NBC radio affiliates in Atlantic City in the fall of 1947, KPRC general manager Jack Harris heard David Sarnoff, founder of the National Broadcasting Corporation (NBC) and head of the Radio Corporation of America (RCA), speak about how the relatively new medium of television was certain to become more important than either radio or newspapers. Although the first electronic television had been invented in 1927 by Philo Taylor Farnsworth and a few broadcast stations were established in the late 1920s and early 1930s, it wasn't until 1938 that the first television sets were commercially produced. The outbreak of World War II, however, put further development and expansion of the television industry in limbo. Television remained out of the view of the vast majority of Americans until the late 1940s, when first NBC and then Dumont, CBS, and ABC established television networks and television sets became widely available at prices the middle class could afford. Sarnoff, one of the most influential and powerful media executives in the United States, advised his audience that radio station owners, particularly those who also owned newspapers, would be wise to consider filing a television station license application with the Federal Communications Commission (FCC) and to add a television station to their media holdings. Of course, Sarnoff's goal was to increase the number of television stations in the country, which not only would expand NBC's new television network and increase revenue from commercials but also would boost the sales of RCA's television sets. Sarnoff's presentation impressed Harris. After he returned to Houston, Harris told the Hobbys about Sarnoff's speech and recommended they give serious thought to entering the television business.[24]

Will, who had worked with Ross Sterling to establish KPRC Radio in the early days of commercial radio, was not averse to business opportunities in new communications media. He expressed an immediate interest in Harris's recommendation. Oveta was interested as well, but she was shocked by his estimate that it could cost as much as $1 million to build a broadcast station from scratch and fill it with professional staff. Aware that she and Will would need bank financing for such an enterprise, she had doubts that their bankers would be interested in taking a risk with such a new industry that some critics had dismissed as a passing fad. As Oveta admitted years later, "Back in those days TV was nothing. There were very few stations in the country."[25]

Harris deepened Oveta's concern when he estimated that the station might operate at a loss for at least the first two or three years. The debt payments during that period would have to come from profits generated by the *Post* and KPRC Radio. He could not say how large the initial losses would be and how long it would take for the station to break even, not to mention turn a profit. There were a number of uncertainties about the immediate future of television, but Harris was utterly convinced that it was going to be huge in the long run and that it was a gamble they should take. Will and Oveta had enormous respect for the man they continued to call "Colonel" Harris, but while they were considering his proposal they also sought advice from other sources. Lyndon Johnson told Oveta that it might take a couple of years before they made any money, but he believed television was soon going to be popular and thus ultimately profitable. His wife, Lady Bird, had already decided to seek a license for a television station in Austin. LBJ's opinion, along with that of Jack Harris and other people the Hobbys respected, convinced the Hobbys, despite Oveta's anxiety about the expense, to file an application for a television broadcast license with the FCC.[26]

When Will and Oveta made their decision, Jack Harris warned that it was possible their application might be delayed or even denied because the FCC had shown a bias in favor of applicants who did not own a newspaper in the same television market. It was known that former Harris County judge Roy Hofheinz and wildcat oilman Glenn McCarthy were submitting their own separate applications, and since neither owned a newspaper, the FCC might prefer their requests over the Hobbys'. Oveta and Will also knew that Jesse Jones was giving serious consideration to applying for a license, although his ownership of the *Houston Chronicle* might also put his application at a disadvantage with the FCC. Their knowledge that Jones might apply for a license also encouraged the Hobbys to submit their application as quickly as possible.[27]

The Hobbys' application to the FCC soon stalled, but not for the reason Harris had feared. On September 30, 1948, while the Hobbys' application was pending, the FCC issued a freeze on issuing new licenses. The commission had already approved one hundred licenses, but its overwhelmed staff was struggling to process an additional seven hundred applications, with many more anticipated. "The FCC put a freeze on [new stations] because they wished to restudy the whole spectrum," Oveta recalled. "We were caught in the freeze as everyone was." The commission also was having difficulty resolving several technical and political problems related to the new broadcast medium. Those problems included designating a standard for color television; reserving channel space for educational, noncommercial stations; reducing interference between channels; opening additional spectrum space; and ensuring that licenses were being distributed evenly across the nation. The commission thought it could end the freeze after six months, but the problems turned out to be more difficult to solve than expected. The outbreak of the Korean War also interfered with the FCC's timeline by taking resources away from the manufacture of television broadcast equipment and home receivers, drastically cutting the supply. As a result, the freeze lasted four years instead of a few months and was not lifted until April 1952.[28]

Early in 1950, while the Hobbys waited on news about their license application, Oveta received a phone call from Houston businessman W. Albert Lee, who explained that he had a business deal in which he thought the Hobbys might have an interest. Oveta knew Lee slightly. He owned nine moderately priced hotels in downtown Houston, and he had been one of the founders of the popular Houston Fat Stock Show. She also knew that Lee owned radio station KLEE, which went on the air in 1947. Soon after KLEE's first broadcast, Lee had applied to the FCC for a television license, which the commission approved three months before the freeze. KLEE-TV went on the air on January 1, 1949, making it the first television station in Houston and only the second in Texas.[29]

With a limited broadcast range and not enough television sets in Houston to attract many advertisers, KLEE-TV soon hemorrhaged money, pushing Lee ever deeper into debt. Aware that the Hobbys' application for a television license had been trapped in the FCC freeze, Lee thought they might be interested in buying a percentage of his television station, which would help him get out from under his debt. "Mr. Lee came to see me and wanted to know if I would be interested in buying half of his [television] station," Oveta later recalled. "We talked a long time. He was losing money and wanted some help really." Oveta told Lee that his offer was interesting but she needed to discuss it with Will and Jack Harris.[30]

Harris warned Will and Oveta about the financial risk, noting that Lee "was losing his shirt . . . about $30,000 a month." The Hobbys, however, were aware of the financial risk when they made their original decision to apply for a license, so they were prepared for operational losses in the short term. Lee's offer presented Will and Oveta with an opportunity to enter the television business without having to wait for the FCC to reopen the licensing system and for less money than it would take to build a new television station. They also hoped that despite their ownership of a newspaper operating in the same market as KLEE-TV, the FCC would view their participation more favorably if they owned only half of the station. They readily accepted Lee's offer to purchase 50 percent of KLEE-TV.[31]

When Albert Lee asked the FCC for approval to split ownership of his television license with Will and Oveta, the FCC rejected the request, not because the Hobbys owned a newspaper but on the grounds that there had to be one owner with at least a 51 percent stake in the license. The agreement between Lee and the Hobbys gave two separate legal entities equal control of KLEE-TV, which to the FCC meant no one was in control. Oveta later recalled that when the commission issued the ruling, she "just dropped" out of the deal. She did not want to go into debt to purchase less than 50 percent of the television station and have no legal control over the budget. "I was terrified of the financial obligation," she later recalled. "The price tag on it, I thought, was enormous. This had to be borrowed capital."[32]

Jack Harris, however, continued to be interested in making a deal with Lee. Jack McGrew, who was Harris's administrative deputy at KPRC Radio, later recalled that he and Harris decided to monitor KLEE's broadcasts to see "what Lee was doing." They purchased two Zenith television receivers. Jack Harris took one home, and Harvey Wheeler, KPRC Radio's chief engineer, took the other set to his house. "The theory," McGrew said, "was that Jack could study the station's operating and programming policies, while Harvey studied its engineering problems and the attempted solutions." After a few weeks McGrew moved Wheeler's receiver over to his home. McGrew was impressed when he saw the neighborhood children flock to his living room to watch the television with his two daughters, convincing him of television's potential to attract youthful viewers.[33]

About this time," McGrew remembered, "[Bill Hobby] became ill and had to be confined to bed for several weeks. Governor asked if he could borrow [one of the televisions] and put it in [Bill's] bedroom so that he might have something to do besides read." Will was soon spending more time watching KLEE-TV's broadcasts than was his son. Impressed with what he was seeing in these early telecasts and still interested in getting into the television business, Will called Jack Harris and asked if it might be time to go back to Albert Lee to see if he would sell all of his ownership in the station. Harris had also continued to monitor KLEE's broadcast, and he was confident that he and his management team could improve programming and make the station profitable. Wheeler told him that Lee's engineers were having some success in their effort to improve broadcast quality. The limited broadcast range was a problem, but Wheeler assured Harris that an investment in the latest equipment would solve that problem. Convinced KLEE-TV could be a successful enterprise, Harris agreed that an offer should be made to buy 100 percent of Lee's station. Harris advised Will that if they did make a deal, the Hobbys should be prepared to absorb at least $250,000 in operating losses before they could break even. That amount, however, was far less than the estimate of $1 million needed to start a station from scratch.[34]

Persuaded by her husband and by Harris to make the effort, Oveta contacted Lee, who said that he was willing to sell his station, but not for less than $740,000 (an amount equal to nearly $8 million in 2018). Oveta, who had been worried about taking on more debt, was stunned when she heard the price. Jack Harris stressed years later that $740,000 was "a lot of money in those days, especially for a new business operating entirely in red ink." Oveta turned to the Hobbys' old friend Judge Jim Elkins for advice. Elkins knew Lee and he was aware of his financial troubles. The judge not only told her that buying the station would be a smart move, he also agreed to finance the purchase.[35]

*Politically powerful Houston attorney and banker and*
*"8F crowd" member James Elkins in October 1946.*

Will, Jack Harris, and the Hobby family attorney Jack Binion agreed that Oveta should be the person to deal with Albert Lee because she was a much tougher negotiator than Will, and Harris would not have the authority to be effective. Jack McGrew later observed that during the negotiations, Oveta found Lee "to be a particularly frustrating person to deal with, but she patiently persevered." Near the end of the negotiations, Will became ill with a serious neurological disorder and had to be hospitalized. Oveta visited him in the hospital and told him she was close to making the purchase and asked for his advice about what to do. "I will rely on your judgment," Will responded.[36]

On March 25, 1950, Oveta and Lee came to final terms for the purchase of KLEE-TV for a price of $740,000. The Hobbys agreed to pay $590,000 in cash, and they assumed responsibility for a $150,000 debt Lee owed to General Electric. The deal was contingent on the FCC granting approval to the Hobbys to take over the broadcast license. Will and Oveta dispatched a letter to Jesse Jones, who was vacationing in Arizona, informing him of their purchase. Although Oveta and Will both signed the letter, it is almost certain that Oveta was the author because the salutation was "Dear Mr. Jones." Will addressed Jones as "Jess" or "Jesse," but Oveta always addressed him formally. Despite Oveta's anxiety about going into debt, she told Jones that it was a good deal. "[KLEE-TV] has been losing money," she admitted, "but it is close to breaking even now and [Jack Harris] thinks he can get it in the black before the end of this year." Almost gloating because of her knowledge that Jones still had plans to get his own license but was trapped by the FCC's freeze, Oveta explained that she and Will were happy there would only be one station in Houston until the FCC decided to end the licensing freeze, which could take months or even a year or more. She added that it was good to close the deal quickly and have the television field to themselves while they worked to make the station profitable. Jones replied that he had read their letter "with much interest." He joked that if the enterprise "turned out all right, I will expect a half interest. If it doesn't, we will talk about it."[37]

Oveta later recalled that she soon realized she had forgotten to tell one of the outside members of the *Houston Post* board that she and Albert Lee had agreed on purchase terms. When she told the board member about the deal, he insisted on talking it over with Will, who had moved from the hospital to recover at home. The board member met with Will and expressed his worries that Lee's price was too high. Will assured him that it would work out. He explained that Oveta was now "running these things" and that he had "never doubted her judgment before. I shan't start now." When Bill Hobby learned that his family now owned KLEE-TV, he sent a letter to his former teacher and mentor at St. Albans, John Davis. "The Hobbys just bought themselves a television station," Bill wrote. "There's only one here, and applications for licenses are frozen, so it's a pretty good bet. The only trouble is that the thing has been in operation for two years and has yet to make one thin dime. In fact, it's lost quite a few dimes. Another trouble is the price. Two meals a day for the next year or so. The folks figured it was one of those things that had to be done, because if we didn't somebody else (guess who?) would." The "who" was obviously Jesse Jones.[38]

*Will Hobby being interviewed by announcer Dick Gottlieb on KPRC's first television broadcast, 1950.*

The FCC approved Will and Oveta's purchase of the KLEE-TV broadcast license on June 1, 1950. The Hobbys immediately changed the station's call letters to KPRC-TV and then on Monday, July 3, made the first broadcast on Channel 2 as the new owners. When the station went on the air that day, Will Hobby appeared on camera with announcer Dick Gottlieb to explain the new call letters and to inform his viewers that it was now part of the *Houston Post* corporate family, which included KPRC Radio. Will declared that it was now "possible for the *Post* to provide our readers with a newspaper to read, our listeners with a radio to hear, and our lookers-on with a telecast to see." He then introduced his "friend and associate, Colonel Jack Harris, [as the] new General Manager of KPRC-TV."[39]

By the time Will Hobby introduced him, Jack Harris had already been hard at work overhauling the station's entire operation. The KLEE-TV studio was in a Quonset hut that lacked air-conditioning and was located behind horse stables in a pasture in what was then far west Houston. Will and Oveta quickly approved the installation of air-conditioning. They also set aside $250,000 as a reserve fund to cover operational losses as the station built an audience and attracted a pool of advertisers. The Hobbys never had to tap the fund. KPRC-TV quickly gained commercial sponsors, and the operation was breaking even financially within the first six months, much earlier than Harris or anyone else had anticipated. The Hobbys made masterful use of the *Houston Post* and KPRC Radio to cross-promote their television station, tools Albert Lee lacked during his ownership of KLEE-TV. Although Lee had a radio station, it rated far behind KPRC Radio in audience share. And nearly every morning when *Houston Post* subscribers opened their newspaper, they saw stories about programs and personalities on KPRC-TV. Lee also lacked the influence and respect and social connections that Will and Oveta had among Houston's power brokers, some of whom were in control of companies that were eager to place commercials on the Hobby television station.

Will and Oveta also had a visionary, innovative, and shrewd general manager. Jack Harris was keenly aware of the critical need to boost television ownership in Houston to increase the number of viewers, which in turn would attract more advertising. A month after the Hobbys took control of the television station, Harris and his management team hosted a three-day television fair at a large nightclub on South Main Street called the Plantation. The idea was to give Houstonians an opportunity to see the wonders of television and to entice them into buying a receiver. Several days before the event, the *Houston Post* ran ads and special features publicizing the fair. KPRC Radio broadcast "public service" announcements encouraging consumers to attend. Advertised as an event held to "formally dedicate KPRC-TV," the publicity campaign announced that the fair would include free musical entertainment featuring the Grand Ole Opry star fiddler and comedian Red Ingle and his band, the Natural Seven, who had released several best-selling records, including *Cigareets, Whuskey, and Wild, Wild Women*. And, of course, a number of retailers had their television sets on display, with helpful employees eager to explain the joys of television viewing.[40]

The promotional effort worked. Harris and his staff reported to the Hobbys that an

*Oveta and Will Hobby in the broadcast control room, KPRC-TV, July 1952.*

estimated fifty thousand curious Houstonians showed up, eager to learn more about television and their options for acquiring sets. The club's stage was used by the entertainers but also for KPRC-TV staff to demonstrate televisions and programming during breaks between performances. Television cameras on site broadcast to television monitors located around the club. Visitors thrilled to see themselves on the screen as they gazed at the cameras. Happy retailers informed Harris that television sales in Houston spiked dramatically, with fifty-three thousand sets sold in a few weeks in December, which was double the usual amount of sales for that span of time. Within months, there were two hundred thousand sets in Houston, and the only station the proud owners could view was KPRC. Harris later recalled, "We made more money for [television] set distributors for quite a while than we made for ourselves. It was not a philanthropic effort. We had to do it to attract advertisers."[41]

Having a monopoly on television broadcasting, which lasted for four years, paid off handsomely for the Hobbys. Jack Harris extended the broadcast hours and initiated new locally produced shows with live audiences, including wrestling matches and beauty pageants. Harris also brought in his veteran news staff from KPRC Radio to broadcast regularly scheduled daily news programs, which was an innovation for local television at the time. Harris acquired old Warner Bros. cartoons, *Three Stooges* and *Little Rascals* shorts, and other programming aimed at kids. "The youngsters would bug their parents until they would buy a set," Harris recalled years later. By the end of 1950, television revenues had surpassed income from both the *Houston Post* and KPRC Radio. KPRC-TV's audience doubled in size during the first year of operation, and by the end of the second year it had doubled again.[42]

By 1953, the Hobbys had spent more than $3 million, financed equally by Jesse Jones's National Bank of Commerce and Judge Elkins's First City National Bank, to replace the old Quonset hut studio with a modern new facility and to fill it with the latest in broadcast technology. That same year three new television stations went on the air and KPRC lost the monopoly that had allowed it to broadcast the most popular programs from the three major networks. As an NBC affiliate, however, KPRC-TV continued to be the dominant television station in the Houston-Galveston market for many years to come.[43]

*Opening ceremony for the new KPRC-TV studio, early 1950s.*

# CHAPTER 31

---

# "I LIKE IKE"

O n the night of December 7, 1949, General of the Army Dwight Eisenhower, who had become president of Columbia University in May 1948, addressed an excited capacity crowd of fifteen thousand people in Sam Houston Coliseum. The occasion was the annual dinner of the Houston Chamber of Commerce, a civic event that normally attracted only a few hundred participants to its usual location, the Rice Hotel ballroom. But when it was announced that the famed leader of the Allied military forces that had defeated the German Army in Western Europe had accepted Jesse Jones's invitation to give the keynote speech at the meeting, the demand for tickets was overwhelming. The chamber decided to move the event to the city's largest auditorium. Will and Oveta joined the other members of Houston's political and business elite at the coliseum to hear Eisenhower speak. His address was advertised as nonpartisan— Eisenhower was refusing to say publicly if he was a Republican or a Democrat—but the speech, which focused on the blessings of capitalism and small government and the country's need to remain active internationally, clearly reflected the basic views of the Republican Party's moderate and internationalist wing in the immediate postwar years.[1]

Eisenhower's visit to Houston was part of a weeklong tour of Texas that he claimed was strictly a vacation, during which he would pay a nostalgic visit to San Antonio and Fort Sam Houston, where he had met his wife, Mamie; go bird hunting on the Texas Gulf Coast; and reconnect with old friends in the Lone Star State, including Oveta Culp Hobby. Immediately following the event at the coliseum, Will and Oveta joined Jesse Jones and his wife, Mary, to cohost a reception in honor of Ike and Mamie Eisenhower at the Joneses' lavish penthouse residence in the Lamar Hotel. It's not known what the Hobbys and Eisenhowers discussed at the reception, but it is hard to imagine that presidential politics was not among the topics of conversation. Leading members of both political parties had tried hard to persuade Ike to run as their candidate for president in 1948, but he had spurned all offers.[2]

---

As Ike visited with his Houston friends at the Joneses' apartment that December night, a faction of moderate Republicans and a number of Southern Democrats, including Will and Oveta and other leaders of the conservative wing of the Texas Democratic Party, were already boosting his nomination as a candidate for president in 1952. Will liked and respected Robert Taft, the unexciting conservative US senator from Ohio who was the leading candidate for the nomination, but as James Clark later explained in his biography of Will, "[Will's] keen political judgment told him that Taft couldn't win and Eisenhower could. He never doubted Ike's political appeal." What was of prime importance to Will was a Republican victory. Oveta was even more enthusiastic for Ike than was Will. She had liked and admired Eisenhower since the day they met at Paddington Station in London in the fall of 1942. She had long held hopes that Eisenhower would eventually be president, and she was determined to work on his behalf in the event that he ever became a candidate, preferably a Republican. She soon got that opportunity.[3]

Despite their switch to the GOP at the presidential level, the Hobbys remained loyal to conservative Democratic candidates in Texas, still an overwhelmingly Democratic state. Although the Hobbys supported the party's conservative wing, they made at least one exception to that preference. In the primary election in 1942 for the US Senate, they endorsed progressive former governor Jimmy Allred instead of the flamboyant and clownish conservative candidate Governor W. Lee "Pappy" O'Daniel. Congressman Lyndon Johnson was also a candidate in that Senate race, but the Hobbys stayed with Allred, who ultimately ran third behind LBJ and the ultimate runoff winner, O'Daniel. Their support of Allred was partially the result of Oveta's longtime friendship with her former beau as well as with his wife, Jo Betsy.[4]

By 1947, Will and Oveta's active support of the national Republican Party had become obvious. In May of that year, Will served as the toastmaster for a dinner hosted by Houston oilmen Hugh Roy Cullen and Jack Porter in honor of Republican Speaker of the House Joe Martin, whose visit to Texas was clearly for partisan purposes. That same month, in a speech in Boston at the opening session of the annual convention of the Advertising Federation of America, Oveta criticized former vice president Henry A. Wallace, who was an aspirant for the 1948 Democratic nomination for president. Wallace was a vocal supporter of the left-wing faction of the party and an advocate for improving relations with the Soviet Union. With the Cold War between the United States and the Soviet Union gaining momentum, Oveta charged that Wallace was trying to "destroy the effectiveness of this country's announced foreign policy. Shall we stick our heads into Henry Wallace's sands, or shall we take our leadership manfully?"[5]

Will and Oveta's negative public reaction to a wave of major labor union strikes that spread across the nation in 1946 and 1947 was further confirmation of their break from the national Democratic Party and its pro-union orientation. Centering in the steel, rail, electrical, mining, and auto industries, the strikes involved more than five million workers. This labor unrest had multiple causes, but the basic issue was the failure of wages to keep up with the dramatic increases in the cost of living while corporate profits soared in the years immediately after the end of the war.

Will and many of the men who were influential in shaping his views on the subject, especially John Henry Kirby, Bronson Cooper, and Ross Sterling, had long records of enmity toward organized labor unions. Will had demonstrated his own opposition to union strike tactics by his actions as governor to break the port strike in Galveston and his sponsorship of the draconian "Hobby Port Law." Over the years, editorials in his newspapers reflected Will's hostility, although in 1935 the *Houston Post* did offer tepid support for the passage of the Wagner Act, which guaranteed the right for workers to organize unions. But that was before Will turned against the New Deal during FDR's second term. By 1940 the *Post* was once again publishing anti-union editorials. No doubt reflecting the discussions he heard at home, fifteen-year-old Bill Hobby contributed a column to the *Post* denouncing the union strikes in 1947. "The labor leaders of the country are deliberately, and with malice aforethought doing as much damage to the nation and its economy as they possibly can," young Bill wrote. "We, the people of Houston, also have experienced the effects of the almost unbelievable selfishness and irresponsibility of the union heads in the building strike." Proud of his son's column, Will sent a transcript to Jesse Jones, whose construction projects had been hit hard by the strikes.[6]

Oveta's views were usually slightly to the left of Will's on the political spectrum, but she basically shared her husband's negative opinion of labor unions, which was also the dominant view of the 8F crowd, especially the Brown and Root Company's Herman and George Brown. Widespread public anger about the labor strikes in 1946 and 1947 gave the new Republican majority in Congress their long hoped for opportunity to reduce the power of the unions. In early June 1947, Congress passed the Taft-Hartley Act, which outlawed various union practices, including secondary and wildcat strikes and closed shops. It also allowed the states to pass right-to-work laws and required union leaders to file sworn affidavits that they weren't members of the Communist Party.[7]

While the bill sat unsigned on President Truman's desk for several days, the Republican Party launched a national campaign urging the public to demand that the president sign it. Oveta joined the campaign. Two days before Oveta embarked on her around-the-world trip, she published an op-ed piece in the *Houston Post*, styled as an "open letter" to President Truman, urging him to sign the bill. She argued that Congress had passed the Taft-Hartley Act because a majority of the American people believed that organized labor had become too powerful. Despite these efforts, President Truman vetoed the act on June 20, 1947. Three days later Congress easily overrode the veto, with more Democrats voting against Truman's veto than for it. Will and Oveta's unhappiness with Truman's veto of the Taft-Hartley bill and what the *Post* called "Trumanism" caused Oveta to publicly charge the administration with corruption and mismanagement.[8]

Will and Oveta also criticized the federal government's claim of ownership of the mineral rights to the so-called tidelands, the submerged oil lands in the Gulf of Mexico extending nearly eleven miles offshore from the Texas and Louisiana coasts. The federal government had recognized Texas's ownership of the tidelands ever since the Annexation Agreement of 1845, but the discovery of extensive oil deposits under the seabed and the development of the offshore oil industry in the 1940s led to the federal government's decision to claim ownership of every state's tideland. State officials in Texas, California, and Louisiana, where most of the offshore oil was known to be located, denounced the federal claim as an attempt to confiscate a valuable revenue source for state government.

The dispute was not trivial. At stake was the amount of money oil companies had to pay in leases and fees. On federal land the oil companies paid a royalty fee 25 percent higher than that charged by the state. The federal government stood to lose millions of dollars in revenue if it lost its claim. The issue became emotional because of its connection to the public schools of Texas. The legislature had passed a law directing the state's tideland oil royalties to be used to help support public education. Although the amount of money allocated was small—a fraction of one cent per child—the oil industry and the politicians who represented it charged that the "feds" were attempting "to rob the little school children" of Texas. The real issue, however, was that the oil industry would have to pay a higher rate in royalties if the federal government prevailed in the dispute. The oil industry's rhetoric was effective. A statewide public opinion poll reported that a majority of Texans considered the dispute over ownership of the tidelands to be one of the most important public issues in the 1948 presidential campaign. Eager for the Republican presidential candidate to carry Texas, the Hobbys recognized the tidelands dispute as a potent issue that could persuade a significant number of Texas's conservative Democrats to vote against Truman. They directed the *Post* to take a strong editorial stance against what the newspaper called an attempt by the Truman administration to "steal" property rightfully owned by the state.[9]

Opposing Truman on almost all fronts except for his internationalist foreign policy, Will and Oveta were pleased when the Republican Party chose New York governor Thomas Dewey over isolationist Ohio US senator Robert Taft as its candidate for the presidency in 1948. Dewey, however, had been reluctant to take a public position on the tidelands issue because of its regional nature and for the reason that most of the states that had no offshore oil favored federal ownership. This was a matter of some concern to the Hobbys. It was generally thought that Dewey favored state ownership of the tidelands, especially because the party's vice presidential candidate was California governor Earl Warren, who actively supported his state's claim of ownership of its submerged land. The issue was important enough to motivate Oveta to travel to Albany, New York, on September 14, 1948, to meet with Dewey to clarify his position. Although Dewey was averse to taking a strong public position one way or the other in the dispute, he managed to assure Oveta he would not continue the federal effort to take ownership of the submerged oil lands. As Oveta left the governor's office, she was met by a contingent of reporters, to whom she declared, "Governor Dewey [is] sympathetic to those who want tideland rights restored to the states." As a result, she believed Dewey could win Texas's twenty-three electoral votes. When she was asked if the *Post* would support Dewey, she smiled and cagily replied, "You wouldn't want me to scoop my own paper, would you?" To no one's surprise, the *Post* soon issued an editorial endorsing the Dewey-Warren presidential ticket, declaring they would "save the Tidelands."[10]

The tidelands dispute was a standard states' rights issue. Will was a fierce defender of states' rights, but Oveta was more likely to take an independent stance, depending on the nature of the dispute. When prosegregation Southern delegates walked out of the 1948 Democratic National Convention in protest of the party's civil rights platform and formed the Dixiecrats as a white supremacy party with South Carolina governor Strom Thurmond as its presidential candidate, a number of Houstonians declared their support, but not Oveta. She abhorred the Dixiecrats and their racism. Historian Debra Sutphen has noted that "Will—perhaps less progressive than his wife on civil rights issues—required greater persuasion to remain separate" from the Dixiecrats. Ed Kilman, the *Post*'s segregationist editorial page editor, shared Will's sympathy for the Dixiecrat campaign. The issue was a good example of the editorial direction the *Post* sometimes took despite Oveta's opposite preferences. Will approved a Kilman editorial in the *Post* that expressed sympathy for Thurmond's states' rights stance without mentioning its racist underpinnings. Another editorial even suggested that a special session of the Texas Legislature should be called to pass a bill authorizing a state referendum to allow Texans to express their views on the Dixiecrats' states' rights position. That idea failed to gain traction, and the editorial campaign was quietly dropped.[11]

Debra Sutphen argues that Will's sympathy for the Dixiecrats stemmed from his strong belief in states' rights, not from racism. He opposed any federal mandates to the states, and that included not only civil rights laws but also any law that Will believed infringed on the powers the Tenth Amendment to the Constitution reserved exclusively for the states. "Both Hobbys," Sutphen claims, "viewed racial bigotry as immoral and unproductive." That they chose to support Governor Dewey, who, according to Truman biographer David McCullough, "held the same or very similar views as Truman" on many issues, including support of civil rights, suggests that the Hobbys' opposition to Truman had little to do with his position on issues of racial justice.[12]

The Hobbys expressed their support for Thomas Dewey's presidential bid mainly through editorials in the *Post*, as well as in speeches Oveta made locally during the campaign. They were both as shocked as most of the nation when Harry Truman overcame the odds and defeated Dewey on November 2, 1948. As was now their habit, Will and Oveta again split their ballots, voting for the Republican presidential candidate while also voting for the Democratic candidates in Texas, including LBJ, who won election to the US Senate.

In the 1948 primary Senate race, the Hobbys had originally supported conservative Houston attorney George Peddy, a former partner in Judge Elkins's law firm and a vocal states' righter. The other candidate was former Texas governor Coke Stevenson, another ultraconservative. Attorney and former state legislator Frank "Posh" Oltorf, who was a lobbyist for the Brown and Root Company and a close associate of LBJ's, later claimed that the *Post*'s support for George Peddy was Ed Kilman's decision and that the Hobbys didn't pay that much attention to the state primary. Oltorf, a native of Marlin, Texas, and a Rice Institute graduate, was Will Hobby's cousin on the Pettus side of his family, and he was close to both Will and Oveta. When LBJ learned that the *Post* had endorsed Peddy, he asked Oltorf to talk to Will. "My father loved him so much," LBJ told Oltorf. "He was in the legislature when Hobby was governor. He supported his program and was very fond of that. Now, that I'm running for [the Senate] everything is Peddy on the [*Post*'s] front page. I think I should get better coverage. Say something for me."[13]

When Oltorf met with Will, he declared, "Governor, Lyndon sent his love to you and Oveta. He said that he'd always remember the deep affection that his father had for you when he was in the legislature and you were governor. He understands that Peddy's a Houstonian and he's an old friend, and that the *Post* would have to be for him during this first primary, but he hopes if he and Stevenson are in the second race that [the *Post*] will help him." "Well, that's mighty nice of Lyndon," Will replied. "Why don't you bring him by for breakfast in the morning?" Oltorf and LBJ met Will and Oveta for breakfast the next day. Afterward, LBJ returned to Austin, leaving Oltorf alone with the Hobbys. Will told Oltorf, "I certainly enjoyed that visit. [LBJ] talks like he knows what he's up to and wants to do. We can sure give a lot of thought to supporting him in the second race, if Peddy's not in it." In the first primary, Peddy won 20 percent of the vote, which forced LBJ into a runoff with Coke Stevenson. The Hobbys were quick to endorse LBJ, and, as Oveta later recalled, they worked "vigorously for him." LBJ beat Stevenson by eighty-seven votes as a result of a highly controversial ballot box in Duval County that Will knew well from his days as governor.[14]

The Truman administration was aware of the Hobbys' opposition. In July 1950, three weeks after the onset of the Korean War, Secretary of Defense Louis Johnson, who had been Truman's chief fundraiser, organized a conference in Washington on the topic of "Womanpower in the Mobilization Effort." Despite Oveta being among the most knowledgeable individuals in the country on this subject, Louis Johnson pointedly left her off the conference invitation list. Journalist Sarah McClendon, a syndicated White House correspondent and native Texan who knew Oveta well, reported that Secretary Johnson's snub infuriated the former director of the WAC. McClendon pointed out that Hobby "had more background to bring to the conference than any other woman there."[15]

Two months after Louis Johnson snubbed Oveta, Truman forced him to resign, not because of his treatment of Oveta but because his tenure in the Pentagon had been a disaster. Truman appointed General George C. Marshall, Hobby's old friend and admirer, as secretary of defense. In August 1951, Marshall corrected Louis Johnson's error by appointing Oveta to his newly formed Defense Advisory Committee on Women in the Services, which Marshall formed to help him develop a strategy to recruit at least eighty thousand women into the military, a difficult challenge Oveta had faced as director of the WAC. Other members of the committee included Nelson Rockefeller's wife, Mary; actress Irene Dunne; Pillsbury heir Mary Lord; and two former comrades from

Oveta's war days: WAVES commanding officer Mildred McAfee and Dorothy Stratton, former director of SPARS.[16]

The committee reported to Anna M. Rosenberg, Marshall's assistant secretary of defense for manpower and personnel, a professional Oveta admired greatly, no matter that Rosenberg was a liberal Democratic activist and a dedicated New Dealer. Rosenberg's appointment to the Defense Department in December 1950 had been controversial because of accusations by notorious anti-Semites and Red Scare activists Gerald L. K. Smith and J. B. Matthews that she was a Communist sympathizer. Rosenberg's nomination survived when a Senate committee cleared her of all charges. Oveta had been among Rosenberg's staunchest defenders. There was much about Rosenberg with which Oveta identified. Both women were talented administrators who had played key roles in the Pentagon during the war. When the accusations were made against Rosenberg, Oveta submitted a letter in her defense to the Senate Armed Services Committee, calling her an "outstanding American patriot." After Rosenberg's confirmation, Oveta, who was well aware of the resistance Rosenberg would have to face from the male leadership in the Pentagon, sent her a brief sympathetic message: "Others will congratulate you. I will pray for you." Rosenberg would eventually be the first woman to receive the Medal of Freedom, the nation's highest civilian award. When the anticommunist hysteria known as the Red Scare took root and spread in the early 1950s, Oveta's McCarthyite critics in Houston would cite her defense of Rosenberg in their attacks on her.[17]

Oveta attended the advisory committee's first meeting in Washington in September 1951. With Oveta taking a leading role and with fresh memories of how the WAC had failed to fill its quota of voluntary enlistees, the committee eventually drafted a report for Marshall recommending that women be included in the military draft. As Oveta later noted, she knew that Congress would reject the recommendation, but she and Rosenberg felt the idea should be considered. Despite the rejection of the proposal to draft women, the committee proved to be useful to the Defense Department and it continues to exist as of this writing.[18]

Will and Oveta opposed nearly every one of Truman's domestic programs, but Oveta, a committed internationalist and supporter of the bipartisan foreign policy forged at the beginning of the Cold War, supported many of Truman's policies in foreign affairs, especially the Truman Doctrine, the Marshall Plan, and the Berlin Airlift. Oveta also accepted an appointment to the board of the Crusade for Freedom, which was officially operated by an organization called the National Committee for a Free Europe but was secretly organized and funded by the Central Intelligence Agency (CIA) during the Truman administration. The Crusade operated Radio Free Europe and Radio Liberty, which broadcast American wire service news reports and CIA-supplied propaganda to Communist countries in Eastern Europe. General Lucius Clay, former military governor of the US occupation zone in West Germany, served as the Crusade's national chairman, while Dwight Eisenhower was one of its spokesmen. To maintain a facade of objectivity, the CIA hid its financial support of the Crusade. The agency funneled unidentified congressional appropriations through a "dummy" foundation established for the purpose. That foundation then passed the money to other independent foundations, which in turn granted it to the Crusade. As a Crusade board member, Oveta obligingly used the Hobby Family Foundation as one of the CIA funding conduits, an arrangement that continued secretly for several years.[19]

Will and Oveta also reluctantly supported Truman's decision on April 11, 1951, to fire General Douglas MacArthur, the commander of UN forces in Korea, for insubordination. The decision caused a public firestorm, especially within the Republican Party. Many of Houston's most influential business leaders denounced MacArthur's dismissal, but the Hobbys published an editorial in the *Post* supporting Truman's decision and criticizing the general while also praising him as a "great" military leader. Oveta's meeting with MacArthur in Tokyo had given her doubts about the general's judgment. The Hobbys' good friend Representative Albert Thomas, Houston's longtime Democratic congressman, praised Will and Oveta for their unpopular stance in the MacArthur controversy. Thomas wrote a letter assuring them they were "rendering the country a real service. It appears that our distinguished soldier wants to involve us in an all-out shooting war with China. In so doing we have everything to lose and nothing to gain."[20]

By 1951 the leaders of the moderate and internationalist wing of the Republican Party, led by Thomas Dewey and Massachusetts senator Henry Cabot Lodge Jr., along with a small but influential group of prominent conservative Texas oilmen, including Sid Richardson, Robert Anderson, and Jack Porter, were urging Dwight Eisenhower to become a candidate for the Republican nomination for president. Oveta eagerly joined in this effort to persuade her friend to enter the race. Her enthusiasm for Ike's possible candidacy not only stemmed from their warm personal relationship and her admiration for his leadership in the war but also from mutually shared views on public policy, which were centered on moderate opposition to "New Deal–style big government," "out of control" congressional spending, "big labor," and the "welfare state." In foreign policy, Oveta also shared Ike's support for the United Nations and his opposition to the isolationist faction of the Republican Party led by Ohio senator Robert Taft, the leading contender for the GOP's 1952 presidential nomination. The fact that Eisenhower also supported Texas's claim of ownership of the tidelands while Taft waffled on the issue enhanced Ike's appeal even more for Oveta's fellow pro-Eisenhower allies in Texas, especially Governor Allan Shivers and other leaders of the conservative wing of the state's Democratic Party.[21]

Eisenhower had taken leave from Columbia University in February 1951 to serve in Paris as the supreme commander of the North Atlantic Treaty Organization (NATO). Oveta and Ike communicated frequently throughout his time at NATO, mainly through her activities as a member of Eisenhower's American Assembly, which he founded at Columbia University in 1950 to serve as a nonpartisan public policy institute. After attending the first board meeting in New York in June, Ike wrote Oveta that he was "especially delighted" she had taken an active role in the assembly, and he urged her to continue her involvement. Recalling the warm reception he had enjoyed in Houston

*Oveta Culp Hobby* (wearing a black hat) *and Jesse Jones* (second from left)
*wait with others as a welcoming delegation at the Houston airport for the
recently dismissed General Douglas MacArthur, June 1951.*

in 1949, he asked Oveta to convey his "warm greetings to Governor Hobby, and Mr. and Mrs. Jones."[22]

As Oveta traveled back and forth from Houston to New York during the winter of 1951, she took time in late February to join Will at a dinner given in their honor by the Houston chapter of the National Conference of Christians and Jews. The conference formally recognized Oveta and Will for their efforts on behalf of racial dignity and justice for the Japanese and African American citizens of Houston during World War II. As a member of Houston's Alien Enemy Hearing Board during the war, Will had vocally opposed the mistreatment of Houstonians of Japanese ancestry. At the *Houston Post*, Oveta had banned derogatory and inappropriate racial references in the newspaper's reporting that had been common practice for decades. The award dinner attracted a crowd of more than nine hundred, which overflowed the Shamrock Hotel's Emerald Room. After Governor Allan Shivers's keynote speech, Oveta gave an eloquent speech stressing the need for tolerance of all religions and the need to judge people as individuals instead of by religion, race, or ethnicity. "The rule of thumb is a simple one . . . like or dislike a person for his own intrinsic qualities—not because he belongs to a different religion—dignify him with individuality."23

Marguerite Johnston attended the awards dinner that night, and she later noted that when it was Will's turn to go to the podium, she wondered, after Oveta's speech, "What was left for him to say?" But Will rose to the occasion. He began by saying, in his well-known, laconic, "just a country boy from East Texas" style, "Unaccustomed as I am to public speakin', and as unaccustomed as I am to a $50 a plate dinner . . ." Johnston observed that after the laughter had died down, Will made a few token statements about brotherhood and then "began a little chat that somehow encompassed all those who had come from Moscow and Killeen and Temple. He tied the hundreds of people in the Shamrock's Emerald Ballroom into a company of friends. [He spoke for] perhaps ten minutes. And he sent them home feeling all warm and appreciated, as though they had been part of a family reunion." The next morning, Johnston told Oveta how well she thought Will had done the night before. "She grinned her delightful grin," Johnston recalled. "Oveta said, 'I may not be a wise woman, but I learned long ago never to follow Will at the podium. NOBODY can top him.'"24

*Will and Oveta Hobby* (middle), *Houston Mayor Oscar Holcombe* (far right) *and friends at Rice University, ca. 1950.*

At a press conference in January 1952, Eisenhower finally confirmed that he was a Republican, which cleared the way for his name to be placed on the ballot in the New Hampshire primary as a candidate for the GOP nomination for president. In June 1952, he resigned his command and returned to the United States. An Eisenhower campaign organization had been in existence for several months, with more than eight hundred "Ike Clubs" operating locally throughout the country and a national group, Citizens for Eisenhower, located in New York City and chaired by Michigan senator Arthur Vandenberg. Among the most active leaders of Citizens for Eisenhower were several close friends of Oveta, including the *New York Herald Tribune* publisher Helen Reid and Mary Pillsbury Lord, daughter of the founder of the Pillsbury Company.[25]

Oveta had been tempted to join her friends in Citizens for Eisenhower when it was organized in February 1952, but for strategic political reasons in Texas she decided to remain publicly unaffiliated with the formal Republican effort to win the nomination for Ike. Although Oveta considered herself a political independent, she continued to self-identify in Texas as a conservative Democrat. Early in the boom for Eisenhower's candidacy, it became clear that the fight with Senator Taft for delegates to the Republican National Convention was going to be difficult and that Texas would be the key battleground state in that contest. The Republican Party in Texas had long been the private patronage machine of a small group of men who decided which GOP candidate for the presidency would receive the vote of the state's delegation at the national convention. Because their interest stemmed from the lucrative patronage benefits they received from Republican presidential appointments, they had little or no interest in the state's local or statewide elections. Their ironfisted control of the party was made possible by the fact that the Republicans had no primary elections in Texas. Delegates were chosen by a few people, typically friends and associates of the clique leaders, who attended precinct caucuses held at odd hours and at inconvenient locations. Led by Republican National Committee member and Fort Worth oilman Henry Zweifel, the members of this political clique strongly supported Robert Taft.

The leadership of the pro-Eisenhower movement in Texas, which included Oveta, was composed largely of conservative Democrats. They understood that their only hope for sending an Eisenhower delegation to the Republican National Convention would be to conduct a major effort to persuade other conservative Democrats, independents, and previously inactive moderate Republicans to organize for Eisenhower at the precinct level. These "one-day Republicans," as the old guard labeled them, would then attend the precinct caucuses and select pro-Eisenhower delegates to the county and state conventions who could elect an Eisenhower delegation to the national convention.[26]

Buoyed by polls indicating that Eisenhower enjoyed widespread popularity in Texas and that he had an excellent chance of winning the state in the presidential election if he succeeded in gaining the GOP nomination, Oveta and Jack Porter took the lead in the campaign to take control of the Republican precinct conventions. A recently passed state law helped make possible Oveta's and her pro-Eisenhower allies' effort. In an incident in

1948, a group of unhappy Republicans in San Antonio announced their intention to oust their dictatorial county chairman by voting against him at the precinct caucus meetings. To fend off this challenge, the besieged chairman held secret caucus meetings attended only by his friends. Other leaders of the state's GOP patronage machine had resorted to this same tactic in the past. The resulting controversy led to a new state law requiring that the date, time, and location of party caucus meetings be published well in advance and that the meetings had to be open to the public, which considerably aided the efforts of the pro-Eisenhower newcomers to the GOP precinct meetings.

On the morning of April 13, 1952, *Houston Post* readers were greeted with a large, two-column front-page headline: "We Like Ike." The editorial announced the Hobbys' support for Dwight Eisenhower to be the Republican Party's presidential nominee, arguing that Eisenhower would stop the nation's "corruption in government, drifting toward socialism, and oppressive taxes to support fantastic spending." The editorial was also the Hobbys' declaration of political war on the Taft faction of the Republican Party. The front-page announcement served as the unofficial launch of the campaign to take over the Republican caucus meetings, scheduled for May 3. Because of the backing of oil interests supporting Texas's claim on its tidelands, the campaign was well funded, making it possible to generate extensive pro-Eisenhower advertising on radio stations across the state and to print and widely distribute campaign flyers and pamphlets, including reprints of the "We Like Ike" editorial from the *Houston Post*.[27]

Nine days after the *Post* published its pro-Eisenhower editorial, the newspaper circulated in its regular edition an eight-page "pull-out" supplement with the headline "Democracy Is Your Job." This special section, which was free of advertising and labeled as a "nonpartisan" political primer, declared that it was every citizen's civic duty to participate in precinct meetings. The supplement was filled with detailed information about how to attend and vote in party precinct conventions. "Organization Is Key to Effective Politics," declared another headline on the first page of the supplement. It was Oveta's thinly veiled effort to instruct pro-Eisenhower Democrats and independents who might have never attended a precinct convention about how to take over the meetings. The supplement also explained that party affiliation was no barrier to voting for Eisenhower delegates in the GOP precinct caucus. Oveta had the *Post*'s "Political Primer" distributed to more than four hundred thousand carefully targeted registered Democrats. The Hobbys also arranged a statewide television broadcast produced by their KPRC-TV station that gave viewers instructions on how precinct conventions worked and why it was crucial to organize support for your cause prior to the meeting. The telecast also explained that Texans could legally cast votes in both the Democratic and Republican precinct elections.[28]

Eisenhower biographer Herbert Parmet determined that Oveta "used her newspaper resources for great partisan effect" during the delegate fight. Eleanor Roosevelt shared that view. "From the start," ER observed, "she threw the support of her newspaper, the *Houston Post*, and the weight of her own considerable influence in her state, behind

General Eisenhower." The Republican regulars who supported Taft resented Oveta's aggressive support of Eisenhower in the Texas primary. They viewed the Hobbys and their Democratic allies as opportunists who simply wanted to deny the presidential nomination to "Mr. Republican" Robert Taft to make the nomination possible for Eisenhower, whom they considered to be a faux Republican (or in current terms, a "Republican in name only," or "RINO"). As one Taft supporter later complained, "Needless to say how we feel about 'Oveta' [Hobby], how did she get on Ike's bandwagon?"[29]

The embittered Taft faction in Texas resorted to the same type of Red Scare campaign tactics that Republican Wisconsin senator Joseph R. McCarthy had been using against President Truman and the Democratic Party since 1950. Taft workers distributed literature throughout Texas written by the anti-Semite and right-wing demagogue Joseph Kamp that featured such headlines as "IKE CODDLED COMMUNISTS WHILE PRESIDENT OF COLUMBIA UNIVERSITY" and "REDS, NEW DEALERS USE IKE IN PLOT TO HOLD POWER." The old-guard leader Henry Zweifel engaged in the same McCarthyite tactics, issuing press releases charging that the Eisenhower Texans, which obviously included the Hobbys (although they weren't named), were acting on behalf of radical labor unions and that they were "so far left that the Texas Democrats don't want them."[30]

Despite the sensational Red Scare tactics, Eisenhower Democrats and independents flooded the GOP precinct meetings, panicking the old-guard leaders, who resorted to rule-breaking maneuvers. In an episode that was repeated in the homes of several other precinct chairmen, Republican national committeeman Henry Zweifel found his Fort Worth living room overrun by strangers who promptly elected a slate of Ike supporters. Stunned, Zweifel led his regular associates out to his front yard, where he convened a second precinct meeting, which elected a Taft slate of delegates.[31]

On May 6, as the meetings moved from the precinct to the county level, party officials were forced to decide between two opposing sets of delegates. To no one's surprise, the leaders of the old patronage machine chose the Taft delegates over Eisenhower's, with the excuse that they were protecting the party from "outside influence" from people who weren't real Republicans. Undaunted, the rejected Eisenhower delegates went to the Republican State Convention in Mineral Wells and demanded to be recognized as official delegates. Oveta made the trip to Mineral Wells by train, but as an observer and strategist, not a delegate. The convention quickly turned chaotic. On May 27, Zweifel's convention officials awarded thirty-four of the spots on the Texas delegation to Taft supporters, four for General MacArthur, and four for Eisenhower. Oveta then joined Eisenhower's delegates as they walked out of the meeting to another hall a block away and held a "rump" convention, where they elected an alternate slate of party delegates to the national convention. After the vote was declared, the delegates began cheering wildly, chanting, "I like Ike! I like Ike!" Clapping her hands, Oveta stood on a folding chair to see the front of the room better and then joined in the chanting. A reporter for the *Houston Press*, who was standing near her, tapped Oveta on the arm and warned her that she was standing on a very unsteady folding chair. She nodded silently, got off the chair, and continued cheering and chanting. Another observer noted that Oveta was visibly swept away by the moment.[32]

As a result of the split at the state convention, two competing delegations from Texas showed up at the Republican National Convention at Chicago's International Amphitheater on Monday, July 7. Oveta remained in Houston, while Jack Porter served as the head of Ike's Texas delegation at the convention. Although she didn't go to Chicago, Oveta publicized the proceedings, which historian Herbert Parmet described as "the center of the battle between the Zweifel and Porter factions." Will and Oveta worked with AT&T to link KPRC-TV to the NBC coaxial cable for a direct connection to broadcast the convention proceedings. It was KPRC-TV's first live network telecast. Oveta also dispatched Brian Spinks, one of her favorite reporters on the *Houston Post* staff, to Chicago to send the newspaper his firsthand accounts of the convention. Oveta gave Spinks an additional task. She loaded him with documents and interview transcripts to submit to the GOP's executive committee backing the claim that Zweifel's machine had stolen the Texas delegation from the pro-Eisenhower group.[33]

The number of delegates needed for the presidential nomination was 604, which both Taft and Eisenhower lacked. The contest was close enough that victory depended on which candidate could win the contested delegates from Texas, Georgia, and three other states. Telegrams from Houston attorney and Eisenhower delegate Dillon Anderson allowed Oveta to monitor the behind-the-scenes maneuvering. She also sent telegrams to the Republican National Committee urging the members to reject Taft's delegates from Texas and to recognize the "fairly and honestly elected" Eisenhower delegates. She assured the committee, "An overwhelming majority of Texas Republicans favor the nomination of General Dwight D. Eisenhower." The decision fell to the credentials committee, which was stacked with Taft partisans, who voted to seat a majority of Taft delegates. The Eisenhower campaign, which had deluged the press with statements complaining about the "Texas Steal" at the state convention in Mineral Wells, made a motion to allow the entire convention, minus the contested delegates, to vote on whether to accept or reject the credentials committee decision. The unprecedented move worked. Eisenhower's Texas delegates were seated, giving Eisenhower the lead in delegate votes for the first time. On July 11, the GOP convention selected Eisenhower to be the party's presidential candidate. California's junior senator, Richard Nixon, was nominated for the vice presidency. Oveta was overjoyed. As Eisenhower biographer Stephen Ambrose noted, "Mrs. Oveta Culp Hobby had helped make Ike's nomination possible." And Eisenhower knew it.[34]

Once Eisenhower secured the Republican nomination, most of the members of the rival factions in Texas united in the campaign to oust the Democrats from the White House. A few Taft diehards who bitterly refused to support Eisenhower switched their support to the Constitutional Party, which had nominated General MacArthur for president, who ignored the nomination and never campaigned.[35]

A month after the GOP convention in Chicago, Oveta and Will traveled by ship to

France, where they toured Paris and the French countryside. Oveta badly needed the time off after working long hours on Ike's nomination fight in Texas, while Will was enjoying a period of relatively good health. After leaving Europe, they met Bill and Jessica at the Greenbrier Hotel near White Sulphur Springs, West Virginia, for their first family vacation in several years. Bill and Jessica stayed in a large private cottage at the Greenbrier, where they remained until the end of August. Bill had taken a break from Rice to attend summer school courses at Columbia University in New York City. In a letter to his former St. Albans teacher, John Davis, Bill reported he had serious doubts that his parents' plan to seclude themselves from the outside world for a couple of weeks was going to happen. He told Davis that although they were "vacationing as much as possible," his parents always made certain a telephone was nearby. Bill added that Eisenhower's upcoming election campaign, which would officially begin after Labor Day, was looming over them. He doubted "they really will stay away from home that long in an election year." His doubts proved to be well placed. While she and Will were staying in the Greenbrier Hotel's luxurious four-bedroom "Top Notch" Cottage, Oveta kept up a steady communication with Eisenhower campaign leaders in New York and with Dillon Anderson, who was drafting a statement about the tidelands issue for the Eisenhower campaign to use.[36]

When the Hobby family's vacation was over at the end of August, Will returned to Houston, while Oveta went directly to New York City to lead the national Democrats for Eisenhower organization, which was an arm of Citizens for Eisenhower. She took an office at the Eisenhower campaign headquarters in the Commodore Hotel and a suite at the Waldorf Astoria, where she stayed while working in Manhattan. Oveta told Senator Arthur Vandenberg, cochair of Citizens for Eisenhower, that it was "wonderful that we will be serving the Boss together." For the next two months she commuted back and forth between Manhattan and Houston as she split her duties between the national campaign and the Texans for Ike organization created by Corpus Christi businessman and conservative Democrat Maston Nixon. In New York, Oveta's main task was to help the Eisenhower campaign break the Democratic Party's grip on Texas and the other Southern states. She oversaw the production of press releases and campaign literature aimed at Southern voters, and she lobbied her newspaper publishing friends in the Southern Newspaper Publishers Association not only to endorse Ike in their editorials but also to persuade their readers that Democrats who voted for Eisenhower were not abandoning their party. Oveta also advised the national campaign about ways to persuade women voters to vote for Ike.[37]

During her trips back to Texas, Oveta focused on the statewide fundraising effort for the campaign, which targeted the state's oilmen, who were activated by the tidelands issue. At one point, Henry Cabot Lodge dispatched the Eisenhower campaign's national finance chairman, multimillionaire Jack Hay "Jock" Whitney, to Texas to help Oveta with some of her more difficult funding targets, which included the eccentric and quarrelsome Dallas oilman H. L. Hunt, a hard-right conservative crusader purported to be the richest man in the United States. At Oveta's request, Whitney went to Dallas to meet with Hunt and other oilmen at the Baker Hotel. At the meeting, Hunt told Whitney he would give the campaign a large contribution, but only on the unusual condition that he be appointed Ike's campaign manager. Whitney went to another room to telephone Oveta to ask how to respond to Hunt's obviously unacceptable demand. Oveta told him to say that he was in no position to make that commitment. That was unacceptable to Hunt, who subsequently gave his money to the Constitution Party's quixotic campaign for Douglas MacArthur.[38]

While Oveta was busy raising money and working for the national campaign, the *Houston Post* was working hard to promote Ike's presidential bid in Texas. From the beginning of September until the election in November, the *Post*'s opinion pages were filled with articles strongly critical of Adlai Stevenson and boosting Eisenhower. Typical examples included headlines such as "Stevenson Wooing of South Indicates Fear of Losing It," "Now's Time for All Good Dems to Come to Aid of GOP," "Ike's Dixie Welcome Significant," "Truman's Whistle-Stop Speeches Bind Adlai Close to Trumanism," and, most ominously, "McCarthy Talk Links Up Record of Adlai's Leftist Associations." The latter was an example of the *Post*'s editorial entrance into the dark world of anticommunist witch-hunting.[39]

Will and Oveta would later openly turn against Joe McCarthy and Houston's local Red Scare warriors, but during the several months leading up to the presidential election in November 1952, Will and Ed Kilman had no qualms about using the Red Scare as a political tactic. Their actions were generally in line with the Eisenhower national campaign strategy of attacking the Truman and Roosevelt administrations on three issues: the Korean War, Communism, and corruption. Of those three issues, Kilman's favorite was the alleged threat of Communist subversion. He filled the *Post*'s editorial pages with Red Scare demagoguery, and he saw "commies" under every bed. Under Kilman's editorship the newspaper repeatedly asked its readers to help root out the subversive elements supposedly pervading not only the federal government but also their own community. In one widely circulated editorial titled "Citizens Can Aid FBI," the *Post* announced that the "home front" was as much an area of conflict as Korea. The *Post* asked Houstonians to watch for "spies" and to notify the FBI if they saw any. Acknowledging that the task would not be easy, as "Communists have been trained in deceit and are not always easy to identify," Kilman's editorial page advised Houstonians to "watch for anyone who can see no virtue in the American Way of Life."[40]

Oveta Hobby was publicly critical of irresponsible Red Scare demagoguery and McCarthy-style accusations, even though her own newspaper was guilty of using them. As the keynote speaker at the annual meeting of the Alabama Press Association in Montgomery on February 1, 1950, Oveta denounced the role local newspapers were playing in encouraging Red Scare extremists. "When sensational charges are made against anyone—not by a jury, not by a district attorney but sometimes by vacant-minded or hysterical people," she declared, "the charges are broadcast from coast to coast and the public instinct is to accept these charges as proof." "For example," she added, "an accusation is made by the

*Oveta Culp Hobby during the Eisenhower presidential campaign in the fall of 1952.*

House Un-American Activities Committee [HUAC] in time for all morning editions. But the denial may reach the wire services only in time for a late evening edition. [I]t is unlikely the late edition denial will be picked up and carried the next day. It all boils down to this: Every newspaper writer is first of all a public servant." She pleaded for her newspaper colleagues to "incessantly ask, 'What is your proof?'" She criticized the press for "giving three or four times the amount of space to unsubstantiated charges" made by the HUAC against the innocent Manhattan Project physicist Dr. Edward Condon as had been given to nuclear physicist Dr. Klaus Fuchs, a self-admitted Soviet spy. She also castigated the press for its "fuzzy-minded habit of labeling all Communists, socialists and liberals together as left wing." Such false assertions, she complained, played "directly into the hands of Russia, which makes capital of it for propaganda purposes."[41]

Oveta delivered her speech in Alabama the same month Senator Joseph McCarthy first startled the nation with his outrageous charges of subversion in the US Department of State. A year earlier Oveta had gone on record in defense of Anna Rosenberg against similar charges. Oveta's son, Bill, also reflected his mother's view of McCarthyism. While he was a student at Rice, Bill wrote a column, Casting Pearls, for the school newspaper, the *Thresher*. In one column Bill pointed out that the US Constitution forbids Congress from passing laws prosecuting anyone for breaking a law before it is passed. "Congressional investigating committees have repeatedly violated the spirit of this clause," he wrote. "They have, in more than one case, condemned a man for sympathizing with Russia at a time when sympathizing with Russia was quite 'legitimate' and in no way considered treasonable." He cited the case of a teacher in Virginia who was attacked because she had attended a Communist Party rally in the 1930s as part of a comparative politics course. "It's unbelievable, but it happened. Thus far have the witch-hunters gone."[42]

Unfortunately, Oveta's criticism of Red Scare demagoguery also left her open to a charge of hypocrisy, for her own newspaper was guilty of practices she denounced in her Alabama speech. Ed Kilman was notorious for insisting in print that liberals were the same as Communists, a practice Oveta overtly condemned. What was little known at the time, however, was that Oveta had tried to remove Kilman as editor of the *Post*'s editorial page, but Will, who was always reluctant to fire anyone, protected his old colleague. Marguerite Johnston would later claim that Oveta had little authority to stop Kilman's demagoguery because of Will's support of his friend. When Johnston complained about Kilman, Oveta shrugged her shoulders in frustration, smiled, and said, "There comes a time in every marriage when a wife knows she has said all she can say about a particular matter."[43]

Unable to move Kilman out, Oveta encouraged other *Post* columnists, including Johnston, to write editorial columns that frequently presented a political view diametrically opposed to the one Kilman was presenting in the newspaper's "official" editorial section. As a result, the *Post* had something of a split personality. Frequently, Ed Kilman would warn readers on one page that "alien Red spies" were subverting every aspect of American life, while on a different page Oveta's favored columnists, Marguerite Johnston and George Fuermann, would extoll tolerance and international brotherhood and take positions that contradicted the editorial page. These contradictory views were partially the result of differences between Will and Oveta in political worldviews. Will was simply more provincial and conservative than Oveta. He had no problem with the views articulated by hard-right conservative Kilman, who considered the New Deal to be outright socialism and whose combative editorial style was to shoot first and ask questions later. This split image, however, was not a balanced one, as Kilman's aggressive Red Scare commentaries grabbed most of the attention because of their sensational and inflammatory nature.[44]

Oveta's public criticism of such journalistic behavior didn't stop Kilman from continuing his Red Scare editorials. One of them, titled "Red Fifth Column," warned Houstonians that because the Communists had gone "underground," it would be even more difficult to ferret them out. Nevertheless, he assured *Post* readers that "whoever helps to expose Red treason now helps to remove [a] menace to his own safety." More Red Scare editorials followed in rapid fashion, with titles such as "Death for Spies" and "French

Red Raps at Door of US." In the editorial titled "Those Who Play with Red Fire in US Do So at Their Peril," Kilman declared that the Communist Party of the United States was a "malign movement" and demanded that it be "suppressed" to prevent "the poisonous growth" from flourishing "at home." In August, Kilman reacted to Senator Pat McCarran's sensational and unsubstantiated charge that there were three to five million illegal "Red" aliens in the United States by writing an editorial titled "Alien Infiltration by Millions Raises Grave National Peril." Instead of following Oveta's dictum of asking, "What is your proof?," Kilman took McCarran at his word and solemnly told Houstonians that many of the "wetbacks from across the Rio Grande River" were subversives who threatened the nation's security. He demanded that the "government crack down with all its might in every possible way on the hordes . . . swarming over the country and coming in by the thousands daily."[45]

Will made few political appearances during the 1952 election campaign, but in his most visible and widely viewed presentation, he used rhetoric similar to his editorial page editor. He joined Governor Allan Shivers and former governors Dan Moody and Coke Stevenson in a statewide radio and television broadcast on October 21 to urge Texas Democrats to split their ballots and vote for Eisenhower while also voting for local and state Democrats. In his speech, Will implied that Adlai Stevenson's victory could lead to a totalitarian state and declared that Eisenhower would save the country "from communism and the dictatorship that goes with communism, a dictatorship that can easily result from an administration too long in power."[46]

The *Houston Chronicle*, led by its editor, Emmet "Soapy Joe" Walter, was even more strident and excessive than the *Post* in its eagerness to spread Senator Joe McCarthy's vicious and unsubstantiated accusations that the Democratic Party was the party of treason and that the Truman administration, especially the State Department, was filled with Soviet spies. This irresponsible journalistic behavior by both newspapers, which was largely motivated by political partisanship instead of any real fear that Communists were ready to seize power, played a significant role in encouraging a local Red Scare in Houston.[47]

In mid-October, Ike invited Oveta to travel with him from New Orleans to Houston on his special campaign train called the Look Ahead. Ike's trip was part of his strategy to loosen the Democratic hold on the "Solid South." On October 13, after she attended Ike's rally in New Orleans's Beauregard Square (now Congo Square), where he pledged his support for Louisiana's claim on its tidelands, Oveta boarded the campaign train for the overnight trip to Houston. On the way, she joined Ike and his wife, Mamie, and their staff for dinner, where she expressed her pleasure over the general's forthright endorsement of state ownership of tidelands. She also shared her impression of the political situation in Texas based on information her political reporters had given her. Because Oveta was a member of the official reception committee that would greet Ike when he arrived in Houston, she also briefed the Eisenhowers on what to expect when they arrived in the city. The Look Ahead pulled into Houston's Southern Pacific passenger depot at seven twenty-five in the morning on October 14, which was also Eisenhower's sixty-second birthday. After Mayor Oscar Holcombe and other civic and business leaders boarded the train to extend an official welcome, Ike and Oveta rode in an automobile procession from the depot to nearby Sam Houston Coliseum, where Ike delivered a campaign speech to a large and enthusiastic crowd. The following day, Oveta had additional time with Ike when she accompanied him to Dallas on the train, where he spoke at another well-attended campaign rally. Oveta was a highly visible presence at the rallies in both cities. After Ike returned to New York City, he wrote a letter to Oveta to express his gratitude for her work on his behalf. "Dear Oveta, I cannot let this day go by without sending you a personal note of appreciation and thanks for your help during the Texas visit," Ike wrote. "You were a good friend to take so much of your time off to be with Mamie and me and make our welcome real and pleasant."[48]

The week after Ike's Texas tour, Oveta was in New York City, where she was one of the featured speakers at an Eisenhower for President rally. Ike, who was campaigning away from New York at the time, sent a telegram to Oveta the next day. "Sherm Adams [governor of New Hampshire and an Eisenhower campaign leader] has reported to me on the fine statement you made in my behalf last night in New York," Ike wrote. "For this, and for taking the job of heading Democrats for Eisenhower and for the time and effort and devotion you are putting into this crusade, my deepest thanks."[49]

Oveta was back in Houston in time to vote with Will for Eisenhower. After her arrival in Houston, she found a telegram on her desk at the *Houston Post* from Ike, who was on a train going from Boston to New York, expressing his thanks for "the really effective help you have been to me personally throughout this campaign." There was nothing left to do but wait on the verdict of the voters. Early in the evening on Election Day, November 4, 1952, Oveta and Will went to the newsroom at the *Post* to read the initial wire service reports on the vote count from New England. Encouraged by the early returns, they went home to their mansion in Shadyside to watch KPRC-TV's coverage of the election returns. By midevening it was obvious, if not official, that Ike would defeat Adlai Stevenson, bringing to an end the twenty-year Democratic reign in Washington. By two thirty in the morning (Houston time) on November 5, Ike's victory was official. He won 55 percent of the ballots cast and 442 electoral votes. Oveta's happiness was doubled when it became apparent that her efforts along with those of the other leaders of the Texas Democrats for Eisenhower had also helped win the state for Ike, the first Republican presidential victory in Texas since 1928. In addition, GOP efforts to break up the Democratic "Solid South" succeeded in Eisenhower victories in Tennessee, Virginia, and Florida.[50]

As had happened during the war, Oveta suffered exhaustion from commuting to New York from Houston on a frequent basis and spending long hours at her desk in the Commodore Hotel in Manhattan and at the *Houston Post*. She finally gave in to her fatigue after the election was decided. Two days after Ike's victory, Bill Hobby wrote to his former teacher, John Davis, that his mother was "slowly recuperating from her exertions of the last few months. She really did a helluva job [in New York] as one of the happy few that fought from the dark pre-convention days." Despite her tiredness, Oveta was soon once again on the road. Nine days after the election, she had recovered sufficiently to travel to Chicago to deliver a major speech to a general session of the American Petroleum Institute, in which she urged the oil and gas industry to do a better job of explaining the vital importance of the industry to the national security of the country. Oveta's speech in Chicago added to her growing list of "first woman" achievements. In this case, she was the first woman to address a general session of the institute.[51]

Because of the prominent role Oveta played in the Eisenhower campaign, there had been speculation in the news media and within GOP leadership circles as far back as the spring of 1952 that if Ike won the election, she would be offered a post in his administration. On April 8 the Hearst newspaper the *New York Journal American* reported, "According to Washington gossip, Oveta Culp Hobby will have an important position if General Eisenhower gets the Presidency." Other Hearst newspapers soon spread the *Journal American* report. Within days after Eisenhower's victory the rumor mill was once again buzzing about Oveta's future.[52]

According to Herbert Parmet, organizing the president-elect's cabinet and other administrative posts "was a process that had gone into full swing almost immediately after Election Day." Eisenhower assigned the job to his old army colleague General Lucius Clay and to Wall Street attorney Herbert Brownell. Working from offices in the Commodore Hotel, Clay and Brownell carefully gathered the names of individuals for Eisenhower's review and selection. New Hampshire governor Sherman Adams, soon to be Ike's White House chief of staff, was also involved in the search for candidates. As Adams later recalled, Eisenhower told them "he would like to have one woman in the group but he said that he had no one particular in mind. Nor did he have any specific Cabinet position reserved for a woman Secretary." Adams, Brownell, and Clay had all worked closely with Oveta in New York during the campaign. They were impressed with her competency and professionalism and they appreciated the critical role she had played in the battle to win Ike the GOP nomination. They also knew that Ike admired and respected her. "Oveta Culp Hobby was an obvious choice," Adams later noted, because of her competence, because of Ike's respect for her, and "because her independent Texas background would add a Southern flavor to the Cabinet." They also liked that Oveta had a public image as a Democrat, which would give a bipartisan aura to her appointment, despite her active support of Republican presidential candidates Willkie and Dewey, not to mention Eisenhower.[53]

Clay informed Eisenhower that he and Brownell recommended Oveta "as a possible appointee to the Cabinet," despite there being no readily obvious place for her. By this time, most of the cabinet secretaries had been selected. But they knew that Eisenhower would ask the newly elected Republican-controlled Congress to authorize a new cabinet-level department, tentatively called the Department of Welfare, that could be a good fit for Oveta. The proposed new department would combine all federal programs and agencies dealing with education, health, and Social Security. During the Truman administration, the Hoover Commission had called for the department's creation, but Congress had rejected the recommendation, largely because Senate Republicans feared that Truman would appoint his Federal Security Agency administrator, Oscar Ewing, to head the new department. Ewing was a tireless advocate for a federal national health insurance system, which the Republicans denounced as socialized medicine and as a plan to turn the United States into a permanent welfare state.[54]

Oveta's experience as an active member of the Hoover Commission, where she had been involved in discussions about the proposed department, made her a logical choice to be its head if Congress agreed to its creation. Ike, however, didn't want to wait on Congress to act before he brought Oveta to Washington, so he and his selection team decided to appoint her head of the massive Federal Security Agency (FSA), which was slated to be among the agencies to be combined into a new department. The FSA administered several key federal programs, including Social Security, the Office of Education, and the Pure Food and Drug Act. With approximately thirty-eight thousand employees and a budget of more than $4.6 billion, the FSA was larger than the Labor, Commerce, and Justice Departments. As head of the FSA, Oveta would be an obvious candidate to be secretary of the new Department of Welfare whenever Congress approved its establishment. Eisenhower liked the idea. When he recalled the episode in his presidential memoir, he wrote that he had known Oveta when she had served as director of the WAC, adding that in that position she "had established a splendid reputation as an administrator and leader." He explained that he was "hopeful of finding a woman of proven ability for a high post in government, and none seemed better fitted for such an appointment than she."[55]

Bringing Oveta into his administration might have been Eisenhower's plan all along, but it was also typical of his delegating management style, honed during the war, to assign duties to others without giving details about his personal preferences. He asked Clay to bring Oveta to New York and offer her the job, which would have the added responsibility of leading the effort to establish the new department. The offer also included the promise that she would participate in cabinet meetings while the department was being planned and that she would eventually be nominated to serve as its first secretary. This arrangement would tap the experience Oveta had gained in organizing and directing the women's corps and working within the federal bureaucracy. It would also take advantage of her political connections with the powerful US House minority leader Sam Rayburn and the Senate's equally influential minority leader, Lyndon B. Johnson. Those connections remained strong despite Oveta's active role in leading Texans for Ike. Oveta's status as editor and publisher of one of the most influential newspapers in Texas was incentive for Rayburn, and most especially LBJ, to remain on Oveta's good side. Ike, who, to the chagrin of Taft Republicans, was not a strongly partisan person, was eager to maintain good relations with both Democratic leaders in Congress, particularly Rayburn, whom he had known for many years. Oveta would help in that effort.[56]

Oveta met with Eisenhower and Lucius Clay at the Eisenhower headquarters in the Commodore Hotel on November 21, where the president-elect offered her the appointment. "I requested her to undertake, immediately upon my inauguration, the duties pertaining to the Federal Security Agency, telling her that pending the creation of the new department she would have Cabinet rank," Eisenhower later wrote. "After some urging she agreed to accept." Reporters surrounded Oveta as she was leaving the Commodore Hotel, asking if Ike had mentioned a possible cabinet post or some other high position in his administration. "It was not mentioned," she answered falsely. She claimed to have only tried to talk Ike into taking a winter vacation in Texas. "He told me it was always a pleasure for him to come to Texas."[57]

Oveta and Will met with the management staffs of the *Houston Post* and KPRC Radio and TV in the *Post* boardroom soon after her return from New York. Will told the staff that his wife had an important announcement to make. Jack McGrew later recalled the moment: "Mrs. Hobby, speaking very softly, explained that Eisenhower had asked her to join his cabinet. She said that she was very reluctant to leave her family—and we were aware that she was especially concerned about Governor—but that she felt that she must accept this new and significant responsibility. As she finished, her eyes filled with tears and her voice almost broke. I had never seen her come close to crying." Will apologized to his editors for not allowing them to have the news scoop but said that Eisenhower's spokesman, James Hagerty, had insisted he would have to make the official announcement from New York City.[58]

Hagerty announced on November 25 that Eisenhower would nominate forty-seven-year-old Oveta Culp Hobby to the FSA post and that she would attend his cabinet meetings. When *U.S. News and World Report* contacted Oveta soon after the news broke, she agreed to an in-depth interview that the magazine subsequently ran as the cover story for its December 26 issue. Although Oveta had much to learn about the complex and diverse FSA, Eisenhower's team had schooled her about the incoming administration's general plan for its reorganization and its mission, especially with respect to the Social Security program. Oveta also did a crash course on the FSA's components and problems. Her preparation was apparent in the interview. Based on what Eisenhower told her, she was comfortable telling *U.S. News and World Report* that the FSA should be reorganized and raised to full cabinet status because of "growing concerns" over the nation's problems in education, health, and welfare. Most important politically, Oveta assured the magazine's readers that the president-elect was committed to expanding the Social Security program, not reducing or eliminating it, as some Taft Republicans were demanding. Her statement about Eisenhower's support for Social Security also reflected her own view. When the interviewer asked about her party affiliation, she answered that her political philosophy was "that of a liberal Republican," which contradicted Oveta's earlier statements that she was a political independent.[59]

Oveta's appointment pleased many of the prominent public figures who knew her. Sherman Adams typified the positive reaction the president-elect's inner circle had to this development. "You are a great girl," Adams wrote Oveta. "I am thrilled that you are coming up to be part of our team." Former president Herbert Hoover wrote her, "No one could be more enthusiastic over your appointment than myself." He reminded Oveta that the Hoover Commission had unsuccessfully tried to persuade Congress to create a cabinet-level department that would pull together under one administrator the various government agencies responsible for Social Security, health, and education. Hoover added that Congress would have passed the bill "but for personal animosities toward the then probable Secretary," a reference to Oveta's predecessor, Oscar Ewing. "With your appointment," Hoover wrote, "that block should now be out of the way." Oveta replied to Hoover that his message had strengthened her "determination to serve well. Frankly, I am not sure that I would have had the courage to take the assignment had it not been for the knowledge that your [Hoover Commission] report would give me guidance."[60]

One of the congratulatory letters most satisfying to Oveta was from General George Marshall, who was now retired after serving as President Truman's secretary of defense. Marshall sent Oveta a heartfelt and uncharacteristically playful message declaring that he was "privately and rather smugly proud" that he had been "involved in the earlier phases" of her career. Marshall added that he "would have liked to have seen you directly in the Cabinet, but, as a matter of fact, there is more to be done, constructively, where you are going than in most Cabinet positions. Your record is rapidly becoming the most notable of any other woman in this country." Eleanor Roosevelt, another woman with a notable record, sent Oveta a congratulatory message, to which Oveta replied, "Mrs. Roosevelt, your thoughtful congratulatory message is so deeply appreciated. I cannot tell you how much it means to me to be remembered by you."[61]

The newspaper industry journal *Editor and Publisher* observed that Ike's cabinet had needed "(1) a woman, (2) a Southerner, and (3) a Democrat." Oveta Culp Hobby's appointment had taken care of all three needs. As an example of Oveta's fame and popularity in the newspaper business, the journal noted that her fellow publishers had given her the "friendly" nickname of the "Hat" because of her habit of wearing especially striking and fashionable hats to meetings and public appearances. "She will give Washington a real style show with her fancy of chic bonnets," the journal added.[62]

Oveta's appointment also drew praise from the Democratic Party's congressional leadership, despite her support of the Republican presidential candidate. Sam Rayburn's private message congratulating Oveta was impishly personal. "Now, I am sure practically all your boy friends have written you congratulating you on the high honor that has been done you by your appointment," he wrote. In a more serious tone, Rayburn added his "sincere congratulations and [I] say to you that I feel that the Office of Federal Security Agency will be administered with a high degree of intelligence and with a splendid patriotism that I know you possess in such high degree." Lyndon Johnson wrote a letter to Republican senator Eugene Millikin of Colorado, who was chairing Oveta's confirmation hearing. Referring to Oveta's support of Eisenhower in the presidential election, LBJ noted, "Texas is a State in which we frequently have our differences and are not overly shy in expressing them. But I think there is one subject upon which every Texan will agree. [You] would have to search far and wide to find anyone better qualified for a position of high responsibility." LBJ placed the text of his letter in the *Congressional Record* and he sent Oveta a copy. When she replied to LBJ's letter, Oveta added, with a figurative wink, "I love your exaggerations."[63]

There was one noteworthy critic of Ike's decision, however, and it came from a somewhat surprising source: Republican senator Margaret Chase Smith of Maine. The senator stated her concerns in a speech at a board meeting of the National Federation of Republican Women on January 16. "There is nothing personal in this," Smith declared. "Mrs. Hobby is a good friend and a most capable woman and will do a good job," but she had been identified in press releases from the Eisenhower headquarters as being "a prominent Democrat." Smith expressed disappointment that the president-elect had chosen a woman whose actual partisan affiliation was in question. She argued that there were many capable longtime Republican women activists who could have been selected. Oveta chose not to respond publicly to Smith's complaint, and after she assumed her position at the FSA, she and Senator Smith remained on good terms.[64]

Oveta also heard much grumbling from right-wing Republican supporters of Senator Joseph McCarthy, some of whom were angered by the revelation that Oveta had donated money to the unsuccessful reelection campaign of her friend William Benton, the Democratic senator from Connecticut. Benton was a vocal critic of McCarthy. The news that the Eisenhower administration planned to establish a new executive branch department that would include supervision of federal health programs brought forth a stream of criticism from McCarthyites and Taft supporters, who feared that the department would lead to socialized medicine. They demanded that Eisenhower withdraw Oveta's nomination, but the Eisenhower team ignored their complaints, as did Oveta. Not only did she feel confident that Eisenhower had her back, she had also taken a clever step on the day her appointment was announced. She called FBI director J. Edgar Hoover, whom she had met during the war, to request a full investigation of her background and her suitability as a candidate to head the FSA. She was well aware of the anger that many members of the far-right wing of the Texas GOP felt toward her as a result of the key role she had played in denying Senator Taft the presidential nomination. A clean report from the FBI, which she was confident she would get (and did get), would be useful if she became a Red Scare target. It might not have been a coincidence that a few days before Oveta called Hoover, the *Houston Post* published an editorial praising the FBI director and his "unceasing fight against communism" and calling for his continuation as head of the bureau. It was known in the newspaper industry that FBI field agents duly clipped newspaper articles and editorials about Hoover and mailed them directly to headquarters in Washington, where they were gathered into compilations that Hoover eagerly read.[65]

Eisenhower's nomination of Oveta attracted little attention from the right wing other than a brief critical mention in the Hearst newspaper chain's pro-McCarthy *New York Journal American*. But Oveta's McCarthyite critics, who were also unhappy with Eisenhower, would not remain silent for long.[66]

# CHAPTER 32

## CREATING HEW

A flight carrying Will, Jessica, and Bill Hobby arrived at Washington National Airport on January 18, 1953, two days before Eisenhower's inauguration. Oveta was already in Washington, where she had settled into a large suite at the Mayflower Hotel that would serve as her home for the next two months. After reuniting at the Mayflower, the Hobbys were driven to the nearby Statler Hotel, where they joined eight thousand other guests at a preinaugural party. The chaotic gathering included Vice President–Elect Richard Nixon, Governors Earl Warren and Thomas Dewey, and other prominent Republican officeholders, as well as Hollywood and Broadway personalities Abbott and Costello, Ethel Merman, Hedda Hopper, and Constance Bennett. The *Chicago Tribune* noted that the guests "walked on one another's feet, knocked hats askew, kicked loose the carpeting, and gaped to see who was wearing what." Typical of Oveta's experiences dating back to her WAC days as one of the only women in a prominent leadership position in the federal government, the *Tribune* photographer had her pose for a photograph with the wives of the cabinet members designate instead of with their husbands.[1]

The following morning, the Hobby family made their way to a room in the Capitol, where the Senate Finance Committee, chaired by Senator Eugene Millikin, had scheduled a hearing to confirm Oveta's nomination as head of the Federal Security Agency. As Will, Bill, and Jessica took seats in the visitors' area in the hearing room, Texas senators Price Daniel and Lyndon B. Johnson escorted Oveta to a chair at the table from where she would answer the committee members' questions. Lady Bird Johnson later recalled that her husband took Oveta "under his wing" and introduced her to all the senators. Sitting in a chair next to Oveta, LBJ asked the committee to confirm her appointment. Assuring his Senate colleagues that she would administer the FSA not only with skill but also in an honest and honorable manner, he added, "Mrs. Hobby is the kind of woman you would want as a trustee of your estate." Recalling the moment years later, Oveta said that LBJ's remark not only "delighted and very much touched me, [it was] a remark that I have never forgotten."[2]

After LBJ's introduction, Oveta submitted her impressive resume to the committee. Aware that Ike's nomination of General Motors chairman Charles Wilson for secretary of defense had been delayed because of Wilson's unwillingness to sell his stock in the company, Oveta presented a detailed statement listing all of her financial assets, adding that she had resigned from her executive position at the *Houston Post*. After only six minutes of discussion, all except one of the committee members indicated their support for confirming Oveta's nomination. Only Republican senator Wallace Bennett of Utah expressed any reluctance to vote yes, not because he had any criticism of Oveta personally, but because he thought the committee had not taken sufficient time to examine her finances closely. He pointed out that the committee had spent hours earlier that morning questioning George Humphrey, the nominee for secretary of the treasury, about his financial interests. After Bennett expressed those concerns, he declined the opportunity to pursue the issue any further. The committee then voted to confirm Oveta's appointment.[3]

After the hearing, Will treated Oveta, Bill, and Jessica to a special brunch to celebrate their shared January 19 birthdays: Oveta's forty-eighth, Bill's twenty-first, and Jessica's sixteenth. The family gathering caught the attention of an Associated Press correspondent, who filed a report on the various happenings in Washington on the day before Eisenhower's inauguration. The reporter noted that the luncheon was one of the most "unusual celebrations of the day" because of the triple birthdays. Afterward, the Hobbys opted out of attending the special events scheduled for the rest of the day. Oveta wanted to spend that time reading informational material about the Federal Security Agency. As she told Inez Robb, a reporter Oveta knew from her Women's Army Corps days, she was working hard to "come to grips with the new job." "I assure you," she said to Robb, "I've been doing a cram course. Every spare moment is spent in reading something I'm supposed to know about." She added that the FSA "really deals with the human side of government. I don't believe there's a person in the nation who isn't touched by it."[4]

At 9:30 a.m. on Inauguration Day, Tuesday, January 20, the Hobbys joined the president-elect and the cabinet-level designees for a communion service at Washington's National Presbyterian Church. As usual, Oveta wore a distinctive and fashionable designer hat. Will's headgear, however, was a dark homburg, which Eisenhower had dictated as the official dress hat for the men in his official party instead of the traditional formal top hat. In his memoir, Sherman Adams recalled that when Ike was told that members of Washington's high society were grumbling that he was breaking tradition, he replied that if they followed historical tradition strictly, they would all have to wear tricornered hats and knee britches. Hearing this comment, General Robert Cutler, who was Ike's personal campaign secretary and close friend, quipped, "If Mrs. Hobby comes in knee britches, I want to be in the front row."[5]

The Hobbys attended the inaugural ceremony at the east portico of the Capitol, and then they were driven to a grandstand on Pennsylvania Avenue to watch the inaugural parade from their reserved seats. The parade lasted several hours longer than scheduled, finally ending at seven o'clock that evening. The Eisenhowers remained until the end, but the exhausted Hobbys left early to rest and dress for a special dinner that preceded the inaugural ball. Jessica had purchased a new strapless evening gown to wear to the ball, but Oveta thought it too daring, especially for a teenage girl, so she brought out a mink stole and instructed her daughter to drape it over her shoulders. With the family now properly attired in formal evening clothes, Oveta herded everyone downstairs to attend a dinner hosted by hotel tycoon Conrad Hilton that included Herbert Hoover, California senators William Knowland and Thomas Kuchel, Attorney General Herbert Brownell, *Los Angeles Times* publisher Norman Chandler, and several Hollywood producers. From there they proceeded to one of the two inaugural balls.[6]

The next morning, the Hobbys went to the White House to attend the swearing-in ceremony for all of Ike's cabinet members except Charles Wilson, whose appointment remained stalled in the Senate. Although Oveta was not yet an official member of the cabinet, the president included her in the ceremony because of his request that she attend cabinet meetings. Ike had Abraham Lincoln's cabinet table moved into the East Room of the White House, and he and the cabinet members and Oveta stood by it as Chief Justice Fred Vinson administered the oaths of office. A *New York Journal American* correspondent reported that the "small, delicately pretty" Oveta had "shadows under her brown eyes. She looked pale and tired from her efforts to enjoy the Inaugural ceremonies with her husband and their two children."[7]

Oveta addressed the women's division of the Republican National Committee (RNC) the day after she took her oath of office. This was the same audience to which Senator Smith had complained only a few days earlier about Ike's appointment of a Democrat instead of a Republican as head of the FSA. Oveta stressed that when she and other women Democrats "signed up as crusaders under General Eisenhower it was not for a mere election. General Eisenhower was not crusading for the presidency—he was . . . crusading for a great moral, philosophical and political transformation of our country." That crusade, she stressed, included Democrats and independents as well as Republicans. Oveta also knew that Senator Taft's supporters on the RNC had publicly demanded that the Eisenhower administration greatly reduce or entirely eliminate many of FDR's and Truman's programs, including the FSA. Oveta explained that many of FDR's and Truman's programs were initiated to meet specific emergencies that no longer existed. She pointed out that while Eisenhower would reassess and reevaluate all of the programs and policies he had inherited, he would not end or alter them in haste. "To junk all at once all that came to us from the preceding administration would be as unfair to the nation as to make permanent legislation which was intended for emergency," Oveta argued. Although she understood that many in her audience would disagree with this "go slow" approach, Oveta refused to tell her audience only what she thought they wanted to hear. "Some of what was done [by Democratic administrations] was sound in policy and shoddy in application; some [was] good in part and wrong in full perspective. Some may have been needed at the time but [is] now obsolescent." She would soon learn that her candid remarks failed to placate the most conservative members of the RNC.[8]

Will flew back to Houston with his son, who would begin his last semester as a senior at Rice. Jessica briefly remained with her mother until she began her junior year at Chatham Hall, an exclusive, Episcopalian, all-girls boarding school located in a small town in southwest Virginia about 250 miles from Washington. Chatham Hall was known for its horseback-riding program, which was a major attraction to the horse-loving Jessica. She had already accumulated a number of ribbons and trophies in Houston for her riding skills. Although the school was a few hours' drive from Washington, it was close enough for Oveta to monitor Jessica's academic progress and her behavior. Oveta, not Will, was the disciplinarian in the family. She made certain her daughter understood that she was expected to excel in her classwork studies, to act appropriately at school, and to stay out of the newspapers. Oveta was well aware that the tabloids were always alert to any misbehavior by the children of presidential cabinet members. Jessica would stay at Chatham Hall for only one year. In the fall of 1953, Oveta transferred her to the exclusive "Miss Hewitt's Classes" (later renamed the Hewitt School), located in a brownstone at Park Avenue and Sixty-Second Street in Manhattan, New York. Jessica graduated in June 1954, with Oveta giving the school's commencement address.[9]

President Eisenhower held his first cabinet meeting on January 23, 1953, and as he had promised, he told Oveta that her presence was not only welcome, it was also required. He intended to make Oveta the second woman in American history to attain a cabinet-level position. The press was characterizing Ike's cabinet as "nine millionaires and a plumber," the latter being Secretary of Labor Martin Durkin. But Durkin's eventual successor as secretary would later say that it was more accurate to refer to Eisenhower's cabinet as ten men and a Hobby.[10]

Unlike many of his predecessors, Eisenhower actively involved his cabinet in the affairs of his office. He held regular meetings with his full cabinet every Friday morning, unless he was traveling. As he noted in the first volume of his presidential memoir, *Mandate for Change*, he expected the members to "consider together questions of general public concern" and to make recommendations "on new government-wide policies and instructions." Stressing that everyone was invited to participate regardless of their own specific responsibilities, he often directed questions to each person at the table.[11]

At cabinet meetings, White House staff provided Oveta with a footstool because the cabinet chairs were too tall for her height. Smoking Parliament cigarettes as the cabinet deliberated with the president, Oveta usually refrained from commenting on matters outside the purview of her department, but there were exceptions. For example, during the crisis in September 1954 caused by Communist China's artillery shelling of the Nationalist Chinese–occupied islands of Quemoy and Matsu, Harold Stassen, Eisenhower's mutual security administrator, blurted out, "We ought to draw a line there, and say to Red China: Cross this, and it's war." Oveta later recalled that she felt the subject was a sensitive national security matter that should not have been discussed at

*Oveta Culp Hobby leaving the first Eisenhower cabinet meeting, January 1953.*

a cabinet meeting. She was appalled that Stassen was giving advice on military strategy to "the man who led our forces in Europe in World War II." She glanced at the president and saw that he was turning red with anger, so she spoke up: "That is exactly what got us into the war in Korea. You never tell an enemy where we draw the line. That enables him to define the battleground." Attorney General Herbert Brownell interjected, "Nothing like a Director of the WACs to explain military strategy!" His remark elicited loud and tension-breaking laughter from all the cabinet members as well as the president, who went on to another topic. Afterward, Eisenhower told Oveta, "You saved my life. I was about to explode." She replied, "Yes, I saw that, so I thought it would be best if I said something dumb." Ike replied, "But you didn't. It wasn't dumb. You never let the enemy pick the battlefield."[12]

Sherman Adams, Eisenhower's chief of staff, later observed that Oveta could always be counted on to "throw out some cautionary suggestion" whenever someone suggested imposing government controls on anything, especially on business. On the other hand, the most conservative members of the cabinet, Secretary of the Interior Douglas McKay, Secretary of Agriculture Ezra Taft Benson, and Secretary of Commerce Sinclair Weeks, were constantly on guard against any liberal social policy ideas that might sneak out of Oveta's department. Emmet J. Hughes, Eisenhower's chief speechwriter and in-house liberal, enjoyed watching the interplay between the rock-ribbed conservatives on the president's cabinet and Oveta. He later wrote that Oveta kept "popping up between them, with impudent grace." Hughes noted that Oveta, "while hardly a secret radical, conscientiously argued on the problems charged to her," which were social welfare programs and policies. These were the areas from which the right wing of the Republican Party wanted the federal government to withdraw completely. According to Hughes, despite Oveta's own conservative viewpoint, she was seen "by the suspicious as harboring egalitarian inclinations not wholly appropriate to a Republican Cabinet." This suspicion partly stemmed from Oveta's past support of the Democratic Party and the fact that her husband was a former Democratic governor of Texas, a history that bothered hard-core members of the GOP. Another factor, however, had to be that she was the only woman on the cabinet, and therefore it was assumed she would take softhearted liberal positions on issues presumed to be of particular concern to women, such as education, health, and welfare.[13]

Oveta's contribution to Eisenhower's first official cabinet meeting was to give him some surprising news. One of the first items on the meeting agenda was the issue of federal employee security regulations, which was a particularly sensitive issue, with Senator Joseph McCarthy eagerly attempting to uncover Communists hiding in the federal government. Early in the discussion, Oveta stated she had learned that half of the security officers in the FSA had never had a background check. Shocked by this revelation and concerned that McCarthy could exploit the information, Eisenhower immediately ordered his cabinet members to have all presidential appointees in their departments undergo FBI background checks. After a few more cabinet meetings,

Eisenhower recorded in his diary that Oveta was performing her duties exactly as he had expected and that he was delighted with her contributions to the cabinet discussions. In turn, Oveta relished her role on the cabinet. Jessica later told historian Debra Sutphen, "Mother rather enjoyed being . . . a big fish in a small pond—the one woman on the Cabinet."[14]

Participating in Eisenhower's Friday morning cabinet meetings was obviously important, but the reason Oveta was in Washington was to take control of the FSA while also planning the proposed new federal department in which the FSA would be the core unit. She had much to do, but first she staged two symbolic events to launch her new job, starting with hosting her first official meeting as FSA director with a member of Congress. With a small group of news photographers and reporters present, Oveta met with her former World War II legislative ally and friend Representative Edith Nourse Rogers, who welcomed Oveta back to Washington. Two days later, Oveta addressed an assembly at a government auditorium of the four hundred FSA staff members who worked in Washington. When Oveta discovered that no previous head of the agency had ever held general meetings of the staff, she decided that such gatherings would be a good way to launch her administration. At this first general meeting, the staff applauded appreciatively when she walked onstage and declared, "I really have nothing important to say, but I know I wouldn't like to work for someone I've never seen and I wouldn't want anyone to work for me who had never seen me, so I asked you to come in."[15]

With these symbolic acts accomplished, Oveta shut her office door and continued an in-depth study of her new domain. Created in 1939 to administer the federal government's social welfare programs, FSA was a sprawling bureaucracy composed of several units, including the Social Security Administration, the Office of Education, the Office of Vocational Rehabilitation, the Food and Drug Administration, and the Public Health Service. A total of 36,800 employees carried out a wide variety of functions, many of them vital to the health and security of millions of Americans. Unfortunately, the FSA wrestled with serious problems caused by the duplication of effort and associated inefficiencies that resulted from the overlapping of responsibilities and duties among its various units, especially at the regional level.[16]

Oveta's first priority was to take control over her agency and sort out the bureaucratic mess. She quickly discovered, however, that she would have little administrative support in carrying out that task. Longtime FSA administrators, especially Social Security Commissioner Arthur Altmeyer and Deputy Commissioner William Mitchell, met her arrival with open hostility and offered little to no cooperation. They suspected that the conservative Republicans on the Senate confirmation committee had approved Oveta's appointment with the understanding that she would fire most of them and then gut the Social Security program. These administrators were mistaken about her plan for Social Security, but the fear that their jobs were in danger was well founded. When President Eisenhower appointed Oveta to her post, he asked her to scrutinize Truman's proposed FSA budget for the coming fiscal year to identify and cut its budgetary "fat," including staff positions she deemed unnecessary. Oveta's efforts to find jobs to eliminate confirmed the suspicions of some of the longtime staff members that she was an uncaring and ruthless hatchet woman for the Republican right wing. Adding to that negative impression was Oveta's preference for formality in her interactions with staff and her vocally expressed outrage at anything she perceived as idleness, unreliability, or disloyalty. Wilbur Cohen, one of the longtime bureaucrats at the FSA who was on the Republican hit list, later described Oveta's behavior in staff meetings as "the way Queen Victoria in her younger days" must have acted.[17]

Oveta's problems were exacerbated by the fact that the FSA had no excess staff to cut. In reality the agency was understaffed, which presented her with the conundrum of being ordered to reduce the size of the FSA while not having enough help to administer the reduction. And those staff members who were in the best position to help weren't inclined to do so, particularly Altmeyer and Mitchell. The dedicated New Dealer Altmeyer, in particular, was openly disdainful of Oveta and her politics. The Social Security commissioner later described Oveta as "almost psychotically obsessed with her power and position." Altmeyer's deputy, William Mitchell, shared his opinion of Oveta. Mitchell had worked as a federal employee with a civil service classification for more than thirty years by the time Oveta assumed her duties at the FSA. In an oral history in 1968, Mitchell accused Oveta of having poor management skills. "Everything had to be spelled out in lengthy memoranda," Mitchell complained, "and had to go through 'X' number of clearance points, studied over by the general counsel and everybody, before any action could be done on anything." Mitchell considered those procedures to be inefficient and wasteful, and he believed her actions were the result of a professional insecurity stemming from Oveta's "recognition of her inadequacies for filling this type of job, to which she had never had any previous exposure."[18]

New Dealers Altmeyer and Mitchell weren't Oveta's only critics. Throughout her two and a half years as a member of the Eisenhower administration, she was a frequent target of Taft Republicans, who thought she was insufficiently conservative, while many on the extreme right accused her of being a closet socialist at best or a traitor at worse. On the other hand, liberal critics such as Altmeyer and Mitchell claimed she was too conservative and a political turncoat because of her support of Eisenhower. Much of this criticism from both the right and the left stemmed from Oveta's being a nonideologue and a political moderate. Altmeyer's and Mitchell's resistance to their recently appointed supervisor, while certainly anchored in political partisanship, also revealed an attitude typical of an old guard in a bureaucracy resistant to a different way of conducting business under a new administrator. George Meany, president of the American Federation of Labor, and Nelson Cruikshank, the federation's chief Washington lobbyist, also claimed that Oveta was incompetent. In an oral history Cruikshank gave years later, he claimed that Oveta was "way over her head. It was just too big a job for her, and too complex." Their unhappiness with Oveta undoubtedly sprang from her antipathy toward labor unions. In reviewing the comments of many of her male detractors, however, it seems more than likely that the words "incompetent," "insecure," and "inadequate" were code words for "woman."[19]

It should be no surprise that Oveta had to learn her job at the FSA and at the Department of Health, Education, and Welfare (HEW), especially the latter, which involved the creation of an entirely new department in the executive branch of the federal government. And it should be no surprise that Oveta made mistakes in dealing with such a complex organization, but that does not equate with incompetence. Debra Sutphen's deeply researched study of Oveta's service in the Eisenhower administration largely disproves the charges that she was incompetent or unfit for her position. Sutphen interviewed several individuals who had worked closely with or for Oveta in the WAC, at HEW, and at the *Houston Post*. They all noted how impressed they were with Oveta's administrative skills. Some of them reacted with incredulity when they heard the claims that Oveta was an incompetent administrator. Those who admired and respected Oveta's administrative talent included Generals George C. Marshall and Alexander Somervell, Herbert Hoover, Eleanor Roosevelt, Jesse H. Jones, and Dwight Eisenhower, each of whom was well positioned to make that determination.[20]

As Oveta struggled to understand FSA's tangled organizational structure and complicated budget, at least one veteran FSA administrator, Rufus Miles, put aside any partisan loyalties he might have had and stepped forward to help her with these daunting tasks. He provided crucial support for Oveta's efforts not only to gain control over the FSA but also to complete the review of FSA's bewildering budget. Miles also helped her develop a deep enough understanding of budget issues to avoid embarrassing herself when she testified at appropriations hearings.[21]

A variety of other pressing administrative obligations complicated Oveta's organizational work and budget preparations. Several members of Congress soon filled her appointments calendar to discuss various legislative proposals they were developing that included making drastic changes in Social Security and the Old Age and Survivors Insurance programs, increasing federal support for education, expanding programs to rehabilitate the disabled, and strengthening federal regulation of food and drugs. And as the only prominent female member of Eisenhower's administration, as well as one of its most articulate, Oveta had to contend with numerous invitations for her to speak to national organizations and groups, as well as requests from news media for interviews. During the first ninety days after Oveta became FSA director, her office documented over two thousand speaking invitations; the vast majority she declined. The number of invitations would increase to five thousand soon after she became HEW secretary. This pattern was thoroughly familiar to Oveta, of course, because of her previous experience as WAC director, when she had dealt with a similar onslaught of requests for her time. As she had done while serving as the "Little Colonel," Oveta did accept interview requests from the leading national magazines and a few influential newspapers with large readerships. Several magazines, including *Life, Time, U.S. News and World Report*, and *Businessweek*, featured Oveta in extensive articles, some of them cover stories.[22]

Working in her office six days a week from 8:00 a.m. until 6:00 or 7:00 p.m. and then a half day on Sundays, Oveta reviewed the extensive administrative records filling a long row of filing cabinets in the FSA's main office as she tried to understand its complex mission and organization and the budget that supported its operations. In the evenings after dinner she hauled stacks of letters back to her suite at the Mayflower, many to be signed and mailed the next morning. During this period the *New York Daily News* published a profile on Oveta that included an anecdote illustrating her intense work habits. One Saturday morning when she had a delay getting to work, Oveta called her office from her hotel suite and asked the switchboard if anyone was in the administrative office. The switchboard operator, who was unaware of her caller's identity, answered that she was sure Mrs. Hobby was in but she wasn't answering her telephone. Oveta asked how she knew that. The operator replied, "Lady, Mrs. Hobby is ALWAYS in."[23]

While Oveta struggled to take control of the FSA, Eisenhower moved forward with his plans to create the new cabinet department he wanted her to administer. On January 27, 1953, only one week after taking office, he issued the first executive order of his presidency, establishing the President's Advisory Committee on Government Organization (PACGO), with Nelson A. Rockefeller as chair. Arthur Flemming, head of the Office of Defense Mobilization, and the president's brother, Pennsylvania State University president Milton Eisenhower, joined Rockefeller as the other members of the committee. The president asked them to make recommendations about how to revive and implement some of the Hoover Commission's proposals that Congress had failed to adopt. But it was understood that their main task was to justify the consolidation of the several agencies, bureaus, and offices loosely operating in and around the FSA into a new cabinet-level department.[24]

Eisenhower asked forty-five-year-old Rockefeller to lead this effort because one of the wealthy New Yorker's pet projects was to establish a department he was calling the Department of Health, Education, and Social Security. In 1949 Rockefeller had directed the privately funded Temple University Survey of Government Organization to study and recommend reorganization plans for the federal government. The president believed that a strong and positive report from Rockefeller's committee, combined with the nomination of the moderately conservative Oveta Culp Hobby as its first secretary, would persuade Congress to authorize the department.[25]

As expected, Rockefeller's PACGO committee submitted a report to Eisenhower recommending the creation of the new department. The president subsequently used the report as the basis of his "Reorganization Plan No. 1," which he sent to Congress on March 11, 1953. The plan called for the creation of the Department of Health, Education, and Welfare to oversee several federal agencies and programs, most of which were already in the FSA. Eisenhower also asked Congress to consider other measures, including strengthening food and drug laws, continuing federal assistance to public schools, and broadening Social Security coverage to include categories of individuals who had not been previously eligible, such as farmers. The president, hoping the news would improve the odds that Congress would approve his plan, announced that Oveta Culp Hobby would be nominated as the secretary of the proposed new department.[26]

The Eisenhower administration expected strong criticism of the proposal to create this new federal department, not only from Senator Robert Taft and his allies in Congress but also from various professional organizations whose members feared federal regulation of their respective professions, businesses, and educational institutions. Among them were the leaders of the pharmaceutical companies and the American Medical Association (AMA), who were obsessed with the fear of a federally controlled national health insurance program, which the AMA labeled as "socialized medicine." In her nationally syndicated column, former war correspondent Doris Fleeson reported that warning flags were being flown from Capitol Hill to remind the president that the plan to establish HEW had become "highly controversial" within the medical profession.[27]

Anticipating this resistance, the Eisenhower administration launched its own lobbying operation a full month before the president submitted his HEW proposal to Congress. Oveta was among the leaders of that effort. On February 15, she appeared as the featured guest on the CBS television network program *State of the Nation*, where she stressed that the FSA, as well as any agency that might take its place while the present administration was in office, had no intention of sponsoring "socialized medicine as it is popularly known." Instead, she pledged that her agency would continue to support critically important medical research and development that would benefit the privately operated medical sector. When she was reviewing her comments in advance of her television appearance, Oveta wrote on her copy of the script, "No compulsory health insurance," as a reminder of the importance of mentioning the issue on the broadcast.[28]

President Eisenhower, Oveta, Rockefeller, and Flemming met with the AMA leadership in an attempt to persuade them to withdraw their opposition to HEW. To lessen AMA fears about socialized medicine, the president agreed that when Congress approved the establishment of HEW, he would appoint as one of the assistant secretaries a physician "recognized as a leader in the medical field" who would essentially be the AMA's representative at HEW. Eisenhower and Oveta followed that meeting with an appearance at a conference of the AMA's house of delegates. Oveta assured the gathering that the administration opposed "compulsory" or "socialized" medicine and that it would continue to consult closely with the medical community on any programs or policies that might affect it. As a result of this effort and the promise that the association would be able to select the new health and medical affairs assistant secretary, the AMA withdrew its official opposition to the legislation. But many individual medical doctors continued to attack the proposal, including a group of physicians in Houston who founded an organization called Doctors for Freedom. Oveta would soon become a target of this group and other right-wing conservatives in her hometown.[29]

Ike also dispatched Oveta to meet with key members of Congress to advocate for the HEW proposal. Newspaper columnist Doris Fleeson observed that the "personality" of the individual who was slated to become secretary of HEW was of "prime importance" to many congressional Republicans. To Fleeson, it was difficult to see how the president could find anyone "better than Mrs. Hobby for the job ahead. It would be interesting to know if he realized how shrewdly he had chosen." She added that Oveta "disarms criticism because she is handsome, well-bred and controlled." According to Fleeson, Oveta's basic strength in the upcoming legislative battle was that she was "instinctively conservative, as are most GOP leaders in Congress, and a team player. Mrs. Hobby will not try to storm Capitol Hill; she will be content to advance as a member of the Eisenhower-Republican team."[30]

Fleeson's observations about Oveta's ability to win over most of the opposition in Congress proved accurate. She spent most of a day at the Capitol meeting with the leaders of both parties to explain the reorganization plan, beginning with the Senate majority leader, Robert Taft, whom she later characterized as being "very interested and very helpful." When she met with Lyndon Johnson, Oveta recalled that her friend listened "very attentively and made very constructive suggestions." Years later, George Reedy, LBJ's press spokesman, recalled the meeting: "Oveta came to Johnson for advice on how to handle herself. We were in the room with her, and there were a couple of advisors." LBJ had a report listing the senators who had voiced opposition to the bill. He placed a check mark by the name of each senator, told Oveta to pay each one a visit, and advised her about how to deal with each senator individually. "And it worked," Reedy said. "I think Oveta was quite grateful to him." LBJ also called Arkansas senator John McClellan, the ranking member of the Government Operations Committee, to come to his office to hear Oveta's argument for creating HEW. She later recalled that LBJ and McClellan were "both very constructive in their suggestions and very constructive on the floor [of the Senate]" when the bill came to a vote.[31]

Oveta learned that senators on both sides of the aisle understood that vital public policy as well as political futures might be at stake over the HEW issue. Republican senators had a special problem, however. As author Cary Reich noted, "On the one hand, HEW was the veritable incarnation of the welfare state that Republicans had incessantly reviled for over twenty years. On the other hand, such enterprises as Social Security were now mainstays of American life; sacred cows that only the most diehard GOP fundamentalists dared pillory. By quickly elevating the department to cabinet status, Eisenhower was freely acknowledging this fact."[32]

The House passed the HEW bill on March 18 by a vote of 329 to 85. It had little difficulty in the House, thanks to the leadership of Oveta's friend, the minority leader Sam Rayburn. Rayburn understood that the creation of HEW would protect Social Security and other New Deal programs, so he rallied the Democratic minority behind it. The Eisenhower administration, however, had more worries about the conservative Republicans in the Senate and their leader, Robert Taft. On the day the bill passed in the House, Oveta testified in its favor at a hearing of the Senate Appropriations Committee. Taft questioned her about the name of this new department, which as far as he was concerned, sent the wrong message to the public about how active the federal government was going to be in providing social, educational, and health services and benefits. Oveta admitted she was not that excited about naming the new department Health, Education, and Welfare, because the title was too complicated and wordy. She preferred the name "Department of General Welfare," a phrase she extracted from the preamble to the Constitution. With her eye on Senator Taft, Oveta was careful to explain that in her view the term meant that it was the government's duty "to *promote* the general welfare rather than to *provide* for the general welfare." Taft, however, protested that even the idea of *promoting* the general welfare was "what I've been trying to get away from."[33]

On March 26, five days before the full Senate was to vote on the HEW bill, Oveta took advantage of a break in the schedule to fly to Houston to preside over a gala celebrating Will's seventy-fifth birthday. The event attracted many of Will's old friends, associates from the *Post* and the KPRC radio and television stations, and several of the city's civic and business elite. Oveta was in bed by midnight, barely got in three hours of sleep, and then flew back to Washington just in time for Eisenhower's weekly 9:30 a.m. cabinet meeting.[34]

Despite Taft's grumbling, the Senate easily passed the HEW bill on March 31, with critical support from Lyndon Johnson. On April 1, 1953, Eisenhower signed the bill creating the first new cabinet department in forty years. Eisenhower's staff secretary Arthur Minnich gave Oveta a large share of the credit for its passage. "Out of her effective selling of the plan came the phrase 'Hobby's Lobby,'" Minnich noted. "Thereafter . . . there was a tendency to suggest that Mrs. Hobby be called in whenever a matter arose which might incur rough going on Capitol Hill." Accordingly, during the first four months that Oveta served as HEW secretary, she testified nine times before congressional commit-tees. Lyndon and Lady Bird Johnson hosted a party in honor of Oveta and the creation of HEW. Will flew to Washington to join Oveta in the celebration. After the party, the Johnsons sent Oveta a large bouquet of flowers. "That was a gloriously delightful party," Oveta wrote the Johnsons. "I want you to know how much all of your kindnesses have meant to Will and me! All of our love to you both."[35]

Because HEW was an entirely new executive branch department, Oveta had to undergo another confirmation hearing, although the process was pro forma. She had strong bipartisan support in both houses of Congress and easily won confirmation. *Life* magazine reported that when she dutifully appeared before the Senate committee for her confirmation hearing, she was "greeted gallantly by many Senators and questioned by none." A Capitol Hill correspondent for the Associated Press wrote that Oveta "had made friends so rapidly in Washington that there seemed little chance of a 'no' vote. Reporters had to beat the bushes to find any opposition" to her appointment as secretary. They did find one, however, and that was Mississippi congressman John Bell Williams. Although as a member of the House Williams couldn't vote on a Senate confirmation, he publicly criticized her appointment with the warning that by creating HEW and placing Oveta at its head, Congress was creating a "tool" that a future president could use to establish socialized medicine. Williams's warning was noted by the right wing of the Republican Party, especially its adherents in Houston.[36]

*Oveta Culp Hobby walking with Will Hobby on the tarmac after his flight landed at National Airport, Washington, DC, April 1953.*

At ten o'clock on Saturday, April 11, 1953, Oveta Culp Hobby became the first secretary of HEW and only the second woman in American history to serve as an official member of a presidential cabinet. President Eisenhower stood by her side in the Oval Office of the White House as a White House assistant administered the oath. Will Hobby and several members of the Texas congressional delegation also attended. At the end of the ceremony, Ike handed Oveta her official commission, rolled up and tied with a ribbon, and proclaimed, "Now you are a real Secretary!" The president took Will by the wrist and drew him close to pose for photographs with him and Oveta. Eisenhower then made a quick exit from the White House to get in a round of golf, while Oveta and Will stepped outside to a paved area where she reenacted her oath taking for the movie reel cameras. While posing, she chatted with reporters, who asked her if she should be addressed as "Madame Secretary," which was the title Roosevelt's secretary of labor, Frances Perkins, had used.

*Oveta Culp Hobby, President Eisenhower,
and Will Hobby at the White House
after Oveta's swearing in as Secretary of
the Department of Health, Education,
and Welfare, April 11, 1953.*

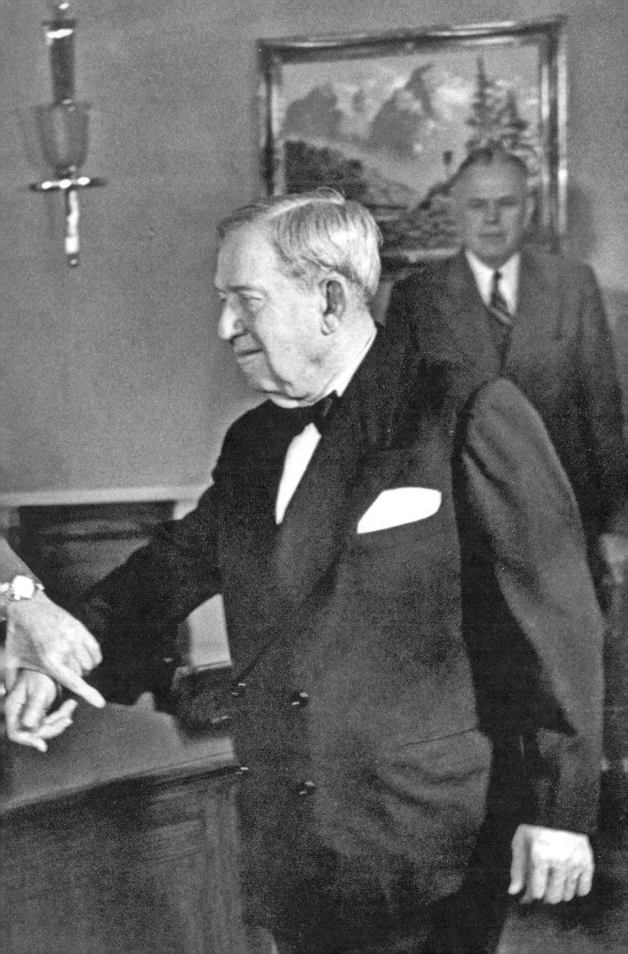

"No," Oveta replied, "that's too formal. Please call me Mrs. Secretary." Walter Trohan, the *Chicago Tribune*'s veteran Washington correspondent, sent a note to Jesse Jones in Houston to tell him how impressed he was with Oveta's performance at the ceremony. Jones responded that he was well acquainted with Oveta's ability to charm and was not surprised to hear that she was being accepted. "It is not hard to get along in Washington if you understand human nature and like people," he told Trohan. "I am glad Mrs. Hobby is taking well. She would, I think, in any situation."[37]

Immediately after reenacting her oath taking for the cameras, Oveta was driven in her government limousine to the huge five-story Federal Security Building on Independence Avenue, located two blocks from the Capitol, where she took an elevator to the top floor to move into a private office forty by twenty-five feet in size. Her glass-topped desk sat on one side of the room, with a silk Stars and Stripes flag hanging from a stand behind it. A conference table and chairs were on the other end of the office. When she entered the room, she found large sprays of lilacs and roses that Nelson Rockefeller had placed on her conference table to welcome her. Rockefeller, who had been operating out of his PACGO office located in the Executive Office Building next door to the White House, had hoped Eisenhower would ask him to head HEW. Despite his disappointment at not getting the job, and against the advice of friends, he had accepted the president's offer to serve as HEW undersecretary, with the announcement of his appointment delayed until after Oveta assumed her new position. Rockefeller told his associates that federal health, education, and welfare policy was one of his strong interests and that he felt obligated to help Oveta organize the new department because of the role he had played in its creation.[38]

Rockefeller biographer Richard Norton Smith claimed that Rockefeller's acceptance of a second-tier appointment was "shrewd, if surprising." Smith argued that Rockefeller, whose long-term goal was the presidency, could see that serving as Oveta's deputy "would broaden his knowledge of the domestic scene" and supplement his strength in international relations, his particular field of interest. Of equal importance to Rockefeller's political ambitions was his belief that by serving in any capacity in the Eisenhower administration, he would demonstrate that he was "a team player among Republicans suspicious of his previous service in Democratic administrations." The latter goal, however, proved elusive. "Ironically," Smith points out, "Rockefeller made more enemies than friends among fiscal conservatives within the administration, to say nothing of an emerging coterie of rightward thinking opinion makers."[39]

Oveta welcomed Rockefeller's appointment. She saw Rockefeller as a badly needed ally who would help her manage the complex bureaucracy that was being consolidated under HEW. According to Cary Reich, Oveta needed an administrator "who grasped the full scope of the department's influence, and someone who could push its program through Congress. No one she knew of fit the bill better than Nelson Rockefeller." In addition, she had gotten to know Rockefeller soon after she became head of the FSA, and they had worked together in the lobbying effort to persuade Congress to authorize

HEW. Oveta announced Rockefeller's appointment as undersecretary a week after she was sworn in as secretary of HEW.[40]

For the remainder of her first day on the job and for a couple of days after, *Life* magazine photographer Hank Walker photographed Oveta as she busily organized her office, met with staff, had lunch with Rockefeller at her conference table, and testified to the House Appropriations Committee about HEW's budget. *Life* used the photographs to illustrate a major story on Oveta's becoming secretary of HEW. The story's headline, "A Lady Takes Over Newest Cabinet Post: Mrs. Secretary . . . finds a woman's job is almost never done," spoke volumes about how unusual it was for a woman to have such an elevated status in a presidential administration in this era. As was typical, *Life* assigned the story to the magazine's fashion editor, Sally Kirkland, instead of a political reporter. Kirkland assured her readers, "As effective as [Oveta] is as an executive, she is still an efficient homemaker who retains her interest in such womanly matters as fashion and family life." In a follow-up letter to Oveta, Kirkland wrote that *Life*'s editors were "delighted . . . at the nice balance between Mme. Secretary, the hard working executive and Mrs. Hobby, the attractive and feminine woman."[41]

In addition to the "lady"-takes-a-job approach, the news media also did profiles on Will, the only male spouse of a department secretary. A headline in the *Washington Star* proclaimed, "Husband of Welfare Boss Genial Texan." The story explained that Will would be the first "cabinet husband" to be "on the Capital social horizon," because the spouse of Frances Perkins, the only other female cabinet member in US history, had been in poor health and was seldom in Washington during Perkins's service on FDR's cabinet. Noting the age difference between Will and Oveta, the *Star* gently hinted at scandal by noting that Will was "very reticent about the circumstances under which he met and married his attractive young bride." When asked how he and Oveta got together, Will answered, "I feel like I have always known her. Her father was in the Texas Legislature when I was governor, and I knew of her then as a very bright girl."[42]

As Oveta organized HEW, she faced intense pressure from conservative Republicans in Congress and on the Republican National Committee for her to purge FDR's and Truman's political appointees from the FSA component of her new cabinet department. Many of those appointees had been in their jobs for more than a decade because of the unprecedented length of FDR's tenure as president. To conservative Republicans in Congress, led by Senator Carl Curtis of Nebraska, the leading opponent of Social Security, the leadership of the FSA was a particular problem. They viewed FSA administrators as liberal New Deal holdovers who had to be removed as quickly as possible. As soon as Oveta assumed her duties at the FSA in late January, Curtis pressured her to remove Social Security Commissioner Altmeyer; his chief assistant, Wilbur Cohen; and Deputy Commissioner Mitchell, among others. All were widely respected administrators but also known to be liberal Democrats and fervent New Dealers. Altmeyer and Mitchell, but not Cohen, had waged bureaucratic war against Oveta from the start of her tenure as director of the FSA, and she was more than eager to be rid of both.

With Eisenhower planning to ask Congress to expand Social Security coverage, Oveta and the president's political operatives in the White House realized that it would be smart political strategy to remove the Social Security administrators as soon as possible, not only to demonstrate the administration's determination to "clean up" the agency, as Curtis demanded, but also to save the program. It was hoped that conservative Republicans would not try to kill Eisenhower's Social Security agenda if bureaucrats acceptable to Republicans were running the program. As a fierce and vocal defender of the New Deal, Altmeyer knew he was a target. For that reason, he announced his retirement effective on May 8, 1953, when he would qualify for full benefits. During the few weeks prior to his retirement, Altmeyer remained persona non grata to Oveta. Larry DeWitt, the official historian of the Social Security program, has written that she excluded Altmeyer from meetings, ignored his memos, and made a point of being cool to him whenever they did have any interaction. Years later, Altmeyer recalled Oveta as a "shy, and uncertain person who found it painful to deal with fellow officers and to make difficult decisions." Although the situation was awkward for Altmeyer, he was comforted by the knowledge that he would soon retire with full benefits, and then Oveta could replace him with someone of her own choosing. When Eisenhower submitted his "Reorganization Plan No. 1" to Congress, Altmeyer was surprised to learn that the plan abolished the position of commissioner *for* Social Security, which was Altmeyer's job, and then called for the creation of a new position called the commissioner *of* Social Security. It was obvious that by this simple maneuver Altmeyer would be out of a job, even if he decided to delay his retirement. In other words, Oveta would not have to take the distasteful action of firing him if he decided to stay. Altmeyer was relieved, however, when he learned that the plan had an effective date of May 11, which was three days after he would qualify for full retirement.[43]

While Congress was considering Eisenhower's "Reorganization Plan No. 1," the administration, eager to get HEW up and running, asked that the effective date for establishing the department be changed from May 11 to April 11. This date change meant that Altmeyer would be forced to retire twenty-seven days before his wife would be eligible for survivor benefits. When the news media made this known to the public, it quickly developed into a major embarrassment for the White House, as well as for Oveta. She contacted Altmeyer, "literally as he was in the process of cleaning out his desk," according to DeWitt, and offered to hire him as a special consultant for one month to allow him to earn his full retirement. Altmeyer refused Oveta's offer, later stating that he "didn't feel justified in taking money for any such make-work proposition or boondoggle." When Cohen got word that his resignation was expected immediately, he refused the demand. "It was extremely humiliating to me," Cohen recalled, "but I made up my mind that I was not going to be kicked around for political reasons by the Republican National Committee." He remained in his post, but he still had a target on his back.[44]

After Altmeyer's departure, Senator Curtis and members of the Republican National Committee pressured Oveta to continue the purge. On May 18, 1953, Barbara Gunderson, a Republican national committeewoman from South Dakota, wrote one of Oveta's assistant administrators. "I have wondered so often if you have been able to make progress in the touchy and crucial matter of getting new 'Eisenhower Stalwarts' into your department," she pointedly asked. Complaining that it seemed to her that the purge had been in a "virtual deep-freeze," Gunderson demanded action and recommended that a prominent South Dakota Republican woman fill one of the vacancies.[45]

Oveta passed the unpleasant task of cleaning house to Nelson Rockefeller. The highest-ranking targets, William Mitchell, Wilbur Cohen, and Jane Hoey, held civil service appointments, which made them much more difficult to remove than the political appointees. Oveta solved that problem by having their job descriptions rewritten to add policy-making responsibilities to their list of duties, which would allow those positions to be removed from civil service protection. The Civil Service Commission approved this plan, and the jobs were reclassified. They were among the twenty-five positions Oveta had reclassified of the thirty-five thousand total positions at HEW. Job reclassification, however, didn't solve other problems related to Cohen's removal. Rockefeller had worked with and respected Cohen long before Eisenhower became president, and he didn't want to be the one to tell Cohen he had to go. John W. Tramburg, a liberal Republican from Wisconsin, was selected to replace Altmeyer as Social Security commissioner. When Tramburg found out Cohen would be dismissed, he sent word to Oveta that he would not accept the appointment unless he received assurances Cohen would be retained. He and Wisconsin native Cohen were old friends who had been professional colleagues years before in their home state. Tramburg told Rockefeller that Cohen probably knew more about the Social Security program than anyone and that he was a valuable asset to HEW.

The news that an attempt was being made to fire Cohen and Mitchell soon came to the attention of their powerful ally, American Federation of Labor (AFL) president George Meany, who was no fan of Oveta. Meany had years earlier negotiated labor contracts with Rockefeller for his private construction projects, and the two men had a grudging admiration for each other. Meany went to Rockefeller's office at HEW and demanded an end to the political purge, pointing out that the powerful AFL would not stand idly by and watch the Eisenhower administration destroy the civil service system. Although conservative Republicans in Congress were hostile to the labor movement, the Eisenhower administration saw Meany and his AFL as important allies in their effort to persuade Congress to expand Social Security coverage. Rockefeller, who had ambitions for elected public office, was also not eager to alienate the AFL. He gave in to Meany's demand. To get around this problem, Rockefeller, who had recommended Tramburg's appointment and who also didn't want to get rid of Cohen, got Oveta's approval to offer Cohen and Mitchell new positions at HEW that were seemingly less influential than their current jobs. Both men accepted the offer and remained at HEW. "I took a demotion of one grade and one thousand dollars a year," Cohen said. "I willingly accepted that as a basis for trying to solve the problem. I never bore any grievance against Nelson [Rockefeller] who, I think, always remained very friendly with me." Cohen also had no hard feelings for Oveta, because he understood that she was under tremendous pressure from Senator Curtis. As it developed, Cohen would provide valuable aid to Oveta as she and her staff developed a bill to create a medical reinsurance program. "When Mrs. Hobby left [HEW], I went to see her," Cohen remembered. "She thanked me for my help." Mitchell would continue in his position until 1959, when he became commissioner of Social Security, while Cohen would eventually become LBJ's secretary of HEW.[46]

Jane Hoey, the sixty-one-year-old director of the Bureau of Public Assistance, was unable to escape the purge. Hoey, a Democrat who had held her job for eighteen years, was a product of the settlement house movement in New York City and one of the architects of Social Security. She was an expert on social welfare issues who had been widely praised for her nonpartisan and competent handling of the job. Oveta asked Nelson Rockefeller to give Hoey the news that she would be removed from her position. Because Hoey was so well respected professionally, Oveta and Rockefeller anticipated that her removal would be controversial. To tamp down any controversy, they decided, as they had with Cohen and Mitchell, to offer her another position at HEW with a lower level of pay and status. They also learned that Hoey would soon be eligible for retirement, so they decided to give her the option of taking retirement rather than suffering a dismissal. When Rockefeller told Hoey about Oveta's decision to place someone else in her job, he explained that the decision "in no way reflects any lack of appreciation of your long record of devoted service in this field. It is simply a question of carrying out the Administration's policy of placing its representatives in key policy making positions throughout the Government. She would be very glad if you would care to stay in the Department in another capacity." Hoey rejected the offer of another job and retired instead. As anticipated, Hoey's removal generated protests from hundreds of social workers across the nation, who bombarded HEW with petitions demanding her reappointment. But because George Meany and the labor unions had no interest in saving Hoey, Oveta was able to ignore the protest and easily rode out the storm.[47]

A few weeks after Oveta's appointment as secretary of HEW was official, she moved from her suite at the Mayflower Hotel to an eight-room apartment at 2101 Connecticut Avenue. Her neighbors included former vice president Alben Barkley, Senator Eugene Millikin, and Supreme Court justice and fellow Texan Tom Clark. The apartment featured five bedrooms, including one for Jessica, who stayed with her mother every weekend. Another room was for Will, who planned to stay with Oveta some weekends and during the summer, and there was one for the live-in maid Oveta had summoned from Houston, who cooked and took care of the apartment. An additional bedroom was reserved for Bill to use as needed after he graduated from Rice that spring. Oveta's favored space in her apartment was a small study, where she placed on a wall above the couch some items from her prized art collection, including paintings by Matisse and Morandi. With the help of a New York decorator, Oveta carefully selected the apartment's Chinese-influenced décor that included rare Chinese antiques. All of the furniture, however, came from the Hobby mansion at Shadyside. Oveta's love affair with Chinese decorative

*Oveta Culp Hobby with her daughter, Jessica, on a shopping
expedition in New York City, April 1953.*

furnishings partly stemmed from her visit with Chiang Kai-shek and his wife in their impressively furnished private quarters in Nanking in 1947. Oveta admired Madame Chiang's style, manner, and political skills. During the war, Betty Bandel had written in her diary that Oveta "hero-worshipped" the First Lady of Nationalist China. Oveta and Madame Chiang reconnected soon after Oveta joined the Eisenhower administration. During her stay in Washington in March 1953, Madame Chiang had a long visit with Oveta and afterward sent her a handwritten note. "I'm sending you some Chinese tea," she told Oveta, "which I hope you will like as much as the tea I gave you in Nanking."[48]

Oveta was soon embarking on weekend excursions to Manhattan to buy a new wardrobe appropriate for work as well as evening socializing. *Life* magazine described one trip to New York during which she purchased six suits and several hats. She also acquired a custom-designed and fashionable leather valise to carry business papers and a red, leather-bound copy of the Anglican Book of Common Prayer. When at home, the book resided on a table by her bed. Another one of her prized purchases was a pale-pink, brocade, full-length evening gown with a matching satin bag by famed celebrity fashion designer Valentina. The writer for *Life* added that Oveta was "easily the most attractive and stylishly dressed member of President Eisenhower's official family," which another writer described as being a "monochromatic landscape larded with gray lawyers and paunchy businessmen." Rockefeller biographer Cary Reich observed that "at forty-eight, [Oveta] looked like a gracefully aging high-fashion model" who always attracted attention wherever she went. Reich also noted that among the HEW administrative staff, "there was fascination with the Hobby style, which included her hats as well as her clothes."[49]

Joan Braden, who would become Oveta's executive assistant, recalled in her memoir the first time she saw Oveta walk out of the elevator and enter the HEW secretary's suite of offices. "Mrs. Hobby, formidable and forbidding, wore a hat, securely fixed upon her head as she grimly strode, aides rushing to keep up with her, through the halls," Braden remembered. "She was beautiful. She was attractive to men. She'd borne two children. She dressed simply but in great style. [She] began to take over the department."[50]

Nelson Cruikshank, the AFL's chief lobbyist, frequently met with Oveta to discuss Social Security issues. He later observed that Oveta "was very feminine in her appearance and all, but you had the feeling there was a solid iron core there. It wasn't all softness and pink." Many others agreed with this perception. Reich has written that "the bows and brocade could never quite conceal the flinty determination that had propelled her from Killeen." Joan Braden observed that Oveta "did not need a man to give her a backbone. [She] was a tougher boss than any man for whom I've ever worked. She had grown up in a man's world, competing against men and competing successfully. The effort had required more self-discipline than most women of her generation ever had to demand of themselves."[51]

# CHAPTER 33

# MRS. SECRETARY AND ROCKY

O veta wasted no time immersing herself in her new job as secretary of the Department of Health, Education, and Welfare (HEW). She moved quickly to pull together the various agencies and institutions that Congress had allocated to HEW and to place them under her administrative control. Although organizing the Women's Army Corps had been a major challenge, most of those problems had been straightforward, with clear right and wrong options. HEW was different. The WAC had been part of a large army bureaucracy, and many decisions had been made for her. At HEW she was in charge of the department's bureaucracy, not controlled by it. She reported to the president, which meant she reported to no one. In significant ways she was entirely on her own.[1]

By the time Oveta sat down to work at her mahogany desk that first week, she had a general knowledge of what had to be done to organize her massive new federal department, but it was a daunting task. Before she could get deeper into the weeds, she had to organize a staff. The legislation creating HEW included an appropriation for additional administrative personnel. Oveta's first hire was Jane Morrow Spaulding, an African American graduate of Fisk University. Henry Cabot Lodge, who was now Eisenhower's UN ambassador, recommended Spaulding to Oveta. Spaulding had been one of the first prominent African American women to announce support for Eisenhower for president. She subsequently held a post as a member of the women's division in the national headquarters of Citizens for Eisenhower in 1952, with the specific duty of organizing black voters nationwide. Oveta met her when they both were working at the presidential campaign headquarters in New York. Spaulding had made a positive impression on Eisenhower's campaign staff, especially Lodge. On April 14 Oveta appointed Spaulding to the position of assistant to the secretary, with general staff responsibilities for education, Social Security, child welfare, and health. With her appointment she became the highest-ranking African American in the federal government.[2]

*Oveta Culp Hobby's second* Time *cover, 1953.*

Nelson Rockefeller set up his office near Oveta's and brought in his own team to help her address the massive task of consolidating several federal agencies under HEW. Joan Braden was one of Rockefeller's assistants who moved over to Oveta's personal staff. Braden later recalled that Rockefeller came to her one morning and said, "Mrs. Hobby wants to see you. It's all right. Just go in and see her." According to Braden, when she met with Oveta the latter "smiled as she told me . . . 'I want you to be my personal assistant, help me organize . . . help me keep track of what's going on, help me with everything.'" Braden agreed.[3]

Rockefeller eventually helped fill a number of other key positions on Oveta's administrative staff, including the assistant secretaries. On Rockefeller's recommendation, Oveta appointed Roswell Perkins to serve as her special assistant to lead a task force to outline Eisenhower's proposed revision of the Social Security system. Only twenty-seven years old, Perkins had been a leader of the Young Republicans for Eisenhower organization in New York City during the presidential campaign. Over a period of six weeks, Perkins gathered a mass of information that eventually proved invaluable to the effort to broaden the existing Social Security system.[4]

*Oveta Culp Hobby with Roswell Perkins and President Eisenhower*
*in the Oval Office of the White House, 1953.*

Oveta, who would later characterize Perkins as a "brilliant" man, decided in January 1954 to recommend him to the White House for the position of HEW assistant secretary in charge of Social Security. Because this position was a presidential appointment, Oveta had to submit Perkins's name to Eisenhower's chief of staff, Sherman Adams, for screening. Adams soon called Oveta with the news that Eisenhower's appointments staff had rejected her request because they thought Perkins was too young. "Well, I'm going to submit his name anyway," Oveta replied. "Let's set up a meeting with the President, and you tell the staff's side and I'll tell mine, we'll let him decide." Adams scheduled the meeting with Eisenhower at a time when Oveta had a full day of appointments that she could not cancel. The stern Vermonter responded that the meeting with the president could not be canceled. "Okay," Oveta answered. "You go to the meeting and you give the staff's side and then you give my side." After a long silence, Adams said, "You mean that?" "Certainly," Oveta replied. "I know you'll make a fair presentation." Oveta then sent more information about Perkins to Adams to use in presenting her side of the issue to Eisenhower. After Adams met with the president, he sent a message to Oveta's office asking her to call him. When she did, Adams told her that he would never "fall into your trap again!" Oveta asked what he meant. Adams explained, "I presented your side first, and the President never even gave me a chance to give the other side. He just said, 'Let me have those papers and I'll sign them.'" Adams had learned that what Oveta wanted, Oveta usually got, especially from Dwight Eisenhower. Perkins was sworn in as assistant secretary, with responsibility for "policy analysis" and for HEW's legislative program. Oveta came to rely heavily on Perkins, and the two shared mutually strong feelings of respect and admiration.[5]

Even though Oveta depended on "Rocky" to fill most of the HEW jobs, she didn't go along with everything he wanted. Oveta set up a schedule for weekly early morning meetings with bureau chiefs. When Rockefeller asked if he could bring his personal assistant, Nancy Hanks, to the meetings, Oveta said no, much to Rockefeller's chagrin. Joan Braden later wrote that Oveta had drawn a line for Rockefeller when he made the request. "[Nelson] had organized this department, brought the people in, and had been the principle player, and now quite suddenly he had a new assertive boss . . . who . . . knew what she wanted people to do and got them to do it. Including Nelson."[6]

In her memoir, Braden cited another incident when Oveta showed Rockefeller who was in charge. On an early summer evening in 1953, Nelson and his wife, Tod, hosted a dinner party at their vast estate on Washington's Foxhall Road for Eisenhower's cabinet members, their wives, and their chief aides. The guests gathered outside the mansion on a terrace that overlooked the lawn. "We all stood there on that lovely spot like so many pasteboard cutouts," Braden recalled. "None of the Cabinet members knew one another well, and none of their wives knew one another at all." They were having trouble even engaging in small talk. It was an awkward moment. "Oveta knew at once what was wrong [with the party]," Braden wrote. The Rockefellers were waiting until dinner to take cocktail orders. Oveta strolled over to Rockefeller and commanded, "Nelson, drinks."

Nelson then asked the waiter to get Oveta a glass of wine. "No," said Oveta, "I don't want a glass of wine, Nelson. I want scotch, bourbon, gin, vodka, and rye. I want it for everybody and I want it now." Braden said that Oveta was smiling politely while she was barking out her order. "Nelson had a look of wonderment on his face," Braden recalled. "He ran into the house" to talk to the kitchen staff. Oveta turned to Braden and pointed out that Secretary of Defense Charlie Wilson was "about to die" for lack of having a drink. When Rockefeller returned with his wife at his side, he announced that they would soon serve dinner and wine would be available then. Oveta turned to Mrs. Rockefeller and said, "Hold dinner. Hold it until everybody has had a drink and don't serve it until the secretary of defense has had two." The Rockefellers followed Oveta's instructions. Braden remembered that after everyone was well into the alcohol, Oveta invited a much happier Secretary Wilson to rise and sing his famous version of "The Face on the Barroom Floor." "He sang lustily and to great applause," Braden said. "Everybody had a splendid time, except perhaps Nelson, who had a learning experience instead." The former "Little Colonel" had made a statement about who was in command.[7]

Although Oveta might have been in charge, Rockefeller occasionally succeeded in showing her that the administrative methods she employed weren't always the best for staff morale. Reich observed that the contrast between the enthusiastic and playful "Rocky" and the "imperious, often remote Hobby—who insisted that her aides rise when she stepped into the room, as though this was still the WACs—could not have been starker." A couple of days before Halloween in 1953, Rockefeller initiated and participated in a pumpkin-carving contest with his secretaries, which was held on the conference table in his office. They were busy carving when the secretary of HEW suddenly opened the door and saw the table covered with pumpkins and the cuttings scattered about. With a shocked look on her face, Oveta asked Rockefeller to step outside the room for a talk. Out in the hall, Oveta, who was visibly angry, lectured Rockefeller about allowing his secretaries to engage in such frivolous activities on government time. When Oveta finished her scolding, Rockefeller calmly explained that the pumpkin carving wasn't the secretaries' idea—it was his. She got the message. The following day, Oveta had a prominent display of the secretaries' carved pumpkins in her office suite.[8]

Despite Rockefeller's tendency to show an attitude of entitlement as a member of one of the wealthiest and most famous families on earth, as well as his obvious inclination to be in control, Rockefeller knew how to behave. "As assertive as he was behind the scenes," Cary Reich claimed, "Rockefeller was scrupulously careful not to be seen to be usurping his boss's authority. No decision was reached without consulting her; no initiative was taken that had not been vetted with her first; no contacts were made with Congress or the executive branch of which she had not been apprised." Roswell Perkins recalled, "Nelson was very respectful, very supportive, courteous, [deferential]. When he wanted to make a point, he would say, 'Well, now, Oveta, I wonder whether we should consider this.' And in private conversation, there were many times when he would say something to me like 'Look, we've got to reframe this, or do something that will put it more in line with what the secretary is looking for.'" When Oveta was preparing to testify at a congressional hearing where she anticipated hostile questions from the Democratic members ("a very scary task," she later recalled), Rockefeller went to her office and recounted the story of Daniel in the lions' den as she listened with a puzzled look on her face. He then gave her Alberto Giacometti's small sculpture of a lion's head, telling her that it was meant to bolster her courage when she faced the committee. "And it did," Oveta admitted when telling the story to one of her granddaughters years later.[9]

When Rockefeller accompanied Oveta to testify at Senate committee hearings, he went out of his way to make it clear that Oveta was his boss and that he was there to help, including walking two paces behind her and lighting her cigarettes. "Rockefeller's friends took this spectacle with slack-jawed wonderment," Reich noted. New York attorney Oscar Ruebhausen, Rockefeller's close friend and advisor, observed that he had "never seen anyone struggle or strain as much as [Rockefeller] did to preserve the ultimate deferential protocol. It was not easy for him at all." Several of Rockefeller's intimates claimed that by playing the second fiddle role publicly, Rockefeller was trying to prove that he was not the "conniving renegade" many Republicans perceived him to be.[10]

Journalist and native Texan Liz Carpenter covered some of the hearings when Oveta testified. She later recalled watching Oveta "looking elegant, calm, assured, her home-work completed for her testimony, explaining her requests and answering questions. At her side was the buoyant Nelson Rockefeller. . . . [W]hat a surge of Texas pride I felt that here was a girl from Killeen saying to the man who inherited Rockefeller Center as his graduation gift from Dartmouth . . . 'Please, Nelson, do pull down the charts.' And while the . . . committee waited, Nelson bounced off to do her bidding."[11]

As long as Rockefeller behaved himself and showed proper deference, Oveta was happy, as well as thankful, to have him and his team at HEW. Oveta "put up with [Rocke-feller's] freewheeling ways," Cary Reich noted, "[because] she needed Rockefeller—needed his gift for presentation, his adept handling of the staff, his unique ability to marshal outside expertise. And his dynamism was what she prized most." Oveta had a healthy understanding of her limits. She fully realized that she was responsible for significant programs dealing with matters about which she had little or no knowledge. Reich also observed, "For once in her life, the proud, supremely competent Oveta Culp Hobby found herself overwhelmed. As capable as she was, nothing in [her] experience prepared her for all this. She had no background in health issues, no background in education issues, no background in welfare issues. But to her credit, rather than continue to stumble along, she took a decisive step." And that step was to delegate to Rockefeller and his team.[12]

Joan Braden, who worked more closely with Oveta than anyone else at HEW, had a different view about her boss than did her colleagues. Braden admitted Oveta had a steep learning curve at first, but she soon developed a firm grasp of the big picture at HEW, even if she lacked knowledge of many critical details. "Oveta never let her strength show," Braden recalled. "It was, rather, revealed. She never raised her voice, never demonstrated anger." That style went a long way with her expert staff, and as a result, they were more than patient and understanding of Oveta's lack of knowledge about her responsibilities.[13]

One major sign that Oveta valued Rockefeller's advice and trusted his judgment was her approval of his proposal to create a council composed of all department heads within HEW. Oveta and Rockefeller generally kept a schedule of weekly meetings with the council, unless they were both traveling. The council made it easy for all the component agencies to be informed on the work of the others to avoid overlapping projects and duplication of effort. Oveta later recalled that the council provided an opportunity for "a general discussion of objectives . . . [that] helped in the preparation of legislation . . . in which one would have an overlap with the other. It was a very rewarding experience." At first, some of the staff saw the council as a way Rockefeller could exert his control over HEW. But Cary Reich noted that at those daily briefings, "it was always Hobby who was the chairperson, and Hobby who asked most of the questions."

The White House had no doubt about who was in charge of HEW. Maxwell Rabb was Eisenhower's special assistant who worked closest with Oveta and the other cabinet members. Years later, when Rabb was asked if it was Rockefeller who ran HEW, he quickly replied, "No way." Allen Drury, a veteran journalist and an astute observer of the presidency, noted in his nationally syndicated column, "There is no doubt who runs [HEW] and there is no doubt she runs it well."[14]

As Oveta settled in as secretary of HEW, her immediate policy challenges included reducing the budgets of the various agencies constituting HEW, which followed Eisenhower's instruction to reduce federal expenditures. The total HEW budget of $1.7 billion was larger than all other cabinet departments, except for Defense and Treasury. Social Security policy presented another challenge. During the presidential campaign, Eisenhower had promised to expand the Social Security program to include farmers, domestic workers, and the self-employed. The president revisited the issue in his first State of the Union address in February by urging Congress to extend coverage "to millions of citizens who have been left out of the Social Security system."[15]

Beyond those general directions, the president gave Oveta no guidance about how far she was supposed to go in cutting budgets or how to expand Social Security coverage. Was she to follow the conservative gospel of balanced budgets and status quo in government programs, or was she to devise new programs in health, education, and Social Security, which would require budget increases? All Oveta had to go on were scattered clues and hints the president provided in meetings and in public pronouncements. The reality was that Eisenhower had little interest in HEW. At press conferences he often had trouble remembering the department's name, sometimes calling it "Health, Welfare, and Whatnot." As a result, Oveta struggled when reporters asked her for specifics about her agenda, forcing her to reply with a few brief generalizations with little or no details. Nevertheless, the president had promised to reduce the federal budget, and Oveta would follow through as best she could.[16]

At Oveta's first press conference after she assumed her duties as secretary of HEW, she announced a $64 million reduction in HEW's $1.7 billion budget. She provided no details about where the cuts would be applied, because she didn't know. She did tell reporters that a cut of that size was necessary to help pay for the Korean War, implying that cuts would be restored once the war was over. "A general peace, of course, would brighten the whole picture," she explained. "If providing for the common defense is no longer our greatest expense, many social gains will be possible." As it turned out, an armistice was reached in Korea three months after Oveta's news conference, but with no end to the Cold War in sight, the defense budget was increased, not reduced.[17]

After Oveta read her prepared statement to the press, reporters pressed her about the administration's plan to expand Social Security coverage. There was little she could say other than to repeat Eisenhower's vaguely stated desire to see it done. At that point, one reporter reminded her of an ongoing controversy over the federal government's insistence that people who employed domestic servants had to pay a Social Security tax. Ironically, the controversy began with a protest from a group of housewives back in Oveta's home state. The women, who lived in Marshall, Texas, attracted national attention when they organized in 1951 and declared that the tax violated the Constitution. When the reporter asked for her own position on the issue, Oveta answered that she supported the tax. He then pointed out that the *Houston Post* had published an editorial in July 1951 in support of the housewives. She quickly repudiated her own newspaper's editorial, claiming that it had appeared when she was away from Houston and that the editorial page editor, presumably Ed Kilman, had been on vacation. The *Post*'s rogue editorial writer remained unidentified, although the opinion stated was in harmony with Kilman's political views. It is doubtful that such an editorial stance would have been taken without Will Hobby's approval and possible encouragement. Somewhat taken aback and embarrassed, Oveta "declared emphatically" that the editorial did not reflect her views. "Domestic servants as a matter of simple human dignity," she stressed, "have a right to contribute to their own security." A subsequent headline in the *Dallas Morning News* proclaimed, "Maid Tax Gets Hobby Backing."[18]

Walter Hornaday, Washington correspondent for the *Dallas Morning News*, asked Oveta one other inconvenient question. Knowing that his readers back home were curious about Oveta's political affiliation after she had led the Democrats for Eisenhower national organization and was now serving in a Republican administration, Hornaday asked if she was now a "permanent, full-fledged Republican." Visibly annoyed, Oveta retorted, "You ask me a specific question and I'll give you a specific answer." He asked her a specific question: "Will you take part in the Republican primary in Texas in 1954 and will you vote Republican?" Oveta explained that she had voted for the Republican presidential candidates from 1940 through 1952, but that she had voted for Democrats at the state and local level in Texas. She reminded her fellow Texan that "we have cross filing in Texas" party primaries and that she would decide her choices when the time came. She then declared her hope that the Republicans would increase their majorities in the House and the Senate in the 1954 congressional election. Hornaday followed with an obvious question. Did that mean, he asked, that she wanted Republicans in Texas to defeat incumbent Democrats, which included her friends LBJ and Sam Rayburn and her hometown congressman Albert Thomas? Seemingly caught off guard, as one observer noted, Oveta "dodged that question" and "loftily dismissed" it "as not a proper one." She "laughingly" told Hornaday that she should take him out and spank him for putting her on the spot back in Texas. Hornaday's newspaper followed with the headline "Mrs. Hobby Faces a Political Problem."[19]

After that unhappy experience, Oveta held no more press conferences for several months and granted no interviews. She would meet with the press only six times during her tenure as secretary of HEW. A columnist for the *New York Post* later concluded, "Mrs. Hobby's newspaper association has not made her notably sympathetic to Washington reporters. She solves the problem of her relations with the press by having no relations." *Newsweek* also criticized Oveta for preaching etiquette to the press while providing "very little real news." At the few press conferences she did have, Oveta carried out a tightly choreographed and controlled routine. As the press strolled into HEW's large conference room, her staff distributed large information packets with a copy of the remarks she would read to them during the meeting. Ahead of Oveta's arrival, her department heads and the top policy experts on their staffs would take their places on either side of the rostrum, waiting to be called on to make statements in support of the secretary's remarks. When Oveta marched into the room, always exactly on time, she would explain that after she delivered her prepared statement, follow-up questions were required to be about specific subjects. Nationally syndicated columnist Peter Edson described the sessions in a story titled "Foot-in-Mouth Trouble Has Not Bothered Mrs. Hobby." Oveta would read her prepared statement "slowly in a mellow contralto that soothes as it edifies." He sarcastically added that it was "always a great help to reporters, to have long handouts read to them. Left to their own wits, they don't read well, obviously. And when the stuff is read at them, there is no chance for slips of the tongue or misquotation." Edson added that reporters could "never catch the little lady from Texas off base. As is proper for a lady [she] has done a better job of keeping her foot out of her mouth than any other member of the Eisenhower Cabinet."[20]

As the *Dallas Morning News* claimed after her first press conference, Oveta might have had a political problem back home, but if she did, it paled in comparison to the problems she was facing getting all of HEW's diverse components in sync with her office. One historian has referred to HEW at this time as an "intricate, sprawling network of fiefdoms," with many units having operated autonomously for years. Oveta later recalled that HEW included such a diverse group that it was exceedingly difficult "to try to weave a thread of common interest and common obligation" among them. "There was some resistance, of course," she observed. "It's only human that there should have been." Oveta soon discerned a theme of "organic unity" amid the mass of unrelated facts, figures, and projects that swirled around in her administrative portfolio. Through HEW's diverse components ran "a common thread of family service," Oveta realized. "Cut one, and you destroy the lifeline of the others."[21]

As Oveta studied her new domain to discern its "organic unity," she found that the work of HEW's thirty-five thousand employees directly affected the lives of more American citizens than any other department of the federal government. The Social Security Administration alone managed a program for sixty-seven million people that distributed $4 billion a year in pension and welfare funds. The health function of Oveta's department directed one of the world's greatest medical research centers, including an institute for cancer research; maintained hospitals for merchant seamen and leprosy patients; supervised the Freedmen's Hospital and St. Elizabeth's Hospital, the latter a major psychiatric hospital; and promoted the federal effort to fluoridate the public water supply. The education component of her portfolio was under heavy pressure as it grappled with the escalating public school needs of the postwar baby boom. Her Office of Education distributed funds to land-grant colleges; had oversight responsibilities for Howard University, the nation's largest institution of higher learning for African Americans; administered a teacher-student exchange program with foreign countries; and supervised the American Printing House in Lexington, Kentucky, which printed and distributed books in braille for the blind and visually impaired. Within this portfolio, Oveta focused much personal attention on her effort to make it possible for Howard University to train more African American physicians, nurses, and dentists because of a national shortage of black health professionals.[22]

Pressuring this huge maze of federal programs was a tireless engine of special interests. Labor unions were monitoring and reacting quickly to any perceived threats to Social Security. The Public Health Service endured constant criticism from the powerful American Medical Association and other health industry lobbies. Pharmaceutical companies and food processors fought against any hint of regulation from the Food and Drug Administration. The Office of Education had to contend with the entire educational establishment, public and private, while also establishing programs at the fast-growing institutions of higher education, ranging from newly established community colleges to long-standing state universities and the private schools of the Ivy League. This tangled web of involvement in many aspects of the nation's domestic affairs naturally made HEW the most controversial cabinet department in Eisenhower's administration. To many conservatives, it was a symbol of dreaded big government and federal interference in the private lives of Americans.[23]

On May 4, 1953, *Time* featured "Mrs. Secretary Hobby" as that issue's cover story. The magazine reported that after assuming her duties at HEW, Oveta had continued to work six and a half days a week, as she had when she was appointed head of the Federal Security Agency. The story also had to mention, of course, that she took a brief break every Saturday afternoon to get her hair done at Elizabeth Arden's salon. As Joan Braden later noted, Oveta cared a lot about how she looked, but she was sensitive about not giving the impression that she spent much time working on her appearance. According to Braden, she was infuriated when she found out that Rockefeller had peeked into her appointment book and told staff that he had found the words "beauty parlor" on the schedule.[24]

For its cover story, *Time* assigned a reporter to follow Oveta around in late April to document one of her "typical" days. *Time* reported that normally Oveta was up at 6:30 a.m. to read through a stack of newspapers while she ate breakfast. The *Houston Post* was airmailed to her every day, and she read it closely and critically. After that latter fact was revealed, a columnist for the *New York Post*, noting that Will Hobby was in "failing health," observed that "for the past several years, she has been the real boss of the [*Houston Post*]. She receives each edition in Washington by air mail, reads it carefully, and keeps a sharp eye on its management," despite her earlier statements that she had suspended her involvement in the newspaper's affairs. She usually walked into her office a little after nine, except on Fridays, when she went directly to the White House to attend the weekly cabinet meeting. Usually arriving early, Oveta had a quiet and private spot near the cabinet room where she studied the meeting agenda and prepared her thoughts. Back at the office, work often continued through lunch, which invariably consisted of cottage cheese or fruit salads, as she met with staff. A heavy smoker, she would puff on Parliament cigarettes off and on throughout the day while working at her desk. Oveta preferred that brand because she believed the company's advertisements claiming its recessed filters strained out the toxins from nicotine. To be safe, she only smoked them halfway down, believing that would help reduce the nicotine intake. Debra Sutphen has noted that it was ironic that the first secretary of HEW was an inveterate smoker and not fond of exercise. Her daughter, Jessica, jokingly recalled that both of her parents lacked an interest in physical exertion, although in her younger years Oveta had been a skilled horsewoman.[25]

Usually around 7:00 p.m., but often later, Oveta walked out of her office with her valise stuffed with work papers. Her chauffeur drove her to her Connecticut Avenue apartment, where she called Will every night before having dinner. After her evening meal, Oveta worked on HEW paperwork. She was rarely in bed before midnight. Without citing a source, the *New York Post* claimed Oveta was "a bad sleeper. If she wakes during the night, she uses the time to make memos in her notebook for the next day's work."[26]

The cover story in *Time* was one of a flurry of articles about Oveta that appeared in the news media in April, May, and June of 1953, including a cover story in *Businessweek*. Being on the covers of these national magazines also earned Oveta an appearance in April on NBC's popular morning television program *Today*. She took advantage of this media coverage not only to promote HEW but also to tamp down conservative anxiety about her new department and to counter the ongoing rumors spread by right-wing Republicans that she was spearheading a move to create a version of the British welfare state. The *Businessweek* cover featured Oveta's portrait over the headline "Secretary Hobby's Credo: Welfare, but No Welfare State," which was a title that transmitted the message Oveta was eager to communicate. In addition, she succeeded in getting the

wire services and the *New York Times* to print prominent stories about her opposition
to socialized medicine. The *New York Times* story quoted her as saying she believed the
"nation's medical needs could be met by expansion and perfection of voluntary systems
of health insurance." Oveta added that her views on the issue were "wholly in line with
those of President Eisenhower."[27]

While Oveta's work organizing HEW attracted largely positive attention from national
news media that spring, she also became entangled in the Eisenhower administration's
first racial controversy, which was over segregated schools on US military bases, mainly
in the Jim Crow South. Because federal education policy was an important component
of her portfolio as secretary of HEW, Oveta was at center stage on this issue.

When Eisenhower assumed office in January 1953, fifteen of the twenty-one military
bases in the country, all in the South, except for one in Oklahoma, had racially segregated
schools. Local school boards in areas in which Jim Crow racial laws were in force administered the educational facilities on these military posts. This local practice violated
(in spirit, if not technically) President Truman's order in 1948 to desegregate the nation's
armed forces. In March 1953 Congressman Adam Clayton Powell Jr., the flamboyant and
brash Democratic congressman representing New York City's Harlem district, sent a letter to the president calling his attention to this situation. He demanded that Eisenhower
order an investigation. Powell sent a copy of his letter to the National Association for the
Advancement of Colored People (NAACP) and other civil rights organizations, which
issued their own statements denouncing the practice. The resulting news media coverage
placed enough pressure on Eisenhower to force him to direct Defense Secretary Charles
Wilson to ask local school authorities to integrate classrooms located on military bases
by the fall of 1953, regardless of local laws or "customs." Eisenhower further directed
that if school officials refused to integrate, the federal government would assume the
funding for those schools and integrate them, with HEW's education commissioner
taking responsibility for their operations.

The president's directive alarmed Oveta, who among other problems was struggling to organize HEW. She wrote Secretary Wilson on April 13, 1953, with a copy to
Eisenhower, offering her opinion that the coming fall might not give the newly created
HEW sufficient time to take charge of these schools. She also argued that there were
other problems to consider. "There is no way," she wrote, "in which local school authorities in these states could operate these schools on an integrated basis unless [the]
[s]tates' laws or constitutions are changed." Oveta pointed out that many children
who lived on military bases attended schools located outside the bases, and to abolish
segregation at these off-base schools would require the federal government to take
control away from local authorities. Such action, she argued, would place the federal
government in conflict with the principle of state and local responsibility for public
education. She also reminded Wilson that the *Brown v. Board of Education of Topeka*
case was pending before the Supreme Court and that it would be best if the Eisenhower
administration took no action until the court ruled on the matter. If the court declared

racial segregation of public schools to be unconstitutional, it would solve the problem of segregated schools on military bases. It would also spare the administration from having to take an action that was certain to be highly controversial and politically damaging, not only to the Republican Party in the South but also in Congress, which Oveta feared might harm HEW's upcoming legislative agenda. Counseling patience and delay, she suggested that HEW continue to study the situation "before any further decisions are made." Oveta's argument swayed Eisenhower, who had long held traditional paternalistic white racist views about African Americans and was basically neutral on the issue of racial segregation, which he felt was a problem best dealt with by the states, not the federal government. He agreed to delay action, moving the deadline from fall 1953 to the beginning of the new school year in fall 1955.[28]

Jane Spaulding, Oveta's special assistant, wound up with a copy of Oveta's April 13 message to Secretary Wilson. Without Oveta's knowledge, Spaulding leaked it to Clarence Mitchell, chief lobbyist for the NAACP, who passed it on to Congressman Powell. The Harlem congressman dispatched a letter to Oveta on May 28 informing her that he had learned that Eisenhower's order "affecting segregation of schools on Army posts has been held up by you particularly at Camp Hood, Texas. Will you be kind enough to tell me the facts in connection with this?" Oveta hastily drafted a response to Powell's letter, but she decided not to send it. The draft remains in her papers at Rice University, labeled "not sent."[29]

Apparently unaware of Jane Spaulding's role in this affair, Oveta seems to have decided that a more effective response to Powell would be a letter from Spaulding denying that Oveta was delaying the integration of schools on military bases. When Spaulding came to work a couple of days after Powell sent his letter, she was surprised to find a typewritten letter on her desk with the title "Statement by Mrs. Jane Morrow Spaulding." An attachment to this letter instructed her to read and sign it. When Spaulding read the text she was upset to see that it criticized Powell for demanding Oveta move quickly to desegregate schools on military bases and that it denied Oveta was trying to delay action. What was worse, however, was an especially insulting statement that Spaulding was expected to offer as her own. The letter presumptuously had her stating that "as a member of the colored race," she had been sorry to read Powell's "misadvised statements" and disappointed that he had demonstrated "such unreasonable impatience." As Debra Sutphen argues, "Though Hobby may not have composed the letter, she almost certainly authorized it." Spaulding refused to sign the prewritten statement, which created "a particularly tense situation" between her and Oveta. Nevertheless, Spaulding continued in her job. After the incident in early June, she continued to serve as HEW's outreach person to the black community, which included speaking to groups about civil rights issues and condemning racial discrimination. Her strongly worded statements on racial matters at these speaking engagements soon attracted the attention of the increasingly annoyed secretary of HEW. Oveta directed a staff member to send a message to Spaulding that she should give "less controversial" speeches, but

Spaulding rejected this advice. At this point, Spaulding's forced departure from HEW was not a question of if but when.[30]

As a result of the in-house dustup between Oveta and Spaulding, Powell's letter went unanswered. If Oveta thought her failure to respond to Congressman Powell would end the matter, she miscalculated. On June 3, Powell sent a telegram to Eisenhower charging Oveta, Secretary of the Navy Robert Anderson (a Texas oilman), and the Veterans Administration's chief medical officer Joel Boone with undermining the president's integration policy. Powell's telegram falsely accused Oveta of "virtually" countermanding Ike's policy on segregation in schools for dependents on army posts by "telling" the secretary of defense to ignore the president's order. Powell provided a copy of this telegram to the *Washington Star*, which subsequently reprinted the text in full with the headline "Hobby Note Flouts Segregation Order, Powell Charges."[31]

Deeply concerned about the potentially awful public relations problems Powell was creating for the administration, Eisenhower's aides persuaded the president to dispatch Max Rabb to meet with Congressman Powell to work out a compromise arrangement that would persuade Powell to suspend his protest campaign. Rabb was a diplomatically skilled, Harvard-trained attorney who was well known as one of the Eisenhower administration's most liberal members in the area of race relations and civil rights. He persuaded Powell to suspend his crusade on this particular issue in return for a conciliatory letter from the president praising Powell's work as a civil rights leader and promising to work with him on the problem of "segregation in federally supported institutions." After Powell received the letter, he followed through with his part of the deal. He held a press conference during which he distributed the letter and extravagantly praised Eisenhower's statement as a "Magna Carta for minorities."[32]

Although this incident soon faded out of the news, it would not be Oveta's last tangle with racial issues as a cabinet member. The relationship between Oveta and Jane Spaulding finally reached a breaking point late in the fall of 1953, when Oveta announced her support for a $1.5 million Hill-Burton grant to a hospital in Houston where African American doctors were not allowed to practice. Oveta justified the grant on highly technical legalistic and procedural grounds. Spaulding, who had been advising African American physicians in Houston on the matter, apparently without Oveta's knowledge, publicly denounced the decision and argued that the grant should not be made until the hospital agreed to end its discriminatory policies. Hovering over this controversy was the fact that the hospital in question was in Oveta's home city, which was an especially sensitive matter for her. Oveta soon made plans to demote Spaulding, who had no civil service protection, to a lesser position at HEW with a lower salary in the hope that Spaulding would get the message and leave the department on her own volition. Oveta's problem with Spaulding would come to a head in January 1954.[33]

With Congressman Powell's recent accusations undoubtedly ringing in her ears, Oveta delivered a commencement address at Ohio Wesleyan University in Delaware, Ohio, on June 10 about the societal cost of racial discrimination. She made a practical economic argument instead of a moral one, declaring that racial "prejudice is costing the nation tax dollars in what must be astronomical amounts," possibly as high as $30 billion a year. This high cost, she argued, was the result of not allowing all people "to reach their full potential" and not permitting them "to earn the salaries their work merits." She told the graduating students that they should work to alleviate this problem, reminding them "that the white man is a pretty small minority in the earth's population today. We are outnumbered two to one in the world."[34]

By the beginning of June 1953, Oveta had become fully aware of the multitasking demands of being head of one of the most complex and controversial departments in the federal government, a job made more difficult by the fact that it was still being organized. At the same time that Oveta was dealing with Congressman Powell and the controversy resulting from her recommendation to delay the integration of schools on military bases, she had to continue her effort to tamp down conservative fears that HEW was a threat to free enterprise and states' rights. As part of that effort she delivered the keynote speech to the American Medical Association's national convention on June 1 at the Waldorf Astoria Hotel in New York City. Oveta wasted no time in addressing the medical profession's anxieties about socialized medicine. She told a standing-room-only audience of physicians and surgeons that HEW shared their professional objective, which was to provide the best medical care possible to the American people, and that it was best left to private health care professionals. She assured her audience that she was opposed to any government program of compulsory health care because it was "undemocratic, economically unsound, and an intrusion by Government into the physician-patient relationship, and a violation of the democratic principle of free choice and consent." She added, however, that it was critical that the medical profession participate actively in the effort to solve the socioeconomic problems caused by inadequate health care. Otherwise, she warned, the solution would be "taken out of our hands and that solution will not be a happy one."[35]

Oveta was quite sensitive about federal involvement in the health care industry. At one point early in her tenure as secretary, she met with the California industrialist Henry J. Kaiser and his aides to hear an elaborate and lengthy presentation about their intention to ask for federal aid for their Kaiser Permanente medical centers, which pioneered prepaid group medical care. The Kaiser plan had been one of the Truman administration's recommendations as a basis for a federal health policy and it was fiercely criticized by the American Medical Association. Kaiser stressed that his plan left physicians in total control of the centers. Oveta had little response during the presentation. When it was over, she remained silent. After a minute or two, Kaiser said he assumed her silence meant she had no objection to his request and that he could so inform Congress. Arthur Altmeyer, who was present at the meeting, later claimed that when Kaiser made that statement, "she said very quietly, and succinctly, 'If you do I shall cut your throat.' This response left Mr. Kaiser speechless." Oveta was stunned that Kaiser assumed she would endorse a plan advocated by the Truman administration and opposed by the American Medical Association. She immediately ended the conference.[36]

On June 3, two days after Oveta addressed the medical association and on the same day that Congressman Powell sent his telegram to Eisenhower criticizing her role in delaying the integration of schools on military bases, she was back in Washington to participate in a live broadcast from the White House. She joined President Eisenhower, Treasury Secretary George Humphrey, Agriculture Secretary Ezra Taft Benson, and Attorney General Herbert Brownell for a special thirty-minute broadcast at prime time over a national radio hookup as well as on all three of the major television networks. The program, which was the first of its kind in the history of the American presidency, was designed to bring attention to the administration's new policy initiatives. The entire presentation was carefully rehearsed and scripted to show the Eisenhower administration on the move more than it actually was.

As planned, Ike asked Oveta to talk briefly about HEW's legislative agenda, which in reality had been bogged down by the organizational problems inherent in creating a massive new federal department. Despite having little of importance to announce, Oveta stated that HEW had submitted three bills to Congress. This was accurate, but two of the bills dealt with relatively minor issues, while the third was an amendment to the Food and Drug Act clarifying a technical problem related to written reports of drug factory inspections. More important, and as scripted, Oveta added that she had appointed a committee of expert consultants to study ways to expand Social Security coverage. Ike then asked his scripted question: "Well now, Mrs. Hobby, tell us something of that trouble we're having with the Food and Drug Act, will you please?" Oveta responded that the Supreme Court had ruled that the language in the Food and Drug Act was contradictory, and as a result, the Food and Drug Administration could no longer inspect drug-manufacturing plants without the company's prior consent. The bill HEW had recently submitted was intended to restore HEW's inspection authority. Oveta stressed that she believed the bill was "vital to the protection of the American people." Eisenhower concluded Oveta's presentation by stating, "Well, I think, Mrs. Hobby, that everybody will agree that you have about as complicated a task as there is in government. You run the biggest insurance business and you run a medical research center and everything in between."[37]

The response to this unusual show from the White House was generally favorable. Eisenhower's personal staff thought Oveta's performance was the high spot of the program. The morning after the broadcast, Ann Whitman, the president's personal secretary and confidant, sent Oveta a handwritten note: "You were superb last night." Many others shared Whitman's favorable view of the job Oveta was doing. Walter Trohan, the Washington correspondent for the *Chicago Tribune*, reported to his friend Jesse Jones that "Mrs. Hobby's appointment is not only popular and politically helpful, but she is doing a good job." Agreeing with these positive assessments, the New York and New England division of B'nai B'rith presented its Woman of the Year award to Oveta in a ceremony in Monticello, New York. Naturally, Will Hobby also agreed with these reviews. When a reporter asked him if he didn't think his wife was the smartest member of the cabinet, the governor gave a characteristic reply: "'Course she is," he said. "But if she weren't, she'd have them thinking she was."[38]

The press also gave Oveta good marks. But the highly respected *New York Herald Tribune* health and science correspondent and columnist Earl Ubell wrote that Oveta was "in for the kind of punishment frequently directed at the pilot of any controversial agency." Her biggest challenge was how to tackle "the many complex and difficult issues her department has to confront." Ubell explained that it was widely rumored the Eisenhower administration had asked Oveta to reduce the HEW budget by nearly $75 million, which would close hospitals, reduce grants for school and hospital construction, and lay off one thousand federal employees scattered throughout the department. "Local Congressmen are already howling," Ubell pointed out. "Mrs. Hobby faces a rough year. She must make friends for the Administration through her . . . program . . . and she mustn't spend too much money."[39]

While the national news media was focused on Oveta and her plans for HEW, she managed to fly to Houston the day after her television appearance to attend her son's graduation from Rice Institute and to take a short break from the pressures in Washington. Bill had earned a bachelor of arts degree cum laude in American history while also working as a reporter on the *Post* three evenings a week. Belying her claims that she was no longer involved in the management of the *Houston Post*, Oveta also joined Will in meetings with their administrative staff to discuss plans to construct a new building for the paper.[40]

Oveta's presence in Texas generated rumors she was evaluating her prospects for running as a candidate for governor in 1954, possibly as a Republican, but more likely as a primary challenger to incumbent governor Allan Shivers. On June 30, the *Austin American-Statesman* reported that an authoritative source had revealed that Oveta planned "to resign from the cabinet and run for governor of Texas." The Austin newspaper claimed the real reason Nelson Rockefeller had agreed to accept the subordinate position at HEW was because he knew Oveta would be a political candidate in 1954 and he expected to take her cabinet post when she resigned. "Mrs. Hobby has a following in Texas," the *Statesman* declared, "and would give Governor Allan Shivers a real race." Popular gossip columnist "Cholly Knickerbocker" picked up the story from Austin and repeated it in his widely syndicated column in the *New York Journal American*. It's unknown how this rumor began, although there was some speculation that Rockefeller might have been the source. But Oveta had no intention of running for governor, especially against her husband's friend Allan Shivers. She released a statement to the press to squelch the rumors. "At no time have I considered resigning and running for governor of Texas," she declared. "The report has no foundation."[41]

By the end of June, Oveta was back in Washington to preside over the dedication ceremony for the National Institutes of Health's new $64 million fourteen-story clinical center in Bethesda, Maryland. The next morning she attended an important cabinet meeting in which the president's budget proposal to Congress was the main agenda item. When it was Oveta's turn to talk about the HEW budget, she "proudly" declared that her administrative team had found areas in which significant reductions could be made. The president smiled enthusiastically at the prospect of Oveta's budget cut. His smile vanished, however, when Oveta reported she had targeted the federal grants for education program for a major reduction. With a shocked expression on his face, Eisenhower complained that he "hadn't heard of this before. I am amazed at the thought of an education cut! This is the most important thing in our society." He explained to Hobby that "every liberal—including me—will disapprove." When Oveta explained that the cuts would be popular with Congress, the president told her it didn't matter. Referring to Congress's recent passage of a bill to increase the appropriation for its own operations, he stated, "We can play some politics. If Congress can increase its expense accounts, we shouldn't cut vital education programs." Cary Reich noted, "A confused Hobby, on that day at least, was forced to come to terms with a 'liberal' Eisenhower. What the next day would bring, she could only guess."[42]

Eisenhower might have been determined to "play some politics" to persuade his Republican majority in Congress to maintain a status quo budget for HEW's education programs, but the ultraconservative members of his own party nevertheless were intent on reducing HEW's appropriations, even if it meant going against the president. They proposed cuts ranging from $10 million to $30 million in excess of those Oveta had recommended. Oveta fought against the additional reductions, especially in the Office of Education, the Food and Drug Administration, and Public Health. Adding to Oveta's burdens was her responsibility for also pushing through the administration's proposal to expand the Social Security program.

In June, the twelve consultants on Roswell Perkins's special task force on Social Security submitted a report to Oveta on the extension of coverage of old-age and survivor insurance. They limited their recommendations to the question of extending the coverage of the insurance system to new groups, which they endorsed, calling for expanding coverage by more than ten million workers while also increasing monthly benefits. Oveta submitted the task force recommendations to the White House in July. Eisenhower accepted the recommendations and on August 1, 1953, he submitted a special message to Congress recommending that additional groups be covered by old age and survivors insurance.[43]

The ultraconservative wing of the Republicans in Congress, led by Senator Carl Curtis of Nebraska, who chaired the subcommittee conducting hearings on Eisenhower's request, not only opposed expansion, they also wanted to pay retirees from current payroll deductions, not from the Social Security trust fund, which is a type of wage loss insurance pool. As the plan's critics pointed out, that system would force Congress to raise the revenue it needed each year through taxation to fund current benefits. Rockefeller and Oveta understood that it would not be long before political pressure forced Congress to ease the tax burden by curtailing the whole program, which was the result right-wing Republican members of Congress intended. Oveta and Rockefeller, who were both strong

*Oveta Culp Hobby and Nelson Rockefeller after their meeting with President Eisenhower in Denver about the Social Security bill, August 1953.*

supporters of the Social Security program, met in late August with Eisenhower, who was on vacation in Denver, to discuss strategy for getting the plan out of Curtis's committee and to a vote in the Senate. Ike assured them that he fully supported the expansion plan and that he would urge the Republican congressional leadership to approve it.[44]

As the budget battles were being fought in Congress, Eisenhower continued to monitor developments from Colorado. After Oveta returned to Washington following her meeting with him in Denver, she received a letter from the president stating his concerns about the budget battles. "I am disturbed . . . that the cuts affect items that are known as 'humanitarian' in their purpose," Eisenhower wrote. He argued that HEW could not "make great savings at this moment, in a more or less blind fashion, and without regard to public opinion," because it would present the administration to the public "as being indifferent to the health, welfare, and educational advantages of the less fortunate of our people." But the president also pointed out the need for substantial reductions in other areas of her budget. The message to Oveta was for her to find cuts in areas that did not directly affect basic needs in human services. Eisenhower's instructions put Oveta in a bind. Somehow she was to reduce her budget while also maintaining the status quo in her most expensive programs. Eventually, Eisenhower was forced to concede defeat and accept the Republican Congress's budget. The president's request to expand Social Security coverage fared no better, as it remained bogged down in Curtis's subcommittee. It would not resurface for another six months.[45]

Near the end of August, Oveta, Will, and Jessica traveled to California for a working vacation. Their first stop was Los Angeles, which the *Los Angeles Times* heavily publicized, printing four separate stories about their activities, each with a photo of Oveta. The *Times* even sent a reporter and a photographer to Houston to accompany the Hobbys on the train to Los Angeles aboard the Southern Pacific's Sunset Limited. "Mrs. Secretary is a tiny and extremely pretty woman who speaks softly, slowly and thoughtfully—but never hesitates over an answer," the *Times* correspondent reported. "Quick to smile, completely captivating in her simple, direct manner, the little lady . . . is feminine to her unpainted finger tips." When the female reporter asked Oveta if she ever noticed any resentment from other women because of her success and prominence, Oveta exclaimed, "Good Lord, no! And I consider myself an expert on this. That old theory is a fictitious legend! After all, I worked with 600,000 women during the war." The reporter asked Will how he and the kids felt about Oveta's work. "I've always had a hard working wife," Will replied. "I do not think the children ever give it a thought."[46]

The Hobbys arrived in LA early in the morning of August 25 and checked into the Beverly Hills Hotel before being driven to the Biltmore Hotel, where Oveta addressed an audience of one thousand attendees at the annual meeting of the Los Angeles chapter of the American Red Cross. As a member of the Red Cross national board of directors, Oveta mainly spoke about the need for citizens to donate blood "to save the lives of recuperating wounded servicemen" returning from Korea. She also took advantage of the opportunity to make a pitch for HEW's plan for expanding Social Security coverage. That night the Hobbys attended a party in their honor at the Beverly Hills home of oilman and developer William T. Sesnon Jr., who was on the American Red Cross board of directors. After the Hobbys stood in a receiving line to greet three hundred guests, they escaped to the patio around the swimming pool, where they sat in chairs under umbrellas and tried to rest. Journalist and syndicated columnist Inez Robb and her friend General Ira Eaker, former commander of the Eighth Air Force during World War II, grabbed chairs at their table and visited with the Hobbys. Robb had met Oveta in 1947 when Robb was in Texas to report on the ship and oil refinery explosions and disaster in Texas City. Oveta had met

Eaker when she commanded the WAC. Robb later reported in her column that Oveta was "much more attractive than her pictures. She's slimmer, too. She's probably the most self-assured woman I've ever met. . . . [S]he moves with an easy grace; she talks with a measured nuance and she gives the impression of one in serious thought." Exhausted by the events of a long day, Will and Oveta left the party early as a band played "Deep in the Heart of Texas."

*Oveta and Will Hobby on the Southern Pacific's Sunset Limited, 1953.*

The hectic schedule continued the following day, as *Los Angeles Times* publisher Norman Chandler and his wife hosted a private luncheon in the Hobbys' honor. Among the guests were Hedda Hopper, Walgreens heir Justin Dart, LA mayor Norris Poulson, automobile tire company heir Leonard Firestone, and Ford Foundation president Paul Hoffman. After Oveta addressed a luncheon on Friday, August 28, hosted by the Pasadena Chamber of Commerce and attended by eight hundred guests, the Hobbys spent the weekend enjoying some private time before they boarded a train late Sunday evening for San Francisco. As they were departing Southern California, the *LA Times* declared that the "charming" Oveta had "completely captivated Los Angeles during her visit here."[47]

The Hobbys spent less time in San Francisco than they had in LA, because the purpose was largely for work, not leisure. Oveta was in the city to speak to the national convention of the American Hospital Association, a powerful lobby for the hospital industry and one of HEW's prime constituencies. In her speech, Oveta once again publicly announced that the Eisenhower administration had no interest in imposing socialized medicine on the country despite the rumors being spread by right-wing Republicans. She did argue, however, that one of the best ways to head off future demands for a federally managed universal health care program was for hospitals to develop programs to mitigate the high costs of major surgery and long stays in the hospital for the middle class. The wealthy can take care of themselves, she stated, and the poor and indigent can count on charity. It was the middle class that needed help in the event of a catastrophic illness. Her comments were among the first hints that the Eisenhower administration was considering some type of national health insurance plan.[48]

Oveta's thoughts as she and Will made their way back to Washington from California at the beginning of September were focused on the next big items on her HEW agenda, the most important being the ongoing effort to persuade Congress to expand Social Security coverage and benefits. She undoubtedly also had thoughts about a major exposé of Red Scare activists in Houston that she had instigated and that she knew the *Houston Post* would soon publish.

# CHAPTER 34

---

# RED SCARE

In the fall of 1953, Oveta embarked on a series of high-profile speaking engagements to educate the public about the importance of the newest department of the executive branch. The tour included a keynote speech at the annual meeting of the Pennsylvania Newspaper Publishers Association in Harrisburg, Pennsylvania, on October 10, 1953. The topic of Oveta's keynote speech diverged from her other presentations during the tour. It focused on the critical importance of freedom of the press to democracy, especially the responsibility of the free press to educate the citizenry about threats to democratic values and to monitor activities of the government at local, state, and federal levels. Although federal secrecy regulations were not part of her HEW responsibilities, she took the opportunity to announce that President Eisenhower would soon revoke President Truman's executive order that had restricted public access to a wide range of government documents. Explaining that Eisenhower's action would "honor the basic tenets of freedom of information," she argued that it would "go far toward removing the barrier between Government and the press" that the Truman administration had erected.[1]

As Oveta spoke to her audience of newspaper publishers, she knew that the following morning, her own newspaper, the *Houston Post*, would print on its front page the first in a series of eleven articles exposing a local movement that she and some of her editors and reporters felt was a threat to basic democratic values. The series, which was the product of months of investigative sleuthing by *Houston Post* reporter Ralph S. O'Leary, charged that members of a coalition of ultraconservative organizations were convinced that Communist subversives were scattered among administrators and teachers in the city's public schools, the Methodist clergy, and the faculty of the University of Houston. The organizations' accusations were fomenting anticommunist hysteria in Houston's churches and schools. The most prominent and active of the organizations included the Houston chapter of the national Minute Women of the U.S.A., the local "Americanism" chapter of the American Legion, the Committee for the Preservation of Methodism, and Doctors for Freedom. Many of the members of these groups had been activists in the anti–civil rights "Dixiecrat" faction of the Democratic Party or were disgruntled right-wing Republicans who had opposed Eisenhower's nomination. O'Leary's exposé would charge that despite Houston being "remarkably free of Communistic influences," this coalition of organizations had initiated a "reign of terror" in the city.[2]

The reign of terror to which O'Leary referred was a local manifestation of the national controversy known as America's second "Red Scare," which permeated nearly every aspect of American society during the post–World War II decade. The Red Scare was characterized by a widespread series of actions by individuals and groups whose intentions were to frighten Americans with false and highly exaggerated charges of Communist subversion for the purpose of political, economic, and psychological profit. Those who carried out the Red Scare relied on tactics that included indiscriminate, often unfounded accusations, inquisitorial investigative methods, and sensationalism, ostensibly in the suppression of Communism. These tactics were named "McCarthyism," for the demagogic Republican senator Joseph R. McCarthy, who was their most famous practitioner.[3]

O'Leary's series, which ran in the *Post* from October 11 through October 21, had its origins in May 1953, when a prominent member of the League of Women Voters met with Rienzi Johnston's grandson, Harry Johnston, the city editor of the *Post*. The woman, whose name was never revealed, gave Johnston a batch of pamphlets, circulars, and broadsides and a list of more than five hundred names, addresses, and telephone numbers of individuals she claimed were members of a secretive local Red Scare pressure group called the Minute Women. She claimed that the group was responsible for most of the recent attacks on teachers, school administrators, and educational institutions in Houston. The informant insisted that her identity remain confidential. She told Johnston that the Minute Women and their backers were more powerful than the Hobbys and the *Houston Post* and that they could have her fired from her job.[4]

Because of a number of Red Scare incidents in Houston beginning as early as 1951, Ralph O'Leary had been pleading with Johnston to let him do an investigative report on the pressure groups that seemed to be responsible for the incidents, but Johnston had refused. Now armed with material provided by the anonymous informant, O'Leary changed Johnston's mind. Johnston took the information to his boss, Managing Editor Arthur Laro. The chubby, curmudgeonly, cigar-chomping Laro recognized that an exposé of these people might appeal to Oveta, who was one of their targets. He also liked to cast the *Post* as having more journalistic courage than the rival *Chronicle*. Laro often reminded *Post* reporters that his creed was "Go beneath the surface of the news and report things that other people either aren't equipped to report—or don't want to." The editor gave O'Leary the green light to do his investigation. Although no written documentation could be found that Laro cleared his decision with Oveta, it is unthinkable that the investigation would have proceeded without her approval. Oveta had been Laro's patron and immediate supervisor at the *Post* before she joined the Eisenhower administration.

*Oveta and Will Hobby with their fellow Houston newspaper publishers and editors,*
*Jesse Jones (left) and his* Houston Chronicle *editor Emmett Walter (standing far left),*
*and George Carmack of the* Houston Press *(standing right).*

There is evidence that Oveta had already encouraged the investigation. In an interview
with this author, Marguerite Johnston later claimed it was Oveta who first suggested to
Laro that the newspaper should do an exposé about the Minute Women. At the *Post*, a
suggestion made by Oveta Culp Hobby was tantamount to an order, even while she was
secretary of HEW and supposedly playing no official role in the paper's management.[5]

George Carmack, editor of the *Houston Press*, later insisted, "Harry [Johnston] was
just a conduit. That was purely Oveta's decision. I don't think the Governor would've
cared much about it. It was a real smart decision. Oveta decided that this was a road that
the *Houston Post* ought to take. Oveta did it for what it would do for the *Post*'s image."
Carmack also believed that a series of highly publicized investigatory reports about anti-
Eisenhower fringe groups was a smart business move on Oveta's part, as Eisenhower was
hugely popular in Houston. Not only would an exposé sell newspapers, it would also give
the *Post* a crusading and progressive image without much risk.

Will Hobby, Jesse Jones, and the editors of their newspapers' editorial pages had
used their respective newspapers as political weapons to help Dwight D. Eisenhower
win Texas in the presidential election. The *Houston Post* even serialized Senator Joseph
McCarthy's book, *McCarthyism: The Fight for America*, and heavily promoted it. While
the *Post* tended to be slightly more moderate than the *Chronicle*, the editorials and
opinion columns of both newspapers encouraged the anticommunist hysteria in which
Houston's Red Scare thrived.

In his study of how the nation's newspapers reported Joe McCarthy's activities, Edwin R. Bayley observed, "It was no wonder that so many people were convinced that McCarthy was exposing Communists. The newspapers said so." And Houston's newspapers were among those saying it. Through their scare stories, the newspapers seemed to verify the charges and claims of the right-wing extremist fringe, conferring respectability and credibility on people whom in earlier years would have been either scorned or laughed at or both. More significantly, press manipulations of anticommunist hysteria served the pragmatic needs of conservative politics: to restore the Republican Party to national power after sixteen years of Democratic control of the presidency. Native Texan and humorist John Henry Faulk, whose career on national television ended when a Red Scare organization, Aware Inc., placed his name on the infamous blacklist despite his being innocent of any subversive activities, later observed that newspapers in Houston encouraged the Red Scare, "shamefully enough, not because they believed that the community was threatened by subversion but because they saw an opportunity to strengthen their political advantages."[6]

In Texas, the deep animosities between moderate Eisenhower Republicans and the smaller, right-wing faction of the party surfaced almost as soon as Eisenhower assumed office in January 1953. The main source of friction between moderates like the Hobbys and the extreme right was their different perceptions of the nature of the Communist threat. For moderates and some of the Taft supporters, the Red Scare was a symbolic partisan issue that could be manipulated to win political office. Once Eisenhower restored the Republican Party to national power, the issue of Communists in government could be muffled if not abandoned. Right-wing Republicans who supported Senator Joe McCarthy and made up the hard core of the Red Scare perceived the Communist issue differently. They were ideological "true believers" who steadfastly believed much of their own Red Scare rhetoric. Already wounded by their intraparty defeat, these activists were shocked when the Eisenhower administration failed to conduct a wholesale purge of the nonexistent "Communist-infested" federal bureaucracy and repeal New Deal reforms such as Social Security.

As a result, Senator McCarthy's claim that "twenty years of treason" had become "twenty-one years of treason" found instant support among a number of groups on the extreme right. One of those groups was the Minute Women of the U.S.A., a national organization founded in 1948 by Suzanne Silvercruys Stevenson, a Belgian-born sculptor who became an American citizen in 1922. Exhibiting all the ideological zeal of the recently converted, Stevenson became obsessed with the idea that the Truman administration was rife with traitors intent on turning the United States into a socialized state. When she announced the formation of the Minute Women, Stevenson declared that "women must mobilize" to defend the "traditional American way of life in a national crusade" that she would personally lead. The Minute Women agenda included preservation of "states' rights," which meant continued racial segregation and support of state claims of ownership of their tidelands; a call for "fairer taxes," which was a demand to repeal the federal income tax; passage of "right to work" laws to destroy the labor movement; and the initiation of a "courageous and enlightened foreign policy," which among many other things called for the American military to remove the Soviet Red Army out of Eastern Europe and for a complete withdrawal from the United Nations. The Minute Women later added to their objectives the passage of a constitutional amendment to severely restrict the president's ability to make treaties with foreign countries. This amendment, which was named for its chief advocate, Senator John Bricker of Ohio, would eventually become a major Minute Women cause célèbre.[7]

The Minute Women soon became self-appointed anticommunist watchdogs in communities throughout the United States. By 1952, the organization had spread from its start in Connecticut to at least twenty-six other states, with a national membership numbered at about fifty thousand. Minute Women activities were overt enough to elicit a stinging editorial response from the New York Times, which declared that the Minute Women displayed "an inexcusable disregard for the principles of freedom of thought and freedom of expression." An editorial in the St. Louis Post-Dispatch noted, "This is a free country and that gives the Minute Women a pretty wide franchise. We have always felt that if you let the lunatic fringe talk, it will quickly expose its lunacy. But we are getting a little worried about the people who do not recognize lunacy when they hear it."[8]

A group of women in Houston organized a local chapter of the Minute Women in 1951. The chapter, which quickly developed into one of the most active local branches in the United States, provided the central leadership role in the conduct of Houston's Red Scare. Their allied organizations included the Committee for the Preservation of Methodism, which claimed that the national Methodist Church hierarchy and many of its ministers were socialists and Communist sympathizers; the Americanism Committee of the American Legion, which focused on movie censorship; the Committee for Sound American Education, which defended racial segregation of public schools and opposed HEW's aid to education programs; and Doctors for Freedom, whose members opposed socialized medicine. Although each one of these groups had special interests, their members essentially had overlapping political agendas.

These Red Scare activists adopted the traditional techniques of political pressure groups. The Minute Women devised a telephone chain system to harass their enemies and initiated massive letter campaigns to influence local affairs. The allied organizations sometimes joined forces to bring in outside speakers, distribute propaganda pamphlets, engage in picketing, heckle and censor "controversial" speakers, and conduct educational workshops and discussion groups. From the fall of 1951 through the summer of 1953, the Minute Women and their allies succeeded in having the programs of several speakers canceled. A few of those targeted persevered and made their appearances, only to have yelling and heckling Red Scare activists disrupt their programs.

By the fall of 1953, Houston's Red Scare seemed to be unopposed and uncontested as its activists falsely accused a growing number of individuals of having unpatriotic opinions or of having once been members of organizations deemed subversive by the

*Minute Women members pack the room at a Houston
Independent School District Board meeting, July 18, 1953.*

House Un-American Activities Committee. The list included the deputy superintendent of the Houston Independent School District and the president of the University of Houston. Liberals in public positions, no matter how moderate their politics, waited in fear, wondering who would be next. This fear was especially true of many of the city's educators, whose morale had fallen as a result of attacks on the public schools and successful campaigns to censor or ban textbooks. At the University of Houston, programmers deleted American history courses from the university's pioneering educational television channel for the fall semester of 1953, due to a fear that Houston's ideological censors might deem comments made by one of the instructors as being "un-American."

While they attacked their political enemies in Houston, local Red Scare activists also turned their sights on the Eisenhower administration, with a special focus on their hometown celebrity, Oveta Culp Hobby, and her much-feared HEW. The Minute Women distributed a circular in Houston that proclaimed, "The whole social security system is alien to America and is more parallel to the USSR than ours." When physician members of Doctors for Freedom met with their patients, they handed them circulars declaring that HEW would be an "ideal vehicle for the complete socialization of medicine" and asked them to write letters denouncing the department to the members of the Texas congressional delegation. Minute Women members initiated a separate letter-writing campaign aimed at the Texas congressional delegation and at the White House. Many of those letters denounced Oveta by name. "[Oveta] Hobby went high under Truman and now Eisenhower," one letter exclaimed. "Anything for advancement—nice business!" Another letter writer from Houston urged Senator Price Daniel to launch an investigation of Oveta's alleged subversive activities. The vast majority of letters received at the White House attacking HEW came from Houston. Individual Minute Women members openly accused Oveta of having Communist sympathies and claimed that HEW was a nefarious "socialistic" plot. As evidence of Oveta's supposedly radical-left political views, some Minute Women cited her staunch defense of the liberal Democrat and New Dealer Anna Rosenberg against Joe McCarthy's allegations that Rosenberg was a Communist fellow traveler. Other Minute Women, aided by allies in Montgomery, Alabama, cited the speech Oveta made in that city in 1950 when she castigated the press for its "fuzzy-minded habit of labeling all Communists, socialists and liberals together as left wing."[9]

The charge that Oveta was "soft on Communism" was ironic in light of the *Houston Post*'s Red Scare editorial campaign during the presidential election campaign. Although Ed Kilman printed those editorials despite Oveta's objections, that in-house disagreement was unknown to the public, and it was widely assumed that the editorials reflected Oveta's opinions. More ironic, however, were some of Oveta's actions as a member of Eisenhower's cabinet. As secretary of HEW, Oveta suspended the federal research grants of nearly thirty scholars working on medical projects, because they were deemed to be "security risks." The scientists were deprived of their financial support without benefit of charges or hearings, on the basis of unsubstantiated and largely scurrilous secret reports from the Federal Loyalty Review Board. Oveta later explained that the scientists were not government employees and none were working on secret projects. In making her decisions, she claimed that her department had been careful to "avoid any undue interference with scientific research." She also dismissed Dr. John P. Peters as a special consultant to the Public Health Service and Kenneth M. Cole as a federal food and drug inspector after they were accused, in separate incidents, of being security risks. The US Supreme Court, in *Peters v. Hobby* (1955) and *Cole v. Young* (1956), later overturned the dismissals, ruling that Oveta had improperly fired both men. Nevertheless, the old resentments over the Taft-Eisenhower nomination battle, Joe McCarthy's criticisms of Eisenhower policies, and a paranoid fear of the new HEW department obscured everything else for the Minute Women and their associates.[10]

Concurrent with the Red Scare attacks back in Houston, Senator McCarthy and his supporters were causing Eisenhower and the national Republican Party hierarchy much alarm. McCarthy's outrageous and irresponsible behavior was rapidly transforming the senator from an asset to a liability in the eyes of Eisenhower Republicans. In the early summer of 1953, veteran journalist William S. White observed in *Look* magazine that "in McCarthy, embarrassed Republican leaders know they have got hold of a red-hot bazooka, useful in destroying the enemy but also quite likely to blister the hands of the forces that employ it. Their private fear is that a lethal rocket may at any moment blast out through the wrong end of the pipe." Eisenhower was becoming increasingly impatient with McCarthy, whom he grew to loathe, as well as with criticism from the right wing of the party. Those critics included a few of his wealthy supporters in Houston, especially oilman Hugh Roy Cullen. In response to one of Cullen's letters giving unsolicited and uninformed advice about how Eisenhower should manage foreign affairs, the president peevishly wrote, "I must say I was surprised by some of your comments. . . . I am astonished by your implied fear that . . . my associates and I might fail to keep up our guard [against Communists]."

Oveta knew how much Eisenhower disliked McCarthy and his rabid followers. It was a dislike she shared with the president. No one in the administration, however, including Eisenhower and Vice President Richard Nixon, was prepared to publicly attack McCarthy and his wealthy supporters, such as Cullen. The support of McCarthy's followers and the money of his wealthy enablers would be needed in the upcoming 1954 congressional elections. In addition, the Republicans in Congress were not ready to abandon their own fearmongering tactics about the threat of Communist subversion. Nevertheless, the Eisenhower administration and its moderate Republican allies in the Senate had lost patience with the rabid local fringe groups on the extreme right. Personal attacks on the president and on Oveta and other members of the administration by a small but vocal pack of troublesome women and their spouses had to be dealt with. As one politically active Houston woman observed, "Oveta doesn't brook back-talk." And while McCarthy could not be attacked, for reasons of political caution, at least his supporters could be, and this would be an indirect assault on the senator himself.[11]

Oveta had long complained to Will about the *Post*'s editor, Ed Kilman, and his Red Scare editorials. Although Oveta had failed earlier to persuade Will to restrain Kilman and moderate his more extreme editorials, she did succeed in keeping the *Post* from endorsing McCarthy's activities. Unlike the *Houston Chronicle*, and contrary to Kilman's editorials, the *Post*'s other editorial writers and columnists were openly critical of McCarthy. One of the *Post*'s columnists frequently referred to the senator as "the loud Wisconsin solon." But McCarthy's virulent attacks on the Eisenhower administration, and by association on Oveta, made Will Hobby much less tolerant of Kilman's reactionary editorials. Will told KPRC's Jack McGrew that he supported President Eisenhower's refusal to openly criticize Joe McCarthy. Will noted that when he was growing up, "popular wisdom in Moscow [Texas] dictated that one didn't willingly engage 'in a pissing contest with a skunk.'"[12]

Now that the extreme right in Houston was targeting Oveta and Eisenhower, Kilman's power over the *Houston Post*'s editorial pages was greatly reduced, to the point where he became something of an editorial figurehead until his retirement in 1961, spending his last years with the *Post* as a columnist writing about Texas folklore, history, and archeology. As a result, the *Post*'s editorial page became more moderate in tone and content.[13]

A controversy over Charlie Chaplin's movie *Limelight* illustrated the change in the *Post*'s editorial policies. The American Legion had waged a Red Scare campaign against the movie industry since the late 1940s. The American Legion's magazine featured numerous articles charging that subversives and un-American influences dominated Hollywood. In one article, author J. B. Matthews, who was a Red Scare polemicist, claimed that three hundred movie personalities had once or still belonged to the Communist Party. Among the accused was Charlie Chaplin, one of the biggest stars in film history. As a result, Red Scare groups harassed the internationally famous comedian and filmmaker to such an extent that in 1952 he moved to Europe, where he remained until his death twenty years later. Following his self-exile, Chaplin continued to make films, *Limelight* being one of them. In March 1953, a movie theater in Houston placed Chaplin's *Limelight* on its screening schedule. The Minute Women and the Americanism Committee of the American Legion immediately denounced the theater's owners for their decision, declaring, "Americans aid and abet Stalin's Communism when they patronize and pay money to see Limelight." The theater immediately canceled Chaplin's movie. The *Houston Post* remained silent throughout this affair.

Three months later, another theater in Houston dared to schedule a screening of Chaplin's film. The Legion's Americanism Committee once again demanded that the movie not be shown. This time, the *Houston Post* reacted. An unsigned *Post* editorial on June 27, 1953, blasted the protesters with the charge that they supported a "false concept of Americanism. . . . [I]t is not the office of the Legion to decide for all the people whether or not the film affects the public welfare." The identity of the editorial's author is unknown, but it is near certain that it was not Kilman. The author might have been either Marguerite Johnston or George Fuermann, the *Post*'s resident liberals. The straightforward denunciation of the Legion's censorship efforts certainly reflected the opinion Oveta had stated several years earlier in a speech she gave at a meeting of the Houston Council of Federated Church Women. She told her audience that if a person objected to the contents of a movie, that person should simply not go see the movie.[14]

In its response to the *Post*'s editorial scolding, the American Legion committee released a statement complaining it was "inconceivable that the *Houston Post* can deny the soundness . . . of the Legion's viewpoint." The Americanism Committee's chairman declared that it was evidence the *Post*, and by implication the Hobbys, must be "tolerant of Communist sympathizers" and "intolerant" of "pro-American views." A large number of letters assailing the Hobbys as "left-wingers" soon arrived in the *Post*'s mail room, most of them personal attacks on Oveta.[15]

Bill Hobby had recently graduated from Rice Institute and was living at home that summer. He was working at the *Post* before he was scheduled to enter the navy in September. In a letter to his St. Albans School mentor, John Davis, Bill reported there had been "a little hassle . . . with the American Legion over the showing of the Charlie Chaplin film 'Limelight.'" Bill explained that the Legion had succeeded in getting the film banned at a local movie house back in March. "Then, two weeks ago, another theatre that had been planning to run the film cancelled it under threat of picketing by the Legion. The next day, we ran a strong editorial condemning the Legion for trying to get the film banned and the theatre for knuckling under to them, and the film was shown. Since then, we have received a very nasty letter from the Legion saying that we are Communists, enemies of home, chastity, the flag and everything else."[16]

The *Post*'s stand in the *Limelight* affair was one of the first indications a change in editorial direction had occurred. Oveta decided it was time to pull the plug on the local Red Scare. The *Post*'s new attitude was made even more obvious on Sunday, October 11, 1953, when Ralph O'Leary's deeply researched exposé made its appearance in the newspaper. O'Leary's editor, Harry Johnston, felt that the story was too complex to be adequately told in one report. He decided to publish the material as an eleven-part series of articles placed prominently on the front page. O'Leary's reporting, richly illustrated with photographs of accusers and accused, was published daily, with the last story appearing on October 21, 1953.

O'Leary wrote the exposé in serial form, with teasers at the end of each article hinting at new revelations to come in the next installment. Armed with Minute Women literature and its membership roll, as well as with the names of activists in the other prominent Red Scare organizations in the city, O'Leary drew from a treasure trove of information about their activities. In addition, the *Post*'s skilled investigative reporter persuaded a few activists, including three Minute Women leaders, to give him candid on-the-record interviews. One of the interviewees told O'Leary she believed the Hobbys ran the *Houston Post* as a "front" for someone else, perhaps even the Communist Party. Another insisted that Oveta held radical "left-wing" beliefs.[17]

O'Leary's exposé, which became known as "The Minute Women Series," was an instant sensation in Houston, and the paper was in great demand for ten days after the initial article. As a flood of mail poured into the offices of the *Post* in reaction to the series, the newspaper made a decision to publish ten thousand special reprint editions. When those copies sold out quickly, the *Post* rushed the printing of another ten thousand copies. The American Federation of Labor and the National Education Association's Defense Committee in Washington, DC, ordered thousands of additional copies to distribute throughout the United States. One group in Connecticut, the home state of the Minute Women founder, requested copies to distribute to the members of that state's legislature. In all, individuals and organizations across the nation requested 120,000 copies of O'Leary's work, an astounding figure for a local newspaper reprint. In Georgia, the *Atlanta Constitution*'s editor and columnist Ralph McGill wrote that the *Post* had provided a public service in the best traditions of journalism and "Americanism." *Time* featured a story on O'Leary's exposé, declaring, "The *Post*'s . . . careful, unhysterical tone was a model of how a newspaper can effectively expose irresponsible vigilantism." The magazine the *Nation* published a three-page condensation of the series titled "Daughters of Vigilantism" in January 1954, which was reprinted and distributed as a pamphlet by critics of Joe McCarthy and his followers.[18]

Houston Post *reporter Ralph S. O'Leary, 1953.*

In Houston, influential civic leaders praised O'Leary's series as a badly needed exposé of the individuals and groups who were engaged in community red-baiting. Philanthropist Nina Cullinan, daughter of the founder of Texaco, publicly declared that the Red Scare had reached a turning point in Houston because of the series and that it had relieved the atmosphere of "repression and fear." Bill Hobby, who was a cadet in a naval officer school in Rhode Island by the time the series appeared, sent O'Leary a letter congratulating him on the exposé: "What a masterful job of reporting, researching, and writing the series was! I think you have done Houston—and the *Post*—a service that will be much noted and long remembered. It was a job that needed to be done in the worst way."[19]

Understandably, O'Leary neglected to discuss the significant role the *Post* and the *Houston Chronicle* played in encouraging the Red Scare in Houston. Reacting to O'Leary's statement that there were few Communists in Texas, a reader wrote a letter to the *Post* reminding the editors that "the only place I ever read . . . there were a lot of communists in Texas was in the columns of the *Houston Post*." O'Leary knew this accusation was true, but the journalist was a realist, grateful to be able to finally go after the activists of the Red Scare, if not its enablers.[20]

The American Newspaper Guild awarded O'Leary its prestigious Heywood Broun Award for "disclosing a growing climate of fear" in Houston. The guild noted that it took courage for the *Houston Post* to print the exposé in an area of the nation in which the "suppressionist spirit is especially strong." O'Leary also won the Sidney Hillman Foundation and the National Headliner Club awards.[21]

Not all reaction was favorable. Someone exploded a small bomb in the doorway of O'Leary's home shortly after the series was published, causing minor damage but no injuries. A less violent protest came from the Republican Women's Club of Harris County (Houston), an organization dominated by Minute Women. The club passed a resolution attacking the *Post* and criticizing its "biased" reporting on Senator McCarthy's activities. The resolution warned that President Eisenhower had swung to the ideological left and had used the *Post* and other papers "under his control" to prepare the public for an even more "radical swing to the left." According to the club, the *Post* had attacked the Minute Women because its members had angered Oveta by opposing the creation of HEW, which was largely accurate. The Republican Party of Harris County, however, which represented the dominant pro-Eisenhower faction, repudiated the club's resolution, claiming that the women represented a small minority of Republicans in Houston.[22]

The *Houston Chronicle*, which remained steadfast in its pro–Red Scare editorial opinions, criticized O'Leary's series and argued that Houstonians were not victims of any "thought control." According to the *Chronicle*, "One gets the idea that a reign of terror has all but paralyzed the clergy and the educators of Houston." The newspaper claimed that it had failed to find any person in the city fearful of speaking up on any issue, declaring that "anti-anticommunists . . . scream 'thought control' at anyone who is sensible enough to reject their weird philosophy."[23]

Despite criticism, the *Post* stayed on its anti–Red Scare and anti-McCarthy track. In the months after publishing the O'Leary series, the *Post* published several editorials critical of McCarthy. One urged the public to support the Eisenhower administration's "effort to prevent [McCarthy] from wrecking its plans for the country's good." The *Post* also published and heavily promoted a series of intensely hostile "analytical and biographical" articles about McCarthy.

In April 1954, Senator McCarthy accepted an invitation to be the keynote speaker at the annual celebration of the Battle of San Jacinto at the battleground near Houston. His appearance was soon threatened when a congressional committee investigating the senator's attack on the US Army scheduled a hearing for the day of the celebration. McCarthy had charged that at the highest levels of the military, Red sympathizers were protecting Russian spies. McCarthy accused Secretary of the Army Robert T. Stevens of trying to blackmail him and his Senate staff by claiming (correctly) that the senator and his counsel, Roy Cohn, had pressured the army to extend privileged treatment to Cohn's close friend, draftee G. David Schine. Under strong pressure from the White House, the Senate decided to launch an investigation of McCarthy's conduct in his attack on Secretary Stevens and the army.

The congressional hearing, which was to be broadcast live on television, required McCarthy's presence. Suspecting that Oveta was somehow behind the scheduling of the hearing to prevent McCarthy's appearance at San Jacinto, a delegation of Minute Women met with conservative Republican oilman Hugh Roy Cullen, who was an enthusiastic supporter of McCarthy. After the women asked Cullen to intervene, he called Senate Minority Leader Lyndon Johnson to request a day's postponement of the hearing. "No reason why they shouldn't do that," Cullen asserted. "We want to get Joe McCarthy [to Houston] because people here want it. This whole state is roused up. Figure it's a double cross and figure Oveta Hobby has done it." LBJ reluctantly agreed to recommend a delay, which was granted by the committee chair, Senator Karl Mundt.[24]

On December 2, 1954, the US Senate voted sixty-seven to twenty-two to condemn Joseph McCarthy for contempt and abuse of Senate committees. In the debate about the resolution, LBJ asserted that McCarthy's description of the committee members investigating his record as the "unwitting handmaidens of Communism" did not deserve to be in the *Congressional Record*. It "would be more appropriate on the wall of a men's room," LBJ declared. Throughout the debate, Houston's Minute Women bombarded LBJ's office with pro-McCarthy mail and telephone calls. Senator Johnson ignored their protests. He led the effort to get the resolution through the Senate. The Senate's condemnation devastated McCarthy and ended his influence, although his humiliation and fall only discredited, but did not destroy, the style and technique that had become known as "McCarthyism." The Wisconsin Republican, a victim of his abuse of alcohol, died on May 2, 1957. Houston's Red Scare groups, already in retreat, shared in McCarthy's downfall. As for the Minute Women and their allies in Houston, Oveta Hobby had played a decisive role in their ultimate collapse. "O'Leary torpedoed the Minute Women," historian Robert Pando has written, "which meant that [Oveta] Hobby had torpedoed the Minute Women."[25]

Although the *Houston Chronicle* strongly criticized the *Post* for publishing the Minute Women series, Jesse Jones was not concerned about the controversy. He had long before turned the newspaper's editorial page over to Emmet Walter, who was even more to the right than the *Post*'s Ed Kilman. The venom spewing from the *Chronicle*'s editorial page was Walter's. Now approaching his eightieth birthday, Jones's health was in decline—he had almost died in July 1953 of complications from gall bladder surgery—and he was little involved in the operations of his newspaper. He essentially left the *Chronicle* under the direction of his nephew, John T. Jones Jr., although he retained a tight grip on his bank and his real estate holdings. Jesse Jones was somewhat amused by the right-wing attack on Oveta, and did not take it seriously. He gently kidded Oveta about it in a letter he sent to her apartment in Washington. Referring to the controversy over Joe McCarthy's invitation to speak at San Jacinto, Jones informed Oveta, tongue firmly in cheek, that his wife "insists that you should make the San Jacinto speech instead of McCarthy. Incidentally the town is almost at war over his invitation."[26]

By the fall of 1953, Will Hobby was seventy-five years old and Jesse Jones was seventy-nine, and the health of both men was fragile. Their close professional and social relationship stretched back a quarter of a century. That friendship had endured its rocky moments, especially during the years that Jones owned the *Post* and Will was its editor. And their relationship was strained during the period when the Hobbys were trying to purchase the *Post* from the "Jones Interests." Oveta had something of a love-hate relationship with Jesse, although she had always kept the negative part of that emotional equation to herself. After all, Jesse Jones was not a man any reasonable person doing business in Houston would want to have as an enemy, if it could be avoided. Jesse Jones was her husband's best friend, and that friendship had only strengthened as Will and Jesse aged. Oveta acted accordingly, always treating Jones with deference, respect, and warmth in their personal exchanges. When Jones entered the hospital in Houston in July 1953, her note to him reflected the "love" part of the feelings she had for the most powerful man in the 8F crowd. "My Pet," she wrote, "I am sorry you are in the hospital. Hope you are out soon. Love, Oveta."[27]

After Oveta joined Eisenhower's cabinet and was spending most of her time in Washington, Will and Jesse became even closer. With both men relying on others to manage most of their various business interests, they had more time to keep each other's company. They frequently had lunch together in Jesse's apartment, and in the late afternoon often played poker, gossiped, swapped jokes, and reminisced while enjoying an alcoholic beverage or two. Jones especially enjoyed the homespun, folksy stories that Will had heard as a youth in rural East Texas. A month after Jones returned home after his near death that summer of 1953, he wrote Oveta, "The Governor comes by about every other day and I am always glad to see him." During one of Will and Jesse's lunches, they placed a telephone call to Oveta's office at HEW, knowing that she would be eating lunch at

*Will Hobby and Jesse Jones at one of their frequent dinner events, early 1950s.*

My Dear Friend
I am honored to be
with you.
Jesse Jones

her desk. Both men picked up phones on their end of the line to be able to talk to Oveta together. The call was strictly for fun. The next morning, Oveta wrote Jones to tell him how much she enjoyed the phone call. She added that Will had called her the night before to tell her of "the fun he had playing poker" with Jones. In October, during one of Will's frequent stays with Oveta at the apartment on Connecticut Avenue in Washington, Jones sent him a letter that hinted at a bit of loneliness: "I am sure you are enjoying Oveta and your stay in Washington, but don't stay away too long."[28]

Jones closely followed Oveta's activities as a member of Eisenhower's cabinet. In late September 1953, when she was on a speaking tour to boost support for the administration's efforts to expand Social Security coverage, Oveta addressed the American

Federation of Labor's national convention in St. Louis. Sitting in his spacious apartment in the Lamar Hotel, Jones listened carefully to her speech, which was broadcast nationally on the radio. As he had often done over the years, Jones offered Oveta his critique of her performance. In a letter written the next day, Jones said he had the "feeling that you did not do yourself justice. Your speech was much too long for the time you had. You are one of our best speakers. Your manner is excellent—and your looks do not hurt any. But you must be more deliberate and take more time. With worlds of love to Jessica and to you and the Governor." Although Jones didn't oppose Social Security expansion, he was a fiscal conservative and was always on guard against what he believed was excessive federal spending. He ended the typed letter to Oveta with a handwritten postscript: "Let's keep a little further to the *right*." Oveta's response came a few days later. "It was sweet of you to listen . . . and to give me the benefit of your suggestions," she wrote Jones. "I agree that the speech was a little too long for the time allotted, and will certainly try to avoid that in the future."[29]

Oveta's other public appearances that fall of 1953 included an address to the Air Force Officers Wives Club of Washington, with Mamie Eisenhower as her guest; an appearance with President Eisenhower and Secretary of Agriculture Ezra Taft Benson at the national convention of the Future Farmers of America in Kansas City; a speech to the National Rehabilitation Association at its annual conference in Miami Beach; and a press conference in New York City, where she told reporters that Americans wanted more Social Security, not less, and that the president's Social Security proposal should "rank high on the priority list" of the next session of Congress. Because of her effectiveness as a speaker, the Eisenhower administration also tapped Oveta to promote programs outside of her portfolio. Her assignments included speaking to a banquet room full of major Republican donors at the Palmer House in Chicago, where she presented a comprehensive overview of the Eisenhower administration's various program initiatives. All totaled, that fall Oveta gave twenty-three "major" speeches and several minor ones. Joan Braden and Roswell Perkins drafted most of those speeches, which would ordinarily have been a major time saver for Oveta, but because of years of experience as a newspaper editor, she developed an unshakable habit of closely editing any drafts other writers produced for her. As historian Debra Sutphen points out, Oveta labored "over each sentence, her keen eye attuned not only to grammatical correctness but to verbal effectiveness."[30]

As had happened during her years leading the Women's Army Corps, Oveta's breakneck schedule, long working hours, and continuing problem with her thyroid condition lowered her resistance to respiratory illnesses. Her smoking habit could only have exacerbated the problem. She became ill in the middle of November and was forced to send Nelson Rockefeller out as a substitute for her remaining speaking engagements. She was unable even to attend a dinner at the Waldorf Astoria in Manhattan where she was to receive the Gold Medal of the National Institute of Social Sciences.[31]

Concerned about her health and exhausting work schedule, Eisenhower sent Oveta a note near the end of November to remind his HEW secretary that he had recently asked her to take "a short breather." He noted that her reply had been that she would take Thanksgiving Day off. "Now I admit that when anyone gets as high ranking as you are," Eisenhower said, "such a person has gotten beyond a place where he or she can be 'ordered about.' But I would deem it a very great personal favor if you would get out of this place no later than tomorrow morning (Wednesday) and not be back before Monday." He added, "[My] purpose in making this request would be defeated if you would lug off with you a brief case full of papers (anyway brief cases belong only to the diplomatic service)." Eisenhower emphasized that his request was "based on purely selfish reasons . . . that are shared by the entire Cabinet. Briefly stated they are nothing more than our conviction that you are absolutely necessary to this Administration, and we want you to get enough . . . recreation and rest in your life that you don't become bored, sick, or just plain tired of your job."[32]

Oveta responded that it was Eisenhower's "usual kind and generous self to write me as you did . . . and I thank you from the bottom of my heart for your consideration. It's always a pleasure and a privilege, Sir, to follow orders from you! But I know you will take into consideration the extenuating circumstances if I delay compliance until later this month, when I truly plan to go away for a good rest. . . . [E]ven had I been away I would have had no peace of mind."[33]

A few days before Christmas, Oveta's dear friend General George Marshall joined Eisenhower in urging her to be careful about overworking. In a handwritten letter, Marshall mentioned that he recently had been ill with a virus that had put him into Walter Reed Hospital. He reported that when Eisenhower visited him in the hospital, "I only made one . . . suggestion regarding his administration. I advised him to curtail your speaking schedule by 75 [percent] and give you orders to leave your office at 5pm and no home work. I feel sure you are working to your self-destruction. Please do restrain yourself or trouble will be on you before you realize it. With my love, affectionately." Oveta replied that she was surprised to learn about Marshall's stay in the hospital and that she would have visited him if she had known. "You are in my thoughts so often," Oveta wrote. "It is so characteristic of you to think of others, even when you are beset with problems of your own. I was touched at your thought of me, and appreciate your wise words of counsel. Of course you are right, and I am striving to organize my work so that I have more time for rest and relaxation." Oveta, who was back in her office after spending a few days in Houston for the Christmas holiday, told Marshall, "I believe I'm making some headway now."[34]

The rest Oveta enjoyed in Houston that Christmas of 1953 was well timed, although her appointment calendar from 1954 shows little sign that she heeded Eisenhower's or Marshall's advice. As the new year began, she was ready to lead Rockefeller and her HEW administrative team in the effort to achieve some of the president's most important goals on his domestic policy agenda, specifically the expansion of Social Security.

# CHAPTER 35

## SOCIAL SECURITY AND RACIAL INTEGRATION

As 1953 approached its end, President Eisenhower renewed the effort to expand Social Security coverage. Roswell Perkins's original proposal had been mired for several months in Carl Curtis's Senate committee, with faint prospect of escaping. To improve its chance of passage, the president asked Oveta to have Perkins's original version revised and improved. He also requested that she develop a legislative agenda for the Department of Health, Education, and Welfare (HEW) that would fulfill some of the promises he had made in early 1953 in his State of the Union address. He left it to Oveta and her administrative team to fill in the details.

Oveta assigned those tasks to Nelson Rockefeller, Roswell Perkins, and other HEW administrators, including Commissioner of Education Samuel Brownell and Surgeon General Leonard Scheele. Brownell was the brother of US attorney general Herbert Brownell and a professional educator. Scheele was a career public health service officer who had served as the head of the National Cancer Institute. Oveta had first met him when she served as the vice chair of the national cancer fund campaign in the late 1940s. Scheele was a pioneer in researching the link between cigarette smoking and lung disease, but he was best known for advocating mass fluoridation of drinking water. He has been credited with raising the post of surgeon general from obscurity.[1]

Oveta's team produced an ambitious legislative agenda of eleven bills that included relatively noncontroversial plans for a new federal program for the rehabilitation of the temporarily disabled and an amendment to the Hill-Burton hospital construction act of 1946 to include funds for long-term facilities, rehabilitation centers, and outpatient departments. They also drafted controversial proposals to expand access to health care through private insurance and to address a severe national shortage of public school classrooms. It was Oveta's job to review and approve these proposals and then to present them to the president and the cabinet for final approval. If the proposals were accepted, Oveta would take responsibility for shepherding the finished products through Congress.[2]

Pushing the legislative agenda was a tough challenge by itself, but at the same time, Oveta also had to develop a budget for HEW for the coming fiscal year. The budget placed another layer of complexity and difficulty on top of her grueling work to win approval of HEW's legislative objectives. The department was new, its budget was evolving, and it was obvious to Oveta it was underfunded. As she later told a subcommittee of the House Appropriations Committee, the size of the HEW allocation was "out of all proportion" to the importance of the department's functions. Oveta also faced the dilemma of how to formulate a budget for HEW's multifarious, massive, and severely underfunded bureaucracy that included new funding for construction of hospitals and other medical facilities, while also trying to follow President Eisenhower's orders to reduce expenditures.[3]

Of the items on HEW's legislative agenda, Social Security initially attracted most of the public's attention. While Roswell Perkins's revised plan retained the proposal to expand coverage to more than ten million people, it also included new provisions to allow individuals to continue to work after they were eligible for Social Security benefits without affecting their payments, an increase in benefits for most Social Security recipients, and a provision for individuals to receive full benefits if they were disabled prior to reaching age sixty-five. The latter provision was linked to one of the administration's other initiatives for HEW: reform of the federal physical rehabilitation program. Rockefeller, Perkins, and their consultants determined that state-level vocational rehabilitation programs and Social Security should be closely connected. Whenever a person applied for Social Security disability benefits, he or she would be referred to their state rehabilitation agency and enrolled in a rehabilitation program. The ultimate goal was to return these individuals to the workforce and get them off federal disability payments. This rehabilitation proposal was drafted as a stand-alone bill, separate from the Social Security expansion act.[4]

Perkins's revisions to the Social Security proposal emphasized the conservative principle of promoting work over welfare by encouraging individuals to continue in their jobs after retirement age. Oveta hoped these revisions would blunt the attempts of Senator Curtis to shrink the size of the existing system or even to dismantle it completely. She also thought it would appeal to conservatives by reducing the need for public assistance programs to the needy aged, dependent children, and the permanently and totally disabled by bringing more individuals into the Social Security system and increasing the size of individual Social Security payments. Her team believed that the need for some measure of public assistance would continue, but an expanded Social Security program would reduce the extent of public assistance payments and substitute them with Social Security benefits. Perkins and his team claimed that the cost to the federal government would be minimal, because a slight increase in the payroll tax would cover most of the extra cost, while funding for public assistance would eventually decline.

The Hill-Burton Act of 1946 established a highly successful program that provided matching funds to state and local entities to construct new hospitals to tend to the medical needs of the fast-growing postwar population. With the act set to expire in 1954, HEW called for its extension. But the department also proposed a change in focus from general hospital construction to the building of nursing facilities, convalescent homes, and rehabilitation centers to provide care to the chronically ill, who by 1953 constituted the vast majority of the hospital population. Nelson Rockefeller was primarily responsible for the overall concept for the vocational rehabilitation bill, but Oveta and Roswell Perkins filled in most of the details.[5]

When Oveta joined the Eisenhower cabinet in early January 1953, public schools in the United States were struggling with a severe shortage of classroom space, the result of the ban on new construction during World War II combined with a massive increase in the student population due to the baby boom. Oveta's education experts in HEW estimated that the current shortage of 340,000 classrooms would increase to over 400,000 within seven years. HEW also estimated that it would cost $10 to $12 billion to construct enough new facilities to solve the problem. Eisenhower had acknowledged the situation during the 1952 election campaign, and he had made a vague pledge to address it—but he didn't say how. He and his advisors had no idea how to solve the shortage, given that opposition to federal aid to education was part of Republican orthodoxy. More than a year after his inauguration, Eisenhower and HEW had shown little interest in solving the problem. As much as the president and his conservative advisors wanted the crisis to go away without federal involvement, it had only worsened as the baby boom accelerated, generating demands from the National Education Association, local school boards, parent lay groups, and other educational organizations for Congress and the White House to come to their aid.[6]

As public pressure intensified, the president turned to Oveta to find a solution. The fiscally conservative Eisenhower viewed public education strictly as a local issue in which the federal government should play little or no role. Oveta shared the president's views on the matter, and she preferred to keep her distance from the topic. She was aware of the virulent opposition to federal aid for education in her home state and in other western and southern states. She was also anxious to avoid entanglement in the question of whether any federal aid plan should also include parochial and other private schools. Education Commissioner Samuel Brownell and his staff developed proposals that reflected both of those concerns. They drafted a bill to make the federal government a facilitator instead of a funder of state-level programs to alleviate classroom shortages. They would ask Congress to allocate funding for the White House to sponsor conferences in each of the forty-eight states plus US territories (including Alaska and Hawaii, which were still seeking statehood) to identify and to gather information about local educational problems. Those findings would be submitted to a national White House conference of educators, who in turn would work with HEW to develop proposals for solutions, none of which would require federal funding. The plan was notable for its emphasis on studying instead of solving problems, and it failed to provide immediate action to address the crisis.[7]

A health reinsurance scheme that Nelson Rockefeller had recommended to Oveta soon after he assumed his position at HEW was the final legislative item. Richard Norton Smith has written that Rockefeller came up with a "complex scheme of government-backed guarantees intended to lure private companies and non-profit organizations into covering many of the 63 million Americans" unable to afford health insurance. The concept of reinsurance, which was to spread risk against catastrophic losses, was a long-established practice in the insurance industry, but private industry itself had always served as the reinsurer, not the federal government. Rockefeller complained to Oveta that the Eisenhower administration "could not sit on its hands on the health insurance issue" and that "it had to do *something*." Citing the intense controversy generated by President Truman's ultimately unsuccessful attempts to establish a compulsory, federally funded, universal health insurance program, Rockefeller argued that no plan would pass Congress unless it worked within the private health system, was voluntary, and gave the government minimal involvement in its management. His argument persuaded Oveta to create a HEW task force to study the issue.[8]

Rockefeller recruited his friend Oscar Ruebhausen, a Democrat who had been involved in developing President Truman's ill-fated federal health insurance plan, to help write a federally sponsored plan to offer low-cost hospitalization and physician services that would work with private insurance. Rockefeller and Ruebhausen drafted a plan to establish a federally funded, $25 million pool of money health insurance companies could tap for any "abnormal losses" they might suffer as a result of broadening coverage to the previously uninsured. Participating companies would pay a percentage of their insurance premiums into the fund over time, ultimately making the program self-sufficient and free of federal support and interference. In its public/private approach, the plan was an early version of the Obama administration's Affordable Care Act of 2010. Although Ruebhausen helped craft the plan, he soon complained that "the whole thing smacked of excessive gimmickry," calling it an impractical "Rube Goldberg" plan. Other critics would complain that the scheme was overly complicated, that it lacked details on a range of critical issues related to implementation and administration, and that it failed to specify standards or require changes within the insurance industry that were believed essential to the plan's success.[9]

Oveta had her own concerns that the reinsurance proposal was another one of Rocky's wild ideas. Perkins recalled that Oveta was sometimes "amused, or skeptical of [Rockefeller's] grand schemes, as many were." But invariably, after offering her critiques, she would be persuaded by the sheer force of his personality. And this project was a good example of that process. She found the idea interesting enough to join Rockefeller and Dr. Chester Keefer, HEW's assistant secretary for health and medical affairs, in their discussion with American Medical Association officials and national health insurance company executives. Reactions were ambivalent at best.

Oveta sent a draft of the proposal to Eisenhower, who distributed it to the cabinet. Treasury Secretary George Humphrey "hit the ceiling" in anger when he read the proposal.

*Nelson Rockefeller talking to Rajkumari Amrit Kaur, minister of health for India, as Oveta Culp Hobby's facial expression reveals the amused skepticism she often had for Rocky's ideas, October 1954.*

Budget Director Joseph Dodge told the secretary not to worry, because he didn't believe the president would support the proposal. It shocked Dodge and the hard-line conservatives on the cabinet when Eisenhower told them he did support the plan. A side effect of this episode was that it fed the suspicions of the most conservative members of the cabinet, including Commerce Secretary Sinclair Weeks, Treasury Secretary Humphrey, Agriculture Secretary Benson, and Interior Secretary Douglas McKay, that Oveta and Rockefeller had established a liberal outpost at HEW.[10]

The HEW team completed the drafts of all of the department's legislative proposals in mid-November, and Oveta quickly approved them. She immediately arranged to present the proposals to the president at the cabinet meeting scheduled for Friday morning, November 20. To prepare for this crucial meeting, Oveta immersed herself in the details, holding sessions with Perkins and Rockefeller to sort out complicated points and to get their advice about how to explain them to the president. Cary Reich has noted that Rockefeller was "convinced of the potency of visual aids" because of his dyslexia. He persuaded Oveta to use a set of his charts to illustrate the new plan clearly and concisely to the president and the cabinet. Rockefeller loved to present complex information on a series of large wall charts with color graphs and information in large print and in outline form, basically a low-tech, predigital version of PowerPoint. A reporter observed that the charts were "Technicolor productions that look like [Salvador] Dali dreams."[11]

Oveta, with Perkins and Rockefeller at her side, presented HEW's legislative agenda to the cabinet, carefully explaining the main points in what the cabinet minutes recorded as a "lengthy presentation," spending most of her time on the revised Social Security proposal. Denouncing the alternate plan Senator Curtis had proposed earlier in the year as a "criminal raid on the Social Security trust fund," she warned that its adoption would have damaging political consequences for the Republican Party in the 1954 congressional election. Oveta stressed that the administration's new proposal was economically sound and that it would be popular with a majority of voters. When she ended her presentation, the cabinet broke into applause. With a wide grin on his face, Eisenhower stated that it was obvious Oveta's fellow cabinet members liked the legislative plan, and more important, it also had his enthusiastic endorsement. The meeting would be one of the high points of Oveta's tenure in the Eisenhower administration.[12]

The week before Christmas Day, Eisenhower asked Oveta to present the administration's full HEW legislative agenda to the Republican congressional leadership. For the congressmen, the surprise of the meeting was a general outline of the medical reinsurance plan, which Oveta explained would be "wholly voluntary," with its implementation dependent on decisions at the state and local level. The Republican leaders reacted to this unexpected news with shock and skepticism. Oveta responded that polls indicated a majority of Americans were dissatisfied with the current status of medical insurance and were demanding reform. Despite the doubts expressed by the congressional leaders, Eisenhower told them he would submit the legislation in mid-January and that when they saw the details, he was confident Congress would support the reinsurance plan.[13]

Oveta's new Social Security plan compelled Senator Curtis to make a countermove. On January 6, he submitted a new proposal to Congress that included a number of tweaks to the current Social Security program, including a few enhancements of benefits. But he retained the proposal to convert Social Security into a pension plan with funding subject to the changeable whims of Congress.[14]

Oveta and Rockefeller convinced Eisenhower to reject Curtis's new plan, pointing out that polls showed a majority of Americans were opposed to dismantling the current Social Security program. Arthur Larson, one of the president's special assistants during this period, later wrote that during the 1952 presidential campaign, when the subject of Social Security came up, Eisenhower often repeated "the old chestnut that, if security is what you want, the most complete security of all is in jail." As soon as Eisenhower took office, however, he recommended the extension of Social Security coverage to ten million people. Larson argues that Eisenhower's change in attitude demonstrated he was "capable of changing his mind if a persuasive case was laid before him by people he respected and trusted. This was particularly true in areas like social security, where he

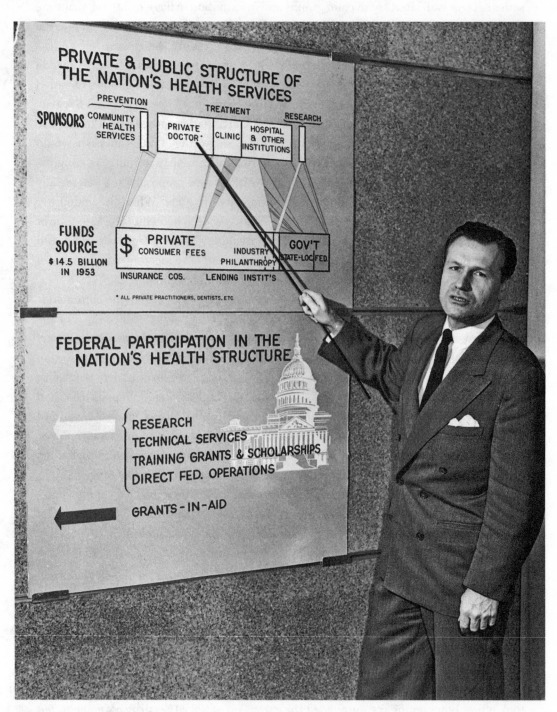

*Nelson Rockefeller explains his medical reinsurance plan with one of his famous charts, 1954.*

was the first to admit that he brought with him no personal expertise to the Presidency." Larson notes that Oveta and Rockefeller were responsible for persuading Eisenhower to throw "his weight behind progressive proposals in the social legislative field."[15]

In his State of the Union address on January 7, 1954, Eisenhower once again called for the expansion of the Social Security program. He also requested the passage of HEW's bills to reform the vocational rehabilitation system, to extend and broaden the Hill-Burton Act, to study the classroom shortage problem, and to create a medical reinsurance program to give more Americans access to health care. He explained that details about the bills would be included in forthcoming special messages to Congress, which he submitted on January 14 and 18. In the matter of health insurance, the president argued that a "limited Government reinsurance service would permit the private and non-profit insurance companies to offer broader protection to more of the many families which want and should have it." Keenly aware of conservative Republican hostility to federal involvement in health care, Eisenhower assured Congress he was "flatly opposed" to socialized medicine. "The great need for hospital and medical services can best be met by the initiative of private plans," Eisenhower declared. "But it is unfortunately a fact that medical costs are rising and already impose severe hardships on many families. The Federal Government can do many helpful things and still carefully avoid the socialization of medicine."[16]

On January 19, while Oveta and her team busily prepared for the upcoming battle in Congress over HEW's ambitious legislative proposals, the president sent happy birthday greetings to Oveta, who turned forty-nine that day. Ever concerned about her health, Eisenhower added that he hoped she could get away from her "busy office long enough to enjoy a truly fine celebration." In a postscript on the note, he also urged her to "take a few hours vacation." Unknown to the president, Oveta, her fellow cabinet members, and Vice President Nixon would surprise him the next day with the gift of a large, custom-made, crystal Steuben cup to commemorate the first anniversary of his inauguration. Oveta took the lead in ordering and getting the cup designed and in arranging the presentation event. She also persuaded her fellow cabinet members to chip in fifty dollars each to pay for it. Eisenhower was delighted when Oveta, Nixon, and the other cabinet members entered his office with the Steuben glass. Nixon made the formal presentation. That same afternoon, Eisenhower sent Oveta a personal note of thanks. "Dear Oveta: Mamie and I will cherish the truly lovely Eisenhower Cup during our lives for which I know you were largely responsible."[17]

The good feelings Oveta had about surprising the president with the commemorative glass cup were somewhat diminished when she returned to her office at HEW and found a letter from Congressman Adam Clayton Powell Jr. Oveta had heard little from Powell since he had accused her in May 1953 of not implementing President Eisenhower's order to integrate schools on military bases. Powell was now confronting her with the charge that African American physicians were being barred from treating their patients at Houston's Jefferson Davis Hospital, the joint city-county medical facility for the indigent. Pointing out that Eisenhower's stated policy was to desegregate any facility that was receiving federal funding, the congressman informed Oveta that the Houston hospital had submitted an application under the Hill-Burton Act for a federal grant to pay for the expansion of its building. If HEW approved funding, the hospital should be required to allow African American doctors to practice there.

For Oveta, Powell's complaint about segregation in a hospital in her hometown was trouble enough, but the congressman also brought up Jane Spaulding's involvement in the controversy, which was a special irritant. "Mrs. Spaulding [who is] one of your assistants," Powell reminded her, had been advising the "colored doctors of Houston on this matter." He told Oveta that he had been "advised that under a contemplated reorganization in [HEW] Mrs. Spaulding will be offered an inferior position considerably below the grade she now holds. This demotion, I learn, would effectively prevent her from following through on the Houston hospital matter." He warned that if any move was made to demote or to oust Spaulding, he would take the matter to the "floor of Congress" and that a "major public controversy" would result.[18]

Apparently searching for some cover in this matter, Oveta asked for a security review on Spaulding to determine if she had any links—past or present—to the Communist Party or to Communist front organizations or any associations with subversive individuals. This request was ironic in light of the *Houston Post*'s Minute Women series. The only "negative" information that came back in the review was insignificant. Spaulding had given false information about her birth year, which was earlier than she had reported. It also appeared that she had somewhat exaggerated the extent of her education.[19]

While this was going on, the Eisenhower administration was working to resolve the Spaulding matter. Concerned about the political fallout that would result if Spaulding was dismissed or resigned in protest, the administration, probably on cabinet secretary Max Rabb's recommendation, created a better-paying job with a higher administrative rank for her at the Foreign Claims Settlement Commission. Two days after Oveta received Powell's letter with its threats, Spaulding submitted her resignation to Oveta. She left quietly, even expressing gratitude to Oveta "for the privilege it has been for me to work with you in pursuance of the great humanitarian goals of the Department." Despite this drama-free departure, Oveta retained hard feelings for Spaulding. She even refused to write and sign a letter to Spaulding acknowledging her resignation. While Oveta was on a trip to New York City, she sent word to Nancy Hanks that she wanted Rockefeller to sign the letter with the excuse that Oveta was away from Washington. Nancy Hanks, who was a critic of Oveta (although not to her face), complained to Rockefeller that Oveta should send Spaulding a telegram under her name from New York instead. When Oveta received this suggestion from Hanks, she vetoed the idea. Oveta even resisted cabinet secretary Max Rabb's recommendation that the acknowledgement letter contain a phrase similar to "With kind regards." Oveta told Rabb that she didn't want to use that phrase unless "she had to." Rockefeller followed orders and signed the acknowledgement letter, but he closed it, "With kind regards."[20]

The quiet exit Spaulding made from HEW lasted less than a week. On January 28,

*Jet* magazine broke the news about Spaulding's departure. The *Jet* story included Clarence Mitchell's charge that Spaulding's job "had been abolished because of differences on racial matters between Mrs. Spaulding and Mrs. Hobby." Other African American leaders were quoted saying Oveta had gotten rid of Spaulding because she opposed the federal grant slated for a partially segregated hospital in Houston and because she had been too forceful an advocate for ending racial segregation of schools on military bases. *Jet* also revealed the heretofore unknown incident when Spaulding had refused to sign the HEW scripted letter to Congressman Powell back in June 1953.[21]

The United Press (UP) picked up *Jet's* story and on January 31 sent the details out on its wire. The UP story added something, however. A White House source (possibly Max Rabb) revealed that Secretary of Defense Charles Wilson was preparing an order to end racial segregation of schools on all military posts by September 1, 1955. The UP claimed that "reliable sources" had told the news service that Oveta "opposed swift action to wipe out segregation and carried her fight to the cabinet level." The wire service report added that its sources also claimed Oveta "was overruled by the President, who instructed Wilson to take decisive action to eliminate the remaining segregated schools." As word of the controversy spread, newspapers nationwide printed stories featuring headlines like one in the *New York Post* declaring, "Oveta's Negro Aide Fired—Fought Bias." A few newspapers published editorials criticizing Oveta as the villain in the episode. One editorial demanded a congressional investigation of Oveta's management of HEW and called the affair "The Mess That Hobby Made."[22]

While the storm of negative news stories raged around her, Oveta finally responded to Congressman Powell's letter of January 18. She addressed his complaint about Jefferson Davis Hospital in Houston. Her explanation was an exercise in legal acrobatics and an excruciatingly narrow and unimaginative interpretation of the Hill-Burton Act. She stated that when Congress passed the original legislation in 1946 authorizing federal funds for hospital construction, it had placed "no provision" in the act permitting the Public Health Service "to refuse Federal aid to a hospital solely on the basis that the hospital will not allow colored doctors to use its facilities for treatment of their patients." The Southern congressional delegation had defeated an amendment that would have prohibited such discrimination. She explained that the Hill-Burton Act prohibited racial discrimination against patients, not doctors. She also pointed out that the act had specifically prohibited federal officers and employees from having "any supervision or control over the administration, personnel, maintenance, or operation of a hospital receiving funds under the Act." Oveta added that the Houston hospital had not yet submitted an application for Hill-Burton funding, but if it did, and the application met the legislation's standards, "the Surgeon General is required . . . to approve it." She concluded with a comment on Jane Spaulding's status: "You will perhaps have heard by now of Mrs. Spaulding's resignation as Assistant to the Secretary . . . to accept a position with the War Claims Commission." Without further comment, she enclosed a HEW press release announcing Spaulding's resignation.[23]

The same day that Oveta responded to Powell, Secretary of Defense Charles Wilson issued a statement defending his cabinet colleague, declaring there was "absolutely no truth to stories" that she had opposed integrated schools on military bases. Oveta also issued a statement to the press claiming there had "never" been "any difference between the President, Secretary Wilson, and myself as to the objectives or the desirability of moving ahead toward the elimination of segregation in schools on military bases at the earliest possible time." On February 12, Secretary Wilson finally issued his order abolishing segregation in all schools on military posts, no matter where they were located.[24]

The Spaulding story soon cooled, but the controversy occasionally resurfaced. In an obvious attempt to calm the storm, Oveta offered Spaulding's former job to Paul Phillips, an African American civic leader, but he declined the offer, resulting in more negative news. A headline in the *New York Post* declared in large print, "Negro Leader Refuses Job of One Fired by Mrs. Hobby." The story had legs even a year later. On June 5, 1955, muckraking journalist Drew Pearson revisited the episode on his Sunday television show. Citing the Spaulding affair, Pearson charged that it proved Oveta was not qualified to be secretary of HEW. "She appointed Mrs. James Spaulding, to her staff as adviser on Negro affairs," Pearson declared, "but when Mrs. Spaulding expressed a desire to see Negro doctors admitted to the staff of a Texas hospital, Mrs. Spaulding suddenly found herself no longer an advisor to Mrs. Hobby. Her firing did not help the administration politically."[25]

HEW did not fully recover from the Spaulding incident as long as Oveta remained as secretary. Historian Debra Sutphen argues that Oveta's role in the controversy "tainted her as a racist" in some eyes. Although Sutphen believes that perception was unfair, she also concludes that the episode "sullied [Oveta's] reputation as a defender of racial equality." Charges that Oveta was racially prejudiced had also surfaced at the beginning of her tenure as leader of the Women's Army Auxiliary Corps. Sutphen and other scholars who have studied Oveta's career provide convincing evidence to moderate that charge significantly. Oveta's statements and, more important, her actions throughout her life, including as editor and publisher of the *Houston Post* and as director of the Women's Army Corps, contradict the charges that she was a racist. It is more likely that Oveta's problems with Spaulding were caused by Oveta's obsession with control, her insistence on loyalty, and her gradualist views on integration.[26]

Nevertheless, Oveta's background, associations, and some of her actions provided plenty of fodder for claims she was racist. Her roots as a Texan who grew up in the Jim Crow South, her conservative political views that included strong but not rigid support for states' rights, and the fact that her husband had a public record throughout his time in elected office as having paternalistic racist views typical of his generation of Texans provided a not unreasonable basis for those charges. Will Hobby's actions and rhetoric as governor during the Shillady beating incident in Austin and Will's accusations that African American opposition to Jim Crow laws was the result of "Bolshevik" agitators instead of horrific racial oppression occurred slightly more than a decade before he and Oveta were married, but memories in the black community were long—for understandable reasons—and assumptions were easily made about his influence over Oveta's views of race.

It appears, however, that Oveta had more influence over her husband in the matter of race than he had over her, and as a result, Will's racial prejudice diminished over time. One of Oveta's confidants, journalist Marguerite Johnston, recalled an episode that illustrated how Will's racial views were changing. In May 1950, Oveta chaired the arrangements committee planning the celebration of the first Armed Forces Day in Houston. When she and the young vice chairman discussed plans for a grand banquet to honor veterans, Oveta realized he had not included African Americans on the guest list. Oveta told him every member of the military would be welcome at the banquet, regardless of race. The young chairman was shocked at this news. "Mrs. Hobby," he asked, "would you eat dinner with a Negro?" "I have many times," Oveta replied. At that point, Will, who had overheard this conversation, walked into Oveta's office. "You're too young to sound like that," he gently chided the young man. "If you were my age, you could get by with it. But you're too young."[27]

Another factor that shaped Oveta's public image in the matter of race relations was that, like Eisenhower and many other members of his administration, Oveta held a "gradualist" view of racial integration, meaning that she supported integration but she also believed effective and lasting change in the matter of race relations could come about only by slow and measured actions. Civil rights activists understandably and reasonably criticized that position.[28]

In early March, Oveta spoke at the eighty-seventh anniversary celebration of the founding of Howard University, the predominately African American school in Washington, DC, which was part of the HEW domain. On the defensive because of the Spaulding controversy a month earlier, Oveta vigorously denounced racial discrimination as "morally and economically wrong." Possibly aware of the mistake she had made in denouncing segregation mainly for its economic costs to society when she had made a speech on the subject a few years earlier while directing the WAC, Oveta declared that the "spiritual losses resulting from prejudice and discrimination are, of course, even more devastating than the economic losses. No one can measure in dollars the cost to human beings who suffer the stigma of ostracism . . . and the anguish of seeing little children hurt and rejected." She assured that the country was "moving and rapidly to a new era in race relations." In reaction to Oveta's clear statement denouncing racial prejudice, Congressman Powell sent her a telegram praising "the excellent address. . . . [T]he reaction to it has been tremendous. I was talking to the head of the History Department . . . who stated that in all of his years at Howard, he had never heard an address delivered by a white person as forthright . . . on the issue as you presented." Oveta responded, undoubtedly with some relief and gratitude, that she had "enjoyed the occasion very much. It provided an opportunity to pay tribute to the splendid work of Howard University and to reaffirm the continuing high interest of the President and myself in Howard. It was gratifying, as well, to have your comments on that section of the speech which dealt with the evil of discrimination."[29]

Two weeks later, on March 14, Oveta was a guest on the NBC television network's *American Forum of the Air*. A reporter who was anticipating the forthcoming Supreme Court decision in the *Brown v. Board of Education* case asked Oveta if the racial integration of schools and the military was "merely a half-way station" to giving African Americans "complete social equality." Oveta responded that she would have to wait for the Supreme Court's decision in the case before she could make any comments about it. But she was quick to stress that integration of the armed services was "only fair and a long-delayed justice. I don't see how you can expect people to wear the uniform of a country and not be treated equally."[30]

Oveta, however, did not view public school integration the same way she viewed integration of the military, because public schools were local institutions not operated by the federal government. Neither she nor the president was pleased with the *Brown* decision, although she never criticized it in public because of her fear of being called a racist. During the 1956 GOP convention in San Francisco, Eisenhower demanded that Herbert Brownell remove the statement from the party platform that the Eisenhower administration supported the *Brown v. Board* decision. The president denied to Brownell that the administration had ever "taken a stand on the matter." Tellingly, he reminded Brownell that the issue "had never come before Cabinet. . . . [C]ould the Attorney General imagine what a storm Mrs. Hobby would raise, had it? The Attorney General agreed that was true."[31]

Oveta expected that the Supreme Court would rule racial segregation of the schools unconstitutional. Despite her personal feelings about federal interference in local school matters, Oveta respected the court as an institution, and she would make her peace with the decision. But she was concerned with how it would be received in Houston. Accordingly, she made certain the *Houston Post* would be prepared for that announcement. At his wife's request, Will told *Post* reporters to seek the opinions of the most respected Jewish, Protestant, and Catholic leaders in Houston about a possible decision voiding racial segregation in the public schools. Oveta later said that she knew the decision would be controversial in Houston, but she thought the *Post* could play a constructive role in the effort to persuade Houstonians to accept it. She anticipated that the leaders, some of whom she and Will knew well, would be supportive of the decision. "My purpose was to present our readers with the opinion of religious leaders," she recalled, which she felt would have more persuasive power in support of desegregation than legal arguments. When the Supreme Court announced its decision in the *Brown* case on May 17, 1954, the *Houston Post* printed a front-page story that included the statements of the religious leaders supporting the decision.[32]

Despite the discomfort the Spaulding affair and the *Brown* case caused Oveta, it was in some ways background noise as she launched a six-month campaign to persuade Congress to pass HEW's legislative proposals. That effort included making frequent trips to

Capitol Hill to testify to congressional committees, going on the road to speak to special interest groups, and appearing on national television. Adhering to her well-ingrained habit of deep preparation, she once again turned to Roswell Perkins for coaching. Working in their new chart-production room at HEW, Rockefeller's staff made additional graphic charts to explain some of the more technical points of the proposed legislation, especially Social Security expansion and medical reinsurance.

In her public statements advocating HEW's legislative proposals, Oveta stressed that because of her acute awareness of having "responsibility for programs affecting 160 million people," she had rejected the "temptation to push ahead pell-mell in the first few months with hastily constructed proposals, just to show people we were doing something." She claimed that her HEW team had subjected the Social Security plan to more than six thousand hours of intensive study, examining it from every angle. Oveta pointed out that HEW had taken a practical approach in devising its entire legislative agenda, characterizing it as "government by common sense." The medical reinsurance plan, for example, was a commonsense measure based on the "traditional American way of individual responsibility and private endeavor" to encourage nonprofit health organizations and private insurance companies to offer "more non-cancelable health insurance policies at prices people can afford to pay."[33]

In reply to a reporter who asked if HEW had developed any proposals with political considerations in mind, Oveta declared that she was opposed to using health, education, and welfare issues for partisan purposes and that she had not approached the program in that way. That statement was not true. She did admit, however, that it would be naïve "to think that [our proposals] will not have a political effect because I think the American people . . . on the domestic side, are more interested in health, education, and welfare matters than in any other phase of the government I can think of."[34]

Of the five major health and welfare proposals HEW sent to Congress in 1954, the vocational rehabilitation bill and the legislation to extend and expand the Hill-Burton Act had the least opposition. Oveta and her team were given friendly receptions when they made detailed presentations to House and Senate committees in support of both bills. As Sutphen notes, Oveta's lobbying for the rehabilitation proposal "turned out to be more formality than challenge," and it became law on August 3. The hospital construction bill, which provided matching federal funds for new facilities in nearly every congressional district in the country and therefore was an attractive bit of pork barrel legislation for every member of the House, was even easier to pass than the vocational bill, although congressional Democrats wanted the allocation to be larger than the amount that was finally approved. It became law on July 12.[35]

HEW's proposal to expand Social Security coverage and increase benefits had more difficulty getting through Congress because of Senator Carl Curtis's opposition and the lobbying of the US Chamber of Commerce and other business organizations. But as Richard Norton Smith has noted, "The so-called Hobby Lobby neutralized Carl Curtis." With crucial help from Rockefeller, Perkins, and HEW's experts on Social Security, Oveta gave highly effective presentations and testimony at congressional hearings in April and June that, along with Eisenhower's strong endorsement, persuaded most of the Republican members to abandon support for Curtis's proposal. Oveta and her "Hobby Lobby" spent three days testifying at House budget committee hearings on the Social Security bill. Once again armed with Rockefeller's charts, Oveta answered questions and exchanged views with committee members, who suggested minor revisions to the bill that Oveta and her team accepted. On June 1, the House approved the revised version of the bill and then dispatched it to the Senate. After an additional ten days of hearings, Congress passed the legislation on August 20 only hours before adjourning. The president signed the bill and the expansion of Social Security coverage became law.[36]

Rockefeller's useful charts eventually caused Oveta much embarrassment. When she presented her budget to the House Appropriations Committee during the summer, the members were unhappy to learn that she had cut $20 million in funding for research in cancer, heart disease, tuberculosis, and mental illness. She also eliminated a federal-state program for the education of the children of migrant farmworkers and cut the school lunch program by 10 percent. To make matters worse, the committee found a line in the budget revealing that while Oveta was practicing strict economy, she had spent $100,000 (equal to nearly $1 million in 2018) to construct a "motion picture room" at her HEW headquarters. Caught off guard by the criticism, Oveta explained that the expenditure was not for a movie theater, but for the chart room in her office suite. One of the committee's Republican members told Oveta he was "astonished at this expenditure, particularly in view of the fact that a number of items for health, welfare, and educational projects were cut at your request." Another member pointed out that Congress had allocated no money for that specific purpose. The committee voted to reprimand Oveta for excessive administrative expenses. It also set a limit of $200,000 that could be transferred in the coming fiscal year from other subagencies to her office, and it banned any transfers during the following fiscal year. This moment was a humiliating one for Oveta. The *New York Post* ran a headline declaring, "Hobby's Face Is Red." The news was not all bad. The committee cut Oveta's budget by an additional $15 million, but that was not as steep a reduction as she had feared, and it was only 1 percent of the total budget. The reduction would have been larger, but the committee restored Oveta's cuts in medical research.[37]

After Oveta suffered through this embarrassing budget hearing, she had to battle with Congress over the two proposals on HEW's legislative agenda that had attracted the most opposition: medical reinsurance and the plan to sponsor conferences to study the nation's classroom shortage. Both had faced powerful opposition as soon as they were proposed, and both became entangled in the briar patch of political ideology.

When the medical reinsurance bill was first proposed in January, Oveta had been optimistic about its chances for passage. She assured her colleagues at HEW that the president's popularity with the nation's voters would make the Republican majority in Congress reluctant to oppose it. The insurance industry and the American Medical

Association (AMA) were the main critics of the reinsurance bill, but Oveta was confident that both could be persuaded to moderate or even drop their objections.

Oveta made the insurance industry her first target in the effort to win over the most powerful opponents to the medical reinsurance bill. In mid-May 1954, she arranged a luncheon for Eisenhower to host at the White House with the chief executive officers of the seventeen largest health insurance companies. The meeting went well, with Eisenhower, Oveta, and Rockefeller making their pitches and answering questions. The president pledged that the reinsurance plan would not lead to federal regulation of the private insurance industry, while Oveta emphasized that the industry would benefit from a vast increase in policyholders without placing it at greater risk. Rockefeller entertained the group with his colorful explanatory charts, his boyish enthusiasm, and his considerable charm. "Much to my pleasure and much to [Eisenhower's]," Oveta later recalled, "they left the White House and . . . passed a resolution to support it."[38]

Oveta's attempts to win over the AMA, however, failed. She and Rockefeller held several meetings with the association's leaders, but they remained hostile. The AMA denounced the proposed legislation as the "first step toward socialized medicine." As Cary Reich has noted, "Even the faintest suggestion of a federal insurance scheme sent Republican hard-liners [in Congress] into apoplectic rage. With the AMA standing foursquare behind them, they railed against any program that hinted of 'socialized medicine.'" Conservative Republicans also feared the bill would create another massive spending program.[39]

During her appearance on the nationally telecast *American Forum of the Air* in March, Oveta was asked if her reinsurance legislation was an attempt to resurrect the Truman administration's failed effort to establish a national health insurance program. "I see no possible connection with a Federal reinsurance plan and compulsory health insurance," she answered. Truman's proposal, she explained, was a compulsory insurance program run by the federal government. The private insurance industry would manage the Eisenhower administration's program, and it would be voluntary. The next morning, Eisenhower sent Oveta a note stating he hadn't seen her television appearance, "but reports have been coming to me that it was extremely effective and worthwhile."[40]

Oveta embarked on a speaking tour to respond to the AMA's opposition, a tactic she had adopted and fine-tuned during the war, when she was countering the attacks on the WACs. Her tour included speeches at a meeting of the New England Hospital Association and the annual convention of the National Association of State Insurance Commissioners in Detroit. Oveta's strong determination to fight the AMA even persuaded her to speak at a National Press Club luncheon on May 11, much to the shock of the Washington press corps, who had been pressing her for several months to appear at their club. She made her case for HEW's entire legislative agenda, with most of her emphasis on the medical reinsurance plan. She argued that she would not have recommended the legislation if she didn't believe it would enable millions of Americans to have access to more and better health care. But she also stressed that the program would be on a voluntary basis. "We believe the American people don't want compulsory health insurance," Oveta stated. "There is very wide acceptance of voluntary health insurance, which means the American people prefer this plan."[41]

As she fought for the medical reinsurance bill in Congress, attended cabinet meetings, and tended to the various administrative matters in her vast department, Oveta also took time in the spring and summer of 1954 to carry out her symbolic public duties as secretary of HEW by making speeches on general issues related to her department. She spoke at the dedication ceremonies for the opening of the new ten-story New York Infirmary in New York City, a hospital founded by the first woman physician in the country and staffed entirely by women. Lamenting the fact that only 6 percent of the country's physicians and only 5 percent of its medical students were women, Oveta urged medical schools to intensify their recruitment of women students. Referring to the extension of the Hill-Burton hospital construction bill, she also stressed that it was up to local communities to decide what kind of hospitals they needed and that it was their responsibility to raise most of the funding.[42]

Oveta's speaking appearances during this period also included a discourse on the power of charity to the Jewish congregation of Tifereth Temple in Cleveland and the opening speech in Washington at the HEW-sponsored East Coast Migrant Project. At the latter event she argued that the federal government could "offer encouragement and advice," but the states were responsible for providing most of the nation's social welfare needs, including the health and education of migrant farm children, who "live in the twilight zone of citizenship." A few editorial columnists noted that Oveta's statement ignored the fact that by its nature, migrant labor was necessarily an interstate, not a state, matter.[43]

During Oveta's appearance at the temple in Cleveland, a congregant asked if she knew Jesse Jones. She replied, "Why, Mr. Jones is one of my oldest and dearest friends." One of Jones's acquaintances in Cleveland told him about her comment, which prompted Jones to write Oveta a letter, declaring that he liked "the 'dearest' business, but why the 'oldest'? With worlds of love, as ever yours, Jesse." His exchange with Oveta prompted Jones to talk to Will Hobby about Oveta's workload. Jones knew from reading the news that Oveta was once again in the eye of the storm, battling for her legislative agenda at multiple hearings on Capitol Hill and traveling on her hectic speaking tour. Jones became concerned about her health because of her thyroid condition, which overwork aggravated. A week after their exchange about Oveta's speech in Cleveland, Jones sent her a short note written in his typically terse and pointed manner, advising her to slow down. "I understand from [Will] that you are playing a heavy schedule," he wrote. "I suppose it never occurs to you to rest occasionally and maybe loaf a little."[44]

A month later, Will spent a few days in Washington with Oveta, who was testifying at hearings on Capitol Hill much of the time while he was in town. When he returned to Houston he had his regularly scheduled lunch with Jones, to whom he confided that Oveta was "working too hard and covering too much ground." Will told his old friend that he was urging Oveta to take a month off and come home to Houston for a rest but that he doubted she would do it, because of her effort to get the HEW bills passed. This increased Jones's worries about Oveta's health. Jones was aware that even if Oveta agreed to take a break, she would get little rest in Houston. He decided that Oveta might be lured into taking time off if she had an unusual and special invitation to travel to France with Will.

With Will's approval, but without telling Oveta, Jones wrote his friend John M. Franklin, the president of the US Steamship Lines in New York City. Franklin's company owned the SS *United States*, the world's fastest and largest passenger liner, which plied a regularly scheduled route between Manhattan and Europe. When Jones was directing the Reconstruction Finance Corporation, he had provided federal aid to Franklin's company. Jones asked Franklin if he could give the Hobbys a complimentary round trip to Europe on the *United States*. Franklin, however, replied that it would be a "mistake for Secretary Hobby to accept free transportation on the ship." He pointed out that under international agreements, his company had to print a list of all passengers who were provided free transportation, and the information would become public knowledge. Although he had the right to grant free transportation, he had never done that for anyone in public office. "I know the financial aspect is of no importance," Franklin wrote. "My suggestion is that they pay the minimum First Class rate and we will work out a very good room or suite for them." Aware that Jones's request had a slight hint of a quid pro quo for giving Reconstruction Finance Corporation support to his company, the shipping magnate assured Jones he had not forgotten that Jones had been a "wonderfully good friend" to his company and had done the SS *United States* "great good." "I understand the situation perfectly," Jones replied, adding that he would pass Franklin's offer on to Will. "[The Hobbys] are exceptionally well off and can afford anything they want. My thought was to probably induce her with a little invitation."[45]

Oveta turned down Franklin's offer, but she did manage to get back to Houston for several days early in June to rest. She finally decided to take time off, acutely aware she faced a hard struggle for the remainder of the summer, not only to save the administration's medical reinsurance plan but also to find a solution to the increasingly difficult and controversial baby boomer classroom-shortage crisis in the nation's public schools.

# CHAPTER 36

# "SOCIALIZED MEDICINE"

B y the time Oveta was back in Washington after her badly needed rest break in Houston, the medical reinsurance bill had moved closer to a vote in Congress. On July 9, 1954, Oveta joined with President Eisenhower to make a fifteen-minute presentation on radio and television about the Department of Health, Education, and Welfare's entire legislative agenda, with a special focus on the health reinsurance plan. President Eisenhower opened the broadcast with a short statement of his full support for HEW's proposed social welfare program, the keystone being the reinsurance plan. After the president's remarks, he introduced Oveta, who focused on the most controversial item on her legislative agenda. Pointing out that sixty-three million Americans had no medical insurance "whatsoever," she explained that the reinsurance plan was designed to "help you get better insurance protection against long-term illness." Oveta stated that the cost to Americans for hospital and medical care in 1952 amounted to $9.4 million, with insurance covering only $1.6 million of that expense. The administration's reinsurance plan would provide funds to protect insurance companies from the risks of providing more affordable policies and allow the industry to pay much of the cost that had not previously been covered. Once again emphasizing that the program would be "wholly voluntary," Oveta assured her audience that despite the claims of the American Medical Association (AMA), the administration remained opposed to socialized medicine.[1]

The House and Senate committees approved the bill, although without enthusiasm, and sent it to both houses of Congress in early July. At this critical stage, however, organized labor became an even more formidable, and somewhat unanticipated, opponent. Labor's hostility was partially the result of HEW bungling. Oveta's team held meetings with the leaders of the American Federation of Labor (AFL) to enlist union support, which was key to getting congressional Democrats behind the bill. When the AFL's lead negotiator, Nelson Cruikshank, insisted on major changes to the proposed legislation to better protect workers from major health costs, Oveta's negotiators broke off the negotiation with a declaration that HEW didn't need their support. This insulting behavior and Oveta's refusal to revise the reinsurance proposal alienated the unions, whose lobbyists launched a campaign with Democratic allies in Congress to kill the bill. They argued that it was a scheme to protect the profits of greedy insurance companies and that it would not lower the cost of individual policies or improve the benefits for persons already insured. As the AFL's Nelson Cruikshank later recalled, American Medical Association and labor union joint opposition to the bill was the "most curious combination of right-wing reactionaries and left-wing liberals that you ever saw."[2]

Sam Rayburn, the Democratic minority leader in the House, rallied his caucus to join with seventy-five Republicans to send the bill back to committee "for further study," effectively killing it. According to Cary Reich, the "infuriated labor leaders decided to play their hole card: the deep-rooted enmity they knew that Sam Rayburn felt toward his fellow Texan Oveta Culp Hobby." Reich claims Rayburn "found Hobby's defection to the Eisenhower camp an unforgivable sin, a betrayal of the Texas Democratic organization that had nurtured her career." Reich's statement reveals his lack of knowledge about political relationships back in the Lone Star State. While Rayburn certainly was unhappy that Will and Oveta had aligned themselves with Eisenhower in 1952, he couldn't have been surprised. The Hobbys had openly supported Republican presidential candidates in every election since 1940. There is no evidence Rayburn's opposition to the medical reinsurance bill was the result of an alleged personal spite toward Oveta. A few months after the 1952 presidential election campaign, when Oveta had committed her "unforgivable sin," Rayburn had been one of Oveta's strongest allies in the fight to create HEW, and he demonstrated his continuing friendship with her until his death in 1961. Rayburn simply disliked the medical reinsurance bill for other reasons. He had supported Truman's federal health insurance proposal and he was not thrilled with Eisenhower's plan for the federal government to be the protector of the private insurance industry's profits. Rayburn told Capitol Hill reporters that the medical reinsurance plan was a "blundering, stupid way" to start a health program.[3]

While Reich's claim that Rayburn held a personal grudge against Oveta was not true, she was stung by Rayburn's harsh statement that the medical reinsurance bill was a stupid blunder, especially because of their long friendship. She told Lyndon Johnson that Rayburn's derogatory speech denouncing the reinsurance bill had "in three minutes" ended their many years of friendship. After LBJ shared her remark with Rayburn, he reported back to Oveta that her comment had "amazed and hurt" Rayburn. Oveta asked LBJ to tell Rayburn that her response to his comment was "Nuts," which had been army general Anthony McAuliffe's famous response to the German demand that he surrender when his troops were surrounded at Bastogne, Belgium, during World War II. It was Oveta's pointed way of telling her fellow Texan that she would not give up the fight in support of the medical reinsurance proposal. Her anger toward Rayburn soon dissipated, however. They would renew their friendship in the coming months, especially after Rayburn regained his speakership in the House.[4]

*Oveta Culp Hobby and Sam Rayburn in Washington, DC, ca. 1942.*

Oveta was not the only person in the Eisenhower administration angered by the defeat of the medical reinsurance bill. The president was outraged when he learned that seventy-five Republican members of the House had voted against it. He complained to his press secretary, James Hagerty, that if any of those congressmen expected help from him in the upcoming election campaign, "they are going to be very much surprised. This was a major part of our liberal program and anyone who voted against it will not have one iota of support from me." The president asked Republican House leader Charles Halleck, "How in the hell is the AMA going to stop socialized medicine if they oppose such bills as this?" Eisenhower predicted that without some other plan to expand access to private-market health insurance, socialized medicine was inevitable "sooner or later and the AMA will have no one to blame but itself." He also expressed his anger to the cabinet, stating, "As far as I'm concerned, the American Medical Association is just plain stupid. This plan of ours would have shown the people how we could improve their health and stay out of socialized medicine." The president vowed to give it another try in the next congressional session. Oveta told the *New York Times* that the reinsurance plan was "a new and novel idea, and many new and novel ideas don't get by the first time. I'm not discouraged. Maybe we can write a better bill. Maybe we can be more specific."[5]

HEW's response to the classroom shortage crisis fared slightly better than its medical reinsurance proposal but did nothing to tamp down the mounting attacks on the Eisenhower administration for its failure to take decisive and immediate action. On April 2, 1954, while the "Hobby Lobby" was defending the HEW budget in Congress and absorbed in the effort to pass its other legislative proposals, the Senate subcommittee on education summoned Oveta and Education Commissioner Samuel Brownell to a hearing to explain their White House conference proposal. Democratic senator Lister Hill of Alabama, who was a thorn in Oveta's side throughout her tenure at HEW, asked why she was proposing conferences to talk about this pressing issue instead of taking immediate action to provide direct federal grant support for the construction of new classrooms. Explaining that public school issues were best addressed at the state and local levels, Oveta told Hill she agreed with him that a serious problem existed and that steps needed to be taken to alleviate it, but that she and he simply differed over how to approach the problem. "I do not believe the people of the United States want the federal government to control education," she stated. She stressed that the public schools could be helped faster "by getting agreement as to what all levels of government can do" and that the White House–sponsored conferences would accomplish that goal. Senator Hill expressed his disappointment over Oveta's plan, pointing out that seven national conferences had already been held to discuss the subject and $7 million had been spent on a study of the classroom problem, with no results. Simply providing money to the states to build new classrooms hardly constituted a federal takeover of public schools.[6]

Liberal newspaper commentators reacted with sarcasm to Oveta's proposal to have a series of conferences. William Shannon, a columnist for the *New York Post*, complained that Oveta was "a devotee of the 'no business' conference at which important people gather, information is exchanged which could just as well be exchanged by letter, and a formal statement is issued. No action is taken but the impression of action is created." Oveta's plan even elicited criticism from two women whose words must have had a special sting. In a speech to the New Jersey Federation of Teachers in early December 1954, her friend and fellow newspaper publisher Agnes Meyer accused Oveta and US commissioner of education Neil McElroy of "hypocrisy" and "inexcusable dilatory procedure" in the matter of federal school aid. In May 1955, Eleanor Roosevelt addressed the issue in her widely syndicated newspaper column. "It was interesting to read the testimony the other day of Secretary Oveta Culp Hobby on aid to education . . . for building schools," the former First Lady declared. "Mrs. Hobby would delay giving funds till a further study is made, which to my mind is a good subterfuge for doing nothing. You can go on examining indefinitely, and nothing is ever accomplished." Despite these criticisms, the Republican-controlled Congress approved funding for the conferences.[7]

Oveta's refusal to propose direct federal aid for school construction also frustrated liberal Republican senators from northeastern states. They joined their Democratic colleagues to push for an allocation of $500 million for direct grants to participating states over a period of two years. Oveta sent a message to the Senate's education committee asking it to reject that proposal and any other aid to education bills until the White House conference could be held, which was more than a year away. The committee ignored Oveta's recommendation and sent the federal aid bill to the Senate floor on July 9.[8]

On August 4, 1954, while the Senate was still debating its bill for federal aid to education, a reporter asked President Eisenhower at a news conference if he favored the legislation. Obviously distracted by the Senate select committee's highly publicized investigation of Senator Joe McCarthy's attack on the army and angered by the recent vote in Congress to significantly reduce his foreign aid request, the president told reporters to "ask Mrs. Hobby" for an answer. When they did, Oveta handed out a report she had prepared for the House Education and Labor Committee criticizing the bill, repeating her argument that school construction was a state and local issue. Residents in the local school districts, she declared, should tax themselves to address the problem. Stating that she opposed any "precipitous" federal action, she repeated her call for forty-eight state education conferences to be held to develop action programs "if any is needed." After Oveta released these statements, a delegation of Republican sponsors of the bill sought an appointment with her. She referred them to Commissioner of Education Samuel Brownell, who explained he had no personal objection to their bill but that he could not speak for the administration. "That was the death of the bill," a reporter later noted, adding that one member of the congressional delegation complained that Oveta had given him "the greatest run-around" he had experienced in his fifteen years in Congress.[9]

Despite the strong support of twenty national educational organizations, led by the National Education Association, procedural maneuvers delayed action on the school bill, resulting in the Senate failing to vote on the measure before adjourning until the new Congress convened in January 1955. In early September 1954, with Congress in adjournment, Oveta took a few days off to return to Houston, where Will had been monitoring the construction of the *Houston Post*'s new $4 million printing plant and office building, located across the street from the old facility on Polk and Dowling Streets. The *Post*'s new 118,000-square-foot home would house massive printing presses placed on special foundations to eliminate vibration. It would also feature spacious, well-furnished, and brightly lit editorial and executive offices and, to the delight of the entire staff, air-conditioning throughout the building. Will directed stoneworkers to chisel a phrase from the Declaration of Independence above the building's main entrance: "Let facts be submitted to a candid world." This was the first Houston Post Building that was entirely Will Hobby's from conception to completion, and it fulfilled a dream he had envisioned for many years. In comfort, efficiency, and size, it was light-years away from the old Larendon Building that had housed the newspaper in 1895, when G. J. Palmer hired seventeen-year-old Will to work as a circulation clerk. According to a longtime *Post* staff member, among the improvements that pleased Will the most were two elevators, which the old building had lacked. During the last few years that the *Post* operated in its former headquarters, Will had been unable to walk up a flight of steep stairs to his office, so sturdy maintenance workers would meet him at the entrance and carry him up in a chair. On one occasion when Will entered the old building, he noticed a young *Post* staff member looking at the stairs as she tried to work up the energy to climb them. When Will asked if she needed help, she replied that she recently had surgery and was unsure if she could make it upstairs. "Just a minute," Will said, "I'll call the boys and they will take you up in my private elevator." To the young staffer's delight, she was carried upstairs in Will's chair. The *Post*'s building project was almost finished by the time Oveta was back in the city. The first edition of the *Post* printed by the new press equipment was circulated on October 11, although a formal dedication ceremony for the new facility would not be held until January 1955.[10]

A few days after Oveta arrived in Houston, she and Will traveled to North Carolina to attend the wedding of their son, Bill, to Diana Poteat Stallings on September 11. The ceremony was held at Forest Home, Diana's family farm near Yanceyville, North Carolina. Bill, who was now an ensign in the navy, had been granted leave in June to attend graduate school at Georgetown University to work on his master's degree in history. It was at Georgetown that he met Diana, a fellow graduate student. After earning her undergraduate degree with Phi Beta Kappa honors from Radcliffe in 1952, Diana had taken a teaching job at Chatham Hall in Virginia while also attending classes at Georgetown. Diana's father, Laurence Stallings, was the noted playwright, screenwriter, photographer, author, and book and drama critic for the *New York World*. Her mother was Helen Poteat, the daughter of the longtime president of Wake Forest College, William Louis Poteat. Will and Oveta were delighted by Bill's relationship with the pretty and intellectual Diana, and they readily accepted Diana into the Hobby family. After the newlyweds found a place to live in Virginia, they continued their studies at Georgetown.[11]

A month after the wedding, journalists Les and Liz Carpenter, whose news service, the Carpenter News Bureau, covered the nation's capital for the *Houston Post*, hosted a Sunday morning brunch party at their home in Northwest Washington in honor of Bill and Diana's marriage. Oveta was late to the party because of a prior commitment to appear on NBC's news program *Meet the Press*. Bill and Diana and the other guests gathered around the Carpenters' television set to watch Oveta talk about her initiatives at HEW. At the end of the broadcast, Oveta raced to the party, where she joined Bill, Diana, and the Carpenters and their guests to gather under a Lone Star flag flying from a pole on the front lawn to sing "Deep in the Heart of Texas" and "The Eyes of Texas."[12]

With November's congressional elections approaching, Oveta did her bit to help the Republican Party raise money for the campaign. The previous May, she was the first woman to deliver the main address at the annual $100-a-plate fundraising dinner for the New York State Republican Committee, held at the Waldorf Astoria Hotel. Her speech followed one given by Vice President Nixon. Joan Braden worked with a public relations representative for the Ford Motor Company who was also one of Nixon's speechwriters to draft Oveta's speech. Braden and Oveta were shocked when Nixon read the first half of Oveta's speech word for word, exactly as they had drafted it. The Ford Motor Company PR man had obviously shared Oveta's speech with the vice president. According to Braden, Oveta remained calm as Nixon read half of her speech. When she went to the podium, she congratulated Nixon on his fine presentation and said she agreed with his comments. Oveta then read the part of her speech Nixon had left out of his talk, which Braden stated was "statistical and therefore dull and boring." Braden noted that Oveta "finished a little early, but without the slightest indication of despair." Oveta never mentioned the incident to Nixon.[13]

One of the few partisan events in which Oveta participated during the election campaign was a television broadcast on Monday night, October 25, in which she urged

*Oveta Culp Hobby appears on NBC's* Meet the Press *television program, October 24, 1954.*

voters to reelect Congressman Robert Kean and to elect former congressman Clifford Case to the US Senate. Both men were liberal New Jersey Republicans facing strong Democratic challengers. Oveta wanted to help Kean, who was an influential member of the House Ways and Means Committee, because he had worked hard to get the Social Security bill passed in the House. Case was known to be a friend of Social Security. The broadcast was part of a hectic day for Oveta. Early that evening she attended a nationally televised special meeting of the cabinet that featured Secretary of State John Foster Dulles discussing the latest developments in Soviet-American relations. Immediately afterward, she hurried to National Airport and boarded a flight to Newark, New Jersey, landing at 9:50 p.m., where she was met by Nelson Rockefeller. A limousine rushed them to a local television station, where Oveta joined a live broadcast at 10:30 p.m. After the fifteen-minute program, she and Rockefeller barely made an 11:15 p.m. flight back to Washington. Both candidates won their elections.[14]

Although Republicans were victorious in New Jersey, losses elsewhere cost the party its control of Congress. Lyndon Johnson became the Senate leader in January 1955, although with only a one-seat majority. Sam Rayburn reclaimed the speakership of the House. Although Oveta was disappointed by the results, it was clear, as her own newspaper pointed out, that the election results could not be seen as a rebuke of Eisenhower. All polls indicated that the president remained popular with the nation's voters. As Eisenhower later noted in his presidential memoir, he resolved to stay the course he had followed during the first two years of his term. He advised Oveta and the other members of his cabinet that they should conduct business as usual, and move forward with the new Democratic majority, working together whenever they found common ground.[15]

Of the members of the administration, Oveta and the secretary of the navy, fellow Texan and Democrat Robert Anderson, were best positioned to help Eisenhower's efforts to work with Democrats. Both of the new leaders of the congressional majority were Texans whom Oveta and Will had known and supported for many years. She believed her relationships with LBJ and Rayburn gave her a decent chance of getting a new version of the medical reinsurance bill passed if it was revised enough to satisfy them.

Oveta was enthusiastic about her work in the coming year, which included overseeing the state and territorial conferences that were studying educational issues. She planned to host the White House conference where those state findings would be evaluated. She nevertheless planned for 1955 to be her last as HEW secretary. She had accepted the cabinet appointment in 1953 with the expectation of serving only two years. She had assumed that would be long enough to organize HEW and help the Eisenhower administration implement conservative management over the federal government's social welfare programs, as well as to minimize federal involvement in education and health care. Will would be seventy-seven in 1955, and although he was having good health days as well as bad, the bad days were outnumbering the good. Oveta understood that the prosperous Hobby business enterprises would need much more of her personal direction sooner than later.

*Oveta Culp Hobby gets
a laugh out of President
Eisenhower after a nationally
televised cabinet meeting,
October 25, 1954.*

When Oveta mentioned her plans to Eisenhower in December 1954, he asked that she stay at her post until the end of his first term in January 1956. After all, he had not yet decided to run for a second term. He confirmed his wish in a note to Oveta sent from Augusta, Georgia, on December 29. Eisenhower stressed to Oveta that it was his "profound hope" that he would continue to have her "invaluable assistance as long as I shall be called upon to bear any governmental responsibility." Oveta agreed to keep Eisenhower's wishes in mind. She would make a decision at whatever time seemed right, even if that meant extending her appointment through a fourth year. In the meantime, she still had goals to accomplish, and she hoped that the coming months would be positive and productive. As it turned out, that would not be the case.[16]

As Oveta planned HEW's 1955 agenda, she was aware that Nelson Rockefeller would not be around to help. Back in mid-November the invaluable but restless Rockefeller had informed her of his intention to resign, effective in January 1955. According to Richard Norton Smith, Rockefeller was "disenchanted with a job too small for his aspirations." In public, Rockefeller's relationship with Oveta was "that of the loyal subordinate," but in private, Rockefeller was frustrated by what he judged to be Oveta's indecisiveness. The evidence is that she was merely cautious while Rockefeller was impulsive. The scion of the Standard Oil fortune was eager for greater things, perhaps to serve as mayor of New York City or governor of New York State, but ultimately the presidency. Elected office would have to wait, however. In the meantime, Rockefeller accepted a position as a member of Eisenhower's staff, and he moved his office to the Executive Office Building at the start of 1955. One of the last assignments Oveta gave Rockefeller was for him to speak as her substitute at HEW's annual Conference of State and Territorial Health Officers in Washington on December 7.[17]

Oveta was forced to skip the conference due to illness. Her work habits had once again compromised her health, although not in a serious way. Nevertheless, her bout of sickness brought another reminder from the president to slow down. In a personal note, Eisenhower expressed his wish that Oveta would "take time off during 1955 for a really good, long rest. I say this selfishly, for I need and depend upon you, and I want you to keep your health and spirits."[18]

After taking a short break during the Christmas and New Year's holidays, Oveta was back in Washington in time for the opening of the Democratic-controlled Congress and to prepare HEW's legislative plans for the new session. Happily for Oveta, Roswell Perkins, the person she had relied on even more than she had on Rockefeller, remained at his HEW post to lend his skilled help. She renewed her close association with Lyndon Johnson, while also patching up her relationship with Rayburn following their quarrel over the original version of the medical reinsurance bill. Contrary to Reich's claim, Perkins noted that Oveta had an "excellent and longstanding" relationship with Speaker Rayburn and that she "saw the opportunity to use her unique status as a bridge between the Administration and Congress." Soon after Congress convened in early January, Oveta hosted a small and elegant black-tie party at the historic F Street Club near George

Washington University. Perkins, who attended the party, later recalled that "[Oveta] was decked out in a red satin dress that displayed her most appealing femininity. Her vivacious style, grace, and charm dominated the occasion. . . . Johnson and Rayburn were given the attention they loved, and the Eisenhower Administration clearly had made a conquest—all masterminded by Oveta." Lady Bird Johnson later remembered that during this period she and her husband had "any number of warm evenings with [Oveta] in Speaker Sam Rayburn's upstairs apartment across from the Anchorage when she was one of six or eight guests. Lively conversation about significant events and personalities were the 'main course' of those gatherings."[19]

Oveta might have smoothed over any discord she had with Rayburn, but to her disappointment the crafty veteran of decades of legislative battles remained opposed to much of Eisenhower's domestic policies, especially the medical reinsurance scheme. A few weeks before the new Congress convened in January 1955, the president told Oveta that he was willing to give the medical reinsurance proposal another try and that her experts should revise the old bill. Led once again by Roswell Perkins, Oveta's team drafted a more realistic bill that included a section requiring HEW to coordinate the reinsurance program with the individual state insurance commissions and a provision specifically prohibiting federal regulation of the insurance industry. The White House submitted the new version of the bill to Congress in February 1955. When Oveta testified at a hearing of the House Interstate Commerce Committee in support of this new version, one of the Republican members asked her if the administration's bill was an "entering wedge" for socialized medicine. "I thought that ghost was laid down," Oveta replied in frustration. "The bill clearly is an attempt to help a man and his family to help themselves." Despite the revisions and her reassurances, Speaker Rayburn and his Democratic colleagues remained unconvinced, and the bill was essentially dead on its arrival to Congress.[20]

The defeat was a bitter one for Oveta. In what was for her an uncharacteristically harsh public statement, she denounced the American Medical Association leadership as a "little group of reactionary men dead set against any change." Others blamed Rockefeller for the bill's demise because of serious conceptual and structural problems even after it was revised. Arthur Larson later argued that the White House shared some of the blame for its failure. He claimed that the administration "made consistently bad judgments" in its attempt to sell the merits of the bill and that it lost "an admirable opportunity to espouse a measure that was not only widely popular but also necessary and sound." Larson thought it significant that the medical reinsurance battle, "although visible during much of the Eisenhower administration as a top-rank controversy," was not mentioned in either volume of Eisenhower's detailed account of his presidency. A decade would pass before a federally funded health insurance program, Medicare, would become reality. It would be another six decades before Congress passed the Affordable Care Act ("Obamacare") in 2010, creating a federally directed universal health insurance plan in coordination with the private sector that had similarities to the Eisenhower administration's reinsurance bill.[21]

After the new Congress convened in January 1955, the Democratic majority focused much of their attention on fulfilling the party's campaign pledge to provide $1 billion per year in outright grants to school districts for classroom construction. To pressure the Democrats to follow through with their promise, a coalition of educational organizations led by the National Education Association swamped Congress with a mass of letters and telegrams urging the members to take action as soon as the new session began. Hobby, Perkins, and Education Commissioner Samuel Brownell ignored this lobbying effort, concentrating instead on organizing the individual state education conferences and the White House conference, the latter being the final stage in the process of studying the school issues.

The Eisenhower administration considered the Democratic plan to be an irresponsible splurge of federal money, one that would bust the administration's conservative budget and involve the federal government in the affairs of local school boards. At the urging of Treasury Secretary George Humphrey, who was having nightmares about "run away and wasteful spending" on such frivolities as public school classrooms, Eisenhower asked Oveta to draft a plan that would offer a reasonably quick solution to the classroom shortage crisis without resorting to a direct grants-in-aid program. The president's goal was to stop the Democrats, whose proposals he considered "an all-out grab under the . . . theory that anything you get from the Federal government is for free." As she had frequently done in the past, Oveta gave this difficult job to Nelson Rockefeller, who at this point had not yet resigned from HEW. Rockefeller enlisted the help of Wall Street bond lawyer John Mitchell, a future attorney general who would later serve time in federal prison for his involvement in the Watergate scandal. Mitchell hurriedly cobbled together a complex loan program that would allow semiautonomous state agencies to issue bonds to finance school construction and then lease the buildings back to local school boards. The lease revenue would pay off the bonds over time, thus avoiding the outright "gift" of federal money. Rockefeller and Mitchell drafted the plan without input from educators or legislators.[22]

Oveta presented Rockefeller and Mitchell's school bond scheme to the president at a cabinet meeting on January 14, 1955. Oveta explained that the long-term cost of the program to the federal government, estimated to be about $15 million, would be relatively low. To get the program off the ground, the federal treasury would have to advance $100 million to the states, but the allocation would be paid back over a three-year period. Treasury Secretary Humphrey opposed the plan because it would compete with the private financial interests in the public securities market. Despite Humphrey's protest, Eisenhower was willing to give the plan his support, although he also expressed his worry that it might not provide relief quickly enough to hard-pressed school districts. He also wanted firm assurances that the states would share responsibility equally with the federal government for the sound fiscal management of the loan program. Sensing a hint of reluctance to act on the president's part, Vice President Nixon and the members of the cabinet who were concerned about political costs to the Republican Party argued it was critical that the administration be identified with an effective school construction plan as soon as possible. It was clear that this was a matter of great interest to a majority of the voters. The president was persuaded to move forward.[23]

Eisenhower submitted what was now known as the Hobby-Brownell bill to Congress on February 8, 1955, declaring it a "sound and equitable" program that would provide funds to build new school facilities "within the framework of local responsibility" and free of federal control of education. But the bill ran into serious trouble as soon as it hit Capitol Hill. Experts in school finance criticized the plan as being overcomplicated, while teachers' lobbies denounced it as "too clever by half." The National Education Association called it a "bankers' bill" and complained that HEW had not sought the advice of professional educators and representatives of school boards. Commissioner Brownell explained that he and the secretary of HEW had been "well aware of their thinking" and therefore had not seen any need to meet with educators.[24]

Upon further review, it was clear the bill contained built-in procedural problems, as well as no real breaks for poor school districts. Hobby-Brownell was a loan program rather than direct federal aid and therefore would pledge the future credit of the state. Every state wanting to participate would have to take legislative action before they could accept the funds, greatly slowing the overall process. The bill did include a provision to establish a federal grants-in-aid program for poverty-stricken school districts unable to pay back loans or make lease payments. But even in those cases, states would be required to match the federal grants, and the combined funding would have to be used to enable poor school districts to sell bonds to the federal government or lease buildings from statewide authorities. The federal funds allocated to the program would have to be paid back eventually through one mechanism or another, and with interest. There would be no "giveaway" school building program.

The Hobby-Brownell bill was pitched as a conservative plan, which it certainly was, but it still met stiff resistance from ultraconservative Republican members of Congress. They considered the bill to be actuarially unsound and an audacious example of a "fiscal sleight of hand." It also became entangled in the issue of whether public funding should be available to parochial schools. Despite these difficulties, Oveta worked hard to get the bill passed. Two days after the White House submitted it to Congress, she held a press conference to promote the bill's benefits and to answer questions to counter criticisms. Downplaying the burdensome and time-consuming approval procedures built into the bill, she argued that it would allow state and local governments to take "quick and effective action" to build new schools. The press conference went relatively smoothly because school construction and complicated funding plans were less than exciting issues to the news media. Oveta's next appearance, however, was much more uncomfortable.[25]

A few days after her press conference at HEW, Oveta testified at a hearing of the Senate Labor Committee. Six of her staff members sat behind her, available to provide additional information if needed. Oveta read a preliminary statement about the bill, stressing that it was comprehensive and flexible. After she finished, Senator Paul Douglas immediately countered that contrary to the secretary's statement, the plan was "highly inflexible." Oveta answered that she considered it flexible because it offered three different methods to pay for new school construction. School districts could sell bonds to the federal government, they could rent school buildings from special state agencies set up to receive construction loans from the federal government, or impoverished school districts could apply for federal grants for half of the cost of new buildings, with the remaining expense covered by selling bonds or having a state agency pay for it. In other words, the bill was essentially a loan plan instead of direct aid. Oveta's explanation merely confirmed Democratic accusations. Strongly condemning the Hobby-Brownell bill, Senator Lister Hill complained, "[It] seemed to offer interminable delay on the one hand and an eager dole on the other." Other Democrats belittled the plan as "an empty hoax" and "an attempt to extinguish a conflagration with a squirt-gun."[26]

Predictably, the National Education Association's response was that the plan was "too little aid and too much control." In a speech at Yale after the Senate hearing, newspaper publisher Agnes Meyer continued to criticize Hobby's focus on states' rights. She called on Congress to discard the complicated loan proposal and simply send the critically needed funding directly to the states as grants-in-aid. Classrooms were jammed beyond capacity, students were being taught in temporary wood shacks, and schools were forced to rotate students through half-day schedules, with one group of students attending morning classes and another group replacing them in the afternoon. Federal grants for schools, Meyer argued, should be seen as an investment in the nation's future, not as a "gimmicky" plan to sell bonds.[27]

A month after her appearance at the Senate committee, Oveta was invited to testify at a hearing of the House Committee on Education and Labor. She told the committee that the Hobby-Brownell bill would ensure that "all of the nation's school children are housed in adequate buildings by 1960." When Oveta finished reading her prepared statement, Congressman Adam Clayton Powell Jr. joined the discussion. He asked Hobby why the Eisenhower administration was now suddenly pushing forward with its school construction plan after arguing that nothing could be done until the White House conference on public education was held. He implied that the Hobby-Brownell bill was a hasty, ill-conceived, and transparent effort to stop the Democratic plan for a federal grants-in-aid program. Powell also pointed out that the Supreme Court had not yet issued instructions to local school districts on the timetable for implementing the *Brown v. Board of Education* decision. The Hobby-Brownell bill's failure to include a desegregation requirement would "squander" federal funds by presiding over the construction of "dual school systems" in segregated areas that would, according to the Supreme Court's ruling, eventually have to integrate. Wouldn't it be prudent, Powell asked, to wait on the court's instructions on timing to avoid building segregated schools that ultimately might have to be abandoned?[28]

According to one observer, Oveta responded with "a rambling and confused reply," followed by a plea to Powell and the other members of the committee to "house the schoolchildren who need it" without waiting for a Supreme Court decision that might take years to implement. Her priorities were clear. Schools needed to be constructed, and newly built segregated schools were better than none at all. Powell reminded Oveta, however, that during the Houston hospital segregation controversy the previous year, Eisenhower had assured him "that no federal funds should be used to support any form of segregation." Powell then declared that he intended to offer an amendment to any bill that came out of the House committee that would ban the allocation of federal funds to any school district that refused to desegregate.[29]

Oveta agreed with Powell that they were in a difficult "interregnum" in the matter of desegregation. She pointed out that no one could predict when the court would announce its decision about how quickly desegregation must occur. Contradicting her previous position, Oveta argued that the classroom shortage had reached a crisis stage, and school construction had to be funded as soon as possible. Not persuaded by Oveta's argument, Powell said he would continue to press the issue. Powell's criticism and threat to amend the bill hopelessly entangled it in the *Brown v. Board of Education* controversy, which damaged its chances for passage into law.[30]

Members of the Southern delegation in Congress were well aware that their states were prepared to abolish their public school systems in order to avoid racial integration. Fearing educational chaos, they had no intention of supporting a bill that required public schools to desegregate to qualify for badly needed funding. The Hobby-Brownell bill had created a formidable coalition of opponents that included segregationist Southern congressmen; liberal Democrats eager to give, not loan, federal money to the states; and right-wing Republicans who opposed any federal involvement in local schools. The latter included some of Eisenhower's cabinet members, who, led by Agriculture Secretary Ezra Taft Benson, urged the president to proceed slowly and cautiously, with the unspoken hope that the bill would die from the lack of Eisenhower's active support. Benson, who later supported the extreme right-wing John Birch Society, demonstrated how blind he was to reality when he advised Eisenhower that there was no need to spend federal money on local schools. He argued, "There are no longer any poor states in this country. Why not let the people spend their own money at home to build their own schools?"[31]

At a cabinet meeting on April 22, 1955, Oveta admitted that the school desegregation controversy had halted the Senate committee's hearings on the Hobby-Brownell bill, and progress on the bill had slowed considerably in the House committee. "My guess is that the chances of any school construction measure being enacted this year are not greater than 50-50," she said. A month later, Oveta reported to the cabinet that it was highly unlikely that the Hobby-Brownell bill would be reported out of the Senate committee, because of Democratic opposition. She accused the Democrats of keeping the administration from getting any credit for good work in the areas of social progress and human welfare. Oveta had fought hard, but the bill was dead. This news undoubtedly pleased Secretary Benson and his conservative colleagues on the cabinet. It also diminished Eisenhower's enthusiasm for further involvement in local school matters. During the remainder of his presidency, Congress only took minor action to facilitate new school construction, and that would not be until 1958. As Sherman Adams later observed, "Whatever would have to be done about the shortage of classrooms Eisenhower left for his successor." Full federal support would not occur until 1965 as part of LBJ's Great Society program.[32]

The favorable political climate in 1954 that had made possible the passage of HEW's Social Security expansion, vocational rehabilitation program, and hospital construction legislation began to fade in 1955 and to disappear almost entirely after Eisenhower was elected to a second term in November 1956 and he became obsessed with balancing the budget and holding down taxes. This strong turn to the right made Eisenhower markedly less interested in HEW's issues, although the effort to end the polio epidemic and the national hysteria it was causing would pull him deeply into the department's health portfolio in the spring and summer of 1955.

# CHAPTER 37

---

# POLIO

During the first half of the twentieth century, polio was the disease most widely feared by the American public. The poliomyelitis epidemic was one of the most significant health issues in American history in terms of public anxiety and even terror, although the virus ranked relatively low as a threat to public health when compared to the annual toll taken by influenza, cancer, heart disease, and automobile accidents. This widespread public fear was due to some extent to the publicity and fundraising machine created by the National Foundation for Infantile Paralysis (NFIP), which became famous for its March of Dimes marketing campaigns with its ubiquitous posters and magazine ads featuring pictures of crippled children. Founded in 1938, the NFIP became one of the most effective organizations of its type in heightening public consciousness in the United States about a specific disease and in raising money to fight it.[1]

Polio is an enterovirus that typically enters the body through the mouth and subsequently affects the gastrointestinal tract, eventually leaving the body when stools are discharged. Individuals are usually infected as a result of poor hygiene, mainly from hand-to-mouth transmission. The vast majority of those infected experienced relatively mild, nonparalytic symptoms that included nausea, fever, malaise, and headache. Many were unaware they even had polio. According to Public Health Service statistics, approximately 2 percent of the individuals infected with polio had much more severe symptoms, most significantly acute paralysis, with an estimated 60 to 90 percent of those victims suffering permanent loss of muscle strength, typically in the legs; a few suffered total body paralysis and death. Many of those who suffered permanent damage were forced to live their lives bedridden, in wheelchairs, burdened with crutches and heavy leg braces, or attached to artificial respiration, with the latter involving the full-body "iron lung," which in the public mind became the gruesome symbol of the disease.[2]

Although the first major polio outbreak occurred in the United States at the beginning of the twentieth century, the first full-scale epidemic was in 1916, when the virus killed around six thousand people. More than twenty-seven thousand were infected in twenty-six states, with New York City being especially hard hit. Even those disturbing numbers fell far short of the toll taken by tuberculosis, which killed on average 110,000 individuals a year during this same period. After 1916, the number of polio cases mysteriously dropped and stayed level until 1943, when infections surged until they reached a high in 1952. The transmission of poliovirus was little understood at the time, and public health officials were unsure of the steps that could be taken to protect against infection. That lack of knowledge fueled an atmosphere of helplessness and near panic among the general public, who viewed the disease as a plague.[3]

Oveta Culp Hobby was well aware of the level of fear that the polio epidemic was generating. Texas was among the states most severely impacted by the epidemic, with Houston and Harris County bearing the brunt, especially in 1943 and in 1952, when more than seven hundred cases were reported. This terror was well covered by the *Houston Post*. During the outbreak in 1943, while Oveta was leading the Women's Army Corps, she recorded a speech for radio broadcast in Texas urging listeners to donate money to the state campaign for the March of Dimes for polio research in honor of Franklin Roosevelt's birthday. In contrast to the public reputation Oveta would later develop as not taking the threat of polio seriously enough, Oveta's radio speech in 1943 bordered on the alarmist. Declaring that hundreds of thousands of Americans had been struck by the disease, she warned that every person in the country was potentially at risk. It was impossible to predict how many more would become ill in the coming year. She asked her radio audience if they had ever seen a victim of polio. "That sight is the most eloquent appeal of all," she stated. "Can you imagine one of your own little ones coming in from play, slightly feverish . . . symptoms of a cold, you might think—then suddenly the vicious infantile paralysis germ strikes—little limbs are stilled—little eyes look out on a sunless, funless world." She warned that such a child faced a long period of treatment, "if there IS a road back. Months, even years, in splints, plaster casts, braces—even the iron lung—months when the tinkling laugh and patter of little feet are heard no more."[4]

In March 1953, after Congress placed the National Institutes of Health under the administration of the newly created HEW, Surgeon General Leonard Scheele informed Oveta that Dr. William G. Workman, head of the National Institutes of Health unit responsible for licensing commercial products, was monitoring various research projects that were attempting to develop a polio vaccine. Two of those projects were especially promising. The NFIP was funding the work of Dr. Jonas Salk, whose lab team at the University of Pittsburgh was researching a dead-virus vaccine that would be administered by injection. Another project was in Ohio, where Dr. Albert Sabin, working independently from Salk, was developing a vaccine from a weakened strain of a live virus to be taken orally. Salk and his research team had developed their vaccine first. In July 1952, Salk had conducted a successful but limited field trial of the vaccine in Pittsburgh that included his own children as well as himself. Convinced that the dead-virus vaccine was safe, Salk persuaded the NFIP to fund a much larger field trial, but Salk's labs were unable to

*Oveta Culp Hobby with March of Dimes polio poster child, ca. 1953.*

produce the volume of vaccine required for the test. As a result, Salk and the foundation turned to the pharmaceutical companies Eli Lilly and Parke-Davis to produce the vaccine in the needed quantity. In April 1953, after these two commercial companies produced a sufficient supply, the NFIP asked HEW's Public Health Service agency for permission to conduct more extensive field trials of the dead-virus vaccine. The agency approved the request on April 25, 1953, and field trials, which would be conducted for about one year, began the next day.[5]

The NFIP-funded trials injected Salk's vaccine into more than 650,000 so-called Polio Pioneer children in forty-four states. An additional 1,180,000 children received placebo injections and served as the control group. In all, more than two million people participated in this unprecedented experiment that historian David Oshinsky has called the "biggest gamble in medical history." The US news media gave Salk's polio vaccine experiment massive coverage, including a story in *Time* featuring Salk on the cover. Salk, who had been an obscure medical researcher laboring away in his Pittsburgh lab, suddenly became a national celebrity to an American public that waited anxiously for some sign of good news about the fight against a dreaded disease.[6]

Five months into the national field trials, the NFIP informed HEW that it had paid the pharmaceutical companies to make enough vaccine to supply the trials, but once the trials were completed the supply would be exhausted. The cost to make enough additional vaccine available to cover the rest of the population for free was beyond NFIP's capability. As a result NFIP asked HEW to seek $35 million from Congress that would make grants-in-aid available to the states. The grants would pay for the manufacture of millions of additional doses of the vaccine and fund a free inoculation for those most vulnerable to the disease.

When the proposal reached Oveta's desk in September 1954, she counseled her Public Health Service administrators to be patient and wait for the results of the field trials, which were months away. Before she involved HEW in any distribution program, she first wanted confirmation that the vaccine was safe and effective. While Oveta understood the anxiety that many Americans had over the certainty that the disease would strike during the coming summer, she was not convinced that a crisis existed that would justify massive federal intervention. She knew that many more children died or were killed every year by influenza and that polio ranked low in any list of dangers to the public's health. As Debra Sutphen has noted, "Frustration and fear did not, in [Oveta's] opinion, constitute an emergency. [Polio's] eradication was of utmost importance, but Hobby would have gone against character had she allowed emotionalism to dictate her actions on this matter."[7]

Oveta believed the vaccination program was best left to the private sector and to the states to manage. Her handling of the issue was also influenced by a number of factors, including the American Medical Association's fierce opposition to federal involvement in health care, the bugaboo of "socialized medicine," and the criticism of local right-wing political pressure groups, such as Houston's Doctors for Freedom and the Minute Women. For these reasons, Oveta decided that HEW should wait another six months for the trials to end and for the results to be evaluated before she would recommend what, if any, role the federal government would play in vaccine distribution.[8]

After the vaccine trials were completed at the end of March 1954, Salk and his team submitted the results to the Vaccine Evaluation Center at the University of Michigan.

Salk's research mentor, Dr. Thomas Francis, had established the center only a few weeks earlier. It took another year for Francis to complete his evaluation of the trial test results. Finally, in early March 1955, Francis told the NFIP that his work was done, but the final report would not be ready for public release until mid-April. The foundation decided that it would announce the results on April 12, 1955, at a press conference in Ann Arbor, Michigan. That date was the tenth anniversary of the death of Franklin D. Roosevelt, polio's most famous victim, who had played a key role in establishing the NFIP.[9]

Up to this point, Oveta had not been directly involved in the Salk vaccine project. But Congress had given the authority to license vaccines to a unit of HEW's Public Health Service. When Francis announced he would release the results of his evaluation at the press conference on April 12, Oveta sent William Workman and a team of other HEW experts to Ann Arbor to monitor the event and meet with polio specialists. If the Francis report was positive, that team would serve as a committee to advise HEW about the immediate licensing of the batch of Salk vaccine that had already been stockpiled by drugmakers.[10]

On the morning of April 12, Thomas Francis presented his evaluation of the Salk vaccine trials to five hundred public officials and leaders of the medical world who were gathered in Rackham Hall at the University of Michigan. Earlier that morning, packets containing the full report, a summary, and a press release were distributed to reporters at a tumultuous press conference. In a chaotic free-for-all, journalists grabbed and snatched the packets out of the hands of the university staff. At one point, the staff had to stand on tables and toss the packets out for reporters to catch. Desperate for a scoop, reporters ignored the detailed findings in the actual report and instead relied entirely on the university's brief press release, with its somewhat misleading heading: "The vaccine works. It is safe, effective, and potent." That heading resulted in a rush of stories declaring the wonderful but incorrect news that the vaccine was 100 percent effective and that it would be immediately available nearly everywhere.[11]

In reality, Thomas Francis had determined that the effectiveness of the Salk vaccinations in the test trials had ranged from 60 percent protection against the most prevalent strain of the virus to about 90 percent against the two other known strains of paralytic poliomyelitis. The happiest finding was that the vaccine provided 94 percent effectiveness against bulbar poliomyelitis, the deadly strain that affected breathing and occasionally caused death. The vaccine proved extraordinarily safe in all cases. Though not perfect, as the press erroneously suggested (it had provided no protection in 40 percent of the cases of the most common polio virus), Salk's vaccine was nevertheless a major advance toward the control and possibly the eventual elimination of the disease as the vaccine was improved.[12]

Immediately after Thomas Francis reported his conclusions, Salk read a paper that he had written before Francis had completed his evaluation. Despite Francis's report that the vaccine was effective in the vast majority of cases but certainly far from all, Salk announced that the vaccine offered the possibility of "100 percent protection" from paralysis, a statement that seemed to validate the press reports. This declaration shocked Francis. He knew that no vaccine had ever been developed that guaranteed 100 percent immunity except in extremely rare ideal conditions.[13]

William Workman had arranged for his committee of experts and public health officials to meet at a hotel in downtown Ann Arbor immediately after the release of the Francis report in order to advise HEW if it should provide immediate licensing for commercial production and distribution. After two hours of discussion, the committee remained uncertain about the effectiveness of the vaccine and whether or not it would provide the best prevention against polio. One of the committee members was Dr. Sabin, who was among the strongest doubters. Despite some concern about the vaccine's actual effectiveness, the data proved that it was safe. The committee members were also convinced of the proven ability of the leading and long-established pharmaceutical companies to follow the federal standards on safety and quality for vaccines. The committee felt great pressure from the impending onset of another polio season and the certainty that an excited public, reacting to the somewhat exaggerated news about the vaccine's effectiveness, would demand access to the vaccine for their children. As a result, they voted unanimously to recommend licensing the vaccine, although some of the yes votes were reluctant ones.[14]

A claim would surface a couple of years later that Oveta had given Workman's advisory committee in Ann Arbor only seventy-five minutes to make up its mind about whether the vaccine should be released. Sociologist Jane Smith repeated the charge in her deeply flawed book *Patenting the Sun* (1990). Smith alleged that Oveta pushed Workman's committee to give "instant" approval for licensing and was "furious" when it took them a while to issue an opinion. Oveta steadfastly denied that allegation, declaring that no "responsible layman would be so presumptuous as to give a scientific group a deadline on a recommendation." Debra Sutphen, in her thoroughly researched dissertation on Oveta's tenure as HEW secretary, points out that there is "no record that Hobby or Scheele were upset that the committee took the time it did to deliberate," "no record of pressure exerted on her or Scheele's part, and no evidence that anyone was coerced to make the decision to license."[15]

Workman immediately telephoned news of the committee's decision to Surgeon General Scheele, who was in Washington anxiously waiting for the phone call. Scheele hurried to Oveta's office to give her the good news. A HEW publicist had scheduled a press conference for 3:00 p.m. that same day without informing Scheele or Oveta. As a result, HEW's conference room was already packed with reporters eagerly waiting for Oveta's reaction to the news. The press had been informed that the conference would feature Oveta signing licenses to allow the six pharmaceutical companies to make and distribute the Salk vaccine to the nation's physicians. Because it took Workman's committee longer to make a decision than HEW's public representative anticipated, the press conference was two hours late.

Finally, at 5:00 p.m., Oveta and Scheele entered the pressroom as the flashbulbs of news photographers popped. Supported by the Workman committee's decision, Oveta sat at a table and signed the licenses with Scheele at her side. An almost giddy Oveta declared to reporters, "It's a great day. It's a wonderful day for the whole world. It's a history-making day!" HEW staff distributed a press release that included Oveta's statement stressing that her authority in this matter was restricted to certifying the safety and effectiveness of the vaccine and ensuring that it be distributed fairly. She also reminded the public that she had no power to impose price controls on the vaccine market. The *New York Times* praised Oveta's quick decision, declaring that she had acted "with the greatest possible speed to make the vaccine available to the public."[16]

David Oshinsky has observed that for "millions of Americans" the news about the Salk vaccine meant "instant access to the most heralded product in recent medical history." Rumors spread that the vaccine had already been distributed to warehouses around the country, "waiting only to be licensed by Oveta Culp Hobby, who had the stamp of approval poised in her hand." The rumor was partially true. More than ten million doses of vaccine had been stockpiled in pharmaceutical warehouses. Before Francis announced the trial test results, NFIP president Basil O'Connor had held private meetings with the six major drug companies, including Eli Lilly and Parke-Davis. O'Connor offered them $9 million of NFIP money (approximately $1 a shot) to make sure stockpiles would be ready after the release of testing results. On the day Francis issued his report, the NFIP announced it would provide the vaccine for no charge to nine million children in the United States. The first inoculations would be administered to the 1.8 million "Polio Pioneers" who had received the inert placebos during the field test. A booster shot would be given to the more than 450,000 children who had been given the real vaccine. The rest of the vaccine was reserved for an additional 7 million schoolchildren in the first and second grades. In all, approximately 30 percent of American kids in the most susceptible age groups could expect to receive the NFIP-purchased vaccine that summer.[17]

Under federal law, the Public Health Service was required to certify the vaccine's effectiveness and safety before it could be distributed, which was a time-consuming process. Only six US pharmaceutical firms were licensed to manufacture the vaccine. With no precedents from which to work, they could only make rough estimates about how much product would be needed. Making the Salk vaccine also proved to be extremely complex. It generally took at least ninety days to go from the culturing of the vaccine to inoculation. Individuals not included in NFIP distribution plans could expect the Salk vaccine sometime in late July, but only if no problems arose in production.[18]

On April 13, Oveta and Surgeon General Scheele appeared before Lister Hill's Senate Subcommittee on Labor and Public Welfare. The committee was holding hearings on a bill to provide grants to the states to increase the number of nurses. Chairman Hill took the opportunity, however, to tell Oveta he was disturbed by something Jonas Salk had said on Edward R. Murrow's *See It Now* television program, broadcast the night before. Salk had implied there would be a shortage of polio vaccine. Oveta told Hill not to worry, that the Public Health Service and every other department of HEW would "work to assure that every young child" in the country would be able to get the vaccine and that a voluntary distribution plan would be announced soon. She also stated that the pharmaceutical companies and the medical profession were working closely together, and their collaboration would ensure that the people who needed the vaccine the most would be able to get it.[19]

Hill replied that he shared Oveta's high regard for the vaccine manufacturers as well as the medical profession, and he was confident a voluntary program would work. He thought, however, that it would help if the president called a White House conference to develop a plan to make certain the vaccine was distributed fairly and that the plan be shared with the public. His constituents had heard rumors the injections would be expensive and only the wealthy would be able to afford them. He also expressed concerns that a black market for the vaccine could develop in the absence of a fair distribution program. A conference hosted by the president could be an effective way to persuade the American people that the government had the problem of vaccine distribution under control. "I am so glad that you say on a voluntary basis," Oveta replied. "If we were to try to put this on a regulatory basis it is entirely possible that many children would thereby have been denied the shots." The hearing ended on a cordial note, with Oveta promising to pass Hill's conference suggestion on to the president at their meeting scheduled for the next day.[20]

After the Senate hearing, Oveta hurried back to her office to call President Eisenhower, who was on a golfing vacation in Augusta, Georgia. She briefed the president about the status of Salk vaccine distribution and gave him an account of her interchange with Senator Hill. When Oveta told Eisenhower that Senator Hill wanted a White House conference on vaccine production and distribution, the president offered an alternative approach. He directed Oveta to have HEW, not the White House, organize and host a meeting of scientists and administrators from pharmaceutical companies to address the manufacturing and distribution problems causing the shortage of the vaccine. That meeting would be followed the next day by a larger meeting of pharmaceutical company representatives, the medical profession, state and local public health authorities, and members of Congress, especially the influential Senator Hill.

President Eisenhower also articulated his idea that the United States should offer every country with which it had diplomatic relations, including the Soviet Union, full information about the vaccine's formula and the scientific reports on its effectiveness and safety. Oveta cautioned Eisenhower that because the vaccine could not be produced quickly, it was not known when or how much vaccine would ultimately be made available to other countries. Noting her concern, the president said that he would direct the Commerce Department to impose strict export controls on the vaccine. Secretary of State John Foster Dulles later announced the United States would make information about the Salk vaccine available to other nations, but the vaccine itself would not be available until the supply could be increased. Later that day, White House spokesman Jim Hagerty told the press that the president had directed the HEW secretary to "set in motion a program of cooperation with the medical authorities and pharmaceutical industries." To head off the usual cries about socialized medicine, Hagerty stressed that the administration was determined to carry out the program with state and municipal officials by voluntary means only.[21]

Oveta moved quickly to carry out Eisenhower's direction. HEW announced it would host a Salk vaccine conference in Washington on April 22. She assigned Dr. Chester Keefer the job of organizing and chairing the scientific meeting on April 20 and 21 as well as the larger conference on April 22. During World War II, Keefer had served on the War Production Board as the "Penicillin Czar" responsible for supply and distribution of the new "wonder drug" to ensure that a sufficient supply was available for the military. Keefer, who had been appointed to his post at HEW on the recommendation of the American Medical Association, was a vocal opponent of federal control of the allocation of vaccines. He soon became a valuable advisor to Oveta as she became entangled in a major controversy about the role of the federal government, and more specifically HEW, in the production and distribution of the Salk vaccine.[22]

By this time, the NFIP had stockpiled approximately ten million doses of the Salk vaccine. "That was the good news and it didn't last long," Oshinsky has noted. The NFIP planned to give this supply to the nation's first and second graders free of charge, which meant most Americans under eighteen would remain unprotected. Only 1 percent of the existing doses of vaccine would remain available after the NFIP received its allocation. It was now obvious that an ample new supply would not be available to the general public for several months. Not surprisingly, with summer rapidly approaching, everyone wanted the vaccine at once. HEW had been surprised by the great demand, which bordered on the hysterical. The simple fact was HEW had failed to plan for that contingency. As news of the short supply hit the public, the Eisenhower administration faced a major controversy. Oveta and Surgeon General Scheele calmly issued assurances to the public that all would be well, but those statements failed to stem the increasing public alarm and belief that the Eisenhower administration had mishandled a major public health situation.[23]

The Eisenhower administration was confident that the big pharmaceutical companies, motivated by the profit incentive, would resolve the supply shortage quickly. The result of the administration's confidence in the private sector was that it had no vaccine distribution plan in place to deal with the problem. When this information became publicly known, it was met with shock and outrage. On April 16, *Businessweek* declared the situation "made to order for panic and hysteria, especially if there are any major polio outbreaks."[24]

Public and legislative pressure on Oveta increased while she was still struggling to get the Hobby-Brownell school construction bill through a House committee. In response to the public outcry over the vaccine shortage, congressional Democrats soon submitted three separate bills demanding the federal government take over the distribution of the Salk vaccine. Nevertheless, the president remained confident that the HEW vaccine distribution conferences scheduled for April 22 would resolve the problem without federal intervention. Eisenhower later recalled, "In spite of these disheartening delays and their attendant confusion, Mrs. Hobby proceeded with the preparation of a comprehensive plan for a national distribution of the vaccine, to go into effect as soon as the National Foundation's free inoculation program for first and second graders ended and vaccine for others became available."[25]

On the two days prior to the April 22 conference on polio vaccine production and distribution, Oveta hosted private meetings at HEW with technical representatives and executive officers from the pharmaceutical companies. She asked the gathering to review the cause for the vaccine shortage and to draft a strategy to solve the problem. At the end of the meeting on April 21, the industry representatives reported to Oveta, Keefer, and HEW's Public Health Service staff that the rigorous and elaborate federal requirements for vaccine testing had played a critical role in causing the shortage. All agreed, however, that the standards should be maintained and production not be rushed because of risks to safety. The pharmaceutical companies were making improvements to, and in one case expanding, their facilities to increase output. That increase of supply would still not be seen for another four months, which meant not until late July or early August. The company representatives also warned that if any lot of vaccine failed to pass federal standards or proved to be compromised at any point during production, the entire schedule would be disrupted and distribution delayed. The most important decision the manufacturers made at the preconference was to suspend production of the vaccine for the commercial market until the NFIP had the amount needed to inoculate all schoolchildren in the first and second grades.

On Friday morning, April 22, Oveta opened the main conference on the Salk vaccine attended by nearly eighty delegates representing the pharmaceutical companies, medical and health professions, state public health agencies, the NFIP, and Congress. She explained that the meeting had two purposes. One was to determine how soon there would be enough vaccine "to take care of the children of America." The second was to arrive at an understanding about how the vaccine would be distributed. "What steps are necessary," she asked, "to assure that vaccine on hand goes to the most susceptible age groups in the population?" She also explained that the conference had been called at the request of President Eisenhower and that she would report its findings "as quickly as possible" to him. Without taking questions, Oveta turned the proceedings over to Dr. Keefer and then headed to the White House to attend a cabinet meeting.[26]

Oveta had banned the news media from the conference, which generated a vigorous protest from the press. Some reporters pointed out the irony of a newspaper editor and publisher restricting news media access to a government-sponsored conference, especially on such a serious public issue. Oveta argued that solutions to the supply problem could not be discussed without manufacturers disclosing proprietary trade information. Public disclosure of that information would violate the trust that existed between the Eisenhower administration and private industry, which could threaten the success of the voluntary

*President Eisenhower and Oveta Culp Hobby at the White House ceremony honoring National Foundation for Infantile Paralysis president Basil O'Connor (far left) and Dr. Jonas Salk (second to left), for developing the Salk polio vaccine, April 22, 1955.*

program. She also claimed the presence of reporters might hamper free and open discussion among the conference participants. The press was somewhat satisfied, however, with Oveta's decision to make the delegates available for interviews during the lunch break. She also announced that HEW would not ask the participants to keep the proceedings confidential. They would be free to talk to the press after the conference ended.[27]

After the cabinet meeting, Oveta hurried to the conference to attend lunch with the delegates and to receive a report from Keefer about the proceedings. She then returned to the White House to attend a ceremony in the Rose Garden honoring Jonas Salk and NFIP president Basil O'Connor. When Oveta arrived at the White House, she was ushered into the Oval Office to give the president a briefing on the polio vaccine conference. She told Eisenhower the conference had accomplished all she had hoped it would. "There was a remarkable degree of cooperation and understanding," Oveta stated. "Every participant immediately shared in the single purpose of getting the polio vaccine to the children of the United States as soon as possible. There was not one dissenting note in the day's activities." After a fifteen-minute discussion, she and Eisenhower walked out to the Rose Garden, where Oveta presided over the event with Eisenhower at her side. After she introduced Salk and O'Connor, Eisenhower presented them both with presidential citations. Salk received his for the role he played in developing the polio vaccine, while NFIP president Basil O'Connor was recognized for his leadership in providing the foundation's support for Salk's work.[28]

The most important result of the April 22 conference was the decision to establish a National Vaccine Advisory Committee to gather information from the pharmaceutical companies and state health agencies about the available supply of vaccine and then to set priorities for distribution to the states. Keefer made it clear to the pharmaceutical companies that HEW would stay out of their way, but the department expected them to take care of any vaccine shortages that might develop. The companies pledged their full cooperation in following the committee's recommendations.[29]

Oveta and her staff immediately prepared for the public meeting on April 27 that would be the follow-up to the April 22 conference. Unlike the previous conference, the citizens' conference, composed of delegates "broadly representative of the American public," would be open to the news media so that plans for vaccine production and distribution could be made available to all. As she prepared for this next conference, Oveta was confident that a voluntary distribution plan for the polio vaccine would soon go into action, solving HEW's polio vaccine problems.[30]

Four days after the April 22 conference, however, it became evident that the Eisenhower administration's polio vaccine problems were not solved. In the early evening of April 26, the day before the citizens' conference meeting, word arrived at HEW that a few of the vaccinated children in California, Idaho, and Chicago had become ill with paralytic polio within about ten days of being inoculated. One had died. This unwelcome news was quickly conveyed to Leonard Scheele. The paralysis had begun in the inoculated arm of each child, and they all had been vaccinated with serum from Cutter Labs in Berkeley, California. HEW's Public Health Service (PHS) scientists met all night in Washington to assess the situation. The matter was urgent. Thousands of children would be inoculated in California later that same day, and many of them would receive vaccine from Cutter Labs. At three o'clock in the morning of April 27, PHS scientists arranged a telephone conference to get advice from four polio experts, including Thomas Francis, about what, if any, action to take. Because of the lack of confirmable information, the experts failed to reach a consensus about what this outbreak meant and exactly what action should be taken in response. The children might have already been infected with polio before they were given the vaccine. It was also understood that the vaccine was not 100 percent effective, with a rate of effectiveness of only 60 percent for one strain. Nonetheless, everyone agreed that HEW had to investigate.[31]

While PHS staff were assessing the vaccination problem and trying to determine a strategy to deal with it, Oveta, unaware of the problem, opened the citizens' conference later that same morning in the HEW auditorium. Turning the meeting over to other members of her staff, she returned to her office to gather her coat and valise to depart on a flight to New York City. The reason for her trip was to be with Will, who was in Presbyterian Hospital with a severe flare-up of his arthritis. As she was leaving the office, Oveta paused at Joan Braden's desk to give instructions about work Braden should handle while Oveta was away from Washington. About this time, according to Braden, Surgeon General Scheele rushed into the office, "literally wringing his hands." Scheele gave Oveta the terrible news that children had become ill with polio after receiving the vaccine. Oveta immediately postponed her trip to New York and then met privately with Scheele to discuss how HEW should respond to the crisis.[32]

HEW lacked the legal authority to order the vaccine off the market, so Oveta approved Scheele's recommendation that he contact Cutter Labs and ask them to recall their vaccine voluntarily, which Cutter's executives agreed to do. Scheele soon dispatched two PHS experts to Cutter's labs in Berkeley to help determine what had gone wrong. In addition, the other pharmaceutical manufacturers agreed to hold back their inventory of undistributed vaccine until PHS could identify the cause of the problem. Because this action resulted in the suspension of already announced vaccination schedules, Scheele notified the news media, stressing that the recall did not "imply that any correlation exists between the vaccine and the occurrence of poliomyelitis."[33]

On April 29, as PHS scientists reviewed Cutter Labs' protocol records and tested vials of Salk vaccine, Dr. Scheele convened an ad hoc committee of experts, including Thomas Francis, Albert Sabin, and Jonas Salk, to discuss the vaccine problem. After two days of reviewing records, conducting talks with pharmaceutical company scientists, and analyzing the information gathered, the committee reached a unanimous conclusion that the surgeon general had acted appropriately when he suspended the use of the Cutter Labs vaccine while allowing the other five manufacturers to continue production and distribution. The committee also urged a reevaluation of federal standards for making the vaccine, a recommendation HEW quickly accepted.[34]

Leaving Dr. Workman in charge, Leonard Scheele broke away from the ad hoc committee's deliberations long enough to accompany Oveta and Dr. Keefer to a session of the president's cabinet at ten o'clock that morning. Warned that the growing controversy about the polio vaccine would be the main subject, Oveta had directed Scheele and his staff to prepare a detailed report on the current status of the Salk vaccine for distribution to the president and the cabinet. The report included information about the mysterious outbreak of polio among a few children in California who had been vaccinated with serum from Cutter Labs.[35]

After the report was circulated, Oveta made a brief opening statement emphasizing that the April 22 polio vaccine conference was "a complete success." She then asked Dr. Keefer to discuss the highlights of the report she had distributed, especially the priority target group for the inoculation program. Keefer explained that of the large number of children who had not received shots as part of the NFIP's campaign, those from the ages of five to nine would be the first group to be inoculated, followed by children from one up to five years old. Private family physicians and pediatricians would perform these vaccinations at a cost of a little more than four dollars (equivalent to thirty-six dollars in 2019) for the initial injection and two boosters for each child. When Eisenhower suggested that the federal government should pay for vaccinating children whose families could not afford the cost of the inoculation, Oveta explained that some of the states had agreed to cover that expense, and other states were considering doing the same. She recommended that the federal government wait to see if every state eventually would assume the cost for vaccinating the indigent. If any of the states failed to take that step, HEW would consider how it could assist them.[36]

Oveta's statement undoubtedly satisfied the archconservative members of the cabinet, especially Ezra Taft Benson and George Humphrey, but the president was not satisfied. He told Oveta that his administration would, indeed, pay the cost of vaccinating children from poor families. "No child must be denied the vaccine for financial reasons," he declared. "If necessary, we would use the President's Emergency Fund, but some source must be found." Eisenhower then asked why a few children had become ill with polio recently. Making reference to the normal polio season, which occurred during the summer, he wondered if it wasn't "a little early [in the year] for them to come naturally." Scheele replied that it was likely the ill children were already infected by the time they received their vaccination. Scheele reminded the cabinet that even if the ill children had not been infected before being vaccinated, the Salk vaccine was not 100 percent effective, and it should be expected that the disease would strike hundreds of children even though they had been inoculated. The meeting concluded with a discussion about the rumors circulating publicly that physicians were telling families the vaccine was in short supply because the federal government was controlling its distribution. Outraged anyone would spread such false information, Eisenhower instructed every member of the cabinet to make public statements denying the rumor, and he declared he would do the same at his next press conference.[37]

Although the inspection of Cutter Labs had not been completed, Dr. Scheele's confident speculations about why a few vaccinated children had become ill with polio seem to have placated the president and Oveta's fellow cabinet members. That afternoon, however, news arrived at HEW that an additional group of vaccinated children had been stricken with polio, three of whom had not received vaccine produced by Cutter Labs. This report convinced HEW to suspend immediately the certification of all the additional lots of vaccine until more information could be gathered from the labs in California. Oveta knew the decision to suspend the certification process, even on a temporary basis, would make the supply shortage even worse. It was certain to generate a negative reaction in the press, the general public, and in Congress. Accordingly, Oveta and Scheele decided to calm the waters by making public appearances during which they could give updates on the current situation and assure the public that HEW was working with the pharmaceutical industry and state public health authorities to solve the problems with manufacturing, supply, and distribution. At this point, Oveta and Scheele intended to downplay the polio outbreak among the small number of vaccinated children because of their strong suspicion that the illnesses were simply confirmation the vaccine was not 100 percent effective. After all, literally millions of children had been vaccinated and only a few dozen had become ill, which seemed to PHS scientists to be proof the vaccine worked.

On Monday, May 2, three days after HEW suspended certification of the remaining vaccine in stock, Scheele appeared on the CBS network television show *Face the Nation*, where he tried to explain the problems with vaccine supply and distribution and assure the public the PHS was working with the pharmaceutical companies to solve those problems. The following day, Scheele joined Oveta at a governors' conference she had arranged to discuss the vaccine supply shortage and distribution issues and to enlist the aid of state officials in the distribution program. In her speech to the delegates, Oveta summarized HEW's work with the pharmaceutical companies, state public health officials, and the medical community to ensure the Salk vaccine was distributed equitably and efficiently. She stressed, however, that it had been HEW's policy to defer to nongovernmental organizations and the private sector on matters related to vaccine development, supply, distribution, and marketing. She assured the governors that as secretary of HEW she had opposed federal direction or control of the nation's health care system.[38]

During the discussion session following Oveta's presentation, several of the governors expressed their support of her opposition to socialized medicine while also criticizing her for failing to develop an effective distribution program for the Salk vaccine. The conservative Republican governor of Wyoming, Milward L. Simpson, complained HEW seemed to have been "going around in circles" in its polio vaccine actions. In response to the governors' criticisms, Oveta agreed to consider a different approach. She assured the governors, "[If] it appears on the basis of our findings that the fight against polio will best be advanced by [federal] legislation, I shall recommend it to the President." She asked the governors to consult with their state officials and then send their recommendations to her about how HEW should address the vaccine distribution issue. Within ten days of the conference's end, Oveta had a response from fifty-one governors of states and territories. Most of the governors called on HEW, in consultation with state officials, to take responsibility for distributing the vaccine to their states and territories, fear of socialized medicine notwithstanding.[39]

The day after Oveta conferred with the nation's governors, PHS confirmed fifty cases of paralytic polio and two cases of nonparalytic polio among children vaccinated with

Salk vaccine. Forty-four of those cases were directly linked to vaccine manufactured by Cutter Labs, with that total eventually rising to more than two hundred. The National Institutes of Health's advisory committee had now seen enough. Its members concluded that PHS regulations governing the production of the Salk vaccine were inadequate. Feeling the force of massive public demand, the pharmaceutical companies and the PHS had issued about half of the vaccine under a guideline known as "release by protocol," which was an inspection system based on the examination of company records documenting the manufacturing process instead of testing each individual lot for the presence of live virus. Release by protocol worked well for most vaccines, but, as it turned out, not for the Salk vaccine. The result was the distribution of several batches of vaccine containing impurities that allowed the live virus to be given to some children. The prime offender was Cutter Labs. Accordingly, the committee recommended to Scheele that he temporarily suspend the entire vaccination program pending a thorough review of the production processes of all six of the manufacturers. With Oveta's agreement, Scheele announced on a network television and radio broadcast on May 8 that he was imposing a temporary halt on all polio vaccinations. In an attempt to reassure the parents of the five million children who had already been inoculated, Scheele stressed that with the exception of those who had received vaccine produced by Cutter Labs, the incidence of polio infection had only been one in seven hundred thousand. He promised those who were still waiting on the vaccine that "in time" there would be "ample and safe vaccine for all who need it and wish it."[40]

Unfortunately, Scheele's statement failed to reassure a large portion of the American public, especially as the news spread that additional children had become ill with paralytic polio. Newspapers described popular reaction as bordering on panic. Fear-stricken parents overwhelmed the White House and HEW with letters, telegrams, and telephone calls demanding action be taken immediately to end the crisis. Not surprisingly, much of the criticism and blame was aimed directly at the secretary of HEW. An editorial in the *New York Post*, one of the newspapers most critical of Oveta in general, charged she "had fantastically bungled the polio vaccine program" by her lack of planning and failure to ensure that enough vaccine had been produced.[41]

In the days immediately after Dr. Francis released his report on the Salk vaccine on April 12, the PHS, the NFIP, Jonas Salk, and the pharmaceutical companies went to great lengths to assure the public that the new vaccine was effective and safe. The news media had essentially declared the end of polio as a public health threat. Suddenly all of those assurances seemed empty and even misleading. Many felt betrayed by the government and the scientists who had promoted the vaccine. The euphoria resulting from the seemingly miraculous development of a serum to banish a dreaded disease quickly turned into anger and fear for many.

Newspaper editorials, opinion columns, and letters to the editor were filled with demands for the federal government to take the entire polio vaccine program away from the private sector, possibly to place it under the control of some other federal agency than HEW. Republican as well as Democratic members of Congress and the leaders of a number of influential civic and professional organizations echoed those demands. To Oveta's shock and frustration, even the American Medical Association, the loudest opponent of federal involvement in health care, issued a statement asking why HEW had not been in control of polio vaccine production and supply of vaccine from the beginning. Despite this intense and widespread criticism, Oveta held fast to her position that the system of voluntary distribution was working. She continued to reject proposals for the federal government to seize control of the vaccine's supply and distribution. President Eisenhower fully backed her stance on the issue.[42]

Oveta's rigid opposition to federal involvement in the health care industry, and the fact that she had official responsibility as secretary of HEW for all actions taken by the department, left her vulnerable to this massive wave of criticism. As head of HEW, however, Oveta served as an administrator, not as an expert on medical science. In that capacity, she had no direct involvement in developing the vaccine or in certifying its safety and effectiveness. That was Surgeon General Scheele's job as head of the PHS, and Oveta never meddled in his work, not only because of her lack of expertise but also because by tradition, as a scientific agency, PHS had been allowed a significant amount of independence in its operations. Over the years, Congress had given independent authority to the surgeon general to monitor and regulate a wide variety of matters related to the nation's public health. Therefore, for legal as well as for practical reasons, Oveta had followed her surgeon general's lead in the areas over which he had authority and expertise. Even if they were aware of these facts, none of it mattered to the news media.

An unabashedly snide column written by William V. Shannon, the Washington correspondent for the *New York Post*, illustrated the negative attitude toward Oveta that some members of the press developed as the polio vaccine controversy grew. Shannon observed that Oveta was being heavily criticized "for her slow, glacial approach to the problem of the distribution of the Salk polio vaccine." Shannon's comments, as well as those of many of Oveta's other critics, exuded sexism. As was the case with some of her other detractors, he seemed to delight in reminding the public that a woman had been in charge of the "bungling." Eisenhower had appointed Oveta to serve as head of HEW, Shannon surmised, because the department was "responsible for . . . concerns of particular interest to women." Shannon offered that it must have come as "some slight surprise to him that Mrs. Hobby has exhibited none of the enthusiasms conventionally associated with women." Instead, Shannon continued, she "had displayed tight-lipped respect for the taxpayer's dollar, hostility to positive government action, and canny caution about sticking her neck out. Neither sentiment nor indignation nor passion for the underdog has disturbed the even tenor of her way." The *New York Post* columnist added, "Self help is her motto. It has paid off in her own life. She sees no reason why it should not in the lives of others. Her record has earned her [the] accolade 'The Secretary of Not-Too-Much Health, Education, and Welfare.' Such criticisms, however, do not disturb Mrs. Hobby."[43]

But the criticism did disturb Oveta, according to her son, Bill. Bill was living near Washington during the polio controversy and saw his mother frequently. "Mother was devastated by the accusations made against her," Bill Hobby later recalled. "It really did hurt her, but she was not the type who would show it. My father at the time was seriously ill and in and out of the hospital, so she was under almost unbearable professional pressure and emotional stress."[44]

Eisenhower inadvertently exacerbated Oveta's problems when he tried to counter news media and congressional criticism of her role in the polio vaccine controversy. At his press conference on May 11, a reporter asked the president why Oveta had not taken early steps to ensure an adequate supply of vaccine. Eisenhower speculated that because there had been such intense pressure on HEW to distribute the vaccine as quickly as possible, scientists at PHS "probably tried to short cut a little bit. I don't know. The report will have to show. I am not a scientist, as you well know." The implication was HEW had been sloppy in handling a matter of great seriousness. "Look, I am speculating on that particular point . . . and I am not making any statement that is to be taken as authoritative," he added. Revealing great irritation with the matter, Eisenhower finally blurted out that he didn't understand the question. "The government would know no more about the factors in this than this body would," he complained. "What would you know what to do with such technical things? I wouldn't." The president's performance not only failed to stem the criticism, it also seemed to confirm the accusations that Oveta was incompetent, as well as making it appear PHS had been reckless.[45]

The news only worsened. The morning after the president's press conference, Scheele informed Oveta as she was preparing for a cabinet meeting that the number of vaccine-caused polio cases had increased to a total of sixty-seven. Nearly all of the cases had resulted in paralysis. Cutter Labs had produced the vaccine in all but ten cases; the other cases had involved vaccine manufactured by Eli Lilly and Wyeth. Especially devastating was the information that five individuals had died after being vaccinated. When Scheele gave Oveta the latest news, he also had to share it with a committee of the House of Representatives during a hearing following his consultation with her. Scheele pointed out that nearly three hundred thousand children had been inoculated with Cutter vaccine, and that there had been a low infection rate relative to the number of vaccinations. He admitted that even one infection was unfortunate, but no vaccine was perfect and the low rate of infection proved it was safe and effective. "No national health emergency confronts this country," Scheele argued.[46]

During the cabinet session that same morning, the Salk vaccine crisis dominated the discussion for the second meeting in a row. Oveta reported PHS was working overtime to manually test every batch of vaccine as it was being produced. That same day PHS would approve eleven lots of Parke-Davis vaccine for distribution. The vaccine program would soon be ready to restart. Oveta admitted that while the process was slow by necessity, the distribution program would continue on a voluntary basis with no federal interference. Undoubtedly in reaction to Eisehower's speculation about PHS scientists possibly taking shortcuts to get the vaccine to the public, Oveta did her own speculating. She suggested the NFIP was responsible for rushing the Salk vaccine into distribution. She believed that the American Medical Association's surprising statement that HEW should have controlled the distribution of the Salk vaccine from the beginning of the program was aimed at the NFIP because of the "bad blood" between the two organizations. The AMA statement, Oveta noted, was something she "never expected to hear" from an organization that had fought hard to defeat HEW's medical reinsurance proposal on the grounds the federal government had no role to play in the nation's health care. Oveta assured the president and the cabinet that great strides had been made in solving the problem of tainted vaccine. She would soon submit a revised distribution plan to the administration that she believed would finally restart the inoculation program.

After Oveta concluded her remarks, the president expressed his confidence in the polio vaccine program. "I'm so glad my grandson has been inoculated," he stated. "I'm just waiting until my granddaughters are old enough." Thanking Eisenhower for his confidence in her work, Oveta blamed the news media for stirring up the controversy. "My profession has caused much of the trouble," she lamented. "And the demagogues," Eisenhower added.[47]

# CHAPTER 38

# "NO ONE COULD HAVE FORESEEN THE PUBLIC DEMAND"

On May 15, 1955, as the Cutter Labs fiasco generated sensational headlines, Senator Lister Hill summoned Oveta to a hearing of his Labor and Public Welfare Committee. He wanted her to answer questions about the worrisome problems besetting the Department of Health, Education, and Welfare's management of the polio vaccine. Anticipating trouble, Oveta brought Surgeon General Leonard Scheele and Roswell Perkins to the hearing. Hill allowed Oveta to give an opening statement before he and his colleagues began their questioning.

Oveta announced she had submitted a detailed vaccine distribution plan to the White House only a few hours before the hearing that called for the vaccine to be distributed directly to the individual states. She stressed that distribution would not occur until the Public Health Service certified each lot as safe. Once the vaccine was distributed, HEW would leave it up to the states to decide on a voluntary basis how best to manage their vaccination efforts. Whatever plan was devised, it would have to be applied equally to all citizens without regard to race, religion, or ethnicity. In addition, no child should be denied a vaccination because of an inability to pay for it. To make that possible, she was requesting an appropriation of $28 million to buy vaccine for the needy, with those funds going directly to the states as block grants, with each state making its own decision about which citizens qualified for free inoculations. "State officials can direct and carry out a distribution plan within any state far more effectively than could federal officials," Oveta argued. She added that federal involvement would likely cause a "delay in getting vaccine to the children." Oveta later recalled that her main concern "was to get this vaccine out as quickly as we could. So by going by the state and regions, we could actually get this vaccine out fast."[1]

It was obvious to the committee members that Oveta's recommendation was based on politics, not fairness. The plan was an obvious signal to the Southern states that the administration was wary of stirring up a battle over states' rights. The Eisenhower administration needed the support of Southern Democrats for the administration's over-all legislative agenda. After Oveta read her statement, Chairman Hill criticized her rigid insistence on making the distribution plan voluntary. He questioned the reliability of a program that had no mechanism for enforcing the plan's requirements. Hill noted that he couldn't find anything in Oveta's plan "that gives you any . . . assurance that the states will go forward and develop a system that will insure that all these recommendations be carried out." Oveta replied, "I cannot believe that the governor of any state or a health officer of any state would not be mindful of his obligations and responsibilities and be eager to assume them." Senator Hill made it clear he found her answer unconvincing.

Another Democratic member of the committee, Herbert Lehman of New York, asked Oveta if her "inaction had led directly to the current shortage." Oveta's reply was one she would soon deeply regret. "Senator, I would assume that this is an incident unique in medical history," she declared. "I think no one could have foreseen the public demand. There has been no drug like this." Not satisfied with Oveta's response, Senator Lehman raised his voice belligerently and continued to demand an explanation for what he perceived to be Oveta's failure to plan for an effective supply and distribution effort. Although the Republican members of the Senate committee came to her defense, the hearing was an emotionally exhausting public relations disaster for Oveta.[2]

In David Oshinsky's view, Oveta "had made the mistake of admitting an obvious truth. The administration's lack of planning was a conscious decision, not an unfortunate oversight. Neither the president nor his advisors viewed the distribution of polio vaccine as a legitimate government function." Oveta, Oshinsky pointed out, "fully expected the process to remain in private hands, with the vaccine going from the manufacturer to the wholesaler to the druggist to the local doctor, who would inoculate the child three times in three paid office visits." That thinking satisfied the pharmaceutical compa-nies, whose executives spread the fear that if the federal government took control over the Salk vaccine, "America would become like Soviet Russia, the ultimate symbol of socialism run amuck."[3]

The news media jumped on Oveta's comment that "no one could have foreseen the public demand." Newspaper editorials mocked the secretary and demanded her resigna-tion. The Hearst newspaper chain's flagship, the *New York Journal American*, declared that the "confusion of heartful hope and heartbreaking disappointment" surrounding the news about the Salk vaccine was "abetted by official indecision and inadequate preparation for evaluation and distribution." One widely published editorial cartoon depicted Oveta as an unfeeling and blind tyrant marching down Pennsylvania Avenue, declaring that "no one could have foreseen the demand," while a crowd of desperate people followed her, carrying signs demanding their children be given the polio vac-cine. Some cartoons portrayed Oveta applying makeup in front of a vanity mirror while babies died. Letters and telegrams poured into the White House denouncing Oveta as insensitive at best and heartlessly cruel at worst. A wide range of political leaders, including former president Harry Truman, former Democratic presidential candidate

Adlai Stevenson, and Minnesota senator Hubert Humphrey joined the chorus of critics lambasting Oveta. Stevenson declared that it didn't require "any special clairvoyance" on Oveta's part "to estimate the demand for the vaccine." Years after her damaging gaffe, Oveta claimed she had meant she had not anticipated "65-year-old women hammering on doctors' doors in New York demanding vaccination for themselves." Unfortunately, if those were her thoughts she kept them to herself at the time. Joan Braden later noted that "imperturbably, [Oveta] took it. She stuck to her maxim with a will of iron: 'Never complain; never explain.'"[4]

Soon after Oveta's disastrous appearance before Senator Hill's committee, Oregon's Republican senator Wayne Morse made a fiery speech on the floor of the Senate demanding that Eisenhower fire Oveta for a level of "gross incompetency that comes close to immorality." He charged that she and Scheele had known "for months that there was going to be a shortage of the vaccine," yet they had made no plans. The senator urged the administration to force Oveta and the surgeon general "to visit the hospital rooms of the boys and girls who have contracted this horrible disease."[5]

In his presidential memoir, Eisenhower recalled, "Democrats roared: Why had not Mrs. Hobby turned up the distribution plan six weeks earlier, when the vaccine was first released? They demanded that I fire her for 'gross incompetence.' I backed her instead." At his press conference on May 18, the president stated he would not waste his time thinking about Morse's accusations, and he quickly added that Oveta had done a "magnificent" job as secretary of HEW. He reminded the reporters that she had been, "when you come down to it, merely the agent of these great scientists and doctors" in their efforts to bring the vaccine to American children as quickly and safely as possible. A reporter asked if Oveta was going to resign for "purely personal reasons." Eisenhower replied that she had placed him on notice many months ago "that conditions might arise that would compel her to leave government. If she has to go, I will be very, very disappointed." If she left the government, he said, it would have nothing to do with the Salk vaccine controversy. He praised Oveta's handling of the program and stressed that she had worked hard to get serum quickly to the children who needed it most. There was now a distribution plan, Eisenhower insisted, and enough vaccine on hand to inoculate every schoolchild in the first and second grades. Aware that some of Oveta's critics had insinuated that Oveta was unqualified for her position because she was a woman, the president declared, "[She is] a symbol of the fact that properly trained women are just as capable of carrying heavy executive jobs as are the men." When another reporter asked Eisenhower about Oveta's statement that no one could have foreseen the public demand for the polio vaccine, he responded, "I don't know to what she is referring. You have to go and ask her the question."[6]

Oveta, however, wasn't available to answer the question. After the disastrous hearing she flew to Houston to be with Will. Although he had been released recently from Presbyterian Hospital in New York City after a stay of more than a week, Oveta's seventy-seven-year-old husband was still suffering from a severe arthritic condition. While in

New York, Will had written his old friend Jesse Jones that he was in "a good deal of pain." That pain increased after Will returned to Houston, and his condition worsened during the summer, causing Oveta to shuttle back and forth from Washington to Houston to oversee her husband's care. Even that need failed to spare her from criticism. While Will was still in a Manhattan hospital in early May, Oveta postponed an appearance before a House committee to be at her husband's bedside. One of the Democratic members of the committee, Isidore Dollinger of New York City, accused her of using her husband's illness to avoid tough questioning by the committee. Chairman J. Percy Priest, also a Democrat, defended Oveta, explaining she had phoned him to offer apologies for her inability to return to Washington for the committee meeting, which had been scheduled early the next morning, and she would be available to testify after she returned to the capital.[7]

During the last two weeks of May, while Oveta remained in Houston, Scheele's Technical Committee on Poliomyelitis Vaccine continued to work with Jonas Salk to refine the vaccine-manufacturing process, testing standards, and record-keeping requirements. Meanwhile, the number of vaccinated children infected with paralytic polio continued to grow, reaching a total of nearly one hundred by the end of the month. The technical committee's new procedures would finally solve the problem, and the tragic incidents would cease after the mass inoculation program was restarted. It was now clear the Salk vaccine was safe and effective, but public confidence would not be restored for months to come.[8]

The vaccine's safety would not become apparent to most of the public until the beginning of the fall of 1955, which meant Oveta continued to be widely criticized. Some of the criticism in and outside of Congress was motivated by political partisanship and would not end until Oveta either resigned or was removed from her post. As a result, the news media reported rumors that Oveta had become a political liability to the Eisenhower administration and the Republican Party and that pressure was mounting on the president to force her resignation.

In late May, the New York Times and the New York Journal American published stories speculating that US ambassador to Italy Clare Boothe Luce, who had been helpful to Oveta when Luce was a member of Congress during the war, would soon replace Oveta as HEW secretary. Ambassador Luce immediately issued a denial she had any interest in the job and insisted she wouldn't take it if offered. At the same time that Luce was issuing her denial, Robert Allen, Washington correspondent for the New York Post, reported an anonymous source at the White House had informed him the undersecretary of the Treasury, Marion B. Folsom, would replace Oveta. Allen wrote that Oveta's "obdurate refusal to assume effective control of the production and distribution of a safe polio vaccine" had frustrated and angered her HEW staff, especially those in the PHS. "It has been an open secret . . . for weeks that high HEW officials urged her to take such decisive measures. But she turned a deaf ear to them." He claimed that as a result, "Mrs. Hobby is widely unpopular in her department. Her ouster will be occasion for much satisfaction in that harried agency." An Associated Press report, referring to a "well-posted source," also claimed Oveta would soon be forced to resign and Folsom would replace her. Hearing these negative reports, Jesse Jones dispatched a note to his friend, *Chicago Tribune* Washington correspondent Walter Trohan, stressing, "We, here [in Houston], are in Mrs. Hobby's corner."9

The evidence suggests Oveta had made a decision sometime in February to resign as secretary of HEW due to Will's growing health issues. Marion Folsom, one of Oveta's allies in her effort to pass the bill expanding Social Security coverage, later claimed she told him in February 1955 of her plans to leave HEW to take care of her sick husband in Houston. She had informed Folsom that she intended to recommend him to the president as her replacement at HEW. Oveta had also told Eisenhower she hoped to stay at her post until the end of 1955, but only if Will's health held steady. Will's health setback in May was severe enough to send Oveta first to New York for a few days and then to Houston for a couple of weeks to manage his care. Despite Will's illness and the increasingly harsh attacks on her competence, humanity, and even her womanhood, Oveta made a decision to stay on the job until she was confident that the vaccine crisis had passed and her good reputation had been restored. She also might have been determined to leave the cabinet on her own terms rather than fuel the perception she was forced out.10

At the beginning of June, Scheele gave Oveta the welcome news that the PHS's technical committee had completed its work and the National Foundation for Infantile Paralysis's inoculation program could resume. With Oveta's approval, the PHS announced on June 6 that the Eli Lilly Company had produced one million shots of polio vaccine that PHS had cleared for immediate distribution. The NFIP promptly distributed the vaccine to be given to first and second graders. But no other batches were approved for distribution. Scheele explained this was because the vaccine required "extraordinary safety safeguards" and manufacturers had to adjust their production procedures to meet the new standards, which would delay production.11

The day after PHS announced resumption of the vaccination program, Oveta and Scheele participated in a nationwide radio and television broadcast. It was an attempt to blunt the expected criticism about the availability of only one million approved injections, which meant millions of other children would have to wait an unknown length of time to receive their vaccinations. Seated in an upholstered office chair, Oveta, unusually tense and grim, opened the program with stiffly delivered remarks. She then turned to Scheele, who described the "difficult and delicate" process of producing the vaccine. Scheele explained it typically took about ninety days to make a batch of vaccine. Any sign of problems would extend that production schedule, which was one reason it was difficult to provide precise information about how much vaccine would soon be available. Admitting there would not be enough vaccine to immunize all children that summer, Scheele decided to take the necessary but extremely controversial step of explaining to the public the actual extent of danger that polio posed to those who would not receive a vaccination for several more months. The surgeon general admitted that polio certainly qualified as "a national health problem" but that in reality influenza and pneumonia killed many more children than did polio. Scheele's statement reflected the long-held belief among many medical researchers that the NFIP had oversold polio as a menace to public health. As one critic complained, "Polio has so few patients and gets so much money." Scheele also explained that the chances were "only one in 7,500 that any individual of any age" would get polio, that only one in 32,000 would suffer permanent paralysis, and that only one in 68,000 cases would be fatal. He did warn, however, that there would be scattered local outbreaks and that "some may be severe." Because of the shortage of vaccine, it was critical that polio vaccination decisions be made at the local level and specifically targeted to vulnerable areas instead of attempting to blanket the entire nation.[12]

It should not have been a surprise to anyone that Scheele's fact-based risk assessment of the polio threat not only failed to tamp down public anxiety but also intensified criticism of him, the PHS, and Oveta. The NFIP, which had spent decades stoking terror about polio to justify its massive fundraising campaigns, immediately countered Scheele's statement. The attacks on Oveta continued. At Eisenhower's press conference the day after Oveta and Scheele's broadcast, reporters once again asked the president about

*Oveta Culp Hobby and Surgeon General Dr. Leonard Scheele holding a nationally televised press conference on the polio vaccine crisis, June 7, 1955.*

Oveta's handling of the polio vaccine crisis. The president stressed that his confidence in Oveta had not diminished. She had been "very wise," he said, to insist on safety and caution in the effort not to distribute the vaccine in "mere haste," because of the potential for "disastrous effects."[13]

Oveta not only did little to blunt the attacks, she also continued to take actions and make comments that congressional Democrats eagerly exploited. When Senator Lister Hill submitted a bill to provide free Salk vaccine shots to all children under the age of nineteen, Oveta announced her opposition at a hearing of the Senate Labor and Public Welfare Committee on June 14. Republican senator Barry Goldwater asked her if she thought Senator Hill's plan would create a popular clamor for federal involvement in other public health programs. "I'm sure there would be a demand for it," she replied. Goldwater then asked, "Is there any other term for that [than] socialized medicine?" After a long pause, Oveta replied, "That's socialized medicine by the back door, not the front door." She estimated the cost for each shot would be in the range of $3.50 to $4.20, plus the fee for a doctor's appointment. "Thus the total cost per child will not be great," she declared, ignoring the reality that the shots would cost parents with four baby boomer children nearly $16, equivalent to almost $150 in 2019, not a small expense, even for a middle-class family. She did offer that vaccinations for children from low-income families might need to be subsidized. The Democrats immediately claimed that her statement was further evidence of her lack of sympathy for the poor and her rigid adherence to a heartless conservatism.[14]

Oveta remained undaunted in the face of such criticism. At a White House press conference the day after her Senate testimony, she refused to back away from her opposition to federally funded polio vaccinations. She told reporters that federal taxation would be necessary to pay for the shots, which would cost parents more in the long run than the private medical fees for the vaccine. This argument was widely criticized as specious. She also repeated her charge that it would be a "back door to socialized medicine." With the economy doing well, Oveta declared, there was "no reason that the rest of us can't pay for vaccine for our children." An editorial in the conservative tabloid *New York Daily News* supported Oveta's position. "Start soaking the taxpayers for shots for all the youngsters, and where do we stop? From there on, the road to Socialist medicine would be downhill. We'd wind up with the medical profession enslaved to the bureaucrats in Washington." Less conservative commentators, however, ridiculed such extreme rhetoric.[15]

During the last two weeks of June, Oveta continued to defend her actions in the polio vaccine supply and distribution affair. In an interview on the Mutual Broadcasting System's national radio program *Reporter's Roundup* on June 20, Oveta said she had no apologies to make. "There is nothing I could have done differently," she argued. When questioned about her statement that no one could have foreseen the popular demand for the vaccine, Oveta responded, "It is a question I asked myself. Why couldn't [the Public Health Service] anticipate the demand?" She said the answer PHS had given her was that there had never been "any such demand in the history of the U.S. It has been a unique situation." Perceiving that perhaps Oveta was blaming Scheele and the PHS for not anticipating the demand, the interviewer asked her to elaborate. She replied that under the law, the PHS was responsible for the safety of vaccine. As secretary of HEW, her only responsibility was to license the vaccine on the recommendation of the surgeon general, whom, she added, is appointed by the president. When asked if anyone in the PHS had been negligent in the matter, she stated evasively that she wasn't qualified to answer the question. Apparently realizing the implications of her comments, Oveta quickly added that she wanted "to make clear that I am not dissatisfied with Dr. Scheele's performance," and that if any blame about the controversy was placed on the PHS, she would be "delighted" to share that blame.[16]

Oregon's Democratic senator Richard Neuberger noted Oveta's remarks. He gave a speech on the floor of the Senate in which he accused Oveta of "disloyalty to a subordinate," claiming she had attempted to shift blame from herself to Surgeon General Scheele for problems with the supply and distribution of the Salk vaccine. Republican senator William Purtell of Connecticut immediately came to Oveta's defense, correctly pointing out that Hobby had praised Scheele and the Public Health Service. Scheele followed up with a statement that Hobby had supported the PHS "fully and unqualifiedly in our recent studies on polio vaccine."[17]

On the same day that Senator Neuberger criticized Oveta, the PHS gave her more bad news. The inoculations scheduled to be given as booster shots to previously vaccinated children had been delayed for at least several weeks, if not months, because the supply was "practically exhausted." The pharmaceutical companies had fallen behind on production because of the rigid new standards. After HEW announced this delay, Joseph Rauh, chairman of the liberal political lobby Americans for Democratic Action, charged Oveta with "fantastic fumbling" of the vaccine program. "The inefficiency of Mrs. Hobby's administration is equaled only by its inhumanity," Rauh said. He called on the president to fire her.[18]

Early in July Oveta realized it was time to give up her post. The intense and exhausting battles over HEW's legislative agenda, which had drawn criticism in Congress from members of both parties and resulted in the defeat of two of her most important initiatives; the heavy travel schedule and public appearances; and the stress of Will's declining health had all taken a major toll. But the coup de grace was the ever-intensifying polio vaccine controversy and the constant and virulent personal attacks by the news media and congressional Democrats.

On July 8, the PHS announced that it had given permission to Wyeth Labs to release a batch of Salk vaccine large enough for about three hundred thousand inoculations. This batch of polio vaccine was the first released since the PHS had stopped distribution on June 6. The vaccine would be administered immediately. Oveta took this promising news with her to a private meeting with Eisenhower in the Oval Office prior to a cabinet meeting. The real purpose of the meeting, however, was to tell the president that she would submit her resignation within a week. Because there is no record of their discussion,

Eisenhower's reaction is unknown. It is obvious, however, that they both agreed not to make Oveta's decision known to the public.

After the cabinet meeting, Oveta tried to avoid reporters by quietly exiting from a side door of the White House while the other cabinet members left through the door normally used for their departures. Despite her effort, a group of reporters spotted Oveta, and they began to pepper her with questions. Rumors she would resign, either voluntarily or not, had circulated around the capital for several weeks. Because those rumors had recently intensified, the press was eager to know if they were accurate and if Will's ill health was a factor. One reporter described Oveta as "good humoredly" denying she had submitted her resignation. She told the reporters Will's arthritic condition had improved and he was "making good progress." She stepped into her limousine and was driven away. Afterward, White House spokesman James Hagerty declared, "There is no resignation before us," which was true in a literal sense. Nevertheless, the Associated Press reported that an unnamed "administration source" said that Oveta's resignation was "virtually certain."[19]

On Wednesday, July 13, President Eisenhower invited members of the news media to a previously unscheduled press conference at the White House. This invitation caught the press by surprise, not only because an unscheduled press conference was an unusual event but because the president would be leaving in a few days for Geneva, Switzerland, to attend a summit with the leaders of the United Kingdom, France, and the Soviet Union. For those reasons, the press conference attracted a larger-than-normal crowd of reporters, photographers, and newsreel camera crews. As soon as the members of the press had settled in, they were surprised to see Oveta walk in with the president. Eisenhower went to the podium and announced that Oveta would leave her post as secretary of HEW on August 1. He then turned to look at Oveta, who was standing at his side. "Well, Oveta, this is a sad day for the Administration," the president lamented. "We are just distressed to lose you. In these last two years and a half, your talents have again been devoted to the service of your country, and most effectively. And I would think I could express the feeling of the Cabinet toward you by quoting the Secretary of the Treasury. Shortly after you had told me that you would have to go, I said to [Humphrey] that we were going to lose you. And his eyes popped open and he said, 'What? The best man in the Cabinet?'" Eisenhower then recalled with fondness the first time he met Oveta, then thirty-seven, on the platform of Paddington Station, when she arrived with Eleanor Roosevelt in London in the fall of 1942.[20]

The *New York Times* reported that Oveta "listened intently, looking directly at the President" as he spoke. When he asked her to step up to the microphone to respond, Oveta, who was fighting back tears, stated, "It is impossible for those who love this country to leave its service without regret, no matter how compelling is the reason to leave." In a reference to her departure from the WAC exactly ten years earlier, she noted, "Once again, I feel that deep sense of sadness that comes when one must step out of active duty." Turning toward the president and with her voice breaking, Oveta said, "[I] truly [feel] God has had His hand on the United States in the kind of leadership you have given us."

Obviously embarrassed by being described as God's agent, Eisenhower quipped, "If I had known that you felt like that, I would never have accepted your letter of resignation." As he closed the ceremony, the president added that no one in his administration would forget her "calm confidence in the face of every kind of difficulty" and her "concern for people everywhere."[21]

As soon as the president and Oveta left the conference room, the press began to chatter about the reasons for Oveta's resignation. The stories they filed and the columns they wrote speculated that Eisenhower had forced her to quit because of the Salk polio vaccine controversies. The evidence strongly counters that claim. During Oveta's remaining two weeks as secretary of HEW, Eisenhower and most of Oveta's fellow cabinet members showered her with praise and emotional expressions of regret that she was leaving Washington. And the deep respect and admiration that Eisenhower had for Oveta was clearly evident at the time of her departure from the cabinet. Soon after she submitted her resignation, Eisenhower sent her a deeply personal message reluctantly accepting her decision, admitting that it was "one of the hardest letters I have ever had to write." There was not the slightest hint of discord. He praised her service as founding director of the WAC and extolled her "great qualities of leadership, perseverance . . . and dedication that difficulties could not shake."[22]

Eisenhower and Oveta's relationship remained mutually warm, respectful, and strong until Eisenhower's death in March 1969. In the first volume of his presidential memoir, which was published in 1963, Eisenhower continued to praise her service in his administration. Noting that Oveta had resigned for "personal reasons," which was a reference to Will's bad health, Eisenhower admitted, "Inevitably there were reports that she was leaving under fire." He denied that accusation and then detailed her achievements. Oveta "had earned the thanks of her fellow citizens," he wrote. As the first secretary of the newly created HEW, "she had organized many disparate units and agencies into an effective team and helped to make the heart of government a visible fact." He added that her fellow members of the cabinet, "without exception," had assured him that they regarded her departure from government "as a loss to the nation—as I did."[23]

In his own memoir, Eisenhower's chief of staff, Governor Sherman Adams, testified that in "all of the anguish of the Salk crisis," there had never been a "serious difference of opinion" between Oveta and the president "that changed his high opinion of her ability as an administrator." Adams claimed that the problems in the polio vaccine program "were largely beyond Mrs. Hobby's control. When Mrs. Hobby resigned, her resignation had no connection with the Salk vaccine controversy. She had explained to the President several months earlier that the illness of her husband would require her to give up her work in Washington." At least in public, Oveta always denied she had been dismissed. And in one of the only documented private references she made to this issue, Oveta told Marguerite Johnston, her longtime confidant at the *Houston Post*, that neither President Eisenhower nor anyone else in the administration had forced her to resign. There is no reason to doubt her.[24]

When she announced her resignation, congressional Republicans issued statements praising her work at HEW, while many of the Democrats in the Senate and the House remained silent. The two most powerful Democrats in Congress, however, did not. Senate Majority Leader Lyndon Johnson, who was at home recovering from a heart attack, placed a statement in the *Congressional Record* in which he expressed his regret that Oveta had resigned. Applauding the job she had done to organize HEW, LBJ pointed out that Oveta had faced difficult problems "and met them with the calm dignity of dedicated selflessness that has been the hallmark of her career." As usual, Speaker Sam Rayburn was more to the point. "Mrs. Hobby is a very capable and fine lady," he said. "She and her husband have been friends of mine over the years. Frankly, I think she has had a very rough ride. She is not a doctor, not a scientist, and she has had to take the advice of someone else on things like vaccine."[25]

Many of the newspaper writers and opinion columnists who had bedeviled Oveta editorially during her tenure at HEW had muted reactions to her resignation, but not all. The *New York Times* and the *New York Herald Tribune* both praised Oveta's role in setting up HEW. "Mrs. Hobby showed talents that should be the envy of many [a] highly placed executive," the Republican-leaning *Herald Tribune* declared. "[She] was a thoughtful and skilled advocate of the President's middle-of-the-road philosophy." The *Times* was more restrained. "Mrs. Hobby's career in office has been at times a somewhat stormy one," its editorial pointed out, "but it cannot be said that she lacked enthusiasm or devotion to the task at hand."[26]

Many of Oveta's former and current colleagues at HEW sent personal letters citing her leadership, acknowledging her accomplishments, and thanking her for personal favors. Rufus Miles, for example, cited her "vision and courage in fighting off the attacks on social security and in obtaining legislation to broaden and strengthen the system." Of the letters Oveta received from HEW associates, three in particular undoubtedly attracted her closest attention, eventually finding prominent places in her HEW scrapbook.[27]

One was from Surgeon General Scheele, whose warm letter countered accusations that Oveta had tried to shift blame to him for problems in the polio vaccine program. Scheele stressed how "deeply" he appreciated "the hundred percent support" Oveta had given him and the Public Health Service "in our hours and days of trial on poliomyelitis vaccine problems. No one could have asked for or received better support." Another special letter came from Roswell Perkins, who had become Oveta's most skilled and valuable ally and advisor at HEW. "My many indebtednesses to you quite overwhelm me," he wrote. "I wonder whether you could possibly ever contribute more to the shaping of the career of an individual than you have in my own case." He thanked her for "the unparalleled opportunities you have given me to work intimately with you. . . . I will forever be grateful." Perkins also noted Oveta's "amazingly rapid perception . . . 'lawyer-like' analytical powers . . . human warmth and sensitivity, and . . . keen sense of public opinion and political affairs." He ended his letter with a statement conveying what Oveta must have felt was the ultimate tribute: "As for your qualities of leadership . . . I regard them as matched only by President Eisenhower."[28]

Perhaps the letter Oveta found to be the most interesting was the one she received from Nelson Rockefeller, with whom she had a somewhat complicated relationship. Writing from his new office in the White House, Rockefeller declared it "a sad day in the annals of the Eisenhower Administration. Your departure is a great loss to the American people." He accurately inventoried her accomplishments, citing the major role she had played "in the crusade that swept the President into office," her distinction as one of Eisenhower's "first appointments to a key position," and her work with Senator Taft and the congressional leadership to establish HEW, "the first new Cabinet post in 42 years." He complimented her on undertaking "one of the biggest organizational and administrative jobs in Government" and her "brilliant record" in developing proposals for sweeping revisions in Social Security. "But the official annals cannot adequately record your warmth, understanding, and selflessness," Rockefeller added, "qualities which make you a truly wonderful person, friend, and associate."[29]

Although Oveta appreciated Rockefeller's praise, she might also have been amused by Rockefeller's flattery. She had been well aware of the frustration Rockefeller had felt as Oveta's second-in-command and the cult of personality that some of the women on his staff, chiefly Nancy Hanks, Rockefeller's longtime assistant (as well as one of his lovers), created around "Rocky." Hanks, a magna cum laude graduate of Duke University who would later serve as the head of the National Endowment for the Arts, took the lead in persuading some people at the time, as well as future biographers, that Rockefeller had been the unofficial secretary of HEW, while Oveta had been a figurehead. Nevertheless, Oveta had managed to work successfully with Rockefeller when he was at HEW, and she wasn't immune to his charms. As she was leaving HEW, Oveta sent him a heartfelt letter expressing her thanks for the role he had played in helping her set up the new department. "Your contribution in ideas, in enthusiasm, in loyalty, and most importantly, in real dedication to the American people, is one which I cannot measure," Oveta wrote. It's also clear that despite the snippy remarks emanating from his acolytes, Rockefeller himself developed an appreciation for Oveta's intelligence and common sense. He was also aware of her close relationship with the president and the political connections she continued to enjoy in elements of both major political parties, including with the Senate majority leader. For personal as well as practical reasons related to his own political aspirations, Rockefeller would maintain a warm and respectful relationship with Oveta for many years into the future.[30]

Oveta attended her last cabinet meeting on July 29, 1955. It was a deeply emotional occasion for her. She had participated in these meetings for two and a half years, and as the only woman in the group and as an Eisenhower favorite, she had been the center of attention at many of them. It had given her the opportunity to meet with Eisenhower and his department secretaries on a regular basis, afforded her access to highly privileged information, and empowered her with direct participation in the executive deliberations

*Oveta Culp Hobby enjoys a light moment with Sam Rayburn at her "going away" party at the Washington home of journalists Les and Liz Carpenter, July 29, 1955.*

of the most powerful country in the world. Because the president had only recently returned from an exhausting trip to Europe and a conference with the new Soviet leadership, the agenda for her last cabinet meeting was light. The meeting was shorter than usual in length, which allowed time for a small ceremony to mark Oveta's departure. Eisenhower surprised Oveta with a large Steuben crystal bowl engraved with an inscription and HEW's official seal as a going-away gift from her fellow cabinet members. After the cabinet members and their aides filed out of the room, Oveta remained with the president. While they visited, someone allowed news photographers into the room before Eisenhower was ready for them. As they entered, the photographers could see tears streaming down Oveta's cheeks. Eisenhower immediately waved them out of the room. "I haven't sent for you yet," he barked. When the photographers were called back in, the *New York Times* reported, Oveta was "somewhat red-eyed but composed."[31]

Oveta left the cabinet meeting at the White House and went directly to Liz and Les Carpenter's home to attend a going-away party, not only in her honor but also for fellow Texan Robert Anderson, who was leaving the Eisenhower administration. Nelson Rockefeller, Herbert Brownell, and Harold Stassen as well as most of the Texas congressional delegation attended the party. The members of the Texas delegation included Oveta's friend Waco congressman W. R. Poage, whose marriage proposals she had declined many years ago. Lady Bird Johnson was there without her husband, who was still recuperating from his heart attack. Lady Bird later recalled that Sam Rayburn pulled up a lawn chair and sat next to Oveta. It was clear that the two were not harboring any bad feelings toward each other, despite some reports in the press. "The Speaker was very courtly toward her, as he was toward most women," Lady Bird noted, "but it was quite easy to be courtly to her because she was such an elegant woman." At one point, Rayburn was overheard telling Oveta, "I love you." To which she responded, "Mr. Speaker, you are a man of many prejudices, but I love your prejudices. Go on being prejudiced." The party at the Carpenters' house was not the end of Oveta's going-away events. The next day Oveta traveled to Gettysburg, Pennsylvania, where the president and the First Lady hosted a farewell picnic at their farm, which was attended by Richard Nixon, cabinet members, presidential aides, and other White House staff and their spouses.[32]

Considering Eisenhower's as well as Oveta's behavior as she left her post, it seems obvious that this was not a situation in which a disenchanted boss had fired a poorly performing employee. The first cabinet meeting attended by Marion B. Folsom, Oveta's replacement as secretary of HEW, was held on August 5. After Ike welcomed the new HEW secretary, Folsom replied, "Everybody is going to be awfully disappointed whenever they look down to this end of the table again." Later in the meeting a heated, expletive-filled discussion occurred, behavior that previously had been avoided in deference to the presence of the only woman member of the cabinet. At the end of the discussion, the president commented that if that was going to be the kind of talk he could expect in future meetings, he needed to "get [Oveta] right back here."[33]

Two weeks after Oveta returned to Houston, Eisenhower flew to Denver for what the White House described as a "work and play" vacation that would last until October. Working from his office at Lowry Air Force Base, the president sent word to Oveta on September 6 that he was appointing her to the committee in charge of the White House Conference on Education to be held in November, the same conference Oveta had planned and arranged while she was still secretary of HEW. Eisenhower wrote that he took "particular pleasure in appointing" her to the committee because of her role in proposing the conference when she was dealing with the classroom shortage bills.

*Oveta Culp Hobby at the party in her honor at the Eisenhowers' Gettysburg farm after her resignation from HEW, July 30, 1955. Left to right: Oveta, President Eisenhower, Richard Nixon, Mamie Eisenhower, and Nelson Rockefeller.*

Significantly, the president added that he had made the appointment "mainly because it brings you officially back to the 'team.'" After she accepted the appointment, Oveta brought in Clint Pace, a political reporter for the *Houston Post*, to serve as the conference coordinator.[34]

Late in the day on September 24, Oveta was stunned when a *Houston Post* editor brought her the wire service teletype copy reporting that Eisenhower had suffered a heart attack early that morning and had been rushed to Fitzsimons Army Hospital in Aurora, Colorado. Like most of the nation, she relied on the continuing flow of wire service reports to keep up with Eisenhower's medical progress. The implications were that his situation was dire. On September 29 she received a detailed, single-spaced, two-page letter from Eisenhower's personal physician, Dr. Howard Snyder, describing the sequence of events when Ike suffered his heart attack, even listing the drugs he administered to the president. Snyder had served as Eisenhower's personal physician since 1945, and he was a confidant of the president. Snyder had gotten to know Oveta when he was among those she had consulted on medical matters during her days at HEW. His message reads like he was writing to someone who still held a high position in the administration. "We will guard him carefully," Snyder assured Oveta, adding ominously, "if and when he returns to his desk as President of the U.S." While Eisenhower was in Denver recuperating, Oveta sent him a box of musical recordings to enjoy. He responded with a letter: "Dear Oveta, Surprisingly, there are a number of compensations for my present enforced inactivity. I am having a fine time listening at intervals to old (and new) favorites. As usual, you intuitively knew what I would like." After a long recuperation, Eisenhower recovered fully and was released from the hospital on November 11. He and Mamie returned to their farm in Gettysburg to continue his rest before going back to the White House. Mamie took the time to send Oveta personal notes reporting on her husband's progress. Six days after arriving at the farm, Mamie wrote Oveta that Ike was "gaining in strength and vigor daily." As evidence of the Eisenhowers' warm feelings for Oveta, Mamie added, "We miss you so much and think of you often."[35]

On August 12, two weeks after she departed from Washington, Oveta's relentless efforts to prevent the federal government from taking control of the polio vaccination program finally succeeded. Congress passed the Poliomyelitis Vaccination Assistance Act of 1955, allocating $30 million for distribution to the states as grants to pay for vaccinating children from low-income families. According to the provisions of the act, federal involvement in the vaccination program would remain restricted to certifying the safety of the vaccine. Supply and distribution would continue on a voluntary basis. This legislation represented a major victory for Oveta in her battle to keep the vaccination program on a voluntary basis.[36]

"I can't help but look back thoughtfully over the last two and a half years—what we've been able to do and what we haven't," Oveta wrote Nelson Rockefeller as she was leaving the Eisenhower administration. "It is still too early to see in any perspective, but at least I feel that important steps have been taken toward bettering the life of the American people." Two decades later, when newly elected president Jimmy Carter appointed Juanita Kreps and Patricia Harris to his cabinet, the *Dallas Times Herald* interviewed Oveta about her memories of being the second woman in American history to serve on a presidential cabinet. Oveta told the interviewer that she believed her most important accomplishments included organizing HEW and expanding Social Security coverage to more Americans, especially to farmers, whose financial hardships during old age she had witnessed as a child growing up in Central Texas. Prior to the expansion, she explained, when a "farmer was disabled or died, there was no money to keep the family together." When asked to name her worst experience, she quickly admitted it was the Salk polio vaccine crisis. "We had to stop the manufacture of Salk vaccine," she recalled, "take it off the market for a while, put it back on the market, because . . . children died from it. . . . That to me was the most heartbreaking thing of all."[37]

Those who have assessed Oveta's performance in the Eisenhower administration have generally agreed that her most important policy achievement was her leadership in getting Congress to expand Social Security coverage, but that victory was largely obscured by the Salk vaccine debacle. In the latter matter, however, those who oppose government involvement in health care have given her much credit for fending off attempts to federalize the vaccination program and for ultimately shepherding it to a successful conclusion. Despite the ups and downs she experienced as head of what was at the time the largest department in the federal government, Oveta always remained proud of her service on the cabinet and her opportunity to work closely with one of the men she most admired in her life: Dwight Eisenhower. "I feel a deep sense of sorrow at leaving the service of a great man," Oveta told Rockefeller. Although she had great pride in her work during World War II, she considered her work at HEW to have been "an experience unparalleled in my life." When an oral history interviewer asked how she felt about those thirty months she served on the cabinet, without hesitation Oveta declared, "I shall always regard it as one of the greatest things that ever happened to me."[38]

## CHAPTER 39

# OVETA COMES HOME

W ill's health and spirits were greatly boosted by Oveta's return to Houston in August 1955. Les Carpenter, the *Houston Post*'s Washington correspondent, visited Houston that fall, and he wrote Oveta that it was "wonderful to see the Governor looking so good and finding him as full as ever of his delightful wit and good sense. He gave the nicest luncheon for us and made the kindest talk." Despite Will's rejuvenation, he was ready once again to pass on to Oveta management of the *Post* and the broadcast entities. Within days after her return to Houston, Will officially transferred all executive responsibilities to his wife, who was eager to reassume direction over their media business after nearly four years' absence. Will assumed the title of chairman of the board of the Houston Post Company, which relieved him from the daily pressures of supervising the family media enterprises. Oveta became president and editor of the *Houston Post*.[1]

When the *Post* announced Will and Oveta's new executive titles, the press release stressed that Oveta had "returned to Houston to resume direction of the newspaper with the Governor." Oveta insisted the statement be worded to reflect that she and Will would be equal partners in managing the *Post*, but in reality the *Post* was now more Oveta's than Will's. The restoration of Will's energy would not last long. His health soon returned to a state of gradual decline, and the long period of coleadership of the family business had come to an unofficial end. Even while she served in the Eisenhower administration, Oveta had received a copy of every edition of the *Houston Post* by airmail, and she continued to monitor and occasionally, as in the case of the Minute Women exposé, direct the managing editor to assign staff to write stories on special topics of interest to her. Nevertheless, her involvement in the daily operations of the *Post* and KPRC had been limited by the demands of her job at the Department of Health, Education, and Welfare.[2]

Oveta's now almost daily presence in the office marked a significant change in the work environment for a news and editorial staff more accustomed to Will's laid-back

---

manner and infrequent involvement in day-to-day operations. His associates recalled that as a manager, Will "had a knack of communicating warmth and friendliness and the ability to ease a tense situation with his humor." A story in the *Dallas Morning News* quoted one of Will's friends: "What kind of modest, good-humored fellow Will Hobby is, his favorite nickname is 'Guv.' He ran the newspaper, in an informal, casual and yet very efficient fashion."[3]

Anecdotes about Will and his easygoing ways were part of *Houston Post* staff lore. Longtime workers in the newspaper's printing operation often told a story about one of Will's excursions in the plant during the Christmas season. A printer in the *Post's* back shop violated a company rule by downing a drink from a bottle of whiskey circulating while he tended the machinery during a press run. Not noticing that Will was standing behind him, the printer passed the whiskey bottle over his shoulder to "Governor," who took a large swig, quietly gave the bottle to the next man, and then went about his business without saying a word.[4]

One can't imagine Oveta silently taking that shot of whiskey in the *Post's* printshop. Except for being "very efficient," Oveta shared few of Will's personal qualities as a business manager. She was not unfriendly to her employees and she occasionally showed warmth and a sense of humor, but "informal," "casual," and "modest," were not terms normally used to describe her behavior in the office. Despite the stark differences in personalities and management styles between Will and Oveta, from every indication it appears that Oveta's return to management went smoothly, with minimal grumbling among the staff. Despite Will's up and down health, he remained a presence at the *Post*, even when he was confined to his home. When his health allowed it, Will went to his office at the *Post*, which was adjacent to Oveta's. And when Will didn't feel well enough to go to the newspaper, he and Oveta often worked together in an office that covered the entire third story of their Shadyside mansion. Until Will's passing in 1964, Oveta organized much of her life around the state of her husband's health, and the two were nearly inseparable.[5]

Oveta's return to full-time duty at the *Post* and her focus on Will did not keep her from paying close attention to national political and public policy developments. She was eager for insider news about the political scene in Washington, which her Capitol correspondents Leslie and Liz Carpenter dutifully and regularly provided. Oveta was particularly curious about Lyndon Johnson's political ambitions and machinations. In December 1955, Les Carpenter reported in lengthy detail about a trip he made to LBJ's ranch in the Texas Hill Country when US senator Estes Kefauver of Tennessee paid a visit. Carpenter wrote Oveta, "[I am] convinced that Lyndon has completely put prospects that he might be nominated President out of his mind." Carpenter added that although LBJ assured him that he would not accept the Democratic Party's nomination for vice president in 1956, Carpenter had reasons "to believe he would." Oveta and LBJ maintained close ties as the senator maneuvered toward a possible presidential bid in 1960. Whenever Lyndon Johnson learned that Oveta was traveling to Washington, he would ask her to meet with him to discuss politics. When the American Society of Newspaper Editors held its annual convention in Washington in 1959, LBJ asked Oveta to "drop by my office in the Capital [*sic*] about 5 PM on Thursday. There'll be a pot of coffee, refreshments and a little time to relax. May I count on seeing you? I'm hoping we can get together for a few minutes of 'Texas talk' while you're here." Oveta accepted the invitation, and over a drink in the majority leader's office she and LBJ discussed his political options for 1960.[6]

As had been the case when Oveta left Washington in 1945, her departure from HEW and return to Houston in 1955 soon generated invitations for her to become involved in other public policy projects and to join the boards of a variety of corporations and organizations. Corporate board memberships that came her way during these years included the board of directors of Mutual of New York in May 1956, where she became the company's first woman board member—another one of her growing list of "firsts." She also received a number of honors to add to her growing collection of official accolades. Among those extended in the fall of 1955 was one given to her in Dallas, where she was declared Woman of the Year on Women's Day at the State Fair of Texas before an audience of five thousand. Three days later she and Will traveled to Austin, where the Texas Heritage Foundation recognized her as the Texian Woman of the Year at a dinner hosted by Edgar H. Perry Sr., a friend of Will's since his days as governor. Lyndon Johnson and Governor Allan Shivers both gave speeches praising Oveta.[7]

Oveta also received numerous invitations to speak, many of which she declined because of Will's poor health or the press of work at the *Post*. Among those she did accept was an invitation from the American Bankers Association to address the association's annual Trust Division Conference in Houston in November 1955. This group might have been of special interest to Oveta because of her and Will's involvement in the banking business. They still controlled a bank in Cleburne in north-central Texas, and Oveta was joining with an investment group of nineteen fellow Houstonians, including prominent attorney George Butler, oilman Michel Halbouty, and heart surgeon Denton Cooley, to apply for a charter for a new state bank in Houston. Addressing an audience of six hundred fellow bankers, Oveta declared that everything possible should be done to maintain world peace for the sake of US domestic stability, pointing out that stability was essential to the health of the banking industry.[8]

Although Oveta's professional reputation in some quarters had been badly battered by the polio vaccine controversy, a Gallup Poll released in January 1956 revealed she had made the poll's list of the top ten most-admired living women in the world in the opinion of the American public. Oveta joined Eleanor Roosevelt, who headed the list, Oveta's friends Clare Boothe Luce and Mamie Eisenhower, Helen Keller, Queen Elizabeth II, Madame Chiang Kai-shek, and Maine's Republican senator Margaret Chase Smith. This had to be exhilarating news for Oveta, who had been deeply wounded by the virulent personal attacks in her last weeks as secretary of HEW.[9]

Oveta's spirits were given another boost in May 1956 when Mary Hardin–Baylor

*Oveta Culp Hobby after receiving an honorary degree from Mary Hardin-Baylor College, May 1956. Joining Oveta are her mother, Emma Culp, and her sister, Juanita.*

College in Killeen gave her an honorary doctorate and asked her to deliver the school's commencement address. By this time, Oveta had already been given fourteen honorary college degrees, some of them from much more prestigious institutions than the little college in her hometown. This honor, however, was special. Oveta's mother, Emma, and her sister Juanita were in the audience and were given recognition by the school's president. With memories of Emma's suffragist days undoubtedly on her mind, Oveta urged the new graduates of the all-female school to make good use of the rights that women of earlier generations were denied. She also advised them to "form a strong purpose in life and to learn how to examine every new idea thoroughly and then courageously adopt or discard it. A purpose gives meaning to life. It is like the hub of a wheel with every spoke fitted into it to make a strong and perfect circle."[10]

While Oveta and Will were in Killeen, Jesse Jones lay dying in Houston's St. Luke's Hospital. Only three months earlier, the Hobbys had joined a throng of one thousand who had gathered at the Rice Hotel to honor Jones for his recent philanthropic gifts to the city's educational and charitable institutions. Jones had endured an emergency gall bladder operation in 1953 and had lingered near death for several days. Although he survived that bout of ill health, he never regained his previous vigor. He and Will had continued their card games and lunches, but with Will's own failing health and Jones's decline, those visits happened less frequently as time passed. During the night of June 1, 1956, four days after Will and Oveta's visit to Killeen, Jesse Jones died of kidney failure at the age of seventy-nine. It was a deeply sorrowful loss for Will. Oveta's feelings must have been more complicated. She had always had something akin to a love/hate relationship with the powerful "Mr. Houston." Other than the expected published personal expressions of praise and condolence and the *Post*'s editorials celebrating his life and achievements, however, there is little evidence documenting her private reaction to Jones's death.[11]

Oveta's active outside interests after her departure from Washington also included an ambitious and complex endeavor by another friend with presidential ambitions: Nelson Rockefeller. In November 1956, her former deputy at HEW assumed the presidency of the Rockefeller Brothers Fund, a $60 million endowment established by his father, John D. Rockefeller Jr., with Nelson and his four brothers (Laurance, Winthrop, David, and John D. Rockefeller III) serving as trustees. The Rockefeller brothers' father created the fund as an entirely separate entity from the famed Rockefeller Foundation. It was established as a philanthropic vehicle for the brothers to support and guide their individual projects, with Nelson's focus being the study of public policy issues.[12]

Nelson Rockefeller's first major program, which he initiated in the spring of 1956, was the Special Studies Project, which had the grandiose purpose of enlisting the talents of 108 of the nation's prominent citizens to identify, study, and recommend strategies for addressing the challenges the United States faced in world affairs in the coming years and to define America's national purpose as it extended its global reach. The prominent citizens Rockefeller recruited included nuclear physicist Edward Teller, RCA founder and NBC head David Sarnoff, economist Arthur Burns, Notre Dame University president Theodore Hesburgh, army general Lucius Clay, former FDR "brain trust" member Adolf Berle Jr., Time-Life publisher Henry Luce, Massachusetts governor Christian Herter, Rockefeller Foundation president Dean Rusk, and other business, academic, cultural, and political leaders. Because the project was launched under the shadow of the ongoing Cold War, half of the issues chosen for study related to some aspect of US foreign policy. More than one hundred experts in a wide variety of public policy issues also joined the project as researchers on selected topics, while a staff, headed by Rockefeller's close associate Nancy Hanks, provided managerial, editorial, and clerical support. To direct the overall project, Rockefeller recruited noted political scientist Henry Kissinger, who took a leave from his faculty position at Harvard. Oveta eagerly accepted Rockefeller's invitation to be a member of the group that would serve as the project's "overall panel." Two other women whom Oveta knew, military defense specialist Anna Rosenberg and attorney and journalist Margaret Hickey, also joined the project. To justify including three women on this otherwise all-male enterprise, Rockefeller explained to his associates the project could benefit from a bit of "the woman's view point."[13]

Oveta attended the organizing forum for the Special Studies Project in May 1956, held at Rockefeller Center in Midtown Manhattan. Because of the substantial number of participants, the meeting took place in a large room in the Radio City Music Hall where the famed Rockettes rehearsed. At this first assembly, Rockefeller and Kissinger explained their hopes for the project. They explained that during the summer they would work with staff to identify subject areas for study and to devise a work plan for the project, which would be conducted by six subpanels of the overall panel. An initial list of issues to study had already been compiled, and research would begin during the summer.[14]

Oveta's active involvement in the Special Studies Project was an opportunity for her to be closely connected to the airy world of policy wonks and academics, public-policy-oriented business and news media figures, and political leaders interested in an intellectual approach to confronting issues of national importance. This experience, among others, also enhanced her intellectual credentials and gave her added confidence when she later assumed a position on the governing board of Rice University, despite not having a college degree. In the coming years, Oveta would also draw heavily from the ideas that freely circulated among the members of the project as she shaped the editorial content and news coverage of the *Post*.

From the start, Nelson Rockefeller made it clear to Oveta that he expected her to play an active role in project deliberations and actions and that he needed her personal counsel. In mid-September 1956, after a summer of project planning, Rockefeller sent Oveta a list of people he was considering for membership on the panels, as well as a draft memorandum outlining the project's organization. "Everything seems to be going extremely well as far as the studies themselves are concerned," Rockefeller told her. "Some 71 papers have been commissioned and are in the works. These will be the basis for the discussions in each of the six areas which the project is to cover." Urging Oveta to review the organizational plan and the study topics closely, Rockefeller said he would soon call to get her reaction and her suggestions. When Rockefeller called her four days later, Oveta gave him a detailed critique. In a letter to Oveta immediately after their phone conversation, Rockefeller enclosed a revised draft of the memorandum that reflected most of Oveta's suggestions, which included her recommendations on word usage. "We changed the word 'beliefs,'" Rockefeller wrote, "but after long discussion decided to keep the word 'develop.'" Referring to the overall panel, Rockefeller told Oveta it "should be tremendously interesting and a lot of fun."[15]

At the end of October, Rockefeller told Oveta that a final decision had been made to have the subpanels meet four or five times between November 1956 and spring 1957. He asked Oveta to participate in subpanel six on the "challenge and opportunity" of the democratic process in the United States. The panel also included James A. Perkins, vice president of the Carnegie Corporation; Justin Dart, founder of the Rexall drugstore chain; and General Lucius Clay, former military governor of the US occupation zone in Germany and a confidant of President Eisenhower's. The subject was of great interest to Oveta. She readily agreed to be on the subpanel, explaining that it was the one she would have selected herself, but she insisted that she was unable to serve as chair. She told Rockefeller she would attend the subpanel dinner at the Plaza Hotel in Manhattan on November 20 and the working meeting the next morning. Pleased by Oveta's acceptance, Rockefeller stressed that he wanted her subpanel to have a special focus on Communism's threat to "the democratic idea" worldwide and "the question of whether the United States could live up to its own values."[16]

Rockefeller and Kissinger presided over the meeting of Oveta's subpanel in New York City in December. Kissinger selected two members of each subpanel to draft "thought" papers identifying challenges the United States faced over the next decade. He stressed that the subpanel members weren't expected to propose specific policy recommendations. Instead, they should "develop the conceptual framework on which policy might be based, sketch longer term trends, and outline alternative means of coping with them." Rockefeller explained that the panels should "have an oral presentation, and then a discussion on the papers." After deliberation, the revised draft papers would eventually be added to the records of the overall panel. Oveta's role in this process was to contribute to the discussions, but she was not expected to write any of the papers. The Special Studies staff, under Nancy Hanks's direction, would collate, revise, and edit the papers. Kissinger, who was skilled at synthesizing complex subjects into understandable texts, would take the edited drafts and author most of the final published reports.[17]

After four months of research and writing by the project panelists, Oveta traveled to New York City on Sunday, April 28, 1957, to attend three days of meetings of the Special Studies overall panel at the Waldorf Astoria. The meeting schedule included one day at the fabled Rockefeller family compound, located twenty miles north of Manhattan in Sleepy Hollow. Oveta played a key role in the redrafting of her subpanel's report. After she returned to Houston, she told Rockefeller, "[I have] never attended a meeting which was better conducted or which drew out its participants as much as did the Overall Panel meetings at Sleepy Hollow. The more I attend the meetings, the more I am convinced that the results may be among the most valuable contributions the Rockefeller interests have made." Rockefeller appreciated Oveta's "tremendous personal contribution. [Y]our presence meant a great deal. Your active participation in the subpanels helped bring the issues into focus in a way that made an important contribution."[18]

Oveta was deeply engaged in the Special Studies Project until the publication of the final overall report in 1961, a date much later than Rockefeller had planned. Will's health was slightly better in 1956 and 1957, when much of the work was done, which made it easier for Oveta to travel to New York to attend most of the panel meetings. Always supportive and proud of his wife, the increasingly frail Will was nevertheless not particularly happy whenever Oveta was away from home. And he had only a general idea about what the Special Studies Project was about. As far as he knew, it was "some accomplishment with Rockefeller Brothers," as he explained to his sister Laura. When Oveta was away for a few days on one of her trips to New York, Will also told Laura "*aside* from" Oveta being in New York, "we are doing well."[19]

When Will's health took a bad turn in 1958 and Oveta was unable to travel to New York, Rockefeller and Kissinger often conferred with her on the telephone. They also sent drafts of reports to Houston, which Oveta carefully critiqued and edited, paying attention to word choices, tone, and content to make certain they accurately reflected the views of the panel members. When she sent a multipage critique of the first draft of the overall report to Kissinger, Oveta stated, "The report is very good and the ideas clearly expressed. It is appropriate that the first chapters should lean rather heavily toward broad philosophy for purposes of orientation. There are, at the same time, sufficient concrete facts to hold the interest of the reader." At one point, she told Rockefeller that Kissinger had called her to fill her in on the status of some of the reports. "He sent me two of them" Oveta said, "and I am very much interested in the one on philosophy which I am now reading." After a panel meeting in New York in September 1957, Kissinger told Oveta "how very helpful you've been to me. Whenever you have thoughts on the report I do hope you will let me have them. And of course if you will permit me, I would like to take the liberty of asking your advice on chapters as we get them finished."[20]

At the end of September 1957, Oveta sent Kissinger clippings of a *Houston Post* news story about the Special Studies Project and an editorial that Bill Hobby wrote praising the project. The clips were attached to a note in which Oveta assured Kissinger, in a statement that likely fudged the truth, that the story and the editorial had "appeared without any influence from me in the *Houston Post*. As you can see, both found your report enormously worthwhile." Following one of the key work sessions conducted in New York in December 1957, Rockefeller wrote Oveta that he was "tremendously grateful to you for your long trip up and back. You certainly were effective in the meeting and thanks to you and Lucius [Clay], I think we have something that will be very exciting." He added that Adolf Berle and Dean Rusk had reviewed her recommendations closely. "We hope to get the final draft out tomorrow to everybody. It really looks terrific." Kissinger agreed with Rockefeller about Oveta's suggestions. "I very much agree with your comments. We have redone some of the pertinent chapters in order to include your suggestions. Your point about including the problem of leisure seemed to me particularly powerful."[21]

In January 1958 the first panel report was published to great acclaim. Doubleday printed four hundred thousand copies in its first run. NBC's *Today Show* promoted the report on the air, distributing two hundred thousand copies to viewers who requested them, while Doubleday shipped the remainder to bookstores and newsstands. Nelson Rockefeller was delighted. He told Oveta how much he appreciated the role she played in the project's first published report. "Your enthusiasm and thoughtfulness every step of the way ensured success of the project before any publication was made."[22]

Oveta had some issues with the next report, which was that of panel six on economic and social policy. She submitted a five-page critique to Kissinger, stating that although it was "a highly readable document, the section on the farm problem" troubled her. She feared that the recommendation that government should initiate a program to encourage small farmers to move to cities could be criticized as "taking an inhumane attitude toward 3 million or so sub-marginal farm families. Someone almost certainly will compare it with the Russian campaign to liquidate the Kulaks." She pointed out that the migration of the farm population to urban areas had been going on for several years and was "likely to continue gradually through the operation of natural forces." She felt a "deliberate governmental program to speed it up is, politically speaking, quite something else. Since most of these people are unskilled, would we not simply be transferring our problems from the country to the city? Perhaps at a much greater cost ultimately than subsidizing and trying to sustain them on the farm." Addressing her largely urban-centered fellow panel members, she also defended the historical role of small farmers and small towns, which "have contributed importantly to the molding of our national character and culture. One might ask: Should we not try to preserve them—to the extent possible—rather than liquidate them?" Kissinger agreed with her comments. "I think you will find a more careful statement of the agricultural problem in the next draft as a result."[23]

Oveta also had a problem with the panel five report, which focused on the utilization of human resources. She complained to Kissinger that it was too philosophically broad, and its discussion of the educational system was inadequate. "The report seems to be addressed more to those with a professional interest in the philosophy of education than to the general public," she stated. Kissinger agreed. He urged her to come to the next meeting in New York to elaborate: "Both Nelson and I feel that your presence would be a tremendous encouragement and assistance." Unfortunately, Will was recovering from major surgery to correct a life-threatening condition, which made it impossible for Oveta to leave Houston.[24]

On March 8, 1958, Will's health had stabilized enough to allow Oveta to travel to New York to attend what she considered to be the final meeting of her subpanel, which had recently finished a draft of its report. Nelson Rockefeller presided as he, Oveta, and her fellow panel members conducted a page-by-page review of the draft. At the end of the meeting, Nelson asked the panel to work with a project staff writer to produce a final version. The completed document was submitted to the overall panel during the summer of 1958, where it remained without further action. Considering her work done, Oveta wrote Nelson: "I don't think I have to tell you that for me, the opportunity to serve on the Panel was one of the most tremendous experiences of my life." She asked for advance copies of all the panel reports before they were distributed to the public, because the *Post* could mine them for editorials. In response Nelson assured Oveta, "Not only was your advice invaluable when we were organizing the studies but your guidance throughout has meant a great deal to me."[25]

Nelson Rockefeller's successful bid for the Republican nomination for governor of New York in the summer of 1958 and his subsequent campaign and ultimate victory in November delayed completion of the Special Studies Project. Laurance Rockefeller replaced his brother as chair of the overall panel, and he and Kissinger were able to get three panel reports completed and published during the winter and spring of 1959. In August 1959, Laurance scheduled a meeting of the overall panel in New York, to be held in September. Kissinger sent a draft of the report on US international objectives to Oveta and her fellow panel members, stressing that it was urgent they review the document and provide a critique in time for the meeting. By then, however, Will Hobby's health had taken yet another bad turn, and Oveta found it difficult to leave Houston, much less provide a thorough review of the new draft.[26]

Oveta missed the September meeting, but she was able to submit her critique of the latest report. She argued that the section on the "Pacific Community" put too much emphasis on defense issues and that it should instead stress the "existing and growing community of interests with Asian and Pacific nations outside the Communist orbit. It has always seemed to me that this is a weakness in our national thinking." Laurance Rockefeller replied that he and Dean Rusk agreed with her recommendation, adding that they were "grateful for all you have done."[27]

The only panel report that remained unfinished was the one on which Oveta and her colleagues had worked. On October 20, 1959, the panel chair, John Dickey, reminded Oveta and her fellow panel members that their work had started three years ago and that "most of us have been through what sometimes seems like countless meetings and drafts in an effort to fulfill the assigned task." Frustrated by the delay in completing their work, Dickey observed that their collective effort "indubitably has demonstrated the difficulty of using the democratic process to write a report on the democratic process." He distributed a draft that he and the project staff believed "creditably reflects the consensus of our efforts" and asked the panelists to let him know if they agreed that "we in good conscience now feel we have met our responsibility." Oveta approved this latest draft, which ended her work in the Special Studies Project.[28]

The Rockefeller Brothers Fund finally published Oveta's panel's report, "The Power of the Democratic Idea," in September 1960, four years after they initiated the project. Authored largely by Roswell Perkins and Charles Frankel, the latter a professor of philosophy at Columbia University, the report reflected the underlying elitist assumptions of the previous five reports with its argument that "governing elites should forge a consensus and then implement policy." As a member of Houston's power elite "8F crowd," that surely was an argument with which Oveta could identify. Her panel's report also declared, "Government, political parties, media of communication, and all other agencies of society . . . do not simply reflect [public opinion]. They form and inform it and give it its direction and mode of expression." This idea was also familiar to Oveta, who believed strongly that the mission of the media of communication—in her case, the *Houston Post*—was not simply to inform but also to lead and direct.[29]

"The Power of the Democratic Idea" was integrated with the other five panel reports into the Special Studies Project's final publication, *Prospect for America*, published by Doubleday in March 1961. *Prospect for America* eventually sold six hundred thousand copies, an astounding number for a "think tank" publication. Oveta was pleased with the final result of more than four years of work. She sent Laurance Rockefeller a telegram: "Delighted with [the book's] sense of concern and challenge. Preface excellent." The *Houston Post* promoted *Prospect for America* by publishing a laudatory book review as well as a column by Marguerite Johnston praising the work of the Special Studies Project.[30]

The Special Studies Project had little influence on the Eisenhower administration. By the time most of the reports were released, Eisenhower's presidency was in its last days. In addition, many members of the administration felt that the Rockefeller reports were critical of the president's record. Ironically, the reports would gain a small measure of influence in John F. Kennedy's administration. The most important results of the project, however, included the elevation of Henry Kissinger to national prominence and the burnishing of Nelson Rockefeller's credentials as a public policy innovator, which proved useful in his successful election campaign in 1958 for governor of New York. It also helped make Rockefeller a viable, if unsuccessful, candidate for the Republican nomination for president.[31]

The completion of the Special Studies Project did not end Oveta's involvement with Rockefeller brothers projects. Before the Special Studies Project closed its offices, she agreed in the summer of 1959 to serve as a member of the advisory council for an environmental conservation project, the awkwardly titled Outdoor Recreation Resources Review Commission, which had been established by Congress in 1958, with Laurance Rockefeller serving as chairman. Congress gave the bipartisan commission the task of determining the nation's present and future outdoor recreational needs. Although this was not one of Oveta's special interests, she enjoyed her relationship with the Rockefeller family and was reluctant to turn down the invitation. She managed to attend a couple of council meetings, and she critiqued the draft of a public survey that was eventually used to gauge public attitudes about various forms of outdoor recreation. She also had one of her *Post* columnists write an article about the commission's work, using the text of a speech Laurance Rockefeller gave to the American Forestry Association. After a

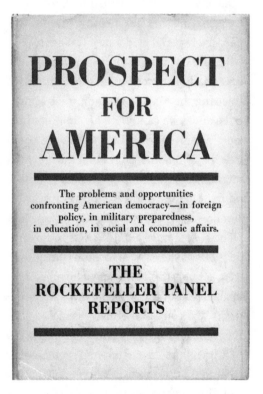

*Cover of the Special Studies Project publication,* Prospect for America, *1961.*

year and a half, however, Oveta resigned from the council. She had missed several meetings and had been unable to find time to review various documents the commission had sent her. "Not only is it impossible for me to attend the Board meetings," Oveta explained to Laurance, "but it is impossible for me to give adequate service in any other way."[32]

Oveta's involvement in the Rockefeller brothers' projects gave her a continuing connection to two of the wealthiest and most interesting men in America, particularly Nelson Rockefeller. Although Oveta had often been frustrated with "Rocky" when he was her second-in-command at HEW, she nevertheless was fascinated by him, and they maintained an informal if not a close relationship for the rest of his life. After he entered the race for governor of New York in 1958, Rockefeller kept Oveta informed about his chances for victory, at one point telling her he was "running just about neck and neck" with his opponent, incumbent governor Averell Harriman. After Rockefeller won the election, Oveta called to congratulate him. They spent several minutes in an affable private conversation reminiscing about their work at HEW and Rocky's hopes for his governorship. When Rockefeller visited Houston in December 1959, Oveta traveled to Houston's International Airport to greet him as he stepped off his flight. She also helped make arrangements for him to meet with local business leaders during the day he spent in the city. After he returned to New York, Rockefeller sent a warm thank you letter to Oveta, stating that her meeting him "at the airport in Houston meant more to me than I can say. I was so glad to see you again."[33]

Despite Oveta's good relationship with Rockefeller over the years, his mercurial ways occasionally annoyed her. In the summer of 1960, Rockefeller released a public statement criticizing the Eisenhower administration's defense policies. He also declared he would not be an active candidate for the Republican presidential nomination that year but he would accept a draft. In a telephone conversation with Eisenhower after Rockefeller made his comments, Oveta told the president she deplored Rockefeller's remarks, adding that she was irritated by Rockefeller's indecision about running for the 1960 presidential nomination. She told Eisenhower it was "sad," because Rockefeller had great potential. Eisenhower agreed with Oveta's assessment.[34]

The *Houston Post* and KPRC's radio and television stations prospered in the mid and late 1950s as the city of Houston continued to experience phenomenal growth. Although Oveta actively directed overall business matters and editorial policy, she delegated daily management of the newspaper to Arthur Laro and the broadcast units to Jack Harris. Oveta's work outside of business included not only continued involvement in the Special Studies Project but also participation in Eisenhower's reelection campaign.

Oveta and the president had remained in touch, often by telephone, ever since she left Washington. Eisenhower's happy birthday message to Oveta in January 1956 conveyed his undiminished admiration. "I am struck once again by the sense of loss I have felt ever since you left Washington," Eisenhower wrote. "We miss you very much." After Eisenhower announced his candidacy for a second term, Oveta kept up a steady stream of messages to boost his efforts. She telephoned the president the morning after he made an evening television broadcast to the nation to explain his veto of a farm bill sponsored by the Democrats, which he claimed was an irresponsible waste of federal funds. Oveta told Eisenhower his speech had been extremely effective and she doubted Congress would overturn his veto, which turned out to be an accurate prediction. Soon after the call, Eisenhower dispatched a note to Oveta. "Many thanks for your enthusiastic telephone call after the talk last night," the president wrote. "Your approval means a great deal to me, especially in a situation as delicate and difficult as was this one."[35]

In the months immediately following the president's heart attack, there had been intense speculation about whether he would run for a second term. Although she was concerned about the president's health, Oveta fervently hoped that he would run again if given the green light by his cardiologist, Dr. Paul Dudley White. The president, who was struggling with his decision, had refused to announce one way or the other. Nevertheless, only one month after Eisenhower's coronary, Republican Party moderates and pro-Eisenhower Democrats resurrected Citizens for Eisenhower, the campaign organization established in 1952 as a bipartisan counterweight to the ultraconservative Taft wing of the Republican establishment and its McCarthyite allies. Oveta played a key role in this effort. She joined the advisory board and worked closely with fellow board members Lucius Clay, Augusta National Golf Club founder Clifford Roberts, and Goldman Sachs partner Sidney Weinberg to set up an office, hire staff, produce campaign literature, and raise funds for the upcoming campaign. Oveta contributed $1,000 to the organization, edited and revised official letters and brochures, and consulted frequently with Clay, Roberts, and Weinberg on campaign strategy, especially on how to retain the votes of Democrats who had supported Eisenhower in 1952.[36]

Oveta conducted her work for Citizens for Eisenhower by correspondence and telephone calls made from her office at the *Houston Post*. She also traveled to Washington in January 1956 to attend a board meeting at the Mayflower Hotel. At that gathering, Oveta, Clay, and Weinberg signed a letter that was distributed to the supporters of the 1952 Citizens for Eisenhower, announcing their conviction that Ike would run for a second term, "provided he finds that his health will permit him to carry the load." The letter stressed it was imperative that the various groups that were organizing on his behalf be consolidated into one organization: Citizens for Eisenhower. "It is not our intent to bring pressure upon [the president] as those of us who will enter into the movement will accept his decision cheerfully," she stated.[37]

Thomas Campbell, an agribusiness tycoon and major fundraiser for the GOP who had dealt with Oveta during her tenure at HEW, wrote her that he was pleased she and other Republican moderates had revived the Citizens organization. "I found it easier to raise money for Citizens for Eisenhower than for the Republican Party, which is still not progressive enough for the present generation." After meeting with Sherman Adams, Campbell told Oveta, "I left Washington feeling that the President would be a candidate for reelection even if he is not one hundred percent well." Campbell's feelings proved to be accurate. Finally given a clean bill of health and under intense pressure to make a decision, Eisenhower declared his candidacy in late February 1956. After Eisenhower's announcement, Oveta returned to New York City in March to discuss campaign strategy with Weinberg and General Clay at lunch at the Sherry-Netherland Hotel. The following day the three leaders hosted a larger meeting of Citizens for Eisenhower.[38]

Eisenhower's nomination for a second term was never in doubt. But he refused to openly endorse the nomination of Richard Nixon as his vice president. Nixon's status remained unresolved until the national convention in San Francisco in August. Whether

Nixon would remain on the ticket was still a question publicly, but in reality the Republican National Committee had decided the issue in Nixon's favor weeks before the convention. Nevertheless, Oveta knew that Eisenhower's preferred running mate was Texas Democrat and former navy secretary Robert Anderson. Eisenhower admired Anderson greatly, but as a lifelong Democrat he was unlikely to be accepted by the conservative wing of the GOP. Eisenhower had talked to Oveta about the possibility of Anderson serving as vice president during his second term in the event that Nixon accepted Eisenhower's offer to serve as secretary of defense, which Nixon declined. Although Oveta was not a fan of Nixon, she remained neutral in the matter. Anderson, however, resisted Eisenhower's overtures.[39]

The preconvention kerfuffle over the vice presidential nomination suggested that the Republican convention, which was to be held August 20 to 23 at the Cow Palace in San Francisco, might have more drama than had been previously anticipated. If that happened, Oveta would be there to see it. She traveled to San Francisco a week early, probably to get a break from Houston's oppressive heat and humidity. Arriving on August 16, she rented an apartment at 840 Powell Street in San Francisco's Nob Hill section.

Oveta was a visible presence around San Francisco during the convention. Her status as the first director of the WAC continued to make her a celebrity among women in the military. Two days after she arrived in the city, a member of the Defense Department's Advisory Committee on Women in the Services hosted a reception at her home in Oveta's honor. A large group of women members of the armed services who were stationed in the Bay Area attended the party, eagerly greeting Oveta as the pioneer who had made their military service possible. The night before the opening of the GOP convention, Oveta rode in a convertible in the Citizens for Eisenhower parade that terminated at the steps of city hall. Immediately after the parade, she was one of the featured speakers at a rally in the nearby civic auditorium. Oveta proclaimed she was supporting Eisenhower's reelection because "in four short years [he] has returned to government the integrity so essential to a government of the people. The things I believed about him in 1952 are the things I know about him in 1956. He has renewed in us our faith in government."[40]

After the convention convened, a chauffeur drove Oveta to the city's Cow Palace, approximately eight miles south of her apartment, where she visited with her former colleagues in the Eisenhower administration, notably White House spokesman and journalist Jim Hagerty and his wife, Marjorie, with whom she had become social friends while a member of the cabinet. Oveta watched the convention's proceedings from her reserved seat in the cavernous Cow Palace, attended the most important receptions and luncheons, and met with General Clay to discuss Citizens for Eisenhower plans for the fall campaign. She also appeared on three national telecasts: a Citizens for Eisenhower presentation, from the civic auditorium; NBC's *Home* program, from the Fairmont Hotel; and CBS's *The Morning Show*, from the Mark Hopkins Hotel.[41]

The anticipated drama over the vice presidential administration ended before it began. The delegates nominated Nixon without a fight. Eisenhower was nominated by acclimation. The entire affair was later described as "quiet and dignified," exactly the way Eisenhower had wanted it to be.[42]

Reporters from Texas newspapers who were desperately searching for stories to send back home during a boring, controversy-free convention noticed Oveta's conspicuous activity. They soon speculated she was organizing support for a campaign to win the US Senate seat that Price Daniel Sr. was vacating after winning the Democratic nomination for governor of Texas. Daniel's victory in the general election was assured in the one-party state. Because two years remained in his Senate term, a special election would be held to fill the vacancy, and the winner would be whomever won the most votes even if it was not a majority. A political columnist for the *Dallas Morning News* reported, "[Oveta's] party label is uncertain, but that wouldn't matter in a special election in which the ballots do not give party affiliation of the candidates." Oveta was likely amused by this speculation but there was no chance that she would be a candidate for any public office, especially one that would require her to leave Will and return to Washington, DC.[43]

After Oveta returned to Houston at the end of August, she focused her attention on helping Eisenhower carry Texas. The president enjoyed a comfortable lead in the polls over his Democratic opponent, Adlai Stevenson, but the specter of Truman's totally unexpected defeat of Thomas Dewey in 1948 still haunted the Republican Party. It was crucial that Eisenhower once again carry Texas, which the Democrats continued to dominate politically. For that reason, as well as for her need to stay close to home for Will's sake, Oveta largely remained in Texas to work on the state campaign, which included a four-day speaking tour of West Texas that Weldon Hart coordinated. Transported on the personal airplane of Eisenhower booster Charles I. Francis, a Houstonian who was Texas Eastern Corporation's general counsel, Oveta went to San Angelo, El Paso, Lubbock, Midland, and Amarillo to urge voters to support Ike. In San Angelo, she praised Eisenhower for being "liberal" in all things that "deal with people" while being "conservative" when spending "the people's money." In El Paso she assailed Eisenhower's Democratic opponent, Adlai Stevenson, for his "irresponsible" demand to ban the testing of hydrogen bombs, calling him "terrifyingly naïve." After the tour, Oveta wrote Dorothy Houghton, a Republican Party activist in Iowa whom Oveta had selected to be cochair of Citizens for Eisenhower: "I do believe, while it is touch and go in Texas, the chances of its remaining in the Eisenhower column are growing increasingly stronger."[44]

Although Oveta remained in Texas for most of the fall of 1956, she did make a few brief campaign trips out of state. In early September, she attended an important outdoor meeting at President Eisenhower's Gettysburg farm with Richard Nixon and the campaign leaders, including representatives from the prominent New York ad agency Batton, Barton, Durstine, and Osborne. Oveta participated in discussions about what issues to emphasize in the campaign and how to plan a voter registration effort targeted at Southerners, especially Texans, who were likely to vote Republican. At one point, when it was stressed that the president should make it clear to voters he was in good physical condition, Eisenhower walked to the podium, smiled, and declared, "I feel fine." Oveta joined with the other attendees to give him an enthusiastic standing ovation. Nevertheless, Eisenhower told the gathering there would be no rerun of the 1952 campaign, when he had conducted an exhausting sweep through every section of the country, often giving several speeches a day. Eisenhower intended to limit himself to a few major speeches delivered on national television. Richard Nixon would assume the burden of traveling the country. The fact was the polls indicated Eisenhower had a commanding lead over Governor Adlai Stevenson. The president also stressed that world conditions required his full attention.[45]

A few weeks after launching the presidential campaign, Hungarians revolted against their Communist government, a rebellion that the Soviet Union brutally suppressed. While the crisis in Eastern Europe was occurring, the Israeli, British, and French militaries attacked Egypt after that country occupied the Suez Canal. Both of these affairs were exceedingly dangerous international crises that fully engaged the administration's attention. Referring to the perilous international situation, Oveta wrote Dorothy Houghton that it would "be particularly interesting to see what effect events in the Middle East during the past couple of days may have. For my own part, nothing could make me feel better than to know that the President is in the White House at this time."[46]

Nixon and his wife, Pat, also went on the campaign trail. At Oveta's urging they made Texas an early destination. They arrived in Houston on September 25, where Nixon gave a campaign speech at a rally at Houston Music Hall in which (as Oveta advised) he toned down his fiercely partisan rhetoric to avoid alienating the conservative Texas Democrats who were needed to carry the state for Eisenhower. Afterward, Will and Oveta hosted the Nixons at an evening reception and dinner at their Shadyside mansion. Their daughter, Jessica, who had a strongly negative view of Nixon, seems to have been charmed by him. Oveta later reported to Bill, who was in Virginia serving in the navy, "I wish you and Diana could have been with us Tuesday night when the Nixon's [*sic*] were at the house. Dick seems even to have converted Jessica." In that same letter, Oveta also commented about a news story in the Communist *People's Daily World* that Bill had mischievously sent his mother, which was highly critical of her. "Thanks for the clipping. I hope you don't believe all you read, but if you do, please judge your poor old mother by the enemies she makes."[47]

Eisenhower easily won reelection on November 6, carrying forty-one of the forty-eight states, including Texas. Shortly before the election and two days after the Israeli invasion of Egypt resulted in the Suez crisis, Oveta had appeared on a national television broadcast from Houston urging voters to reelect Ike "as the world's best hope for peace. This is not the time to experiment in leadership. This is the time to use the best we have—the best in experience, the best in leadership and the best in courage." After Eisenhower's win, Oveta wrote him an effusive letter expressing her delight with the result, declaring that his "overwhelming victory will stand as a tribute to this Nation's common sense." A few days later, the president sent Oveta a thank you note that reflected his nostalgic feelings for his native state. "Dear Oveta," he wrote, "I was delighted that Texas again reaffirmed its confidence in the principles for which I stand. Although I would not like to be quoted, Texas was one state that in my heart I really wanted to carry." As preparations were being made for his inauguration to a second term, Eisenhower sent Oveta and Will a note stating his "hopes that you will be the personal guests of Mamie and myself for the various functions." Will's precarious state of health, however, prevented the Hobbys from attending the inauguration.[48]

As the years passed during Eisenhower's second term, Will's health problems and Oveta's involvement in the Special Studies Project, as well as her need to focus on managing the Hobby media properties, made it difficult for her to carry out her responsibilities as a volunteer on public service boards and committees. In January 1957, she accepted an invitation from University of Texas Board of Regents chairman Tom Sealy to serve on its Committee of 75. The committee's purpose was to celebrate the university's seventy-fifth anniversary in 1958 by producing a "realistic and attainable" plan for the institution's next twenty-five years. Sealy warned Oveta that acceptance meant "some work and personal sacrifice on your part. It is an invitation to public service of the highest order." When Oveta attended the first meeting in April 1957 in Austin, the committee chairman, Humble Oil general counsel Rex Baker, assigned her to the task force on the "Scope and Size of the University System." The committee decided to examine the University of California system of higher education as a potential model for Texas.[49]

Despite Oveta's willingness to participate in this endeavor, her increasingly complicated obligations at home and at work made it difficult for her to contribute. She was forced to miss an important meeting in March because of Will's ill health and another in June 1957 because of a Special Studies Project gathering in New York City. By an almost Herculean effort, she managed to attend a critical meeting in Austin on October 26. Because she had little time to study the committee's lengthy reports and communications, Oveta asked *Houston Post* reporter Brian Spinks to provide her with brief summaries. Spinks also accompanied her to the October meeting in Austin to help him understand the proceedings enough to give Oveta informed reports. In the end, Oveta's contribution to her task force was minimal. Although her name was on the Committee of 75's final official report, there was little, if any, of Oveta's thinking in it.[50]

Even though Oveta's main focus during Eisenhower's second term was on the *Houston Post*, she accepted invitations to serve on the boards of a small number of nonprofit organizations of special personal significance. They included the advisory committee of the George C. Marshall Research Foundation in Lexington, Virginia, whose namesake had been deeply supportive of Oveta's tenure as head of the Women's Army Corps. She also joined the board of St. Albans School. In accepting the latter invitation, Oveta wrote she had "just cause to be grateful to St. Albans as my son was in the school's care during those busy years of WWII." She also directed the Hobby Family Foundation to make a gift to the newly constructed Sam Rayburn Library. She flew with George and Herman Brown in the Brown and Root Company plane to Bonham, Texas, to attend the library's dedication on October 1, 1957. At the buffet luncheon, Oveta ate her meal from a television tray while sitting on the porch of Rayburn's two-story house, located near the library. A *Life* magazine photographer who documented the event took pictures of Oveta busily chatting with guests at the Rayburn home, who included former Supreme Court justice Tom Clark, independent oilman Sid Richardson, John Connally, Speaker Rayburn, Lyndon Johnson, and former president Truman.[51]

Throughout 1957, the Hobbys' businesses continued to flourish. In October 1957 the *Houston Post*'s circulation department gave Will and Oveta the happy news that for the first time in twenty years, the *Post* had passed the *Houston Chronicle* in weekday circulation. The *Chronicle* maintained its lead in Sunday circulation, but within two years the *Post* passed the *Chronicle* in that category as well. The pressure from the *Post*'s rapid growth, Will's fragile health, and Oveta's public policy efforts and other activities in which she was involved convinced Oveta it was time for her son and daughter-in-law to move to Houston to help her with the newspaper.[52]

Bill Hobby had given serious consideration to a career in naval intelligence, but Oveta persuaded him to come home to be groomed to eventually take over the newspaper. Bill later said he came back to Houston because he felt it was his duty and responsibility to help his mother "run the family business." Consequently, Bill left active duty in the navy on January 19, 1957. The plan was for Bill, who had turned twenty-five, to get more experience as a reporter. Before entering the navy he had worked part-time at the *Post*, and he had written columns for Rice Institute's school newspaper, but his parents understandably felt he needed more seasoning as a journalist. Accordingly, after he and Diana moved to Houston, where they settled in a house near Rice University, Will and Oveta sent him to Austin to cover sessions of the Texas Legislature for the *Post*'s capitol bureau. Bill quickly moved up the company job ladder. In July 1959, after a year of basic reporting, he was promoted to associate editor of the *Post*. Oveta gave Diana Hobby the job of *Houston Post* book page editor, a position Oveta had once held. This job was one for which Diana, who was a voracious reader and intellectual, was well prepared and one in which she excelled. She continued as book page editor until the early 1970s.[53]

Another significant change came to the *Post* in February 1958, when the Hobbys hired star reporter and editor Jack Donahue away from the *Houston Press*. Donahue, a native Texan and graduate of Baylor University, made an immediate impact on the quality of the newspaper's investigative reporting. Soon after joining the *Post*, he filed a series of reports from Caracas, Venezuela, on the status of US oil companies in that country. A revolution had overthrown the previous government, which had been friendly to corporate oil interests—a subject of great interest to Houston's oil companies. Donahue also initiated a series on Houston's unsolved crimes, offering a $5,000 reward to readers who provided information resulting in a conviction. When Donahue asked for Oveta's approval for the series, she replied that it had "an aura of the common about it. Cloak it with a mantle of decency." To satisfy Oveta's requirement, Donahue began each story in the series with a quotation from J. Edgar Hoover or some other famed crime fighter about the importance of citizen involvement in law enforcement. Donahue then "shot

*Oveta Culp Hobby having a private talk with Treasury Secretary Robert Anderson
at the opening of the Sam Rayburn Library, Bonham, Texas, October 10, 1957.*

the works," as he later recalled, by writing the rest of the story in the tabloid manner he had learned at the *Houston Press*. In July 1959, after a stint on the *Post's* editorial staff, Donahue became the newspaper's managing editor.[54]

Donahue's work, along with those of other staffers, such as business editor Sam Weiner, political correspondent Felton West, and editorial writers George Fuermann and Marguerite Johnston, enhanced the *Post's* growing reputation for quality journalism. Beginning in 1953 with Ralph S. O'Leary's famed exposé of Red Scare activists, the *Post* accumulated sixty-five statewide and national journalistic awards in five years. This record attracted national attention. In a 1958 story, *Time* magazine lauded the *Houston Post's* "alert, far-ranging news coverage and a thoughtful, middle-of-the-road Republican editorial page" that had given it "a reputation as the Southwest's most readable daily." After the death of Jesse Jones, the *Post's* chief competitor, the *Houston Chronicle*, became even more deeply mired in a right-wing ideological outlook, attacking the United Nations and the Eisenhower administration's foreign policy and espousing a rigid opposition to racial integration and the civil rights movement. The *Chronicle's* editorial position had become so far right that by contrast it gave the *Post* a progressive reputation. *Time* declared that the *Chronicle* "often sounds like an oil-belt echo of the *Chicago Tribune*."[55]

Despite her focus on other matters, Oveta did manage to keep her pipeline to the White House open, occasionally offering advice or helping with various matters. For example, at the request of Postmaster General Arthur Summerfield, she contacted her friends in Congress, including Albert Thomas, W. R. Poage, Lyndon Johnson, and Sam Rayburn, to urge their support of the president's plan to reorganize the Department of Defense. When she heard that Eisenhower was hosting a labor-management conference, she sent a message to the White House to encourage the president to add consumer issues to his meeting agenda. Labor Secretary James Mitchell responded, "You can be sure that your idea will get to the President." On another occasion, when Eisenhower announced a plan to slow the rate of inflation, Oveta informed him in a personal message that he had her "complete support" and promised "to do whatever I can to be of help in this crucial fight by getting the facts before the people and the Congress. I assure you of my very best efforts." Her efforts in this case were made on the editorial pages of the *Houston Post*.[56]

Oveta also helped Eisenhower when he was forced to confront a major civil rights crisis in Little Rock, Arkansas, in September 1957, when Governor Orval Faubus ordered the state's National Guard to block nine African American students from enrolling at the city's Central High School. While Eisenhower abhorred racial discrimination, his approach to school desegregation was delay and gradualism, believing that only the passage of time would change hearts, not court orders. He opposed federal involvement in the matter, preferring instead to allow local school authorities to take steps aligned with federal court decisions and local conditions. The irresponsible actions of Governor Faubus and racist mobs in Little Rock eventually compelled him to enforce court orders and support the rule of law. On October 24, nearly two months after the crisis began, Eisenhower reluctantly directed the secretary of defense to nationalize the Arkansas National Guard and to fly the 101st Airborne Division to Little Rock, where they deployed around the high school to allow the African American students to enroll and attend classes.[57]

The president was eager to remove the troops as soon as possible, but Governor Faubus refused to guarantee the students' safety once the troops were withdrawn. Eisenhower sought the support of moderate Southern leaders in his attempt to resolve the stalemate. On October 19, he called Oveta for advice on how to get more support from the South that would help him end the crisis. As she had done while HEW secretary when confronting major problems such as the classroom shortage in the public schools and the polio vaccine crisis, Oveta advised Eisenhower to arrange a White House conference with Southern business leaders and public officials to consider a solution. Eisenhower, however, thought nothing could be accomplished at such a conference because there were few moderates in the South whom he could call on to attend. He complained that the only prominent Southerner who had rallied to his side was Ralph McGill, columnist and editor of the *Atlanta Constitution*, who was outspoken in his support of the president's actions.[58]

After her telephone discussion with Eisenhower, Oveta contacted George Champion, executive vice president (later president) of Chase Manhattan Bank. Champion was a leader of the religiously liberal New York Protestant Council, which sponsored evangelist Billy Graham's historic crusade in New York City in the summer of 1957. Oveta asked Champion to talk to Graham about making a special nationwide television broadcast calling for Americans to support peaceful racial integration. Oveta knew Eisenhower had approached Graham in 1956 to enlist the help of Southern churches to promote better race relations, but Graham had given the president an evasive answer and had advised him to stay "out of this bitter racial situation." His gradualist views on racial integration matched Eisenhower's exactly. Nevertheless, Oveta believed Graham might still be persuaded to help Eisenhower defuse the Little Rock controversy. Speaking to the press earlier, Graham had recommended that the white citizens of Little Rock should comply with the order of the federal court. "It is the duty of every Christian, when it does not violate his relationship to God, to obey the law. I would urge them to do so in this case."

After Champion communicated Oveta's request to Graham, the evangelist distributed a sermon "encouraging love across the color line" that was broadcast on radio stations in Arkansas. In addition, he issued a statement that "called for Christians in Little Rock 'to obey the law'" and declared that "all thinking southerners" were distressed by the mob violence in the city. His offer to conduct services in Little Rock, however, was discouraged by the city's clergy, who were afraid it might further enflame the situation. Graham waited until the controversy cooled considerably before he held a racially integrated revival in Little Rock a year later. Eight of the nine African American students protected by federal troops eventually graduated from Central High School in May 1958, but it would take more than two years of heated struggle and controversy before Little Rock schools were integrated and, even then, only at a token level.[59]

Oveta's effort to calm the racial tensions in Little Rock by enlisting Billy Graham's help was not only motivated by her desire to help the president out of his quandary, it was also driven by her dislike of racial bigotry and hatred. As she had declared in her speech at Ohio Wesleyan University four years earlier, racial discrimination was practiced at high cost to society by preventing black citizens from reaching "their full potential." Oveta duly noted the serious damage Governor Faubus and his segregationist supporters had inflicted on Little Rock's image and business environment. She would later draw on that experience when Houston faced a similar situation.[60]

# CHAPTER 40

—

# TACTFUL TEXAN

W hile Oveta was serving on Eisenhower's cabinet, Will was collaborating, in between bouts of illness, on his biography with veteran journalist and book author James A. Clark, whom Will had known for nearly forty years. Will had first met Clark in 1915 in Beaumont when Clark was a seven-year-old hanging out in front of the *Beaumont Enterprise* offices, just as Will had once hung around the *Houston Post* in his youth. Will, who was in his first term as lieutenant governor and was back home in Beaumont between legislative sessions, gave Clark a job selling copies of the *Enterprise* on the street. Clark eventually became a copy boy and cub reporter and briefly worked as Will's assistant at the *Enterprise* while attending South Park Junior College. After a stint at the *Galveston News*, Clark worked as a reporter for the *Beaumont Journal*. Clark eventually held a variety of other jobs in journalism and public relations. In 1952 he and petroleum geologist Michel Halbouty coauthored *Spindletop*, the story of the historic oil discovery near Beaumont. Two years later, Clark published *Three Stars for the Colonel*, a biography of General Ernest O. Thompson, a longtime member of the Texas Railroad Commission. Impressed with *Spindletop*, Will approached Clark in September 1952 about writing his biography. At the time, Clark was working on *Three Stars for the Colonel* and writing a column about the oil industry for the *Houston Post*. Clark eagerly accepted the offer from his old friend.

Will promised he would spend as much time as necessary to answer questions and tell his story to Clark, but he had one restriction: "Don't write anything that will hurt any man who can't defend himself." Oveta had her own restriction. The book was to be about Will, not her. As Clark later wrote in his foreword, "There is little in this book about Governor's wonderful wife out of deference to Mrs. Hobby's own wish." Clark readily agreed to those restrictions and then secured a contract from Random House, the publisher of *Spindletop*.[1]

Will answered Clark's questions and dictated stories to him in work sessions that

—

began in 1952 and continued off and on for five years. Clark recruited two of Will's former employees to gather information from the newspaper clip files at the *Beaumont Enterprise* and from Will's gubernatorial papers in the Texas State Archives in Austin. They interviewed Raymond Brooks, Will's secretary when he was governor. Brooks also served as one of Clark's researchers. Ed Kilman's wife, Alice, conducted research in the *Houston Post*'s news clipping morgue, and she drew material from the manuscript of her husband's history of the *Houston Post*, which had been published as a series in the *Post* a few years earlier. Will suggested that Clark use his nickname "Guv" as the title, but Clark and Oveta talked him into accepting the advice of Random House's editors, who insisted that "Texan" be in the title for marketing purposes. With Will's agreement, the book was titled *The Tactful Texan: A Biography of Governor Will Hobby*.[2]

When Clark completed a first draft of Will's biography in 1957, he turned it over to Will and Oveta to review and correct. By this time, Bill and Diana Hobby had moved back to Houston, and Will shared the manuscript with them. Bill later recalled that he and Diana thought that Clark's "manuscript was unreadable." Bill called Weldon Hart, a veteran journalist who had served as chief of the *Austin Statesman*'s capitol news bureau, and asked him to "reorganize and rewrite" Clark's text. A confidant and advisor to Governor Allan Shivers, Hart had served as state director of the Democrats for Eisenhower organization in 1952 and 1956, where he worked closely with Oveta. At the time Bill called on Hart to help, Hart was running his own public relations firm in Austin.[3]

Hart did additional research, included his own memories of working with Will when Will was governor and later editor of the *Post*, and thoroughly revised Clark's manuscript. Bill gave the new draft to his mother, who asked Marguerite Johnston to help her make additional revisions. During this process, Oveta sent a page-by-page list of revisions to Clark and Hart. She complained about the "perfunctory" treatment of Willie Hobby, whom Oveta referred to as "Miss Willie." She told Clark, "It seems to me that the same kind of amplification should be given to her qualities that are given to [Will's] brother Edwin at the time he died." She also wanted more emphasis placed on Will's service on the Alien Enemy Hearing Board, noting that it was "one of the most important [jobs] done in this area throughout WWII. His was the voice of sanity and balance which kept incredible injustices from being done to foreign-born or Americans of Oriental ancestry."[4]

Even though Oveta wanted little of the book to be about her, Clark and Hart obviously couldn't leave her out entirely. And understandably, Oveta closely reviewed those sections, especially discussions of her relationship with Will. She disliked a statement in the manuscript implying she had left Will alone to manage the *Post* and care for the children when she moved to Washington to work in the War Department and that the "Hobby Team" endured a temporary suspension during those years. She told Clark the statement was "not quite valid. The team prevailed though the two parties were in separate cities." As for the children, they "lived in Houston or in Washington as the team could best see their case. Governor himself went through a serious illness in Washington, where the family was together." About her resignation from the Women's Army Corps, Oveta asked Clark to make a "slight expansion here to explain why [Oveta] resigned before war's end—since some WACs felt they had been deserted and the fact that Governor felt it was best for her health that she resign as well as that he needed her at home." She also insisted that Will never gave up his direction of the *Post*, even when he was sick. Oveta suggested the entire passage dealing with President Roosevelt's dismissal of Jesse Jones and the *Post*'s editorial denouncing of it should be cut. Will's version of the dismissal was removed, but the *Post*'s editorial reaction remained in the book, possibly at the insistence of the editor at Random House, who was eager for material of national interest.[5]

In January 1958 Clark submitted the final manuscript of *The Tactful Texan*, along with a selection of photographs to illustrate the book, to Robert Loomis, a newly hired editor at Random House. In his more than fifty years with Random House, Loomis would earn a reputation as one of the top editors in the book-publishing business, working with a wide range of famed authors, including William Styron and Maya Angelou. Loomis hurriedly edited Clark and Hart's manuscript, with the goal of getting the book out in time for Will's eightieth birthday in March. He proved to be a tough editor, ruthlessly striking out the word "very" wherever he found it and writing in tiny handwriting in the margins of the manuscript the comment "we know" whenever he read something he thought was boring. He disliked the photos the Hobbys selected for the book, but after some back and forth discussion with Clark, he eventually decided not to push the issue.[6]

A sudden illness almost took Will away before he could see the publication of his biography. On January 27, while Loomis was editing the manuscript and Oveta was deeply involved with the Special Studies Project, "Governor" underwent major surgery on his throat and nearly died. Will remained in the hospital during most of the first half of February. Oveta told friends that Will was "frighteningly ill." While he was struggling to recover, he received the news that his older sister Mary, who had stood vigil with Will by their younger brother Paul's deathbed many years before, had died in Dallas at the age of eighty-seven.[7]

*Tactful Texan*, with 203 pages of text, appeared in print in time for Will's birthday in late March 1958, with the author's credit "by James Clark, with Weldon Hart." Oveta had a large number of complimentary copies of *Tactful Texan* distributed to her wide circle of friends and associates, with a printed note from Will tucked inside. Nelson Rockefeller sent Oveta a handwritten letter declaring, "Tod and I were thrilled to get the book from Will!" She also shipped out more than 1,100 complimentary copies to grade school, high school, and college libraries throughout Texas. The biography generated mixed reviews, however, with some complaining that it was an exercise in hagiography, citing Clark's unabashed declarations in his foreword that "William Pettus Hobby is a great man" and that "this book probably is not objective. It is hard for one who knows him to be objective about Will Hobby." Other reviewers criticized it as a light and superficial account of the numerous significant events in Will's life. A review in the University of Texas's student newspaper, the *Daily Texan*, pointed out that it was an authorized biography that told

A Biography of Governor Will Hobby

★

# The Tactful Texan

by James A. Clark

with Weldon Hart

*Cover of Will Hobby's authorized biography, published in 1958.*

"more of his times" than it did about Hobby: "In this book, he remains a name, never a personality." In a more favorable review for the *Dallas Morning News*, William Ruggles's only complaint was that Clark had overlooked "one telling point in the [1914] campaign. Will Hobby was known and liked by newspaper editors and publishers the state over. They helped mightily."[8]

Will failed to regain his health in time for the release of his biography. The aftereffects of surgery, combined with his chronic and severe arthritis, kept him bedridden at the mansion in Shadyside for much of the spring and summer of 1958. Two events that year, however, did give Will some happiness in the midst of these troubles. In February, Will and Oveta's twenty-one-year-old daughter, Jessica, married twenty-eight-year-old Henry Catto, who was a partner in his family's insurance agency in San Antonio. In October, Will's daughter-in-law, Diana, gave birth to the Hobbys' first grandchild, whom she and Bill named Laura Poteat Hobby, after Will's favorite sister.[9]

Unlike her brother, Bill, Jessica decided not to take a job at the *Houston Post* when she embarked on her own career. After a brief job at a small weekly newspaper in one of Houston's suburbs, she tried her hand at operating a ski lodge in Arizona, but that was a financial bust. "I didn't make a penny's profit," she later admitted. After that unsuccessful venture, she moved back to Houston, where she lived with her parents. She met Henry during San Antonio's annual Fiesta celebrations in April 1957. Catto later recalled he was "smitten" with Jessica the moment he met her. "She was gorgeous; blonde with sparkling blue eyes, an hourglass figure, and an impish sense of fun." Catto was soon making frequent treks from San Antonio to Houston to see Jessica. "I was intimidated by her family," he recalled. He found Will "relaxing and charming," but not Oveta, at least not in their first meeting. He did note, however, that Oveta was "beautiful and articulate, telling stories of her extraordinary life in a modulated voice from which all trace of her Texas upbringing had been eradicated. She viewed this candidate for son-in-law with at best a raised eyebrow. On the other hand, the governor would bid me Sunday night farewell with 'Come back again soon!'" Henry and Jessica's wedding was held in Houston on February 15, 1958, a few weeks after Will's throat surgery. Henry later noted that "the Governor" was disabled, but "he recovered sufficiently to give away the bride." Oveta wrote Lyndon Johnson that Will had been "dangerously ill" but that he "recovered beautifully in time" for Jessica's wedding ceremony, "only to go back to the hospital three days later for another acute spell."[10]

Early in the fall of 1958, Will seemed to be gaining strength. He was on his feet most of the time and he felt well enough to go on frequent drives around town with his chauffeur. On Saturday evening, November 29, after taking one of his auto tours, he was struck with severe pain in his abdomen. An ambulance rushed him to nearby Hermann Hospital, where he had emergency surgery the next morning to remove a hemorrhaging stomach ulcer. His survival was in doubt the night after his surgery. Oveta, Bill, and Jessica (who drove over from San Antonio) spent the night at the hospital, monitoring his condition.[11]

Will once again survived major surgery, but this bout of illness robbed him of his mobility and finally ended his active involvement in the Hobby businesses. He spent the rest of his life as an invalid. For a few months after Will's surgery, Oveta tried to remain upbeat about Governor's prognosis. The news in April 1959 that Jessica had given birth to a baby girl named Heather helped lift Will's spirits. Oveta sent a positive report on Will's health to their friend Malcolm Wilkey, a Houston attorney whom Eisenhower had recently appointed assistant attorney general. "Governor is much better now," Oveta wrote, "though still not his best, but so happy over the birth of our daughter Jessica's baby that it is hard to convince him he is not ready for all challenges." Three months later, however, Oveta was forced to admit that Will's condition was not improving and was unlikely to improve in the future. Melvin Hattwick, a noted advertising psychologist whom Oveta had met during her wartime service in Washington, invited her to give a speech to an organization with which he was associated. Oveta replied, "In the past year, Governor's prolonged and at moments acute illness has taught me that my time is not my own to commit. Compelled as I was to cancel out on some engagements just when the cancellation must have been hardest on those who had to cope with it, I have long since realized that the only fair thing for me to do is to take on no additional commitments of any kind now."[12]

The year 1959 proved to be especially difficult for Oveta. While she was trying to cope with Will's invalidism and its impact on her daily life, as well as continuing to contribute to the Special Studies Project, her seventy-eight-year-old mother, Emma, died suddenly from a heart attack on September 1 while on a five-week-long visit to Houston. Emma had led an active life in Killeen, fishing, gardening, and driving her Buick. When she developed heart problems in 1955, she moved to Fort Worth to live with her daughter Juanita. She had lived for twenty-five years after the death of Ike Culp. Emma Elizabeth Hoover Culp was buried next to her husband in Killeen Cemetery. Several years prior to her death, the City of Killeen had named Culp Avenue in Ike and Emma's honor.[13]

As the 1950s were ending, the continuing growth and success of the *Houston Post* and KPRC television were among the bright spots in Oveta's life, otherwise made stressful by Will's condition and saddened by her mother's death. Bill continued to expand his role at the *Post*, which the *Dallas Morning News*, in a story about the newspaper's increasing editorial influence, characterized as "very much a Hobby enterprise." The Dallas newspaper pointed out Oveta's role as president and editor and Bill's role as an associate editor, with "his desk in the midst of the busy city room." Diana Hobby, the story added, was editing "one of the better book sections in the Southwest."[14]

During the first five months of 1959, Bill spent much of his time in Austin, following in Oveta's public service footsteps. Lieutenant Governor Ben Ramsey appointed him legislative parliamentarian, but in the Texas Senate, not in the House, where his mother had worked. Later that year Bill covered President Eisenhower's state visit to India, with his reports given special attention in the *Post*. In May 1960, Bill continued his administrative ascent at the *Post* by assuming the position of managing editor, replacing Jack Donahue. Arthur Laro had earlier resigned from the *Post* to be executive editor of the *Los Angeles*

*Mirror-News*, and Donahue soon followed him to California to take an assistant editor's position at the same newspaper. Laro's and Donahue's departures gave Will and Oveta the opportunity to promote Bill to the job for which he had been groomed ever since his return to Houston after leaving the navy in 1957. In June, a month after Bill's move up the executive ladder at the *Post*, Diana gave birth to their second child, Paul.[15]

Bill was twenty-eight years old when he became managing editor of the *Post*. To counter potential criticism that he was too young to lead the newspaper, the *Post* included in the announcement of his promotion that his father had only been twenty-six when he assumed the same job. In a feature about Bill's new position, *Time* noted that Will and Oveta's son had taken command "over a healthy paper." The *Post*'s daily circulation now led the *Houston Chronicle* by nearly twenty-thousand subscriptions. The *Houston Press* was far behind the *Post* and the *Chronicle*, with only half the number of subscribers. The *Post*'s Sunday circulation also passed the *Chronicle* to become the largest in Texas, although the Hobbys' newspaper continued to trail the *Chronicle* in advertising revenue. *Time*, which had long shown an interest in Oveta's career, observed that the *Post*'s "blanket news coverage and lively writing have made it the equal of any paper in the Southwest." But this positive statement also included a gratuitous negative jab, as *Time* added its opinion that "Bill Hobby is taking command of a paper made outstanding by others—who have left." *Time* added, however, that under Oveta's guidance, "Bill Hobby is likely to continue putting out one of the Southwest's better newspapers."[16]

The *Post*'s success compelled Will and Oveta to move forward with a $2.5 million expansion of the printing plant. At the same time that Bill was assuming his duties as managing editor in May 1960, contractors began work on the three-story addition needed to house the *Post*'s new high-speed color presses. The new space trebled the size of the pressroom and made it possible for the newspaper to handle the rapidly increasing circulation more efficiently. Oveta presided over the ground-breaking ceremony, which was held in a parking lot next to the Post Building on May 11. The new presses became operational in June 1961.[17]

While the Hobbys were busily expanding the *Houston Post*'s facilities, African American students at Texas Southern University (TSU), inspired by the success of peaceful protests against segregated lunch counters in Greensboro, North Carolina, organized to overthrow Jim Crow practices in the South's largest city. Eldrewey Stearns, a twenty-eight-year-old army veteran and student at the TSU Law School, assumed a leadership role in the protests. Stearns, a native of Galveston, had been badly beaten by Houston police in 1959 for allegedly smarting off to a white officer after a traffic stop, although Stearns alleged the actual cause was the discovery of a white woman's photo in his wallet. In late March, Stearns led a group of approximately one hundred TSU students in a sit-in demonstration at a grocery store lunch counter in south Houston. The store's management closed the lunch counter to keep from serving the students. On March 25, 1960, Stearns led a student group to Houston City Hall, where they picketed and sang church songs. Afterward, they entered the city hall cafeteria and asked to be served.

To their shock, white Houston city councilman and future mayor Louie Welch joined them at the counter and ordered the manager to serve the students, who were subsequently sold coffee and food. With Oveta's approval, the *Houston Post* ran the story on the front page. A large number of angry white Houstonians immediately flooded city hall with mail and telephone calls denouncing the desegregation of the lunch counter. When Houston mayor Lewis Cutrer warned that in the future any African American individuals who tried to be served at the lunch counter would be arrested, the chief of police, Carl Shuptrine, informed the mayor that because the African American customers would be breaking no laws, his officers would not make the arrests.

Encouraged by this success, the TSU students targeted grocery stores, theaters, bus stations, department stores, and other businesses in Houston. The specter of Little Rock, where the school integration controversy had damaged the business community, hung over Houston's merchants. With growing anxiety, the city's Retail Merchants' Association advised their members to respond to the protests in a manner that would allow the business community to "continue to grow and prosper free of the disorder and violence which took their toll on business and community life in Little Rock."[18]

Many Houstonians feared that if the protests continued, violence would likely result. In August 1960, Robert Dundas, vice president of Foley's department store in downtown Houston, was among the first of Houston's business leaders to seek a resolution to the racial tension. Dundas was an old-school political fixer and lobbyist who had close connections with the 8F crowd and other power elites in the city. He had been a teenager in 1917 when the Camp Logan riot occurred, and the memory of that horrific event was etched in his mind. He had gone with his father to the city morgue and seen the bodies of the people who had been killed in the riot. He was determined to do whatever he could to prevent a similar tragedy. Dundas wanted to desegregate Foley's restaurant, but he feared that if his department store was the first to break the color barrier, it would bear the brunt of white racist anger and lose customers. He decided to convince the owners and managers of other downtown lunch counters that if they all desegregated at the same time, white protesters would be unable to single out an individual business for reprisal. After a series of private talks, Dundas persuaded most of the downtown lunch counter operators to join with Foley's to end racial segregation in downtown Houston. Retailers soon quietly removed the "Colored" and "White" signs over water fountains and on restroom doors. The retail executives insisted, however, that they would desegregate only if the news media agreed not to cover the event. They were aware that news coverage in other Southern cities had led to violence by white racists. It was hoped that suppressing the story would allow Houston to avoid a similar fate.[19]

Dundas explained his strategy to Oveta and to Jesse Jones's nephew, John T. Jones, who had succeeded his uncle as publisher of the *Houston Chronicle*. Oveta was determined to prevent another Little Rock situation in Houston. She and John Jones agreed to block stories about the desegregation decision from their papers and their news broadcasts. The *Houston Press*, which was owned by the Scripps-Howard newspaper chain, initially refused Dundas's request. Foley's, however, was one of the *Press*'s most important advertisers. After Dundas threatened to stop buying ads, editor George Carmack buckled under the pressure and agreed not to cover the event. Other radio and television stations fell in line, largely due to Foley's advertising power.[20]

Oveta immediately informed her photographers, reporters, and editors that no pictures of or stories about any African Americans seated at a lunch counter would be published in the *Post*. "I said we will have no undue publicity on the lunchroom desegregation," she later recalled. "We [would] not give the [white] goons any incentive to come to a restaurant. No photographers, no feature stories, nothing, unless it became a matter for the police blotter." *Post* reporters, including city editor Ralph O'Leary and civil rights specialist Blair Justice, pleaded with Oveta to reverse her decision. It was a big story, they argued, and the *Post* had an obligation to report it. Oveta ignored their pleas. Nevertheless, news about the decision to desegregate was quietly spread by word of mouth throughout Houston's African American community. On August 25, 1960, Dundas made a point to greet a contingent of TSU students when they arrived at Foley's lunch counter and asked for service. The operators of the other Houston lunch counters followed Foley's lead on that same date.[21]

When the national press learned about the coordinated news blackout in Houston, a number of newspapers and news magazines printed editorials criticizing the decision. The liberal *Texas Observer*, understanding that raising public awareness of segregation practices was a key part of the strategy of civil rights activists, declared, "We are still blinking our eyes—we can't believe it! The entire Houston press—newspapers, radio, and TV—entering into an overt conspiracy to suppress a major news development they had covered fully up to the time of its climax! Inflammatory reporting is one thing, but truthful reporting is another." Hobby-friendly *Time* magazine, however, was less critical. In a story with the headline "Blackout in Houston," *Time* emphasized the public safety and security motivations, as well as the economic reasons behind the decision, quoting an anonymous Houstonian that the retail stores desired "to integrate the lunch counters at the least possible cost. They wanted to lose neither Negro nor white business. They felt that not publicizing the event was their safest course of action." The influential weekly news magazine reported that when angry Houstonians called Oveta to protest the decision, she "blandly replied that the blackout had been taken as 'another public service of the *Post* to insure public safety.'" For Oveta, the concept was simple. As her Special Studies panel had made clear in its recently published report, the mission of "media of communication," in her case, the *Houston Post*, was not simply to inform but also "to lead and direct."[22]

On May 9, 1960, two days before Oveta dedicated the *Post*'s new printing plant, she received a telephone call from the president of the United States. For Oveta, a call from Dwight Eisenhower was not unusual, but the timing of the call and its surprising purpose were. Eisenhower was in the middle of a serious crisis caused by the downing of American CIA pilot Francis Gary Powers and his U-2 spy plane over the Soviet Union on May

1. The Eisenhower administration had claimed that the U-2 was a weather plane on a routine mission when it "accidentally" wandered over Soviet airspace and was brought down by a missile. On May 7, however, the Soviets revealed that the pilot was alive and in custody. Moreover, the wreckage of the U-2 had been found, including its camera and exposed film with photographs of Soviet missile sites. Eisenhower had been caught in a lie, but he had not yet admitted it publicly. This humiliating story was dominating the headlines of the nation's newspapers, including the *Houston Post*.

Oveta thought it odd that the president was calling her during this international crisis and wondered if it was to seek her advice about public relations damage control. When Oveta took the president's call, he made no mention of the U-2 crisis but instead went directly to the subject of the 1960 presidential campaign. Eisenhower was not yet resigned to the prospect of Richard Nixon's nomination as the Republican Party's presidential candidate. Nixon's only viable rival at this point was Nelson Rockefeller, about whom Eisenhower had serious reservations because of what the president saw as his wild ideas and his liberal views on federal spending. Eisenhower preferred Robert Anderson, a Democrat who was now serving as secretary of the treasury. He asked Oveta to persuade Texas Republicans to organize a campaign to select Anderson as the state's favorite-son candidate, which he hoped might lead to his nomination for president at the Republican Party's national convention in Chicago in July. He stunned Oveta by telling her that if she thought his plan for an Anderson nomination wouldn't work, she should seriously consider the possibility of entering the presidential race herself. Oveta politely declined, but that didn't persuade the president.

After their phone conversation ended, he immediately put his thoughts in writing in a letter to Oveta. "It occurs to me that if [Anderson] should object," Eisenhower wrote, "then we ought to be the first to name a lady as the 'favorite *son*.' How about it? In any event we ought to be having some real activity—the kind that will remind people that there are ladies as well as other leaders, such as Bob, who believe in moderate government, fiscal responsibility, and official and personal integrity. If you have any good hot ideas, I would like to hear them." If Oveta replied to Eisenhower's letter, no copy exists in her papers. Oveta understood that if the president's thoughts became public, a major controversy would erupt that might be detrimental to Nixon's candidacy and hurt GOP chances in November. She wrote a note to her assistant directing her to lock the letter in her safe. The episode is solid evidence of Eisenhower's trust in Oveta's judgment as well as his admiration for her.[23]

As the campaign for the Republican nomination continued into the summer, Eisenhower once again sought Oveta's counsel. He telephoned on June 11 to get her reaction to Nixon's campaign tactics. Eisenhower, who had become more optimistic about Nixon than he had been only a month earlier, told Oveta he believed that his vice president was growing in stature and that he was winning the respect of more voters. Oveta, however, told Eisenhower that Nixon "was not easy." Noting he would soon be giving an important campaign speech, she hoped Nixon would not "make the kind of talk that will drive intelligent independent voters away." Oveta warned Eisenhower that the vice president's extreme partisanship "was driving away independents and Texas Democrats," whom Nixon had to win over if he had any hope of carrying Texas in the general election. She urged Eisenhower to tell Nixon that his speeches needed to be constructive and nonpartisan. The president took Oveta's advice seriously. He dictated a letter to Nixon giving him Oveta's advice, and added a note: "Personally I concur." Oveta would continue during the campaign to urge Nixon to be less politically strident in his rhetoric. After he gave a more moderate campaign speech in Dallas, she sent him a note that it was "toned and turned just right."[24]

Eisenhower delivered his political farewell speech to the Republican Party's national convention on July 26. Nixon had been in Houston the month before to speak to the Texas Press Association Convention at Oveta's invitation, and she had handed Nixon a page of written suggestions that she felt Eisenhower might want to include in his convention address the following month. She asked Nixon to personally deliver it to the president, who incorporated some of her ideas into his speech. After the convention was over, Oveta arranged for an editorial in the *Houston Post* giving Eisenhower's speech high praise, and she had the text printed in the newspaper. She sent a copy to the White House. As usual when he wrote Oveta, the president's response was warm, personal, and clearly sincere. "I am so pleased that you liked the talk and highly complimented by the editorial that you sent to me," the president wrote. "Because I knew of your interest in it (Dick Nixon had forwarded to me your suggestions), I was particularly anxious to know your reaction. And, I might add, that reaction was more than I had dared hope." Oveta's letter conveying the editorial also included her offer to help the president in any way she could during his last days in office. "Certainly I shall keep in mind your offer," Eisenhower stated. "What would probably do the most good of all would be the opportunity for a good, long, uninterrupted talk with you one of these days. If you are in Washington, do not fail to get in touch with me."[25]

Eisenhower's trusted assistant, Ann Whitman, also wrote Oveta to tell her how much she liked the editorial in the *Houston Post*. "[The president] worked personally very hard on [his speech] and was eager, because of the interest he knew you had, to know *your* reaction. He was so pleased by your letter, by the editorial, and the fact that you had seen fit to run the speech in full."[26]

Despite Oveta's highly visible public efforts on behalf of Richard Nixon's campaign, she was careful to protect her relationship with Lyndon Johnson, who she knew had his own presidential aspirations. As early as January 1960, the *Post* endorsed LBJ as its preferred candidate for the Democratic nomination for president, although Johnson had not yet entered the presidential race. During a trip to Houston in April 1960, which included a visit with Oveta, LBJ held a press conference where he stated he was flattered by calls for him to be a candidate for president but that it was more important he focus on his duties as the Senate majority leader rather than on partisan activities. The Senate was in session and considering important legislation. "Somebody must keep the store," he declared. The *Post* responded with an editorial praising Johnson for staying in the Senate to take care of legislative affairs instead of traveling around the country campaigning and being an absent senator, an indirect dig at Senator John F. Kennedy, who was deeply involved in the primaries. The *Post* added that LBJ was "known and acknowledged to be the hardest working member of the U.S. Senate, in season and out." This was another gibe at Kennedy, who had a reputation as an indifferent member of the Senate who was frequently absent from the chamber. LBJ was grateful for the positive editorial. Fully aware of who was responsible, Johnson winked rhetorically, "I hope you will tell the author of the editorial how much I appreciate the generous references to me."[27]

LBJ eventually declared his candidacy for the nomination but lost to Kennedy and accepted his invitation to join the ticket as his vice presidential running mate. Although the Democratic ticket now included the Hobbys' old friend Lyndon Johnson, Oveta's loyalty to the Eisenhower administration was stronger than her ties to LBJ. Nevertheless, Johnson made a personal appeal to Oveta to come over to his side. On August 18, he telephoned her, wanting "to see if there is any way possible of getting you to help me down there" in the presidential campaign. Afterward, LBJ's secretary, with a tone of finality, simply noted in his daily diary that "Mrs. Hobby said she could not support Kennedy-Johnson." Six days later the *Houston Post* published an editorial on its front page endorsing Nixon for president and Henry Cabot Lodge for vice president. The newspaper would reiterate that support with another editorial the day before the election. Tellingly, the *Post* editorials criticizing Kennedy never mentioned LBJ. Lady Bird Johnson later recalled that in 1960 "Oveta was not for [Lyndon]; I mean she didn't come out for him. And I guess by this time Oveta must have been a real Republican. She was, and remained our friend, always. But, it was clear-cut for her, she could not come out for us." Oveta's decision, however, was not based on a negative view of her friend Lyndon or on any positive feelings for Nixon, but rather on her dislike of Kennedy and her knowledge that Eisenhower viewed the presidential election of 1960 as a referendum on his administration.[28]

Although the old party loyalties were fraying, Houston was still a Democratic city in 1960, and the *Post*'s endorsement of Nixon, who lacked Eisenhower's nonpartisan appeal, generated mailbags full of hostile letters criticizing Oveta's support. She ignored the most negative letters and didn't bother to answer them, but one accusing her of opposing John F. Kennedy because he was a Catholic touched a sensitive spot. She replied, "No one who has known me even casually would ever form the opinion that I might be anti-Catholic." Pointing out that she had campaigned for the Catholic Al Smith in 1928, Oveta explained that for many years she had worked actively with the National Conference of Christians and Jews, which included many Catholic members. "The *Post* through the years has fought prejudice," she wrote. "Among its employees are a large number of Catholics and Jews, as well as Protestants." Her critics also came from the opposite theological direction. When a Church of Christ preacher toured Houston giving sermons urging voters to reject Kennedy because of his Catholicism, Oveta approved a news story in the

*Will and Oveta Hobby attending a formal occasion at Rice Institute, 1960.*

*Post* that placed the preacher in unfavorable light. Bill Hobby told *Time*, "We soon got all sorts of hell from ministers of his denomination." A delegation of local Church of Christ preachers soon appeared at the Post Building, demanding that the newspaper print an apology or they would call for an advertising boycott. Oveta and Bill ignored the threat and refused the request. There was no noticeable loss in advertising.[29]

As the presidential campaign reached its final days, Oveta arranged for Rice University to invite Eisenhower to deliver a nonpartisan speech at the university on Monday night, October 24. After Eisenhower accepted the invitation, Oveta wrote to express how much she looked forward to seeing him and that she and Will would be honored if he would spend the night at their Shadyside mansion. "I, too, am looking forward eagerly to seeing you," Eisenhower responded. He assured Oveta that while he was in the city, "certainly we shall be able to arrange a 'quiet' visit." For security reasons, however, the Secret Service vetoed the idea of the president staying at the Hobbys' home. He stayed instead at the Shamrock Hotel. "Governor and I are deeply disappointed that you cannot be our guests," Oveta wrote Eisenhower. "We will give way gracefully only if you will remember that from January 1961, forevermore, you have a standing invitation to visit us on Remington Lane."[30]

Oveta took charge of the local arrangements for Eisenhower's visit. She worked by telephone with White House staffer Tom Stephens to plan the president's schedule and to determine with whom he wanted to meet and be seen. She told Stephens she would arrange for Mayor Lewis Cutrer to be at the airport to greet the president. Because the event would be advertised as nonpartisan, Oveta vetoed efforts by state and local Republican candidates, including US Senate candidate John Tower, to be prominently visible at Eisenhower's side. Oveta explained to the White House, "We ought not to have any candidates in the motorcade," and added that John Tower presented "some problems for a lot of people," alluding to Tower's extreme right-wing rhetoric and personal criticism of her friend Lyndon Johnson. She also had to referee a petty dispute between Albert Fay and Thad Hutcheson, rival leaders of Houston's regular Republican Party apparatus who were jockeying for prominent places on the platform with Eisenhower when he was given his official welcome to Houston. "As to Fay and Hutcheson," Stephens told Oveta, "the President thought that could be left [to you] to do whatever would keep peace and harmony." Oveta decided to place them with the two other party officials on the platform and in the motorcade, with the justification that they weren't political candidates.

The president arrived at Houston International Airport at 4:25 p.m. on October 24 with his press spokesman, Jim Hagerty. They traveled by helicopter to a large open parking lot in downtown Houston next to Sam Houston Coliseum. A crowd of several thousand assembled in front of a platform where a welcoming committee awaited his arrival. Those seated on the platform included Oveta and her close friend George Brown; former governor Allan Shivers, who was leading the Texas Democrats for Nixon and Lodge organization; and several officials of the Texas Republican Party. After the ceremony, Eisenhower and Hagerty were driven to the massive, green-roofed Shamrock Hotel, where the president posed in a private room for pictures with various Republican aspirants for Congress, including John Tower. Oveta returned home to prepare for the event at Rice later that night.[31]

When Eisenhower arrived on the Rice campus, Oveta, George Brown, and Rice president Carey Croneis met him at the front door of the university gymnasium and then accompanied him to the speaker's platform, where he addressed an audience of eight thousand students, faculty, school administrators, and special guests. Before the president began his speech, he acknowledged Oveta, his "good friend and wise counselor of many years." Despite the White House's statement that his speech would be "nonpolitical," Eisenhower touted the accomplishments of his administration with the clear implication that Nixon would continue that record. He also countered Senator Kennedy's claims (without naming the Democratic candidate) that the nation's military defenses had fallen behind those of the Soviet Union. The president received a standing ovation when he declared that the South was a longtime staunch defender of states' rights, "to its great and everlasting credit." Civil rights leaders later criticized Eisenhower's remarks because white supremacists in the South were invoking the states' rights argument in defense of racial segregation. After the speech, Eisenhower invited Oveta, former governor Shivers, and Continental Oil Company board chairman L. F. McCollum to his hotel suite for a private talk.[32]

The next morning, Oveta hosted a breakfast for Eisenhower at the Shamrock Hotel that included twenty-three other guests, including her son, Bill, and 8F crowd associates George Brown, Judge James Elkins, and Gus Wortham, as well as *Houston Chronicle* publisher John T. Jones and *Houston Press* editor George Carmack. After breakfast, Eisenhower departed from the Shamrock grounds by helicopter to the airport for his flight back to Washington. Afterward, he wrote Oveta: "Quite the nicest part of being in Houston was the opportunity to see you again and to get your always refreshing, always intelligent and always interesting viewpoint on many of the problems that concern us both. Thank you so much for all you did to make my visit there successful."[33]

A few days before the general election, the polls indicated a very tight race in Texas between Nixon and Kennedy. At Oveta's urging, Nixon traveled to Houston on the night of November 3 to speak at Miller Theater, an amphitheater in Hermann Park. Oveta headed the reception committee that greeted the vice president's airplane when it landed at Houston Municipal Airport a few minutes before 8:00 p.m. After a press conference at the airport, Nixon, Oveta, and the rest of their party traveled in a motorcade down the Gulf Freeway and on to Hermann Park. At Oveta's request, Department of Health, Education, and Welfare secretary Arthur Flemming accompanied her in a convertible car provided by the reception committee. After exiting the freeway, attendants lowered the car tops and the motorcade drove slowly past crowds lined up on the street sidewalks. At the amphitheater, Oveta was assigned a prominent chair on the stage behind the podium from where Nixon delivered his speech. A KPRC-TV crew filmed Nixon's talk for broadcast on the station's 10:00 p.m. evening news as well as for distribution to other television stations around Texas in the following days. Nixon's visit lasted less than two and a half hours, with the vice president's plane lifting off at about 10:30 p.m. As Oveta was driven home by her chauffeur, she felt encouraged enough by the size and enthusiasm of the crowds on the streets to harbor hope that Nixon might prevail in Texas.[34]

Those hopes evaporated late in the night of November 8, when the returns revealed that although Nixon had won Harris County, he would lose Texas and the nation in one of the closest presidential elections in US history. Oveta had supported Nixon during the campaign largely out of loyalty to Eisenhower. Her main regret about the election results was that Eisenhower had seen the campaign as a referendum on his presidency, and she knew from reports of friends in the administration that he had taken the defeat personally and was depressed.

On November 30, Oveta traveled to Washington to attend Eisenhower's final thank you dinner in the White House with Nixon, White House staff, and current and former cabinet members and other administration officials. After dinner, the Marine Orchestra and the Air Force "Singing Strings" band performed while many of the guests danced and visited informally, reminiscing about their experiences as key players in the Eisenhower presidency. Oveta took the opportunity one last time before Ike became a private citizen to thank him for his support during her days as Department of Health, Education, and Welfare secretary. Eisenhower in turn thanked Oveta for her service dating all the way back to when they had first met in London over a quarter of a century before, when she was still the "Little Colonel" and he was the "Supreme Commander, Allied Expeditionary Force."

Ike and Oveta would maintain their close relationship after Eisenhower was no longer president. Four days before leaving office, Ike sent Oveta his warm greetings for a happy birthday, adding that he intended to stay in touch with her. "In the years to come," he stressed, "Mamie and I hope to see you often." It was a hope that would be fulfilled.[35]

# CHAPTER 41

# THE DEATH OF WILL HOBBY

On January 20, 1961, the inauguration of John F. Kennedy left Oveta Culp Hobby with no special ties to the White House for the first time since FDR's second term. At the start of Kennedy's presidency, it appeared Oveta would have some influence in his administration and in Congress through her longtime relationships with the new vice president, Lyndon B. Johnson, and Sam Rayburn, who had retained his position as Speaker of the House. But a deeply frustrated LBJ soon found himself with little influence as the odd man out in the Kennedy administration, while cancer would kill Rayburn before year's end. Sam Rayburn's death was a particularly hard loss for the Hobbys. When Rayburn entered his final illness, Oveta sent him a letter of appreciation and farewell. "Will and I . . . were talking about you over dinner last night," she wrote, "counting up the years and the achievements with the pride of old friends, and I can't quite tell you how deeply it made us realize how much we of America owe to you." Rayburn responded, "You and Will have always been fine and kind to me. You have really been my friends and I have in every way tried to reciprocate. Thank you and Will for the great friendship you have given me over the years." Rayburn died two months later.[1]

Oveta's cabinet service in the previous administration, the prominent national role she had played as an Eisenhower Republican in 1952 and 1956, and her newspaper's endorsement of Richard Nixon for president ensured she would not play a part in JFK's "New Frontier." Nor did she really expect to have a role. She did attend a meeting at the White House in the autumn of 1961 at the invitation of presidential spokesman Pierre Salinger, but the occasion was something of a press promotion and of little import. When JFK came to Houston on September 11, 1962, to give his famed "We Choose the Moon" speech at Rice University Stadium and to tour NASA, Oveta was celebrating the recent birth of another grandchild, Andrew Purefoy Hobby, Bill and Diana's third child. Nevertheless, she was among the local dignitaries who greeted JFK when he arrived at Ellington Field on Air Force One. She had an opportunity to chat briefly with the president as they stood on the tarmac, but there was nothing of substance to that brief encounter.[2]

Oveta might have been exiled from the White House during JFK's presidency but for her ties to LBJ, yet her relationship with one former president remained strong. At the beginning of October 1961, Dwight Eisenhower wrote Oveta he had been invited to San Antonio to campaign for Republican congressional candidate John Goode. He told Oveta he had been pleasantly surprised to learn that Henry Catto was a Republican candidate for the Texas Legislature. He would be happy to help her son-in-law's campaign. It was Henry's second race for the legislature, after losing a bid a year earlier in the general election. Jessica had been surprised when Henry decided to announce as a Republican, because he had not previously identified with either major political party. His decision caused Jessica some concern because she was a staunch Democrat who disliked the extreme right-wingers in the Republican Party. Nevertheless, she happily campaigned for her husband. Will Hobby approved of Henry's decision to run for the legislature, but when Will learned his son-in-law was running as a Republican, he asked Henry if he had lost his mind. Because the Democratic Party still dominated Texas politics, running for public office as a Republican was considered folly.[3]

In his letter to Oveta, Ike stressed that he was eager to see her again. "It seems probable that I shall make a trip down there at the very end of the month," Eisenhower wrote. "Will there be any chance that you might be in town?" Because of a long-planned trip to New York City, Oveta was unable to go to San Antonio to see Ike. Jessica and Henry, however, greeted Eisenhower at the airport and took advantage of the moment for a campaign photo op. Despite Eisenhower's endorsements, both Goode and Catto lost their races. As Henry Catto later observed, "Ike or no, it was no go." After the election, Oveta wrote Eisenhower: "You were generous to make the trip to San Antonio. . . . Jessica and Henry were ecstatic over your visit and the time they spent with you. Jessica said that one of the worst things about Henry's losing his race was that they were afraid that you would be disappointed." Ike responded, "Your daughter is charming—and she particularly interested me because I detected in her so many of your wonderful characteristics. And I enjoyed greatly being with her husband. Of course I was disappointed in the outcome of the election."[4]

Ike and Oveta remained close, and they continued their frequent communications until Ike's death. In December 1961, Oveta directed the Hobby Family Foundation to donate $5,000 to the Eisenhower Presidential Library in Abilene, Kansas. That same month, Ike wrote Oveta, "Failing to think of anything that I considered suitable for a Christmas present for one I owe so much (I mean a gift that I can afford!), I have to resort to the only alternative I can think of—which is to send you once again assurances of my personal devotion and my lasting gratitude for your friendship. Merry Christmas." Immediately before Christmas, Oveta shipped a box of golf balls to Ike as a gift. "When friends start concentrating on giving me gifts that indicate a serious preoccupation with sports," Ike responded, "I think I can truthfully say that I have finally 'retired.' I am delighted to have two dozen of my favorite golf balls—I assure you that at the rate I have been using them in my two days here at El Dorado, that they will come in most handy.[5]

A month later Ike, who was still golfing in Palm Desert, California, wrote Oveta to apologize for a note he had sent to the *Houston Chronicle* congratulating the newspaper on its sixtieth anniversary, which the *Chronicle* eagerly published. He explained to Oveta that he had sent the note "at the suggestion of the Republican National Committee" and that he had not paid close enough attention to the matter. He became upset when he realized he had endorsed Oveta's business competitor. He was eager to assure her, "there is only one paper in Houston—or for that matter in all Texas—that could inspire from me a voluntary salute. And you know the identity of that one!" He added that he was playing golf every day with the golf balls Oveta had shipped to him.[6]

Oveta and Ike's communications remained steady throughout the first half of the decade. During the race for governor of Texas in the fall of 1962, the Republican National Committee led Ike astray once again by persuading him to write Oveta to ask her to endorse GOP candidate Jack Cox instead of Democrat John Connally. Cox had worked with Oveta to elect pro-Eisenhower delegates to represent Texas at the Texas Republican Convention in 1952. "It is not for me to advise you about things about which you are more intimately acquainted than I," Eisenhower wrote. "Whatever you decide to do will have my approval." Despite Eisenhower's message, the *Houston Post* endorsed Connally, who went on to defeat Cox.[7]

After the election, Oveta, understandably concerned about declining Ike's request, wrote him a detailed justification for her decision not to endorse Cox. She explained that Cox had made unacceptable racial comments when he had met with her and the other members of the *Post*'s editorial board. Oveta also disliked statements he had made on the campaign trail. "He was the only major Republican candidate we failed to endorse," Oveta told Ike. It was troubling enough that Cox had revealed a lack of knowledge about significant issues, but he had also stated his strong support for Mississippi governor Ross Barnett's attempt to prevent African American veteran James Meredith from enrolling at the University of Mississippi. Oveta pointed out that "most of the schools in Texas have moved smoothly" to desegregate, but Dallas was among those school districts that had continued to take delaying action, for which she blamed Dallas resident Cox and his supporters in the city's business community. Little Rock continued to be on Oveta's mind. She believed if he had become governor, Cox could have created "a crisis similar to that which occurred in . . . Little Rock" and in Oxford, Mississippi, where riots had broken out when James Meredith enrolled as the first black student at Ole Miss. Eisenhower was true to his word. Oveta's refusal to endorse Cox had no effect on their relationship.[8]

In October 1962, Ike, while working on his presidential memoir, *Mandate for Change*, asked Oveta if she had a copy of the memorandum she composed for his administration to submit to Congress in 1953 to justify the creation of the Department of Health, Education, and Welfare (HEW). In a handwritten postscript he added, "It's been far too long since Mamie and I have seen you. I hope, most earnestly, that the Governor is doing well." Oveta found her copy of the memorandum and sent it to Ike, who summarized it in his memoir. After *Mandate for Change* was published in early November 1963, Ike sent an autographed copy to Oveta. "It is a book which Will and I shall treasure throughout our lives," she responded. "I feel that we all owe you a tremendous debt for writing this book because only you know the full story which you have told here." This incident made her realize that Ike lacked a large number of important records documenting her tenure as secretary of HEW. As a result, Oveta eventually agreed to give thirty linear feet of her 1952 campaign and HEW papers plus 117 scrapbooks to the Eisenhower Presidential Library in Abilene, Kansas, to ensure the record would be as complete as possible. At the same time, she also donated her Women's Army Corps papers to the Library of Congress.[9]

Although she had no meaningful connection to the Kennedys during LBJ's frustrating years as vice president, Oveta continued to be close to LBJ and Lady Bird. She was a frequent guest of the Johnsons at parties they hosted at the LBJ Ranch, often flying with George and Alice Brown in the Brown and Root Company plane to attend events such as a barbecue honoring United Nations officials the spring before President Kennedy was assassinated. When Oveta visited LBJ at his ranch, she often brought him tear sheets of positive editorials she had recently published in the *Post* about his good work as vice president. To make certain his parties at the ranch in honor of dignitaries were given special coverage in her newspaper, Oveta occasionally brought a *Post* reporter with her.[10]

During his vice presidency LBJ made other efforts to preserve his ties with Will and Oveta. In 1963 he was frequently in Houston to visit the Manned Spacecraft Center in nearby Clear Lake in his role as chairman of the National Aeronautics and Space Center, one of the few programs in JFK's administration on which he had influence. "My husband was then confined to his room," Oveta recalled. "The Vice President always came to see him when he came to Houston." Lady Bird Johnson later noted her husband "was a great admirer of former Governor Hobby and looked to him for counsel. Even after [Oveta] was the star in the family and Governor Hobby had declined into old age, [Lyndon] would seek him out and ask his advice and sort of pay special deference to him, which was . . . recognized and appreciated by them."[11]

Will was buoyed by LBJ's visits. They talked politics and reminisced about the days when Will was governor of Texas and LBJ's father was in the legislature. During LBJ's visit early on the morning of August 13, 1963, accompanied by Jack Valenti, the vice president pulled up a chair next to Will's bed and leaned close so he could hear Will's weak voice. Oveta and Bill were also in the room. "Mr. Johnson began talking rapidly," Oveta said, "and when [he] stopped for breath, Governor asked, 'Well, Lyndon, how's the President treating you?' William [Bill] and I whooped with laughter. Mr. Johnson looked at [Bill] and said, 'Your father always goes right for the jugular!' But he turned to Governor and said President Kennedy was treating him well. And then he started talking about Robert Kennedy, and what he said, I could never repeat in any kind of company." Before leaving, LBJ gave Will a silk robe as a "get well" gift.[12]

After he returned to Washington, LBJ wrote Oveta, "What an uncommon man [Will] is! It was so good to find him lucid and interested. I pray for him." Enclosed in his letter was a personal note to Will: "You looked so handsome in those pajamas that when I came upon a pair of pajamas I had from Hong Kong, I decided they should go to the man who wears them so well. I'm delighted they have an 'LBJ' embroidered on the pocket because there isn't anyone except Lady Bird I would rather share that name [with], and also because it will prove to some of those Houston fat cat critics that I am a man who is willing to give the shirt off his back at all times!" The warm and personal attention LBJ paid to Will in his last months made its mark on Oveta. She sent LBJ a personal note after the August 1963 meeting, telling him she was deeply touched by his visit and that it had meant much to Will, who "has mentioned it to me many times since."[13]

Like most Americans, Oveta's life was changed by the tragic murder of President Kennedy in Dallas on November 22, 1963. President Kennedy, First Lady Jackie Kennedy, Vice President Johnson, and Lady Bird Johnson had traveled to Texas to raise money for JFK's 1964 reelection campaign and to unify the bitterly divided Texas Democratic Party. After delivering a speech in San Antonio, the Kennedys and the Johnsons flew to Houston, where JFK spoke at a sold-out testimonial dinner honoring Congressman Albert Thomas. Because Oveta was out of the country, Bill Hobby and *Houston Post* columnist and advertising agency executive Jack Valenti met the presidential party at Houston's municipal airport. Valenti was a friend and an occasional advisor to LBJ. After the dinner that night, Valenti went to Fort Worth with JFK and LBJ. The next day, Kennedy was assassinated while riding in a motorcade in downtown Dallas.[14]

In an oral history interview recorded for the LBJ Library nearly five years after the assassination, Oveta observed, "This country was blessed that [LBJ] was vice president when this tragedy occurred, because no one comes to mind that I think could have picked up as easily and as effectively as he picked up." As an old friend of the new president, Oveta was among those who understood that LBJ was well prepared by skill and experience to do whatever was necessary to calm a grieving nation and to keep the ship of state on a safe course moving forward. Two days after the assassination, an editorial in the *Houston Post*, "New Leader of Free World Well Prepared," expressed the solid confidence Oveta had in Johnson's leadership. Bill Hobby sent the editorial to President Johnson, whose response signified that Oveta's links to the White House had been restored. "These have been somber hours," LBJ wrote Bill. "I wanted you to know that your letter and editorial comforted me greatly. How I wish I had the wise counsel of your father right now, for he was always a beneficial influence in my life." LBJ's lament about Will Hobby was a reference to Will being near death and inaccessible by December 1963. He added, "I am going to lean on you, Bill, for much help in the months ahead." LBJ was true to his word, but the Hobby he would lean on the most would be Bill's mother.[15]

By the begining of 1964 it was clear to all that Will Hobby had begun his final decline. He had long ago stopped going to his office at the *Post* and he rarely left his bed at the mansion on Remington Lane. When he did it was only with the help of his attendants, and he usually remained in his room. Despite his condition, Will still managed to enjoy the times when handymen and painters from the *Post* came to the mansion to make repairs to the aging structure. He had his nurse show the workers into his room, and then, with his head and shoulders propped up on pillows, he would invite them to play poker with him. "It was always for low stakes," one of the staff recalled. "They'd play for pocket change—or [would] join him in watching and placing small bets on a TV ball game. This would often go on for hours with little work getting accomplished. Mrs. Hobby would come home and, understanding that it was Governor's doing, would never say a word [to the workers], but you could sense her intense disapproval."[16]

During those last few months of Will's life, Oveta remained close to home, making few excursions to the outside world. One exception to that routine was when her old acquaintance Clare Boothe Luce was honored with a dinner at Houston's Rice Hotel ballroom in January 1964. Oveta invited Luce to stay with her at the Shadyside mansion during her two-night stay in Houston. Oveta gave the speech introducing Luce at the Rice Hotel dinner. "Our friendship began during the years of World War II when she was a distinguished member of Congress and I the inexperienced director of the WAC," Oveta explained. "I was often called up to Capitol Hill to answer the questions of Congress, and I soon learned that whenever I appeared before a committee which included Mrs. Luce in its membership she saw to it that I got fair play, that I received the opportunity to present my facts as best I could. Our friendship stems from that time." During the two nights Luce was an overnight guest at 2 Remington Lane, Oveta savored the opportunity to have late-night chats with her friend, who was a tireless gossip and entertaining conversationalist. After Luce returned home, she wrote Oveta, "I think you know that the delicious, warm, unforgettable, part of my trip were my late conversations, over a chaste glass of milk with you."[17]

Early in 1964, Oveta, sensing that the end was growing ever closer for Will, arranged to have one of the regularly scheduled meetings of the *Houston Post*'s editorial board at the mansion on Remington Lane. She had attendants carry Will downstairs from his bedroom, still in his pajamas, to sit in on the meeting. The board members were struck by his frail appearance. "His ears . . . seemed so thin they were almost translucent," one recalled years later. "But he seemed to enjoy himself thoroughly. . . . [H]e was among friends and associates with whom he had worked, in some cases, for many years. Most of us would not see him again."[18]

In early February, the Harris County Commissioners Court voted to name a new sixty-five-foot-long ferryboat to be used at the Lynchburg automobile crossing of the Houston Ship Channel after the former governor. Oveta christened the *William P. Hobby* when the boat was launched at the Todd Shipyards on Greens Bayou. Appropriately, given the intertwined careers of both men, a second new ferryboat, named the *Ross Sterling*, was launched at the same time to operate in tandem with the *William P. Hobby*. Jack Harris arranged to broadcast the launching ceremony live on KPRC-TV so Will could watch from his bed.[19]

*Oveta Culp Hobby and Clare Boothe Luce, 1964.*

A few days after the ferryboat launching, Will's condition worsened. His physician told Oveta that Will had pneumonia and it was not likely he would survive. She spent several days and nights at his bedside anticipating his death, but he rallied and survived the pneumonia, although it left him in a precariously weak state. It was an extremely difficult emotional and physical time for Oveta, leaving her exhausted and depressed. During a phone conversation with President Johnson on February 14, George Brown told him about Will's latest health crisis. "He's very critical," Brown reported. "Wasn't supposed to live. . . . [H]e's over that, but he's still awful weak. . . . Damn near died." Brown told the president that this latest bout had taken a heavy toll on Oveta. "That's what got her down, staying up with him day and night," Brown said. "I mean he was just touch and go for several days. She's been under the weather for about two weeks and is just getting up. [She was] lonesome last night and called me, and we just talked about a half hour about everything, over the phone."[20]

The end for the eighty-six-year-old Will Hobby finally came on the night of June 7, 1964, when he suffered a massive stroke. His physician, Mavis Kelsey, pronounced him dead at 10:30 p.m., as Bill and Oveta sat at his bedside. Jessica was in San Antonio and was unable to get to Houston in time. Bill immediately telephoned the news to the *Post's* night desk, and the morning edition's front page was redone to announce Will's passing in a headline. Bill sent a letter with the news of his father's death to his former teacher, John Davis, acknowledging what many who were close to "Governor" must have felt: that Will's health "had been such for several years that his passing could not have been other than a release for him."[21]

Will's death was met with an outpouring of condolences to Oveta, and his life was praised and celebrated widely. Governor Connally declared a week of official mourning and ordered the lowering of the flags over all state buildings to half-mast. Houston mayor Louie Welch directed that the flags over city property also be lowered. In an editorial about Will's death, the *Houston Chronicle* observed, "Governor Hobby was a warm and gracious man, with a lively mind, and deft but gentle wit. [He] played an important part in the building of Houston, and he has left his mark on it." In its obituary for Will, the *New York Times* noted, "Mr. Hobby found himself Governor—in the midst of a war, a drought and a political scandal. Nevertheless, Governor Hobby pressed successfully for a progressive legislative program, including women's suffrage and drought relief."[22]

President Johnson released an official statement from the White House declaring, "Texas and the Nation are diminished by the loss of Governor Hobby. Throughout the last 30 years he was a wise, charitable, and loyal friend to me." But no statement came from Dwight Eisenhower. A few days later, Oveta discovered that one of her staff members had not followed through with her assignment to send a telegram notifying the Eisenhowers about Will's death. She quickly dispatched a letter explaining to Ike why he hadn't received the notice. She assured him, "Throughout the years of our friendship you and Mamie have both consistently shown your warm interest in his welfare. [Will] always valued your concern."[23]

Will's death had been anticipated for several weeks, which made it possible for Oveta to have all arrangements made early enough for the funeral service to be held the day after his death. Accordingly, Will's funeral was held on June 8 at 11:00 a.m. in the 1,500-seat, 125-year-old Episcopalian Christ Church Cathedral. The cathedral was filled to capacity, forcing approximately two hundred people to stand along the interior walls, while another large group waited outside. A white-and-purple-robed choir followed a gold cross down the center aisle to the altar as the cathedral bell chimed. Pallbearers and executives of the *Houston Post* and KPRC followed Will's flag-draped casket. Because Will had complained to Oveta that most eulogies were pompous, none were delivered at his service. Although Will had never been actively religious, he had identified as a Methodist when asked, and he had always supported ecumenism. Hence, Methodist bishop Paul Martin was called on to assist Episcopalian canon H. Douglas Fontain with the service. Following Episcopalian tradition, there were no flowers in the church and Will Hobby's name was not mentioned in the service.[24]

Will Hobby was buried at the historic 1871 Glenwood Cemetery on the north bank of Buffalo Bayou in Houston. A silk US flag that had been displayed in his office at the *Post* for more than thirty years draped his casket. Before the casket was lowered into the grave, Jack Harris and funeral director George Lewis Jr. removed the flag and presented it to Oveta, who then handed it to Jessica and Bill. Will Hobby was buried next to his

*Front page of the* Houston Post, *June 7, 1964.*

first wife, Miss Willie, who had died all those many years ago. The plot on the other side of Will's grave was reserved for Oveta.[25]

On July 2, less than one month after Will's death, the Houston City Council honored his legacy in an especially noteworthy way. The City of Houston was building a new international airport north of the city that would eventually be named Houston Intercontinental. The plan was to keep the old airport open and available to private aviation, but to avoid confusion it needed a new name. The council voted to change the name of Houston International Airport to William P. Hobby Airport. Will's passing gave the council not only an opportunity to have an appropriate name but also a way to honor one of Houston's most important leaders. Other namings also honored Will's legacy. In October 1964, newspaper publisher Houston Harte funded a permanent historical marker for the Texas Historical Commission to place at Will's birthplace in Moscow, Texas. In January 1965, the Houston Independent School District named an elementary school in Will's honor.[26]

As Oveta continued in her role as chairman and CEO of the Hobby enterprises, she was ever mindful of the role Will had played in her success. In an overly modest moment, Oveta told Marguerite Johnston, "Every lovely or interesting thing that has happened to me fell in my lap. I have never had to fight for anything. And, of course, it was Governor who made it all possible."[27]

At the time of Will Hobby's death, the *Houston Post* was continuing to prosper along with the boomtown it covered. It now had one of the largest circulations in Texas, with more than 220,000 subscribers at a time when the city's population was slightly less than one million. As the *Post* grew in size, its influence in the Texas news media industry increased. Oveta Culp Hobby and the Hobbys' friend *San Antonio Express-News* publisher Houston Harte were arguably the most influential newspaper publishers in the state, especially as the *Houston Chronicle*'s Jesse Jones and the *Fort Worth Star-Telegram*'s Amon Carter Sr. passed from the scene and the *Dallas Morning News*' ailing Edward "Ted" Dealy and his editors wandered in the wilderness of the extreme right wing. As a result, Oveta was much in demand as a speaker at news industry gatherings, and her declared opinions, which often stressed the importance to democracy of a free press, carried weight within the profession. One of her favored lines when addressing her colleagues in the news business was, "The facts and events of each day become the material which a citizen uses in his daily work of self-government. News is the homework of a free man." When Oveta addressed the annual meeting of the Texas Associated Press Managing Editors in Houston in January 1963, she reminded the editors that a newspaper was more than a business. "In a free society such as ours, there is no greater responsibility resting on any group of men and women than the editing of honest, meaningful newspapers, large and small," she said. "The test is to do all of this accurately, honestly, and with the greatest possible speed."[28]

In February 1963 the Hobbys expanded their media holdings by outbidding four rivals to purchase the morning *Galveston News*, the afternoon *Galveston Tribune*, and the afternoon *Texas City Sun* from Galveston's Moody Foundation. The purchase was made over the objection of business leader and philanthropist Mary Moody Northen, whose father, W. L. Moody, had founded the newspapers. "This has broken my heart," Northen declared after the other stockholders outvoted her. "My father told me never to dispose of these papers." *Time* published a story about the purchase, declaring that the *Post* "has of recent years quietly tended to patiently building up . . . its reputation as one of the best in the Southwest." *Time* noted that with Will too ill to provide leadership, Oveta had managed the paper "with the same crispness that she brought to her work as wartime director of the WACs and as first U.S. Secretary of Health, Education and Welfare." The purchase made the *Post* the dominant newspaper in the fast-growing upper Texas Gulf Coast region, but *Time* declared, "Crew-cut Post Managing Editor William P. Hobby Jr., 30, Oveta's boy, was quick to hush speculation that it was out for more. 'Much as I like the sound of the phrase,' said he, 'this is not the start of an empire.'" The *Post*'s domination would be short lived. The newspaper lost its lead when the *Houston Chronicle* bought the *Houston Press* from the Scripps-Howard chain and closed it down in March 1964. The *Chronicle* grabbed the *Press*'s subscribers, which increased its circulation to over 250,000. It added the *Press*'s most popular syndicated features, and it took a lead over the *Post* that it never lost.[29]

Two months after purchasing the Galveston newspapers, Oveta acted quickly to tamp down grumbling in the island city about Houstonians taking control of a treasured local business institution. Accompanied by Bill, who had recently been elected to the Texas Press Association's board of directors, she addressed a sold-out Galveston Chamber of Commerce luncheon at the Jack Tar Hotel on April 1. Oveta assured the Galveston business community that the *Post* would work with the chamber of commerce "to bring additional people and payrolls to Galveston and shall continue to try to make this city attractive to visitors, to new residents and new business." The Hobbys soon merged the Texas City and Galveston newspapers to form the *News-Sun Today* and expanded its coverage to include the booming area around the Manned Spacecraft Center in Clear Lake City. As subscription numbers peaked in 1967, Oveta sold the *News-Sun* for a hefty profit.[30]

After Will's death, Oveta assumed the position of chairman of the *Houston Post* board and chief executive officer. She appointed Bill Hobby president and executive editor and Jack Harris executive vice president of the Houston Post Company and president of its broadcast division. In 1967, James Crowther joined the *Post* as vice president and general counsel of the newspaper. A native of Ohio, Crowther had practiced law for eight years at Butler and Binion, the firm that had represented the Hobby family since the end of World War II. Crowther would soon become one of the most important figures in the Hobby family business.[31]

Crowther later noted that if Oveta had been forced to "choose between being the publisher and the editor, I believe she would have chosen to be the editor." He noted that by wearing both hats, Oveta was in a position to resolve conflicts between the paper's news and business interests. He argued that describing her management style as "demanding" was too strong but noted she was firm in her insistence on quality and loyalty. "She had this fire, this desire, this will to succeed," Jim Crowther observed. "Being average was not in her makeup." Oveta insisted to her editors that the *Post* be known for the high quality of its reporting and that it be "a good corporate citizen." And whenever the newspaper made mistakes, they would be made "very, very slowly," a line that expressed her deliberate approach to issues. It was also a phrase she borrowed from a statement that President Eisenhower made to his cabinet in its first meeting of his presidency.[32]

Oveta's insistence on excellence paid off in 1965, when one of her reporters, Gene Goltz, won the *Post* its first Pulitzer Prize for an exposé of city hall corruption in Pasadena, the major oil-refining center on the Houston Ship Channel. It was the first Pulitzer won by any Houston newspaper. Some credit for the prize-winning story belongs to William Woestendiek, who had become the *Post*'s managing editor in 1964 after serving as an editor for *Newsday*. Woestendiek was a self-assertive and outspoken journalist who encouraged and supported aggressive investigative reporting. He demanded his reporters follow the news wherever it took them, no matter how controversial or threatening to the city's power elite. He would later claim that was not what Oveta had in mind when she insisted on quality. Woestendiek's first sense that he and Oveta had differing definitions of investigative journalism and editorial freedom was in 1966, when the *Post* fired politically liberal editorial cartoonist Thomas Darcy, whom Woestendiek had hired the year before. Darcy, whose cartoon style and political outlook was similar to that of the *Washington Post*'s Herblock, described his own work as "not for the amusement of the comfortable." He was an early critic of the Vietnam War, and he frequently drew unflattering cartoons of Oveta's good friend LBJ, which Woestendiek claimed was the reason Oveta ordered Darcy's dismissal.[33]

Darcy's firing signified that not all was well at the *Post* in the mid-1960s, despite its newly won Pulitzer. Tension between Woestendiek on one side and Oveta and Bill Hobby on the other escalated as Woestendiek claimed that Oveta was killing important editorial op-ed columns critical of LBJ. The brash managing editor also alleged Bill Hobby had censored a number of stories written by his investigative reporters that the Hobbys feared would anger their key advertisers, citing as an example a story about local housewives picketing the Weingarten grocery stores because of high prices. The family-owned grocery chain's elderly founder and patriarch, Joe Weingarten, had been an old friend of Will Hobby's.[34]

Woestendiek's complaints and criticism of Oveta led to a predictable result: she fired him. The *Post* story, however, said he had resigned. She later charged that Woestendiek was "not a competent managing editor" and that he was trying to get rid of longtime and highly valued members of the *Post*'s news staff to replace them with people who would be loyal to him. Whether it was a prime factor or not, it was also known that Woestendiek, who was married, was having an affair with one of his female staff members, whom he later wed. A few years after Woestendiek's dismissal, an anonymous *Post* "insider" told

*Texas Monthly* that Woestendiek was fired because he "popped off" to Oveta one too many times. Woestendiek, however, said he was fired because his philosophy of what a newspaper should be differed radically from Oveta's.[35]

Not long after he was fired, Woestendiek gave a lecture at Rice University about the journalism profession, in which he also gave his views about the state of newspaper reporting in Houston. To no one's surprise, the outspoken editor was highly critical of both the *Post* and the *Chronicle*. "A newspaper should be a watchdog," he declared. "In Houston they are lap-dogs." The city's largest retail businesses, he charged, had too much influence at both newspapers "over areas . . . which should be managed by the staff and owners with no regard to the advertisers." He also complained there was too much advertising in both papers, which resulted in not enough space for hard news. He acknowledged that newspapers were businesses but pointed out they had the unique status of being protected by the First Amendment, which meant they had significant public responsibilities. Obviously referring to Oveta Hobby, "the owners," he said, "decide what they consider good for the public and select what they print and where it goes accordingly." Their editorial policies, Woestendiek stated, "could be summed up in three words: don't make waves." Peace was soon restored in the *Post*'s newsroom and the paper moved forward successfully, but it remained behind the *Houston Chronicle* in circulation.[36]

It seems obvious that the trouble between Oveta and her forceful and opinionated managing editor was a classic example of the kind of clash that can occur in a news organization between the social and business interests of the owner-publisher and the crusading mission of the editorial and news side of the enterprise. Undoubtedly, Woestendiek's strong muckraking drive, his professional ambitions, and his willingness to print critical stories and editorials about Oveta's friends in the business and the political elite (especially LBJ) were destined to conflict with Oveta's controlling nature, her deliberative management philosophy, and her desire for the *Post* to be a "good corporate citizen." And, of course, the *Post*'s editorials were understood to be the opinions of the owner and the editorial board, not the managing editor. The accuracy of Oveta's charges against Woestendiek are difficult to determine, although several years later when he was managing editor of the *Cleveland Plain Dealer*, he had a similar conflict with his publisher that had the same result: his dismissal. Woestendiek eventually ended his career as dean of the School of Journalism at the University of Southern California. He died in 2015.[37]

Although Oveta kept her primary focus on the *Houston Post*, in the years immediately after Will's death she didn't neglect her radio and television stations. One of her executives recalled that as she walked through the halls at KPRC, she stopped in each office doorway and talked briefly with the people there. "The conversations were not pro forma, either—she knew each person well enough to make her comments and questions meaningful." She also held weekly Monday morning meetings with KPRC executives to review broadcast ratings and to discuss other business and programming issues. She was always eager to know about any new developments in the broadcast industry at large. KPRC's Jack McGrew noted that Oveta's "interest in what was going on in the broader

*Oveta Culp Hobby with Jack McGrew, KPRC Radio station manager*
*(left) and Jack Harris, KPRC-TV station manager, 1960.*

world of both television and radio was very keen." She read the broadcast industry publications, she wanted her executives to be active in national professional organizations,
and she expected them to keep her posted about what they were hearing at their national
conventions.[38]

KPRC-TV and KPRC Radio were the cash cows of the Hobby media operations, due
largely to the skills of station executives Jack Harris and Jack McGrew and news director Ray Miller. The city's continuing prosperity also helped. Harris had earned much
respect from his professional peers nationally for his innovative direction of the stations.
Miller was also widely respected in the broadcast news industry and was an active and
influential member of the Radio-Television News Directors Association. For several years
in the 1960s and 1970s Miller hosted *The Last Word*, a locally influential late Sunday
night television interview program that was often the only place Houstonians could hear
in-depth discussions about current local, state, and national news. "Fortunately, we've
had good management," Oveta noted in an interview she gave in 1969. "We're very proud
of that station. We are very proud of all its public service awards, and the constructive
part it has played in the community."[39]

As an affiliate of NBC, a pioneer in color television, KPRC-TV was the first station
in Houston to broadcast all of its local programs in color, the only station in Texas

with a full-time Austin news bureau, and the first to use portable live mini-cameras. Oveta's programming team at KPRC-TV also made the station one of the state's leaders in attractive locally produced special programs, an initiative Oveta eagerly supported. When the Texas Legislature passed legislation in 1968 to establish the official "Texas Tourist Trails" to attract out-of-state vacationers, her staff developed the idea of filming a thirty-minute special program titled "More Than a State of Mind," to bring attention to the newly designated roads. The staff wanted lame-duck Texas governor John Connally to narrate the film, but he was resistant. The governor's reluctance disappeared, however, after Oveta called and made a personal plea for him to participate in the program. KPRC's most successful local production would be the *Eyes of Texas* travelogue program created and initially hosted by Ray Miller but later hosted by popular KPRC news anchor Ron Stone.[40]

Under Oveta's active direction, KPRC was also the first television station in Houston to hire a female reporter. In 1967, Kay Bailey, a twenty-four-year-old recent graduate of the University of Texas Law School, was unable to find a job as a lawyer because of the informal sexist policies then in place at Houston's law firms. As she later remembered, "My [male] law school classmates were going right to work, while I was still looking." In frustration, she abandoned her search for a job as an attorney and instead decided to seek employment as a television reporter, despite having no journalism experience or background. "I dropped in cold, without an appointment, to KPRC-TV," Bailey recalled. She asked the receptionist if she could talk to someone about a job as a news reporter. The receptionist called news director Ray Miller. "To everyone's surprise," Bailey said, "Ray Miller . . . came out to visit with a person who didn't have an appointment. Ray later told me he was intrigued because no one with a law degree had ever applied for a job at KPRC before." Miller didn't have a position available, but he asked her not to take another job until he could work something out. He went to Jack Harris and recommended that a place be found for her on the reporting staff. Harris, who had great respect for Miller's judgment, took the idea to Oveta, who not only liked the prospect of a young woman with a law degree working for KPRC-TV but also was enthusiastic about her television station being the first in the city to have a woman news reporter. Because of Bailey's legal training and her undergraduate degree in government, Miller sent her to Austin to cover the legislature. After nearly five years of reporting from Austin and covering politics in Houston when the legislature was not in session, Bailey was elected in 1972 as a Republican state representative from an affluent district in west Houston.[41]

Oveta's decision to hire Kay Bailey sight unseen because she liked the idea of hiring Houston's first woman television reporter demonstrates her firm belief in equal rights for women; yet she was never comfortable with making a personal show of that belief, and she disliked bringing special attention to a particular woman's work or professional status. To her it was irrelevant that a professional person in any field happened to be a woman. It was her view that if too much was made of female achievement, it would not become a common thing. Jim Crowther once asked Oveta if she would like to change her title on the *Post*'s masthead from chairman to chairperson or chairwoman. "No," Oveta replied. "They know I'm a woman."[42]

Oveta revealed her thinking on this topic in a speech she gave in 1963 to the male-dominated International Management Congress. She warned business leaders they could "ill afford much longer to ignore almost entirely the brainpower possibilities of the other half of the human race. Women still have a long way to go before they are accepted without comment being made that they are women." She argued that most women in business simply wanted "to be taken for granted, to be judged on merit, to be a woman without italics or quotation marks around the word, to be allowed to do her job without prejudice or preference, and to receive the advancement and financial reward that her efforts justify."[43]

Oveta never publicly associated with the women's liberation movement, and she never self-identified as a feminist. When biographer Debra Sutphen asked several individuals who were close to Oveta how they thought Oveta viewed the issue of women's rights, none of them believed Oveta ever considered herself a feminist. "All seemed in general agreement that the term 'feminist' implied a belligerent support for women's causes," Sutphen reported. "It was a term that she rejected as extremist and unnecessarily confrontational." Oveta's daughter thought it would be more accurate to describe her mother as "a great defender of women" rather than a "feminist."[44]

Feminist or not, Oveta's behavior and the actions she took, beginning in childhood, from her deep admiration as a youth for her mother's work on behalf of women's suffrage to her fierce advocacy for the WAC, provide ample evidence that her support for equal rights for women was deeply embedded in her core beliefs. Oveta's experience as leader of the Women's Army Corps solidified her views. She stressed in one of her newspaper interviews that she believed the turning point in women's personal liberation took place the day women entered the armed services. An undated (ca. 1972) quote transcribed in her papers at Rice University can stand as the final word on her view of women's rights: "It is true, I was the first woman to do several jobs that were once open only to men. . . . It annoys me a little that people pull back and say, 'Well, a woman did that.' Why not a woman? I think we ought to get this out of the whole lexicon of thinking and writing, surprised when a woman does something. I'd like to live long enough to see people not be surprised by the fact that a woman succeeded in something."[45]

Benefitting from expert executive managers and Houston's boomtown economy, which was given an extra boost by the National Aeronautics and Space Administration's decision in 1961 to locate its Manned Spacecraft Center in nearby Clear Lake City, the *Houston Post* and KPRC Radio and television enjoyed a steady increase in profits throughout the 1960s. With her media company in good hands and free of the responsibility of managing the care of an invalid husband, Oveta was open to invitations from LBJ's White House to take on special presidential assignments that would draw her back to Washington and government service.

# CHAPTER 42

# L B J

W hen her friends of many years, Lyndon and Lady Bird Johnson, moved into the White House after JFK's assassination, Oveta's connections to the presidency were fully restored. Those links were further strengthened when journalist and fellow Texan Liz Carpenter, an old friend of Oveta's, became Lady Bird's press secretary. Oveta's connection to Lyndon and Lady Bird was also enhanced by her warm friendship with fellow Houstonians George and Alice Brown, who were especially close to the Johnsons. George and his late brother, Herman, had long played crucial roles in LBJ's rise as a politician.[1]

Oveta's bond with LBJ was of a far different nature from the one she had with Ike. For Oveta, Eisenhower had always been the inspirational supreme commander of Allied forces, someone she had held in awe ever since their first meeting in 1942. He was her leader and she was his follower. In some respects, Ike was a mentor and role model for Oveta, and although he was only fifteen years older than Oveta, he was also something of a father figure. They had a warm and mutually respectful relationship, but it was more reserved and formal than the one she had with Lyndon Johnson. Oveta had known LBJ, who was three years younger than she, since he was a young man who eagerly sought Will's blessing and support for his first congressional race in the late 1930s. Oveta's sister, Lynn, had dated LBJ's brother, Sam, when Lynn lived with her sister in Houston in 1934 and Sam was employed at a bank in the city. But Oveta and LBJ also shared a significant link that went even further back in their past. Not only was LBJ's father, Sam Johnson, a political ally of Will Hobby's when Sam was in the legislature and Will was governor, he also was a legislative ally of Ike Culp, and the three men forged friendships during their service in state government.[2]

Oveta and the Johnsons had been in the same social circles in Washington when Oveta was directing the Women's Army Corps and later when she was secretary of the Department of Health, Education, and Welfare (HEW). LBJ had led support for her nomination as director of the Federal Security Agency, and he had been an ally during the trying days of the Salk vaccine controversy. During Oveta's tenure on Eisenhower's cabinet, her relationship with Johnson, who was the Democrats' leader in the Senate, was politically important and served to strengthen their personal ties. "[LBJ] got along as well with Oveta as did anybody else," recalled George Reedy, Johnson's press spokesman. "And he got along even better with her after she got in the cabinet than he did before." LBJ was Oveta's peer, someone with whom she could comfortably discuss the nuts and bolts of politics as well as exchange gossip about mutual acquaintances while enjoying a drink and a cigarette. He was Oveta's gregarious friend, not an awe-inspiring mentor like Ike. Nevertheless, she deeply respected his political skill, and she enjoyed and appreciated the attention LBJ gave her once he was in the White House. "Lyndon always liked women," Lady Bird later observed, but he "was crazy about Oveta." The First Lady stated that one of several reasons her husband respected Oveta was because "she lived up to every obligation and every potential of growth that she had," and she "surely did live up to her obligations to the Governor" during his years as an invalid.[3]

*Oveta Culp Hobby with Lyndon B. Johnson*
*and Supreme Court Justice Tom Clark, October 1957.*

The frequency and duration of Oveta's contacts with the Johnsons increased notably after November 22, 1963. Oveta accepted nearly every one of the invitations she received to join them at their ranch in Texas or in Washington, DC. According to official records, Oveta made no fewer than fifteen visits to the White House while LBJ was president, and thirteen of those visits included overnight stays, for a total of sixteen nights. She went to the ranch at least four times, spending the night twice. In addition, she and the president frequently spoke on the telephone.

When one listens to LBJ and Oveta's telephone conversations (the president had his calls recorded), the sincere warmth of their relationship is clearly apparent, even when LBJ's propensity for opportunistic flattery is taken into account. They freely called each other "dear," with LBJ tossing in an occasional "darling." On one occasion when LBJ telephoned Oveta to invite her to his ranch in the Texas Hill Country, he told her he would send an air force jet to pick her up and that she could bring "whoever you like." When Oveta asked whom he would like to see, LBJ emphatically answered, "You!" Oveta chuckled and said, "Oh, I know, but who would you like for me to bring?" "Nobody else," LBJ replied. "I'd just like to see you, really. . . . Just come by yourself. I don't like having a lot of people supervising us anyway."[4]

Oveta's eager acceptance of these invitations probably reflected her desire to recapture the deep satisfaction she had enjoyed as a player in Washington during the war and later as a member of the Eisenhower cabinet. Her daughter, Jessica, believed that her mother loved those years when she had presence in the halls of power in Congress as well as in the White House. Jessica felt that Oveta missed those times, despite the various difficulties she had often faced and the negative impact on her health. In addition, as a newspaper publisher, Oveta also had an understandable craving for behind-the-scenes information and insider gossip about politics, governance, and public policy sausage-making. Her relationship with the Johnsons restored some of her access to presidential power, and her visits with the president and the First Lady often included time for private and candid insider talks that occasionally gave the *Houston Post* news scoops.

And LBJ surely had reasons beyond friendship for maintaining a close relationship with Oveta, including the obvious benefit of making it more likely that one of the leading news media organizations in Texas would be friendly to his political agenda. LBJ was well aware of the growing strength of the Republican Party in Texas. His former seat in the US Senate had been filled by Republican John Tower, and the GOP was hoping to mount a successful campaign against Texas's incumbent Democratic senator Ralph Yarborough in the general election in 1964. LBJ was facing his own election campaign in 1964, and the assumption was that if he won, he would run again in 1968. Winning Texas was critical to his chances for a victory that was far from a sure thing. Having the support of Oveta Culp Hobby, the woman who had openly supported and worked for Republican presidential candidates in every election since 1936 while continuing to support Democrats in Texas would not hurt his effort to carry his home state. One visible signal he could send that he had Oveta on his side was to associate her with his administration, even if it was only for special projects or missions, such as membership on a temporary commission, task force, or policy study group. Their long friendship was the paramount reason, of course, for their relationship to deepen after November 22, 1963, but it would be naïve to ignore the possibility that mutual interests were also a factor, especially with Lyndon Johnson.

In March 1964 Oveta agreed to write a review of Ruth Montgomery's biography of Lady Bird, *Mrs. LBJ*, for the *Chicago Tribune*. A few days after the *Tribune* published her highly laudatory piece, Oveta republished it in the *Houston Post*. The review was an opportunity to heap well-deserved praise on the First Lady. "No one can write about Mrs. Johnson," Oveta wrote, "without giving way to a few adjectives—warm, thoughtful, gracious, efficient, serene." Oveta sent a clipping of the book review to the White House, something she would continue to do whenever the *Post* published its dependably positive stories, columns, and editorials about the Johnson administration. Lady Bird was pleased. "Unaccustomed as I am to so many printed words about me," Lady Bird responded, "I find it very pleasant when they come from a pen as generous as yours." The president was equally pleased. "Lady Bird let me read your review of the book," he wrote Oveta. "You are kind, my good friend, and you are gracious, and for those expressions of loyalty, we are both grateful to you. Every now and then, Jack Valenti passes to me editorials from the *Post*. Invariably they are cheering words to read. Let me hear from you. Your advice and your counsel are always welcome here." LBJ added a handwritten PS: "Love and a special hug." Oveta's praises didn't stop with the review. Several days later she had the *Post* publish an editorial, essentially based on her book review, commending Lady Bird on her performance as First Lady during the early months of the new administration.[5]

It was a presidential election year, and it was obvious LBJ would easily win his party's nomination. Alabama governor George C. Wallace was Johnson's only active primary opponent, but Wallace's campaign was largely a self-promotional publicity effort that posed no real threat to the president. Oveta's former deputy at HEW, Governor Nelson Rockefeller, was the leading candidate for the Republican Party's presidential nomination for most of the spring. His effort eventually failed, however, largely because of the scandal resulting from his divorce and remarriage. Rockefeller's fall opened the field for Arizona senator Barry Goldwater, the leader of the party's rapidly growing right wing. Goldwater's nomination made Oveta's decision to support Lyndon Johnson even more firm because she abhorred Goldwater's hyperpartisan right-wing conservatism and his legislative record as a senator.

Oveta never had to consider whom she would support for president in 1964. That she had not supported a Democratic presidential candidate in nearly thirty years was irrelevant in this case. Months before the Republicans had nominated Goldwater, Oveta was passing to LBJ and his key supporters in Houston information she was picking up from her Republican friends about how the party planned to attack Johnson during the campaign. In February 1964, when LBJ asked George Brown if Republican leaders in Houston were taking on "a little hope and a little life" in their effort to defeat him, Brown replied, "Well, these down here are. This is what I get from Oveta." She had told Brown about Republican plans to investigate LBJ's radio and television station ownership in Austin, which legally were in Lady Bird's name. "They tell [Oveta] that they're going to demand to see the accounts of the . . . stations up there for the last 20 years, to see how many people advertised who did not do business in [Austin], trying to prove that it's a payoff to you." LBJ asked Brown who was behind the investigation. Brown replied that Oveta didn't know. "She's been hearing rumors from Republican circles that's what they're really going to get, find some meat on the bone. And it isn't there."[6]

In late July, as the time for the Democratic National Convention at Atlantic City drew near, LBJ called George Brown again to get an update on the political situation in Houston. "It looks pretty bad in the South, from what reports I pick up," Johnson said. "Is it that bad in Houston?" Brown believed it wasn't as bad for the Democrats as the pundits were saying. "Oveta is going to give you a good plug here," Brown added. "I mean a good [editorial]. She'll come out at what she thinks is the most opportune time." Brown told LBJ that Bill Hobby had been quoted in a news magazine story that he believed the president would carry Texas by a sixty-five to thirty-five margin.[7]

That same morning Oveta, who might have been encouraged by Brown, called the president to assure him of her support, but she wanted him to know she would soon be leaving the country for a badly needed vacation after Will's death in early June. She was embarking on a three-week-long sailing trip around the islands in the Aegean Sea. Referring to LBJ's public statements after Will's death, Oveta said, "I didn't want to leave without telling you myself how much your kindness meant. And number two, when I announce that I am going to support you, [whether] you would rather have it done, you know, in an interview or just the paper [*Houston Post*] or what." LBJ replied that he preferred that she conduct an interview "any time you're up this way." Oveta responded that she thought LBJ's media advisors should give him their opinion, but he said no. "I haven't got many, honey. I really don't have anyone that I can rely on very much now . . . but I'd say your judgment is better than anybody's I've got." Oveta stressed that she wanted him to get "some mileage" out of her announcement and that she needed his advice about what to say. "I'd tell them that . . . you had faith in this program as being best for America, and you believe it's going to be a prudent one," LBJ stated. "And you believe it's going to be one of progress, and you don't believe it'll be deeply partisan, and that you think it'll be based on what's good for the country, and . . . I assure you that that's the standard I'm going to use." "Well, now, I know that," Oveta answered. "You know I know that." LBJ also promised Oveta that he wasn't going to conduct "a mean or vicious" campaign. "I want to tell you how proud I am of you for not being mean and vicious," she replied. "And I know how hard at times it is. But I'm really proud of you. And I hope you can sustain this for some time." "I'm going to if the good Lord just keeps his arm around me," he replied. "And I'm not going to do anything . . . that you'd ever have to [be embarrassed by]." Oveta assured the president, "Oh, you don't have to tell me that. I have that faith and confidence in you."

As their conversation continued, Oveta expressed her fear about white backlash in the South against LBJ because of the civil rights bill. LBJ shared her concern, observing that there was "such a deep, bitter, unbelievable feeling of hatred and of denial among so many of those people." He added he was also worried that many African American voters, despite his work to pass the civil rights bill, would not vote for him because "they can never excuse themselves for voting for any . . . 'white southerner.'" To which Oveta replied, "Yeah. Yeah. I know that's true!" The president also pointed out that the Goldwater campaign was trying to frighten white voters by using examples of black extremism, such as the Black Muslims and the "Mississippi extremists," in their campaign literature. The president's mention of "Mississippi extremists" was an apparent reference to the members of the recently organized Mississippi Freedom Democratic Party, who were demanding to be seated at the Democratic National Convention as their state party's official delegation instead of the members of Mississippi's whites-only establishment delegation. LBJ was afraid the Mississippi Freedom protest would further inflame white Democrats in the South.

The president also expressed his worries about fundraising. He claimed that the Goldwater campaign had raised $3 million, including $350,000 from white Southerners who had responded to the GOP's racial scare tactics. One donor in Mississippi had contributed $50,000. "Good Lord!" Oveta exclaimed. "I didn't think there was that much money in the whole state!" LBJ explained it was critical that he match or exceed Goldwater's fundraising totals. Accordingly, he had held a meeting of the country's leading businessmen to assure them his administration was probusiness and to appeal for their financial backing. Oveta told LBJ she had heard that the reaction to his meeting with the business community was "tremendous" and that their support was essential. "After all, they employ the people that [make] the country go." "They sure do," LBJ replied. "And they're giving me the jobs that give me this prosperity." Oveta responded, "I think they've got it now. I really do. I'm not just talking about Democrats; I'm talking about Republicans as well." She felt LBJ would attract more Republicans "as the campaign heats up. I think some of it will improve as Goldwater talks. This man, you know, has got a real penchant for saying the wrong thing." She also advised LBJ that she had only "one piece of advice to give you. And I don't care whom you have for vice president—minus one. I guess you can guess that one," she said, referring to Robert F. Kennedy. "Please get a man that, if we get into trouble during that time, and you have to be in Washington, that could carry the load for you campaign-wise. If somebody should try to embarrass us during that campaign time and you had to be in Washington, you've got to have a man who can carry the fight." The president gave assurances he would follow her advice.

Before Oveta ended the call, Jack Valenti came on the phone to tell her that John Cowles, the influential publisher of the *Minneapolis Tribune*, the *Minneapolis Star Journal*, the *Des Moines Register*, *Look* magazine, and several other publications, had met privately with LBJ the day before and had pledged his support, which was the first time he had ever supported a Democratic presidential candidate. "Thank God!" Oveta declared. She had recently met with Cowles at his headquarters in Des Moines, Iowa, to make a pitch for him to back LBJ against Goldwater. She had long been a friend of the Cowles family. "The President feels that you, more than any single person, had more to do with that," Valenti said, "and he's very grateful to you for it." "Oh . . . I don't know that I did," Oveta replied. "Well, he considers it so," Valenti stated, "because he knows that you made that trip and that you talked to him."[8]

Oveta returned from her trip abroad the week prior to LBJ's nomination as the Democratic Party's candidate for president on August 26, 1964. Two days later, he called Oveta to invite her to a luncheon with his vice presidential running mate, Minnesota senator Hubert Humphrey, at the LBJ Ranch on August 29. During the call, Oveta told the president that she was publishing the *Post*'s endorsement for his election in a couple of days. She wanted to have a news story about Humphrey's visit to the ranch and the coming campaign to accompany the editorial. She asked if she could bring her new managing editor, Bill Woestendiek, with her when she came to the ranch to interview them (Oveta's problems with Woestendiek lay in the future). If LBJ had no objection, she would also send a *Houston Post* photographer to take photographs for Woestendiek's story. The photos would be featured prominently with the story. Obviously aware the *Post*'s article would be supportive, LBJ gave his consent.[9]

The next morning, LBJ sent a small air force JetStar to Houston to pick up Oveta, George and Alice Brown, the Gus Worthams, and Woestendiek at the Brown and Root Company's airplane hangar. Bill Hobby was unable to come because Diana was pregnant (Kate, their fourth child, was born on November 27) and in the hospital recovering from an operation on the small veins in her legs. Shortly after Oveta and her party landed at the ranch, Dan Hardy, the *Post*'s photographer, arrived and took pictures of LBJ and Humphrey as they rode hatless on horseback through a ranch pasture while dressed in business suits. The photo op was an exclusive for the *Post*. Oveta was delighted. "Thank you, dear," she later told the president in a phone call. "I'm very grateful." After lunch, the Houstonians flew back to their home city.[10]

On August 30, the day after Oveta's visit to the LBJ Ranch, the *Post* published its editorial along with Woestendiek's news story and the photographs, with the *Post* distributing the latter over the UPI wire. Bill Hobby wrote the editorial, which had a headline declaring, "For a Better USA—Vote for LBJ." Bill pulled a quote from the Democratic Party's 1964 platform as one of the *Post*'s reasons for opposing Goldwater, who had voted against the Civil Rights Act of 1964: "We are firmly pledged to continue the nation's march toward the goals of equal opportunity and equal treatment for all Americans regardless of race, creed, color, or national origin." LBJ, who had received his copy late that same morning, was delighted. He tried to call Oveta, but she was at the cemetery visiting Will's grave. He finally located her at Bill's house. "I just wanted to tell you that I didn't think it could have been better," the president enthused. Telling LBJ that Bill had written the editorial, she handed her son the telephone receiver. The president complimented Bill on the editorial and the photographs that ran with it. He was so happy with the coverage that he asked Bill to send him several copies of the newspaper. Hubert Humphrey also spoke with Bill, telling him the photo of him on horseback was "the finest picture I've ever taken," adding that he wanted Bill to send copies to the newspapers in Minneapolis and Saint Paul.

When LBJ and Oveta got back on the phone, LBJ said she should be pleased the *Post* got the photo scoop on Time-Life, which was now demanding access for their photographers to take similar photographs on the ranch, a request LBJ ignored. Oveta told LBJ the *Kansas City Star*, which was a solidly Republican newspaper, had published an editorial that morning also endorsing him. She thought it was important enough for her to reprint, along with others "that I really think are great," in the *Post*. Oveta offered to go to Los Angeles to see Otis Chandler, the publisher of the *Los Angeles Times*, to try to persuade him to support Johnson, "if you think it would do any good"; that trip proved unnecessary, however. Oveta also recommended LBJ "round up" his staff to compile all the favorable newspaper editorials and publish them in a campaign pamphlet. "It would be very useful to you," she stressed. As they ended their conversation, the president reminded Oveta about a meeting the following week at the White House to publicly announce the formation of a women's section of the National Citizens Committee for Johnson and Humphrey. LBJ emphasized it was time "to get our women going," to which Oveta replied, "Well, I think we ought to get these women going pretty soon."[11]

Aware that Barry Goldwater's hard-line, right-wing campaign rhetoric had given LBJ an opportunity to draw voters away from the alienated Eisenhower wing of the GOP, the president organized a bipartisan national committee for that purpose. He also wanted a women's subcommittee, hence his reference to getting "our women going." Oveta helped lead that effort. She agreed to recruit some of the key members, as well as to cochair the group, which was given the name National Citizens Committee for Johnson and Humphrey. She brought to the cause two of her former colleagues in the Eisenhower administration, Arthur Larson and Max Rabb. Her successor as HEW secretary, Marion Folsom, and former Treasury secretary and fellow Texan Robert Anderson had joined the organization earlier. Oveta's work with the committee meant she would have the unusual experience of having led national bipartisan presidential campaign efforts for both political parties.

Oveta was at the White House on October 1 to join twenty-two other prominent Democratic, Republican, and politically independent women to announce the formation of the women's subcommittee of the National Citizens Committee for Johnson and Humphrey. Oveta led the women in signing a formal statement endorsing LBJ's election. They also pledged to appear on radio and television shows to talk about why they were supporting the president. The subcommittee included actors Ethel Merman and Betty Furness, diplomat and past president of the League of Women Voters Anna Lord Strauss, novelist Katherine Anne Porter, and women's rights activist and author Betty Friedan. LBJ invited the women to the Cabinet Room, where he spoke "off record" for nearly an hour instead of the scheduled fifteen minutes.[12]

Oveta later explained to reporters she was supporting LBJ because "he is a progressive man who desires a more meaningful life for all" and because he "will try unusual ways to bring peace and stability to all the world." After spending the night at the White House in the Queens' Bedroom, Oveta met with Robert Anderson, her former colleague in the Eisenhower administration, to draft a statement she planned to release in her name explaining why she was supporting Johnson for president after favoring Republican candidates in the past. *Houston Post* White House correspondent Grace Halsell, who duly covered Oveta's activities during this trip, was given time on Johnson's schedule to interview him about his longtime relationship with the Hobbys.[13]

Oveta made a few speeches for the Johnson-Humphrey ticket during the crucial month of October, including a heavily publicized appearance in Cleveland. After the election, George Brown jokingly told LBJ he had carried Ohio only because Oveta "made that talk in Cleveland." To which LBJ, replied, "She did right well, didn't she?" On October 31, 1964, four days before the election, Oveta traveled to New York City to join three other women in the Louis XVI Room of the Waldorf Astoria Hotel to videotape a conversation with LBJ, which was distributed as a political advertisement for broadcast on television stations across the country. After the taping, Oveta accompanied the president to Madison Square Garden, where a huge rally was being staged for Robert F. Kennedy's US Senate campaign as well as for LBJ.[14]

As expected, LBJ won a landslide victory over Senator Goldwater on November 3. Johnson won every state except for Arizona and five Deep South states: Louisiana, Mississippi, Alabama, Georgia, and South Carolina. The morning after the election, the victorious president called Oveta. When she answered the phone, she said firmly, "Sir, you should be asleep." Ignoring her admonition but obviously sleep deprived, LBJ said he was calling to thank her for her support "and to tell you how much I love you." Responding, Oveta teased that his victory speech the night before "was almost as good as I could have done, maybe it's the best speech you ever gave." On a high from his overwhelming election victory, LBJ replied, "Well, you're a noble woman, and a great one. You don't normally find courage and compassion and brains all wrapped up in a pretty figure, but you got it and I got to see more of you darling. . . . [Y]ou mean everything in the world to me and I know the Governor would be so happy with us." He added that he wished that "Governor had been here" to help him celebrate. Oveta responded that she had held an election-night party with George and Alice Brown and other friends at her mansion. To commemorate LBJ's victory, she went to Will's private stock and opened a bottle of rare, thirty-year-old scotch whisky that "Governor" had kept for especially important occasions, "because I knew that's what he would do." Before hanging up, the president asked Oveta to tell "your sweet boy [Bill] . . . I'm mighty proud of him." He closed by asking her to come to the White House the next time she came to the East Coast and to "quit being a little modest girl now because there are too few of us left and those that are got to stay a little closer together." "We will do that," Oveta replied.[15]

Two days later, Oveta attended a barbecue at the LBJ Ranch in honor of Gustavo

Díaz Ordaz, president-elect of Mexico. A month later, Oveta traveled to Washington for another meeting with LBJ. Soon after she arrived, Oveta accompanied the president to see ailing congressman Albert Thomas, who had recently been released from the Bethesda Naval Hospital after cancer surgery. After a brief visit with Thomas at his home, LBJ took Oveta to the West Wing lobby to show her Frederick Remington's painting *Aiding a Comrade*, which the White House had recently borrowed from the Hogg Collection at the Museum of Fine Arts, Houston. There are indications that during Oveta's three-day White House stay, LBJ asked her if she would be available to help his administration in some capacity, even if only temporarily. Based on later events, she apparently said yes. After she returned to Houston, Oveta wrote LBJ a letter hinting they had discussed in-depth matters of importance to them both. "[I am] deeply grateful for the generous amount of time you gave me last Tuesday," Oveta wrote. "It meant much to me to have the visit with Albert Thomas, and your thoughtfulness in taking me to see him touched me."[16]

Oveta was unable to attend LBJ's inauguration in January 1965, but her increasingly close relationship with the president began to involve her more directly in the workings of his administration. In early February, the Justice Department appointed Oveta to the governing board of General Aniline and Film Company, which had been seized as enemy property during World War II because of allegations that it was a front for the German industrial giant IG Farben. Her fellow board members included MCA's Lew Wasserman, influential Washington power broker Clark Clifford, and Federated Department Stores vice chairman Maurice Lazarus.[17]

Oveta didn't see the Johnsons again until late Friday afternoon, April 9, 1965, when they paid an unscheduled visit to her Shadyside mansion on their way to attend the official opening of the Houston Astrodome, which featured an exhibition game between the Houston Astros and the New York Yankees. Astrodome promoter, owner of the Astros, and former Houston mayor Roy Hofheinz was an old friend of the Johnsons. He had managed LBJ's 1941 and 1948 US Senate campaigns in Houston, and he was also a good friend of Jack Valenti. At Hofheinz's urgent behest, Valenti lobbied the president to go to Houston for the stadium's spectacular opening. Almost at the last minute, LBJ decided to make the trip to Houston. He and Lady Bird rounded up Valenti, presidential aide Horace Busby, and Peace Corps director Sargent Shriver and his wife, Eunice Kennedy Shriver, to go with them. An hour after Air Force One lifted off, LBJ learned they would land early. The president decided they would have time to visit Oveta, whose mansion was near the Astrodome. He called Oveta from Air Force One about an hour before they were to arrive in Houston.

Despite the incredibly short warning, Oveta managed to assemble all of her household staff and to summon some of her employees at the *Post* to hurriedly put together a reception for the Johnsons. She also persuaded George and Alice Brown, Houston attorney George Butler, Lloyd and B. A. Bentsen, Jim Elkins Jr., heart surgeon Denton Cooley, and several other friends of the Johnsons and Jack Valenti to rush to her house for the party. The US House of Representatives had passed the Medicare bill the day before the Johnsons came to Houston and the president was pumped up about it. When Oveta introduced the president to Dr. Cooley, LBJ told him not to be worried about socialized medicine. "The fact is," LBJ declared, "not only is Medicare going to save our elderly citizens, it will also make you and all of your fellow doctors rich. You will no longer have to treat our old folks as charity patients. We're going to pay you for it."[18]

Lady Bird later recorded the visit in her audio diary. "We went directly to Mrs. Hobby's, a small cocktail party arranged in mid-air on an hour's notice, a home that bespoke culture, charm, intellectual grace every step of the way. Oveta's house is full of paintings—some great—all charming. She has done so much with her life." After an hour passed, the Secret Service rushed the Johnsons and their companions to the Astrodome, where Roy Hofheinz awaited them. "I have tried to put on paper 'what honor and grace' came to our house when the two of you and your friends arrived," Oveta wrote Lady Bird after the visit. "Both of you have always been cherished guests in our home. What a joy it would have been to Will to have welcomed you to our house." Lady Bird replied that she and Lyndon "both remember so fondly the wonderful party at your house—and you with only an hour notice! There were so many people there that we enjoy being with and [had] not seen in a long time. . . . I am so glad I got to see the paintings and hear you tell about them."[19]

Three months after the president's surprise drop-in to her Shadyside mansion, Oveta was in Washington on a business trip when she paid LBJ a visit at the Oval Office in the White House. While they chatted, the president suddenly got the idea to take her on a dinner cruise on the Potomac River in the presidential yacht, the *Honey Fitz*. He escorted Oveta upstairs to the family quarters to tell Lady Bird. "What about dinner on the boat?" he asked. Lady Bird wrote in her diary that his idea was "a delightful surprise." The White House staff scrambled to call several other guests to join the Johnsons on the cruise, including journalist Marianne Means and Senators Richard Russell, George Smathers, William Fulbright, and Warren Magnuson. In addition, two out of town visitors, Tennessee governor Buford Ellington and Brown and Root lawyer and lobbyist Ed Clark of Austin, joined the party. After gathering at the naval shipyard, the *Honey Fitz* cruised for four hours, during which the guests ate dinner on television trays. "The evening was superb," Lady Bird noted in her diary. "The views [were] a balm to the spirit (but the river full of floating debris) and the talk good. There was a big comfortable chair at the very end of the Honey Fitz—that's Lyndon's favorite of the boat—and Lyndon ensconces himself there. . . . Tonight it was Oveta Hobby who was with him much of the time." Oveta, who accepted the president's invitation for her to stay overnight, returned to the White House with the Johnsons in the presidential limousine.[20]

Six weeks later, LBJ treated Oveta to another boat ride, although one that was drastically different from the genteel trip on the *Honey Fitz*. Oveta, Bill and Diana Hobby, and George and Alice Brown flew to the LBJ Ranch in the Brown and Root airplane to celebrate Labor Day. That afternoon Lady Bird took Oveta and Alice Brown to the president's birthplace house, which had been restored to the way it had appeared when

LBJ was born in 1908. Because most of the furnishings had disappeared or been replaced over the years, Lady Bird had worked with friends to find furniture and decorations typical of a modest farmhouse in that era. Oveta and Alice had donated some of the items, and Lady Bird was eager to show them "their handiwork." Oveta's gift had been several items she had stored in the attic at her mansion, including one of her father's desks and a Victorian sofa. Lady Bird told Oveta the sofa was "just right" and that Lyndon's mother "would just have loved it." She wrote in her diary that she "loved taking Oveta and Alice down to the little house. . . . We enjoyed it, with that warm, conspiratory [*sic*], self-congratulatory wave that women have when they have worked together on a project." The First Lady also wanted to take Oveta and Alice to Johnson City to see another house where Lyndon had lived when he was young, which had also been restored. The president, however, preferred to take everyone to the Haywood Ranch property he owned on Lake LBJ to go boating. Originally known as Granite Shoals Lake, the Lower Colorado River Authority had renamed the lake for Johnson in April of that year.[21]

The trip to the lake included Lady Bird, Oveta, Bill and Diana Hobby, Jack Valenti, KTBC-TV general manager J. C. Kellam, federal judge Homer Thornberry, and entertainment lawyer Arthur Krim, who observed, as he later recalled in an oral history interview, that Oveta "seemed to be very friendly with the President." The size of the party required transportation on two helicopters. Soon after they arrived, Oveta and Diana were treated to a wild speedboat ride on the lake for a couple of hours, with the president at the wheel and a stopover at a beach house on the lakeshore, while the other members of the party remained on a larger party boat. After sunset, the party boat with Lady Bird and the other guests docked at the beach house, where a "hot and plentiful" fried fish dinner was served. As the boat was docking, Lady Bird heard "a stir of excitement and then squeals of laughter." A Secret Service agent told her, "The President has Mrs. Hobby and Diana in the little [amphibious] car." Without telling Oveta and Diana that the blue convertible was an amphibious vehicle, Lyndon drove them down a steep road that led straight to the lake and then yelled, "Oh, oh, our brakes don't work," as the car plunged into lake. The water quickly rose to within three or four inches below the windows. He then hit the motor switch and they drove around in the lake. Oveta had known the car was amphibious, but she hadn't warned her daughter-in-law. Lady Bird wrote in her diary that Oveta and Diana "squealed and Lyndon enjoyed himself hugely. The little boy . . . still lives in this 57 year-old man, and manifests itself, no doubt to the horror of the Secret Service, from time to time."[22]

Once everyone was on board the big party boat, Bill Hobby told his wife and his mother that at LBJ's request, he and Arthur Krim had tried to follow the amphibious vehicle as it headed down to the lake, but they took the wrong gravel road and missed seeing them go into the river. When LBJ saw Krim back on the party boat, he called out, "Where the hell were you?" Krim replied that he and Bill Hobby had been unable to find Johnson and his amphibious car. "Damn it," LBJ responded. "I wanted . . . to see what [Bill Hobby] would do if he saw the President and his mother about to drown."[23]

The next day, which was Tuesday and Election Day, Oveta flew with the Johnsons, Jack Valenti, and White House aide Jake Jacobsen by helicopter to Johnson City, where LBJ voted. Bill and Diana Hobby had flown back to Houston with the Browns the night before. The helicopter then took them to Bergstrom Air Force Base in Austin, where they boarded Air Force One and flew to Washington

At lunch the following day, the president, who knew Will and Oveta had been involved in the establishment at the University of Houston of the nation's first educational television station, asked Oveta for her assessment of how well that station had turned out. She gave the endeavor high marks. He then told her the Carnegie Corporation of New York was forming a commission to study and produce a report on how a network of noncommercial public television stations could be organized and what that network's mission would be. He believed there was great need for a public television network, and he planned to use the commission report as justification for Congress to pass legislation providing federal support for the network's creation. The president told Oveta he needed someone he could trust to serve on the commission and to report to him about its progress. J. C. Kellam, his loyal longtime general manager at Lady Bird Johnson's television station in Austin, had agreed to serve, but LBJ wanted an additional representative. "I want that person to be you," he declared. The president explained that the commission's work would not begin until early in 1966, which would give Oveta time to arrange her schedule. Oveta was easily swayed by the famous "Johnson treatment," and she quickly agreed.[24]

After her lunch with the president on September 8, Oveta flew to Dallas, where she was scheduled to give a speech the next day to 750 people at an "Amazing Women" luncheon at the Statler Hilton Hotel. Sponsored by Oveta's friend Stanley Marcus, head of the Neiman-Marcus clothing store, and the Community Council of Greater Dallas, the purpose of the event was to attract women to volunteer for work at more than seventy charitable, educational, and social service organizations in the city. When a reporter from the *Dallas Morning News* interviewed Oveta after she arrived at Love Field, she took the opportunity to make a statement about male-female equality. Pointing out that the "status of women has improved a great deal in the past few years," she explained that employers were accepting job applications from more women than they once had. "Every day you see women in vocations [that] you would have never thought about having a woman [in] a few years ago," she said, a statement obviously inspired by her experience as head of the Women's Army Corps. "In my own organization I no longer think of any difference in being a woman employee. I hope no one else there does. There's not any difference [between men and women] in skill in gathering facts and writing them."[25]

A month after her appearance in Dallas, Oveta gave a speech in Houston that was noteworthy for demonstrating her deep interest in and knowledge about the issues and problems she believed the nation would face in the coming decades. Addressing six hundred executives at the annual management meeting of the American Chamber of Commerce at the Rice Hotel on October 12, she accurately predicted economic, sociological, educational, and governing problems that would plague the United States severely in the coming century. Long before the birth of the digital age, she warned that technological advancements would soon create serious problems that couldn't be ignored. "Automation will give us a new concept of work that will require us to educate youth to confront," she declared. Unusually liberal in tone as well as surprising in light of Houston's involvement in the manned spacecraft program, Oveta also questioned current government budget priorities. "It hurts to see that we can spend billions on outer space but cannot adequately support the charity hospital," she said. Her statement was not a criticism of the space program per se but a complaint about the failure of local government to play a stronger role in support of social welfare needs. In reference to complaints from the business community about LBJ's Great Society initiatives and the growth of the federal government, she explained that Washington had taken the initiative in handling many local problems because city and county governments, which could handle such problems better and at less cost, had failed to do so. Finally, Oveta warned that the country needed "statesmen of business and labor rather than representatives of special interests in the challenging period ahead." It was an impressive analysis of serious issues the country would eventually confront.[26]

Two days after she addressed the meeting of the National Chamber of Commerce, Oveta attended Dwight Eisenhower's seventy-fifth birthday party at the Augusta National Golf Club in Georgia on October 14. Cliff Roberts had built the Eisenhowers a seven-room, two-story house near the tenth tee. At Augusta, Oveta not only had the opportunity to see many of her former colleagues, but she also had a chance to spend some private time with Ike and Mamie. She gave one of the speeches at the birthday dinner, proclaiming, "Perhaps not since George Washington has a man offered for President, served two terms and retired with no measurable loss in the confidence given him by the American people." After Oveta returned to Houston, she wrote Eisenhower, "I can't tell you how much pleasure it gave me to see you again and to be with so many old friends on such a happy occasion." A month later, Oveta was shocked by the news that Ike had suffered another heart attack while he and Mamie were still in Augusta. Ike was rushed to a nearby army hospital and then two weeks later transferred to Walter Reed Medical Center in Bethesda, Maryland. Mamie sent a handwritten note to Oveta. "There is not much to tell you about my husband's condition," she wrote. "I assume you have been listening to the telecasts. You can be sure when he is better I will be better also. We have no immediate plans but are going from day to day." Ike recovered from this setback and eventually returned to the golf course, but the end was near.[27]

# CHAPTER 43

# PBS AND VIETNAM

I n May 1961, Newton Minow, the newly appointed chairman of the Federal Communications Commission, shocked attendees at a convention of the National Association
of Broadcasters with the charge that television was a "vast wasteland" filled with
excessive violence and frivolity. He urged broadcasters to fulfill their obligation to the
"public interest" with high-quality educational, cultural, and current-affairs programming and to respect "decency and decorum" in entertainment offerings. Minow's speech
annoyed and even angered many broadcasters, including KPRC's Jack Harris, who was
at the conference. But Harris's boss, Oveta Culp Hobby, was among those who agreed
with much of Minow's assessment.[1]

Minow's speech was a boost for those demanding publicly funded alternatives to
commercial television broadcasting. Those demands led Congress in 1962 to pass the
Educational Television Facilities Act, which provided grants to construct and equip
local educational television stations. By 1964, however, supporters of noncommercial
television saw the need for a national public television network. They persuaded John
Gardner, president of the Carnegie Corporation, to fund a study that might provide
justification for such a network. Because federal funding would ultimately be needed
to establish a national program, Carnegie staff contacted the Johnson administration
to see if the White House would support their efforts with a presidential commission.
LBJ's initial reaction was guarded. Because Lady Bird owned a commercial television
station in Austin, he was concerned that the administration's direct involvement in
the study would fuel suspicions of self-dealing. He had no objection, however, to a
privately funded study sponsored by the Carnegie Corporation, which would give him
political protection.[2]

The Carnegie board approved Gardner's request in April 1965 to create a commission
to examine how a public-supported television network could provide instructional programming, including in-class educational material as well as programs on public affairs

and policy, the arts and culture, and science and technology for the general viewing audience. In November 1965 Carnegie publicly announced the project and the appointment of former MIT president James R. Killian Jr. as commission chair and fourteen other members, including former Harvard president James B. Conant, novelist Ralph Ellison, Polaroid Corporation president Edwin Land, and concert pianist Rudolf Serkin. By the time of this announcement in November, John Gardner had taken a leave of absence as Carnegie's president to serve as LBJ's secretary of HEW. The acting president, Alan Pifer, accepted LBJ's recommendation for Oveta Culp Hobby and J. C. Kellam to serve as LBJ's representatives on the commission. Gardner, who continued to monitor the Carnegie Commission's progress from his post at HEW, was especially pleased that Oveta accepted the appointment. Gardner had gotten to know Oveta when they both worked on Nelson Rockefeller's Special Studies Project.[3]

Oveta took her appointment to the commission seriously. "We worked very hard for a year on that study," she later recalled. She devoted a considerable amount of time in 1966 to the commission's activities, including attending its eight formal meetings and participating in some of the commission's fact-finding visits to local educational television stations. She worked closely with her fellow commission members and the commission's professional staff of researchers and writers to shape a report supporting the president's goal to create a publicly funded national television network. The president wanted a final report by January 1967, in time for him to include its findings in his State of the Union address and to submit a bill to the new Ninetieth Congress.[4]

A month after Oveta's appointment to the Carnegie Commission, the president invited her to go with him on an exhausting excursion that began in Austin and ended at the White House. On December 12, LBJ sent a plane to Houston to fly Oveta as its only passenger to a private terminal at the Austin Municipal Airport, where he and Arthur Krim and Krim's wife waited for her in the presidential limousine. From the airport they drove to the campus of the University of Texas to pick up Lady Bird, who had been visiting their daughter Lynda at her sorority house. After spending a few minutes talking to Lynda and her sorority sisters, they drove to the nearby Governor's Mansion, where John and Nellie Connally were hosting a dinner party in the president's honor. After dinner, Oveta and the Krims went with the Johnsons back to Bergstrom Air Force Base, where they flew on Air Force One to Washington, landing at one thirty in the morning. After they arrived by helicopter at the White House, Oveta accompanied the Johnsons upstairs, where she retired to the Queens' Bedroom. Thoroughly exhausted, she finally got to bed by 2:30 a.m.[5]

On the last morning after Oveta's busy three-night stay at the White House, LBJ asked her to meet with him privately to discuss a matter of importance. Curious about his request, she changed her return flight reservation and met with him in the Oval Office. Johnson began the meeting by expressing his desire to provide humanitarian aid to South Vietnam to help alleviate that country's problems of extreme poverty, illiteracy, poor health conditions, and other social and economic ills. He believed such aid would defeat the Viet Cong as thoroughly as military action. Accordingly, he had asked HEW Secretary John Gardner to lead a task force to South Vietnam to study conditions in the country and then write a plan to guide an effective humanitarian aid program that could bring a version of his "Great Society" to Southeast Asia. The president told Oveta if he could get the official cooperation of the South Vietnamese leadership in this humanitarian effort, he wanted her to serve on the task force. As the person who had organized HEW and served as its first secretary, she was especially well qualified for the assignment. Surprised by the president's request, Oveta expressed her concern that taking on another assignment as significant as the one he was proposing would not allow her to give the Carnegie Commission her full attention once it began its work early in 1966. After LBJ stated his complete confidence in her ability to tend to both assignments with diligence and skill, she promised to give his invitation serious thought.[6]

Two months after meeting with Oveta, President Johnson joined leaders of the government of South Vietnam in Honolulu to discuss military strategy. Among the several initiatives the Vietnamese leaders agreed to support was the fact-finding tour of their country by Gardner's presidential task force. After he returned from Hawaii, LBJ telephoned Oveta to give her the news and to plead with her to join the task force, arguing it couldn't be done without her. "Your country needs you and your President needs you," he stressed. He told her that John Gardner had been delighted to know she might be on the team, because he was one of her greatest admirers. LBJ's flattery and cajoling was nothing new for Oveta, so that was not what persuaded her to accept the assignment. What did the trick was her deep curiosity and serious concerns about US actions in Southeast Asia. Despite her business responsibilities and her work with the Carnegie Commission, Oveta welcomed the opportunity to cross the Pacific to get a firsthand look. She accepted the appointment.[7]

Oveta and her fourteen fellow task force members, including Surgeon General William Stewart; Dr. James Cain of the Mayo Clinic; General James Earl Rudder, president of Texas A&M University; and representatives from the Public Health Service and the construction industry, had their first meeting with Secretary Gardner at HEW headquarters on March 10. Gardner, who had earned a PhD in psychology at the University of California at Berkeley, was a liberal Republican who had long been a member of Nelson Rockefeller's circle of public intellectuals. He was the type of man Oveta liked and respected: strong-minded but reserved, well educated, patrician, and low-key in manner. Gardner was the only Republican in LBJ's cabinet. He was also a busy man. At the same time he took on the Vietnam assignment, Gardner was deep into the launch of the newly established Medicare program.

Gardner told the group they had been selected because of their special knowledge of issues relevant to the mission. When they were in South Vietnam, their job would be to assess problems related to those specialties. Oveta was an exception, however. Because of her experience as a former secretary of HEW, her role was to help in the assessment of the overall situation in Vietnam. After they returned to the States at the end of the fact-finding tour, they would write a report of their findings and recommendations to submit to the president.[8]

After the meeting at HEW, Oveta and her fellow task force members met with the president at the White House. In a rousing speech to the group, LBJ emphasized that their mission was not military in nature, but humanitarian. He wanted the military action in South Vietnam to be more than a war against Communism; he also wanted to wage war on ignorance, disease, and hunger. Oveta spent that night at the White House, where she and the Mayo Clinic's Dr. Cain joined the president and Lady Bird for dinner. The morning after their dinner, on March 11, Lady Bird wrote in her diary that when the president joined them at 9:15 p.m., he was "not in a hurry very much to go to dinner. He enjoys Oveta Hobby very much." She noted that Oveta and Dr. Cain were leaving for Vietnam the next morning after being in briefings all day, and they were enthusiastic and hopeful about the trip. After enjoying a couple of scotches with Oveta and the Cains, the president launched into a lengthy and enthusiastic lecture about what he hoped the mission would accomplish. "I want to do something about the conditions that cause this war." The first thing he mentioned was his intention to improve Vietnamese hygiene, which he curiously expressed as making sure "that everyone there got a bath. It is simple to wash. I am sure Procter and Gamble can get us the soap." The president explained that sores caused by lack of cleanliness and skin diseases were "a major scourge of the country." He then talked about providing preventative health services, including a mass inoculation program, because the Vietnamese "die at 35" as a result of poor medical care. LBJ told Oveta he also wanted to improve the Vietnamese educational system and see that everyone learned "the simple three R's." Another of his goals was to improve Vietnamese agriculture by sharing American "know-how" and technology with them. "We are going to give them 200 pound hogs for their 100 pound hogs," LBJ declared. "Our sweet potato vines produce twice as many pounds of sweet potatoes as their vines do."[9]

The president stressed that the only reason the United States was in Vietnam was "to keep these people from being eaten up. I want to get out of there more than anybody, including the Marines." Looking straight at Oveta, LBJ said that since he had become president, the man who had helped him the most on Vietnam and asked for the least in return was President Eisenhower. He also discussed Vietnamese president Ngo Dinh Diem's murder in November 1963. Lady Bird wrote in her diary afterward that the subject always made her "uncomfortable." She explained that her husband regarded the coup "as a hideous turning point in the war and a black spot in our national life." As they finally sat down at the dinner table, President Johnson criticized the antiwar liberals who were raising questions about his Vietnam military policy. Showing his increasing frustration with the Democrats on the left and comfortable in his understanding that Oveta was no liberal, he declared, "I'm not a liberal. I'm a progressive. The liberal believes in controlling your mind, like a Communist does. I do not believe in that." Oveta responded that she shared his view about liberals, especially their criticism of his Vietnam policy. "There is something sick in the liberal viewpoint in all this," she said, which undoubtedly pleased the president. When LBJ gave the blessing before they ate, Lady Bird wrote, Oveta "made a sweet, grave little addition of asking help for [Lyndon]. We had a merry dinner, and then by midnight, we were in bed."[10]

Oveta departed Washington for South Vietnam on Saturday, March 12. US ambassador Henry Cabot Lodge, Oveta's friend from the 1952 presidential campaign and her colleague in the Eisenhower administration, greeted Gardner, Oveta, and their mission colleagues when they arrived in Saigon. After Gardner held a press conference at the airport to answer questions about his mission, Lodge met privately with the task force members and told them they would not be able to travel to the area around Da Nang because of the Buddhist Uprising, which the South Vietnamese Army (ARVN) was trying to suppress. He claimed that the southern section of the country was the most important area to inspect. Following Lodge's advice, the task force split into smaller groups that traveled by land, air, and water throughout the south. They inspected hospitals and schools and noted health and living conditions in the villages, occasionally within sight and sound of ARVN military operations against the Viet Cong. They learned that the US development mission was the largest in the world at that time, with almost one thousand American men and women civilians operating an economic assistance program that cost the United States $500 million a year. They met with Vietnamese individuals who represented, in Oveta's words, both the "high and humble," including soldiers, priests, doctors, and teachers. She later described the extensive water pollution, lack of clean drinking water, and the rampant infectious diseases as "something incredible."[11]

LBJ had stressed that political and military issues were not within their purview, but the task force members were unable to ignore the current war as well as the long history of Vietnam as a battleground. In addition, the task force learned that life in Vietnam was, as Oveta acknowledged later, "a complicated fabric of racial differences, religious disputes, and social upheaval of a degree rarely seen." Despite her awareness of these complexities, Oveta accepted the Johnson administration's simple explanation that the war was being fought, as she would later state, "to prevent a nation from being submerged in a tide of Communism it does not want." Privately, however, Oveta questioned that simple public explanation. She seriously doubted the ability of the government of South Vietnam to survive, later admitting, "What that nation will eventually be like it is impossible to say."[12]

After Oveta and her colleagues returned to the United States on March 21, they worked for a week on their individual reports before submitting them to Secretary Gardner, who wrote the final task force document for the White House. Although Oveta had much experience in task force studies, she and her colleagues had a difficult job summarizing their findings because of the complexity of the situation in South Vietnam. Gardner's final report to the president urged an extensive American investment in the health, education, and welfare of the people of South Vietnam, not only for humanitarian reasons but also as the most effective way to win the war against Communism.

With her mission completed, Oveta wrote a letter to LBJ telling him that her tour of Vietnam "was the most fascinating I have ever undertaken." She thanked him for the opportunity "to see first-hand the health, education, and welfare installations of the Republic of South Viet Nam. I hope our report will be useful." Oveta also told him how much she admired John Gardner, who was "as fine an administrator as I have ever seen. His devotion to you and your objectives is heartwarming." But Gardner's view of the Vietnam War eventually changed to one of opposition, leading him to resign from HEW in March 1968. He later founded the citizen's advocacy group Common Cause.[13]

Several days after she returned to Houston, Oveta spoke about her Vietnam travels to a Rice University Associates dinner. She acknowledged the country's long history of turmoil and warfare, including the periods when it was a French colonial possession and when the Japanese Army occupied the country during World War II. "The struggle for freedom within its borders is not new," she told the dinner guests, who, like most Americans, probably knew little about Vietnam. She also indicated her belief in the so-called domino theory of combatting Communism, a term that President Eisenhower had coined. "The war now being fought is a war that not only carries with it great implications for the Vietnamese people, but for the entire Free World." She concluded with the observation that there was "a unifying theme in the vast panorama of Vietnam, it is the Vietnamese people themselves . . . their longing for freedom and their hatred of Communism."[14]

Oveta's work on the Vietnam task force was over, but her labors for President Johnson continued. Not only did she remain involved with the Carnegie Commission's study on educational television, she also accepted a presidential appointment to yet another commission. On July 2, only three months after her tour of Vietnam, LBJ telephoned Oveta and persuaded her to serve on a special White House commission to examine the nation's military draft. As wariness about the Vietnam War spread and criticism of the draft as racially and economically biased grew, LBJ responded by creating the National Advisory Commission on Selective Service to conduct a "sweeping study of the fairness and effectiveness of the draft." He especially wanted the commission to review and evaluate the deferment process, particularly for college students. The president appointed Burke Marshall, a former assistant attorney general, to head the twenty-member commission, which, along with Oveta, included former CIA director John McCone, former marine corps commandant General David Shoup, and Yale University president Kingman Brewster.

Unlike the case with the Vietnam task force, membership on the selective service advisory commission required little travel, except for one special trip to Gettysburg, Pennsylvania, in the fall of 1966. Dwight Eisenhower, who had recovered from the heart attack he had suffered a year earlier, agreed to meet with Oveta and her colleagues at his farm to share his assessment of the current state of the draft and his recommendations for any changes to the system. Not surprisingly, the general made a forceful argument in support of conscription and the system then in place. He saw no need for any changes.

Afterward, Oveta sent a note to Ike, writing, "You must know how deeply we all appreciated your kindness in letting us call on you for advice and to be able once again to be guided by your good judgment and sound counsel. It doesn't seem that a year could have passed since that tremendously special celebration in Augusta." Ike was equally pleased by the visit and the opportunity to see Oveta. "I cannot tell you what a lift I got out of the meeting with you and your committee," he wrote. "I think I enjoyed the meeting more than any other I have had for a long, long time. I shall be very interested to see a copy of your report when it is made."[15]

Oveta's main responsibility on the selective service advisory commission was to evaluate and respond to the written reports compiled by commission staff members, which were mailed to her in Houston. Her special focus was on public opinion about the draft as perceived from her position as a newspaper publisher. Reporters at the *Houston Post* helped by sending her information they picked up in conversations with random people on the street and from local high school counselors, college deans, and leaders of youth organizations. As was the case with the public-television study, President Johnson told the selective service commission members that he wanted their report in time for him to include draft reform on his list of legislative goals in his State of the Union address in January 1967. Veteran journalist Harry Middleton was recruited to write the national advisory commission's final report. Impressed with Middleton's work on the report, LBJ appointed him to his speechwriting staff. Middleton would later serve for more than thirty years as the director of the LBJ Presidential Library in Austin.[16]

The findings of neither the selective service group nor the public-television task force had been released, however, by the time the president gave his State of the Union address on January 10, 1967. When the Carnegie Commission completed its work at the end of 1966, a draft copy of its report was sent to the White House in time for President Johnson to know its contents before he gave his address, but not soon enough for the report to be published and distributed. Nevertheless, in his speech to Congress, LBJ referred to the work of both commissions and his plan to submit bills based on their work. "We should modernize our Selective Service System," the president stated. "The National Commission on Selective Service will shortly submit its report. I will send you new recommendations to meet our military manpower needs. But let us resolve that this is to be the Congress that made our draft laws as fair and as effective as possible." Turning to his public-television initiative, the president declared that he would also seek congressional authorization to "develop educational television into a vital public resource to enrich our homes, [to] educate our families, and to provide assistance in our classrooms. We should insist that the public interest be fully served through the public's airwaves." After Johnson delivered his State of the Union address, the only telephone calls he accepted at the White House late that night were from Oveta and Supreme Court justice Abe Fortas. Oveta called at 11:15 p.m. to give him her detailed and highly favorable reaction to the speech.[17]

The Carnegie Commission published and distributed more than fifty thousand copies of its report, *Public Television: A Program for Action*, on January 26, 1967. The report attracted widespread attention from the news media. Shortly thereafter, President Johnson submitted a bill to Congress that incorporated most of the report's proposals. In November, the Public Broadcasting Act of 1967 became law. It created the Corporation for Public Broadcasting, which in turn led to the establishment of not only the Public Broadcasting System but also National Public Radio. The selective service report soon followed, and it eventually resulted in Congress passing the Military Selective Service Act of June 1967 as an amendment to the Selective Service Act of 1948. The 1967 act broadened presidential authority to revise deferment classifications to expand the size of the draft pool, and it gave local selective service boards more discretion in making draft decisions on an individual basis instead of being restricted by blanket requirements.[18]

At LBJ's request Oveta trekked to the White House for a meeting during the afternoon of January 31, 1967. LBJ escorted her to his small workspace adjacent to the Oval Office, where they met for fifteen minutes. The president's mood was somber. Earlier in the day, he and Lady Bird had attended the funeral services at Arlington Cemetery for astronauts Gus Grissom and Roger Chaffee, who had died horrifically in an oxygen-fed fire in their capsule on the launchpad in Florida during a test. After a brief chat about the accident and a discussion about how she felt it would affect public opinion in Houston about NASA, LBJ asked Oveta to accept a fourth major assignment for his administration, this time as a member of the advisory board for the US Information Agency, the federal government's overseas publicity operation to counter anti-American propaganda. He was aware of Oveta's longtime interest in the issue, and he wanted her to draw on the experience she had gained as a member of the US delegation to the UN Conference on Freedom of Information in Geneva in 1948. The president's somber mood might have made it difficult for Oveta to turn him down, but this was another area of genuine interest to her. She accepted this new appointment, but it did not require much of her time or attention.[19]

The Vietnam War was the topic when Bill Hobby joined several other Texas newspaper editors for a meeting at the White House with the president and army general William Westmoreland in April 1967. LBJ brought General Westmoreland back from Vietnam in an attempt to persuade the news media that despite all appearances the United States was winning the war militarily but that antiwar protests on the home front were a major threat to victory. The meeting accomplished LBJ's goal, at least in regard to the *Houston Post*. After Bill Hobby returned to Houston, he got Oveta's approval to publish an editorial denouncing the antiwar movement as "giving aid and comfort to the enemy." Dusting off language formerly used by the late Joe McCarthy and his followers, the editorial declared that Americans who opposed the war included "outright Communists, Communist sympathizers and peacenik extremists. Whatever their motivation, they too, are enemies of freedom, and in many ways much more dangerous than the Viet Cong and North Vietnamese." For Oveta and the *Post*, this Red Scare–style rhetoric was a startling retreat from the days of the Minute Women exposé. Bill sent a copy of the editorial to the White House the day before it was published, where it was received with predictable approval.[20]

Meanwhile, Oveta continued her close relationship with the president and First Lady. Two weeks after the *Post*'s editorial, Oveta called Lady Bird Johnson to offer a Waterford chandelier as a gift to the White House. Oveta's close friend Alice Brown was working with Lady Bird in her effort to redecorate the executive mansion, and she enlisted Oveta's help in the project. James Ketchum, the White House curator, later recalled that Oveta "would come and spend the night and say, 'What this room needs is a decent chandelier.'" She would go back to Houston and find one to offer. Lady Bird accepted the gift, stating that she was "grateful and happy" to receive the "delicate and charming" chandelier because it would be "a beautiful addition to the Queen's Room, where I shall like it all the more because that is 'your' room when you are here." Oveta sincerely admired and liked Lady Bird. "Mrs. Johnson is a star," she later stated in an oral history interview. "She worked as hard at her job as I can imagine anyone working. She's a lady in every variation of the word. And she has an integrity of mind and purpose that I've never seen equaled."[21]

In the midst of maintaining a hectic schedule and tending to her duties as a member of an impressive list of committees, task forces, commissions, and boards, Oveta was named to the Rice University Board of Trustees on June 17, 1967. She was the first woman member ever to serve on Rice's board, adding to her list of "first woman" accomplishments. According to Bill Hobby, Oveta was appointed to the board largely because of her close friendship with George Brown, who felt it was time to have a woman member. Bill later noted that Brown was "dragging Rice, kicking and screaming, into the 20th century." In the early 1960s, Brown had been responsible for going to court to change founder William Marsh Rice's will, which had imposed racial segregation on the university.[22]

Oveta returned to the White House in November 1967 as a special guest of honor at President Johnson's signing ceremony for a congressional bill to provide equal promotion opportunities for women in the military. "As our good friends Senator Margaret Chase Smith and Mrs. Hobby and many others can testify, women in uniform have had to fight on more than one battlefield of war," LBJ said. "I well recall when one of my male colleagues in the House of Representatives, back in 1942 when we were debating the bill to create the WAAC, had this to say: 'What has become of the manhood of America?'" Oveta stayed at the White House that night as well as the following night, when she had a late evening dinner with Lyndon, Lady Bird, and Oveta's old friend from Dallas Judge Sarah Hughes, who also stayed overnight. Former Speaker and vice president "Cactus Jack" Garner had died that morning, and President Johnson, Judge Hughes, and Oveta swapped stories about the irascible Texan who had once been among the most powerful men in Washington. After dinner, they all went downstairs to the Oval Office, where the president showed them a photograph of him sitting with Garner, Harry Truman, and Sam Rayburn on the front porch of Garner's home in Uvalde, Texas, during the celebration of Cactus Jack's ninetieth birthday in 1959.[23]

*Oveta Culp Hobby and President Lyndon B. Johnson at the*
*White House ceremony honoring women in the military.*

On December 12, 1967, Central Texas College, a newly established two-year public school located between Killeen and Copperas Cove, held an event to celebrate the naming of the school's library in Oveta's honor. LBJ flew in a helicopter from his ranch to speak at the dedication ceremony. When the presidential helicopter landed in an open area in front of the college's main building, LBJ walked the short distance to greet Oveta, who was waiting on the front steps with college officials and Lieutenant General George Mather, commander of the nearby Fort Hood army base. The audience of five thousand was composed largely of soldiers in uniform who were also students at the college, which is on land completely surrounded by Fort Hood. After LBJ gave a speech lauding Oveta's accomplishments, he and the other dignitaries walked to the new library building as he shook hands with members of the crowd along the way. Oveta cut a ribbon to open the library, and she and LBJ took a quick tour of the building. Immediately after, the president bid Oveta goodbye and then departed by helicopter to Fort Hood's parade ground to review a formation of young men who would soon be dispatched to Vietnam.[24]

*Oveta Culp Hobby and President Lyndon B. Johnson at the dedication of the
Oveta Culp Hobby Library at Central Texas College, Killeen, December 1967.*

By the end of 1967, Oveta Culp Hobby's service on a wide range of important presidential task forces, commissions, and committees had restored her celebrity almost to the level it had occupied during her service as director of the Women's Army Corps and as HEW secretary, when her portrait had graced the covers of most of the major news magazines. Her name was frequently mentioned in the press and in popular journals. Earlier in the year *Harper's Bazaar* had placed Oveta on its list of "100 American Women of Accomplishment."[25]

LBJ gave Oveta her final presidential assignment in mid-February 1968, when he appointed her to a four-year term on the newly created board of the Corporation for Public Broadcasting (CPB). The CPB was created as a conduit for financial assistance for the noncommercial educational television and radio broadcasting systems Congress had authorized the year before. It was a natural fit for Oveta because of her work on the report that had led to the CPB as well as her experience as the operator of television and radio stations. Her colleagues on the CPB board included individuals whom Oveta knew from other associations, including John D. Rockefeller III, whom she had gotten to know through her relationship with his brothers, Nelson and Laurance; former *Houston Post* employee Jack Valenti; and Dwight Eisenhower's brother, Milton, the emeritus president of Johns Hopkins University who had been president of Pennsylvania State University when Oveta was HEW secretary. Oveta would play an active role on the board in the next four years as it guided the creation of the Public Broadcasting Service and National Public Radio as program distributors to local broadcast affiliates.[26]

On the evening of March 31, 1968, Lyndon Johnson stunned the country when he announced on a prime-time, nationwide television broadcast, "I shall not seek, and I will not accept, the nomination of my party for another term as your president." Despite her close relationship and frequent contact with Lyndon and Lady Bird, Oveta had received no hint that the president was contemplating such an action. "I was shocked," she later recalled. "I certainly didn't know it before I heard it on TV. But in looking back I wasn't so shocked." Two hours after the president made his announcement, Oveta and George Brown, who had watched the broadcast together at 2 Remington Lane, called LBJ from Houston, but there is no recording or transcript of the conversation, which lasted less than three minutes. Two days after LBJ's shocking announcement Oveta directed the *Post* to publish an editorial, "Johnson Bows Out," which admitted that the president's decision was "unexpected . . . but it was hardly surprising" considering the "formidable" burdens of the office, especially when "personal insults and abuse are heaped upon the President and members of his family" and he was denied the "understanding, sympathy and support of many members of his own party." The editorial gave one hint about who had directed its message: "If there was anything really surprising about his announcement to *those who know him personally*, it was the timing" (emphasis added). Oveta also directed that the *Post* publish LBJ's entire withdrawal speech in the same issue in which the editorial appeared.[27]

The year 1968 was one of tumult and shock. Only two days after the *Post* published its editorial reaction to Johnson's decision not to run for reelection, Dr. Martin Luther King Jr. was assassinated in Memphis. On April 6, Oveta approved a *Post* editorial, probably written by George Fuermann, strongly condemning the "senseless" murder— "an evil from which no good can possibly come"—and lamenting the loss of Dr. King from the civic life of the nation. "No sane American . . . can fail to sense our shame." Two months later, Sirhan Sirhan murdered Senator Robert F. Kennedy. In the days immediately following that tragedy the *Post* was filled with news about the assassination, with headlines such as "Nation Shocked, Sad, Angered by Shooting of Sen. Kennedy" and "Happy Victory Speech—Then Sorrow." Four days after Kennedy's shooting, the *Post* published an editorial with the headline "Nation of Guns," deploring the nation's lax attitude toward and inadequate regulation of guns that had resulted in the United States "having the highest rate of slaughter—by accident and by murder—of any civilized nation in the world." The *Post* cited the gun laws of the United Kingdom as a model for the United States to follow.[28]

A month after Oveta was shocked by LBJ's announcement he would not run for a second term, she was hit hard by another event. In April, Dwight Eisenhower suffered his third heart attack while he was in California and was hospitalized at March Air Force Base near Riverside. He was soon transferred to Walter Reed. In August, Mamie wrote Oveta, "Thank you for the telegram you sent after Ike's last heart attack. This was a massive one and will require a long siege in the hospital—already it has been three months but I do not care if he just gets well. [I] am happy the doctors let me stay here at Walter Reed. Shared [with] Ike your message—He was pleased."[29]

Oveta consulted with Houston heart surgeon Denton Cooley about Ike's prognosis. After Dr. Cooley contacted colleagues at Walter Reed, he told Oveta the damage to Eisenhower's heart was extensive and irreparable. His death was likely within a few months. With Cooley's confirmation that the former president did not have long to live, Oveta sent a telegram to Ike at Walter Reed Hospital on his seventy-eighth birthday. "Happy Birthday, My Dear Mister President," she wrote. "I hope you have some idea of the love and affection the people of the United States have for you." Mamie kept Oveta informed about Ike's condition during these last months of his life. In November, she wrote Oveta, "The General is progressing steadily, but slowly, and we are delighted with the progress he has made. He has a few bad days, but most are good and I feel very fortunate that I am able to be nearby at all times." In the final weeks of his life, Ike managed to get a letter off to Oveta to wish her a happy birthday and apologized that his note was brief but was "sincere to say the least." He managed to scribble a PS: "My love to your charming daughter and my best to her husband." Oveta's visit with Ike at Gettysburg in October 1966 was the last time she saw him.[30]

On March 28, 1969, Oveta received a telegram containing a long-dreaded announcement: "Mrs. Eisenhower and son, John, have asked me to inform you of the death of the Honorable Dwight David Eisenhower." Oveta flew to Washington to attend Ike's funeral at the National Cathedral on Monday, March 31, 1969. After the service, which was attended by Charles de Gaulle, Prince Charles, the shah of Iran, and the king of Belgium, among many other dignitaries, Oveta attempted to visit with Mamie but she was unable to make her way through the throng surrounding her. Disappointed, Oveta nevertheless placed her card in the hand of one of Mamie's attendants and urged her to show it to Mamie to make certain she knew Oveta had attended the funeral. Oveta maintained contact with Mamie after Ike's passing. Four months after his death, Oveta wrote the former First Lady, "I have thought of you so many, many times these past few weeks. . . . I well know how difficult these next months will be for you. If there is anything at all I can do for you, I am at your service." Oveta well knew what Mamie was going through because she had been widowed a few years earlier.[31]

Oveta's interactions with the Johnsons were much reduced during LBJ's last ten months as president. This probably stemmed from his fevered efforts to force Hanoi into concessions at the negotiating table and end the war in Vietnam and his increasing isolation from the societal tumult surrounding the White House during much of 1968.

Oveta's few visits with the president and Lady Bird after March 31 included two occasions in April 1968: a dinner at the LBJ Ranch with the Johnsons and a large group of other guests and a private dinner party at the White House a week later that included Vice President Humphrey, Ford Foundation president McGeorge Bundy, and novelist John Steinbeck and his wife. Oveta stayed overnight after the dinner, but she lost the Queens' Bedroom to the Steinbecks. It would be her last overnight stay at the White House during the LBJ presidency. She also saw the Johnsons when she was visiting at George Brown's ranch near Concan in the Texas Hill Country in August. Lyndon, Lady Bird, and Luci arrived by helicopter for lunch and they spent the afternoon visiting. Afterward, LBJ took the Browns and Oveta with him back to the LBJ Ranch by helicopter, where they drove around the ranch, including a nostalgic stop at LBJ's birthplace. After a couple of hours, Oveta and the Browns departed the ranch on a Jetstream aircraft. This might have been the last time Oveta saw LBJ while he was president.[32]

After LBJ left office in January 1969, Oveta continued to have little contact with the former president, who rarely left his ranch, except to go to Austin to monitor progress on his presidential library. She did have the opportunity to visit with the Johnsons in December 1970, when she attended a party at the LBJ Ranch in honor of former Mexican president Miguel Alemán. In April 1971, Bill Hobby went to the ranch to get LBJ's advice about running for lieutenant governor of Texas. Johnson told Bill he would support him, but only if George Christian, LBJ's former press secretary, decided not to run. As it turned out, Christian did not enter the race. Afterward, Oveta wrote LBJ, "William appreciated your seeing him and all the wonderful advice you gave him. I appreciated it, too." LBJ replied, "You and the Governor did a wonderful job on Bill. I want to help any way in the world I can, and will again the next time he passes this way." In May 1971 Oveta attended the opening of the LBJ Presidential Library in Austin. It was a hectic event attended by a large crowd, including President Richard Nixon. Security was extraordinarily tight and the area was cordoned off from a major gathering of antiwar protestors. Oveta's contact with the Johnsons and with Nixon was brief by necessity. She later wrote Lyndon and Lady Bird (whom she called "Bird") a brief letter: "I was truly thrilled by the beauty of the library and the magnificent setting, a handsome addition to the University and a treasure for the State and nation."[33]

LBJ's health was more seriously in decline than many of his friends realized and he made few public appearances. Nevertheless, LBJ's bond with Oveta remained strong. He went to the trouble in March 1972 of traveling to Houston to be at Oveta and Bill's side at the formal opening of the new KPRC-TV studios located near the new Houston Post Building. The last time Oveta saw Lyndon Johnson before his death was on January 16, 1973, when Bill took his oath of office as lieutenant governor during the inaugural ceremony on the south steps of the Texas Capitol. The former president accepted Bill's invitation to attend the celebration. Bill later recalled that after the ceremony, LBJ "was mobbed by well-wishers. It was a great last hurrah." At the luncheon at the Governor's

Mansion following the inauguration, Oveta sat next to LBJ and they exchanged memories of their long relationship.

Six days later, on January 22, 1973, Lyndon Johnson died from a heart attack he suffered on his ranch. In a statement issued immediately after she got the news, Oveta declared, "President Johnson loved his country and served it well. The nation has lost a great patriot." The *Post* published a front-page editorial the day after LBJ's death that catalogued his achievements as president, including the Great Society legislation, especially Medicare, civil rights bills, and federal aid to education. Little mention was made of the war in Southeast Asia, other than the claim that it was a war "he had inherited" and the observation that it had been "a divisive force in the country." The editorial concluded with a statement that LBJ "gave most of the years of his life to public service. As he finds his place in history, it will be an honorable place and an honored one."[34]

# CHAPTER 44

---

# MANAGING THE HOUSTON POST

In the weeks following Lyndon Johnson's withdrawal from the presidential campaign in March 1968, Oveta restored her ties to the Republican Party, throwing her support behind Richard Nixon. Although she had never been enthusiastic about Nixon as a person, his political positions were much closer to hers than were those of Hubert Humphrey. Another factor in her decision to return to the GOP was her outrage at what she considered to be the Democratic Party's disgraceful treatment of LBJ. In addition, she believed the antiwar movement and the political and social violence that had engulfed the country had paralyzed the Democrats, who she felt were now incapable of governing.

Bill Hobby, who continued to identify as a Democrat and who aspired to enter electoral politics in Texas, did not share Oveta's support for Nixon, nor did her more liberal daughter, Jessica. But Oveta's son-in-law, Henry Catto, was on the Nixon team. He had worked in Nixon's campaign in 1960 and he accepted a position as finance chairman of the 1968 Citizens for Nixon organization. Oveta agreed to serve as vice chair of the Eisenhower Team for Nixon-Agnew, but it was largely a token gesture. She was little involved in the ebb and flow of the campaign. She was even a no-show for Nixon's campaign visit to Houston on September 7, 1968. The former vice president had wanted Oveta to make a public appearance with him and his wife, Pat, but inexplicably his staff members were unable to find her. As he was leaving Houston, Nixon sent Oveta a handwritten note. "It seems we've been unsuccessful in reaching you by phone," he lamented, "so I am dropping you this note to tell you how sorry Pat and I are that we missed seeing you. I hope we shall soon meet again—in New York, Houston, or *maybe* Washington D.C.!" That the Nixon team had found it impossible to reach Oveta or that no one at the *Houston Post* knew her whereabouts seems strange, given that Oveta's staff members were known for their efficiency. Was she impossible to find on purpose? It's likely. Oveta was still closely connected to LBJ and it might have been that she was avoiding an awkward situation. The president obviously knew Oveta was supporting Nixon, and it clearly had no effect

---

on their relationship—that was politics, after all. But openly campaigning with Nixon in Houston might have been something Oveta thought went too far.[1]

In late October, Oveta published an editorial in the *Post* endorsing Richard Nixon for president. Nixon wrote Oveta that her "unreserved editorial endorsement" was "uniquely defining and I want you to know how much I value it. With your depth of experience your comments have added meaning. . . . It is awfully good to have your support and confidence."[2]

As Election Day approached, KPRC-TV made arrangements for its coverage of the vote returns. Because the presidential election was expected to be extremely close, Jack Harris organized a reporting team that could stay on the air all night if necessary. In late October, however, Harris was alarmed by news reports that NBC, the network with which KPRC was affiliated, planned to mine data from early voting returns to make projections of probable winners in each state and, if possible, to declare either Nixon or Humphrey the next president long before the polls had closed in many states west of the Mississippi River, including Texas. Harris was disturbed that NBC's early projections might deter voters from going to the polls and make them think that the winner had already been decided.

Harris met with Oveta and Bill Hobby to tell them about NBC's plan and his concerns about its impact on the vote in KPRC's broadcast area. Oveta agreed that NBC's plan was a bad idea. She told Harris that they should "make every effort" to dissuade NBC from feeding these reports to KPRC-TV for broadcast before the polls closed in Texas. Oveta decided to call Robert Sarnoff, president of RCA, the corporate owner of NBC, to express her opposition to NBC's election coverage plan. She was unable to reach Sarnoff, but his aide called her back that afternoon. Oveta shared her concerns with the aide and asked that they be passed on to Sarnoff and to Julian Goodman, NBC's president. The next day, Don Mercer, NBC vice president for station relations, called Harris to ask for more information about KPRC's concerns. Harris told Mercer he and Oveta felt it was not in the public interest "to take any chance of influencing people who had not yet voted by giving early and possibly dramatic predictions from other areas." He stressed that Oveta was urging the network to refrain from making such projections until the polls had closed throughout the country, or at least in Texas. Mercer assured Harris that NBC planned to use projections "with utmost caution," but he agreed to pass Harris's concerns on to Julian Goodman. On October 28, Mercer sent Harris a letter stating NBC would use "extreme caution in their projections and reminders to the public that the polls were still open in various parts of the country."[3]

Harris took NBC's response to Oveta and Bill, who told Harris to ask the network to send KPRC silent visual or audio cues before the network issued any projections prior to the polls closing in Texas so that KPRC could switch to commercials or give local returns instead. NBC responded that technical issues would prevent them from sending any cues. Harris felt the message was a "run-around" and that it was "obvious NBC could give such cues." When Harris informed Oveta about NBC's intransigence, she told Harris to sit in the KPRC control room the night of the election to make decisions about whether or not to pull away from NBC if they gave any sign that they were going to announce a winner before the polls closed in Texas. As it turned out, NBC was unable to make any early victory projections because of the extremely close vote.[4]

Richard Nixon defeated Hubert Humphrey, with the race undecided until the day after voting had ended. Nixon's inaugural committee sent a special invitation to Oveta, but she did not attend, possibly out of respect for LBJ as well as for Humphrey. Despite her support for Nixon, Oveta was never involved in his administration and she made few visits to the Nixon White House. One was on August 13, 1969, when she attended the White House dinner honoring the Apollo 11 astronauts, partly because of her longtime support of the Manned Spacecraft Center near Houston. She later thanked First Lady Pat Nixon for the invitation, stating she would "always remember it as one of the truly magnificent evenings of a lifetime." On April 10, 1970, she attended a state dinner in honor of German chancellor Willy Brandt. Afterward, she told Pat Nixon that the "White House has never looked lovelier, with the cherry trees and azaleas so breathtakingly beautiful, the whole effect like a charming fairyland."[5]

Oveta's overall support of Nixon remained tepid throughout his first term as president, although she strongly supported his foreign policy initiatives, especially his trip to the People's Republic of China in February 1972. When Nixon ran for a second term, she decided to publish an editorial in the *Post* endorsing Nixon's reelection. As her confidant Marguerite Johnston later admitted, Oveta's decision "was not for love of Nixon" but instead was based on her strong opposition to the liberal platform of Democratic presidential candidate Senator George McGovern, as well as her continuing loyalty to Dwight Eisenhower's legacy. Oveta asked George Fuermann to draft the editorial. Marguerite Johnston recalled that when Fuermann read his draft aloud at an editorial board meeting, it was "the most backed-into, back-handed, not so much half-hearted as no hearted-at-all editorial you ever heard." Oveta sat quietly for a moment looking around the table at her editorial board members and then said, "None of you wants to support him, do you? All of you are against me?" Fuermann replied, "Well, no, Mrs. Hobby. There is a very conservative assistant editor who is going to vote for Nixon, and I think some people in the back shop are." After staring quietly for a moment, she then asked Fuermann to draft a "reasonable editorial to run on page one and I will sign it." Marguerite Johnston noted that she and her fellow board members "were grateful [Oveta] had spared them from having to make the endorsement."[6]

Oveta's editorial lauded Nixon for his diplomatic initiatives with China and the Soviet Union, his reduction of American troop levels in Vietnam, and his attempts to reduce inflation and stabilize the dollar. There was no mention of Nixon's controversial domestic agenda that aimed to attract conservative Southern Democrats to the GOP, his administration's attacks on the press, or his attempts to stack the Supreme Court with appointees who had anti–civil rights records. His opponent, Senator George McGovern, was not mentioned, nor was there any reference to the June break-in at the Democratic

Party office in the Watergate apartment and office complex. It's unknown how much, if any, of the text Oveta revised, but it clearly reflected her views by referring only to that portion of Nixon's record that many Democrats also supported. The editorial, simply titled "For Nixon," was published on the front page of the *Post* on October 29, 1972, with Oveta prominently listed as the author. When Nixon read the editorial, he wrote a "Dear Oveta" letter. "I want you to know how much I appreciate . . . the support of the *Houston Post*," Nixon wrote. "Your confidence means a great deal to me and it is deeply gratifying to receive your high marks."[7]

The endorsement of Nixon's reelection was not the first time Oveta signed a *Post* editorial. Only a year earlier, in June 1971, she had asked for an editorial critical of the *New York Times* decision to publish the Pentagon Papers, a top secret Defense Department history of American involvement in Vietnam from 1945 to 1967 that former analyst Daniel Ellsberg had illegally leaked to the press. It's likely that her experience with the HEW Vietnam task force and her close friendship with Johnson were among the reasons for her negative opinion of the *Times'* controversial decision. Oveta's past stances had always been solidly in support of press freedoms, but she viewed publication of the Pentagon Papers as endangering national security. Prior to her meeting with the editorial board to discuss the issue, George Fuermann, who thought the *Times'* decision was a good one, knew that Bill Hobby also supported the *Times*. Bill agreed to go with Fuermann to persuade Oveta that the *Post* shouldn't take a critical position in the matter. They presented their case, but Oveta was not persuaded, telling them that the *Times* had gone too far. She asked them to draft the editorial; however, she relieved the editorial board of any responsibility for her own opinion of the issue and signed the editorial to make it obvious that this was her personal view.[8]

Oveta's last known communication with Richard Nixon while he was president was in February 1973, as the Senate investigation of the Watergate break-in gained steam. Oveta, who many months earlier had grown wary of the Vietnam War (a wariness that was gradually becoming evident on the *Post*'s editorial page), published an editorial praising Nixon's recent announcement that US troops would soon be withdrawn from South Vietnam. The spirit of the editorial was more about hopes that the war would soon end rather than any endorsement of Nixon's conduct of the war. Nixon saw the editorial and wrote his thanks to Oveta for printing it. The president noted that he and Oveta "have not, of course, always seen eye-to-eye over the Vietnam issue but I am pleased to know that I have your confidence and good wishes." In her reply, Oveta thanked Nixon for his "very kind letter. It was most gracious of you to comment so generously on the *Houston Post* editorial. It conveyed only a small measure of the admiration and appreciation we feel for your dedicated efforts to achieve an honorable peace."[9]

During the spring and summer of 1974, the *Houston Post* provided extensive coverage of the growing Watergate scandal as more information surfaced and Nixon's criminal complicity in the cover-up became known, but the paper expressed no strong editorial positions about the president's behavior. And then on the morning of August 9, 1974, a headline on the front page of the *Houston Post* screamed, "NIXON RESIGNS." News of the resignation covered the entire front page and continued with stories scattered throughout the rest of the news sections, including the Associated Press's transcript of the entire text of Nixon's resignation speech.[10]

The first *Post* editorial related to the resignation appeared on August 10, but it ignored Nixon and focused instead on the new president, Gerald R. Ford. Titled "Measure of the Man," the editorial praised him for his "decency" and called on him to restore the faith of the American people in their government. That edition was also filled with news of the continuing story (front-page headline: "Ford Says 'Nightmare Over'"), with editorial commentary provided by syndicated columnists. Another pro-Ford editorial was published on August 15, 1974: "Reassurance at the Top." The *Post* editorials made no mention of Richard Nixon by name, only making reference to the "previous administration." By Thursday, August 15, Watergate was off the front page. It was clear that Oveta, who controlled the editorial page, was done with Richard Nixon, much to the relief of several of her editorial writers.[11]

Oveta remained publicly silent about the Watergate affair until a couple of years after Nixon resigned, when a magazine writer asked her opinion about the role the *Washington Post* had played in Nixon's downfall. "As an editor, I might have done something differently in covering the story," she said, "but I still would have pursued it just as diligently as the *Washington Post* did. Obstruction of justice is a serious matter." She was also asked to comment on Attorney General John Mitchell's telephone call to *Washington Post* publisher Katharine Graham in which he threatened that if her newspaper didn't back off, she would "get her tit caught in a wringer." Oveta replied that her "reaction would have been the same as hers. If anything, the phone call would have made me more determined to publish. Blackmail is an ugly word, and the people of the U.S. needed to know what kind of Attorney General they had."[12]

In the late 1960s, the *Post* continued to be profitable enough for Oveta to decide to build an expensive and impressive new headquarters and printing plant, but she had no specific location in mind. Bill Hobby later recalled, "When we were looking for a new location for the *Post*, I happened to drive by some land located at the intersection of the Southwest Freeway and the just finished Loop 610 Freeway. I noticed a for-sale sign and realized that the telephone number was that of Rice University." He contacted the university to find out the price. Bill later learned that George Brown had built a street connecting the twenty-one-acre property to existing road thruways at no cost to the university to enhance its value. When he decided the price seemed reasonable, Bill took the idea to Oveta. After she inspected the site and consulted with her business advisors, she agreed to buy the property. It would be another three years before the building was designed and constructed.[13]

Although Bill was much involved in the building project, Oveta remained in charge. One longtime employee recalled that during the planning, she "would go into detail about everything from the number of telephones within a given department to the

*The newly constructed Houston Post Building,*
*ca. early 1970s, known by staff as "Fort Hobby."*

---

spending of millions for new presses and other high-tech printing systems. Amazingly, she understood the basics of utility rate structures and how to achieve allowable discounts." At one point she even brought in experts on color dynamics and the effects of different colors on workers. She also wanted the newspaper's operations to be as modern and efficient as possible and eventually made it one of the first fully computerized newspapers in the country.[14]

After many months of planning, including working out a design by the firm of Wilson, Morris, Crain, and Anderson, who were the architects of the Astrodome, the *Post*'s new campus was finally ready for occupancy late in 1970. The complex consisted of seven buildings, most of which were connected, containing a total of more than 440,000 square feet. The main four-story building, where Oveta's office was located, fronted one of Houston's busiest freeways. It was among the first of many notable buildings that were quickly springing up in the adjacent area, including the Galleria shopping mall and a large Neiman-Marcus department store. An architectural guide to Houston published not long after the complex opened described the new Post Building as an example of the brutalist style of architecture, with its "rectangular box around which concrete silos have been picturesquely arrayed." The guide also refers to the building as an early local example of "freeway" architecture that "projects a formal image that is strong, yet simple enough to be apprehended from a speeding car." With its eight turreted, exposed-concrete modules that some compared to grain elevators, Houstonians soon began referring to the *Post*'s new home as "Fort Hobby." Obviously, Oveta did not describe her new building in such a jocular manner. Soon after the complex opened, a magazine writer who was writing a profile on Oveta commented to her that the "striking" design was "surely her proudest innovation." Oveta answered, "It's fabulous isn't it? It's a great place."[15]

All of the *Post*'s operations were moved to the new location on the Southwest Freeway, except for the presses, which remained at the old plant at Polk and Dowling Streets. An article in *Women's Wear Daily* published a few weeks after the staff moved into the building observed that the newsroom was "not a typical newspaper office. It is carpeted [and] airy," with reporters working behind "yellow and blue Lucite partitions that look like enormous Polaroid wraparound sunglasses and sit[ting] on chrome furniture. The total look is more Madison Avenue, less 'Front Page.'" The same was true of the publisher's office, which was also unusual for the time—or in some respects, for any time. Located on the third floor, Oveta's meticulously planned and designed office was actually a suite of three rooms. The main room, which served as her work and meeting space, had twenty-foot ceilings, burnished hardwood floors, a wall of bookshelves, a fireplace, and antique oak wall paneling taken from an English manor. The paneling had been a much-treasured gift from Will, so she had it carefully removed panel by panel from her old office and placed on the walls of her new office.

Oveta filled her office with nineteenth-century tables and chairs, pewter ashtrays, and an oriental rug. A Chinese tapestry was suspended from hooks on a wall. Her massive mahogany desk was located in a corner of the room. A US flag from her days as head of the Women's Army Corps and an official HEW banner hung from tall flag stands positioned in front of the floor-to-ceiling windows near her desk. A bust of Dwight Eisenhower in his army uniform sat on top of an antique chest of drawers. Another relic from the WAC, a bust of the goddess Athena, sat atop a table next to the fireplace mantel. "Mrs. Hobby's office was an entry into another world," one of her editors later recalled.[16]

The size of Oveta's new office, as well as its furnishings, signified the occupant's authority, experience, and prestige. And her deportment when meeting with staff and visitors from the outside underscored that image. After a writer for *Houston Town and Country* magazine interviewed Oveta in her office in the 1970s, he reported she exuded "charm by the buckets-full as she moves away from her desk and invites me to sit opposite her in a high backed brocaded chair. Coffee is served in china cups and saucers, cigarettes offered from a leather box. Taken together, all these things add up to an impression of graciousness rarely achieved in today's business world. Mrs. Hobby's personal appearance can only be described as tastefully conservative." Her deportment was the same whether she was with an employee or a visitor. One of her reporters later recalled Oveta "combined the roles of executive and hostess with practiced ease. She greeted visitors

*Oveta Culp Hobby in her office at the* Houston Post, *ca. early 1980s.*

at her office door. She knew every guest's name and something personal about him. A white-jacketed male served [beverages]. In the small dining room just off her office, we drank coffee from fine china."[17]

Harry Hurt III, who wrote an insightful profile of Oveta for *Texas Monthly* at the time, observed that when he first met Oveta he was struck by her presence and the ambience she had created in her impressive office. "Mrs. Hobby is much prettier and thinner than her recent photographs suggest. She is the kind of woman who imparts the sense that she is in love with life. At the same time, she always seems to be in total control—of herself, of her company, of her situation." He noted that after interviewing several people who knew Oveta, he realized that she "inspires hatred as well as love, fear as well as admiration." His interviewees had described Oveta variously as "temperamental, autocratic, old-fashioned. But even those who dislike Oveta Hobby seem to have an overriding respect for her, a special kind of awe. She is regal, but not condescending, dignified, but not stuffy, cordial but never weak."[18]

When she moved into her new headquarters, Oveta spun KPRC-TV and Radio out of the Houston Post Company and organized the broadcast properties under the name Channel Two Company. Sensitive to growing public concerns about the growth of media conglomerations, Oveta explained in an interview with *Women's Wear Daily* that the reorganization would make her media holdings "look less like a concentration of the media, which we never wanted it to look like. It is our policy not to discuss the paper's editorial policies on radio or television or vice versa." She felt it was better to have a separate board of directors for each company. She was now editor, chairman, and chief executive officer of the *Post* and chairman of the Channel Two Company and KPRC Radio.[19]

As head of both the *Houston Post* and the Channel Two Company, Oveta held her administrative conferences in her office in the Post Building. Not much of a memo writer, she preferred to have face-to-face talks with her top executives as often as possible, which resulted in much of her day being taken up with departmental meetings. She held consultations at least once a week with executive vice president and general counsel Jim Crowther and KPRC-TV station chief Jack Harris, the two most influential members of her executive team. Crowther can be best characterized as Oveta's consigliere and right-hand man. He sat on all the major *Post* boards, including the editorial board, and met personally with Oveta more often than any other *Post* executive. Oveta also held editorial board meetings in her office. Those were scheduled twice a week, every Monday and Thursday morning. The board also included the main news writers and Bill Hobby, when he was not in Austin. Before Oveta arrived at these meetings, some of the junior reporters would be downstairs gazing out the windows watching for the arrival of her limousine. Oveta's chauffeur, Cecil McBride, drove her to the office each morning at about nine thirty, and he would wait in the *Post* lobby or by the car until it was time for her to leave. Gossip columnist Marge Crumbaker was one of those staff members who often watched for Oveta's arrival. "I admired the way she alighted from her chauffeured limousine, carrying nothing—no purse, no briefcase," Crumbaker later recalled. "These mundane things apparently were assigned to others."[20]

As Oveta made her way to the editorial meeting, the participants arrived ahead of her and took their assigned seats at a long, polished table. The chair Oveta had used when she attended Eisenhower's cabinet meetings was placed at the head of the table. A silver coffeepot, china cups, and silver spoons were available on a nearby chest. Coffee was self-serve, with one exception: one of the editors would pour a cup of coffee and place it where she sat. When Mrs. Hobby walked into the room everyone stood (a formality dating back to her days as commander of the women's corps), and one of the editors held her chair while she was getting seated. After taking a sip of coffee, she would light the first of the many Parliament-brand cigarettes she chain-smoked as the editors began a brief roundup of the morning's news developments pulled from the wire services. She would fold her tortoiseshell glasses carefully and rest them in her lap while she listened silently to the reports. Her editorial writers presented the topics they wanted to address as editorials, which often provoked a lively discussion. At this stage of the meeting everyone would begin to loosen up, including Oveta. Ed Hunter, who was the managing editor and later executive editor, remembered an incident at an editorial meeting that was typical of the kind of sly little remarks Oveta often made once the session became less formal. Hunter was a conservative who frequently clashed with the more liberal Marguerite Johnston over editorials. Once, when he disagreed with a position Johnston was taking, he looked at Oveta and declared that he didn't "want to get into a fight with Marguerite over this, but. . . ." At that point Oveta interrupted "with a smile and a wink" and said, "Oh, that's all right. You and Marguerite go ahead and get into a fight." Her remark brought forth boisterous laughter.[21]

During the editorial discussions, Oveta would reject some of the proposals, while putting others on hold. She often approved editorials silently, with a wave of her hand. Typically, once that business was concluded Oveta turned to the city editor and inquired, using a favorite phrase of hers, what he was hearing "on the street." After the editor shared whatever information he had, Oveta sometimes brought up some bit of news gossip she had picked up, usually from her anonymous but well-connected friends, such as George Brown, attorney and *Houston Post* board member George Butler, or federal judge Woodrow Seals. Occasionally something would remind her of a small incident that happened in her past, usually of a humorous nature, and she would share the story with her editors. When someone brought up Nelson Rockefeller's name after he became Gerald Ford's vice president, it reminded Oveta of the time early in his tenure as Oveta's deputy at HEW when Rockefeller was briefly trying to play down his great wealth by traveling by taxi instead of limousine. After she and Rockefeller had dinner in a restaurant, he had to borrow money from her because he had none on him to pay his cab fare home. At another meeting, Jesse Jones's name was mentioned, triggering a story from Oveta about the multimillionaire and his wife Mary's frugal ways. When she was with Mary Jones at the Mayflower Hotel in Washington during the war, they decided to go to lunch at a club that was several blocks away. As they walked out to the front of the hotel, Oveta went toward the cabstand, but Mary stopped her and said that a cab was too expensive. They could walk to the club. "I think cabs then would have cost a quarter," Oveta recalled. "So we walked. I'll never forget it because I was wearing a new pair of shoes." Ed Hunter later noted, "Who could forget those delicious little tidbits, sidebars, that came out of those board meetings!"[22]

Although Oveta ruled the editorial page with an iron hand, set the general policy and tone of the newspaper, and paid attention to the quality and general content of the *Post*'s overall news coverage, she normally remained aloof from the day-to-day operation of the newsroom. There were exceptions, however, but they typically related to newsroom developments that had larger implications for the *Post* as a company. During the 1970s, for example, prosecutors in the Harris County district attorney's office called *Post* reporter Jon Standifer to testify in a criminal case. The DA's office demanded that Standifer give them the name of the confidential source for the story he had written about the crime, but Standifer didn't want to reveal the source. He met with Oveta, who advised him that the choice was his to make, "because you are the one who will go to jail. But we'll litigate it as far as you want to." That gave Standifer confidence that Oveta had his back, but it developed that his testimony wasn't needed. On another occasion in the early 1970s, Mickey Herskowitz, who had been a reporter and sports columnist at the *Post* since 1954, wrote a column critical of FBI Director J. Edgar Hoover. "[Hoover] was still an icon to most of America, including the River Oaks neighborhood where Mrs. Hobby's closest friends lived," Herskowitz remembered. "When I returned from a trip, one of the editors showed me a note in Mrs. Hobby's handwriting. 'Tell that young man that the next time he writes something like this, I expect him to stay here and answer my telephone.'"[23]

When *Post* reporter and gossip columnist Marge Crumbaker learned it was likely that wheeler-dealer Roy Hofheinz would soon lose control of his business empire, including the Astrodome, the Astros baseball team, and the AstroWorld amusement park, she asked her editor, Ed Hunter, if she could write a story about Hofheinz's problems, which were unknown to the public at that point. Knowing this was a news story that required Oveta's approval, Hunter and Crumbaker went to Oveta to ask her permission. After a lengthy discussion, Oveta conceded that Crumbaker had sufficient material to do the story or even a series of stories. Oveta then explained what she perceived as the "backbreaking task that was bearing down on Hofheinz," Crumbaker later recalled. "'Roy Hofheinz is trying his best,' she concluded, oh so softly. 'We won't be running a story. I never like to kick a man when he's down.'"[24]

In the 1970s, Oveta increasingly was the subject of rumors that she had ceded control of the *Post* to Bill Hobby and that she spent most of her time focused on her social and intellectual life. When a magazine writer confronted Oveta with one of those rumors shortly after she celebrated her sixty-sixth birthday in 1971, she was quick to dismiss it. "I know about every single thing that goes into this paper. Regardless of what some people think, I am still the chief executive and I make the decisions around here." When she was told there were "persistent rumors" that every time Vernon Wiley, her chauffeur of thirty-eight years, delivered her to the *Post* she rode up to her office in her private elevator to spend the rest of the day reading, she declared, "That's ridiculous! I still run this paper. Everything from management reports to technical questions flow up here. Do you want to see my calendar? There is hardly any empty space on it. And these are not social functions. My business life is the office. My social life is my family. Actually, I consider the *Post* my third child, besides Jessica and William."[25]

Unfounded concerns about age-related health issues that might be plaguing Oveta were occasionally expressed in letters from her former colleagues in the Women's Army Corps and at HEW. In answer to a letter from one of Oveta's old comrades in the army, Mabel "Georgia" Sorrells, asking about her health, Oveta's assistant Peggy Buchanan answered that her boss was in the office for meetings every morning. "She is Editor, Chairman, and Chief Executive Officer of the Post, Chairman of Channel Two Television and KPRC Radio in Houston," Buchanan wrote. "She also serves on various civic and cultural boards, and has recently agreed to serve on the Overseers Board of Harvard Graduate School of Business. All of this sounds as though it would be enough to make anyone ill, but she thrives on it; it is only the secretaries who run down and pant for breath now and then." As Buchanan finished typing the letter, Oveta walked into her office, picked up her former colleague's letter, and burst out laughing. She told Buchanan to tell Sorrells, "You are dear to write, but I am still flying the flag and going strong." Buchanan typed Oveta's remarks on the letter as a postscript and then added, "And so indeed she is."[26]

Oveta was speaking truthfully. Her health was excellent, she continued to work long hours, and she was in control. Throughout the 1970s, her active direction of the *Post* was well known among her publishing peers, and knowledgeable observers of the nation's press placed her in the "trinity of American women newspaper executives," along with the *Washington Post*'s Kay Graham and the *New York Post*'s Dorothy Schiff.

Oveta lived alone in her twenty-seven-room mansion at 2 Remington Lane for nearly seven years after Will's death, although she continued to have staff on the property twenty-four hours a day. Over time, the fifty-year-old structure's repair and maintenance problems became more frequent, and the cost of upkeep escalated. Despite its impressive qualities, it was obvious the house was a victim of changing times and fashion, but an expensive renovation and modernization project made no sense to Oveta. Consequently, in 1970, Oveta decided to demolish the mansion and develop the seven-acre site, perhaps with two or more new houses, one of which might serve as her new residence. She apparently also considered constructing a high-rise apartment building on the site. While a seventeen-story condominium had been built on Hermann Drive near Remington Lane in 1957, it's difficult to know how seriously Oveta considered the idea.

Whatever the ultimate plan, Oveta needed the approval of the Shadyside homeowners' association to redevelop the property. The original deed restrictions had expired in 1967, but the association had adopted a new set of rules that only allowed single-family residences. The new rules were to be in effect in perpetuity. Oveta made a request to the association for an exception to the deed restrictions, but it was denied. Oveta then filed a lawsuit against her neighbors, initiating a legal battle that eventually went to the Texas Supreme Court, which ruled that the restrictions were legal and therefore enforceable.

After her loss in court, Oveta was legally unable to subdivide her property or construct apartments on it. Accordingly, she decided to demolish the mansion and build and move into an entirely new three-story house at 3202 Huntingdon Place in a neighborhood near the exclusive River Oaks subdivision. She hired famed Texas architect O'Neil Ford to design it. Ford had some of the interior classical ornamentation removed from the mansion and incorporated into her new home, which was built around an outdoor patio garden. Once the house was ready, Oveta emptied the mansion, had it demolished, and filled in the swimming pool, all without informing her neighbors. The demolition was carried out in the middle of the night while the neighbors slept. Some of them believed she acted in a fit of pique. Marguerite Johnston later stated that Oveta's actions were not done to spite the neighbors but for safety reasons, although why a nighttime demolition was safer than one in daylight was left unexplained. Oveta claimed the mansion was too deteriorated to restore and would have had to be razed anyway. She donated the property to Rice University to sell for its financial benefit. It was not the first gift of real estate she had made to Rice. She and Will had given the university a property on Alameda Road in Houston's Southmore Addition in 1962. She eventually donated the Huntingdon house and lot to Rice in December 1976 while retaining a life estate that allowed her to continue to live there.[27]

On July 6, 1971, Bill Hobby, who was now thirty-nine years old, announced at a press conference in the Texas Senate Chamber in the capitol that he would seek nomination as the Democratic Party's candidate for lieutenant governor of Texas in the 1972 primary. This was the same position his father had held early in the century, before James Ferguson's removal from office cast Will into the governor's chair. Bill's announcement surprised many Democratic Party leaders and officeholders outside the *Houston Post*'s circulation area, where he was not well known, although his family name had widespread recognition because of his parents' public careers. Oveta supported Bill's decision. She helped fund his campaign and agreed to make speeches for him. On his fortieth birthday on January 19, 1972 (Oveta's sixty-seventh), Bill opened his campaign headquarters in an office on the Southwest Freeway located near the Houston Post Building. His mother was a highly visible presence at the opening, which included bands, singers, beer, and balloons bearing Hobby's campaign slogans. More than one thousand people crowded into the headquarters to celebrate the opening and to watch Bill blow out the candles on his birthday cake. In a brief talk, Bill stressed that the most important issues in the campaign were constitutional reform and restoring confidence in state government after the Sharpstown State Bank corruption scandal that had resulted from federal charges of bribery and influence peddling in the state legislature and among elected state officials.[28]

Three months later, Bill was at Oveta's side as they celebrated another opening: the newly constructed KPRC-TV broadcast center. Oveta persuaded Lyndon Johnson to leave his seclusion on the ranch to travel to Houston to be the featured guest at the opening. The event was officially nonpartisan, but LBJ's highly publicized presence sent a message to the public about his friendship with Bill and Oveta. LBJ remained popular with many Texans despite his rejection by the antiwar wing of the national Democratic Party. The new broadcast center was another one of Oveta's prized accomplishments. Jack Harris had convinced her the facility was necessary for KPRC-TV to make maximum use of rapidly developing new broadcast technology and to remain competitive in the Houston market. Oveta was enthusiastic about the project from the beginning. She played the decisive role in selecting the site, and she closely examined blueprints and specifications with her executive staff and the architects, frequently making suggestions that were based on her experience in planning the construction of the Houston Post Building. The architects built an elaborate scale model of the facility that Oveta kept in her office to proudly show staff and visitors.[29]

Bill's entry into electoral politics raised a question about how the *Post* would cover the campaign of one of its executive officers. Oveta made the not-surprising decision to editorially promote her son's candidacy while maintaining neutrality in news coverage. Accordingly, the *Post* published four highly laudatory front-page editorials in support of Bill's bid for lieutenant governor. The goal of neutrality in news coverage, however, proved to be somewhat elusive. *Time* later pointed out that there were two "curious things about the *Post*'s quadruple blessing of Hobby: the paper declined to take a stand on any of the other statewide contests, and it neglected to mention Hobby's position as president and executive editor of the newspaper." The *Houston Journalism Review*, an upstart new publication produced by local journalists independent of their employers, later published an article analyzing the *Post*'s coverage of Bill Hobby's campaign in June 1972. The coauthors, *Houston Post* reporters Susan Caudill and Darrell Hancock, claimed Hobby had received more coverage in the *Post* than all of the other candidates combined. "Most of the articles were unattributed," the article pointed out. "And that is only counting the articles about Bill Hobby the candidate. Four months after his announcement, the *Post* was still printing news about Bill Hobby . . . neglecting to mention his political aspirations."[30]

With the Democratic primary scheduled for early May, Bill Hobby campaigned full-time in March and April. Several other individuals entered the race, but only three were serious contenders, each one an incumbent state senator: Wayne Connally (former governor John Connally's brother), Joe Christie, and Ralph Hall. Because of his connections to his brother's political network and his family's name recognition, Connally was considered by many pundits to be the favorite. Bill's brother-in-law, Henry Catto, later recalled the family's concerns about Connally. "We feared that the vaunted Connally political machine would prove too tough," he admitted, adding, "Jessica returned to San Antonio [from her residence in Virginia] to campaign for [Bill] in the city's Spanish-speaking neighborhoods." Jessica spoke fluent Spanish.[31]

Jessica was not the only family member working for Bill's campaign. Oveta went on the road in April to make appearances in conservative urban areas of the state, especially the western and northwestern sections, where the Republican Party was gaining strength. Transported by private plane, her six-city tour began on April 11 in Fort Worth and then continued with stops in Dallas, San Angelo, Midland, Lubbock, and Amarillo. In Fort Worth, she attended a campaign brunch at the city's tony River Crest Country Club and then held a press conference at Bill's campaign headquarters. This pattern of country club appearances and press conferences was followed in every city. She was back in Houston by April 14. After her visit to Dallas, the *Dallas Times Herald* described Oveta as having "bobbed blonde hair swept back from her still-flawless face" and proudly wearing her Distinguished Service Medal pinned to her lapel. The story also noted that despite her age, Oveta was "still a bundle of energy." Oveta told the Dallas paper that she "did not feel her association with a Republican administration will hurt her son's campaign" and that "she doesn't expect to influence him in any way. We are a close knit family, but we do our own thing. Bill is his own man. He will have his own thoughts." When Oveta was asked about her son's qualifications for the job he was seeking, she gave a detailed answer about his budgeting and legislative skills, adding that as a working reporter he was "familiar with the needs of the people of the state" and that he would provide a "fresh face. He is free of political strings and obligations." Referring to the Sharpstown scandal, Oveta declared, "Dishonesty anywhere is indefensible. Corruption in the highest levels of state government is offensive to every Texan who believes in government by and for the people. He will go to Austin not to seek career and fortune, but to discharge a public trust."[32]

The day after Oveta left Dallas, Bill's main opponent, Wayne Connally, spoke at the Dallas Club, where he implied Bill knew his campaign was failing and had called for his mother to save him. "I'm a little bit surprised [Oveta] has come out and decided to actually campaign for him," Connally declared. "I'll have to assume they have a strong and serious concern about the way Bill Hobby is doing the job campaigning alone. This is not totally unexpected since she has always maintained that type of leadership at the *Houston Post*." The latter statement was a continuation of Connally's ongoing claim that Oveta wouldn't turn over control of the *Post* to Bill because of her lack of confidence in his abilities.[33]

Diana Hobby joined Oveta in Dallas to accompany her mother-in-law to San Angelo, where Oveta appeared on a morning television program. Later in the afternoon, Diana returned to Houston while Oveta flew on to Midland, where she claimed Bill had "wanted to serve the people of Texas since he was a little boy . . . listening to his father and me discussing the problems and challenges of government." She stressed that Bill's platform was focused on revising the state constitution: "The time has come to modernize state government to give the executive branch more responsibility," Oveta argued. Recalling her late husband's views, she stated, "The power of the executive branch began to erode with the impeachment of Ferguson. . . . As things now stand, the office of governor can be blamed for things over which the governor actually has no authority to do anything about." She also emphasized Bill's support for education, adding that too many students had dropped out of school without a marketable skill and that Texas had more people working for poverty-level incomes than any other state. She noted, "Bill wants to help them become contributing members of society. . . . [W]e have to have more vocational schools and colleges." Oveta finished her tour with a brief visit to Lubbock and an overnight stay in Amarillo.[34]

When the primary election votes were reported the night of May 6, 1972, Bill Hobby placed first with a plurality of 33.2 percent of the vote, while Wayne Connally came in second with 28.8 percent, which threw them into a primary runoff election campaign. With the public polls indicating Bill would prevail over Connally, Oveta took a less visible role in the second campaign. She did, however, make a campaign trip on May 25 to Corpus Christi, largely in response to an invitation from a close friend and Bill Hobby supporter, Ed Harte, the publisher of the *Corpus Christi Caller-Times*. When a reporter told her Wayne Connally had accused Bill of being contradictory and dishonest and of flip-flopping on school busing and the enforcement of drug laws, Oveta replied, "It's that season of the year for making political statements. What Mr. Connally says is his business. I believe in freedom of speech. I know of no dishonest statement made by Bill." Oveta stressed that Bill had "always been and is now against forced busing. I'm sorry that Mr. Connally is so misinformed." As for the drug laws, she stated Bill believed "we must go hard on the heroin pushers and some way we must find a way to protect our children." Bill, however, did support reducing marijuana possession from a felony

*Oveta Culp Hobby and Diana Hobby celebrate Bill Hobby's*
*victory in the Democratic primary election of 1972.*

to a misdemeanor. "When you write a felony on a young man, it is there for life," Oveta pointed out, "and he is restricted from many, many professions. On a first time offense for a young man or young woman who is experimenting, a felony is rather harsh."[35]

Bill handily defeated Wayne Connally in the runoff to secure the Democratic nomination for lieutenant governor. As had been the case with his father's campaigns, Bill benefitted from the Hobby family connections with other Texas newspaper publishers, especially Houston Harte, who controlled the influential Harte-Hanks newspaper chain, which included daily newspapers in San Angelo, Corpus Christi, Harlingen, Abilene, and San Antonio. Oveta was particularly pleased that Will's old newspaper the *Beaumont Enterprise* endorsed Bill. After the election, she wrote Bill Hartman, the publisher: "I think you must know a little of what it meant to the Hobbys to know the *Beaumont Enterprise* was standing with us in the campaign. The endorsement and strong support you gave to Bill was a source of pride and encouragement to us."[36]

After Bill's victory, the *Houston Journalism Review* published an editorial expressing concern about journalists and newspaper publishers being elected to public offices that their newspapers were supposed to be covering objectively, citing Bill Hobby as example number one. The *Review* declared it "almost beyond the realm of possibility that the *Post* will be able to do critical, fair, investigative reporting of the lieutenant governor's performance." Acknowledging Hobby's statement that he would take a leave of absence as president and executive editor of the *Houston Post*, the editorial noted, "The fact that his mother is chairman of the board and editor and that he very well may return to the paper in the future will not be lost on the *Post* management and news staff. Pressures or not, reporters inevitably will fear reprisals for writing stories critical of Hobby and his political allies."[37]

A comprehensive analysis of how the *Houston Post* covered Bill Hobby's tenure as lieutenant governor has not been done, but this author's sampling of *Post* news stories during those years indicated nothing especially biased. It should be no surprise, however, that the *Post*'s overall coverage was positive. It can be reasonably assumed that this was not only because his family owned the newspaper, but also because he was one of the most popular and respected lieutenant governors in Texas history and had a lengthy record of legislative achievements with no hint of corruption.

Bill Hobby's nomination in the Democratic primary assured him of victory in the general election on November 7 because he had no Republican opponent. He won 93 percent of the vote. Uvalde rancher and banker Dolph Briscoe Jr. was elected governor, although he had a Republican opponent, Houstonian Hank Grover, who ran an unexpectedly close race. Bill and Diana and their four children moved to Austin after the election. As he had promised, Bill took an official leave of absence from the *Post* during the months the legislature was in session, including special sessions, and he announced he would no longer participate in the editorial decisions of the newspaper.

Oveta attended Bill's inauguration on January 16, 1973, which featured the presence of her friends Lyndon and Lady Bird Johnson, whom Bill had persuaded to come. She also attended the celebratory opening day of the state Senate on January 17, when Bill gaveled his first session to order. Bill's wife, Diana, and their four children were also present, as was his sister, Jessica. Henry Catto was away in El Salvador, where he had been serving as the US ambassador since September 1971. At the opening session of the legislature, A. M. Aikin, dean of the Senate, presented Bill with a portrait of his father, which the Texas State Library loaned to him to display in his office. In his introductory remarks, Bill noted that his grandfather Edwin Hobby had served in the Senate in the 1870s. Afterward the members of the House and the Senate assembled in a joint session in the House chamber to hear the newly elected governor, Dolph Briscoe, give his first official speech. At the joint session, Speaker Price Daniel Jr., who was the presiding officer, called attention to Oveta's presence, noting she had been parliamentarian of the House from 1926 to 1931. She stood and received a prolonged standing ovation. Oveta Culp Hobby had traveled a long distance over many years from her childhood home in Killeen to this point in time.[38]

# CHAPTER 45

# "BUT THINK OF THE WAVE SHE LEAVES. . . ."

I n the mid-1970s, a writer for a Houston magazine asked Oveta if she would share her favorite memories with the magazine's readers. "Really, there's never been that much time to look back," she replied. "I've so many things to look ahead to. You just tell people that Oveta Culp Hobby is not at the reminiscing stage yet." Her actions at the time confirmed those forward-looking intentions as she led the Hobby enterprises into their first foray outside of the Houston-Galveston region.[1]

In spring of 1975, Oveta learned that her friends at Harte-Hanks Newspapers had purchased a television station in Jacksonville, Florida. At her weekly meeting with Jack Harris she noted it appeared the Hartes had made a "good buy" and mused she might have missed an attractive investment opportunity. Jack Harris admitted he had known the station was on the market, but he'd had no idea Oveta was open to buying more television properties. Oveta confirmed she was interested in "good prospects." Harris responded that he believed Houston's American General Corporation, founded by Oveta and Will's longtime friend Gus Wortham, who was now retired, might be interested in selling WLAC-TV, the CBS affiliate in Harris's hometown, Nashville, Tennessee. When American General bought the Life and Casualty Insurance Company of Tennessee in 1968, WLAC-TV and Radio had been among the company's assets. Because the television and radio stations were unrelated to its core business, American General was open to selling them. Oveta asked Harris to confirm his information. If accurate, she wanted to investigate the possibilities. This was an important enough prospect that Bill Hobby took time away from his duties in Austin to go with Harris to pay "a clandestine visit to Nashville" to tour the station and analyze the market. Other Hobby company executives followed with their own visits to Nashville. Liking what they saw, they recommended to Oveta that the family make an offer to American General to buy the television station but not WLAC Radio.[2]

Oveta was directly involved in negotiations with American General's management, which continued through the summer of 1975, interrupted only by Oveta's brief stay in Houston Methodist Hospital for an undisclosed but apparently benign ailment. When she informed American General's board she was interested in the television property but not the radio station, the board agreed to spin the latter out of the deal. Oveta and American General reached an agreement in October to sell WLAC-TV to the Hobbys' broadcast entity, the Channel Two Television Company, for a reported $17 million. Negotiating with American General proved to be much easier than getting the Federal Communications Commission to approve the purchase. The FCC held up the sale for several weeks. Among the issues was the FCC rule prohibiting television and radio stations in the same city sharing the same call letters but having different owners. Jack Harris received FCC approval to change the television station's WLAC call letters to WTLV, which removed one obstacle to approval.

But other obstacles remained, chiefly the FCC's "for the good of the community" public-interest standard. That was a vital element in FCC decisions to grant licenses to new stations and to approve the purchase of existing ones. As a result, it was essential that the purchaser of a television station cultivate the goodwill of the local civic and business leadership. The FCC's interest in keeping ownership local meant that many, if not most, television stations were still locally owned in the 1970s. But the FCC was gradually letting go of that provision, which would soon open the gates for national media corporations to buy locally owned broadcast properties and integrate them into larger companies with corporate headquarters in cities far away from the local station. The same process was happening in the newspaper and radio industries.

In the mid-1970s, however, the FCC was still paying attention to local reactions when an out-of-town entity sought to purchase one of a city's television stations, which were often considered community institutions. Local protests to the FCC could cause the commission to stop the purchase. Aware of this issue, Jack Harris persuaded Oveta, Bill, and Jessica to make a well-publicized goodwill visit to Nashville in late June 1976 to assure local viewers the family would be thoughtful owners who would be considerate of local interests and concerns. Harris's publicity team sent advance notice to the city's two daily newspapers, the *Banner* and the *Tennessean*, that the prospective new owners of WLAC-TV would be arriving at the Nashville Airport and that Oveta Culp Hobby, the famed "Little Colonel" of the WAC and member of Eisenhower's cabinet, had "agreed" to be available for interviews about her plans for the television station. Both newspapers took the bait. Their reporters conducted friendly interviews with Oveta, whose civic-boosterish quotes were featured in stories about the visit of these Texans who hoped to be soon managing WLAC. Instead of a business reporter the *Tennessean* sent its women's editor to interview Oveta, which was no surprise to Oveta. The editor reported that Oveta's "natural, genuine friendliness immediately puts one at ease." The headline in the next day's *Tennessean* proudly proclaimed, "Mrs. Hobby Finds City Progressive." Oveta played her role. She assured Nashville's citizens, in boosterism rhetoric Will would have approved, that her family knew their city was "unique in every respect. It's the center of the music world, an educational center, an Athens of the South. You still have a frontier spirit and there is a warmth among the people which is a gift." She explained that the Hobby family had "looked at many major television stations" and they had discovered that WLAC "is a wonderful station . . . [and] the personnel is just the best. We plan to spend a great deal of time here. We want to learn the community. We want to learn its desires, its needs."[3]

After the airport news conference, Oveta, Bill, and Jessica, accompanied by Jack Harris and Jack McGrew, attended a luncheon in their honor at Commerce Union Bank, one of the city's largest financial institutions, where they visited with the leaders of important community organizations, including the local chapters of the League of Women Voters, the Council of Jewish Women, and the National Council of Negro Women. Oveta gave brief remarks in which she told the leaders that they should be "proud" of the contributions they were making to the American "way of life." That evening the Hobbys had an early dinner with Tennessee governor Ray Blanton at the Belle Meade Country Club, followed by a charity show at the city auditorium starring Jerry Lewis and Roy Clark. When recalling the trip years later, McGrew noted, "Nashville's civic and business leaders were both flattered and charmed by [Oveta's] participation in the process." By coincidence, Oveta's friend Ed Harte, publisher of the *Corpus Christi Caller-Times*, was seated in the first-class section of an airliner that stopped in Nashville on the way to Houston when Oveta boarded on her return home. She invited him to sit in an empty seat beside her in the smoking section of first class, where she talked about her experience in Nashville and the prospects for the television station. He later recalled that "a sherry [was] on her tray, and a cigarette pack at the ready."[4]

The FCC decision remained unmade for several months. That August, Oveta complained to a friend that she had been "in the midst of negotiations for a television station in Nashville and [we] are still in the process of going through the intricacies involved in getting it settled. It is no simple matter doing business these days." When the FCC eventually approved the purchase, the Hobby family quickly assumed ownership and management of the station. Oveta's growing, privately held communications empire now had three thousand employees and was estimated in 1978 to have a value of at least $200 million and earnings of about $18 million a year in pretax profits.[5]

Beginning in January 1973, Bill Hobby's attention was focused on his full-time duties as lieutenant governor of Texas. The necessary result was that he was less involved in managing the Hobby media properties than he had been previously, although he did participate in major decisions affecting the family business. Oveta surely took pride in Bill's successful performance as the new lieutenant governor, but an incident near the end of his first term did not please her. Early in the morning of June 20, 1974, Bill was arrested in Austin on a DWI charge. The arrest of a lieutenant governor was newsworthy, although there had been no car wreck. Reporters at the *Post* came to work that morning wondering how the paper was going to handle this news. A regular meeting of the editorial board was scheduled for the usual time, but some of the editors assumed it would be postponed. It wasn't. Oveta insisted on keeping her set schedule despite the news from Austin. Before she took her seat in the boardroom, she calmly declared to her editors, "I know what's on all of your minds. I want you to run a story and I want you to put it on page one." She then sat, spoke no more of the incident, and conducted the meeting as though nothing had happened. Bill Hobby pleaded no contest to the charge and was given a one-hundred-dollar fine and a probated thirty-day jail sentence. Oveta later claimed she never castigated Bill for the arrest. "I never dressed him down," she said. "He is a grown man. I personally approve his admission of [guilt] and admire him for it. I don't expect anyone to be a saint. I've made too many mistakes in my own life."[6]

Despite the DWI episode, in 1974 Bill won the Democratic nomination with 70 percent of the vote and ran unopposed in the general election, the first time the terms in office for statewide elected officeholders would be four instead of two years. Oveta was a visible presence at Bill's inauguration in January 1975. An hour prior to the event, Bill invited some friends to his office for a coffee reception that Oveta also attended. The group included former KPRC-TV reporter and future US senator Kay Bailey, who was beginning her second term in the legislature. "We had a wonderful visit," Bailey later recalled. "At the age of seventy, [Oveta] was just as active and informed as ever, and had the bearing of a venerable personage. I thanked her for giving me an unprecedented opportunity six years earlier. She said she had watched my career and was proud of what I had been able to do."[7]

Bill would be reelected three more times, becoming the longest-serving lieutenant governor in Texas history and one of the most influential. Oveta attended Bill's inauguration to his third term in 1979, but health issues kept her away from Bill's last two inaugural ceremonies in 1983 and 1987. "William is being inaugurated as lieutenant governor in Austin today for his fourth term," Oveta wrote in 1983 to an old friend from WAC days, Helen Gruber. "I had to cancel plans to attend when I came down with a wretched cold, and now the weather has turned to cold rain, so it is just as well I did not try to make the trip.[8]

Oveta did not take as prominent a role in her son's other reelection campaigns as she had in 1972, but she remained an important source of funding for his political races. Texas state senator Don Adams, Bill's close friend and campaign manager in 1982, later recalled that early in the campaign Oveta telephoned and asked him to come to Houston for a meeting at her office at the *Post*. For the first time since his election in 1972, Bill had a Republican opponent, George Strake, a wealthy Houston oilman who was perceived to be a serious threat to Bill's reelection. Strake had a highly professional campaign operation, deep pockets, and the advantage of the rapidly growing strength of the Republican Party in Texas. Bill defeated Strake, but the campaign was expensive. According to Adams, when he met with Oveta she asked, "Senator, do you have any idea what this campaign's going to cost?" He replied that it would be about $4 million. "The worst thing that could happen to William is to lose this race because of money," she responded. "I want to introduce you to Jim Crowther, our general counsel." When they met with Crowther, Oveta told him that whenever "Senator Adams calls and asks for money, send it." Adams later claimed that after that meeting, he would call Crowther whenever the campaign needed more money. "I'd tell him that I needed another million dollars," Adams stated. "He would send it right away. It was the best campaign manager's job that you could have."[9]

After the FCC relaxed its criteria for approving broadcast mergers, the Hobbys acquired television stations in Meridian, Mississippi (1981), and Tucson, Arizona (1982). In 1983 they purchased two of the Cowles Media Company stations, one in Des Moines, Iowa, and the other in Daytona Beach–Orlando, Florida. Gardner Cowles Jr. was an old friend of Oveta's, and they worked together on the deal. The Hobbys made their last media acquisition in 1986, when they bought KSAT-TV in San Antonio, Henry Catto's hometown. Oveta was involved in the negotiations to acquire those four television stations in the early 1980s, and she maintained her regular schedule at the *Post*, but she was cutting back on other civic activities to spend more time on traveling for leisure, studying art, and working with her collection. For more than fifty years Oveta had maintained a heavy speechmaking schedule, but she gradually reduced the number of those engagements in the late 1970s.[10]

Not surprisingly, Will's death in 1964 had permanently affected how Oveta conducted her social relations in the years that followed. "Though [Oveta] had many friends who were men, she did not turn to them in widowhood," Marguerite Johnston later observed. "After Governor died, she went to dinner parties and other social functions in the company of married couples—the [George and Alice] Browns [and] the Leonard F. McCollums in particular." McCollum was a geologist who had built the Continental Oil Company into a major corporation after World War II. But after Leonard McCollum's wife died, Oveta never again accepted his invitations to be her escort to social events. "In all the years after Governor's death, she never let an unattached male escort her," Johnston said. "She always took another woman with her . . . whenever she had to drive a male dignitary to an event where he was to speak." Whenever she agreed to accompany a male friend at a party or at a dinner, she always arranged to meet him at the affair. Her chauffeur drove her to the event and would wait with the car until she was ready to return home.[11]

Oveta's conservative behavior in her relationships with men didn't mean she was a judgmental prude. When the brash wildcat oilman Glenn McCarthy included his long-time mistress in his party at the huge banquet that famously opened the Shamrock Hotel, some of Oveta's friends were offended, especially because McCarthy's wife was also at the party. Oveta's response to her shocked friends was if his mistress "was giving her life to McCarthy, she should be included in the perks." Oveta didn't extend this tolerant attitude to Nelson Rockefeller, however, not necessarily because he had a mistress—that behavior was not news—but because he had committed the sin of abandoning his dutiful wife of many years. Oveta told a friend that Rockefeller had severely disappointed her when he divorced his wife, Tod, and married Margaretta "Happy" Murphy. When the press quoted Rockefeller as saying that his new marriage had made him "very happy," Oveta was indignant. Her comment to friends was in the form of a question: "How could he be 'very happy' considering the hurt he had dealt his family?"[12]

George and Alice Brown's daughter, Isabel Brown Wilson, told Robert Pando that while Oveta "preferred formality in her relationships . . . she [also] loved to tell a good story over drinks with her mostly male friends and colleagues." Wilson described Oveta as "a discreet flirt" who could tell bawdy but not obscene jokes and stories. From his interviews with Oveta's friends, Pando concluded, "She tossed back her share of scotch but there is not a single hint that she ever tossed back more than her share." When Oveta went to a party, always wearing designer or custom-tailored fashions, she walked straight to where the men were gathered discussing politics and financial matters and joined in the conversation. Jim Crowther, the *Post*'s general legal counsel, described her as "a cool, poised, composed, sophisticated woman with a sense of humor. She was very self-controlled. When she walked into a room, she filled it." Despite Oveta's authoritative and self-confident demeanor, she retained what were culturally defined at the time as traditionally feminine traits. "There was a softness that cared for people," Crowther noted, "but she did not want the world to see it."[13]

After a speech to the Retail Merchants Association in Houston in March 1980, however, Oveta reduced her speaking schedule drastically, making only two or three speeches before she withdrew from public appearances entirely in the mid-1980s. A speech Oveta gave at an awards dinner in March 1983 and another at the Goodwill Industries Distinguished Citizen Awards two months later were among her last.[14]

She was spending more time with George and Alice Brown, often traveling on vacation trips with them. They dined together nearly every Sunday night, a ritual that began in the late 1960s. Those dinners, which included a changing set of guests, were marked by lively conversation about politics, business developments in Houston, and gossip. The Browns' daughter, Isabel Wilson, later recalled that a guest "needed to be a good conversationalist and 'in the know' to be invited back with regularity." Dinner would be followed by a spirited game of pitch, a card game also known as high-low-jack. They typically invited three to five guests, to make a table of six or eight. Wilson said that she "had never seen three people enjoy a game more than Oveta and my parents. They never played for money, but as Oveta said, 'just blood.'"[15]

With Oveta taking a smaller role in the Hobby media enterprises, her daughter, Jessica, now forty-six years old, and son-in-law, Henry Catto, became more involved in the family business. The Cattos had been living with their four children in McLean, Virginia, throughout most of the 1970s while Henry served in a series of posts in the federal government, including stints as chief of protocol for Presidents Nixon and Ford. He was serving as assistant secretary of defense for public affairs in the Reagan administration when he resigned from his position in January 1983 to return to Texas. Jessica remained in Washington, where she was the publisher of the *Washington Journalism Review*, a media watchdog magazine she and Henry acquired in 1979 by assuming its $50,000 debt. Oveta was proud of Jessica's work with the review. When one of Oveta's old friends

*Oveta Culp Hobby with her close friends Alice (left)
and George Brown (right) at Rice University, 1967.*

told her she enjoyed reading it, Oveta replied, "I am glad you enjoy Jessica's [magazine]. I think she is doing a fine job and seems to have the talent to make it work. She and Henry enjoy the Washington life, but, fortunately, can escape now and then to Aspen to recoup." Jessica eventually joined with her husband to take an executive position with her family's business while maintaining a residence in San Antonio, Texas, and a ranch in Aspen, Colorado.[16]

Another reason for Henry Catto's return to Texas might have been the declining fortunes of the family's flagship property, the *Houston Post*. The *Post* continued to fall behind the *Houston Chronicle* in circulation, and by 1983 the *Chronicle* led the *Post* in daily subscriptions by more than forty thousand. In an article in *Houston City Magazine* published that year, Joel Barna wrote, "Clearly the *Post* is the financial dog of the Hobby family's properties, returning far less on the capital invested—and with every downward tick in its advertising market share, the *Post* becomes less valuable. The family will obviously need cash to cover inheritance taxes. So the time to sell the *Post* is now." Industry analysts speculated the paper could sell for as much as $225 million. Barna had accurately described the unpromising situation the Hobbys faced with the *Post*. An additional factor was a change in family interests, especially on the part of the Cattos, who had never been particularly involved in the management of the newspaper, although Jessica held a titular position as vice president. Bill remained an enthusiast, but he was deeply focused on his position as lieutenant governor. His power and influence had increased with each passing session. He was serving a fourth term, and he had one eye on the governor's office. He was also a realist and could see that the *Post* was likely to continue to be a losing proposition.

Bill later wrote an opinion column for the *Houston Chronicle* about the problems newspapers were facing in the 1980s. He explained in detail the difficult economics of the newspaper business: the high cost of labor, printing equipment ("used only a few hours a day"), and newsprint, yet the cost to readers of single copies as well as for subscriptions was almost free. He pointed out that the price of newsprint, which was 40 percent of total expenses, had gone up precipitously in recent years. Because the *Post* had a smaller circulation than the *Chronicle*, it could not charge as much for advertising as its competitor could. In addition, the *Chronicle*'s owner was the philanthropic foundation the Houston Endowment, which gave the *Chronicle* significant tax advantages over the *Post*. Bill explained that those negative factors kept the *Post* from being profitable. Despite nostalgia and respect for Will and Oveta's legacy, the Hobby family, including Oveta, saw no point in trying to sustain a business that apparently would continue to drain their financial resources long into the future. As Barna had predicted, it was time to get out while they could sell for a significant price.[17]

An unspoken factor in the decision to put the newspaper on the market was Oveta's age. At seventy-eight, she was beginning to have more frequent bouts of ill health, suffering from colds and other minor respiratory problems. In a letter to her brother Evetts, Oveta referred to her respiratory problems, undoubtedly exacerbated by many years of chain-smoking. "I wish I could talk with you on the telephone," she lamented, "but I know my voice is not yet strong enough for you to hear me well, and it would be difficult for you."[18]

In late July 1983, Oveta announced that the *Houston Post* was for sale. A buyer quickly surfaced and a deal was made much sooner than the family had anticipated. Sun Media, a Canadian company that published the conservative Canadian tabloid the *Toronto Sun*, made an offer on October 12. After a couple of days of negotiation, Oveta accepted Sun Media's offer of $130 million, with $100 million of it to be paid in cash. The selling price was considerably less than the estimated market value of between $175 and $225 million. The deal excluded the *Post*'s downtown printing plant, which the *Sun* agreed to lease, and a portion of the site occupied by the *Post*'s headquarters on the Southwest Freeway. The Hobbys agreed to turn control over to Sun Media early in November. Oveta later told her friend Henry Taub that the sale "was more sudden than we had anticipated."[19]

On Monday, October 17, Oveta asked the *Post*'s news and editorial staff to assemble in the newsroom for an announcement. Wearing one of her famous hats and elbow-length gloves, Oveta entered the newsroom with Bill and Jessica. They introduced *Toronto Sun* publisher Douglas Creighton and informed the staff that the paper had been sold to the Sun Media Company, which would start publishing the *Post* in early November. After the sale was announced, Creighton told the UPI news agency he would not make the *Post* a tabloid. Instead, he would concentrate on publishing more color pictures and defining the editorial-page policy "more clearly." He added that the *Post* was an attractive acquisition because of its extensive computerization and its capacity for color printing.[20]

Oveta chaired her last meeting of the *Post*'s editorial board on November 10, 1983. This final gathering proceeded as normal, with the board members suggesting editorial topics. When all the proposals had been discussed, Oveta asked if anything else should be brought up. There were no responses. Al Shire, a longtime *Post* staffer and editor, later recalled, "Mrs. Hobby looked down at the table and said, hesitantly: 'I hope . . . I hope I can say this.' She looked to her left at the wall. 'I think all of you know how much your friendship means to me.' Her voice broke halfway through the sentence, and she strained to get the last few words out." At that point Marguerite Johnston said, "We know that, dear." Straining to keep her composure, Oveta said softly, "You are my friends," and then she stopped and took a deep breath. "There were tears in her eyes," Shire remembered. "She took off her glasses and wiped her eyes. There was a long silence." Eventually, Oveta was able to speak. "You are, well, in a way, my family." George Fuermann said, "That's true. Outside of the Army, I've never worked for anyone else." Oveta laughed and replied, "Well, don't let *that* get around." That broke the tension and Oveta regained her composure. In a reference to the many stories she had related to the editors at the end of these meetings over the years, Oveta said, "I'll tell you one more story. There was a man at the *Dallas Morning News* who had worked for the Belo organization his entire life, and much was made of that fact at his retirement. When he got up to speak, he said, 'The reason I never worked for anyone else was that no one else ever asked me!'"[21]

Thus ended nearly a century of Hobby family association with the *Houston Post*, first as employees and eventually as owners, beginning with the hiring of seventeen-year-old Will Hobby as a clerk in 1895. This abrupt change in Oveta's life affected her deeply. Her own association with the paper stretched back more than fifty years. The hurried nature of the entire affair only added to her sense of loss. She had little time to clear out of the Post Building, which included removing not only all of her furniture, rugs, memorabilia, framed pictures, and art but also her office's wood flooring, antique wall paneling, and mantelpiece. She placed the wood and marble material that had been physically attached to the building's structure into storage, with the eventually unfulfilled hope that it would "grace another Hobby office." She told a friend, "[It was] a monumental task to vacate

*Oveta Culp Hobby during a light moment at the meeting with* Houston
Post *staff when she announced she was selling the newspaper, 1983.*

the premises of the *Post* in such a short time. It will take us some time to sort ourselves
out." Soon after the deal was completed, Oveta told Lalo Galaviz, a longtime member of
her household staff, that selling the *Post* was one of the hardest decisions of her life. She
admitted to Mickey Herskowitz, the *Post*'s nationally known sports columnist, "The last
weeks at the *Post* were such difficult, emotionally draining ones, parting and breaking
ties with longtime friends and associates." *Houston Chronicle* president Richard "Dick"
Johnson, whose own paper was soon to be sold to the Hearst Corporation, wrote Oveta:
"It doesn't seem like it, but for almost thirty years, I have spent every day waking up to
[do] battles with the *Post*—and you—and suffering over the cuts and bruises. It hasn't
quite settled on me yet that you are no longer at the *Post*. I don't really know if it ever
will. You have been a tough competitor, Mrs. Hobby, and I have always held you and your
family in the highest esteem."[22]

With the money from the sale, combined with the estimated value of her broadcast properties as well as her real estate and other assets, Oveta Culp Hobby was now
one of the nation's wealthiest women. The Hobbys' radio and television stations were

subsidiaries of Channel Two Television Company. When the *Post* was sold, the Hobbys' retained their broadcast properties and reorganized their family's business interests, taking the name H&C Communications Inc. (the letters standing for Hobby and Catto). H&C and the Hobby Family Foundation moved into an office suite at 3050 Post Oak Boulevard near the Galleria shopping mall. Oveta assumed the title of chairman of H&C's executive committee. Henry Catto became vice chairman of H&C's broadcast group. "Rumors to the contrary," Oveta told her friend Mike Stude, Herman Brown's son, "I did not retire when we sold the *Post*, only shifted gears from newspaper to broadcast. I am hardly the type to be a lady of leisure; I wouldn't know how to act!"[23]

Oveta might have been determined not to retire or to be a "lady of leisure," but in reality, as she entered her eighties, she began to withdraw from public view. Running the *Houston Post* had taken up much of her time, but the *Post* was now gone. She continued to monitor her broadcast properties, but H&C's locally based executives Jack Harris and Jack McGrew ran KPRC-TV and Radio and they needed little direction.

After Oveta sold the *Post*, she began to lead a much more private life largely centered on her grandchildren. By the time the *Post* was sold, she had resigned from most of her directorships. Any board memberships she retained were in name only and essentially honorific. She received an honorary degree from the University of Houston in May 1984, which turned out to be her last major public appearance. With George Brown's death in 1983 and then Alice Brown's in 1984, Oveta withdrew even more from life outside her condominium in the high-rise Huntingdon Building on Kirby Drive. Her reclusiveness was also the result of increasingly frequent bouts of illness and the frailties of old age. In a letter Oveta wrote to a friend in April 1984, she complained she had been plagued with "ails . . . these many moons."[24]

When Oveta's granddaughter Heather Catto announced her wedding plans in the spring of 1985, Oveta was unable to attend because of her physical ailments. "I loved your dear note telling me your hope that I would be at your wedding, and my heart aches with longing to be there," Oveta lamented. "I know you understand that I am just not strong enough to travel, but you cannot possibly know how much it would mean to me to be there when you marry." A year later, Oveta had to decline an invitation to participate in an event held on her eighty-first birthday, when the City of Killeen unveiled a historical marker at her birthplace, a white frame house at 319 Young Street. A celebratory program at the First Baptist Church followed the unveiling ceremony. Her old friend Liz Carpenter gave a speech about Oveta's life and accomplishments, and Bill Hobby, who represented his mother, read a message she asked him to deliver in her absence.[25]

Among the few things interrupting Oveta's self-imposed isolation during the last ten years of life were her regular trips to the hairdresser, visits to the doctor, and occasional expeditions to the H&C Communications office on San Felipe Street. After being driven to the office by her longtime butler and chauffeur Cecil McBride, Oveta, dressed as always in hat, gloves, and fashionable clothes, would walk through the offices to say hello and to chat briefly with staff. After she had seen everyone, McBride would escort her to the car and drive her back to the Huntingdon, which was located near the H&C office. By the late 1980s these visits grew fewer in number until they ceased entirely in the early 1990s.[26]

Marguerite Johnston watched as Oveta's withdrawal from society "came gradually, almost unnoticeably." In 1993 the family arranged for nurses to be with her twenty-four hours a day, the hairdresser started coming to the residence, doctors and dentists paid house calls, and cooks prepared special meals. After she received an invitation to dinner from Houston's prominent banker and civic leader Ben Love and his wife, Margaret, Oveta wrote, "As you probably are aware, I am no longer able to leave my home." Similar messages were dispatched to other friends.[27]

Nevertheless, until the last few months of her life, Oveta remained engaged and mentally aware. During this period only immediate family members were welcome to come to her hideaway at the Huntingdon. For all others, including even close, longtime associates, such as Marguerite Johnston, the telephone was Oveta's favored and exclusive instrument for keeping contact. Oveta spent hours every day on the phone, starting in the morning with calls to her longtime personal assistant, Peggy Buchanan (whom she always addressed as "Mrs. Buchanan" despite a thirty-six-year working relationship), and to other staff to instruct them on the tasks she wanted performed that day, including the ongoing work of documenting and cataloguing her extensive art, silver, and jewelry collections. The rest of the day, Oveta spent her time watching C-SPAN, reading (until her eyesight began to fail), and making phone calls to friends and family. Marguerite Johnston later described those telephone conversations as "warm" and "lively" chats about state and national politics and developments in her city. As always, "[Oveta] liked to ask 'What's happening on the street?'"[28]

Ed Harte was one of those friends on Oveta's telephone list. "I never saw Mrs. Hobby in her declining years," Harte recalled. "But feeling the need to communicate with her, I initiated what became a fascinating affair via telephone. I would make a list of topics— current events of special interest, books of recent vintage, and memoirs and biographies of people she had known. It soon became clear to me that she really liked to visit on the telephone, and that she was absolutely current on world and national events. If she [was] feeling good, almost any topic would suffice to launch her on an interesting dissertation, enriched by personal recollections as she pored through the experiences of a life conducted at the summits of power."[29]

Marguerite Johnston noted that when Oveta withdrew and "she saw no one but family, doctors, and staff, many of her friends were hurt at first. Gradually they granted her the right to withdraw and the friendships continued." Oveta's grandson Paul observed that in her last years, "she was basically a recluse, and explained that fact by saying that late in life privacy was the only compliment she was willing to pay herself. [She] took great pains with her own appearance because of her high standards. . . . [H]er personal vanity was for its own sake. If she were alone on a desert island, I am sure that she would have taken the same care with her appearance as if she had been on Fifth Avenue." Lady Bird Johnson, who was one of Oveta's few peers still living, noted in an interview she gave less than a year before Oveta died that Oveta had become "entirely a recluse, and I don't know why. It could be because she's such a proud woman, and when one gets very old and loses any of your capacity—for instance, I think she is in a wheelchair, but the world's not going to see her in a wheelchair. She was always a dominant person and in [her] advanced eighties she isn't, so she lives apart from the world."[30]

A few especially notable developments occurred outside the walls of Oveta's high-rise retreat that were of special concern to her in the last three years of her life. In early 1992, Peggy Buchanan coordinated an effort to try to persuade the army to promote Oveta to the rank of brigadier general on the retired list as part of the celebration of the fiftieth anniversary of the founding of the Women's Army Auxiliary Corps. It is unclear who first thought of this way to honor Oveta or whether or not Oveta knew about the request prior to it being made. Buchanan called Henry Catto to see if he would ask his good friend President George H. W. Bush to approve the promotion. Catto, who had reentered government service in 1989 when President Bush appointed him ambassador to the United Kingdom, enthusiastically agreed to do whatever he could, responding that it would be "a fitting tribute to a gallant lady and a symbol of how far the military had come in recognizing women."[31]

After Catto wrote President Bush a letter explaining the proposal, he decided to make it a bipartisan effort by getting support from Democratic senator Lloyd Bentsen, an old friend of the Hobby family. Bentsen agreed to help, telling Catto, "Stars would look good on her and would be much deserved." Catto also called General Colin Powell, who was then serving as the chairman of the Joint Chiefs of Staff. Powell's response, however, was restrained. He explained there were sensitive precedent issues involved in making such a promotion. Nevertheless, he assured Catto he would look into it. In mid-June 1992, Rose Zamaria, one of President Bush's closest assistants, called Catto and gave him the bad news that a promotion could not be approved. "The president had talked with Secretary of Defense Cheney and the secretary of the Army," Catto recalled, "and the problems were simply too great. Though disappointed, I felt we had had a hearing at the highest possible levels." President Bush confirmed this decision in a letter to Senator Bentsen, with the explanation that his "thoughtful recommendation" could not be approved because Oveta had not been eligible for promotion when she left the army in 1945. Bentsen released a statement to the press that he was "very disappointed Mrs. Hobby has been denied a promotion, which was long overdue." Oveta's reaction to this decision is unknown. She surely must have been disappointed, but given her previous experience with the army brass as director of the women's corps, she could not have been surprised.[32]

One of the last events honoring Oveta's family while she was still living occurred on February 13, 1993, when a large swimming pool at the Peaceable Kingdom Retreat for Children on the Lampasas River near Killeen was dedicated in memory of Oveta's parents, Ike and Emma Culp. The Hobby Family Foundation paid for the pool. Bill Hobby, who had left the lieutenant governor's post in January 1991 after serving five terms, once again represented his mother and gave the dedicatory address. Oveta's brother Reverend

Texas Evetts Culp, who was a retired Baptist preacher, gave the invocation. He and his sister Lynn Culp Loving also gave recollections of their parents. Their older sister Juanita Culp Harris had died in 1977, and their brother J. R. Culp in 1991. Evetts died six months after the swimming pool dedication.[33]

One of the most significant and poignant developments in Oveta's life during these last years was the sale of KPRC Radio and the KPRC and KSAT television stations. The latter properties generated a combined total of more than $23 million in net income in the last year of H&C ownership. The first property to be sold was KPRC Radio, which

*Oveta Culp Hobby with KPRC-TV's Jack Harris, ca. mid-1980s.*

Sunbelt Broadcasting bought in 1993. That sale ended more than six decades of the Hobbys' association with the pioneering radio station, including five decades of ownership. Several months later, after what Henry Catto later described as "a great deal of debate" within and between the Hobby and Catto families, H&C Communications sold its flagship Houston television station along with its station in San Antonio to the Washington Post Company. "Jessica and her brother Bill decided to sell the family television company, both having doubts about the industry's future and the best way of running things," Catto noted in his memoir. "I hated to see it happen. I loved the years spent working for H&C, and I had thought I might return to it if . . . my government career ended. That, however, was not to be." Following negotiations that began near the end of 1993, the *Washington Post* agreed to pay H&C $253 million and to assume the stations' $4 million in liabilities. The deal was closed on January 31, 1994, and finalized on April 22. The liquidation of these long-held Hobby broadcast venues occurred during the last two years of Oveta's life. No record could be found documenting any role she might have played in the decision to let the properties go, but Oveta was mentally alert and still actively engaged (at least from her residence in the Huntingdon) in family matters until only a few months before she died. It can be reasonably assumed that Bill and Jessica consulted with her in the matter and that she approved.[34]

On April 18, 1995, the *Houston Post* ceased operations, an event that signified the end of Will and Oveta's most important business legacy. Ten years earlier, in September 1985, only two years after it purchased the *Post* from the Hobbys, Sun Media sold the newspaper for $150 million to MediaNews Group, a newspaper chain owned by Dean Singleton and Richard Scudder. Singleton also owned the *Dallas Times Herald*. Before buying the *Post*, Singleton had tried to acquire the *Houston Chronicle* from the Houston Endowment, but the Hearst Corporation outbid him. With the *Post* continuing to lose money despite major staff layoffs and other cost reductions, Singleton and Scudder shut the paper down and sold the newspaper's remaining assets to the Hearst Corporation. Five days after the last issue of the *Post* was printed and distributed, the *Houston Chronicle* published Bill Hobby's op-ed piece, "A Requiem for the *Houston Post*," about the closing of his family's former newspaper. "The *Houston Post* is dead," he lamented. It was "not just a business," he wrote, "but a voice, a personality, that was a vital part of Houston for more than a century." He explained that the decision to close the newspaper was the result of difficult economic conditions, including the rapid growth of competing alternative news sources, the loss of advertising, and the ever-increasing cost of operations. Nevertheless, the end of the *Post* was an especially sad development to Bill. He ended his editorial with a heartfelt sentence: "Please forgive the lump in my throat."[35]

On Monday April 17, 1995, the day after Easter and the day before the *Post* printed its last issue, Oveta had a severe, debilitating stroke. She had observed her ninetieth birthday three months earlier. The day before she suffered the stroke, Oveta and her sister Lynn had one of their weekly telephone conversations. This one was nearly two hours in length. "She was in a wonderful frame of mind," Lynn noted. "We talked about

Governor, and about the great-grandchildren who gave her so much joy, and about things that happened when I lived in Houston. I felt a great relief, she sounded so happy. It was my last real visit with her."[36]

The stroke was severe but not immediately fatal. Nevertheless, the end grew close. Peggy Buchanan reported the news to one of Oveta's friends, adding that Oveta had "long foreseen the possibility that she might be bedridden and had nurses on hand and the necessary equipment that allows her to be in her home. She is receiving excellent care and is improving." Still hopeful, Buchanan told Mattie Treadwell, Oveta's former WAC comrade, "Mrs. Hobby is holding her own. She is getting much better care than if she were in the hospital. She is still not out of the woods but her progress is encouraging."[37]

Marguerite Johnston later said that only after Oveta suffered the stroke did she find it difficult to enjoy life. It became even harder a couple of months after the stroke when she essentially lost her ability to read. Nonetheless, this woman who had always demonstrated such determination, willpower, and ability to control her circumstances did not let go easily. Even in these extreme conditions, she managed to communicate and relate to those around her. "I had a good visit with [Oveta] Friday," Peggy Buchanan told one of Oveta's friends in early June. "First time she had been out of her room. The nurse had her in her living room. Her doctor feels she has improved as much as is possible." One day Oveta looked at Buchanan and declared, "I'm bored as hell." Buchanan immediately moved her into a wheelchair and took her through the condominium, stopping for a few minutes for Oveta to gaze out the floor-to-ceiling window from on high at the sprawling city she and Will had helped to transform.[38]

By July, however, Oveta probably knew that death would soon come. She began to lose what little zest she had been able to summon since her stroke. She gave up trying to dictate letters to her friends because, as Peggy Buchanan noted, she was simply not able to do it. "Her condition just makes it impossible to verbalize much." She also lost interest in food, surviving mainly on Ensure with ice cream and small pieces of fruit. As the end approached, she asked Peggy Buchanan to summon to the Huntingdon one of her close associates of many years, Marguerite Johnston. Because it had been years since Johnston had seen Oveta, she "had no idea" how she would look. "But suddenly one day, near the end, I got a call that I could come now," Johnston recalled. "I drove immediately to the Huntingdon and was taken to her room. She was stretched out on a chaise lounge. Her skin, her hair, her hands, her gown, all creamy white. She could have been carved in ivory and she was utterly beautiful. I shall always be grateful that I was allowed that last vision."[39]

During these last weeks, Oveta asked her nurses to sing hymns to her. One of the nurses also read Bible verses to her, especially one of her favorites, Psalm 91. Traditionally invoked in times of hardship and known as the Soldier's Prayer, the ninety-first psalm was an apt one for the former "Little Colonel" whose most cherished heroes had been George C. Marshall and Dwight Eisenhower. Before Oveta went to sleep at night, she asked her nurses to join her in saying her prayers out loud. Oveta "would say her prayers . . . and some of them were the warmest I've ever heard," one nurse recalled. "She would say, 'Oh Lord, I thank you for everybody in this house. I thank you for life and longevity.' It was deep and moving. You could tell she was at peace." When the nurses told Peggy Buchanan they were surprised at Oveta's knowledge of the Bible and hymns, she explained that Oveta had been raised in "a devout Baptist family."[40]

On August 12, Oveta somehow found enough strength to dictate to Peggy Buchanan a few brief letters. One was to her younger sister Lynn. "I miss our telephone talks," she said in what proved to be a goodbye. "I love you very much." Four days later Oveta Culp Hobby was dead, killed by another stroke.[41]

When Will and Oveta's longtime competitor, the *Houston Chronicle*, reported the news of Oveta's death, it printed an editorial declaring she was "a woman of iron will and strong convictions who kept a firm and steady control over her life and all she met in it. Her influence was virtually unlimited, ranging from those as close to her as her son . . . through the millions reached through her communications empire, the untold numbers of women in the U.S. military, all Americans who've benefitted through her work in organizing HEW, and generations of Houstonians—of the past, of the moment, and of the future. Truly, her death marks the end of an era." *Houston Chronicle* publisher Dick Johnson issued a separate statement in which he said that Oveta was "a tough competitor, but always with dignity. She was an overachiever, but always with total charm and grace."[42]

The news of Oveta's death was reported by the wire services and printed in the nation's leading newspapers. The *New York Times* published its own version of an obituary, including photographs that filled half of a page. Although Oveta had outlived most of her old friends and associates, letters of praise and remembrance still poured into the H&C office, with a large number of them from former WACs. Many of the letters came from prominent and influential friends. For example, a letter from former US senator and secretary of the treasury Lloyd Bentsen noted that news of Oveta's passing "brought back a flood of memories of the times I would go out to an editorial meeting of the *Houston Post*, and she would sit at one end of the table and I would sit at the other end and the staff remained an audience. Her questions were incisive, provocative and penetrating."[43]

Six years before her death and to the surprise of no one who knew her, Oveta had carefully planned every facet of her funeral. Peggy Buchanan wrote down the details as Oveta dictated them. It was to be a "simple ceremony" held at Palmer Memorial Episcopal Church, with her grandsons and "grandsons-in-law" serving as pallbearers. She wanted her daughter-in-law, Diana, to select the music. Buchanan's notes also included, "Scripture: Passages from Ecclesiastes 3 (A time to be born, and a time to die . . .)," "Closed wooden casket not [to] be opened at any time," "Burial: Next to Governor," "Private Burial service," and "Flag ceremony, using Mrs. Hobby's flag." Oveta told Buchanan that the flag should be presented and placed in her son's and daughter's hands and that the ceremony "should be rehearsed." She wanted Jack Harris and Jim Crowther to perform the flag ceremony. Marguerite Johnston was to give the funeral eulogy, which would "last until dark." The notes include Oveta's instruction to Johnston to "do whatever you do." After Oveta's death, Johnston asked Bill Hobby how long she should speak, no doubt wondering what "until dark" really meant. Bill responded, "Oh, Mother said, 'Marguerite can run on all afternoon if she wants to.'"[44]

Oveta's instructions were followed. On Friday, August 18, a standing-room crowd of approximately 375 attended the funeral service at Palmer Memorial Church, followed by the burial at Glenwood Cemetery. The biographical portion of Marguerite Johnston's eulogy was based mainly on the obituary she and Oveta had drafted years before. After she presented a full description of Oveta's accomplishments, however, Johnston concluded with a statement entirely of her own construction. She said of Oveta,

> We are the lucky ones privileged to know her, to enjoy her, to love her, each of us sure that she cared about us too. We probably know more, care more, and are better people for having known her. But think of the wave she leaves, spreading out across the world—the 100,000 women in uniform, their children, their friends. The hundreds of millions affected by her work as first Secretary of Health, Education, and Welfare. The generations who read the *Houston Post*. We say farewell to one of the greatest leaders the United States has ever produced. And we, here today, were fortunate enough to have known her.[45]

# EPILOGUE

A quarter of a century after her death, Oveta Culp Hobby continues to be celebrated as the person who took on the formidable task of creating and commanding the Women's Army Corps in World War II. She was also the second
woman to serve in a presidential cabinet, and she was the organizer and first secretary
of the Department of Health, Education, and Welfare. Those unique accomplishments
will never be superseded. As a result, Oveta Culp Hobby has taken a permanent place
among the ranks of the most influential women in American history. The statement
in which she declared that her WACs were "women who stepped up" was chosen to
be carved in stone in 2004 on one of the main walls of the World War II Memorial
on the National Mall in Washington, DC. Her words on the memorial join those of
Franklin D. Roosevelt, Harry S. Truman, Dwight D. Eisenhower, Chester Nimitz, and
Douglas MacArthur.

On April 15, 2011, the US Postal Service issued an seventy-eight-cent Oveta Culp
Hobby stamp in the Distinguished Americans series. The stamp art, by illustrator and
painter Sterling Hundley of Richmond, Virginia, was based on an undated black-and-
white photograph of Oveta in her WAC uniform, wearing the famed "Hobby hat." The
stamp was yet another recognition of Oveta's many "firsts."[1]

Will Hobby's name, however, since his death in 1964, has not been well remembered,
despite Will's accomplishments as governor of Texas, his key role in developing what
will soon be the third-largest city in the United States, and his actions as a pioneer of
American journalism and broadcasting. Millions of air passengers know the Hobby
name because of the commercial airport in Houston titled in Will's honor, but some
assume it is named for Oveta. Many Texans who recall that Will and Oveta's son, William
"Bill" P. Hobby Jr., was lieutenant governor of the state from 1973 to 1991, think the
airport is named for him instead of his father.

Although he was not nationally well known, Will Hobby was a significant figure in

Texas history. Will first gained statewide attention as a young and progressive editor and publisher of the *Beaumont Enterprise* who skillfully used his newspaper to promote the city and to gain support for developing its deepwater port. He held public office during one of the most tumultuous periods in the history of the state's politics. He made a quietly smooth transition into the governor's office after the tumult of the impeachment of James Ferguson. He maneuvered successfully through heated political struggles over prohibition and women's suffrage and oversaw Texas's ratification of the Eighteenth and Nineteenth amendments to the US Constitution. He managed the impact of World War I on his state while enduring major scandals in the Texas Rangers and related violence on the Mexican border. All of these achievements and more were in addition to confronting the normal problems of legislating and governing.

Will's gubernatorial record was not free of serious blemishes. Among them were the Hobby Loyalty Act, a wartime-inspired assault on civil liberties; and the Hobby Open Port Law, an attack on the labor-union movement. His mixed responses as governor to the racial violence of the horrific "Red Summer" in 1919 and his unfortunate handling of the Shillady incident surely were influenced by his father's and uncle's history as fire-breathing secessionists and fierce Confederates who fought to preserve the institution of slavery. The Civil War might have freed the enslaved, but it did not end the widespread and deeply embedded belief in the "Lost Cause" and in white supremacy, beliefs that were highly influential in the era Will served as governor. He was adamantly opposed to the Ku Klux Klan, however, and he abhorred lynching and violence. Much influenced by Oveta and the passing of time, Will did soften his racial prejudice toward African Americans, if not his paternalism.

Will left office in 1921 as one of the most popular governors in the state's history because of his laudably progressive legislative accomplishments, especially his support of suffrage and education. It is likely that he could have gone on to the US Senate if he had chosen to run for that office. His name was even touted in the press as a possible candidate for the Democratic nomination for vice president in 1920. Given the dominant business forces and the cultural and social conditions at the time, those aspects of Will's record that many (including this author) now view as regrettable—the restriction of civil liberties during wartime, the anti-unionism, and the support of Jim Crow laws and traditions—actually enhanced his image for many white Texans. The reality is that Will Hobby was a man of his time and place, which is not an excuse but an explanation.[2]

After Will left elected office to reassume his role as a member of the Fourth Estate, he built Ross Sterling's *Houston Post-Dispatch* into a profitable newspaper, eventually became its owner, and made it one of the state's most influential newspapers in an era when the views expressed on the editorial page could change minds and sway votes. As a result, Will became a political power broker whose influence stemmed not only from his newspaper's stance on elections but also from his active membership in Houston's informal civic power-elite group known as the "8F crowd." The leading politicians in his state, including John Nance Garner, Sam Rayburn, Lyndon B. Johnson, and several governors and members of the legislature, assiduously sought his counsel and endorsement almost until the day of his death.

When Will and Oveta wed, she was already on a path to becoming a person of political influence, a path that like Will's was paved by talent paired with her family's connections. Will and Oveta were born into families rich in public service heritage, and each came early to journalism and politics. Both had learned how important a network of powerful connections could be. For example, Will's early successes, and political actions, were profoundly shaped by his family's connections within the Peach Tree Village community, while Oveta's were helped by being visibly at her father's side during his service in the Texas Legislature, which brought her to the attention of the leaders of state government, her future husband, and a circle of women activists who helped foster her career.

Oveta's marriage to Will soon placed her in the thick of Houston's social and political elite as she partnered with her husband not only to develop the *Houston Post* and KPRC Radio but also to bring television to Houston with KPRC-TV. At that time, for a woman to hold the highest position at the *Houston Post* and at Houston's most popular radio and television stations was remarkable in and of itself. Her position at the *Post* and her ability to pursue her many other "firsts" are inextricably linked to her husband and his political and journalistic clout, as well as to his strong support for and encouragement of her career. Likewise, Will's charismatic, ambitious, and gifted wife enhanced his own circle of influence, not only at the *Post* and his other business enterprises but also in the broader political arena. Their devotion to each other and their family was matched by their mutual dedication to examining and influencing the workings of government, as both journalists and public officials. From Will sitting at the metaphorical feet of Colonel Rienzi Johnston and Ross Sterling to Oveta's regular calls with Dwight Eisenhower and LBJ, the power and influence of the "Hobby Team" would reach to the highest offices in the nation.

As their daughter, Jessica, later noted, "My mother, in most respects, led a charmed and charming life. . . . She walked the corridors of power with eagerness and commitment." It is safe to say that Oveta and Will shared that eagerness and commitment to a larger good.[3]

Will and Oveta's commitment to public service was and continues to be carried forward by their children and grandchildren. Before her death in 2009, Jessica was deeply involved in the environmental movement, among other public-spirited activities. She and her husband, Henry, used their Woody Creek ranch in Aspen, Colorado, as a humanities and scientific center, hosting such nonprofit organizations as the Aspen Writers' Foundation and the Aspen Center for Environmental Studies. Bill's record-breaking eighteen years of service as lieutenant governor of Texas are regarded by many students of state government as the best performance of anyone who has held that powerful office. His five victories and no defeats in his election bids are ample testimony to his popularity. In the years after he left office in 1991, Bill devoted much of his time to the cause of education, including being a member of the Texas Higher Education Coordinating Board, teaching at the University of Texas at Austin's LBJ School of Public Affairs for seven years, and serving for two years as chancellor of the University of Houston at a time when that school desperately needed stable and skilled administrative oversight. He also supported the establishment of the Hobby School of Public Affairs at the University of Houston, which grows in stature with each passing year.[4]

Will and Oveta's eight grandchildren have made their own contributions to public service. Like their grandmother and mother, most of Jessica's children have been engaged to varying degrees in environmental and humanist causes. Heather Catto Kohout was an active supporter of the humanities and environmental protection before her death in 2014. She and her husband, Martin, founded Madroño Ranch, a writer's retreat near Medina, Texas. John Catto is a photojournalist and Emmy-winning filmmaker whose subject matter has focused on environmental as well as social issues. Isa Catto is an artist and writer who has contributed a regular column to the *Chronicle of Philanthropy*. Will Catto has served as president and CEO of the Catto Charitable Foundation.[5]

Bill and Diana Hobby's children are Laura Hobby Beckworth, Paul Hobby, Kate Hobby Gibson, and Andrew Hobby. Laura is an attorney who has been a community

*US postage stamp honoring Oveta Culp Hobby, 2011.*

volunteer in both Houston and Austin. She has served as chair of the University of Texas at Austin Development Board and sat on the advisory committees of the Lady Bird Johnson Wildflower Center and Austin's KLRU public television station. The University of Texas Law School honored Laura in 2005 with its Award for Community Service. Paul began his public service as assistant US attorney for the Southern District of Texas. He left that post to serve as chief of staff to Lieutenant Governor Bob Bullock from 1991 to 1994, after which he narrowly lost a bid to be the nominee for lieutenant governor in the Democratic primary in 1998. He has also served as a member of the Texas General Services Commission and the Texas Ethics Commission. Paul and Laura are also directors of the Hobby Family Foundation in Houston, which has supported a wide variety of public programs, educational institutions, and other areas of public service. The foundation's major gifts include $21.4 million to Rice University's Fondren Library and significant foundational support for the Hobby Center for the Performing Arts in downtown Houston. Paul and Laura were actively involved in the fundraising, planning, and initial direction of the Hobby Center, which is named in honor of their father. Their sister, Kate Hobby Gibson, is a farm and ranch broker whose public service interests include the Texas Nature Conservancy. Texas State University graduate Andrew Hobby has worked as a reporter, photojournalist, and editor for various news enterprises.[6]

This dual biography of Will Hobby and Oveta Culp Hobby documents two lives marked by remarkable success in business, politics, government, and good works. Their lives reflected a shared purpose: to use their considerable talents and influence to benefit their communities, their state, and their country. That purpose was fulfilled, and it continues as a legacy for their descendants. As Paul Hobby observed, "I have had some good examples of public service in my family and I'm proud of that. I was raised to think that those folks who can do public service should do public service. The whole ethic was, 'If something is not right, either go change it, or hush up.' I know I was obliged to give something back."[7]

# ACKNOWLEDGMENTS

T he publication of *The Governor and the Colonel* marks the closing of a professional circle for me as a historian, one that began more than fifty years ago with
my doctoral dissertation on the Red Scare, which focused on the role Houston's
three major daily newspapers played in encouraging and abetting the anticommunist
hysteria that plagued the city from the late 1940s until the mid-1950s. That research
necessarily led me to examine the news and editorial pages of the *Houston Post* from
those years, which in turn, first brought Will and Oveta Hobby to my close attention.
Their ambiguous relationship to the Red Scare was a key issue in that study. After much
additional research, *Texas Monthly* magazine's book division published a revised and
expanded version of my dissertation, retitled as *Red Scare*, in 1985. The University of
Texas Press issued a reprint in 2014.

After the publication of *Red Scare*, I assumed that was the end of my interest in the
Hobby family as a historian, but the story of their lives continued to intersect with my
future professional interests in unexpected ways. In 2007, at the urging of former Texas
governor Dolph Briscoe Jr., I edited and annotated former Texas governor Ross Sterling's
memoir, *Ross Sterling, Texan*, which was an "as told to" work by Ed Kilman, the longtime
*Houston Post* editor and friend of Will Hobby's. Sterling and Kilman each played key
roles in the lives of Will and Oveta Hobby.

In 2015, nearly thirty years after the initial publication of *Red Scare*, Will and Oveta's
son, William P. "Bill" Hobby Jr., lieutenant governor of Texas from 1973 until 1991, asked
me if I would write a book about his family. I had met Bill a few years earlier when he
emailed me that he had finally read *Red Scare*, as well as *Ross Sterling, Texan*, and had
liked both, although he felt that perhaps only 80 percent of the information about his
parents in *Red Scare* was accurate. I responded that I was much pleased and surprised
that he liked my book despite it not being particularly favorable toward his parents and
their newspaper. I also told him that 80 percent wasn't bad given that his late mother

had never replied to my requests for an interview. That exchange led to our friendship. Not long after, the Briscoe Center published Bill's delightful memoir, *How Things Really Work*, for which I wrote a preface.

Obviously, I accepted Bill's offer to write this book. After *Red Scare* was published, I had not planned professionally to revisit the history of the couple that became known as "The Hobby Team," but I was both honored and flattered by Bill's invitation and his stated desire that I tell the story objectively and based on original sources. This request that I be objective, as well as critical whenever necessary, was reiterated by two of Bill's children, Paul Hobby and Laura Hobby Beckworth, both of whom have been supportive of my effort. It soon occurred to me that I had nearly forty-five years of intermittent and unplanned professional experiences related directly and indirectly to the history of the Hobby family. In addition to *Red Scare* and *Ross Sterling, Texan*, I had already written two other books that included important references to the Hobbys, specifically a biography of Houston oilman J. R. Parten and an "as told to" memoir by Dolph Briscoe Jr., respectively. Because of that body of work, I had a general knowledge of the history and a clear understanding of the family's historical significance.

The first person I must thank in these acknowledgements is Bill Hobby, the best lieutenant governor who has ever served the citizens of Texas, although he would claim that his father deserves that honor. Thank you, Bill, for your support and encouragement.

No author can claim sole credit for a book of this complexity and length, and this one is no exception. I have benefitted greatly from the research of Dr. Dolph Briscoe IV, known to his friends and family as "DB." Early in this project he spent many weeks searching through sources in several special collections, including the Texas State Library and the Briscoe Center (the latter named for his grandfather, who was governor of Texas from 1973 until 1979) for information that has proved critical to my work. DB is a promising young historian who is now on the history faculty of Texas A&M–San Antonio.

Erin Purdy, the talented former chief oral historian and associate director of the Briscoe Center, also made significant contributions to this project. Erin read the entire manuscript and made numerous edits and suggestions that have much improved the text. I've also benefitted greatly from the discussions Erin and I have had about Will and Oveta.

The Briscoe Center's director of special projects, Alison Beck, my professional colleague and friend of more than forty years, contributed her skills as the photo editor and tenacious pursuer of image-use permissions. I appreciate not only Alison's contributions to *The Governor and the Colonel* but also all that she has done to help build the Briscoe Center over the years.

Dr. Nancy Beck Young, a much-published scholar of American political and legislative history and former chair of the University of Houston Department of History, uncovered and shared with me a number of important documents related to Will and Oveta Hobby during her research on a biography of John Nance Garner.

I also gratefully acknowledge the help of Delores Chambers, Bill Hobby's executive assistant. Journalist Saralee Tiede, Bill Hobby's former chief of staff and the coauthor of his book, *How Things Really Work*, read early drafts of the manuscript and made valuable suggestions for improvement. My thanks also go to presidential historian Mark Updegrove, CEO of the Lyndon B. Johnson Foundation, and to Mark Lawrence, director of the LBJ Presidential Library and Museum, for their help with the story of Lyndon and Lady Bird Johnson's relationship with the Hobbys.

As the director of a history research center that makes its archival, artifact, and library collections available for primary research, I am keenly aware of the essential services the reference staffs of special collections provide to all historians, including me. I am especially indebted for the valuable and cheerful help provided to me by Rice University Historian Dr. Melissa Kean; Amanda Focke, the Head of Special Collections at Rice's Woodson Research Center; and the other skilled professionals at Woodson, where the main body of Oveta Culp Hobby's papers are housed. I am equally indebted to reference archivists in the Manuscripts Division of the Library of Congress and at the Dwight D. Eisenhower Presidential Library, where there are other significant collections of Oveta Culp Hobby's Papers. A major portion of the original sources for Will Hobby's history are in the archives and library of the Briscoe Center, where I received help from my professional colleagues Catherine Best, Hal Richardson, Amy Bowman, Evan Hocker, and Ben Wright. Echo Uribe, the center's highly efficient associate director for administration, aided by her assistant, Marla Henley, took care of a million and one logistical matters and kept me on a straight path. I owe a major debt to Dr. Holly Taylor, the talented, patient, and unflappable editor who heads the Briscoe Center's publication program. Abby Webber did an outstanding job of copyediting, Helen Novielli was efficient and thorough with the proofreading, and Derek George applied his formidable talent to the design. I convey my sincere thanks to them all.

I owe much to my friend Dave Hamrick, former director of the University of Texas Press, who was a valued advisor from the beginning until the end of my work on this book. Robert Devens, Hamrick's successor as director, was a source of encouragement for me when he was managing editor at UT Press.

My thanks also go to the staffs of the University of Houston's M. D. Anderson Library Special Collections; the South Texas College of Law Special Collections; the Dallas Historical Society; the Texas State Library, which houses Will Hobby's official gubernatorial papers; the Herbert Hoover, Franklin D. Roosevelt, Harry S. Truman, and Lyndon B. Johnson Presidential Libraries; the Rockefeller Archive Center in Tarrytown, New York; the Mudd Library, Princeton University; the George C. Marshall Research Library in Lexington, Virginia; the National Archives; the Tyrrell Historical Library in Beaumont, Texas; and the Ralph Steen Library, Stephen F. Austin University.

I have relied heavily on three outstanding doctoral dissertations about Oveta Culp Hobby: Robert T. Pando's "Oveta Culp Hobby: A Study of Power and Control"; Debra Lynn Sutphen's "Conservative Warrior: Oveta Culp Hobby and the Administration of America's Health, Education, and Welfare, 1953–1955"; and Kelli Cardenas Walsh's

"Oveta Culp Hobby: A Transformational Leader from the Texas Legislature to Washington, D.C." All are required reading for anyone interested in Oveta's life. I have also depended on the work of many other authors too numerous to list here, but each is listed in the bibliography.

Dr. Greg Fenves, the former president of the University of Texas at Austin, approved my request to take official time to work on this book and encouraged me to make it a formal project of the Briscoe Center. Accordingly, all sales income, including author's royalties, earned by *The Governor and the Colonel* will go directly into the center's publication support fund.

Finally, but most important, is the love, support, encouragement, and patience that my wife, Suzanne, has unselfishly given me, without which this work would not have been possible.

# NOTES

1. In his dissertation on the life of Oveta Culp Hobby, Robert Pando noted, "It is unclear when Oveta Culp and Will Hobby became romantically linked, and under what circumstances. Published feature stories and biographical sketches give only vague, often contradictory details." Pando, "Oveta Culp Hobby," 49–50.

## CHAPTER 1

1. The roots of the Hobby family are in England and Wales. Before English-language spellings were standardized in the mid-eighteenth century, the family name was written in various ways, including Hoby, Hobye, Hubby, Hobbie, and Hobbei. There are competing theories about the origins of the family name. The most convincing is that the family was associated with the village of Hoby, a parish in Leicestershire, England. The family included a number of notable members, including members of Parliament, several barons, and the English ambassadors to France and the Holy Roman Empire. Most of these Hobbys were collateral ancestors of Will Hobby. Of that group, perhaps the most prominent was Sir Philip Hoby (Hobby), son of William Hoby of Leominster in Herefordshire. Sir Philip conducted diplomatic missions for Henry VIII in France and the Netherlands and served on Edward VI's privy council. Records suggest that William Hobby, who migrated to Massachusetts Bay Colony in the mid-seventeenth century, was the first in the long line of Will P. Hobby's family in America. William

was born in Wales in 1635. He, his wife, Anne, and their children migrated to New England in 1668. With his relatives on the English-controlled island of Jamaica, William founded a business importing sugar and molasses to Boston, where the molasses was distilled into rum, a major commodity in the African slave trade. William and Anne's son, John, migrated with his parents to New England when he was only seven years old. Known as "Captain" John Hobby, he married Anne Wensley. He died in 1711 in Boston, two years before his father's death. One of Captain Hobby's children was Wensley Hobby, who was six years old when his father died. Wensley's son, Wensley Hobby Jr., moved from Boston to Middletown, Connecticut, in the 1760s. The 1780 census shows Wensley Jr. had one son and a daughter. He also owned two enslaved people. Van Dusen, *Middletown and American Revolution*; family genealogical records in the William P. Hobby (hereafter WPH) Sr. Papers, Dolph Briscoe Center for American History (hereafter DBCAH).

2. Anna Slade Hobby and her first husband, Captain Danelly, had two children at the time of his death. It is not known if those children lived with their mother and step-father, Alfred Hobby. One of the children was John Danelly, who eventually settled in Galveston, where he served as a judge. Family genealogical records in the WPH Sr. Papers, DBCAH.

3. Family genealogical records in the WPH Sr. Papers, DBCAH.

4. Huson, "Hobby, Alfred Marmaduke"; Torget, *Seeds of Change*, 264–265.

5. Neighbors, "Old Town of Saint Mary's," 28; Wood, "Founding of Saint Mary's," 71; US Census, 1860, Texas, schedule 1, Refugio County, "St Maries," p. 21.

6. Neighbors, "Old Town of Saint Mary's," 28

7. Dunn, "KGC in Texas"; Buenger, *Secession and the Union*, 156.

8. For example, see Edwin Hobby to C. A. Russell, April 14, 1861, Charles Arden Russell Papers, DBCAH; Neighbors, "Old Town of Saint Mary's," 58.

9. Neighbors, "Old Town of Saint Mary's," 34.

10. Campbell, *Gone to Texas*, 241–242.

11. Campbell, 242–243.

12. "Alfred Marmaduke Hobby," Legislative Reference Library of Texas, lrl.texas.gov/legeLeaders /members/memberdisplay.cfm?memberID =4926; Huson, "Hobby, Alfred Marmaduke"; Williams, "Kinney, Henry Lawrence."

13. Campbell, *Gone to Texas*, 244.

14. Alfred and Edwin's youngest brother, Barney Hobby, would eventually also serve in the Confederate Army, but no information has been found about his experiences other than that he was a veteran. *Dallas Morning News*, September 2, 1904; Neighbors, "Old Town of Saint Mary's," 47–48; Huson, "Hobby, Alfred Marmaduke"; Buenger, *Secession and Union*, 144, 174, 176.

15. Delaney, "Corpus Christi, Battle of"; Ed Kilman, "History of the *Houston Post*," Oveta Culp Hobby (hereafter OCH) Papers, Woodson Research Center, Rice University (hereafter Rice).

16. In September 1862 a detachment of Alfred Hobby's soldiers captured the Union naval commander John W. Kittredge when he landed with a few of his men near Corpus Christi. Alfred was not present when Kittredge was captured, but he escorted the Union naval officer to General Bee's headquarters in San Antonio. Kittredge was soon paroled, and he departed from Texas. Delaney, "Corpus Christi, Battle of"; Clark, *Tactful Texan*, 20–22; genealogical file, WPH Sr. Papers, DBCAH.

17. Alwyn Barr, "Battle of Galveston"; Huson, "Hobby, Alfred Marmaduke."

18. While Alfred and Edwin were stationed on the island, several prominent local women formed the "Ladies of Galveston" to host a gala ball on July 4 in honor of General Magruder; his adjutant, Colonel Andrew Dickinson; and Colonel Alfred M. Hobby. At the gala, Alfred met Emma Gertrude Stiles Menard, an attractive woman whose husband was a member of the founding family of Galveston. Family lore claims that Gertrude was a widow when she met Alfred, but burial records indicate that Gertrude's husband, Adolphe, did not die until February 1867. Gertrude and Adolphe had a daughter named Mary, who was about four years old when Gertrude met Alfred. Neighbors, "Old Town of Saint Mary's," 47–48; Marriage Records of Galveston County, vol. F, p. 181; "Mary Desile Menard," Find a Grave, added April 15, 2014, https://www .findagrave.com/cgi-bin/fg.cgi?page=gr&GRid =128010963.

19. A round of grapeshot fired from a Union gunboat on the Red River ripped the top of Tom Green's head off as he led a charge of dismounted cavalry. During the war, Edwin's brother Alfred wrote several patriotic poems, including "The Sentinel's Dream of Home," which was widely published in Southern newspapers. Barr, "Green, Thomas"; Allardice, *Confederate Colonels*, 197; Ellinger, "Southern War Poetry."

20. Marriage Records of Galveston County, vol. F, p. 181. Alfred and Edwin's younger brother, Barney, also mustered out of the Confederate Army and moved to Galveston, where he married a local woman named Louise Watts in 1868. Neighbors, "Old Town of Saint Mary's," 47–48. Gertrude Menard's daughter, Mary, now eight years old, took Alfred Hobby's last name. She lived with Gertrude and Alfred until her death in August 1873 at the age of fourteen. Mary Hobby's 1873 headstone at her grave in Galveston's Old Catholic Cemetery is inscribed with the words "Our Daughter"; "Mary Desile Menard," Find a Grave, added April 15, 2014, https://www .findagrave.com/cgi-bin/fg.cgi?page=gr&GRid =128010963. After his marriage, Alfred wrote a biography of David G. Burnet that was published in 1871. He later published two volumes of poetry and a book, *Frontier from the Saddle*. After Gertrude's daughter, Mary, died, Alfred sold his business in Galveston and he and his wife moved to Grant County in the southwest corner of New Mexico, where the discovery of silver deposits attracted a large number of prospectors and led to the founding of Silver City. Alfred opened a small mercantile store in the village of San Lorenzo, located in the foothills of the Mogollon Mountains. Living conditions

were primitive and Apaches periodically raided the settlement. Alfred and Gertrude remained in the territory for about eight years, until he was killed in a wagon accident in nearby Silver City on February 5, 1881. He died childless. Gertrude returned to Texas, where she died in Ellis County in 1927 at the age of eighty-six. Many years after Alfred's death, the Texas Historical Commission erected a historical marker on the Refugio Courthouse lawn commemorating his adventure-filled life. *Houston Post*, April 23, 1940.

21. During the Civil War, Dr. Pettus and his seventeen-year-old son, William, both volunteered for service in the Confederate Army, the father in the Sixteenth Infantry Brigade and the son in Waul's Texas Legion. Rock and Smith, *Southern and Western Texas*, 208; US Census,1860, schedule 4, Production of Agriculture, Texas, Fort Bend County, p. 5, line 39; Early, *Texas Baptist History*, 59; Baylor University, The Alumni Directory, 1854-1917, 12; Pando, "Oveta Culp Hobby," 26; Raymond Barnett to Laura Aline Hobby, April 3, 1954, WPH Sr. Papers, DBCAH.

22. In his legal history of Texas, Michael Ariens explains that the bar licensing statute of the nineteenth century was based on procedures followed during the Texas Republic and readopted during statehood in 1846, 1873, and 1891. Edwin Hobby was licensed under the 1846 statute, which required that the applicant be twenty-one, a citizen, and furnish testimonials as to good character. District court judges were given license-granting authority. The statute authorized district judges to appoint panels consisting of three lawyers who would examine each applicant in their districts and then approve or disapprove the candidates by a vote of at least two to one. According to Ariens, getting approval was "extraordinarily easy." The prevailing sentiment in Jacksonian America was that any man meeting the age requirement and having "proof" of good character should be allowed to practice law. If he proved to be incompetent he would be unable to attract clients. The flaw in such wishful thinking eventually became evident, although little was done until 1903, when the Texas Legislature passed a bill requiring that candidates pass a written exam. The evidence is clear, however, that Edwin Hobby was not only a competent lawyer but also a legal scholar. His book on Texas land law became a standard

reference on the subject. The Texas Bar Association admitted Edwin as a member in 1891, and he was invited to address the organization at its meeting in Galveston in 1894. His speech was titled "The Legal Profession, Its Value, Importance and Influence." Ariens, *Lone Star Law*, 182; Texas Bar Association, *Proceedings*, 81–92; Marriage Records of Fort Bend County, vol. B, p. 81; Genealogical Records and Notes, WPH Sr. Papers, DBCAH.

23. Abernethy, "Big Thicket"; E. Haynes, *Polk County*, 151.

24. Peach Tree Village eventually become a ghost town after the Trinity and Sabine Railroad line was routed through the nearby town of Chester in 1883. Martin, "Peach Tree Village."

25. Martin; Clark, *Tactful Texan*, 7.

26. "Samuel Bronson Cooper," in *Biographical Directory of US Congress*, bioguideretro.congress.gov; Wooster, "Cooper, Samuel Bronson"; "Samuel Bronson Cooper," campaign biographical sketch, typescript, John Henry Kirby Papers, University of Houston Special Collections (hereafter UH).

27. "Samuel Bronson Cooper," in *Biographical Directory of US Congress*, bioguideretro.congress.gov; Wooster, "Cooper, Samuel Bronson"; "Samuel Bronson Cooper," campaign biographical sketch, typescript, John Henry Kirby Papers, UH.

28. Bronson Cooper and John Henry Kirby attended a one-room school in Peach Tree Village for an unknown period before enrolling in the Woodville school. In 1913, Kirby built a church in Peach Tree Village in memory of his parents. On May 11 of that year, he hosted a dedication ceremony at the village that Will Hobby attended along with five thousand other guests. Samuel Bronson Cooper and Texas governor Oscar Colquitt gave the dedication speeches. Will published an editorial in the *Beaumont Enterprise* lauding the event. "Peach Tree Village Hall, Dedicated by John Henry Kirby as a memorial to the Memory of His Father and Mother," pamphlet, Kirby Lumber Company Records, East Texas Research Center (hereafter ETRC), Stephen F. Austin State University; Lasswell, *John Henry Kirby*, 13, 32; Clark, *Tactful Texan*, 15; King, *Early History*, 5; Daniell, *Personnel of Texas Government*, 475–476; Sterling and Kilman, *Ross Sterling*, 5, 129.

29. Edwin Hobby's mother, Anna Slade Hobby, died at Edwin and Dora's home in Moscow in 1877. Two years before his death, Dr. Pettus had begun

to withdraw from his various enterprises. He rented out his plantation, but he and his wife, Mary, had continued to live in the two-story house on the property. After Dr. Pettus's death, Mary sold thirty-seven acres of the plantation to their son, William, for five dollars. William had studied medicine at the University of Virginia and the University of Maryland and then returned to Fort Bend County, where he worked as a physician. He eventually acquired the entire Pettus plantation. In 1877 William moved to Georgetown, Texas, where he opened a new medical practice. Deed Records of Fort Bend County, bk. H, pp. 340–342; US Census, 1870, Texas, schedule 1, Tyler County, p. 8; Mrs. B. W. Merritt to Laura Hobby, October 12, 1936, WPH Sr. Papers, DBCAH; Daniell, *Personnel of Texas Government*, 475–476; Clark, *Tactful Texan*, 165.

30. Edwin's partners would also make successful bids for political office. William Nicks later served as district attorney, county judge, and district judge. Bronson Cooper would be appointed Tyler County attorney in 1876, followed by two terms in the Texas Senate and then six terms in US Congress. Cardwell, *Sketches of Legislators*; Campbell, *Gone to Texas*, 284–285; Truett, *Circling Back*, 93.

31. Democratic efforts to regain control of Texas state government in this period were greatly aided by the Panic of 1873, which plunged the United States into a deep economic depression that lasted through most of the 1870s. The financial collapse, which had multiple causes, was a political disaster for the Grant administration and the Republican Party. For the effects of the Panic of 1873 on Reconstruction, see Foner, *Reconstruction*. Former Confederates organized paramilitary units similar to the Travis Guards and Rifles throughout the South as means of enforcing white supremacy. Campbell, *Gone to Texas*, 284–285.

32. Spaw, *Texas Senate*, 199.

33. *Texas Senate Journal*, Fourteenth Legislature, 1874–1875.

34. Campbell, *Gone to Texas*, 285; During Edwin's first term in the Senate, the Constitution of 1869 required annual sessions of the legislature. *Texas Senate Journal*, Fourteenth Legislature, 1873.

35. Although heavily amended, the Constitution of 1876 remains in effect as of 2019. Although Edwin played a leadership role in the effort to produce a new constitution, he did not run for election as a delegate to the convention. For the passage of the 1876 Texas Constitution, see Campbell, *Gone to Texas*, 285.

36. US Census, 1880, schedule 1, Texas, Polk County, Moscow, p. 3, lines 40–46; Spaw, *Texas Senate*, 243.

37. "True and Correct Copy" of William Pettus Hobby's birth certificate, issued on September 28, 1942, by J. H. McKee, County Clerk, Polk County, Texas, WPH Sr. Family Papers, DBCAH; US Census, 1880, schedule 1, Texas, Polk County, Moscow, p. 3, lines 40–46; Clark, 5; Spaw, 243, 267; *Texas Senate Journal*, Sixteenth Legislature, 1879.

38. Edwin Hobby continued to serve in the Senate through the remainder of the regular session and until the end of the called session, which met from June 10 to July 10, 1879. Despite his pending resignation, Edwin was as active in the special session as he had been in all of his previous sessions, chairing the Rules Committee, raising points of order on procedural matters, and offering amendments to proposed bills and resolutions. Spaw, *Texas Senate*, 267; *Texas Senate Journal*, Sixteenth Legislature, 1879; *Galveston News*, October 7, 1917.

39. Spaw, *Texas Senate*, 267; *Texas Senate Journal*, Sixteenth Legislature, 1879

40. E. Hobby, *Treatise on Texas Land Law*.

41. When Edwin's son Will was governor of Texas, one of his father's old friends, James Stovall, recalled that for several years Edwin would spend Sunday nights at the Stovall family farm on the Neches River in Angelina County whenever he held court on Mondays in the county. "We thought a great deal of [Edwin]," Stovall stated, "so much that my brother named his first boy Edwin Hobby Stovall." James Stovall to WPH, undated letter in WPH Sr. Papers, DBCAH; D. White, "Alabama Indians," 322.

42. Morgan, "Kirby, John Henry"; Wooster, "Cooper, Samuel Bronson"; Lasswell, *John Henry Kirby*, 42.

43. Although Cooper left the Texas Senate in 1884, he continued to nurse his political ambitions and worked to maintain his political ties. In October 1884, he organized a large political rally in Woodville in support of the presidential campaign of Grover Cleveland, which attracted a crowd composed mainly of former Confederate soldiers and officials. As its master of ceremonies, Cooper gave a fiery introduction for the

featured speaker, US senator Richard Coke. Many years later, John Henry Kirby recalled Bronson Cooper "was then in his early thirties. On this day his long black coat, flowing hair and aesthetic form was particularly pleasing. He had endeared himself to those grizzled Confederates as their representative in the Senate of Texas, where he secured an enactment granting to disabled Confederate soldiers and their widows their first pension." Cooper's efforts on behalf of the successful Cleveland campaign led to his 1885 appointment to the financially lucrative position of collector of internal revenue for the Galveston district, an office he held for nearly four years as he continued to live in Woodville. In 1892, Cooper would leverage his political connections into winning a seat in Congress. "Samuel Bronson Cooper," in *Biographical Directory of US Congress*; Lasswell, *John Henry Kirby*, 37, 42; Clark, *Tactful Texan*, 15; King, *Early History*, 5; Daniell, *Personnel of Texas Government*, 476; D. White, *East Texas*, 585–586.

44. Clark, *Tactful Texan*, 5, 7.

45. E. Haynes, *History of Polk County*; J. Johnston, "Some Old Poems," 271.

46. Clark, *Tactful Texan*, 5–7.

47. Barr, *Reconstruction to Reform*, 140, 214; Clark, *Tactful Texan*, 7, 8.

48. Bradley, *Edison to Enron*.

49. Morrison & Fourmy, *Houston Directory*, 1890–1891, p. 221.

50. Lasswell, *John Henry Kirby*, 59–60; Clark, *Tactful Texan*, 8.

51. Clark, *Tactful Texan*, 9; Texas Bar Association, *Proceedings*, 39; Morrison & Fourmy, *Houston Directory*, 1894–1895; King, *Early History*, 6–7; Davis and Grobe, *Encyclopedia of Texas*, 206–209; Lasswell, *John Henry Kirby*, 52.

52. For Kirby's financial woes, see Samuel Bronson Cooper to John Henry Kirby, May 27, 1896, John Henry Kirby Papers, UH.

53. Edwin's street railway company seems not to have succeeded, because a streetcar system did not operate in Ardmore for another ten years. In September 1895 Edwin became ill during one of his visits back home in Houston. The illness was concerning enough to cause Bronson Cooper to rush to the side of his dear friend. Edwin recovered sufficiently to allow him to return to his post in the Indian Territory, but his daughter Mary went back with him, which suggests the family continued to have worries about his

health. *Houston Post*, October 8, 1895; *Daily Ardmoreite*, October 16, 1895.

54. WPH's Post Card column, *Houston Post*, August 10, 1954; Kilman, "History of the *Houston Post*," OCH Papers, Rice; Clark, 9.

55. Kilman, "History of the *Houston Post*," OCH Papers, Rice; Clark, *Tactful Texan*, 9.

56. Clark, 9-10; M. Johnston, Houston, 105.

57. Clarkson would eventually be promoted to business manager of the *Post* and later to secretary-treasurer. He later became Will's right-hand man at the *Post* and remained with the newspaper until the late 1940s, contributing more than fifty years of service. Clarkson died in May 1956 and left an estate valued at $400,000. Kilman, "History of the Houston Post," OCH Papers, Rice; Clarkson, A. E., www.findagrave.com.

58. Clark, *Tactful Texan*, 10; Kilman, "History of the *Houston Post*," OCH Papers, Rice.

59. Daugherty, *Hiding Man*, 71; Clark, *Tactful Texan*, 12–13; Patterson, "Porter, William Sydney"; M. Johnston, *Houston*, 105.

60. *Houston Post*, August 10, 1954; Clark, *Tactful Texan*, 13; M. Johnston, *Houston*, 105.

61. Clark, *Tactful Texan*, 13–14; Kilman, "History of the *Houston Post*," OCH Papers, Rice.

62. Anonymous, "Johnston, Rienzi Melville"; Clark, *Tactful Texan*, 12.

63. Ed Kilman, "History of the *Houston Post*," OCH Papers, Rice; Sterling and Kilman, *Ross Sterling*, 78.

64. "Old" Rice Hotel refers to the building demolished in 1911 and replaced with a "new" Rice Hotel. Kilman, "History of the *Houston Post*," OCH Papers, Rice; anonymous, "Johnston, Rienzi Melville"; Sterling and Kilman, *Ross Sterling*, 78; *Houston Press*, April 20, 1941; WPH's Post Card column, *Houston Post*, August 10, 1954.

65. Ed Kilman, "History of the *Houston Post*," OCH Papers, Rice; Clark, *Tactful Texan*, 14; Fitzgerald, *Governors*, 38.

66. Notes in WPH Sr. biographical file, DBCAH; Morrison & Fourmy, *Houston Directory*, 1898.

67. Glenwood would eventually be the gravesite of several prominent Texans, including some of Edwin's descendants. *Houston Daily Post*, November 2, 1899; Reid, *Spartan Band*.

CHAPTER 2

1. Mary Pettus soon moved to Georgetown, Texas, to live with her son William, whose medical

practice was prospering. She died there in April 1910 and was buried in the Odd Fellows Cemetery in Williamson County. Morrison & Fourmy, *Houston Directory*, 1900–1901, 1903–1904; Clark, *Tactful Texan*, 14; A. E. Clarkson to Helon Johnston, September 2, 1954, OCH Papers, Rice.

2. Ed Kilman, "History of the *Houston Post*," OCH Papers, Rice; Clark, *Tactful Texan*, 14.

3. Campbell, *Gone to Texas*, 338–340; Clark, *Tactful Texan*, 14–15.

4. Feder, "Disaster Reporting"; *Houston Daily Post*, September 10, 1900; Ed Kilman, "History of the *Houston Post*," OCH Papers, Rice.

5. Clark, *Tactful Texan*, 17; Ed Kilman, "History of the *Houston Post*," OCH Papers, Rice; Wooster, "Lucas, Anthony Francis"; King, *Early History*, 9.

6. A. E. Clarkson's financial notes, James Clark Papers, Rice; Clark, *Tactful Texan*, 15, 16.

7. Clark, *Tactful Texan*, 16

8. *Houston Post*, May 4, 1901

9. By 1901, Kirby owned homes in Houston; Saranac, New York; and his native Peach Tree Village; as well as a vacation camp called Kamp Kill Kare near Seabrook, between Houston and Galveston. He also maintained hotel suites in New Orleans and New York City. Clark, *Tactful Texan*, 15; Morgan, "Kirby, John Henry"; Lasswell, *John Henry Kirby*, xi, 33; Dressman, *Gus Wortham*, 44.

10. *Houston Post*, November 13, 1901; Ed Kilman, "History of the *Houston Post*," OCH Papers, Rice; Clark, *Tactful Texan*, 16.

11. Clark, *Tactful Texan*, 17; M. Johnston, *Houston*, 114.

12. Clark, *Tactful Texan*, 16–17; Ed Kilman, "History of the *Houston Post*," OCH Papers, Rice; Anonymous, "Ousley, Clarence N.", Handbook of Texas Online, accessed June 20, 2020 http://www.tshaonline.org/handbook/online/articles/fou02

13. Ed Kilman, "History of the *Houston Post*," OCH Papers, Rice

14. Clark, *Tactful Texan*, 17; Ed Kilman, "History of the *Houston Post*," OCH Papers, Rice.

15. Clark, *Tactful Texan*, 19–20; Ed Kilman, "History of the *Houston Post*," OCH Papers, Rice.

16. Ed Kilman, "History of the *Houston Post*," OCH Papers, Rice; Champagne et al., *Austin/Boston Connection*, 22.

17. Clark, *Tactful Texan*, 19; WPH's Post Card column, *Houston Post*, August 10, 1954; Ed Kilman, "History of the *Houston Post*," OCH Papers, Rice.

18. Clark, *Tactful Texan*, 19; WPH's Post Card column, *Houston Post*, August 10, 1954; Ed Kilman, "History of the *Houston Post*," OCH Papers, Rice.

19. *Houston Daily Post*, August 16 and 17, 1904; Morrison & Fourmy, *Houston Directory*, 1903–1904, 1905–1906.

20. Clark, *Tactful Texan*, 20–22; Anonymous, "John M. Pinckney," Handbook of Texas Online, accessed June 20, 2020; Ed Kilman, "History of the *Houston Post*," OCH Papers, Rice.

21. Ed Kilman, "History of the *Houston Post*," OCH Papers, Rice.

22. Fitzgerald, *Governors*, 38; Clark, *Tactful Texan*, 22.

23. Houston's city auditorium was named after Winnie Davis, Confederate president Jefferson Davis's daughter. *Houston Post*, March 4, 1906; Ed Kilman, "History of the *Houston Post*," OCH Papers, Rice.

24. In 1901 US senators were still chosen by the state legislatures. The Seventeenth Amendment, which established the direct popular election of US senators (which the antiprogressive Joe Bailey opposed) would be adopted in 1913. Gould, *Progressives and Prohibitionists*, 22; Acheson, *Joe Bailey*, 234; Barr, *Reconstruction to Reform*, 226; Clark, *Tactful Texan*, 23; Champagne et al., *Austin/Boston Connection*, 23–24.

25. Gould, *Progressives and Prohibitionists*, 19–20; Holcomb, "Bailey, Joseph Weldon"; "Joseph Bailey," biographical file, DBCAH.

26. Gould, *Progressives and Prohibitionists*, 19–20; Champagne et al., *Austin/Boston Connection*, 26–27; "Joseph Bailey," biographical file, DBCAH.

27. Clark, *Tactful Texan*, 23.

28. *Houston Post*, October 7, 1906.

29. Claude Bowers in Champagne et al., *Austin/Boston Connection*, 17; Clark, *Tactful Texan*, 24–25.

30. *Houston Post*, October 7, 1906.

31. *Houston Post*, October 7, 1906; Clark, *Tactful Texan*, 23.

32. Gould, *Progressives and Prohibitionists*, 19–24; "Joseph Bailey," biographical file, DBCAH; Barr, *Reconstruction to Reform*.

33. Lasswell, *John Henry Kirby*, 120–121.

34. Clark, *Tactful Texan*, 26–28; Stratton, *Story of Beaumont*, 112.

35. Clark, *Tactful Texan*, 26–28; Stratton, *Story of Beaumont*, 112.

36. Kirby's support for Will to take over the *Enterprise* might also have been motivated by his perception that the former owners had been

unfriendly to him. He had complained to the newspaper's editor about an editorial it had printed about him: "I have been advertised in the *Enterprise* as being . . . unfriendly to Beaumont." He charged that the editorial had been made "for political purposes or vicious reasons." After Will took control of the *Enterprise*, Will performed as Kirby had hoped, with stories and editorials favorable to Kirby and his business and political interests. From the beginning of Will's ownership of the newspaper until Will was elected lieutenant governor in 1914, Kirby fed Will a steady stream of material, including a few of Kirby's speeches, for Will to publish as editorials, often word for word as Kirby had written them. The editorials included one in 1907 urging Kirby to run for governor. At one point in 1913, when Kirby felt that Will was not giving Bronson Cooper enough positive attention in the *Enterprise*, Kirby complained that the paper was "not giving our friend Bronson Cooper as much publicity as he is entitled to. I want you to do him the justice to see that proper credit is accorded him." Kirby to F. W. Greer, September 12, 1905, John Henry Kirby Papers, UH; Kirby to WPH, August 26, 1907, August 21, 1906, October 18, 1909, June 28, 1912, and February 20, 1913, Kirby Lumber Company Records, ETRC; Clark, *Tactful Texan*, 27–28.

37. Clark, 28; Ed Kilman, "History of the *Houston Post*," OCH Papers, Rice; A. J. Peeler Company, *Blue Book of Texas*.

38. Clark, *Tactful Texan*, 26–29; Ed Kilman,"History of the *Houston Post*," OCH Papers, Rice; *Beaumont Enterprise*, June 11, 1907.

39. Clark, *Tactful Texan*, 28.

CHAPTER 3

1. Isaac, "Beaumont, TX"; Clark and Halbouty, *Spindletop*; Stratton, *Story of Beaumont*, 113.

2. Jones Advertising, *Souvenir*, 3, 34–35, 60; East, *Jefferson County*, 139–140, 151.

3. Isaac, "Beaumont, TX"; Stratton, *Story of Beaumont*, 81; Jones Advertising, *Souvenir*, 3, 34–35, 60; East, *Jefferson County*, 139–140, 151.

4. Brownell, *Urban Ethos*, 59.

5. WPH to Kirby, September 6, 1907, and Kirby to Wiess, September 5, 1907, John Henry Kirby Papers, UH.

6. Wooster, "Sabine-Neches Waterway"; S. B. Cooper Sr. to Kirby, February 9, 1900, John Henry Kirby Papers, UH.

7. Storey, "Port Arthur, TX,"; Kleiner, "Orange, TX."

8. S. B. Cooper Sr. to Kirby, February 9, 1900, and Kirby to Cooper, January 2, 1906, and February 8, 1906, John Henry Kirby Papers, UH; East, *Jefferson County*, 157–158; Clark, *Tactful Texan*, 29; Barr, *Reconstruction to Reform*, 234.

9. The project for a deepwater port on the Neches River had a history with the Hobby family. Thirty years earlier, Will's father, Edwin, had proposed legislation to improve navigation on the Sabine River and other waterways in southeast Texas while he was in the Texas Senate. Kirby to WPH, August 26, 2007, John Henry Kirby Papers, UH; Clark, *Tactful Texan*, 29; Stratton, *Story of Beaumont*, 145.

10. Clark, *Tactful Texan*, 28; Ed Kilman, "History of the *Houston Post*," OCH Papers, Rice.

11. Stratton, *Story of Beaumont*, 93.

12. Kirby to WPH, August 26, 1907, and WPH to Kirby, August 29, 1907, John Henry Kirby Papers, UH.

13. Kirby to Wiess, September 5, 1907, and WPH to Kirby, September 6, 1907, John Henry Kirby Papers, UH.

14. Ed Kilman, "History of the *Houston Post*," OCH Papers, Rice; Clark, *Tactful Texan*, 31.

15. Clark, 31–32; Stratton, *Story of Beaumont*, 145.

16. Clark, *Tactful Texan*, 32.

17. Kirby, who had complained to Cooper that he was running a terrible campaign, was among the few who were not surprised by Cooper's defeat. "There is no one in the world who understands my friend better than I do," Kirby told Will Hobby. "He feels humiliated . . . for the reason that he knows that whatever the cause or causes which contributed to his defeat the main reason therefor lies with himself. No man of my acquaintance ever frittered away so great an opportunity as he has done." Cooper to Kirby, January 30, 1908, and Kirby to WPH, September 8, 1908, John Henry Kirby Papers, UH.

18. McDaniel, "First Congressman," 140; Clark, *Tactful Texan*, 35.

19. Clark, 35.

20. Kirby to F. W. Greer, September 12, 1905, John Henry Kirby Papers, UH; East, *Jefferson County*, 158; Duffy, "Link, John Wiley."

21. Clark, *Tactful Texan*, 34–35.

22. Sibley, *Port of Houston*; *Texas House Journal*, Thirty-First Legislature; Clark, *Tactful Texan*, 34–35.

23. Cooper to Kirby, February 9, 1909, John Henry Kirby Papers, UH.

24. Culberson's alcohol problem would force him to give up his leadership position in 1910. Wagner, "Culberson, Charles Allen"; Clark, *Tactful Texan*, 36.

25. Clark, 36–37.

26. It would take Houston another two years to create its district. Clark, 36–37; Sibley, *Port of Houston*.

27. WPH to Kirby, August 12, 1909, John Henry Kirby Papers, UH; East, *Jefferson County*, 159; Clark, *Tactful Texan*, 37.

28. Clark, 38–39.

29. Clark, 39.

30. Clark, 39–40.

31. *Beaumont Enterprise*, July 30 and August 1, 1910.

32. Clark, *Tactful Texan*, 39–40.

33. WPH to Colquitt, July 16, 1910, Oscar B. Colquitt Papers, DBCAH; Clark, *Tactful Texan*, 39–40; *Beaumont Enterprise*, October 20, 1910.

34. Clark, *Tactful Texan*, 40–41.

35. Clark, 41.

CHAPTER 4

1. Beaumont Chamber of Commerce, *Beaumont*, 4; Clark, *Tactful Texan*, 43.

2. Beaumont Chamber of Commerce, *Beaumont*, 10.

3. Beaumont Chamber of Commerce, 10.

4. Morrison & Fourmy, *Beaumont Directory*, 1910–1911, p. 137; letterhead, WPH to Colquitt, July 16, 1910, Oscar B. Colquitt Papers, DBCAH; Clark, *Tactful Texan*, 42–44, 56.

5. Unidentified news clippings, Rienzi M. Johnston Papers, Rice.

6. Gould, *Progressives and Prohibitionists*, 86–87; Colquitt to WPH, November 29, 1911, Oscar B. Colquitt Papers, DBCAH; Campbell, *Gone to Texas*, 345–346; Rhoades, "Texas Gubernatorial Election."

7. Gould, *Progressives and Prohibitionists*, 42–43. For the progressive movement and prohibition, see Robert H. Wiebe, *The Search for Order, 1877–1920* (Hill and Wang, 1967); Richard Hofstadter, *The Age of Reform: From Bryan to F.D.R.* (Vintage, 1955); and Timberlake, *Prohibition and Progressive Movement*.

8. Clark, *Tactful Texan*, 51; Fitzgerald, *Governors*, 40; *Beaumont Enterprise*, July 21, 1911; Kirby to WPH, June 11, 1912, Kirby Lumber Company Records, ETRC.

9. Gould, *Progressives and Prohibitionists*, 86–87; Campbell, *Gone to Texas*, 346; Rhoades, "Texas Gubernatorial Election of 1912."

10. One of the blind spots in the progressive agenda was the lack of interest in addressing racial injustice, which most progressives simply ignored or, in some cases, made worse. Gould, *Progressives and Prohibitionists*, 86–87; Rhoades, "Texas Gubernatorial Election of 1912."

11. Gould, *Progressives and Prohibitionists*, 91.

12. Gould, 80, 82; *Beaumont Enterprise*, July 3, 1911.

13. Champagne et al., *Austin/Boston Connection*, 29; Colquitt to C. W. Nugent, December 26, 1912, Oscar B. Colquitt Papers, DBCAH.

14. Miscellaneous genealogical information in WPH Sr. Papers, DBCAH; John F. Worley Directory Company, *Dallas Directory*, 1910, 1914; Clark, *Tactful Texan*, 45.

15. A. J. Peeler Company, *Blue Book of Texas*, 152, 157–158; East, *Jefferson County*, 53.

16. *Austin American-Statesman*, November 27, 1927; Hinman, *Washington Sketch Book*, 23; Wolz, "Kidd-Key College."

17. *Austin American-Statesman*, November 27, 1927; Hinman, *Washington Sketch Book*, 23; N. Patterson, "Mrs. William Pettus Hobby"; Cooper to Kirby, May 27, 1896, and November 17, 1900, John Henry Kirby Papers, UH.

18. *Austin American-Statesman*, November 27, 1927; Willie Cooper to Kirby, April 4, 1900, John Henry Kirby Papers, UH.

19. Leach, *Sun Country Banker*, 21; Hinman, *Washington Sketch Book*, 23; *Austin American-Statesman*, November 27, 1927.

20. *Austin American-Statesman*, November 27, 1927; unidentified and undated news clipping in Willie's scrapbook, WPH Sr. Papers, DBCAH.

21. Morrison & Fourmy, *Beaumont Directory*, 1904, p. 89; Leach, *Sun Country Banker*, 24; unidentified and undated news clipping in Willie's scrapbook, WPH Sr. Papers, DBCAH; Clark, *Tactful Texan*, 61.

22. After losing his seat in Congress for the last time, Cooper gave serious thoughts to running for governor of Texas. Although John Henry Kirby told Cooper that he would endorse him for governor, Kirby also argued that a campaign would cost at least $25,000 and implied he wouldn't pay the cost. Despite Kirby's discouragement, Cooper, hoping to attract supporters, had letters published in a few newspapers proclaiming his views on current public issues. He gave up the quest

when his letters failed to elicit any responses. Cooper admitted to Kirby he was "somewhat humiliated" that his letters failed to attract much attention, even criticism. Kirby to Cooper, March 30, 1909, and Cooper to Kirby, June 9, 1909, John Henry Kirby Papers, UH.

23. Cooper was a friend of Teddy Roosevelt, and when Roosevelt was leaving the presidency in 1909 he urged his successor, Taft, to find Cooper a federal appointment. Senator Joe Bailey also lobbied Taft on Cooper's behalf. Wooster, "Cooper, Samuel Bronson."

24. Bronson Cooper had faced financial ruin off and on for the past twenty years (at one point complaining to Kirby during his last term in office that he had "grocery bills at home yet unpaid, and I have got to practice frugality in order to keep my home credit"), but John Henry Kirby had often rescued his mentor, even when Kirby himself was in financial trouble. Before Cooper received his federal appointment, Kirby had assured Will that he would give Cooper "at least business enough to keep the wolf from the door and will increase the amount as and when I have the opportunity." Cooper to Kirby, January 30, 1908, October 31, 1908, February 9, 1909, and May 23, 1896, and Kirby to Cecil A. Lyon, August 3, 1909, John Henry Kirby Papers, UH.

25. Leach, *Sun Country Banker*, 24; Farrell and Silverthorne, *First Ladies*, 296; Daniel, Daniel, and Blodgett, *Governor's Mansion*, 155; Clark, *Tactful Texan*, 61; *Austin American-Statesman*, November 27, 1927; A. J. Peeler Company, *Blue Book of Texas*.

CHAPTER 5

1. Gould, *Progressives and Prohibitionists*, 126–133.

2. The brewing and liquor industries were the main targets of the prohibition progressives. James Timberlake, a historian of the prohibition movement, has noted, "What aroused special hostility was [their] arrogant and ruthless practice of gross political corruption to influence and control politicians and elections." In Texas the brewing industry spent millions of dollars from 1900 to 1911 to fight prohibition, much of it in clear violation of election laws. Timberlake, *Prohibition and Progressive Movement*, 106–107, 109–111, 120–121; Gould, *Progressives and Prohibitionists*, 131; McKay, *Texas Politics*, 54.

3. While Kirby was being urged to run as a dry candidate for governor, he wrote Joe Bailey a letter in June 1913 to inform him of his decision to not join the race. He urged Bailey to run instead. Kirby to Bailey, June 27, 1913, Kirby Lumber Company Records, ETRC; Gould, *Progressives and Prohibitionists*, 131; Acheson, *Joe Bailey*, 375; McKay, *Texas Politics*, 54; Johnston to Colquitt, May 25, 1914, Oscar B. Colquitt Papers, DBCAH; Lasswell, *John Henry Kirby*, 146.

4. Clark, *Tactful Texan*, 49; McKay, *Texas Politics*, 58; quote from Rienzi Johnston's obit in Johnston Papers, Rice; Ed Kilman, "History of the *Houston Post*," OCH Papers, Rice.

5. Osofsky, *Burden of Race*, 181–184.

6. Ed Kilman, "History of the *Houston Post*," OCH Papers, Rice; Clark, *Tactful Texan*, 46–47.

7. Ed Kilman, "History of the *Houston Post*," OCH Papers, Rice; Clark, *Tactful Texan*, 46–47.

8. WPH to Duff, March 31, 1919, Governor WPH Sr. Papers, Texas State Library and Archives Commission (hereafter TSLAC).

9. When Will purchased the *Waco Morning News*, Kirby suggested he should also buy the *Austin American-Statesman*, which was in financial trouble. Will declined. Kirby to WPH, June 28, 1912, and January 15, January 31, and March 13, 1914, Kirby Lumber Company Records, ETRC; *Dallas News*, May 31, 1914; Ed Kilman, "History of the *Houston Post*," OCH Papers, Rice; Clark, *Tactful Texan*, 44.

10. Transcript of Rawlins's testimony in the *Texas House Journal*, August 1911.

11. Fitzgerald, *Governors*, 40; Clark, *Tactful Texan*, 45–47.

12. Rawlins Colquitt to Oscar Colquitt, May 31, 1914, Oscar B. Colquitt Papers, DBCAH; Clark, *Tactful Texan*, 47.

13. *Dallas News*, May 31, 1914; *Coleman Democratic-Voice*, June 15, 1914.

14. Rawlins Colquitt to Oscar Colquitt, June 5, 1914, Oscar B. Colquitt Papers, DBCAH.

15. Clark, *Tactful Texan*, 48–49.

16. Gould, *Progressives and Prohibitionists*, 228.

17. N. Patterson, "Mrs. William Pettus Hobby"; Farrell and Silverthorne, *First Ladies*, 297; Daniel, Daniel, and Blodgett, *Governor's Mansion*, 154–155.

18. *El Paso Herald*, August 29, 1919.

19. Clark, *Tactful Texan*, 48–51.

20. Ed Kilman, "History of the *Houston Post*," OCH Papers, Rice.

21. Kirby to WPH, June 5, 1914, Kirby Lumber

Company Records, ETRC; Clark, *Tactful Texan*, 48–51; miscellaneous undated clippings in Willie's scrapbook, including one from the *Hamilton Herald*, WPH Sr. Papers, DBCAH; Ed Kilman, "History of the *Houston Post*," OCH Papers, Rice.

22. Miscellaneous undated news clippings, including from the *Temple Mirror*, in Willie Hobby's scrapbook, WPH Sr. Papers, DBCAH; Fitzgerald, *Governors*, 40; Ed Kilman, "History of the *Houston Post*," OCH Papers, Rice; anonymous, "Mayes, William Harding."

23. Ed Kilman,"History of the *Houston Post*," OCH Papers, Rice.

24. Telegram, Edwin Hobby to Willie Cooper, July 27, 1914, WPH Sr. Papers, DBCAH; Kirby to WPH, July 14, 1914, Kirby Lumber Company Records, ETRC. As Lewis Gould observed, "The disaster of the 1914 Democratic primary marked the nadir of the prohibitionist fortunes." Gould, *Progressives and Prohibitionists*, 145; *Houston Post*, July 28, 1914; Clark, *Tactful Texan*, 53.

25. Clark, *Tactful Texan*, 54.

26. Clark, 57–58; Edwin Hobby to Sadie Webb, August 1, 1914, WPH Sr. Papers, DBCAH.

27. Clark, *Tactful Texan*, 54.

28. Clark, *Tactful Texan*, 57-58.

29. *Beaumont Enterprise*, January 11, 1915; Clark, *Tactful Texan*, 58.

CHAPTER 6

1. Quintus Watson became acting lieutenant governor when William Mayes resigned as lieutenant governor the previous summer. Mayes, who was a newspaper publisher, left the office to join the faculty of the University of Texas to establish its Department of Journalism. Anonymous, "Mayes, William Harding,"; *Temple Daily Telegram*, January 20, 1915; *Texas House Journal*, Thirty-Fourth Legislature, regular session, 1915, p. 125.

2. *Texas House Journal*, Thirty-Fourth Legislature, regular session, 1915, p. 125.

3. *Texas House Journal*, Thirty-Fourth Legislature, regular session, 1915, pp. 125–127; *Houston Post*, January 20, 1915; Clark, *Tactful Texan*, 59.

4. Kirby to WPH, January 15, 1915, Kirby Lumber Company Records, ETRC; *Texas Senate Journal*, Thirty-Fourth Legislature, regular session, 1915.

5. Constitution of the State of Texas, article IV, section 16; WPH to Ed S. Henry, January 25, 1915, Governor WPH Sr. Papers, TSLAC; Clark, *Tactful Texan*, 60.

6. Kirby to WPH, January 15, 1915, Kirby Lumber Company Records, ETRC; *Texas Senate Journal*, Thirty-Fourth Legislature, regular session, 1915.

7. *Texas Senate Journal*, Thirty-Fourth Legislature, regular session, 1915.

8. Daniel, Daniel, and Blodgett, *Governor's Mansion*, 154; Clark, *Tactful Texan*, 61–62.

9. National Child Labor Committee, "Child Labor," 15; Clark, *Tactful Texan*, 67; Gould, *Progressives and Prohibitionists*, 190–191; Lundberg, "Bear Fight," 20–21.

10. Clark, *Tactful Texan*, 60–61.

11. Undated and unidentified news clippings in Willie's scrapbook, WPH Sr. Papers, DBCAH.

12. News clip of editorial, ca. May 1918, *New Orleans Item*, in WPH Sr. biography file, DBCAH; Clark, *Tactful Texan*, 61–62.

13. Clark, 61–62.

14. Miscellaneous undated newspaper clippings in Willie Hobby's scrapbook, WPH Sr. Papers, DBCAH.

15. Clark, *Tactful Texan*, 61–62; undated news clip from *Austin Statesman*, ca. May 1918, WPH Sr. biography file, DBCAH.

16. Daniel, Daniel, and Blodgett, *Governor's Mansion*, 154; quote from unidentified news clipping in Willie Hobby's scrapbook, WPH Sr. Papers, DBCAH.

17. Clark, *Tactful Texan*, 60; Steen, "Ferguson, James Edward."

18. Unidentified and undated newspaper clippings in Willie Hobby's scrapbook, WPH Sr. Papers, DBCAH.

19. Unidentified news clippings in Willie's scrapbook, WPH Sr. Papers, DBCAH; Crawford, "Texas Woman's Fair."

20. Clark, *Tactful Texan*, 62–63.

21. *Beaumont Enterprise*, April 16, 1916; Clark, *Tactful Texan*, 63.

22. Clark, 63–64.

23. In January 1913, the Texas Women's Press Association requested that the University of Texas establish a School of Journalism and that William H. Mayes be named as organizer and director. Mayes, who was then lieutenant governor of Texas and a qualified journalist, officially founded the Journalism School in 1914. Undated and unidentified newspaper clipping, but probably *Austin American-Statesman*, ca. June 1916, William H. Mayes biographical file, DBCAH.

24. WPH to Greer, July 29, 2016, John Henry Kirby Papers, UH.

25. Lundberg, "Bear Fight," 25; Gould, *Progressives and Prohibitionists*, 194.

26. Undated and unidentified newspaper clippings in WPH Sr. Papers, DBCAH; Gould, *Progressives and Prohibitionists*, 194.

27. Clark, *Tactful Texan*, 66.

28. Gould, *Progressives and Prohibitionists*, 181; Wagner, "Culberson, Charles Allen"; Hughes and Harrison, "Charles A. Culberson," 41–48.

29. WPH to Ferguson, November 22, 1916, James Edward Ferguson Collection, DBCAH.

CHAPTER 7

1. *Texas House Journal*, Thirty-Fifth Legislature, regular session, 1917, p. 139.

2. Ed Kilman, "History of the *Houston Post*," OCH Papers, Rice.

3. A sea of ink has been used to print all of the articles and books published about the Ferguson affair, but the definitive history of the episode remains Lewis Gould's *Progressives and Prohibitionists*, published in 1973. My account of the affair is based on Gould's work.

4. Gould.

5. Gould.

6. Gould.

7. Clark, *Tactful Texan*, 69.

8. McAdoo to James Ferguson, February 13, 1917, McAdoo to WPH, February 16, February 24, and March 4, 1917, William Gibbs McAdoo Papers, Library of Congress (hereafter LOC).

9. Clark, *Tactful Texan*, 69; WPH to Dora Hobby, March 24, 1917, WPH Sr. Papers, DBCAH.

10. Gould, *Progressives and Prohibitionists*; *Dallas News*, June 17, 1917.

11. Gould, *Progressives and Prohibitionists*.

12. Canada to Ellis, July 25, 1917, Alexander Caswell Ellis Papers, DBCAH.

13. Gould, *Progressives and Prohibitionists*; WPH to Love, June 18, 1917, Thomas Love Papers, Dallas Historical Society (hereafter DHS).

14. Ellis to W. S. Sutton, August 6, 1917, Alexander Caswell Ellis Papers, DBCAH; Gould, *Progressives and Prohibitionists*.

15. Canada to Ellis, July 25, 1917, Alexander Caswell Ellis Papers, DBCAH.

16. Edwin Hobby to Love, July 28, 1917, Thomas Love Papers, DHS.

17. Edwin Hobby to Love, July 28, 1917, Thomas Love Papers, DHS.

18. WPH to Love, August 2 and August 6, 1917, Thomas Love Papers, DHS.

19. WPH to Love, August 6, 1917, Thomas Love Papers, DHS.

20. When a newspaper reporter told Willie that many people thought she was "the more politic of the Hobbys," she "threw her head back and laughed. 'Well, I am not so sure of that. But you know that I have lived this sort of life since I was a girl. My father was a [congressman] and we lived in Washington. I love the life. Perhaps it is bred in the bone.'" *El Paso Herald*, August 29, 1919; undated clipping of editorial in the *Temple Mirror*, ca. August 1917, in Willie Hobby's scrapbook, WPH Sr. Papers, DBCAH.

21. Gould, *Progressives and Prohibitionists*.

22. Gould.

23. Will to Dora, August 27, 1917, WPH Sr. Papers, DBCAH.

24. "Governor's Call for Special Session of the 35th Legislature," August 29, 1917, pp. 301–393, WPH Sr. Papers, DBCAH; *Texas Senate Journal*, Thirty-Fifth Legislature, p. 861; Clark, *Tactful Texan*, 72.

25. Texas Legislature, *Record of Proceedings*, 10; Clark, *Tactful Texan*, 71–72.

26. Kirby to WPH, September 11, 1917, Kirby Lumber Company Records, ETRC; undated newspaper clip, *San Antonio Express*, Rienzi M. Johnston Papers, Rice; Hogg to WPH, September 18, 1917, Will C. Hogg Papers, DBCAH.

27. WPH to Andrews, September 19, 1917, Frank Andrews Papers, Special Collections, South Texas College of Law Houston (hereafter STCL); WPH to Love, September 21, 1917, Thomas Love Papers, DHS; WPH to Dora Hobby, September 14, 1917, WPH Sr. Papers, DBCAH.

28. Gould, *Progressives and Prohibitionists*, 217–218.

29. Gould, 217–218; Hogg to Shelby, September 7, 1917, Will C. Hogg Papers, DBCAH.

30. Undated news clip from *Dallas Times Herald*, ca. fall 1917, in WPH Sr. biographical file, DBCAH.

CHAPTER 8

1. Anne Austin column, *Waco Daily News*, November 22, 1917, clipping in Willie Hobby's scrapbook, WPH Sr. Papers, DBCAH.

2. B. Hobby, *How Things Really Work*.

3. Gould, *Progressives and Prohibitionists*, 221; Clark, *Tactful Texan*.

4. Gould, *Progressives and Prohibitionists*, 229.

5. *Galveston News*, October 7, 1917.

6. *Galveston News*, October 7, 1917.

7. *Galveston News*, October 7, 1917.

8. Newspaper clip, unidentified newspaper, October 1917, in WPH Sr. biographical file, DBCAH; Gould, *Progressives and Prohibitionists*, 229.

9. After Will became governor, Kirby was quick to remind him that he had known Will when he was a mere "office boy. Please keep in mind that I will come to Austin at any time that you think I can be of service to you in any matter however unimportant." Kirby to WPH, October 8, 1917, Kirby Lumber Company Records, ETRC; Gould, *Progressives and Prohibitionists*, 228.

10. Love to WPH, October 8, 1917, Thomas Love Papers, DHS.

11. WPH to Love, October 22, 1917, Thomas Love Papers, DHS.

12. WPH to Love, November 16, 1917, Thomas Love papers, DHS.

13. Love to Edwin Hobby, December 31, 1917, Thomas Love Papers, DHS.

14. WPH to Love, December 31, 1917, and Love to WPH, January 7, 1918, Thomas Love Papers, DHS.

15. In a letter Kirby had written to Will a few years earlier, he referred to Bill Haywood as a "lawless character" who was "promoting discord and trouble" in the lumber industry. As for Will's relationship with labor unions, according to Kirby, he was "blacklisted and boycotted by the Timber Workers" in East Texas. Kirby to WPH, June 28, 1912, Kirby Lumber Company Records, ETRC. For more on Kirby and labor unions, see Morgan, "Gospel of Wealth," 186–197; Maroney, "Vignettes," 91.

16. Maroney, "Oil Field Strike"; Sterling and Kilman, "Ross Sterling," 64.

17. Miscellaneous newspaper clips, including *Austin Statesman*, November 9, 1917, in WPH Sr. biographical file, DBCAH.

18. Gould, *Progressives and Prohibitionists*, 236.

19. Jackson, "Petticoat Politics," 7.

20. Farrell and Silverthorne, *First Ladies*, 299; Daniel, Daniel, and Blodgett, *Governor's Mansion*, 157; unidentified and undated news clippings from Willie Hobby's scrapbook, WPH Sr. Papers, DBCAH.

21. "James A. Elkins," biographical file, DBCAH; Hyman, *Craftsmanship and Character*, 52–53.

22. Sterling and Kilman, *Ross Sterling*, 64.

23. Farrell and Silverthorne, *First Ladies*, 300.

24. Will Hogg to Woodward, December 10, 1917,

WPH to Hogg, December 29, 1917, Hogg to D. W. Bowser, January 30, 1918, and Hogg to WPH, May 23, 1918, Will C. Hogg Papers, DBCAH.

25. Crane to WPH, January 10, 1918, Martin McNulty Crane Papers, DBCAH.

26. John J. Pleasant to Crane, February 15, 1918, Martin McNulty Crane Papers, DBCAH.

27. *Austin Statesman*, January 20, 1919.

28. Brochure in Alexander Caswell Ellis Papers, DBCAH; "Names of the Men Present at the Meeting in Dallas, January 19, 1918," typescript, Minnie Fisher Cunningham Papers, UH.

29. Typescript, Minnie Fisher Cunningham Papers, UH.

CHAPTER 9

1. Will Hogg to WPH, January 31, 1918, WPH Sr. Papers, DBCAH.

2. WPH to Thomas Perkins, February 1, 1918, Governor WPH Sr. Papers, TSLAC.

3. R. L. Pillow to WPH, January 22, 1918, WPH Sr. Papers, DBCAH.

4. WPH to Andrews, January 12, 1918, Frank Andrews Papers, STCL.

5. Will Hogg to WPH, January 31, 1918, Governor WPH Sr. Papers, TSLAC.

6. WPH to Joseph Bailey, February 1, 1918, WPH Sr. Papers, DBCAH; Love to WPH, January 26, 1918, and WPH to Love, February 9, 1918, Thomas Love Papers, DHS.

7. Telegram, Baker to WPH, *Texas House Journal*, vol. 35, part 4, p. 8; telegram, Baker to WPH, February 12, *Texas House Journal*, vol. 35, part 4, p. 53; McArthur and Smith, *Minnie Fisher Cunningham*, 60.

8. Crane to WPH, February 2, 1918, and WPH to Crane, February 9, 1918, Martin McNulty Crane Papers, DBCAH.

9. Clark, *Tactful Texan*, 81; WPH to Andrews, January 12, 1918, Frank Andrews Papers, STCL; WPH to Terrell, February 6, 1918, and WPH to Bailey, February 13, 1918, Governor WPH Sr. Papers, TSLAC.

10. Love to WPH, February 21, 1918, Thomas Love Papers, DHS; Crane to WPH, February 23, 1918, Martin McNulty Crane Papers, DBCAH.

11. McArthur and Smith, *Minnie Fisher Cunningham*, 60; WPH to Hogg, February 14, 1918, and WPH to John Davis, January 21, 1918, Governor WPH Sr. Papers, TSLAC; Crane to WPH, May 2, 1918, Martin McNulty Crane Papers, DBCAH; M. Johnston, *Houston*, 207.

12. McArthur and Smith, *Minnie Fisher Cunningham*, 61–62; Farrell and Silverthorne, *First Ladies*, 298.

13. M. Johnston, *Houston*, 207; *Texas House Journal*, vol. 35, part 4, p. 2; McArthur and Smith, *Minnie Fisher Cunningham*, 61–62; McArthur, *New Woman*, 138.

14. McArthur and Smith, *Minnie Fisher Cunningham*, 61–62.

15. McArthur and Smith, *Minnie Fisher Cunningham*, 61–62.

16. *Houston Chronicle*, undated clipping, but ca. 1929, WPH Sr. biographical file, DBCAH; WPH to Cooper, March 25, 1918, Governor WPH Sr. Papers, TSLAC.

17. Frank Andrews and former Speaker Chester Terrell drafted the zoning bills for Will. WPH to Crane, February 28, 1918, Martin McNulty Crane Papers, DBCAH; Clark, *Tactful Texan*, 81; *Austin American*, March 2, 1918; Gould, *Progressives and Prohibitionists*, 233.

18. Clark, *Tactful Texan*, 94; Acheson, *Joe Bailey*, 384–385; Alonzo [illegible last name] to Hogg, May 7, 1918, Will C. Hogg Papers, DBCAH.

19. Crane to WPH, March 6, 1918, Martin McNulty Crane Papers, DBCAH; Love to Edwin Hobby, March 14, 1918, Thomas Love Papers, DHS; Jackson, "Petticoat Politics," 6.

20. Hochschild, "Dissent," 82; *General and Special Laws of the State of Texas*, Thirty-Fifth Legislature, first called session, 1918, pp. 12–15.

21. Stone, *Perilous Times*, 146–232.

22. Stone, 146–232.

23. WPH to Baker, April 19, 1918, Governor WPH Sr. Papers, TSLAC; Love to Edwin Hobby, March 14, 1918, Thomas Love Papers, DHS.

24. WPH to Cooper, March 25, 1918, Governor WPH Sr. Papers, TSLAC; WPH to Crane, April 4, 1918, Martin McNulty Crane Papers, DBCAH; Love to Edwin Hobby, March 14, 1918, Thomas Love Papers, DHS.

25. *Houston Post*, April 2, 1918; *Beaumont Enterprise*, March 26, 1918; Gould, *Progressives and Prohibitionists*, 235; Clark, *Tactful Texan*, 84–85; Jackson, "Petticoat Politics," 6; Crane to WPH, April 2, 1918, Martin McNulty Crane Papers, DBCAH.

26. Throughout April and early May, Ferguson was campaigning hard and attracting large crowds, while the Will Hobby campaign was relatively inactive. "We have been trying to engineer the Liberty Loan here," Martin Crane complained to Will Hogg. "[Ferguson] has spoken . . . while we have remained silent." Crane to WPH, April 16, 1918 and WPH to Crane, April 20, 1918, Martin McNulty Crane Papers, DBCAH; Crane to Hogg, May 7, 1918, Will C. Hogg Papers, DBCAH; Clark, *Tactful Texan*, 86.

27. Farrell and Silverthorne, *First Ladies*, 300; unidentified (except for *American Statesman*) and undated newspaper clippings, WPH Sr. biographical file, DBCAH.

28. Daniel, Daniel, and Blodgett, *Governor's Mansion*, 156; N. Patterson, "Mrs. William Pettus Hobby"; Farrell and Silverthorne, *First Ladies*, 300.

29. Unidentified (except for *American Statesman*) and undated newspaper clippings, WPH Sr. biographical file, DBCAH; Daniel, Daniel, and Blodgett, *Governor's Mansion*, 156; McArthur, *New Woman*, 135.

30. WPH to Crawford, April 24, 1918, Governor WPH Sr. Papers, TSLAC; George Bailey to Will Hogg, May 8, 1918, Will C. Hogg Papers, DBCAH.

31. WPH to Hogg, April 25, 1918, Bailey to Hogg, May 8, 1918, Hogg to WPH, May 23, 1918, Will C. Hogg Papers, DBCAH.

32. Hogg to WPH, May 23, 1918, Will C. Hogg Papers, DBCAH.

CHAPTER 10

1. Gould, *Progressives and Prohibitionists*, 239.

2. Clark, *Tactful Texan*, 87–92; Walter Crawford to Will Hogg, May 9, 1918, Will C. Hogg Papers, DBCAH; Gould, *Progressives and Prohibitionists*, 239.

3. One source claims that 80 percent of the state's newspapers supported Will's election in 1918; J. W. Mahan to W. B. Smylie, March 30, 1918. Sam Harbin, Secretary of the Texas Press Association, wrote the *Fort Worth Star-Telegram*'s James Upshur Vincent, "I have known Hobby a long time, have always known him to be a 'four square' man. Hobby is not a fanatic on any subject." Even Marcellus Foster's *Houston Chronicle* declared its strong support for Will's election. Harbin to Vincent, February 22, 1918, and Marcellus Foster to Walter Crawford, May 22 and June 10, 1918, WPH Sr. Papers, DBCAH; Edmund Travis to Will Hogg, May 8, 1918, Will C. Hogg Papers, DBCAH; W. W. Woodson to E. C. Barker, May 1, 1918, Eugene C. Barker Papers, DBCAH; *El Paso Herald Tribune*, August 29, 1919.

4. Carlton to Will Hogg, June 15, 1918, Will C. Hogg Papers, DBCAH.

5. Anecdote from notes in WPH Sr. Papers, DBCAH.

6. "Ed Hunter," in Shire, *Oveta Culp Hobby*, 30; Clark, *Tactful Texan*, 87; typescript copy of editorial, *New York Herald*, June 1, 1918, WPH Sr. Papers, DBCAH.

7. Walter Crawford to Will Hogg, May 16, 1918; W. L. Moody to Will Hogg, May 17, 1918; George W. Littlefield to Will Hogg, May 17, 1918, Will C. Hogg Papers, DBCAH.

8. In January 1917, the German foreign office sent a diplomatic message, known as the "Zimmerman Telegram," to its ambassador in Mexico to present to the Mexican government offering American territory and financial support if it declared war on the United States in the event the United States entered the European war against Germany. The Mexican government, led by Venustiano Carranza, briefly considered Germany's proposal to declare war on the United States, but reality quickly set in. Mexico was in the middle of a civil war, it was militarily weak, and it lacked any ability to occupy territory the size of Texas, which had a population of four million people, many of them rural people in South Texas who were almost as heavily armed as the Mexican Army. For more information about this diplomatic incident and its repercussions, see Barbara Tuchman, *The Zimmerman Telegram* (1958).

9. Harris and Sadler, *Texas Rangers*, 342–343, 396, 504.

10. Harris and Sadler, 328–329, 504.

11. Harris and Sadler, 398; Utley, *Lone Star Lawmen*, 74.

12. Ivey, *Texas Rangers*, 180; Utley, *Lone Star Lawmen*, 74; Harris and Sadler, *Texas Rangers*, 398, 399, 402; Swanson, *Cult of Glory*, 268–269.

13. Three of the eight Rangers who Will decided to dismiss had already left the Rangers at the time he fired the other five. Swanson, *Cult of Glory*, 269; Utley, *Lone Star Lawmen*, 74–75; *New York Times* (hereafter *NYT*), May 23, 1918; Harris and Sadler, *Texas Rangers*, 398–399.

14. Harris and Sadler, 398–399.

15. Harris and Sadler, 398–399.

16. Harris and Sadler, 398–399.

17. Will also admitted that "a certain amount of politics" was part of the problem, as the long-established custom of making Ranger appointments from the governor's office augmented the use of Rangers for political purposes; while that practice had not begun with the Hobby administration, it certainly increased with the creation of the Loyalty Rangers during Will's first year as governor. Harris and Sadler, *Texas Rangers*, 328–329, 332, 463; Looney, "Texas Rangers," 5–10.

18. Clark, *Tactful Texan*, 111.

19. Harris and Sadler, *Texas Rangers*, 342–343, 396, 504.

20. Ivey, *Texas Rangers*, 180; Looney, "Texas Rangers," 72–75.

21. Harris and Sadler, *Texas Rangers*, 400–402.

22. Utley, *Lone Star Lawmen*, 74–75; *NYT*, May 23, 1918; Harris and Sadler, *Texas Rangers*, 398–399.

23. Ivey, *Texas Rangers*, 180; Looney, "Texas Rangers," 72–75.

24. The King Ranch's Caesar Kleberg, the *patrón* of Kleberg County, was also supporting Hobby. J. T. Canales to Hobby Campaign Committee, July 15, 1918, Oscar Dancy to Walter Crawford, July 10, 1918, and Walter Crawford to Oscar Dancy, July 13, 1918, WPH Sr. Papers, DBCAH.

25. Voter fraud was also uncovered in Starr and Hidalgo counties, but unlike Duval County, the fraud was in Will Hobby's favor. In 1948, Duval County would attract national notoriety for the role it played in LBJ's election to the US Senate. Charles Flato to Walter Crawford, July 15, 1918, WPH Sr. Papers, DBCAH; Harris and Sadler, *Texas Rangers*, 424–425; Clark, *Tactful Texan*, 112.

26. Clark, 112, 117; Utley, *Lone Star Lawmen*, 81.

27. For an example of the work performed by the speakers' committee, see several letters in series 4 of the Minnie Fisher Cunningham (hereafter MFC) Papers, UH. Crawford to MFC, June 7, 1918, Crawford to MFC, June 27, 1918, MFC to Mrs. E. E. Thompson, June 12, 1918, R. Lee Kempner to MFC, June 12, 1918, MFC Papers, UH; Annie Webb Blanton to Jasper Collins, June 13, 1918, and Blanton to Walter Crawford, July 2, 1918, WPH Sr. Papers, DBCAH.

28. McArthur and Smith, *Minnie Fisher Cunningham*, 64; MFC to Walter Crawford, June 6, 1918, MFC Papers, UH.

29. Edwin Hobby, who was working full time on his brother's campaign, focused a significant amount of his time on the women's vote. He sent a steady stream of letters out to the women

county leaders, boosting their efforts. "A word to the good women of your community," Edwin declared in one of the letters, "will be of untold benefit and we are especially anxious that they take a prominent part in this election." Edwin Hobby to Mrs. O. D. Wilkes, July 11, 1918; WPH Sr. Papers, DBCAH; "Hobby Rally," flyers, MFC Papers, UH.

30. Crane to Crawford, July 12, 1918, Martin McNulty Crane Papers, DBCAH.

31. J. C. Jones to Ferguson, June 22, 1918, James Edward Ferguson Collection, DBCAH; typescript of stenographic report by J. A. Lord, May 22, 1918, MFC Papers, UH.

32. Brochure, James Edward Ferguson Collection, DBCAH.

33. "Made by German," circular, MFC Papers, UH; Gould, *Progressives and Prohibitionists*, 192; Nicholas, "Academic Dissent," 220–229.

34. Gould, *Progressives and Prohibitionists*, 241; Clark, *Tactful Texan*, 90, 93.

35. F. C. Davis to Walter Crawford, July 16, 1918, WPH Sr. Papers, DBCAH; Caro, *Path to Power*, 73.

36. Will's campaign donors also included Dallas bankers Nathan Adams and Royal Ferris, Wichita Falls railroad tycoon Frank Kell, San Antonio banker and philanthropist George W. Brackenridge, the King Ranch's Caesar Kleberg, Kerrville rancher Charles Schreiner, Galveston entrepreneur R. L. Kempner, Houston oilmen J. S. Cullinan and Lee Blaffer, and Houston attorneys Jacob Wolters, James A. Baker, and James A. Elkins. Elkins paid suffrage activist and attorney Hortense Clark's expenses for traveling throughout Texas to speak on Will's behalf at Women for Hobby club meetings. Elkins to R. W. Brahan, July 13, 1918, and undated clipping, *San Antonio Express News*, WPH Sr. Papers, DBCAH; Clark, *Tactful Texan*, 102; Walter Crawford to E. E. Clark, June 20, 1918, Will C. Hogg Papers, DBCAH; M. Edmonson to Thomas Love, June 1918, H. L. Flewellen to J. W. Mahan Jr., Secretary of the WPH Campaign Committee, June 18, 1918, John Terrell to J. W. Mahan, June 20, 1918, Thomas Love Papers, DHS.

37. Gould, *Progressives and Prohibitionists*, 240–241.

38. Clark, *Tactful Texan*, 95; typescript of notes taken during interview with WPH conducted by "J.D.M.," October 1, 1952, WPH Sr. Papers, DBCAH.

39. Gould, *Progressives and Prohibitionists*, 242–243; Crawford to Andrews, July 25, 1918, Frank Andrews Papers, STCL.

40. Clark, *Tactful Texan*, 94; Farrell and Silverthorne, *First Ladies*, 301; Gould, *Progressives and Prohibitionists*, 245–246.

41. After the election, Cunningham wrote Walter Crawford: "Congratulations! It is to be supposed that we will hear no more of this person Ferguson, since the people not only 'spoke,' but shouted on Saturday." MFC to Crawford, July 30, 1918, MFC Papers, UH; Gould, *Progressives and Prohibitionists*, 245; telegram, Mr. and Mrs. R. H. Kirby to MFC, July 28, 1918, MFC Papers, UH.

42. McArthur and Smith, *Minnie Fisher Cunningham*, 66; Crane to WPH, July 29, 1918, Martin McNulty Crane Papers, DBCAH; Gould, *Progressives and Prohibitionists*, 245–246.

43. WPH to Andrews, August 16, 1920, Governor WPH Sr. Papers, TSLAC.

44. Clark, *Tactful Texan*, 96; Farrell and Silverthorne, *First Ladies*, 301–302.

45. W. C. Connor to WPH (copy), August 5, 1918, Frank Andrews Papers, STCL; unidentified news clippings in Willie Hobby's scrapbook, and pamphlet, "Memorial Proceedings Before the Board of United States General Appraisers in Honor of Honorable Sam Bronson Cooper," September 19, 1918, WPH Sr. Papers, DBCAH.

CHAPTER 11

1. Clark, *Tactful Texan*, 98–99.

2. McArthur and Smith, *Minnie Fisher Cunningham*, 66.

3. Clark, *Tactful Texan*, 99.

4. Clark, 99.

5. Clark, 99–100; WPH to Woodrow Wilson (copy), September 22, 1918, Thomas Love Papers, DHS.

6. Andrews to WPH, September 12, 1918, Frank Andrews Papers, STCL.

7. Ed Kilman, "History of the *Houston Post*," OCH Papers, Rice; Clark, *Tactful Texan*, 107; Love to WPH, December 28, 1918, Thomas Love Papers, DHS.

8. WPH to Dora Hobby, September 30, 1918, WPH Sr. Papers, DBCAH; Clark, *Tactful Texan*, 100.

9. *Washington Times*, October 14, 1918; Clark, *Tactful Texan*, 100–101; WPH to Love, October 15, 1918, and Love to WPH, October 19, 1918, Thomas Love Papers, DHS.

10. *Austin American*, October 14, 1918.

11. Clark, *Tactful Texan*, 100, 102; Ed Haltom to Harry Weinberger, December 1919, Harry Weinberger Papers, Yale University Library (hereafter Yale).

12. *Houston Post*, November 12, 1918.

13. John C. Townes Jr. to WPH, November 18, 1918, and December 2, 1918, copies enclosed in WPH's letter to Andrews, December 13, 1918, Frank Andrews Papers, STCL.

14. John C. Townes Jr. to WPH, November 18, 1918, and December 2, 1918, Frank Andrews Papers, STCL.

15. Clark, *Tactful Texan*, 104; Farrell and Silverthorne, *First Ladies*, 300, 302.

16. *Texas House Journal*, Thirty-Sixth Legislature, regular session, 1919, p. 127; Ed Kilman, "History of the *Houston Post*," OCH Papers, Rice; M. Johnston, *Houston*, 196.

17. Clark, *Tactful Texan*, 112, 117; Utley, *Lone Star Lawmen*, 81.

18. Clark, *Tactful Texan*, 112, 117; Utley, *Lone Star Lawmen*, 81.

19. Clark, *Tactful Texan*, 117; Looney, "Texas Rangers," 5–10.

20. Looney, 5–10; *Austin Statesman*, February 19, 1919.

21. Ivey, *Texas Rangers*; Looney, "Texas Rangers," 72–75; Swanson, *Cult of Glory*, 271

22. *Texas House Journal*, Thirty-Sixth Legislature, regular session, 1919, p. 128.

23. *Texas House Journal*, Thirty-Sixth Legislature, regular session, 1919, p. 128.

24. Clark, *Tactful Texan*, 106–109.

25. Fitzgerald, *Governors*, 38.

26. Typescript of notes taken during interview with WPH conducted by "J.D.M.," October 1, 1952, WPH Sr. Papers, DBCAH.

27. W. L. Dean to WPH, January 2, 1918, Governor WPH Sr. Papers, TSLAC; *Congressional Record*, vol. 110 (1964), 14243.

28. Gould, *Progressives and Prohibitionists*, 254–255; McArthur and Smith, *Minnie Fisher Cunningham*, 75, 78.

29. Gould, *Progressives and Prohibitionists*, 254–255; McArthur and Smith, *Minnie Fisher Cunningham*, 75, 78.

30. Clipping from *Austin Statesman*, March 4, 1919, WPH Sr. Papers, DBCAH; Daniel, Daniel, and Blodgett, *Governor's Mansion*, 156; Farrell and Silverthorne, *First Ladies*, 302; *Governor's Mansion Historical Gazette*, vol. 2 (2010).

31. Will to Dora Hobby, March 12, 1919, WPH. Sr. Papers, DBCAH.

32. Hunt, "Mineral Wells"; typescript of notes taken during interview with WPH conducted by "J.D.M.," October 1, 1952, WPH Sr. Papers, DBCAH.

33. Daniel, Daniel, and Blodgett, *Governor's Mansion*, 156–157; Farrell and Silverthorne, *First Ladies*, 303; *Austin American-Statesman*, November 21, 1920; WPH to Henderson M. Jacoway, September 9, 1919, Governor WPH Sr. Papers, TSLAC; Leach, *Sun Country Banker*, 34, 38, 41.

34. Daniel, Daniel, and Blodgett, *Governor's Mansion*, 156–157; Farrell and Silverthorne, *First Ladies*, 303; Leach, *Sun Country Banker*, 50; Willie Hobby obituary, January 14, 1929, unidentified newspaper, WPH Sr. biographical file, DBCAH.

35. *Dallas News*, November 5, 1920.

36. Florence Stratton was born in Brazoria, Texas, in March 1881. She attended normal college in Troy, Alabama, and was valedictorian of her 1900 graduating class. She moved to Beaumont in 1903, where she taught school before she joined the staff of the *Beaumont Journal*. *Galveston News*, October 27, 1920, and January 29, 1938; Stratton, *Story of Beaumont*.

37. Will made the appearance in Houston as a favor to W. C. Munn, his friend and major supporter. Munn organized a welcoming committee, which included Frank Andrews and other members of Houston's civic and business elite, to meet Will and Willie as they arrived at the train station. The committee then escorted them to Munn's store, where they had breakfast, followed by Will's speech to a large crowd gathered on the Exposition floor. *Houston Post*, April 24, 1919; James A. Harley to Frank Andrews, April 17, 1919, and Andrews to Hill, April 18, 1919, Frank Andrews Papers, STCL.

38. Gould, *Progressives and Prohibitionists*, 254.

39. Gould, 255; Jackson, "Petticoat Politics," 8–9; newspaper clip, unidentified newspaper, June 15, 1919, WPH Sr. biographical file, DBCAH; Clark, *Tactful Texan*, 118.

40. An unidentified and undated newspaper clipping about the adoption of the Nineteenth Amendment in Willie Hobby's scrapbook features a formal portrait of Willie with a caption stating, "Worked for equal suffrage in Washington and New York." It also mentioned she was

present at the Capitol when the US Congress passed the bill. "Texas Women Leaders for Equal Suffrage," Willie Hobby Scrabook, WPH Sr. Papers, DBCAH; Gould, *Progressives and Prohibitionists*, 256.

41. Gould, 255–256; Clark, *Tactful Texan*, 118.

42. Gould, *Progressives and Prohibitionists*, 255–256; Clark, *Tactful Texan*, 118.

43. Clark, 119; *Congressional Record*, Senate (1964), 14243.

### CHAPTER 12

1. Hochschild, "Dissent," 82; Nicholas, "Academic Dissent," 215–230.

2. *Austin American-Statesman*, September 28, 1919; Nicholas, "Academic Dissent," 225.

3. WPH to Cohen, February 14, 1920, and E. L. Doheny to Cohen, February 17, 1920, Henry Cohen Papers, DBCAH.

4. Kennedy, *Over Here*, 279, 281–282; Hine, *Black Victory*, 88–89; Hochschild, "Dissent," 84.

5. For the definitive account of the Houston race riot, see R. Haynes, *Night of Violence*.

6. Swanson, *Cult of Glory*, 296; Harris and Sadler, *Texas Rangers*, 466.

7. Harris and Sadler.

8. Durham, "Longview Race Riot"; Harris and Sadler, *Texas Rangers*, 466.

9. *Dallas Morning News*, July 12–19, 1919; Durham, "Longview Race Riot"; *Longview Daily Leader*, July 11, 1919; Swanson, *Cult of Glory*, 296; Tuttle, "'Heathen' Land."

10. Harris and Sadler, *Texas Rangers*, 468.

11. Rucker and Upton, *American Race Riots*, 92–93; *NYT*, July 28, 1919.

12. WPH to Palmer, July 29, 1919, Governor WPH Sr. Papers, TSLAC.

13. Harris and Sadler, *Texas Rangers*, 468; Swanson, *Cult of Glory*, 297.

14. According to Doug Swanson, Shillady "never recovered physically or mentally from the beating" and soon resigned from the NAACP. Swanson, *Cult of Glory*, 298; NAACP, "Mobbing of Shillady"; *Austin American-Statesman*, August 22, 1919; Schmidt, *Red Scare*, 180; *NYT*, August 23, 1919; Hine, *Black Victory*.

15. *Austin American-Statesman*, September 28, 1919; Gould, *Progressives and Prohibitionists*, 253.

### CHAPTER 13

1. Daniel, Daniel, and Blodgett, *Governor's Mansion*, 66; WPH to King, August 14, 1919, and WPH to Jacoway, September 9, 1919, Governor WPH Sr. Papers, TSLAC.

2. WPH to George F. Howard, May 10, 1920, Governor WPH Sr. Papers, TSLAC; WPH to "Barney" Baruch, February 5, 1921, Bernard M. Baruch Papers, Special Collections, Princeton University Library (hereafter Princeton).

3. Governor Allan Shivers, who served from 1949 to 1957, would be the first to break the two-term tradition. Daniel, Daniel, and Blodgett, *Governor's Mansion*, 66; Clark, *Tactful Texan*, 126.

4. Clark, 124, 126.

5. *El Paso Herald*, August 29, 1919.

6. *El Paso Herald*, August 29, 1919; Gould, *Progressives and Prohibitionists*, 261; Link, *Wilson*.

7. Clark, *Tactful Texan*, 125; WPH to Kirby, March 31, 1919, Governor WPH Sr. Papers, TSLAC; Kirby to WPH, April 4, 1919, Kirby Lumber Company Records, ETRC.

8. Gould, *Progressives and Prohibitionists*, 262–267; Clark, *Tactful Texan*, 127.

9. Clark, 126–127.

10. Dexter Hamilton to Crane, February 21, 1920, and Crane to Mrs. A. N. McCallum, March 13, 1920, Martin McNulty Crane Papers, DBCAH; Clark, *Tactful Texan*, 126–127.

11. Andrews to WPH, March 22, 1920, Frank Andrews Papers, STCL; Gould, *Progressives and Prohibitionists*, 263.

12. Clark, *Tactful Texan*, 128–129; Gould, *Progressives and Prohibitionists*, 266–269; WPH to George F. Howard, May 10, 1920, Governor WPH Sr. Papers, TSLAC.

13. Clark, *Tactful Texan*, 130–132; Jackson, "Petticoat Politics," 26; *Texas House Journal*, Thirty-Sixth Legislature, fourth called session, 1920.

14. *San Antonio Express*, April 16, 1920; Fitzgerald, *Governors*.

15. *Austin American-Statesman*, undated news clip, WPH Sr. biographical file, DBCAH; Daniel, Daniel, and Blodgett, *Governor's Mansion*, 87.

16. Brown, *Little Brown Jug*, 16–17; Gould, *Progressives and Prohibitionists*, 277; Holcomb, "Bailey, Joseph Weldon."

17. Clark, *Tactful Texan*, 120.

18. *Austin American-Statesman*, March 15, 1920; Clark, *Tactful Texan*, 121.

19. Clark, 121.

20. This discussion of the Galveston labor strike of 1920 is based primarily on Angel, "Controlling the Workers"; Maroney, "Galveston Longshoremen's Strike"; and Abel, "Closed Shop" (2013).

Readers interested in more information about the episode should consult these scholars' excellent work.

21. Wakstein, "Open-Shop Movement," 460–475; Abel, "Closed Shop" (2013), 188.

22. Clark, *Tactful Texan*, 133; Maroney, "Galveston Longshoremen's Strike"; Abel, "Closed Shop" (2013), 189.

23. Abel, 190–191.

24. In one of his letters to Will, Kirby wrote that the Industrial Workers of the World "is a criminal organization." John Henry Kirby to WPH, June 28, 1912, Kirby Lumber Company Records, ETRC. List of donors is from an undated news clip from the *San Antonio Express*, WPH Sr. Papers, DBCAH.

25. Clark, *Tactful Texan*, 132–133; Abel, "Closed Shop" (2013), 193–194, 196.

26. Clark, *Tactful Texan*, 133; Abel, "Closed Shop" (2013), 192–194.

27. Clark, *Tactful Texan*, 133; see also Maroney, "Galveston Longshoremen's Strike."

28. Hobby's declaration of martial law and his order to Texas National Guard units to occupy Galveston was not a unique incident in the United States during this period of postwar labor unrest. Other cities were placed under martial law, including Gary, Indiana, and Cleveland, Ohio, and strikes were ruthlessly suppressed. Hochschild, "Dissent," 82–84; Clark, *Tactful Texan*, 133; Abel, "Closed Shop" (2013), 193–194.

29. Abel, 188, 197; WPH to Cope, June 10, 1920, Governor WPH Sr. Papers, TSLAC.

30. Abel, "Closed Shop" (2013), 200.

31. Abel, 201; Clark, *Tactful Texan*, 134; Gantt, *Chief Executive*, 157.

32. Abel, "Closed Shop" (2013), 202–203.

33. Abel, 197, 203, 204; *Houston Post*, September 1, 1920; Clark, *Tactful Texan*, 135.

34. Clark, 135.

35. *Galveston News*, September 20, 1920; undated news clip, *Houston Chronicle*, WPH Sr. Papers, DBCAH; *Texas House Journal*, Thirty-Sixth Legislature, fourth called session, 1920.

36. WPH to Sid Compton, September 14, 1920, Governor WPH Sr. Papers, TSLAC.

37. Abel, "Closed Shop" (2013), 201–202, 205; Clark, *Tactful Texan*, 135.

38. WPH to W. D. Cope, September 21, 1920, Governor WPH Sr. Papers, TSLAC.

39. *Texas House Journal*, Thirty-Sixth Legislature, fourth called session, 1920; *Dallas Dispatch*, September 24, 1920; WPH to Sid Compton, September 14, 1920, Governor WPH Sr. Papers, TSLAC.

40. After the special session adjourned, Will and Willie traveled to Dallas on October 23 to attend the marriage of Will's sister Mary to Joseph Amis, a pharmacist from Fort Worth. The wedding ceremony took place at Edwin Hobby's home. *Galveston News*, October 27, 1920; *Houston Post*, October 4, 1920; Clark, *Tactful Texan*, 136–137.

41. Ed Kilman, "History of the *Houston Post*," OCH Papers, Rice; Abel, "Closed Shop" (2013), 210.

CHAPTER 14

1. *Fort Worth Record*, September 9, 1920.

2. *Louisville (KY) Herald*, October 7, 1920.

3. Hindman, "Diplomacy by Proxy," 179; unidentified newspaper clip, August 31, 1919, in WPH Sr. biographical File, DBCAH; Clark, *Tactful Texan*, 140.

4. *Austin American-Statesman*, September 28, 1919; Clark, *Tactful Texan*, 140.

5. Harris and Sadler, *Texas Rangers*, 491.

6. Harris and Sadler, *Texas Rangers*, viii, 143, 384, 503, and "Reyes Conspiracy," 325–348.

7. Harris and Sadler, "Reyes Conspiracy," 335.

8. Hall, *Álvaro Obregón*; Krause, *Harding*, 395–413.

9. *El Paso Times*, October 7, 1920; Harris and Sadler, "Reyes Conspiracy," 325–348; Clark, *Tactful Texan*, 140.

10. *El Paso Times*, October 7, 1920; Clark, *Tactful Texan*, 141.

11. Walter, "Octaviano Ambrosio Larrazolo," 101; Hall, "Schizophrenic Border," 132–133.

12. The popular cartoon strip *Mutt and Jeff* featured Mutt, who was tall, and Jeff, who was very short. Historian Linda Hall writes that Will Hobby "did not indicate which was to be Mutt and which Jeff, but the sentiment was clear." Hall also notes that Will's comment was "inappropriate" given Mexican feelings about American treatment of Mexico historically but that "more important, [Will Hobby] advocated immediate recognition." Hall, "Schizophrenic Border," 132–133; *El Paso Herald*, October 9, 1920.

13. Hindman, "Diplomacy by Proxy," 202, 204; *Commerce and Finance*, vol. 9, October 27, 1920, p. 1544; *Dallas Morning News*, October 17, 1920.

14. Clark, *Tactful Texan*, 141–142; *Houston Post*, October 18, 1920; *Houston Chronicle*, October 20, 1920.

15. *Dallas Morning News*, October 17 and 19, 1920; *Houston Post*, October 20, 1920; Clark, *Tactful Texan*, 141.

16. WPH to Obregón, October 21, 1920, Governor WPH Sr. Papers, TSLAC; *Houston Post*, October 22, 1920; Clark, *Tactful Texan*, 141–142.

17. *Fort Worth Star-Telegram*, October 31, 1920; *Waco Times-Herald*, October 31, 1920; *San Antonio Light*, October 29, 1920.

18. Among those who responded to Will's call for donations was John Henry Kirby. The cost estimate for building the hospital proved to be low. Eventually the Texas Department of Health assumed responsibility for the project and completed the hospital's construction. Kirby to WPH, October 21, 1920, Kirby Lumber Company Records, ETRC; *Beaumont Journal*, November 3, 1920; Clark, *Tactful Texan*, 138–139.

19. The senators traveling with Harding were Joseph Frelinghuysen, Frederick Hale, and Davis Elkins. Will Hobby's entourage also included Chester Bryan, Harris County judge; H. A. Wroe, president of the American National Bank in Austin; Mr. and Mrs. Harry Wiess; and Will's secretary, Raymond Brooks. Caesar and Robert Kleberg boarded the train at the King Ranch's Norias station. *NYT*, November 10, 1920; Russell, *Blooming Grove*, 420, 438; Krause, *Harding*, 135–136; *Brownsville Herald*, November 17, 1920.

20. *Brownsville Herald*, November 17, 1920.

21. Farrell and Silverthorne, *First Ladies*, 304; *Dallas News*, November 17, 1920.

22. *Dallas News*, November 17, 1920; Clark, *Tactful Texan*, 139.

23. Krause, *Harding*, 135–136; Torres to Chapa, November 24, 1920, Francisco A. Chapa Family Papers, Special Collections, University of Texas at San Antonio Libraries (hereafter UTSA).

24. Hall, "Schizophrenic Border," 53–54; Russell, *Blooming Grove*, 634–636.

25. *Dallas News*, November 17, 1920.

26. Undated and unidentified news clipping in Willie Hobby's scrapbook, WPH Sr. Papers, DBCAH; Russell, *Blooming Grove*, 421; P. Payne, *Dead Last*.

27. Telegram, Torres to Chapa, November 24, 1920, and telegram, Ralph Soape to Chapa, November 19, 1920, Francisco A. Chapa Family Papers, UTSA.

28. *NYT*, November 27, 1920.

29. *Dallas News*, December 2, 1920; undated news clips from unidentified newspapers in Willie Hobby's scrapbook, WPH Sr. Papers, DBCAH.

30. *Dallas News*, December 2, 1920; undated news clips from unidentified newspapers in Willie Hobby's scrapbook, WPH Sr. Papers, DBCAH.

31. *Dallas News*, December 2, 1920; Daniel, Daniel, and Blodgett, *Governor's Mansion*, 90, 136; Clark, *Tactful Texan*, 150.

32. Undated news clips from unidentified newspapers in Willie Hobby's scrapbook, WPH Sr. Papers, DBCAH; *Dallas News*, December 3, 1920; Farrell and Silverthorne, *First Ladies*, 295.

33. *Austin American-Statesman*, December 5, 1920.

34. Almaráz, *Knight without Armor*, 359.

35. The Coolidge-Obregón treaty was unpopular in Mexico because it was seen as a sellout to American oil companies and a violation of the country's sovereignty. Obregón served as president until 1924, but during his last year in office he was forced to suppress a rebellion by his former ally (and Willie Hobby's seatmate at Obregón's inauguration) Adolfo de la Huerta, who barely escaped execution to find asylum in Los Angeles, California. After retiring to Sonora to manage his agricultural holdings, Obregón ran again for president of Mexico in 1928 and won, but he was assassinated before he took the oath of office. Edwin Hobby to McAdoo, December 20, 1920, William Gibbs McAdoo Papers, LOC; Hall, "Schizophrenic Border."

36. Undated news clips from unidentified newspaper in Willie Hobby's scrapbook, WPH Sr. Papers, DBCAH; Clark, *Tactful Texan*, 149.

37. The so-called Brackenridge Tract remains university property, although debates about its future use continue. *Austin American-Statesman*, April 27, 1958; Brown, *Little Brown Jug*, 31–32.

38. Typescript of notes taken during interview with WPH conducted by "J.D.M.," October 1, 1952, WPH Sr. Papers, DBCAH; Farrell and Silverthorne, *First Ladies*, 303; Daniel, Daniel, and Blodgett, *Governor's Mansion*, 156–157; Clark, *Tactful Texan*, 150.

39. Weldon Hart, typescript notes, ca. 1954, James Clark Papers, Rice; Clark, *Tactful Texan*, 144–146.

40. Brown, *Little Brown Jug*, 26; Clark, *Tactful Texan*, 144–146; B. Hobby, *How Things Really Work*, 10; Weldon Hart, typescript notes, ca. 1954, James Clark Papers, Rice.

41. Bill Hobby, interview; B. Hobby, *How Things Really Work*, 10.

42. Crane to WPH, August 5, 1920, Martin McNulty Crane Papers, DBCAH; Raymond Brooks, *Austin American-Statesman*, April 27, 1958; Schmelzer, "Campbell, Thomas Mitchell."

CHAPTER 15

1. Morrison & Fourmy, *Beaumont Directory*, 1923; Bill Hobby, interview; *Fourth Estate*, January 17, 1920.
2. Clark, *Tactful Texan*, 151–152.
3. Baruch to WPH, February 10, 1921, and WPH to Baruch, February 5, 1921, Bernard M. Baruch Papers, Princeton.
4. Stratton, *Story of Beaumont*, 114; Ed Kilman, "History of the *Houston Post*," OCH Papers, Rice; Clark, *Tactful Texan*, 151.
5. Clark, 151.
6. Clark, 151–152.
7. Clark, 152.
8. Clark, 152; Hardin, "Hobby, TX."
9. Rienstra and Linsley, *Historic Beaumont*, 62–63; Alexander, *Crusade for Conformity*, 5–9, 10, 31.
10. Alexander, *Crusade for Conformity*, 17, 18, 31.
11. Wagner, "Culberson, Charles Allen"; Brown, *Little Brown Jug*, 112–114, 116.
12. Wagner, "Culberson, Charles Allen"; Brown, *Little Brown Jug*, 112–114, 116.
13. Brown, *Little Brown Jug*, 112–114, 116; news clipping from unidentified newspaper, 1921, WPH Sr. biographical file, DBCAH.
14. Rienstra and Linsley, *Historic Beaumont*, 62–63; Alexander, *Crusade for Conformity*, 17–19, 31, 78–79.
15. Clark, *Tactful Texan*, 152–153.
16. Jim Mapes's wife, Kathryn, continued to own and manage the *Enterprise* and the *Journal* until she died in 1948. In 1983 the two newspapers were combined into one. Clark, *Tactful Texan*, 152–153; Kleiner, "Beaumont Enterprise"; Wooster, "Crawford, Walter Joshua."
17. Clark, *Tactful Texan*, 153.
18. *Best's Insurance News*, July 10, 1922, p. 34; John Henry Kirby to WPH, September 1, 1921, Kirby Lumber Company Records, ETRC.
19. Frank Andrews to WPH, February 3 and May 19, 1922, and WPH to Andrews, February 6, 1922, WPH Sr. Papers, DBCAH.
20. Andrews continued to be Will Hobby's attorney until Andrews's death in December 1936. Frank Andrews to New York Life Insurance Company, July 8, 1936, and WPH to Andrews, July 22, 1936, WPH Sr. Papers, DBCAH; Baker, "Andrews, Frank"; Clark, *Tactful Texan*, 152–153; WPH to Frank Andrews, September 18, 1922, Andrews to WPH, October 10 and 20, 1922, and Andrews to Ralph Kimball, October 20, 1922, WPH Family Papers, DBCAH.
21. Hyman, *Craftsmanship and Character*, 56, 160–164.
22. Unidentified news clippings in Willie Hobby's scrapbook, September 29, 1922, WPH Sr. Papers, DBCAH; Morrison & Fourmy, *Houston Directory*, 1925; Brown, *Little Brown Jug*, 99–104, 179; McKay, *Texas Politics*, 112.
23. WPH to Baruch, March 30 and September 30, 1925, Baruch to WPH, November 20, 1925, WPH to Baruch, November 15, 1926, and Baruch to WPH, November 29, 1926, Bernard M. Baruch Papers, Princeton; W. Haynes, *Stone That Burns*.
24. Farrell and Silverthorne, *First Ladies*, 305–306; Anna Pennybacker to WPH, ca. January 1929, in *Tributes in Memory of Willie Cooper Hobby* (Houston: Will Hobby, 1929).
25. Typescript of notes from James Clark's interview with Wright Morrow, ca. 1954, James Clark Papers, Rice; Sterling and Kilman, *Ross Sterling*, 60.
26. Sterling and Kilman, *Ross Sterling*, 61; Ed Kilman, "History of the *Houston Post*," OCH Papers, Rice.
27. Sterling paid $1,150,000 for the *Post*. Watson issued a statement explaining, "I have chosen to ignore offers from Eastern publishers to the end that ownership of *Post* control may remain here in Houston in the hands of men known for their civic activities and home-interest." Undated clipping, *Houston Chronicle*, Willie Hobby's scrapbook, WPH Sr. Papers, DBCAH; Sterling and Kilman, *Ross Sterling*, 62–63; *Fourth Estate*, August 2, 1924; *NYT*, July 30, 1924.
28. Will's happiness about returning to his old newspaper was tempered by the fact that Walter Crawford had died suddenly from a massive stroke only five months earlier. Crawford was one of Will's best friends and closest political operatives who, seventeen years earlier, had been the person most responsible for Will's move to Beaumont to become the editor of the *Enterprise*. Kleiner, "Beaumont Enterprise"; Wooster, "Crawford, Walter Joshua"; *Houston Post*, July 30, 1924; Sterling and Kilman, *Ross Sterling*, 64; Ed Kilman, "History of the *Houston Post*," OCH Papers, Rice.

29. Clark, *Tactful Texan*, 159–160; unidentified news clippings, Rienzi Johnston Papers, Rice; Ed Kilman, "History of the *Houston Post*," OCH Papers, Rice; *NYT*, March 29, 1989.

30. Sterling and Kilman, *Ross Sterling*, 64–65; Ed Kilman, "History of the *Houston Post*," OCH Papers, Rice.

31. *Houston Post-Dispatch*, August 1, 1924.

32. Clark, *Tactful Texan*, 156–157; *Houston Post-Dispatch*, August 1, 1924.

33. Clark, *Tactful Texan*, 156–157; *Houston Post-Dispatch*, August 1, 1924.

34. Sterling and Kilman, *Ross Sterling*, 64; Hall, "Schizophrenic Border," 136; *Houston Post-Dispatch*, September–December 1924.

35. Brown, *Little Brown Jug*, 211–238.

36. Sterling and Kilman, *Ross Sterling*, 67; Clark, *Tactful Texan*, 157.

37. Sterling and Kilman, *Ross Sterling*, 67.

38. Sterling and Kilman.

39. Clark, *Tactful Texan*, 157–158; Brown, *Little Brown Jug*, 250–251.

CHAPTER 16

1. Sterling and Kilman, *Ross Sterling*, 60.

2. Sterling and Kilman, 68–69.

3. Sterling and Kilman, 69; Clark, *Tactful Texan*, 158.

4. Clark, 158.

5. Sterling and Kilman, *Ross Sterling*, 69; Clark, *Tactful Texan*, 158.

6. Sterling and Kilman, *Ross Sterling*, 69–70.

7. M. Johnston, *Houston*, 244; Sterling and Kilman, *Ross Sterling*, 70.

8. Sterling and Kilman, 69–70.

9. According to historian Norman Brown, despite all the rumors, "no clear-cut evidence was ever offered" that the Fergusons sold pardons. Brown, *Little Brown Jug*, 270–271, 273, 284–292; Sterling and Kilman, *Ross Sterling*, 79; Clark, *Tactful Texan*, 159.

10. Sterling and Kilman, *Ross Sterling*, 79; Brown, *Little Brown Jug*, 299, 301.

11. Brown, 309; Sterling and Kilman, *Ross Sterling*, 79; *Houston Post-Dispatch*, August 24, 1926.

12. Brown, *Little Brown Jug*, 326, 331; Ed Kilman, "History of the *Houston Post*," OCH Papers, Rice.

13. Brown, *Little Brown Jug*, 340, 358; Sterling and Kilman, *Ross Sterling*, 80, 89; Ed Kilman, "History of the *Houston Post*," OCH Papers, Rice.

14. Morrison & Fourmy, *Houston Directory*, October 1927; Ed Kilman, "History of the *Houston Post*," OCH Papers, Rice.

15. Two years prior to Edwin's death, his wife, Sadie, took her own life after suffering for several years with what was diagnosed as "nervous trouble," which in that era was the term often used to describe a mental illness such as acute anxiety or bipolar disorder. *Dallas Morning News*, November 23, 1927; Leach, *Sun Country Banker*, 56; Clark, *Tactful Texan*, 160.

16. Brown, *Little Brown Jug*, 406.

17. Fenberg, *Unprecedented Power*, 136–137, 140–141.

18. Clark, *Tactful Texan*, 162–163; Timmons, *Jesse H. Jones*, 146.

19. Final Report, Committee on Arrangements, National Democratic Convention, July 24, 1928, Will C. Hogg Papers, DBCAH; Clark, *Tactful Texan*, 162.

20. *Houston Post-Dispatch*, June 28 and 29, 1928; Walsh, "Oveta Culp Hobby" (2006), 57; Fenberg, *Unprecedented Power*, 152–157; Pando, "Oveta Culp Hobby," 46–47.

21. *Houston Post-Dispatch*, June 28 and 29, 1928; Walsh, "Oveta Culp Hobby" (2006), 57; Fenberg, *Unprecedented Power*, 152–157; Hogg to Ike Ashburn, May 30, 1928, Will C. Hogg Papers, DBCAH.

22. Fenberg, *Unprecedented Power*, 161; Timmons, *Jesse H. Jones*, 147; Clark, *Tactful Texan*, 163; McKay, *Texas Politics*, 160–161.

23. McKay, 160–161, 165; Clark, *Tactful Texan*, 164.

24. McKay, *Texas Politics*, 176–177; Clark, *Tactful Texan*, 164.

25. Clark, 165.

26. Morrison & Fourmy, *Houston Directory*, 1929–1930, p. 970; Anchorage Foundation, *Braeswood*, 6; Drexel Turner, *Houston Chronicle*, August 21, 2013.

27. *Houston Post-Dispatch*, January 15, 1929; Farrell and Silverthorne, *First Ladies*, 306; Pennybacker to WPH, in *Tributes in Memory of Willie Cooper Hobby* (Houston: Will Hobby, 1929).

28. *Texas Senate Journal*, Forty-First Legislature, regular session, 1929, pp. 60, 150; *Brownwood Bulletin*, January 16, 1929; *Houston Chronicle*, January 15, 1927.

29. *Tributes in Memory of Willie Cooper Hobby* (Houston: Will Hobby, 1929).

30. With Willie's death, Florence Stratton drifted away from Will, although she continued to write a popular column, Susie Spindletop's Weekly Letter, for the *Beaumont Enterprise* until the mid-1930s. In 1931, she published *The White Plume, or O. Henry's Own Short Story*, a book

about William Sydney Porter's early love life. She died in New Orleans in 1938. Paul, "Florence Stratton," *Rediscovering Southeast Texas* (blog), October 10, 2012, https://www.rediscovering setx.com/2012/10/10/florence-stratton/; *Houston Post-Dispatch*, January 15, 1929; Farrell and Silverthorne, *First Ladies*, 303, 306; *Tributes in Memory of Willie Cooper Hobby* (Houston: Will Hobby, 1929).

CHAPTER 17

1. Walsh, "Oveta Culp Hobby" (2006), 23; Pando, "Oveta Culp Hobby," 49–50.
2. Bill Hobby, interview; Pando, "Oveta Culp Hobby," 50; Walsh, "Oveta Culp Hobby" (2006), 38.
3. That Oveta and her two children were all born on January 19 was such an oddity that the popular comic strip *Ripley's Believe It or Not!* featured the fact in its nationally syndicated cartoon published on August 28, 1942, after she had gained fame as commander of the WAAC. Clipping in OCH Papers, Dwight D. Eisenhower Presidential Library (hereafter DDEPL); *Texas House Journal*, January 18, 1905, p. 123; Bill Hobby, interview; *Time*, May 4, 1953, pp. 24–27.
4. *Time*, May 4, 1953, pp. 24–27; Marguerite Johnston, "The Early Years," in Shire, *Oveta Culp Hobby*, 55.
5. Texas State Historical Association, "Baptist Church," 85; genealogical records in the William P. Hobby Jr. (hereafter Bill Hobby) Papers, DBCAH.
6. Genealogical records, Bill Hobby Papers, DBCAH; Paddock, *Central and Western Texas*, 607–608.
7. Genealogical records, Bill Hobby Papers, DBCAH; Bell County Historical Commission, *Bell County*, 2:623; Paddock, *Central and Western Texas*, 607–608.
8. The Culp home was located at the corner of Eighth Street and Rancier Avenue in Killeen. *Killeen Herald*, May 26, 1905; Bell County Historical Commission, *Bell County*, 2:142, 151, 623; Walsh, "Oveta Culp Hobby" (2006), 9; Paddock, *Central and Western Texas*, 607–608; genealogical records, Bill Hobby Papers, DBCAH; Wharton, *Many Flags*, 183; Pando, "Oveta Culp Hobby," 17.
9. *Time*, May 4, 1953, p. 25; Pando, "Oveta Culp Hobby," 18.
10. *NYT*, August 17, 1995; Liz Carpenter, "Tribute to Oveta Culp Hobby," typescript of speech, January 19, 1986, Bill Hobby Papers, DBCAH.
11. *Time*, May 4, 1953, p. 25.
12. News clip from *Killeen Daily Herald*, March 5, 1972, Bill Hobby Papers, DBCAH; news clip from *Killeen Daily Herald*, May 1, 1983, and Peggy Buchanan to Mattie Treadwell, July 12, 1995, OCH Papers, Rice; Pando, "Oveta Culp Hobby," 20.
13. *Time*, May 4, 1953, p. 24; Marguerite Johnston, "The Early Years," in Shire, *Oveta Culp Hobby*, 55; Pando, "Oveta Culp Hobby," 19.
14. *Time*, May 4, 1953, p. 24; Marguerite Johnston, "The Early Years," in Shire, *Oveta Culp Hobby*, 55; Pando, "Oveta Culp Hobby," 19.
15. Marguerite Johnston, "The Widening Wake," in Shire, *Oveta Culp Hobby*, 77.
16. Blair, "Woman Soldier," 40–41; Pando, "Oveta Culp Hobby," 44; Marguerite Johnston's notes, OCH Papers, Rice.
17. Blair, "Woman Soldier," 40–41; Pando, "Oveta Culp Hobby," 44; Marguerite Johnston's notes, OCH Papers, Rice.
18. Marguerite Johnston, "The Widening Wake," 77; Blair, "Woman Soldier," 40–41; Pando, "Oveta Culp Hobby," 25.
19. Blair, "Woman Soldier," 40–41; Marguerite Johnston, "The Early Years," in Shire, *Oveta Culp Hobby*, 56; Hurt, "Great Ladies," 146–147.
20. Pando, "Oveta Culp Hobby," 20; Liz Carpenter, typescript of speech, "Tribute to Oveta Culp Hobby," January 19, 1986, Bill Hobby Papers, DBCAH; Lynn Culp Loving, "My Sister, Oveta," in Shire, *Oveta Culp Hobby*, v.
21. Pando, "Oveta Culp Hobby," 44; Marguerite Johnston's notes, OCH Papers, Rice.
22. Pando, "Oveta Culp Hobby," 25.
23. Liz Carpenter, "Tribute to Oveta Culp Hobby," typescript of speech, January 19, 1986, Bill Hobby Papers, DBCAH.
24. Portrait of Ike and Emma Culp in Shire, *Oveta Culp Hobby*, 22.
25. Pando, "Oveta Culp Hobby," 21–22.
26. Pando, "Oveta Culp Hobby."
27. Lynn Culp Loving, "My Sister, Oveta," in Shire, *Oveta Culp Hobby*, v; Blair, "Woman Soldier," 41.
28. Lynn Culp Loving, "My Sister, Oveta," in Shire, *Oveta Culp Hobby*, v; *Time*, May 4, 1953, p. 25; *NYT*, August 17, 1995; Walsh, "Oveta Culp Hobby" (2006), 15; Marguerite Johnston to Hope Stoddard, ca. August 1968, and November 4, 1968, OCH Papers, Rice.
29. Wharton, *Many Flags*, 183.
30. OCH to Mashburn, April 2, 1984, OCH Papers,

Rice; Walsh, "Oveta Culp Hobby" (2006), 13; Liz Carpenter, "Tribute to Oveta Culp Hobby," typescript of speech, January 19, 1986, Bill Hobby Papers, DBCAH.

31. Pando, "Oveta Culp Hobby," 23–24; Liz Carpenter, "Tribute to Oveta Culp Hobby," typescript of speech, January 19, 1986, Bill Hobby Papers, DBCAH.

32. *NYT*, August 17, 1995; Blair, "Woman Soldier," 41; OCH to "Miss Mashburn," April 2, 1984, OCH Papers, Rice; Walsh, "Oveta Culp Hobby," (2006), 15; Pando, "Oveta Culp Hobby," 24.

33. Thomason found Oveta a job with the House Jurisprudence and Judiciary Committee. R. E. Thomason, interview, LBJPL.

34. *Texas House Journal*, Thirty-Sixth Legislature, second called session, July 11, 1919, pp. 376–377.

35. For example, see *Texas House Journal*, Thirty-Sixth Legislature, p. 662.

36. Marguerite Johnston, "The Early Years," in Shire, *Oveta Culp Hobby*, 56; Pando, "Oveta Culp Hobby," 24.

37. Pando, "Oveta Culp Hobby," 25; Marguerite Johnston, "The Early Years," in Shire, *Oveta Culp Hobby*, 56; *Time*, May 4, 1953, p. 25.

38. Pando, "Oveta Culp Hobby," 24; *Time*, May 4, 1953, p. 25.

39. Pando, "Oveta Culp Hobby," 25–26; OCH to Miss Mashburn, April 2, 1984, OCH Papers, Rice; Marguerite Johnston, "The Early Years," in Shire, *Oveta Culp Hobby*, 56.

40. When the banking laws were published, Oveta Culp's work was acknowledged on the title page. Charles O. Austin, *State Banking Laws of Texas* (Austin, 1927); Pando, "Oveta Culp Hobby," 29; Walsh, "Oveta Culp Hobby" (2006), 10; OCH to Miss Mashburn, April 2, 1984, OCH Papers, Rice; *Time*, May 4, 1953; Bill Hobby, interview; Hurt, "Great Ladies," 147.

41. *Time*, May 4, 1953.

42. *Time*, May 4, 1953; J. R. Parten, interview.

43. Jesse Ziegler to mother, 1933, Jesse D. Ziegler Papers, DBCAH.

44. Duggan, "Poage, William Robert"; Bob Poage to Oveta Culp, February 20, 1931, OCH Papers, Rice.

45. Undated news clip, OCH Papers, Rice.

46. Ike Culp to Oveta, January 19, 1926, OCH Papers, Rice.

CHAPTER 18

1. McArthur, "Sterling, Florence M."

2. McArthur.

3. In the late 1960s, Oveta claimed she did not move to Houston because of Flo Sterling's invitation, but the evidence is contradictory. She acknowledged, however, that her first residence in the city was Sterling's home. In addition, when Oveta ran for a seat in the Texas Legislature in 1930, Sterling wrote an editorial endorsing Oveta's candidacy, declaring that as the two had an "unusual relation of intimacy it had given Sterling an opportunity to see and study her, as is seldom afforded." In her 1954 book *Ladies of Courage*, Eleanor Roosevelt wrote, "In Houston, [Oveta] lived with the sister of Ross Sterling, millionaire oil man who later became Governor of Texas" (228). See also Marguerite Johnston to Hope Stoddard, ca. August 1968, and November 4, 1968; Sterling quote is in the *Houston Mirror*, undated news clip, OCH Papers, Rice; Clark, *Tactful Texan*, 172; Walsh, "Oveta Culp Hobby" (2015), 321.

4. Pando, "Oveta Culp Hobby," 27; Morrison & Fourmy, *Houston Directory*, 1926, p. 673; Walsh, "Oveta Culp Hobby" (2006), 27.

5. Collier, "Woman's Viewpoint"; McArthur, "Sterling, Florence M."

6. Walsh, "Oveta Culp Hobby" (2006), 16; *Houston Post-Dispatch* circular to staff, December 12, 1925, OCH Papers, Rice; *Time*, May 4, 1953; *NY Daily News*, March 21, 1953; Marguerite Johnston's notes, OCH Papers, Rice.

7. Al Shire, "That Reminds Me," in Shire, *Oveta Culp Hobby*, 71; B. Scott, *Such Interesting People*, 19–20.

8. Walsh, "Oveta Culp Hobby" (2015), 333; OCH to Miss Mashburn, April 2, 1984, OCH Papers, Rice.

9. Bill Hobby, interview; *San Angelo Standard-Times*, April 16, 1972.

10. Robert Pando confirmed that the biographical sketches Oveta prepared for her official government personnel documents were accurate. Pando, "Oveta Culp Hobby," 24; *Time*, February 14, 1944; *Austin Directory*, May 1927.

11. Walsh, "Oveta Culp Hobby" (2015), 322.

12. Pando, "Oveta Culp Hobby," 29.

13. Blair, "Woman Soldier," 43–48; Pando, "Oveta Culp Hobby," 27–28; Walsh, "Oveta Culp Hobby" (2006), 39; OCH to Miss Mashburn, April 2, 1984, OCH Papers, Rice.

14. John Henry Kirby to WPH, September 6, 1914, and WPH to Kirby, September 10, 1914, C. Read Granberry Papers, DBCAH.

15. *Texas House Journal*, Thirty-Ninth Legislature, first called session, p. 4; Associated Press, undated news clip, OCH Papers, Rice.

16. Walsh, "Oveta Culp Hobby" (2006), 20; Bill Hobby, interview.

17. *Texas House Journal*, Thirty-Ninth Legislature, first called session, p. 4; Bill Hobby, interview.

18. Blair, "Woman Soldier," 43–48; Pando, "Oveta Culp Hobby," 27–28; Ed Kilman, "History of the *Houston Post*," OCH Papers, Rice; *Houston Post-Dispatch*, January 14, 1927, and June 25, 1930; Walsh, "Oveta Culp Hobby" (2006), 30.

19. Pando, "Oveta Culp Hobby," 30; Blair, "Woman Soldier," 43–48.

20. Morrison & Fourmy, *Houston Directory*, 1928; *Austin Directory*, 1929–1930.

21. Walsh, "Oveta Culp Hobby" (2006), 16–17; Pando, "Oveta Culp Hobby," 47; Sutphen, "Conservative Warrior," 11–12.

22. Gano, "Sharp, Walter Benona."

23. Marguerite Johnston, typescript, Bill Hobby Papers, DBCAH; Sutphen, "Conservative Warrior," 12; Walsh, "Oveta Culp Hobby" (2015), 321.

24. Sutphen, "Conservative Warrior," 11–12; Marguerite Johnston, typescript, Bill Hobby Papers, DBCAH.

25. Pando, "Oveta Culp Hobby," 38–39; Marguerite Johnston, typescript, Bill Hobby Papers, DBCAH.

26. Marguerite Johnston, typescript, Bill Hobby Papers, DBCAH; OCH to Mrs. Charles Dunbar Jr., ca. 1933, OCH Papers, Rice; Pando, "Oveta Culp Hobby," 47–48.

27. Walsh, "Oveta Culp Hobby" (2006), 21, 23.

28. Walsh, 30–31; Pando, "Oveta Culp Hobby," 47.

29. "Minutes of the Executive Committee Meeting, June 8, 1928," pp. 2–3, Will C. Hogg Papers, DBCAH.

30. West, "Thru the Lorgnon," 10; Walsh, "Oveta Culp Hobby" (2006), 30–31, and "Oveta Culp Hobby" (2015), 322.

31. Biles, *New Deal*, 23; Pando, "Oveta Culp Hobby," 48–49.

32. Shire, *Oveta Culp Hobby*, 57; OCH to Mrs. Joe P. Lehman, August 30, 1960, OCH Papers, Rice; Pando, "Oveta Culp Hobby," 49; Sutphen, "Conservative Warrior," 12.

33. *Houston Telephone Directory*, 1928; Morrison & Fourmy, *Houston Directory*, 1928; West, "Thru the Lorgnon"; *Houston Post-Dispatch*, June 24, 1930.

## CHAPTER 19

1. Pando, "Oveta Culp Hobby," 50; Walsh, "Oveta Culp Hobby" (2006), 28; M. Johnston, *Houston*, 286.

2. WPH to Oveta Culp, November 23 and December 1, 1929, WPH Sr. Papers, DBCAH; Sutphen, "Conservative Warrior," 13.

3. Sterling and Kilman, *Ross Sterling*, 93.

4. Dolph Briscoe Jr., interview; Sterling and Kilman, *Ross Sterling*, 73–74.

5. Sterling and Kilman, 74.

6. "James Young," in US Congress, *Biographical Directory*; Pando, "Oveta Culp Hobby," 50.

7. News clipping from unidentified newspaper, 1929, OCH Papers, DDEPL.

8. Walsh, "Oveta Culp Hobby" (2006), 33; Pando, "Oveta Culp Hobby," 50; La Forte, "Hughes, Sarah Tilghman."

9. Al Shire, "That Reminds Me," in Shire, *Oveta Culp Hobby*, 71; news clip, unidentified newspaper, ca. May 1930, OCH Papers, Rice.

10. *Houston Post-Dispatch*, June 24, 1930.

11. Benham, "Moore, Helen Edmunds"; Helen Moore to Oveta Culp, June 24, 1930, OCH Papers, Rice.

12. Walsh, "Oveta Culp Hobby" (2006), 26; unidentified news clipping, OCH biographical file, DBCAH; Walsh, "Oveta Culp Hobby" (2006), 35–36.

13. Johnson, *Texas and Texans*; Al Shire, "That Reminds Me," in Shire, *Oveta Culp Hobby*, 71; Pando, "Oveta Culp Hobby," 51.

14. Helen Moore to Oveta Culp, June 24, 1930, and undated news clipping from *Houston Mirror*, OCH Papers, Rice.

15. Pando, "Oveta Culp Hobby," 51; Walsh, "Oveta Culp Hobby" (2006), 26; Al Shire, "That Reminds Me," in Shire, *Oveta Culp Hobby*, 71.

16. The vote was 7,026 votes for Mathis and 4,594 for Oveta. Unidentified news clipping, OCH Papers, Rice; Al Shire, "That Reminds Me," in Shire, *Oveta Culp Hobby*, 57; Pando, "Oveta Culp Hobby," 51.

17. McKay, *Texas Politics*, 190; Sterling and Kilman, *Ross Sterling*, 94.

18. Sterling and Kilman, 99, 107; Helen Moore to Oveta, ca. June 1930, OCH Papers, Rice.

19. Sterling and Kilman, *Ross Sterling*, 114; McKay, *Texas Politics*, 202.

20. Sterling and Kilman, *Ross Sterling*, 120; McKay, *Texas Politics*, 207–208.

21. Sterling and Kilman, *Ross Sterling*, 127.

22. Sterling and Kilman, 125.

23. Sterling and Kilman, 129.

24. Will and Oveta's marriage does have the aura of a business deal, at least for Oveta, whose tangible affection for Will might have been enhanced by his prominence as a well-connected former governor and editor of one of the leading newspapers in Texas. Her friend journalist Liz Carpenter later observed, "Oveta courted power; she courted older men. That's why she was close to Jesse Jones and the [George] Browns." But this is speculation and will remain as such until and if new evidence ever surfaces to clarify Will and Oveta's relationship when they married. It should be stressed, however, that it is clear Will was in love and that Oveta obviously had deep respect and a fondness for Will that eventually deepened into love. Until further evidence appears, one is wise to keep in mind an observation Oveta made years later about Lyndon and Lady Bird Johnson: "I don't suppose anyone would really know how a husband and wife talk things out." *Texas House Journal*, Forty-Second Legislature, regular session, p. 46; Hurt, "Great Ladies," 148; Blair, "Woman Soldier," 41; Liz Carpenter and OCH interviews, LBJ Presidential Library (hereafter LBJPL).

25. Leach, *Sun Country Banker*, 114, 261.

26. Kohout, "Young, Samuel Doak"; Leach, *Sun Country Banker*, 114, 261; Bill Hobby, interview.

27. *Waco News-Tribune*, February 14, 1931; Bob Poage to Oveta, February 20, 1931, OCH Papers, Rice.

28. Walsh, "Oveta Culp Hobby" (2006), 40; Sterling and Kilman, *Ross Sterling*, 128, 130; Clark, *Tactful Texan*, 169.

29. Walsh, "Oveta Culp Hobby" (2015), 324; Pando, "Oveta Culp Hobby," 52; Sutphen, "Conservative Warrior," 14–15; Hurt, "Great Ladies," 148.

30. Pando, "Oveta Culp Hobby," 53; news clip in unidentified newspaper, 1931, C. Read Granberry Papers, DBCAH; Susan Barnes, in Shire, *Oveta Culp Hobby*, 5.

31. *Temple Daily Telegram*, February 24, 1931; *Time*, May 4, 1953.

32. Pando, "Oveta Culp Hobby," 51–52; Bill Hobby, interview.

33. Jessie Ziegler to mother, February 25 and March 10, 1931, Jessie D. Ziegler Papers, DBCAH.

34. M. Johnston, *Houston*, 286; Morrison & Fourmy, *Houston Directory*, 1929–1930, p. 970; Anchorage Foundation, *Braeswood*, 6; Drexel Turner, *Houston Chronicle*, August 21, 2013.

CHAPTER 20

1. Schlesinger, *Old Order*, 3.

2. Buenger and Pratt, *Good Business*, 90.

3. *Austin American-Statesman*, August 17, 1995; Clark, *Tactful Texan*, 168–174.

4. Blair, "Woman Soldier," 41.

5. Ziegler letters to her mother, April 6 and 7, 1931, Jessie D. Ziegler Papers, DBCAH; *Houston Post-Dispatch*, April 22, 1931.

6. Ziegler to mother, April 9, 1931, Jessie D. Ziegler Papers, DBCAH; Sterling and Kilman, *Ross Sterling*, 152.

7. Ziegler to mother, April 9, 1931, Jessie D. Ziegler Papers, DBCAH.

8. Weldon Hart, typescript of notes about WPH and typescript of notes of James Clark's interview with Wright Morrow, ca. 1954, James Clark Papers, Rice.

9. Weldon Hart, typescript notes, Wright Morrow interview, James Clark Papers, Rice.

10. "Robert Lee Henry," in US Congress, *Biographical Directory*; Ziegler to mother, October 31, 1931, Jessie D. Ziegler Papers, DBCAH; Clark, *Tactful Texan*, 169.

11. Clark, 169–170; Sterling and Kilman, *Ross Sterling*, 128, 161.

12. Sterling and Kilman, 182.

13. Leach, *Sun Country Banker*, 104.

14. Sterling and Kilman, *Ross Sterling*, 182–183.

15. Sterling and Kilman, 182–183; Fenberg, *Unprecedented Power*, 182–183.

16. Buenger and Pratt, *Good Business*, 98, 102–104; Timmons, *Jesse H. Jones*, 157–158.

17. Buenger and Pratt, *Good Business*, 98, 102–104; Timmons, *Jesse H. Jones*, 157–158.

18. Timmons, *Jesse H. Jones*, 156–161; Fenberg, *Unprecedented Power*, 182–183; Sterling and Kilman, *Ross Sterling*, 182–183; Ziegler to mother, October 31, 1931, Jessie D. Ziegler Papers, DBCAH.

19. Timmons, *Jesse H. Jones*, 159.

20. Buenger and Pratt, *Good Business*, 102–103; Timmons, *Jesse H. Jones*, 156–161; Ziegler to mother, October 31, 1931, Jessie D. Ziegler Papers, DBCAH; WPH to Advisory Committee, October 29, 1931, Jesse H. Jones Papers, DBCAH; Sterling and Kilman, *Ross Sterling*, 182–183.

21. Will's offer was to buy 4,412 shares of stock in the *Houston Post-Dispatch* from the Sterling Trust at $125 per share. He already owned 117 shares, which would give him a total of 4,529

shares. WPH to Advisory Committee, October 29, 1931, Jesse H. Jones Papers, DBCAH; Ziegler to mother, October 31, 1931, Jessie D. Ziegler Papers, DBCAH; Timmons, *Jesse H. Jones*, 156–161; *Time*, December 14, 1931.

22. WPH to Advisory Committee, November 2, 1931, Jesse H. Jones Papers, DBCAH; Timmons, *Jesse H. Jones*, 156–161; M. Johnston, *Houston*, 288; legal records, April 1931, OCH Papers, Rice.

23. Bascom Timmons, who wrote an authorized biography of Jesse Jones, admitted that the *Houston Post-Dispatch* was "purchased in the name of J. E. Josey," whose brother Robert Josey was "a close friend of Jones." Timmons's account of the deal, however, implies that Jones soon sold the paper to Will Hobby, failing to mention that the sale didn't occur until several years after Jones bought it. Timmons, *Jesse H. Jones*, 160–161; Weldon Hart, typescript of notes on history of the *Houston Post*, ca. 1954, James Clark Papers, Rice; *Time*, December 14, 1931; Clark, *Tactful Texan*, 171; Sterling and Kilman, *Ross Sterling*, 182–183; Bill Hobby, interview; Charles Marsh to E. M. House, November 29, 1932, Edward Mandell House Papers, Yale.

24. J. E. Josey to Advisory Committee, November 28, 1931, Jesse H. Jones Papers, DBCAH.

25. Sterling and Kilman, *Ross Sterling*, 182–183; Buenger and Pratt, *Good Business*, 75.

26. J. E. Josey to Sterling, December 23, 1931, Ross Sterling Papers, DBCAH.

27. Sterling and Kilman, *Ross Sterling*, 183; Clark, *Tactful Texan*, 170–171; Ed Kilman, "History of the *Houston Post*," OCH Papers, Rice; *Houston Post*, February 1, 1932.

28. Clark, *Tactful Texan*, 171; Ed Kilman, "History of the *Houston Post*," OCH Papers, Rice.

29. Clark, *Tactful Texan*, 171; undated news clipping, *Houston Chronicle*, 1932, WPH Sr. Papers, DBCAH.

30. Undated news clipping, *Houston Chronicle*, 1932, WPH Sr. Papers, DBCAH; *Dallas Morning News*, February 18, 1932; news clipping, March 4, 1932, OCH Papers, Rice.

31. John Henry Kirby to Oveta Hobby, January 21, 1932, James V. Allred to WPH, January 22, 1932, Bob Poage to Will and Oveta Hobby, January 20, 1932, WPH Sr. Papers, DBCAH.

32. Florence Sterling to Oveta and WPH, January 27, 1932, Thomas Love to WPH, January 20, 1932, Tom Connally to Bill Hobby, January 19,

1932, Ross Sterling and Dan Moody to WPH, January 20, 1932, WPH Sr. Papers, DBCAH; Ziegler to WPH, January 19, 1932, Jessie D. Ziegler Papers, DBCAH; Clark, *Tactful Texan*, 171; M. Johnston, *Houston*, 286.

33. Ziegler to mother, March 14, 1932, Jessie D. Ziegler Papers, DBCAH.

34. *New York Daily News*, March 21, 1953; Sutphen, "Conservative Warrior," 17, 21; Pando, "Oveta Culp Hobby," 54; Ziegler to mother, August 18, 1932, Jessie D. Ziegler Papers, DBCAH.

35. Hurt, "Great Ladies," 225; Sutphen, "Conservative Warrior," 17; Ziegler to mother, July 14, 1932, Jessie D. Ziegler Papers, DBCAH.

36. Hurt, "Great Ladies," 225; Sutphen, "Conservative Warrior," 17; Ziegler to mother, July 14, 1932, Jessie D. Ziegler Papers, DBCAH.

37. Clark, *Tactful Texan*, 172; Ziegler to mother, August 18 and September 3, 1932, Jessie D. Ziegler Papers, DBCAH; Hurt, "Great Ladies," 225.

38. Clark, *Tactful Texan*, 172; Ziegler to mother, August 18 and September 3, 1932, Jessie D. Ziegler Papers, DBCAH; Sutphen, "Conservative Warrior," 17; Hurt, "Great Ladies," 225.

39. Clark, *Tactful Texan*, 172; Pando, "Oveta Culp Hobby," 54; Marguerite Johnston, "Oveta Culp Hobby," OCH Papers, Rice.

40. Sterling and Kilman, *Ross Sterling*, 196, 198–213; Clark, *Tactful Texan*, 173–174; Brown, *Little Brown Jug*, 432.

41. Ziegler to mother, September 3 and 30, 1932, Jessie D. Ziegler Papers, DBCAH.

42. Pando, "Oveta Culp Hobby," 58; T. H. Williams, *Huey Long*, 531–533; Hurt, "Great Ladies," 225.

43. T. H. Williams, *Huey Long*, 763; *Houston Press*, October 1, 1932.

44. *Houston Chronicle*, October 2, 1932; T. H. Williams, *Huey Long*, 763; B. Hobby, *How Things Really Work*, 14–16; Sterling and Kilman, *Ross Sterling*, 204–213.

45. Pando, "Oveta Culp Hobby," 58; B. Hobby, *How Things Really Work*, 14–16; Hurt, "Great Ladies," 225.

46. Al Shire, "That Reminds Me," in Shire, *Oveta Culp Hobby*, 72; B. Hobby, *How Things Really Work*, 14–16; Pando, "Oveta Culp Hobby," 58.

47. *Shreveport Times*, October 2, 1932.

CHAPTER 21

1. Marguerite Johnston, biographical notes, OCH Papers, Rice; Bill Hobby, interview.

2. George Lynn to McAdoo, April 12 and 18, 1932, and WPH to Stuart R. Smith, July 1, 1932, William Gibbs McAdoo Papers, LOC.

3. Sutphen, "Conservative Warrior," 18; Clark, *Tactful Texan*, 172–180; Eleanor Roosevelt (hereafter ER) to OCH, October 10, 1932, OCH Papers, Rice.

4. Ziegler to mother, August 18, 1932, Jessie D. Ziegler Papers, DBCAH; Bill Hobby, interview.

5. Legal agreement between WPH and Eddie Clarkson and Jack Josey, December 30, 1932, WPH Sr. Papers, DBCAH.

6. Weldon Hart, typescript of biographical notes about WPH, ca. 1954, James Clark Papers, Rice.

7. Okrent, *Last Call*; Michael Lerner, "Prohibition: Unintended Consequences," PBS, 2011, https://www.pbs.org/kenburns/prohibition/unintended-consequences/.

8. Clark, *Tactful Texan*, 171–172; Ed Kilman, "History of the *Houston Post*," OCH Papers, Rice.

9. WONPR to OCH, March 14, 1933, OCH Papers, Rice; Okrent, *Last Call*, 224, 290, 341, 346, 350.

10. WONPR to OCH, March 14, 1933, OCH Papers, Rice.

11. Fenberg, *Unprecedented Power*, 205; Jones to Hobby, April 9, 1933, Jesse H. Jones Papers, Rice; Clark, *Tactful Texan*, 174; OCH to Florence Rodgers, April 19, 1933, OCH Papers, Rice.

12. Marguerite Johnston, biographical notes, OCH Papers, Rice.

13. Kerr, "Prohibition."

14. *Houston Post*, May 14, 1933.

15. M. H. Jacobs to Mrs. F. C. White, October 18, 1933, OCH Papers, Rice.

16. Sutphen, "Conservative Warrior," 16–17, 21–22; *Time*, May 4, 1953; Marguerite Johnston, biographical notes, OCH Papers, Rice.

17. Sutphen, "Conservative Warrior," 16–17, 21–22; *Time*, May 4, 1953; Shire, *Oveta Culp Hobby*, 45; Lynn Culp Loving, "My Sister, Oveta," in Shire, *Oveta Culp Hobby*, v–vi.

18. Lynn Culp Loving, "My Sister, Oveta," in Shire, *Oveta Culp Hobby*, v; Sam Houston Johnson, interview, October 1, 1976, LBJPL.

19. Lynn Culp Loving, "My Sister, Oveta," in Shire, *Oveta Culp Hobby*, v; Bill Hobby, interview.

20. Ziegler to mother, July 10, 1933, Jessie D. Ziegler Papers, DBCAH.

21. OCH, "A Plea for Tolerance," *Houston Post*, August 15, 1936.

22. OCH to WPH, August 14, 1936, OCH Papers, Rice.

23. OCH to WPH, August 14, 1936, OCH Papers, Rice.

24. Pando, "Oveta Culp Hobby," 60; *Houston Post*, October 5, 1934; Clark, *Tactful Texan*, 180–181.

25. Clark, 179; Pando, "Oveta Culp Hobby," 58.

26. Will and Oveta's son, Bill, would serve on the University of Houston Board of Regents in the mid-1960s and as chancellor from 1995 to 1997. The university is now home to the Hobby School for Public Policy. *Houston Post*, March 10, 1938; Pando, "Oveta Culp Hobby," 59; Bill Hobby, interview.

27. OCH, "Political Education for Women," typescript, OCH Papers, Rice; Walsh, "Oveta Culp Hobby" (2006), 34–36.

28. OCH, "Movie Censorship," January 5, 1938, typescript, OCH Papers, Rice.

29. OCH, undated MS of foreword to *Mr. Chairman*, OCH Papers, Rice.

30. *Houston Post*, March 22, 1936.

31. Timmons, *Jesse H. Jones*, 269–270; Fenberg, *Unprecedented Power*, 257–259.

32. J. Payne, "Steamboat House," 10–11; Clark, *Tactful Texan*, 176–177.

33. OCH to Jesse Jones, March 11, 1936, OCH Papers, Rice.

CHAPTER 22

1. Pando, "Oveta Culp Hobby," 57.

2. White House diaries for June 11–12, 1936, "Franklin Roosevelt Day by Day," Franklin D. Roosevelt Presidential Library and Museum, accessed March 26, 2020, www.fdrlibrary.marist.edu/daybyday; *Houston Post*, June 11 and 12, 1936; Clark, *Tactful Texan*, 177.

3. The City of Dallas removed the statue of Robert E. Lee from the park in 2017 in response to protests against memorials on public property commemorating Confederate leaders. White House diaries, June 11–12, 1936; Clark, *Tactful Texan*, 177; Fenberg, *Unprecedented Power*, 261–262.

4. Fenberg, 261–262; Clark, *Tactful Texan*, 177; Timmons, *Jesse H. Jones*, 270–271; Pando, "Oveta Culp Hobby," 57; M. Johnston, *Houston*, 303–304; "Plane Crash," Jesse H. Jones Papers, Rice.

5. *Washington Post*, June 13, 1936; *Houston Chronicle*, June 13 and 14, 1936; Clark, *Tactful Texan*, 177; Jones to Ed Hefley, July 3, 1936, and Dr. J. L. Goforth to Jones, June 18, 1936, "Airplane Accident," Jesse H. Jones Papers, LOC.

6. Fenberg, *Unprecedented Power*, 262; ER to OCH, June 13, 1936, OCH Papers, Rice.

7. Hefley, who received a number of honors for his

heroic actions in saving the lives of his passengers, continued his career as a distinguished professional pilot for more than forty years, including a stint as a test pilot for B-24 bombers during World War II and several years as Henry Ford II's personal pilot. He died at the age of eighty-five. *Houston Chronicle*, June 14, 1936; Fenberg, *Unprecedented Power*, 262; Jones to Arthur Hays Sulzberger, June 22, 1936, and Jones to Dr. J. L. Goforth, June 22, 1936, Jesse H. Jones Papers, LOC.

8. Clark, *Tactful Texan*, 177; OCH and WPH to Jones, June 11, 1937, Jesse H. Jones Papers, LOC; "Cecil McBride," in Shire, *Oveta Culp Hobby*, 36.

9. OCH to Tom Bonner, July 1 and 18, 1936, and Richard Waldo to OCH, August 7, 1936, OCH Papers, Rice.

10. Wakefield to OCH, October 2, 1936, OCH Papers, Rice; *Austin American-Statesman*, October 11, 1936.

11. Oveta offered a revised version of her columns to the McClure Newspaper Syndicate for national syndication, but McClure declined the offer. OCH to Abe Merritt, September 14, 1937, H. L. Mills to Blair, September 8, 1938, W. W. Kemmerer to OCH, July 10, 1936, OCH to J. O. Webb, January 13, 1937, OCH to H. L. Mills, October 18, 1937, and H. L. Mills to Senator Clay Cotton, October 18, 1937, OCH Papers, Rice.

12. Bonner to OCH, February 19 and August 31, 1937, Walter Woodul to Senator Clay Cotton, September 13, 1937, Tom Bonner to OCH, October 13, 1937, OCH Papers, Rice.

13. OCH to Bonner, May 10, May 28, and June 10, 1941, OCH to Roger Warren, February 18, 1941, Bonner to OCH, March 14, 1940, Stone to OCH, September 25, 1940, Helon Johnson to OCH, October 12, 1943, OCH Papers, Rice.

14. Mrs. F. A. Kling, OCH's secretary, to Tom Bonner, January 18, 1937, OCH Papers, Rice; Clark, *Tactful Texan*, 179; *Time*, May 4, 1953; Pando, "Oveta Culp Hobby," 42; Bill Hobby, interview.

15. WPH to Jones, telegram, March 14, 1933, WPH to Jones, April 20, 1933, Jones to WPH, April 26, 1933, WPH to Jones, July 18, 1933, and Jones to WPH, July 19, 1933, Jesse H. Jones Papers, Rice.

16. Pando, "Oveta Culp Hobby," 41–43; *Time*, May 4, 1953; Sutphen, "Conservative Warrior," 24.

17. Pando, "Oveta Culp Hobby," 41–43.

18. As Robert Pando convincingly argues, the rumor "requires a suspension of logic—why would a married woman name her child after a lover who was the child's father? Why would her husband agree to such a name?" The rumor that Jesse Jones was Jessica Hobby's biological father even made its way into Oveta's FBI file, where it is mentioned several times. That a report of the rumor is in her FBI file is hardly proof that it was true. FBI files on individuals are notorious for being filled with unsubstantiated claims, false accusations, and hearsay. The file actually supports the opposite conclusion because it documents that even the FBI could find no substantive evidence to support the rumor, and if they had uncovered such evidence it is certain they would have reported it to FBI director J. Edgar Hoover, who had an insatiable appetite for salacious information. Because Oveta would eventually serve in two critically important federal positions, including one job during World War II that had sensitive national security concerns, an investigation into her background would have been thorough. Rumors were also spread that Oveta had affairs with Dwight Eisenhower and Nelson Rockefeller. Those rumors have even less credence than the one about her and Jones. Pando argues that a "thoughtful review of Hobby's focused and disciplined life effectively rules out behavior that was reckless or off-target." In the absence of any credible evidence, Pando's is certainly a valid conclusion. Sutphen, "Conservative Warrior," 24; Hurt, "Great Ladies," 220; Pando, "Oveta Culp Hobby," 41–43; *Time*, May 4, 1953.

19. OCH to Tom Bonner, February 6, 1937, Bonner to OCH, February, 19, 1937, and OCH to Bonner, April 12, 1937, OCH Papers, Rice.

20. Clark, *Tactful Texan*, 179; OCH, speech typescript, April 21, 1937, OCH Papers, Rice; *Houston Post*, April 22, 1937.

21. Bill Hobby, interview; "Cecil McBride," in Shire, *Oveta Culp Hobby*, 35.

22. Clark, *Tactful Texan*, 178; *Houston Chronicle*, August 17, 1995.

23. Clark, *Tactful Texan*, 181; Sutphen, "Conservative Warrior," 23; Hurt, "Great Ladies," 225.

24. "*Houston Post* Prospectus," March 1938, and Ed Kilman, "History of the Houston Post," OCH Papers, Rice.

25. *New York Daily News*, March 21, 1953; *Houston Chronicle*, August 17, 1995; Sutphen, "Conservative Warrior," 107; Hurt, "Great Ladies," 226.

CHAPTER 23

1. In the 1940s the Internal Revenue Service challenged the Houston Printing Company's tax returns for the late 1930s. Will Hobby filed a response to the IRS explaining why the paper had earned no profits during those years. A copy of the response, which provides documentation for the business relationship between the Hobbys and the "Jones Interests," is in the OCH Papers at Rice. Apparently the Hobbys either won their case or were able to reach a modest settlement. There is no evidence the Hobbys experienced any consequential tax penalties. "Petition to the Internal Revenue Service," ca. 1946, OCH Papers, Rice; Timmons, *Jesse H. Jones*, 160–161.

2. Hurt, "Great Ladies," 225–226; Pando, "Oveta Culp Hobby," 62; "Petition to the Internal Revenue Service," ca. 1946, OCH Papers, Rice.

3. Weldon Hart's typescript notes on history of *Houston Post*, James Clark Papers, Rice; "Petition to the Internal Revenue Service," ca. 1946, OCH Papers, Rice.

4. Risedorf, "Morse, Robert Emmett"; E. R. Lindley to OCH, February 3, 1939, OCH Papers, Rice; Walsh, "Oveta Culp Hobby" (2006), 11; Ed Kilman, "History of the *Houston Post*," OCH Papers, Rice.

5. Oddly, neither James Clark, Hobby's biographer, nor Jesse Jones's two biographers, Bascom Timmons and Steven Fenberg, had much to say about how Jones handled the sale of the *Post* and KPRC to the Hobbys, despite it being a significant event in the history of news media in Texas, as well as an insight into Jesse Jones's business practices and character. Timmons simply repeated Jones's self-serving justification for selling the properties, while Fenberg failed to mention it in his 584-page celebration of Jones's life, except as a bare reference in a photograph caption. Purchase agreement, Jesse H. Jones Papers, DBCAH; Fenberg, *Unprecedented Power*, 342.

6. Al Shire, "That Reminds Me," in Shire, *Oveta Culp Hobby*, 74; Timmons, *Jesse H. Jones*, 160–161; Hurt, "Great Ladies," 225–226; M. Johnston, *Houston*, 331–332.

7. Hurt, "Great Ladies," 226; Marguerite Johnston, "The Widening Wake," in Shire, *Oveta Culp Hobby*, 78; Marguerite Johnston to Isabel Ross, ca. 1968, OCH Papers, Rice.

8. *Time*, May 4, 1953; *NY World Telegram*, April 22, 1941; Ed Kilman, "History of the *Houston Post*," OCH Papers, Rice.

9. Bill Hobby, interview; Weldon Hart, typescript notes, James Clark Papers, Rice.

10. Bill Hobby, interview; OCH to Laura Remer, April 15, 1938, and Marguerite Johnston, typescript, both in Bill Hobby Papers, DBCAH; "Cecil McBride," and "Vernon Wiley," in Shire, *Oveta Culp Hobby*, 35–36, 51.

11. Weldon Hart, typescript notes, James Clark Papers, Rice; *NY World Telegram*, April 22, 1941; "Prospectus," OCH Papers, Rice; Hurt, "Great Ladies," 226.

12. Walsh, "Oveta Culp Hobby" (2015), 324–325; Sutphen, "Conservative Warrior," 24–25; *New York Daily News*, March 22, 1953; Shire, "That Reminds Me," in Shire, *Oveta Culp Hobby*, 68.

13. McGrew to Bill Hobby, January 12, 1991, Bill Hobby Papers, DBCAH.

14. McGrew, "Reminiscences," typescript, ca. 1995, Bill Hobby Papers, DBCAH.

15. Pando, "Oveta Culp Hobby," 61; Bill Hobby, interview.

16. Perez, "Florence, Fred Farrel"; B. Hobby, *How Things Really Work*, 38; Hyman, *Craftsmanship and Character*, 56, 160–164; M. Johnston, *Houston*, 198–199; Bill Hobby, interview; R. J. MacBean to WPH, March 14, 1945, OCH Papers, Rice; J. A. Phillips to WPH, March 28, 1949, Jesse H. Jones Papers, DBCAH.

17. Fenberg, *Unprecedented Power*, 329–330, 353; Timmons, *Jesse H. Jones*, 276.

18. WPH to A. A. Berle, April 16, 1940, speech files, 1940, Adolf A. Berle Papers, Franklin D. Roosevelt Presidential Library (hereafter FDRPL); Fenberg, *Unprecedented Power*, 333; Ed Kilman, "History of the *Houston Post*," OCH Papers, Rice.

19. Brands, *Traitor to His Class*, 556, 768; Ed Kilman, "History of the *Houston Post*," OCH Papers, Rice.

20. Clark, *Tactful Texan*, 181; *Houston Post*, January 26, 1938; *Washington Herald*, April 23, 1939; Walsh, "Oveta Culp Hobby" (2006), 40.

21. Brands, *Traitor to His Class*, 68–75; OCH, "Calling the Shots," in Shire, *Oveta Culp Hobby*, 62.

22. Weldon Hart, typescript notes prepared for book *Tactful Texan*, James Clark Papers, Rice; B. Hobby, *How Things Really Work*, 5.

23. Clark, *Tactful Texan*, 180.

24. OCH, "It Can Happen Here," pamphlet, March 31, 1937, OCH Papers, Rice.

25. Oveta's declaration that she would "never again say . . . I am a Republican," like most "never

again" statements people make, was eventually forgotten when she later declared she was a
Republican while serving on President Eisenhower's cabinet. OCH, "Calling the Shots," in
Shire, *Oveta Culp Hobby*, 62.

26. Lewis, *Wendell Willkie*, xi–xvi.

27. Clark, *Tactful Texan*, 183.

28. OCH, interview, July 11, 1969, LBJPL; WPH to
Lyndon B. Johnson (hereafter LBJ), April 15,
1937, LBJ Congressional Papers, LBJPL; Caro,
*Path to Power*, 443.

29. Clark, *Tactful Texan*, 184; Fenberg, *Unprecedented Power*, 366–367.

30. Martha Cross to OCH, September 1, 1940, and
OCH to Mrs. Henry Breckinridge, September
23, 1940, OCH Papers, Rice; Kirkland, *Hogg
Family*, 34; Hyman, *Craftsmanship and
Character*, 197.

31. Burrough, *Big Rich*, 137.

32. OCH to Cross, November 4, 1940, and OCH to
Mrs. Henry Breckinridge, September 23 and
November 4, 1940, OCH Papers, Rice; *Louisville
Courier-Journal*, September 21, 1940.

33. OCH to Cross, November 4, 1940, OCH Papers,
Rice.

34. Bill Hobby, school paper, ca. October 1940,
Bill Hobby Papers, DBCAH.

35. Brands, *Traitor to His Class*, 574.

36. OCH to Mrs. Ashton, November 11, 1940, and
OCH to Willkie, November 12, 1940, OCH
Papers, Rice.

CHAPTER 24

1. The Hobbys' vocal support of FDR for reasons
of national defense was an easy move for them
to make. Willkie's foreign policy positions as a
presidential candidate differed little from FDR's.
As internationalists, the Hobbys (especially
Oveta) disdained the America First movement
led by aviation hero Charles A. Lindbergh. It
was FDR's domestic policies, his attempt to pack
the Supreme Court, and his breaking of the two-
term tradition that fueled their opposition to his
reelection. Clark, *Tactful Texan*, 184; Sutphen,
"Conservative Warrior," 24.

2. Bill Hobby, interview; Jack McGrew to Bill
Hobby, January 12, 1991, Bill Hobby Papers,
DBCAH; Salazar, "Steiner, Thomas Casper";
B. Hobby, *How Things Really Work*, 12–13.

3. Ralph Bowen to OCH, February 1, 1941, OCH
to Mrs. G. A. Atchley, December 18, 1940, OCH
to Bowen, February 7, 1941, and Bill Hobby to

OCH, ca. February 1941, Bill Hobby Papers,
DBCAH; Bill Hobby, interview.

4. M. Johnston, *Houston*, 337; OCH, interview,
July 11, 1969, LBJPL; Edy, *War Correspondent*,
65–66; Pando, "Oveta Culp Hobby," 77–78.

5. The story about Oveta in the *Washington Herald*
featured the headline "Woman Solves Puzzle
for 120 Men Editors," which was about the stir
she created in the Press Club Auditorium "as
she clarified a point in parliamentary procedure
which had stumped 120 men." A journalist for
one of the Washington newspapers described
Oveta as looking "scarcely older than a debu-
tante" and that she was "extremely bashful"
when talking to reporters, because, she declared,
"there is nothing to say about me." *Washington
Herald*, April 23, 1939; *NY World Telegram*,
April 22, 1941; R. Ernest Dupuy, June 8, 1941,
Marguerite Johnston Barnes Papers, Rice; OCH,
interview, July 11, 1969, LBJPL.

6. Sutphen, "Conservative Warrior," 25–26; OCH,
interview, July 11, 1969, LBJPL.

7. Sutphen, "Conservative Warrior," 25–26.

8. R. Ernest Dupuy to OCH, July 10, 1941, OCH
Papers, Rice.

9. OCH to R. Ernest Dupuy, July 12, 1941, OCH
Papers, Rice; OCH, "Outline of Suggested Plan
for Women's Branch of the Bureau of Public
Relations," OCH Papers, LOC.

10. OCH appointment letter, July 29, 1941, and
OCH to Mrs. Paul P. Manship, August 8,
1941, OCH Papers, LOC; Treadwell, *Women's
Corps*, 21; Pando, "Oveta Culp Hobby," 77–78;
M. Johnston, *Houston*, 336–337.

11. *Time*, August 11, 1941; *Houston Post*, July 31,
1941; *NY Sun*, August 12, 1941; *NY Herald
Tribune*, August 2, 1941; Ed Kilman, "History
of the *Houston Post*," and clip of AP wire story,
August 2, 1941, both in OCH Papers, Rice; Edy,
*War Correspondent*, 66; *Bulletin of the American
Society of Newspaper Editors*, September 1, 1941.

12. In the years after World War II, the story of how
Oveta became involved with the War Department
became enmeshed in faulty memories. When
recalling the meeting many years later, Oveta
said that General Alexander Surles was then
serving as head of the army's Bureau of Public
Relations, that he chaired the meeting, and that
he guided the events that immediately followed,
including making the offer for her to take charge
of the Women's Interest Section. But General
Surles was still at Fort Knox, Kentucky, in June

and July. Oveta also claimed that she declined General Surles's offer to appoint her to serve as the administrative head of the new women's section, citing the need to help her aging husband and to take care of her two young children, as well as her heavy workload at the *Post*. According to this version, Surles telephoned Oveta soon after she returned to Houston and asked her to reconsider the decision to come to Washington to work for the War Department, and she again declined the offer. Marguerite Johnston's published version of this story claims that after Oveta hung up the phone after rejecting Surles's offer, Will told her she needed to take the job, saying, "You shouldn't have made him have to ask you a second time." According to Johnston, Oveta then called General Surles and accepted his offer. The evidence suggests that the story Oveta told Johnston was either a bit embellished or the product of a hazy memory. She obviously consulted with Will, and it is obvious that he approved. But the record shows that it was General Richardson who offered the job to Oveta and that she never rejected the offer. In some ways, these may only be minor corrections to Oveta's version of the story about her appointment, but the important point is that Oveta's version made it seem that she didn't want the appointment but accepted only after being begged by the army and scolded by Will to take it, which is misleading. Pando, "Oveta Culp Hobby," 77; "Alexander D. Surles 1911," West Point Association of Graduates, accessed March 28, 2020, https://www.westpointaog.org/memorial-article?id=9c6aa096-4636-4962-956d-84f225657f89.

13. Ed Kilman, "History of the *Houston Post*," OCH Papers, Rice.

14. Lynn Culp Loving, "My Sister, Oveta," in Shire, *Oveta Culp Hobby*, vi.

15. Treadwell, *Women's Corps*, 21; *Washington Post*, August 10, 1941; *NY Herald Tribune*, October 14, 1941; *Pathfinder*, January 17, 1942; Pogue, *George C. Marshall*, 106; Moore, *To Serve My Country*, 37; "Agenda," Meeting of Advisory Council, Women's Interest Section, WD Bureau of Public Relations, October 13, 1941, OCH Papers, Rice.

16. *Pathfinder*, January 17, 1942; *NY Daily Mirror*, April 7, 1942.

17. Dupuy to OCH, memorandum, October 18, 1941, OCH Papers, LOC.

18. *Vogue*, July 1, 1942.

19. Many years after the war, Oveta took umbrage when a writer described her work with the Women's Interest Section as being a "press agent." She explained that her job was an educational one on a "woman-to-woman level." While it is true that she was not a press agent per se, her work was not purely educational either. She claimed that the bureau "handled the press," but that was a misleading statement, as the record documents. See typescript draft of a letter from Marguerite Johnston to Miss Hope E. Stoddard, OCH Papers, Rice; Moore, *To Serve My Country*, 37; Pando, "Oveta Culp Hobby," 78–79.

20. Velma Soule, memorandum to Dupuy, OCH Papers, LOC; Pando, "Oveta Culp Hobby," 79; *Pathfinder*, January 17, 1942.

21. M. Johnston, *Houston*, 337; *NY Daily Mirror*, April 7, 1942.

22. *NY Sun*, October 17, 1941; Edy, *War Correspondent*, 66.

23. Pogue, *George C. Marshall*, 106–114; Walsh, "Oveta Culp Hobby" (2006), 45–47.

24. Treadwell, *Women's Corps*, 18–19; Pogue, *George C. Marshall*, 105; Walsh, "Oveta Culp Hobby," 6–8.

25. Treadwell, *Women's Corps*, 18, 20–22; Walsh, "Oveta Culp Hobby" (2006), 6–8; Pogue, *George C. Marshall*, 105.

26. Pogue, 106; Treadwell, *Women's Corps*, 18, 20–22; Pando, "Oveta Culp Hobby," 80.

27. Eleanor Roosevelt's papers at the FDR Library contain a file of the several memoranda she and Oveta exchanged in the period from January until September 1942 during the effort to win congressional approval for the WAAC and then to organize the corps. When FDR received a recommendation about where to locate the first women officers training camp, he sent a typed note to Eleanor suggesting she "take this up with Mrs. Hobby who has been selected to run the Women's Division in the War Department." FDR to ER, March 31, 1942, Correspondence with Government Departments, OCH file, ER Papers, FDRPL; Pogue, *George C. Marshall*, 106; Treadwell, *Women's Corps*, 18, 20–22; Pando, "Oveta Culp Hobby," 80.

28. *Chicago Tribune*, December 8, 1941; M. Johnston, *Houston*, 337; Pando, "Oveta Culp Hobby," 80; "Itemized Schedule of Travel," and Florence B. Bovett to OCH, June 12, 1942, OCH Papers, LOC.

29. Treadwell, *Women's Corps*, 29–30; Edy, *War*

Correspondent, 67; Moore, *To Serve My Country*, 37; Pando, "Oveta Culp Hobby," 78–79; *Pathfinder*, January 17, 1942; Marshall to Stimson, March 18, 1942, George C. Marshall Papers, George C. Marshall Research Library (hereafter GCMRL).

30. *Pathfinder*, January 17, 1942.

31. M. Johnston, *Houston*, 337–338; Treadwell, *Women's Corps*, 21; Walsh, "Oveta Culp Hobby" (2006), 50.

32. *NY Daily News*, March 21, 1953; Marshall to Stimson, March 18, 1942, George C. Marshall Papers, GCMRL; Pogue, *George C. Marshall*, 107–108; *Houston Post*, May 16, 1942; Marguerite Johnston, "Oveta Culp Hobby," OCH Papers, Rice.

33. *Washington Post*, January 22, 1942; Treadwell, *Women's Corps*, 25; Young, *Why We Fight*, 107; *NYT*, June 27, 1942.

34. Marshall to Stimson, March 18, 1942, George C. Marshall Papers, GCMRL; "Itinerary for Canadian Trip," March 5–11, 1942, OCH Papers, LOC; Treadwell, *Women's Corps*, 28–33.

35. Treadwell, 28–29; Walsh, "Oveta Culp Hobby" (2006), 52.

36. M. Johnston, *Houston*, 338; Pogue, *George C. Marshall*, 108; Johnston to Hope Stoddard, ca. August 1968 and November 4, 1968, Marguerite Johnston Barnes Papers, Rice.

37. OCH, interview, July 11, 1969, LBJPL; Marshall to Stimson, March 18, 1942, and Stimson to Roosevelt, March 18, 1942, George C. Marshall Papers, GCMRL; Treadwell, *Women's Corps*, 28–33.

38. *NY Daily Mirror*, April 7, 1942; *NY Journal American*, April 16, 1942.

39. *NY Journal American*, April 16, 1942; Pando, "Oveta Culp Hobby," 84.

40. Pando, 84–85.

41. Treadwell, *Women's Corps*, 30–41.

42. Pogue, *George C. Marshall*, 108–109; Treadwell, *Women's Corps*, 45; *NYT*, May 15, 1942.

43. *Houston Post*, May 16, 1942; *NY Sun*, *NYT*, and *NY Daily News*, May 16, 1942; *Rocky Mountain News*, June 13, 1942; Treadwell, *Women's Corps*, 45–46; Pogue, *George C. Marshall*, 109; Stimson to OCH, May 15, 1942, OCH Papers, Rice; *Brooklyn Eagle*, June 7, 1942; *NY Journal American*, May 13, 1942; Cook, *Eleanor Roosevelt*, 428.

44. Footage of Oveta taking the oath of office can be viewed on several channels on YouTube. Treadwell, *Women's Corps*, 46–47; "The Diaries of Henry Lewis Stimson," microfilm edition, reel 7, vol. 39, May 16, 1942, Yale.

45. Treadwell, *Women's Corps*, 30, 48, 49; Laas, *Bridging Two Eras*, xvii; *NY Journal American*, May 22, 1942; *San Antonio Express*, May 16, 1942.

46. Pogue, *George C. Marshall*, 109; Ed Kilman, "History of the *Houston Post*," OCH Papers, Rice.

47. *NY Journal American*, May 22, 1942.

48. *Tulsa Daily World*, May 19, 1942, and *Portland (ME) Press Herald*, May 22, 1942, OCH scrapbook, OCH Papers, LOC.

49. *Atlanta Journal*, May 17, 1942; *Washington Star*, May 23, 1942; Treadwell, *Women's Corps*, 48–49.

50. *Washington Post*, May 25, 1942.

51. Treadwell, *Women's Corps*, 50; Pogue, *George C. Marshall*, 110.

CHAPTER 25

1. Treadwell, *Women's Corps*, 48.

2. Treadwell, 49.

3. *Time*, June 15, 1942; Pogue, *George C. Marshall*, 265; Jordan, *American Warlords*, 286–287.

4. Treadwell, *Women's Corps*, 31, 50–53.

5. Pando, "Oveta Culp Hobby," 150; Treadwell, *Women's Corps*, 39.

6. Treadwell, 36–38.

7. Treadwell, 38, 65; Pando, "Oveta Culp Hobby," 105–107.

8. Pando, 106–108.

9. Pando, 106–108; Reich, *Nelson A. Rockefeller*, 514.

10. Moore, *To Serve My Country*, 37–39; Laas, *Bridging Two Eras*, xvii.

11. Treadwell, *Women's Corps*, 35–36, 56–57; *Life*, June 8, 1942.

12. *Life*, June 8, 1942; Treadwell, *Women's Corps*, 54–57; Pando, "Oveta Culp Hobby," 71; V. Williams, *WACs*, 36.

13. *Vogue*, July 1, 1942; *NYT Magazine*, May 24, 1942; *Life*, June 8, 1942; Treadwell, *Women's Corps*, 54–57.

14. *Life*, June 8, 1942; Treadwell, *Women's Corps*, 54–57.

15. *NYT*, May 15 and 16, 1942; Moore, *To Serve My Country*, 16; Pando, "Oveta Culp Hobby," 94.

16. It is likely that Oveta's meeting with Dr. Bethune was also motivated by her awareness that ER was both an admirer of Bethune and a vocal advocate for including African American women in the WAAC. Moore, *To Serve My Country*, 56–57, 241; Walsh, "Oveta Culp Hobby" (2006), 14–15; Pando, "Oveta Culp Hobby," 93–94.

17. Pando, 94–95; Treadwell, *Women's Corps*, 73,

599; Moore, *To Serve My Country*, 56–65, 73; Walsh, "Oveta Culp Hobby" (2006), 136–139.

18. OCH to Betty Apgar, June 19, 1942, OCH to Cora Toole Alderson, May 23, 1942, and OCH to Frank C. Adams, June 29, 1942, OCH Papers, LOC; Helon Johnson to OCH, June 18, 1942, OCH Papers, Rice; Laura Hobby, interview.

19. *Rocky Mountain News*, June 13, 1942.

20. "World War II Enemy Alien Control Program Overview," National Archives, last modified July 12, 2018, https://www.archives.gov/research/immigration/enemy-aliens-overview; Clark, *Tactful Texan*, 185.

21. Treadwell, *Women's Corps*, 63; Pando, "Oveta Culp Hobby," 69.

22. Colonel Don Carlos Faith was promoted to brigadier general in December 1942. He would later be awarded the Distinguished Service Medal for his oversight of the WAAC training program. "Don Carlos Faith," www.arlingtoncemetery.net/dfaith.htm; Treadwell, *Women's Corps*, 59, 66; Bugbee, *Officer and Lady*, 19–20.

23. Treadwell, *Women's Corps*, 66.

24. *Washington Evening Star*, *NY Journal American*, and *NYT*, August 24, 1942.

25. Moore, *To Serve My Country*, 80–81; Treadwell, *Women's Corps*, 599.

26. Basil Walters to OCH, September 17, 1943, OCH Papers, LOC.

27. Treadwell, *Women's Corps*, 82–83.

28. OCH to Lillie Cullen, August 22, 1942, OCH Papers, LOC; Treadwell, *Women's Corps*, 71–72.

29. Treadwell, 75; Bugbee, *Officer and Lady*, 30–34.

30. Treadwell, *Women's Corps*, 85–87.

31. Marshall to Somervell, September 17, 1942, George C. Marshall Papers, GCMRL; Treadwell, *Women's Corps*, 85–87.

32. Treadwell, 166.

33. Treadwell, 76; Pogue, *George C. Marshall*, 110; Bugbee, *Officer and Lady*, 33–34.

34. Cook, *Eleanor Roosevelt*, 438–440; Lash, *Eleanor and Franklin*, 658.

35. Marshall to OCH, September 16, 1942, George C. Marshall Papers, GCMRL.

36. Treadwell, *Women's Corps*, 91; Marshall to Somervell, September 17, 1942, George C. Marshall Papers, GCMRL.

37. Treadwell, *Women's Corps*, 91; *Houston Post*, October 2, 1942; Lash, *Eleanor and Franklin*, 658; Rayburn to Mrs. Palmer Hutcheson, October 1, 1942, OCH Papers, Rice.

38. *NYT*, May 25, 1997.

39. Roosevelt, *This I Remember*, 260–262.

40. Roosevelt.

41. Bugbee, *Officer and Lady*, 3.

42. Roosevelt, *This I Remember*, 260–262; Lash, *Eleanor and Franklin*, 658; Bugbee, *Officer and Lady*, 41–42; Dwyer, *Strained Relations*, 63–64.

43. Roosevelt, *This I Remember*, 260–262; Lash, *Eleanor and Franklin*, 658; Bugbee, *Officer and Lady*, 41–42.

44. Lash, *Eleanor and Franklin*, 658; Bugbee, *Officer and Lady*, 41–42.

45. Lash, *Eleanor and Franklin*, 659; Roosevelt, *This I Remember*, 262; Cook, *Eleanor Roosevelt*, 440–441; *NY Journal American*, October 24, 1942.

46. Cook, *Eleanor Roosevelt*, 441; Lash, *Eleanor and Franklin*, 659; "America's First Lady in Britain Aka Mrs Roosevelt in Britain," YouTube video, British Pathée News Reel, uploaded April 13, 2014, https://www.youtube.com/watch?v=FHJIjPgGiU0.

47. Cook, *Eleanor Roosevelt*, 441; OCH, "first draft typescript of a speech to be given at a celebration of Eisenhower's 75th birthday in Augusta, Georgia, on August 27, 1965," OCH Papers, Rice; Bugbee, *Officer and Lady*, 42–43.

48. Bugbee, 44.

49. ER, "My Day," October 27, 1942; Cook, *Eleanor Roosevelt*, 441; Lash, *Eleanor and Franklin*, 661; Treadwell, *Women's Corps*, 84.

50. Bugbee, *Officer and Lady*, 43; Moore, *To Serve My Country*, 82.

51. Bugbee, *Officer and Lady*, 43; transcript of President Eisenhower's remarks at White House event on July 13, 1955, OCH Papers, Rice.

52. Bugbee, *Officer and Lady*, 44–45.

53. Roosevelt, *This I Remember*, 268; Cook, *Eleanor Roosevelt*, 444.

54. *NY Sun*, October 30, 1942.

55. *NY Herald Tribune*, October 26, 1942; OCH tribute book, 3.

56. Bugbee, *Officer and Lady*, 52.

57. Cook, *Eleanor Roosevelt*, 444; *NYT*, November 2, 1942.

58. Bugbee, *Officer and Lady*, 42, 48–50.

59. Bugbee, 3, 41, 45.

60. OCH to ER, November 21, 1942, ER Papers, FDRPL.

CHAPTER 26

1. Treadwell, *Women's Corps*, 110.

2. Treadwell, 110, 100; Pando, "Oveta Culp Hobby," 172.

3. Transcript of Bandel letter, November 19, 1942, and Helon Johnson to Lois Hill, November 20, 1942, OCH Papers, Rice.

4. Treadwell, *Women's Corps*, 97–98; Al Shire, "That Reminds Me," in Shire, *Oveta Culp Hobby*, 65; *NY Herald Tribune*, November 21, 1942.

5. Treadwell, *Women's Corps*, 100–101; Pando, "Oveta Culp Hobby," 172; *NY Journal American*, January 22, 1953.

6. Bugbee, *Officer and Lady*, 53; V. Williams, *WACs*, 31–32.

7. Marshall to Stratemeyer, November 27, 1942, George C. Marshall Papers, GCMRL.

8. Bugbee, *Officer and Lady*, 50; Treadwell, *Women's Corps*, 50.

9. In the early 1980s, when Oveta was asked about the pregnancy dispute, she denied it had happened. "There was never any such battle at all. There was never any question of giving a dishonorable discharge for pregnancy because it could have been done only if soldiers were discharged from the Army for fathering a child." Her response is puzzling because it contradicts the army's official history of the WAC, which Oveta read and approved before it was published. It also contradicts Eleanor Roosevelt's version of the issue in her book *Ladies of Courage*, 226–227. See also Marguerite Johnston to Isabel Ross, OCH Papers, Rice; Treadwell, *Women's Corps*, 73, 500–501.

10. When Eisenhower learned that General Bedell Smith had succeeded in having the five WAACs assigned to Algiers, Eisenhower sent him a message stating, "I cannot tell you how delighted I am that you have got the Wack [WAAC] business all buttoned up." The reference to the "Wack" was standard language within all ranks of the army at the time. Chandler, *Papers of Eisenhower*, 693–694; Bugbee, *Officer and Lady*, 49; General Marshall to Military Committee, House of Representatives, December 3, 1942, George C. Marshall Papers, GCMRL.

11. Treadwell, *Women's Corps*, 106; ER to OCH, invitation, OCH Papers, LOC.

12. Chandler, *Papers of Eisenhower*, 1155.

13. Pogue, *George C. Marshall*, 111; Treadwell, *Women's Corps*, 106.

14. Pogue, *George C. Marshall*, 111; Treadwell, *Women's Corps*, 106.

15. Pogue, *George C. Marshall*, 111; Treadwell, *Women's Corps*, 113, 116.

16. *Houston Post*, December 23, 1942; OCH to Julia and Bill Bertner, January 4, 1943, and OCH to Olga and Harry Wiess, January 5, 1943, both in OCH Papers, LOC.

17. Lynn Culp Loving, "My Sister, Oveta," in Shire, *Oveta Culp Hobby*, vi–vii.

18. Bugbee, *Officer and Lady*, 60; Treadwell, *Women's Corps*, 30, 118.

19. Bugbee, *Officer and Lady*, 55.

20. Bugbee, 53; Pando, "Oveta Culp Hobby," 72–73.

21. Dwight Eisenhower to Mamie Eisenhower, January 18, 1944, transcript of letter, item 111, Swann auction catalog, sale 2413, May 5, 2016.

22. Treadwell, *Women's Corps*, 360–361; Pogue, *George C. Marshall*, 57–58, 65, 104.

23. Treadwell, *Women's Corps*, 360–361; Pogue, *George C. Marshall*, 57–58, 65, 104.

24. Bugbee, *Officer and Lady*, 62.

25. *NYT*, February 3, 1943.

26. "Three Weeks Trip," itinerary, OCH Papers, LOC; Bugbee, *Officer and Lady*, 67, 69; OCH to ER, November 21, 1942, and ER to OCH, November 24, 1942, ER Papers, FDRPL; Roosevelt, *This I Remember*, 282; ER to OCH, February 23, 1943, OCH Papers, Rice.

27. "Three Weeks Trip," itinerary, OCH Papers, LOC; *Houston Post*, February 15 and 17, 1943.

28. "Three Weeks Trip," itinerary, OCH Papers, LOC; *NYT*, March 3, 1943; Ed Kilman, "History of the *Houston Post*," OCH Papers, Rice; *Houston Post*, February 19, 1943; *San Francisco Examiner*, March 3, 1943.

29. Bugbee, *Officer and Lady*, 71; *Time*, May 10, 1943; Pogue, *George C. Marshall*, 108; R. E. Thomason, interview, LBJPL.

30. Bugbee, 73–74; Helon Johnson to OCH, March 31, 1943, OCH Papers, Rice.

31. Treadwell, *Women's Corps*, 195.

32. Meyer, *Creating GI Jane*, 6–10.

33. *Time*, January 17, 1944; Treadwell, *Women's Corps*, 193–195.

34. Treadwell, 193, 216, 574–576.

35. Itinerary, War Writers' Board Tour, April 15–17, 1943, OCH Papers, LOC; Bugbee, *Officer and Lady*, 98; Treadwell, *Women's Corps*, 574–576.

36. Treadwell, 574–576; Bugbee, *Officer and Lady*, 98.

37. Itinerary, War Writers' Board Tour, April 15–17, 1943, OCH Papers, LOC.

38. *Temple Daily Telegram*, May 13, 1943; "Director's Engagements," May 1943, OCH Papers, LOC; Ed Kilman, "History of the *Houston Post*," OCH Papers, Rice.

39. Appendix to the *Congressional Record*, May 17, 1943, A2461–2465.

40. Betty Bandel to OCH, May 15, 1943, OCH Papers, LOC.

41. "Director's Engagements," May 1943, OCH Papers, LOC; Ed Kilman, "History of the *Houston Post*," OCH Papers, Rice.

42. *NYT*, May 31, 1943.

43. Treadwell, *Women's Corps*, 216–217; "Itinerary, Clergymen's Tour," June 2–4, 1943, OCH Papers, LOC.

44. "Visit to Training Center," Fort Oglethorpe, June 12, 1943, OCH Papers, LOC.

45. "Director's Engagements, Trip to Los Angeles, California, June 20 to June 24, 1943," OCH Papers, LOC; "Women at War (1943)," synopsis, IMDb, https://imdb.com/title/tt0036544/.

46. *NY Daily News*, June 8, 1943; Treadwell, *Women's Corps*, 201–204; V. Williams, *WACs*, 4; Starbird, *Army Shoes*, 5.

47. Treadwell, *Women's Corps*, 193, 204.

48. Treadwell, 203–205, 218; Pogue, *George C. Marshall*, 112; Marshall to OCH, June 15, 1943, George C. Marshall Papers, GCMRL; *NY Journal American*, June 9, 1943.

49. Treadwell, *Women's Corps*, 217–218; Pando, "Oveta Culp Hobby," 112.

50. Treadwell, *Women's Corps*, 205.

51. Pogue, *George C. Marshall*, 111–112.

52. Treadwell, *Women's Corps*, 205, 218; Pfau, *Miss Yourlovin*, 97–151.

53. *NYT*, June 21, 1943; *NY World Telegram*, June 30, 1943.

54. Moore, *To Serve My Country*, 39–40; Treadwell, *Women's Corps*, 205.

55. Roosevelt, *Ladies of Courage*, 226; Pando, "Oveta Culp Hobby," 69; Treadwell, *Women's Corps*, 205.

56. Helon Johnson to OCH, July 2, 1943, OCH Papers, Rice; *NY Post*, July 6, 1943.

57. Pando, "Oveta Culp Hobby," 73; H. B. Lewis to OCH, July 5, 1943, OCH Papers, Rice; *NYT*, July 6, 1943.

CHAPTER 27

1. Treadwell, *Women's Corps*, 87, 722; Pando, "Oveta Culp Hobby," 73; Chandler, *Papers of Eisenhower*, 1229–1230.

2. Treadwell, *Women's Corps*, 483–484, 489–491.

3. *Time*, January 17, 1944; Treadwell, *Women's Corps*, 235, 270, 490.

4. "Trip to Mitchel Field, New York, 6 July 1943,"

itinerary, OCH Papers, LOC; *NYT*, July 7, 1943; *NY Post*, July 24, 1943.

5. *NY Post*, July 24, 1943.

6. "Trip to San Antonio, Texas and Houston, Texas, July 15–20 and Appearance at Advertising Club of New York, July 21," OCH Papers, LOC; "Travel Schedule," OCH Papers, Rice; *NYT*, July 22, 1943.

7. "Itinerary, August 2–7, 1943," OCH Papers, LOC; notes, and Ed Kilman, "History of the *Houston Post*," both OCH Papers, Rice.

8. *Austin American*, September 15, 1943.

9. OCH to Charles Cushing, September 18, 1943, OCH Papers, Rice; Bugbee, *Officer and Lady*, 129–130; *Chattanooga Times*, September 23, 1943.

10. OCH to Mary Hobby Amis, September 30, 1943, OCH Papers, LOC; WPH to J. E. Josey, September 25, 1943, copy in Jesse H. Jones Papers, LOC; "Director's Engagements," October and November 1943, OCH Papers, LOC.

11. "Director's Engagements," October and November 1943, OCH Papers, LOC; *Dallas News*, October 24, 1943; *NY Journal American*, October 18, 1943.

12. Helon Johnson to OCH, October 5, 1943, and OCH to Johnson, October 7, 1943, OCH Papers, Rice.

13. Treadwell, *Women's Corps*, 235–236; Walsh, "Oveta Culp Hobby" (2006), 82.

14. Treadwell, *Women's Corps*, 227–231.

15. Treadwell, 233.

16. Pando, "Oveta Culp Hobby," 74; Treadwell, *Women's Corps*, 220–221, 233; *Time*, December 27, 1943.

17. *Time*, December 27, 1943.

18. Treadwell, *Women's Corps*, 246–247; *Time*, January 17, 1944.

19. Treadwell, *Women's Corps*, 246–247.

20. Treadwell, 270–272.

21. Bugbee, *Officer and Lady*, 140–141; Kimbrough, "Giles, Benjamin Franklin"; undated clipping from *Houston Post*, OCH Papers, Rice.

22. Helon Johnson to OCH, December 6, 1943, OCH Papers, Rice; Bugbee, *Officer and Lady*, 138–139.

23. Bugbee, 68.

24. Multiple letters and dates, Helon Johnson to OCH and OCH to Helon Johnson, OCH Papers, Rice.

25. Helon Johnson to OCH, March 31, October 12, November 29, and ca. December 1943, OCH Papers, Rice.

26. Helon Johnson to OCH, March 31, October 12,

November 29, and ca. December 1943, OCH Papers, Rice.

27. Bugbee, *Officer and Lady*, 139; *NYT*, January 10, 1944; Reich, *Nelson A. Rockefeller*, 514.

28. *Time*, January 17, 1944.

29. Clark, *Tactful Texan*, 185; AP, *Cincinnati Enquirer*, May 15, 1944.

30. *Time*, January 17, 1944.

31. *Time*, January 17, 1944.

32. Bugbee, *Officer and Lady*, 142.

33. Bugbee, 142; Clark, *Tactful Texan*, 185.

34. Bugbee, *Officer and Lady*, 140–141; *Rochester Democrat and Chronicle*, November 18, 1943; *NYT*, January 19 and 20, 1944.

35. Bugbee, *Officer and Lady*, 139, 144; *NYT*, February 4, 1944; Al Shire, "That Reminds Me," in Shire, *Oveta Culp Hobby*, 73–74.

36. Bugbee, *Officer and Lady*, 142.

37. Bugbee, 142–143, 144.

38. Bugbee, 139, 144; *NYT*, February 4, 1944.

39. Al Shire, "That Reminds Me," in Shire, *Oveta Culp Hobby*, 73–74; OCH, typescript of speech to Congressional Club, February 4, 1944, OCH Papers, Rice.

40. Al Shire, "That Reminds Me," in Shire, *Oveta Culp Hobby*, 73–74.

41. *NYT*, February 14, 1944.

42. Helon Johnson to OCH, February 17, 1944, OCH Papers, Rice.

CHAPTER 28

1. Oveta always publicly rejected the term "Hobby's Army" whenever newspaper reporters used it during interviews. Treadwell, *Women's Corps*, 268, 277.

2. Treadwell, 272.

3. Pogue, *George C. Marshall*, 113–114; *NYT*, February 4, 1944; Marshall to Herman W. Steinkraus, February 15, 1944, George C. Marshall Papers, GCMRL; Anna Wilson to OCH, ca. March 1944, OCH Papers, LOC; Treadwell, *Women's Corps*, 272.

4. Forrest Pogue's three-volume biography of General Marshall is the definitive source on his life and career. Aaron L. Friedberg, "Mission Impossible," *NYT Book Review*, June 10, 2018.

5. As Sutphen has pointed out, while Oveta was working in Washington, both during the war and after, she "moved gracefully among the all-male cliques of political power, as comfortable talking politics with President Roosevelt or House Majority Leader Sam Rayburn as she had been discussing the flooding of Buffalo Bayou with Houston's businessmen." Sutphen, "Conservative Warrior," 16–17, 21–22; Al Shire, "That Reminds Me," in Shire, *Oveta Culp Hobby*, 72; Roosevelt, *Ladies of Courage*; *Time*, May 4, 1953.

6. Treadwell, *Women's Corps*, 272–274; Pogue, *George C. Marshall*, 110.

7. Treadwell, *Women's Corps*, 272–274.

8. Treadwell, 272–274.

9. Treadwell, 272–274.

10. Treadwell, 272–274.

11. Marshall, memorandum for the Bureau of Public Relations, January 26, 1944, George C. Marshall Papers, GCMRL; Treadwell, *Women's Corps*, 274.

12. Treadwell, 275–277.

13. Treadwell, 719; *NYT*, July 4, 1944; *NY Journal American*, July 9, 1944; *Time*, July 10, 1944; Anna W. Wilson to OCH, July 12, 1944, and Helen Barr to OCH, July 20, 1944, OCH Papers, LOC.

14. Treadwell, *Women's Corps*, 713.

15. Treadwell, 719; Walsh, "Oveta Culp Hobby" (2006), 155; Marshall to OCH, July 27, 1944, George C. Marshall Papers, GCMRL.

16. B. Hobby, *How Things Really Work*, 20; OCH to George C. Beach, October 26, 1944, OCH Papers, LOC; Treadwell, *Women's Corps*, 719; Miller White to OCH, ca. August 1944, OCH Papers, LOC; *Dallas Morning News*, October 16, 1944.

17. Pando, "Oveta Culp Hobby," 96; Treadwell, *Women's Corps*, 722.

18. ER to OCH, May 4, 1944, ER Papers, FDRPL; Cook, *Eleanor Roosevelt*, 518, 518n, 647.

19. Treadwell, *Women's Corps*, 599; Moore, *To Serve My Country*, 105.

20. Treadwell, *Women's Corps*, 721; Harry Johnston to OCH, April 27, 1944, OCH Papers, LOC; Pogue, *George C. Marshall*, 108.

21. Treadwell, *Women's Corps*, 721; Walsh, "Oveta Culp Hobby" (2006), 163; M. G. White to George C. Marshall, December 19, 1944, OCH Papers, Rice.

22. Treadwell, *Women's Corps*, 721; Walsh, "Oveta Culp Hobby" (2006), 163; *NYT*, January 1 and 9, 1945; *NY Herald Tribune*, January 10, 1945; Sutphen, "Conservative Warrior," 31–32; OCH to "Miss Mashburn," April 2, 1984, OCH Papers, Rice; Mary McLeod Bethune to OCH, January 2, 1945, OCH Papers, LOC.

23. M. G. White to OCH, ca. August 1971, and

OCH to M. G. White, August 12, 1971, OCH Papers, Rice.

24. In December 1943, an anonymous writer sent an unsigned memorandum to the Democratic National Committee accusing Oveta of disloyalty to the Roosevelt administration because of the *Houston Post*'s editorial attacks on the president. The memo had a clip of one of the *Post*'s anti-Roosevelt editorials that had appeared that month. The *Post* editorial denounced the administration's efforts to outlaw the poll tax and declared that the "moving forces behind [abolishing the tax] are the Negro leaders, the radical and Communistic press and the C.I.O. lobbyists." To what degree Oveta was involved in or approved the attacks on FDR is unknown, but she had to have been aware of the editorials. A copy of each morning's *Houston Post* was airmailed and delivered to Oveta's desk at the Pentagon every day. It's possible that this was an area in which Oveta simply deferred to Will, if for no other reason than she had no time to be involved. The months prior to the 1944 presidential campaign were extremely busy and tense ones for Oveta and the WAC. Clipping of *Houston Post* editorial, ca. December 1943, in "Correspondence with State Leaders—Texas, 1940–1948," Democratic National Committee files, FDRPL; Clark, *Tactful Texan*, 185–186.

25. Winik, *FDR*, 508–509; B. Hobby, *How Things Really Work*, 13; Bill Hobby, interview.

26. Lelyveld, *His Final Battle*, 264.

27. Fenberg, *Unprecedented Power*, 507.

28. Timmons, *Jesse H. Jones*, 356–357; Fenberg, *Unprecedented Power*, 510; B. Hobby, *How Things Really Work*, 13.

29. Clark, *Tactful Texan*, 187; Timmons, *Jesse H. Jones*, 352–358.

30. Fenberg, *Unprecedented Power*, 519–520.

31. *NY Herald Tribune*, May 17, 1945; OCH to H. Johnson, May 5, 1945, and Ed Kilman, "History of the *Houston Post*," OCH Papers, Rice; Clark, *Tactful Texan*, 188; Treadwell, *Women's Corps*, 720.

32. Treadwell, 726; M. Johnston, *Houston*, 339–340.

33. Treadwell, *Women's Corps*, 720–721; Adjutant General's Office to OCH, July 11, 1945, "Orders," official military personnel file for OCH, Office of Military Personnel files, 1912–1998, RG 319, National Archives (hereafter NA).

34. Colonel Boyce later married and took her

husband's last name, which was Long. Nicholas Westray, "Westray Battle Long," *Dictionary of North Carolina Biography*, 94–95; Treadwell, *Women's Corps*, 722.

35. Adjutant General's Office to OCH, July 11, 1945, "Orders," official military personnel file for OCH, Office of Military Personnel files, 1912–1998, RG 319, NA.

36. *Washington Post*, August 1, 1945; Bugbee, *Officer and Lady*, 183.

37. *NYT*, July 19, 1945; *Time*, July 23, 1945; Treadwell, *Women's Corps*, 722–723; M. Johnston, *Houston*, 339–340; *Washington Post*, August 1, 1945.

38. *Washington Post*, August 1, 1945.

39. *NY Herald Tribune*, July 14, 1945.

40. Treadwell, *Women's Corps*, 723.

41. Treadwell, 724–725.

42. Treadwell, 724–725; Bugbee, *Officer and Lady*, 187.

43. Treadwell, *Women's Corps*, 75–77, 733, 742, 746–749; Pando, "Oveta Culp Hobby," 74–75.

44. Pando, "Oveta Culp Hobby," 117–118; Walsh, "Oveta Culp Hobby" (2015), 328.

45. M. Johnston, *Houston*, 339; Mattie Treadwell to Katherine Schultz, November 16, 1994, OCH Papers, Rice.

46. Walsh, "Oveta Culp Hobby" (2006), 173–174.

47. Ruth C. Streeter to OCH, ca. 1980s, OCH Papers, Rice.

CHAPTER 29

1. Carleton, *Red Scare*, 12–13.

2. In response to President Truman's message, Oveta wrote, "I hope you know how much it means to have one's Commander-in-Chief say 'well done.' Our thoughts and prayers are with you constantly." Truman to Sam Taub, September 14, 1945, and OCH to Truman, October 20, 1945, PPF file 1922, Harry S. Truman Papers, Harry S. Truman Presidential Library (hereafter HSTPL); *NYT*, May 15, 1949; Marshall to OCH, September 18, 1945, George C. Marshall Papers, GCMRL; Clark, *Tactful Texan*, 188.

3. *Austin American-Statesman*, September 14, 1945; Clark, *Tactful Texan*, 188; OCH, "Calling the Shots," in Shire, *Oveta Culp Hobby*, 64; Pando, "Oveta Culp Hobby," 102; OCH speech files, OCH Papers, Rice; Walsh, "Oveta Culp Hobby" (2006), 167.

4. *Daily Texan*, August 23, 1945; Allen Kander correspondence with OCH, OCH Papers, Rice.

5. OCH to Helon Johnson, February 9, 1945, OCH Papers, Rice.

6. Will made Laro a director of the Houston Post Company in 1950. *Houston Post*, December 20, 1950; Clark, *Tactful Texan*, 187–189.

7. *NY Herald Tribune*, September 25, 1945.

8. *Time*, May 30, 1960, p. 64; Bill Hobby, interview; "3 Are Elected as Directors of Houston Post," *Editor and Publisher*, December 30, 1950.

9. J. A. Phillips to WPH, March 28, 1949, Jesse H. Jones Papers, DBCAH; Scott, *Interesting People*, 176; "3 Are Elected as Directors of Houston Post," *Editor and Publisher*, December 30, 1950; "Houston Post" files, OCH Papers, Rice; Clark, *Tactful Texan*, 187–188; *Houston Chronicle*, December 14, 1955; anonymous, "Lewis, Judd Mortimer."

10. J. A. Phillips to WPH, March 28, 1949, Jesse H. Jones Papers, DBCAH.

11. Jake Butler to Jones, May 31, 1949, with addendum from Emmet Walter, Jesse H. Jones Papers, DBCAH.

12. "Arnold Rosenfeld," in Shire, *Oveta Culp Hobby*, 42; David Westheimer quote from unidentified magazine clip, OCH Papers, Rice.

13. Scott, *Interesting People*, 179.

14. Clark, *Tactful Texan*, 193; "Leon Hale" and "Arnold Rosenfeld," in Shire, *Oveta Culp Hobby*, 23, 42.

15. David Westheimer quote from unidentified magazine clip, OCH Papers, Rice.

16. *Time*, May 4, 1953; undated clip of AP story, OCH Papers, Rice.

17. *Time*, May 4, 1953; undated clip of AP story, OCH Papers, Rice.

18. A native of Newton, Mississippi, and a graduate of Millsaps College, Peggy Buchanan worked for Oveta from 1960 until the latter's death in 1995. She also served as treasurer of the Hobby Foundation. She died in 2007. *Houston Chronicle*, October 23, 2007; "Peggy Buchanan," in Shire, *Oveta Culp Hobby*, 10; Clark, *Tactful Texan*, 193; Pando, "Oveta Culp Hobby," 3; *Editor and Publisher*, February 24, 1951; undated clip of AP story, OCH Papers, Rice; *Time*, May 4, 1953.

19. Gunn, "Tips, Kern"; "3 Are Elected as Directors of Houston Post," *Editor and Publisher*, December 30, 1950; Harris, Huhndorff, and McGrew, *Fault*; OCH speech, typescript, OCH speech files, OCH Papers, Rice.

20. William Simpson, "An Appraisal of Interior Furnishings for the Estate of William P. Hobby,"

November 1, 1964, WPH Sr. Papers, DBCAH; OCH to Emma Culp, June 18, 1946, Bill Hobby Papers, DBCAH.

21. M. Johnston, *Houston*, 194; *Time*, May 4, 1953.

22. Jack McGrew to Bill Hobby, January 15, 1991, Bill Hobby Papers, DBCAH; *Time*, May 4, 1953; "Cecil McBride," in Shire, *Oveta Culp Hobby*, 36.

23. *Time*, May 4, 1953; Paul Hobby, "Consistent, But Complicated," ix, and Susan Barnes, 5, in Shire, *Oveta Culp Hobby*.

24. For a full discussion of the lives and careers of Herman and George Brown, see Pratt and Castaneda, *Builders*; M. Johnston, *Houston*, 386–387; Carleton, *Red Scare*, 70–71; Pando, "Oveta Culp Hobby," 129.

25. Carleton, *Red Scare*, 12–15.

26. *Life*, October 21, 1946, pp. 108–117; *New Yorker*, March 13, 1948.

27. Carleton, *Red Scare*, 12–15; Pando, "Oveta Culp Hobby," 131–132.

28. T. White, "Texas," 10–17.

29. Carleton, *Red Scare*, 71.

30. OCH to Elkins, February 12, 1945, OCH Papers, Rice; Carleton, 70–71.

31. Texas Eastern's pipelines, known as Big Inch and Little Inch, were built by the federal government during World War II and purchased by the company after the war. Carleton, *Breed So Rare*, 399, 402–403, and *Red Scare*, 7.

32. Carleton, *Red Scare*, 70–71.

33. Carleton, 70.

34. Clark, *Tactful Texan*, 198.

35. Clark, 189; Jones to E. M. Antrim, June 4, 1946, Jesse H. Jones Papers, DBCAH.

36. Clark, *Tactful Texan*, 188–189.

37. Mellinger, "Newspaper Editors," 21; O. Hobby, *Around the World*, 1.

38. O. Hobby, 1.

39. O. Hobby, 1.

40. O. Hobby, 1–2.

41. O. Hobby, 8–10.

42. O. Hobby, 16, 18, 23.

43. O. Hobby, 25, 29.

44. O. Hobby, 31–34.

45. O. Hobby, 43.

46. O. Hobby, 46–47.

47. O. Hobby, 54.

48. O. Hobby, 50–54.

49. O. Hobby, 55.

50. O. Hobby, 62–65.

51. *Honolulu Star-Bulletin*, June 30, 1947; O. Hobby, *Around the World*, 55, 62–65.

52. O. Hobby, 67; *Oakland Tribune*, June 30, 1947; "PAA Clipper 'America' Circles Globe," *Sky Writer* (Pan American Airways newsletter), July 1947.

53. Because *Around the World in 13 Days* was a private printing that Oveta distributed to friends and associates, it has no cataloging information, including the name of the publisher and the date of publication, but it was likely printed in late 1947; O. Hobby, *Around the World*, 67.

## CHAPTER 30

1. Mirroring Will's illnesses were those of some of his longtime associates, including his mentors. John Henry Kirby had died in 1940, while Ross Sterling would die in 1949. *Texas Parade*, March 1953, p. 18.

2. "Posh" Oltorf to Bill Hobby, March 28, 2002, Bill Hobby Papers, DBCAH.

3. *Dallas Morning News*, March 17, 1949; Clark, *Tactful Texan*, 190–191; Ed Kilman, "History of the *Houston Post*," OCH Papers, Rice; *Houston Post*, April 22, 1948.

4. "C of C Highway Group Honors Chairman Hobby," *Houston* (magazine), July 1950, p. 16; *Houston Post*, June 10, 1950.

5. Clark, *Tactful Texan*, 190; Pando, "Oveta Culp Hobby," 10–13.

6. *Dallas News*, October 11, 1948; various undated news clips in OCH scrapbook, OCH Papers, Rice; Pando, "Oveta Culp Hobby," 134.

7. Pando, "Oveta Culp Hobby," 39, 134, 138–139; *NYT*, March 1, 1948.

8. News clip from unidentified newspaper, March 13, 1945, "Freedom of Information Conference, United Nations," Harry S. Truman Papers, HSTPL; Clark, *Tactful Texan*, 189.

9. "Re: William Benton," Memorandum to Files, February 18, 1948, PPF file, Harry S. Truman Papers, HSTPL; Canham, "Freedom of Information," 584–598; Chafee, "Legal Problems," 545–583.

10. "Foreign Relations of the United States, 1948, General; the United Nations, Volume I, Part 1: Document 189," US Department of State, Office of the Historian, accessed March 11, 2020, https://history.state.gov/historicaldocuments/frus1948v01p1/d189; US Department of State, *Department of State Bulletin*, March 21, 1948, p. 378; Canham, "Freedom of Information," 584–598.

11. Ed Kilman, "History of the *Houston Post*," OCH Papers, Rice; Pando, "Oveta Culp Hobby," 137–138; *Houston Post*, June 13, 1948; *Houston Chronicle*, May 23, 1948.

12. Herbert Hoover to OCH, May 14, 1948, OCH Papers, Rice; Pemberton, "Hoover Commission."

13. OCH to Herbert Hoover, May 17, 1948, OCH Papers, Rice.

14. Pando, "Oveta Culp Hobby," 140–141; Pemberton, "Hoover Commission."

15. Pemberton, 1.

16. Pemberton, 1; Pando, "Oveta Culp Hobby," 63; Ed Kilman, "History of the *Houston Post*," OCH Papers, Rice.

17. Pemberton, "Hoover Commission," 1.

18. *NY Herald Tribune*, December 13, 1949; OCH quote in AP wire story, December 15, 1950.

19. Ed Kilman, "History of the *Houston Post*," OCH Papers, Rice; Pando, "Oveta Culp Hobby," 63, 141–142; *NY Daily News*, April 27, 1950.

20. Adamczyk, *Readers Guide*.

21. The OCH Papers at Rice contain a file of correspondence between Oveta and Treadwell about the project. For examples, see Treadwell to OCH, July 14, 1948, Treadwell to OCH, April 21, 1950, OCH to Treadwell, July 10, 1950, Helon Johnson to OCH, July 12, 1950, Treadwell to OCH, July 13, 1950, and OCH to Treadwell, July 26, 1950, OCH Papers, Rice; Treadwell, *Women's Corps*, xiii, 29.

22. *Houston Post*, December 12, 1950; Treadwell to OCH, November 16, 1950, and Treadwell to Katherine Schultz, November 16, 1994, OCH Papers, Rice; Treadwell, *Women's Corps*, xiv.

23. In his foreword, General Ward candidly noted the army "was shocked by the advent of a women's corps in its midst. The Army did not always understand the WAC—its needs and temperament, and the many other things that man, being the son of woman, should have known but did not, much to his continued embarrassment." Treadwell, xiii.

24. Harris, Huhndorff, and McGrew, *Fault*, 5–6.

25. OCH, interview, July 11, 1969, LBJPL.

26. Harris, Huhndorff, and McGrew, *Fault*, 5–6; OCH, interview, July 11, 1969, LBJPL.

27. Harris, Huhndorff, and McGrew, *Fault*, 6–7.

28. Barnouw, *Image Empire*.

29. *Fort Worth Star-Telegram* publisher Amon Carter's WBAP-TV was the first television station in Texas. Its first broadcast was in September 1948. "The History of Channel 5," NBC DFW, October 8, 2008, https://www

.nbcdfw.com/on-air/about-us/The_History_Of
_Channel_5.html; "W. Albert Lee," biographical
files, DBCAH.

30. OCH, interview, July 11, 1969, LBJPL.

31. OCH, interview, July 11, 1969, LBJPL; Harris,
Huhndorff, and McGrew, *Fault*, 7.

32. OCH, interview, July 11, 1969, LBJPL.

33. McGrew to Bill Hobby, January 15, 1991, Bill
Hobby Papers, DBCAH.

34. Harris, Huhndorff, and McGrew, *Fault*, 7.

35. Harris, Huhndorff, and McGrew, 7; M. Johnston,
*Houston*, 386.

36. McGrew to Bill Hobby, January 15, 1991, Bill
Hobby Papers, DBCAH; OCH, interview, July 11,
1969, LBJPL; Pando, "Oveta Culp Hobby," 127.

37. James Elkins to OCH, March 27, 1950, and
Purchase Contract, March 27, 1950, OCH
Papers, Rice; Will and Oveta to Jones, March 25,
1950, and Jones to Will and Oveta, March 25,
1950, Jesse H. Jones Papers, DBCAH.

38. Pando, "Oveta Culp Hobby," 127; OCH, inter-
view, July 11, 1969, LBJPL; Bill Hobby to John
Davis, March 25, 1950, Bill Hobby Papers,
DBCAH; Bill Hobby, interview.

39. Typescript of Will Hobby's remarks, speech files,
OCH Papers, Rice; Dick Gottlieb, interview.

40. *Houston Post*, July 2, 1950; Dick Gottlieb,
interview.

41. Jack McGrew to Bill Hobby, January 15, 1991,
Bill Hobby Papers, DBCAH; Harris, Huhndorff,
and McGrew, *Fault*, 7–10; *Houston Chronicle*,
March 2, 1986.

42. *Houston Chronicle*, March 2, 1986; Harris,
Huhndorff, and McGrew, *Fault*, 7–10.

43. President, National Bank of Commerce, to
Houston Post Company, June 25, 1953, Jesse H.
Jones Papers, DBCAH.

CHAPTER 31

1. *Houston Post*, December 8, 1949.

2. *Houston Post*, December 8, 1949; Clark, *Tactful
Texan*, 195; Timmons, *Jesse H. Jones*, 381;
Fenberg, *Unprecedented Power*, 555.

3. *Houston Post*, December 8, 1949; *Galveston
Daily News*, December 9, 1949; Clark, *Tactful
Texan*, 195; Timmons, *Jesse H. Jones*, 381;
Fenberg, *Unprecedented Power*, 555.

4. J. R. Parten, interview; McKay, *Texas Politics*,
355–390; G. Green, *Establishment*, 32–38.

5. *NY Sun*, May 26, 1947, in OCH file, *NY Herald
Tribune* Morgue, DBCAH.

6. Pando, "Oveta Culp Hobby," 150–151; *Houston

Post*, January 3, 1940; transcript of Bill Hobby's
column, Jesse H. Jones Papers, DBCAH.

7. For George and Herman Brown's antilabor
views, see Caro, *Path to Power*, 369–373;
Lichtenstein, *State of the Union*, 115–117.

8. Lichtenstein, 115–117; *Houston Post*, June 15,
1947; McCullough, *Truman*, 565–566.

9. Sutphen, "Conservative Warrior," 32; Clark, *Tactful Texan*, 190; Carleton, *Red Scare*, 229–230,
*Breed So Rare*, 410.

10. *NY Herald Tribune*, September 15, 1948; Clark,
*Tactful Texan*, 194.

11. Clark, 190; Sutphen, "Conservative Warrior," 33.

12. McCullough, *Truman*, 672; Sutphen, "Conservative Warrior," 33–34n, 672.

13. B. Hobby, *How Things Really Work*, 26; Frank
"Posh" Oltorf, interview, LBJPL.

14. Clark, *Tactful Texan*, 190; Ed Kilman, "History
of the *Houston Post*," OCH Papers, Rice; "Posh"
Oltorf and Morris Roberts interviews, both
LBJPL.

15. Pando, "Oveta Culp Hobby," 136.

16. Pando, 136; Marshall to OCH, undated carbon
copy, OCH Papers, Rice.

17. Committee on Armed Services, "Nomination of
Anna Rosenberg," 333–371; *American Magazine*,
1953, vol. 155, p. 108; Reeves, *Joe McCarthy*,
360–361; Oshinsky, *Conspiracy So Immense*,
203–205; Pando, "Oveta Culp Hobby," 136.

18. Telegram, George Marshall to OCH, August 18,
1951, OCH Papers, Rice; McCullough, *Truman*,
741–742.

19. Pando, "Oveta Culp Hobby," 143–146; Cone,
"Right to Deceive," 148–156.

20. McCullough, *Truman*, 843; *Houston Post*, April
12, 1951; Albert Thomas to WPH and OCH,
April 18, 1951, OCH Papers, Rice.

21. Ambrose, *Eisenhower, Vol. I*, 525, 527.

22. H. Brownell, *Advising Ike*, 107; Parmet, *Eisenhower*, 223; news clip in OCH file, *NY Journal
American* Morgue, DBCAH; Jacobs, "American
Assembly," 455–468; DDE to OCH, June 12,
1951, OCH Papers, Rice.

23. *Houston Magazine*, March 1951; Clark, *Tact-
ful Texan*, 185; E. R. McWilliams to WPH
and OCH, February 25, 1951, and "Speech to
National Conference of Christians and Jews,"
February 28, 1951, OCH Papers, Rice; Sutphen,
"Conservative Warrior," 45.

24. Marguerite Johnston, typescript, Bill Hobby
Papers, DBCAH.

25. Eisenhower, *Mandate for Change*, 20, 27, 28.

26. *Life*, May 19, 1952, p. 34; Parmet, *Eisenhower*, 76.

27. *Houston Post*, April 13, 1952.

28. *Houston Post*, April 13 and 22, 1952; *Time*, November 24, 1952, p. 20; Keith McCanse to OCH, May 9, 1952, OCH Papers, DDEPL; Parmet, *Eisenhower*, 76.

29. Eleanor Roosevelt, who supported Adlai Stevenson in 1952, later observed, "Had Oveta Hobby been born and brought up in the North, she undoubtedly would be a Republican. . . . [I]t can be assumed that she would belong to the progressive wing." Roosevelt, *Ladies of Courage*, 224–225; Parmet, *Eisenhower*, 76; Carleton, *Red Scare*, 229.

30. Parmet, *Eisenhower*, 77; Carleton, *Red Scare*, 229.

31. Parmet, *Eisenhower*, 76; Ambrose, *Eisenhower, Vol. I*, 536; *Time*, May 4, 1953.

32. H. Brownell, *Advising Ike*, 112; *Houston Post*, May 28, 1952; *Houston Press*, November 26, 1952; Pando, "Oveta Culp Hobby," 115.

33. Pando, 155; Parmet, *Eisenhower*, 79; Clark, *Tactful Texan*, 196.

34. Eisenhower campaign leader Herbert Brownell later noted, "[Oveta] was a powerhouse for gathering Eisenhower support in her state." H. Brownell, *Advising Ike*, 112; Clark, *Tactful Texan*, 196; Dillon Anderson to OCH, July 1, 1952, and OCH to M. S. McCorquodale, June 30, 1952, OCH Papers, DDEPL; Parmet, *Eisenhower*, 98–100; Ambrose, *Eisenhower, Vol. II*, 24.

35. Carleton, *Red Scare*, 229.

36. OCH to Sam Rayburn, August 18, 1952; Rayburn Papers, BCAH; Bill Hobby to John Davis, August 7, 1952, Bill Hobby Papers, DBCAH; WPH to Jones, August 22, 1952, Jesse H. Jones Papers, DBCAH; OCH to Mary Lord, September 4, 1952, and Dillon Anderson to OCH, August 20, 1952, OCH Papers, DDEPL.

37. OCH to Mrs. Walter Williams and Mrs. Oswald Lord, September 4, 1952, OCH Papers, DDEPL; DDE to OCH, October 25, 1952, and OCH to Arthur Vandenburg, telegram, OCH Papers, Rice; Parmet, *Eisenhower*, 147; *Houston Chronicle*, October 21, 1952; Pando, "Oveta Culp Hobby," 154–156.

38. Pando, 157; *Time*, May 4, 1953; Al Shire, "That Reminds Me," in Shire, *Oveta Culp Hobby*, 69.

39. *Houston Post*, September 5, 11, 26, and 30, and October 1 and 29, 1952.

40. Carleton, *Red Scare*, 85–86.

41. *Austin American-Statesman*, February 12, 1950;

*NYT*, May 6, 1950; *Editor and Publisher*, May 6, 1950; Pando, "Oveta Culp Hobby," 142.

42. Undated clip, *Rice Thresher* 37, no. 16, Bill Hobby Papers, DBCAH.

43. Carleton, *Red Scare*, 85–88.

44. Carleton, 85–88.

45. Carleton, 87–88.

46. Clark, *Tactful Texan*, 197; Carleton, *Red Scare*, 171.

47. Carleton, 81, x.

48. *Houston Post*, October 14 and 15, 1952; Branyan and Larsen, *Eisenhower Administration*, 123–125; Parmet, *Eisenhower*, 223; *Dallas Morning News*, October 15 and 16, 1952; Joe Ingraham to OCH, October 12, 1952, and DDE to OCH, October 16, 1952, OCH Papers, Rice.

49. DDE to OCH, October 23, 1952, OCH Papers, Rice.

50. DDE to OCH, November 3, 1952, and miscellaneous undated notes, OCH Papers, Rice; Clark, *Tactful Texan*, 197; Ambrose, *Eisenhower, Vol. I*, 571; Parmet, *Eisenhower*, 144.

51. Bill Hobby to John Davis, November 7, 1952, Bill Hobby Papers, DBCAH; OCH, typescript copy of speech to the API, November 13, 1952, Jesse H. Jones Papers, DBCAH.

52. *NY Journal American*, April 8, 1952.

53. Parmet, *Eisenhower*, 168; Adams, *First-Hand Report*, 62; Sutphen, "Conservative Warrior," 47–50.

54. Eisenhower, *Mandate for Change*, 92; Sutphen, "Conservative Warrior," 47–50.

55. Eleanor Roosevelt observed, "[Eisenhower] had a chance during the war to observe just how good an administrator Oveta Hobby is." Roosevelt, *Ladies of Courage*, 225; Eisenhower, *Mandate for Change*, 92.

56. Eisenhower, 92, 493; Parmet, *Eisenhower*, 16–17, 286–287; Ambrose, *Eisenhower, Vol. I*, 515.

57. Eisenhower, *Mandate for Change*, 92; *Austin American*, November 22, 1952.

58. Jack McGrew to Bill Hobby, January 15, 1991, Bill Hobby Papers, DBCAH; Bill Hobby, interview.

59. *U.S. News and World Report*, December 26, 1952; Reich, *Nelson A. Rockefeller*, 527.

60. Sherman Adams to OCH, December 5, 1952, OCH Papers, Rice; Hoover to OCH, November 28, 1952, and OCH to Hoover, December 26, 1952, "Mrs. Oveta Culp Hobby Correspondence File," Herbert Hoover Papers, Herbert Hoover Presidential Library (hereafter HHPL).

61. George C. Marshall to OCH, December 5, 1952, OCH Papers, Rice; OCH to ER, February 6, 1953, OCH file, Eleanor Roosevelt Papers, FDRPL.

62. *Editor and Publisher*, undated clip in OCH file, *NY Herald Tribune* Morgue, DBCAH; *NYT*, November 26, 1952.

63. Lyndon and Lady Bird Johnson, telegram to OCH, November 26, 1952; LBJ to Eugene D. Millikin, January 14, 1953, and OCH to LBJ, January 23, 1953, "Famous Names File," LBJ Senate Papers, LBJPL; Sam Rayburn to OCH, December 13, 1952, OCH Papers, Rice.

64. *NYT*, January 17, 1952; Sutphen, "Conservative Warrior," 50–51.

65. Pando, "Oveta Culp Hobby," 166; Carleton, *Red Scare*, 83–84.

66. *NY Journal American*, November 30, 1952.

CHAPTER 32

1. OCH to Sherman Adams, telegram, December 30, 1952, OCH Papers, DDEPL; *Chicago Tribune*, January 19, 1953.

2. Lady Bird Johnson and OCH interviews, LBJPL; Sutphen, "Conservative Warrior," 52.

3. Committee on Finance, "Nominations"; Pando, "Oveta Culp Hobby," 159; Sutphen, "Conservative Warrior," 52–53.

4. *Austin American-Statesman*, January 20, 1953; *NY Journal American*, January 22, 1953.

5. Eisenhower, *Mandate for Change*, 100; Adams, *First-Hand Report*, 67; Sherman Adams to OCH, December 29, 1952, OCH Papers, DDEPL.

6. Eisenhower, *Mandate for Change*, 102; *Time*, May 4, 1953; *LA Times*, January 20, 1953.

7. Eisenhower, *Mandate for Change*, 108; *NY Journal American*, January 22, 1953.

8. *Dallas News*, January 23, 1953.

9. OCH to Charlotte Comfort, June 11, 1954, OCH Papers, DDEPL; Hurt, "Great Ladies," 228; *NYT*, June 3, 1954.

10. *NY Daily News*, January 23, 1954.

11. Parmet, *Eisenhower*, 176; Eisenhower, *Mandate for Change*, 133–134.

12. Sutphen, "Conservative Warrior," 329; Al Shire, "That Reminds Me," in Shire, *Oveta Culp Hobby*, 70.

13. Adams, *First-Hand Report*, 5; Hughes, *Ordeal of Power*, 67.

14. Eisenhower, *Mandate for Change*, 309, and *Diaries*, 227; Sutphen, "Conservative Warrior," 21.

15. Pando, "Oveta Culp Hobby," 168; Miles,

*Department of Health*, 17; *Dallas Morning News*, January 25, 1953; *San Antonio Express*, March 29, 1953.

16. Sutphen, "Conservative Warrior," 63–64.

17. Sutphen, 55, 81; Berkowitz, *Mr. Social Security*, 91.

18. Altmeyer, *Formative Years*; Sutphen, "Conservative Warrior," 84; William Mitchell, interview, Columbia University Oral History Collection (hereafter Columbia).

19. Nelson Cruikshank, interview, Columbia; Reich, *Nelson A. Rockefeller*, 522–526; Sutphen, "Conservative Warrior," 85.

20. Sutphen, 81–83.

21. Sutphen, 15, 54, 84–85.

22. *Life*, April 27, 1953; *Time*, May 4, 1953; *Businessweek*, May 16, 1953; Sutphen, "Conservative Warrior," 54–58.

23. *NY Daily News*, March 21, 1953; Sutphen, "Conservative Warrior," 60.

24. Sutphen, 66.

25. Oveta declared in a speech in Chicago in the spring of 1953, "Although I am basically a newspaper woman, I also have been associated, until I resigned all my connections to become Federal Security Administrator, with a radio and a television outlet." OCH, "The Newspaper," speech to the Economic Club of Chicago, March 23, 1953; Reich, *Nelson A. Rockefeller*, 499–500, 503; R. Smith, *His Own Terms*, 218–219.

26. *NY Herald Tribune*, March 13, 1953; R. Smith, *His Own Terms*, 220–221.

27. Doris Fleeson column, OCH file, *NY Journal American* Morgue, DBCAH.

28. *NYT*, February 16, 1953; Pando, "Oveta Culp Hobby," 173–174.

29. Sutphen, "Conservative Warrior," 69–70; Reich, *Nelson A. Rockefeller*, 507; R. Smith, *His Own Terms*, 220; Doris Fleeson column, OCH file, *NYJournal American* Morgue, DBCAH; Carleton, *Red Scare*, 150.

30. Doris Fleeson column, OCH file, *NY Journal American* Morgue, DBCAH.

31. George Reedy and OCH interviews, LBJPL.

32. Reich, *Nelson A. Rockefeller*, 517.

33. Within a month after Oveta's testimony Taft would be diagnosed with cancer, and he would be dead by July 1953. Undated news clip in OCH file, *NY Journal American* Morgue, DBCAH; Reich, *Nelson A. Rockefeller*, 517; *NYT*, April 27, 1953; *San Antonio Express*, March 29, 1953; *NY Herald Tribune*, October 8, 1953; OCH, interview, July 11, 1969, LBJPL.

34. *Time*, May 4, 1953.

35. Sutphen, "Conservative Warrior," 13, 72; OCH to Johnsons, April 21, 1953, OCH Papers, Rice.

36. *Dallas News*, March 19, 1953; *NY Herald Tribune*, April 2, 1953; *Life*, April 27, 1953, p. 36.

37. Parmet, *Eisenhower*, 191; *NYT*, April 12, 1953; *Life*, April 27, 1953, pp. 36–38; *Time*, May 4, 1953; Jesse Jones to Walter Trohan, May 5, 1953, "Jesse H. Jones File," Walter Trohan Papers, HHPL.

38. Reich, *Life of Rockefeller*, 511; R. Smith, *His Own Terms*, 221.

39. Reich, *Life of Rockefeller*, 511; R. Smith, *His Own Terms*, 221.

40. Reich, *Life of Rockefeller*, 507; R. Smith, *His Own Terms*, 220–221.

41. Sally Kirkland to OCH, April 15, 1953, OCH Papers, DDEPL; *Life*, April 27, 1953, pp. 36–39.

42. *Washington Star*, April 19, 1953.

43. Altmeyer, *Formative Years*, 221; Wilbur Cohen, interview, December 8, 1968, LBJPL; DeWitt, "Never a Finished Thing."

44. DeWitt.

45. Barbara Gunderson to Jack Beardwood, May 18, 1953, HEW bound volumes, vol. 13, Nelson A. Rockefeller Papers, Rockefeller Archive Center (hereafter RAC).

46. Wilbur Cohen, interview, December 8, 1968, LBJPL; Berkowitz, *Mr. Social Security*, 87; *NYT*, November 15, 1953; Reich, *Nelson A. Rockefeller*, 522–525.

47. Rockefeller to Jane Hoey, October 27, 1953, and "List of Letters Submitted to HEW on the Dismissal of Jane Hoey—All Critical," HEW bound volumes, vol. 13, Nelson A. Rockefeller Papers, RAC; Wilbur Cohen, interview, December 8, 1968, LBJPL; *NYT*, November 4, 1953; "Hoey, Jane M.," VCU Libraries Social Welfare History Project, accessed March 29, 2020, http://www.socialwelfarehistory.com/people/hoey-jane-m/.

48. *Washington Star*, April 19, 1953; *Life*, April 27, 1953.

49. *Life*, April 27, 1953; Reich, *Nelson A. Rockefeller*, 516–517.

50. Braden, *Just Enough Rope*, 66.

51. Nelson Cruikshank, interview, Columbia; Reich, *Nelson A. Rockefeller*, 515; *Texas Parade*, 18; Braden, *Just Enough Rope*, 66–67.

## CHAPTER 33

1. Reich, *Nelson A. Rockefeller*, 516–517.

2. J. Smith, "Jane Spaulding," 611; "Jane Morrow Spaulding," press release, April 14, 1953, HEW bound volumes, vol. 13, Nelson A. Rockefeller Papers, RAC; Sutphen, "Conservative Warrior," 126; *Life*, April 27, 1953.

3. Braden, *Just Enough Rope*, 63–64.

4. Press release, March 16, 1954, HEW bound volumes, vol. 13, Nelson A. Rockefeller Papers, RAC; Sutphen, "Conservative Warrior," 150.

5. Press release, March 16, 1954, HEW bound volumes, vol. 13, Nelson A. Rockefeller Papers, RAC; Reich, *Nelson A. Rockefeller*, 520–521; *NYT*, January 23, 1954; Al Shire, "That Reminds Me," in Shire, *Oveta Culp Hobby*, 75.

6. Braden, *Just Enough Rope*, 66–67.

7. Braden, 65–66.

8. Reich, *Nelson A. Rockefeller*, 529.

9. R. Smith, *His Own Terms*, 222–223; OCH to Heather Catto, January 9, 1979, OCH Papers, Rice.

10. Reich, *Nelson A. Rockefeller*, 521–522; R. Smith, *His Own Terms*, 222–223.

11. Liz Carpenter, speech typescript, "Tribute to Oveta Culp Hobby," January 19, 1986, Bill Hobby Papers, DBCAH.

12. Reich, *Nelson A. Rockefeller*, 518.

13. Braden, *Just Enough Rope*, 67.

14. Sutphen, "Conservative Warrior," 88; Reich, *Nelson A. Rockefeller*, 521; *NYT*, August 15, 1953; OCH, interview, July 11, 1969, LBJPL; *Minneapolis Star*, January 21, 1954.

15. *Time*, May 4, 1953.

16. Oshinsky, *Conspiracy So Immense*, 217–218; Reich, *Nelson A. Rockefeller*, 517.

17. *Austin American*, April 28, 1953.

18. *NY World Telegram*, April 27, 1953; *Houston Post*, July 31, 1951; *Dallas Morning News*, April 28, 1953.

19. Reich, *Nelson A. Rockefeller*, 516; *NY World Telegram*, April 27, 1953; *Dallas News*, May 4, 1953.

20. *NY Post*, April 30, 1955; *Newsweek*, May 11, 1953; Pando, "Oveta Culp Hobby," 164; Peter Edson column, unidentified newspaper, ca. February 1955, OCH biographical file, DBCAH.

21. *Time*, May 4, 1953; Reich, *Nelson A. Rockefeller*, 516; OCH, interview, July 11, 1969, LBJPL.

22. *NYT*, August 2, 1953.

23. Reich, *Nelson A. Rockefeller*, 516–517.

24. Braden, *Just Enough Rope*, 67.

25. *Time*, May 4, 1953; *NY Post*, April 30, 1955; Sutphen, "Conservative Warrior," 75.

26. *Time*, May 4, 1953; *NY Journal American*, September 20, 1953; *NY Post*, April 30, 1955.

27. J. Stewart Hunter to OCH, May 2, 1953, and

Richard Pinkham to OCH, May 5, 1953, OCH Papers, DDEPL; *Businessweek*, May 16, 1953; *NYT*, May 10, 1953.

28. *NYT*, April 15, 1953; OCH to Eisenhower, April 13, 1953, Federal Security Agency Records, RG 235, NA; Ambrose, *Eisenhower, Vol. II*, 125–127; Sutphen, "Conservative Warrior," 113.

29. Adam Clayton Powell Jr. to OCH, May 28, 1953, and OCH to Powell, undated and unsent, OCH Papers, Rice.

30. "Confidential Memorandum on Mrs. Jane M. Spaulding," unidentified author, and John Grindle to Rockefeller, January 18, 1954, both in HEW bound volumes, vol. 13, Nelson A. Rockefeller Papers, RAC; J. Smith, "Jane Spaulding," 611; *Jet*, January 28, 1954, pp. 3–4; Sutphen, "Conservative Warrior," 127–128.

31. Sutphen, "Conservative Warrior," 113–115; Parmet, *Eisenhower*, 419.

32. Sutphen, "Conservative Warrior," 105; Eisenhower, *Mandate for Change*, 236.

33. "Confidential Memorandum on Mrs. Jane M. Spaulding," unidentified author, HEW bound volumes, vol. 13, Nelson A. Rockefeller Papers, RAC; J. Smith, "Jane Spaulding," 611; Sutphen, "Conservative Warrior," 130–132.

34. *Dallas News*, June 10, 1953.

35. Dwight H. Murray to OCH, June 2, 1953, OCH Papers, DDEPL; *NYT*, June 2, 1953.

36. Altmeyer's status as an objective witness has to be questioned, but his quote of Oveta's response to Kaiser provides some credence to his version of the anecdote. Oveta had an unusual habit of using the phrase "I shall" instead of the more common "I will." Kaiser's health care plan was the basis for the highly successful Kaiser Permanente, the nation's first health maintenance organization (HMO). Altmeyer, *Formative Years*, 212; Foster, *Henry J. Kaiser*, 231–232.

37. "Television and radio broadcast by President Dwight Eisenhower and selected cabinet members, June 3, 1953, all networks," and Ann Whitman to OCH, June 4, 1953, OCH Papers, Rice; Walter Trohan to Jones, and Jones to Trohan, May 5, 1953, Jesse H. Jones Papers, DBCAH; *NYT*, May 27, 1953; *Time*, May 4, 1953.

38. Whitman to OCH, June 4, 1953, OCH Papers, Rice; *NY Herald Tribune*, June 7, 1953.

39. *NY Herald Tribune*, June 7, 1953.

40. Bill Hobby to John Davis, July 6, 1953, Bill Hobby Papers, DBCAH; Bill Hobby, interview.

41. *Austin American-Statesman*, June 30, 1953;

*NY Journal American*, July 31, 1953; *NYT*, July 7, 1953.

42. *NY Journal American*, July 2, 1953; Ambrose, *Eisenhower, Vol. II*, 115; Reich, *Nelson A. Rockefeller*, 517.

43. *NY Daily News*, August 21, 1953; R. Smith, *His Own Terms*, 230; Eisenhower, *Mandate for Change*, 295.

44. Berkowitz, *Mr. Social Security*, 890; Rockefeller to Eisenhower, August 28, 1953, OCH Papers, Rice; R. Smith, *His Own Terms*, 230.

45. For more on Senator Curtis's antagonistic view of Social Security, see Altmeyer, *Formative Years*, 214, 221–222. Eisenhower to OCH, August 20, 1953, OCH Papers, DDEPL; Pando, "Oveta Culp Hobby," 170.

46. *LA Times*, August 25, 1953.

47. John Grindle Jr. to Chester Lund, August 17, 1953, OCH Papers, DDEPL; *LA Times*, August 26, 27, and 28, 1953.

48. *NYT*, September 1, 1953.

CHAPTER 34

1. *Editor and Publisher*, October 17, 1953.

2. For a detailed study of the anti-Communist hysteria in Houston in the early 1950s, see Carleton, *Red Scare*.

3. There are numerous studies of McCarthyism and the Red Scare, but I have relied largely on Thomas C. Reeves's *Life and Times of Joe McCarthy*; David Oshinsky's *A Conspiracy So Immense*; David Caute's *Great Fear*; Robert Griffith's *Politics of Fear*; and Athan Theoharis's *Seeds of Repression*.

4. Carleton, *Red Scare*, 235.

5. *Time*, November 2, 1953; Marguerite Johnston and George Fuermann interviews.

6. Bayley, *Joe McCarthy*, 76; Faulk quote in Carleton, *Red Scare*, x, 233.

7. Carleton, 111–113.

8. *NYT*, November 19, 1953; *St. Louis Post-Dispatch*, November 7, 1953.

9. Carleton, *Red Scare*, 230–231.

10. *NYT*, April 29, 1954; Carleton, *Red Scare*, 231.

11. For Eisenhower's views of McCarthy and the president's strategy for handling him, see Nichols, *Ike and McCarthy*; Sutphen, "Conservative Warrior," 6; for Eisenhower's comments to Cullen and for "back-talk" quote, see Carleton, *Red Scare*, 232, 233.

12. Carleton, 228, 232; McGrew to Bill Hobby, January 15, 1991, Bill Hobby Papers, DBCAH.

13. Marguerite Johnston, interview, January 17, 1984; Terry, "Kilman, Edward Wolf."

14. Carleton, *Red Scare*, 233–234.

15. Carleton, 234.

16. Bill Hobby to John Davis, July 5, 1953, Bill Hobby Papers, DBCAH.

17. Carleton, *Red Scare*, 234.

18. Carleton, 238.

19. Carleton, 238.

20. Carleton, 238–239.

21. Carleton, 238.

22. Carleton, 240.

23. Carleton, 241; *Houston Chronicle*, December 1, 1953.

24. Carleton, *Red Scare*, 267–268.

25. From the perspective of 2020, it is obvious that the Minute Women and their allied foot soldiers were precursors of the Tea Party, the latter shorn of the fear of Communism but retaining the fear of big government and the racist underpinnings. Pando, "Oveta Culp Hobby," 149–150.

26. Fenberg, *Unprecedented Power*, 557, 565, 570; Jones to OCH, April 8, 1954, Jesse H. Jones Papers, DBCAH.

27. OCH to Jones, July 10, 1953, Jesse H. Jones Papers, DBCAH.

28. Jones to OCH, August 17, 1953, Jones to WPH, October 3, 1953, and OCH to Jones, February 26, 1954, Jesse H. Jones Papers, DBCAH.

29. *Dallas News*, September 25, 1953; Jones to OCH, September 25, 1953, and OCH to Jones, October 5, 1953, Jesse H. Jones Papers, DBCAH.

30. *Dallas News*, October 10 and November 8, 1953; *NYT*, October 17, 1953; *NY Journal American*, October 28, 1953; *Dallas News*, November 8, 1953; Sutphen, "Conservative Warrior," 83–84.

31. *NYT*, November 20–21, 1953.

32. DDE to OCH, November 24, 1953, OCH Papers, Rice.

33. OCH to DDE, Dwight D. Eisenhower Papers, DDEPL.

34. Marshall to OCH, December 22, 1953, and OCH to Marshall, January 7, 1954, OCH Papers, Rice.

CHAPTER 35

1. "Former U.S. Surgeon General Leonard A. Scheele, 85, Dies," *Washington Post*, January 10, 1993; R. Smith, *His Own Terms*, 230.

2. R. Smith, 230–234.

3. *NYT*, April 16, 1954; Sutphen, "Conservative Warrior," 154.

4. Sutphen, 155–156.

5. Sutphen, 163–164.

6. Sutphen, 189.

7. Sutphen, 191–192; Sundquist, *Politics and Policy*, 158.

8. Sutphen, "Conservative Warrior," 174; Beland, *Social Security*, 126; Reich, *Nelson A. Rockefeller*, 530; R. Smith, *His Own Terms*, 231.

9. Sutphen, "Conservative Warrior," 174–181; Reich, *Nelson A. Rockefeller*, 530–531.

10. Roswell Perkins, interview, Columbia; Sutphen, "Conservative Warrior," 175; Reich, *Nelson A. Rockefeller*, 531; Hughes, *Ordeal of Power*, 67.

11. Reich, *Nelson A. Rockefeller*, 519; R. Smith, *His Own Terms*, 222–223.

12. Minutes, cabinet meeting, November 20, 1954, DDEPL; Reich, *Nelson A. Rockefeller*, 527; Sutphen, "Conservative Warrior," 151.

13. Sutphen, 174; Brian Spinks, MS, OCH Papers, Rice.

14. Sutphen, "Conservative Warrior," 174; Brian Spinks, MS, p. 5, OCH Papers, Rice; *U.S. News and World Report*, December 11, 1953.

15. Larson, *Eisenhower*, 138–140.

16. Sutphen, "Conservative Warrior," 157–158; Reich, *Nelson A. Rockefeller*, 527.

17. DDE to OCH, January 19, 1954, Harold Stassen to OCH, September 23, 1953, John M. Gates to OCH, September 24, 1953, OCH to Thomas Gates, January 19, 1954, and DDE to OCH, January 20, 1954, OCH Papers, Rice.

18. Powell to OCH, January 18, 1954, OCH Papers, Rice; "Confidential Memorandum on Mrs. Jane M. Spaulding," unidentified author, n.d., HEW bound volumes, vol. 13, Nelson A. Rockefeller Papers, RAC; Sutphen, "Conservative Warrior."

19. Rockefeller to Maxwell Rabb, January 20, 1954, and "Jane Morrow Spaulding," security review, unidentified author, January 19, 1954, both in HEW bound volumes, vol. 13, Nelson A. Rockefeller Papers, RAC; Sutphen, "Conservative Warrior," 133–134.

20. Memorandum, Nancy Hanks to Rockefeller, January 22, 1954, and press release, January 22, 1954, both in HEW bound volumes, vol. 13, Nelson A. Rockefeller Papers, RAC; Sutphen, "Conservative Warrior," 130–135.

21. John Grindle to Rockefeller, January 18, 1954, HEW bound volumes, vol. 13, Nelson A. Rockefeller Papers, RAC; *Jet*, January 28, 1954, pp. 3–4.

22. *NY Daily News*, February 1, 1954; *NY Post*, February 2, 1954; Sutphen, "Conservative Warrior," 135.

23. OCH to Adam Clayton Powell, February 1, 1954, OCH Papers, Rice.

24. Sutphen, "Conservative Warrior," 136.

25. *NY Post*, February 18, 1954; Sutphen, "Conservative Warrior," 136; transcript of broadcast, enclosed in John T. Jones to Jesse H. Jones, June 13, 1955, Jesse H. Jones Papers, DBCAH.

26. Spaulding worked for the Foreign Claims Settlement Commission until the end of December 1954, when she lost her job as the result of a major reduction of commission staff. The Eisenhower administration then appointed her as a consultant to the Foreign Operations Administration on social welfare issues in India and other undeveloped countries. She died in 1965. Smith, *Notable Black Women*, 611. On Oveta's racial views, see Sutphen, "Conservative Warrior"; Walsh, "Oveta Culp Hobby" (2006); Pando, "Oveta Culp Hobby."

27. Marguerite Johnston, typescript, Bill Hobby Papers, DBCAH; Pando, "Oveta Culp Hobby," 98.

28. Sutphen, "Conservative Warrior," 76–77, 107–109; Duram, *Moderate among Extremists*, 28, 132.

29. *NYT*, March 3, 1954; telegram, Powell to OCH, March 4, 1954, and OCH to Powell, March 12, 1954, OCH Papers, Rice.

30. "American Forum of the Air," transcript, March 14, 1954, OCH Papers, Rice; OCH to Julian Bartolini, March 15, 1954, OCH Papers, DDEPL.

31. Duram, *Moderate among Extremists*, 133.

32. *Houston Post*, May 18, 1954; OCH, interview by Marguerite Johnston, transcript, Marguerite Johnston Barnes Papers, Rice.

33. Sutphen, "Conservative Warrior," 157–158; *NYT*, March 24, 1954.

34. Sutphen, "Conservative Warrior," 157–158.

35. *NYT*, February 5 and March 18, 1954; *NY Herald Tribune*, March 31, 1954; Obermann, *Vocational Rehabilitation*, 348–350; Sutphen, "Conservative Warrior," 166–168.

36. The major opponents of HEW's Social Security bill included the National Association of Manufacturers, the American Farm Bureau, and the American Medical Association. Altmeyer, *Formative Years*, 241–243; *NYT*, April 2 and June 25, 1954; R. Smith, *His Own Terms*, 233; Sutphen, "Conservative Warrior," 158–160.

37. *NY Post*, September 5 and 12, 1954; Reich, *Nelson A. Rockefeller*, 519; *NYT*, June 5, 1954.

38. Reich, *Nelson A. Rockefeller*, 531–532; OCH, interview, July 11, 1969, LBJPL.

39. Reich, *Nelson A. Rockefeller*, 530–531.

40. OCH, interview, July 11, 1969, LBJPL; Adams, *First-Hand Report*, 306; *Dallas News*, March 22, 1954; DDE to OCH, March 15, 1954, and "American Forum of the Air," transcript, OCH Papers, Rice.

41. Arthur Schroeder to OCH, May 11, 1954, DDEPL; *NY Herald Tribune*, April 1 and May 12, 1954; *NYT*, June 11, 1954.

42. *NY World Telegram*, May 19, 1954; *NY Journal American*, May 21, 1954.

43. Oveta's speech in Cleveland was titled "The Spiritual Pillars of a Free Society." Abba Hillel Silver to OCH, April 1, 1954, OCH Papers, DDEPL; *NYT*, February 12, March 29, and May 18, 1954; *NY Herald Tribune*, April 13, 1954; *NY Journal American*, June 28, 1954.

44. Jones to OCH, April 1, 1954, and Jones to OCH, April 8, 1954, Jesse H. Jones Papers, DBCAH.

45. Jones to John M. Franklin, May 13, 1954, Franklin to Jones, May 25, 1954, and Jones to Franklin, May 28, 1954, Jesse H. Jones Papers, DBCAH.

CHAPTER 36

1. OCH, "TV Speech, Washington, DC, July 9, 1954," transcript, OCH Papers, DDEPL; *NYT*, July 10, 1954.

2. Sutphen, "Conservative Warrior," 181–182; Reich, *Nelson A. Rockefeller*, 532; Nelson Cruikshank, interview, Columbia.

3. *NYT*, August 13, 1954; *NY Post*, September 5, 1954; Reich, *Nelson A. Rockefeller*, 532.

4. Sutphen, "Conservative Warrior," 185–186; Bill Hobby, interview.

5. Sutphen, "Conservative Warrior," 185–186; *NYT*, August 13, 1954.

6. Pando, "Oveta Culp Hobby," 172; *NYT*, April 2, and December 5, 1954.

7. *NY Post*, April 30, 1955; *NYT*, December 5, 1954; *Washington Daily News*, May 17, 1954; Sundquist, *Politics and Policy*, 159.

8. Sundquist, 160–161.

9. *NYT*, August 5, 1954; *Atlanta Constitution*, August 4, 1954; Nichols, *Ike and McCarthy*, 289–290; *NY Post*, September 5, 1954; Sundquist, *Politics and Policy*, 160–161; Cross, *Political Education*, 13–14.

10. Weldon Hart, typescript notes prepared for the book *Tactful Texan*, James Clark Papers, Rice.

11. Bill Hobby, interview; *Houston Chronicle*, July 4, 2014; Brittain, *Laurence Stallings*.

12. Clark, *Tactful Texan*, 199; Lawrence E. Spivak to OCH, October 11, 1954, OCH Papers, DDEPL; unidentified and undated clip in Diana Hobby folder, Bill Hobby Papers, DBCAH.

13. OCH's annotated speech text, and Judy Weiss and Jane Todd to OCH, May 22, 1954, OCH Papers, DDEPL; *NY Herald Tribune*, April 26, 1954; Braden, *Just Enough Rope*, 58–59.

14. *NYT*, October 26, 1954.

15. Eisenhower, *Mandate for Change*, 440, 442.

16. DDE to OCH, December 29, 1955, OCH Papers, Rice.

17. R. Smith, *His Own Terms*, 233–234; *NYT*, December 8, 1954.

18. DDE to OCH, January 18, 1955, OCH Papers, Rice.

19. "Lady Bird Johnson," 31, and "Roswell Perkins," 38, in Shire, *Oveta Culp Hobby*.

20. Sutphen, "Conservative Warrior," 188; Adams, *First-Hand Report*, 306; *NYT*, March 3, 1955.

21. The Kerr-Mills Act of 1960, which was passed during the last days of the Eisenhower administration, created a pool of federal funds to allocate to states on a voluntary basis to help pay for medical care for the elderly. The act's provisions drew heavily on the failed medical reinsurance plan. Larson, *Eisenhower*, 139–140; Sutphen, "Conservative Warrior," 188; Wilbur Cohen, interview, LBJPL.

22. R. Smith, *His Own Terms*, 232; Cross, *Political Education*, 14; Sutphen, "Conservative Warrior," 197–198.

23. Branyan and Larsen, *Eisenhower Administration*, 435; Adams, *First-Hand Report*, 308–311.

24. Sutphen, "Conservative Warrior," 197–198.

25. R. Smith, *His Own Terms*, 232–233; Cross, *Political Education*, 14; Adams, *First-Hand Report*, 308–311.

26. *NYT*, February 11, 1955; Sutphen, "Conservative Warrior," 198.

27. *NYT*, February 17, 1955.

28. Sutphen, "Conservative Warrior," 200–202.

29. Sutphen, 200–202; *NYT*, February 17, 1955; *Houston Post*, March 30, 1955; *NY Daily News*, March 31, 1955.

30. Sutphen, "Conservative Warrior," 200–202.

31. Sutphen, 198–199.

32. Adams, *First-Hand Report*, 310–311; R. Smith, *His Own Terms*, 232–233; Duram, *Extremists*, 206–207; Cross, *Political Education*, 14.

CHAPTER 37

1. Oshinsky, *Polio*, 47. My discussion of the Salk vaccine controversy is based largely on Oshinsky; and Sutphen, "Conservative Warrior," pp. 231–277.

2. The iron lung, now rarely used, has been replaced by the ventilator. Neumann, "Polio," 479–480.

3. Neumann, 481; Sutphen, "Conservative Warrior," 208–212.

4. Neumann, "Polio," 481; Wooten, *Polio Years*; OCH, typescript of speech, 1943, OCH Papers, Rice.

5. Oshinsky, *Polio*, 174–187.

6. Sutphen, "Conservative Warrior," 225–226, 239; Oshinsky, *Polio*, 188–189.

7. Sutphen, "Conservative Warrior," 230–231.

8. Oshinsky, *Polio*, 219; Carleton, *Red Scare*, 231.

9. Oshinsky, *Polio*, 201.

10. Sutphen, "Conservative Warrior," 234–235.

11. Sutphen, 231–232.

12. Sutphen, 232.

13. Oshinsky, *Polio*, 205.

14. Sutphen, "Conservative Warrior," 235.

15. Sutphen, 237–238; *Austin American-Statesman*, December 13, 1957; Anna J. Kendall to OCH, January 14, 1958, and OCH to Kendall, January 21, 1958, OCH Papers, Rice.

16. *NY Herald Tribune*, April 13, 1955; *NYT*, April 14, 1955.

17. Oshinsky, *Polio*, 200, 217; Sutphen, "Conservative Warrior," 239–240.

18. Sutphen, 240.

19. Sutphen, 244–245; Oshinsky, *Polio*, 209–213.

20. Sutphen, "Conservative Warrior," 244–238.

21. *NY Daily News*, April 14, 1955; Eisenhower, *Mandate for Change*, 495; *NYT*, April 15, 1955.

22. Sutphen, "Conservative Warrior," 89, 249–250; *NYT*, April 15, 1955.

23. Oshinsky, *Polio*, 218.

24. *Businessweek*, April 16, 1955.

25. Eisenhower, *Mandate for Change*, 495.

26. Sutphen, "Conservative Warrior," 256–258; OCH, "Remarks," April 22, 1955, DDEPL.

27. "Minutes of Cabinet Meeting," April 29, 1955, President's Cabinet Series, DDEPL; Oshinsky, *Polio*, 220.

28. Oshinsky, 215–216.

29. Eisenhower, *Mandate for Change*, 495.

30. Sutphen, "Conservative Warrior," 259–260.

31. Oshinsky, *Polio*, 225.

32. John T. Jones to Jesse Jones, April 28, 1955, Jesse H. Jones Papers, DBCAH; Sutphen,

"Conservative Warrior," 262; Braden, *Just Enough Rope*, 60–62.

33. Oshinsky, *Polio*, 225.

34. Sutphen, "Conservative Warrior," 266–267.

35. "Minutes of Cabinet Meeting," April 29, 1955, President's Cabinet Series, DDEPL.

36. "Minutes of Cabinet Meeting," April 29, 1955.

37. "Minutes of Cabinet Meeting," April 29, 1955.

38. Sutphen, "Conservative Warrior," 273.

39. Sutphen, 274.

40. Sutphen, 276; *NY Daily News*, May 3, 1955; *NYT*, May 9, 1955.

41. *NY Post*, May 13, 1955.

42. Sutphen, "Conservative Warrior," 292–293; Eisenhower, *Mandate for Change*, 496.

43. *NY Post*, April 30 and May 13, 1955.

44. Bill Hobby, interview.

45. *NYT*, May 12, 1955; Sutphen, "Conservative Warrior," 284–285.

46. Sutphen, 284.

47. "Minutes of Cabinet Meeting," May 13, 1955, DDEPL.

CHAPTER 38

1. *Houston Post*, May 17, 1955; Sutphen, "Conservative Warrior," 294–297; OCH, interview, July 11, 1969, LBJPL.

2. Branyan and Larsen, *Eisenhower Administration*, 575–583; Sutphen, "Conservative Warrior," 301–303.

3. Oshinsky, *Polio*, 219.

4. *NY Journal American*, May 17, 1955; *NYT*, May 17, 1955; *NY Herald Tribune*, May 16, 1955; Oshinsky, *Polio*, 218; Sutphen, "Conservative Warrior," 303–312; Marguerite Johnston to Isabel Ross, ca. 1968, OCH Papers, Rice; Braden, *Just Enough Rope*, 60–62.

5. *NY Journal American*, May 17, 1955.

6. Branyan and Larsen, *Eisenhower Administration*, 581–582; Eisenhower, *Mandate for Change*, 496; *Austin American-Statesman*, May 19, 1955; Sutphen, "Conservative Warrior," 306–308.

7. *NY Journal American*, May 17, 1955; WPH to Jones, telegram, May 4, 1955, Jesse H. Jones Papers, DBCAH; Sutphen, "Conservative Warrior," 307.

8. Sutphen, "Conservative Warrior," 310; Oshinsky, *Polio*, 237.

9. Morris, *Price of Fame*, 412; *NYT*, May 26, 1955; *NY Journal American*, May 28 and 29, 1955; *NY Post*, May 28, 1955; Jones to Walter Trohan, June 1, 1955, Walter Trohan Papers, HHPL.

10. Marion Folsom, interview, DDEPL; Sutphen, "Conservative Warrior," 306–307.

11. *NY Daily News*, June 7, 1955; *NY Herald Tribune*, May 17, 1955.

12. "A Special Report on Polio" (orig. broadcast June 7, 1955), YouTube video, Library of Congress, uploaded September 27, 2018, https://www.youtube.com/watch?v=nkr269ube9k; *New York Herald Tribune*, June 8, 1955; Oshinsky, *Polio*, 240.

13. *NYT*, June 9, 1955.

14. *NYT*, June 15, 1955; *NY Journal American*, June 14, 1955.

15. *NYT*, June 17, 1955; *NY Daily News*, June 16, 1955.

16. Pando, "Oveta Culp Hobby," 164–165; *NYT*, June 21, 1955.

17. *NYT*, June 22, 1955.

18. *NY Journal American*, June 21, 1955; *NYT*, June 27, 1955.

19. *NY Post*, July 8, 1955; *NY Herald Tribune*, July 9, 1955; *NY Journal American*, July 8, 1955.

20. *NYT*, July 14, 1955; OCH to DDE, July 13, 1955, OCH Papers, Rice.

21. *NYT*, July 14, 1955.

22. DDE to OCH, July 13, 1955, OCH Papers, Rice.

23. Eisenhower, *Mandate for Change*, 497.

24. Adams, *First-Hand Report*, 308; Marguerite Johnston to Isabel Ross, undated carbon copy, OCH Papers, Rice. David Oshinsky strongly implies that Oveta was forced to resign, although he doesn't make a direct claim. "The political fallout from Cutter was enormous," he writes. "In July 1955, Oveta Culp Hobby stepped down from her cabinet post and returned to Texas." Historian Jill Lepore, in her error-filled book *These Truths*, states, "In the end, after a related scandal, Hobby was *forced to resign*" (my emphasis). Lepore does not identify the scandal, but it is assumed she refers to the Cutter Labs affair. Lepore cites Oshinsky as her source. Oshinsky, *Polio*, 238; Lepore, *These Truths*, 570.

25. *NYT*, July 14, 1955; *NY Herald Tribune*, July 14, 1955.

26. *NYT*, July 14, 1955; *NY Herald Tribune*, July 14, 1955.

27. Rufus Miles to OCH, July 22, 1955, OCH Papers, Rice.

28. Scheele to OCH, July 25, 1955, and Roswell Perkins to OCH, July 26, 1955, OCH Papers, Rice.

29. Rockefeller to OCH, July 28, 1955, OCH Papers, Rice.

30. OCH to Rockefeller, July 28, 1955, HEW bound volumes, vol. 13, Nelson A. Rockefeller Papers, RAC; *NYT*, January 8, 1983; Sutphen, "Conservative Warrior," 301.

31. *NYT*, July 30, 1955; Sutphen, "Conservative Warrior," 329.

32. *Washington Post*, July 30, 1955; Lady Bird Johnson, interview, LBJPL; *NYT*, July 31, 1955; DDE to OCH, September 5, 1956, OCH Papers; Sutphen, "Conservative Warrior," 325–326.

33. Sherman Adams to OCH, August 5, 1955, OCH Papers, Rice.

34. After the White House Conference on Education was over, Clint Pace returned to Houston to work as Oveta's administrative assistant until he resigned in 1957 to take an executive position at Procter and Gamble. DDE to OCH, September 6, 1955, OCH Papers, Rice; *NYT*, September 7, 1955.

35. *NYT*, September 25, 1955; Snyder to OCH, September 29, 1955, DDE to OCH, October 17, 1955, and Mamie Eisenhower to OCH, November 17, 1955, all in OCH Papers, Rice.

36. O. Anderson, "Polio Vaccine Act," 1349.

37. OCH to Rockefeller, July 28, 1955, HEW bound volumes, vol. 13, Nelson A. Rockefeller Papers, RAC; *Dallas Times Herald*, January 31, 1977.

38. Nelson Cruikshank, interview, Columbia; Sutphen, "Conservative Warrior," 184; R. Smith, *His Own Terms*, 231; Reich, *Nelson A. Rockefeller*, 532–533; Larson, 139–140; Adams, *First-Hand Report*, 306; OCH, interview, LBJPL; OCH to Rockefeller, July 28, 1955, HEW bound volumes, vol. 13, Nelson A. Rockefeller Papers, RAC.

CHAPTER 39

1. After she left Washington, Oveta replicated her HEW office at the *Post*, including her office desk, cabinet chair, and a flag Ike had given her. Pando, "Oveta Culp Hobby," 183; Les Carpenter to OCH, December 7, 1955, OCH Papers, Rice.

2. *Houston Post*, press release, 1961, and Marguerite Johnston to Isabel Ross, ca. 1968, OCH Papers, Rice.

3. *Dallas Morning News*, August 17, 1959; *Houston Post*, June 8, 1964.

4. Weldon Hart, undated typescript report for "Tactful Texan" MS, James Clark Papers, Rice.

5. OCH obituary, *NYT*, August 17, 1995; Hurt, "Great Ladies," 228–229.

6. Les Carpenter to OCH, December 7, 1955, and February 25, 1957, LBJ to OCH, April 7, 1959, and Helon Johnson to LBJ, April 9, 1959, OCH Papers, Rice.

7. Louis Dawson to OCH, May 23, 1956, OCH Papers, Rice; *NY Journal American*, October 19, 1955; *Dallas Morning News*, July 12, 1956; *Austin American*, October 22, 1955.

8. *Dallas Morning News*, November 5, 1955, and May 15, 1956.

9. *Houston Post*, January 24, 1956.

10. *Dallas Morning News*, May 29, 1956.

11. Timmons, *Jesse H. Jones*, 388–390; Fenberg, *Unprecedented Power*, 580–581.

12. R. Smith, *His Own Terms*, 253; Ferguson, *Kissinger*, 390–391.

13. R. Smith, *His Own Terms*, 253–254; Ferguson, *Kissinger*, 387–399.

14. R. Smith, *His Own Terms*, 253–254; Andrew, "Cracks in Consensus," 536, 547.

15. N. Rockefeller to OCH, September 14 and 18, 1956, "Membership—Hobby, Oveta Culp," Rockefeller Brothers Fund Records, Special Studies Project (hereafter cited as Special Studies), RAC.

16. N. Rockefeller to OCH, October 31, 1956, and OCH to Rockefeller, November 5, 1956, Special Studies, RAC.

17. N. Rockefeller to OCH, October 31, November 20, and December 5, 1956, Henry Kissinger to OCH, November 29, 1956, and OCH to N. Rockefeller, December 12, 1956, Special Studies, RAC; Andrew, "Cracks in Consensus," 536; R. Smith, *His Own Terms*, 255; Ferguson, *Kissinger*, 390–391.

18. OCH to N. Rockefeller, May 13, 1957, and Rockefeller to OCH, May 14, 1957, Special Studies, RAC.

19. WPH to Laura Hobby, September 17, 1957, WPH Sr. Papers, DBCAH.

20. Nancy Hanks to Helon Johnson, August 28, 1957, N. Rockefeller to OCH, August 28, 1957, Kissinger to OCH, September 10, 1957, Helon Johnson to Kissinger, August 23, 1957, OCH to N. Rockefeller, August 26, 1957, Kissinger to OCH, September 15, 1957, Special Studies, RAC.

21. Adolph Berle was an economist and lawyer who had been a close advisor to FDR during the early days of the New Deal. OCH to Kissinger, October 1, 1957, Kissinger to OCH, November 23, 1957, OCH to Kissinger, December 13, 1957, N. Rockefeller to OCH, December 26, 1957, and Kissinger to OCH, January 9, 1958, Special Studies, RAC.

22. N. Rockefeller to OCH, January 24, 1958, Special Studies, RAC.

23. N. Rockefeller to OCH, January 24, 1958, OCH to Kissinger, February 7, 1958, and Kissinger to OCH, February 12, 1958, Special Studies, RAC.

24. OCH to Kissinger, February 12, 1958, and Kissinger to OCH, February 12, 1958, Special Studies, RAC.

25. John Dickey to OCH, October 20, 1959, OCH to N. Rockefeller, March 24, 1958, OCH to Kissinger, April 26, 1958, and N. Rockefeller to OCH, June 25, 1958, Special Studies, RAC.

26. Laurance Rockefeller to OCH, August 10, 1959, Helon Johnson to Nancy Hanks, September 9, 1959, OCH to L. Rockefeller, September 15, 1959, OCH to Nancy Hanks, September 25, 1959, and L. Rockefeller to OCH, October 28, 1959, Special Studies, RAC; Ferguson, *Kissinger*, 394.

27. Laurance Rockefeller to OCH, August 10, 1959, Helon Johnson to Nancy Hanks, September 9, 1959, OCH to L. Rockefeller, September 15, 1959, OCH to Nancy Hanks, September 25, 1959, and L. Rockefeller to OCH, October 28, 1959, Special Studies, RAC.

28. John S. Dickey to OCH, October 20, 1959, and Laurance Rockefeller to OCH, April 12, 1960, Special Studies, RAC.

29. Nancy Hanks to Helon Johnson, July 22, 1960, Special Studies, RAC; Ferguson, *Kissinger*, 387–399; Andrew, "Cracks in Consensus," 548.

30. Laurance Rockefeller to OCH, November 22, 1960, OCH to L. Rockefeller, November 28, 1960, L. Rockefeller to OCH, January 27, 1961, and OCH to Nancy Hanks, February 9, 1961, Special Studies, RAC.

31. Andrew, "Cracks in Consensus," 548; Ferguson, *Kissinger*, 394–395.

32. OCH to Laurance Rockefeller, June 4, 1959, OCH to L. Rockefeller, November 6, 1959, OCH to L. Rockefeller, May 4, 1960, Carl O. Gustafson to Norman Wengert, May 10, 1960, and OCH to L. Rockefeller, February 8, 1961, Outdoor Recreation Resources Review Commission, Advisory Council, Laurance S. Rockefeller Papers, RAC.

33. N. Rockefeller to OCH, September 30, 1958, January 14, 1959, and December 21, 1959, OCH Papers, Rice.

34. Transcript of telephone conversation, OCH to DDE, June 11, 1960, Dwight D. Eisenhower Papers, DDEPL.

35. DDE to OCH, January 16 and April 17, 1956, OCH Papers, Rice.

36. Helon Johnson to Peter Clayton, December 30, 1955, OCH Papers, Rice.

37. James Murphy to OCH, January 9, 1956, and printed letter to "Citizens" from Lucius Clay, OCH, and Sidney Weinberg, January 17, 1956, OCH Papers, Rice.

38. Thomas D. Campbell to OCH, February 14, 1956, and Lucius Clay to OCH, telegram, March 13, 1956, OCH Papers, Rice.

39. DDE to OCH, May 9, 1960, OCH Papers, Rice; Parmet, *Eisenhower*, 417–432.

40. *San Francisco Examiner*, August 19 and 20, 1956; OCH, typescript of speech, "Remarks Made at Civic Auditorium in San Francisco," August 19, 1956, OCH Papers, Rice.

41. OCH to James Hagerty, August 2, 1956, OCH Papers, Rice.

42. Ambrose, *Eisenhower, Vol. II*, 326; Parmet, *Eisenhower*, 457.

43. Clint Pace to M. W. Shelton, September 21, 1956, OCH Papers, Rice; *Dallas Morning News*, August 26, 1956.

44. *Houston Post*, October 23, 1956; Clint Pace to OCH, October 18, 1956, Dorothy Houghton to OCH, April 26, 1956, and OCH to Dorothy Houghton, October 30, 1958, OCH Papers, Rice; *Austin American*, October 22, 1956.

45. OCH to N. Rockefeller, September 5, 1956, Nelson A. Rockefeller Papers, RAC; DDE to OCH, telegram, September 5, 1956, and Clint Pace to OCH, September 5, 1956, OCH Papers, Rice.

46. OCH to Dorothy Houghton, October 30, 1958, OCH Papers, Rice; Parmet, *Eisenhower*, 461; Ambrose, *Eisenhower, Vol. II*, 437.

47. *Houston Post*, September 26, 1956; OCH to Bill Hobby, September 28, 1956, Bill Hobby Papers, DBCAH.

48. OCH, speech typescript, October 31, 1956, OCH to DDE, November 13, 1956, DDE to OCH, November 15, 1956, DDE to OCH, December 22, 1956, and DDE to OCH, January 16, 1957, OCH Papers, Rice.

49. Tom Sealy to OCH, January 22, 1957, and OCH to Tom Sealy, January 23, 1957, OCH Papers, Rice.

50. Clint Pace to L. F. McCollum, May 28, 1957, OCH to Jack Curlin, telegram, ca. March 1957, OCH to W. D. Blunk, March 6, 1957, Brian Spinks to OCH, September 19, 1957, minutes, meeting of Task Force III, University of Texas Committee of 75, October 26, 1957, Jack V. Curlin to OCH, October 22, 1957, OCH to W. D. Blunk, January 8, 1958, and W. D. Blunk to OCH, March 6, 1958, OCH Papers, Rice.

51. OCH to unidentified, 1957, and OCH to Omar Bradley, March 10, 1960, OCH Papers, Rice.

52. *Time*, May 30, 1960.

53. Paul Hobby, interview, August 4, 2017; Bill Hobby, interview; *Houston Chronicle*, July 8, 2014.

54. *Time*, May 30, 1960.

55. *Time*, May 30, 1960.

56. OCH to Arthur Summerfield, June 11, 1958, Summerfield to OCH, May 29, 1958, James Mitchell to OCH, November 16, 1959, and OCH to Fred Seaton, March 6, 1959, OCH Papers, Rice.

57. Duram, *Moderate among Extremists*, 157–158; Ambrose, *Eisenhower, Vol. II*, 497–498; Parmet, *Eisenhower*, 439.

58. Duram, *Moderate among Extremists*, 143–167; telephone call, Eisenhower diary, October 19, 1957, Whitman File, Dwight D. Eisenhower Papers, DDEPL.

59. Hitchcock, "Billy Graham"; Miller, *Republican South*, 52–54; Ambrose, 308; Duram, *Moderate among Extremists*, 167.

60. *Dallas News*, June 10, 1953.

CHAPTER 40

1. Random House published Clark's biography of E. O. Thompson, *Three Stars for the Colonel*, in 1954. John McCall to Raymond Brooks, October 2, 1952, and John McCall to WPH, September 26, 1952, WPH Sr. Papers, DBCAH; Bill Hobby, interview; Palmer, "Clark, James Anthony"; Clark, *Tactful Texan*, 10, x, xi.

2. Clark, x, xi; *Dallas News*, August 17, 1959.

3. Bill Hobby, interview.

4. OCH notes and typescript of "Tactful Texan" MS, OCH Papers, Rice.

5. Clark, *Tactful Texan*, 187; OCH notes on MS for "Tactful Texan," OCH Papers, Rice.

6. *NYT*, May 8, 2011; Robert D. Loomis to James Clark, January 29, 1958.

7. When Nelson Rockefeller saw the story about Will's surgery in the *New York Daily News*, he immediately sent a telegram expressing his deep concern. *NY Daily News*, January 28, 1958; LBJ to OCH, January 31, 1958, OCH Papers, Rice; Helon Johnson to Rockefeller, February 11, 1958, Family and Friends, Nelson A. Rockefeller Papers, RAC; *Dallas Morning News*, February 20, 1958.

8. Clark, *Tactful Texan*, x, xi; N. Rockefeller to OCH, June 25, 1958, Special Studies, RAC;

"[*Tactful Texan*] Distribution List," 1958, WPH Sr. Papers, DBCAH; *Daily Texan*, April 24, 1958; *Dallas Morning News*, June 1, 1958.

9. Bill Hobby, interview. Laura Hobby was born on October 25, 1958.

10. In 1997 I played a small role in the effort to get the University of Texas Press to publish Henry Catto's memoir. In one of our meetings, Henry talked fondly about Oveta, but he also recalled that during the period he and Jessica were dating, it was Oveta, not Will, who played the stern and suspicious parent. News clip, unidentified publication, August 7, 1970, Bill Hobby Papers, DBCAH; Catto, *Ambassadors at Sea*, 7; OCH to LBJ, ca. March 1958, OCH Papers, Rice.

11. Albert Thomas to OCH, January 30, 1958, OCH Papers, Rice; *Dallas Morning News*, February 20, 1958; *Houston Press*, December 1, 1958; *Houston Post*, December 1, 1958.

12. OCH to Malcolm Wilkey, April 13, 1959, and OCH to Melvin Hattwick, July 7, 1959, OCH Papers, Rice.

13. Only nine months before Emma's death, Oveta's brother I. W. Culp died of a heart attack in Houston at the age of fifty-two. *Killeen Herald*, September 2, 1959; *Austin American-Statesman*, September 23, 1959; *Time*, May 4, 1953, p. 25.

14. *Dallas Morning News*, December 3, 1958, and August 17, 1959.

15. *Dallas Morning News*, August 17, 1959, and May 17, 1960; *Time*, May 30, 1960, p. 64; Hurt, "Great Ladies," 229.

16. *Time*, May 30, 1960, p. 64; Hurt, "Great Ladies," 229.

17. *Houston Post*, May 11, 1960; "Report on the new printing plant," OCH Papers, Rice.

18. Anderson, "Eldrewey Stearns," 24–25; Cole, *No Color Is My Kind*, 43, 54–57.

19. Pando, "Oveta Culp Hobby," 184–185.

20. Bill Hobby, interview; Anderson, "Eldrewey Stearns," 26; Pando, "Oveta Culp Hobby," 184–185.

21. Cole, *No Color Is My Kind*, 43, 54–57; Pando, "Oveta Culp Hobby," 184–185.

22. *Texas Observer*, September 2, 1960, p. 52; *Time*, September 12, 1960, p. 68.

23. Ann Whitman's notes on telephone call from DDE to OCH, May 9, 1960, Ann Whitman Name Series, DDEPL; DDE to OCH, May 9, 1960, OCH Papers, Rice.

24. Frank, *Ike and Dick*, 197; transcript of telephone

conversation, DDE to OCH, June 11, 1960, DDEPL; OCH to Nixon, September 22, 1960, OCH Papers, Rice; Ambrose, *Eisenhower, Vol. II*, 595.

25. Nixon to OCH, June 24, 1960, and DDE to OCH, August 6, 1960, OCH Papers, Rice.
26. Whitman to OCH, August 9, 1960, OCH Papers, Rice.
27. *Houston Post*, January 9, April 25, August 24, and November 7, 1960; LBJ to OCH, May 5, 1960, OCH Papers, Rice.
28. "Senator Lyndon B. Johnson, Daily Diary," August 18, 1960, LBJ Senate Papers, LBJPL; *Houston Post*, August 24, 1960; *NY Journal American*, August 25, 1960; Lady Bird Johnson and OCH interviews, LBJPL.
29. Bill Hobby, interview; OCH to Mrs. Joe P. Lehman, August 30, 1960, OCH Papers, Rice; *Time*, September 19, 1960.
30. Carey Croneis to OCH, October 13, 1960, OCH to DDE, ca. October 1960, and DDE to OCH, October 14, 1960, OCH Papers, Rice.
31. Transcript, "Telephone Conversation between Mrs. Hobby and Mr. Tom Stephens of the White House," October 19, 1960, OCH Papers, Rice; *Houston Post*, October 25, 1960.
32. "Monday, October 24, 1960," typescript of event schedule, OCH Papers, Rice; *Houston Post*, October 25, 1960.
33. *Houston Post*, October 15, 1960; "Guest List for Breakfast, October 25, Suite 1303, Shamrock Hotel," and Eisenhower to OCH, October 27, 1960, OCH Papers, Rice; presidential appointment book, October 24, 1960, DDEPL.
34. *Houston Post*, November 4, 1960; itinerary, "Arrangements to Greet Vice President Nixon, Thursday, November 3, 1960," OCH Papers, Rice.
35. Presidential appointment book, November 30, 1960, DDEPL; DDE to OCH, January 16, 1961, OCH Papers, Rice.

CHAPTER 41

1. Dudley Dougherty, interview, December 27, 1971, LBJPL; Sam Rayburn to OCH, September 15, 1961, and OCH to Rayburn, September 14, 1961, OCH Papers, Rice.
2. Pierre Salinger to OCH, October 23, 1961, and JFK to OCH, September 21, 1962, OCH Papers, Rice.
3. Catto, *Ambassadors at Sea*, 8–10.
4. Catto, 9–10, and photograph with Goode and Eisenhower in photo insert of Catto's memoir; OCH to DDE, November 8, 1961, and DDE to OCH, November 21, 1961, OCH Papers, Rice.
5. Benjamin Fairbanks to OCH, December 5, 1961, and DDE to OCH, December 15, 1961, and DDE to OCH, December 22, 1961, OCH Papers, Rice.
6. DDE to OCH, January 6, 1962, OCH Papers, Rice.
7. DDE to OCH, September 25, 1962, OCH Papers, Rice; *Houston Post*, October 21, 1962.
8. OCH to DDE, December 14, 1962, OCH Papers, Rice.
9. DDE to OCH, October 16, 1962, DDE to OCH, November 6, 1962, OCH to DDE, November 11, 1963, DDE to OCH, December 10, 1963, OCH to W. D. Aeschbacher, September 14, 1964, OCH to John E. Wickman, November 25, 1969, Edwin A. Thompson to OCH, December 12, 1969, and B. Hunter Loftin to OCH, March 26, 1970, OCH Papers, Rice.
10. "Partial List of Guests to the Vice President and Mrs. Johnson's Barbecue for United Nations Visitors, LBJ Ranch, April 27, 1962," and LBJ to OCH, May 8, 1963, OCH Papers, Rice.
11. OCH and Lady Bird Johnson interviews, LBJPL.
12. Al Shire, "That Reminds Me," in Shire, *Oveta Culp Hobby*, 69; "Vice President Lyndon B. Johnson, Daily Diary," August 13, 1963, LBJ Vice Presidential Papers, LBJPL.
13. LBJ to OCH, August 19, 1963, LBJ to OCH, September 2, 1963, and OCH to LBJ, September 17, 1963, OCH Papers, Rice.
14. When the news of Kennedy's murder was transmitted over the United Press wire service to the *Houston Post*, Bill Hobby immediately ordered and oversaw the printing of an extra edition of the paper. Bill Hobby, interview.
15. OCH, interview, July 11, 1969, LBJPL; *Houston Post*, November 24, 1963; LBJ to Bill Hobby, December 9, 1963, OCH Papers, Rice.
16. "Brawley Marze," in Shire, *Oveta Culp Hobby*, 34.
17. OCH, typescript of her introduction of Clare Boothe Luce at the Institute of International Education dinner honoring Luce, January 15, 1964, and Luce to OCH, January 19, 1964, OCH Papers, Rice.
18. Notes with quotes from unidentified *Post* staffer, OCH Papers, Rice.
19. *Houston Post*, February 7, 20, and 27, 1964.
20. LBJ and George Brown telephone call, February 14, 1964, LBJPL.

21. *Houston Post*, June 7, 1964; Bill Hobby, interview, August 31, 2015; Bill Hobby to John Davis, July 1, 1964, Bill Hobby Papers, DBCAH.

22. *Austin American-Statesman*, June 8, 1964; *Houston Chronicle*, June 8, 1964; *NYT*, June 8, 1964.

23. LBJ, "Statement on the Death of William P. Hobby, Sr.," June 8, 1964, and OCH to Eisenhower, June 18, 1964, both in OCH Papers, Rice.

24. *Houston Post*, June 8, 1964; *Houston Chronicle*, June 9, 1964; Walsh, "Oveta Culp Hobby" (2006), 33.

25. Will's friend and business associate Ross Sterling was also buried at Glenwood. After Will's funeral, George H. W. Bush, at that time president of the Zapata Off-Shore Company of Houston and a Republican candidate for the US Senate against the incumbent, Ralph Yarborough, sent a two-page handwritten letter to Oveta, who had endorsed his candidacy. "Dear Mrs. Hobby," Bush wrote, "I had intended to write to you about your wonderful help on the recent campaign. It meant so much to me—then came Gov. Hobby's death. I am so sorry. I was at the funeral, and I am so pleased I went. It was impressive to see so many people pay their respects . . . your bearing reflecting courage and typical of one who has served her country and yet has kept the family's importance paramount." George H. W. Bush to OCH, WPH Sr. Papers, DBCAH.

26. *Austin American-Statesman*, October 26, 1964; *Houston Post*, October 28, 1964, and January 22, 1965.

27. *Houston Chronicle*, August 16, 1995.

28. *Houston Post*, August 23, 1962; *Dallas Times Herald*, January 28, 1963.

29. *Time*, March 1, 1963, p. 40; Hurt, "Great Ladies," 229.

30. *Houston Post*, April 2, 1963; Hurt, "Great Ladies," 229.

31. Bill Hobby, interview; *Houston Chronicle*, July 7, 2005.

32. *Houston Chronicle*, August 16, 1995; "Jim Crowther," in Shire, *Oveta Culp Hobby*, 15.

33. *Texas Monthly*, October 1978; Bagdikian, "Houston's Shackled Press."

34. *Texas Monthly*, October 1978.

35. *Texas Monthly*, October 1978.

36. *Rice Thresher* 54, no. 24, April 13, 1967.

37. *LA Times*, January 19, 2015.

38. Hurt, "Great Ladies," 236; McGrew to Bill

Hobby, January 15, 1991, Bill Hobby Papers, DBCAH.

39. Harris, Huhndorff, and McGrew, *Fault*, 55.

40. OCH, interview, LBJPL; Harris, Huhndorff, and McGrew, *Fault*, 55.

41. Kay Bailey married attorney Ray Hutchison, who was a legislative colleague. Later, as Kay Bailey Hutchison, she served as state treasurer of Texas and was the first woman US senator from Texas, from 1993 to 2013. Hutchison, *Unflinching Courage*, 315–316.

42. Pando, "Oveta Culp Hobby," 2; "Jim Crowther," in Shire, *Oveta Culp Hobby*, 15; *Houston Chronicle*, August 16, 1995; Sutphen, "Conservative Warrior," 106.

43. *Houston Post*, September 20, 1963.

44. Sutphen, "Conservative Warrior," 29.

45. "Oveta Culp Hobby," undated notes in Marguerite Johnston Barnes Papers, Rice.

CHAPTER 42

1. The relationship between LBJ and George and Herman Brown is detailed in Caro, *Path to Power*.

2. Sam Houston Johnson, interview, October 1, 1976, LBJPL.

3. George Reedy and Lady Bird Johnson interviews, LBJPL.

4. The contacts between Oveta and LBJ are detailed in his official presidential daily diary, as well as in their taped telephone conversations, both available at the LBJ Library. LBJ and OCH phone conversation, August 28, 1964, LBJPL; Sutphen, "Conservative Warrior," 21.

5. Walter Simmons to OCH, March 27, 1964, Lady Bird Johnson to OCH, April 6, 1964, LBJ to OCH, April 7 and 15, 1964, OCH Papers, Rice.

6. LBJ and George Brown phone conversation, July 29, 1964, LBJPL.

7. LBJ and George Brown phone conversation, July 29, 1964, LBJPL.

8. LBJ and OCH phone conversation, July 29, 1964, LBJPL.

9. "President's Daily Diary," August 28 and 29, 1964, and LBJ and OCH phone conversation, August 28, 1964, LBJPL.

10. *Houston Post*, August 30, 1964; LBJ and OCH phone conversation, August 30, 1964, LBJPL.

11. *Houston Post*, August 30, 1964; LBJ and OCH phone conversation, August 30, 1964, LBJPL.

12. "President's Daily Diary," August 28, 1964, and LBJ to OCH, September 14, 1964, LBJPL.

13. LBJ was so impressed with the vivacious Halsell that he soon hired her to be one of his speechwriters. Halsell later gained fame for her 1969 book *Soul Sister*. OCH to LBJ, October 8, 1964, OCH to Lady Bird Johnson, October 8, 1964, and LBJ to OCH, October 15, 1964, OCH Papers, Rice; *Washington Post*, October 2, 1964; Walter Jenkins to Jack Valenti, October 6, 1964, "Presidential Daily Diary," October 1 and 3, 1964, "Lady Bird Johnson's Daily Diary," October 1, 1964, and interview with Ruth Prokop, LBJPL.

14. "President's Daily Diary," October 31, 1964, and LBJ and George Brown phone conversation, November 5, 1964, LBJPL.

15. LBJ and OCH phone conversation, November 4, 1964, LBJPL.

16. Social Secretary, White House, to OCH, November 6, 1964, *Houston Post* to White House, telegram, November 9, 1964, and OCH to LBJ, December 18, 1964, OCH Papers, Rice; "President Lyndon B. Johnson, Daily Diary," December 15, 1964, LBJPL; *Houston Post*, December 16, 1964.

17. *Houston Post*, February 4, 1965.

18. "Lady Bird Johnson's Audio Diary and Annotated Transcript," April 9, 1965, LBJPL; Denton Cooley, interview.

19. "Lady Bird Johnson's Audio Diary and Annotated Transcript," April 9, 1965, LBJPL; OCH to Lyndon and Lady Bird Johnson, May 3, 1965, and Lady Bird Johnson to OCH, May 7, 1965, OCH Papers, Rice.

20. "President Lyndon B. Johnson, Daily Diary," July 20, 1965, and "Lady Bird Johnson's Audio Diary and Annotated Transcript," July 20, 1965, LBJPL.

21. "Lady Bird Johnson Audio Diary and Transcript," September 6, 1965, LBJPL.

22. "Lady Bird Johnson Audio Diary and Transcript," September 6, 1965, and Arthur Krim, interview, May 17, 1982, LBJPL.

23. Arthur Krim, interview, May 17, 1982, LBJPL.

24. "President Lyndon B. Johnson, Daily Diary," September 4 and 6, 1965, and "Lady Bird Johnson Audio Diary and Transcript," September 6, 1965, LBJPL.

25. *Dallas Morning News*, September 10, 1965.

26. *Houston Post*, October 13, 1965.

27. Ambrose, *Eisenhower, Vol. II*, 669; Eisenhower to OCH, October 20, 1965, OCH, typescript of speech at Eisenhower celebration, October 27, 1965, OCH to Dwight and Mamie Eisenhower, October 29, 1965, and Mamie Eisenhower to OCH, November 18, 1965, OCH Papers, Rice.

CHAPTER 43

1. Minow, "Television," 395–406.

2. Schindler, "America's System."

3. Schindler.

4. Schindler; OCH, interview, LBJPL.

5. "President Lyndon B. Johnson, Daily Diary," December 12, 13, and "Lady Bird Johnson's Daily Diary," December 13, 1965, LBJPL.

6. "Lady Bird Johnson's Daily Diary," December 15, 1965, LBJPL; OCH to Lady Bird Johnson, December 29, 1965, OCH Papers, Rice; OCH, interview, LBJPL.

7. "President Lyndon B. Johnson, Daily Diary," February 28 and March 6, 1966, and OCH, interview, LBJPL.

8. "President Lyndon B. Johnson, Daily Diary," March 5, 1966, LBJPL; *Houston Post*, April 20 1966; *NYT*, February 18, 2002.

9. "Lady Bird Johnson's Daily Diary," March 10, 11, and 12, 1966, LBJPL.

10. OCH, interview, "Lady Bird Johnson's Daily Diary," March 10, 11, and 12, 1966, and "President Lyndon B. Johnson, Daily Diary," March 11, 1966, LBJPL.

11. *Houston Post*, April 20, 1966; OCH, interview, LBJPL.

12. *Houston Post*, April 20, 1966; Sutphen, "Conservative Warrior," 333.

13. OCH to LBJ, April 26, 1966, OCH Papers, Rice; *Houston Post*, April 21, 1966; *NYT*, February 18, 2002.

14. *Houston Post*, April 21, 1966; OCH, interview, LBJPL.

15. OCH to DDE, October 11, 1966, and DDE to OCH, October 14, 1966, OCH Papers, Rice.

16. *Houston Post*, April 21, 1966; OCH, interview, LBJPL.

17. Schindler, "America's System"; "President Lyndon B. Johnson, Daily Diary," January 10, 1967, LBJPL.

18. Schindler, "America's System."

19. "President Lyndon B. Johnson, Daily Diary," January 10 and 31, 1967, and OCH, interview, both LBJPL.

20. *Houston Post*, April 27, 1967; Bill Hobby to LBJ, April 26, 1967, OCH Papers, Rice.

21. Lady Bird Johnson to OCH, May 10, 1967, OCH Papers, Rice; OCH and James Ketchum interviews, LBJPL.

22. Brown's action, which had Oveta's support but

was opposed by several influential Rice alums, had economic as well as racial fairness motivations. Federal funding for a wide range of programs was being denied to racially segregated educational institutions. Rice was deeply involved in NASA programs and that involvement was threatened by the university's racial policies. On September 26, 1962, the Rice Board of Governors unanimously passed a resolution to desegregate. *Houston Post*, June 18, 1967; Bill Hobby, interview.

23. "President Lyndon B. Johnson, Daily Diary," November 6 and 7, 1967, and "Lady Bird's Daily Diary," November 7, 1967, LBJPL; "Remarks upon Signing Bill Providing Equal Opportunity in Promotions for Women in the Armed Forces," November 8, 1967, American Presidency Project, https://www.presidency.ucsb.edu; photo of LBJ shaking hands with OCH, http://www.gettyimages.com/pictures/at-bill-signing-ceremony-washington-president-johnson-today-news-photo-515038986.

24. *Houston Post*, December 13, 1967; "President Lyndon B. Johnson, Daily Diary," December 12, 1967, LBJPL.

25. Oveta's memberships included the Carnegie Commission on Educational Television, the National Advisory Commission on Selective Service, the University of Texas Committee of 75, the board of directors of the General Aniline and Film Company, the board of advisors to the Committee for Economic Development, the President's Commission on Employment of the Physically Handicapped, the visiting committee of Harvard's Graduate School of Education, the board of trustees of Rice University, the advisory board of the George C. Marshall Research Foundation, the board of trustees of the Houston Symphony Society, the national council of the Metropolitan Opera, and the national council of the Eleanor Roosevelt Memorial Foundation, among other appointments—all while also overseeing the *Houston Post* and KPRC Radio and TV. *Houston Post*, August 28, 1967.

26. *Houston Post* and *Dallas Morning News*, February 18, 1968; "President Lyndon B. Johnson, Daily Diary," February 17, 1968, LBJPL; LBJ to OCH, March 13, 1968, OCH Papers, Rice.

27. OCH, interview, and "President Lyndon B. Johnson, Daily Diary," March 31, 1968, LBJPL; *Houston Post*, April 2, 1968.

28. *Houston Post*, April 6, and June 6 and 9, 1968.

29. Mamie Eisenhower to OCH, August 15, 1968, OCH Papers, Rice.

30. Many years later, when I was working with Dr. Cooley on his memoir, *100,000 Hearts*, he told me he believed Eisenhower would have been a "great candidate for a heart transplant," but the first transplant had just been performed in December 1967. The procedure was too new to consider that option seriously, but there can be no doubt that Cooley would have loved to have been the first surgeon to transplant a heart into a former president. Denton Cooley, interview; OCH to DDE, October 14, 1968, Mamie Eisenhower to OCH, November 26, 1968, and DDE to OCH, January 19, 1969, OCH Papers, Rice.

31. In June 1971 Oveta helped organize a luncheon at the Hotel Pierre in New York City to honor Mamie and to raise money for the "Eisenhower Agricultural Program" in South Korea. Oveta directed the Hobby Foundation to contribute $1,000 for the event, and she was given a seat at the head table. Mamie died in 1979. Unidentified individual to OCH, telegram, March 28, 1969, OCH to Mamie Eisenhower, ca. April 1969, OCH to Mamie Eisenhower, July 21, 1969, Roswell Perkins to OCH, April 30, 1971, and Howard A. Rusk to OCH, March 30, 1971, OCH Papers, Rice.

32. "President Lyndon B. Johnson, Daily Diary," and "Lady Bird Johnson's Daily Diary," both April 20 and 26, and August 11, 1968, LBJPL.

33. OCH to LBJ, December 9, 1970, OCH to LBJ, April 20, 1971, LBJ to OCH, April 29, 1971, and OCH to Lyndon and Lady Bird Johnson, May 27, 1971, OCH Papers, Rice.

34. Bill Hobby, "Days of Pomp and Ceremony," typescript, January 25, 1973, Bill Hobby Papers, DBCAH; B. Hobby, *How Things Really Work*, 30; *Houston Post*, January 23, 1973.

CHAPTER 44

1. Catto, *Ambassadors at Sea*, 13; Nixon to OCH, September 7, 1968, OCH Papers, Rice.

2. Nixon to OCH, October 19, 1968, Nixon to OCH, October 30, 1968, and telegram, Nixon to OCH, October 30, 1968, OCH Papers, Rice.

3. Jack Harris, "Recap of Discussions Concerning NBC Election Coverage," November 4, 1968, OCH Papers, Rice.

4. Jack Harris, "Recap of Discussions Concerning NBC Election Coverage," November 4, 1968, OCH Papers, Rice.

5. Telegram, OCH to White House Social Secretary, August 1, 1969, OCH to Patricia Nixon, August 26, 1969, and OCH to Patricia Nixon, April 14, 1970, OCH Papers, Rice; Sutphen, "Conservative Warrior," 334.

6. Marguerite Johnston, interview; "George Fuermann," in Shire, *Oveta Culp Hobby*, 20–21.

7. "George Fuermann," 20–21; *Houston Post*, October 29, 1972; Richard Nixon to OCH, November 3, 1972, OCH Papers, Rice.

8. "George Fuermann," in Shire, *Oveta Culp Hobby*, 20–21.

9. *Houston Post*, January 25, 1973; Richard Nixon to OCH, February 13, 1973, and OCH to Nixon, February 27, 1973, OCH Papers, Rice.

10. *Houston Post*, August 9, 1974.

11. *Houston Post*, August 10 and 15, 1974; Bill Hobby, interview.

12. Oveta and Kay Graham were friends. Oveta had known Kay's parents, Eugene and Agnes Meyer, as well as Kay's husband, Philip Graham. In her memoir, *Personal History*, Kay wrote that soon after Phil died in 1963, Oveta paid her a visit at Kay's *Newsweek* office in New York City. Kay recalled that Oveta advised her about the obligations of a news executive, including speechmaking. When Kay, who was intensely shy, protested that she was uncomfortable with speaking in public and that she had no intention of making any speeches, Oveta told her she had no choice, stressing she would have to learn to do things like that. "[Oveta] herself hadn't known many things but had learned. I realized . . . that she might be right, and that speechmaking might indeed be in my future." Graham, *Personal History*, 344–345; Shannon, "They Built Houston," 21–23.

13. *Women's Wear Daily*, January 11, 1971.

14. Bill Hobby, interview.

15. "Brawley Marze," in Shire, *Oveta Culp Hobby*, 34–35; Marguerite Johnston, typescript, 1995, Bill Hobby Papers, DBCAH.

16. Papademetriou, *Architectural Guide*; Hurt, "Great Ladies," 144, 146; *Women's Wear Daily*, January 1971.

17. A set of professionally shot photographs of Oveta's office are filed in her papers at Rice University. *Women's Wear Daily*, January 1971; Hurt, "Great Ladies," 144, 146; "Arnold Rosenfeld," in Shire, *Oveta Culp Hobby*, 42.

18. Shannon, "They Built Houston"; "Arnold Rosenfeld," in Shire, *Oveta Culp Hobby*, 42.

19. "Campbell Geeslin" in Shire, *Oveta Culp Hobby*, 22; Hurt, "Great Ladies," 144, 146.

20. Hurt, "Great Ladies," 233–234; "Marge Crumbaker," in Shire, *Oveta Culp Hobby*, 16.

21. Al Shire, "That Reminds Me," 67, and "Ed Hunter," 29, in Shire, *Oveta Culp Hobby*.

22. Al Shire, "That Reminds Me," 67, 71, 74, and "Ed Hunter," 29, in Shire, *Oveta Culp Hobby*.

23. "Mickey Herskowitz," in Shire, *Oveta Culp Hobby*, 28; *Houston Chronicle*, August 17, 1995.

24. "Marge Crumbaker," in Shire, *Oveta Culp Hobby*, 17.

25. *Women's Wear Daily*, January 1971.

26. Peggy Buchanan to Mabel Sorrells, April 25, 1978, OCH Papers, Rice.

27. OCH biographical clipping file, DBCAH.

28. *Houston Chronicle*, January 20, 1972; *Dallas Times Herald*, January 20, 1972.

29. Jack McGrew to Bill Hobby, January 15, 1991, Bill Hobby Papers, DBCAH.

30. *Time*, June 19, 1972; Caudill and Hancock, "Guild and Post."

31. Catto, *Ambassadors at Sea*, 79.

32. *Dallas Times Herald*, April 12, 1972; *Houston Post*, April 12, 1972.

33. *Dallas Times Herald*, April 13, 1972.

34. *Midland Reporter-Telegram*, April 13, 1972; *Amarillo Daily News*, April 14, 1972.

35. *Houston Post*, May 7, 1972; *Corpus Christi Caller-Times*, May 25, 1972.

36. OCH to Bill Hartman, June 22, 1972, and Harold S. Taxel to OCH, June 27, 1972, Bill Hobby Papers, DBCAH.

37. *Houston Journalism Review*, July 1972.

38. Catto, *Ambassadors at Sea*, 44, 84; *Houston Post*, January 18, 1973.

CHAPTER 45

1. Shannon, "They Built Houston."

2. Harris, Huhndorff, and McGrew, *Fault*, 118–119; Bill Hobby, interview.

3. *Nashville Banner*, June 24, 1976; *Tennessean*, June 25, 1976.

4. *Tennessean*, June 25, 1976; "Ed Harte," in Shire, *Oveta Culp Hobby*, 26.

5. OCH to Kaye McDermott, August 11, 1976, OCH Papers, Rice; Harris, Huhndorff, and McGrew, *Fault*, 118–122; Hurt, "Great Ladies," 233–234.

6. Hurt, "Great Ladies," 143, 237.

7. Hutchison, *Unflinching Courage*, 315–316.

8. OCH to Helen Gruber, February 11, 1983, OCH Papers, Rice.

9. B. Hobby, *How Things Really Work*, 53–54; Don Adams, interview by Patty Hart.

10. Harris, Huhndorff, and McGrew, *Fault*, 118–122; Hurt, "Great Ladies," 233–234; speech files, OCH Papers, Rice.

11. Hurt, "Great Ladies," 233–234; "Pat Bowman," 9, and "Isabel Brown Wilson," 52–53, in Shire, *Oveta Culp Hobby*; Johnston quote in OCH note files, Marguerite Johnston Barnes Papers, Rice.

12. Undated notes in Marguerite Johnston Barnes Papers, Rice.

13. Pando, 2; "Jim Crowther," in Shire, 15; Sutphen, 106.

14. Texas A&M University also honored Oveta by naming a new four story dormitory after her in October 1980. "Speech Files," OCH Papers, Rice.

15. Hurt, "Great Ladies," 233–234; "Pat Bowman," 9, and "Isabel Brown Wilson, 52–53, in Shire, *Oveta Culp Hobby*.

16. In May 1987 the Cattos donated the *Washington Journalism Review* to the University of Maryland, where the name was changed to the *American Journalism Review*. The university closed the publication in July 2015 for financial reasons. Catto, *Ambassadors at Sea*, 218; *NYT*, December 21, 2011; Robertson, "Life and Times"; OCH to Helen Gruber, February 11, 1983, OCH Papers, Rice.

17. Barna, "Oveta Posts Notice," 116; Bill Hobby, "A Requiem for the *Houston Post*," *Houston Chronicle*, April 23, 1995.

18. OCH to Evetts Culp, October 13, 1983, OCH Papers, Rice.

19. Barna, "Oveta Posts Notice," 116; *NYT*, July 30, 1983; OCH to Henry Taub, January 13, 1984, OCH Papers, Rice; *USA Today*, July 22, 1983; *Advertising Age*, October 24, 1983, p. 6.

20. Photograph of announcement meeting in Shire, *Oveta Culp Hobby*, 42; *Houston Post*, October 20, 1983.

21. Al Shire, "That Reminds Me," in Shire, *Oveta Culp Hobby*, 76.

22. OCH to Woodrow Seals, March 27, 1984, OCH to Henry Taub, January 13, 1984, OCH to Mickey Herskowitz, February 17, 1984, and Richard J. V. Johnson to OCH, April 3, 1984, OCH Papers, Rice; "Lalo Galaviz," in Shire, *Oveta Culp Hobby*, 21.

23. In 1994 *Forbes* magazine estimated Oveta's fortune at $400 million; Sutphen, "Conservative Warrior," 333; OCH to Mike Stude, February 11, 1984, OCH Papers, Rice.

24. Speech files, OCH Papers, Rice; OCH to "Virginia," April 9, 1984, OCH Papers, Rice.

25. Bill Hobby, interview; Woodrow Seals to OCH, April 13, 1984, OCH to Heather Catto, May 13, 1985, and OCH to Jessica and Henry Catto, August 23, 1985, OCH Papers, Rice; *Houston Post*, January 19, 1986.

26. Sutphen, "Conservative Warrior," 331.

27. Marguerite Johnston, "The Widening Wake," in Shire, *Oveta Culp Hobby*, 80; OCH to Michael K. McGuire, January 18, 1995, OCH to Margaret and Ben Love, January 17, 1995, and Peggy Buchanan to Michael Sharlot, February 14, 1995, OCH Papers, Rice.

28. Sutphen, "Conservative Warrior," 1, 2; Jessica Catto, "An Exciting Life, Well-Lived," in Shire, *Oveta Culp Hobby*, iii; Pando, "Oveta Culp Hobby," 187.

29. "Ed Harte," in Shire, *Oveta Culp Hobby*, 26.

30. Paul Hobby, "Consistent, But Complicated," in Shire, *Oveta Culp Hobby*, viii–xi; Lady Bird Johnson, interview, November 5, 1994, LBJPL.

31. Catto, *Ambassadors at Sea*, 359; *Austin American-Statesman*, June 14, 1992.

32. Catto, *Ambassadors at Sea*, 359.

33. Program, 1990s, and news clip from Hobby family genealogical file, Bill Hobby Papers, DBCAH.

34. Henry Catto served as the American ambassador to the United Kingdom from 1989 until 1991, when Bush appointed him director of the US Information Agency, a post he held until 1993. On August 2, 1990, Henry and Jessica were hosting a meeting at their ranch in Aspen between President Bush and Margaret Thatcher when Iraq invaded Kuwait. The Cattos were active in the Aspen Institute, where they established the Catto Fellowship for a Sustainable Future. Jessica became a fervent environmentalist and she and Henry provided support for the Aspen Center for Environmental Studies. Jessica died in 2009 and Henry in 2011. Catto, *Ambassadors at Sea*, 357; *NYT*, December 21, 2011.

35. *NYT*, September 11, 1987; *Houston Chronicle*, April 23, 1995.

36. Lynn Culp Loving, "My Sister, Oveta," in Shire, *Oveta Culp Hobby*, vii.

37. Peggy Buchanan to Mrs. M. A. Wright, May 10, 1995, and Peggy Buchanan to Mattie Treadwell, May 2, 1995, OCH Papers, Rice.

38. Marguerite Johnston, "The Widening Wake," in Shire, *Oveta Culp Hobby*, 80; Peggy Buchanan

to Mrs. John [Allene] Wolfe, June 5, 1995, OCH Papers, Rice.

39. Peggy Buchanan to Mrs. John [Allene] Wolfe, August 15, 1995, OCH Papers, Rice; "Notes," Marguerite Johnston Barnes Papers, Rice.

40. "Peggy Fontenette," in Shire, *Oveta Culp Hobby*, 20; Peggy Buchanan to Mattie Treadwell, July 12, 1995, OCH Papers, Rice.

41. Lynn Culp Loving, "My Sister, Oveta," in Shire, *Oveta Culp Hobby*, vii; *Houston Chronicle* and *Austin American-Statesman*, August 17, 1995.

42. *Houston Chronicle* and *Austin American-Statesman*, August 17, 1995.

43. *NYT*, August 17, 1995; Sutphen, "Conservative Warrior," 335; Lloyd Bentsen to Bill Hobby, August 29, 1995, Bill Hobby Papers, DBCAH.

44. "Mrs. Hobby's wishes regarding services at the time of her death," September 19, 1989, OCH Papers, Rice; Marguerite Johnston, "The Widening Wake," in Shire, *Oveta Culp Hobby*, 77.

45. *Austin American-Statesman*, April 19, 1995; Pando, "Oveta Culp Hobby," 187–188; Marguerite Johnston, "The Widening Wake," in Shire, *Oveta Culp Hobby*, 80.

EPILOGUE

1. The stamp was designed by Phil Jordan of Falls Church, Virginia. "Oveta Culp Hobby,"

US Stamp Gallery, accessed March 27, 2020, usstampgallery.com.

2. Unfortunately, from my perspective as this book goes to press in 2020, anti-unionism, the restriction of civil liberties because of war and the fear of terrorism, and racism have returned to levels approximating those of Will Hobby's years as governor.

3. Jessica Catto, "An Exciting Life, Well-Lived," in Shire, *Oveta Culp Hobby*, iii.

4. Bill Hobby's wife, Diana, died on July 4, 2014. *Houston Chronicle*, July 5, 2014; B. Hobby, *How Things Really Work*, 164–175; "Hobby School of Public Affairs," University of Houston, accessed March 27, 2020, uh.edu/hobby.

5. "Heather Catto Kohout," *Austin American-Statesman*, October 20, 2014; John Catto, Alpenglow Pictures, alpenglowpictures.com; Isa Catto Studio, isacatto.com.

6. "Laura Beckworth," Headliners Foundation, https://headlinersfoundation.org/bio-laura -beckworth; "Paul W. Hobby," Texas Undergraduate Studies, https://ugs.utexas.edu/support /advisory-council/paul-hobby; "Kate Gibson," Republic Ranches, https://republicranches.com /about/; Andrew Hobby, LinkedIn; Bill Hobby, interview.

7. Paul Hobby, interview.

# BIBLIOGRAPHY

ARCHIVES AND MANUSCRIPTS

DBCAH: Dolph Briscoe Center for American
History, University of Texas at Austin, TX
    Eugene C. Barker Papers
    Liz Carpenter Papers
    Henry Cohen Papers
    Oscar B. Colquitt Papers
    Martin McNulty Crane Papers
    Alexander Caswell Ellis Papers
    James Edward Ferguson Collection
    Lewis Gould Papers
    C. Read Granberry Papers
    William (Bill) P. Hobby Jr. Papers
    William P. Hobby Sr. Papers
    Will C. Hogg Papers
    Jesse H. Jones Papers
    *New York Herald Tribune* Morgue
    *New York Journal American* Morgue
    *New York Times* Morgue
    *Newsweek* Research Archive
    J. R. Parten Papers
    Sam Rayburn Papers
    Charles Arden Russell Papers
    Ross Sterling Papers
    Jessie D. Ziegler Papers
DDEPL: Dwight D. Eisenhower Presidential
Library, Abilene, KS
    Stephen Benedict Papers
    Dwight D. Eisenhower Presidential Papers
    Oveta Culp Hobby Papers
DHS: Dallas Historical Society, TX
    Thomas Love Papers
ETRC: East Texas Research Center, Stephen F.
Austin State University, Nacogdoches, TX

Kirby Lumber Company Records
FDRPL: Franklin D. Roosevelt Presidential Library,
Hyde Park, NY
    Adolf A. Berle Papers
    Democratic National Committee Papers
    Eleanor Roosevelt Papers
GCMRL: George C. Marshall Research Library,
Lexington, VA
    George C. Marshall Papers
HHPL: Herbert Hoover Presidential Library,
West Branch, IA
    Herbert Hoover Papers
    Walter Trohan Papers
HSTPL: Harry S. Truman Presidential Library,
Independence, MO
    Harry S. Truman Papers
LBJPL: LBJ Presidential Library, Austin, TX
    Lady Bird Johnson Papers
    Lyndon B. Johnson Papers
LOC: Library of Congress, Washington, DC
    Oveta Culp Hobby Papers
    Jesse H. Jones Papers
    William Gibbs McAdoo Papers
Miami: Special Collections, Merrick Library,
University of Miami, FL
    Pan American World Airways Records
NA: National Archives, Washington, DC
    Records of the Army Staff, RG 319
Princeton: Special Collections, Princeton University
Library, Princeton, NJ
    Bernard M. Baruch Papers
RAC: Rockefeller Archive Center, Tarrytown, NY
    Nelson A. Rockefeller Papers
    Laurance S. Rockefeller Papers

Rice: Woodson Research Center, Rice University, Houston, TX
    Marguerite Johnston Barnes Papers
    James Clark Papers
    Oveta Culp Hobby Papers
    Hobby Family Foundation Records
    Rienzi M. Johnston Papers
    Jesse H. Jones Papers
    Gus Wortham Papers
STCL: Special Collections, South Texas College of Law Houston, Houston, TX
    Frank Andrews Papers
TSLAC: Texas State Library and Archives Commission, Austin, TX
    Governor William P. Hobby Sr. Papers
UH: Special Collections, University of Houston, TX
    Minnie Fisher Cunningham Papers
    John Henry Kirby Papers
UTSA: Special Collections, University of Texas at San Antonio Libraries, San Antonio, TX
    Francisco A. Chapa Family Papers
Yale: Yale University Library, New Haven, CT
    Edward Mandell House Papers
    Harry Weinberger Papers

## ORAL HISTORIES

By the author
    Dolph Briscoe Jr.
    Delores Chambers
    Denton Cooley
    Laura Hobby
    Paul Hobby
    William "Bill" P. Hobby Jr.
    Marguerite Johnston
    J. R. Parten
    Saralee Tiede
By Patty Hart
    Don Adams
Columbia: Columbia University Oral History Collection, New York, NY
    Nelson Cruikshank
    William Mitchell
    Roswell Perkins
    Leonard A. Scheele
    Charles I. Schottland
DDEPL: Dwight D. Eisenhower Presidential Library, Abilene, KS
    Marion Folsom
HMRC: Houston Metropolitan Research Center, Houston, TX
    Dick Gottlieb

LBJPL: LBJ Presidential Library, Austin, TX
    Liz Carpenter
    Wilbur Cohen
    Dudley Dougherty
    Oveta Culp Hobby
    Claudia "Lady Bird" Johnson
    Sam Houston Johnson
    James Ketchum
    Arthur Krim
    Frank "Posh" Oltorf
    George Reedy
    Morris Roberts
    R. E. Thomason

## WORKS CITED

Abel, Joseph. "Opening the Closed Shop: The Galveston Longshoremen's Strike of 1920–1921." In *Texas Labor History*, edited by Bruce A. Glasrud and James C. Maroney, 185–218. College Station: Texas A&M University Press, 2013.

———. "Opening the Closed Shop: The Galveston Longshoremen's Strike, 1920–1921." Master's thesis, Texas A&M University, 2004.

Abernethy, Frances E. "Big Thicket." *Handbook of Texas Online*. Uploaded June 12, 2010. https://tshaonline.org/handbook/online/articles/gkb03.

Acheson, Sam Hanna. *Joe Bailey: The Last Democrat*. New York: Macmillan, 1932.

Adams, Sherman. *First-Hand Report: The Story of the Eisenhower Administration*. New York: Harper, 1961.

Adamczyk, Richard D. *United States Army in World War II: Readers Guide*. Washington, DC: US Government Printing Office, 1992.

A. J. Peeler Standard Blue Book Company. *The Standard Blue Book of Texas, 1908–09: Edition de Luxe of Beaumont*. Houston: A. J. Peeler Standard Blue Book Company, 1908.

Allardice, Bruce S. *Confederate Colonels: A Biographical Register*. Columbia: University of Missouri Press, 2008.

Alexander, Charles C., *Crusade for Conformity: The Ku Klux Klan in Texas, 1920–1930*. Houston: Texas Gulf Coast Historical Society, 1962.

Almaráz, Felix D., Jr. *Knight without Armor: Carlos Eduardo Castañeda, 1896–1958*. College Station: Texas A&M University Press, 1999.

Altmeyer, Arthur J. *The Formative Years of Social Security: A Chronicle of Social Security Legislation and Administration, 1934–1954*. Madison: University of Wisconsin Press, 1966.

Ambrose, Stephen E. *Eisenhower, Volume I: Soldier,*

*General of the Army, President-Elect, 1890-1952.* New York: Simon and Schuster, 1983.

———. *Eisenhower, Volume II: The President.* New York: Simon and Schuster, 1984.

Anchorage Foundation of Texas. *Braeswood: An Architectural History.* Houston: Old Braeswood Civic Club, 1988.

Anderson, Michael. "Eldrewey Stearns and Houston's Student Civil Rights Movement." *Houston History* 14, no. 2 (Spring 2017): 23–27.

Anderson, Otis. "The Polio Vaccine Assistance Act of 1955." *American Journal of Public Health* (October 1955): 1349.

Andrew, John, III. "Cracks in the Consensus: The Rockefeller Brothers Fund Special Studies Project and Eisenhower's America." *Presidential Studies Quarterly* 28, no. 3 (Summer 1998): 535–552.

Angel, William D., Jr. "Controlling the Workers: The Galveston Dock Workers' Strike of 1920 and Its Impact on Labor Relations in Texas." *East Texas Historical Journal* 23, no. 2 (Fall 1985): 14–27.

Anonymous. "Johnston, Rienzi Melville." *Handbook of Texas Online.* Last modified April 12, 2017. https://tshaonline.org/handbook/online/articles/fjo38.

———. "Lewis, Judd Mortimer." *Handbook of Texas Online.* Last modified May 15, 2017. https://tshaonline.org/handbook/online/articles/fle43.

———. "Mayes, William Harding." *Handbook of Texas Online.* February 13, 2020. https://tshaonline.org/handbook/online/articles/fma89.

———. "Ousley, Clarence N." *Handbook of Texas Online.* Last modified April 30, 2019. https://tshaonline.org/handbook/online/articles/fou02.

———. "Pinckney, John M." *Handbook of Texas Online.* Last modified February 13, 2020. https://tshaonline.org/handbook/online/articles/fpi24.

Ariens, Michael. *Lone Star Law: A Legal History of Texas.* Lubbock: Texas Tech University Press, 2011.

Bagdikian, Ben H. "Houston's Shackled Press." *Atlantic Monthly,* August 1966.

Baker, Erma. "Andrews, Frank." *Handbook of Texas Online.* Last modified August 29, 2016. https://tshaonline.org/handbook/online/articles/fan17.

Barna, Joel. "Oveta Posts Notice." *Houston City Magazine,* November 1983.

Barnouw, Erik. *The Image Empire: A History of Broadcasting in the United States, Vol. III—from 1953.* New York: Oxford University Press, 1970.

Barr, Alwyn. "Battle of Galveston," *Handbook of Texas Online.* Last modified June 20, 2020, http://www.tshaonline.org/handbook/online/articles/qeg01.

———. "Green, Thomas." *Handbook of Texas Online.* Last modified November 11, 2019. https://tshaonline.org/handbook/online/articles/fgr38.

———. *Reconstruction to Reform: Texas Politics, 1876–1906.* Austin: University of Texas Press, 1971.

Bayley, Edwin R. *Joe McCarthy and the Press.* Madison: University of Wisconsin Press, 1981.

Baylor University, *The Alumni Directory, 1854-1917.* Waco, 1917.

Beaumont Chamber of Commerce. *Beaumont: A Gateway to the Marts of the World.* Beaumont, TX: Beaumont Chamber of Commerce, 1910.

Beland, Daniel. *Social Security: History and Politics from the New Deal to the Privatization Debate.* Lawrence: University Press of Kansas, 2005.

Bell County Historical Commission. *Story of Bell County, Texas.* 2 vols. Austin: Eakin Press, 1988.

Benham, Priscilla Myers. "Moore, Helen Edmunds." *Handbook of Texas Online.* Uploaded June 15, 2010. https://tshaonline.org/handbook/online/articles/fmo83.

Berkowitz, Edward D. *Mr. Social Security: The Life of Wilbur J. Cohen.* Lawrence: University Press of Kansas, 1995.

Biles, Roger. *The South and the New Deal.* Lexington: University Press of Kentucky, 2015.

Blair, Emily Newell. "Woman Soldier Number One." *Liberty,* August 1, 1942.

Blevins, Cameron. "Space, Nation, and the Triumph of Region: A View of the World from Houston." *Journal of American History* 101, no. 1 (June 2014): 122–147.

Bradley, Robert L., Jr. *Edison to Enron: Energy Markets and Political Strategies.* Salem, MA: Scrivener, 2011.

Braden, Joan. *Just Enough Rope: An Intimate Memoir.* New York: Villard, 1989.

Brands, H. W. *Traitor to His Class: The Privileged Life and Radical Presidency of Franklin Delano Roosevelt.* New York: Random House, 2008.

Brannon-Wranosky, Jessica, and Bruce A. Glasrud, eds. *Impeached: The Removal of Texas Governor James E. Ferguson.* College Station: Texas A&M University Press, 2017.

Branyan, Lawrence H, and Robert L. Larsen. *The Eisenhower Administration, 1953–1961: A Documentary History.* Vol. 1. New York: Random House, 1971.

Brittain, Joan T. *Laurence Stallings*. Boston: Twayne, 1975.

Brown, Norman D. *Biscuits, the Dole, and Nodding Donkeys*. Austin: University of Texas Press, 2019.

———. *Hood, Bonnet, and Little Brown Jug: Texas Politics, 1921–1928*. College Station: Texas A&M University Press, 1984.

Brownell, Blaine A. *The Urban Ethos in the South, 1920–1930*. Baton Rouge: Louisiana State University Press, 1975.

Brownell, Herbert, with John P. Burke. *Advising Ike: The Memoirs of Attorney General Herbert Brownell*. Lawrence: University Press of Kansas, 1993.

Bryant, Keith L., Jr. "Arthur E. Stilwell and the Founding of Port Arthur: A Case of Entrepreneurial Error." *Southwestern Historical Quarterly* 75, no. 1 (July 1971): 19–40.

Bryce, Robert. "Do Not Go Gentle." *Houston Press*, September 10–16, 1998.

Buenger, Walter L. "Between Community and Corporation: The Southern Roots of Jesse H. Jones and the Reconstruction Finance Corporation." *Journal of Southern History* 56, no. 3 (August 1990): 481–510.

———. *Secession and the Union in Texas*. Austin: University of Texas Press, 1984.

Buenger, Walter L., and Joseph A. Pratt. *But Also Good Business: Texas Commerce Banks and the Financing of Houston*. College Station: Texas A&M University Press, 1986.

Bugbee, Sylvia J., ed. *An Officer and a Lady: The World War II Letters of Lt. Col. Betty Bandel, Women's Army Corps*. Hanover, NH: University Press of New England, 2004.

Burka, Paul. "Bill Hobby: A Lesson in Public Service." *Texas Monthly*, September 1997.

Burrough, Bryan. *The Big Rich: The Rise and Fall of the Greatest Texas Oil Fortunes*. New York: Penguin, 2009.

Campbell, Randolph B. *Gone to Texas: A History of the Lone Star State*. New York: Oxford University Press, 2003.

Canham, Erwin D. "International Freedom of Information." *Law and Contemporary Problems* 14, no. 4 (Fall 1949): 584–598.

Cardwell, John. *Sketches of Legislators and State Officers, Fifteenth Legislature, 1876–1878*. Austin: Democratic Statesman Steam Print, 1876.

Carleton, Don. *A Breed So Rare: The Life of J. R. Parten, Liberal Texas Oil Man, 1896–1992*. Austin: Texas State Historical Association, 1998.

———. *Red Scare: Right-Wing Hysteria, Fifties Fanaticism, and Their Legacy in Texas*. Austin: University of Texas Press, 2014.

Caro, Robert A. *Means of Ascent: The Years of Lyndon Johnson II*. New York: Knopf, 1990.

———. *The Path to Power: The Years of Lyndon Johnson I*. New York: Knopf, 1982.

Cates, Meryl. "Favorite Recipes of Famous Women." *Paris Review*, February 17, 2016.

Catto, Henry E., Jr. *Ambassadors at Sea: The High and Low Adventures of a Diplomat*. Austin: University of Texas Press, 1998.

Caudill, Susan, and Darrell Hancock. "The Guild and the Post." *Houston Journalism Review*, June 1972.

Caute, David. *The Great Fear: The Anti-communist Purge under Truman and Eisenhower*. New York: Simon and Schuster, 1978.

Chafee, Zechariah, Jr. "Legal Problems of Freedom of Information in the United Nations." *Law and Contemporary Problems* 14, no. 4 (Fall 1949): 545–583.

Champagne, Anthony, Douglas B. Harris, James W. Riddlesperger Jr., and Garrison Nelson. *The Austin/Boston Connection: Five Decades of House Democratic Leadership, 1937–1989*. College Station: Texas A&M University Press, 2009.

Chandler, Alfred D., Jr. *The Papers of Dwight David Eisenhower: The War Years*. Baltimore, MD: Johns Hopkins University Press, 1970.

Clark, James A. *The Tactful Texan: A Biography of Governor Will Hobby*. New York: Random House, 1958.

Clark, James A., and Michel T. Halbouty. *Spindletop*. New York: Random House, 1952.

Cole, Thomas R. *No Color Is My Kind: The Life of Eldrewey Stearns and the Integration of Houston*. Austin: University of Texas Press, 1997.

Collier, Jo. "The Woman's Viewpoint." *Handbook of Texas Online*. Uploaded February 24, 2017. https://tshaonline.org/handbook/online/articles/edwom.

Cook, Blanche Wiesen. *Eleanor Roosevelt, Volume 3: The War Years and After, 1939–1962*. New York: Viking Press, 2016.

Committee on Armed Services. "Nomination of Anna M. Rosenberg to be Assistant Secretary of Defense: Hearing before the Committee on Armed Services, United States Senate, Eighty-First Congress, Second Session." Washington, DC: US Government Printing Office, 1950.

Committee on Finance. "Nominations: Hearing before the Committee on Finance, United States

Senate, Eighty-Third Congress, First Session, on Nominations of George M. Humphrey, Secretary of the Treasury-Designate, Oveta Culp Hobby, Federal Security Administrator-Designate." Washington, DC: US Government Printing Office, 1953.

Cone, Stacey. "Presuming a Right to Deceive: Radio Free Europe, Radio Liberty, the CIA, and the News Media." *Journalism History* 24, no. 4 (Winter 1999): 148–156.

Crawford, Ann Fears, and Crystal Sasse Ragsdale. *Women in Texas: Their Lives, Their Experiences, Their Accomplishments.* Austin: Eakin Press, 1982.

Crawford, Audrey Y. "The Texas Woman's Fair: Women, Fairs, and the Growth of Houston in the Progressive Era." Master's thesis, University of Houston, 2002.

Cross, Christopher T. *Political Education: Setting the Course for State and Federal Policy.* New York: Teachers College Press, 2014.

Daniel, Jean Houston, Price Daniel, and Dorothy Blodgett. *The Texas Governor's Mansion: A History of the House and Its Occupants.* Austin: Texas State Library and Archives Commission, 1984.

Daniell, Lewis E. *Personnel of the Texas State Government, with Sketches of Representative Men of Texas.* San Antonio: Maverick Printing House, 1892.

Daugherty, Tracy. *Hiding Man: A Biography of Donald Barthelme.* New York: St. Martin's Press, 2009.

Davis, Ellis A., and Edwin H. Grobe, eds. *The Encyclopedia of Texas, Volume I.* Dallas: Texas Development Bureau, 1926.

Davis, J. William. "Lieutenant Governor." *Handbook of Texas Online.* Last modified November 25, 2019. https://tshaonline.org/handbook/online/articles/mbl01.

Delaney, Norman C. "Corpus Christi, Battle of." *Handbook of Texas Online.* Last modified March 4, 2011. https://tshaonline.org/handbook/online/articles/qec03.

DeWitt, Larry. "Never a Finished Thing: A Brief Biography of Arthur Joseph Altmeyer—the Man FDR Called 'Mr. Social Security.'" Social Security History, US Social Security Administration. Accessed February 13, 2020. https://www.ssa.gov/history/bioaja.html.

Dressman, Fran. *Gus Wortham: Portrait of a Leader.* College Station: Texas A&M University Press, 1994.

Duffy, Winifred A. "Link, John Wiley." *Handbook of Texas Online.* Last modified May 15, 2017. https://tshaonline.org/handbook/online/articles/fli24.

Duggan, Laura Woolsey. "Poage, William Robert." *Handbook of Texas Online.* Last modified April 25, 2018. https://tshaonline.org/handbook/online/articles/fpo50.

Dunn, Roy Sylvan. "The KGC in Texas, 1860–1861." *Southwestern Historical Quarterly* 70, no. 4 (April 1967): 543–573.

Duram, James C. *A Moderate among Extremists: Dwight D. Eisenhower and the School Desegregation Crisis.* Chicago: Nelson-Hall, 1981.

Durham, Kenneth R., Jr. "The Longview Race Riot of 1919." *East Texas Historical Journal* 18, no. 2 (1980): 13–24.

Dwyer, T. Ryle. *Strained Relations: Ireland at Peace and the USA at War, 1941.* Dublin, Ireland: Gill and Macmillan, 1988.

Earley, Charity Adams. *One Woman's Army: A Black Officer Remembers the WAC.* College Station: Texas A&M University Press, 1989.

Early, Joseph E., Jr. *A Texas Baptist History Sourcebook: A Companion to McBeth's "Texas Baptists."* Denton: University of North Texas Press, 2004.

East, Lorecia. *History and Progress of Jefferson County.* Dallas: Royal Publishing Company, 1961.

Edy, Carolyn M. *The Woman War Correspondent, the U.S. Military, and the Press: 1846–1947.* Lanham, MD: Lexington Books, 2017.

Eisenhower, Dwight D. *The Eisenhower Diaries.* Edited by Robert H. Ferrell. New York: W. W. Norton, 1981.

———. *Mandate for Change, 1953–1956: The White House Years.* New York: Doubleday, 1963.

Ellinger, Esther Parker. "The Southern War Poetry of the Civil War." PhD diss., University of Pennsylvania, 1918.

Farrell, Mary D., and Elizabeth Silverthorne. *First Ladies of Texas: The First One Hundred Years, 1836–1936.* Belton, TX: Stillhouse Hollow Publishers, 1976.

Feagin, Joe R. *Free Enterprise City: Houston in Political-Economic Perspective.* New Brunswick, NJ: Rutgers University Press, 1988.

Feder, Lester. "Disaster Reporting through the Ages." *Columbia Journalism Review*, December 18, 2008.

Fenberg, Steven. *Unprecedented Power: Jesse Jones, Capitalism, and the Common Good.* College Station: Texas A&M University Press, 2011.

Ferguson, Niall. *Kissinger: 1923-1968; The Idealist.* New York: Penguin, 2015.

Fitzgerald, Hugh Nugent. *Governors I Have Known.* Austin: Austin American-Statesman, 1927.

Foner, Eric. *Reconstruction: America's Unfinished Revolution, 1863-1877.* New York: Harper, 1988.

Foster, Mark S. *Henry J. Kaiser: Builder in the American West.* Austin: University of Texas Press, 1989.

Frank, Jeffrey. *Ike and Dick: Portrait of a Strange Political Marriage.* New York: Simon and Schuster, 2013.

Fuermann, George. *Houston: Land of the Big Rich.* New York: Doubleday, 1951.

———. *Reluctant Empire: The Mind of Texas.* New York: Doubleday, 1957.

Gano, R. C. "Sharp, Walter Benona." *Handbook of Texas Online.* Last modified March 8, 2019. https://tshaonline.org/handbook/online/articles/fsh06.

Gantt, Fred, Jr. *The Chief Executive in Texas: A Study in Gubernatorial Leadership.* Austin: University of Texas Press, 1964.

Gardner, William H. "Mr. and Mrs. Texas." *Texas Parade,* March 1953.

Gould, Lewis L. *Progressives and Prohibitionists: Texas Democrats in the Wilson Era.* Austin: University of Texas Press, 1973.

Graham, Katharine. *Personal History.* New York: Vintage, 1997.

Green, George Norris. *The Establishment in Texas Politics: The Primitive Years, 1938-1957.* Westport, CT: Praeger, 1979.

Green, James R. *Grass-Roots Socialism: Radical Movements in the Southwest, 1895-1943.* Baton Rouge: Louisiana State University Press, 1978.

Griffith, Robert. *The Politics of Fear: Joseph R. McCarthy and the Senate.* Lexington: University Press of Kentucky, 1970.

Guinn, Jack. *The Caperberry Bush.* Boston: Little, Brown, 1954.

Gunn, Sylvia. "Tips, Kern." *Handbook of Texas Online.* Last modified July 20, 2017. https://tshaonline.org/handbook/online/articles/fti05.

Hall, Linda. *Álvaro Obregón: Power and Revolution in Mexico, 1911-1920.* College Station: Texas A&M University Press, 2000.

———. "Creating a Schizophrenic Border: Migration and Perception, 1920-1925." In *The Mexican Revolution: Conflict and Consolidation, 1910-1940,* edited by Douglas W. Richmond and Sam W. Haynes, 89-116. College Station: Texas A&M University Press, 2013.

Hanson, Joyce A. *Mary McLeod Bethune and Black Women's Political Activism.* Columbia: University of Missouri Press, 2003.

Hardin, Stephen L. "Hobby, TX." *Handbook of Texas Online.* Uploaded June 15, 2010. https://tshaonline.org/handbook/online/articles/hvh75.

Harris, Charles, III, and Louis R. Sadler. "The 1911 Reyes Conspiracy: The Texas Side." *Southwestern Historical Quarterly* 83, no. 4 (April 1980): 325-348.

———. *The Texas Rangers and the Mexican Revolution: The Bloodiest Decade, 1910-1920.* Albuquerque: University of New Mexico Press, 2004.

Harris, Jack, Paul Huhndorff, and Jack McGrew. *The Fault Does Not Lie with Your Set: The First Forty Years of Houston Television.* Austin: Eakin Press, 1989.

Hatfield, Thomas M. *Rudder: From Leader to Legend.* College Station: Texas A&M University Press, 2011.

Haynes, Emma R. *The History of Polk County.* N.p.: Haynes, 1937.

Haynes, Robert V. *A Night of Violence: The Houston Riot of 1917.* Baton Rouge: Louisiana State University Press, 1976.

Haynes, William. *The Stone That Burns: The Story of the American Sulphur Industry.* New York: Van Nostrand, 1942.

Hearn, Hilton Waldo. "W. Albert Lee: Pioneer of Houston Television." Master's thesis, University of Texas at Austin, 1971.

Henderson, Aileen Kilgore. *Stateside Soldier: Life in the Women's Army Corps: 1944-1945.* Columbia: University of South Carolina Press, 2001.

Hindman, Ewell James. "The United States and Álvaro Obregón: Diplomacy by Proxy." PhD diss., Texas Tech University, 1972.

Hine, Darlene Clark. *Black Victory: The Rise and Fall of the White Primary in Texas.* Columbia: University of Missouri Press, 2003.

Hinman, Ida. *Washington Sketch Book: A Society Souvenir.* Washington, DC: Hartman and Cadick, 1895.

Hitchcock, William I. "The President Who Made Billy Graham 'America's Pastor.'" *Washington Post,* February 28, 2018.

Hobby, Bill. "Journalism: Literature's Fourth Dimension." *Texas Quarterly,* Winter 1959.

———. "A Lesson from the Sports Page." *Reporter,* September 18, 1958.

Hobby, Bill, with Saralee Tiede. *How Things Really Work: Lessons from a Life in Politics.* Austin: Dolph Briscoe Center for American History, 2010.

Hobby, Edwin. *A Treatise on Texas Land Law*. St. Louis, MO: Gilbert Book Co., 1883.

Hobby, Oveta Culp. *Around the World in 13 Days*. Houston, TX: Houston Post, ca. 1947.

——. "Child Health Day, May 1, 1953." *Public Health Reports* 68, no. 1 (April 1953): 396.

——. "A Dedication to the Health of Future Generations." *Public Health Reports* 69, no. 7 (July 1954): 627–629.

——. "Federal-State Relations and Grants-in-Aid." *Public Health Reports* 69, no. 1 (January 1954): 88–91.

——. *Mr. Chairman: Rules, and Examples in Story Form, of Parliamentary Procedure Written Expressly for Use in Schools and Clubs*. Oklahoma City: Economy, 1936.

——. "My Current Reading." *Saturday Review*, April 24, 1948.

——. "Schools Remain a Local Responsibility." *Phi Delta Kappan* 35, no. 5 (February 1954): 204–206.

——. "The Tyranny of Freedom." *Phi Delta Kappan* 36, no. 6 (March 1955).

Hochschild, Adam. "When Dissent Became Treason." *New York Review of Books*, September 28, 2017.

Holcomb, Bob C. "Bailey, Joseph Weldon." *Handbook of Texas Online*. Uploaded June 12, 2010. https://tshaonline.org/handbook/online/articles/fba10.

Hughes, Emmet John. *The Ordeal of Power: A Political Memoir of the Eisenhower Years*. New York: Atheneum, 1963.

Hughes, Pollyanna B., and Elizabeth B. Harrison. "Charles A. Culberson: Not a Shadow of Hogg." *East Texas Historical Journal* 11, no. 2 (1973): 41–52.

Hunt, William R. "Mineral Wells, TX." *Handbook of Texas Online*. Uploaded June 15, 2010. https://tshaonline.org/handbook/online/articles/hem04.

Hurt, Harry, III. "The Last of the Great Ladies." *Texas Monthly*, October 1978.

Huson, Hobart. "Hobby, Alfred Marmaduke." *Handbook of Texas Online*. Uploaded June 15, 2010. https://tshaonline.org/handbook/online/articles/fho02.

Hutchison, Kay Bailey. *American Heroines: The Spirited Women Who Shaped Our Country*. New York: Harper, 2004.

——. *Unflinching Courage: Pioneering Women Who Shaped Texas*. New York: HarperCollins, 2013.

Hyman, Harold M. *Craftsmanship and Character: A History of the Vinson & Elkins Law Firm of Houston, 1917–1997*. Athens: University of Georgia Press, 1998.

Isaac, Paul E. "Beaumont, TX." *Handbook of Texas Online*. Last modified November 7, 2018. https://tshaonline.org/handbook/online/articles/hdb02.

Ivey, Darren L. *The Texas Rangers: A Registry and History*. Jefferson, NC: McFarland, 2010.

Jackson, Emma Louise Moyer. "Petticoat Politics: Political Activism among Texas Women in the 1920s." PhD diss., University of Texas, 1980.

Jacobs, Travis Beal. "Eisenhower, the American Assembly, and 1952." *Presidential Studies Quarterly* 22, no. 3 (Summer 1992): 455–468.

John F. Worley Directory Company. *Worley's Dallas City Directory*. Dallas: 1910, 1914.

Johnson, Frank White. *A History of Texas and Texans*. Vol. 4. Chicago: American Historical Society, 1914.

Johnston, J. N. "Some Old Poems in History." *Texas School Journal*, May 1904.

Johnston, Marguerite. *Houston: The Unknown City, 1836–1946*. College Station: Texas A&M University Press, 1991.

Jones Advertising Company. *Souvenir: Beaumont, Texas*. Dallas: Jones Advertising Company, 1903.

Jordan, Jonathan W. *American Warlords: How Roosevelt's High Command Led America to Victory in World War II*. New York: New American Library, 2016.

Kazin, Michael. *War against War: The American Fight for Peace, 1914–1918*. New York: Simon and Schuster, 2017.

Kean, Melissa. *Desegregating Private Higher Education in the South: Duke, Emory, Rice, Tulane, and Vanderbilt*. Baton Rouge: Louisiana State University Press, 2008.

Keith, Gary A. *Eckhardt: There Once Was a Congressman from Texas*. Austin: University of Texas Press, 2007.

Kennedy, David M. *Over Here: The First World War and American Society*. New York, Oxford University Press, 2004.

Kerr, K. Austin. "Prohibition." *Handbook of Texas Online*. Last modified May 6, 2019. https://tshaonline.org/handbook/online/articles/vap01.

Kilgore, Linda Elaine. "The Ku Klux Klan and the Press in Texas: 1920–1927." Master's thesis, University of Texas, 1964.

Kimbrough, Anne Giles. "Giles, Benjamin Franklin." *Handbook of Texas Online*. Uploaded June 15,

2010. https://tshaonline.org/handbook/online /articles/fgiff.

King, John O. *The Early History of the Houston Oil Company of Texas, 1901–1908*. Houston: University of Houston, 1959.

Kirkland, Kate Sayen. *The Hogg Family and Houston: Philanthropy and the Civic Ideal*. Austin: University of Texas Press, 2009.

Kleiner, Diana J. "Beaumont Enterprise." *Handbook of Texas Online*. Uploaded June 12, 2010. https://tshaonline.org/handbook/online/articles /eeb04.

———. "Orange, TX." *Handbook of Texas Online*. Last modified April 30, 2019. https://tshaonline .org/handbook/online/articles/heo01.

Kohout, Martin Donell. "Young, Samuel Doak, Sr." *Handbook of Texas Online*. Last modified April 12, 2019. https://tshaonline.org/handbook /online/articles/fyo21.

Krause, S. Joseph. *Harding, His Presidency and Love Life Reappraised*. Bloomington, IN: AuthorHouse, 2013.

Krauze, Enrique. *Mexico: Biography of Power*. Translated by Hank Heifetz. New York: HarperCollins, 1998.

Laas, Virginia Jeans, ed. *Bridging Two Eras: The Autobiography Emily Newell Blair, 1877–1951*. Columbia: University of Missouri Press, 1999.

La Forte, Robert S. "Hughes, Sarah Tilghman." *Handbook of Texas Online*. Last modified January 14, 2020. https://tshaonline.org/handbook /online/articles/fhu68.

Larson, Arthur. *Eisenhower: The President Nobody Knew*. New York: Scribner, 1968.

Lash, Joseph P. *Eleanor and Franklin*. New York: W. W. Norton, 1971.

Lasswell, Mary. *John Henry Kirby: Prince of the Pines*. Austin: Encino Press, 1967.

Leach, Joseph. *Sun Country Banker: The Life and the Bank of Samuel Doak Young*. El Paso, TX: Mangan Books, 1989.

Lelyveld, Joseph. *His Final Battle: The Last Months of Franklin Roosevelt*. New York: Knopf, 2016.

Lepore, Jill. *These Truths: A History of the United States*. New York: W. W. Norton, 2018.

Lewis, David Levering. *The Improbable Wendell Willkie: The Businessman Who Saved the Republican Party and His Country, and Conceived a New World Order*. New York: Liveright, 2018.

Lichtenstein, Nelson. *State of the Union: A Century of American Labor*. Princeton, NJ: Princeton University Press, 2013.

Limmer, E. A., ed. *Story of Bell County, Texas*. Vol. 2. Austin: Eakin Press, 1988.

Link, Arthur S. *Wilson: The New Freedom*. Princeton, NJ: Princeton University Press, 1956.

Looney, Wesley Hall. "The Texas Rangers in a Turbulent Era." Master's thesis, Texas Tech University, 1971.

Lundberg, John R. "The Great Texas 'Bear Fight': Progressivism and the Impeachment of James E. Ferguson." In *Impeached: The Removal of Texas Governor James E. Ferguson*, edited by Jessica Brannon-Wranosky and Bruce A. Glasrud. College Station: Texas A&M University Press, 2017.

Maroney, James C. "East Texas Labor Vignettes." *East Texas Historical Journal* 51, no. 2 (September 2013): 81–88.

———. "The Galveston Longshoremen's Strike of 1920." *East Texas Historical Journal* 16, no. 1 (Spring 1978): 34–38.

———. "The Texas-Louisiana Oil Field Strike of 1917." In *Essays in Southern Labor History: Selected Papers, Southern Labor History Conference, 1976*, edited by Gary M. Fink and Merl E. Reed, 161–172. Westport, CT: Greenwood Press, 1977.

Martin, Howard N. "Peach Tree Village." *Handbook of Texas Online*. Last modified May 1, 2019. https://tshaonline.org/handbook/online/articles /hvp24.

McArthur, Judith N. *Creating the New Woman: The Rise of Southern Women's Progressive Culture in Texas, 1893–1918*. Urbana: University of Illinois Press, 1998.

———. "Sterling, Florence M." *Handbook of Texas Online*. Last modified February 22, 2020. https://tshaonline.org/handbook/online/articles /fstbq.

McArthur, Judith N., and Harold L. Smith. *Minnie Fisher Cunningham: A Suffragist's Life in Politics*. New York: Oxford University Press, 2003.

McComb, David G. *Galveston: A History*. Austin: University of Texas Press, 1986.

———. *Houston: The Bayou City*. Austin: University of Texas Press, 1969.

McCullough, David. *Truman*. New York: Touchstone, 1992.

McDaniel, Dennis K. "The First Congressman Martin Dies of Texas." *Southwestern Historical Quarterly* 102, no. 2 (October 1998): 131–161.

McKay, Seth S. *Texas Politics, 1906–1944*. Lubbock: Texas Tech Press, 1952.

Mellinger, Gwyneth. "American Society of Newspaper Editors." In *Encyclopedia of American*

*Journalism*, edited by Stephen L. Vaughn, 21. New York: Routledge, 2008.

Meyer, Leisa D. *Creating GI Jane: Sexuality and Power in the Women's Army Corps during World War II*. New York: Columbia University Press, 1996.

Miles, Rufus, Jr. *The Department of Health, Education, and Welfare*. New York: Praeger, 1974.

Miller, Steven P. *Billy Graham and the Rise of the Republican South*. Philadelphia: University of Pennsylvania Press, 2009.

Minow, Newton. "Television and Public Interest." *Federal Communications Law Journal* 55, no. 3 (May 2003): 395–406.

Moore, Brenda L. *To Serve My Country, to Serve My Race: The Story of the Only African American WACs Stationed Overseas during World War II*. New York: New York University Press, 1996.

Morden, Bettie J. *The Women's Army Corps, 1945–1978*. Washington, DC: US Army Center of Military History, 1990.

Morgan, George T., Jr. "The Gospel of Wealth Goes South: John Henry Kirby and Labor's Struggle for Self-Determination, 1901–1916." *Southwestern Historical Quarterly* 75, no. 2 (October 1971): 186–197.

———. "Kirby, John Henry." *Handbook of Texas Online*. Last modified April 18, 2017. https://tshaonline.org/handbook/online/articles/fki33.

———. "No Compromise—No Recognition: John Henry Kirby, the Southern Lumber Operators' Association, and Unionism in the Piney Woods, 1906–1916." *Labor History* 10, no. 2 (Spring 1969): 193–204.

Morris, Sylvia Jukes. *Price of Fame: The Honorable Clare Boothe Luce*. New York: Random House, 2014.

Morrison & Fourmy Directory Company. *Austin City Directory*. 1927, 1929–1930.

———. *City of Beaumont Directory*. 1904, 1910–1911, 1923.

———. *General Directory of the City of Houston*. 1890–1891, 1894–1895, 1900–1901, 1903–1904, 1925, 1926, 1928, 1929–1930.

NAACP (National Association for the Advancement of Colored People). "Mobbing of John R. Shillady, Secretary of the National Association for the Advancement of Colored People, at Austin, Texas, Aug. 22, 1919." New York: NAACP, October 1919.

National Child Labor Committee. "Proceedings of the Twelfth Annual Conference on Child Labor." *Child Labor Bulletin* 5, no. 1 (February 1916).

Neighbors, Camille Y. "The Old Town of Saint Mary's." Master's thesis, Southwest Texas State Teachers College, 1942.

Neumann, Donald A. "Polio: Its Impact on the United States and the Emerging Profession of Physical Therapy." *Journal of Orthopaedic and Sports Physical Therapy* 34, no. 8 (August, 2004): 479–492.

Nicholas, William E. "World War I and Academic Dissent in Texas." *Arizona and the West* 14, no. 3 (Autumn 1972): 215–230.

Nichols, David A. *Ike and McCarthy: Dwight Eisenhower's Secret Campaign against Joseph McCarthy*. New York: Simon and Schuster, 2017.

Obermann, Carl Esco. *A History of Vocational Rehabilitation in America*. Minneapolis, MN: T. S. Denison, 1965.

Okrent, Daniel. *Last Call: The Rise and Fall of Prohibition*. New York: Scribner, 2010.

Oshinsky, David M. *A Conspiracy So Immense: The World of Joe McCarthy*. New York: Simon and Schuster, 1983.

———. *Polio: An American Story*. New York: Oxford University Press, 2005.

Osofsky, Gilbert. *The Burden of Race: A Documentary History of Negro-White Relations in America*. New York: Harper and Row, 1967.

"Oust Jane Spaulding from Top U.S. Job." *Jet*, January 28, 1954.

"Oveta Culp Hobby's New Job." *Businessweek*, May 16, 1953.

Paddock, B. B. *A History of Central and Western Texas*. Vol. 2. Chicago: Lewis Publishing, 1911.

Palmer, Jerrell Dean. "Clark, James Anthony." *Handbook of Texas Online*. Last modified October 24, 2016. https://tshaonline.org/handbook/online/articles/fcl52.

Pando, Robert T. "Oveta Culp Hobby: A Study of Power and Control." PhD diss., Florida State University, 2008.

Pando, Robert, and Patricia Pando. "Giving as a Hobby: A Family Legacy." *Houston History* 7, no. 2 (Spring 2010): 10–13.

Papademetriou, Peter. *Houston: An Architectural Guide*. Houston: Houston Chapter, American Institute of Architects, 1972.

Parmet, Herbert S. *Eisenhower and the American Crusades*. New York: Macmillan, 1972.

Patterson, Connie. "Porter, William Sydney." *Handbook of Texas Online*. Last modified May 6, 2019.

https://tshaonline.org/handbook/online/articles/fpo20.

Patterson, Norma. "Mrs. William Pettus Hobby." *Holland's Magazine,* June 1920.

Payne, John W. "Steamboat House: Sam Houston's Last Home." *East Texas Historical Journal* 28, no. 2 (October 1990): 3–15.

Payne, Phillip G. *Dead Last: The Public Memory of Warren G. Harding's Scandalous Legacy.* Athens: Ohio University Press, 2009.

Pemberton, William E. "Truman and the Hoover Commission." *Whistle Stop* 19, no. 3 (1991).

Perez, Joan Jenkins. "Florence, Fred Farrel." *Handbook of Texas Online.* Last modified May 24, 2016. https://tshaonline.org/handbook/online/articles/ffl14.

Pfau, Ann Elizabeth. *Miss Yourlovin: GIs, Gender, and Domesticity during World War II.* New York: Columbia University Press, 2008.

Pogue, Forrest C. *George C. Marshall: Organizer of Victory, 1943–1945.* New York: Viking Press, 1973.

Pratt, Joseph A., and Christopher J. Castaneda. *Builders: Herman and George R. Brown.* College Station: Texas A&M University Press, 1998.

Reese, Marsia Hart. "Landmark Restoration." *Austin Home and Gardens,* March 1986.

Reeves, Thomas C. *The Life and Times of Joe McCarthy: A Biography.* New York: Stein and Day, 1982.

Reich, Cary. *The Life of Nelson A. Rockefeller: Worlds to Conquer, 1908–1958.* New York: Doubleday, 1996.

Reid, Thomas. *Spartan Band: Burnett's 13th Texas Cavalry in the Civil War.* Denton: University of North Texas Press, 2005.

Rhoades, Lida. "The Texas Gubernatorial Election of 1912." Master's thesis, Texas Tech University, 1948.

Rienstra, Ellen Walker, and Judith Walker Linsley. *Historic Beaumont: An Illustrated History.* San Antonio: HPN Books, 2002.

Risedorf, Jordan. "Morse, Robert Emmett." *Handbook of Texas Online.* Uploaded February 14, 2017. https://tshaonline.org/handbook/online/articles/fmors.

Robertson, Lori. "The Life and Times of AJR." *American Journalism Review,* November 2002.

Rock, James L., and W. I. Smith. *Southern and Western Texas Guide for 1878.* St. Louis, MO: A. H. Granger, 1878.

Roosevelt, Eleanor. *Ladies of Courage.* New York: Putnam, 1954.

———. *This I Remember.* New York: Harper, 1949.

Rossinow, Doug. *Visions of Progress: The Left-Liberal Tradition in America.* Philadelphia: University of Pennsylvania Press, 2009.

Rucker, Walter C., and James N. Upton, eds. *Encyclopedia of American Race Riots.* Vol. 1. Westport, CT: Greenwood, 2007.

Russell, Francis. *The Shadow of Blooming Grove: Warren G. Harding in His Times.* New York: McGraw-Hill, 1968.

Salazar, Stephanie M. "Steiner, Thomas Casper [Buck]." *Handbook of Texas Online.* Last modified April 12, 2019. https://tshaonline.org/handbook/online/articles/fstdp.

Schindler, Steven. "America's System of Public Broadcasting and Public Radio." New York: Carnegie Corporation, 1965.

Schlesinger, Arthur M., Jr. *The Age of Roosevelt: The Crisis of the Old Order, 1919–1933.* Boston: Houghton Mifflin, 1957.

Schmelzer, Janet. "Campbell, Thomas Mitchell." *Handbook of Texas Online.* Last modified September 17, 2019. https://tshaonline.org/handbook/online/articles/fca37.

Schmidt, Regin. *Red Scare: FBI and the Origins of Anticommunism in the United States.* Copenhagen: Museum Tusculanum Press, 2000.

Scott, Bess Whitehead. *You Meet Such Interesting People.* College Station: Texas A&M University Press, 2008.

Scott, Janelle D. "Local Leadership in the Woman Suffrage Movement: Houston's Campaign for the Vote 1917–1918." *Houston Review* 12, no. 1 (1990): 3–23.

Shannon, Michael. "They Built Houston." *Houston Town and Country,* April 1976.

Shesol, Jeff. "Lyndon Johnson's Unsung Role in Sending Americans to the Moon." *New Yorker,* July 20, 2019.

Shire, Al, ed. *Oveta Culp Hobby.* Houston: William P. Hobby and Jessica Hobby Catto, 1997.

Sibley, Marilyn McAdams. *The Port of Houston: A History.* Austin: University of Texas Press, 1968.

Smith, Jessie Carney, ed. "Jane Spaulding." In *Notable Black American Women, Book II.* Detroit, MI: Gale, 1996.

Smith, Richard Norton. *On His Own Terms: A Life of Nelson Rockefeller.* New York: Random House, 2014.

Spaw, Patsy McDonald, ed. *The Texas Senate: Volume II, Civil War to the Eve of Reform, 1861–1889.* College Station: Texas A&M Press, 1999.

Starbird, Ethel A. *When Women First Wore Army Shoes: A First-Person Account of Service as a Member of the Women's Army Corps during WWII*. Bloomington, IN: iUniverse, 2010.

Steen, Ralph W. "Ferguson, James Edward." *Handbook of Texas Online*. Last modified October 2, 2019. https://tshaonline.org/handbook/online/articles/ffe05.

Sterling, Ross S., and Ed Kilman. *Ross Sterling, Texan: A Memoir by the Founder of Humble Oil and Refining Company*. Edited and revised by Don Carleton. Austin: University of Texas Press, 2007.

Stone, Geoffrey R. *Perilous Times: Free Speech in Wartime*. New York: W. W. Norton, 2004.

Storey, John W. "Port Arthur, TX." *Handbook of Texas Online*. Last modified May 6, 2019. https://tshaonline.org/handbook/online/articles/hdp05.

Straight, Michael. *Nancy Hanks: An Intimate Portrait*. Durham, NC: Duke University Press, 1988.

Stratton, Florence. *The Story of Beaumont*. Houston: Hercules Printing, 1925.

Swanson, Doug J. *Cult of Glory: The Bold and Brutal History of the Texas Rangers*. New York: Viking, 2020.

Sundquist, James L. *Politics and Policy: The Eisenhower, Kennedy, and Johnson Years*. Washington, DC: Brookings Institution Press, 1968.

Sutphen, Debra Lynn. "Conservative Warrior: Oveta Culp Hobby and the Administration of America's Health, Education, and Welfare, 1953–1955." PhD diss., Washington State University, 1997.

Terry, Margaret Kilman. "Kilman, Edward Wolf." *Handbook of Texas Online*. Last modified April 17, 2017. https://tshaonline.org/handbook/online/articles/fki46.

Texas Legislature. *Record of Proceedings of the High Court of Impeachment on the Trial of Hon. James E. Ferguson, Governor, August 1–September 29, 1917*. Austin: A. C. Baldwin, 1917.

*Texas House Journal*. Various dates. https://texashistory.unt.edu/explore/collections/TXHRJ/.

*Texas Senate Journal*. Various dates. https://texashistory.unt.edu/explore/collections/TXSJ/.

Theis, David. "2001 Gold Medal." *Rice Owlmanac*, summer 2001.

Timberlake, James H. *Prohibition and the Progressive Movement, 1900–1920*. New York: Macmillan, 1970.

Texas Bar Association. *Proceedings of the Thirteenth Annual Session of the Texas Bar Association [. . .] for the Year 1894–95*. Austin: Texas Bar Association, 1894.

Texas State Historical Association. "The Records of an Early Texas Baptist Church." *Quarterly of the Texas State Historical Association* 11, no. 2 (October 1907): 85–156.

Theoharis, Athan. *Seeds of Repression: Harry S. Truman and the Origins of McCarthyism*. New York: Times Books, 1971.

Timmons, Bascom N. *Jesse H. Jones: The Man and the Statesman*. New York: Henry Holt, 1956.

Torget, Andrew J. *Seeds of Empire: Cotton, Slavery, and the Transformation of the Texas Borderlands, 1800–1850*. Chapel Hill: University of North Carolina Press, 2015.

Treadwell, Mattie E. *United States Army in World War II: The Women's Army Corps*. Washington, DC: US Army Center of Military History, 1954.

Truett, Joe C. *Circling Back: Chronicle of a Texas River Valley*. Iowa City: University of Iowa Press, 1996.

Turner, Alan. "What Lurks in the Old Hobby Mansion?" *Houston Chronicle*, August 21, 2013.

Tuttle, William M., Jr. "Violence in a 'Heathen' Land: the Longview Race Riot of 1919." *Phylon* 33, no. 4 (1972): 324–333.

Utley, Robert M. *Lone Star Lawmen: The Second Century of the Texas Rangers*. New York Oxford University Press, 2007.

Van Dusen, Albert. *Middletown and the American Revolution*. Middletown, CT: Rockfall, 1950.

Wagner, Robert L. "Culberson, Charles Allen." *Handbook of Texas Online*. Last modified February 24, 2016. https://tshaonline.org/handbook/online/articles/fcu02.

Wakstein, Allen M. "The Origins of the Open-Shop Movement, 1919–1920." *Journal of American History* 51, no. 3 (December 1964): 460–475.

Walsh, Kelli Cardenas. "Oveta Culp Hobby: Ability, Perseverance, and Cultural Capital in a Twentieth-Century Success Story." In *Texas Women: Their Histories, Their Lives*, edited by Elizabeth Hayes Turner, Stephanie Cole, and Rebecca Sharpless, 318–337. Athens: University of Georgia Press, 2015.

———. "Oveta Culp Hobby: A Transformational Leader from the Texas Legislature to Washington, D.C." PhD diss., University of South Carolina, 2006.

Walter, Paul A. "Octaviano Ambrosio Larrazolo." *New Mexico Historical Review* 7, no. 2 (April 1932): 101.

Weatherford, Doris. *American Women and World War II*. New York: Castle Books, 2008.

Weigand, Cindy. *Texas Women in World War II*. Lanham, MD: Rowman and Littlefield, 2003.

West, Ruth. "Thru the Lorgnon." *Houston Gargoyle*, August 14, 1928.

Westray, Nicholas. "Westray Battle Long." In *Dictionary of North Carolina Biography*, vol. 4, edited by William Powell, 94–95. Chapel Hill: University of North Carolina Press, 1991.

Wharton, Clarence R. *Texas under Many Flags*. Vol. 5. Chicago: American Historical Society, 1930.

Williams, Amelia W. "Kinney, Henry Lawrence." *Handbook of Texas Online*. Uploaded June 15, 2010. https://tshaonline.org/handbook/online /articles/fki29.

Williams, T. Harry. *Huey Long*. New York: Knopf, 1970.

Williams, Vera S. *WACs: Women's Army Corps*. Osceola, WI: Motorbooks, 1997.

Winik, Jay. *1944: FDR and the Year that Changed History*. New York: Simon and Schuster, 2015.

White, Dabney. "Alabama Indians." *Frontier Times* 10, no. 7 (April 1933).

——, ed. *East Texas: Its History and Its Makers*. Vol. 2. New York: Lewis Publishing, 1940.

White, Theodore. "Texas: Land of Wealth and Fear." *Reporter*, May 25, 1954.

Wolz, Larry. "Kidd-Key College." *Handbook of Texas Online*. Last modified November 12, 2019. https://tshaonline.org/handbook/online /articles/kbk02.

Wooster, Robert. "Cooper, Samuel Bronson." *Handbook of Texas Online*. Last modified September 17, 2019. https://tshaonline.org/handbook /online/articles/fco61.

——. "Crawford, Walter Joshua." *Handbook of Texas Online*. Uploaded June 12, 2010. https:// tshaonline.org/handbook/online/articles/fcr12.

——. "Lucas, Anthony Francis." *Handbook of Texas Online*. Last modified July 27, 2016. https:// tshaonline.org/handbook/online/articles/flu04.

——. "Sabine-Neches Waterway and Sabine Pass Ship Channel." *Handbook of Texas Online*. Uploaded June 15, 2010. https://tshaonline.org /handbook/online/articles/rrs02.

US Congress. *Biographical Directory of the United States Congress*. bioguideretro.congress.gov.

Wooten, Heather Green. *The Polio Years in Texas: Battling a Terrifying Unknown*. College Station: Texas A&M University Press, 2009.

Young, Nancy Beck. *Why We Fight: Congress and the Politics of World War II*. Lawrence: University Press of Kansas, 2013.

# ILLUSTRATION CREDITS

---

# INDEX

reinsurance plan, 590–591; and Social Security, 532, 569–570; and "The Minute Women Series," 564. *See also* unions and unionism.

*American Forum of the Air*, 584, 587

American General Corporation, 452, 455, 744–745

Americanism Committee. *See* American Legion.

American Legion: accusing *Post* of Communist sympathies, 563; Americanism Committee, 555, 559, 563; fundraising for veterans' hospital, 184–185, 789; and Red Scare, 555

American Legion Memorial hospital, 184–185, 789

American Medical Association (AMA): criticism of Public Health Service, 542; Eisenhower on, 593; fear of socialized medicine, 520; and national health care program, 547; and polio vaccine, 610, 623, 625; and reinsurance plan, 586–588, 590–592, 601; and Social Security bill, 816

American Newspaper Publishers Association, 312, 324, 472–473

American Red Cross: Ferguson's challenge to Will, 132; fundraising for, 467; Oveta's speech to, 552; and Rogers, 331; and WAAC, 399; and Willie, 119

American Society of Newspaper Editors, 305, 457

Amis, Joseph, 788

Amis, Mary Hobby (sister): birth of, 11; death of, 667; in Dallas, 58; and father's illness, 775; and Kirby, 38; marriage of, 788; and Paul's death, 32

amphibious vehicle, 708

Anderson, Louise, 382

Anderson, Robert: and desegregation, 546; and Eisenhower, 492, 597, 656; and Oveta, 639, 705; as presidential candidate, 674; and Sam Rayburn Library, *661*

Andrews, Frank, 65; advising Will, 96; and Bailey, 166; and Bailey *vs.* Crane debate, 35; and Christie and Hobby, 201–202; drafting legislation for Will, 194, 783; and Great War veterans, 142; and prohibition, 111, 194, 783; and Will, 32; as Will's attorney, 790; and Will's campaign, 104, 107–108, 133; and Will's speech at W. C. Munn's, 151, 786; and Wortham, 139

Annexation Agreement of 1845, 488

anti-Communist hysteria. *See* Red Scare.

anti-German hysteria. *See* German Americans.

anti-prohibition movement: and acquittal, 31, 66; and Ferguson, 64–65; and gubernatorial race of 1918, 135; and Johnston, 30, 65, 86; Kirby and, 30, 216, 779; and Ousley, 30; and prohibition zoning, 111, 112; and Smith, 216; in South Texas and cities, 57, 127; and Will, 66–67, 70, 72, 84, 110, 115–116, 133, 135. *See also* prohibition.

Anti-Saloon League, 56

antisemitism, 198, 491, 497. *See also* racism.

antitrust laws, Texas, 34–35, 36, 72, 176

anti-unionism, 170–171, 172, 828. *See also* unions and unionism.

antiwar movement, 714–715, 718, 724, 726. *See also* Vietnam War.

Apalachee Bay, 4

Apollo 11, 728

Arabian-American Oil Company (Aramco), 458–459

Armed Forces Day, 583

Armed Forces Radio Network interview, 409

Army, U.S.: and attitudes toward women in military, 405; bureaucracy of, 372, 375, 474; and change, 373; and creation and expansion of WAAC, 338–339, 358; and failure to understand WAC, 809; hostility to WAACs and WACs, 392–393, 418, 421; and oil laborer's strike, 103; opposition to formation of WAAC, 331; Oveta as consultant, 324–331, *327*; rejection of Oveta's recommendations, 372; and Women's Army Auxiliary Corps (WAAC), 331–332; and women's uniforms, 338. *See also* Services of Supply; War Department; Women's Army Auxiliary Corps (WAAC); Women's Army Corps (WAC); Women's Interest Section.

Army Air Corps, US, 375–376

Army Corps of Engineers: and beans, 472; and dredging Neches River, 47, 51–52

Army Ground Forces, 422

army protocol, 329–330, 355, 364, 365–366

Army Service Forces. *See also* Services of Supply.

Arnold, Henry "Hap," 375–376, 407, 428

*Around the World in 13 Days*, 463, *463*, 809

Associated Press Managing Editors Association, 81–82, 85, 690

Astrodome, 706, 707, 731, 736

Athena, 348, 446, 732

Atkinson, Cordelia. *See* Hoover, Cordelia Atkinson.

Atlantic Union Committee, 467

atomic bomb, 460

*A Treatise on Texas Land Law*, 14

Augusta National Golf Club, 710

Austin, Anne, 98

Austin, Charles O., 240

Austin, TX: and Bill, 323, 660, 670, 742; Bill's DWI charge, 746–747; and Brackenridge Tract, 192; and constitutional convention, 12–13; gun battle in, 143; and KGC, 5; and Lady Bird's television station, 701, 711; LBJ Presidential Library, 717, 724; McKinley's visit, 28; and Oveta, 240, 248,

250, 267, 276; Oveta and father, 237, 238–239; and secession, 5, 12–13; and Shillady's beating, 159, 582; and Spanish flu, 141; and United Daughters of the Confederacy convention, 150; wedding night in, 265; and Will, 323; and Will and Willie, 80, 135; Will's visits to Oveta, 256, 261

*Austin American-Statesman*, 301, 549, 779. *See also Austin Statesman.*

*Austin Statesman:* and Johnston, 23; and Marsh and Fentress, 198; and Oveta, 240; and war garden, 118; and Willie, 119; Will's flight at Kelly Field, 103. *See also Austin American-Statesman.*

automobile committees, 131

Auxiliary Territorial Service (ATS), 369, 410

## B

baby boom, 542, 574

babysitting, 294

background investigations, 509, 515, 798

Bailey, George McLelland: and Bronson Cooper's funeral, 136; and editorial battle with *Chronicle*, 208; and Fergusons, 213, 214; and *Houston Post*, 30–31, 34, 204, 208; and Will's gubernatorial campaign, 119

Bailey, Joseph: antitrust lawsuit, 34–35; and Beaumont deepwater channel, 46, 49, 50, 51, 52; and Chapa's pardon, 180; and Cooper, 779; corruption and misconduct accusations, 35, 36, 107; and Crane, 34–37, 106–107; criticism of Will's administration, 162; death of, 168; and gubernatorial campaigns, 165–166, 168; and Kirby, 779; opposition to Will, 115, 118; as orator, 34, 35; politics of, 34; and prohibition, 115, 228, 779; and US Senate, 32, 34, 36, 55, 58, 776; Will's criticism of, 162, 164

Bailey, Kay, 695–696, 747, 823

Bailey *vs.* Crane debate, 34–37

Baker, James A. Sr., 35, 785

Baker, Newton, 92, 108, 111, 115

Ball, Tom: and Bailey *vs.* Crane debate, 35; gubernatorial campaign, 65, 71; Houston navigation district, 49; and Oveta, 259; and prohibition, 65, 83; and Will, 69

Bandel, Betty: on British food, 371; and chocolate bars, 368–370; dinner with ER, 377; and field hospital, 413; on Hobby children and home, 373; letter to Oveta, 389; new hairdo, 384–385; and North Africa, 412–413; and outdoor showers, 415; overseas tour, 362–371, 407, 409–416, *411*; and overseas tour, 363; and Oveta, 380, 385, 412; on Oveta, 359, 361, 370, 380; with Oveta,

*360*; and Oveta's resignation from WAC, 433, 434; Thanksgiving, 376; and WAC, 357–358, 379–380, 399, 435, 473; and *The Women's Army Corps*, 473

bandits, Mexican, 123, 124, 180, 182, 189

banking industry: and "8F crowd," 453; and Elkins, 313; First City National Bank, 312; and Hobbys, 645; Hobbys' investment in, 197, 240, 311, 645; Houston National Bank, 269, 270–272, 273; and Jones, 270–273, 294; Oveta as bank auditor, 240–241, 242, 793; Reconstruction Finance Corporation (RFC), 283–284, 287, 307, 314, 428, 429, 589; and Sam Young, 262; Sterling as "jazz banker," 273

Baptist church: and Culp family, 229, 230–231, 233; Ike Culp as minister, 229; and Oveta and Will's wedding, 264–265; and Oveta's faith, 232, 264–265, 760; Texas Evetts Culp as minister, 232, 756–757

Barnes, Marguerite Johnston. *See* Johnston, Marguerite.

Barron, Wingate, 253

Baruch, Bernard: and Democratic National Convention, 217; and Texas Gulf Sulphur, 202–203; as War Industries Board chairman, 140; and Will, 140, 197, 202–203

Battle, William J., 78, 86–87

Battle of the Flowers Fiesta, 151

Baxter, Norman, 429

Baylor Academy, 238, 239

Baylor College. *See* Mary Hardin-Baylor College.

Baylor University, 342, 388–389

Baytown-La Porte Tunnel, 466

Beaumont, TX: in 1907, 39–40; in 1920, 196; Chamber of Commerce, 41, 49, 51, 52, 54; city charter referendum, 44–45; city hall building, 197; city projects, 54; competition of, 42; and deepwater channel, 12, 41–42, 46, 49–50, 52, 53; economy of, 37, 39, 45; and KKK, 198; and Neches River dredging, 41–42; and Panic of 1907, 45; port of, 46, 53, 82, 777; prominent citizens, 41; and Southwestern Open Shop Association, 170; and 1928 State Democratic Party convention, 216

Beaumont Chamber of Commerce: and city development, 41; and deepwater port, 49, 51, 52; and Southeast Texas Fair, 54

*Beaumont Enterprise:* advertising, 40–41, 43–44; and *Beaumont Journal*, 37, 196, 198, 790; and Bill, 742; bond petition drive, 50; and Bronson Cooper, 50; building of, *43*; circulation of, 43–44, 55; city boosting, 40, 43, 54–55; and

christening ceremony, 379

Christie, George, 201–202, 268–269

Christie, Joe, 739

Christie and Hobby, 201–202, 268–269

Christmas Day pardons, 193

Christmas holidays: with Dora, 142, 192; and Emma Culp's charitable work, 235; gift for Eisenhower, 682–683; with *Houston Post* staff, 220; of 1929, 255; Oveta's return home for, 379, 571, 600; presents for Hobby children, 409; Will's visits to *Houston Post* plant, 644

Chupadera Ranch, 255, 271

Church of Christ, 677

*Cigareets, Whuskey, and Wild, Wild, Women*, 482

cigarettes: Chesterfield, 252; Ike's sharing of, 367; Parliament, 513, 543, 734; Rockefeller lighting, 538. *See also* smoking.

Citizens for Eisenhower, 495, 499, 533, 655, 656

Citizens for Nixon, 726

City National Bank, 313, 452, 484

Civil Rights Act of 1964, 702, 703, 725

civil rights movement: Civil Rights Act of 1964, 702, 703, 725; and Dixiecrats, 489; and Eisenhower, 679; media and public awareness, 673; and Rabb, 546; and racial integration, 583. *See also* desegregation; racism.

Civil Service Commission, 529

Civil War, 6–8, 10, 23, 229, 772, 773

Claridge's Hotel, 365, 366, 412

Clark, Edward (TX governor), 6

Clark, Mark, *414*, 417

Clark, James A., 665–669, 799

Clarkson, A. E. "Eddie," 21–22, 25, 284, 775

classroom shortage, 542, 572, 579, 593–594, 602–606

Clay, Lucius: and Citizens for Eisenhower, 655, 656; and Crusade for Freedom, 491; and Eisenhower's cabinet, 505; and Oveta's appointment, 506–507; and Special Studies Project, 647, 648, 650

Clayton, Will, 217, 429, 470

closed-shop contracts, 169–170, 172, 176. *See also* unions and unionism.

Cohen, Henry, 154

Cohen, Wilbur, 517, 527, 528, 529–530

Coke, Richard, 11, 12, 13, 774

Cold War: and Crusade for Freedom, 491–492; and foreign policy, 486, 491; and HEW budget, 540; and Special Studies Project, 647; and UN Conference on Freedom of Information, 468. *See also* Communism.

colonel's pin, 342

color dynamics, 731

Colquitt, Oscar B.: as anti-prohibition, 57, 65, 66; and Chapa, 180; *vs.* Culberson, 84; and deepwater channel, 52; and Germany, 84; as governor, 52, 55–58, 63, 75; influence on Will, 63, 102; and Johnston, 58; and Moody's inauguration, 215; and Peach Tree Village church, 773; racism of, 57; and Sturgeon, 65; and Will, 55–56, 63, 84

Colquitt, Rawlins: in Galveston, 81; and Willie and Will's wedding, 79; and Will's campaign, 66–67, 68, 71; and Will's handling of prohibition, 116

Columbia University, 68, 469, 485, 492, 499

Command and General Staff School, 372, 381

Commercial National Bank, 18

Commission of Appeals, 17, 99

Commission on the Organization of the Executive Branch, 469–473

Committee of 75, 659, 825

Committee of Public Safety, 6

Communism: and China, 460, 513, 515; and Czechoslovakia, 468; and domino theory, 716; fear of, 141–142, 556; and freedom of information, 468–469; Hungarian revolt, 658; and labor unions, 487; and Oveta's concerns with, 456; and race riots, 158; and Spaulding, 580; and Special Studies Project, 648; and Vietnam War, 714, 715. *See also* Red Scare.

Communist Party, 487, 502, 503, 563. *See also* Red Scare.

Confederate Army, 7, 23, 122, 229, 772

Confederate Navy, 7

Confederate Veterans Association, 182

Conference on Freedom of Information, 464, 467–468, 718

confirmation hearings, 510–511, 522

Congress, U.S.: and appropriations increase for, 550; and classroom shortage, 593, 602–606; congressional testimony, 334–335, 384, 385, 392, 399, 521–522, 527, 538, 573, 584–586, 601, 603–604, 632; and educational television, 711; and Eisenhower administration, 597; and HEW, 505, 520–522, 527, 573, 584–586; and Hobby-Brownell bill, 603–604; and Hoover Commission, 471–472, 473; and McCarthy, 567; and Neutrality Act, 321; and Nineteenth Amendment, 786; Oveta's confirmation hearings, 510–511, 522; and polio vaccine, 624, 632; and public television, 718; and reinsurance plan, 584–586, 601; and Reorganization Plan No. 1, 519–520; and Rockefeller, 538, 585–586; and Rogers Bill, 331–336, 384; and WAAC, 374, 384, 385, 392; and WAC, 384, 399, 407, 435; and Will, 216

Drug Administration, 542; and Gardner, 713, 716; job reclassification, 529; and labor unions, 542; learning curve, 518; legislative agenda, 548, 572–577, 584–586, 606; and medical research, 542; and Minute Women, 560–561; and nomination as secretary, 506; and Office of Education, 516, 550; organic unity in, 541–542; organization of, 533, 541–542; Oveta's reflection on, 641–642; Oveta's resignation from, 597, 633–639, *638*, 818; Oveta's swearing in, 523–526, *524–525*; and pharmaceutical companies, 542; and polio vaccine, 610, 612–618, 620–624; and political appointees, 527, 528–529; politics of legislation, 585; and Public Health Service, 542; and Rayburn, 591; and Red Scare, 561, 566; and reinsurance plan, 575–576; and research grants, 561; and Rockefeller, 519, 586; and Social Security bill, 816; and Spaulding, 533, 581, 582; and special interests, 542; symbolic duties of secretary, 588. *See also* Federal Security Agency (FSA); polio vaccine; reinsurance plan; Social Security.

depression, Will's, 216

depressions, economic: Panic of 1873, 774; Panic of 1893, 20, 28; Panic of 1907, 45. *See also* Great Depression.

desegregation: *Brown v. Board of Education*, 544–545, 584, 604, 605; and Dallas schools, 683; and Hobby-Brownell bill, 604–605; of Houston lunch counters, 671–673; and Little Rock, 662–664; and military bases, 544–546, 582. *See also* segregation.

Deutser, Bernard, 41, 79, 196

Dewey, Thomas, 464, 469, 470, 488–489, 492, 510

Dhahran, Saudi Arabia, 458–459

Díaz, Porfirio, 179, 180

Díaz Ordaz, Gustavo, 706

Dies, Martin Sr., 46–47, 49, 51, 52–53

discrimination: and African Americans, 425–426, 579–580, 581; and German Americans, 126–127; Jefferson Davis Hospital, 579–580, 581; and military training camps, 350; and Oveta's speech on, 583–584; and *Post's* use of derogatory language, 306; and Powell, 579–580; and Spaulding, 580–581; and WAAC, 339, 352–353; and WAC, 425–426. *See also* desegregation; segregation.

Distinguished Americans stamp series, 762, *765*, 828

Distinguished Service Medal, 426–428

Dixiecrats, 445, 489

doctors, 542, 547, 579–580, 581, 588. *See also* American Medical Association (AMA).

Doctors for Freedom, 520, 556, 559, 560–561, 610

Doctors Hospital, 434

dollar bill and Short Snorter Club, 363, 367

domestic servants and Social Security tax, 540

domino theory, 716

Donahue, Jack, 660, 662, 670–671

Douglas, Lewis, 458

Douglas, Paul, 603–604

draft, military. *See* selective service.

Driskill Hotel, 94, 147

drought, 98, 102

drug laws, enforcement of, 741–742

dry-goods stores, 3

dual primary bill, 116

Dudley, Ray: and *Houston Dispatch*, 203; and *Houston Post-Dispatch*, 204; and KPRC, 211; Lewis on, 27; and Will, 206

Duff, R. C., 41, 66, 79

Duncan, Elspeth, 367–368

Dundas, Robert, 672–673

Dupuy, Ernest, 324–325, 326, 329–330, 331, 333

Duval County, 127–128, 490, 784

D.W.C 28 campaign, 50–51

DWI charge, 746–747

E

eagle, colonel's, 343

East Coast Migrant Project, 588

Economy Publishing Company, 296, 301–302

editorials, importance of, 70

education: and Bill, 740, 764; *Brown v. Board of Education*, 544–545, 584, 604, 605; classroom shortage, 572, 574, 579, 593–594, 602–606; desegregation of schools, 544–546, 662–665, 683; federal aid for, 550, 574, 594, 602–606, 725; and FSA, 516; and Hobby-Brownell bill, 602–606; and LBJ, 725; and Little Rock schools, 662–665; and migrant farmworkers' children, 586, 588; National Education Association, 564, 574, 594, 602, 603, 604; Nixon on school construction, 602–603; and school bond scheme, 602; state funding for public schools, 77, 87, 167; as state responsibility, 588, 594; states' rights movement, 604, 605; and television, 709, 711–712; Texas Higher Education Coordinating Board, 764; White House Conference on Education, 574, 593, 639–641. *See also* public schools.

educational television, 709, 711–712

Educational Television Facilities Act, 711

efficiency: in government, 472; and Hoover Commission, 469–470; and lack in FSA, 516; and Oveta, 443, 446–447

Eichelberger, Robert, 461

"8F crowd": and Eisenhower, 679; influence and connections of, 450–456; and Jones, 568; and labor unions, 487; and Will, 763

Eighteenth Amendment: ratification of, 112, 115, 138; repeal of, 285–288; and Smith, 219; and US Congress, 102, 104. *See also* prohibition.

Eighteenth Texas Legislature, 14–15

Eighth Army Air Force bases, 410, *411*

Eisenhower, Dwight "Ike": advising LBJ on Vietnam, 714; and AMA, 520; and *Brown v. Board of Education* decision, 584; and budget battles, 551–552; bust of, 732; cabinet meetings, 513, 515–516, 639; cabinet of, 300, 505–507; as candidate for heart transplant, 825; and cigarettes, 367; and Columbia University, 485; and Crusade for Freedom, 491; death of, 723; and decision to run again, 655; and desegregation of schools, 544, 664–665; and domino theory, 716; and education policy, 550, 574, 602, 605–606, 639–641; endorsement of *Houston Chronicle*, 683; farewell speech, 675; as faux Republican, 497; on federal aid for education, 594; as fiscal conservative, 574; flag gifted to Oveta, 819; and freedom of the press, 555; gift for Oveta, 639; golf balls, 682–683; and Goode, 682; heart attacks, 641, 655, 710, 716, 723; and HEW, 519, 539, 550, 572; honoring Salk and O'Connor, *617*, 617–618; and Hungarian revolt, 658; inauguration of, 510–512, 659; lack of partisanship, 506; and McCarthy, 562; meeting Oveta, 365, 367, 410; memoir, 683–684; and military draft, 716–717; and NATO, 492; and newspapers as political weapons, 557; and Nixon, 655–656, 674–675; and non-fraternization rule, 398–399; official dress hat, 511; opposing socialized medicine, 579; and Oveta, 410, 486, 492–493, 504, 513, 515, 536, 570–571, 579, *598–599*, 600, 634–635, 641, 654, 658–659, 679, 680, 682–684, 717, 723, 811; and Oveta for president, 674; Oveta's admiration of, 697, 759; Oveta's loyalty to, 728; on Oveta's performance, 515–516; and Oveta's resignation, 600, 633–635; Oveta's support for, 811; and Oveta's swearing in, 523, *524–525*; with Perkins and Oveta, *535*; physical condition of, 657–658; at picnic, 639, *640*; and polio vaccine, 614–616, 619, 620, 623–625, 628, 631–632; political affiliation of, 485, 495; popularity of, 495, 597; presidential campaigns of, 464, 485, 492, 503–504, 656–657; and presidential election of 1960, 674–675, 678, 680; racism of, 545; and reinsurance plan, 576, 579, 587, 592–593,

601; and Reorganization Plan No. 1, 519–520; resignation from UN, 495; at Rice University, 678–679; rumors of affair with Oveta, 798; and second Hoover Commission, 473; and second term, 606; and segregation, 605; seventy-fifth birthday party, 710; and Social Security, 539, 550, 570, 572, 577, 579, 586; and Suez Canal crisis, 658; supporting Oveta, 623, 628; television broadcasts, 548; and tidelands mineral rights, 492; tour of Texas, 485; and U-2 spy plane crisis, 673–674; visit to India, 670; and WAACs, 356, 366, 367, 377, 380–381, 804; and WACs, 398–399, 410–411, 435; and White House Conference on Education, 639–641; White House farewell dinner, 680; and Will's death, 688; and World War II memorial, 438

Eisenhower, Mamie: and 1952 presidential campaign, 503; admiration of, 645; appearance with Oveta, 570; and death of husband, 723; and Eisenhower's health, 641; and Eisenhower's presidential campaign, 503; and farewell picnic for Oveta, 639; and Ike's heart attack, 710; meeting husband, 485; and Oveta, 570, 641, 723, 825; at picnic, *640*; and top ten most admired women, 645

Eisenhower administration. *See* Department of Health, Education, and Welfare (HEW); education; polio vaccine; reinsurance; Social Security.

Eisenhower Agricultural Program, 825

Eisenhower Presidential Library, 682, 684

election fraud, 127–128, 490, 784

election returns: of gubernatorial race, 134; monitoring 1952 election, 504; of 1914 lieutenant governor campaign, 71–72; Parr *vs.* Glasscock, 128; tabulation bureau, 82; and Texas Associated Press, 82

elections. *See* political campaigns; individual candidates.

elections, primary, 108–109, 114–115

Eli Lilly, 609, 613, 624, 630

Elizabeth II, Queen, 361, 365, 366, 645

Elkins, James Anderson "Jim": and anti-unionism, 171; and Christie and Hobby, 202; as district attorney, 105–106; and 8F crowd, 452, 454–455; and Eisenhower, 679; as Hobbys' banker, 313, 454–455, 478; and Houston mayoral race, 455; and Huntsville, 294; image of, *478*; and Wilkie campaign, 318–319; and Will, 105–106, 108, 313, 785

Ellington Field, 390, 440, 681

El Paso National Bank, 269–270

Emerson, Faye, 390

epidemic, Spanish flu, 140–141

Espionage Act, 116–117

Evans, Silliman, 241

Evetts, J. H., 229, 230

extremism, black, 702

*Eyes of Texas* travelogue, 695

F

*Face the Nation,* 621

Faith, Don Carlos, 355, 373, 803

Fall, Albert, 186, 187–188

Farley, James, 314, 317

farmers: and agricultural cooperatives, 127; and Federal Farm Loan Act, 88–89; Future Farmers of America, 570; loan programs for, 145; and price fixing, 138; and Social Security, 642, 816; and Special Studies Project, 650–651; tenant, 64, 69, 72, 101. *See also* cotton farming.

Farmers and Laborers Protective Association, 127

farm problem, 650–651

Farrar, Roy M., 255, 271, 273

Faubus, Orval, 662–663

Federal Bureau of Investigation (FBI), 158, 391, 509, 515, 736, 798

Federal Communications Commission (FCC): and broadcast mergers, 748; and KPRC Radio, 302, 323; and local ownership of television stations, 745; and Minow, 711; and purchase of KLEE-TV, 477, 482; and purchase of WLAC-TV, 745, 746; and shared call letters, 745; and television station licenses, 474, 475–476, 477, 745

Federal Farm Loan Act, 88–89

Federal Farm Loan Bank, 88–89, 92

Federal Land Bank, 88–91, 92, 93

Federal Loan Administration, 314

Federal Loyalty Review Board, 561

federal price fixing, 138–139

Federal Security Agency (FSA): budget of, 516–517, 518; confirmation hearing, 510–511; and congressmen, 518; crash course on, 507, 511; evaluation of programs, 512–513; and general staff meeting, 516; hostility from administrators, 516, 517–518; inefficiency in, 516; and LBJ, 697–698; learning curve, 517; meeting with Rogers, 516; Oveta as head, 506–509, 517–518, 697–698; Oveta's work schedule, 518; programs of, 506; and Social Security Administration, 516; and Taft supporters, 512. *See also* Department of Health, Education, and Welfare (HEW).

Federal Security Building, 526

"feminine wiles," 420

femininity: and competence, 436; and Oveta, 337,

373, 527, 601, 623, 749; and WAAC uniform, 385; and WACs, 400–401, 422, 436

feminism, 695–696, 709

Fentress, E. S., 198

Ferguson, James E. "Pa": and Battle, 86–87; and Chapa, 180; corruption accusations, 83, 213; and Culberson, 84; Cunningham on, 785; and demagoguery, 65, 88, 120–121, 260; and Federal Land Bank, 89; feud with University of Texas, 86–87, 89, 781; and Fuller, 92, 93; as governor, 74, 78, 92, 99; gubernatorial campaigns, 64, 71, 72, 101, 103–104, 119, 134, 783; and *Houston Post-Dispatch,* 260; impeachment of, 90–91, 92–94, 740; inauguration of, 75, 86; indictments of, 87, 91, 92, 103–104; loan, mystery, 93–94, 96, 107–108, 120, 132, 135; and Mayfield, 200; at Moody's inauguration, 215; *vs.* Morris, 83; at O'Daniel inauguration, *309;* oratory style of, 64; and *patrones,* 127; politics of, 64, 69, 72, 87, 101; popular dislike of, 85; and populist reforms, 64; and public schools, 87; at reception honoring Hobbys, 80; resignation of, 96; reward for arrest of Will and Carter, 213; and Selective Service Act, 99; special legislative sessions, 78, 92; and Sterling, 214, 260; and tenant farmers, 64, 72, 101; and Travis County, 87, 91, 92; US senate campaign, 199–200; and West Texas A&M College, 89–90; and wife's administration, 213; and Will, 68, 119, 122, 187, 197, 200, 214, 268, 304; and women's vote, 132, 135

Ferguson, Miriam "Ma": as governor, *209,* 213, 247, 248, 791; on Governor's Mansion, 104; gubernatorial campaigns, 208–209, 213–215, 259, 260, 277, 278; at Moody's inauguration, 215; and prohibition, 287; reception for Hobbys, 80; reward for arrest of Will and Carter, 213; selling pardons, 791; special legislative session, 247, 248; and Sterling, 277

*Ferguson Forum,* 103–104

ferryboat, 686

Fifteenth Texas Legislature, 13

First City National Bank, 313, 452, 484

First National Bank of Killeen, 229

Fitzgerald, Hugh Nugent, 34, 146, *195*

flags and flag ceremonies: Alamo presentation, 294–295; forgetting to salute, 355; gift from Ike, 819; Oveta's funeral, 760; in Oveta's offices, 526, 732, 819; and Pan Am, 458; WAC company flags, 400, 403–404; and Will's death, 688; and Will's funeral, 688–689

Flemming, Arthur, 519, 520, 679

flood control, 292, 308, 440

and Eisenhower's inauguration, 510, 511–512; as environmentalist, 764, 827; and family business, 745, 746, 749–752, 758; and father, 321–322, 356, 669; and father's death and funeral, 688–689; and horses, 465, 513; and *Houston Post,* 749–750, 751, 752; inauguration gown, 512; marriage of, 669; and mother, 304, 432, 512, 513, *531;* on mother, 420, 543, 696, 699; on mother's charmed life, 764; naming of, 302–303; and Nixon, 658, 726; and Oveta's funeral, 760; on parents' dislike of exercise, 543; and Republican party, 682; rumors about parentage, 302–303, 798; vacations, 499, 552; in Washington, DC, 353, 402, 403, 407, 530; and *Washington Journalism Review,* 749–750, 827; and WLAC-TV, 745, 746

Hobby, Oveta Culp: birth of, 228; death of, 760; and 1933 Mother's Day edition of *Post,* 288; in 1940s, *471;* administrative skills of, 517; admiration of Eisenhower, 697; Aegean sailing trip, 701; affair rumors, 304, 798; after Will's death, 748–749; and Allred, 241; American Society of Newspaper Editors, 457; 100 American Women of Accomplishment, 721; ancestry of, 228; and "8F crowd", 450–456, *451,* 453; on antiwar movement, 714–715; appearance of, 337–338, 400–401, 532, 542–543, 732, 754, 755, 759; and army, 324–331, *327,* 328–330, 365–366, 375, 474; *Around the World in 13 Days,* 463, *463;* art and art collection, 450, 461, 530, 748, 755; as arts patron, 450; assistant to city attorney, 253; and authoritarianism, 320, 321; bag, 447; and Bailey, 695–696; balancing roles, 245, 288; and Bandel, 357–358, *360,* 380, 389; bedridden, 277–278, 759; and Bethune, 352–353, 802; and Bill, 274–275, 276, 278, 294, 418, 595, 738, 739–743, *741,* 746–748; and Bill's DWI charge, 746–747; birthdays, 275, 412, 511, 579, 792; board memberships and volunteer service, 305, 457, 467, 492, 645, 653, 659, 706, 719, 737, 825; and Browns, 749, *750;* and Buchanan, 808; on budget priorities, 710; and Bureau of Public Relations, 325, 333–334, 339–341, 423, 432, 800–801; and Bush, 823; business reputation of, 312; camel ride, 415, *416;* campaign for legislature, 251, 253, 257–259, *258,* 657, 793, 794; career in banking, 240–241, 242, 793; and Catto, 669, 821; celebrity of, 287, 439, 456, 466–467, 656, 721; and censorship, 293, 563, 692; and Central Texas College, 720, *721;* at ceremony honoring women in military, *720;* character of, 230, 232–233, 234, 235–236, 278,

359, 380, 436, 582, 693, 733–735; charm of, 525; childhood, *231,* 232–235; and chocolate bars, 369–370; and CIA, 491–492; and cigarettes and smoking, 252, 367, 513, 538, 543, 734; and colonel's insignia, 350; and Committee of 75, 659; and Communism, 456; community projects, 291–292; congressional testimony (*see* Congress, U.S.); and Congressional Wives Club, 417; continuing recognition of, 762; and Cowles, 703; and Cox, 683; and criticism, 312; criticism of, 517–518, 621, 623–624, 632, 675–676; and Crusade for Freedom, 491–492; and dating, 235–236, 241–242, 254–265, 748; and debt, 479; dedication of *William B. Ogden,* 383–384; Distinguished Service Medal, 426–428, *427;* and Dixiecrats, 489; and draft for women, 405, 407; and driving, 311; on duty of media, 652, 690; ease in all-male cliques, 806; editing of speeches, 570; education of, 238, 239, 240, 245–246, 288, 290, 342, 793; and efficiency, 443, 446–447; and Eisenhower, 356–357, 364, 365, 367, 371, 410, 485–509, *535,* 536, 570–571, 579, *598–599,* 600, 634–635, *640,* 641, 654, 658–659, 678–679, 680, 682–684, 710, 717, 723, 811; and Eisenhower administration (*see* classroom shortage; Department of Health, Education, and Welfare (HEW); polio vaccine; reinsurance plan; Social Security); and Eisenhower Presidential Library, 684; on Eisenhower's calm, 367; and Eisenhower's campaigns, 485–509, 654, 655–658, 811; and Eisenhower's inauguration, 510, 511–512; and Eisenhower's memoir, 683–684; and Elizabeth Arden salon, 542; emotional toll of service, 417, 432; end of life, 754–756, 759–761; engagement of, 261–262; enjoyment of roles in Washington, 516, 699; and ER, 283, 371, *383,* 430, 801; on ethics of war, 460; and face to face meetings, 734; on failure of local government, 710; and fair reporting, 446; and fashion, 450, 749; and father, 230, 234, 237–240, 242, 290; as father's favorite, 230; favorite quotes and phrases, 452–453, 472; FBI file, 509, 798; and FDR, 315, 386–387, *388,* 429, 430, 806; feelings for Will, 794–795; and feminine wiles, 420; and femininity, 337, 373, 527, 601, 623, 749; and feminism, 695–696, 709; and ferryboat, 686; and Fields, 337; on fighting for WAACs, 373; on firing of MacArthur, 492; and Florence Sterling, 243–245, 793; on following Will at podium, 494; and food, 369–370, 371, 409, 458; on foreign requests for U.S. funds, 462; friendships with men, 748; and FSA, 506–507, 515–519;

fundraising, 467, 596; and gender equality, 709; and George Brown, 452; and Glenn McCarthy, 562; on Glenn McCarthy's mistress, 748; good cheer of, 370; and government personnel documents, 793; and Graham, 826; grandchildren, 670, 681, 754, 765–766; and grandmother, 232–234; and Great Depression, 266–267; guest information sheets, 449; and Harris, 447, *694, 757*; and hats, 235, 312, 508; and H&C executive committee, 754; health of, 373, 401–402, 418, 423–424, 432, 434–435, 456, 504, 570–571, 588, 747, 751, 754; and Heather's wedding, 754; on her army experience, 437; on her career, 812; and HEW (*see* classroom shortage; Department of Health, Education, and Welfare (HEW); polio vaccine; reinsurance plan; Social Security); on HEW accomplishments, 641–642; and Hobby enterprises, 690; and "Hobby hat," 349, 351, 355; and "Hobby's Army" nickname, 806; homes of (*see* Connecticut Avenue apartment; Glen Haven Home; Shadyside Mansion); honeymoon of, 265; honorary degrees, 390, 402, 466, 645–646, *646,* 754; on honorary *vs.* earned degrees, 246; and Hoover Commission, 469–473; horseback riding, 276–277, 543; as hostess, 448–450, *449,* 732–733; and *Houston Post,* 284, 288, 291, 305–306, 310–312, 408, 426, 441, 443, 445, 493, 543, 556–557, 643, 671–673, 691–692, 730–732, 735–736, 752–753; *Houston Post* and language used, 306, 311; and *Houston Post-Dispatch,* 250, 267; *Houston Post* editorial board, 734–735, 752; and Hughes, 256; importance of appearance, 252; influence of, 685, 690, 737, 761; injured hand, 282; international worldview of, 457, 463–464, 468; on intolerance, 291; and Japanese newsreel, 461; and Jessica, 304, 407–408, 512, 513, *531*; and JFK, 675, 681–682, 685; and Johnsons, 240, 712; Jolly Entertainers, 234–235; and Jones, 303, 430, 479, 568–570, 588, 646–647, 795; and Joseph McCarthy, 453; as journalist, 457, 462; and Juanita, 233, 234, *646*; and Kaiser health plan, 547, 814; and Kilman, 502, 562; and KPRC, 312–313, 408, *482,* 727–728, 738; and Ku Klux Klan, 258–259; and labor unions, 487; and Lady Bird Johnson, 700, 719; land inherited, 455; last letters of, 760; and LBJ, 318, 490, *698,* 698–710, 722; LBJ as peer, 698; and LBJ birthplace restoration, 708; and LBJ Presidential Library, 724; on LBJ's preparation to lead after JFK's death, 685; and LBJ's visits to Will, 684; and League of Women Voters, 244, 245,

246, 256, 267, 268; legacy of, 762–763; as legislative committee clerk, 237–238, 240, 793; lifestyle of, 288, 445–446; "Little Colonel" nickname, 357; and Long, 279, 280–281; on looking forward instead of back, 744; "looking the part," 337, 341–342; with Luce, *687*; and MacArthur, 461, 462, *493*; and Madame Chiang, 460, 532; and Mamie Eisenhower, 723, 825; management style of, 443, 445, 517, 644, 692; and Marguerite Johnston, 442, 468, 759; on marriage, 795; and Marshall, 332, 334, 338, 341, 419; Mary Hardin-Baylor College honorary doctorate, 645–646, *646*; meeting king and queen, 365; on meeting Will, 227, 245; in mid-1930s, *289*; and military draft, 716–717; as a modern woman, 246; monitoring *Post* from Washington, 441; and mother, 228, 234, 236, 264, *646*; motherhood, 245, 268, 274–275, 276–277, 278, 288, 296, 322, 362, 395, 408, 417; and *Mr. Chairman,* 293, 296, 300–302, 304; naming of, 228; and Nashville, 745–746; on nation's future challenges, 710; networking, 250; and Nixon, 658, 674–675, 726–727, 728–729; on not retiring, 754; offices of, 311, 732–733, *733,* 738, 752–753; opposing permanent WAC, 435; overseas, 361–371, 409–416, *411, 414*; and Pan Am flight around the world, 457–464; as parliamentarian, 247–250, *249,* 253, 255–256, 261, 264, 308–309; and parliamentary procedure, 301, 798; and Pearl Harbor bombing, 333; and Pentagon Papers, 729; performing, 234–235, 290, 390; and Perkins, *535,* 536, 600; personal impact of WAC service, 436; personal library, 236, 244; photographs, autographed, 399; plane crash, 297–300, *298*; and polio vaccine (*see* polio vaccine); political affiliation of, 314–315, 318, 319, 486, 495, 508, 509, 540–541, 591, 657, 799–800, 811; political conventions, 248, 251, 497–498; and politics, 234, 240, 242, 245, 253; portrait of, *263*; and *Post* staff Christmas gifts, 403; and prohibition, 285–288; as public figure, 288, 471–472; and publicity, 249; public speaking, 295, 330–331, 456, 467, 555, 570, 587–588, 690, 748; on purchase of *Post,* 310; on purpose of life, 646; and Queen's Bedroom, 705, 712, 719, 724; racism and racial justice, 353, 425–426, 489, 493–494, 544–547, 581, 582–584, 605, 663–664; and Rayburn, 591, *592,* 600–601, 806; reading habits of, 236, 247, 252, 366; recruitment of, 336–337, 800–801; and Red Scare, 500–502, 556–557, 560–561, 562, 566, 568; religious faith of, 264–265, 447,

visits to Will, 684; as lieutenant governor, 742–743, 746–748, 764; on *Limelight* censorship, 563–564; on McCarthyism, 501–502; on "Minute Women Series," 566; and mother, 278, 353, 356, 413, 432; on mother, 504–505, 624; and mother's funeral, 760, 761; move to Austin, 742; naval career, 566, 660; and Nixon, 726; Oveta on, 739–740; on Oveta's uniform, 356; and Pentagon Papers, 729; political campaigns, 738, *741*, 742; and political campaigns, 739–740; rabbit hunting, 322; representing Oveta, 756–757; and Rice Institute, 465, 513, 549, 563, 660; and Rice University, 719; on rumors of mother's affair, 304; St. Albans School, 424, 429, 465, 659; and television, 477, 479, 738, 744, 745, 746, 758; as Texas Senate parliamentarian, 670; *Time* magazine on, 691; and University of Houston, 797; and Vietnam War, 718–719; and *Waco Morning News,* 779; wedding of, 595; and Will's biography, 666; and Will's health, 669; and Woestendiek, 692

Hobby, William Pettus, Sr. "Will": birth of, 13; death of, 688, *689*, 748; in 1908, *48*; as "accidental governor," 98; on achievements as governor, 166; as acting governor, 83, 94–95; and Alien Enemy Hearing Board, 354, 493; ancestry of, 3–24, 771, 773; appearance of, 303, 311, 356; approval to marry Oveta, 261–262; arranging Oveta's release from job, 264; arthritis, 628–629, 669; Associated Press Managing Editors Association, 81–82, 85; and Austin, 135; Austin on, 98; and Bailey, 162, 164; and Bailey-Crane debate, 35, 36, 37; and Bandel's hairdo, 384–385; and Banking Commission, 240–241; and bankruptcy threat, 266–267; and battle with *Chronicle,* 208; and Beaumont, 40, 54, 196–198; and *Beaumont Enterprise,* 37, 43, 67, 196, 201, 215, 763; and *Beaumont Journal,* 197–198; and Beaumont newspapers, 201; bedridden, 684–685; and Bill, 294, *322,* 323; and Bill's wedding, 595; biography of, 665–666, 669; birthdays, 522, 667; and Bronson Cooper, 136, 137; and brother Edwin, 215–216; and Brown, 452; and Browne, 25; and Bush, 823; business opportunities, 197, 200–201; as "cabinet husband," 527; cast of *This Is the Army,* 356; and Catto, 682, 821; Catto on, 669; cavalry parade, 188; and centennial celebrations, 294; character of, 121, 284–285, 354; childhood of, 15; and children, 254, 321–322, 325, 336, 356, 408; and Christie, 201–202; and Christie and Hobby, 269; and civil rights, 489; clemency petitions, 354; and

Colquitt, 55–56, 84; community projects of, 291, 305–306; Confederate Veterans Association convention, 182; and Connecticut Avenue apartment, 530; connections of, 58, 67, 70; and conservative allies, 55, 100, 113, 115–116, 133; and Cordelia Hoover's funeral, 233; and court summons, 169; and Crawford, 790; on criticism, 312; criticism of, 193, 194; decision not to run again, 161–162, 166; decision to be newspaperman, 21; and deepwater channel, 49–53; deer-hunting trip, 255; deferring to Oveta, 445; depression of, 216; and drafting of bills, 146; dream job, 216; and educational television, 709; education of, 15, 17, 20–21, 22; and "8F crowd," 452; and Eisenhower, 503, 504; and Eisenhower inauguration, 510–512; and election returns, 82; and elevators, 595; engagements, 62–63, 66, 261–262; entry into politics, 25; on eulogies, 688; on famous wife, 356; and FDR, 283, 296–297, 428–430; and FDR's dismissal of Jones, 430; and Federal Land Bank, 88–89, 92, 93; and Ferguson, 85, 93, 187, 199–200, 304; and Fergusonism, 208–209; and Fergusons, 213–214; and Ferguson's impeachment, 90–91, 94–96; and ferryboat, 686; final decline of, 685–688; finances of, 161–162, 268–269; flight, 103; and flood control, 292, 440; and Fort Sam Houston, 103; and Fuller, 91–92; fundraising (*see* fundraising); funeral of, 688–690; and Galveston labor strike, 171, 173; and García collection, 191; and Garner, 282–283; and Glenn McCarthy, 453; golf, 149, 150; as governor, 83, 94–95, 98–109, 116–117, 135, 137, 139, 145–146, 151, 155–156, 158–160, 172, 179, 193–194; and grandchildren, 670, 681, 765–766; groundbreakings, *165,* 466; gubernatorial campaigns, 99–108, 119–135, 166, 783, 785; gubernatorial record of, *194,* 763; and Harding, 185, *186,* 789; health and *Houston Post,* 644; health and Oveta's career, 597, 643, 649; health of, 267, 304, 441, 445, 448, 465, 543, 628–629, 633, 669, 685–686; and Hempstead shooting story, 32–34; and HEW bill passage, 522; and Hightower, 193; and highway development, 261, 305–306; and highways, 466; Hobby Loyalty Act, 116–117; and Hobby Team, 291; homes of (*see* Calder Avenue; Glen Haven home; Shadyside mansion); honeymoon, 265; and Hoover commission, 469; hospitalization of, 479; and Houston, 18–20, 200–201, 292, 440; and Houston mayoral race, 455; on Houston National Bank sale, 271; and *Houston Post,* 21–22, 24, 27, 29–38, 274, 276,

283–284, 305, 310–311, 441, 443, *444*, 445, 540, 549, 557, 584, 594–595, 665, 763, 807; and Houston Post Company, 643; and *Houston Post-Dispatch*, 204, 206–207, 272, 274, 798–799; and *Houston Post-Dispatch* financial soundness, 207; and *Houston Post-Dispatch* purchase, 269–270, 272, 313, 442, 795; and *Houston Post-Dispatch* stock, 204, 284; and *Houston Post* hired by, 24, 752; and *Houston Post* shares, 25; humor of, 452; and Ike Culp, 238, 245, 290–291; importance of, 762–763; inaugural ball, 147–149; inauguration of, 75–76, 86, 96, 145, 147–179; investments of, 202; and Japanese Houstonians, 493; and Jones, 217, 283–284, 302–303, 314, *454*, 568–569, 646; on journalism career, 83; and Kilman, 502, 503, 562; and Kirby, 28–29, 777, 782; and KKK, 198, 199–200; and labor strikes, 102; and labor unions, 487, 782; and Larrazolo, 182; last meeting with editorial board, 686; and LBJ, 318, 490, 684–685; on LBJ's future, 318; and League of Nations, 164–165, 456; legacy of, 762–763; as lieutenant governor, 75–85, 88; lieutenant governor campaigns, 62–63, 67, 69–72, *71*, 82, 83, 88; as lobbyist, 49, 51, 138–139, 152; and Long's visit, 279–281; loss of mobility, 669–670; and "Lost Cause," 763; love for Oveta, 254, 794–795; and Loyalty Rangers, 125–126; and MacArthur, 492; management style of, 284–285, 311, 445, 643–644; as man of his time and place, 763; marriage to Oveta, 261, 262; and martial law, 156, 158, 171–174, 788; and McKinley's speech, 28; and Mexico, 179–180, 182–183, 188–191; and milk truck, 311; and Moody, 214, 215; and mother, 148–149, 198, 200; and navigation district, 47–48; and Neff, 190; new career, 201; newspapers' support of, 67–68, 70, 118, 121, 783; and New York, 203; and Nineteenth Amendment, 151–152; and Obregón, 179, 180–184, 188–191; at O'Daniel's inauguration, *309*; offices of, 311, 448; and oil labor strike, 103; at Old Settlers Ranching Festival, *163*; as orator, 121–122; and Oveta, 341, 402, 432, *494*, *523*, 543, *553*, 568–569, 588–589; on Oveta, 312, 326, 328, 339, 353–354, 446, 548–549; and Oveta driving, 311; as Oveta's adviser, 260, 312, 336; and Oveta's book, 302; and Oveta's campaign for office, 259; as Oveta's hero, 252; and Oveta's resignation from WAC, 433, 434; and Oveta's swearing in, *340*, 394–395, 523, *524–525*; and Oveta's trip overseas, 362; and Oveta's visits, 373, 379, 382; and Oveta's

wardrobe, 328; and paneling in Oveta's office, 732; and parties, 448; and Peach Tree Village, 773; as personality, 134; philanthropy, 466; plane crash, 297–300, *298*; pneumonia, 687; as political adviser, 216, 305, 311, 318, 763–764; political affiliation of, 209, 219, 314–315, 318, 319, 486, 591; and political conventions, 25, 137–138, 167–168, 217, 251; popularity of, 85, 97; and Porter, 22; and Porvenir massacre, 124; *Post* name change, 274; powerful allies of, 32; proclamation calling for donations, 178–179; and progressive movement, 68, 82, 106–107, 164; and prohibition, 57, 83–84, 99, 102, 110, 285; and prohibition zoning, 111–112, 115, 783; proposal to Oveta, 261; pursuit of Oveta, 227, 245, 254–265, 527; qualifications for office, 76; and race riots, 155–156; racism of, 159–160, 489, 582–583, 763; on radio and newspapers, 211; as reader, 15; and Red Scare tactics, 500, 562; and Red Summer, 158, 159–160; reevaluation of life, 200; religious beliefs of, 265, 688; at Rice Institute, *677*; and Rice University, 738; and Rienzi Johnston, 24, 30, 34, 55, 143; on role of government, 164–165, 315; on role of lieutenant governor, 76; and Roosevelt campaign, 283; and rumors of Oveta-Jones affair, 303–304; salary of, 37, 310; and Sam Jr.'s campaign, 81; and Sanders kidnapping attempt, 174; and San Jacinto day celebrations, 267–268, 304, 466; and Savannah's wedding, 192–193; and seating of Parr, 143; as Senate president pro tem, 94; and shaving, 311; and Shillady, 159; and Smith-Robinson ticket, 219; social life of, 58–59; and Spanish flu, 141, 142; and Special Studies Project, 651; and states' rights movement, 489, 582; and Sterling, 215, 220, 255, 260–261, 270; and Sterling administration, 261; and Sterling campaigns, 219–220, 256, 257, 259–261, 278; stomach ulcer, 669; and stories, 15, 17, 121–122, 185–186, 465; success of, 55; success of marriage to Oveta, 264; sued, 173; and suffrage movement, 68, 69, 109, 112–113, 115, 138, 151; and suffrage referendum act, 147, *148*; supporting Oveta's career, 264, 288, 325, 333, 339, 432, 436, 438, 507, 801; surgeries, 402, 432, 667; and Taft, 486; and television, 211, 477, *480–481*, 482, *482*; at Texas Cotton Palace Festival, 184; and Texas Democratic Party, 37, 67, 178; and Texas Rangers, 124, 125, 144; on Texas Rangers, 125, 784; and Texas Technical College, 190; and Theodore Roosevelt, 32; and tidelands mineral rights, 487–488; as toastmaster, 465–466; at

Hoover, J. Edgar, 509, 660, 736, 798

Hoover Commission, 469–473, 506, 519

Horowitz, Will, 210

House Bill 5, 143–145

House Bill 15, 116–117

house lot, 220

House Un-American Activities Committee (HUAC), 500–502, 559–560. *See also* Communism; Red Scare.

*Houston* (ship), 379

Houston, Sam, 5, 6, 104, 294, 465

Houston, TX: in 1890s, 17; in 1900s, 27; in 1920s, 200–201, 266; 1935 flood, 292; airport, 690; Astrodome opening, 706; and Beaumont, 42; bird's-eye view of, *18–19*; Chamber of Commerce, 305–306, 362, 466, 485; and city auditorium, 776; and Civil War, 7, 8; convention center, 217; and Democratic Party national convention, 216, 217, 251–252; and desegregation, 671–673; and Edwin Hobby, 8, 17; and "8F crowd," 450–456, *451*; Federal Land Bank, 88–89; and flood control, 292, 440; and Great Depression, 200–201, 266; and hurricane, 26, 27; and JFK's "We Choose the Moon" speech, 681; and Lamar Hotel, 294; mayoral campaign of 1900, 25; and Minute Women, 556, 559, 566–568; navigation district, 49, 778; newspaper competition in, 442–443; Nixon's campaign visit to, 679; and Oveta, 242, 243–244, 246, 250, 439–440, 793; and polio outbreak, 608; *Post* reporting on unsolved crimes, 660, 662; postwar era, 439, 442, 452, 465–466; race riots, 155, 672; as rail center, 19; Red Scare in, *555–571*; and space program, 684, 696; and Sterling campaign, 260; and Texas Woman's Fair, 81; W. C. Munn's department store, 151, 786; and Willie, 200–201, 203; as Will's hometown, 17, 200–201

Houston Astros, 706, 736

Houston Central High School, 21

Houston Chamber of Commerce, 305–306, 362, 466, 485

*Houston Chronicle:* accusing *Post* of Klan sympathies, 208; advertising, 671; on Bailey *vs.* Crane debate, 36; and Bill's birth, 275; and Bill's op-ed on the shutdown of *Post,* 758; blocking news of lunch counter desegregation, 672–673; circulation of, 660, 671, 750; as combination morning and afternoon paper, 198; competition with *Post,* 208, 443, 751, 753; criticism of Minute Women series, 566, 568; editorials, 568; Eisenhower's endorsement of, 683; and Foster, 30; and Hearst Corporation, 753, 758; and *Houston Press,* 691;

and John T. Jones Jr., 568; and KTRH, 213; McCarthy and McCarthyism, 503, 557, 562; on Oveta, 760; on poll tax, 175; right-wing ideology of, 662; and Schacher, 300; success of, 210; and taxes, 442; on Willie's influence, 115; on Will's death, 688; and Will's gubernatorial campaign, 783; Woestendiek's criticism of, 693

Houston City Hall lunch counter, 671–672

Houston Country Club, 290

*Houston Dispatch,* 203–204. *See also Houston Post; Houston Post-Dispatch.*

Houston East and West Texas Railway, 19

Houston Endowment, 751

Houston Independent School District, 301, 302, 560, 690

Houston Museum of Fine Arts, 290, 466, 706

Houston National Bank, 269–273

Houston Normal School, 20–21

*Houston Post:* active selling of, 443; and advertising, 142, 308, 442, 671, 677; and African American community, 306; as anti-Catholic, 675–676; awards of, 662; and Bailey *vs.* Crane debate, 35, 36; bias of, 742; and Bill, 294, 351, 549, 742; and *Brown v. Board of Education,* 584; buildings for, 21, 22, 206, 549, 594–595, 730–732; and call for unity, 321; ceasing operations, 758; changes to, 324, 441–442; and Church of Christ, 677; circulation of, 204, 283, 408, 442, 660, 671, 690, 750–751; and Communism, 500; computerization of, 731, 752; and Connally, 683, 740; and "court-packing" plan, 316; and coverage of Bill's campaign, 739; declining prosperity of, 750–751; and desegregation of Houston lunch counters, 672–673; and Dewey, 488–489; and draft commission, 717; editorial board, 675, 686, 728, 729, 734–735, 746–747, 752; editorial policy, 563–564; editorials, 23, 43, 274, 502–503, 540, 703, 722, 729; and Eisenhower, 496–497, 675; fair and accurate reporting, 437; and FDR, 316, 429, 430; financial struggles of, 751; and Ford, 730; and Fuermann's editorials, 502, 722; and Galveston hurricane, 26–27; and Governor's Race of 1932, 278; and Great Depression, 269–274; and Hempstead shooting story, 33–34; Hobby family's sale of, 751–753; Hobbys considering sale of, 440–441; Hobbys' purchase of, 307–308, 309–310; and "Hobby Team," 291; and Hoover, 509; and Hoover Commission, 469, 470; and *Houston Chronicle,* 751, 753; and *Houston Dispatch,* 203; and Houston Post Building, 730–732; improvement of, 311–312; influence of, 690; international outlook of, 457; and investigative reporting, 660; IRS challenge of tax returns, 798–799; and JFK, 675, 822; and Jones, 308, 430, 796; and Josey, 272–274, 276; and Kilman, 502–503, 561, 562; and KPRC, 442, 482; and Lady Bird Johnson, 700; Larendon Building, 21, 22, 595; and LBJ, 675, 684, 685, 692, 703–704, 722, 725; and *Limelight,* 563–564; and loans for Hobbys' purchase, 272, 284, 309–310, 313, 442; losing money, 307–308, 310; and lunch counter desegregation, 672–673; and MacArthur's firing, 492; and Marguerite Johnston, 502, 563, 735; and McCarthy, 562, 567; and McCarthyism, 502, 557; Minute Women exposé series, 555–571; modernization of, 283, 308, 311; Mother's Day edition, 288; name change, 274; neighboring Will's school, 21; and news blackout, 672–673; news coverage increased, 442, 443; and Nixon, 675, 727, 728–729; opposing views in *Houston Post,* 502–503; and Oveta, 277, 292, 305–306, 446, 511, 643, 691, 692, *753;* Oveta's management of, 643–644; Oveta's office, 732–733, *733,* 738, 819; and Oveta's personal views, 729; and Oveta's status as national figure, 456; photographs of LBJ and Humphrey, 703; policy on political statements, 318; on precinct meetings, 496; and printing plant, 594–595, 671, 732, 751–752; profits of, 312, 441, 442–443, 448, 465, 730; prosperity of, 654; and Pulitzer Prize, 692; and Red Scare, 500, 502–503, 554, 561, 566, 718; and release of Pentagon Papers, 729; repayment of loans, 442; reputation of, 662; and Rienzi Johnston, 21, 23–24, 70, 86, 96, 142–143; and Robert Kennedy, 722; and Roosevelt administration, 807; and Roy Watson, 23, 142, 204, 790; and salaries, 310; sent to Oveta in Washington, 543, 807; serialization of *McCarthyism: The Fight for America,* 557; and Social Security and domestic servants, 540; special edition, 822; and Special Studies Project, 650, 652; and Spindletop oil strike, 27; split personality of, 502; staff Christmas gifts, 403; staff of, 274, 276, 356, 448–450; and Sterling Trust, 795; streamlining of, 305; and Sunday book page, 288; and taxes, 442; and *Texas* battleship, 466; and U-2 spy plane crash, 674; and unsolved crime reporting, 660, 662; and Vietnam War, 718; and WAAC, 342; and Wagner Act, 487; during war years, 440–441; and Watergate, 729–730; Watson's sale of, 204; wedding of Kirby's daughter, 37; and Will, 21–22, 24, 27, 29–38; and Willie and Will's wedding, 79; and Will's campaigns, 70; and Will's death, 688, *689;* Will's decreased

role at, 445; Will's editorial board last meeting, 686; Will's editorials for, 43, 274, 540; Will's first job with, 22, 752; Will's loyalty to, 37; Will's purchase of shares, 25; Will's unhappiness at, 283–284; and Woestendiek, 692–693; women's special interests, 311–312. *See also Houston Dispatch; Houston Post-Dispatch.*

Houston Post Building, 730–732, 752–753

Houston Post Company, 442, 643, 691, 734, 808

*Houston Post-Dispatch:* advertising in, 269; backing Butte for governor, 209; buildings of, 206, 211, 212; circulation of, 212, 269; editorials, 208, 213–214; first issue of, 206–207; and Governor's race of 1926, 214; and Great Depression, 269–275; merger of *Post* and *Dispatch,* 204; name change of, 274; and Oveta, 245, 250, 267; and Oveta's appointment as parliamentarian, 249; and Oveta's campaign for office, 251, 257; Oveta's resignation from, 248; plans for, 220; profitable, 210; and radio giveaway, 211–212; and Sterling, 204, 206–207, 260, 271–273; and Sterling's loss of Houston National Bank, 271; and support for Moody, 214; taxes of, 558–559, 798–799. *See also Houston Dispatch; Houston Post.*

Houston Post-Dispatch Building, 206, 211, 212

Houston Post Foundation, 466

*Houston Press:* blocking news of lunch counter desegregation, 672–673; as competition, 273; and *Houston Chronicle,* 691; and Scripps-Howard, 173, 273, 442, 672, 691; tabloid style of, 662; and taxes, 442; and Wolters' attempts to silence, 173–174

Houston Printing Company: and bond issue to *Houston Post-Dispatch,* 269; Hobbys' purchase of, 307–310; and Jones, 274, 283, 284, 307; and Josey, 274, 283, 310; and Sterling, 204, 271–272; tax returns, 798–799; and Watson, 142; Will's stock in, 284

Houston Ship Channel, 49, 315, 466, 686, 692

Houston Symphony, 290, 466

Howard University, 353, 542, 583–584

Hubbard, Richard, 12, 13

Huerta, Adolfo de la, 182, 189, 789

Huerta, Victoriano, 181

Hughes, Emmet J., 515

Hughes, Howard Sr., 27, 201, 250

Hughes, Sarah T., 256–257, 719

Humble Oil Company: and Baker, 452; and Christie and Hobby, 201–202; and Edgar Townes, 141; and labor strikes, 103; oil lease for Oveta's land, 455; orchestra, 212; and Sterling, 210, 269, 271; Will's connection to, 27

Humphrey, George, 511, 575–576, 602, 620

Humphrey, Hubert: LBJ's running mate, 703; and 1968 presidential election, 728; and polio vaccine, 628; politics of, 726; on *Post* endorsement, 703; at White House, 724

Hunt, H. L., 499–500

Huntingdon Place home, 737, 754

Huntress, Frank G., 187

hurricanes: of 1915, 81; Galveston 1900, 26–27, 30; Hurricane Harvey, 292

Hurt, Harry III, 240, 261, 304, 733

Hutchison, Kay Bailey. *See* Bailey, Kay.

hydrogen bombs, 657

**I**

"I Am So Glad" poem, 294

Ickes, Harold, 348

Ike Clubs, 495

*Îl de France*, 426

inaugural balls, 147–149, 511–512

income taxes, federal, 558–559, 798–799

India, 459

Indian Territory, 20, 21, 22, 24, 775

Industrial Workers of the World (IWW), 102, 788

influence-peddling scheme, 187

influenza, 140–141, 147, 610, 630–631

initiative reform, 57, 58

insurance, 201–202, 518, 575–576, 587. *See also* health care and health insurance.

Internal Revenue Service (IRS), 135, 798–799

International and Great Northern Railroad (I&GN), 188–189

International Longshoremen's Association (ILA), 169

Interstate Trust Company, 202

Intracoastal Canal, 43, 54

Ireland, John, 12

Ireland, Northern, 370, 371, 457, 458

Ireland, Republic of, 362, 363

iron lung, 607

Isaacs, Stella. *See* Reading, Lady Stella Isaacs .

Italy, 413–415

*It Can't Happen Here*, 316

**J**

Jackson, General, 192–193

Jackson, Savannah, 192–193, 222

Jacoway, Henderson M., 60, 79, 161

Jacoway, Margaret Cooper, 60, 79, 149

Japan, 321, 333, 435, 460–462, 716

Japanese Americans, 354, 493, 666

Jefferson Davis Hospital, 579–580, 581

Jim Crow laws: and *Houston Post*, 31; and lunch

counters, 671; reviving support for, 763; and schools, 544; in Texas, 57, 582–583; and WAAC, 350, 425

*John Henry Kirby* (yacht), 46

Johnson, Dick, 753, 760

Johnson, Gail Borden, 21

Johnson, Helen: and Hobby children, 409, 417; and Hobby household, 408–409; and Houston Post Company, 442; as Oveta's assistant, 326, 394–395, 403, 408–409, 441; sending food to Oveta, 395; as Will's executive secretary, 408

Johnson, James Weldon, 155

Johnson, Lady Bird: and Bill, 742; boating trip, 708–709; and Carpenter, 697; on dinner cruise, 707; and HEW bill, 522; and JFK assassination, 685; on LBJ and Oveta, 675, 698; on LBJ and Will, 684; Montgomery's biography of, 700; and Oveta, 601, 639, 684, 706–707, 712, 714, 719; on Oveta's withdrawal from society, 755–756; and restoration of LBJ's birthplace, 708; television station of, 475, 701, 711; and Vietnam, 714; visit to Brown ranch, 724

Johnson, Lyndon Baines (LBJ): and Bill, 724–725, 738, 742; birthplace of, 708; boating trip at Lake LBJ, 708–709; and Browns, 452, 701; campaign tactics of, 701–702; and Central Texas College library, 720, *721*; and congressional campaigns, 318, 486, 489–490; and Corporation for Public Broadcasting board, 721; and Darcy's cartoons, 692; decision not to run for second term, 722; declining health of, 724; and dinner cruise, 707; and flattery, 699; fundraising concerns, 702; Great Society program, 606, 710, 713, 725; and Halsell, 705, 824; heart attacks, 636, 725; and HEW, 521, 522; and Hobbys, 684–685; honoring Oveta, 645; inauguration of, 706; isolation of, 724–725; and JFK, 684, 685; and Lady Bird's radio station, 701; and McCarthy, 567; and Medicare, 707; and Middleton, 717; and Oveta, 342, 506, 508–509, 510–511, 600–601, 639, 644–645, 697–710, *698*, 712, 721; on Oveta, 636; as Oveta's peer, 698; and Oveta's political affiliation, 541; pajamas, 685; popularity in Texas, 738; and *Post*, 675, 703–704; presidential campaigns, 675–676, 699–701; and public television, 711, 712, 717, 718, 721; as senator, 597, 675–676; and space program, 684; surprise visit, 706–707; sworn in as president, 256; telephone conversations with Oveta, 699; and television, 475, 738; and Tower, 678; and vaccine crisis, 698; as vice president, 681; and Vietnam, 712–717, 723, 725; visit to Brown ranch, 724; and voter fraud, 784;

and Will, 133, 318, 684–685, 763–764; on Will's
death, 688; and Woestendiek, 693; and women
in military, 719, *720*
Johnson, Richard "Dick," 753
Johnson, Sam, 290, 697
Johnson, Sam Ealy, 133, 240, 318, 697
Johnson administration: Civil Rights Act of 1964,
702, 703, 725; and draft, 718; Great Society
program, 606, 710, 713, 725; Medicare, 707; and
military draft, 716–717; and public television,
709, 717, 718, 721; and US Information Agency,
718; and Vietnam, 712–717
Johnston, Harry, 143, 206
Johnston, Harry Jr., 206, 441–442, 556; as assistant
editor, 441
Johnston, Marguerite: editorials of, 502, 563, 662;
and eulogy for Oveta, 760–761; on Hobbys and
Kilman, 502; and Hunter, 735; and Oveta, 442,
468, 755, 759, 760–761; on Oveta, 436, 728,
752, 755, 759, 761; and *Post*, 442, 557, 563, 662,
735, 752; praise for *Prospect for America*, 652;
and UN conference, 467, 468; on Will, 494; and
Will's biography, 666
Johnston, Rienzi M.: in 1913, *31*; as acting governor, 140; background of, 23; and Bailey, 34, 35;
and Ball, 65; and Beaumont, 49; and Bronson
Cooper, 136; and Browne, 25; death of, 206,
214; editorials of, 23–24, 70, 96; and Edwin
Hobby, 24; and Ferguson, 65, 88, 95, 96; and
Garner, 53; and *Houston Post*, 21, 23, 142–143;
and *Houston Post-Dispatch* board of directors,
206; and labor unions, 102; nickname of, 23;
pension, 142; politics of, 23–24, 25, 30, 32, 57,
65–66, 106, 108, 109, 112, 113, 116; and Porter,
22; and prohibition, 57, 65–66, 106, 108, 112,
116; relationship with Will, 55, 143; and Spanish
flu, 141; and state prison commission, 143; and
Sturgeon, 65; supporting Parr's seating, 143; as
Texas state senator, 86, 95; as trustee for Watson,
23; as US senator, 58; waning influence of, 168;
as Will's mentor, 24, 30, 34, 37, 102; and Will's
newspaper career, 25, 27, 28, 29, 34, 38; and
Will's political career, 25–26, 63, 66, 70, 71, 104,
108, 116, 119, 133; and Will's wedding, 79; and
women's suffrage, 109, 113
Jolly Entertainers, 234–235
Jones, Alfred, 196, 198
Jones, Jesse Holman: affair of, 303; and Alamo
centennial celebration, 294–295; appearance of,
303; with architect, *285*; and Bailey *vs.* Crane
debate, 35; and banking industry, 270–273, 294;
and breakfast, 252; and *Chronicle* and KTRH

radio, 272–273; and control of *Post*, 283; critique
of Oveta's speeches, 569–570; and Cullen, 453;
death of, 646–647, 662, 690; declining health,
568; and deer-hunting trip, 255; and Democratic National Convention 1928, 216; and "8F
crowd," 452, *454*; and Eisenhower, 485; eulogy
for Schacher, 300; and FDR, 296, 308, 318,
428–429, 430, 667; on FDR, 430; and Federal
Loan Administration, 314; and Franklin, 589;
at fundraising rally, 379; and Hobbys, 302–303,
479; and Hoover Commission, 470; and *Houston
Chronicle*, 213, 557, 662; and Houston National
Bank, 270–272; and Houston politics, 455; and
Houston Printing Company, 307; and KTRH
radio, 272–273; and labor unions, 487; and loan
to Wortham, 455; and MacArthur, *493*; marriage of, 303; "Mr. Houston," 303; and Oveta,
287, 294, 305, 548, 568–570, 588–589, 630,
798; on Oveta's charm, 525; and plane crash,
297–300, *298*; poker games, 453; politics of,
570; and *Post*, 271–273, 304, 307, 308, 309–310,
796, 799; presidential ambitions, 216–218, 251,
314; and Reconstruction Finance Corporation,
283–284, 287, 307, 314, 428, 589; and Red
Scare, 568; repayment of, 313; rumors of affair
with Oveta, 303–304, 798; and sale of *Post* to
Hobbys, 308, 309–310, 799; and Sam Houston
Hall dedication, 217; as secretary of commerce,
428; and Sterling Trust, 271; and television
industry, 475; in Washington, 453; and Will, 217,
314, *454*, 568–569, 646
Jones, John T., 568, 672–673, 679
Jones, Mary Gibbs, 217, 303, 485, 735
Josey, J. E. "Jack": death of, 442; excuses of, 273–
274; as Jones's surrogate, 272–273, 276, 796;
and Oveta, 288, 305; and *Post*, 272–273, 274,
276, 283–284, 305, 310, 796; and State Teachers
College of Texas, 390; and Sterling, 274
J. Walter Thompson advertising agency, 420

**K**

Kaiser, Henry J., 547, 814
Kamp, Joseph, 497
Keasby, Lindely M., 132
Keefer, Chester, 575, 615, 616, 618, 620
Kellam, J. C., 708–709, 712
Kemp, Joseph, 189, 191
Kennedy, John F. (JFK): assassination of, 685, 822;
criticism of Eisenhower, 679; and Hughes, 256;
inauguration of, 681; and LBJ, 684; and Oveta,
675; presidential campaign, 676; "We Choose
the Moon" speech, 681–682

Mapes, Kathryn, 780

March, Charles, 198

March of Dimes, 607, 608, *609*

Marcus, Stanley, 709

Marshall, George Catlett: advising on congressional testimony, 334; and Air Corps, 375–376; and All-States Plan, 404; and American Red Cross, 467; and belongings of WAAC volunteers in North Africa, 381; character of, 419–420; and Eisenhower, 376, 377–378; and first WAAC officer graduates, 357; letter to army commanding officers, 422–423; and Meek Report, 420–422; and Oveta, 336, 338, 341, 355, 419, 420–423, 426, 432, 440, 508, 571; on Oveta, 335; and Oveta's Distinguished Service Medal, 427, 428; as Oveta's hero, 759; and Oveta's resignation, 424, 432; and Oveta's speech to Congressional Wives Club, 417; and Oveta's swearing in, 339–341, 395, *397–398*; photograph of, 446; and Potsdam Conference, 433; respect for Oveta, 381; and Rogers bill, 331–332, 333–334, 335; as Secretary of Defense, 490; and Somervell, 348; and WAAC, 336, 351, 358, 361–362, 365, 376, 377–379, 381, 391–392; and WAC, 407, 419, 421–423, 432, 436; and *The Women's Army Corps*, 474; women's clubs meeting, 328, *329*; and women's draft, 405, 407

martial law, 156, 158, 171–172, 788

Mary Hardin-Baylor College: banquet at, 388; and Baylor Academy, 239; and Dora's education, 8; honorary doctorate, 645–646, *646*; Oveta's attendance at, 239, 245

Massey, Otis, 388

Mather, George, 720

Mathis, John Sr., 258–259, 794

Matthews, J. B., 491, 563

Mayes, William "Will," 70, 83, 780

Mayfield, Earle B.: and gubernatorial campaigns, 99, 106, 118, 251, 259–260; and KKK, 199–200; and prohibition, 100, 106; and senate campaigns, 199–200, 219; as senator, 216

Mayflower Hotel, 287

McAdoo, William Gibbs: and Federal Land Bank, 88, 89, 92, 93; and Ferguson, 92; and Mexican government, 191; and presidential campaigns, 166, 167; for vice president, 282–283; and war bonds, 101

McAfee, Mildred, 382, 491

McAlister, Hill, 294

McBride, Cecil, 300, 311, 323, 450, 754–755

McCarthy, Glenn, 439, 453, *454*, 475, 748

McCarthy, Joseph R.: campaign tactics of, 497; and Eisenhower policies, 561; and Hobbys, 500, 561; as liability, 561–562; and newspapers, 558, 564; and Nixon, 562; *Post* criticism of, 566, 567; and Red Scare, 454, 501, 515; and Rosenberg, 561; and San Jacinto celebrations, 567; Senate investigation, 567, 594; and Stevens, 567; and "The Minute Women Series," 564

McCarthyism: and criticism of Oveta, 509; and *Houston Chronicle*, 503, 557, 562; and Minute Women, 558, 567; Oveta's opposition to, 500–502; and *Post*, 557; and Republican Party, 509, 558, 561–562. *See also* Red Scare.

*McCarthyism: The Fight for America*, 557

McCloy, John J., 334, 425

McFaddin, W. P., 41, 54

McGrew, Jack: on Hobby Team, 445; and KLEE broadcasts, 477; and KPRC, 312–313, 447, 694, 754; and Oveta, 693–694, *694*; parties at Hobby mansion, 448, 449–450; and television, 477

McKay, Douglas, 515, 576

McKay, John, 68

McKinley, William, 28

McKinne, Sarah Elizabeth, 3

McLean, Evalyn Walsh, 185, 186–187

McLean, Ned, 185, 186

McNair, Lesley J., 421

Meany, George, 517, 529, 530

Medal of Freedom, 491

media, news : duty and obligations of, 468, 470, 555, 652, 673; focus on Oveta's appearance, 328, 335, 337–338; frivolous questions, 355; misreporting Oveta's education, 246; obligations of, 693; and Oveta's resignation from HEW, 634–635; and Oveta's resignation from WAC, 433–434; Oveta's scolding of, 561; and polio vaccine, 610, 611, 616–617, 622–624, 627–628; and rumors of Oveta-Jones affair, 303–304; and Texas Legislature, 12; and WAAC training, 354–355. *See also* newspapers; press conferences.

media corporations, national, 745

MediaNews Group, 758

medical research, 520, 542, 586. *See also* polio.

Medicare bill, 601, 707, 725

Meek, Samuel W., 420–421

Meek Report, 420–422

memorial, World War II, *437*, 437–438

Menard, Gertrude Stiles, 8

Meredith, James, 683

Metcalf, Charles, 113–114

Mewhinney, Hubert, 470

Mexican Americans, 123, 124, 126, 127–128

Mexican War, 122

Neches River: bridge, 54; dredging of, 41–42, 46–47, 50, 51–52; and Peach Tree Village, 9; shipbuilding factories, 197. *See also* Sabine-Neches deepwater channel.

Neches-Sabine deepwater channel. *See* Sabine-Neches deepwater channel.

Neff, Pat: and Allred, 241; as governor, 178, 239; and gubernatorial campaign, 161, 168; at inauguration of O'Daniel, *309*; in Mexico City, 191; at Moody's inauguration, 215; and Oveta, 388–389; at Texas Cotton Palace Festival, 184

New Deal programs: and HEW bill, 521; and Hoover Commission, 469, 470–471; and Japan, 461–462; and Kilman, 502; and Somervell, 348; and Wilkie, 317; and Will, 487

"New Freedom," 164

New Orleans, 45–46, 78–80

newspapers: black publications and race riots, 158–159; combination morning and afternoon papers, 198; and competition from radio, 211; duty of, 690; and endorsements of LBJ, 703; and Hobbys' wedding, 79–80; Houston news blackout, 673; and McCarthyism, 503, 557, 558, 562; and Mexico, 184; and Minute Women, 559; morning paper advantages, 443; role and responsibilities of, 428, 673, 693; and Sanders' kidnapping attempt, 174; supporting Moody, 214–215; as watchdogs, 693; and Will, 103; and Willie, 93, 118–119; and Will's campaigns, 67–68, 70, 118, 121, 783; and Will's open door policy, 139. *See also* media, news; specific newspapers.

newsreels, 339, 355, 369, 461, 523

New York City: and Coopers, 62; and polio outbreaks, 608; promoting Texas businesses in, 72; shopping excursions to, 532; visit to, 203, 356

*New York Herald Tribune:* on Oveta, 326, 428, 434, 549, 636; Oveta on role of post-war newspapers, 428; and Reid, 457, 464, 495

*New York Journal American:* and Hearst newspaper chain, 627; on Oveta, 505, 509, 512, 549; and WAC, 337, 403, 629

New York Municipal Airport. *See* LaGuardia Airport.

*New York Times*, 72, 688, 760

Nicks, William Perry, 11, 774

Nineteenth Amendment, 138, 147, 151–152, 174–175, 243, 786. *See also* women's suffrage movement.

Niños Héroes, 190

Nixon, Richard: and Catto, 749; and classroom shortage, 602–603; diplomatic policy of, 728–729; and Eisenhower, 579, 674–675; fundraising speech, 596; inauguration of, 728; and LBJ Presidential Library, 724; and LBJ's

inauguration, 510; and McCarthy, 562; and Oveta, 726–727, 728–729; partisanship of, 658, 674–675; at picnic, 639, *640*; presidential campaigns, 674–675, 679, 726–728; and Supreme Court, 728; as vice-presidential candidate, 498, 655–657, 658; and Vietnam, 729; and Watergate, 729–730

Nixon administration, 728

non-fraternization rule, WAAC, 398–399

North Africa: allied landing in, 367; Anderson, 382; and Boyce, 432; U-boat attack, 377, 410; and WAACs serving in, 367, 376–378, 380, 382, 389, 410, 804; and WAC inspection tour, 412–413

North Atlantic Trade Organization (NATO), 492

**O**

Obregón, Álvaro, 179–184, 187–192, 207, 789

O'Connor, Basil, 613, *617*, 617–618

O. Henry. *See* Porter, William Sydney.

oil industry: and Beaumont, 39; and Coolidge-Obregón treaty, 789; and Dhahran, 458–459; and Great Depression, 266; and labor strikes, 102–103; and Mexico, 187, 192, 789; and postwar boom, 453; and Red River, 168; and Saudi Arabia, 458–459; Spindletop Oil strike, 27; and Venezuela, 660

Oilman's Reciprocal Association, 201–202

Oklahoma-Texas border dispute, 168–169

Old Age and Survivors Insurance programs, 518

O'Leary, Ralph S.: in 1953, *565*; and Minute Women exposé series, 555–556, 564, 566; and news blackout, 673; and *Post*, 662

Oltorf, Frank "Posh," 452, 489–490

101st Airborne Division, 663

Open Shop Association, 176

open shop movement, 170–171, 172, 176. *See also* unions and unionism.

Orange, TX, 47, 49, 53, 54

Ousley, Clarence, 30, 65, 140, 199

Oveta Culp Hobby stamp, 762, *765*, 828

**P**

pajamas, 685, 686

Pallas Athena, 348, 446, 732

Palmer, A. Mitchell, 158, 159

Palmer, George J., 23, 27, 142

Panama Canal, 52

Pan American Airways (Pan Am) flight, 457–463

Pan-American Round Table, 179

paneling, oak, 732, *733*, 752

Panic of 1873, 774

Panic of 1893, 20

616, 622; vaccine conferences, 614, 616–618; voluntary distribution plan, 618, 624–625, 626. *See it Now,* 613

political campaigns: and "8F crowd," 455; and KKK, 199–200; and Loyalty Rangers, 126–127; and *patrones,* 127–128, 134, 180, 784; and prohibition, 64–65, 70, 83–84, 106, 110–111, 780; and radio, 213; women voters, 108–109, 128–132, 134–135, 499, 784–785. *See also* individual candidates.

Polk County, TX, 13, 71–72

poll tax: and 1918 gubernatorial race, 128; and returning soldiers, 151; and voting rights, 31; and women's suffrage, 114, 174–175, 176, 239. *See also* voter suppression.

Populist Party, 17

pork barrel politics, 53

Port Arthur, 42, 50, 55, 170

Porter, Jack, 486, 492, 495–496, 498

Porter, William Sydney, 22, 452, 791

Port of Beaumont, 46, 53, 82, 777. *See also* Sabine-Neches deepwater channel.

Porvenir massacre, 124–125

Powell, Adam Clayton Jr., 544–546, 579–580, 581, 583–584, 604–605

"The Power of the Democratic Idea, 652. *See also* Special Studies Project.

Powers, Francis Gary, 673–674

precinct conventions and Texas Republican Party, 495–498

prepaid group medical care, 547

President's Advisory Committee on Government Organization (PACGO), 519–520, 526

press. *See* media, news; newspapers.

press conferences: choreographing of, 541; with ER, 417; and HEW, 540–541, 611, 612–613, 634–635; in Los Angeles, 382; on Pan Am flight around the world, 463; and polio vaccine, 611, 612–613; and Social Security, 570; and WAAC, 355, 368–370; and WAC, 400, 404–405, 416, 433–434

primary suffrage bill, 114–115, 134

"The Private Life of a Can of Beans" speech, 472

Proctor, Frederick C., 73, 102

progressive movement: campaign finance, 69; and Ferguson, 64–65; and Love, 58; and Moody, 214–215; and "New Freedom," 164; and prohibition, 56–57; proposed reforms, 57; racism and racial injustice, 778; referendum reform, 57, 58; and Thirty-Fourth Legislature, 77–78; and Will, 68, 69, 82, 106–107, 164; and Wilson, 58; and women, 256

prohibition: arguments of, 56; and Bailey, 779; and

Ball, 65; and brewing industry, 779; as campaign issue, 64–65, 70, 83–84, 106, 110–111, 780; and Chupadera Ranch hunting trips, 255; and Cox, 167; and "Dean Law," 152; and Edwin Hobby, 72; Eighteenth Amendment, 102, 104, 112, 115, 138, 219, 285–288; and Ferguson, 64; and Ike Culp, 236; and Kirby, 779; local *vs.* state issue, 101–102; movement in Texas, 56–57; opposition to, 30, 216, 779; prohibition zones, 111–112, 115, 783; referendums on, 72, 146–147, 152, 286; repeal of, 285–288; and Sheppard, 58; special legislative sessions, 107, 110; state amendment, 146–147; and Sturgeon, 65; and Texas Democratic Party, 137–138; Texas Federation of Anti Prohibition Clubs, 287; Texas state amendment, 67, 71; and University of Texas, 86; and Utah, 287; and Will, 57, 68, 70, 72, 83–84, 98, 100–101, 102, 111–112, 133, 135; and Wilson, 58, 167; and women's suffrage, 146–147; zoning bill, 115. *See also* anti-prohibition movement.

prohibition zones, 111–112, 115, 783

Prokosch, Eduard, 153–154

propaganda, 153, 468–469, 491, 497. *See also* Red Scare.

*Prospect for America,* 652, 653. *See also* Special Studies Project.

prostitution, 113, 115, 117, 173, 385–386, 391–394

protests, 671–673, 724, 797

Public Broadcasting Act of 1967, 718. *See also* public television.

Public Broadcasting Service, 722

Public Broadcasting System, 718

Public Health Service (PHS): and AMA criticism, 542; budget cuts, 550; certification of polio vaccine, 613, 623, 626; distribution of polio vaccine, 613–614, 630; and FSA, 516; and Hill-Burton Act, 581; independence of, 623; and polio in vaccinated children, 618–619, 621–622; and polio vaccine, 633; and Red Scare, 561; and safety of polio vaccine, 618, 619, 622, 633; testing of polio vaccine, 622, 624; and Wyeth labs, 633

publicity campaigns: for integration of WAAC with regular army, 382–384, 386–389, 390–394; and Meek Report, 420–421; Somervell's undermining of, 421; for WAAC recruitment, 374; and WAC, 399, 400–404; of Women's Interest Section, 325, 330–331

Public National Bank, 270–271, 273

public school attendance, mandatory, 77

public schools: assistance for, 101; and classroom shortages, 542, 572, 574, 593–594, 602–606; desegregation of, 544–546; and federal aid, 594;

and Hobby's plane crash, 299; landing in Republic of Ireland, 364; meeting king and queen, 365, 366; most admired women, 645; and Oveta, 296, 315, 371, 430, 801; on Oveta, 366, 394, 420, 508, 811; and Oveta and Lady Reading's relationship, 370; with Oveta and Munson, *383*; on *Post* support of Eisenhower, 496–497; thanks from, 283; and trip to UK, 362–363; and visit to ATA, 369; visit to Fort Des Moines, 382; and visit to UK, 361–371; and WAAC, 332, 377, 392; and WAC recruiting problems, 417; and Women's Interest Section, 328

Roosevelt, Franklin D. (FDR): and Berle, 819; and Bill, 319–320; and conservative Democrats, 317; at Cotton Bowl, 297, *297*; "court-packing" plan, 315–316; death of, 430; failing health of, 429; "Happy Warrior" nomination speech, 283; and Hobby team, 314–316, 800; and Japan, 321; and Jones, 287, 308, 428, 430; and Marshall, 419; and Oveta, 337, *388*, 806; and plane crash, 299; and polio, 611; presidential campaigns, 282–283, 296, 314; and Rogers bill, 338; and Sabin, 286–287; and sending ER to United Kingdom, 361; and Smith's nomination, 218; as vice president candidate, 167–168; and WAAC, 338, 374, 381, 386–387, 392; and WAC Bill, 394; and World War II memorial, 438

Roosevelt, Theodore, 31, 32, 50, 58, 60–61, 317, 779

Rosenberg, Anna M., 491, 561, 647

Rosenberg, Henry, 82

roses, yellow, 450

*Ross Sterling* ferryboat, 686

Rough Riders, 32, 122

Ruebhausen, Oscar, 575

runoff elections. *See* political campaigns; individual candidates.

Russell, Charles Arden, 5, 6

Russell, Lee M., 189


**S**

Sabin, Albert, 608, 612, 619

Sabin, Pauline Morton, 286–287, 288

Sabine Lake, 42

Sabine-Neches deepwater channel: deepening of, 197; dredging of, 46–47; federal funding for, 42–43, 49–53; and navigation bill, 12; and navigation district, 47, 49; opening of, 46; and Theodore Roosevelt, 50

Sabine River, 12, 777

Sakowitz Bros., 207

Saks Fifth Avenue, 350

Salk, Jonas: ceremony honoring, *617*, 617–618; and

manufacturing polio vaccine, 629; and polio vaccine, 608–612, 613, 619, 622

Salk vaccine. *See* polio vaccine.

saluting flag, 355

Sam Houston Hall, 216, 217, 260

Sam Rayburn Library, 659–660

San Antonio, TX, 80, 103, 132–133, 151, 294–295

Sanders, G. V., 173–174

*San Jacinto* (ship), 379

San Jacinto celebrations: and McCarthy, 567; and Oveta, 267–268; Will presiding at, 267–268, 304, 466

Sappington, H. O., 170, 171, 173

Sarnoff, David, 474–475, 647

Satterwhite, Lee, 239, 247, 248, *249*

Saudi Arabia, 458–459

Sayers, Joseph "Joe," 28, 80, 215

Schacher, Eugene, 298, 299–300

Scheele, Leonard: career of, 572; and HEW legislative agenda, 572; and NIH, 608; on Oveta's resignation from HEW, 636; and polio vaccine, 612–613, 615, 618–624, 626, 630–631, *631*

school bond program, 602–604

school lunch program, 586

Schreiner, Charles, 185, 785

Scobey, Frank, 185, 186, 187

Scripps-Howard, 173, 273, 442, 672, 691

Seagler, R. E., 240

Secession Convention, 5–6, 12–13, 465

Security Union Casualty Company, 201, 202–203

segregation: and Committee for Sound American Education, 559; in hospitals, 579–580; and *Houston Post*, 31; and Minute Women, 558; and Rice University, 719; and Spaulding, 580–581. *See also* desegregation; racism.

Selective Service: and Great War, 98–99; peacetime draft law, 323–324; Selective Service acts, 98–99, 321, 718; White House commission on, 716–717; for women, 374, 405, 407, 491; and Women's Interest Section, 330; World War II, 321

Services of Supply: and bras, 358–359; and clothing similar to WAAC uniforms, 386; and supplies for WAACs, 374; toiletry kits for WAACs, 369; and WAAC chain of command, 347; and winter uniforms, 359–360. *See also* Army, U.S.

Sesnon, William T. Jr., 552

Seventeenth Amendment, 84

Seventeenth Texas Legislature, 14–15

Shadyside mansion: 1964 election-night party, 705; business events at, 448–450; demolition of, 737–738; Eisenhower invited to, 678; home office, 644; hosting LBJ's surprise visit, 706–707;

Tejanos. *See* Mexican Americans.

television, public, 709, 711–712, 716, 717–718, 721–722

television appearances: and Eisenhower, 548; and Eisenhower campaign, 630–631, *631*, 656, 658; and HEW, 520; *The Last Word*, 694; and March of Dimes, 608; *Meet the Press*, 595, *596*; and polio vaccine, 630–631; *Reporter's Roundup*, 632–633; *Today Show*, 543, 650

television fair, 482–483

television industry: and 1954 elections, 596–597; Channel Two Television Company, 734, 745, 748, 753–754; and children, 477, 484; Dumont network, 474; educational television, 709, 711–712; and FCC, 474, 475–476, 477, 745; and Glenn McCarthy, 475; and Hofheinz, 475; and Johnsons, 701; and Lady Bird Johnson, 475, 701, 711; and LBJ, 475, 711, 712, 717, 718, 721, 738; and NBC, 474–475; startup costs, 474–475, 477–478; and University of Houston, 709; and WBAP-TV, 809; and Will, 475, 477, 709. *See also* KPRC-TV; television, public.

television sets, 474, 476, 482–483

Teller, Edward, 647

temperance oath, 232–233

Temple High School, 237, 238

tenant farmers, 64, 72, 101. *See also* farmers.

Tennessee Legislature, 152

Terrell, Chester, 112, 247, 783

TESA (Texas Equal Suffrage Association), 128, 131–132, 257

Texas: antitrust laws, 35; centennial celebrations, 294–295, 313; constitution of, 11, 12–13, 76–77, 112, 740, 774; domination of Democrats, 657; and Mexico, 179–192, 294; and Nixon, 680; and polio epidemic, 608; and prohibition, 286, 287–288; and secession, 5–6, 12–13, 465; and Spanish flu epidemic, 141; and Washington, DC, 140

Texas A&M University, 145, 827

Texas Banking and Insurance department, 240

Texas Bar Association, 773

*Texas* battleship, 466

Texas Brewers Association, 56, 93–94

Texas Centennial Exposition, 313

Texas Cotton Palace Festival, 184

Texas Democratic Women's Club, 251

Texas Eastern Corporation, 455, 808

Texas Equal Suffrage Association (TESA), 128, 131–132, 257

Texas Federation of Anti Prohibition Clubs, 287

Texas Gulf Coast, 12, 39, 202–203, 439. *See also* Galveston; Gulf of Mexico.

Texas League of Women Voters, 256, 267, 268. *See also* League of Women Voters.

Texas Legislature, 239; Alfred Hobby and, 6; Bill as senate parliamentarian, 670; Burton's seating, 12; conscription act, 6; and Edwin Hobby, 11–14; emergency appropriations bill of 1920, 167; and Ferguson's impeachment, 91, 92–94; and Ike Culp, 228–229, 236–238, 242; and local taxing districts, 47; and Love, 117–118; and Nineteenth Amendment, 151–152; and open port law, 175–177; and Oveta, 237–238, 239–240, 247–250, *249*, 253, 255–256, 261, 264, 308–309, 743; parliamentarian duties, 247; poll tax, 239; presidents pro tem, 12, 13, 14, 75, 94, 140, 142; and prohibition, 92–94, 101–102, 107, 112, 286; and reporters, 12; senate terms, 13; sessions of, 13, 14–15, 77–78, 107, 112–114, 151, 175–177, 239–240, 248; and Texas Rangers, 143–144; and "Texas Tourist Trails," 695; and US Senators, 776; Will's proposals for, 145–146

*Texas Monthly* profile of Oveta, 240, 261, 304, 733

Texas National Guard, 156, 168–169, 180, 275, 788

Texas-Oklahoma border dispute, 168–169

Texas Press Association, 63, 691

Texas Railroad Commission, 145, 146

Texas Rangers: in 1920, *144*; and Confederate Army, 122; criminal actions of, 123–124; and elections, 127–128; and Ferguson, 92; and frontier justice, 122–124, 143–144; and Galveston labor strike, 170, 175–176; and Hanson, 125, 143, 158; and Harley, 123–124, 144; and Harry Johnston, 143; and Hempstead shooting, 33; and House Bill 5, 143–144; and Mexican border, 123; and Obregón's visit, 183; and political use of, 784; and Porvenir massacre, 124; and race riots, 155–156, 158; reform of, 144–145; reputation of, 145; and Rodriguez, 123–124; screening of, 123, 145; service of, 122–123; and Texas Legislature, 143–144; violence and criminal actions of, 98, 122–123, 143–144; and voter suppression, 128; Will on, 125; and Will's campaigns, 122, 124, 127–128, 194. *See also* Loyalty Secret Service Department (Loyalty Rangers).

"Texas Regulars," 429

Texas Southern University (TSU), 671–673

Texas Technical College, 190

"Texas Tourist Trails," 695

Texas Woman's Fair, 81

Texas Woman Suffrage Association, 108–109

Texas Women's Democratic League, 128, 132, 243

textbooks, banned, 560

U.S. Marine Corps Women's Reserve (women marines), 437
U.S. Postal Service, 762, *765*, 828

## V

vaccine, polio. *See* polio vaccine.
Vaccine Evaluation Center, 610–611
Valenti, Jack, 685, 702–703, 706, 708–709, 722
Valentina (fashion designer), 532
Vance, Myrtle, 65
Vandenberg, Arthur, 495, 499
Venezuela, 660
veterans, Confederate, 14–15, 182, 774–775
veterans, Great War, 141, 142, 145, 151
veterans' hospital, 184–185, 789
vice laws, 113
Vietnam War, 692, 712–716, 718–719, 723, 725, 729
Vinson, Robert E., 87, 91, 135, 154
vocational rehabilitation, 516, 573, 574, 579, 585
voter fraud, 127–128, 490, 784
voters, Catholic, 259
voter suppression, 31, 57, 126–127, 128, 175

## W

WAAC. *See* Women's Army Auxiliary Corps (WAAC).
WAC. *See* Women's Army Corps.
*Waco Morning News*, 66, 779
Wagner Act, 177, 487
Wakefield, Paul, 300–301
Waldron, A. E., 51
Walker's Station, TX, 8
Wallace, Henry A., 314, 320, 342, 430, 486
wallpaper, airplanes, 373
Walter, Emmet "Soapy Joe," 443, 455, 503, 568
Walter Reed General Hospital, 423, 424, 571, 710, 723
Walters, Lemuel, 156
war bonds: Liberty Loan drive and Will, 118, 119, 138, 783; selling of, 101; and women's corps anniversary parade, 431–432
Ward, Hortense, 128, 245
Ward, Orlando, 473, 809
War Department: and chain of command, 338, 347; code name for ER, 362; and news stories on Oveta, 324, 800; and Oveta, 324–331, 433–444; preclearance of speeches, 417; and WAAC, 331, 374, 380, 381, 392, 404; and Will, 103; "woman" problem, 323–324. *See also* Army; Women's Army Auxiliary Corps (WAAC); Women's Army Corps (WAC); Women's Interest Section.
Wardlaw, L. J., 219

war garden, 118
War Manpower Commission (WMC), 404
Washington, DC: and Bill, 465; Connecticut Avenue apartment, 530, 532, 543, 569; Jessica in, 353, 402, 403, 407, 530; and Jones, 284–285, 302–303; Oveta in, 328–330, 379–380, 432, 468–469; and race riots, 154, 158; Texas influence in, 140; Westchester Apartments, 402, 422; Will as lobbyist, 49–52, 72, 137, 139–140; and Willie, 60–62, 140; Will's visits to Oveta, 256, 376, 569; women's clubs meeting, 328; WONPR conference, 287
*Washington Journalism Review*, 749–750, 827
*Washington Post*, 730
Washington Post Company: purchase of KPRC and KSAT, 758
Watergate, 728–730
water power, 197
Watson, J. L., 21, 23
Watson, Roy, 23, 142, 204, 790
WAVES (Women Accepted for Volunteer Emergency Service), 378, 382, 399, 420–421, 491
WBAP, 211, 312, 809
Weed, James, 53
Weeks, Sinclair, 515
Welch, Louie, 455, 672, 688
Wells, Jim, 127, 134
Werlein, Shepard Halsey, 79
West, Harriet, 353, 357, 435
West, Jim "Silver Dollar," 271, 273, 318–319, 453
Westchester Apartments, 402, 422
Westheimer, David, 443, 445
Westmoreland, William, 718
West Texas A&M College, 89–90
WEV radio, 210
Wheeler, Harvey, 477
White, Miller G., 424, 426–427, 428, 433
White, Theodore, 453
White House, 705, 712, 719, 724
"White Man's Union," 57
white supremacy: and civil rights bill, 702; and desegregation, 672–673; and Dixiecrats, 489; and Eisenhower, 545; and *Houston Post*, 31; and "Lost Cause," 17; and paramilitary units, 11, 774; and race riots, 158–159; and Red Summer, 154–160; and states' rights movement, 17, 679; and Texas Democratic Party, 11; and Texas Legislature, 14; and Will, 159–160. *See also* racism; states' rights movement.
Whitman, Ann, 675
Whitney, Jack Hay "Jock," 499–500
widows, Confederate, 14–15

of Oveta, 403, 446; advisory board, 422; African Americans, 404, 425–426; and African Americans, 426; All-States Plan , 403–404; and anniversary celebrations, 410, *431*, 431–432, 756; Army's failure to understand, 809; awards and medals received, 413, 435; band, 461; and Bandel, 433, 434, 435, 473; and Boyce, 432–433, 434, 435, 440; and combat, 410; and command over men, 394; commissioning of officers, 394; commissions for prominent women, 407, 421; and Congress, 384, 399, 407, 435; and Congressional Wives Club, 416–417; conversion from WAAC, 398–405; and cultural attitudes, 405; and dating, 398–399, 420; demobilization of, 424, 432, 435; documenting history of, 473–474; and Eisenhower, 398–399, 410–411, 435; and ER, 417, 425; and FDR, 394; as feminine and professional, 385, 400–401, 422, 436; Fifth Army and WACs, 413–416; and flags, 400, 403–404; Fort Des Moines, 473; Fort Oglethorpe, 407; and Gallup Polls, 404, 405, 407, 421; and Germany, 392, 405; as "Hobby's Army," 806; hostility from servicemen, 418, 421; in Italy, 413–415, 417; jobs of, 405, 407, 412; mail from family members, 399; and Maloney, 413; and Marshall, 407, 419, 422–423, 432, 436; and McCloy, 425; and media, 399, 433–434; and Meek Report, 420–422; merit based commissions, 421; military benefits, 394; military benefits for, 394; morale of, 423–424, 434–435; and *New York Journal American*, 403, 629; non-fraternization rule, 398–399; and North Africa, 410, 412–413; numbers of, 418; opposition to, 435; overseas deployment, 404, 409–410, 412, 425–426, 432; overseas inspection tour, 407, 409–416; and Oveta's image, 400–401; Oveta's impact on, 436–437; Oveta's resignation from, 425, 432–435; Oveta's role with, 398–400, 407; Oveta's swearing in, 394–395, *397–398*; Oveta's workload, 400; in Pacific bases, 432; and Pallas Athena, 446; and permanent WAC, 435; and promotion for Oveta, 756; public image and publicity campaigns, 382–384, 399, 400–405, 412, 416, 433–434; and Purple Heart medals, 435; racism in, 425–426; radio broadcasts: promoting WAAC and WAC, 393, 403, 409; and rations, 414–415; and recruitment, 403–404, 405, 413, 418, 421–422, 437; and Rogers, 379, 380, 394, 435–436; slander campaign, 421–422, 437; and Somervell, 398, 407, 421, 422; standards for recruits, 404; and Stimson, 436; success of, 435; and Surles, 422; and *Time*

magazine, 405, 410, 411–412; Treadwell, Mattie, 436, 473–474, 759; in Tunisia, 415; uniform of, 413, 420–421; and war fatigue, 423–424, 425; and *The Women's Army Corps*, 473–474; and women's rights, 696. *See* Women's Army Auxiliary Corps (WAAC).

*The Women's Army Corps,* 473–474

Women's Army Corps (WAC) bill, 331–336, 338–339, 382, 384, 392

Women's Interest Section: advisory councils for, 328, 382, 383, 390; and anti-slander campaign, 393; and ER, 328; focus on individuals, 330; job offer to Oveta, 800–801; and Newell, 350; and Oveta, 324–331, 800–801; question and answer sessions, 330–331; and recruitment of WAACs, 350; role and mission of, 325, 330, 333; staff for, 328; and women reporters, 325

women's liberation movement, 695–696, 709

Women's Organization for National Prohibition Reform (WONPR), 286–288

women's suffrage movement: anti-suffrage movement, 30, 151; and Ike Culp, 236; and Japan, 461; and opposition to, 151; and *patrones*, 127; and poll tax, 239; and primary elections, 108–109, 114–115, 151; and prohibition, 146–147; and referendums, 147, 148, 150–151; registration of women voters, 128, 131, 135, 236; and Rienzi Johnston, 30; state amendment for, 147; and Texas legislature, 77, 112–113; Texas Woman Suffrage Association, 108–109; and University of Texas, 86; and wage gap, 69; and Will, 68, 69, 98, 164; and Willie, 68–69, 81; and Will's gubernatorial campaign, 108–109, 128–132, 134–135, 784–785. *See also* Cunningham, Minnie Fisher; Nineteenth Amendment.

Women's Voluntary Service, British, 361, 370

women voters, 108–109, 128–132, 134–135, 499, 784–785

Wood, William, 12

Woodul, Walter: as assistant adjunct general, 139; and Oveta's book, 302; and senate campaign, 219; and Sterling administration, 261; Texas Rangers and Will's campaign, 122

Woodville: and Cooper, 773, 774–775; and Hobby family, 10–11, 17, 205; and Kirby, 773; as Tyler county seat, 9; and Willie, 60

Workman, William G., 608, 611, 612, 619

World War I. *See* Great War.

World War II: construction ban, 574; documenting history of, 473–474; and Germany, 313, 321, 331, 361, 368, 413, 431; Japan, 321, 333, 435, 460–462, 716; Pearl Harbor bombing, 332–333;

and Philippines, 459; rationing, 311, 369–370, 395, 409; and service of *Post* staff, 403; before US entry, 321. *See also* Women's Army Auxiliary Corps (WAAC); Women's Army Corps (WAC); Women's Interest Section.

World War II memorial, *437*, 437–438, 762

Wortham, Gus, 452, 455, 679, 744

Wortham, John L., 65, 139

Wortham, Louis J., 79

Writers' War Board, 384, 386

Wroe, H. A., 189, 191

WSM Radio, 447

WTLV-TV, 744–746

Wyeth labs, 624, 633

**X**

xenophobia, 153–154. *See also* racism.

**Y**

Yarborough, Ralph, 699

Yates, Paul, 214

*You Never Can Tell,* 290

Young, James, 256, 260

Young, Sam, 149–150, 261–262, 269–270

Young and Rubicam, 404, 420

Young Men's Democratic Club of Houston, 32

**Z**

Zamaria, Rose, 756

Ziegler, Jessie: on Bill's birth, 275–276; on Oveta's appearance, 267, 276; and State Highway Commission, 290; as Sterling's secretary, 267; on Will's probable resignation from *Post,* 283

Zimmerman, G. E., 211

Zweifel, Henry, 495, 497, 498